THE DEBATE ON
THE CONSTITUTION

PART ONE

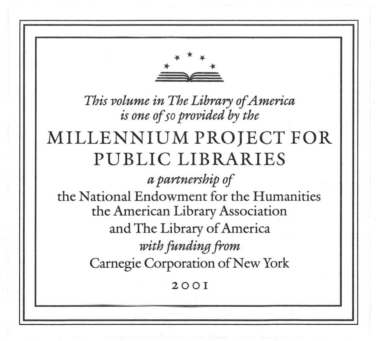

The Debate on the Constitution

Federalist and Antifederalist Speeches, Articles,
and Letters During the Struggle over Ratification

PART ONE

DEBATES IN THE PRESS AND IN PRIVATE CORRESPONDENCE

September 17, 1787–January 12, 1788

DEBATES IN THE STATE RATIFYING CONVENTIONS

Pennsylvania, November 20–December 15, 1787
Connecticut, January 3–9, 1788
Massachusetts, January 9–February 7, 1788

THE LIBRARY OF AMERICA

The paper used in this publication meets the
minimum requirements of the American National Standard for
Information Sciences—Permanence of Paper for Printed
Library Materials, ANSI Z39.48—1984.

Distributed to the trade in the United States
by Penguin Putnam Inc.
and in Canada by Penguin Books Canada Ltd.

Library of Congress Catalog Number: 92–25449
For cataloging information, see end of Index.
ISBN 0–940450–42–9

———
Fifth Printing
The Library of America—62

Manufactured in the United States of America

BERNARD BAILYN
SELECTED THE CONTENTS AND WROTE
THE HEADINGS AND NOTES FOR THIS VOLUME

The Debate on the Constitution: Part One
is kept in print
by a gift in honor of

JOHN C. WHITEHEAD

from
The Andrew W. Mellon Foundation
to the Guardians of American Letters Fund,
established by The Library of America
to ensure that every volume in the series
will be permanently available.

The publishers wish to thank
The Lynde and Harry Bradley Foundation
for funding the publication of The Debate on the Constitution.

The publishers also express their appreciation to
John P. Kaminski and Gaspare J. Saladino, editors of
The Documentary History of the Ratification of the Constitution,
and the State Historical Society of Wisconsin, the publisher,
for editorial assistance, the use of archival materials, and
permission to reprint extensive excerpts.

Contents

DEBATES IN THE STATE
RATIFYING CONVENTIONS

Pennsylvania Ratifying Convention, November 20–December 15, 1787

DEBATES IN THE PRESS
AND IN PRIVATE
CORRESPONDENCE

September 17, 1787–January 12, 1788

"I AGREE TO THIS CONSTITUTION, WITH ALL ITS FAULTS"

Benjamin Franklin's Speech at the Conclusion of the Constitutional Convention

Philadelphia, September 17, 1787

I confess that I do not entirely approve of this Constitution at present, but Sir, I am not sure I shall never approve it: For having lived long, I have experienced many Instances of being oblig'd, by better Information or fuller Consideration, to change Opinions even on important Subjects, which I once thought right, but found to be otherwise. It is therefore that the older I grow the more apt I am to doubt my own Judgment and to pay more Respect to the Judgment of others. Most Men indeed as well as most Sects in Religion, think themselves in Possession of all Truth, and that wherever others differ from them it is so far Error. Steele, a Protestant, in a Dedication tells the Pope, that the only Difference between our two Churches in their Opinions of the Certainty of their Doctrine, is, the Romish Church is infallible, and the Church of England is never in the Wrong. But tho' many private Persons think almost as highly of their own Infallibility, as that of their Sect, few express it so naturally as a certain French lady, who in a little Dispute with her Sister, said, I don't know how it happens, Sister, but I meet with no body but myself that's *always* in the right. *Il n'y a que moi qui a toujours raison.*

In these Sentiments, Sir, I agree to this Constitution, with all its Faults, if they are such: because I think a General Government necessary for us, and there is no *Form* of Government but what may be a Blessing to the People if well administred; and I believe farther that this is likely to be well administred for a Course of Years, and can only end in Despotism as other Forms have done before it, when the People shall become so corrupted as to need Despotic Government,

3

being incapable of any other. I doubt too whether any other Convention we can obtain, may be able to make a better Constitution: For when you assemble a Number of Men to have the Advantage of their joint Wisdom, you inevitably assemble with those Men all their Prejudices, their Passions, their Errors of Opinion, their local Interests, and their selfish Views. From such an Assembly can a perfect Production be expected? It therefore astonishes me, Sir, to find this System approaching so near to Perfection as it does; and I think it will astonish our Enemies, who are waiting with Confidence to hear that our Councils are confounded, like those of the Builders of Babel, and that our States are on the Point of Separation, only to meet hereafter for the Purpose of cutting one another's Throats. Thus I consent, Sir, to this Constitution because I expect no better, and because I am not sure that it is not the best. The Opinions I have had of its Errors, I sacrifice to the Public Good. I have never whisper'd a Syllable of them abroad. Within these Walls they were born, & here they shall die. If every one of us in returning to our Constituents were to report the Objections he has had to it, and endeavour to gain Partizans in support of them, we might prevent its being generally received, and thereby lose all the salutary Effects & great Advantages resulting naturally in our favour among foreign Nations, as well as among ourselves, from our real or apparent Unanimity. Much of the Strength and Efficiency of any Government, in procuring & securing Happiness to the People depends on Opinion, on the general Opinion of the Goodness of that Government as well as of the Wisdom & Integrity of its Governors. I hope therefore that for our own Sakes, as a Part of the People, and for the Sake of our Posterity, we shall act heartily & unanimously in recommending this Constitution, wherever our Influence may extend, and turn our future Thoughts and Endeavours to the Means of having it well administred. —

On the whole, Sir, I cannot help expressing a Wish, that every Member of the Convention, who may still have Objections to it, would with me on this Occasion doubt a little of his own Infallibility, and to make *manifest* our *Unanimity*, put his Name to this Instrument. —

Then the Motion was made for adding the last Formula, viz Done in Convention by the unanimous Consent &c —which was agreed to and added—accordingly.

"Z" Replies to Franklin's Speech

Independent Chronicle (Boston), December 6, 1787

Mess'rs. ADAMS & NOURSE, When I read Dr. FRANKLIN's address to the President of the late Convention, in the last Monday's Gazette, I was at a loss to judge, till I was informed by mere accident, from which of the contending parties it went to the press. "I confess," says the Doctor, (and observe the Printers tell us it was *immediately* before his signing) "I confess that I do not entirely approve of this Constitution at present." Surely, I thought, no zealous fœderalist, in his right mind, would have exposed his cause so much as to publish to the world that this great philosopher *did not* entirely approve the Constitution at the very moment when his "hand marked" his approbation of it; especially after the fœderalists themselves had so often and so loudly proclaimed, that he had *fully* and *decidedly* adopted it. The Doctor adds, "I am not sure I shall never approve it." This then is the only remaining hope of the fœderalists, so far as the Doctor's judgment is or may be of any service to their cause, that one time or another he *may* approve the new Constitution.

Again, says the Doctor, "In these sentiments I agree to this Constitution, with all its faults, if they are such; because I think a general government necessary for us, and there is no FORM of government but what may be a blessing to the people, if well administered." But are we to accept a form of government which we do not entirely approve of, merely in hopes that it *will* be administered well? Does not every man know, that nothing is more liable to be abused than power. Power, without a check, in *any* hands, is tyranny; and such powers, in the hands of even *good men*, so infatuating is the nature of it, will probably be wantonly, if not tyrannically exercised. The world has had experience enough of this, in every stage of it. Those among us who cannot entirely approve the *new* Constitution as it is called, are of opinion, in

6

order that any form may be well administered, and thus be made a blessing to the people, that there ought to be at least, an express reservation of certain inherent unalienable rights, which it would be equally sacrilegious for the people to *give away*, as for the government to *invade*. If the rights of conscience, for instance, are not sacredly reserved to the people, what security will there be, in case the government should have in their heads a predilection for any *one* sect in religion? what will hinder the civil power from erecting a national system of religion, and committing the law to a set of lordly priests, reaching, as the great Dr. *Mayhew* expressed it, from the desk to the skies? An *Hierarchy* which has ever been the grand engine in the hand of civil tyranny; and tyrants in return will afford them opportunity enough to vent their rage on *stubborn hereticks*, by *wholesome severities*, as they were called by national religionists, in a country which has long boasted its freedom. It was doubtless for the peace of *that* nation, that there should be an *uniformity* in religion, and for the same *wise* and *good* reason, the act of uniformity remains *in force* to these enlightened times.

The Doctor says, he is "*not* sure that this is *not* the best Constitution that we may expect." Nor can he be sure that it might not have been made *better* than it now is, if the Convention had adjourned to a distant day, that they might have availed themselves of the sentiments of the people at large. It would have been no great condescension, even in that *august* Body, to have shown so *small* a testimony of regard to the judgment of their constituents. Would it not be acting more like men who wish for a *safe* as well as a *stable* government, to propose such amendments as would meliorate the form, than to approve it, as the Dr. would have us, "with all its faults, if they are such." *Thus* the Doctor consents, and hopes the Convention will "act *heartily* and *unanimously* in recommending the Constitution, wherever their influence may extend, and turn their future tho'ts and endeavors to the means of having it well administered." Even a bad form of government may, in the Doctor's opinion, be well administered—for, says he, there is *no* form of government, but what may be made a blessing to the people, *if* well administered. He evidently, I think, builds his hopes, that the Constitution proposed, will be a blessing to the people,—not on the *principles* of the government itself, but on the *possibility*, that, with *all its faults*, it *may* be well administered;—and concludes, with wishing, that others, *who had objections* to it, would yet, like him, doubt of their own infallibility, and put their names to the instrument, to make an *Unanimity* MANIFEST! No wonder he *shed a tear*, as it is said he did, when he gave *his* sanction to the *New* Constitution.

Alexander Hamilton's Conjectures About the New Constitution

September 1787

The new constitution has in favour of its success these circumstances—a very great weight of influence of the persons who framed it, particularly in the universal popularity of General Washington,—the good will of the commercial interest throughout the states which will give all its efforts to the establishment of a government capable of regulating protecting and extending the commerce of the Union—the good will of most men of property in the several states who wish a government of the union able to protect them against domestic violence and the depredations which the democratic spirit is apt to make on property; and who are besides anxious for the respectability of the nation—the hopes of the Creditors of the United States that a general government possessing the means of doing it will pay the debt of the Union. a strong belief in the people at large of the insufficiency of the present confederation to preserve the existence of the Union and of the necessity of the union to their safety and prosperity; of course a strong desire of a change and a predisposition to receive well the propositions of the Convention.

Against its success is to be put, the dissent of two or three important men in the Convention; who will think their characters pledged to defeat the plan—the influence of many *inconsiderable* men in possession of considerable offices under the state governments who will fear a diminution of their consequence power and emolument by the establishment of the general government and who can hope for nothing there—the influence of some *considerable* men in office possessed of talents and popularity who partly from the same motives and partly from a desire of *playing a part* in a convulsion for their own aggrandisement will oppose the quiet adoption of the new government—(some considerable men out of office, from motives of ambition may be disposed to act the same part)—add to these causes the disinclination of the people to taxes and of course to a strong government—the opposition of all men much in debt who will not wish to see a government established one object of which is to restrain this means of cheating Creditors—the democratical jealousy of the people which may be alarmed at the appearance of institutions that may seem calculated to place the power of the community in few hands and to raise a few individuals to stations of great preeminence—and the influence of some foreign powers who from different motives will not wish to see an energetic government established throughout the states.

In this view of the subject it is difficult to form any judgment whether the plan will be adopted or rejected. It must be essentially matter of conjecture. The present appearances and all other circumstances considered the probability seems to be on the side of its adoption.

But the causes operating against its adoption are powerful and there will be nothing astonishing in the Contrary—

If it do not finally obtain, it is probable the discussion of the question will beget such struggles animosities and heats in the community that this circumstance conspiring with the *real necessity* of an essential change in our present situation will produce civil war. Should this happen, whatever parties prevail it is probable governments very different from the present in their principles will be established—A dismemberment of the Union and monarchies in different portions of it may be expected. It may however happen that no civil war will take place; but several republican confederacies be established between different combinations of particular states.

A reunion with Great Britain, from universal disgust at a state of commotion, is not impossible, though not much to be feared. The most plausible shape of such a business would be the establishment of a son of the present monarch in the supreme government of this country with a family compact.

If the government is adopted, it is probable general Washington will be the President of the United States—This will ensure a wise choice of men to administer the government and a good administration. A good administration will conciliate the confidence and affection of the people and perhaps enable the government to acquire more consistency than the proposed constitution seems to promise for so great a

Country—It may then triumph altogether over the state governments and reduce them to an entire subordination, dividing the large states into smaller districts. The *organs* of the general government may also acquire additional strength.

If this should not be the case, in the course of a few years, it is probable that the contests about the boundaries of power between the particular governments and the general government and the *momentum* of the larger states in such contests will produce a dissolution of the Union. This after all seems to be the most likely result.

But it is almost arrogance in so complicated a subject, depending so entirely on the incalculable fluctuations of the human passions, to attempt even a conjecture about the event.

It will be Eight or Nine months before any certain judgment can be formed respecting the adoption of the Plan.

"A Revolution Effected by Good Sense and Deliberation"

Daily Advertiser (New York), September 24, 1787

The result of the deliberations of the National Convention is now laid before the public, and I congratulate each patriot heart on the important disclosure. The causes which have all pressed, as it were to a point, to render a thorough reform indispensably necessary, have been long the subject of general speculation. The Casuist has disputed—the Orator has harangued—and the Essayist has reasoned on them. Indeed, the necessity of the Convention has been generally admitted, and almost universally *felt*. We have now offered to us a Constitution, which, if happily received, will disappoint our enemies, render us safe and happy at home, and respected abroad. Heaven, in mercy to us, has furnished this auspicious event, in order to snatch us from impending ruin, and to re-establish this favored land on the substantial basis of liberty, honor and virtue. The means of wiping opprobrium from our country are now in our power; let us neither reject nor forego them. It will be the duty of all honest, well-disposed men, friends to peace and good government, as well in this State as throughout the Union, to cultivate and diffuse, as far as their walk may extend, a spirit of submission to the counsels of this great patriot band; who have sought to procure, and have been anxious in their endeavors to establish, our liberty, and aggrandize our fame. If the New Constitution is not as perfect in every part as it might have been, let it be considered, that it is much more so than the most friendly and sanguine expected; and, at the same time, let it be remembered, that "the *mutual deference and concession*," and that "*spirit of amity*," from which this Constitution has resulted, ought to have a strong operation on the minds of all generous Americans, and have due influence with every *State Convention*, when they come to deliberate upon its adoption.

Every good American, when he reflects, will exult with joy

that his countrymen have calmly resorted to so temperate and wise a measure as the late Convention; not only on account of the advantages, which, by the blessing of Heaven, we are likely to derive from it; but also as it furnishes a valuable precedent, if it shall be found necessary hereafter. It will likewise teach foreign nations to reflect, that, tho' discord may rear its Hydra head, and state jealousies for a while prevail, yet the enlightened Americans will not consent that the fair fabric of Liberty, which they have established with their blood, shall be endangered by anarchy at home, or destroyed by violence from abroad. The conflict which America lately sustained in the cause of Freedom, will be historiated as an important lesson to distant nations and future ages. Let the present epoch be recorded as a lesson to future generations in these United States, as having given birth to *a revolution*, effected by good sense and deliberation: Let it be stiled the reign of reason, the triumph of discretion, virtue and public spirit!

Perhaps the greatest, if not the only difficulty, which will arise against the adoption of this New Federal System of Government, will be made by those ambitious citizens, in the different States, who either *now are in power*, or who will practise their political wiles on the ignorant and unsuspicious part of the people, in order to obtain their own *private purposes*. It is a lamentable consideration, that men of this stamp too frequently, by the folly and blindness of the people, are put in the exercise of such offices as give them a very dangerous degree of influence—Hence the social compact is often violated, and sometimes dissolved.

Let difficulties, if any unhappily arise, be no longer laid to *our charge*—and let us all, who are friends to order and good government, in the language of scriptural injunction, *"watch and pray."*—Watch, and, *with open front,* manfully oppose every ambitious demagogue, however *high in office,* who may attempt to form combinations, with a wicked intent to destroy the labors of those distinguished worthies; and *pray the Governor of the world* to avert, and finally disappoint their nefarious purposes.—If the change, which genius and patriotism has presented to us, as the most advisable to be received, should be rejected, and if (which God avert) such evil-minded men should prevail, what is the alternative? Gorgon-headed anarchy, or a miserable aristocratic domination; all the wretchedness and wickedness of an aristocracy, without a single particle of its dignity.

Certain it is, we have no reason to fear (whatever pseudo-patriots may insinuate) a well digested system, which reconciles in a great measure, various interests, and embraces the happiness of the whole; which has been approved by the most dignified and patriotic citizens in the Union; and which at once gives a power that will be efficient and adequate to the support and happiness of the Confederation; and, at the same time, so guards and checks the administration of it, that there will be little danger of running into a lawless Democracy, on the one hand, or of the Sovereign authority degenerating into Tyranny, on the other.—In short, a system, which it will be wise in us to accept with gratitude—the rejection of which might, perhaps, be dreadful.

David Redick to William Irvine

Philadelphia, September 24, 1787

The new plan of government proposed by the convention has made a bustle in the city & its vicinity. all people, almost, are for Swallowing it down at once without examining its tendencies.——

I have thought it unsafe within the wind of hurricane to utter a Sylable about it: but to you Sir I may venture to Say that in my oppinion the day on which we adopt the present proposed plan of government, from that moment we may Justly date the loss of American liberty. perhaps my fears hath contributed principlely to this oppinion. I will change the moment that I See better. My dear Sir why is not the liberty of the press provided for? why will the Congress have power to alter the plan or mode of chusing Representatives? why will they have power to lay direct Taxes? why will they have power to keep Standing Armies in time of peace? why will they have power to make laws in direct contradiction to the forms of government established in the Several States? why will they have power to collect by law ten Dollars for ever German or Irishman which may come to Settle in America? why is the Trial by Jury destroyd in Civil causes before Congress? and above all I cannot imagine why the people in this city are So verry anxious to have it adopted instantly before it can be digested or deliberatly considered. If you were only here to See and hear those people, to observe the means they are useing to effect this purpose, to hear the tories declare they will draw their Sword in its defence, to See the quaquers runing about Signing declarations and Petitions in favor of it befor the have time to examine it, to See Gentlemen runing into the Country and neibouring towns haranguing the Rabble. I Say were you to See and hear these things as I do you would Say, with me that: the verry Soul of confidence itself ought to change into distrust. If this goverment be a good

15

one or even a tollorable one the Necessities and the good Sense of America will lead us to adopt it. if otherwise give us time and it will be amended and then adopted. but I think the measures pursued here is a Strong evidence that these people know it will not bear an examination and therefor wishes to adopt it first and consider it afterward. I hope Congress will be verry deliberate and digest it thoroughly before they Send it recommended to the States. I Sincerely hope that Such Gentlemen as were Members of Convention, and who have Seats in Congress may not be considered as verry proper Judges of their own Works.——

I pray a spirit of Wisdom and a Spirit of integrity prevade Congress, more especially at this time.

Strictures on the Proposed Constitution

Freeman's Journal (Philadelphia), September 26, 1787

The writer of the following Remarks has the happiness and respectability of the United States much at heart—and it is with pleasure he has seen a system promulged by the late Convention, which promises to ensure those blessings: But as perfection is not the lot of human nature, we are not to expect it in the new Federal Constitution. Candour must confess, however, that it is a well wrought piece of stuff, and claims, upon the whole, the approbation of all the States. Our situation is critical, and demands our immediate care. It is therefore to be hoped that every State will be speedy in calling a Convention—*speedy*; because the business is momentous, and merits the utmost deliberation.

The following strictures on the proposed Constitution, are submitted with diffidence. Excepting a single instance, they regard points of an inferior magnitude only;—and as the writer is not possessed of any of the reasons which influenced the Convention, he feels the more diffident in offering these.

REMARKS.

Art. 1. *Sect.* 2. (3d clause) "The number of Representatives shall not exceed one for every 30,000."—If we consider the *vast* extent and *increasing* population of the United States, it will appear that a Representation upon this principle (though proper to *begin* with) cannot last very long. It must grow far too unwieldly for business—and the Constitution must therefore be mended, and patched with new work. Let your government be invariably fixed; so far, at least, as human foresight can go—and age will secure it respect and veneration from the multitude. In framing a government, we should consider a century to come as but a day, and leave the least possible for posterity to mend. Errors sanctified by long usage are not easily relinquished. Their age attaches the people, and renders a reform difficult. There is even danger in reforming the errors of a government, but there is more in letting them alone.—Hence we ought to aim at PERMANENCY in every part of a Constitution intended to endure. *In America Representation ought to be in a ratio with population*—and this should be provided for in the government of the United States.

Sect. 4. (1st clause) "The *times, places* and manner of holding elections for senators and representatives, shall be prescribed in each State by the Legislature thereof; but the Congress may at any time by law make or *alter* such regulations, except as to the places of chusing senators."—A general uniformity of acting in confederations (whenever it can be done with convenience) must tend to federalize (allow me the word) the sentiments of the people. The *time*, then, might as well have been fixed in Convention—not subject to *alteration* afterwards. Because a day may be chosen by Congress which the Constitution or laws of a State may have appropriated to *local* purposes, not to be subverted or suspended. Leaving the *places* subject to the alteration of Congress, may also lead to improper consequences, and (*humanum est errare*) tempt to sinister views.—Who in Pennsylvania would think it adviseable to elect Representatives on the shore of Lake Erie; or even at Fort Pitt?

Second clause. "The Congress shall assemble *at least once* in every year, and such meeting shall be on the first Monday in *December.*"—Here is a kind of solecism; as the late period of assembling hardly admits of a prorogation and re-assembling in the same year: But as probably a *Federal* year is meant, it should have been so expressed. *December* is an objectionable month, too, for the Representatives of so many distant States to meet in—the depth of winter forbids the convenience of water, and the communication by land is expensive, inconvenient, and often obstructed at this season: Much time would necessarily be lost in bringing the members together.

Sect. 9. (22d clause) "No *Capitation* or other direct tax shall be laid, unless" &c.—I confess here a great disappointment. When I began to read this clause, I did not doubt that the poll-tax would share the fate of ex post facto laws and bills of attainder. I am sorry to find myself mistaken: For a Capitation Tax is *impolitic* and *unjust*; it is a tax upon population, and falls indiscriminately upon the poor and the rich; the helpless, who cannot work, and the robust, who can. The poll-taxes of the Eastern States, have forced many thousands of their valuable citizens to emigrate, and made those disaffected who staid behind.

Art. 3. *Sect.* 2. (3d clause) "The trial of all crimes, except in cases of impeachment, shall be by *Jury.*"—I sincerely wish the Convention had said, *a "Jury" of* THIRTEEN, *a* MAJORITY *of whom shall determine the verdict.* Is it not extravagantly absurd to expect that twelve men shall have but one opinion among them upon the most difficult case? Common sense revolts at the idea,—while conscience shudders at the prostitution of an oath thus sanctified by law! Starve, or be perjured! say our Courts. The monstrous attachment of the people to an English Jury shews how far the force of prejudice can go—and the encomiums which have been so incessantly lavished upon it should caution us against borrowing from others, without the previous conviction of our own minds.

"An American Citizen" [Tench Coxe] I

Independent Gazetteer (Philadelphia), September 26, 1787

It is impossible for an honest and feeling mind, of any nation or country whatever, to be insensible to the present circumstances of America. Were I an East Indian, or a Turk, I should consider this singular situation of a part of my fellow creatures, as most curious and interesting. Intimately connected with the country, as a citizen of the union, I confess it entirely engrosses my mind and feelings.

To take a proper view of the ground on which we stand, it may be necessary to recollect the manner in which the United States were originally settled and established.—Want of charity in the religious systems of Europe and of justice in their political governments were the principal moving causes, which drove the emigrants of various countries to the American continent. The Congregationalists, Quakers, Presbyterians and other British dissenters, the Catholics of England and Ireland, the Hugonots of France, the German Lutherans, Calvinists, and Moravians, with several other societies, established themselves in the different colonies, thereby laying the ground of that catholicism in ecclesiastical affairs, which has been observable since the late revolution: Religious liberty naturally promotes corresponding dispositions in matters of government. The Constitution of England, as it stood on paper, was one of the freest at that time existing in the world, and the American colonies considered themselves as entitled to the fullest enjoyment of it. Thus when the ill-judged discussions of latter times in England brought into question the rights of this country, as it stood connected with the British crown, we were found more strongly impressed with their importance and accurately acquainted with their extent, than the wisest and most learned of our brethren beyond the Atlantic. When the greatest names in Parliament insisted on the power of that body over the commerce of the colonies, and even the right to bind us in all cases whatsoever, America, seeing that it was only another form of tyranny, insisted upon the immutable truth, that taxation and representation are inseparable, and while a desire of harmony and other considerations induced her into an acquiescence in the commercial regulations of Great Britain, it was done from the declared necessity of the case, and with a cautious, full and absolute saving of our voluntarily suspended rights. The Parliament was persevering, and America continued firm till hostilities and open war commenced, and finally the late revolution closed the contest forever.

'Tis evident from this short detail and the reflections which arise from it, that the quarrel between the United States and the Parliament of Great Britain did not arise so much from objections to the form of government, *though undoubtedly a better one by far is now within our reach*, as from a difference concerning certain important rights resulting from the essential principles of liberty, which the Constitution preserved to all the subjects actually residing within the realm. It was not asserted by America that the people of *the Island of Great Britain* were slaves, but that *we*, though possessed absolutely of the same rights, were not admitted to enjoy *an equal degree of freedom*.

When the declaration of independence completed the separation between the two countries, new governments were necessarily established. Many circumstances led to the adoption of the republican form, among which was the predilection of the people. — In devising the frames of government it may have been difficult to avoid extremes opposite to the vices of that we had just rejected; nevertheless many of the State constitutions, we have chosen, are truely excellent. Our misfortunes have been, *that in the first instance we adopted no national government at all,* but were kept together by common danger only, *and that in the confusions of a civil war we framed a Federal Constitution now universally admitted to be inadequate to the preservation of liberty, property, and the union.* — The question is not then how far our State Constitutions are good or otherwise — the object of our wishes is *to amend and supply the evident and allowed errors and defects of the Federal Government.*

—Let us consider awhile, that which is now proposed to us—let us compare it with the so much boasted British form of government, and see how much more it favors the people and how completely it secures their rights, remembring at the same time that we did not dissolve our connexion with that country so much on account of its constitution as the perversion and mal-administration of it.

In the first place let us look at the nature and powers of the head of that country, and those of the ostensible head of ours.

The British King is the great Bishop or Supreme Head of an established church, with an immense patronage annexed. In this capacity he commands a number of votes in the House of Lords, by creating Bishops, who, besides their great incomes, have votes in that assembly, and are judges in the last resort. They have also many honorable and lucrative places to bestow, and thus from their wealth, learning, dignities, powers and patronage give a great lustre and an enormous influence to the crown.

In America our President will not only be *without* these influencing advantages, *but they will be in the possession of the people at large, to strengthen their hands in the event of a contest with him.* All religious funds, honors and powers, are in the gift of numberless, unconnected, disunited, and contending corporations, wherein the principle of perfect equality universally prevails. In short, danger from ecclesiastical tyranny, that long standing and still remaining curse of the people—that sacrilegious engine of royal power in some countries, can be feared by no man in the United States. In Britain their king is for life—In America our president will always be *one of the people* at the end of four years. In that country the king is hereditary and may be an idiot, a knave, or a tyrant by nature, or ignorant from neglect of his education, yet cannot be removed, for *"he can do no wrong."* In America, as the president is to be one of the people at the end of his short term, so will he and his fellow citizens remember, *that he was originally one of the people; and that he is created by their breath*—Further, he cannot be an idiot, probably not a knave or a tyrant, for those whom nature makes so, discover it before the age of thirty-five, until which period he cannot be elected. It appears we have not admitted that he can do no wrong, but have rather pre-supposed he may and will sometimes do wrong, by providing for *his impeachment, his trial, and his peaceable and complete removal*.

In England the king has a power to create members of the upper house, who are judges in the highest court, as well as legislators. Our president not only cannot make members of the upper house, but their creation, like his own, is by *the people* through their representatives, and a member of assembly may and will be as certainly dismissed at the end of his year for electing a weak or wicked senator, as for any other blunder or misconduct.

The king of England has legislative power, while our president can only use it when the other servants of the people are divided. But in all great cases affecting the national interests or safety, his modified and restrained power must give way to the sense of two-thirds of the legislature. In fact it amounts to no more, than a serious duty imposed upon him to request both houses to reconsider any matter on which he entertains doubts or feels apprehensions; and here the people have a strong hold upon him *from his sole and personal responsibility*.

The president of the upper house (or the chancellor) in England is appointed by the king, while our vice-president, who is chosen *by the people* through the electors and the senate, *is not at all dependant on the president*, but may exercise equal powers on some occasions. In all royal governments an helpless infant or an unexperienced youth, may wear the crown. *Our president must be matured by the experience of years*, and being born among us, his character at thirty-five must be fully understood. Wisdom, virtue, and active qualities of mind and body can alone make him the first servant of a free and enlightened people.

Our president will fall very far short indeed of any prince in his annual income, which will not be hereditary, but *the absolute allowance of the people passing through the hands of their other servants from year to year as it becomes necessary*. There will be no burdens on the nation to provide for his heir or other branches of his family. 'Tis probable, from the state of property in America and other circumstances, that many citizens will *exceed* him in shew and expence, those dazzling trappings of kingly rank and power. He will have no authority to make a treaty without *two-thirds of the senate*, nor can he appoint ambassadors or other great officers *without their approbation*, which will remove the idea of *patronage and influence*, and of personal obligation and dependance. The appointment of even the inferior officers may be taken out of his hands by an act of Congress at any time; he can create no nobility or titles of honor, nor take away offices during good behaviour. *His person is not so much protected as that of a member of the house of representatives; for he may be proceeded against like any other man in the ordinary course of law.* He appoints no officer of the separate states. He will have no influence *from placemen in the legislature*, nor can he prorogue or dissolve it. He will have no power *over the treasures of the state*; and lastly, as he is *created* through the electors by the people at large, *he must ever look up to the support of his creators.* From such a servant with powers so limited and transitory, there can be no danger, especially when we consider the solid foundations on which our national liberties are immovably fixed by the other provisions of this excellent constitution. Whatever of dignity or authority he possesses, *is a delegated part of their Majesty and their political omnipotence, transiently vested in him by the people themselves for their own happiness.*

"An American Citizen" [Tench Coxe] II

Independent Gazetteer (Philadelphia), September 28, 1787

We have seen that the late honorable Convention, in designating the nature of the chief executive office of the United States, *have deprived it of all the dangerous appendages of royalty*, and provided for *the frequent expiration of its limited powers* —As our President bears *no resemblance to a King*, so we shall see the Senate have *no similitude to nobles*.

First then not being hereditary, their *collective* knowledge, wisdom and virtue are not precarious, *for by these qualities alone are they to obtain their offices*; and they will have none of the *peculiar* follies and vices of those men, *who possess power merely because their fathers held it before them*, for they will be educated (under equal advantages and with equal prospects) among and on a footing with the other sons of a free people—If we recollect the characters, who have, at various periods, filled the seats of Congress, we shall find this expectation *perfectly reasonable*. Many *young* men of genius and *many characters of more matured abilities, without fortunes*, have been honored with that trust. *Wealth has had but few representatives there, and those have been generally possessed of respectable personal qualifications*. There have also been many instances of persons, not eminently endowed with mental qualities, who have been sent thither *from a reliance on their virtues, public and private*—As the Senators *are still to be elected by the legislatures of the states*, there can be no doubt of *equal safety and propriety* in their future appointment, especially as no further pecuniary qualification is required by the constitution.

They can hold *no other office* civil or military under the United States, nor can they join *in making provisions for themselves*, either by creating new places or encreasing the emoluments of old ones. As their sons are not to succeed them, they will not be induced to aim at an increase or perpetuity of their powers, at the expence of the liberties of the people of which those sons will be a part. They possess *a much smaller share of the judicial power* than the upper house in Britain, for they are not, as there, the highest court in civil affairs. Impeachments *alone* are the cases cognizable before them, and in what other place could matters of that nature be so properly and safely determined? The judges of the federal courts will owe their appointments to the president and senate, therefore may not feel so perfectly free *from favor, affection and influence*, as the upper house, who receive their power from the people, through their state representatives, and are immediately responsible to those assemblies, and finally to the nation at large—Thus we see when a daring or dangerous offender is brought to the bar of public justice, the people *who alone can impeach him by their immediate representatives*, will cause him to be tried, *not by judges appointed in the heat of the occasion*, but by two thirds of *a select body, chosen a long time before, for various purposes by the collected wisdom of their state legislatures.* From a pretence or affection of extraordinary purity and excellence of character *their word of honor* is the sanction, under which these high courts in other countries, have given their sentence—but with us, like the other judges of the union, like the rest of the people *of which they are never to forget they are a part* it is required, that they be on oath.

No ambitious, undeserving or unexperienced *youth* can acquire a seat in this house by means of the most enormous wealth or most powerful connections, *till thirty years have ripened his abilities and fully discovered his merits to his country* —a more rational ground of preference surely than mere property.

The senate though more independent of the people as to *the free exercise of their judgement and abilities*, than the house of representatives, by the longer term of their office, must be older and more experienced men and the public treasures, *the sinews of the state*, cannot be called forth by their original motion. They may *restrain the profusion or errors* of the house of representatives, *but they cannot take the necessary measures to raise a national revenue.*

The people, through the electors, *prescribe* them such a president as shall be *best qualified to controul them.*

They can only, by conviction on impeachment, *remove and*

incapacitate a dangerous officer, but the punishment of him as a criminal *remains within the province of the courts of law to be conducted under all the ordinary forms and precautions*, which exceedingly diminishes the importance of their judicial powers. They are *detached*, as much as possible, from *local* prejudices in favour of their respective states, by having *a separate and independent vote*, for the sensible and conscientious use of which, every member will find *his person, honor and character* seriously bound—He cannot shelter himself, *under a vote in behalf of his state*, among his immediate colleagues. As there are only *two*, he cannot be voluntarily or involuntarily governed *by the majority of the deputation*—He will be obliged, by wholsome provisions, *to attend his public duty*, and thus in great national questions *must give a vote* of the honesty of which, he will find it necessary to convince his constituents.

The senate *must always receive the exceptions of the president* against any of their legislative acts, which, without *serious deliberation and sufficient reasons*, they will seldom disregard. They will also feel a considerable check *from the constitutional powers of the state legislatures*, whose rights they will not be disposed to infringe, since they are the bodies *to which they owe their existence*, and are moreover to remain *the immediate guardians of the people*.

And lastly the senate will feel *the mighty check of the house of representatives*—a body *so pure in its election*, so intimately connected, by its interests and feelings, *with the people at large*, so guarded against *corruption and influence*—so much, from its nature, *above all apprehensions*, that it *must ever be able to maintain the high ground assigned to it by the federal constitution*.

"An American Citizen" [Tench Coxe] III

Independent Gazetteer (Philadelphia), September 29, 1787

In pursuing the consideration of the new federal constitution, it remains now to examine the nature and powers of the house of representatives—*the immediate delegates of the people.*

Each member of this truly popular assembly will be chosen by about six thousand electors, *by the poor as well as the rich.* No decayed and venal borough will have an *unjust* share in their determinations—No old *Sarum* will send thither a representative *by the voice of a single elector**—As we shall have no royal ministries to purchase votes, so we shall have no votes for sale. *For the suffrages of six thousand enlightened and independent Freemen are above all price*—When the encreasing population of the country shall render the body too large at the rate of one member for every thirty thousand persons, they will be returned at the greater rate of one for every forty or fifty thousand, which will render the electors still more incorruptible. For this regulation is only designed to prevent a *smaller number* than thirty thousand from having a representative. Thus we see a provision follows, that no state shall have less than one member; for if a new and greater number should hereafter be fixt on, which shall exceed the whole of the inhabitants of any state, such state, without this wholesome provision, would lose its voice in the house of representatives—A circumstance which the constitution renders *impossible.*

The people of England, whose house of commons is filled with military and civil officers and pensioners, say their liberties would be perfectly secured by triennial parliaments. *With us no placemen can sit among the representatives of the people, and two years are the constitutional term of their existence.* Here again, lest wealth, powerful connexions, or even *the unwariness of the people* should place in this important trust an un-

---

*This is the case with that British borough.

deserving, unqualified or inexperienced youth, the wisdom of the convention has proposed *an absolute incapacity till the age of twenty-five*. At twenty-one a young man is made the guardian of his *own* interests, *but he cannot for a few years more be entrusted with the affairs of the nation*. He must be an inhabitant of the state that elects him, that he may be intimately acquainted with their *particular* circumstances—The house of representatives is not, *as the senate*, to have a president chosen *for them* from *without* their body, *but are to elect their speaker from their own number*—They will also appoint *all their other officers*. In great state cases, they will be *the grand inquest of the nation*, for they possess *the sole and uncontroulable power of impeachment*. They are neither *to wait the call* nor *abide the prorogations and dissolutions of a perverse or ambitious prince*, for they are to meet at least once in every year, and sit on adjournments to be agreed on between themselves and the other servants of the people. Should they differ in opinion, the president who is a temporary fellow servant and not their hereditary master, has *a mediatorial power* to adjust it for them, *but cannot prevent their constitutional meeting within the year*. They can compel the attendance of their members, that their public duty may not be *evaded* in times of difficulty or danger—The vote of each representative can be always known, as well as the proceedings of the house, *that so the people may be acquainted with the conduct of those in whom they repose so important a trust*. As was observed of the senators, they cannot make *new* offices *for themselves*, nor increase, *for their own benefit*, the emoluments of old ones, *by which the people will be exempted from needless additions to the public expences on such sordid and mercenary principles*—They are not to be restrained from *the firm and plain language*, which becomes the independent representatives of freemen, *for there is to be a perfect liberty of speech*. Without their consent *no monies can be obtained, no armies raised, no navies provided*. They *alone* can originate bills for drawing forth the revenues of the union, and *they will have a negative upon every legislative act of the other house*—So far, in short, as the sphere of federal jurisdiction extends, they will be controulable *only by the people*, and in contentions with the other branch, so far as they shall be right, *they must ever finally prevail*.

Such, my countrymen, are some of *the cautionary provisions* of the frame of government your faithful convention have submitted to your consideration—such *the foundations of peace, liberty and safety*, which have been laid by their unwearied labors—They have guarded you against *all servants* but those "whom choice and common good ordain," against *all masters* "save preserving Heaven."

"Cato" I

New York Journal, September 27, 1787

To the CITIZENS *of the* STATE *of* NEW-YORK.

The Convention, who sat at Philadelphia, have at last delivered to Congress that system of general government, which they have declared best calculated to promote your safety and happiness as citizens of the United States. This system, though not handed to you formally by the authority of government, has obtained an introduction through divers channels; and the minds of you all, to whose observation it has come, have no doubt been contemplating it; and alternate joy, hope, or fear have preponderated, as it conformed to, or differed from, your various ideas of just government.

Government, to an American, is the science of his political safety—this then is a moment to you the most important—and that in various points—to your reputation as members of a great nation—to your immediate safety, and to that of your posterity. In your private concerns and affairs of life you deliberate with caution, and act with prudence; your public concerns require a caution and prudence, in a ratio, suited to the difference and dignity of the subject. The disposal of your reputation, and of your lives and property, is more momentous than a contract for a farm, or the sale of a bale of goods; in the former, if you are negligent or inattentive, the ambitious and despotic will entrap you in their toils, and bind you with the cord of power from which you, and your posterity, may never be freed; and if the possibility should exist, it carries along with it consequences that will make your community totter to its center: in the latter, it is a mere loss of a little property, which more circumspection, or assiduity, may repair.

Without directly engaging as an advocate for this new form of national government, or as an opponent—let me conjure you to consider this a very important crisis of your safety and character—You have already, in common with the rest of your countrymen, the citizens of the other states, given to the world astonishing evidences of your greatness—you have fought under peculiar circumstances, and was successful against a powerful nation on a speculative question—you have established an original compact between you and your governors, a fact heretofore unknown in the formation of the governments of the world—your experience has informed you, that there are defects in the fœderal system, and, to the astonishment of mankind, your legislatures have concerted measures for an alteration, with as much ease as an individual would make a disposition of his ordinary domestic affairs: this alteration now lies before you, for your consideration; but beware how you determine—do not, because you admit that something must be done, adopt any thing—teach the members of that convention, that you are capable of a supervision of their conduct. The same medium that gave you this system, if it is erroneous, while the door is now open, can make amendments, or give you another, if it is required.— Your fate, and that of your posterity, depends on your present conduct—do not give the latter reason to curse you, nor yourselves cause of reprehension; as individuals you are ambitious of leaving behind you a good name, and it is the reflection, that you have done right in this life, that blunts the sharpness of death; the same principles would be a consolation to you, as patriots, in the hour of dissolution, that you would leave to your children a fair political inheritance, untouched by the vultures of power, which you had acquired by *an unshaken* perseverance in the cause of liberty—but how miserable the alternative—you would deprecate the ruin you had brought on yourselves—be the curse of posterity, and the scorn and scoff of nations.

Deliberate, therefore, on this new national government with coolness; analize it with criticism; and reflect on it with candour: if you find that the influence of a powerful few, or the exercise of a standing army, will always be directed and exerted for your welfare alone, and not to the agrandizement of themselves, and that it will secure to you and your posterity happiness at home, and national dignity and respect from abroad, adopt it—if it will not, reject it with indignation—better to be where you are, for the present, than insecure forever afterwards. Turn your eyes to the United Netherlands, at this moment, and view their situation; compare it with what yours may be, under a government substantially similar to theirs.

Beware of those who wish to influence your passions, and to make you dupes to their resentments and little interests—personal invectives can never persuade, but they always fix prejudices which candor might have removed—those who deal in them have not your happiness at heart. Attach yourselves to measures, not to men.

This form of government is handed to you by the recommendations of a man who merits the confidence of the public; but you ought to recollect, that the wisest and best of men may err, and their errors, if adopted, may be fatal to the community; therefore, in principles of *politics*, as well as in religious faith, every man ought to think for himself.

Hereafter, when it will be necessary, I shall make such observations, on this new constitution, as will tend to promote your welfare, and be justified by reason and truth.

Sept. 26, 1787.

Reply to "Cato" I: "Cæsar" I

Daily Advertiser (New York), October 1, 1787

The Citizens of the State of New-York have received yesterday, from Cato (an ally of *Pompey*, no doubt) an introductory discourse on the appearance of the New System for the Government of the United States: this, we are told, will be followed by such observations, on the constitution proposed to the Union, "as will promote our welfare and be justified by reason and truth." There is, in this preparatory lecture, little that is necessary to be dwelt on just now; and if Cato had not possessed his future investigations, in such terms as wore a *questionable shape*, they should have passed unheeded.

Cato tells us that he will not *directly engage as an advocate*, for this new form of Government—or as an *opponent*. Here Cato, without any dispute, acts prudently. It will be wise in him to rest a while; since he has given a *preface*, which, with small address, can easily be made to work on either side. When the sentiments of the Confederated States come to be generally known, it will be time enough to proceed—Cato will then *start fair*. A little caution, however, he thinks necessary to be given in the mean time. "Do not" says this prudent Censor, in addressing the Citizens, "because you admit that *something* must be done, adopt *any thing*." What, in the name of common sense, does this injunction import? I appeal to men of understanding, whether it is not obviously the language of distrust, calculated, as far as such a thing can influence, to prejudice the public opinion against the New Constitution; and, in effect, by a periphrastic mode of speech, recommending the rejection of it?—"*Teach* the Members of the Convention (Cato *very modestly* goes on) that you are capable of a supervision of their conduct; the same medium that gave you this system, if it is erroneous, while the door is now open, can make amendments, *or give you another.*" O excellent thought, and happily advised! Be clamorous, my friends—be

34

discontented—assert your prerogative—for ever assert the power and *Majesty of the People!!!*—I am not willing to suspect any man's intentions, when they aim at giving information; but when they come abroad, couched in such *magisterial* terms, I own I feel some indignation. If this demagogue had talents to throw light on the subject of Legislation, why did he not offer them when the Convention was in session? If they had been judged useful, no doubt they would have been attended to. But *is this now a time* for such insinuations? Has not the wisdom of America been drawn, as it were, into a focus, and the proferred Constitution sent forth with an unanimity, that is unequalled in ancient or modern story? And shall we now wrangle and find fault with that *excellent Whole*, because, perhaps, some of its parts *might have been* more perfect?—There is neither virtue nor patriotism in such conduct. Besides, how can Cato say, "That the door is *now open* to receive any amendments, or to give us *another Constitution*, if required." I believe he has advanced *this* without proper authority. I am inclined to believe that the *door of recommendation is shut, and cannot be opened by the same men*; that the Convention, in one word, is *dissolved*: if so, we must reject, IN TOTO, or *vice versa*; just take it as it is; and be thankful. I deny the similarity betwixt the present Constitution and that of the United Netherlands.—Cato would here draw a very melancholy picture, but it won't apply. In my humble opinion, it has a much greater affinity with a Government, which, in all human probability, will remain when the History of the Seven Provinces shall be forgotten.—Cato tells us (what all America knows by this time) that the New Constitution comes sanctioned with the approbation of General Washington; and, though he appears to have some reverence for that great patriot chief, yet he very sagaciously observes, that the BEST AND WISEST MAN MAY ERR; and thence asserts, that every man in *politics*, as well as in religion, ought to judge for himself. This paragraph needs no comment, and, for that reason, I shall not touch it; but, with all deference to Cato's penetration, I would recommend to him, instead of entering into fruitless discussion of what has come from so many *clear heads, and good hearts*, to join his Fellow Citizens, and endeavour to reconcile this *excellent Constitution* to the *weak*, the *sus-*

picious, and the *interested*, who will be chiefly opposed to it; that we may enjoy the blessings of it as soon as possible. I would also advise him to give his vote (as he will probably be one of the *Electors*) to the American Fabius: it will be more healthy for this country, and *this state*, that he should be induced to accept of the Presidency of the New Government, than that he should be solicited again to accept of the command of *an army*.

Cato, it appears, intends to adventure on perilous ground; it will therefore become him to be cautious on what terms he takes the field. "He advises us to attach ourselves to measures, and not to men." In this instance he advises well; and I heartily recommend to *himself*, not to forget the force of that important admonition: for Cato, in his future *marches*, will very probably be *followed* by CÆSAR.

Friday.

Rebuttal to "Cæsar" I: "Cato" II

New York Journal, October 11, 1787

To the CITIZENS *of the* STATE *of* NEW-YORK.

> "*Remember, O my friends! the laws, the rights,*
> "*The generous plan of power deliver'd down,*
> "*By your renown'd Forefathers;*
> "*So dearly bought, the price of so much blood!*
> "*O let it never perish in your hands!*
> "*But piously transmit it to your children.*"

The object of my last address to you was to engage your dispassionate consideration of the new Fœderal government; to caution you against precipitancy in the adoption of it; to recommend a correction of its errors, if it contained any; to hint to you the danger of an easy perversion of some of its powers; to solicit you to separate yourselves from party, and to be independent of and uninfluenced by any in your principles of politics: and, that address was closed with a promise of future observations on the same subject which should be justified by reason and truth. Here I intended to have rested the introduction, but a writer under the signature of CÆSAR, in Mr. Childs's paper of the 1st instant, who treats you with passion, insult, and threat has anticipated those observations which would otherwise have remained in silence until a future period. It would be criminal in me to hesitate a moment to appear as your advocate in so interesting a cause, and to resist the influence of such doctrines as this Cæsar holds.—I shall take no other cognizance of his remarks on the *questionable* shape of my future, or the *equivocal* appearance of my past reflections, than to declare, that in my past I did not mean to be misunderstood (for Cæsar himself declares, that it is obviously the language of distrust) and that in my future there will not be the semblance of doubt. But, what is the language of Cæsar—he redicules your prerogative, power, and majesty—he talks of this *proferred constitution* as the tender mercy of a benevolent sovereign to deluded subjects, or, as his tyrant name-sake, of his proferred grace to the virtuous Cato:—he shuts the door of free deliberation and discussion, and declares, that you must receive this government in manner and form as it is *proferred*—that you cannot revise nor amend it, and lastly, to close the scene, he insinuates, that it will be more healthy for you that the American Fabius should be induced to accept of the presidency of this new government than that, in case you do not acquiesce, he should be solicited to command an army to impose it on you. Is not your indignation roused at this absolute, imperious stile?—For what did you open the veins of your citizens and expend their treasure?—For what did you throw off the yoke of Britain and call yourselves independent?—Was it from a disposition fond of change, or to procure new masters?—if those were your motives, you have your reward before you—go,—retire into silent obscurity, and kiss the rod that scourges you—bury the prospects you had in store, that you and your posterity would participate in the blessings of freedom, and the employments of your country—let the rich and insolent alone be your rulers—perhaps you are designed by providence as an emphatic evidence of the mutability of human affairs, to have the shew of happiness only, that your misery may seem the sharper, and if so, you must submit. But, if you had nobler views, and you are not designed by heaven as an example—are you now to be derided and insulted?—is the power of thinking, on the only subject important to you, to be taken away? and if per chance you should happen to dissent from Cæsar, are you to have Cæsar's principles crammed down your throats with an army?—God forbid!

In democratic republics the people collectively are considered as the sovereign—all legislative, judicial, and executive power, is inherent in and derived from them. As a people, your power and authority have sanctioned and established the present government—your executive, legislative, and judicial acknowledge it by their public acts—you are again solicited to sanction and establish the future one—yet this Cæsar mocks your dignity and laughs at the majesty of the people.

Cæsar, with his usual dogmatism, enquires, if I had talents to throw light on the subject of legislation, why did I not offer them when the Convention was in session?—he is answered in a moment—I thought with him and you, that the wisdom of America, in that Convention, was drawn as it were to a Focus—I placed an unbounded confidence in some of the characters who were members of it, from the services they had rendered their country, without adverting to the ambitious and interested views of others. I was willingly led to expect a model of perfection and security that would have astonished the world. Therefore, to have offered observation, on the subject of legislation, under these impressions, would have discovered no less arrogance than Cæsar. The Convention too, when in session, shut their doors to the observations of the community, and their members were under an obligation of secrecy—Nothing transpired—to have suggested remarks on unknown and anticipated principles would have been like a man groping in the dark, and folly in the extreme. I confess, however, I have been disappointed, and Cæsar is candid enough to make the same declaration, for he thinks it *might* have been more perfect.

But to call in dispute, at this time, and in the manner Cæsar does, the right of free deliberation on this subject, is like a man's propounding a question to another, and telling him, at the same time, that if he does not answer agreeable to the opinion of the propounder, he will exert force to make him of the same sentiment:—to exemplify this, it will be necessary to give you a short history of the rise and progress of the Convention, and the conduct of Congress thereon. The states in Congress suggested, that the articles of confederation had provided for making alterations in the confedcration —that there were defects therein, and as a mean to remedy which, a Convention of delegates, appointed by the different states, was resolved expedient to be held for the sole and express purpose of revising it, and reporting to Congress and the different legislatures such alterations and provisions therein as should (when agreed to in Congress and confirmed by the several states) render the fœderal constitution adequate to the exigencies of government. This resolution is sent to the different states, and the legislature of this state, with others, appoint, in conformity thereto, delegates for the purpose, and in the words mentioned in that resolve, as by the resolution of Congress, and the concurrent resolutions of the senate and assembly of this state, subjoined, will appear. For the sole and express purpose aforesaid a Convention of delegates is formed at Philadelphia:—what have they done? have they revised the confederation, and has Congress agreed to their report?—neither is the fact.—This Convention have exceeded the authority given to them, and have transmitted to Congress a new political fabric, essentially and fundamentally distinct and different from it, in which the different states do not retain separately their sovereignty and independency, united by a confederated league—but one entire sovereignty—a consolidation of them into one government—in which new provisions and powers are not made and vested in Congress, but in an assembly, senate, and president, who are not known in the articles of confederation.—Congress, without agreeing to, or approving of, this system *proferred* by the Convention, have sent it to the different legislatures, not for their confirmation, but to submit it to the people; not in conformity to their own resolution, but in conformity to the resolution of the Convention made and provided in that case. Was it then, from the face of the foregoing facts, the intention of Congress, and of this and the other states, that the essence of our present national government should be annihilated, or that it should be retained and only had an increase of substantial necessary power? Congress, sensible of this latter principle, and that the Convention had taken on themselves a power which neither they nor the other states had a right to delegate to them, and that they could not agree to, and approve of this consolidated system, nor the states confirm it—have been silent on its character; and though many have dwelt on their unanimity, it is no less than the unanimity of opinion that it originated in an assumption of power, which your voice alone can sanctify. This new government, therefore, founded in usurpation, is referred to your opinion as the origin of power not heretofore delegated, and, to this end, the exercise of the prerogative of free examination is essentially necessary; and yet you are unhesitatingly to acquiesce, and if you do not, the American Fabius, if we may believe Cæsar, is to command an army to impose it. It is not my view to rouse your passions, I only wish to excite you to, and assist you in, a cool and deliberate discussion of the subject, to urge you to behave like sensible freemen. Think, speak, act, and assert your opinions and rights—let the same good sense govern you with respect to the adoption of a future system for the administration of your public affairs that influenced you in the formation of the present.—Hereafter I do not intend to be diverted by either Cæsar, or any other—My object is to take up this new form of national government—compare it with the experience and the opinions of the most sensible and approved political authors—and to shew, that its principles, and the exercise of them, will be dangerous to your liberty and happiness.

James Madison to George Washington

New York, September 30, 1787

I found on my arrival here that certain ideas unfavorable to the Act of the Convention which had created difficulties in that body, had made their way into Congress. They were patronised chiefly by Mr. R.H.L. and Mr. Dane of Massts. It was first urged that as the new Constitution was more than an Alteration of the Articles of Confederation under which Congress acted, and even subverted these articles altogether, there was a Constitutional impropriety in their taking any positive agency in the work. The answer given was that the Resolution of Congress in Feby. had recommended the Convention as the best mean of obtaining a firm *national Government*; that as the powers of the Convention were defined by their Commissions in nearly the same terms with the powers of Congress given by the Confederation on the subject of alterations, Congress were not more restrained from acceding to the new plan, than the Convention were from proposing it. If the plan was within the powers of the Convention it was within those of Congress; if beyond those powers, the same necessity which justified the Convention would justify Congress; and a failure of Congress to Concur in what was done, would imply either that the Convention had done wrong in exceeding their powers, or that the Government proposed was in itself liable to insuperable objections; that such an inference would be the more natural, as Congress had never scrupled to recommend measures foreign to their constitutional functions, whenever the public good seemed to require it; and had in several instances, particularly in the establishment of the new Western Governments, exercised assumed powers of a very high & delicate nature, under motives infinitely less urgent than the present state of our affairs, if any faith were due to the representations made by Congress themselves, ecchoed by 12 States in the Union, and confirmed by the general voice of the people.—An attempt was made in the next place by R.H.L. to amend the Act of the Convention before it should go forth from Congress. He proposed a bill of Rights—provision for juries in civil cases & several other things corresponding with the ideas of Col. M—He was supported by Mr. Me— Smith of this State. It was contended that Congress had an undoubted right to insert amendments, and that it was their duty to make use of it in a case where the essential guards of liberty had been omitted. On the other side the right of Congress was not denied, but the inexpediency of exerting it was urged on the following grounds. 1. that every circumstance indicated that the introduction of Congress as a party to the reform, was intended by the States merely as a matter of form and respect. 2. that it was evident from the contradictory objections which had been expressed by the different members who had animadverted on the plan, that a discussion of its merits would consume much time, without producing agreement even among its adversaries. 3. that it was clearly the intention of the States that the plan to be proposed should be the act of the Convention with the assent of Congress, which could not be the case, if alterations were made, the Convention being no longer in existence to adopt them. 4. that as the Act of the Convention, when altered would instantly become the mere act of Congress, and must be proposed by them as such, and of course be addressed to the Legislatures, not conventions of the States, and require the ratification of thirteen instead of nine States, and as the unaltered act would go forth to the States directly from the Convention under the auspices of that Body—Some States might ratify one & some the other of the plans, and confusion & disappointment be the least evils that could ensue. These difficulties which at one time threatened a serious division in Congs. and popular alterations with the yeas & nays on the journals, were at length fortunately terminated by the following Resolution— "Congress having recd. the Report of the Convention lately assembled in Philada., Resold. *unanimously* that the said Report, with the Resolutions & letter accompanying the same, be transmitted to the several Legislatures, in order to be submitted to a Convention of Delegates chosen in each State by the people thereof, in conformity to the Resolves of the Convention made & provided in that case." Eleven States were present, the absent ones R.I. & Maryland. A more direct approbation would have been of advantage in this & some other States, where stress will be laid on the agency of Congress in the matter, and a handle taken by adversaries of any ambiguity on the subject. With regard to Virginia & some other States, reserve on the part of Congress will do no injury. The circumstance of unanimity must be favorable every where.

The general voice of this City seems to espouse the new Constitution. It is supposed nevertheless that the party in power is strongly opposed to it. The Country must finally decide, the sense of which is as yet wholly unknown. As far as Boston & Connecticut has been heard from, the first impression seems to be auspicious. I am waiting with anxiety for the eccho from Virginia but with very faint hopes of its corresponding with my wishes.

P.S. a small packet of the size of 2 vol. 8o. addressed to you lately came to my hands with books of my own from France. Genl. Pinkney has been so good as to take charge of them. He set out yesterday for S. Carolina & means to call at Mount Vernon.

Richard Henry Lee to George Mason

New York, October 1, 1787

I have waited until now to answer your favor of Septr. 18th from Philadelphia, that I might inform you how the Convention plan of Government was entertained by Congress. Your prediction of what would happen in Congress was exactly verified—It was with us, as with you, this or nothing; & this urged with a most extreme intemperance—The greatness of the powers given & the multitude of Places to be created, produces a coalition of Monarchy men, Military Men, Aristocrats, and Drones whose noise, impudence & zeal exceeds all belief—Whilst the Commercial plunder of the South stimulates the rapacious Trader. In this state of things, the Patriot voice is raised in vain for such changes and securities as Reason and Experience prove to be necessary against the encroachments of power upon the indispensable rights of human nature. Upon due consideration of the Constitution under which we now Act, some of us were clearly of opinion that the 13th article of the Confederation precluded us from giving an opinion concerning a plan subversive of the present system and eventually forming a New Confederacy of Nine instead of 13 States. The contrary doctrine was asserted with great violence in expectation of the strong majority with which they might send it forward under terms of much approbation. Having procured an opinion that Congress was qualified to consider, to amend, to approve or disapprove— the next game was to determine that tho a right to amend existed, it would be highly inexpediant to exercise that right, but merely to transmit it with respectful marks of approbation—In this state of things I availed myself of the Right to amend, & moved the Amendments copy of which I send herewith & called the ayes & nays to fix them on the journal—This greatly alarmed the Majority & vexed them extremely—for the plan is, to push the business on with great dispatch, & with as little opposition as possible; that it may be adopted before it has stood the test of Reflection & due examination—They found it most eligible at last to transmit it merely, without approving or disapproving; provided nothing but the transmission should appear on the Journal— This compromise was settled and they took the opportunity of inserting the word *Unanimously*, which applied only to simple transmission, hoping to have it mistaken for an Unanimous approbation of the thing—It states that Congress having Received the Constitution unanimously transmit it &c.—It is certain that no Approbation was given—This constitution has a great many excellent Regulations in it and if it could be reasonably amended would be a fine System—As it is, I think 'tis past doubt, that if it should be established, either a tyranny will result from it, or it will be prevented by a Civil war—I am clearly of opinion with you that it should be sent back with amendments Reasonable and Assent to it with held until such amendments are admitted—You are well acquainted with Mr. Stone & others of influence in Maryland—I think it will be a great point to get Maryld. & Virginia to join in the plan of Amendments & return it with them—If you are in correspondence with our Chancelor Pendleton it will be of much use to furnish him with the objections, and if he approves our plan, his opinion will have great weight with our Convention, and I am told that his relation to Judge Pendleton of South Carolina has decided weight in that State & that he is sensible & independent— How important will it be then to procure his union with our plan, which might probably be the case, if our Chancelor was to write largely & pressingly to him on the subject; that if possible it may be amended there also. It is certainly the most rash and violent proceeding in the world to cram thus suddenly into Men a business of such infinite Moment to the happiness of Millions. One of your letters will go by the Packet, and one by a Merchant Ship. My compliments if you please to Your Lady & to the young Ladies & Gentlemen

Suppose when the Assembly recommended a Convention to consider this new Constitution they were to use some words like these—It is earnestly recommended to the good people of Virginia to send their most wise & honest Men to this Convention that it may undergo the most intense consideration before a plan shall be without amendments adopted that admits of abuses being practised by which the best interests of this Country may be injured and Civil Liberty greatly endanger'd.—This might perhaps give a decided Tone to the business—

Please to send my Son Ludwell a Copy of the Amendments proposed by me to the new Constitution sent herewith—

Rev. James Madison to James Madison

c. October 1, 1787

I was greatly indebted to you for your Favour by Mr. Blair.
I do not know whether I should be justifiable in making any
observations upon what I suppose, may be considered as the
Chef d'œuvre of continental Wisdom. Yet to you I will
venture a few.—The general Plan for a federal Government,
that is, ye Idea of a Division of ye Power of ye united States
into three Branches, is certainly most wise & fortunately conceived. If any Circumstance can induce a ready Compliance
amongst ye Bulk of ye People of America, with federal Measures, it will be, that they flow from a Form of Govt. to wch.
they are so strongly attached, and in wch. they will consider
themselves as justly represented. This was a great Point
gained, & I think may promise a Durability to the Union,
wch. it's warmest Friends scarce hoped for. I doubt not also,
but under the new Constitution, national Faith, a great &
important Object certainly, will be effectually restored—I
doubt not but it will be ye Means of giving Stability &
Vigour to ye State Govts., & prevent those frequent Vacilla-
tions from one iniquitous or absurd Scheme to another, wch.
has destroyed all Confidence amongst Individuals. It will
create ye Habit of Obedience to the Laws, & give them that
Energy wch. is unquestionably essential to a free Govt.—
These & many other happy Effects, may reasonably be expected from a Govt. so wisely conceived in it's general Plan,
& wch. must possess Vigour & Energy sufft. to execute the
Measures adopted under it—With all these Advantages then,
ought any one to raise Objections against it? Should we not,
under the Consciousness, that it is impossible to form a Constitution agreable to ye Minds of all, rest satisfied with this,
wch. promises so many Advantages? I confess, under these
Considerations, I feel myself as a Citizen, strongly inclined to

add my Voice of Approbation to that of ye many who so highly extol ye Labours of ye Convention.—But, I must also declare that it appears to me to possess a Defect, wch. perhaps threatens Ruin to Republicanism itself. Is it not my Friend, received by all, as a political Axiom—that it is essential to every free Govt., that ye Legislative & executive Departments should be entirely distinct & independent? Upon what Principle was it, that this fundamental Axiom in Politics has been disregarded—since, it appears almost a Certainty, that where those Powers are united, Govt. must soon degenerate into a Tyranny.—A sole Executive, who may be for Life, with almost a Negative upon ye Legislature;—ye Senate, a principal Part of ye Legislature, wch may also be for Life, occasionally a Part of ye Executive—these appear to me to be most unfortunate Features in the new Constn. I may be deceived, but they present to my Mind so strong a Stamp of Monarchy or Aristocracy, that, I think, many Generations would not pass before one or other wd. spring from the new Constn. provided, it were to continue in its present Form. It is true it may be amended—the only Danger is in permitting that to be received, wch may never be amended—It is not ye Quantum of Power, proposed to be given to ye new Congress, of wch. I complain. I am persuaded, if it be wisely exercised, it must be most happy for ye States both individually & collectively, to have a Power equally restrictive & energetic lodged in ye supreme Council—I only complain & lament that that Power was not distributed in such a Manner as might preserve, instead of, threaten Destruction to ye Liberties of America.

Yet, after all, so greatly do I respect ye Framers of that Constitution, so beneficial must it's Effects be in many important Instances—that, I shd. rejoice to see it adopted,—*provided*, it's Continuance was limited to a certain fixed Period—revivable or not, as ye States might determine. We shd. then feel it's good Effects, without running ye Risque of ye Dangers it seems to threaten.—But I fear I shall only tire you with my Observations—So Adieu.

"*Southwark*"

Pennsylvania Gazetteer (Philadelphia), October 3, 1787

Messrs. HALL & SELLERS,

The following comparison of the characters and conduct of the tories, and the antifœderal junto, may serve to shew that they are animals of the same breed, and should be equally despised by all true friends to their country.

1st. The principal tories were *officers of government*—so are the antifœderalists: Witness, Messrs. Bryan, J. B. Smith, Nicholson, &c.

2d. The tories said, the *time* for opposing Great-Britain was not come—the antifœderalists say, "more time for considering the new government is necessary, than is allowed by the resolves of the Assembly."

3d. The tories said our grievances were all *imaginary* in the year 1776—the antifœderalists say the same of the defects of our present governments, and of the universal distress and complaints of the people.

4th. The tories tried to prevent an appeal to the people, by calling a Convention to form a new government in Pennsylvania in the year 1776—the antifœderalists are trying every art to prevent an *appeal to the people*, to alter the present constitution of Pennsylvania, so as to make it fit the new fœderal government.

5th. The tories despised the proceedings of conventions and town-meetings, and called them nothing but *mobs*—the antifœderalists despise the convention of the United States, and call the petitions and resolves of our citizens the acts of mobs and fools.

6th. The tories thought they alone were inspired with a knowledge in government—the antifœderalists entertain the same exalted opinion of themselves.

7th. The tories were deserted by all their friends who were honest—the antifœderalists, in like manner, have been deserted by the party which they once led, and now stand alone, like four or five dead and rotten trees in an old field.

It is to be hoped the antifœderalists will end their career, as some of the tories, whom they resemble in so many particulars, have done, viz.—in poverty—in exile—or in that state of *dependance* which is inflicted upon treason in Pennsylvania.

"Centinel" [Samuel Bryan] I

Independent Gazetteer (Philadelphia), October 5, 1787

MR. OSWALD, *As the Independent Gazetteer seems free for the discussion of all public matters, I expect you will give the following a place in your next.*

TO THE FREEMEN OF PENNSYLVANIA.

Friends, Countrymen and *Fellow Citizens*, Permit one of yourselves to put you in mind of certain *liberties* and *privileges* secured to you by the constitution of this commonwealth, and to beg your serious attention to his uninterested opinion upon the plan of federal government submitted to your consideration, before you surrender these great and valuable privileges up forever. Your present frame of government, secures you to a right to hold yourselves, houses, papers and possessions free from search and seizure, and therefore warrants granted without oaths or affirmations first made, affording sufficient foundation for them, whereby any officer or messenger may be commanded or required to search your houses or seize your persons or property, not particularly described in such warrant, shall not be granted. Your constitution further provides "that in controversies respecting property, and in suits between man and man, the parties have a right *to trial by jury, which ought to be held sacred.*" It also provides and declares, "*that the people have a right of* FREEDOM OF SPEECH, *and of* WRITING *and* PUBLISHING *their sentiments, therefore* THE FREEDOM OF THE PRESS OUGHT NOT TO BE RESTRAINED." The constitution of Pennsylvania is *yet* in existence, *as yet* you have the right to *freedom of speech*, and of *publishing your sentiments.* How long those rights will appertain to you, you yourselves are called upon to say, whether your *houses* shall continue to be your *castles*; whether your *papers*, your *persons* and your *property*, are to be held sacred and free from *general warrants*, you are now to determine. Whether the *trial by jury* is to continue as your birth-right, the freemen of Pennsylvania, nay, of all America, are now called upon to declare.

Without presuming upon my own judgement, I cannot think it an unwarrantable presumption to offer my private opinion, and call upon others for their's; and if I use my pen with the boldness of a freeman, it is because I know that *the liberty of the press yet remains unviolated*, and *juries yet are judges*.

The late Convention have submitted to your consideration a plan of a new federal government—The subject is highly interesting to your future welfare—Whether it be calculated to promote the great ends of civil society, *viz.* the happiness and prosperity of the community; it behoves you well to consider, uninfluenced by the authority of names. Instead of that frenzy of enthusiasm, that has actuated the citizens of Philadelphia, in their approbation of the proposed plan, before it was possible that it could be the result of a rational investigation into its principles; it ought to be dispassionately and deliberately examined, and its own intrinsic merit the only criterion of your patronage. If ever free and unbiassed discussion was proper or necessary, it is on such an occasion.—All the blessings of liberty and the dearest privileges of freemen, are now at stake and dependent on your present conduct. Those who are competent to the task of developing the principles of government, ought to be encouraged to come forward, and thereby the better enable the people to make a proper judgment; for the science of government is so abstruse, that few are able to judge for themselves; without such assistance the people are too apt to yield an implicit assent to the opinions of those characters, whose abilities are held in the highest esteem, and to those in whose integrity and patriotism they can confide; not considering that the love of domination is generally in proportion to talents, abilities, and superior acquirements; and that the men of the greatest purity of intention may be made instruments of despotism in the hands of the *artful and designing*. If it were not for the stability and attachment which time and habit gives to forms of government, it would be in the power of the enlightened and aspiring few, if they should combine, at any time to destroy the best establishments, and even make the people the instruments of their own subjugation.

The late revolution having effaced in a great measure all former habits, and the present institutions are so recent, that their exists not that great reluctance to innovation, so remarkable in old communities, and which accords with reason, for the most comprehensive mind cannot foresee the full operation of material changes on civil polity; it is the genius of the common law to resist innovation.

The wealthy and ambitious, who in every community think they have a right to lord it over their fellow creatures, have availed themselves, very successfully, of this favorable disposition; for the people thus unsettled in their sentiments, have been prepared to accede to any extreme of government; all the distresses and difficulties they experience, proceeding from various causes, have been ascribed to the impotency of the present confederation, and thence they have been led to expect full relief from the adoption of the proposed system of government; and in the other event, immediately ruin and annihilation as a nation. These characters flatter themselves that they have lulled all distrust and jealousy of their new plan, by gaining the concurrence of the two men in whom America has the highest confidence, and now triumphantly exult in the completion of their long meditated schemes of power and aggrandisement. I would be very far from insinuating that the two illustrious personages alluded to, have not the welfare of their country at heart; but that the unsuspecting goodness and zeal of the one, has been imposed on, in a subject of which he must be necessarily inexperienced, from his other arduous engagements; and that the weakness and indecision attendant on old age, has been practised on in the other.

I am fearful that the principles of government inculcated in Mr. Adams's treatise, and enforced in the numerous essays and paragraphs in the news-papers, have misled some well designing members of the late Convention.—But it will appear in the sequel, that the construction of the proposed plan of government is infinitely more extravagant.

I have been anxiously expecting that some enlightened

patriot would, ere this, have taken up the pen to expose the futility, and counteract the baneful tendency of such principles. Mr. Adams's *sine qua non* of a good government is three balancing powers, whose repelling qualities are to produce an equilibrium of interests, and thereby promote the happiness of the whole community. He asserts that the administrators of every government, will ever be actuated by views of private interest and ambition, to the prejudice of the public good; that therefore the only effectual method to secure the rights of the people and promote their welfare, is to create an opposition of interests between the members of two distinct bodies, in the exercise of the powers of government, and balanced by those of a third. This hypothesis supposes human wisdom competent to the task of instituting three co-equal orders in government, and a corresponding weight in the community to enable them respectively to exercise their several parts, and whose views and interests should be so distinct as to prevent a coalition of any two of them for the destruction of the third. Mr. Adams, although he has traced the constitution of every form of government that ever existed, as far as history affords materials, has not been able to adduce a single instance of such a government; he indeed says that the British constitution is such in theory, but this is rather a confirmation that his principles are chimerical and not to be reduced to practice. If such an organization of power were practicable, how long would it continue? not a day—for there is so great a disparity in the talents, wisdom and industry of mankind, that the scale would presently preponderate to one or the other body, and with every accession of power the means of further increase would be greatly extended. The state of society in England is much more favorable to such a scheme of government than that of America. There they have a powerful hereditary nobility, and real distinctions of rank and interests; but even there, for want of that perfect equallity of power and distinction of interests, in the three orders of government, they exist but in name; the only operative and efficient check, upon the conduct of administration, is the sense of the people at large.

Suppose a government could be formed and supported on such principles, would it answer the great purposes of civil society; If the administrators of every government are actuated by views of private interest and ambition, how is the welfare and happiness of the community to be the result of such jarring adverse interests?

Therefore, as different orders in government will not produce the good of the whole, we must recur to other principles. I believe it will be found that the form of government, which holds those entrusted with power, in the greatest responsibility to their constituents, the best calculated for freemen. A republican, or free government, can only exist where the body of the people are virtuous, and where property is pretty equally divided, in such a government the people are the sovereign and their sense or opinion is the criterion of every public measure; for when this ceases to be the case, the nature of the government is changed, and an aristocracy, monarchy or despotism will rise on its ruin. The highest responsibility is to be attained, in a simple struction of government, for the great body of the people never steadily attend to the operations of government, and for want of due information are liable to be imposed on.— If you complicate the plan by various orders, the people will be perplexed and divided in their sentiments about the source of abuses or misconduct, some will impute it to the senate, others to the house of representatives, and so on, that the interposition of the people may be rendered imperfect or perhaps wholly abortive. But if, imitating the constitution of Pennsylvania, you vest all the legislative power in one body of men (separating the executive and judicial) elected for a short period, and necessarily excluded by rotation from permanency, and guarded from precipitancy and surprise by delays imposed on its proceedings, you will create the most perfect responsibility, for then, whenever the people feel a grievance they cannot mistake the authors, and will apply the remedy with certainty and effect, discarding them at the next election. This tie of responsibility will obviate all the dangers apprehended from a single legislature, and will the best secure the rights of the people.

Having premised thus much, I shall now proceed to the examination of the proposed plan of government, and I trust, shall make it appear to the meanest capacity, that it has none of the essential requisites of a free government; that it is neither founded on those balancing restraining powers, recommended by Mr. Adams and attempted in the British constitution, or possessed of that responsibility to its constituents, which, in my opinion, is the only effectual security for the liberties and happiness of the people; but on the contrary, that it is a most daring attempt to establish a despotic aristocracy among freemen, that the world has ever witnessed.

I shall previously consider the extent of the powers intended to be vested in Congress, before I examine the construction of the general government.

It will not be controverted that the legislative is the highest delegated power in government, and that all others are subordinate to it. The celebrated *Montesquieu* establishes it as a maxim, that legislation necessarily follows the power of taxation. By sect. 8, of the first article of the proposed plan of government, "the Congress are to have power to lay and collect taxes, duties, imposts and excises, to pay the debts and provide for the common defence and *general welfare* of the United States; but all duties, imposts and excises, shall be uniform throughout the United States." Now what can be more comprehensive than these words; not content by other sections of this plan, to grant all the great executive powers of a confederation, and a STANDING ARMY IN TIME OF PEACE, that grand engine of oppression, and moreover the absolute controul over the commerce of the United States and all external objects of revenue, such as unlimited imposts upon imports, &c.—they are to be vested with every species of *internal* taxation;—whatever taxes, duties and excises that they may deem requisite for the *general welfare*, may be imposed on the citizens of these states, levied by the officers of Congress, distributed through every district in America; and the collection would be enforced by the standing army, however grievous or improper they may be. The Congress may construe every purpose for which the state legislatures now lay taxes, to be for the *general welfare*, and thereby seize upon every object of revenue.

The judicial power by 1st sect. of article 3 "shall extend to all cases, in law and equity, arising under this constitution, the laws of the United States, and treaties made or which shall be made under their authority; to all cases affecting ambassadors, other public ministers and consuls; to all cases of admiralty and maritime jurisdiction, to controversies to which the United States shall be a party, to controversies between two or more states, between a state and citizens of another state, between citizens of different states, between citizens of the same state claiming lands under grants of different states, and between a state, or the citizens thereof, and foreign states, citizens or subjects."

The judicial power to be vested in one Supreme Court, and in such Inferior Courts as the Congress may from time to time ordain and establish.

The objects of jurisdiction recited above, are so numerous, and the shades of distinction between civil causes are oftentimes so slight, that it is more than probable that the state judicatories would be wholly superceded; for in contests about jurisdiction, the federal court, as the most powerful, would ever prevail. Every person acquainted with the history of the courts in England, knows by what ingenious sophisms they have, at different periods, extended the sphere of their jurisdiction over objects out of the line of their institution, and contrary to their very nature; courts of a criminal jurisdiction obtaining cognizance in civil causes.

To put the omnipotency of Congress over the state government and judicatories out of all doubt, the 6th article ordains that "this constitution and the laws of the United States which shall be made in pursuance thereof, and all treaties made, or which shall be made under the authority of the United States, shall be the *supreme law of the land*, and the judges in every state shall be bound thereby, any thing in the constitution or laws of any state to the contrary notwithstanding."

By these sections the all-prevailing power of taxation, and such extensive legislative and judicial powers are vested in the general government, as must in their operation, necessarily absorb the state legislatures and judicatories; and that such was in the contemplation of the framers of it, will appear from the provision made for such event, in another part of it; (but that, fearful of alarming the people by so great an innovation, they have suffered the forms of the separate governments to remain, as a blind.) By sect. 4th of the 1st article, "the times, places and manner of holding elections for senators and representatives, shall be prescribed in each state by the legislature thereof; *but the Congress may at any time, by law, make or alter such regulations, except as to the place of chusing senators.*" The plain construction of which is, that when the state legislatures drop out of sight, from the necessary operation of this government, then Congress are to provide for the election and appointment of representatives and senators.

If the foregoing be a just comment—if the United States are to be melted down into one empire, it becomes you to consider, whether such a government, however constructed, would be eligible in so extended a territory; and whether it would be practicable, consistent with freedom? It is the opinion of the greatest writers, that a very extensive country cannot be governed on democratical principles, on any other plan, than a confederation of a number of small republics, possessing all the powers of internal government, but united in the management of their foreign and general concerns.

It would not be difficult to prove, that any thing short of despotism, could not bind so great a country under one government; and that whatever plan you might, at the first setting out, establish, it would issue in a despotism.

If one general government could be instituted and maintained on principles of freedom, it would not be so competent to attend to the various local concerns and wants, of every particular district; as well as the peculiar governments, who are nearer the scene, and possessed of superior means of information, besides, if the business of the *whole* union is to be managed by one government, there would not be time. Do we not already see, that the inhabitants in a number of larger states, who are remote from the seat of government, are loudly complaining of the inconveniencies and disadvantages they are subjected to on this account, and that, to enjoy the comforts of local government, they are separating into smaller divisions.

Having taken a review of the powers, I shall now examine the construction of the proposed general government.

Art. I. sect. I. "All legislative powers herein granted shall be vested in a Congress of the United States, which shall consist of a senate and house of representatives." By another section, the president (the principal executive officer) has a conditional controul over their proceedings.

Sect. 2. "The house of representatives shall be composed of members chosen every second year, by the people of the several states. The number of representatives shall not exceed one for every 30,000 inhabitants."

The senate, the other constituent branch of the legislature, is formed by the legislature of each state appointing two senators, for the term of six years.

The executive power by Art. 2, Sec. 1. is to be vested in a president of the United States of America, elected for four years: Sec. 2. gives him "power, by and with the consent of the senate to make treaties, provided two thirds of the senators present concur; and he shall nominate, and by and with the advice and consent of the senate, shall appoint ambassadors, other public ministers and consuls, judges of the Supreme Court, and all other officers of the United States, whose appointments are not herein otherwise provided for, and which shall be established by law, &c." And by another section he has the absolute power of granting reprievs and pardons for treason and all other high crimes and misdemeanors, except in case of impeachment.

The foregoing are the outlines of the plan.

Thus we see, the house of representatives, are on the part of the people to balance the senate, who I suppose will be composed of the *better sort*, the *well born*, &c. The number of the representatives (being only one for every 30,000 inhabitants) appears to be too few, either to communicate the requisite information, of the wants, local circumstances and sentiments of so extensive an empire, or to prevent corruption and undue influence, in the exercise of such great powers; the term for which they are to be chosen, too long to preserve a due dependence and accountability to their constituents; and the mode and places of their election not sufficiently ascertained, for as Congress have the controul over both, they may govern the choice, by ordering the *representatives* of a *whole* state, to be *elected* in *one* place, and that too may be the most *inconvenient*.

The senate, the great efficient body in this plan of government, is constituted on the most unequal principles. The smallest state in the union has equal weight with the great states of Virginia, Massachusetts, or Pennsylvania. — The Senate, besides its legislative functions, has a very considerable share in the Executive; none of the principal appointments to office can be made without its advice and consent. The term and mode of its appointment, will lead to permanency; the members are chosen for six years, the mode is under the controul of Congress, and as there is no exclusion by rotation, they may be continued for life, which, from their extensive means of influence, would follow of course. The President, who would be a mere pageant of state, unless he coincides with the views of the Senate, would either become the head of the aristocratic junto in that body, or its minion; besides, their influence being the most predominant, could the best secure his re-election to office. And from his power of granting pardons, he might skreen from punishment the most treasonable attempts on the liberties of the people, when instigated by the Senate.

From this investigation into the organization of this government, it appears that it is devoid of all responsibility or accountability to the great body of the people, and that so far from being a regular balanced government, it would be in practice a *permanent* ARISTOCRACY.

The framers of it; actuated by the true spirit of such a government, which ever abominates and suppresses all free enquiry and discussion, have made no provision for the *liberty of the press*, that grand *palladium of freedom*, and *scourge of tyrants*; but observed a total silence on that head. It is the opinion of some great writers, that if the liberty of the press, by an institution of religion, or otherwise, could be rendered *sacred*, even in *Turkey*, that despotism would fly before it. And it is worthy of remark, that there is no declaration of personal rights, premised in most free constitutions; and that trial by *jury* in *civil* cases is taken away; for what other construction can be put on the following, viz. Article III. Sect. 2d. "In all cases affecting ambassadors, other public ministers and consuls, and those in which a State shall be party, the Supreme Court shall have *original* jurisdiction. In all the other cases above mentioned, the Supreme Court shall have *appellate* jurisdiction, both as to *law and fact?*" It would be a novelty in jurisprudence, as well as evidently improper to allow an appeal from the verdict of a jury, on the matter of fact; therefore, it implies and allows of a dismission of the jury in civil cases, and especially when it is considered, that jury trial in criminal cases is expresly stipulated for, but not in civil cases.

But our situation is represented to be so *critically* dreadful, that, however reprehensible and exceptionable the proposed plan of government may be, there is no alternative, between the adoption of it and absolute ruin.—My fellow citizens, things are not at that crisis, it is the argument of tyrants; the present distracted state of Europe secures us from injury on that quarter, and as to domestic dissentions, we have not so much to fear from them, as to precipitate us into this form of government, without it is a safe and a proper one. For remember, of all *possible* evils, that of *despotism* is the *worst* and the most to be *dreaded*.

Besides, it cannot be supposed, that the first essay on so difficult a subject, is so well digested, as it ought to be;—if the proposed plan, after a mature deliberation, should meet the approbation of the respective States, the matter will end; but if it should be found to be fraught with dangers and inconveniencies, a future general Convention being in possession of the objections, will be the better enabled to plan a suitable government.

"WHO'S HERE SO BASE, THAT WOULD A BONDMAN BE?
"IF ANY, SPEAK; FOR HIM HAVE I OFFENDED.
"WHO'S HERE SO VILE, THAT WILL NOT LOVE HIS COUNTRY?
"IF ANY, SPEAK; FOR HIM HAVE I OFFENDED."

James Wilson's Speech at a Public Meeting

Philadelphia, October 6, 1787

Mr. Wilson then rose, and delivered a long and eloquent speech upon the principles of the Fœderal Constitution proposed by the late convention. The outlines of this speech we shall endeavour to lay before the public, as tending to reflect great light upon the interesting subject now in general discussion.

Mr. Chairman and Fellow Citizens, Having received the honor of an appointment to represent you in the late convention, it is perhaps, my duty to comply with the request of many gentlemen whose characters and judgments I sincerely respect, and who have urged, that this would be a proper occasion to lay before you any information which will serve to explain and elucidate the principles and arrangements of the constitution, that has been submitted to the consideration of the United States. I confess that I am unprepared for so extensive and so important a disquisition; but the insidious attempts which are clandestinely and industriously made to pervert and destroy the new plan, induce me the more readily to engage in its defence; and the impressions of four months constant attention to the subject, have not been so easily effaced as to leave me without an answer to the objections which have been raised.

It will be proper however, before I enter into the refutation of the charges that are alledged, to mark the leading descrimination between the state constitutions, and the constitution of the United States. When the people established the powers of legislation under their separate governments, they invested their representatives with every right and authority which they did not in explicit terms reserve; and therefore upon

63

every question, respecting the jurisdiction of the house of assembly, if the frame of government is silent, the jurisdiction is efficient and complete. But in delegating fœderal powers, another criterion was necessarily introduced, and the congressional authority is to be collected, not from tacit implication, but from the positive grant expressed in the instrument of union. Hence it is evident, that in the former case every thing which is not reserved is given, but in the latter the reverse of the proposition prevails, and every thing which is not given, is reserved. This distinction being recognized, will furnish an answer to those who think the omission of a bill of rights, a defect in the proposed constitution: for it would have been superfluous and absurd to have stipulated with a fœderal body of our own creation, that we should enjoy those privileges, of which we are not divested either by the intention or the act, that has brought that body into existence. For instance, the liberty of the press, which has been a copious source of declamation and opposition, what controul can proceed from the fœderal government to shackle or destroy that sacred palladium of national freedom? If indeed, a power similar to that which has been granted for the regulation of commerce, had been granted to regulate literary publications, it would have been as necessary to stipulate that the liberty of the press should be preserved inviolate, as that the impost should be general in its operation. With respect likewise to the particular district of ten miles, which is to be made the seat of fœderal government, it will undoubtedly be proper to observe this salutary precaution, as there the legislative power will be exclusively lodged in the president, senate, and house of representatives of the United States. But this could not be an object with the convention, for it must naturally depend upon a future compact, to which the citizens immediately interested will, and ought to be parties; and there is no reason to suspect that so popular a privilege will in that case be neglected. In truth then, the proposed system possesses no influence whatever upon the press, and it would have been merely nugatory to have introduced a formal declaration upon the subject—nay, that very declaration might have been construed to imply that some degree of power was given, since we undertook to define its extent.

Another objection that has been fabricated against the new constitution, is expressed in this disingenuous form—"the trial by jury is abolished in civil cases." I must be excused, my fellow citizens, if upon this point, I take advantage of my professional experience to detect the futility of the assertion. Let it be remembered then, that the business of the Fœderal Convention was not local, but general; not limited to the views and establishments of a single state, but co-extensive with the continent, and comprehending the views and establishments of thirteen independent sovereignties. When therefore, this subject was in discussion, we were involved in difficulties which pressed on all sides, and no precedent could be discovered to direct our course. The cases open to a trial by jury differed in the different states, it was therefore impracticable on that ground to have made a general rule. The want of uniformity would have rendered any reference to the practice of the states idle and useless; and it could not, with any propriety, be said that "the trial by jury shall be as heretofore," since there has never existed any fœderal system of jurisprudence to which the declaration could relate. Besides, it is not in all cases that the trial by jury is adopted in civil questions, for causes depending in courts of admiralty, such as relate to maritime captures, and such as are agitated in courts of equity, do not require the intervention of that tribunal. How then, was the line of discrimination to be drawn? The convention found the task too difficult for them, and they left the business as it stands, in the fullest confidence that no danger could possibly ensue, since the proceedings of the supreme court, are to be regulated by the congress, which is a faithful representation of the people; and the oppression of government is effectually barred, by declaring that in all criminal cases the trial by jury shall be preserved.

This constitution, it has been further urged, is of a pernicious tendency, because it tolerates a standing army in the time of peace.—This has always been a topic of popular declamation; and yet, I do not know a nation in the world, which has not found it necessary and useful to maintain the appearance of strength in a season of the most profound tranquility. Nor is it a novelty with us; for under the present articles of confederation, congress certainly possesses this reprobated power, and the exercise of that power is proved at this moment by her cantonments along the banks of the Ohio. But what would be our national situation were it otherwise? Every principle of policy must be subverted, and the government must declare war, before they are prepared to carry it on. Whatever may be the provocation, however important the object in view, and however necessary dispatch and secrecy may be, still the declaration must precede the preparation, and the enemy will be informed of your intention, not only before you are equipped for an attack, but even before you are fortified for a defence. The consequence is too obvious to require any further delineation, and no man, who regards the dignity and safety of his country, can deny the necessity of a military force, under the controul and with the restrictions which the new constitution provides.

Perhaps there never was a charge made with less reasons than that which predicts the institution of a baneful aristocracy in the fœderal senate. This body branches into two characters, the one legislative, and the other executive. In its legislative character it can effect no purpose, without the cooperation of the house of representatives, and in its executive character, it can accomplish no object, without the concurrence of the president. Thus fettered, I do not know any act which the senate can of itself perform, and such dependance necessarily precludes every idea of influence and superiority. But I will confess that in the organization of this body, a compromise between contending interests is descernible; and when we reflect how various are the laws, commerce, habits, population, and extent of the confederated states, this evidence of mutual concession and accommodation ought rather to command a generous applause, than to excite jealousy and reproach. For my part, my admiration can only be equalled by my astonishment, in beholding so perfect a system, formed from such heterogeneous materials.

The next accusation I shall consider, is that which represents the fœderal constitution as not only calculated, but designedly framed, to reduce the state governments to mere corporations, and eventually to annihilate them. Those who have employed the term corporation upon this occasion, are not perhaps aware of its extent. In common parlance, indeed, it is generally applied to petty associations for the ease and conveniency of a few individuals; but in its enlarged sense, it will comprehend the government of Pennsylvania, the existing union of the states, and even this projected system is nothing more than a formal act of incorporation. But upon what pretence can it be alledged that it was designed to annihilate the state governments? For, I will undertake to prove that upon their existence, depends the existence of the fœderal plan. For this purpose, permit me to call your attention to the manner in which the president, senate, and house of representatives, are proposed to be appointed. The president is to be chosen by electors, nominated in such manner as the legislature of each state may direct; so that if there is no legislature, there can be no electors, and consequently the office of president cannot be supplied. The senate is to be composed of two senators from each state, chosen by the legislature; and therefore if there is no legislature, there can be no senate. The house of representatives, is to be composed of members chosen every second year by the people of the several states, and the electors in each state shall have the qualifications requisite for electors of the most numerous branch of the state legislature,—unless therefore, there is a state legislature, that qualification cannot be ascertained, and the popular branch of the fœderal constitution must likewise be extinct. From this view, then it is evidently absurd to suppose, that the annihilation of the separate governments will result from their union; or, that having that intention, the authors of the new system would have bound their connection with such indissoluble ties. Let me here advert to an arrangement highly advantageous, for you will perceive, without prejudice to the powers of the legislature in the election of senators, the people at large will acquire an additional privilege in returning members to the house of representatives—whereas, by the present confederation, it is the legislature alone that appoints the delegates to Congress.

The power of direct taxation has likewise been treated as an improper delegation to the fœderal government; but when we consider it as the duty of that body to provide for the national safety, to support the dignity of the union, and to discharge the debts contracted upon the collective faith of the states for their common benefit, it must be acknowledged, that those upon whom such important obligations are imposed, ought in justice and in policy to possess every means requisite for a faithful performance of their trust. But why should we be alarmed with visionary evils? I will venture to predict, that the great revenue of the United States must, and always will be raised by impost, for, being at once less obnoxious, and more productive, the interest of the government will be best promoted by the accommodation of the people. Still however, the objects of direct taxation should be within reach in all cases of emergency; and there is no more reason to apprehend oppression in the mode of collecting a revenue from this resource, than in the form of an impost, which, by universal assent, is left to the authority of the fœderal government. In either case, the force of civil institutions will be adequate to the purpose; and the dread of military violence, which has been assiduously disseminated, must eventually prove the mere effusion of a wild imagination, or a factious spirit. But the salutary consequences that must flow from thus enabling the government to receive and support the credit of the union, will afford another answer to the objections upon this ground. The State of Pennsylvania particularly, which has encumbered itself with the assumption of a great proportion of the public debt, will derive considerable relief and advantage; for, as it was the imbecility of the present confederation, which gave rise to the funding law, that law must naturally expire, when a competent and energetic fœderal system shall be substituted—the state will then be discharged from an extraordinary burthen, and the national creditor will find it to be his interest to return to his original security.

After all, my fellow citizens, it is neither extraordinary or unexpected, that the constitution offered to your consideration, should meet with opposition. It is the nature of man to pursue his own interest, in preference to the public good; and I do not mean to make any personal reflection, when I add, that it is the interest of a very numerous, powerful, and respectable body to counteract and destroy the excellent work produced by the late convention. All the offices of government, and all the appointments for the administration of justice and the collection of the public revenue, which are transferred from the individual to the aggregate sovereignty of the states, will necessarily turn the stream of influence and emolument into a new channel. Every person therefore, who either enjoys, or expects to enjoy, a place of profit under the present establishment, will object to the proposed innovation; not, in truth, because it is injurious to the liberties of his country, but because it affects his schemes of wealth and consequence. I will confess indeed, that I am not a blind admirer of this plan of government, and that there are some parts of it, which if my wish had prevailed, would certainly have been altered. But, when I reflect how widely men differ in their opinions, and that every man (and the observation applies likewise to every state) has an equal pretension to assert his own, I am satisfied that any thing nearer to perfection could not have been accomplished. If there are errors, it should be remembered, that the seeds of reformation are sown in the work itself, and the concurrence of two thirds of the congress may at any time introduce alterations and amendments. Regarding it then, in every point of view, with a candid and disinterested mind, I am bold to assert, that it is the best form of government which has ever been offered to the world.

> Mr. Wilson's speech was frequently interrupted with loud and unanimous testimonies of approbation, and the applause which was reiterated at the conclusion, evinced the general sense of its excellence, and the conviction which it had impressed upon every mind.

Reply to Wilson's Speech:
"A Democratic Federalist"

Pennsylvania Herald (Philadelphia), October 17, 1787

The arguments of the Honorable Mr. Wilson, expressed in the speech he made at the state-house on the Saturday preceding the general election (as stated in the Pennsylvania Herald,) although extremely *ingenious* and the best that could be adduced in support of so bad a cause, are yet extremely *futile*, and will not stand the test of investigation.

In the first place, Mr. Wilson pretends to point out a leading discrimination between the State Constitutions, and the Constitution of the United States.—In the former, he says, every power which is not *reserved* is *given*, and in the latter, every power which is not *given* is *reserved*: And this may furnish an answer, he adds, to those who object, that a bill of rights has not been introduced in the proposed Federal Constitution. If this doctrine is true, and since it is the only security that we are to have for our natural rights, it ought at least to have been clearly expressed in the plan of government. The 2d. section of the present articles of confederation says: *Each State retains its sovereignty, freedom and independance,* AND EVERY POWER, JURISDICTION AND RIGHT WHICH IS NOT BY THIS CONFEDERATION EXPRESSLY, DELEGATED TO THE UNITED STATES IN CONGRESS ASSEMBLED.—This declaration (for what purpose I know not) is entirely omitted in the proposed Constitution. And yet there is a material difference between this Constitution and the present confederation, for Congress in the latter are merely an executive body; it has no power to raise money, it has no *judicial jurisdiction*. In the other, on the contrary, the federal rulers are vested with each of the three essential powers of government—their laws are to be *paramount* to the laws of the different States, what then will there be to oppose to their encroachments? Should they ever pretend to tyrannize over the people, their *standing army,* will silence every popular effort, it will be theirs to explain the powers which have been granted to them; Mr. Wilson's distinction will be forgot, denied or explained away, and the liberty of the people will be no more.

It is said in the 2d. section of the 3d. article of the Federal Plan: "The judicial power shall extend to ALL CASES in *law* and *equity*, arising under this constitution." It is very clear that under this clause, the tribunal of the United States, may claim a right to the cognizance of all offences against the *general government*, and *libels* will not probably be excluded. Nay, those offences may be by them construed, or by law declared, *misprision of treason*, an offence which comes literally under their express jurisdiction.—Where is then the safety of our boasted liberty of the press? And in case of a *conflict of jurisdiction* between the courts of the United States, and those of the several Commonwealths, is it not easy to foresee which of the two will obtain the advantage?

Under the enormous power of the new confederation, which extends to the *individuals* as well as to the *States* of America, a thousand means may be devised to destroy effectually the liberty of the press—There is no knowing what corrupt and wicked judges may do in process of time, when they are not restrained by express laws. The case of *John Peter Zenger* of New-York, ought still to be present to our minds, to convince us how displeasing the liberty of the press is to men in high power—At any rate, I lay it down as a general rule, that wherever the powers of a government extend to the lives, the persons, and properties of the subject, all their rights ought to be clearly and expressly defined—otherwise they have but a poor security for their liberties.

The second and most important objection to the federal plan, which Mr. Wilson pretends to be made *in a disingenuous form*, is the entire *abolition of the trial by jury in civil cases*. It seems to me that Mr. Wilson's pretended answer, is much more *disingenuous* than the objection itself, which I maintain to be strictly founded in fact. He says "that the cases open to trial by jury differing in the different States, it was therefore impracticable to have made a general rule." This answer is extremely futile, because a reference might easily have been made to the *common law of England*, which obtains through

every State, and cases in the maritime and civil law courts
would of course have been excepted. I must also directly contradict Mr. Wilson when he asserts that there is no trial by
jury in the courts of chancery—It cannot be unknown to a
man of his high professional learning, that whenever a difference arises about a matter of fact in the courts of equity in
America or England, the fact is sent down to the courts of
common law to be tried by a jury, and it is what the lawyers
call a *feigned issue*. This method will be impracticable under
the proposed form of judicial jurisdiction for the United
States.

But setting aside the equivocal answers of Mr. Wilson, I
have it in my power to prove that under the proposed Federal
Constitution, *the trial of facts in civil cases by a jury of the
Vicinage* is entirely and effectually abolished, and will be absolutely impracticable. I wish the learned gentleman had explained to us what is meant by the *appellate* jurisdiction as to
law and *fact* which is vested in the superior court of the
United States? As he has not thought proper to do it, I shall
endeavour to explain it to my fellow citizens, regretting at the
same time that it has not been done by a man whose abilities
are so much superior to mine. The word *appeal*, if I understand it right, in its proper legal signification includes the *fact*
as well as the *law*, and precludes every idea of a trial by
jury—It is a word of *foreign growth*, and is only known in
England and America in those courts which are governed by
the civil or ecclesiastical law of the *Romans*. Those courts have
always been considered in England as a grievance, and have
all been established by the usurpations of the *ecclesiastical* over
the *civil* power. It is well known that the courts of chancery in
England were formerly entirely in the hands of *ecclesiastics*,
who took advantage of the strict forms of the common law,
to introduce a foreign mode of jurisprudence under the specious name of *Equity*. Pennsylvania, the freest of the American
States has wisely rejected this establishment, and knows not
even the name of a court of chancery—And in fact, there can
not be any thing more absurd than a distinction between LAW
and EQUITY. It might perhaps have suited those barbarous
times when the law of England, like almost every other
science, was perplexed with quibbles and *Aristotelian* dis-

tinctions, but it would be shameful to keep it up in these more enlightened days. At any rate, it seems to me that there is much more *equity* in a trial by jury, than in an appellate jurisdiction from the fact.

An *appeal* therefore is a thing unknown to the common law. Instead of an appeal from facts, it admits of a second, or even third trial by different juries, and mistakes in points of *law*, are rectified by superior courts in the form of a *writ of error*—and to a mere common lawyer, unskilled in the forms of the *civil law* courts, the words *appeal from law and fact*, are mere nonsense, and unintelligible absurdity.

But even supposing that the superior court of the United States had the authority to try facts by *juries of the vicinage*, it would be impossible for them to carry it into execution. It is well known that the supreme courts of the different states, at stated times in every year, go round the different counties of their respective states to try issues of fact, which is called *riding the circuits*. Now, how is it possible that the supreme continental court, which we will suppose to consist at most of five or six judges, can travel at least twice in every year, through the different counties of America, from New-Hampshire to Kentuckey, and from Kentuckey to Georgia, to try facts by juries of the vicinage. Common sense will not admit of such a supposition. I am therefore right in my assertion, that *trial by jury in civil cases, is, by the proposed constitution entirely done away, and effectually abolished.*

Let us now attend to the consequences of this enormous innovation, and daring encroachment, on the liberties of the citizens. Setting aside the oppression, injustice, and partiality that may take place in the trial of questions of property between man and man, we will attend to one single case, which is well worth our consideration. Let us remember that all cases arising under the new constitution, and all matters between *citizens of different states*, are to be submitted to the new jurisdiction. Suppose therefore, that the military officers of congress, by a wanton abuse of power, imprison the free citizens of America, suppose the excise or revenue officers (as we find in Clayton's Reports, page 44 Ward's case)—that a constable, having a warrant to search for stolen goods, pulled down the clothes of a bed in which there was a woman, and searched under her shift,—suppose, I say, that they commit similar, or greater indignities, in such cases a trial by jury would be our safest resource, heavy damages would at once punish the offender, and deter others from committing the same: but what satisfaction can we expect from a lordly court of justice, always ready to protect the officers of government against the weak and helpless citizen, and who will perhaps sit at the distance of many hundred miles from the place where the outrage was committed?—What refuge shall we then have to shelter us from the iron hand of arbitrary power?—O! my fellow citizens, think of this while it is yet time, and never consent to part with the glorious privilege of trial by jury, but with your lives.

But Mr. Wilson has not stopped here—he has told us that a STANDING ARMY, that *great support of tyrants*, not only was not dangerous, but that it was *absolutely necessary.*—O! my much respected fellow citizens! and are you then reduced to such a degree of insensibility, that assertions like these will not rouse your warmest resentment and indignation? Are we then, after the experience of past ages, and the result of the enquiries of the best and most celebrated patriots have taught us to dread a standing army above all earthly evils, are we then to go over all the thread-bare common place arguments that have been used without success by the advocates of tyranny, and which have been for a long time past so gloriously refuted! Read the excellent *Burgh* in his political disquisitions, on this hackneyed subject, and then say, whether you think that a standing army is necessary in a free country? Even Mr. Hume, an *aristocratical* writer, has candidly confessed, that *an army is a mortal distemper in a government, of which it must at last inevitably perish* (2d Burgh 349) and the Earl of Oxford (*Oxford* the friend of France, and the *pretender*, the attainted *Oxford*) said in the British parliament, in a speech on the mutiny bill; that "while he had breath, he would speak for the liberties of his country, and against courts martial and a standing army in peace as dangerous to the constitution," (*Ibid* page 455). Such were the speeches even of the enemies to liberty, when Britain had yet a right to be called free. But, says Mr. Wilson, "It is necessary to maintain the appearance of strength even in times of the most profound tranquillity."

And what is this more than a thread-bare hackneyed argument, which has been answered over and over in different ages, and does not deserve even the smallest consideration?— Had we a standing army, when the British invaded our peaceful shores? Was it a standing army that gained the battles of Lexington, and Bunker's Hill, and took the ill fated Burgoyne? Is not a well regulated militia sufficient for every purpose of internal defence? And which of you, my fellow citizens, is afraid of any invasion from foreign powers, that our brave militia would not be able immediately to repel?

Mr. Wilson says that *he does not know of any nation in the world which has not found it necessary to maintain the appearance of strength in the season of the most profound tranquility*; if by this *equivocal* assertion, he has meant to say that there is no nation in the world without *a standing army in time of peace*, he has been mistaken. I need only adduce the example of Switzerland, which, like us, is a *republic*, whose *thirteen* cantons, like our thirteen States, are under a *federal government*, and which besides is surrounded by the most powerful nations in Europe, all jealous of its liberty and prosperity: And yet that nation has preserved its freedom for many ages, with the sole help of a militia, and has never been known to have a standing army, except when in actual war.—Why should we not follow so glorious an example, and are we less able to defend our liberty without an army, than that brave but small nation, which with its militia alone has hitherto defied all Europe?

It is said likewise, that *a standing army is not a new thing in America*—*Congress even at this moment have a standing army on foot.*—I answer, that *precedent* is not *principle*—Congress have no right to keep up a standing army in time of peace: —If they do, it is an infringement of the liberties of the people—*wrong* can never be justified by *wrong*—but it is well known that the assertion is groundless, the few troops that are on the banks of the Ohio, were sent for the express purpose of repelling the invasion of the savages, and protecting the inhabitants of the frontiers.—It is our misfortune that we are never at peace with those inhuman butchers of their species, and while they remain in our neighbourhood, we are always, with respect to them, in a state of war—as soon as the danger is over, there is no doubt but Congress will disband their handful of soldiers: — it is therefore not true, that Congress keep up a standing army in a time of peace and profound security.

The objection to the enormous powers of the President and Senate is not the least important of all, but it requires a full discussion and ample investigation—I shall take another opportunity of laying before the public my observations upon this subject, as well as upon every other part of the new constitution. At present I shall only observe, that it is an established principle in America, which pervades every one of our State Constitutions, that *the legislative and executive powers ought to be kept forever separate and distinct from each other*, and yet in this new constitution we find there are TWO EXECUTIVE BRANCHES, each of which has *more or less controul over the proceedings of the legislature*. This is an innovation of the most dangerous kind upon every known principle of government, and it will be easy for me to convince my fellow citizens that it will, in the first place, create a *Venetian* aristocracy, and, in the end, produce an *absolute monarchy*.

Thus I have endeavoured to answer to the best of my abilities, the principal arguments of Mr. Wilson—I have written this in haste, in a short interval of leisure from my usual avocations. I have only traced the outlines of the subject, and I hope some abler hand will second my honest endeavours.

Reply to Wilson's Speech: "Centinel" [Samuel Bryan] II

Freeman's Journal (Philadelphia), October 24, 1787

To the PEOPLE of PENNSYLVANIA.

FRIENDS, COUNTRYMEN, *and* FELLOW-CITIZENS, As long as the liberty of the press continues unviolated, and the people have the right of expressing and publishing their sentiments upon every public measure, it is next to impossible to enslave a free nation. The state of society must be very corrupt and base indeed, when the people in possession of such a monitor as the press, can be induced to exchange the heavenborn blessings of liberty for the galling chains of despotism.—Men of an aspiring and tyrannical disposition, sensible of this truth, have ever been inimical to the press, and have considered the shackling of it, as the first step towards the accomplishment of their hateful domination, and the entire suppression of all liberty of public discussion, as necessary to its support.—For even a standing army, that grand engine of oppression, if it were as numerous as the abilities of any nation could maintain, would not be equal to the purposes of despotism over an enlightened people.

The abolition of that grand palladium of freedom, the liberty of the press, in the proposed plan of government, and the conduct of its authors, and patrons, is a striking exemplification of these observations. The reason assigned for the omission of a *bill of rights*, securing the *liberty of the press*, and *other invaluable personal rights*, is an insult on the understanding of the people.

The injunction of secrecy imposed on the members of the late Convention during their deliberations, was obviously dictated by the genius of Aristocracy; it was deemed impolitic to unfold the principles of the intended government to the people, as this would have frustrated the object in view.

The projectors of the new plan, supposed that an ex parte

discussion of the subject, was more likely to obtain unanimity in the Convention; which would give it such a sanction in the public opinion, as to banish all distrust, and lead the people into an implicit adoption of it without examination.

The greatest minds are forcibly impressed by the immediate circumstances with which they are connected; the particular sphere men move in, the prevailing sentiments of those they converse with, have an insensible and irresistible influence on the wisest and best of mankind; so that when we consider the abilities, talents, ingenuity and consummate address of a number of the members of the late Convention, whose principles are despotic, can we be surprised that men of the best intentions have been misled in the difficult science of government? Is it derogating from the character of the *illustrious and highly revered* WASHINGTON, to suppose him fallible on a subject that must be in a great measure novel to him?—As a patriotic hero, he stands unequalled in the annals of time.

The new plan was accordingly ushered to the public with such a splendor of names, as inspired the most unlimited confidence; the people were disposed to receive upon trust, without any examination on their part, what would have proved either a *blessing* or a *curse* to them and their posterity.—What astonishing infatuation! to stake their happiness on the wisdom and integrity of any set of men! In matters of infinitely smaller concern, the dictates of prudence are not disregarded! The celebrated *Montesquieu*, in his Spirit of Laws, says, that "slavery is ever preceded by sleep." And again, in his account of the rise and fall of the Roman Empire, page 97, "That it may be advanced as a general rule, that in a free State, whenever a perfect calm is visible, the spirit of liberty no longer subsists." And Mr. *Dickinson*, in his Farmer's Letters, No. XI. lays it down as a maxim, that "A perpetual jealousy respecting liberty is absolutely requisite in all free States."

"Happy are the men, and happy the people, who grow wise by the misfortunes of others. Earnestly, my dear countrymen, do I beseech the author of all good gifts, that you may grow wise in this manner, and I beg leave to recommend to you in general, as the best method of obtaining this wisdom, diligently to study the histories of other countries. You will there find all the arts, that can possibly be practised by cunning rulers, or false patriots among yourselves, so fully delineated, that changing names, the account would serve for your own times."

A *few* citizens of Philadelphia (too few, for the honour of human nature) who had the wisdom to think *consideration* ought to precede *approbation*, and the fortitude to avow that they would take time to judge for themselves on so momentous an occasion, were stigmatized as enemies to their country; as monsters, whose existence ought not to be suffered, and the destruction of them and their houses recommended, as meritorious. — The authors of the new plan, conscious that it would not stand the test of enlightened patriotism, tyrannically endeavoured to preclude all investigation. — If their views were laudable; if they were honest, — the contrary would have been their conduct, they would have invited the freest discussion. Whatever specious reasons may be assigned for secrecy during the framing of the plan, no good one can exist, for leading the people blindfolded into the implicit adoption of it. Such an attempt does not augur the public good — It carries on the face of it an intention to juggle the people out of their liberties.

The virtuous and spirited exertions of a few patriots, have at length roused the people from their fatal infatuation to a due sense of the importance of the measure before them. The glare and fascination of names is rapidly abating, and the subject begins to be canvassed on its own merits; and so serious and general has been the impression of the objections urged against the new plan, on the minds of the people, that its advocates, finding mere declamation and scurrility will no longer avail, are reluctantly driven to defend it on the ground of argument. Mr. *Wilson*, one of the deputies of this State in the late Convention, has found it necessary to come forward. From so able a lawyer, and so profound a politician, what might not be expected, if this act of Convention be the heavenly dispensation which some represent it. Its divinity would certainly be illustrated by one of the principal instruments of the Revelation; for this gentleman has that transcendent merit! — But if, on the other hand, this able advocate has failed to vindicate it from the objections of its adversaries, must we not consider it is as the production of *frail* and *interested* men.

Mr. *Wilson* has recourse to the most flimsey sophistry in his attempt to refute the charge that the new plan of general government will supersede and render powerless the state governments. His quibble upon the term *Corporation*, as sometimes equivalent to communities which possess sovereignty, is unworthy of him. The same comparison in the case of the British parliament assuming to tax the colonies, is made in the Xth of the Farmer's Letters, and was not misunderstood in 1768 by any. He says that the existence of the proposed federal plan depends on the existence of the State governments, as the senators are to be appointed by the several legislatures, who are also to nominate the electors who chuse the President of the United States; and that hence all fears of the several States being melted down into one empire, are groundless and imaginary.—But who is so dull as not to comprehend, that the *semblance* and *forms* of an ancient establishment, may remain, after the *reality* is gone.—*Augustus*, by the aid of a great army, assumed despotic power, and notwithstanding this, we find even under Tiberius, Caligula and Nero, princes who disgraced human nature by their excesses, the shadows of the ancient constitution held up to amuse the people. The senate sat as formerly; consuls, tribunes of the people, censors and other officers were annually chosen as before, and the forms of republican government continued. Yet all this was in *appearance* only.—Every *senatus consultum* was dictated by him or his ministers, and every Roman found himself constrained to submit in all things to the despot.

Mr. *Wilson* asks, "What controul can proceed from the federal government to shackle or destroy that *sacred palladium* of national freedom, the *liberty of the press*?" What!—Cannot Congress, when possessed of the immense authority proposed to be devolved, restrain the printers, and put them under regulation.—Recollect that the omnipotence of the federal legislature over the State establishments is recognized by a special article, viz.—"that this Constitution, and the laws of the United States which shall be made in pursuance thereof, and all treaties made, or which shall be made, under the authority of the United States, shall be the *supreme law* of the land; and the judges in every State shall be bound thereby, any thing in the *Constitutions* or laws of any State to the contrary notwithstanding."—After such a declaration, what security does the *Constitutions* of the several States afford for the *liberty of the press and other invaluable personal rights*, not provided for by the new plan?—Does not this sweeping clause subject every thing to the controul of Congress?

In the plan of Confederation of 1778, now existing, it was thought proper by Article the 2d, to declare that "each State retains its sovereignty, freedom and independence, and every power, jurisdiction and right, which is not by this Confederation expressly delegated to the United States in Congress assembled." *Positive* grant was not *then* thought sufficiently descriptive and restraining upon Congress, and the omission of such a declaration *now*, when such great devolutions of power are proposed, manifests the design of reducing the several States to shadows. But Mr. Wilson tells you, that every right and power not specially granted to Congress is considered as withheld. How does this appear? Is this principle established by the proper authority? Has the Convention made such a stipulation? By no means. Quite the reverse; the *laws* of Congress are to be "the *supreme law* of the land, any thing in the *Constitutions* or laws of any State to the contrary notwithstanding;" and consequently, would be *paramount* to all *State* authorities. The lust of power is so universal, that a speculative unascertained rule of construction would be a *poor* security for the liberties of the people.

Such a body as the intended Congress, unless particularly inhibited and restrained, must grasp at omnipotence, and before long swallow up the Legislative, the Executive, and the Judicial powers of the several States.

In addition to the respectable authorities quoted in my first number, to shew that the right of *taxation* includes all the powers of government, I beg leave to adduce the Farmer's Letters, see particularly letter 9th, in which Mr. Dickinson has clearly proved, that if the British Parliament assumed the power of taxing the colonies, *internally*, as well as *externally*, and it should be submitted to, the several colony legislatures would soon become contemptible, and before long fall into disuse.—Nothing, says he, would be left for them to do, higher than to frame bye-laws for empounding of cattle or the yoking of hogs.

By the proposed plan, there are divers cases of judicial authority to be given to the courts of the United States, besides the two mentioned by Mr. *Wilson.*—In maritime causes about property, jury trial has not been usual; but in suits in *equity*, with all due deference to Mr. *Wilson*'s professional abilities, (which he calls to his aid) jury trial, as to facts, is in full exercise. Will this jurisperitus say that if the question in equity should be, did *John Doe* make a will, that the chancellor of England would decide upon it? He well knows that in this case, there being no mode of jury trial before the chancellor, the question would be referred to the court of king's bench for discussion according to the common law, and when the judge in equity should receive the *verdict*, the fact so established, could never be re-examined or controverted. Maritime causes and those appertaining to a court of equity, are, however, but *two* of the many and extensive subjects of federal cognizance mentioned in the plan. This jurisdiction will embrace all suits arising under the laws of impost, excise and other revenue of the United States. In England if goods be seized, if a ship be prosecuted for non-compliance with, or breach of the laws of the customs, or those for regulating trade, in the court of exchequer, the claimant is secured of the transcendent privilege of Englishmen, *trial by a jury of his peers.* Why not in the United States of America? This jurisdiction also goes to all cases under the laws of the United States, that is to say, under all statutes and ordinances of Congress. How far this may extend, it is easy to foresee; for upon the decay of the state powers of legislation, in consequence of the loss of the *purse strings*, it will be found necessary for the federal legislature to make laws upon every subject of legislation. Hence the state courts of justice, like the barony and hundred courts of England, will be eclipsed and gradually fall into disuse.

The jurisdiction of the federal court goes, likewise, to the laws to be created by treaties, made by the President and Senate, (a species of legislation) with other nations; "to all cases affecting foreign ministers and consuls; to controversies wherein the United States shall be a party; to controversies between citizens of different states," as when an inhabitant of *New-York* has a demand on an inhabitant of *New-Jersey.*—This last is a very invidious jurisdiction, implying an improper distrust of the impartiality and justice of the tribunals of the states. It will include all legal debates between foreigners in Britain, or elsewhere, and the people of this country.—A reason hath been assigned for it, viz. "That large tracts of land, in neighbouring states, are claimed under royal or other grants, disputed by the states where the lands lie, so that justice cannot be expected from the state tribunals."—Suppose it were proper indeed to provide for such case, why include all cases, and for all time to come? Demands as to land for 21 years would have satisfied this. A London merchant shall come to America, and sue for his supposed debt, and the citizen of this country shall be deprived of jury trial, and subjected to an appeal (tho' nothing but the *fact* is disputed) to a court 500 or 1000 miles from home; when if this American has a claim upon an inhabitant of England, his adversary is secured of the privilege of jury trial.—This jurisdiction goes also to controversies between any state and its citizens; which, though *probably* not intended, may hereafter be set up as a ground to divest the states, severally, of the trial of criminals; inasmuch as every charge of felony or misdemeanour, is a controversy between the state and a citizen of the same: that is to say, the state is plaintiff and the party accused is defendant in the prosecution. In all doubts about jurisprudence, as was observed before, the paramount courts of Congress will decide, and the judges of the state, being *sub graviore lege*, under the paramount law, must acquiesce.

Mr. *Wilson* says, that it would have been impracticable to have made a general rule for jury trial in the civil cases assigned to the federal judiciary, because of the want of uniformity in the mode of jury trial, as practised by the several states. This objection proves too much, and therefore amounts to nothing. If it precludes the mode of common law in civil cases, it certainly does in criminal. Yet in these we are told "the oppression of government is effectually barred by declaring that in all criminal cases *trial by jury* shall be preserved." Astonishing, that provision could not be made for a jury in civil controversies, of 12 men, whose verdict should be unanimous, *to be taken from the vicinage*; a precaution which is omitted as to trial of crimes, which may be any where in the state within which they have been committed. So that an inhabitant of *Kentucky* may be tried for treason at *Richmond*.

The abolition of jury trial in civil cases, is the more considerable, as at length the courts of Congress will supersede the state courts, when such mode of trial will fall into disuse among the people of the United States.

The northern nations of the European continent, have all lost this invaluable privilege: *Sweden*, the last of them, by the artifices of the *aristocratic* senate, which depressed the king and reduced the house of commons to insignificance. But the nation a few years ago, preferring the absolute authority of a monarch to the *vexatious* domination of the *well-born* few, an end was suddenly put to their power.

"The policy of this right of juries, (says judge Blackstone) to decide upon *fact*, is founded on this: That if the power of judging were entirely trusted with the magistrates, or any select body of men, named by the executive authority, their decisions, in spite of their own natural integrity, would have a biass towards those of their own rank and dignity; for it is not to be expected, that the *few* should be attentive to the rights of the *many*. This therefore preserves in the hands of the people, that share which they ought to have in the administration of justice, and prevents the encroachments of the more powerful and wealthy citizens."

The attempt of governor *Colden*, of New-York, before the revolution to re-examine the *facts* and re-consider the *damages*, in the case of *Forsey* against *Cunningham*, produced about the year 1764, a flame of patriotic and successful opposition, that will not be easily forgotten.

To manage the various and extensive judicial authority, proposed to be vested in Congress, there will be one or more inferior courts immediately requisite in each state; and laws and regulations must be forthwith provided to direct the judges—here is a wide door for inconvenience to enter. Contracts made under the acts of the states respectively, will come before courts acting under new laws and new modes of proceeding, not thought of when they were entered into.—An inhabitant of Pennsylvania residing at Pittsburgh, finds the goods of his debtor, who resides in Virginia, within the reach of his attachment; but no writ can be had to authorise the marshal, sheriff, or other officer of Congress, to seize the property, about to be removed, nearer than 200 miles: suppose that at Carlisle, for instance, such a writ may be had, mean while the object escapes. Or if an inferior court, whose judges have ample salaries, be established in every county, would not the expence be enormous? Every reader can extend in his imagination, the instances of difficulty which would proceed from this needless interference with the judicial rights of the separate states, and which as much as any other circumstance in the new plan, implies that the dissolution of their forms of government is designed.

Mr. *Wilson* skips very lightly over the danger apprehended from the standing army allowed by the new plan. This grand machine of power and oppression, may be made a fatal instrument to overturn the public liberties, especially as the funds to support the troops may be granted for *two* years, whereas in Britain, the grants ever since the revolution in 1688, have been *from year to year*. A standing army with regular provision of pay and contingencies, would afford a strong temptation to some ambitious man to step up into the throne, and to seize absolute power. The keeping on foot a hired military force *in time of peace*, ought not to be gone into, unless *two thirds* of the members of the federal legislature agree to the necessity of the measure, and adjust the numbers employed. Surely Mr. *Wilson* is not serious when he adduces the instance of the troops now stationed on the Ohio, as a proof of the propriety of a standing army.—They are a mere occasional armament for the purpose of restraining divers hostile tribes of savages. It is contended that under the present confederation, Congress possess the power of raising armies at pleasure; but the opportunity which the states severally have of withholding the supplies necessary to keep these armies on foot, is a sufficient check on the *present* Congress.

Mr. *Wilson* asserts, that never was charge made with less reason, than that which predicts the institution of a *baneful aristocracy* in the federal Senate.—In my first number, I stated that this body would be a very unequal representation of the several states, that the members being appointed for the long term of six years, and there being no exclusion by rotation, they might be continued for life, which would follow of course from their extensive means of influence, and that possessing a considerable share in the *executive* as well as *legislative*, it would become a *permanent aristocracy*, and swallow up the other orders in the government.

That these fears are not imaginary, a knowledge of the history of other nations, where the powers of government have been injudiciously placed, will fully demonstrate. Mr. *Wilson* says, "the senate branches into two characters; the one legislative and the other executive. In its legislative character it can effect no purpose, without the co-operation of the house of representatives, and in its executive character it can accomplish no object without the concurrence of the president. Thus fettered, I do not know any act which the senate can of itself perform, and such dependence necessarily precludes every idea of influence and superiority." This I confess is very specious, but experience demonstrates, that checks in government, unless accompanied with *adequate* power and *independently* placed, prove *merely nominal*, and will be *inoperative*. Is it probable, that the president of the United States, limited as he is in power, and dependent on the will of the senate, in appointments to office, will either have the *firmness* or *inclination* to exercise his prerogative of a conditional controul upon the proceedings of that body, however injurious they may be to the public welfare: it will be his interest to coincide with the views of the senate, and thus become the head of the aristocratic junto. The king of England is a constituent part in the legislature, but although an hereditary monarch, in possession of the whole executive power, including the unrestrained appointment to offices, and an immense revenue, enjoys but in *name* the prerogative of a negative upon the parliament. Even the king of England, circumstanced as he is, has not dared to exercise it for near a century past. The check of the house of representatives upon the senate will likewise be rendered nugatory for want of due weight in the democratic branch, and from their constitution *they* may become so *independent* of the *people* as to be indifferent of its interests: nay as Congress would have the controul over the mode and

place of their election, by ordering the representatives of a
whole state to be elected at *one* place, and that too the most
inconvenient, the ruling power may govern the *choice*, and thus
the house of representatives may be composed of the *creatures*
of the senate. Still the *semblance* of checks, may remain but
without *operation*.

This mixture of the legislative and executive moreover
highly tends to corruption. The chief improvement in government, in modern times, has been the compleat separation of
the great distinctions of power; placing the *legislative* in different hands from those which hold the *executive*; and again
severing the *judicial* part from the ordinary *administrative*.
"When the legislative and executive powers (says Montesquieu) are united in the same person, or in the same body of
magistrates, there can be no liberty."

Mr. *Wilson* confesses himself, not satisfied with the organization of the federal senate, and apologizes for it, by alledging
a sort of compromise. It is well known, that some members of
convention, apprized of the mischiefs of such a compound of
authority, proposed to assign the supreme executive powers
to the president and a small council, made personally responsible for every appointment to office, or other act, by having
their opinions recorded; and that without the concurrence of
the majority of the quorum of this council, the president
should not be capable of taking any step. Such a check upon
the chief magistrate would admirably secure the power of pardoning, now proposed to be exercised by the president alone,
from abuse. For as it is placed he may shelter the traitors
whom he himself or his coadjutors in the senate, have excited
to plot against the liberties of the nation.

The delegation of the power of taxation to Congress, as far
as duties on imported commodities, has not been objected to.
But to extend this to excises, and every species of internal
taxation, would necessarily require so many ordinances of
Congress, affecting the body of the people, as would perpetually interfere with the State laws and personal concerns of
the people. This alone would directly tend to annihilate the
particular governments; for the people fatigued with the
operations of two masters would be apt to rid themselves of
the weaker. But we are cautioned against being alarmed with

imaginary evils, for Mr. *Wilson* has predicted that the great revenue of the United States, will be raised by impost. Is there any ground for this? Will the impost supply the sums necessary to pay the interest and principal of the foreign loan, to defray the great additional expence of the new constitution; for the policy of the new government will lead it to institute numerous and lucrative civil offices, to extend its influence and provide for the swarms of expectants; (the people having in fact no controul upon its disbursements) and to afford pay and support for the proposed standing army, that darling and long wished for object of the *well-born* of America; and which, if we may judge from the principles of the intended government, will be no trifling establishment, for cantonments of troops in every district of America, will be necessary to compel the submission of the people to the arbitrary dictates of the ruling powers? I say will the impost be adequate? By no means.—To answer these there must be excises and other indirect duties imposed, and as land taxes will operate too equally to be agreeable to the wealthy aristocracy in the senate who will be possessed of the government, *poll taxes* will be substituted as provided for in the new plan; for the doctrine then will be, *that slaves ought to pay for wearing their heads*.

As the taxes necessary for these purposes, will drain your pockets of every penny, what is to become of that virtuous and meritorious class of citizens the public creditors. However well disposed the people of the United States may be to do them justice, it would not be in their power; and, *after waiting year after year*, without prospect of the payment of the interest or principal of the debt, they will be constrained to sacrifice their certificates in the purchase of waste lands in the far distant wilds of the western territory.

From the foregoing illustration of the powers proposed to be devolved to Congress, it is evident, that the general government would necessarily annihilate the particular governments, and that the security of the personal rights of the people by the state constitutions is superseded and destroyed; hence results the necessity of such security being provided for by a bill of rights to be inserted in the new plan of federal government. What excuse can we then make for the omission of this grand palladium, this barrier between *liberty* and *oppression*. For universal experience demonstrates the necessity of the most express declarations and restrictions, to protect the rights and liberties of mankind, from the silent, powerful and ever active conspiracy of those who govern.

The new plan, it is true, does propose to secure the people of the benefit of personal liberty by the *habeas corpus*; and trial by jury for all crimes, except in case of impeachment: but there is no declaration, that all men have a natural and unalienable right to worship Almighty God, according to the dictates of their own consciences and understanding; and that no man ought, or of right can be compelled to attend any religious worship, or erect or support any place of worship, or maintain any ministry, contrary to, or against his own free will and consent; and that no authority can or ought to be vested in, or assumed by any power whatever, that shall in any case interfere with, or in any manner controul, the right of conscience in the free exercise of religious worship: that the trial by jury in civil causes as well as criminal, and the modes prescribed by the common law for safety of life in criminal prosecutions shall be held sacred; that the requiring of excessive bail, imposing of excessive fines and cruel and unusual punishments be forbidden; that monopolies in trade or arts, other than to authors of books or inventors of useful arts, for a reasonable time, ought not to be suffered; that the right of the people to assemble peaceably for the purpose of consulting about public matters, and petitioning or remonstrating to the federal legislature ought not to be prevented; that *the liberty of the press be held sacred*; that the people have a right to hold themselves, their houses, papers and possessions free from search or seizure; and that therefore warrants without oaths or affirmations first made, affording a sufficient foundation for them, and whereby any officer or messenger may be commanded or required to search suspected places, or to seize any person or his property, not particularly described, are contrary to that right and ought not to be granted; and that standing armies in time of peace are dangerous to liberty, and ought not to be permitted but when absolutely necessary; all which is omitted to be done in the proposed government.

But Mr. *Wilson* says, the new plan does not arrogate perfection, for it provides a mode of alteration and correction, if found necessary. This is one among the numerous deceptions attempted on this occasion. True, there is a mode prescribed for this purpose. But it is barely possible that amendments may be made. The fascination of power must first cease, the nature of mankind undergo a revolution, that is not to be expected on this side of eternity. For to effect this (Art. 6.) it is provided, that if *two thirds* of both houses of the federal legislature shall propose them; or when two thirds of the several states by their legislatures, shall apply for them, the federal assembly shall call a convention for proposing amendments, which when ratified by three fourths of the state legislatures, or conventions, as Congress shall see best, shall controul and alter the proposed confederation. Does history abound with examples of a voluntary relinquishment of power, however injurious to the community? No; it would require a general and successful rising of the people to effect any thing of this nature.—This provision therefore is mere sound.

The opposition to the new plan (says Mr. Wilson) proceeds from interested men, *viz.* the officers of the state governments. He had before denied that the proposed transfer of powers to Congress would annihilate the state governments. But he here lays aside the masque, and avows the fact. For, the truth of the charge against *them* must entirely rest on such consequence of the new plan. For if the state establishments are to remain unimpaired, why should officers peculiarly connected with them, be interested to oppose the adoption of the new plan? Except the collector of the impost, judge of the admiralty, and the collectors of excise (none of whom have been reckoned of the opposition) they would otherwise have nothing to apprehend.—But the charge is unworthy and may with more propriety be retorted on the expectants of office and emolument under the intended government.

The opposition is not so partial and interested as Mr. *Wilson* asserts. It consists of a respectable yeomanry throughout the union, of characters far removed above the reach of his unsupported assertions. It comprises many worthy members of the late convention, and a majority of the present Congress, for a motion made in that honorable body, for their *approbation* and *recommendation* of the new plan, was after two days animated discussion, prudently withdrawn by its advocates, and a simple *transmission** of the plan to the several states could only be obtained; yet this has been palmed upon the people as the approbation of Congress; and to strengthen the deception, the bells of the city of Philadelphia were rung for a whole day.

Are Mr. W——n, and many of his coadjutors in the late C———n, the disinterested patriots they would have us believe? Is their conduct any recommendation of their plan of government? View them the foremost and loudest on the floor of Congress, in our Assembly, at town meetings, in sounding its eulogiums:—View them preventing investigation and discussion, and in the most despotic manner endeavouring to compel its adoption by the people, with such precipitancy as to preclude the possibility of a due consideration, and then say whether the motives of these men can be pure.

My fellow citizens, such false detestable *patriots* in every nation, have led their blind confiding country, shouting their applauses, into the jaws of *despotism* and *ruin*. May the wisdom and virtue of the people of America, save them from the usual fate of nations.

*Upon the last motion being made, those who had strenuously and successfully opposed Congress giving any countenance of approbation or recommendation to this system of oppression, said,—"We have no objection to transmit the new plan of government to the several states, that they may have an opportunity of judging for themselves on so momentous a subject." Whereupon it was unanimously agreed to, in the following words, *viz.* "Congress having received the report of the Convention lately assembled in Philadelphia, *resolved unanimously*, That the said report, with the resolutions and letter accompanying the same, be *transmitted* to the several legislatures, in order to be submitted to a convention of delegates, chosen in each state by the people thereof, in conformity to the resolves of the Convention, made and provided in that case."

Reply to Wilson's Speech: *"Cincinnatus"* [*Arthur Lee*] I

New York Journal, November 1, 1787

MR. GREENLEAF, A speech made to the citizens of Philadelphia, and said to be by Mr. WILSON, appears to me to abound with sophistry, so dangerous, as to require refutation. If we adopt the new Constitution, let us at least understand it. Whether it deserves adoption or not, we can only determine by a full examination of it, so as clearly to discern what it is that we are so loudly, I had almost said, indecently called upon to receive. Such an examination is the object of the papers which I am to entreat you to lay before the public, in answer to Mr. Wilson, and under the signature of——Cincinnatus.

Sir, You have had the graciousness, Sir, to come forward as the defender and panegyrist of the plan of a new Constitution, of which you was one of the framers. If the defence you have thought proper to set up, and the explanations you have been pleased to give, should be found, upon a full and fair examination, to be fallacious or inadequate; I am not without hope, that candor, of which no gentleman talks more, will render you a convert to the opinion, that some material parts of the proposed Constitution are so constructed—that a *monstrous aristocracy springing from it, must necessarily swallow up the democratic rights of the union, and sacrifice the liberties of the people to the power and domination of a few*.

If your defence of this new plan of power, has, as you say, been matured by four months constant meditation upon it, and is yet so very weak, as I trust will appear, men will begin to think, that—the thing itself is indefensible. Upon a subject so momentous, the public has a right to the sentiments of every individual that will reason: I therefore do not think any apology necessary for appearing in print; and I hope to avoid, at least, the indiscriminate censure which you have, with so much candor and liberality, thrown on those who will not worship *your idol*—"that they are industriously endeavouring to prevent and destroy it, by insidious and clandestine attempts." Give me leave just to suggest, that perhaps these clandestine attempts might have been owing to the terror of *your mob*, which so nobly endeavoured to prevent all freedom of action and of speech. The *reptile Doctor* who was employed to blow the trumpet of persecution, would have answered the public reasoning of an opponent, by hounding on him the rage of a deluded populace.

It was to such men, and under such impressions, that you made the speech which I am now to examine; no wonder then that it was received with loud and unanimous testamonies of their approbation. They were vociferating through you the panegyric of their own intemperate opinions.

Your first attempt is to apologize for so very obvious a defect as—the omission of a declaration of rights. This apology consists in a very ingenious discovery; that in the state constitutions, whatever is not reserved is given; but in the congressional constitution, whatever is not given, is reserved. This has more the quaintness of a conundrum, than the dignity of an argument. The conventions that made the state and the general constitutions, sprang from the same source, were delegated for the same purpose—that is, for framing rules by which we should be governed, and ascertaining those powers which it was necessary to vest in our rulers. Where then is this distinction to be found, but in your assumption? Is it in the powers given to the members of convention? no—Is it in the constitution? not a word of it:—And yet on this play of words, this dictum of yours, this distinction without a difference, you would persuade us to rest our most essential rights. I trust, however, that the good sense of this free people cannot be so easily imposed on by professional figments. The confederation, in its very outset, declares—that what is not expressly given, is reserved. This constitution makes no such reservation. The presumption therefore is, that the framers of the proposed constitution, did not mean to subject it to the same exception.

You instance, Sir, the liberty of the press; which you would persuade us, is in *no* danger, though not secured, because there is no express power granted to regulate literary publications. But you surely know, Sir, that where general powers are expressly granted, the particular ones comprehended within them, must also be granted. For instance, the proposed Congress are empowered—to define and punish offences against the law of nations—mark well, Sir, if you please—to *define* and punish. Will you, will any one say, can any one even think that does not comprehend a power to define and declare all publications from the press against the conduct of government, in making treaties, or in any other foreign transactions, an offence against the law of nations? If there should ever be an influential president, or arbitrary senate, who do not choose that their transactions with foreign powers should be discussed or examined in the public prints, they will easily find pretexts to prevail upon the other branch to concur with them, in restraining what it may please them to call—the licentiousness of the press. And this may be, even without the concurrence of the representative of the people; because the president and senate are empowered to make treaties, and these treaties are declared the supreme law of the land.

What use they will make of this power, is not now the question. Certain it is, that such power is given, and that power is not restrained by any declaration—that the liberty of the press, which even you term, the sacred palladium of national freedom, shall be forever free and inviolable. I have proved that the power of restraining the press, is necessarily involved in the unlimited power of defining offences, or of making treaties, which are to be the supreme law of the land. You acknowledge, that it is not expressly excepted, and consequently it is at the mercy of the powers to be created by this constitution.

Let us suppose then, that what has happened, may happen again: That a patriotic printer, like Peter Zenger, should incur the resentment of our new rulers, by publishing to the world,

transactions which they wish to conceal. If he should be prosecuted, if his judges should be as desirous of punishing him,
at all events, as the judges were to punish Peter Zenger, what
would his innocence or his virtue avail him? This constitution
is so admirably framed for tyranny, that, by clear construction, the judges might put the verdict of a jury out of the
question. Among the cases in which the court is to have appellate jurisdiction, are—controversies, to which the United
States are a party:—In this appellate jurisdiction, the judges
are to determine, *both law and fact*. That is, the court is both
judge and jury. The attorney general then would have only to
move a question of law in the court below, to ground an
appeal to the supreme judicature, and the printer would be
delivered up to the mercy of his judges. Peter Zenger's case
will teach us, what mercy he might expect. Thus, if the president, vice-president, or any officer, or favorite of state, should
be censured in print, he might effectually deprive the printer,
or author, of his trial by jury, and subject him to something,
that will probably very much resemble the—Star Chamber of
former times. The freedom of the press, the sacred palladium
of public liberty, would be pulled down;—all useful knowledge on the conduct of government would be withheld from
the people—the press would become subservient to the purposes of bad and arbitrary rulers, and imposition, not information, would be its object.

The printers would do well, to publish the proceedings of
the judges, in Peter Zenger's case—they would do well to
publish lord Mansfield's conduct in, the King against Woodfall;—that the public mind may be properly warned of the
consequences of agreeing to a constitution, which provides
no security for the freedom of the press, and leaves it controversial at least—whether in matter of libels against any of our
intended rulers; the printer would even have the security of
trial by jury. Yet it was the jury only, that saved Zenger, it was
a jury only, that saved Woodfall, it can only be a jury that will
save any future printer from the fangs of power.

Had you, Mr. Wilson, who are so unmerciful against what
you are pleased to call, the disingenuous conduct of those
who dislike the constitution; had you been ingenuous enough
to have stated this fairly to our fellow citizens; had you said

to them—gentlemen, it is true, that the freedom of the press is not provided for; it is true, that it may be restrained at pleasure, by our proposed rulers; it is true, that a printer sued for a libel, would not be tried by a jury; all this is true, nay, worse than this is also true; but then it is all necessary to what I think, *the best form of government that has ever been offered the world.*

To have stated these truths, would at least have been acting like an honest man; and if it did not procure you such unanimous testimonies of approbation, what you would have received, would have been *merited.*

But you choose to shew our fellow citizens, nothing but what would flatter and mislead them. You exhibited, that by a rush-light only, which, to dissipate its darkness, required the full force of the meridian sun. When the people are fully apprized of the chains you have prepared for them, if they choose to put them on, you have nothing to answer for. If they choose to be tenants at will of their liberties, by the new constitution; instead of having their freehold in them, secured by a declaration of rights; I can only lament it. There was a time, when our fellow citizens were told, in the words of Sir Edward Coke—For a man to be tenant at will of his liberty, I can never agree to it—*Etiam si* Dominus *non sit molestus, tamen miserremum est,* posse, *se vebit*—Though a despot may not act tyrannically; yet it is dreadful to think, that if he *will,* he *may.* Perhaps you may also remember, Sir, that our fellow citizens were then warned against those—"smooth words, with which the most dreadful designs may be glossed over." You have given us a lively comment on your own text. You have varnished over the iron trap that is prepared, and *bated with some illustrious names, to catch the liberties of the people.*

Reply to Wilson's Speech: "An Officer of the Late Continental Army" [William Findley?]

Independent Gazetteer (Philadelphia), November 6, 1787

MR. OSWALD,

By inserting the following in your impartial paper, you will oblige yours, &c.

To the Citizens of Philadelphia.

Friends, Countrymen, Brethren and Fellow Citizens,

The important day is drawing near when you are to elect delegates to represent you in a Convention, on the result of whose deliberations will depend, in a great measure, your future happiness.

This convention is to determine whether or not the commonwealth of Pennsylvania shall adopt the plan of government proposed by the late convention of delegates from the different states, which sat in this city.

With a heart full of anxiety for the preservation of your dearest rights, I presume to address you on this important occasion—In the name of sacred liberty, dearer to us than our property and our lives, I request your most earnest attention.

The proposed plan of continental government is now fully known to you. You have read it I trust with the attention it deserves—You have heard the objections that have been made to it—You have heard the answers to these objections.

If you have attended to the whole with candor and un-biassed minds, as becomes men that are possessed and deserving of freedom, you must have been alarmed at the result of your observations. Notwithstanding the splendor of names which has attended the publication of the new constitution, notwithstanding the sophistry and vain reasonings that have been urged to support its principles; alas! you must at least have concluded that great men are not always infallible, and that patriotism itself may be led into essential errors.

The objections that have been made to the new constitution, are these:

1. It is not merely (as it ought to be) a CONFEDERATION of STATES, but a GOVERNMENT of INDIVIDUALS.

2. The powers of Congress extend to the *lives*, the *liberties* and the *property* of every citizen.

3. The *sovereignty* of the different states is *ipso facto* destroyed in its most essential parts.

4. What remains of it will only tend to create violent dissentions between the state governments and the Congress, and terminate in the ruin of the one or the other.

5. The consequence must therefore be, either that the *union* of the states will be destroyed by a violent struggle, or that their sovereignty will be swallowed up by silent encroachments into a universal aristocracy; because it is clear, that if two different *sovereign powers* have a co-equal command over the *purses* of the citizens, they will struggle for the spoils, and the weakest will be in the end obliged to yield to the efforts of the strongest.

6. Congress being possessed of these immense powers, the liberties of the states and of the people are not secured by a bill or DECLARATION OF RIGHTS.

7. The *sovereignty* of the states is not expressly reserved, the *form* only, and not the SUBSTANCE of their government, is guaranteed to them by express words.

8. TRIAL BY JURY, that sacred bulwark of liberty, is ABOLISHED IN CIVIL CASES, and Mr. W——, one of the convention, has told you, that not being able to agree as to the FORM of establishing this point, they have left you deprived of the SUBSTANCE. Here are his own words—*The subject was involved in difficulties. The convention found the task* TOO DIFFICULT *for them, and left the business as it stands.*

9. THE LIBERTY OF THE PRESS is not secured, and the powers of congress are fully adequate to its destruction, as they are to have the trial of *libels*, or *pretended libels* against the United States, and may by a cursed abominable STAMP ACT (as the *Bowdoin administration* has done in Massachusetts) pre-

clude you effectually from all means of information. *Mr. W—— has given you no answer to these arguments.*

10. Congress have the power of keeping up a STANDING ARMY in time of peace, and Mr. W—— has told you THAT IT WAS NECESSARY.

11. The LEGISLATIVE and EXECUTIVE powers are not kept separate as every one of the American constitutions declares they ought to be; but they are mixed in a manner entirely novel and unknown, even to the constitution of Great Britain; because,

12. In England the king only, has a *nominal negative* over the proceedings of the legislature, which he has NEVER DARED TO EXERCISE since the days of *King William,* whereas by the new constitution, both the *president general* and the *senate* TWO EXECUTIVE BRANCHES OF GOVERNMENT, have that negative, and are intended to *support each other in the exercise of it.*

13. The representation of the lower house is too small, consisting only of 65 members.

14. That of the *senate* is so small that it renders its extensive powers extremely dangerous: it is to consist only of 26 members, two-thirds of whom must concur to conclude any *treaty or alliance* with foreign powers: Now we will suppose that five of them are absent, sick, dead, or unable to attend, *twenty-one* will remain, and eight of these (*one-third,* and *one* over) may prevent the conclusion of any treaty, even the most favorable to America. Here will be a fine field for the intrigues and even the *bribery* and *corruption* of European powers.

15. The most important branches of the EXECUTIVE DEPARTMENT are to be put into the hands of a *single magistrate,* who will be in fact an ELECTIVE KING. The MILITARY, the land and naval forces are to be entirely at his disposal, and therefore:

16. Should the *senate,* by the intrigues of foreign powers, become devoted to foreign influence, as was the case of late in *Sweden,* the people will be obliged, as the *Swedes* have been, to seek their refuge in the arms of the *monarch* or PRESIDENT GENERAL.

17. ROTATION, that noble prerogative of liberty, is entirely

excluded from the new system of government, and great men may and probably will be continued in office during their lives.

18. ANNUAL ELECTIONS are abolished, and the people are not to re-assume their rights until the expiration of *two, four* and *six* years.

19. Congress are to have the power of fixing the *time, place* and *manner* of holding elections, so as to keep them forever subjected to their influence.

20. The importation of slaves is not to be prohibited until the year 1808, and SLAVERY will probably resume its empire in Pennsylvania.

21. The MILITIA is to be under the immediate command of congress, and men *conscientiously scrupulous of bearing arms*, may be compelled to perform military duty.

22. The new government will be EXPENSIVE beyond any we have ever experienced, the *judicial* department alone, with its concomitant train of *judges, justices, chancellors, clerks, sheriffs, coroners, escheators, state attornies and solicitors, constables, &c.* in every state and in every country in each state, will be a burden beyond the utmost abilities of the people to bear, and upon the whole.

23. A government partaking of MONARCHY and aristocracy will be fully and firmly established, and liberty will be but a name to adorn the *short* historic page of the halcyon days of America.

These, my countrymen, are the objections that have been made to the new proposed system of government; and if you read the system itself with attention, you will find them all to be founded in truth. But what have you been told in answer? I pass over the sophistry of Mr. W——, in his equivocal speech at the state house. His pretended arguments have been echoed and re-echoed by every retailer of politics, and *victoriously* refuted by several patriotic pens. Indeed if you read this famous speech in a cool dispassionate moment, you will find it to contain no more than a train of pitiful sophistry and evasions, unworthy of the man who spoke them. I have taken notice of some of them in stating the objections, and they must, I am sure, have excited your *pity* and *indignation*. Mr. W—— is a man of sense, learning and extensive information, unfortunately for him he has never sought the more solid fame of *patriotism*. During the late war he narrowly escaped the effects of popular rage, and the people seldom arm themselves against a citizen in vain. The whole tenor of his political conduct has always been strongly tainted with the spirit of *high aristocracy*, he has never been known to join in a truly popular measure, and his talents have ever been devoted to the patrician interest. His lofty carriage indicates the lofty mind that animates him, a mind able to conceive and perform great things, but which unfortunately can see nothing great out of the pale of power and worldly grandeur; despising what he calls the inferior order of the people, popular liberty and popular assemblies offer to his exalted imagination an idea of meanness and contemptibility which he hardly seeks to conceal—He sees at a distance the pomp and pageantry of courts, he sighs after those stately palaces and that apparatus of human greatness which his vivid fancy has taught him to consider as the supreme good. Men of sublime minds, he conceives, were born a different race from the rest of the sons of men, to them, and them only, he imagines, high heaven intended to commit the reins of earthly government, the remaining part of mankind he sees below at an immense distance, they, he thinks were born to serve, to administer food to the ambition of their superiors, and become the footstool of their power—Such is Mr. W———, and fraught with these high ideas, it is no wonder that he should exert all his talents to support a form of government so admirably contrived to carry them into execution—But when the people, who possess collectively a mass of knowledge superior to his own, inquire into the principles of that government on the establishment or rejection of which depend their dearest concerns, when he is called upon by the voice of thousands to come and explain that favorite system which he holds forth as an object of their admiration, he comes—he attempts to support by reasoning what reason never dictated, and finding the attempt vain, his great mind, made for nobler purposes, is obliged to stoop to mean evasions and pitiful sophistry; himself not deceived, he strives to deceive the people, and the treasonable attempt delineates his true character, beyond the reach of the pencil of a *West* or *Peale*, or the pen of a *Valerius*.

And yet that speech, weak and insidious as it is, is the only attempt that has been made to support by argument that political monster THE PROPOSED CONSTITUTION. I have sought in vain amidst the immense heap of trash that has been published on the subject, an argument worthy of refutation, and I have not been able to find it. If you can bear the disgust which the reading of those pieces must naturally occasion, and which I have felt in the highest degree, read them, my fellow citizens, and say whether they contain the least shadow of logical reasoning, say (laying your hands upon your hearts) whether there is any thing in them that can impress unfeigned conviction upon your unprejudiced minds.

One of them only I shall take notice of, in which I find that argument is weakly attempted. This piece is signed "AN AMERICAN CITIZEN" and has appeared with great pomp in four succeeding numbers in several of our newspapers. But if you read it attentively, you will find that it does not tell us what the new constitution IS, but what it IS NOT, and extolls it on the sole ground that it does not contain ALL the principles of tyranny with which the European governments are disgraced.

But where argument entirely failed, nothing remained for the supporters of the new constitution but to endeavor to inflame your passions—The attempt has been made and I am sorry to find not entirely without effect. The great names of WASHINGTON and FRANKLIN, have been taken in vain and shockingly prostituted to effect the most infamous purposes. What! because our august chieftain has subscribed his name in his capacity of president of the convention to the plan offered by them to the states, and because the venerable sage of Pennsylvania, has *testified* by his signature that *the majority of the delegates of this state* assented to the same plan, will any one infer from this that it has met with their entire approbation, and that they consider it as the master piece of human wisdom? I am apt to think the contrary, and I have good reasons to ground my opinion on.

In the first place we have found by the publication of *Charles Cotesworth Pinckney*, Esquire, one of the *signing* members of the convention, who has expressed the most pointed disapprobation of many important parts of the new plan of government, that all the members whose names appear at the bottom of this instrument of tyranny have not concurred in its adoption. Many of them might conceive themselves bound by the opinion of the majority of their state, and leaving the people to their own judgment upon the form of government offered to them, might have conceived it impolitic by refusing to sign their names, to offer to the world the lamentable spectacle of the disunion of a body on the decisions of whom the people had rested all their hopes. We KNOW, and the long sitting of the convention tells us, that, (as it is endeavoured to persuade us) concord and unanimity did not reign exclusively among them. The thick veil of secrecy with which their proceedings have been covered, has left us entirely in the dark, as to the *debates* that took place, and the unaccountable SUPPRESSION OF THEIR JOURNALS, the highest insult that could be offered to the majesty of the people, shews clearly that the whole of the new plan was entirely the work of an *aristocratic majority*.

But let us suppose for a moment that the proposed government was the unanimous result of the deliberations of the convention—must it on that account preclude an investigation of its merits? Are the people to be dictated to without appeal by any set of men, however great, however dignified? Freedom spurns at the idea and rejects it with disdain—We appeal to the collective wisdom of a great nation, we appeal to their general sense which is easily to be obtained through the channel of a multitude of free presses, from the opinions of *thirty-nine* men, who secluded from the rest of the world, without the possibility of conferring with the rest of their fellow-citizens, have had no opportunity of rectifying the errors into which they may have been led by the *most designing* among them. We have seen names not less illustrious than those of the members of the late convention, subscribed to the present *reprobated* articles of confederation, and if those patriots have erred, there is no reason to suppose that a succeeding set should be more free from error. Nay the very men, who advocate so strongly the new plan of government, and support it with the infallibility of Doctor Franklin, affect to despise the present constitution of Pennsylvania, which was dictated and avowed by that venerable patriot—They are conscious that he does not entirely approve of the new plan, whose principles are so different from those he has established in our ever-glorious constitution, and there is no doubt that it is the reason that has induced them to leave his respected name out of the *ticket* for the approaching election.

Now then my fellow-citizens, my brethren, my friends; if the sacred flame of liberty be not extinguished in your breasts, if you have any regard for the happiness of yourselves, and your posterity, let me entreat you, earnestly entreat you by all that is dear and sacred to freemen, to consider well before you take an awful step which may involve in its consequences the ruin of millions yet unborn—You are on the brink of a dreadful precipice;—in the name therefore of holy liberty, for which I have fought and for which we have all suffered, I call upon you to make a solemn pause before you proceed. One step more, and perhaps the scene of freedom is closed forever in America. Let not a set of aspiring despots, *who make us* SLAVES and *tell us 'tis our* CHARTER, wrest from you those invaluable blessings, for which the most illustrious sons of America have bled and died—but exert yourselves, like men, like freemen and like Americans, to transmit unimpaired to your latest posterity those rights, those liberties, which have ever been so dear to you, and which it is yet in your power to preserve.

Philadelphia, November 3, 1787.
An Officer of the late Continental Army.

Rebuttal to "An Officer of the Late Continental Army": "Plain Truth"

Independent Gazetteer (Philadelphia), November 10, 1787

FRIEND OSWALD,

Seeing in thy paper of yesterday, twenty-three objections to the new plan of federal government, I am induced to trouble the public once more; and shall endeavour to answer them distinctly, and concisely. That this may be done with candour, as well as perspicuity, I request thee to reprint them as they are stated by *"an officer of the late continental army,"* and to place my answers in the same order.

I shall pass over every thing that is not in point, and leave the strictures on friend W—— to those who are acquainted with him: I will only observe that "his lofty carriage," is very likely to be the effect of habit; for I know by experience that a man who wears spectacles, must keep his head erect to see through them with ease, and to prevent them from falling off his nose.

Now for the Objections.

"1. It is not merely (as it ought to be) a CONFEDERATION of STATES, but a GOVERNMENT of INDIVIDUALS."

Answer 1. It is more a government *of the people*, than the present Congress ever was, because, the members of Congress have been hitherto chosen by the legislatures of the several states. The proposed representatives are to be chosen "BY THE PEOPLE." If therefore it be not a confederation of *the states*, it is a popular compact, something more in favour of liberty. Art. 1. Sect. 2.

"2. The powers of Congress extend to the *lives*, the *liberties* and the *property* of every citizen."

2. Is there a government on earth, where the life, liberty and property of a citizen, may not be forfeited by a violation of the laws of God and man? It is only when justified by such crimes, that the new government has such power; and all

crimes (except in cases of impeachment) are expressly to be TRIED BY JURY, *in the state where they may be committed.* Art. 3. Sect. 2.

"3. The *sovereignty* of the different states, is *ipso facto* destroyed in its most essential parts."

3. Can the sovereignty of each state in all its parts exist, if there be a sovereignty over the whole. Is it not nonsense in terms, to suppose an united government *of any kind*, over 13 co-existent sovereignties? "It is obviously impracticable in the federal government of these states, to secure all the rights of independent sovereignty to each, and yet provide for the interest and safety of all." *President's letter.*

"4. What remains of it, will only tend to create violent dissentions between the state governments and the Congress, and terminate in the ruin of the one or the other."

4. No such dissention can happen, unless some state oppose the interests of the whole collectively; and it is to overcome such opposition by a majority of 12 to 1, "to ensure domestic tranquility, to provide for the common defence, promote the general welfare, and secure the blessings of liberty," that the union is now, and has ever been thought indispensable. (*Introduction to the new plan.*)

"5. The consequence must therefore be, either that the *union* of the states will be destroyed by a violent struggle, or that their sovereignty will be swallowed up by silent encroachments into a universal aristocracy; because it is clear, that if two different *sovereign powers* have a co-equal command over the *purses* of the citizens, they will struggle, for the spoils, and the weakest will be in the end obliged to yield to the efforts of the strongest."

5. The preceding petition being eradicated, this *consequence* falls to the ground. It may be observed however, that the revenue to be raised by Congress, is not likely to interfere with the taxes of any state. Commerce is the source to which they will naturally apply, because that is one great and uniform object, and they cannot attend to detail: The burden too, will in this way be scarcely felt by the people. All foreigners who may sell merchandise at a loss (and that often has been, and often will be the case in an extensive degree) will pay the impost in addition to that loss, and the duties on all

that may be sold at a profit, will be eventually paid by the consumers: Thus the taxes will be insensibly included in the price, and every man will have the power of refusal, by not consuming the taxed luxuries.

"6. Congress being possessed of these immense powers, the liberties of the states and of the people, are not secured by a bill or DECLARATION of RIGHTS."

6. Notwithstanding all that has been written against it, I must recur to friend W——'s definition on this subject. A state government is designed for ALL CASES WHATSOEVER, consequently what is not reserved, is tacitly given. A federal government is expressly only for FEDERAL PURPOSES, and its power is consequently bounded by the terms of the compact. In the first case a Bill of Rights is indispensable, in the second it would be at best useless, and if one right were to be omitted, it might injuriously grant by implication, what was intended to be reserved.

"7. The *sovereignty* of the states is not expressly reserved, the *form* only, and not the SUBSTANCE of their government, is guaranteed to them by express words."

7. When man emerged from a state of nature, he surely did not reserve the natural right of being the judge of his wrongs, and the executioner of the punishments he might think they deserved. A renunciation of such rights, is the price he paid for the blessings of good government; and for the same reason, state sovereignty (as I have before observed) is as incompatible with the federal union, as the natural rights of human vengeance is, with the peace of society.

"The United States shall guarantee to every state, a republican form of government." That is, they shall guarantee it against monarchical or aristocratical encroachments; Congress can go no further, for the states would justly think themselves insulted, if they should presume to interfere in other alterations which may be individually thought more consistent with the good of the people. Art. 4. Sect. 4.

"8. TRIAL BY JURY, that sacred bulwark of liberty, is ABOLISHED IN CIVIL CASES, and Mr. W——, one of the convention, has told you, that not being able to agree as to the FORM of establishing this point, they have left you deprived of the SUBSTANCE. Here is his own words—*The subject was*

involved in difficulties. The convention found the task TOO DIFFI-
CULT *for them, and left the business as it stands."*

8. Trial by jury has been seen to be expressly preserved in
criminal cases. In civil cases, the federal court is like a court of
chancery, except that it has original jurisdiction only in state
affairs; in all other matters it has "appellate jurisdiction both
as to law and fact, *with such exceptions and under such regulations as congress shall make." Art.* 3. *sect.* 2. Nobody ever complained that trials in chancery were not by jury. A court of
chancery "may issue injunctions in various stages of a cause,
saith Blackstone, and stay oppressive judgement." Yet courts
of chancery are every where extolled as the most equitable;
the federal court has not such an extent of power, and what it
has is to be always under the *exceptions and regulations of the
United states in Congress.*

Friend W—— has well observed that it was impossible to
make one imitation of thirteen different models, and the matter seems now to stand, as well as human wisdom can permit.

"9. THE LIBERTY OF THE PRESS is not secured, and the
powers of congress are fully adequate to its destruction, as
they are to have the trial of *libels*, or *pretended libels* against the
United States, and may by a cursed abominable STAMP ACT (as
the *Bowdoin administration* has done in Massachusetts) preclude you effectually from all means of information. *Mr.
W—— has given you no answer to these arguments."*

9. The liberty of the press in each state, can only be in
danger from the laws of that state, and it is every where well
secured. Besides, as the new congress can only have the defined powers given, it was needless to say any thing about
liberty of the press, liberty of conscience, or any other liberty
that a freeman ought never to be deprived of. It is remarkable
in this instance, that among all the cases to which the federal
jurisdiction is to extend (*art.* 3) not a word is said of *"libels or
pretended libels."* Indeed in this extensive continent, and
among this enlightened people, no government whatever
could controul the press: For after all that is said about "balance of power," there is one power which no tyranny on earth
could subdue if once roused by this great and general grievances, that is THE PEOPLE. This respectable power has preserved the press in Great Britain in spite of government; and

none but a madman could ever think of controuling it in America.

"10. Congress have the power of keeping up a STANDING ARMY in time of peace, and Mr. W—— has told you THAT IT IS NECESSARY."

10. The power here referred to is this, "to raise and support armies, *but no appropriation of money to that use shall be for a longer term than two years.*"—*Art.* 1, *sect.* 8. Thus the representatives of the people have it in their power to disband this army every two years, by refusing supplies. Does not every American feel that no standing army in the power of congress to raise, could support despotism over this immense continent, where almost every citizen is a soldier? If such an apprehension came, in my opinion, within the bounds of possibility, it would not indeed become my principles to oppose this objection.

"11. The LEGISLATIVE and EXECUTIVE powers are not kept separate as every one of the American constitutions declares they ought to be; but they are mixed in a manner entirely novel and unknown, even to the constitution of Great Britain."

11. The first article of the constitution defines the legislative, the second, the executive, and the third the judicial powers; this does not seem like *mixing* them. It would be strange indeed if a professed democratist should object, that the president's power is made subject to "the advice and consent of two-thirds of the senate." *Art.* 2. *sect.* 2.

"12. In England, the king only has a *nominal negative* over the proceedings of the legislature, which he has NEVER DARED TO EXERCISE since the days of *King William*, whereas by the new constitution, both the *president general* and the *senate*, TWO EXECUTIVE BRANCHES OF GOVERNMENT, have that negative, and are intended to *support each other in the exercise of it.*"

12. Whoever will read the 7th section of the 4th article, will feel that the president has only a *conditional* negative, which is effectual or not as two-thirds of the senate and two-thirds of the representatives may on reconsideration determine. If the "*two executive branches*" (as they are here called) should agree in the negative, it would not be novel, as to the power of the

senate; for I believe every senate on the continent, and every upper house in the world, may refuse concurrence and quash a bill before it arrives at the executive department: The king of England has an *unconditional* negative, and has often exercised it in his former colonies.

"13. The representation of the lower house is too small, consisting only of 65 members."

13. The congress on the old plan had but 13 voices, and of these, some were frequently lost by equal divisions. If 65 voices be yet too few, it must follow that the new plan has made some progress towards perfection.

"14. That of the *senate* is so small that it renders its extensive powers extremely dangerous: it is to consist only of 26 members, two-thirds of whom must concur to conclude any *treaty or alliance* with foreign powers: Now we will suppose that five of them are absent, sick, dead, or unable to attend, *twenty one* will remain, and eight of these (*one-third*, and *one* over) may prevent the conclusion of any treaty, even the most favorable to America. Here will be a fine field for the intrigues and even the *bribery* and *corruption* of European powers."

14. This like the former objection is mere matter of opinion. The instance as to supposed vacancies does not apply, for "if vacancies happen by resignation *or otherwise* during the recess of the legislature of any state, the executive thereof may make temporary appointments until the meeting of the legislature which shall then fill such vacancies." *Art.* 1 *sec.* 3. This provision expressly implies that accidental vacancies shall be *immediately* filled.

"15. The most important branches of the EXECUTIVE DEPARTMENT are to be put into the hands of a *single magistrate*, who will be in fact an ELECTIVE KING. The MILITARY, the land and naval forces are to be entirely at his disposal."

15. It was mentioned as a grievance in the 12th objection that this supposed "elective king," had his powers clogged by the conjunction of another branch; here he is called a "*single magistrate*." Yet the new constitution provides that he shall act "by and with the advice and consent of the senate." *Art.* 2. *sec.* 2, and can in no instance act alone, except in the cause of humanity by granting reprieves or pardons.

"16. Should the *senate*, by the intrigues of foreign powers, become devoted to foreign influence, as was the case of late in *Sweden*, the people will be obliged, as the *Swedes* have been, to seek their refuge in the arms of the *monarch* or PRESIDENT GENERAL."

16. The comparison of a little kingdom to a great republic, cannot be just. The revolution in Sweden, was the affair of a day, and the success of it was owing to its confined bounds. To suppose a similar event in this extensive country, 3000 miles distant from European intrigues, is, in the nature of things, a gross absurdity.

"17. ROTATION, that noble prerogative of liberty, is entirely excluded from the new system of government, and great men may and probably will be continued in office during their lives."

17. How can this be the case, when at stated periods the government reverts to the people, and to the representatives of the people, for a new choice in every part of it.

"18. ANNUAL ELECTIONS are abolished, and the people are not to re-assume their rights until the expiration of *two, four* and *six* years."

18. Annual changes in a federal government would beget confusion; it requires years to learn a trade, and men in this age are not legislators by inspiration: One third of the senate as well as all the representatives are to be elected every *two* years. *Art*. 1. *sec*. 3.

"19. Congress are to have the power of fixing the *time, place* and *manner* of holding elections, so as to keep them forever subjected to their influence."

19. Congress are not to have power to fix the place of choosing senators; and the time place and manner of electing representatives are to be fixed by each state itself. Congress indeed are to have controul to prevent undue influence in elections, which we all know but too often happens through party zeal. *Art*. 1. *sec*. 4.

"20. The importation of slaves is not to be prohibited until the year 1808, and SLAVERY will probably resume its empire in Pennsylvania."

20. This is fully answered in my letter to Timothy, but it may not be amiss to repeat that Congress will have no power to meddle in the business 'til 1808. All that can be said against

this offending clause is, that we may have no alteration in this respect for 21 years to come, but 21 years is fixed as a period when we may be better, and in the mean time we cannot be worse than we are now. *Article* I. *section* 9.

"21. The MILITIA is to be under the immediate command of Congress, and men *conscienciously scrupulous of bearing arms*, may be compelled to perform military duty."

21. Congress may "provide for *calling forth* the militia," "and may provide for organizing, arming and disciplining it."—But the states respectively can only *raise it*, and they expressly reserve the right of "appointment of officers and of training it."—Now we know that men conscienciously scrupulous by sect or profession are not *forced* to bear arms in any of the states, a pecuniary compensation being accepted in lieu of it.—Whatever may be my sentiments on the present state of this matter is foreign to the point: But it is certain that whatever redress may be wished for, or expected, can only come from *the state Legislature*, where, and where only, the dispensing power, or enforcing power, is *in the first instance* placed. *Article* I. *section* 8.

"22. The new government will be EXPENSIVE beyond any we have ever experienced, the *judicial* department alone, with its concomitant train of *judges, justices, chancellors, clerks, sheriffs, coroners, escheators, state attornies and solicitors, constables, &c.* in every state and in every country in each state, will be a burden beyond the utmost abilities of the people to bear."

22. This mighty expence would be paid by about one shilling a man throughout the states. The other part of this objection is not intelligible, nothing is said in the new constitution of a judicial department in *"states* and *counties,"* other than what is already established.

"23. A government partaking of MONARCHY and aristocracy will be fully and firmly established, and liberty will be but a name to adorn the *short* historic page of the halcyon days of America."

23. The 5th article expressly provides against every danger, by pointing out a mode of amendment when necessary. And liberty will thus be a name to adorn the *long* historic page of American virtue and happiness.

Thus I have answered all the objections, and supported my

answers by fair quotations from the new constitution; and I particularly desire my readers to examine all the references with accurate attention. If I have mistaken any part, it will, I trust, be found to be an error of judgment, not of will, and I shall thankfully receive any candid instruction on the subject.—One quotation more and I have done.—"In all our deliberations on this subject (saith GEORGE WASHINGTON) we kept steadily in our view, that which appears to us the greatest interest of every true American, the consolidation of our union, in which is involved our prosperity, felicity, safety, perhaps our national existence. This important consideration, seriously and deeply impressed on our minds, led each state in the Convention to be less rigid on points of inferior magnitude, than might have been otherwise expected; and thus the constitution which we now present, is the result of a spirit of amity, and of that mutual deference and concession which the peculiarity of our political situation rendered indispensable."

Philadelphia, November 7, 1787.

Reply to Wilson's Speech:
"Cincinnatus" [Arthur Lee] V

New York Journal, November 29, 1787

Sir, In my former observations on your speech, to your fellow-citizens, explanatory and defensive of the new constitution; it has appeared, by arguments to my judgment unanswerable, that by ratifying the constitution, as the convention proposed it, the people will leave the liberty of the press, and the trial by jury, in civil cases, to the mercy of their rulers—that the project is to burthen them with enormous taxes, in order to raise and maintain armies, for the purposes of ambition and arbitrary power—that this power is to be vested in an aristocratic senate, who will either be themselves the tyrants, or the support of tyranny, in a president, who will know how to manage them, so as to make that body at once the instrument and the shield of his absolute authority.— Even the Roman Emperors found it necessary to have a senate for this purpose. To compass this object, we have seen powers, in every branch of government, in violation of all principle, and all safety condensed in this aristocratic senate: we have seen the representative, or democratic branch, weakened exactly in proportion to the strengthing the aristocratic, or, what means the same thing, and will be more pleasing to your ear, Mr. Wilson, the republican branch. We have seen with what cunning the power of impeachment is apparently given to the representative of the people, but really to the senate; since, as they advise these measures of government, which experience has shewn, are the general matters of impunity the executive officers will be sure of impeachment when they act in conformity to their will. Impeachment will therefore have no terrors, but for those who displease or oppose the senate.

Let us suppose that the privy councils who advise the executive government in England, were vested with the sole power of trying impeachments; would any man say that this would not render that body absolute; and impeachment to all popular purposes, negatory? I shall appeal to those very citizens, Mr. Wilson, whom you was misleading, for the propriety of what I am going to observe. They know that their constitution was democratic—that it secured the powers of government in the body of the people. They have seen an aristocratical party rise up against this constitution, and without the aid of such a senate, but from the mere influence of wealth, however unduly obtained, they have seen this aristocracy, under the orignatical title of republicans, procure such a preference in the legislature, as to appoint a majority of the state members in the late convention, out of their body. Had such a senate, as they have now proposed, been part of your constitution, would the popular part of it, have been in effect more than a name. Can your fellow citizens then doubt that these men planned this senate, to effect the very purpose which has been the constant object of their endeavors, that is to overthrow the present constitution. And can you, O citizens of Philadelphia, so soon forget the constitution which you formed, for which you fought, which you have solemnly engaged to defend—can you so soon forget all this, as to be the willing ministers of that ambition, which aims only at making you its footstool—the confirmers of that constitution, which gives your aristocratic enemies their wish, and must trample your state constitution in the dust. Reflect a moment—who wish to erect an aristocracy among you—Mr. Wilson and his party; who were your delegates in framing the constitution now proposed to you—Mr. Wilson, and his party; who harangues you to smooth its passage to your approbation—Mr. Wilson; who have you chosen to approve of it in your state convention—Mr. Wilson.—O sense where is your guard! shame where is your blush! the intention of a state convention is, that a work of so great moment to your welfare, should undergo an examination by another set of men, uninfluenced by partiality or prejudice in its favor. And for this purpose you are weak enough to send a man, who was in the former convention, and who has not only signed his approbation of it, but stands forward as an agitator for it: is this man unprejudiced? would any man who did not suffer party to overcome all sense of rectitude, solicit or accept so improper a trust? He knows, in the line of his profession, that the having given an opinion upon the same question is a constant ground of challenge to a juryman. And does he think that this question is of less importance and ought less to be guarded against partiality and prejudice, than a common jury cause? He knows that a conscientious man will not sit as a juryman twice on the same cause: and is he in this most momentous cause, less conscientious than a common juryman? What are we to expect from the work of such hands? But you must permit me to lay before you, from your own transactions, farther proofs of Mr. Wilson's consistency, and of his sacred attention to your rights, when he counsels you to adopt the new constitution.

You know that he was one of the convention that formed, and recommended to you, your state constitution. Read what is there laid down as a fundamental principle of liberty—"As standing armies, in the time of peace, *are dangerous to liberty*, they ought not to be kept up." Read now what this identical Mr. Wilson says to you in his speech—"This constitution, it has been farther urged, is of a pernicious tendency, because it tolerates a standing army in time of peace. This has always been a topic of popular declamation, and yet I do not know a nation in the world, which has not found it necessary and useful to maintain the appearance of strength, in a season of the most profound peace." What a change of tone is here.— Formerly the mischief of standing armies was of sufficient moment, to find a place in a most solemn recognition of the fundamental rights of the people; standing armies were dangerous to liberty; but *now* they are only a topic of popular declamation, and are both useful and necessary in a season of the most profound tranquility:—O citizens of Philadelphia! do you hear, do you read, do you reflect? can you believe that the man means either wisely or honestly, who thus palpably contradicts himself, who treats with such levity, what your constitution declares to be one of your most sacred rights; and who betrays so little knowledge of ancient and modern history, as not to know, that some of the freest republics in the world, never kept up a standing army in time of peace!

Can you, O deluded men, not see that the object of all this, is to fix upon you, with your own consent, a strong government that will enable a few proud, intriguing, aristocratical men, to make you the instruments of their avarice and ambition, and trample upon your privileges at pleasure. Your privileges, did I say, I beg your pardon; after a surrender of every thing on your part, into the hands of a few, their pleasure will be your only privileges.

I beg you will pardon me, Mr. Wilson, for this digression: it is not a pleasant one, and I wish the cause of it had never existed. We will return, if you please, to your speech. "When we reflect, you say, how various are the laws, commerce, habits, population, and extent, of the confederated states, this evidence of mutual concession and accommodation ought rather to command a generous applause, than to excite a jealousy and reproach. For my part, my admiration can only be equalled by my astonishment in beholding so perfect a system formed from such heterogeneous materials." What a rhapsody is here; it certainly must have excited equal admiration and astonishment in your audience, and called forth those loud and unanimous testimonies of applause which Doctor Panegyric tells us, accompanied your speech. Nil admirari, Mr. Wilson, is a wise lesson, and when you recover from your admiration and astonishment which are always incompatible with truth and reason; I shall ask you what union in the world is so similar in their laws, commerce, habits, population and extent? Is there such difference between Rhode-Island and Virginia, as between Holland and Overyssel; between Massachusetts and Georgia, as between Berne and Switzs? Do not the several states harmonize in trial by jury of the vicinage; taxation by representation; habeas corpus; religious toleration; freedom of the press; separation of the legislative, executive and judicial functions. Are not these the great principles on which every constitution is founded? In these the laws and habits of the several states are uniform. But I suppose, because the citizens of New-York are not in the habit of being so ostentatious as those of Philadelphia, nor its merchants, of being such speculators in commerce as to fill the papers with bankruptcies; because in Carolina they are in the habit of eating rice, and in Maryland of eating homony;

therefore the materials are heterogeneous, out of which this perfect, system; his subject of amazement, was formed.

What was this wonder working concession and accommodation? If they consisted in giving up, or hazarding any of the above fundamental principles of liberty, which I confess seems probable, because some furious spirits in the convention, and such there were, insisted upon it, such conduct may command your generous applause; but trust me, sir, when the people come to feel that their rights have been so basely betrayed by those they trusted, it will command a general execration: And here I cannot avoid remarking on what I have heard and for the truth of which I appeal to you. It is that a member of the late convention said, not very honorably distinguished for his moral or political virtue, admonished his associates that, unless they carried the constitution through before there was time for considering it, there would be no probability of its being adopted. When I couple this profligate declaration, with the equally profligate measures taken by some persons to force it down in Philadelphia, and with the indecent speed with which others posted to Congress, and then to their several states, to hurry it forward—I confess I cannot help apprehending that such advice has not only been given, but followed.

You would next induce us, Mr. Wilson, to believe, that the state sovereignties will not be annihilated, if the general one be established as the convention recommends. Your reason for this is as curious as it is conclusive. Because the state legislatures must nominate the electors of the President once in four years, and chuse a third of the Senate once in two years; therefore they will continue to be sovereign. Sovereignty then consists in electing the members of a sovereignty; to make laws—preside over the administration of justice—command the militia, or force of the state—these I suppose, do not constitute its sovereignty, for these are totally taken away, and yet you are clear the sovereignty remains. Did you think, Sir, that you was speaking to men or to children, when you hazarded such futile observations. Nor are they compensated by the very profound erudition you display in defining the meaning of the word corporation. In common *parlance* we should call this egregious pedantry. Such is the anxiety manifested by the framers of the proposed constitution, for the utter extinction of the state sovereignties, that they were not content with taking from them every attribute of sovereignty, but would not leave them even the name.—Therefore, in the very commencement they prescribe this remarkable declaration —*We the People of the United States.* When the whole people of America shall be thus recognized by their own solemn act, as the people of the United States, I beseech you Sir, to tell us over whom the sovereignty, you say you leave to the several states, is to operate. Did the generous confidence of your fellow citizens, deserve this mockery of their understandings; or inebriated with so unusual a thing as popularity, did you think that every rhapsody you uttered, would be received as reason? That you may not expose yourself again on this subject, give me leave to recommend to you to read Mr. Locke, in whom you will find that sovereignty consists in three things—the legislative, executive, and negociating powers, all which your constitution takes absolutely away from the several states. In Barbeyrac's Puffendorf, you will find these words, "La souvèraintee entant quelle prescrit des regles generales pour la conduite de la vie civile, s'appelle pouvoir legislatif—entant qu'elle prononce sur les demeles des citoiens, conformement a ces regles, pouvoir judiciaire—entant q'uelle arme les citoiens contre un ennemie etranger, ou qu'elle leur ordonne de mettre fin aux acts d'hostilitès; pouvoir de faire la guerre et la paix; entant qu'elle se choisit des Ministres pour lui aider a prendre soin des affaires publiques; pouvoir d'etablir des magistrats. The sovereignty, inasmuch as it prescribes general rules for the conduct of civil life, is called the legislative power—in deciding controversies among its citizens, conformably to those laws it is called the judiciary power—in arming its citizens against a foreign enemy, or ordering them to cease hostilities; it has the power of war and peace—the appointment of officers to aid it in the case of the public, is the power of establishing magistrates." Now, Sir, all these attributes of sovereignty, being vested exclusively in your new government, is it not a mockery of common sense to tell us, the state sovereignties are not annihilated? and yet you undertake to prove, that upon their existence depends the existence of the fœderal plan—and when this mighty undertaking is explained, it is because they must meet once in two years to elect part of the federal sovereignty. O fie! O fie! Mr. Wilson! you had yet some character to lose, why would you hazard it in this manner?

On the subject of taxation, in which powers are to be given so largely by the new constitution, you lull our fears of abuse by venturing to predict "that the great revenue of the United States must and always will be raised by impost"—and you elevate our hopes by holding out, "the reviving and supporting the national credit." If you have any other plan for this, than by raising money upon the people to pay the interest of the national debt, your ingenuity will deserve our thanks. Supposing however, that raising money is necessary to payment of the interest, and such payment requisite to support the credit of the union; let us see how much will be necessary for that end, and how far the impost will supply what we want.

	Dollars.
The arrearages of French and Spanish interest amount now to—	1,500,000
Interest and instalments of do. for 1788,	850,227
Support of government, and its departments, for 1788,—	500,000
Arrears and anticipations of 1787,—	300,000
Interest of domestic debt,—	500,000
	4,650,227

The new Congress then, supposing it to get into operation towards October, 1788, will have to provide for this sum, and for the additional sum of 3,000,000 at least for the ensuing year; which together will make the sum of 7,650,227.

Now let us see how the impost will answer this: Congress have furnished us with their estimate of the produce of the whole imports of America at five per cent. and that is 800,000 dollars: there will remain to provide for, by other taxes, 6,850,227.

We know too, that our imports diminish yearly, and from the nature of things must continue to diminish; and consequently that the above estimate of the produce of the impost, will in all probability, fall much short of the supposed sum.

But even without this, it must appear, that you was either intentionally misleading your hearers, or very little acquainted with the subject when you ventured to predict, that the great revenue of the United States would always flow from the impost. The estimate above is from the publications of Congress, and I presume is right. But the sum stated, is necessary to be raised by the new government, in order to answer the expectations they have raised, is not all. The state debts, independent of what each owes to the United States, amount to about 30,000,000 dollars; the annual interest of this is 1,800,000.

It will be expected, that the new government will provide for this also; and such expectation is founded, not only on the promise you hold forth, of its reviving and supporting public credit among us, but also on this unavoidable principle of justice, that is the new government takes away the impost, and other substantial taxes, from the produce of which the several states paid the interest of their debt, or funded the paper with which they paid it. The new government must find ways and means of supplying that deficiency, or in other words of paying the interest in hard money, for in paper as now, it cannot, without a violation of the principles it boasts, attempt to pay. The sum then which it must annually raise in specie, after the first year, cannot be less than 4,800,000: at present, there is not one half of this sum in specie raised in all the states; and yet the complaints of intolerable taxes has produced one rebellion, and will be mainly operative in the adoption of your constitution.—How you will get this sum is inconceivable, and yet get it you must, or lose all credit. With magnificent promises you have bought golden opinions of all sorts of people, and with gold you must answer them.

"An Old Whig" [*George Bryan et al.*] I

Independent Gazetteer (Philadelphia), October 12, 1787

Mr. PRINTER, I am one of those who have long wished for a federal government, which should have power to protect our trade and provide for the general security of the United States. Accordingly, when the constitution proposed by the late convention made its appearance, I was disposed to embrace it almost without examination; I was determined not to be offended with trifles or to scan it too critically. "We want something: let us try this; experience is the best teacher: if it does not answer our purpose we can alter it: at all events it will serve for a beginning." Such were my reasonings;—but, upon further reflection, I may say that I am shaken with very considerable doubts and scruples, I want a federal constitution; and yet I am afraid to concur in giving my consent to the establishment of that which is proposed. At the same time I really wish to have my doubts removed, if they are not well founded. I shall therefore take the liberty of laying some of them before the public, through the channel of your paper.

In the first place, it appears to me that I was mistaken in supposing that we could so very easily make trial of this constitution and again change it at our pleasure. The conventions of the several states cannot propose any alterations—they are only to give their *assent* and *ratification*. And after the constitution is once ratified, it must remain fixed until two thirds of both the houses of Congress shall deem it necessary to propose amendments; or the legislatures of two thirds of the several states shall make application to Congress for the calling a convention for proposing amendments, which amendments shall not be valid till they are ratified by the legislatures of three fourths of the several states, or by conventions in three fourths thereof, as one or the other mode of ratification may be proposed by Congress.—This appears to me to be only a cunning way of saying that no alteration shall ever be made; so that whether it is a good constitution or a bad constitution, it will remain forever unamended. Lycurgus, when he promulgated his laws to the Spartans, made them swear that they would make no alterations in them until he should return from a journey which he was then about to undertake: — He chose never to return, and therefore no alterations could be made in his laws. The people were made to believe that they could make trial of his laws for a few months or years, during his absence, and as soon as he returned they could continue to observe them or reject at pleasure. Thus this celebrated Republic was in reality established by a trick. In like manner the proposed constitution holds out a prospect of being subject to be changed if it be found necessary or convenient to change it; but the conditions upon which an alteration can take place, are such as in all probability will never exist. The consequence will be that, when the constitution is once established, it never can be altered or amended without some violent convulsion or civil war.

The conditions, I say, upon which any alterations can take place, appear to me to be such as never will exist — two thirds of both houses of Congress or the legislatures of two thirds of the states, must agree in desiring a convention to be called. This will probably never happen; but if it should happen, then the convention may agree to the amendments or not as they think right; and after all, three fourths of the states must ratify the amendments. — Before all this labyrinth can be traced to a conclusion, ages will revolve, and perhaps the great principles upon which our late glorious revolution was founded, will be totally forgotten. If the principles of liberty are not firmly fixed and established in the present constitution, in vain may we hope for retrieving them hereafter. People once possessed of power are always loth to part with it; and we shall never find two thirds of a Congress voting or proposing any thing which shall derogate from their own authority and importance, or agreeing to give back to the people any part of those privileges which they have once parted with — so far from it; that the greater occasion there may be for a reformation, the less likelihood will there be of accomplishing it. The greater the abuse of power, the more obstinately is it always persisted in. As to any expectation of two thirds of the legislatures concurring in such a request, it is if possible, still more remote. The legislatures of the states will be but forms and shadows, and it will be the height of arrogance and presumption in them, to turn their thoughts to such high subjects. After this constitution is once established, it is too evident that we shall be obliged to fill up the offices of assemblymen and councillors, as we do those of constables, by appointing men to serve whether they will or not, and fining them if they refuse. The members thus appointed, as soon as they can hurry through a law or two for repairing highways or impounding cattle, will conclude the business of their sessions as suddenly as possible; that they may return to their own business.—Their heads will not be perplexed with the great affairs of state—We need not expect two thirds of them ever to interfere in so momentous a question as that of calling a Continental convention.—The different legislatures will have no communication with one another from the time of the new constitution being ratified, to the end of the world. Congress will be the great focus of power as well as the great and only medium of communication from one state to another. The great, and the wise, and the mighty will be in possession of places and offices; they will oppose all changes in favor of liberty; they will steadily pursue the acquisition of more and more power to themselves and their adherents. The cause of liberty, if it be now forgotten, will be forgotten forever.—Even the press which has so long been employed in the cause of liberty, and to which perhaps the greatest part of the liberty which exists in the world is owing at this moment; the press may possibly be restrained of its freedom, and our children may possibly not be suffered to enjoy this most invaluable blessing of a free communication of each others sentiments on political subjects—Such at least appear to be some men's fears, and I cannot find in the proposed constitution any thing expressly calculated to obviate these fears; so that they may or may not be realized according to the principles and dispositions of the men who may happen to govern us hereafter. One thing however is calculated to alarm our fears on this head;—I mean the fashionable language which now prevails so much and is so frequent in the mouths of some who formerly held very different opinions;—THAT COMMON PEOPLE HAVE NO BUSINESS TO TROUBLE THEMSELVES ABOUT GOVERNMENT. If this principle is just the consequence is plain that the common people need no information on the subject of politics. Newspapers, pamphlets and essays are calculated only to mislead and inflame them by holding forth to them doctrines which they have no business or right to meddle with, which they ought to leave to their superiors. Should the freedom of the press be restrained on the subject of politics, there is no doubt it will soon after be restrained on all other subjects, religious as well as civil. And if the freedom of the press shall be restrained, it will be another reason to despair of any amendments being made in favor of liberty, after the proposed constitution shall be once established. Add to this, that under the proposed constitution, it will be in the power of the Congress to raise and maintain a standing army for their support, and when they are supported by an army, it will depend on themselves to say whether any amendments shall be made in favor of liberty.

If these reflections are just it becomes us to pause, and reflect previously before we establish a system of government which cannot be amended; which will entail happiness or misery on ourselves and our children. We ought I say to reflect carefully, we ought not by any means to be in haste; but rather to suffer a little temporary inconvenience, than by any precipitation to establish a constitution without knowing whether it is right or wrong, and which if wrong, no length of time will ever mend. Scarce any people ever deliberately gave up their liberties; but many instances occur in history of their losing them forever by a rash and sudden act, to avoid a pressing inconvenience or gratify some violent passion of revenge or fear. It was a celebrated observation of one of our Assemblies before the revolution, during their struggles with the proprietaries, that "those who would give up essential liberty to purchase a little temporary safety deserve neither liberty nor safety."

For the present I shall conclude with recommending to my countrymen not to be in haste, to consider carefully what we are doing. It is our own concern; it is our own business; let us give ourselves a little time at least to read the proposed constitution and know what it contains; for I fear that many, even of those who talk most about it have not even read it, and many others, who are as much concerned as any of us, have had no opportunity to read it. And it is certainly a suspicious circumstance that some people who are presumed to know most about the new constitution seem bent upon forcing it on their countrymen without giving them time to know what they are doing.

Hereafter I may trouble you further on some other parts of this important subject; but I fear this letter is already too long.

"Marcus"

Daily Advertiser (New York), October 15, 1787

The INTERESTS *of this* STATE.

It is the Interest of the Merchants to encourage the New Constitution, because Commerce may then be a national object, and nations will form treaties with us.

It is the Interest of the Mechanics to join the mercantile interest; because it is not their interest to quarrel with their *bread and butter*.

It is the Interest of the Farmer, because the prosperity of Commerce gives vent to his produce, raises the value of his lands, and commercial duties will alleviate the burthen of his taxes.

It is the Interest of the Landholder, because thousands in Europe, with moderate fortunes, will migrate to this country, if an efficient Government gives them a prospect of tranquillity.

It is the Interest of all Gentlemen and Men of Property, because they will see many low Demagogues reduced to their *tools*, whose upstart dominion insults their feelings, and whose passion for popularity will dictate laws,* which ruin the minority of the Creditors, and please the majority of Debtors.

It is the Interest of all Public Creditors, because they will see the credit of the States rise, and their Securities appreciate.

It is the Interest of the American Soldier, as the military profession will then be respectable, and the Floridas may be conquered in a campaign. The spoils of the West-Indies and South-America may enrich the next generation of Cincinnati.

It is the Interest of the Lawyers who have ability and genius, because the dignities in the Supreme Court will interest professional ambition, and create emulation which is not felt now. The dignities of the State Court, a Notary or the prosecutor of a bond will not aspire to, which has cheapened their

*Citation Laws.

value. Men also have enjoyed them without professional knowledge, and who are only versed in the abstract and learned science of the *plough*.

It is the Interest of the Clergy, as civil tumults excite every bad passion—the soul is neglected, and the Clergy starve.

It is the interest of all men, whose education has been liberal and extensive; because there will be a theatre for the display of talents, which have no influence in State Assemblies, where eloquence is treated with contempt, and reason overpowered by a *silent vote*.

It is *not* the Interest of those who enjoy State consequence, which would be lost in the Assemblies of the States. These insects and worms are only seen on their own dunghill. There are minds whose narrow vision can look over the concerns of a State or Town, but cannot extend their short vision to Continental concerns. Manners are essential in such a Government, and where the Union is represented, care should be taken to impress the other States with respectable opinions, and if this becomes a principle they must remain at home, and not presume to these national dignities.

New-York, Oct. 13.

"A Citizen of America" [Noah Webster]

Philadelphia, October 17, 1787

Of all the memorable æras that have marked the progress of men from the savage state to the refinements of luxury, that which has combined them into society, under a wise system of government, and given form to a nation, has ever been recorded and celebrated as the most important. Legislators have ever been deemed the greatest benefactors of mankind—respected when living, and often deified after their death. Hence the fame of Fohi and Confucius—of Moses, Solon and Lycurgus—of Romulus and Numa—of Alfred, Peter the Great, and Mango Capac; whose names will be celebrated through all ages, for framing and improving constitutions of government, which introduced order into society and secured the benefits of law to millions of the human race.

This western world now beholds an æra important beyond conception, and which posterity will number with the age of Czar of Muscovy, and with the promulgation of the Jewish laws at Mount Sinai. The names of those men who have digested a system of constitutions for the American empire, will be enrolled with those of Zamolxis and Odin, and celebrated by posterity with the honors which less enlightened nations have paid to the fabled demi-gods of antiquity.

But the origin of the AMERICAN REPUBLIC is distinguished by peculiar circumstances. Other nations have been driven together by fear and necessity—their governments have generally been the result of a single man's observations; or the offspring of particular interests. In the formation of our constitution, the wisdom of all ages is collected—the legislators of antiquity are consulted—as well as the opinions and interests of the millions, who are concerned. In short, it is an *empire of reason*.

In the formation of such a government, it is not only the

right, but the indispensable *duty* of every citizen to examine the principles of it, to compare them with the principles of other governments, with a constant eye to our particular situation and circumstances, and thus endeavor to foresee the future operations of our own system, and its effects upon human happiness.

Convinced of this truth, I have no apology to offer for the following remarks, but an earnest desire to be useful to my country.

In attending to the proposed Federal Constitution, the first thing that presents itself to our consideration, is the division of the legislative into two branches. This article has so many advocates in America, that it needs not any vindication.*— But it has its opposers, among whom are some respectable characters, especially in Pennsylvania; for which reason, I will state some of the arguments and facts which incline me to favor the proposed division.

On the first view of men in society, we should suppose that no man would be bound by a law which he had not given his consent. Such would be our first idea of political obligation. But experience, from time immemorial, has proved it to be impossible to unite the opinions of all the members of a community, in every case; and hence the doctrine, that the opinions of a *majority* must give law to the *whole State*: a doctrine as universally received, as any intuitive truth.

Another idea that naturally presents itself to our minds, on a slight consideration of the subject, is, that in a perfect government, all the members of a society should be present, and each give his suffrage in acts of legislation, by which he is to be bound. This is impracticable in all large states; and even, were it not, it is very questionable whether it would be the *best* mode of legislation. It was however practised in the free states of antiquity; and was the cause of innumerable evils. To avoid these evils, the moderns have invented the doctrine of *representation*, which seems to be the perfection of human government.

---

*A division of the legislature has been adopted in the new constitution of every state, except Pennsylvania and Georgia.

Another idea, which is very natural, is, that to complete the mode of legislation, all the representatives should be collected into *one body*, for the purpose of debating questions and enacting laws. Speculation would suggest the idea; and the desire of improving upon the systems of government in the old world, would operate powerfully in its favor.

But men are ever running into extremes. The passions, after a violent constraint, are apt to rush into licentiousness; and even the reason of men, who have experienced evils from the *defects* of a government, will sometimes coolly condemn the *whole system*.

Every person, moderately acquainted with human nature, knows that public bodies, as well as individuals, are liable to the influence of sudden and violent passions, under the operation of which, the voice of reason is silenced. Instances of such influence are not so frequent, as in individuals; but its effects are extensive in proportion to the numbers that compose the public body. This fact suggests the expediency of dividing the powers of legislation between two bodies of men, whose debates shall be separate and not dependent on each other; that, if at any time, one part should appear to be under any undue influence, either from passion, obstinacy, jealousy of particular men, attachment to a popular speaker, or other extraordinary causes, there might be a power in the legislature sufficient to check every pernicious measure. Even in a small republic, composed of men, equal in property and abilities, and all meeting for the purpose of making laws, like the old Romans in the field of Mars, a division of the body into two independent branches, would be a necessary step to prevent the disorders, which arise from the pride, irritability and stubbornness of mankind. This will ever be the case, while men possess passions, easily inflamed, which may bias their reason and lead them to erroneous conclusions.

Another consideration has weight: A single body of men may be led astray by one person of abilities and address, who, on the first starting a proposition, may throw a plausible appearance on one side of the question, and give a lead to the whole debate. To prevent any ill consequence from such a circumstance, a separate discussion, before a different body of men, and taken up on new grounds, is a very eligible expedient.

Besides, the design of a senate is not merely to check the legislative assembly, but to collect wisdom and experience. In most of our constitutions, and particularly in the proposed federal system, greater age and a longer residence are required to qualify for the senate, than for the house of representatives. This is a wise provision. The house of representatives may be composed of new and unexperienced members—strangers to the forms of proceeding, and the science of legislation. But either positive constitutions, or customs, which may supply their place, fill the senate with men venerable for age and respectability, experienced in the ways of men, and in the art of governing, and who are not liable to the bias of passions that govern the young. If the senate of Rhode Island is an exception to this observation, it is a proof that the mass of the people are corrupted, and that the senate should be elected less frequently than the other house: Had the old senate in Rhode Island held their seats for three years; had they not been chosen, amidst a popular rage for paper money, the honor of that state would probably have been saved. The old senate would have stopped the measure for a year or two, till the people could have had time to deliberate upon its consequences. I consider it as a capital excellence of the proposed constitution, that the senate can be wholly renewed but once in six years.

Experience is the best instructor—it is better than a thousand theories. The history of every government on earth affords proof of the utility of different branches in a legislature. But I appeal only to our own experience in America. To what cause can we ascribe the absurd measures of Congress, in times past, and the speedy recision of those measures, but to the want of some check? I feel the most profound deference for that honorable body, and perfect respect for their opinions; but some of their steps betray a great want of consideration—a defect, which perhaps nothing can remedy, but a division of their deliberations. I will instance only their *resolution* to build a *Federal Town*. When we were involved in a debt, of which we could hardly pay the interest, and when Congress could not command a shilling, the very proposition was extremely absurd. Congress themselves became ashamed of the resolution, and rescinded it with as much silence as possible. Many other acts of that body are equally reprehensible—but respect forbids me to mention them.

Several states, since the war, have experienced the necessity of a division of the legislature. Maryland was saved, from a most pernicious measure, by her senate. A rage for paper money, bordering on madness, prevailed in their house of delegates—an emission of £.500,000 was proposed; a sum equal to the circulating medium of the state. Had the sum been emitted, every shilling of specie would have been driven from circulation, and most of it from the state. Such a loss would not have been repaired in seven years—not to mention the whole catalogue of frauds which would have followed the measure. The senate, like honest, judicious men, and the protectors of the interests of the state, firmly resisted the rage, and gave the people time to cool and to think. Their resistance was effectual—the people acquiesced, and the honor and interest of the state were secured.

The house of representatives in Connecticut, soon after the war, had taken offence at a certain act of Congress. The upper house, who understood the necessity and expediency of the measure, better than the people, refused to concur in a remonstrance to Congress. Several other circumstances gave umbrage to the lower house; and to weaken or destroy the influence of the senate, the representatives, among other violent proceedings, resolved, not merely to remove the seat of government, but to make every county town in the state the seat of government, by rotation. This foolish resolution would have disgraced school boys—the senate saved the honor of the state, by rejecting it with disdain—and within two months, every representative was ashamed of the conduct of the house. All public bodies have these fits of passion, when their conduct seems to be perfectly boyish; and in these paroxisms, a check is highly necessary.

Pennsylvania exhibits many instances of this hasty conduct. At one session of the legislature, an armed force is ordered, by a precipitate resolution, to expel the settlers at Wioming from their possessions—at a succeeding session, the same people are confirmed in their possessions. At one session, a charter is wrested from a corporation—at another, restored. The whole state is split into parties—every thing is decided by party—any proposition from one side of the house, is sure to be damned by the other—and when one party perceives the other has the advantage, they play truant—and an officer or a mob hunt the absconding members in all the streets and alleys in town. Such farces have been repeated in Philadelphia—and *there alone*. Had the legislature been framed with some check upon rash proceedings, the honor of the state would have been saved—the party spirit would have died with the measures proposed in the legislature. But now, any measure may be carried by party in the house; it then becomes a law, and sows the seeds of dissension throughout the state.*

A thousand examples similar to the foregoing may be produced, both in ancient and modern history. Many plausible things may be said in favor of pure democracy—many in favor of uniting the representatives of the people in a single house—but uniform experience proves both to be inconsistent with the peace of society, and the rights of freemen.

The state of Georgia has already discovered such inconveniences in its constitution, that a proposition has been made for altering it; and there is a prospect that a revisal will take place.

People who have heard and read of the European governments, founded on the different ranks of *monarch, nobility and people*, seem to view the *senate* in America, where there is no

*I cannot help remarking the singular jealousy of the constitution of Pennsylvania, which requires that a bill shall be published for the consideration of the people, before it is enacted into a law, except in extraordinary cases. This annihilates the legislature, and reduces it to an advisory body. It almost wholly supersedes the uses of *representation*, the most excellent improvement in modern governments. Besides the absurdity of constituting a legislature, without supreme power, such a system will keep the state perpetually embroiled. It carries the spirit of discussion into all quarters, without the means of reconciling the opinions of men, who are not assembled to hear each others arguments. They debate with themselves—form their own opinions, without the reasons which influence others, and without the means of information. Thus the warmth of different opinions, which, in other states, dies in the legislature, is diffused through the state of Pennsylvania, and becomes personal and permanent. The seeds of dissension are sown in the constitution, and no state, except Rhode Island, is so distracted by factions.

difference of ranks and titles, as a useless branch—or as a servile imitation of foreign constitutions of government, without the same reasons. This is a capital mistake. Our senates, it is true, are not composed of a different order of men; but the same reasons, the same necessity for distinct branches of the legislature exists in all governments. But in most of our American constitutions, we have all the advantages of checks and balance, without the danger which may arise from a superior and independent order of men.

It is worth our while to institute a brief comparison between our American forms of government, and the two *best constitutions* that ever existed in Europe, the *Roman* and the *British*.

In England, the king or supreme executive officer, is hereditary. In America, the president of the United States, is elective. That this is an advantage will hardly be disputed.

In ancient Rome, the king was elective, and so were the consuls, who were the executive officers in the republic. But they were elected by the body of the people, in their public assemblies; and this circumstance paved the way for such excessive bribery and corruption as are wholly unknown in modern times. The president of the United States is also elective; but by a few men—chosen by the several legislatures—under their inspection—separated at a vast distance—and holding no office under the United States. Such a mode of election almost precludes the possibility of corruption. Besides, no state however large, has the power of chusing a president in that state; for each elector must choose at least one man, who is not an inhabitant of that state to which he belongs.

The crown of England is hereditary—the consuls in Rome were chosen annually—both these extremes are guarded against in our proposed constitution. The president is not dismissed from his office, as soon as he is acquainted with business—he continues four years, and is re-eligible, if the people approve his conduct. Nor can he canvass for his office, by reason of the distance of the electors; and the pride and jealousy of the states will prevent his continuing too long in office.

The age requisite to qualify for this office is thirty-five years.* The age requisite for admittance to the Roman consulship was forty-three years. For this difference, good reasons may be assigned—the improvements in science, and particularly in government, render it practicable for a man to qualify himself for an important office, much earlier in life, than he could among the Romans; especially in the early part of their commonwealth, when the office was instituted. Besides it is very questionable whether any inconvenience would have attended an admission to the consulship at an earlier age.

The powers vested in the president resemble the powers of the supreme magistrates in Rome. They are not so extensive as those of the British king; but in one instance, the president, with concurrence of the senate, has powers exceeding those of the Roman consuls; I mean in the appointment of judges and other subordinate executive officers. The prætors or judges in Rome were chosen annually by the people. This was a defect in the Roman government. One half the evils in a state arise from a lax execution of the laws; and it is impossible that an executive officer can act with vigor and impartiality, when his office depends on the popular voice. An annual popular election of executive officers is the sure source of a negligent, partial and corrupt administration. The independence of the judges in England has produced a course of the most just, impartial and energetic judicial decisions, for many centuries, that can be exhibited in any nation on earth. In this point therefore I conceive the plan proposed in America to be an improvement on the Roman constitution. In all free governments, that is, in all countries, where *laws govern*, and not *men*, the supreme magistrate should have it in his power to execute any law, however unpopular, without hazarding his person or office. The laws are the sole *guardians* of right, and when the magistrate dares not act, every person is insecure.

Let us now attend to the constitution and powers of the senate.

The house of lords in England is wholly independent on the people. The lords spiritual hold their seats by office; and

*In the decline of the republic, bribery or military force obtained this office for persons who had not attained this age—Augustus was chosen at the age of twenty; or rather obtained it with his sword.

the people at large have no voice in disposing of the ecclesiastical dignities. The temporal lords hold their seats by hereditary right, or by grant from the king: And it is a branch of the king's prerogative to make what peers he pleases.

The senate in Rome was elective; but a senator held his seat for life.*

The proposed senate in America is constituted on principles more favorable to liberty: The members are elective, and by

*I say the senate was *elective*—but this must be understood with some exceptions; or rather, qualifications. The constitution of the Roman senate has been a subject of enquiry, with the first men in modern ages. Lord Chesterfield requested the opinion of the learned Vertot, upon the manner of chusing senators in Rome; and it was a subject of discussion between Lord Harvey and Dr. Middleton. The most probable account of the manner of forming the senate, and filling up vacancies, which I have collected from the best writers on this subject, is here abridged for the consideration of the reader.

Romulus chose one hundred persons, from the principal families in Rome, to form a council or senate; and reserved to himself the right of nominating their successors; that is, of filling vacancies. "Mais comme Romulus avoit lui-même choisi les premiers senateurs, il se reserva le droit de nommer, a son gré, leurs successeurs."—Mably, sur les Romains. Other well informed historians intimate that Romulus retained the right of nominating the president only. After the union of the Sabines with the Romans, Romulus added another hundred members to the senate, but by *consent of the people*. Tarquin, the *ancient*, added another hundred; but historians are silent as to the manner.

On the destruction of Alba by Hostilius, some of the principal Alban families were added to the senate, *by consent of the senate and people*.

After the demolition of the monarchy, Appius Claudius was admitted into the senate by *order of the people*.

Cicero testifies that, from the extinction of the monarchy, all the members of the senate were admitted by *command of the people*.

It is observeable that the first creation of the senators was the act of the monarch; and the first patrician families claimed the sole right of admission into the senate. "Les familles qui descendoient des deux cent senateurs que Romulus avoit créés,—se crurent seules en droit d'entrer dans le senat." Mably.

This right however was not granted in its utmost extent; for many of the senators, in the Roman commonwealth, were taken from plebeian families. For sixty years before the institution of the *censorship*, which was A. U. C. 311, we are not informed how vacancies in the senate were supplied. The most probable method was this; to enrol, in the list of senators, the different magistrates; viz. the consuls, prætors, the two quæstors of patrician families, the five tribunes (afterwards ten) and the two ædiles of plebeian families: The office of quæstor gave an immediate admission into the senate. The tribunes were admitted two years after their creation. This enrolment seems to have

the separate legislatures: They hold their seats for six years—they are thus rendered sufficiently dependent on their constituents; and yet are not dismissed from their office as soon as they become acquainted with the forms of proceeding.

It may be objected by the larger states, that the representation in the senate is not equal; the smallest states having the privilege of sending the same number of senators as the largest. To obviate this objection, I would suggest but two or three ideas.

1. If each state had a representation and a right in deciding questions, proportional to its property, three states would almost command the whole. Such a constitution would gradually annihilate the small states; and finally melt down the whole United States into one undivided sovereignty. The free states of Spain and the heptarchy in England, afford striking examples of this.

---

been a matter of course; and likewise their confirmation by the people in their comitia or assemblies.

On extraordinary occasions, when the vacancies of the senate were numerous, the consuls used to nominate some of the most respectable of the equestrian order, to be chosen by the people.

On the institution of the censorship, the censors were invested with full powers to inspect the manners of the citizens,—enrol them in their proper ranks according to their property,—make out lists of the senators and leave out the names of such as had rendered themselves unworthy of their dignity by any scandalous vices. This power they several times exercised; but the disgraced senators had an appeal to the people.

After the senate had lost half its members in the war with Hannibal, the dictator, M. Fabius Buteo, filled up the number with the magistrates, with those who had been honored with a civic crown, or others who were respectable for age and character. One hundred and seventy new members were added at once, with *the approbation of the people*. The vacancies occasioned by Sylla's proscriptions amounted to three hundred, which were supplied by persons, nominated by Sylla and *chosen by the people*.

Before the time of the Gracchi, the number of senators did not exceed three hundred. But in Sylla's time, so far as we can collect from indirect testimonies, it amounted to about five hundred. The age necessary to qualify for a seat in the senate is not exactly ascertained; but several circumstances prove it to have been about thirty years.

See Vertot, Mably, and Middleton on this subject.

In the last ages of Roman splendor, the property requisite to qualify a person for a senator, was settled by Augustus at eight hundred sestertia—more than six thousand pounds sterling.

Should it be said that such an event is desireable, I answer; the states are all entitled to their respective sovereignties, and while they claim independence in internal jurisdiction, the federal constitution ought to guarantee their sovereignty.

2. Another consideration has weight—There is, in all nations, a tendency towards an accumulation of power in some point. It is the business of the legislator to establish some barriers to check that tendency. In small societies, a man worth £.100,000 has but one vote, when his neighbors, who are worth but fifty pounds, have each one vote likewise. To make property the sole basis of authority, would expose many of the best citizens to violence and oppression. To make the number of inhabitants in a state, the rule of apportioning power, is more equitable; and were the United States one indivisible interest, would be a perfect rule for representation. But the detached situation of the states has created some separate interests—some local institutions, which they will not resign nor throw into the hands of other states. For these peculiar interests, the states have an *equal* attachment—for the preservation and enjoyment of these, an *equal* sovereignty is necessary; and the sovereignty of each state would not be secure, had each state, in both branches of the legislature, an authority in passing laws, proportioned to its inhabitants.

3. But the senate should be considered as representing the confederacy in a body. It is a false principle in the vulgar ideas of representation, that a man delegated by a particular district in a state, is the representative of that district only; whereas in truth a member of the legislature from any town or county, is the representative of the whole state. In passing laws, he is to view the whole collective interest of the state, and act from that view; not from a partial regard to the interest of the town or county where he is chosen.

The same principle extends to the Congress of the United States. A delegate is bound to represent the true local interest of his constituents—to state it in its true light to the whole body—but when each provincial interest is thus stated, every member should act for the *aggregate interest* of the whole confederacy. The design of representation is to bring this collective interest into view—a delegate is not the legislator of a single state—he is as much the legislator of the whole confederacy as of the particular state where he is chosen; and if he gives his vote for a law which he believes to be beneficial to his own state only, and pernicious to the rest, he betrays his trust and violates his oath. It is indeed difficult for a man to divest himself of local attachments and act from an impartial regard to the general good; but he who cannot for the most part do this, is not a good legislator.

These considerations suggest the propriety of continuing the senators in office, for a longer period, than the representatives. They gradually lose their partiality, generalize their views, and consider themselves as acting for the whole confederacy. Hence in the senate we may expect union and firmness—here we may find the *general good* the object of legislation, and a check upon the more partial and interested acts of the other branch.

These considerations obviate the complaint, that the representation in the senate is not equal; for the senators represent the whole confederacy; and all that is wanted of the members is information of the true situation and interest of each state. As they act under the direction of the several legislatures, two men may as fully and completely represent a state, as twenty; and when the true interest of each state is known, if the senators perform the part of good legislators, and act impartially for the whole collective body of the United States, it is totally immaterial where they are chosen.*

*It is a capital defect of most of the state-constitutions, that the senators, like the representatives, are chosen in particular districts. They are thus inspired with local views, and however wrong it may be to entertain them, yet such is the constitution of human nature, that men are almost involuntarily attached to the interest of the district which has reposed confidence in their abilities and integrity. Some partiality therefore for constituents is always expectable. To destroy it as much as possible, a political constitution should remove the grounds of local attachment. Connecticut and Maryland have wisely destroyed this attachment in their senates, by ordaining that the members shall be chosen in the *state at large*. The senators hold their seats by the suffrages of the state, *not of a district*; hence they have no particular number of men to fear or to oblige.—They represent *the state*; hence that union and firmness which the senates of those states have manifested on the most trying occasions, and by which they have prevented the most rash and iniquitous measures.

It may be objected, that when the election of senators is vested in the people, they must choose men in their own neighborhood, or else those with

The house of representatives is the more immediate voice of the separate states—here the states are represented in proportion to their number of inhabitants—here the separate interests will operate with their full force, and the violence of parties and the jealousies produced by interfering interests, can be restrained and quieted only by a body of men, less local and dependent.

It may be objected, that no separate interests should exist in a state; and a division of the legislature has a tendency to create them. But this objection is founded on mere jealousy, or a very imperfect comparison of the Roman and British governments, with the proposed federal constitution.

The house of peers in England is a body originally and totally independent on the people—the senate in Rome was mostly composed of patrician or noble families, and after the first election of a senator, he was no longer dependent on the people—he held his seat for life. But the senate of the United States can have no separate interests from the body of the people; for they live among them—they are chosen by them—they *must* be dismissed from their place once in six years and *may* at any time be impeached for mal-practices—their property is situated among the people, and with their persons, subject to the same laws. No title can be granted, but the temporary titles of office, bestowed by the voluntary election of the people; and no pre-eminence can be acquired but by the same means.

The separation of the legislature, divides the power—checks—restrains—amends the proceedings—at the same

---

whom they are unacquainted. With respect to representatives, this objection does not lie; for they are chosen in small districts; and as to senators, there is, in every state, a small number of men, whose reputation for abilities, integrity and good conduct will lead the people to a very just choice. Old experienced statesmen should compose the senate; and people are generally, in this free country, acquainted with their characters. Were it possible, as it is in small states, it would be an improvement in the doctrine of representation, to give every freeman the right of voting for every member of the legislature, and the privilege of choosing the men in any part of the state. This would totally exclude bribery and undue influence; for no man can bribe a state; and it would almost annihilate partial views in legislation. But in large states it may be impracticable.

time, it creates no division of interest, that can tempt either branch to encroach upon the other, or upon the people. In turbulent times, such restraint is our greatest safety—in calm times, and in measures obviously calculated for the general good, both branches must always be unanimous.

A man must be thirty years of age, before he can be admitted into the senate—which was likewise a requisite in the Roman government. What property was requisite for a senator in the early ages of Rome, I cannot inform myself; but Augustus fixed it at eight hundred sestertia—between six and seven thousand pounds sterling. In the federal constitution, money is not made a requisite—the places of senators are wisely left open to all persons of suitable age and merit, and who have been citizens of the United States for nine years; a term in which foreigners may acquire the feelings and acquaint themselves with the interests, of the native Americans.

The house of representatives is formed on very equitable principles; and is calculated to guard the privileges of the people. The English house of commons is chosen by a small part of the people in England, and continues for seven years. The Romans never discovered the secret of representation—the whole body of citizens assembled for the purposes of legislation—a circumstance that exposed their government to frequent convulsions, and to capricious measures. The federal house of representatives is chosen by the people qualified to vote for state-representatives,* and continues two years.

*It is said by some, that no property should be required as a qualification for an elector. I shall not enter into a discussion of the subject; but remark that in most free governments, some property has been thought requisite, to prevent corruption and secure government from the influence of an unprincipled multitude.

In ancient Rome, none but the free citizens had the right of a suffrage in the *comitia* or legislative assemblies. But in Sylla's time the Italian cities demanded the rights of the Roman citizens; alledging that they furnished two-thirds of the armies, in all their wars, and yet were despised as foreigners. Vell. Paterc. lib. 2. cap. 15. This produced the *Marsic* or *social* war, which lasted two years, and carried off 300,000 men. Ibm. It was conducted and concluded by Pompey, father of Pompey the Great, with his lieutenants Sylla and Marius. But most of the cities eventually obtained the *freedom of Rome*; and were of course entitled to the rights of suffrage in the comitia. "Paulatim deinde recipiendo in civitatem, qui arma aut non ceperant aut deposuerant maturiùs, vires refectae sunt." Vell. Paterc. 2. 16.

Some may object to their continuance in power *two years*. But I cannot see any danger arising from this quarter. On the contrary, it creates less trouble for the representatives, who by such choice are taken from their professions and obliged to attend Congress, some of them at the distance of at least seven hundred miles. While men are chosen by the people, and responsible to them, there is but little danger from ambition or corruption.

If it should be said that Congress may in time become triennial, and even septennial, like the English parliaments, I answer, this is not in their power. The English parliament had power to prolong the period of their existence—but Congress will be restrained by the different legislatures, without whose constitutional concurrence, no alteration can be made in the proposed system.

The fourth section, article 1, of the new constitution declares, that "The times, places, and manner of holding elections for senators and representatives, shall be prescribed in each state by the legislature thereof; *but the Congress may at any time by law make or alter such regulations, except as to the places of chusing senators.*" Here let us pause—What did the

---

But Rome had cause to deplore this event, for however reasonable it might appear to admit the allies to a participation of the rights of citizens, yet the concession destroyed all freedom of election. It enabled an ambitious demagogue to engage and bring into the assemblies, whole towns of people, slaves and foreigners;—and every thing was decided by faction and violence. This Montesquieu numbers among the causes of the decline of the Roman greatness. De la grandeur des Romains, c. 9.

Representation would have, in some measure, prevented these consequences; but the admission of every man to a suffrage will ever open the door to corruption. In such a state as Connecticut, where there is no conflux of foreigners, no introduction of seamen, servants, &c. and scarcely an hundred persons in the state, who are not natives, and very few whose education and connexions do not attach them to the government; at the same time, few men have property to furnish the means of corruption, very little danger could spring from admitting every man of age and discretion to the privilege of voting for rulers. But in the large towns of America, there is more danger. A master of a vessel may put votes in the hands of his crew, for the purpose of carrying an election for a party. Such things have actually taken place in America. Besides, the middle states are receiving emigrations of poor people, who are not at once judges of the characters of men, and who cannot be safely trusted with the choice of legislators.

convention mean by giving Congress power to *make regulations*, prescribed by the legislatures? Is this expression accurate or intelligible? But the word *alter* is very intelligible, and the clause puts the election of representatives *wholly*, and the senators *almost wholly*, in the power of Congress.

The views of the convention I believe to be perfectly upright—They might mean to place the election of representatives and senators beyond the reach of faction—They doubtless had good reasons, in *their* minds, for the clause—But I see no occasion for any power in Congress to interfere with the choice of their own body—They will have power to suppress insurrections, as they ought to have; but the clause in *Italics* gives *needless* and *dangerous* powers—I hope the states will reject it with decency, and adopt the whole system, without altering another syllable.

The method of passing laws in Congress is much preferable to that of ancient Rome or of modern Britain. Not to mention other defects in Rome, it lay in the power of a single tribune to obstruct the passing of a law. As the tribunes were popular magistrates, the right was often exercised in favor of liberty; but it was also abused, and the best regulations were prevented, to gratify the spleen, the ambition, or the resentment of an individual.

The king of Great-Britain has the same power, but seldom exercises it. It is however a dangerous power—it is absurd and hazardous to lodge in *one man* the right of controlling the will of a state.

Every bill that passes a majority of both houses of Congress, must be sent to the president for his approbation; but it must be returned in ten days, whether approved by him or not; and the concurrence of two thirds of both houses passes the bill into a law, notwithstanding any objections of the president. The constitution therefore gives the supreme executive a check, but no negative, upon the sense of Congress.

The powers lodged in Congress are extensive; but it is presumed that they are not too extensive. The first object of the constitution is to *unite* the states into one *compact society*, for the purpose of government. If such *union* must exist, or the states be exposed to foreign invasions, internal discord, reciprocal encroachments upon each others property—to weakness and infamy, which no person will dispute; what powers must be collected and lodged in the supreme head or legislature of these states. The answer is easy: This legislature must have exclusive jurisdiction in all matters in which the states have a mutual interest. There are some regulations in which all the states are equally concerned—there are others, which in their operation, are limited to one state. The first belong to Congress—the last, to the respective legislatures. No one state has a right to supreme control, in any affair in which the other states have an interest; nor should Congress interfere in any affair which respects one state only. This is the general line of division, which the convention have endeavored to draw, between the powers of Congress and the rights of the individual states. The only question therefore is, whether the new constitution delegates to Congress any powers, which do not respect the general interest and welfare of the United States. If these powers intrench upon the present sovereignty of any *state*, without having for an object the *collective interest* of the whole, the powers are too extensive. But if they do not extend to all concerns, in which the states have a mutual interest, they are too limited. If in any instance, the powers, necessary for protecting the *general* interest, interfere with the constitutional rights of an *individual* state, such state has assumed powers that are inconsistent with the safety of the United States, and which ought instantly to be resigned. Considering the states as individuals, on equal terms, entering into a social compact, no state has a right to any power which may prejudice its neighbors. If therefore the federal constitution has collected into the federal legislature no more power than is necessary for the *common defence and interest*, it should be recognized by the states, however particular clauses may supersede the exercise of certain powers by the individual states.

This question is of vast magnitude. The states have very high ideas of their separate sovereignty; altho' it is certain, that while each exists in its full latitude, we can have no *Federal Sovereignty*. However flattered each state may be by its independent sovereignty, we can have no union, no respectability, no national character, and what is more, no national justice, till the states resign to one *supreme head* the exclusive power of *legislating, judging and executing*, in all matters of a general nature. Every thing of a private or provincial nature, must still rest on the ground of the respective state-constitutions.

After examining the limits of the proposed congressional powers, I confess I do not think them too extensive—I firmly believe, that the life, liberty and property of every man, and the peace and independence of each state, will be more fully secured under such a constitution of federal government, than they will under a constitution with more limited powers; and infinitely more safe, than under our boasted distinct sovereignties. It appears to me that Congress will have no more power than will be necessary for our union and general welfare; and such power they must have, or we are in a wretched state. On the adoption of this constitution, I should value real estate twenty per cent. higher than I do at this moment.

I will not examine into the extent of the powers proposed to be lodged in the supreme federal head; the subject would be extensive and require more time than I can bestow upon it. But I will just take up some objections, that have been made to particular points of the new constitution.

Most of the objections I have yet heard to the constitution, consist in mere insinuations unsupported by reasoning or fact. They are thrown out to instil groundless jealousies into the minds of the people, and probably with a view to prevent all government; for there are, in every society, some turbulent geniuses whose importance depends solely on faction. To shew the insidious and detestable nature of these insinuations, it is necessary to mention, and remark on a few particulars.

1. The first objection against the constitution is, that the legislature will be more expensive than our present confederation. This is so far from being true, that the money we actually lose by our present weakness, disunion and *want of government* would support the civil government of every state in the confederacy. Our public poverty does not proceed from the expensiveness of Congress, nor of the civil list; but from want of power to command our own advantages. We pay more money to foreign nations, in the course of business, and merely for *want of government*, than would, under an efficient

government, pay the annual interest of our domestic debt. Every man in business knows this to be *truth*; and the objection can be designed only to delude the ignorant.

2. Another objection to the constitution, is the division of the legislature into two branches. Luckily this objection has no advocates but in Pennsylvania; and even here their number is dwindling. The factions that reign in this state, the internal discord and passions that disturb the government and the peace of the inhabitants, have detected the errors of the constitution, and will some time or other produce a reformation. The division of the legislature has been the subject of discussion in the beginning of this essay; and will be deemed, by nineteen-twentieths of the Americans, one of the principal excellencies of the constitution.

3. A third insinuation, is that the proposed federal government will annihilate the several legislatures. This is extremely disingenuous. Every person, capable of reading, must discover, that the convention have labored to draw the line between the federal and provincial powers—to define the powers of Congress, and limit them to those general concerns which *must* come under federal jurisdiction, and which *cannot* be managed in the separate legislatures—that in all internal regulations, whether of civil or criminal nature, the states retain their sovereignty, and have it guaranteed to them by this very constitution. Such a groundless insinuation, or rather mere surmise, must proceed from dark designs or extreme ignorance, and deserves the severest reprobation.

4. It is alledged that the liberty of the press is not guaranteed by the new constitution. But this objection is wholly unfounded. The liberty of the press does not come within the jurisdiction of federal government. It is firmly established in all the states either by law, or positive declarations in *bills of right*; and not being mentioned in the federal constitution, is not—and cannot be abridged by Congress. It stands on the basis of the respective state-constitutions. Should any state resign to Congress the exclusive jurisdiction of a certain district, which should include any town where presses are already established, it is in the power of the state to reserve the liberty of the press, or any other fundamental privilege, and make it

an immutable condition of the grant, that such rights shall never be violated. All objections therefore on this score are *"baseless visions."*

5. It is insinuated that the constitution gives Congress the power of levying internal taxcs at pleasure. This insinuation seems founded on the eighth section of the first article, which declares, that "Congress shall have power to lay and collect taxes, duties, imposts and excises, to pay the debts and provide for the common defence and general welfare of the United States."

That Congress should have power to collect duties, imposts and excises, in order to render them uniform throughout the United States, will hardly be controverted. The whole objection is to the right of levying internal taxes.

But it will be conceded that the supreme head of the states must have power, competent to the purposes of our union, or it will be, as it now is, a *useless body*, a mere expense, without any advantage. To pay our public debt, to support foreign ministers and our own civil government, money must be raised; and if the duties and imposts are not adequate to these purposes, where shall the money be obtained? It will be answered, let Congress apportion the sums to be raised, and leave the legislatures to collect the money. Well this is all that is intended by the clause under consideration; with the addition of a federal power that shall be sufficient to oblige a delinquent state to comply with the requisition. Such power must exist somewhere, or the debts of the United States can never be paid. For want of such power, our credit is lost and our national faith is a bye-word.

For want of such power, one state now complies fully with a requisition, another partially, and a third absolutely refuses or neglects to grant a shilling. Thus the honest and punctual are doubly loaded—and the knave triumphs in his negligence. In short, no honest man will dread a power that shall enforce an equitable system of taxation. The dis-honest are ever apprehensive of a power that shall oblige them to do what honest men are ready to do voluntarily.

Permit me to ask those who object to this power of taxation, how shall money be raised to discharge our honest debts; debts which are universally acknowledged to be just?

Have we not already experienced the inefficacy of a system without power? Has it not been proved to demonstration, that a voluntary compliance with the demands of the union can never be expected? To what expedient shall we have recourse? What is the resort of all governments in cases of delinquency? Do not the states vest in the legislature, or even in the governor and council, a power to enforce laws, even with the militia of the states? And how rarely does there exist a necessity of exerting such a power? Why should such a power be more dangerous in Congress than in a legislature? Why should more confidence be reposed in a member of one legislature than of another? Why should we choose the best men in the state to represent us in Congress, and the moment they are elected arm ourselves against them as against tyrants and robbers? Do we not, in this conduct, act the part of a man, who, as soon as he has married a woman of unsuspected chastity, locks her up in a dungeon? Is there any spell or charm, that instantly changes a delegate to Congress from an honest man into a knave—a tyrant? I confess freely that I am willing to trust Congress with any powers that I should dare lodge in a state-legislature. I believe life, liberty, and property would be as safe in the hands of a federal legislature, organized in the manner proposed by the convention, as in the hands of any legislature, that ever has been, or ever will be chosen in any particular state.

But the idea that Congress can levy taxes *at pleasure* is false, and the suggestion wholly unsupported. The preamble to the constitution is declaratory of the purposes of our union; and the assumption of any powers not necessary to *establish justice, insure domestic tranquility, provide for the common defence, promote the general welfare, and to secure the blessings of liberty to ourselves and our posterity*, will be unconstitutional, and endanger the existence of Congress. Besides, in the very clause which gives the power of levying duties and taxes, the purposes to which the money shall be appropriated are specified, viz. *to pay the debts and provide for the common defence and general welfare of the United States**. For these purposes, money

---

*The clause may at first appear ambiguous. It may be uncertain whether we should read and understand it thus—"The Congress shall have power to

must be collected, and the power of collection must be lodged, sooner or later, in a federal head; or the common defence and general welfare must be neglected.

The states, in their separate capacity, cannot provide for the *common* defence; nay in case of a civil war, a state cannot secure its own existence. The only question therefore is, whether it is necessary to unite, and provide for our *common defence and general welfare*. For this question being once decided in the affirmative, leaves no room to controvert the propriety of constituting a power over the whole United States, adequate to these general purposes.

The states, by granting such power, do not throw it out of their own hands—they only throw, each its proportion, into a common stock—they merely combine the powers of the several states into one point, where they *must* be collected, before they *can* be exerted. But the powers are still in their own hands; and cannot be alienated, till they create a body independent of themselves, with a force at their command, superior to the whole yeomanry of the country.

6. It is said that there is no provision made in the new constitution against a standing army in time of peace. Why do not people object that no provision is made against the introduction of a body of Turkish Janizaries; or against making the Alcoran the rule of faith and practice, instead of the Bible? The answer to such objections is simply this—*no such provision is necessary*. The people in this country cannot forget their apprehensions from a British standing army, quartered in America; and they turn their fears and jealousies against themselves. Why do not the people of most of the states ap-

---

lay and collect taxes, duties, imposts and excises, *in order to pay the debts*," &c. or whether the meaning is—"The Congress shall have power to lay and collect taxes, duties, imposts and excises, and *shall have power to pay the debts*," &c. On considering the construction of the clause, and comparing it with the preamble, the last sense seems to be improbable and absurd. But it is not very material; for no powers are vested in Congress but what are included under the general expressions, of *providing for the common defence and general welfare of the United States*. Any powers not promotive of these purposes, will be unconstitutional; — consequently any appropriations of money to any other purpose will expose the Congress to the resentment of the states, and the members to impeachment and loss of their seats.

prehend danger from standing armies from their own legislatures? Pennsylvania and North Carolina, I believe, are the only states that have provided against this danger at all events. Other states have declared that "no standing armies shall be kept up without the consent of the legislature." But this leaves the power entirely in the hands of the legislature. Many of the states however have made *no provision* against this evil. What hazards these states suffer! Why does not a man pass a law in his family, that no armed soldier shall be quartered in his house by his consent? The reason is very plain: no man will suffer his liberty to be abridged, or endangered—his disposition and his power are uniformly opposed to any infringement of his rights. In the same manner, the principles and habits, as well as the power of the Americans are directly opposed to standing armies; and there is as little necessity to guard against them by positive constitutions, as to prohibit the establishment of the Mahometan religion. But the constitution provides for our safety; and while it gives Congress power to raise armies, it declares that no appropriation of money to their support shall be for a longer term than two years.

Congress likewise are to have power to provide for organizing, arming and disciplining the militia, but have no other command of them, except when in actual service. Nor are they at liberty to call out the militia at pleasure—but only, to execute the laws of the union, suppress insurrections and repel invasions. For these purposes, government must always be armed with a military force, if the occasion should require it; otherwise laws are nugatory, and life and property insecure.

7. Some persons have ventured to publish an intimation, that by the proposed constitution, the trial by jury is abolished in *all civil cases*. Others very modestly insinuate, that it is in *some cases* only. The fact is, that trial by jury is not affected in *any case*, by the constitution; except in cases of impeachment, which are to be tried by the senate. None but persons in office in or under Congress can be impeached; and even after a judgement upon an impeachment, the offender is liable to a prosecution, before a common jury, in a regular course of law. The insinuation therefore that trials by jury are to be abolished, is groundless and beyond conception, wicked. It

must be wicked, because the circulation of a barefaced falsehood, respecting a privilege, dear to freemen, can proceed
only from a depraved heart and the worst intentions.

8. It is also intimated as a probable event, that the federal
courts will absorb the judiciaries of the several states. This is a
mere suspicion, without the least foundation. The jurisdiction
of the federal courts is very accurately defined and easily understood. It extends to the cases mentioned in the constitution, and to the execution of the laws of Congress, respecting
commerce, revenue and other general concerns.

With respect to all other civil and criminal actions, the
powers and jurisdiction of the several judiciaries of each state,
remain unimpaired. Nor is there any thing novel in allowing
appeals to the supreme court. Actions are mostly to be tried
in the state where the crimes are committed—But appeals are
allowed under our present confederation, and no person complains; nay, were there no appeal, every man would have reason to complain, especially when a final judgement, in an
inferior court, should affect property to a large amount. But
why is an objection raised against an appellate jurisdiction in
the supreme court, respecting *fact* as well as *law*? Is it less safe
to have the opinions of two juries than of one? I suspect
many people will think this no defect in the constitution. But
perhaps it will destroy a material requisite of a good jury, viz.
their vicinity to the cause of action. I have no doubt, that
when causes were tried, in periods prior to the Christian æra,
before twelve men, seated upon twelve stones, arranged in a
circular form, under a huge oak, there was great propriety in
submitting causes to men *in the vicinity*. The difficulty of collecting evidence, in those rude times, rendered it necessary
that juries should judge mostly from their own knowledge of
facts or from information obtained out of court. But in these
polished ages, when juries depend almost wholly on the testimony of witnesses; and when a complication of interests, introduced by commerce and other causes, renders it almost
impossible to collect men, in the vicinity of the parties, who
are wholly disinterested, it is no disadvantage to have a cause
tried by a jury of strangers. Indeed the latter is generally the
most eligible.

But the truth is, the creation of all inferior courts is in the power of Congress; and the constitution provides that Congress may make such exceptions from the right of appeals as they shall judge proper. When these courts are erected, their jurisdictions will be ascertained, and in small actions, Congress will doubtless direct that a sentence in a subordinate court shall, to a certain amount, be definitive and final. All objections therefore to the judicial powers of the federal courts appear to me as trifling as any of the preceding.

9. But, say the enemies of slavery, negroes may be imported for twenty-one years. This exception is addressed to the quakers; and a very pitiful exception it is.

The truth is, Congress cannot prohibit the importation of slaves, during that period; but the laws against the importation into particular states, stand unrepealed. An immediate abolition of slavery would bring ruin upon the whites, and misery upon the blacks, in the southern states. The constitution has therefore wisely left each state to pursue its own measures, with respect to this article of legislation, during the period of twenty-one years.

Such are the principal objections that have yet been made by the enemies of the new constitution. They are mostly frivolous, or founded on false constructions, and a misrepresentation of the true state of facts. They are evidently designed to raise groundless jealousies in the minds of well meaning people, who have little leisure and opportunity to examine into the principles of government. But a little time and reflection will enable most people to detect such mischievous intentions; and the spirit and firmness which have distinguished the conduct of the Americans, during the conflict for independence, will eventually triumph over the enemies of our union, and bury them in disgrace or oblivion.

But I cannot quit this subject, without attempting to correct some erroneous opinions respecting *freedom* and *tyranny*, and the principles by which they are supported. Many people seem to entertain an idea, that liberty consists in *a power to act without any control*. This is more liberty than even the savages enjoy. But in civil society, political liberty consists in *acting conformably to the sense of a majority of the society*. In a free government, every man binds himself to obey the *public voice*, or the opinions of a majority; and the *whole society* engages to

protect each individual. In such a government a man is *free* and
safe. But reverse the case; suppose every man to act without
control or fear of punishment—every man would be free, but
no man would be sure of his freedom one moment. Each
would have the power of taking his neighbor's life, liberty or
property; and no man would command more than his own
strength to repel the invasion. The case is the same with
states. If the states should not unite into one compact society,
every state may trespass upon its neighbor, and the injured
state has no means of redress but its own military force.

The present situation of our American states is very little
better than a state of nature—Our boasted state sovereignties are so far from securing our liberty and property, that
they, every moment, expose us to the loss of both. That state
which commands the heaviest purse and longest sword, may
at any moment, lay its weaker neighbor under tribute; and
there is no superior power now existing, that can regularly
oppose the invasion or redress the injury. From such liberty,
O Lord, deliver us!

But what is tyranny? Or how can a free people be deprived
of their liberties? Tyranny is the exercise of some power over
a man, which is not warranted by law, or necessary for the
public safety. A people can never be deprived of their liberties, while they retain in their own hands, a power superior to
any other power in the state. This position leads me directly
to enquire, in what consists the power of a nation or of an
order of men?

In some nations, legislators have derived much of their
power from the influence of religion, or from that implicit
belief which an ignorant and superstitious people entertain of
the gods, and their interposition in every transaction of life.
The Roman senate sometimes availed themselves of this engine to carry their decrees and maintain their authority. This
was particularly the case, under the aristocracy which succeeded the abolition of the monarchy. The augurs and priests
were taken wholly from patrician families.* They constituted
a distinct order of men—had power to negative any law of

---

*"Quod nemo plebeius auspicia haberet, ideoque decemviros connubium
diremisse, ne incerta prole auspicia turbarentur." Tit. Liv. lib. 4. cap. 6.

the people, by declaring that it was passed during the taking of the auspices.* This influence derived from the authority of opinion, was less perceptible, but as tyrannical as a military force. The same influence constitutes, at this day, a principal support of several governments on the Eastern continent, and perhaps in South America. But in North America, by a singular concurrence of circumstances, the possibility of establishing this influence, as a pillar of government, is totally precluded.

Another source of power in government is a military force. But this, to be efficient, must be superior to any force that exists among the people, or which they can command; for otherwise this force would be annihilated, on the first exercise of acts of oppression. Before a standing army can rule, the people must be disarmed; as they are in almost every kingdom in Europe. The supreme power in America cannot enforce unjust laws by the sword; because the whole body of the people are armed, and constitute a force superior to any band of regular troops that can be, on any pretence, raised in the United States. A military force, at the command of Congress, can execute no laws, but such as the people perceive to be just and constitutional; for they will possess the *power*, and jealousy will instantly inspire the *inclination*, to resist the execution of a law which appears to them unjust and oppressive. In spite of all the nominal powers, vested in Congress by the constitution, were the system once adopted in its fullest latitude, still the actual exercise of them would be frequently interrupted by popular jealousy. I am bold to say, that *ten* just and constitutional measures would be resisted, where *one* unjust or oppressive law would be enforced. The powers vested in Congress are little more than *nominal*; nay *real* power cannot be vested in them, nor in any body, but in the *people*. The source of power is in the *people* of this country, and cannot for ages, and probably never will, be removed.

In what then does *real* power consist? The answer is short and plain—in *property*. Could we want any proofs of this,

*Auguriis certe sacerdotisque augurum tantus honos accessit, ut nihil belli domique postea, nisi auspicato, gereretur: concilia populi, exercitus vocati, summa rerum, ubi aves non admisissent, dirimerentur. Liv. lib. 1. cap. 37.

which are not exhibited in this country, the uniform testimony of history will furnish us with multitudes. But I will go no farther for proof, than the two governments already mentioned, the Roman and the British.

Rome exhibited a demonstrative proof of the inseparable connexion between property and dominion. The first form of its government was an elective monarchy—its second, an aristocracy; but these forms could not be permanent, because they were not supported by property. The kings at first and afterwards the patricians had nominally most of the power; but the people, possessing most of the lands, never ceased to assert their privileges, till they established a commonwealth. And the kings and senate could not have held the reigns of government in their hands so long as they did, had they not artfully contrived to manage the established religion, and play off the superstitious credulity of the people against their own power. "Thus this weak constitution of government," says the ingenious Mr. Moyle, speaking of the aristocracy of Rome, "not founded on the true *center of dominion*, *land*, nor on any standing foundation of authority, nor rivetted in the esteem and affections of the people; and being attacked by strong passion, general interest and the joint forces of the people, mouldered away of course, and pined of a lingering consumption, till it was totally swallowed up by the prevailing faction, and the nobility were moulded into the mass of the people."* The people, notwithstanding the nominal authority of the patricians, proceeded regularly in enlarging their own powers. They first extorted from the senate, the right of electing *tribunes*, with a negative upon the proceedings of the senate.† They obtained the right of proposing and debating laws; which before had been vested in the senate; and finally advanced to the power of enacting laws, without the authority of the senate.‡ They regained the rights of election in their comitia, of which they had been deprived by Servius Tullius.§ They procured a permanent body of laws, collected from the Grecian institutions. They

*Essay on the Roman government.
†Livy, 2. 33.
‡Livy, 3. 54.
§Livy, 3. 33.

destroyed the influence of augurs, or diviners, by establishing the *tributa comitia*, in which they were not allowed to consult the gods. They increased their power by large accessions of conquered lands. They procured a repeal of the law which prohibited marriages between the patricians and plebeians.* The Licinian law limited all possessions to five hundred acres of land; which, had it been fully executed, would have secured the commonwealth.†

The Romans proceeded thus step by step to triumph over the aristocracy, and to crown their privileges, they procured the right of being elected to the highest offices of the state. By acquiring *the property* of the plebeians, the nobility, several times, held most of the power of the state; but the people, by reducing the interest of money, abolishing debts, or by forcing other advantages from the patricians, generally held the power of governing in their own hands.

In America, we begin our empire with more popular privileges than the Romans ever enjoyed. We have not to struggle against a monarch or an aristocracy—power is lodged in the mass of the people.

On reviewing the English history, we observe a progress similar to that in Rome—an incessant struggle for liberty from the date of Magna Charta, in John's reign, to the revolution. The struggle has been successful, by abridging the enormous power of the nobility. But we observe that the power of the people has increased in an exact proportion to their acquisitions of property. Wherever the right of primogeniture is established, property must accumulate and remain in families. Thus the landed property in England will never be sufficiently distributed, to give the powers of government wholly into the hands of the people. But to assist the struggle for liberty, commerce has interposed, and in conjunction with manufactures, thrown a vast weight of property into the democratical scale. Wherever we cast our eyes, we see this truth, that *property* is the basis of *power*; and this, being established as a cardinal point, directs us to the means of preserving our freedom. Make laws, irrevocable laws in every state, destroying

*Livy, 4. 6.
†Livy, 6. 35. 42. "Ne quis plus quingenta jugera agri possideret."

and barring entailments; leave real estates to revolve from hand to hand, as time and accident may direct; and no family influence can be acquired and established for a series of generations—no man can obtain dominion over a large territory—the laborious and saving, who are generally the best citizens, will possess each his share of property and power, and thus the balance of wealth and power will continue where it is, in the *body of the people.*

A general and tolerably equal distribution of landed property is the whole basis of national freedom: The system of the great Montesquieu will ever be erroneous, till the words *property or lands in fee simple* are substituted for *virtue,* throughout his *Spirit of Laws.*

Virtue, patriotism, or love of country, never was and never will be, till mens' natures are changed, a fixed, permanent principle and support of government. But in an agricultural country, a general possession of land in fee simple, may be rendered perpetual; and the inequalities introduced by commerce, are too fluctuating to endanger government. An equality of property, with a necessity of alienation, constantly operating to destroy combinations of powerful families, is the very *soul of a republic*—While this continues, the people will inevitably possess both *power* and *freedom*; when this is lost, power departs, liberty expires, and a commonwealth will inevitably assume some other form.

The liberty of the press, trial by jury, the Habeas Corpus writ, even Magna Charta itself, although justly deemed the palladia of freedom, are all inferior considerations, when compared with a general distribution of real property among every class of people.* The power of entailing estates is more

---

*Montesquieu supposed *virtue* to be the principle of a republic. He derived his notions of this form of government, from the astonishing firmness, courage and patriotism which distinguished the republics of Greece and Rome. But this *virtue* consisted in pride, contempt of strangers and a martial enthusiasm which sometimes displayed itself in defence of their country. These principles are never permanent—they decay with refinement, intercourse with other nations and increase of wealth. No wonder then that these republics declined, for they were not founded on fixed principles; and hence authors imagine that republics cannot be durable. None of the celebrated writers on government seem to have laid sufficient stress on a general possession of real property in fee-simple. Even the author of the *Political Sketches,*

dangerous to liberty and republican government, than all the constitutions that can be written on paper, or even than a standing army. Let the people have property, and they *will* have power—a power that will for ever be exerted to prevent a restriction of the press, an abolition of trial by jury, or the abridgement of any other privilege. The liberties of America therefore, and her forms of government, stand on the broadest basis. Removed from the fears of a foreign invasion and conquest, they are not exposed to the convulsions that shake other governments; and the principles of freedom are so general and energetic, as to exclude the possibility of a change in our republican constitutions.

But while *property* is considered as the *basis* of the freedom of the American yeomanry, there are other auxiliary supports; among which is the *information of the people*. In no country, is education so general—in no country, have the body of the people such a knowledge of the rights of men and the principles of government. This knowledge, joined with a keen sense of liberty and a watchful jealousy, will guard our constitu-

---

in the *Museum* for the month of September, seems to have passed it over in silence; although he combats Montesquieu's system, and to prove it false, enumerates some of the principles which distinguish our governments from others, and which he supposes constitute the support of republics.

The English writers on law and government consider Magna Charta, trial by juries, the Habeas Corpus act, and the liberty of the press, as the bulwarks of freedom. All this is well. But in no government of consequence in Europe, is freedom established on its true and immoveable foundation. The property is too much accumulated, and the accumulations too well guarded, to admit the *true principle of republics*. But few centuries have elapsed, since the body of the people were vassals. To such men, the smallest extension of popular privileges, was deemed an invaluable blessing. Hence the encomiums upon trial by juries, and the articles just mentioned. But these people have never been able to mount to the source of *liberty, estates in fee*, or at least but partially; they are yet obliged to drink at the streams. Hence the English jealousy of certain rights, which are guaranteed by acts of parliament. But in America, and here alone, we have gone at once to the *fountain of liberty*, and raised the people to their true dignity. Let the lands be possessed by the people in fee-simple, let the fountain be kept pure, and the streams will be pure of course. Our jealousy of *trial by jury, the liberty of the press*, &c. is totally groundless. Such rights are inseparably connected with the *power* and *dignity* of the people, which rest on their *property*. They cannot be abridged. All *other* nations have wrested *property* and *freedom* from *barons* and *tyrants*; *we* begin our empire with full possession of property and all its attending rights.

tions, and awaken the people to an instantaneous resistance of encroachments.

But a principal bulwark of freedom is the *right of election*. An equal distribution of property is the *foundation* of a republic; but *popular elections* form the great *barrier* which defends it from assault, and guards it from the slow and imperceptible approaches of corruption. Americans! never resign that right. It is not very material whether your representatives are elected for one year or two—but the *right*, is the Magna Charta of your governments. For this reason, expunge that clause of the new constitution before mentioned, which gives Congress an influence in the election of their own body. The *time, place* and *manner* of chusing senators or representatives are of little or no consequence to Congress. The number of members and the time of meeting in Congress are fixed; but the *choice* should rest solely with the several states. I repeat it—reject the clause with decency, but with unanimity and firmness.

Excepting that clause, the constitution is good—it guarantees the *fundamental principles* of our several constitutions—it guards our rights—and while it vests extensive powers in Congress, it vests no more than are necessary for our union. Without powers lodged somewhere in a single body, fully competent to lay and collect equal taxes and duties—to adjust controversies between different states—to silence contending interests—to suppress insurrections—to regulate commerce—to treat with foreign nations, our confederation is a cobweb—liable to be blown asunder by every blast of faction that is raised in the remotest corner of the United States.

Every motive that can possibly influence men ever to unite under civil government, now urges the unanimous adoption of the new constitution. But in America, we are urged to it by a singular necessity. By the local situation of the several states, *a few* command *all* the advantages of commerce. Those states which have no advantages, made equal exertions for independence, loaded themselves with immense debts, and now are utterly unable to discharge them; while their richer neighbors are taxing them for their own benefit, merely because they *can*. I can prove to a demonstration that Connecticut, which has the heaviest internal or state debt, in proportion to its number of inhabitants, of any in the union, cannot discharge its debt, on any principles of taxation ever yet practised. Yet the state pays in duties, at least 100,000 dollars annually, on goods consumed by its own people, but imported by New York. This sum, could it be saved to the state by an equal system of revenue, would enable that state gradually to sink its debt.*

New Jersey and some other states are in the same situation, except that their debts are not so large, in proportion to their wealth and population.

The boundaries of the several states were not drawn with a view to independence; and while this country was subject to Great Britain, they produced no commercial or political inconveniences. But the revolution has placed things on a different footing. The advantages of some states, and the disadvantages of others are so great—and so materially affect the business and interest of each, that nothing but an equalizing system of revenue, that shall reduce the advantages to some equitable proportion, can prevent a civil war, and save the national debt. Such a system of revenue is the *sine qua non* of public justice and tranquillity.

It is absurd for a man to oppose the adoption of the constitution, because *he* thinks some part of it defective or exceptionable. Let every man be at liberty to expunge what *he* judges exceptionable, and not a syllable of the constitution will survive the scrutiny. A painter, after executing a masterly piece, requested every spectator to draw a pencil over the part that did not please him; but to his surprise, he soon found the *whole piece* defaced. Let every man examine the most perfect building by his *own* taste, and like some microscopic critics, condemn the *whole* for small deviations from the rules of architecture, and not a part of the *best* constructed fabric would escape. But let *any* man take a *comprehensive view* of the whole, and he will be pleased with the general beauty and proportions, and admire the structure. The same remarks apply to the new constitution. I have no doubt that *every* member of the late convention has exceptions to *some part* of the system proposed. Their constituents have the same, and if *every*

*The state debt of Connecticut is about 3,500,000 dollars, its proportion of the federal debt about the same sum. The annual interest of the whole 420,000 dollars.

objection must be removed, before we have a national government, the Lord have mercy on us!

Perfection is not the lot of humanity. Instead of censuring the small faults of the constitution, I am astonished, that so many clashing interests have been reconciled—and so many sacrifices made to the *general interest*! The mutual concessions made by the gentlemen of the convention, reflect the highest honor on their candor and liberality; at the same time, they prove, that their minds were deeply impressed with a conviction, that such mutual sacrifices are *essential to our union*. They *must* be made sooner or later by every state; or jealousies, local interests and prejudices will unsheath the sword, and some Cæsar or Cromwell will avail himself of our divisions, and wade to a throne through streams of blood.

It is not our duty as freemen, to receive the opinions of any men, however great and respectable, without an examination. But when we reflect that some of the greatest men in America, with the venerable FRANKLIN and the illustrious WASHINGTON at their head; *some* of them the *fathers* and *saviors* of their country, men who have labored at the helm during a long and violent tempest, and guided us to the haven of peace—and *all* of them distinguished for their abilities, their acquaintance with ancient and modern governments, as well as with the temper, the passions, the interests and the wishes of the Americans;—when we reflect on these circumstances, it is impossible to resist impressions of respect, and we are almost impelled to suspect our own judgements, when we call in question any part of the system, which they have recommended for adoption. Not having the same means of information, we are more liable to mistake the nature and tendency of particular articles of the constitution, or the reasons on which they were admitted. Great confidence therefore should be reposed in the abilities, the zeal and integrity of that respectable body. But after all, if the constitution should, in its future operation, be found defective or inconvenient, two-thirds of both houses of Congress or the application of two-thirds of the legislatures, may open the door for amendments. Such improvements may then be made, as experience shall dictate.

Let us then consider the *New Federal Constitution*, as it

really is, an *improvement* on the *best* constitutions that the world ever saw. In the house of representatives, the people of America have an equal voice and suffrage. The choice of the men is placed in the freemen or electors at large; and the frequency of elections, and the responsibility of the members, will render them sufficiently dependent on their constituents. The senate will be composed of older men; and while their regular dismission from office, once in six years, will preserve their dependence on their constituents, the duration of their existence will give firmness to their decisions, and temper the factions which must necessarily prevail in the other branch. The president of the United States, is elective, and what is a capital improvement on the best governments, the mode of chusing him excludes the danger of faction and corruption. As the supreme executive, he is invested with power to enforce the laws of the union and give energy to the federal government.

The constitution defines the powers of Congress; and every power not expressly delegated to that body, remains in the several state-legislatures. The sovereignty and the republican form of government of each state is guaranteed by the constitution; and the bounds of jurisdiction between the federal and respective state-governments, are marked with precision. In theory, it has all the energy and freedom of the British and Roman governments, without their defects. In short, the privileges of freemen are interwoven into the very feelings and habits of the Americans; *liberty* stands on the immoveable basis of a general distribution of property and diffusion of knowledge; but the Americans must cease to contend, to fear, and to hate, before they can realize the benefits of independence and government, or enjoy the blessings, which heaven has lavished, in rich profusion, upon this western world.

"Brutus" I

New York Journal, October 18, 1787

To the CITIZENS *of the* STATE *of* NEW-YORK.

When the public is called to investigate and decide upon a question in which not only the present members of the community are deeply interested, but upon which the happiness and misery of generations yet unborn is in great measure suspended, the benevolent mind cannot help feeling itself peculiarly interested in the result.

In this situation, I trust the feeble efforts of an individual, to lead the minds of the people to a wise and prudent determination, cannot fail of being acceptable to the candid and dispassionate part of the community. Encouraged by this consideration, I have been induced to offer my thoughts upon the present important crisis of our public affairs.

Perhaps this country never saw so critical a period in their political concerns. We have felt the feebleness of the ties by which these United-States are held together, and the want of sufficient energy in our present confederation, to manage, in some instances, our general concerns. Various expedients have been proposed to remedy these evils, but none have succeeded. At length a Convention of the states has been assembled, they have formed a constitution which will now, probably, be submitted to the people to ratify or reject, who are the fountain of all power, to whom alone it of right belongs to make or unmake constitutions, or forms of government, at their pleasure. The most important question that was ever proposed to your decision, or to the decision of any people under heaven, is before you, and you are to decide upon it by men of your own election, chosen specially for this purpose. If the constitution, offered to your acceptance, be a wise one, calculated to preserve the invaluable blessings of liberty, to secure the inestimable rights of mankind, and promote human happiness, then, if you accept it, you will lay a lasting foundation of happiness for millions yet unborn; generations to come will rise up and call you blessed. You may rejoice in the prospects of this vast extended continent becoming filled with freemen, who will assert the dignity of human nature. You may solace yourselves with the idea, that society, in this favoured land, will fast advance to the highest point of perfection; the human mind will expand in knowledge and virtue, and the golden age be, in some measure, realised. But if, on the other hand, this form of government contains principles that will lead to the subversion of liberty—if it tends to establish a despotism, or, what is worse, a tyrannic aristocracy; then, if you adopt it, this only remaining assylum for liberty will be shut up, and posterity will execrate your memory.

Momentous then is the question you have to determine, and you are called upon by every motive which should influence a noble and virtuous mind, to examine it well, and to make up a wise judgment. It is insisted, indeed, that this constitution must be received, be it ever so imperfect. If it has its defects, it is said, they can be best amended when they are experienced. But remember, when the people once part with power, they can seldom or never resume it again but by force. Many instances can be produced in which the people have voluntarily increased the powers of their rulers; but few, if any, in which rulers have willingly abridged their authority. This is a sufficient reason to induce you to be careful, in the first instance, how you deposit the powers of government.

With these few introductory remarks, I shall proceed to a consideration of this constitution.

The first question that presents itself on the subject is, whether a confederated government be the best for the United States or not? Or in other words, whether the thirteen United States should be reduced to one great republic, governed by one legislature, and under the direction of one executive and judicial; or whether they should continue thirteen confederated republics, under the direction and controul of a supreme federal head for certain defined national purposes only?

This enquiry is important, because, although the government reported by the convention does not go to a perfect and entire consolidation, yet it approaches so near to it, that it must, if executed, certainly and infallibly terminate in it.

This government is to possess absolute and uncontroulable power, legislative, executive and judicial, with respect to every object to which it extends, for by the last clause of section 8th, article 1st, it is declared "that the Congress shall have power to make all laws which shall be necessary and proper for carrying into execution the foregoing powers, and all other powers vested by this constitution, in the government of the United States; or in any department or office thereof." And by the 6th article, it is declared "that this constitution, and the laws of the United States, which shall be made in pursuance thereof, and the treaties made, or which shall be made, under the authority of the United States, shall be the supreme law of the land; and the judges in every state shall be bound thereby, any thing in the constitution, or law of any state to the contrary notwithstanding." It appears from these articles that there is no need of any intervention of the state governments, between the Congress and the people, to execute any one power vested in the general government, and that the constitution and laws of every state are nullified and declared void, so far as they are or shall be inconsistent with this constitution, or the laws made in pursuance of it, or with treaties made under the authority of the United States.—The government then, so far as it extends, is a complete one, and not a confederation. It is as much one complete government as that of New-York or Massachusetts, has as absolute and perfect powers to make and execute all laws, to appoint officers, institute courts, declare offences, and annex penalties, with respect to every object to which it extends, as any other in the world. So far therefore as its powers reach, all ideas of confederation are given up and lost. It is true this government is limited to certain objects, or to speak more properly, some small degree of power is still left to the states, but a little attention to the powers vested in the general government, will convince every candid man, that if it is capable of being executed, all that is reserved for the individual states must very soon be annihilated, except so far as they are barely necessary to the organization of the general government. The powers of the general

legislature extend to every case that is of the least importance—there is nothing valuable to human nature, nothing
dear to freemen, but what is within its power. It has authority
to make laws which will affect the lives, the liberty, and property of every man in the United States; nor can the constitution or laws of any state, in any way prevent or impede the
full and complete execution of every power given. The legislative power is competent to lay taxes, duties, imposts, and
excises;—there is no limitation to this power, unless it be said
that the clause which directs the use to which those taxes, and
duties shall be applied, may be said to be a limitation: but this
is no restriction of the power at all, for by this clause they are
to be applied to pay the debts and provide for the common
defence and general welfare of the United States; but the legislature have authority to contract debts at their discretion;
they are the sole judges of what is necessary to provide for the
common defence, and they only are to determine what is for
the general welfare; this power therefore is neither more nor
less, than a power to lay and collect taxes, imposts, and excises, at their pleasure; not only the power to lay taxes unlimited, as to the amount they may require, but it is perfect
and absolute to raise them in any mode they please. No state
legislature, or any power in the state governments, have any
more to do in carrying this into effect, than the authority of
one state has to do with that of another. In the business
therefore of laying and collecting taxes, the idea of confederation is totally lost, and that of one entire republic is embraced.
It is proper here to remark, that the authority to lay and collect taxes is the most important of any power that can be
granted; it connects with it almost all other powers, or at least
will in process of time draw all other after it; it is the great
mean of protection, security, and defence, in a good government, and the great engine of oppression and tyranny in a
bad one. This cannot fail of being the case, if we consider the
contracted limits which are set by this constitution, to the late
governments, on this article of raising money. No state can
emit paper money—lay any duties, or imposts, on imports,
or exports, but by consent of the Congress; and then the net
produce shall be for the benefit of the United States: the only
mean therefore left, for any state to support its government

and discharge its debts, is by direct taxation; and the United States have also power to lay and collect taxes, in any way they please. Every one who has thought on the subject, must be convinced that but small sums of money can be collected in any country, by direct taxes, when the fœderal government begins to exercise the right of taxation in all its parts, the legislatures of the several states will find it impossible to raise monies to support their governments. Without money they cannot be supported, and they must dwindle away, and, as before observed, their powers absorbed in that of the general government.

It might be here shewn, that the power in the federal legislative, to raise and support armies at pleasure, as well in peace as in war, and their controul over the militia, tend, not only to a consolidation of the government, but the destruction of liberty.—I shall not, however, dwell upon these, as a few observations upon the judicial power of this government, in addition to the preceding, will fully evince the truth of the position.

The judicial power of the United States is to be vested in a supreme court, and in such inferior courts as Congress may from time to time ordain and establish. The powers of these courts are very extensive; their jurisdiction comprehends all civil causes, except such as arise between citizens of the same state; and it extends to all cases in law and equity arising under the constitution. One inferior court must be established, I presume, in each state, at least, with the necessary executive officers appendant thereto. It is easy to see, that in the common course of things, these courts will eclipse the dignity, and take away from the respectability, of the state courts. These courts will be, in themselves, totally independent of the states, deriving their authority from the United States, and receiving from them fixed salaries; and in the course of human events it is to be expected, that they will swallow up all the powers of the courts in the respective states.

How far the clause in the 8th section of the 1st article may operate to do away all idea of confederated states, and to effect an entire consolidation of the whole into one general government, it is impossible to say. The powers given by this article are very general and comprehensive, and it may receive a construction to justify the passing almost any law. A power to make all laws, which shall be *necessary and proper*, for carrying into execution, all powers vested by the constitution in the government of the United States, or any department or officer thereof, is a power very comprehensive and definite, and may, for ought I know, be exercised in such manner as entirely to abolish the state legislatures. Suppose the legislature of a state should pass a law to raise money to support their government and pay the state debt, may the Congress repeal this law, because it may prevent the collection of a tax which they may think proper and necessary to lay, to provide for the general welfare of the United States? For all laws made, in pursuance of this constitution, are the supreme law of the land, and the judges in every state shall be bound thereby, any thing in the constitution or laws of the different states to the contrary notwithstanding.—By such a law, the government of a particular state might be overturned at one stroke, and thereby be deprived of every means of its support.

It is not meant, by stating this case, to insinuate that the constitution would warrant a law of this kind; or unnecessarily to alarm the fears of the people, by suggesting, that the federal legislature would be more likely to pass the limits assigned them by the constitution, than that of an individual state, further than they are less responsible to the people. But what is meant is, that the legislature of the United States are vested with the great and uncontroulable powers, of laying and collecting taxes, duties, imposts, and excises; of regulating trade, raising and supporting armies, organizing, arming, and disciplining the militia, instituting courts, and other general powers. And are by this clause invested with the power of making all laws, *proper and necessary*, for carrying all these into execution; and they may so exercise this power as entirely to annihilate all the state governments, and reduce this country to one single government. And if they may do it, it is pretty certain they will; for it will be found that the power retained by individual states, small as it is, will be a clog upon the wheels of the government of the United States; the latter therefore will be naturally inclined to remove it out of the way. Besides, it is a truth confirmed by the unerring experience of ages, that every man, and every body of men, invested with power, are ever disposed to increase it, and to acquire a superiority over every thing that stands in their way. This disposition, which is implanted in human nature, will operate in the federal legislature to lessen and ultimately to subvert the state authority, and having such advantages, will most certainly succeed, if the federal government succeeds at all. It must be very evident then, that what this constitution wants of being a complete consolidation of the several parts of the union into one complete government, possessed of perfect legislative, judicial, and executive powers, to all intents and purposes, it will necessarily acquire in its exercise and operation.

Let us now proceed to enquire, as I at first proposed, whether it be best the thirteen United States should be reduced to one great republic, or not? It is here taken for granted, that all agree in this, that whatever government we adopt, it ought to be a free one; that it should be so framed as to secure the liberty of the citizens of America, and such an one as to admit of a full, fair, and equal representation of the people. The question then will be, whether a government thus constituted, and founded on such principles, is practicable, and can be exercised over the whole United States, reduced into one state?

If respect is to be paid to the opinion of the greatest and wisest men who have ever thought or wrote on the science of government, we shall be constrained to conclude, that a free republic cannot succeed over a country of such immense extent, containing such a number of inhabitants, and these encreasing in such rapid progression as that of the whole United States. Among the many illustrious authorities which might be produced to this point, I shall content myself with quoting only two. The one is the baron de Montesquieu, spirit of laws, chap. xvi. vol. i. "It is natural to a republic to have only a small territory, otherwise it cannot long subsist. In a large republic there are men of large fortunes, and consequently of less moderation; there are trusts too great to be placed in any single subject; he has interest of his own; he soon begins to think that he may be happy, great and glorious, by oppressing his fellow citizens; and that he may raise himself to grandeur on the ruins of his country. In a large republic, the public good is sacrificed to a thousand views; it is subordinate to exceptions, and depends on accidents. In a small one, the interest of the public is easier perceived, better understood, and more within the reach of every citizen; abuses are of less extent, and of course are less protected." Of the same opinion is the marquis Beccarari.

History furnishes no example of a free republic, any thing like the extent of the United States. The Grecian republics were of small extent; so also was that of the Romans. Both of these, it is true, in process of time, extended their conquests over large territories of country; and the consequence was, that their governments were changed from that of free governments to those of the most tyrannical that ever existed in the world.

Not only the opinion of the greatest men, and the experience of mankind, are against the idea of an extensive republic, but a variety of reasons may be drawn from the reason and nature of things, against it. In every government, the will of the sovereign is the law. In despotic governments, the supreme authority being lodged in one, his will is law, and can be as easily expressed to a large extensive territory as to a small one. In a pure democracy the people are the sovereign, and their will is declared by themselves; for this purpose they must all come together to deliberate, and decide. This kind of government cannot be exercised, therefore, over a country of any considerable extent; it must be confined to a single city, or at least limited to such bounds as that the people can conveniently assemble, be able to debate, understand the subject submitted to them, and declare their opinion concerning it.

In a free republic, although all laws are derived from the consent of the people, yet the people do not declare their consent by themselves in person, but by representatives, chosen by them, who are supposed to know the minds of their constituents, and to be possessed of integrity to declare this mind.

In every free government, the people must give their assent to the laws by which they are governed. This is the true criterion between a free government and an arbitrary one. The former are ruled by the will of the whole, expressed in any manner they may agree upon; the latter by the will of one, or a few. If the people are to give their assent to the laws, by persons chosen and appointed by them, the manner of the choice and the number chosen, must be such, as to possess, be disposed, and consequently qualified to declare the sentiments of the people; for if they do not know, or are not disposed to speak the sentiments of the people, the people do not govern, but the sovereignty is in a few. Now, in a large extended country, it is impossible to have a representation, possessing the sentiments, and of integrity, to declare the minds of the people, without having it so numerous and unwieldly, as to be subject in great measure to the inconveniency of a democratic government.

The territory of the United States is of vast extent; it now contains near three millions of souls, and is capable of containing much more than ten times that number. Is it practicable for a country, so large and so numerous as they will soon become, to elect a representation, that will speak their sentiments, without their becoming so numerous as to be incapable of transacting public business? It certainly is not.

In a republic, the manners, sentiments, and interests of the people should be similar. If this be not the case, there will be a constant clashing of opinions; and the representatives of one part will be continually striving against those of the other. This will retard the operations of government, and prevent such conclusions as will promote the public good. If we apply this remark to the condition of the United States, we shall be convinced that it forbids that we should be one government. The United States includes a variety of climates. The productions of the different parts of the union are very variant, and their interests, of consequence, diverse. Their manners and habits differ as much as their climates and productions; and their sentiments are by no means coincident. The laws and customs of the several states are, in many respects, very diverse, and in some opposite; each would be in favor of its own interests and customs, and, of consequence, a legislature, formed of representatives from the respective parts, would not only be too numerous to act with any care or decision, but would be composed of such heterogenous and discordant principles, as would constantly be contending with each other.

The laws cannot be executed in a republic, of an extent equal to that of the United States, with promptitude.

The magistrates in every government must be supported in the execution of the laws, either by an armed force, maintained at the public expence for that purpose; or by the people turning out to aid the magistrate upon his command, in case of resistance.

In despotic governments, as well as in all the monarchies of Europe, standing armies are kept up to execute the commands of the prince or the magistrate, and are employed for this purpose when occasion requires: But they have always proved the destruction of liberty, and is abhorrent to the spirit of a free republic. In England, where they depend upon the parliament for their annual support, they have always been complained of as oppressive and unconstitutional, and are seldom employed in executing of the laws; never except on extraordinary occasions, and then under the direction of a civil magistrate.

A free republic will never keep a standing army to execute its laws. It must depend upon the support of its citizens. But when a government is to receive its support from the aid of the citizens, it must be so constructed as to have the confidence, respect, and affection of the people. Men who, upon the call of the magistrate, offer themselves to execute the laws, are influenced to do it either by affection to the government, or from fear; where a standing army is at hand to punish offenders, every man is actuated by the latter principle, and therefore, when the magistrate calls, will obey: but, where this is not the case, the government must rest for its support upon the confidence and respect which the people have for their government and laws. The body of the people being attached, the government will always be sufficient to support and execute its laws, and to operate upon the fears of any faction which may be opposed to it, not only to prevent an opposition to the execution of the laws themselves, but also to compel the most of them to aid the magistrate; but the people will not be likely to have such confidence in their rulers, in a republic so extensive as the United States, as necessary for these purposes. The confidence which the people have in their rulers, in a free republic, arises from their knowing them, from their being responsible to them for their conduct, and from the power they have of displacing them when they misbehave: but in a republic of the extent of this continent, the people in general would be acquainted with very few of their rulers: the people at large would know little of their proceedings, and it would be extremely difficult to change them. The people in Georgia and New-Hampshire would not know one another's mind, and therefore could not act in concert to enable them to effect a general change of representatives. The different parts of so extensive a country could not possibly be made acquainted with the conduct of their representatives, nor be informed of the reasons upon which measures were founded. The consequence will be, they will have no confidence in their legislature, suspect them of ambitious views, be jealous of every measure they adopt, and will not support the laws they pass. Hence the government will be nerveless and inefficient, and no way will be left to render it otherwise, but by establishing an armed force to execute the laws at the point of the bayonet—a government of all others the most to be dreaded.

In a republic of such vast extent as the United-States, the legislature cannot attend to the various concerns and wants of its different parts. It cannot be sufficiently numerous to be acquainted with the local condition and wants of the different districts, and if it could, it is impossible it should have sufficient time to attend to and provide for all the variety of cases of this nature, that would be continually arising.

In so extensive a republic, the great officers of government would soon become above the controul of the people, and abuse their power to the purpose of aggrandizing themselves, and oppressing them. The trust committed to the executive offices, in a country of the extent of the United-States, must be various and of magnitude. The command of all the troops and navy of the republic, the appointment of officers, the power of pardoning offences, the collecting of all the public revenues, and the power of expending them, with a number of other powers, must be lodged and exercised in every state, in the hands of a few. When these are attended with great honor and emolument, as they always will be in large states, so as greatly to interest men to pursue them, and to be proper objects for ambitious and designing men, such men will be ever restless in their pursuit after them. They will use the power, when they have acquired it, to the purposes of gratifying their own interest and ambition, and it is scarcely possible, in a very large republic, to call them to account for their misconduct, or to prevent their abuse of power.

These are some of the reasons by which it appears, that a free republic cannot long subsist over a country of the great extent of these states. If then this new constitution is calculated to consolidate the thirteen states into one, as it evidently is, it ought not to be adopted.

Though I am of opinion, that it is a sufficient objection to this government, to reject it, that it creates the whole union into one government, under the form of a republic, yet if this objection was obviated, there are exceptions to it, which are so material and fundamental, that they ought to determine every man, who is a friend to the liberty and happiness of mankind, not to adopt it. I beg the candid and dispassionate attention of my countrymen while I state these objections— they are such as have obtruded themselves upon my mind upon a careful attention to the matter, and such as I sincerely believe are well founded. There are many objections, of small moment, of which I shall take no notice—perfection is not to be expected in any thing that is the production of man—and if I did not in my conscience believe that this scheme was defective in the fundamental principles—in the foundation upon which a free and equal government must rest—I would hold my peace.

The Weaknesses of Brutus Exposed:
"A Citizen of Philadelphia" [Pelatiah Webster]

Philadelphia, November 8, 1787

The long piece signed BRUTUS, (which was first published in a New-York paper, and was afterwards copied into the Pennsylvania Packet of the 26th instant) is wrote in a very good stile; the language is easy, and the address is polite and insinuating: but the sentiments, I conceive, are not only unsound, but wild and chimerical; the dreary fears and apprehensions, altogether groundless; and the whole tendency of the piece, in this important crisis of our politics, very hurtful. I have therefore thought it my duty to make some animadversions on it; which I here offer, with all due deference, to the Author and to the Public.

His first question is, *Whether a confederated government is best for the United States?*

I answer, If Brutus, or any body else, cannot find any benefit resulting from the union of the Thirteen States; if they can do *without* as well as *with* the respectability, the protection, and the security, which the States might derive from that union, I have nothing further to say: but if that union is to be supported in any such manner as to afford respectability, protection, or security to the States, I say it must be done by an adequate government, and cannot be otherwise done.

This government must have a supreme power, *superior to and able to controul* each and all of its parts. 'Tis essential to all governments, that such a power be somewhere existing in it; and if *the place* where the proposed Constitution has fixed it, does not suit Brutus and his friends, I will give him leave to stow it away in any *other place that is better*: but I will not consent to have it *annihilated*; neither will I agree to have it

176

cramped and pinched for room, so as to lessen its energy; for that will *destroy* both its nature and use.

The supreme power of government ought to be *full, definite, established,* and *acknowledged.* Powers of government too limited, or uncertain and disputed, have ever proved, like *Pandora*'s box, a most fruitful source of quarrels, animosities, wars, devastation, and ruin, in all shapes and degrees, in all communities, states, and kingdoms on earth.

Nothing tends more to the honour, establishment, and peace of society, than public decisions, grounded on principles of right, natural fitness, and prudence; but when the powers of government are *too limited*, such decisions can't be made and enforced; so the mischief goes without a remedy: dreadful examples of which we have felt, in instances more than enough, for seven years past.

Further, where the powers of government are not *definite* but *disputed*, the administration dare not make decisions on the footing of impartial justice and right; but must temporise with the parties, lest they lose friends or make enemies: and of course the *righteous* go off injured and disgusted, and the *wicked* go grumbling too; for 'tis rare that any sacrifices of a court can satisfy a prevailing party in the state.

'Tis necessary in States, as well as in private families, that controversies should have a just, *speedy*, and effectual decision, that right may be done before the contention has *time* to grow up into habits of malignity, resentment, ill nature, and ill offices. If a controversy happens between two states, must it continue undecided, and daily increase, and be more and more aggravated, by the repeated insults and injuries of the contending parties, 'till they are ripe for the decision of the sword? or must the weaker states suffer, without remedy, the groundless demands and oppressions of their stronger neighbours, because they have no avenger, or umpire of their disputes?

Or shall we institute a supreme power with full and effectual authority to controul the animosities, and decide the disputes of these strong contending bodies? In the one proposed to us, we have perhaps every chance of a *righteous judgment*, that we have any reason to hope for; but I am clearly of opinion, that even a *wrongful decision*, would, in most cases, be preferable to the continuance of such destructive controversies.

I suppose that neither Brutus nor any of his friends would wish to see our government *embroiled abroad*; and therefore will admit it necessary to institute some federal authority, sufficient to punish *any individual or State*, who shall violate our treaties with foreign nations, insult their dignity, or abuse their citizens, and compel due reparation in all such cases.

I further apprehend, that Brutus is willing to have the *general* interest and *welfare* of the States well provided for and supported, and therefore will consent that there shall exist in the states, an authority to *do* all this *effectually*; but he seems grieved that Congress should be the *judges of this general welfare* of the states. If he will be kind enough to point out any other more suitable and proper judges, I will consent to have them admitted.

Indeed I begin to have hopes of Brutus, and think he may come right at last; for I observe (after all his fear and tremblings about the new government) the constitution he *defines and adopts*, is the very same as that which the federal convention have proposed to us, *viz.* "that the Thirteen States should continue thirteen confederated republics under the *direction and controul* of a supreme federal head, for certain defined national purposes, only." Where we may observe,

1. That the new Constitution leaves all the Thirteen States, complete republics, as it found them, but all confederated under the direction and controul of a federal head, for certain defined national purposes only, *i. e.* it leaves all the dignities, authorities, and internal police of each State in free, full, and perfect condition; unless when national purposes make the controul of them by the federal head, or authority, necessary to the general benefit.

2. These powers of controul by the federal head or authority, are *defined* in the new constitution, as minutely as may be, in their principle; and any detail of them which may become necessary, is committed to the wisdom of Congress.

3. It extends the controuling power of the federal head to no one case, to which the jurisdiction or power of definitive decision of any one state, can be competent. And,

4. In every such case, the controuling power of the federal head, is absolutely necessary to the support, dignity, and benefit of the national government, and the safety of individuals; neither of which can, by any possibility, be secured without it.

All this falls in pretty well with Brutus's sentiments; for he does not think that the new Constitution in *its present state* so very bad, but fears that it will not preserve its purity of institution; but if adopted, will immediately verge to, and terminate in *a consolidation*, i. e. a destruction of the state governments. For argument, he suggests the avidity of power natural to rulers; and the eager grasp with which they hold it when obtained; and their strong propensity to abuse their power, and encroach on the liberties of the people.

He dwells on the vast powers vested in Congress by the new Constitution, *i. e.* of levying taxes, raising armies, appointing federal courts, *&c.*; takes it for granted, that all these powers will be abused, and carried to an oppressive excess; and then harrangues on the dreadful case we shall be in, when our *wealth* is all devoured by taxes, our *liberty* destroyed by the power of the army, and our *civil rights* all sacrificed by the unbounded power of the federal courts, *&c.*

And when he has run himself out of breath with this dreary declamation, he comes to the conclusion he set out with, *viz.* That the Thirteen States are too big for a republican government, which requires *small territory*, and can't be supported in *more extensive nations*; that in large states liberty will soon be swallowed up, and lost in the magnitude of power requisite in the government, *&c.*

If any conclusion at all can be drawn from this baseless assemblage of gloomy thoughts, I think it must be *against any union at all*; against *any kind of federal government*. For nothing can be plainer than this, *viz.* that *the union can't by any possibility be supported with success, without adequate and effectual powers of government?*

We must have *money* to support the union, and therefore the power of raising it must be lodged somewhere; we must have *a military force*, and of consequence the power of raising and directing it must exist; civil and criminal causes of national concern will arise, therefore there must be somewhere a power of appointing *courts* to hear and determine them.

These powers must be vested in Congress; for nobody pretends to wish to have them vested in any other body of men.

The Thirteen States have a territory very extensive, and inhabitants very numerous, and every day rapidly increasing; therefore the powers of government necessary to support their union must be great in proportion. If the ship is large, the mast must be proportionably great, or it will be impossible to make her sail well. The federal powers must extend to every part of the federal territory, *i. e.* to the utmost limits of the Thirteen States, and to every part of them; and must carry with them, sufficient authority to secure the execution of them; and these powers must be vested in Congress, and the execution of them must be under their direction and controul.

These powers are *vast*, I know, and the trust is of the most *weighty kind* that can be committed to human direction; and the execution and administration of it will require the greatest *wisdom, knowledge, firmness,* and *integrity* in that august body; and I hope they will have all the *abilities and virtues* necessary to their important station, and will *perform their duty well*; but if they fail, the fault is in them, not in the constitution. The best constitution possible, even a divine one, badly administered, will make a bad government.

The members of Congress will be the best we can get; they will all of them derive their appointment from the States, and if the States are not wise enough to send *good and suitable* men, great *blame*, great *sin* will lie at their door. But I suppose nobody would wish to mend this fault by taking away the election of the people, and directing the appointment of Congress to be made in any other way.

When we have gotten the best that can be obtained, we ought to be quiet and cease complaining. 'Tis not in the power of human wisdom to do more; 'tis the fate of human nature to *be imperfect and to err*; and no doubt but Congress, with all their *dignity of station and character*, with all their *opportunities* to gain *wisdom and information*, with all their *inducements to virtue and integrity*, will err, and abuse or misapply their powers in more or less instances. I have no expectation that they will make *a court of angels*, or be any thing more than *men*: 'tis probable many of them will be *insufficient* men, and some of them may be *bad men*.

The greatest wisdom, care, and caution, has been used in the *mode* of their appointment; in the *restraints and checks* under which they must act; in the numerous *discussions and deliberations* which all their acts must pass through, before they can receive the stamp of authority; in the terrors of *punishment* if they misbehave. I say, in all *these ways* the greatest care has been used to procure and form a good Congress.

The *dignity and importance* of their station and character will afford all the inducements to virtue and effort, which can influence a mind *capable* of their force.

Their own *personal reputation*, with the eyes of all the world on them,—the *approbation of their fellow citizens*, which every man in public station naturally wishes to enjoy,—and the *dread of censure and shame*, all contribute very forceable and strong inducements to noble, upright and worthy behavior.

The *particular interest* which every member of Congress has in every public order and resolution, is *another strong motive* to right action. For every act to which any member gives his sanction, if it be raising an *army*, levying a *tax*, instituting a *court*, or any other act to bind the *States*,—such act will equally bind *himself, his nearest connections, and his posterity*.

Another mighty influence to the noblest principle of action will be *the fear of God before their eyes*; for while they sit in the place of God, to give law, justice, and right to the States, they must be *monsters indeed* if they do not regard *his law*, and imitate *his character*.

If all this will not produce a Congress fit to be trusted, and worthy of the public confidence, I think we may give the matter up as impracticable. But still we must make ourselves as easy as we can, under a *mischief* which admits *no remedy*, and bear with patience an *evil* which can't be *cured*: for a government we must have; there is no safety without it; though we know it will be imperfect, we still must prefer it to anarchy or no government at all. 'Tis the height of folly and madness to reject a necessary convenience, because it is not a perfect good.

* * *

Upon this statement of facts and principles (for the truth and reality of which, I appeal to every candid man,) I beg leave to remark,

1. That the federal Convention, in the constitution proposed to us, have exerted their utmost to produce *a Congress worthy of the public confidence*, who shall have *abilities* adequate to their important duty, and shall act under every possible inducement to execute it *faithfully*.

2. That this affords every chance which the nature of the thing will admit, of a wise and upright administration.

3. Yet all this notwithstanding, 'tis very possible that Congress *may err, may abuse, or misapply* their powers, which no precaution of human wisdom can prevent.

4. 'Tis *vain*, 'tis *childish*, 'tis *contentious* to object to a constitution thus framed and guarded, on pretence that the commonwealth may suffer by a bad administration of it; or to *withhold* the *necessary powers* of government, from the supreme rulers of it, least they should *abuse* or *misapply* those powers. This is an objection which will operate with equal force against every institution that can be made in this world, whether of policy, religion, commerce, or any other humane concern, which can require regulations: for 'tis not possible to form any institution however necessary, wise, and good, whose uses may not be lessened or destroyed by bad management.

If Brutus, or any body else, can point out any *checks*, cautions, or *regulations*, which have been hitherto omitted, which will make Congress more *wise*, more *capable*, more *diligent*, or more *faithful*, I am willing to attend to them. But to set Congress at the head of the government, and object to their being vested with full and sufficient power to manage all the great departments of it, appears to me *absurd*, quite *wild*, and *chimerical*: it would produce a plan which would destroy itself as it went along, would be a sort of counter position of contrary parts, and render it impossible for rulers to render those services, and secure those benefits to the States, which are the only great ends of their appointment.

The constitution under Brutus's corrections, would stand thus, *viz.* Congress would have power to *raise money*, but must not direct the *quantity*, or *mode of levying* it; they might raise *armies*, but must not judge of the *number* of soldiers necessary, or direct their destination; they ought to provide for the *general welfare*, but must not be judges of what that welfare *consists in*, or in *what manner* 'tis to be provided for; they might controul the several States, for *defined national purposes*, but must not be judges of *what purposes* would come within that *definition*, &c.

Any body with half an eye, may see what sort of administration the constitution, thus corrected, would produce, *e. g.* it would require much greater trouble to leave the work *undone*, than would be necessary to get it *well done*, under a constitution of sufficient powers. If any one wishes to view more minutely this blessed operation, he may see a lively sample of it, in the last seven years practice of our federal government.

5. Brutus all along founds his objections, and fears on *extreme cases* of abuse or misapplication of supreme powers, which may *possibly* happen, under the administration of a wild, weak, or wicked Congress; but 'tis easy to observe that all institutions are liable to *extremes*, but ought not *to be judged by them*; they do not often appear, and perhaps never may; but if they should happen in the cases supposed, (which God forbid,) there is *a remedy pointed out, in the Constitution itself.*

'Tis not supposeable that such abuses could arise to any ruinous height, before they would affect the States so much, that at least *two-thirds* of them would unite in pursuing a remedy, in the mode prescribed by the Constitution, which will always be liable to amendment, whenever any mischiefs or abuses appear in the government, which the Constitution in its present state, can't reach and correct.

6. Brutus thinks we can never be too much afraid of the *encroaching avidity of rulers*; but 'tis pretty plain, that however great the natural *lust of power in rulers* may be, the *jealousy of the people in giving it*, is about equal; these two opposite passions, will always operate in opposite directions to each other, and like *action and reaction* in natural bodies, will ever tend to a good ballance.

At any rate, the Congress can never *get* more power than the people will *give*, nor *hold* it any longer than they will *permit*; for should they assume tyrannical powers, and make incroachments on liberty without the consent of the people, they would soon attone for their temerity, with shame and disgrace, and probably with their heads.

But 'tis here to be noted, that all the danger does not arise from the extreme of power *in the rulers*; for when the ballance verges to the contrary extreme, and the power of the rulers becomes too much *limited and cramped*, all the nerves of government are weakened, and the administration must unavoidably sicken, and lose that energy which is absolutely necessary for the support of the State, and the security of the people. For 'tis a truth worthy of great attention, that laws are not made so much for the *righteous* as for the *wicked*, who never fail to shelter themselves from punishment, whenever they can, under the *defects of the law, and the weakness of government*.

I now come to consider the grand proposition which Brutus sets out with, concludes with, and interlards all along, and which seems to be the great gift of his performance, viz. *That a confederation of the Thirteen States into one great republic is not best for them:* and goes on to prove by a variety of arguments, that *a republican form of government is not compatible, and cannot be convenient to so extensive a territory as the said States possess.* He begins by taking one assumption for granted (for I can't see that his arguments prove it at all) *viz.* That the Constitution proposed will melt down and destroy the *jurisdiction* of the particular States, and *consolidate* them all into one great republic.

I can't see the least reason for this sentiment; nor the least tendency in the new Constitution to produce this effect. For the Constitution does not suffer the federal powers to controul in the least, or so much as to interfere in the internal policy, jurisdiction, or municipal rights of any particular State; except where great and manifest *national purposes and interests* make that controul necessary. It appears very evident to me, that *the Constitution gives an establishment, support, and protection* to the *internal* and *separate police* of each State, under the superintendency of the federal powers, which it could not possibly enjoy in an independent state. Under the confederation each State derives strength, firmness, and permanency from its compact with the other States. Like a stave in a cask well bound with hoops, it stands *firmer*, is not so easily *shaken, bent*, or *broken*, as it would be were it set up by itself alone, without any connexion with its neighbours.

There can be no doubt that each State will receive from the union great *support and protection* against the *invasions and inroads* of foreign enemies, as well as against *riots and insurrections* of their own citizens; and of consequence, the course of their internal administration will be secured by this means against any *interruption or embarrassment* from either of these causes.

They will also derive their share of benefit from the respectability of the union abroad, from the treaties and alliances which may be made with foreign nations, *&c.*

Another benefit they will receive from the controul of the supreme power of the union is this, *viz.* they will be restrained from making *angry, oppressive, and destructive laws*, from declaring *ruinous wars* with their neighbours, from fomenting *quarrels and controversies*, &c. all which ever *weaken* a state, tend to its fatal *disorder*, and often end in its dissolution. *Righteousness exalts* and strengthens *a nation*; *but sin is a reproach* and weakening of *any people*.

They will indeed have the privilege of oppressing *their own citizens* by bad laws or bad administration; but the moment the mischief extends beyond their own State, and begins to affect the citizens of other States strangers, or the national welfare,—the salutary controul of the supreme power will check the evil, and restore *strength and security*, as well as *honesty and right*, to the offending state.

It appears then very plain, that the natural effect and tendency of the supreme powers of the union is to give *strength, establishment, and permanency* to the internal police and jurisdiction of each of the particular States; not to *melt down and destroy*, but to *support and confirm* them all.

By what sort of assurance, then, can *Brutus* tell us that the new Constitution, *if executed, must certainly and infallibly terminate in a consolidation of the whole, into one great republic, subverting all the State authorities*. His only argument is, that the federal powers *may be corrupted, abused*, and *misapplied*,

'till this effect shall be produced. 'Tis true, that the constitution, like every other on earth, committed to human management, *may be corrupted by a bad administration*, and be
made to operate to the *destruction* of the very capital benefits
and uses, which were the great end of its institution. The
same argument will prove with equal cogency, that the constitution of each particular State, may be corrupted in practice,
become tyranical and inimical to liberty. In short the argument proves *too much*, and therefore proves *nothing*: 'tis
empty, childish, and futile, and a serious proposal of it, is, I
conceive, an affront to the human understanding.

But after all, supposing this event should take place, and by
some strange fatality, the several States should be melted
down, and merged in the great commonwealth, in the form
of counties, or districts; I don't see why *a commonwealth mode
of government, would not be as suitable and convenient for the
great State, as any other form whatever*; I cannot see any sufficient ground or reason, for the position pretty often and
boldly advanced, *that a republican form of government can never
be suitable for any nation of extensive territory, and numerous
population*: for if Congress can be chosen by the several States,
though under the form and name of *counties, or election districts*, and be in every respect, instituted as directed by the
new constitution, I don't see but we shall have as suitable a
national council, as wise a *legislative*, and as strong and safe
an *executive power*, as can be obtained under any form of government whatever; let our territory be ever so extensive or
populous.

The most despotic monarch that can exist, must have his
councils, and officers of state; and I can't see any one circumstance of their being appointed under a monarchy, that can
afford any chance of their being any wiser or better, than ours
may be. 'Tis true indeed, the despot may, if he pleases, act
without any advice at all; but when he does so, I conceive it
will be very rare that the nation will receive greater advantages from his unadvised edicts, than may be drawed from the
deliberate acts and orders of our supreme powers. All that can
be said in favour of *those*, is, that they will have less chance
of delay, and more of secrecy, than *these*; but I think it probable, that the latter will be grounded on better information,

and greater wisdom; will carry more weight, and be better supported.

The Romans rose, from small beginnings, to a very great extent of territory, population, and wisdom; I don't think their constitution of government, was near so good as the one proposed to us, yet we find their power, strength, and establishment, were raised to their utmost height, under *a republican form of government*. Their State received very little acquisition of territory, strength, or wealth, after their government became imperial; but soon began to weaken and decay.

The *Carthagenians* acquired an amazing degree of strength, wealth, and extent of dominion, under *a republican form of government*. Neither *they* or *the Romans*, owed their dissolation to any causes arising from *that kind of government*: 'twas the *party rage*, animosity, and violence of their citizens, which destroyed them both; it weakened them, 'till *the one* fell under the power of their enemy, and was thereby reduced to ruin; *the other* changed their form of government, to a monarchy, which proved in the end, equally fatal to them.

The same causes, if they can't be restrained, will weaken or destroy any nation on earth, let their form of government be what it will; witness the *division and dissolution* of the Roman empire; the late *dismemberment* of *Poland*; the intestine divisions, rage, and wars of *Italy*, of *France*, of *Spain*, and of *England*.

No form of government can preserve a nation which can't controul the party rage of its own citizens; when any one citizen can rise *above the controul* of the laws, *ruin* draws near. 'Tis not possible for any nation on earth, to hold their strength and establishment, when the dignity of their government is lost, and this dignity will forever depend on the *wisdom* and *firmness* of the officers of government, aided and supported by the *virtue* and *patriotism* of their citizens.

On the whole, I don't see but that any form of government may be safe and practicable, where the controuling authority of the supreme powers, is strong enough to effect the ends of its appointment, and at the same time, sufficiently *checked* to keep it within due bounds, and limit it to the objects of its duty; and I think it appears, that the constitution proposed to us, has all these qualities in as great perfection, as any form we can devise.

But after all, the *grand secret of forming a good government*, is, *to put good men into the administration*: for *wild, vicious, or idle men*, will ever make a bad government, let its principles be ever so good; but *grave, wise, and faithful men*, acting under a good constitution, will afford the best chance of security, peace, and prosperity, to the citizens, which can be derived from civil police, under the present disorders, and uncertainty of all earthly things.

Philadelphia, Nov. 4, 1787.

FINIS.

A Political Dialogue

Massachusetts Centinel (Boston), October 24, 1787

Mr. GRUMBLE. Sad times! neighbour *Union*, sad times!

Mr. UNION. Why, what is the matter, neighbour *Grumble*?

Mr. GRUMBLE. Why, all our liberties are going to be swallowed up; *the whole country* is in a confederacy to ruin us—I remember the glorious times when every man had a right to speak what he thought.

Mr. UNION. Why, who hinders you now?

Mr. GRUMBLE. Who?—Why every body:—When this report of the Convention came to hand, I thought I would go and talk about it to my neighbours; so I went to the Barber's shop, and taking up the paper, so says I, "it seems this monster which is to devour the liberties of the people is come forth."—Immediately the whole shop was in alarm—Mr. *Razor*'s hand trembled so with indignation, that I thought he would have cut my throat—and the whole shop looked as if they did not care if he had. What's that you say, said a surly *Ship-Carpenter*, do you mean that I and my family should starve? Let us come at him, said a *Blacksmith, Painter, Rope-Maker, Sail-Maker, Corker,* and *Joiner*—the Federal Constitution is the only thing which can save us, and our children, from starving.—Out of the shop with the rascal, said half a dozen different tradesmen. It was in vain I applied to a *Merchant* for protection, he assured me that for want of a Federal Government he had sunk a fortune by importing cargoes under the State imposts, and was undersold by goods from Connecticut—and even my friend *Simon Meek*, the Quaker, who delights in healing quarrels, would not interfere, but cooly told me—*"Friend Grumble, whilst we are in the flesh, we should be obedient to the powers which may be ordained over us."* In fine, I was driven from the shop in the plight of the Israelitish ambassadours.—I ran with my complaint to our reverend

Pastor, who told me that to be bound by this law of equity, was perfect freedom, and bid me beware of the leaven of the Pharisees.—The *Doctor* who tends my sick child, was in the same story—and the honest man from the country, who brings me my winter's cyder, *vowed* it would have been *right cute* if they had kicked me out of the shop, for *his town* thought the new Constitution was altogether up to the *notch*. In a word, every man I have conversed with, has been ready to knock my brains out, if I said a word against it—Do you call these liberty times?

Mr. UNION. Well, but neighbour, what are your objections to the new Constitution?

Mr. GRUMBLE. Why, as to the matter, I can't say I have any, but then what vexes me is, that they won't let me say a word against it—it shews, neighbour, there is some trick in it.

Mr. UNION. But neighbour this is indeed a country of liberty, and every man may speak his mind, especially on a subject which is presented to you, for your consideration—but if all orders and degrees of people oppose your speaking against this proposed constitution, the conclusion is, that the whole people, both see the necessity, and give their warmest approbation of it. And indeed, neighbour, it is no wonder, when we consider the horrours of our present situation—the decay of our trade and manufactures—the scarcity of money—the failure of publick credit—the distraction of our publick affairs, and the distress of individuals, which have all arisen from a want of this very Federal Government—it is no wonder, I say, if men who are so deeply interested, should not be able to sit patiently, and hear revilings against the only remedy which can be applied with success, to our present grievances.

No man is intended to be deprived of a freedom of speech, but the few individuals who oppose the Federal Government, must not be surprised to find, that the *Merchant* and *Trader*, who have been ruined for the want of an efficient Federal Government to regulate trade—will resent it—that the *Landholder* who has been taxed so high that the produce of his farm would scarcely pay its rates—will resent it:—And out of the abundance of the heart, the long train of industrious

Tradesmen, who are now spending their past earnings, or selling their tools for a subsistence—will resent it—nay, the whole body of an almost ruined people, will despise and execrate the wretch who dares blaspheme the POLITICAL SAVIOUR OF OUR COUNTRY.

James Madison to Thomas Jefferson

NEW YORK Octr. 24. 1787.

DEAR SIR

My two last, though written for the two last Packets, have unluckily been delayed till this conveyance. The first of them was sent from Philada. to Commodore Jones in consequence of information that he was certainly to go by the Packet then about to sail. Being detained here by his business with Congress, and being unwilling to put the letter into the mail without my approbation which could not be obtained in time, he detained the letter also. The second was sent from Philada. to Col. Carrington, with a view that it might go by the last packet at all events in case Commodore Jones should meet with further detention here. By ill luck he was out of Town, and did not return till it was too late to make use of the opportunity. Neither of the letters were indeed of much consequence at the time, and are still less so now. I let them go forward nevertheless as they may mention some circumstances not at present in my recollection, and as they will prevent a chasm in my part of [   ] correspondence which I have so many motives to cherish by an exact punctuality.

Your favor of June 20. has been already acknowledged. The last Packet from France brought me that of August 2d. I have recd. also by the Mary Capt. Howland the three Boxes for W.H. B.F. and myself. The two first have been duly forwarded. The contents of the last are a valuable addition to former literary remittances and lay me under additional obligations, which I shall always feel more strongly than I express. The articles included for Congress have been delivered & those for the two Universities and for General Washington have been forwarded, as have been the various letters for your friends in Virginia and elsewhere. The parcel of rice referred to in your letter to the Delegates of S. Carolina has met with some accident. No account whatever can be gathered concerning it. It probably was not shipped from France. Ubbo's book I find was not omitted as you seem to have apprehended. The charge for it however is, which I must beg you to supply. The duplicate vol. of the Encyclopedie, I left in Virginia, and it is uncertain when I shall have an opportunity of returning it. Your Spanish duplicates will I fear be hardly vendible. I shall make a trial wherever a chance presents itself. A few days ago I recd. your favor of the 15 of Augst. via L'Orient & Boston. The letters inclosed along with it were immediately sent on to Virga.

You will herewith receive the result of the Convention, which continued its Session till the 17th. of September. I take the liberty of making some observations on the subject which will help to make up a letter, if they should answer no other purpose.

It appeared to be the sincere and unanimous wish of the Convention to cherish and preserve the Union of the States. No proposition was made, no suggestion was thrown out, in favor of a partition of the Empire into two or more Confederacies.

It was generally agreed that the objects of the Union could not be secured by any system founded on the principle of a confederation of sovereign States. A *voluntary* observance of the federal law by all the members, could never be hoped for. A *compulsive* one could evidently never be reduced to practice, and if it could, involved equal calamities to the innocent & the guilty, the necessity of a military force both obnoxious & dangerous, and in general, a scene resembling much more a civil war, than the administration of a regular Government.

Hence was embraced the alternative of a Government which instead of operating, on the States, should operate without their intervention on the individuals composing them: and hence the change in the principle and proportion of representation.

This ground-work being laid, the great objects which presented themselves were 1. to unite a proper energy in the Executive and a proper stability in the Legislative departments, with the essential characters of Republican Government. 2. to draw a line of demarkation which would give to the General Government every power requisite for general purposes, and

leave to the States every power which might be most beneficially administered by them. 3. to provide for the different
interests of different parts of the Union. 4. to adjust the clashing pretensions of the large and small States. Each of these
objects was pregnant with difficulties. The whole of them together formed a task more difficult than can be well concieved
by those who were not concerned in the execution of it. Adding to these considerations the natural diversity of human
opinions on all new and complicated subjects, it is impossible
to consider the degree of concord which ultimately prevailed
as less than a miracle.

The first of these objects as it respects the Executive, was
peculiarly embarrassing. On the question whether it should
consist of a single person, or a plurality of co-ordinate members, on the mode of appointment, on the duration in office,
on the degree of power, on the re-eligibility, tedious and reiterated discussions took place. The plurality of co-ordinate
members had finally but few advocates. Governour Randolph
was at the head of them. The modes of appointment proposed were various, as by the people at large—by electors
chosen by the people—by the Executives of the States—by
the Congress, some preferring a joint ballot of the two
Houses—some a separate concurrent ballot allowing to each
a negative on the other house—some a nomination of several
canditates by one House, out of whom a choice should be
made by the other. Several other modifications were started.
The expedient at length adopted seemed to give pretty general satisfaction to the members. As to the duration in office,
a few would have preferred a tenure during good behaviour—a considerable number would have done so, in case an
easy & effectual removal by impeachment could be settled. It
was much agitated whether a long term, seven years for example, with a subsequent & perpetual ineligibility, or a short
term with a capacity to be re-elected, should be fixed. In favor
of the first opinion were urged the danger of a gradual degen-
eracy of re-elections from time to time, into first a life and
then a heriditary tenure, and the favorable effect of an incapacity to be reappointed, on the independent exercise of the
Executive authority. On the other side it was contended that
the prospect of necessary degradation, would discourage the

most dignified characters from aspiring to the office, would take away the principal motive to the faithful discharge of its duties—the hope of being rewarded with a reappointment, would stimulate ambition to violent efforts for holding over the constitutional term—and instead of producing an independent administration, and a firmer defence of the constitutional rights of the department, would render the officer more indifferent to the importance of a place which he would soon be obliged to quit for ever, and more ready to yield to the incroachmts. of the Legislature of which he might again be a member. The questions concerning the degree of power turned chiefly on the appointment to offices, and the controul on the Legislature. An *absolute* appointment to all offices—to some offices—to no offices, formed the scale of opinions on the first point. On the second, some contended for an absolute negative, as the only possible mean of reducing to practice, the theory of a free Government which forbids a mixture of the Legislative & Executive powers. Others would be content with a revisionary power to be overruled by three fourths of both Houses. It was warmly urged that the judiciary department should be associated in the revision. The idea of some was that a separate revision should be given to the two departments—that if either objected two thirds; if both three fourths, should be necessary to overrule.

In forming the Senate, the great anchor of the Government, the questions as they came within the first object turned mostly on the mode of appointment, and the duration of it. The different modes proposed were, 1. by the House of Representatives 2. by the Executive, 3. by electors chosen by the people for the purpose. 4. by the State Legislatures. On the point of duration, the propositions descended from good-behavior to four years, through the intermediate terms of nine, seven, six, & five years. The election of the other branch was first determined to be triennial, and afterwards reduced to biennial.

The second object, the due partition of power, between the General & local Governments, was perhaps of all, the most nice and difficult. A few contended for an entire abolition of the States; some for indefinite power of Legislation in the Congress, with a negative on the laws of the States: some for such a power without a negative: some for a limited power of legislation, with such a negative: the majority finally for a limited power without the negative. The question with regard to the Negative underwent repeated discussions, and was finally rejected by a bare majority. As I formerly intimated to you my opinion in favor of this ingredient, I will take this occasion of explaining myself on the subject. Such a check on the States appears to me necessary 1. to prevent encroachments on the General authority. 2. to prevent instability and injustice in the legislation of the States.

1. Without such a check in the whole over the parts, our system involves the evil of imperia in imperio. If a compleat supremacy some where is not necessary in every Society, a controuling power at least is so, by which the general authority may be defended against encroachments of the subordinate authorities, and by which the latter may be restrained from encroachments on each other. If the supremacy of the British Parliament is not necessary as has been contended, for the harmony of that Empire; it is evident I think that without the royal negative or some equivalent controul, the unity of the system would be destroyed. The want of some such provision seems to have been mortal to the antient Confederacies, and to be the disease of the modern. Of the Lycian Confederacy little is known. That of the Amphyctions is well known to have been rendered of little use whilst it lasted, and in the end to have been destroyed by the predominance of the local over the federal authority. The same observation may be made, on the authority of Polybius, with regard to the Achæan League. The Helvetic System scarcely amounts to a Confederacy, and is distinguished by too many peculiarities, to be a ground of comparison. The case of the United Netherlands is in point. The authority of a Statholder, the influence of a Standing army, the common interest in the conquered possessions, the pressure of surrounding danger, the guarantee of foreign powers, are not sufficient to secure the authority and interests of the generality, agst. the antifederal tendency of the provincial sovereignties. The German Empire is another example. A Hereditary chief with vast independent resources of wealth and power, a federal Diet, with ample parchment authority, a regular Judiciary establishment,

the influence of the neighbourhood of great & formidable Nations, have been found unable either to maintain the subordination of the members, or to prevent their mutual contests & encroachments. Still more to the purpose is our own experience both during the war and since the peace. Encroachments of the States on the general authority, sacrifices of national to local interests, interferences of the measures of different States, form a great part of the history of our political system. It may be said that the new Constitution is founded on different principles, and will have a different operation. I admit the difference to be material. It presents the aspect rather of a feudal system of republics, if such a phrase may be used, than of a Confederacy of independent States. And what has been the progress and event of the feudal Constitutions? In all of them a continual struggle between the head and the inferior members, until a final victory has been gained in some instances by one, in others, by the other of them. In one respect indeed there is a remarkable variance between the two cases. In the feudal system the sovereign, though limited, was independent; and having no particular sympathy of interests with the great Barons, his ambition had as full play as theirs in the mutual projects of usurpation. In the American Constitution The general authority will be derived entirely from the subordinate authorities. The Senate will represent the States in their political capacity; the other House will represent the people of the States in their individual capacity. The former will be accountable to their constituents at moderate, the latter at short periods. The President also derives his appointment from the States, and is periodically accountable to them. This dependence of the General, on the local authorities, seems effectually to guard the latter against any dangerous encroachments of the former: Whilst the latter, within their respective limits, will be continually sensible of the abridgment of their power, and be stimulated by ambition to resume the surrendered portion of it. We find the representatives of Counties and corporations in the Legislatures of the States, much more disposed to sacrifice the aggregate interest, and even authority, to the local views of their Constituents: than the latter to the former. I mean not by these remarks to insinuate that an esprit de corps will not exist in the national Government or that opportunities may not occur, of extending its jurisdiction in some points. I mean only that the danger of encroachments is much greater from the other side, and that the impossibility of dividing powers of legislation, in such a manner, as to be free from different constructions by different interests, or even from ambiguity in the judgment of the impartial, requires some such expedient as I contend for. Many illustrations might be given of this impossibility. How long has it taken to fix, and how imperfectly is yet fixed the legislative power of corporations, though that power is subordinate in the most compleat manner? The line of distinction between the power of regulating trade and that of drawing revenue from it, which was once considered as the barrier of our liberties, was found on fair discussion, to be absolutely undefinable. No distinction seems to be more obvious than that between spiritual and temporal matters. Yet wherever they have been made objects of Legislation, they have clashed and contended with each other, till one or the other has gained the supremacy. Even the boundaries between the Executive, Legislative & Judiciary powers, though in general so strongly marked in themselves, consist in many instances of mere shades of difference. It may be said that the Judicial authority under our new system will keep the States within their proper limits, and supply the place of a negative on their laws. The answer is, that it is more convenient to prevent the passage of a law, than to declare it void after it is passed; that this will be particularly the case, where the law aggrieves individuals, who may be unable to support an appeal agst. a State to the supreme Judiciary; that a State which would violate the Legislative rights of the Union, would not be very ready to obey a Judicial decree in support of them, and that a recurrence to force, which in the event of disobedience would be necessary, is an evil which the new Constitution meant to exclude as far as possible.

2. A constitutional negative on the laws of the States seems equally necessary to secure individuals agst. encroachments on their rights. The mutability of the laws of the States is found to be a serious evil. The injustice of them has been so frequent and so flagrant as to alarm the most stedfast friends of Republicanism. I am persuaded I do not err in saying that the

evils issuing from these sources contributed more to that uneasiness which produced the Convention, and prepared the public mind for a general reform, than those which accrued to our national character and interest from the inadequacy of the Confederation to its immediate objects. A reform therefore which does not make provision for private rights, must be materially defective. The restraints agst. paper emissions, and violations of contracts are not sufficient. Supposing them to be effectual as far as they go, they are short of the mark. Injustice may be effected by such an infinitude of legislative expedients, that where the disposition exists it can only be controuled by some provision which reaches all cases whatsoever. The partial provision made, supposes the disposition which will evade it. It may be asked how private rights will be more secure under the Guardianship of the General Government than under the State Governments, since they are both founded on the republican principle which refers the ultimate decision to the will of the majority, and are distinguished rather by the extent within which they will operate, than by any material difference in their structure. A full discussion of this question would, if I mistake not, unfold the true principles of Republican Government, and prove in contradiction to the concurrent opinions of theoretical writers, that this form of Government, in order to effect its purposes, must operate not within a small but an extensive sphere. I will state some of the ideas which have occurred to me on this subject. Those who contend for a simple Democracy, or a pure republic, actuated by the sense of the majority, and operating within narrow limits, assume or suppose a case which is altogether fictitious. They found their reasoning on the idea, that the people composing the Society, enjoy not only an equality of political rights; but that they have all precisely the same interests, and the same feelings in every respect. Were this in reality the case, their reasoning would be conclusive. The interest of the majority would be that of the minority also; the decisions could only turn on mere opinion concerning the good of the whole, of which the major voice would be the safest criterion; and within a small sphere, this voice could be most easily collected, and the public affairs most accurately managed. We know however that no Society ever did or can consist of so homogeneous a mass of Citizens. In the savage State indeed, an approach is made towards it; but in that State little or no Government is necessary. In all civilized Societies, distinctions are various and unavoidable. A distinction of property results from that very protection which a free Government gives to unequal faculties of acquiring it. There will be rich and poor; creditors and debtors; a landed interest, a monied interest, a mercantile interest, a manufacturing interest. These classes may again be subdivided according to the different productions of different situations & soils, & according to different branches of commerce, and of manufactures. In addition to these natural distinctions, artificial ones will be founded, on accidental differences in political, religious or other opinions, or an attachment to the persons of leading individuals. However erroneous or ridiculous these grounds of dissention and faction, may appear to the enlightened Statesman, or the benevolent philosopher, the bulk of mankind who are neither Statesmen nor Philosophers, will continue to view them in a different light. It remains then to be enquired whether a majority having any common interest, or feeling any common passion, will find sufficient motives to restrain them from oppressing the minority. An individual is never allowed to be a judge or even a witness in his own cause. If two individuals are under the biass of interest or enmity agst. a third, the rights of the latter could never be safely referred to the majority of the three. Will two thousand individuals be less apt to oppress one thousand, or two hundred thousand, one hundred thousand? Three motives only can restrain in such cases. 1. a prudent regard to private or partial good, as essentially involved in the general and permanent good of the whole. This ought no doubt to be sufficient of itself. Experience however shews that it has little effect on individuals, and perhaps still less on a collection of individuals, and least of all on a majority with the public authority in their hands. If the former are ready to forget that honesty is the best policy; the last do more. They often proceed on the converse of the maxim: that whatever is politic is honest. 2. respect for character. This motive is not found sufficient to restrain individuals from injustice, and loses its efficacy in proportion to the number which is to divide the praise or the blame. Besides as it has reference to public opinion, which is that of the majority, the Standard is fixed by those whose conduct is to be measured by it. 3. Religion. The inefficacy of this restraint on individuals is well known. The conduct of every popular Assembly, acting on oath, the strongest of religious ties, shews that individuals join without remorse in acts agst. which their consciences would revolt, if proposed to them separately in their closets. When Indeed Religion is kindled into enthusiasm, its force like that of other passions is increased by the sympathy of a multitude. But enthusiasm is only a temporary state of Religion, and whilst it lasts will hardly be seen with pleasure at the helm. Even in its coolest state, it has been much oftener a motive to oppression than a restraint from it. If then there must be different interests and parties in Society; and a majority when united by a common interest or passion can not be restrained from oppressing the minority, what remedy can be found in a republican Government, where the majority must ultimately decide, but that of giving such an extent to its sphere, that no common interest or passion will be likely to unite a majority of the whole number in an unjust pursuit. In a large Society, the people are broken into so many interests and parties, that a common sentiment is less likely to be felt, and the requisite concert less likely to be formed, by a majority of the whole. The same security seems requisite for the civil as for the religious rights of individuals. If the same sect form a majority and have the power, other sects will be sure to be depressed. Divide et impera, the reprobated axiom of tyranny, is under certain qualifications, the only policy, by which a republic can be administered on just principles. It must be observed however that this doctrine can only hold within a sphere of a mean extent. As in too small a sphere oppressive combinations may be too easily formed agst. the weaker party; so in too extensive a one, a defensive concert may be rendered too difficult against the oppression of those entrusted with the administration. The great desideratum in Government is, so to modify the sovereignty as that it may be sufficiently neutral between different parts of the Society to controul one part from invading the rights of another, and at the same time sufficiently controuled itself, from setting up an interest adverse to that of the entire Society. In absolute monarchies, the Prince may be tolerably neutral towards different classes of his subjects, but may sacrifice the happiness of all to his personal ambition or avarice. In small republics, the sovereign will is controuled from such a sacrifice of the entire Society, but is not sufficiently neutral towards the parts composing it. In the extended Republic of the United States, The General Government would hold a pretty even balance between the parties of particular States, and be at the same time sufficiently restrained by its dependence on the community, from betraying its general interests.

Begging pardon for this immoderate digression I return to the third object abovementioned, the adjustment of the different interests of different parts of the Continent. Some contended for an unlimited power over trade including exports as well as imports, and over slaves as well as other imports; some for such a power, provided the concurrence of two thirds of both House were required; Some for such a qualification of the power, with an exemption of exports and slaves, others for an exemption of exports only. The result is seen in the Constitution. S. Carolina & Georgia were inflexible on the point of the slaves.

The remaining object created more embarrassment, and a greater alarm for the issue of the Convention than all the rest put together. The little States insisted on retaining their equality in both branches, unless a compleat abolition of the State Governments should take place; and made an equality in the Senate a sine qua non. The large States on the other hand urged that as the new Government was to be drawn principally from the people immediately and was to operate directly on them, not on the States; and consequently as the States wd. lose that importance which is now proportioned to the importance of their voluntary compliances with the requisitions of Congress, it was necessary that the representation in both Houses should be in proportion to their size. It ended in the compromise which you will see, but very much to the dissatisfaction of several members from the large States.

It will not escape you that three names only from Virginia are subscribed to the Act. Mr. Wythe did not return after the death of his lady. Docr. MClurg left the Convention some time before the adjournment. The Governour and Col. Mason refused to be parties to it. Mr. Gerry was the only other member who refused. The objections of the Govr. turn principally on the latitude of the general powers, and on the connection established between the President and the Senate. He wished that the plan should be proposed to the States with liberty to them to suggest alterations which should all be referred to another general Convention, to be incorporated into the plan as far as might be judged expedient. He was not inveterate in his opposition, and grounded his refusal to subscribe pretty much on his unwillingness to commit himself, so as not to be at liberty to be governed by further lights on the subject. Col. Mason left Philada. in an exceeding ill humour indeed. A number of little circumstances arising in part from the impatience which prevailed towards the close of the business, conspired to whet his acrimony. He returned to Virginia with a fixed disposition to prevent the adoption of the plan if possible. He considers the want of a Bill of Rights as a fatal objection. His other objections are to the substitution of the Senate in place of an Executive Council & to the powers vested in that body—to the powers of the Judiciary—to the vice President being made President of the Senate—to the smallness of the number of Representatives—to the restriction on the States with regard to ex post facto laws—and most of all probably to the power of regulating trade, by a majority only of each House. He has some other lesser objections. Being now under the necessity of justifying his refusal to sign, he will of course muster every possible one. His conduct has given great umbrage to the County of Fairfax, and particularly to the Town of Alexandria. He is already instructed to promote in the Assembly the calling a Convention, and will probably be either not deputed to the Convention, or be tied up by express instructions. He did not object in general to the powers vested in the National Government, so much as to the modification. In some respects he admitted that some further powers would have improved the system. He acknowledged in particular that a negative on the State laws, and the appointment of the State Executives ought to be ingredients; but supposed that the public mind would not now bear them, and that experience would hereafter produce these amendments.

The final reception which will be given by the people at large to the proposed System can not yet be decided. The Legislature of N. Hampshire was sitting when it reached that State and was well pleased with it. As far as the sense of the people there has been expressed, it is equally favorable. Boston is warm and almost unanimous in embracing it. The impression on the Country is not yet known. No symptoms of disapprobation have appeared. The Legislature of that State is now sitting, through which the sense of the people at large will soon be promulged with tolerable certainty. The paper money faction in Rh. Island is hostile. The other party zealously attached to it. Its passage through Connecticut is likely to be very smooth and easy. There seems to be less agitation in this State than any where. The discussion of the subject seems confined to the newspapers. The principal characters are known to be friendly. The Governour's party which has hitherto been the popular & most numerous one, is supposed to be on the opposite side; but considerable reserve is practised, of which he sets the example. N. Jersey takes the affirmative side of course. Meetings of the people are declaring their approbation, and instructing their representatives. Penna. will be divided. The City of Philada., the Republican party, the Quakers, and most of the Germans espouse the Constitution. Some of the Constitutional leaders, backed by the western Country will oppose. An unlucky ferment on the subject in their Assembly just before its late adjournment has irritated both sides, particularly the opposition, and by redoubling the exertions of that party may render the event doubtful. The voice of Maryland I understand from pretty good authority, is, as far as it has been declared, strongly in favor of the Constitution. Mr. Chase is an enemy, but the Town of Baltimore which he now represents, is warmly attached to it, and will shackle him as far as they can. Mr. Paca will probably be, as usual, in the politics of Chase. My information from Virginia is as yet extremely imperfect. I have a letter from Genl. Washington which speaks favorably of the impression within a circle of some extent; and another from Chancellor

Pendleton which expresses his full acceptance of the plan, and the popularity of it in his district. I am told also that Innis and Marshall are patrons of it. In the opposite scale are Mr. James Mercer, Mr. R. H. Lee, Docr. Lee and their connections of course, Mr. M. Page according to Report, and most of the Judges & Bar of the general Court. The part which Mr. Henry will take is unknown here. Much will depend on it. I had taken it for granted from a variety of circumstances that he wd. be in the opposition, and still think that will be the case. There are reports however which favor a contrary supposition. From the States South of Virginia nothing has been heard. As the deputation from S. Carolina consisted of some of its weightiest characters, who have returned unanimously zealous in favor of the Constitution, it is probable that State will readily embrace it. It is not less probable, that N. Carolina will follow the example unless that of Virginia should counterbalance it. Upon the whole, although, the public mind will not be fully known, nor finally settled for a considerable time, appearances at present augur a more prompt, and general adoption of the Plan than could have been well expected.

When the plan came before Congs. for their sanction, a very serious effort was made by R. H. Lee & Mr. Dane from Masts. to embarrass it. It was first contended that Congress could not properly give any positive countenance to a measure which had for its object the subversion of the Constitution under which they acted. This ground of attack failing, the former gentleman urged the expediency of sending out the plan with amendments, & proposed a number of them corresponding with the objections of Col. Mason. This experiment had still less effect. In order however to obtain unanimity it was necessary to couch the resolution in very moderate terms.

Mr. Adams has recd. permission to return, with thanks for his Services. No provision is made for supplying his place, or keeping up any representation there. Your reappointment for three years will be notified from the Office of F. Affrs. It was *made without a negative eight states* being *present. Connecticut however put in a blank ticket* the *sense of* that *state having been declared against embassies. Massachusets betrayed some scruple* on *like ground.* Every *personal consideration* was *avowed* & *I beleive with sincerity* to have *militated against these scruples.* It seems to be understood that letters to & from the foreign Ministers of the U.S. are not free of Postage: but that the charge is to be allowed in their accounts.

The exchange of our French for Dutch Creditors has not been countenanced either by Congress or the Treasury Board. The paragraph in your last letter to Mr. Jay, on the subject of applying a loan in Holland to the discharge of the pay due to the foreign Officers has been referred to the Board since my arrival here. No report has yet been made. But I have little idea that the proposition will be adopted. Such is the state & prospect of our fiscal department that any new loan however small, that should now be made, would probably subject us to the reproach of premeditated deception. The balance of Mr. Adams' last loan will be wanted for the interest due in Holland, and with all the income here, will, it is feared, not save our credit in Europe from further wounds. It may well be doubted whether the present Govt. can be kept alive thro' the ensuing year, or untill the new one may take its place.

Upwards of 100,000 Acres of the surveyed lands of the U.S. have been disposed of in open market. Five million of unsurveyed have been sold by private contract to a N. England Company, at ⅔ of a dollar per acre, payment to be made in the principal of the public securities. A negociation is nearly closed with a N. Jersey Company for two million more on like terms, and another commenced with a Company of this City for four million. Col. Carrington writes more fully on this subject.

You will receive herewith the desired information from Alderman Broome in the case of Mr. Burke. Also the Virga. Bill on crimes & punishments. Sundry alterations having been made in conformity to the sense of the House in its latter stages, it is less accurate & methodical than it ought to have been. To these papers I add a Speech of Mr. C. P. on the Missippi. business. It is printed under precautions of secrecy, but surely could not have been properly exposed to so much risk of publication. You will find also among the Pamplets & papers I send by Commodore Jones, another printed speech of the same Gentleman. The Musæum, Magazine, & Philada.

Gazettes, will give you a tolerable idea of the objects of present attention.

The summer crops in the Eastern & Middle States have been extremely plentiful. Southward of Virga. They differ in different places. On the whole I do not know that they are bad in that region. In Virginia the drought has been unprecedented, particularly between the falls of the Rivers & the Mountains. The Crops of Corn are in general alarmingly short. In Orange I find there will be scarcely subsistence for the inhabitants. I have not heard from Albemarle. The crops of Tobo. are every where said to be pretty good in point of quantity; & the quality unusually fine. The crops of wheat were also in general excellent in quality & tolerable in quantity.

Novr. 1. Commodore Jones having preferred another vessel to the packet, has remained here till this time. The interval has produced little necessary to be added to the above. The Legislature of Massts. has it seems taken up the Act of the Convention, and have appointed or probably will appoint an early day for its State Convention. There are letters also from Georgia which denote a favorable disposition. I am informed from Richmond that the New Election-law from the Revised Code produced a pretty full House of Delegates, as well as a Senate, on the first day. It had previously had equal effect in producing full meetings of the freeholders for the County elections. A very decided majority of the Assembly is said to be zealous in favor of the New Constitution. The same is said of the Country at large. It appears however that individuals of great weight both within & without the Legislature are opposed to it. A letter I just have from Mr. A. Stuart, names Mr. Henry, Genl. Nelson, W. Nelson, the family of Cabels, St. George Tucker, John Taylor and the Judges of the Genl. Court except P. Carrington. The other opponents he describes as of too little note to be mentioned, which gives a negative information of the Characters on the other side. All are agreed that the plan must be submitted to a Convention.

We hear from Georgia that that State is threatened with a dangerous war with the Creek Indians. The alarm is of so serious a nature, that law-martial has been proclaimed, and they are proceeding to fortify even the Town of Savannah.

The idea there, is that the Indians derive their motives as well as their means from their Spanish neighbours. Individuals complain also that their fugitive slaves are encouraged by East Florida. The policy of this is explained by supposing that it is considered as a discouragement to the Georgians to form settlements near the Spanish boundaries.

There are but few States on the spot here which will survive the expiration of the federal year; and it is extremely uncertain when a Congress will again be formed. We have not yet heard who are to be in the appointment of Virginia for the next year. With the most affectionate attachment I remain Dear Sr. Your Obed friend & servant

Js. MADISON Jr.

Thomas Jefferson Replies to Madison

PARIS, Dec. 20. 1787.

DEAR SIR

My last to you was of Oct. 8. by the Count de Moustier. Yours of July 18. Sep. 6. & Oct. 24. have been successively received, yesterday, the day before & three or four days before that. I have only had time to read the letters, the printed papers communicated with them, however interesting, being obliged to lie over till I finish my dispatches for the packet, which dispatches must go from hence the day after tomorrow. I have much to thank you for. First and most for the cyphered paragraph respecting myself. These little informations are very material towards forming my own decisions. I would be glad even to know when any individual member thinks I have gone wrong in any instance. If I know myself it would not excite ill blood in me, while it would assist to guide my conduct, perhaps to justify it, and to keep me to my duty, alert. I must thank you too for the information in Thos. Burke's case, tho' you will have found by a subsequent letter that I have asked of you a further investigation of that matter. It is to gratify the lady who is at the head of the Convent wherein my daughters are, & who, by her attachment & attention to them, lays me under great obligations. I shall hope therefore still to receive from you the result of the further enquiries my second letter had asked. The parcel of rice which you informed me had miscarried accompanied my letter to the Delegates of S. Carolina. Mr. Bourgoin was to be the bearer of both and both were delivered together into the hands of his relation here who introduced him to me, and who at a subsequent moment undertook to convey them to Mr. Bourgoin. This person was an engraver particularly recommended to Dr. Franklin & mr. Hopkinson. Perhaps he may have mislaid the little parcel of rice among his baggage. I am much pleased that the sale of Western lands is so succesful. I hope they will absorb all the Certificates of our Domestic debt speedily in the first place, and that then offered for cash they will do the same by our foreign one.

The season admitting only of operations in the Cabinet, and these being in a great measure secret, I have little to fill a letter. I will therefore make up the deficiency by adding a few words on the Constitution proposed by our Convention. I like much the general idea of framing a government which should go on of itself peaceably, without needing continual recurrence to the state legislatures. I like the organization of the government into Legislative, Judiciary & Executive. I like the power given the Legislature to levy taxes, and for that reason solely approve of the greater house being chosen by the people directly. For tho' I think a house chosen by them will be very illy qualified to legislate for the Union, for foreign nations &c. yet this evil does not weigh against the good of preserving inviolate the fundamental principle that the people are not to be taxed but by representatives chosen immediately by themselves. I am captivated by the compromise of the opposite claims of the great & little states, of the latter to equal, and the former to proportional influence. I am much pleased too with the substitution of the method of voting by persons, instead of that of voting by states: and I like the negative given to the Executive with a third of either house, though I should have liked it better had the Judiciary been associated for that purpose, or invested with a similar and separate power. There are other good things of less moment. I will now add what I do not like. First the omission of a bill of rights providing clearly & without the aid of sophisms for freedom of religion, freedom of the press, protection against standing armies, restriction against monopolies, the eternal & unremitting force of the habeas corpus laws, and trials by jury in all matters of fact triable by the laws of the land & not by the law of Nations. To say, as mr. Wilson does, that a bill of rights was not necessary because all is reserved in the case of the general government which is not given, while in the particular ones all is given which is not reserved, might do for the Audience to whom it was addressed, but is surely a gratis dictum, opposed by strong inferences from the body of the instrument, as well as from the omission of the clause of our present confederation which had declared that in express terms. It was a hard conclusion to say because there has been no uniformity among the states as to the cases triable by jury, because some have been so incautious as to abandon this mode of trial therefore the more prudent states shall be reduced to the same level of calamity. It would have been much more just & wise to have concluded the other way that as most of the states had judiciously preserved this palladium, those who had wandered should be brought back to it, and to have established general right instead of general wrong. Let me add that a bill of rights is what the people are entitled to against every government on earth, general or particular, & what no just government should refuse or rest on inference. The second feature I dislike, and greatly dislike, is the abandonment in every instance of the necessity of rotation in office, and most particularly in the case of the President. Experience concurs with reason in concluding that the first magistrate will always be re-elected if the constitution permits it. He is then an officer for life. This once observed it becomes of so much consequence to certain nations to have a friend or a foe at the head of our affairs that they will interfere with money & with arms. A Galloman or an Angloman will be supported by the nation he befriends. If once elected, and at a second or third election outvoted by one or two votes, he will pretend false votes, foul play, hold possession of the reins of government, be supported by the states voting for him, especially if they are the central ones lying in a compact body themselves & separating their opponents: and they will be aided by one nation of Europe, while the majority are aided by another. The election of a President of America some years hence will be much more interesting to certain nations of Europe than ever the election of a king of Poland was. Reflect on all the instances in history antient & modern, of elective monarchies, and say if they do not give foundation for my fears. The Roman emperors, the popes, while they were of any importance, the German emperors till they became hereditary in practice, the kings of Poland, the Deys of the Ottoman dependancies. It may be said that if elections are to be attended with these disorders, the seldomer they are renewed the better. But experience shews that the only way to prevent disorder is to render them uninteresting by frequent changes. An incapacity to be elected a second time would have been the only effectual preventative. The power of removing him every fourth year by the vote of the people is a power which will not be exercised. The king of Poland is removeable every day by the Diet, yet he is never removed. Smaller objections are the Appeal in fact as well as law, and the binding all persons Legislative Executive & Judiciary by oath to maintain that constitution. I do not pretend to decide what would be the best method of procuring the establishment of the manifold good things in this constitution, and of getting rid of the bad. Whether by adopting it in hopes of future amendment, or, after it has been duly weighed & canvassed by the people, after seeing the parts they generally dislike, & those they generally approve, to say to them 'We see now what you wish. Send together your deputies again, let them frame a constitution for you omitting what you have condemned, & establishing the powers you approve. Even these will be a great addition to the energy of your government.' At all events I hope you will not be discouraged from other trials, if the present one should fail of it's full effect. I have thus told you freely what I like & dislike: merely as a matter of curiosity, for I know your own judgment has been formed on all these points after having heard every thing which could be urged on them. I own I am not a friend to a very energetic government. It is always oppressive. The late rebellion in Massachusets has given more alarm than I think it should have done. Calculate that one rebellion in 13 states in the course of 11 years, is but one for each state in a century & a half. No country should be so long without one. Nor will any degree of power in the hands of government prevent insurrections. France, with all it's despotism, and two or three hundred thousand men always in arms has had three insurrections in the three years I have been here in every one of which greater numbers were engaged than in Massachusets & a great deal more blood was spilt. In Turkey, which Montesquieu supposes more despotic, insurrections are the events of every day. In England, where the hand of power is lighter than here, but heavier than with us they happen every half dozen years. Compare again the ferocious depredations of their insurgents with the order, the moderation & the almost self extinguishment of ours. After all, it is my principle that the will of the Majority should always prevail. If they approve the proposed Convention in all it's parts, I shall concur in it chearfully, in hopes that they will amend it whenever they shall find it work wrong. I think our governments will remain virtuous for many centuries; as long as they are chiefly agricultural; and this will be as long as there shall be vacant lands in any part of America. When they get piled upon one another in large cities, as in Europe, they will become corrupt as in Europe. Above all things I hope the education of the common people will be attended to; convinced that on their good sense we may rely with the most security for the preservation of a due degree of liberty. I have tired you by this time with my disquisitions & will therefore only add assurances of the sincerety of those sentiments of esteem & attachment with which I am Dear Sir your affectionate friend & servant

TH: JEFFERSON

P.S. The instability of our laws is really an immense evil. I think it would be well to provide in our constitutions that there shall always be a twelvemonth between the ingrossing a bill & passing it: that it should then be offered to it's passage without changing a word: and that if circumstances should be thought to require a speedier passage, it should take two thirds of both houses instead of a bare majority.

"Cato" III

New York Journal, October 25, 1787

To the CITIZENS *of the* STATE *of* NEW-YORK.

In the close of my last introductory address, I told you, that my object in future would be to take up this new form of national government, to compare it with the experience and opinions of the most sensible and approved political authors, and to show you that its principles, and the exercise of them will be dangerous to your liberty and happiness.

Although I am conscious that this is an arduous undertaking, yet I will perform it to the best of my ability.

The freedom, equality, and independence which you enjoyed by nature, induced you to consent to a political power. The same principles led you to examine the errors and vices of a British superintendence, to divest yourselves of it, and to reassume a new political shape. It is acknowledged that there are defects in this, and another is tendered to you for acceptance; the great question then, that arises on this new political principle, is, whether it will answer the ends for which it is said to be offered to you, and for which all men engage in political society, to wit, the mutual preservation of their lives, liberties, and estates.

The recital, or premises on which this new form of government is erected, declares a consolidation or union of all the thirteen parts, or states, into one great whole, under the firm of the United States, for all the various and important purposes therein set forth. — But whoever seriously considers the immense extent of territory comprehended within the limits of the United States, together with the variety of its climates, productions, and commerce, the difference of extent, and number of inhabitants in all; the dissimilitude of interest, morals, and policies, in almost every one, will receive it as an intuitive truth, that a consolidated republican form of government therein, can never *form a perfect union, establish justice, insure domestic tranquility, promote the general welfare, and se-cure the blessings of liberty to you and your posterity,* for to these objects it must be directed: this unkindred legislature there-fore, composed of interests opposite and dissimilar in their nature, will in its exercise, emphatically be, like a house di-vided against itself.

The governments of Europe have taken their limits and form from adventitious circumstances, and nothing can be ar-gued on the motive of agreement from them; but these ad-ventitious political principles, have nevertheless produced effects that have attracted the attention of philosophy, which has established axioms in the science of politics therefrom, as irrefragable as any in Euclid. It is natural, says Montesquieu, *to a republic to have only a small territory, otherwise it cannot long subsist: in a large one, there are men of large fortunes, and conse-quently of less moderation; there are too great deposits to intrust in the hands of a single subject, an ambitious person soon becomes sensible that he may be happy, great, and glorious by oppressing his fellow citizens, and that he might raise himself to grandeur, on the ruins of his country. In large republics, the public good is sacrificed to a thousand views; in a small one the interest of the public is easily perceived, better understood, and more within the reach of every citizen; abuses have a less extent, and of course are less pro-tected*—he also shews you, that the duration of the republic of Sparta, was owing to its having continued with the same extent of territory after all its wars; and that the ambition of Athens and Lacedemon to command and direct the union, lost them their liberties, and gave them a monarchy.

From this picture, what can you promise yourselves, on the score of consolidation of the United States, into one govern-ment—impracticability in the just exercise of it—your free-dom insecure—even this form of government limited in its continuance—the employments of your country disposed of to the opulent, to whose contumely you will continually be an object—you must risque much, by indispensibly placing trusts of the greatest magnitude, into the hands of individ-uals, whose ambition for power, and agrandisement, will op-press and grind you—where, from the vast extent of your ter-ritory, and the complication of interests, the science of govern-ment will become intricate and perplexed, and too misterious for you to understand, and observe; and by which you are to be conducted into a monarchy, either limited or despotic; the latter, Mr. Locke remarks, *is a government derived from neither nature, nor compact.*

Political liberty, the great Montesquieu again observes, *consists in security, or at least in the opinion we have of security*; and this *security* therefore, or the *opinion*, is best obtained in moderate governments, where the mildness of the laws, and the equality of the manners, beget a confidence in the people, which produces this security, or the opinion. This moderation in governments, depends in a great measure on their limits, connected with their political distribution.

The extent of many of the states in the Union, is at this time, almost too great for the superintendence of a republican form of government, and must one day or other, revolve into more vigorous ones, or by separation be reduced into smaller, and more useful, as well as moderate ones. You have already observed the feeble efforts of Massachusetts against their insurgents; with what difficulty did they quell that insurrection; and is not the province of main at this moment, on the eve of separation from her. The reason of these things is, that for the security of the *property* of the community, in which expressive term Mr. Lock makes life, liberty, and estate, to consist—the wheels of a free republic are necessarily slow in their operation; hence in large free republics, the evil sometimes is not only begun, but almost completed, before they are in a situation to turn the current into a contrary progression: the extremes are also too remote from the usual seat of government, and the laws therefore too feeble to afford protection to all its parts, and insure *domestic tranquility* without the aid of another principle. If, therefore, this state, and that of N. Carolina, had an army under their controul, they never would have lost Vermont, and Frankland, nor the state of Massachusetts suffer an insurrection, or the dismemberment of her fairest district, but the exercise of a principle which would have prevented these things, if we may believe the experience of ages, would have ended in the destruction of their liberties.

Will this consolidated republic, if established, in its exercise beget such confidence and compliance, among the citizens of these states, as to do without the aid of a standing army—I deny that it will.—The malcontents in each state, who will not be a few, nor the least important, will be exciting factions against it—the fear of a dismemberment of some of its parts, and the necessity to enforce the execution of revenue laws (a fruitful source of oppression) on the extremes and in the other districts of the government, will incidentally, and necessarily require a permanent force, to be kept on foot—will not political security, and even the opinion of it, be extinguished? can mildness and moderation exist in a government, where the primary incident in its exercise must be force? will not violence destroy confidence, and can equality subsist, where the extent, policy, and practice of it, will naturally lead to make odious distinctions among citizens?

The people, who may compose this national legislature from the southern states, in which, from the mildness of the climate, the fertility of the soil, and the value of its productions, wealth is rapidly acquired, and where the same causes naturally lead to luxury, dissipation, and a passion for aristocratic distinctions; where slavery is encouraged, and liberty of course, less respected, and protected; who know not what it is to acquire property by their own toil, nor to œconomise with the savings of industry—will these men therefore be as tenacious of the liberties and interests of the more northern states, where freedom, independence, industry, equality, and frugality, are natural to the climate and soil, as men who are your own citizens, legislating in your own state, under your inspection, and whose manners, and fortunes, bear a more equal resemblance to your own?

It may be suggested, in answer to this, that whoever is a citizen of one state, is a citizen of each, and that therefore he will be as interested in the happiness and interest of all, as the one he is delegated from; but the argument is fallacious, and, whoever has attended to the history of mankind, and the principles which bind them together as parents, citizens, or men, will readily perceive it. These principles are, in their exercise, like a pebble cast on the calm surface of a river, the circles begin in the center, and are small, active, and forcible, but as they depart from that point, they lose their force, and vanish into calmness.

The strongest principle of union resides within our domestic walls. The ties of the parent exceed that of any other; as we depart from home, the next general principle of union is amongst citizens of the same state, where acquaintance, habits, and fortunes, nourish affection, and attachment; enlarge the circle still further, &, as citizens of different states, though we acknowledge the same national denomination, we lose the ties of acquaintance, habits, and fortunes, and thus, by degrees, we lessen in our attachments, till, at length, we no more than acknowledge a sameness of species. Is it therefore, from certainty like this, reasonable to believe, that inhabitants of Georgia, or New-Hampshire, will have the same obligations towards you as your own, and preside over your lives, liberties, and property, with the same care and attachment? Intuitive reason, answers in the negative.

In the course of my examination of the principals of consolidation of the states into one general government, many other reasons against it have occurred, but I flatter myself, from those herein offered to your consideration, I have convinced you that it is both presumptious and impracticable consistent with your safety. To detain you with further remarks, would be useless—I shall however, continue in my following numbers, to anilise this new government, pursuant to my promise.

"Publius," The Federalist I
[Alexander Hamilton]

Independent Journal (New York), October 27, 1787

To the People of the State of New-York.

After an unequivocal experience of the inefficacy of the sub-sisting Fœderal Government, you are called upon to deliber-ate on a new Constitution for the United States of America. The subject speaks its own importance; comprehending in its consequences, nothing less than the existence of the UNION, the safety and welfare of the parts of which it is composed, the fate of an empire, in many respects, the most interesting in the world. It has been frequently remarked, that it seems to have been reserved to the people of this country, by their conduct and example, to decide the important question, whether societies of men are really capable or not, of estab-lishing good government from reflection and choice, or whether they are forever destined to depend, for their politi-cal constitutions, on accident and force. If there be any truth in the remark, the crisis, at which we are arrived, may with propriety be regarded as the æra in which that decision is to be made; and a wrong election of the part we shall act, may, in this view, deserve to be considered as the general misfor-tune of mankind.

This idea will add the inducements of philanthropy to those of patriotism to heighten the sollicitude, which all considerate and good men must feel for the event. Happy will it be if our choice should be decided by a judicious estimate of our true interests, unperplexed and unbiassed by considerations not connected with the public good. But this is a thing more ar-dently to be wished, than seriously to be expected. The plan offered to our deliberations, affects too many particular interests, innovates upon too many local institutions, not to in-volve in its discussion a variety of objects foreign to its merits, and of views, passions and prejudices little favourable to the discovery of truth.

Among the most formidable of the obstacles which the new Constitution will have to encounter, may readily be distinguished the obvious interests of a certain class of men in every State to resist all changes which may hazard a diminution of the power, emolument and consequence of the offices they hold under the State-establishments—and the perverted ambition of another class of men, who will either hope to aggrandise themselves by the confusions of their country, or will flatter themselves with fairer prospects of elevation from the subdivision of the empire into several partial confederacies, than from its union under one government.

It is not, however, my design to dwell upon observations of this nature. I am well aware that it would be disingenuous to resolve indiscriminately the opposition of any set of men (merely because their situations might subject them to suspicion) into interested or ambitious views: Candour will oblige us to admit, that even such men may be actuated by upright intentions; and it cannot be doubted, that much of the opposition which has made its appearance, or may hereafter make its appearance, will spring from sources, blameless at least, if not respectable, the honest errors of minds led astray by preconceived jealousies and fears. So numerous indeed and so powerful are the causes, which serve to give a false bias to the judgment, that we upon many occasions, see wise and good men on the wrong as well as on the right side of questions, of the first magnitude to society. This circumstance, if duly attended to, would furnish a lesson of moderation to those, who are ever so much persuaded of their being in the right, in any controversy. And a further reason for caution, in this respect, might be drawn from the reflection, that we are not always sure, that those who advocate the truth are influenced by purer principles than their antagonists. Ambition, avarice, personal animosity, party opposition, and many other motives, not more laudable than these, are apt to operate as well upon those who support as upon those who oppose the right side of a question. Were there not even these inducements to moderation, nothing could be more illjudged than that intolerant spirit, which has, at all times, characterised political parties. For, in politics as in religion, it is equally absurd to aim at making proselytes by fire and sword. Heresies in either can rarely be cured by persecution.

And yet however just these sentiments will be allowed to be, we have already sufficient indications, that it will happen in this as in all former cases of great national discussion. A torrent of angry and malignant passions will be let loose. To judge from the conduct of the opposite parties, we shall be led to conclude, that they will mutually hope to evince the justness of their opinions, and to increase the number of their converts by the loudness of their declamations, and by the bitterness of their invectives. An enlightened zeal for the energy and efficiency of government will be stigmatised, as the off-spring of a temper fond of despotic power and hostile to the principles of liberty. An overscrupulous jealousy of danger to the rights of the people, which is more commonly the fault of the head than of the heart, will be represented as mere pretence and artifice; the bait for popularity at the expence of public good. It will be forgotten, on the one hand, that jealousy is the usual concomitant of violent love, and that the noble enthusiasm of liberty is too apt to be infected with a spirit of narrow and illiberal distrust. On the other hand, it will be equally forgotten, that the vigour of government is essential to the security of liberty; that, in the contemplation of a sound and well informed judgment, their interest can never be separated; and that a dangerous ambition more often lurks behind the specious mask of zeal for the rights of the people, than under the forbidding appearance of zeal for the firmness and efficiency of government. History will teach us, that the former has been found a much more certain road to the introduction of despotism, than the latter, and that of those men who have overturned the liberties of republics the greatest number have begun their career, by paying an obsequious court to the people, commencing Demagogues and ending Tyrants.

In the course of the preceeding observations I have had an eye, my Fellow Citizens, to putting you upon your guard against all attempts, from whatever quarter, to influence your decision in a matter of the utmost moment to your welfare by any impressions other than those which may result from the evidence of truth. You will, no doubt, at the same time, have collected from the general scope of them that they proceed from a source not unfriendly to the new Constitution. Yes, my Countrymen, I own to you, that, after having given it an attentive consideration, I am clearly of opinion, it is your interest to adopt it. I am convinced, that this is the safest course for your liberty, your dignity, and your happiness. I affect not reserves, which I do not feel. I will not amuse you with an appearance of deliberation, when I have decided. I frankly acknowledge to you my convictions, and I will freely lay before you the reasons on which they are founded. The consciousness of good intentions disdains ambiguity. I shall not however multiply professions on this head. My motives must remain in the depository of my own breast: My arguments will be open to all, and may be judged of by all. They shall at least be offered in a spirit, which will not disgrace the cause of truth.

I propose in a series of papers to discuss the following interesting particulars—*The utility of the* UNION *to your political prosperity*—*The insufficiency of the present Confederation to preserve that Union*—*The necessity of a government at least equally energetic with the one proposed to the attainment of this object*—*The conformity of the proposed Constitution to the true principles of republican government*—*Its analogy to your own state constitution*—and lastly, *The additional security, which its adoption will afford to the preservation of that species of government, to liberty and to property.*

In the progress of this discussion I shall endeavour to give a satisfactory answer to all the objections which shall have made their appearance that may seem to have any claim to your attention.

It may perhaps be thought superfluous to offer arguments to prove the utility of the UNION, a point, no doubt, deeply engraved on the hearts of the great body of the people in every state, and one, which it may be imagined has no adversaries. But the fact is, that we already hear it whispered in the private circles of those who oppose the new constitution, that the Thirteen States are of too great extent for any general system, and that we must of necessity resort to seperate confederacies of distinct portions of the whole.* This doctrine will, in all probability, be gradually propagated, till it has votaries enough to countenance an open avowal of it. For nothing can be more evident, to those who are able to take an enlarged view of the subject, than the alternative of an adoption of the new Constitution, or a dismemberment of the Union. It will therefore be of use to begin by examining the advantages of that Union, the certain evils and the probable dangers, to which every State will be exposed from its dissolution. This shall accordingly constitute the subject of my next address.

*The same idea, tracing the arguments to their consequences, is held out in several of the late publications against the New Constitution.

"John Humble"

Independent Gazetteer (Philadelphia), October 29, 1787

The humble address of the *low born* of the United States of America, to their fellow slaves scattered throughout the world—greeting.

Whereas it hath been represented unto us that a most dreadful disease hath for these five years last past infected, preyed upon, and almost ruined the government and people of this our country; and of this malady we ourselves have had perfect demonstration, not mentally, but bodily, through every one of the five senses: For although our sensations in regard to the mind be not just so nice as those of the *well born*; yet our feeling, through the medium of the plow, the hoe, and the grubbing axe, is as accute as any nobleman's in the world. And whereas a number of skilful physicians having met together at Philadelphia last summer, for the purpose of exploring, and if possible removing the cause of this direful desease, have, through the assistance of John Adams, Esquire, in the profundity of their great political knowledge, found out and discovered, that nothing but a new government consisting of three different branches, namely, *king*, *lords*, and *commons*, or in the American language, *president*, *senate*, and *representatives*, can save this our country from inevitable destruction.—And whereas it hath been reported that several of our *low born* brethern have had the horrid audacity to think for themselves in regard to this new system of government, and, *dreadful thought!* have wickedly began to doubt concerning the perfection of this evangelical constitution, which our political doctors have declared to be a panacea, which (by inspiration) they know will infallibly heal every distemper in the confederation, and finally terminate in the salvation of America.

Now we the *low born*, that is, all the people of the United States except 600 or thereabouts, *well born*, do by this our humble address, declare, and most solemnly engage, that we will allow and admit the said 600 *well born*, immediately to establish and confirm this most noble, most excellent and truely divine constitution: And we further declare that without any equivocation or mental reservation whatever we will support and maintain the same according to the best of our power, and after the manner and custom of all other slaves in foreign countries, namely by the sweat and toil of our body: Nor will we at any future period of time ever attempt to complain of this our *royal* government, let the consequences be what they may.—And although it appears to us that a *standing army*, composed of the purgings of the jails of Great Britain, Ireland and Germany, shall be employed in collecting the *revenue* of this our king and government; yet, we again in the most solemn manner declare, that we will abide by our present determination of non-assistance and passive obedience; so that we shall not dare to molest or disturb those military gentlemen in the service of our royal government. And (which is not improbable,) should any one of those soldiers when employed on duty in collecting the *taxes*, strike off the arm (with his sword,) of one of our *fellow slaves*, we will conceive our case remarkably fortunate if he leaves the other arm on.—And moreover because we are aware that many of our fellow slaves shall be unable to pay their *taxes*, and this incapacity of theirs is a just cause of impeachment of treason; wherefore in such cases we will use our utmost endeavours, in conjunction with the *standing army*, to bring such attrocious offenders before our *federal judges*, who shall have power without *jury* or *trial*, to order the said miscreants for immediate execution; nor will we think their sentence severe unless after being hanged they are also to be both *beheaded* and *quartered*.—And finally we shall henceforth and forever, leave all *power*, *authority*, and *dominion* over our *persons* and *properties* in the hands of the *well born*, who were designed by Providence to *govern*. And in regard to the *liberty of the press* we renounce all claim to it forever more, Amen; and we shall in future be perfectly contented if our *tongues* be left us to lick the feet of our well born masters.

Done on behalf of three millions of
low born American slaves.
JOHN HUMBLE, Secretary.

"Americanus" [*John Stevens, Jr.*] I

Daily Advertiser (New York), November 2, 1787

Cato has at length opened his batteries on the Constitution, submitted to us by the late Convention. He begins with an endeavor to impress us with this idea, that "the axioms of Montesquieu, Locke, &c. in the science of politics, are as irrefragable as any in Euclid." And can we possibly believe Cato to be really in earnest? Wretched indeed would be our political institution, had we been governed by the "axioms" of European writers on politics, in the formation of them. As we are placed in a situation totally new, instead of absurdly hunting for precedents in the old world, we must think, we must reason, for ourselves. Every American breast, retaining the least degree of spirit, must spurn, with indignation, at this insidious attempt to shackle our understandings.

Montesquieu, it seems, tells us, that *a Republic must have only a small territory*. But how, I would ask, would he, or Locke, or any other political writer in Europe, be warranted in insisting on this assertion as *an irrefragable axiom*? Had they formed any conceptions of a republican Government instituted upon the plan of the Constitution now under consideration? Because the wretched attempts that have been made in the old world, to constitute Republican Governments, have necessarily failed of attaining the desired purpose, are we to be told the thing is "impracticable," when attempted upon principles as different, as light is from darkness? Montesquieu's maxim may be just, for aught I know, when applied to such republican Governments as Sparta. This commonwealth affords us a striking instance of the absurdities mankind are capable of when they blindly submit themselves to the guidance of *passion* and *prejudice*. Had we not the undoubted evidence of history, it could never be believed, at this time of day, that such a monstrous political prodigy could really have existed. This institution was founded upon Montesquieu's principle of Republican Government, viz. virtue: by virtue, here, is not meant morality; but an enthusiastic attachment to the political system of the country we inhabit. By the force of this mistaken principle, however, the Government, which Lycurgus established in Sparta, was supported for ages. It is unnecessary for me to attempt a delineation of this wonderful institution, against which the feelings of humanity, every generous sentiment of the human heart, revolt with horror. And what is the tendency of Cato's reasoning, but to form Governments, like that of Sparta, in every State in the Union? Should we be able to support separate independent sovereignties (which, with submission to Cato, I think would be "impracticable") we should soon become mere nests of hornets. The austere hostile spirit of Lacedemon, must be substituted in the place of that benign temper of universal philanthropy which the Constitution offered to us is so eminently calculated to diffuse; and which is so congenial to the habits and sentiments of Americans. Away with this Spartan virtue and black broth; we'll have none of them: and Cato must not think to cram them down our throats, by telling us it is the prescription of a great political doctor. The "axioms" of Montesquieu, or any other great man, tho' Cato shall deem them "as irrefragable as any in Euclid," shall never persuade me to quarrel with my bread and butter.

"A Republic must have only a small territory, otherwise it cannot long subsist." But I utterly deny the truth of this "axiom" of the celebrated civilian. This ought not to be deemed arrogant in me, or in any man, at this time of day, and on this side the Atlantic. The learned Frenchman formed his principles of Government in conformity to the lights he possessed. Had he been an American, and now living, I would stake my life on it, he would have formed different principles. A collection of smaller States, united under one federal head, by a Constitution of Government similar to the one at present under consideration, is capable of a greater degree of real permanent liberty, than any combination of power I can form an idea of. The grand evil which all popular governments have hitherto labored under, is an inveterate tendency to faction. We are naturally inclined, without the aid of reason and experience, to suppose that in a free government every man should have a right to a personal vote on every measure. This is the rock on which all Democratic Governments have split. And, indeed, were we to admit this principle in the formation of a Republic, Mr. Montesquieu's maxim would be perfectly just; for it would be utterly "impracticable" for a people to exercise this right, who were not confined to a "small territory." But reason and experience have at length convinced us of the impropriety of the people themselves interfering, in any shape, in the administration of Government. The powers of Government must, of necessity, be delegated. It was the English who first discovered the secret, of which the ancients were totally ignorant, of Legislation by Representation. This is the hinge on which all Republican Governments must move. But we must proceed a step farther. It has also been discovered, that faction cannot be expelled even from a *Representative* body, while possessed *singly* of the whole of the Legislative power. Hence two distinct Legislative bodies have been contrived, farther to check this turbulent spirit. But even this, too, has been found insufficient. To give, therefore, the last finish to this beautiful model of Republican Government, it has been found necessary to place one more check, by giving the Executive and Judicial a revisory power. But, so prone is the spirit of man to party and faction, that even this admirable system will not prevent their mischivous efforts, in a state possessing a "small territory." The next expedient, then, is to unite a number of these lesser communities under one Federal Head. The chain of dependence, thus lengthened, will give a permanency, consistency, and uniformity to a *Federal* Government, of which that of a *single* State is, in its nature, incapable. The gusts of passion, which faction is ever blowing up in *"a small territory,"* lose their force before they reach the seat of *Federal* Government. Republics, limited to *a small territory*, ever have been, and, from the nature of man, ever will be, liable to be torn to pieces by faction. When the citizens are confined within a narrow compass, as was the case of Sparta, Rome, &c. it is within the power of a factious demagogue to scatter sedition and discontent, instantaneously, thro' every part of the State. An artful declaimer, such as Cato, for instance, by infusing jealousy and rage into the minds of the people, may do irreparable mischief to a small State. The people, thrown suddenly into passion, whilst this paroxysm, whilst this fit of insanity continues, commit a thousand enormities; and it is well if the Government itself escapes from total subversion. Had the commotion, which Shays excited in Massachusetts, happened in a state of *small territory*, what would have been the probable consequences? Before the people had recovered from their madness, perhaps all would have been lost.

"The employments of your country, disposed of to the opulent, to whose contumely you will continually be an object."—"You must risque much, by indispensibly placing trusts of the greatest magnitude in the hands of individuals, whose ambition for power and aggrandizement will oppress and grind you." This is *argumentum ad populum*. Cato knows better: he knows that the powers vested, by this Constitution, in the Federal Government, are incapable of abuse.

The different powers are so modified and distributed, as to form mutual checks upon each other. The State Legislatures form a check on the Senate and House of Representatives, infinitely more effectual than that of the people themselves on their State Legislatures. The people, so far from entertaining a jealousy of, in fact place the highest confidence in, *their* Representatives; who, by giving false colorings to bad measures, are too often enabled to abuse the trust reposed in them. But widely different is the situation in which the Federal Representatives stand, in respect to the State Legislatures. Here the mutual apprehensions of encroachments, must for ever keep awake a jealous, watchful spirit, which will not suffer the smallest abuse to pass unnoticed. The Senate and House of Representatives form mutual checks on each other, and the President on both. Cato's apprehensions of Monarchy are chimerical, in the highest degree; and calculated in the same manner as what he says of the rich oppressing and grinding the poor—to catch the attention of the unwary multitude.

Elbridge Gerry to the Massachusetts General Court

Massachusetts Centinel (Boston), November 3, 1787

Hon. Mr. GERRY's objections to signing the National Constitution.

(The following Letter, on the subject of the American Constitution, from the Hon. ELBRIDGE GERRY, Esq. one of the Delegates representing this Commonwealth in the late Federal Convention, to the Legislature, was on Wednesday last read in the Senate and sent down to the House of Representatives, where it was yesterday read and sent up. As it contains opinions on a subject of the first importance to our country at this day, we have obtained a copy of it for insertion—and are happy to have it in our power thus early to communicate it to the publick.)

NEW-YORK, 18th October, 1787.

GENTLEMEN, I have the honour to inclose, pursuant to my commission, the constitution proposed by the federal Convention.

To this system I gave my dissent, and shall submit my objections to the honourable Legislature.

It was painful for me, on a subject of such national importance, to differ from the respectable members who signed the constitution: But conceiving as I did, that the liberties of America were not secured by the system, it was my duty to oppose it.—

My principal objections to the plan, are, that there is no adequate provision for a representation of the people—that they have no security for the right of election—that some of the powers of the Legislature are ambiguous, and others indefinite and dangerous—that the Executive is blended with

231

and will have an undue influence over the Legislature—that the judicial department will be oppressive—that treaties of the highest importance may be formed by the President with the advice of two thirds of a *quorum* of the Senate—and that the system is without the security of a bill of rights. These are objections which are not local, but apply equally to all the States.

As the Convention was called for "the *sole* and *express* purpose of revising the Articles of Confederation, and reporting to Congress and the several Legislatures such alterations and provisions as shall render the Federal Constitution adequate to the exigencies of government and the preservation of the union," I did not conceive that these powers extended to the formation of the plan proposed, but the Convention being of a different *opinion*, I acquiesced in *it*, being fully convinced that to preserve the union, an efficient government was indispensibly necessary; and that it would be difficult to make proper amendments to the articles of Confederation.

The Constitution proposed has few, if any *federal* features, but is rather a system of *national* government: Nevertheless, in many respects I think it has great merit, and by proper amendments, may be adapted to the "exigencies of government," and preservation of liberty.

The question on this plan involves others of the highest importance—1st. Whether there shall be a dissolution of the *federal* government? 2dly. Whether the several State Governments shall be so altered, as in effect to be dissolved? and 3dly. Whether in lieu of the *federal* and *State* Governments, the *national* Constitution now proposed shall be substituted without amendment? Never perhaps were a people called on to decide a question of greater magnitude—Should the citizens of America adopt the plan as it now stands, their liberties may be lost: Or should they reject it altogether Anarchy may ensue. It is evident therefore, that they should not be precipitate in their decisions; that the subject should be well understood, lest they should refuse to *support* the government, after having *hastily* accepted it.

If those who are in favour of the Constitution, as well as those who are against it, should preserve moderation, their discussions may afford much information and finally direct to an happy issue.

It may be urged by some, that an *implicit* confidence should be placed in the Convention: But, however respectable the members may be who signed the Constitution, it must be admitted, that a free people are the proper guardians of their rights and liberties—that the greatest men may err—and that their errours are sometimes, of the greatest magnitude.

Others may suppose, that the Constitution may be safely adopted, because therein provision is made to *amend* it: But cannot *this object* be better attained before a ratification, than after it? And should a *free* people adopt a form of Government, under conviction that it wants amendment?

And some may conceive, that if the plan is not accepted by the people, they will not unite in another: But surely whilst they have the power to amend, they are not under the necessity of rejecting it.

I have been detained here longer than I expected, but shall leave this place in a day or two for Massachusetts, and on my arrival shall submit the reasons (if required by the Legislature) on which my objections are grounded.

I shall only add, that as the welfare of the union requires a better Constitution than the Confederation, I shall think it my duty as a citizen of Massachusetts, to support that which shall be finally adopted, sincerely hoping it will secure the liberty and happiness of America.

I have the honour to be, Gentlemen, with the highest respect for the honourable Legislature and yourselves, your most obedient, and very humble servant, E. GERRY.

Reply to Elbridge Gerry:
"A Landholder" [Oliver Ellsworth] IV

Connecticut Courant (Hartford), November 26, 1787

To the Landholders and Farmers.
Remarks on the objections made by the Hon. ELBRIDGE GERRY,
to the new Constitution.

To censure a man for an opinion in which he declares himself honest, and in a matter of which all men have a right to judge, is highly injurious; at the same time, when the opinions even of honourable men are submitted to the people, a tribunal before which the meanest citizen hath a right to speak, they must abide the consequence of public stricture. We are ignorant whether the honorable gentleman possesses state dignities or emoluments which will be endangered by the new system, or hath motives of personality to prejudice his mind and throw him into the opposition; or if it be so, do not wish to evade the objections by such a charge. As a member of the general Convention, and deputy from a great state, this honorable person hath a right to speak and be heard. It gives us pleasure to know the extent of what may be objected or even surmised, by one whose situation was the best to espy danger, and mark the defective parts of the constitution, if any such there be. Mr. Gerry, tho' in the character of an objector, tells us "he was fully convinced that to preserve the union an efficient government was indispensibly necessary, and that it would be difficult to make proper amendments to the old articles of confederation" therefore by his own concession there was an indispensible necessity of a system, in many particulars entirely new. He tells us further "that if the people reject this altogether, anarchy may ensue" and what situation can be pictured more awful than a total dissolution of all government. Many defects in the constitution had better be risked than to fall back into that state of rude violence, in which every man's hand is against his neighbour, and there is no judge to decide between them or power of justice to control. But we hope to shew that there are no such alarming defects in the proposed structure of government, and that while a public force is created, the liberties of the people have every possible guard.

Several of the honorable Gentleman's objections are expressed in such vague and indecisive terms, that they rather deserve the name of insinuations, and we know not against what particular parts of the system they are pointed. Others are explicit, and if real deserve serious attention. His first objection is "that there is no adequate provision for a representation of the people". This must have respect either to the number of representatives, or to the manner in which they are chosen. The proper number to constitute a safe representation is a matter of judgment, in which honest and wise men often disagree. Were it possible for all the people to convene and give their personal assent, some would think this the best mode of making laws, but in the present instance it is impracticable. In towns and smaller districts where all the people may meet conveniently and without expence this is doubtless preferable. The state representation is composed of one or two from every town and district, which composes an assembly not so large as to be unwieldy in acting, nor so expensive as to burden the people. But if so numerous a representation were made from every part of the United States, with our present population, the new Congress would consist of three thousand men; with the population of Great Britain to which we may arrive in half a century, of ten thousand; and with the population of France, which we shall probably equal in a century and half, of thirty thousand.

Such a body of men might be an army to defend the country in case of foreign invasion, but not a legislature, and the expence to support them would equal the whole national revenue. By the proposed constitution the new Congress will consist of nearly one hundred men. When our population is equal to Great Britain of three hundred men, and when equal to France of nine hundred. Plenty of Lawgivers! why any gentleman should wish for more is not conceivable.

Considering the immense territory of America, the objection with many will be on the other side; that when the whole is populated it will constitute a legislature unmanagable by its numbers. Convention foreseeing this danger, have so worded the article, that if the people should at any future time judge necessary, they may diminish the representation.

As the state legislatures have to regulate the internal policy, of every town and neighbourhood, it is convenient enough to have one or two men, particularly acquainted with every small district of country, its interests, parties and passions. But the foederal legislature can take cognizance only of national questions and interests, which in their very nature are general, and for this purpose five or ten honest and wise men chosen from each state; men who have had previous experience in state legislation, will be more competent than an hundred. From an acquaintance with their own state legislatures, they will always know the sense of the people at large, and the expence of supporting such a number will be as much as we ought to incur.

If the Hon. gentleman, in saying "there is no adequate provision for a representation of the people" refers to the manner of choosing them, a reply to this is naturally blended with his second objection "that they have no security for the right of election" it is impossible to conceive what greater security can be given, by any form of words, than we here find.

The federal representatives are to be chosen by the votes of the people. Every freeman is an elector. The same qualifications which enable you to vote for state representatives, give you a federal voice. It is a right you cannot lose, unless you first annihilate the state legislature, and declare yourselves incapable of electing, which is a degree of infatuation improbable as a second deluge to drown the world.

Your own assemblies are to regulate the formalities of this choice, and unless they betray you, you cannot be betrayed. But perhaps it may be said, Congress have a power to control this formality as to the time and places of electing, and we allow they have: But this objection which at first looks frightful was designed as a guard to the privileges of the electors. Even state assemblies may have their fits of madness and passion, this tho' not probable is still possible.

We have a recent instance in the state of Rhode-Island, where a desperate junto are governing, contrary to the sense of a great majority of the people. It may be the case in any other state, and should it ever happen, that the ignorance or rashness of the state assemblies, in a fit of jealousy should deny you this sacred right, the deliberate justice of the continent, is enabled to interpose, and restore you a federal voice. This right is therefore more inviolably guarded than it can be by the government of your state, for it is guaranteed by the whole empire. Tho' out of the order in which the Hon. gentleman proposes his doubts, I wish here to notice some questions which he makes. The proposed plan among others he tells us involves these questions "whether the several state governments, shall be so altered as in effect to be dissolved? Whether in lieu of the state governments the national constitution now proposed shall be substituted?" I wish for sagacity to see on what these questions are founded. No alteration in the state governments, is even proposed, but they are to remain identically the same that they now are. Some powers are to be given into the hands of your federal representatives, but these powers are all in their nature general, such as must be exercised by the whole or not at all, and such as are absolutely necessary; or your commerce, the price of your commodities, your riches and your safety will be the sport of every foreign adventurer. Why are we told of the dissolution of our state governments, when by this plan they are indissolubly linked. They must stand or fall, live or die together. The national legislature consists of two houses, a senate and house of Representatives. The senate is to be chosen by the assemblies of the particular states; so that if the assemblies are dissolved, the senate dissolves with them. The national representatives are to be chosen by the same electors, and under the same qualifications, as choose the state representatives; so that if the state representation be dissolved, the national representation is gone of course.

State representation and government is the very basis of the congressional power proposed. This is the most valuable link in the chain of connexion, and affords double security for the rights of the people. Your liberties are pledged to you by your own state, and by the power of the whole empire. You have a voice in the government of your own state, and in the government of the whole. Were not the gentleman on whom the remarks are made very honourable, and by the eminence of office raised above a suspicion of cunning, we should think he had, in this instance, insinuated merely to alarm the fears of the people. His other objections will be mentioned in some future number of the LANDHOLDER.

A Further Reply to Elbridge Gerry: "A Landholder" [Oliver Ellsworth] V

Connecticut Courant (Hartford), December 3, 1787

To the Landholders and Farmers.
Continuation of Remarks on the Hon. ELBRIDGE GERRY's
Objections to the new Constitution.

It is unhappy both for Mr. Gerry and the public, that he was not more explicit in publishing his doubts. Certainly this must have been from inattention, and not thro' any want of ability; as all his honourable friends allow him to be a politician even of metaphysical nicety.

In a question of such magnitude, every candid man will consent to discuss objections, which are stated with perspicuity; but to follow the honourable writer into the field of conjecture, and combat phantoms, uncertain whether or not they are the same which terrified him, is a task too laborious for patience itself. Such must be the writer's situation in replying to the next objection, *"that some of the powers of the Legislature are ambiguous, and others indefinite and dangerous."* There are many powers given to the legislature, if any of them are dangerous, the people have a right to know which they are, and how they will operate, that we may guard against the evil. The charge of being ambiguous and indefinite may be brought against every human composition, and necessarily arises from the imperfection of language. Perhaps no two men will express the same sentiment in the same manner, and by the same words; neither do they connect precisely the same ideas with the same words. From hence arises an ambiguity in all languages, with which the most perspicuous and precise writers are in a degree chargeable. Some persons never attain to the happy art of perspicuous expression, and it is equally true that some persons thro' a mental defect of their own, will judge the most correct and certain language of others to be indefinite and ambiguous. As Mr. Gerry is the first and only man who has charged the new Constitution with ambiguousness, is there not room to suspect that his understanding is different from other men's, and whether it be better or worse, the Landholder presumes not to decide.

It is an excellency of this Constitution that it is expressed with brevity, and in the plain common language of mankind.

Had it swelled into the magnitude of a volume, there would have been more room to entrap the unwary, and the people who are to be its judges, would have had neither patience nor opportunity to understand it. Had it been expressed in the scientific language of law, or those terms of art which we often find in political compositions, to the honourable gentleman it might have appeared more definite and less ambiguous; but to the great body of the people altogether obscure, and to accept it they must leap in the dark.

The people to whom in this case the great appeal is made, best understand those compositions which are concise and in their own language. Had the powers given to the legislature, been loaded with provisos, and such qualifications, as a lawyer who is so cunning as even to suspect himself, would probably have intermingled; there would have been much more danger of a deception in the case. It would not be difficult to shew that every power given to the legislature is necessary for national defence and justice, and to protect the rights of the people who create this authority for their own advantage; but to consider each one particularly would exceed the limits of my design.

I shall therefore select two powers given them, which have been more abused to oppress and enslave mankind, than all the others with which this or any legislature on earth is cloathed. The right of taxation or of collecting money from the people; and of raising and supporting armies.

These are the powers which enable tyrants to scourge their subjects; and they are also the very powers by which good rulers protect the people, against the violence of wicked and overgrown citizens, and invasion by the rest of mankind. Judge candidly what a wretched figure the American empire will exhibit in the eye of other nations, without a power to array and support a military force for its own protection. Half a dozen regiments from Canada or New-Spain, might lay

whole provinces under contribution, while we were disputing, who has power to pay and raise an army. This power is
also necessary to restrain the violence of seditious citizens. A
concurrence of circumstances, frequently enables a few disaffected persons to make great revolutions, unless government is vested with the most extensive powers of self-defence.
Had Shays, the malecontent of Massachusetts, been a man of
genius, fortune and address, he might have conquered that
state, and by the aid of a little sedition in the other states, and
an army proud by victory, became the monarch and tyrant of
America. Fortunately he was checked, but should jealousy
prevent vesting these powers, in the hands of men chosen by
yourselves, and who are under every constitutional restraint,
accident or design will in all probability raise up some future
Shays to be the tyrant of your children.

A people cannot long retain their freedom, whose government is incapable of protecting them.

The power of collecting money from the people, is not to
be rejected because it has sometimes been oppressive.

Public credit is as necessary for the prosperity of a nation as
private credit is for the support and wealth of a family.

We are this day many millions poorer, than we should have
been had a well arranged government taken place at the conclusion of the war. All have shared in this loss, but none in so
great proportion as the landholders and farmers.

The public must be served in various departments.

Who will serve them without a meet recompence? Who
will go to war and pay the charges of his own warfare? What
man will any longer take empty promises of reward from
those, who have no constitutional power to reward or means
of fulfilling them? Promises have done their utmost, more
than they ever did in any other age or country. The delusive
bubble has broke, and in breaking it has beggared thousands,
and left you an unprotected people; numerous without force,
and full of resources but unable to command one of them.
For these purposes there must be a general treasury, with a
power to replenish it as often as necessity requires. And where
can this power be more safely vested, than in the common
legislature, men chosen by yourselves from every part of the
union, and who have the confidence of their several states;

men who must share in the burdens they impose on others; men who by a seat in Congress are incapable of holding any office under the States, which might prove a temptation to spoil the people for increasing their own income.

We find another objection to be "that the executive is blended with and will have an undue influence over the legislative." On examination you will find this objection unfounded. The supreme executive is vested in a President of the United States, every bill that hath passed the senate and representatives, must be presented to the President, and if he approve it becomes law. If he disapproves, but makes no return within ten days it still becomes law. If he returns the bill with his objections, the senate and representatives consider it a second time, and if two thirds of them adhere to the first resolution it becomes law notwithstanding the presidents dissent. We allow the president hath an influence, tho' strictly speaking he hath not a legislative voice; and think such an influence must be salutary. In the president, all the executive departments meet, and he will be a channel of communication between those who make and those who execute the laws. Many things look fair in theory which in practice are impossible. If lawmakers in every instance, before their final decree, had the opinion of those who are to execute them; it would prevent a thousand absurd ordinances, which are solemnly made, only to be repealed and lessen the dignity of legislation in the eyes of mankind.

The vice-president is not an executive officer, while the president is in discharge of his duty; and when he is called to preside his legislative voice ceases. In no other instance is there even the shadow of blending or influence between the two departments. We are further told "that the judicial department, or those courts of law, to be instituted by Congress, will be oppressive."

We allow it to be possible, but from whence arises the probability of this event. State judges may be corrupt, and juries may be prejudiced and ignorant, but these instances are not common; and why shall we suppose they will be more frequent under a national appointment and influence, when the eyes of a whole empire are watching for their detection.

Their courts are not to intermeddle with your internal

policy, and will have cognizance only of those subjects which are placed under the control of a national legislature. It is as necessary there should be courts of law and executive officers, to carry into effect the laws of the nation; as that there be courts and officers to execute the laws made by your state assemblies. There are many reasons why their decisions ought not to be left to courts instituted by particular states.

A perfect uniformity must be observed thro' the whole union or jealousy and unrighteousness will take place; and for a uniformity one judiciary must pervade the whole. The inhabitants of one state will not have confidence in judges appointed by the legislature of another state, in which they have no voice. Judges who owe their appointment and support to one state, will be unduly influenced, and not reverence the laws of the union. It will at any time be in the power of the smallest state by interdicting their own judiciary, to defeat the measures, defraud the revenue, and annul the most sacred laws of the whole empire. A legislative power, without a judicial and executive under their own control, is in the nature of things a nullity. Congress under the old confederation had power to ordain and resolve, but having no judicial or executive of their own, their most solemn resolves, were totally disregarded. The little state of Rhode-Island was purposely left by Heaven to its present madness, for a general conviction in the other states, that such a system as is now proposed is our only preservation from ruin. What respect can any one think would be paid to national laws, by judicial and executive officers who are amenable only to the present assembly of Rhode-Island. The rebellion of Shays and the present measures of Rhode-Island ought to convince us that a national legislature, judiciary and executive must be united, or the whole is but a name; and that we must have these or soon be hewers of wood and drawers of water for all other people.

In all these matters and powers given to Congress, their ordinances must be the supreme law of the land or they are nothing. They must have authority to enact any laws for executing their own powers, or those powers will be evaded by the artful and unjust, and the dishonest trader will defraud the public of its revenue.

As we have every reason to think this system was honestly

planned, we ought to hope it may be honestly and justly executed. I am sensible that speculation is always liable to error. If there be any capital defects in this constitution, it is most probable that experience alone will discover them. Provision is made for an alteration if on trial it be found necessary.

When your children see the candor and greatness of mind, with which you lay the foundation, they will be inspired with equity to finish and adorn the superstructure.

Letters from the "Federal Farmer" to "The Republican"

New York, November 8, 1787

LETTER I.

OCTOBER 8th, 1787.

DEAR SIR, My letters to you last winter, on the subject of a well-balanced national government for the United States, were the result of free enquiry; when I passed from that subject to enquiries relative to our commerce, revenues, past administration, &c. I anticipated the anxieties I feel, on carefully examining the plan of government proposed by the convention. It appears to be a plan retaining some federal features; but to be the first important step, and to aim strongly to one consolidated government of the United States. It leaves the powers of government, and the representation of the people, so unnaturally divided between the general and state governments, that the operations of our system must be very uncertain. My uniform federal attachments, and the interest I have in the protection of property, and a steady execution of the laws, will convince you, that, if I am under any biass at all, it is in favor of any general system which shall promise those advantages. The instability of our laws increase my wishes for firm and steady government; but then, I can consent to no government, which, in my opinion, is not calculated equally to preserve the rights of all orders of men in the community. My object has been to join with those who have endeavoured to supply the defects in the forms of our governments by a steady and proper administration of them. Though I have long apprehended that fraudulent debtors, and embarrassed men, on the one hand, and men, on the other, unfriendly to republican equality, would produce an uneasiness among the people, and prepare the way, not for cool and deliberate reforms in the governments, but for changes calculated to promote the interests of particular orders of men. Acquit me, sir, of any agency in the formation of the new system; I shall be satisfied with seeing, if it should be adopted, a prudent administration. Indeed I am so much convinced of the truth of Pope's maxim, that—"That which is best administered is best," that I am much inclined to subscribe to it from experience. I am not disposed to unreasonably contend about forms. I know our situation is critical, and it behoves us to make the best of it. A federal government of some sort is necessary. We have suffered the present to languish; and whether the confederation was capable or not originally of answering any valuable purposes, it is now but of little importance. I will pass by the men, and states, who have been particularly instrumental in preparing the way for a change, and, perhaps, for governments not very favourable to the people at large. A constitution is now presented, which we may reject, or which we may accept, with or without amendments; and to which point we ought to direct our exertions, is the question. To determine this question, with propriety, we must attentively examine the system itself, and the probable consequences of either step. This I shall endeavour to do, so far as I am able, with candour and fairness; and leave you to decide upon the propriety of my opinions, the weight of my reasons, and how far my conclusions are well drawn. Whatever may be the conduct of others, on the present occasion, I do not mean, hastily and positively to decide on the merits of the constitution proposed. I shall be open to conviction, and always disposed to adopt that which, all things considered, shall appear to me to be most for the happiness of the community. It must be granted, that if men hastily and blindly adopt a system of government, they will as hastily and as blindly be led to alter or abolish it; and changes must ensue, one after another, till the peaceable and better part of the community will grow weary with changes, tumults and disorders, and be disposed to accept any government, however despotic, that shall promise stability and firmness.

The first principal question that occurs, is, Whether, considering our situation, we ought to precipitate the adoption of the proposed constitution? If we remain cool and temperate, we are in no immediate danger of any commotions; we are in a state of perfect peace, and in no danger of invasions; the state governments are in the full exercise of their powers; and our governments answer all present exigencies, except the regulation of trade, securing credit, in some cases, and providing for the interest, in some instances, of the public debts; and whether we adopt a change, three or nine months hence, can make but little odds with the private circumstances of individuals; their happiness and prosperity, after all, depend principally upon their own exertions. We are hardly recovered from a long and distressing war: The farmers, fishmen, &c. have not yet fully repaired the waste made by it. Industry and frugality are again assuming their proper station. Private debts are lessened, and public debts incurred by the war, have been, by various ways, diminished; and the public lands have now become a productive source for diminishing them much more. I know uneasy men, who wish very much to precipitate, do not admit all these facts; but they are facts well known to all men who are thoroughly informed in the affairs of this country. It must, however, be admitted, that our federal system is defective, and that some of the state governments are not well administered; but, then, we impute to the defects in our governments, many evils and embarrassments which are most clearly the result of the late war. We must allow men to conduct on the present occasion, as on all similar one's. They will urge a thousand pretences to answer their purposes on both sides. When we want a man to change his condition, we describe it as miserable, wretched, and despised; and draw a pleasing picture of that which we would have him assume. And when we wish the contrary, we reverse our descriptions. Whenever a clamor is raised, and idle men get to work, it is highly necessary to examine facts carefully, and without unreasonably suspecting men of falshood, to examine, and enquire attentively, under what impressions they act. It is too often the case in political concerns, that men state facts not as they are, but as they wish them to be; and almost every man, by calling to mind past scenes, will find this to be true.

Nothing but the passions of ambitious, impatient, or disorderly men, I conceive, will plunge us into commotions, if time should be taken fully to examine and consider the system proposed. Men who feel easy in their circumstances, and such as are not sanguine in their expectations relative to the consequences of the proposed change, will remain quiet under the existing governments. Many commercial and monied men, who are uneasy, not without just cause, ought to be respected; and, by no means, unreasonably disappointed in their expectations and hopes; but as to those who expect employments under the new constitution; as to those weak and ardent men who always expect to be gainers by revolutions, and whose lot it generally is to get out of one difficulty into another, they are very little to be regarded: and as to those who designedly avail themselves of this weakness and ardor, they are to be despised. It is natural for men, who wish to hasten the adoption of a measure, to tell us, now is the crisis—now is the critical moment which must be seized, or all will be lost: and to shut the door against free enquiry, whenever conscious the thing presented has defects in it, which time and investigation will probably discover. This has been the custom of tyrants and their dependants in all ages. If it is true, what has been so often said, that the people of this country cannot change their condition for the worse, I presume it still behoves them to endeavour deliberately to change it for the better. The fickle and ardent, in any community, are the proper tools for establishing despotic government. But it is deliberate and thinking men, who must establish and secure governments on free principles. Before they decide on the plan proposed, they will enquire whether it will probably be a blessing or a curse to this people.

The present moment discovers a new face in our affairs. Our object has been all along, to reform our federal system, and to strengthen our governments—to establish peace, order and justice in the community—but a new object now presents. The plan of government now proposed, is evidently calculated totally to change, in time, our condition as a people. Instead of being thirteen republics, under a federal head, it is clearly designed to make us one consolidated government. Of this, I think, I shall fully convince you, in my following letters on this subject. This consolidation of the states has been the object of several men in this country for some time past. Whether such a change can ever be effected in any manner; whether it can be effected without convulsions and civil wars; whether such a change will not totally destroy the liberties of this country—time only can determine.

To have a just idea of the government before us, and to shew that a consolidated one is the object in view, it is necessary not only to examine the plan, but also its history, and the politics of its particular friends.

The confederation was formed when great confidence was placed in the voluntary exertions of individuals, and of the respective states; and the framers of it, to guard against usurpation, so limited and checked the powers, that, in many respects, they are inadequate to the exigencies of the union. We find, therefore, members of congress urging alterations in the federal system almost as soon as it was adopted. It was early proposed to vest congress with powers to levy an impost, to regulate trade, &c. but such was known to be the caution of the states in parting with power, that the vestment, even of these, was proposed to be under several checks and limitations. During the war, the general confusion, and the introduction of paper money, infused in the minds of people vague ideas respecting government and credit. We expected too much from the return of peace, and of course we have been disappointed. Our governments have been new and unsettled; and several legislatures, by making tender, suspension, and paper money laws, have given just cause of uneasiness to creditors. By these and other causes, several orders of men in the community have been prepared, by degrees, for a change of government; and this very abuse of power in the legislatures, which, in some cases, has been charged upon the democratic part of the community, has furnished aristocratical men with those very weapons, and those very means, with which, in great measure, they are rapidly effecting their favourite object. And should an oppressive government be the consequence of the proposed change, posterity may reproach not only a few overbearing, unprincipled men, but those parties in the states which have misused their powers.

The conduct of several legislatures, touching paper money, and tender laws, has prepared many honest men for changes in government, which otherwise they would not have thought of—when by the evils, on the one hand, and by the secret instigations of artful men, on the other, the minds of men were become sufficiently uneasy, a bold step was taken, which is usually followed by a revolution, or a civil war. A general convention for mere commercial purposes was moved for—the authors of this measure saw that the people's attention was turned solely to the amendment of the federal system; and that, had the idea of a total change been started, probably no state would have appointed members to the convention. The idea of destroying, ultimately, the state government, and forming one consolidated system, could not have been admitted—a convention, therefore, merely for vesting in congress power to regulate trade, was proposed. This was pleasing to the commercial towns; and the landed people had little or no concern about it. September, 1786, a few men from the middle states met at Annapolis, and hastily proposed a convention to be held in May, 1787, for the purpose, generally, of amending the confederation—this was done before the delegates of Massachusetts, and of the other states arrived—still not a word was said about destroying the old constitution, and making a new one—The states still unsuspecting, and not aware that they were passing the Rubicon, appointed members to the new convention, for the sole and express purpose of revising and amending the confederation—and, probably, not one man in ten thousand in the United States, till within these ten or twelve days, had an idea that the old ship was to be destroyed, and he put to the alternative of embarking in the new ship presented, or of being left in danger of sinking—The States, I believe, universally supposed the convention would report alterations in the confederation, which would pass an examination in congress, and after being agreed to there, would be confirmed by all the legislatures, or be rejected. Virginia made a very respectable appointment, and placed at the head of it the first man in America:—In this appointment there was a mixture of political characters; but Pennsylvania appointed principally those men who are esteemed aristocratical. Here the favourite moment for changing the government was evidently discerned by a few men, who seized it with address. Ten other states appointed, and tho' they chose men principally connected with commerce and the judicial department, yet they appointed many good republican characters—had they all attended we should now see, I am persuaded, a better system presented. The non-attendance of eight or nine men, who were appointed members of the convention, I shall ever consider as a very unfortunate event to the United States.—Had they attended, I am pretty clear that the result of the convention would not have had that strong tendency to aristocracy now discernable in every part of the plan. There would not have been so great an accummulation of powers, especially as to the internal police of the country, in a few hands, as the constitution reported proposes to vest in them—the young visionary men, and the consolidating aristocracy, would have been more restrained than they have been. Eleven states met in the convention, and after four months close attention, presented the new constitution, to be adopted or rejected by the people. The uneasy and fickle part of the community may be prepared to receive any form of government; but, I presume, the enlightened and substantial part will give any constitution, presented for their adoption, a candid and thorough examination: and silence those designing or empty men, who weakly and rashly attempt to precipitate the adoption of a system of so much importance—We shall view the convention with proper respect—and, at the same time, that we reflect there were men of abilities and integrity in it, we must recollect how disproportionably the democratic and aristocratic parts of the community were represented.—Perhaps the judicious friends and opposers of the new constitution will agree, that it is best to let it rest solely on its own merits, or be condemned for its own defects.

In the first place, I shall premise, that the plan proposed, is a plan of accommodation—and that it is in this way only, and by giving up a part of our opinions, that we can ever expect to obtain a government founded in freedom and compact. This circumstance candid men will always keep in view, in the discussion of this subject.

The plan proposed appears to be partly federal, but principally however, calculated ultimately to make the states one consolidated government.

The first interesting question, therefore, suggested, is, how far the states can be consolidated into one entire government on free principles. In considering this question extensive objects are to be taken into view, and important changes in the forms of government to be carefully attended to in all their consequences. The happiness of the people at large must be the great object with every honest statesman, and he will direct every movement to this point. If we are so situated as a people, as not to be able to enjoy equal happiness and advantages under one government, the consolidation of the states cannot be admitted.

There are three different forms of free government under which the United States may exist as one nation; and now is, perhaps, the time to determine to which we will direct our views. 1. Distinct republics connected under a fœderal head. In this case the respective state governments must be the principal guardians of the peoples rights, and exclusively regulate their internal police; in them must rest the balance of government. The congress of the states, or federal head, must consist of delegates amenable to, and removeable by the respective states: This congress must have general directing powers; powers to require men and monies of the states; to make treaties; peace and war; to direct the operations of armies, &c. Under this federal modification of government, the powers of congress would be rather advisory or recommendatory than coercive. 2. We may do away the several state governments, and form or consolidate all the states into one entire government, with one executive, one judiciary, and one legislature, consisting of senators and representatives collected from all parts of the union: In this case there would be a compleat consolidation of the states. 3. We may consolidate the states as to certain national objects, and leave them severally distinct independent republics, as to internal police generally. Let the general government consist of an executive, a judiciary and balanced legislature, and its powers extend exclusively to all foreign concerns, causes arising on the seas, to commerce, imports, armies, navies, Indian affairs, peace and war, and to a few internal concerns of the community; to the coin, post-offices, weights and measures, a general plan for the militia, to naturalization, *and, perhaps to bankruptcies*, leaving the internal police of the community, in other respects, exclusively to the state governments; as the administration of justice in all causes arising internally, the laying and collecting of internal taxes, and the forming of the militia according to a general plan prescribed. In this case there would be a compleat consolidation, *quoad* certain objects only.

Touching the first, or federal plan, I do not think much can be said in its favor: The sovereignty of the nation, without coercive and efficient powers to collect the strength of it, cannot always be depended on to answer the purposes of government; and in a congress of representatives of foreign states, there must necessarily be an unreasonable mixture of powers in the same hands.

As to the second, or compleat consolidating plan, it deserves to be carefully considered at this time by every American: If it be impracticable, it is a fatal error to model our governments, directing our views ultimately to it.

The third plan, or partial consolidation, is, in my opinion, the only one that can secure the freedom and happiness of this people. I once had some general ideas that the second plan was practicable, but from long attention, and the proceedings of the convention, I am fully satisfied, that this third plan is the only one we can with safety and propriety proceed upon. Making this the standard to point out, with candour and fairness, the parts of the new constitution which appear to be improper, is my object. The convention appears to have proposed the partial consolidation evidently with a view to collect all powers ultimately, in the United States into one entire government; and from its views in this respect, and from the tenacity, of the small states to have an equal vote in the senate, probably originated the greatest defects in the proposed plan.

Independant of the opinions of many great authors, that a free elective government cannot be extended over large territories, a few reflections must evince, that one government and general legislation alone never can extend equal benefits to all parts of the United States: Different laws, customs, and opinions exist in the different states, which by a uniform system of laws would be unreasonably invaded. The United States contain about a million of square miles, and in half a century will, probably, contain ten millions of people; and from the center to the extremes is about 800 miles.

Before we do away the state governments, or adopt measures that will tend to abolish them, and to consolidate the states into one entire government several principles should be considered and facts ascertained:—These, and my examination into the essential parts of the proposed plan, I shall pursue in my next.

LETTER II.

OCTOBER 9, 1787.

DEAR SIR, The essential parts of a free and good government are a full and equal representation of the people in the legislature, and the jury trial of the vicinage in the administration of justice—a full and equal representation, is that which possesses the same interests, feelings, opinions, and views the people themselves would were they all assembled—a fair representation, therefore, should be so regulated, that every order of men in the community, according to the common course of elections, can have a share in it—in order to allow professional men, merchants, traders, farmers, mechanics, &c. to bring a just proportion of their best informed men respectively into the legislature, the representation must be considerably numerous—We have about 200 state senators in the United States, and a less number than that of federal representatives cannot, clearly, be a full representation of this people, in the affairs of internal taxation and police, were there but one legislature for the whole union. The representation cannot be equal, or the situation of the people proper for one government only—if the extreme parts of the society cannot be represented as fully as the central—It is apparently impracticable that this should be the case in this extensive country—it would be impossible to collect a representation of the parts of the country five, six, and seven hundred miles from the seat of government.

Under one general government alone, there could be but one judiciary, one supreme and a proper number of inferior courts. I think it would be totally impracticable in this case, to preserve a due administration of justice, and the real benefits of the jury trial of the vicinage—there are now supreme courts in each state in the union; and a great number of county and other courts subordinate to each supreme court—most of these supreme and inferior courts are itinerant, and hold their sessions in different parts every year of their respective states, counties and districts—with all these moving courts, our citizens, from the vast extent of the country must travel very considerable distances from home to find the place where justice is administered. I am not for bringing justice so near to individuals as to afford them any temptation to engage in law suits; though I think it one of the greatest benefits in a good government, that each citizen should find a court of justice within a reasonable distance, perhaps, within a day's travel of his home; so that, without great inconveniences and enormous expences, he may have the advantages of his witnesses and jury—it would be impracticable to derive these advantages from one judiciary—the one supreme court at most could only set in the centre of the union, and move once a year into the centre of the eastern and southern extremes of it—and, in this case, each citizen, on an average, would travel 150 or 200 miles to find this court—that, however, inferior courts might be properly placed in the different counties, and districts of the union, the appellate jurisdiction would be intolerable and expensive.

If it were possible to consolidate the states, and preserve the features of a free government, still it is evident that the middle states, the parts of the union, about the seat of government, would enjoy great advantages, while the remote states would experience the many inconveniences of remote provinces. Wealth, officers, and the benefits of government would collect in the centre: and the extreme states, and their principal towns become much less important.

There are other considerations which tend to prove that the idea of one consolidated whole, on free principles, is ill-founded—the laws of a free government rest on the confidence of the people, and operate gently—and never can extend their influence very far—if they are executed on free principles, about the centre, where the benefits of the government induce the people to support it voluntarily; yet they must be executed on the principles of fear and force in the extremes—This has been the case with every extensive republic of which we have any accurate account.

There are certain unalienable and fundamental rights, which in forming the social compact, ought to be explicitly ascertained and fixed—a free and enlightened people, in forming this compact, will not resign all their rights to those who govern, and they will fix limits to their legislators and rulers, which will soon be plainly seen by those who are governed, as well as by those who govern: and the latter will know they cannot be passed unperceived by the former, and without giving a general alarm—These rights should be made the basis of every constitution; and if a people be so situated, or have such different opinions that they cannot agree in ascertaining and fixing them, it is a very strong argument against their attempting to form one entire society, to live under one system of laws only.—I confess, I never thought the people of these states differed essentially in these respects; they having derived all these rights, from one common source, the British systems; and having in the formation of their state constitutions, discovered that their ideas relative to these rights are very similar. However, it is now said that the states differ so essentially in these respects, and even in the important article of the trial by jury, that when assembled in convention, they can agree to no words by which to establish that trial, or by which to ascertain and establish many other of these rights, as fundamental articles in the social compact. If so, we proceed to consolidate the states on no solid basis whatever.

But I do not pay much regard to the reasons given for not bottoming the new constitution on a better bill of rights. I still believe a complete federal bill of rights to be very practicable. Nevertheless I acknowledge the proceedings of the convention furnish my mind with many new and strong reasons, against a complete consolidation of the states. They tend to convince me, that it cannot be carried with propriety very far—that the convention have gone much farther in one respect than they found it practicable to go in another; that is, they propose to lodge in the general government very extensive powers—*powers* nearly, if not altogether, complete and unlimited, over the purse and the sword. But, in its organization, they furnish the strongest proof that the proper limbs, or parts of a government, to support and execute those powers on proper principles (or in which they can be safely lodged) cannot be formed. These powers must be lodged somewhere in every society; but then they should be lodged where the strength and guardians of the people are collected. They can be wielded, or safely used, in a free country only by an able executive and judiciary, a respectable senate, and a secure, full, and equal representation of the people. I think the principles I have premised or brought into view, are well founded—I think they will not be denied by any fair reasoner. It is in connection with these, and other solid principles, we are to examine the constitution. It is not a few democratic phrases, or a few well formed features, that will prove its merits; or a few small omissions that will produce its rejection among men of sense; they will enquire what are the essential powers in a community, and what are nominal ones, where and how the essential powers shall be lodged to secure government, and to secure true liberty.

In examining the proposed constitution carefully, we must clearly perceive an unnatural separation of these powers from the substantial representation of the people. The state governments will exist, with all their governors, senators, representatives, officers and expences; in these will be nineteen-twentieths of the representatives of the people; they will have a near connection, and their members an immediate intercourse with the people; and the probability is, that the state governments will possess the confidence of the people, and be considered generally as their immediate guardians.

The general government will consist of a new species of executive, a small senate, and a very small house of representatives. As many citizens will be more than three hundred miles from the seat of this government as will be nearer to it, its judges and officers cannot be very numerous, without making our government very expensive. Thus will stand the state and the general governments, should the constitution be adopted without any alterations in their organization: but as to powers, the general government will possess all essential ones, at least on paper, and those of the states a mere shadow of power. And therefore, unless the people shall make some great exertions to restore to the state governments their powers in matters of internal police; as the powers to lay and collect, exclusively, internal taxes, to govern the militia, and to hold the decisions of their own judicial courts upon their own laws final, the balance cannot possibly continue long; but the state governments must be annihilated, or continue to exist for no purpose.

It is however to be observed, that many of the essential powers given the national government are not exclusively given; and the general government may have prudence enough to forbear the exercise of those which may still be exercised by the respective states. But this cannot justify the impropriety of giving powers, the exercise of which prudent men will not attempt, and imprudent men will, or probably can, exercise only in a manner destructive of free government. The general government, organized as it is, may be adequate to many valuable objects, and be able to carry its laws into execution on proper principles in several cases; but I think its warmest friends will not contend, that it can carry all the powers proposed to be lodged in it into effect, without calling to its aid a military force, which must very soon destroy all elective governments in the country, produce anarchy, or establish despotism. Though we cannot have now a complete idea of what will be the operations of the proposed system, we may, allowing things to have their common course, have a very tolerable one. The powers lodged in the general government, if exercised by it, must intimately effect the internal police of the states, as well as external concerns; and there is no reason to expect the numerous state governments, and their connections, will be very friendly to the execution of federal laws in those internal affairs, which hitherto have been under their own immediate management. There is more reason to believe, that the general government, far removed from the people, and none of its members elected oftener than once in two years, will be forgot or neglected, and its laws in many cases disregarded, unless a multitude of officers and military force be continually kept in view, and employed to enforce the execution of the laws, and to make the government feared and respected. No position can be truer than this,—That in this country either neglected laws, or a military execution of them, must lead to a revolution, and to the destruction of freedom. Neglected laws must first lead to anarchy and confusion; and a military execution of laws is only a shorter way to the same point—despotic government.

LETTER III.

OCTOBER 10th, 1787.

DEAR SIR, The great object of a free people must be so to form their government and laws and so to administer them as to create a confidence in, and respect for the laws; and thereby induce the sensible and virtuous part of the community to declare in favor of the laws, and to support them without an expensive military force. I wish, though I confess I have not much hope, that this may be the case with the laws of Congress under the new Constitution. I am fully convinced that we must organize the national government on different principles, and make the parts of it more efficient, and secure in it more effectually the different interests in the community; or else leave in the state governments some powers proposed to be lodged in it—at least till such an organization shall be found to be practicable. Not sanguine in my expectations of a good federal administration, and satisfied, as I am, of the impracticability of consolidating the states, and at the same time of preserving the rights of the people at large, I believe we ought still to leave some of those powers in the state governments, in which the people, in fact, will still be represented—to define some other powers proposed to be vested in the general government, more carefully, and to establish a few principles to secure a proper exercise of the powers given it. It is not my object to multiply objections, or to contend about inconsiderable powers or amendments. I wish the system adopted with a few alterations; but those, in my mind, are essential ones; if adopted without, every good citizen will acquiesce, though I shall consider the duration of our governments, and the liberties of this people, very much dependant on the administration of the general government. A wise and honest administration, may make the people happy under any government; but necessity only can justify even our leaving open avenues to the abuse of power, by wicked, unthinking, or ambitious men. I will examine, first, the organization of the proposed government in order to judge; 2d. with propriety, what powers are improperly, at least prematurely lodged in it. I shall examine, 3d, the undefined powers; and 4th, those powers, the exercise of which is not secured on safe and proper ground.

First. As to the organization—the house of representatives, the democrative branch, as it is called, is to consist of 65 members; that is, about one representative for fifty thousand inhabitants, to be chosen biennially—the federal legislature may increase this number to one for every thirty thousand inhabitants, abating fractional numbers in each state.—Thirty-three representatives will make a quorum for doing business, and a majority of those present determine the sense of the house.—I have no idea that the interests, feelings, and opinions of three or four millions of people, especially touching internal taxation, can be collected in such a house.—In the nature of things, nine times in ten, men of elevated classes in the community only can be chosen—Connecticut, for instance, will have five representatives—not one man in a hundred of those who form the democrative branch in the state legislature, will on a fair computation, be one of the five—The people of this country, in one sense, may all be democratic; but if we make the proper distinction between the few men of wealth and abilities, and consider them, as we ought, as the natural aristocracy of the country, and the great body of the people, the middle and lower classes, as the democracy, this federal representative branch will have but very little democracy in it, even this small representation is not secured on proper principles.—The branches of the legislature are essential parts of the fundamental compact, and ought to be so fixed by the people, that the legislature cannot alter itself by modifying the elections of its own members. This, by a part of Art. 1. Sect. 4. the general legislature may do, it may evidently so regulate elections as to secure the choice of any particular description of men.—It may make the whole state one district—make the capital, or any place in the state, the place or places of election—it may declare that the five men (or whatever the number may be the state may chuse) who shall have the most votes shall be considered as chosen—In this case it is easy to perceive how the people who live scattered in the inland towns will bestow their votes on different men—and how few men in a city, in any order or profession, may unite and place any five men they please highest among those that may be voted for—and all this may be done constitutionally, and by those silent operations, which are not immediately perceived by the people in general.—I know it is urged, that the general legislature will be disposed to regulate elections on fair and just principles:—This may be true—good men will generally govern well with almost any constitution: But why in laying the foundation of the social system, need we unnecessarily have a door open to improper regulations?—This is a very general and unguarded clause, and many evils may flow from that part which authorises the congress to regulate elections—Were it omitted, the regulations of elections would be solely in the respective states, where the people are substantially represented; and where the elections ought to be regulated, otherwise to secure a representation from all parts of the community, in making the constitution, we ought to provide for dividing each state into a proper number of districts, and for confining the electors in each district to the choice of some men, who shall have a permanent interest and residence in it; and also for this essential object, that the representative elected shall have a majority of the votes of those electors who shall attend and give their votes.

In considering the practicability of having a full and equal representation of the people from all parts of the union, not only distances and different opinions, customs, and views, common in extensive tracts of country, are to be taken into view, but many differences peculiar to Eastern, Middle, and Southern States. These differences are not so perceivable among the members of congress, and men of general information in the state, as among the men who would properly form the democratic branch. The Eastern states are very democratic, and composed chiefly of moderate freeholders: they have but few rich men and no slaves; the Southern states are composed chiefly of rich planters and slaves; they have but few moderate freeholders, and the prevailing influence, in them, is generally a dissipated aristocracy: The Middle states partake partly of the Eastern, and partly of the Southern character.

Perhaps, nothing could be more disjointed, unweildly and incompetent to doing business with harmony and dispatch, than a federal house of representatives properly numerous for the great objects of taxation, &c. collected from the several states; whether such men would ever act in concert; whether they would not worry along a few years, and then be the means of separating the parts of the union, is very problematical?—View this system in whatever form we can, propriety brings us still to this point, a federal government possessed of general and complete powers, as to those national objects which cannot well come under the cognizance of the internal laws of the respective states, and this federal government, accordingly, consisting of branches not very numerous.

The house of representatives is on the plan of consolidation, but the senate is entirely on the federal plan; and Delaware will have as much constitutional influence in the senate, as the largest state in the union; and in this senate are lodged legislative, executive and judicial powers: Ten states in this union urge that they are small states, nine of which were present in the convention.—They were interested in collecting large powers into the hands of the senate, in which each state still will have its equal share of power. I suppose it was impracticable for the three large states, as they were called, to get the senate formed on any other principles:—But this only proves, that we cannot form one general government on equal and just principles—and proves, that we ought not to lodge in it such extensive powers before we are convinced of the practicability of organizing it on just and equal principles. The senate will consist of two members from each state, chosen by the state legislature, every sixth year. The clause referred to, respecting the elections of representatives, empowers the general legislature to regulate the elections of senators also, "except as to the places of chusing senators."—There is, therefore, but little more security in the elections than in those of representatives:—Fourteen senators make a quorum for business, and a majority of the senators present give the vote of the senate, except in giving judgment upon an impeachment, or in making treaties, or in expelling a member, when two thirds of the senators present must agree.—The members of the legislature are not excluded from being elected to any military offices, or any civil offices, except those created, or the emoluments of which shall be increased by themselves: two-thirds of the members present, of either house, may expel a member at pleasure.—The senate is an independent branch of the legislature, a court for trying impeachments, and also a part of the executive, having a negative in the making of all treaties, and in appointing almost all officers.

The vice-president is not a very important, if not an unnecessary part of the system—he may be a part of the senate at one period, and act as the supreme executive magistrate at another—The election of this officer, as well as of the president of the United States seems to be properly secured; but when we examine the powers of the president, and the forms of the executive, shall perceive that the general government, in this part, will have a strong tendency to aristocracy, or the government of the few. The executive is, in fact, the president and senate in all transactions of any importance; the president is connected with, or tied to the senate; he may always act with the senate, never can effectually counteract its views: The president can appoint no officer, civil or military, who shall not be agreeable to the senate; and the presumption is, that the will of so important a body will not be very easily controuled, and that it will exercise its powers with great address.

In the judicial department, powers ever kept distinct in well balanced governments, are no less improperly blended in the hands of the same men—in the judges of the supreme court is lodged, the law, the equity and the fact. It is not necessary to pursue the minute organical parts of the general government proposed.—There were various interests in the convention, to be reconciled, especially of large and small states; of carrying and non-carrying states: and of states more and states less democratic—vast labour and attention were by the convention bestowed on the organization of the parts of the constitution offered; still it is acknowledged, there are many things radically wrong in the essential parts of this constitution—but it is said, that these are the result of our situation:—On a full examination of the subject, I believe it; but what do the laborious inquiries and determinations of the convention prove? If they prove any thing, they prove that we cannot consolidate the states on proper principles: The organization of the government presented proves, that we cannot form a general government in which all power can be safely lodged; and a little attention to the parts of the one proposed will make it appear very evident, that all the powers proposed to be lodged in it, will not be then well deposited, either for the purposes of government, or the preservation of liberty. I will suppose no abuse of powers in those cases, in which the abuse of it is not well guarded against—I will suppose the words authorising the general government to regulate the elections of its own members struck out of the plan, or free district elections, in each state, amply secured.— That the small representation provided for shall be as fair and equal as it is capable of being made—I will suppose the judicial department regulated on pure principles, by future laws, as far as it can be by the constitution, and consist with the situation of the country—still there will be an unreasonable accumulation of powers in the general government, if all be granted, enumerated in the plan proposed. The plan does not present a well balanced government: The senatorial branch of the legislative and the executive are substantially united, and the president, or the first executive magistrate, may aid the senatorial interest when weakest, but never can effectually support the democratic, however it may be oppressed;—the excellency, in my mind, of a well balanced government is that it consists of distinct branches, each sufficiently strong and independant to keep its own station, and to aid either of the other branches which may occasionally want aid.

The convention found that any but a small house of representatives would be expensive, and that it would be impracticable to assemble a large number of representatives. Not only the determination of the convention in this case, but the situation of the states, proves the impracticability of collecting, in any one point, a proper representation.

The formation of the senate, and the smallness of the house, being, therefore, the result of our situation, and the actual state of things, the evils which may attend the exercise of many powers in this national government may be considered as without a remedy.

All officers are impeachable before the senate only—before the men by whom they are appointed, or who are consenting to the appointment of these officers. No judgment of conviction, on an impeachment, can be given unless two thirds of the senators agree. Under these circumstances the right of impeachment, in the house, can be of but little importance: the house cannot expect often to convict the offender; and, therefore, probably, will but seldom or never exercise the right. In addition to the insecurity and inconveniences attending this organization beforementioned, it may be observed, that it is extremely difficult to secure the people against the fatal effects of corruption and influence. The power of making any law will be in the president, eight senators, and seventeen representatives, relative to the important objects enumerated in the constitution. Where there is a small representation a sufficient number to carry any measure, may, with ease, be influenced by bribes, offices and civilities; they may easily form private juntoes, and out-door meetings, agree on measures, and carry them by silent votes.

Impressed, as I am, with a sense of the difficulties there are in the way of forming the parts of a federal government on proper principles, and seeing a government so unsubstantially organized, after so arduous an attempt has been made, I am led to believe, that powers ought to be given to it with great care and caution.

In the second place it is necessary, therefore, to examine the extent, and the probable operations of some of those extensive powers proposed to be vested in this government. These powers, legislative, executive, and judicial, respect internal as well as external objects. Those respecting external objects, as all foreign concerns, commerce, impost, all causes arising on the seas, peace and war, and Indian affairs, can be lodged no where else, with any propriety, but in this government. Many powers that respect internal objects ought clearly to be lodged in it; as those to regulate trade between the states, weights and measures, the coin or current monies, post-offices, naturalization, &c. These powers may be exercised without essentially effecting the internal police of the respective states: But powers to lay and collect internal taxes, to form the militia, to make bankrupt laws, and to decide on appeals, questions arising on the internal laws of the respective states, are of a very serious nature, and carry with them almost all other powers. These taken in connection with the others, and powers to raise armies and build navies, proposed to be lodged in this government, appear to me to comprehend all the essential powers in the community, and those which will be left to the states will be of no great importance.

A power to lay and collect taxes at discretion, is, in itself, of very great importance. By means of taxes, the government may command the whole or any part of the subject's property. Taxes may be of various kinds; but there is a strong distinction between external and internal taxes. External taxes are impost duties, which are laid on imported goods; they may usually be collected in a few seaport towns, and of a few individuals, though ultimately paid by the consumer; a few officers can collect them, and they can be carried no higher than trade will bear, or smuggling permit—that in the very nature of commerce bounds are set to them. But internal taxes, as poll and land taxes, excise, duties on all written instruments, &c. may fix themselves on every person and species of property in the community; they may be carried to any lengths, and in proportion as they are extended, numerous officers must be employed to assess them, and to enforce the collection of them. In the United Netherlands the general government has compleat powers, as to external taxation; but as to internal taxes, it makes requisitions on the provinces. Internal taxation in this country is more important, as the country is so very extensive. As many assessors and collectors of federal taxes will be above three hundred miles from the seat of the federal government as will be less. Besides, to lay and collect internal taxes, in this extensive country, must require a great number of congressional ordinances, immediately operating upon the body of the people; these must continually interfere with the state laws, and thereby produce disorder and general dissatisfaction, till the one system of laws or the other, operating upon the same subjects, shall be abolished. These ordinances alone, to say nothing of those respecting the militia, coin, commerce, federal judiciary, &c. &c. will probably soon defeat the operations of the state laws and governments.

Should the general government think it politic, as some administrations (if not all) probably will, to look for a support in a system of influence, the government will take every occasion to multiply laws, and officers to execute them, considering these as so many necessary props for its own support. Should this system of policy be adopted, taxes more productive than the impost duties will, probably, be wanted to support the government, and to discharge foreign demands, without leaving any thing for the domestic creditors. The internal sources of taxation then must be called into operation, and internal tax laws and federal assessors and collectors spread over this immense country. All these circumstances considered, is it wise, prudent, or safe, to vest the powers of laying and collecting internal taxes in the general government, while imperfectly organized and inadequate; and to trust to amending it hereafter, and making it adequate to this purpose? It is not only unsafe but absurd to lodge power in a government before it is fitted to receive it? It is confessed that this power and representation ought to go together. Why give the power first? Why give the power to the few, who, when possessed of it, may have address enough to prevent the increase of representation? Why not keep the power, and, when necessary, amend the constitution, and add to its other parts this power, and a proper increase of representation at the same time? Then men who may want the power will be under strong inducements to let in the people, by their representatives, into the government, to hold their due proportion of this power. If a proper representation be impracticable, then we shall see this power resting in the states, where it at present ought to be, and not inconsiderately given up.

When I recollect how lately congress, convention, legislatures, and people, contended in the cause of liberty, and carefully weighed the importance of taxation, I can scarcely believe we are serious in proposing to vest the powers of laying and collecting internal taxes in a government so imperfectly organized for such purposes. Should the United States be taxed by a house of representatives of two hundred members, which would be about fifteen members for Connecticut, twenty-five for Massachusetts, &c. still the middle and lower classes of people could have no great share, in fact, in taxation. I am aware it is said, that the representation proposed by the new constitution is sufficiently numerous; it may be for many purposes; but to suppose that this branch is sufficiently numerous to guard the rights of the people in the administration of the government, in which the purse and sword is placed, seems to argue that we have forgot what the true meaning of representation is. I am sensible also, that it is said that congress will not attempt to lay and collect internal taxes; that it is necessary for them to have the power, though it cannot probably be exercised.—I admit that it is not probable that any prudent congress will attempt to lay and collect internal taxes, especially direct taxes: but this only proves, that the power would be improperly lodged in congress, and that it might be abused by imprudent and designing men.

I have heard several gentlemen, to get rid of objections to this part of the constitution, attempt to construe the powers relative to direct taxes, as those who object to it would have them; as to these, it is said, that congress will only have power to make requisitions, leaving it to the states to lay and collect them. I see but very little colour for this construction, and the attempt only proves that this part of the plan cannot be defended. By this plan there can be no doubt, but that the powers of congress will be complete as to all kind of taxes whatever—Further, as to internal taxes, the state governments will have concurrent powers with the general government, and both may tax the same objects in the same year; and the objection that the general government may suspend a state tax, as a necessary measure for the promoting the collection of a federal tax, is not without foundation.—As the states owe large debts, and have large demands upon them individually, there clearly would be a propriety in leaving in their possession exclusively, some of the internal sources of taxation, at least until the federal representation shall be properly encreased: The power in the general government to lay and collect internal taxes, will render its powers respecting armies, navies and the militia, the more exceptionable. By the constitution it is proposed that congress shall have power "to raise and support armies, but no appropriation of money to that use shall be for a longer term than two years; to provide and maintain a navy; to provide for calling forth the militia to execute the laws of the union; suppress insurrections, and repel invasions: to provide for organizing, arming, and disciplining the militia: reserving to the states the right to appoint the officers, and to train the militia according to the discipline prescribed by congress;" congress will have unlimited power to raise armies, and to engage officers and men for any number of years; but a legislative act applying money for their support can have operation for no longer term than two years, and if a subsequent congress do not within the two years renew the appropriation, or further appropriate monies for the use of the army, the army, will be left to take care of itself. When an army shall once be raised for a number of years, it is not probable that it will find much difficulty in getting congress to pass laws for applying monies to its support. I see so many men in America fond of a standing army, and especially among those who probably will have a large share in administering the federal system; it is very evident to me, that we shall have a large standing army as soon as the monies to support them can be possibly found. An army is a very agreeable place of employment for the young gentlemen of many families. A power to raise armies must be lodged some where; still this will not justify the lodging this power in a bare majority of so few men without any checks; or in the government in which the great body of the people, in the nature of things, will be only nominally represented. In the state governments the great body of the people, the yeomanry, &c. of the country, are represented: It is true they will chuse the members of congress, and may now and then chuse a man of their own way of thinking; but it is impossible for forty, or thirty thousand people in this country, one time in ten to find a man who can possess similar feeling, views, and interests with themselves: powers to lay and collect taxes and to raise armies are of the greatest moment; for carrying them into effect, laws need not be frequently made, and the yeomanry, &c. of the country ought substantially to have a check upon the passing of these laws; this check ought to be placed in the legislatures, or at least, in the few men the common people of the country, will, probably, have in congress, in the true sense of the word, "from among themselves." It is true, the yeomanry of the country possess the lands, the weight of property, possess arms, and are too strong a body of men to be openly offended—and, therefore, it is urged, they will take care of themselves, that men who shall govern will not dare pay any disrespect to their opinions. It is easily perceived, that if they have not their proper negative upon passing laws in congress, or on the passage of laws relative to taxes and armies, they may in twenty or thirty years be by means imperceptible to them, totally deprived of that boasted weight and strength: This may be done in a great measure by congress, if disposed to do it, by modelling the militia. Should one fifth, or one eighth part of the men capable of bearing arms, be made a select militia, as has been proposed, and those the young and ardent part of the community, possessed of but little or no property, and all the others put upon a plan that will render them of no importance, the former will answer all the purposes of an army, while the latter will be defenceless. The state must train the militia in such form and according to such systems and rules as Congress shall prescribe: and the only actual influence the respective states will have respecting the militia will be in appointing the officers. I see no provision made for calling out the *posse commitatus* for executing the laws of the union, but provision is made for Congress to call forth the militia for the execution of them—and the militia in general, or any select part of it, may be called out under military officers, instead of the sheriff to enforce an execution of federal laws, in the first instance and thereby introduce an entire military execution of the laws. I know that powers to raise taxes, to regulate the military strength of the community on some uniform plan, to provide for its defence and internal order, and for duly executing the laws, must be lodged somewhere; but still we ought not to lodge them, as evidently to give one another of them in the community, undue advantages over others; or commit the many to the mercy, prudence, and moderation of the few. And so far as it may be necessary to lodge any of the peculiar powers in the general government, a more safe exercise of them ought to be secured, by requiring the consent of two-thirds or three-fourths of Congress thereto—until the federal representation can be increased, so that the democratic members in Congress may stand some tolerable chance of a reasonable negative, in behalf of the numerous, important, and democratic part of the community.

I am not sufficiently acquainted with the laws and internal police of all the states to discern fully, how general bankrupt laws, made by the union, would effect them, or promote the public good. I believe the property of debtors, in the several states, is held responsible for their debts in modes and forms very different. If uniform bankrupt laws can be made without producing real and substantial inconveniences, I wish them to be made by Congress.

There are some powers proposed to be lodged in the general government in the judicial department, I think very unnecessarily, I mean powers respecting questions arising upon the internal laws of the respective states. It is proper the federal judiciary should have powers co-extensive with the federal legislature — that is, the power of deciding finally on the laws of the union. By Art. 3. Sect. 2. the powers of the federal judiciary are extended (among other things) to all cases between a state and citizens of another state — between citizens of different states — between a state or the citizens thereof, and foreign states, citizens or subjects. Actions in all these cases, except against a state government, are now brought and finally determined in the law courts of the states respectively; and as there are no words to exclude these courts of their jurisdiction in these cases, they will have concurrent jurisdiction with the inferior federal courts in them; and, therefore, if the new constitution be adopted without any amendment in this respect, all those numerous actions, now brought in the state courts between our citizens and foreigners, between citizens of different states, by state governments against foreigners, and by state governments against citizens of other states, may also be brought in the federal courts; and an appeal will lay in them from the state courts, or federal inferior courts, to the supreme judicial court of the union. In almost all these cases, either party may have the trial by jury in the state courts; excepting paper money and tender laws, which are wisely guarded against in the proposed constitution; justice may be obtained in these courts on reasonable terms; they must be more competent to proper decisions on the laws of their respective states, than the federal courts can possibly be. I do not, in any point of view, see the need of opening a new jurisdiction to these causes—of opening a new scene of expensive law suits—of suffering foreigners, and citizens of different states, to drag each other many hundred miles into the federal courts. It is true, those courts may be so organized by a wise and prudent legislature, as to make the obtaining of justice in them tolerably easy; they may in general be organized on the common law principles of the country: But this benefit is by no means secured by the constitution. The trial by jury is secured only in those few criminal cases, to which the federal laws will extend—as crimes committed on the seas against the laws of nations, treason and counterfeiting the federal securities and coin: But even in these cases, the jury trial of the vicinage is not secured, particularly in the large states, a citizen may be tried for a crime committed in the state, and yet tried in some states 500 miles from the place where it was committed; but the jury trial is not secured at all in civil causes. Though the convention have not established this trial, it is to be hoped that congress, in putting the new system into execution, will do it by a legislative act, in all cases in which it can be done with propriety. Whether the jury trial is not excluded in the supreme judicial court, is an important question. By Art. 3. Sect. 2. all cases affecting ambassadors, other public ministers, and consuls, and in those cases in which a state shall be party, the supreme court shall have jurisdiction. In all the other cases before mentioned, the supreme court shall have appellate jurisdiction, both as to LAW and FACT, with such exception, and under such regulations, as the congress shall make. By court is understood a court consisting of judges; and the idea of a jury is excluded. This court, or the judges, are to have jurisdiction on appeals, in all the cases enumerated, as to law and fact; the judges are to decide the law and try the fact, and the trial of the fact being assigned to the judges by the constitution, a jury for trying the fact is excluded; however, under the exceptions and powers to make regulations, Congress may, perhaps, introduce the jury, to try the fact in most necessary cases.

There can be but one supreme court in which the final jurisdiction will centre in all federal causes—except in cases where appeals by law shall not be allowed: The judicial powers of the federal courts extends in law and equity to certain cases: and, therefore, the powers to determine on the law, in equity, and as to the fact, all will concentre in the supreme court:—These powers, which by this constitution are blended in the same hands, the same judges, are in Great-Britain deposited in different hands—to wit, the decision of the law in the law judges, the decision in equity in the chancellor, and the trial of the fact in the jury. It is a very dangerous thing to vest in the same judge power to decide on the law, and also general powers in equity; for if the law restrain him, he is only to step into his shoes of equity, and give what judgment his reason or opinion may dictate; we have no precedents in this country, as yet, to regulate the divisions as in equity in Great-Britain; equity, therefore, in the supreme court for many years, will be mere discretion. I confess in the constitution of the supreme court, as left by the constitution, I do not see a spark of freedom or a shadow of our own or the British common law.

This court is to have appellate jurisdiction in all the other cases before mentioned: Many sensible men suppose that cases before-mentioned respect, as well the criminal cases as the civil ones, mentioned antecedently in the constitution, if so an appeal is allowed in criminal cases—contrary to the usual sense of law. How far it may be proper to admit a foreigner or the citizen of another state to bring actions against state governments, which have failed in performing so many promises made during the war, is doubtful: How far it may be proper so to humble a state, as to bring it to answer to an individual in a court of law, is worthy of consideration; the states are now subject to no such actions; and this new jurisdiction will subject the states, and many defendants to actions, and processes, which were not in the contemplation of the parties, when the contract was made; all engagements existing between citizens of different states, citizens and foreigners, states and foreigners; and states and citizens of other states were made the parties contemplating the remedies then

existing on the laws of the states—and the new remedy proposed to be given in the federal courts, can be founded on no
principle whatever.

LETTER IV.

OCTOBER 12th, 1787.

DEAR SIR, It will not be possible to establish in the federal
courts the jury trial of the vicinage so well as in the state
courts.

Third. There appears to me to be not only a premature
deposit of some important powers in the general government—but many of those deposited there are undefined, and
may be used to good or bad purposes as honest or designing
men shall prevail. By Art. 1, Sect. 2, representatives and direct
taxes shall be apportioned among the several states, &c.—
same art. sect. 8, the Congress shall have powers to lay and
collect taxes, duties, &c. for the common defence and general
welfare, but all duties, imposts and excises, shall be uniform
throughout the United States: By the first recited clause, direct taxes shall be apportioned on the states. This seems to
favour the idea suggested by some sensible men and writers,
that Congress, as to direct taxes, will only have power to
make requisitions; but the latter clause, power to lay and collect taxes, &c. seems clearly to favour the contrary opinion,
and, to my mind, the true one, that Congress shall have
power to tax immediately individuals, without the intervention of the state legislatures; in fact the first clause appears to
me only to provide that each state shall pay a certain portion
of the tax, and the latter to provide that Congress shall have
power to lay and collect taxes, that is to assess upon, and to
collect of the individuals in the state, the states quota; but
these still I consider as undefined powers, because judicious
men understand them differently.

It is doubtful whether the vice president is to have any
qualifications; none are mentioned; but he may serve as president, and it may be inferred, he ought to be qualified therefore as the president; but the qualifications of the president
are required only of the person to be elected president. By art.
the 2, sect. 2. "But the Congress may by law vest the appoint-

ment of such inferior officers as they think proper in the president alone, in the courts of law, or in the heads of the departments:" Who are inferior officers? May not a Congress disposed to vest the appointment of all officers in the president, under this clause, vest the appointment of almost every officer in the president alone, and destroy the check mentioned in the first part of the clause, and lodged in the senate. It is true, this check is badly lodged, but then some check upon the first magistrate in appointing officers, ought, it appears by the opinion of the convention, and by the general opinion, to be established in the constitution. By art. 3, sect. 2, the supreme court shall have appellate jurisdiction as to law and facts with such exceptions, &c. to what extent it is intended the exceptions shall be carried—Congress may carry them so far as to annihilate substantially the appellate jurisdiction, and the clause be rendered of very little importance.

4th. There are certain rights which we have always held sacred in the United States, and recognized in all our constitutions, and which, by the adoption of the new constitution, its present form will be left unsecured. By article 6, the proposed constitution, and the laws of the United States, which shall be made in pursuance thereof; and all treaties made, or which shall be made under the authority of the United States, shall be the supreme law of the land; and the judges in every state shall be bound thereby; any thing in the constitution or laws of any state to the contrary notwithstanding.

It is to be observed that when the people shall adopt the proposed constitution it will be their last and supreme act; it will be adopted not by the people of New-Hampshire, Massachusetts, &c. but by the people of the United States; and whenever this constitution, or any part of it, shall be incompatible with the antient customs, rights, the laws or the constitutions heretofore established in the United States, it will entirely abolish them and do them away: And not only this, but the laws of the United States which shall be made in pursuance of the federal constitution will be also supreme laws, and whenever they shall be incompatible with those customs, rights, laws or constitutions heretofore established, they will also entirely abolish them and do them away.

By the article before recited, treaties also made under the

authority of the United States, shall be the supreme law: It is not said that these treaties shall be made in pursuance of the constitution—nor are there any constitutional bounds set to those who shall make them: The president and two thirds of the senate will be empowered to make treaties indefinitely, and when these treaties shall be made, they will also abolish all laws and state constitutions incompatible with them. This power in the president and senate is absolute, and the judges will be bound to allow full force to whatever rule, article or thing the president and senate shall establish by treaty, whether it be practicable to set any bounds to those who make treaties, I am not able to say: If not, it proves that this power ought to be more safely lodged.

The federal constitution, the laws of congress made in pursuance of the constitution, and all treaties must have full force and effect in all parts of the United States; and all other laws, rights and constitutions which stand in their way must yield: It is proper the national laws should be supreme, and superior to state or district laws; but then the national laws ought to yield to unalienable or fundamental rights—and national laws, made by a few men, should extend only to a few national objects. This will not be the case with the laws of congress: To have any proper idea of their extent, we must carefully examine the legislative, executive and judicial powers proposed to be lodged in the general government, and consider them in connection with a general clause in art. 1. sect. 8. in these words (after enumerating a number of powers) "To make all laws which shall be necessary and proper for carrying into execution the foregoing powers, and all other powers vested by this constitution in the government of the United States, or in any department or officer thereof."—The powers of this government as has been observed, extend to internal as well as external objects, and to those objects to which all others are subordinate; it is almost impossible to have a just conception of these powers, or of the extent and number of the laws which may be deemed necessary and proper to carry them into effect, till we shall come to exercise those powers and make the laws. In making laws to carry those powers into effect, it will be expected, that a wise and prudent congress will pay respect to the opinions of a free people, and bottom their laws on those principles which have been considered as essential and fundamental in the British, and in our government: But a congress of a different character will not be bound by the constitution to pay respect to those principles.

It is said, that when the people make a constitution, and delegate powers, that all powers not delegated by them to those who govern, is reserved in the people; and that the people, in the present case, have reserved in themselves, and in there state governments, every right and power not expressly given by the federal constitution to those who shall administer the national government. It is said, on the other hand, that the people, when they make a constitution, yield all power not expressly reserved to themselves. The truth is, in either case, it is mere matter of opinion, and men usually take either side of the argument, as will best answer their purposes: But the general presumption being, that men who govern, will, in doubtful cases, construe laws and constitutions most favourably for encreasing their own powers; all wise and prudent people, in forming constitutions, have drawn the line, and carefully described the powers parted with and the powers reserved. By the state constitutions, certain rights have been reserved in the people; or rather, they have been recognized and established in such a manner, that state legislatures are bound to respect them, and to make no laws infringing upon them. The state legislatures are obliged to take notice of the bills of rights of their respective states. The bills of rights, and the state constitutions, are fundamental compacts only between those who govern, and the people of the same state.

In the year 1788 the people of the United States make a federal constitution, which is a fundamental compact between them and their federal rulers; these rulers, in the nature of things, cannot be bound to take notice of any other compact. It would be absurd for them, in making laws, to look over thirteen, fifteen, or twenty state constitutions, to see what rights are established as fundamental, and must not be infringed upon, in making laws in the society. It is true, they would be bound to do it if the people, in their federal compact, should refer to the state constitutions, recognize all parts not inconsistent with the federal constitution, and direct their federal rulers to take notice of them accordingly; but this is not the case, as the plan stands proposed at present; and it is absurd, to suppose so unnatural an idea is intended or implied, I think my opinion is not only founded in reason, but I think it is supported by the report of the convention itself. If there are a number of rights established by the state constitutions, and which will remain sacred, and the general government is bound to take notice of them—it must take notice of one as well as another; and if unnecessary to recognize or establish one by the federal constitution, it would be unnecessary to recognize or establish another by it. If the federal constitution is to be construed so far in connection with the state constitutions, as to leave the trial by jury in civil causes, for instance, secured; on the same principles it would have left the trial by jury in criminal causes, the benefits of the writ of habeas corpus, &c. secured; they all stand on the same footing; they are the common rights of Americans, and have been recognized by the state constitutions: But the convention found it necessary to recognize or re-establish the benefits of that writ, and the jury trial in criminal cases. As to EXPOST FACTO laws, the convention has done the same in one case, and gone further in another. It is a part of the compact between the people of each state and the rulers, that no EXPOST FACTO laws shall be made. But the convention, by Art. 1. Sect. 10. have put a sanction upon this part even of the state compacts. In fact, the 9th and 10th Sections in Art. 1. in the proposed constitution, are no more nor less, than a partial bill of rights; they establish certain principles as part of the compact upon which the federal legislators and officers can never infringe. It is here wisely stipulated, that the federal legislature shall never pass a bill of attainder, or EXPOST FACTO law; that no tax shall be laid on articles exported, &c. The establishing of one right implies the necessity of establishing another and similar one.

On the whole, the position appears to me to be undeniable, that this bill of rights ought to be carried farther, and some other principles established, as a part of this fundamental compact between the people of the United States and their federal rulers.

It is true, we are not disposed to differ much, at present,

about religion; but when we are making a constitution, it is to be hoped, for ages and millions yet unborn, why not establish the free exercise of religion, as a part of the national compact. There are other essential rights, which we have justly understood to be the rights of freemen; as freedom from hasty and unreasonable search warrants, warrants not founded on oath, and not issued with due caution, for searching and seizing men's papers, property, and persons. The trials by jury in civil causes, it is said, varies so much in the several states, that no words could be found for the uniform establishment of it. If so the federal legislation will not be able to establish it by any general laws. I confess I am of opinion it may be established, but not in that beneficial manner in which we may enjoy it, for the reasons beforementioned. When I speak of the jury trial of the vicinage, or the trial of the fact in the neighbourhood,—I do not lay so much stress upon the circumstance of our being tried by our neighbours: in this enlightened country men may be probably impartially tried by those who do not live very near them: but the trial of facts in the neighbourhood is of great importance in other respects. Nothing can be more essential than the cross examining witnesses, and generally before the triers of the facts in question. The common people can establish facts with much more ease with oral than written evidence; when trials of facts are removed to a distance from the homes of the parties and witnesses, oral evidence becomes intolerably expensive, and the parties must depend on written evidence, which to the common people is expensive and almost useless; it must be frequently taken ex-parte, and but very seldom leads to the proper discovery of truth.

The trial by jury is very important in another point of view. It is essential in every free country, that common people should have a part and share of influence, in the judicial as well as in the legislative department. To hold open to them the offices of senators, judges, and officers to fill which an expensive education is required, cannot answer any valuable purposes for them; they are not in a situation to be brought forward and to fill those offices; these, and most other offices of any considerable importance, will be occupied by the few.

The few, the well born, &c. as Mr. Adams calls them, in judicial decisions as well as in legislation, are generally disposed, and very naturally too, to favour those of their own description.

The trial by jury in the judicial department, and the collection of the people by their representatives in the legislature, are those fortunate inventions which have procured for them in this country, their true proportion of influence, and the wisest and most fit means of protecting themselves in the community. Their situation, as jurors and representatives, enables them to acquire information and knowledge in the affairs and government of the society; and to come forward, in turn, as the centinels and guardians of each other. I am very sorry that even a few of our countrymen should consider jurors and representatives in a different point of view, as ignorant, troublesome bodies, which ought not to have any share in the concerns of government.

I confess I do not see in what cases the Congress can, with any pretence of right, make a law to suppress the freedom of the press; though I am not clear, that Congress is restrained from laying any duties whatever on printing and from laying duties particularly heavy on certain pieces printed, and perhaps Congress may require large bonds for the payment of these duties. Should the printer say, the freedom of the press was secured by the constitution of the state in which he lived, Congress might, and perhaps, with great propriety, answer, that the federal constitution is the only compact existing between them and the people; in this compact the people have named no others, and therefore Congress, in exercising the powers assigned them, and in making laws to carry them into execution, are restrained by nothing beside the federal constitution, any more than a state legislature is restrained by a compact between the magistrates and people of a county, city, or town of which the people, in forming the state constitution, have taken no notice.

It is not my object to enumerate rights of inconsiderable importance; but there are others, no doubt, which ought to be established as a fundamental part of the national system.

It is worthy of observation, that all treaties are made by foreign nations with a confederacy of thirteen states—that the western country is attached to thirteen states—thirteen states have jointly and severally engaged to pay the public debts.—Should a new government be formed of nine, ten, eleven, or twelve states, those treaties could not be considered as binding on the foreign nations who made them. However, I believe the probability to be, that if nine states adopt the constitution, the others will.

It may also be worthy our examination, how far the provision for amending this plan, when it shall be adopted, is of any importance. No measures can be taken towards amendments, unless two-thirds of the Congress, or two-thirds of the legislatures of the several states shall agree.—While power is in the hands of the people, or democratic part of the community, more especially as at present, it is easy, according to the general course of human affairs, for the few influential men in the community, to obtain conventions, alterations in government, and to persuade the common people they may change for the better, and to get from them a part of the power: But when power is once transferred from the many to the few, all changes become extremely difficult; the government, in this case, being beneficial to the few, they will be exceedingly artful and adroit in preventing any measures which may lead to a change; and nothing will produce it, but great exertions and severe struggles on the part of the common people. Every man of reflection must see, that the change now proposed, is a transfer of power from the many to the few, and the probability is, the artful and ever active aristocracy, will prevent all peaceable measures for changes, unless when they shall discover some favorable moment to increase their own influence. I am sensible, thousands of men in the United States, are disposed to adopt the proposed constitution, though they perceive it to be essentially defective, under an idea that amendment of it, may be obtained when necessary. This is a pernicious idea, it argues a servility of character totally unfit for the support of free government; it is very repugnant to that perpetual jealousy respecting liberty, so absolutely necessary in all free states, spoken of by Mr. Dickinson.—However, if our countrymen are so soon changed, and the language of 1774, is become odious to them, it will be in vain to use the language of freedom, or to attempt to rouse them to free enquiries: But I shall never believe this is the case with them, whatever present appearances may be, till I shall have very strong evidence indeed of it.

LETTER V.

OCTOBER 13th, 1787.

DEAR SIR, Thus I have examined the federal constitution as far as a few days leisure would permit. It opens to my mind a new scene; instead of seeing powers cautiously lodged in the hands of numerous legislators, and many magistrates, we see all important powers collecting in one centre, where a few men will possess them almost at discretion. And instead of checks in the formation of the government, to secure the rights of the people against the usurpation of those they appoint to govern, we are to understand the equal division of lands among our people, and the strong arm furnished them by nature and situation, are to secure them against those usurpations. If there are advantages in the equal division of our lands, and the strong and manly habits of our people, we ought to establish governments calculated to give duration to them, and not governments which never can work naturally, till that equality of property, and those free and manly habits shall be destroyed; these evidently are not the natural basis of the proposed constitution.—No man of reflection, and skilled in the science of government, can suppose these will move on harmoniously together for ages, or even for fifty years. As to the little circumstances commented upon, by some writers, with applause—as the age of a representative, of the president, &c.—they have, in my mind, no weight in the general tendency of the system.

There are, however, in my opinion, many good things in the proposed system. It is founded on elective principles, and the deposits of powers in several hands, is essentially right.— The guards against those evils we have experienced in some states in legislation are valuable indeed: but the value of every feature in this system is vastly lessened for the want of that one important feature in a free government, a representation of the people. Because we have sometimes abused democracy, I am not among those men who think a democratic branch a nuisance; which branch shall be sufficiently numerous, to admit some of the best informed men of each order in the community into the administration of government.

While the radical defects in the proposed system are not so soon discovered, some temptations to each state, and to many classes of men to adopt it, are very visible. It uses the democratic language of several of the state constitutions, particularly that of Massachusetts; the eastern states will receive advantages so far as the regulation of trade, by a bare majority, is committed to it: Connecticut and New-Jersey will receive their share of a general impost:—The middle states will receive the advantages surrounding the seat of government:—The southern states will receive protection, and have their negroes represented in the legislature, and large back countries will soon have a majority in it.—This system promises a large field of employment to military gentlemen, and gentlemen of the law; and in case the government shall be executed without convulsions, it will afford security to creditors, to the clergy, salary-men and others depending on money payments. So far as the system promises justice and reasonable advantages, in these respects, it ought to be supported by all honest men; but whenever it promises unequal and improper advantages to any particular states, or orders of men, it ought to be opposed.

I have, in the course of these letters observed, that there are many good things in the proposed constitution, and I have endeavoured to point out many important defects in it. I have admitted that we want a federal system—that we have a system presented, which, with several alterations, may be made a tolerable good one—I have admitted there is a well founded uneasiness among creditors and mercantile men. In this situation of things, you ask me what I think ought to be done? My opinion in this case is only the opinion of an individual, and so far only as it corresponds with the opinions of the honest and substantial part of the community, is it entitled to consideration. Though I am fully satisfied that the state conventions ought most seriously to direct their exertions to altering and amending the system proposed before they shall adopt it—yet I have not sufficiently examined the subject, or formed an opinion, how far it will be practicable for those conventions to carry their amendments. As to the idea, that it will be in vain for those conventions to attempt amendments, it cannot be admitted; it is impossible to say whether they can or not until the attempt shall be made: and when it shall be determined, by experience, that the conventions cannot agree in amendments, it will then be an important question before the people of the United States, whether they will adopt or not the system proposed in its present form. This subject of consolidating the states is new; and because forty or fifty men have agreed in a system, to suppose the good sense of this country, an enlightened nation, must adopt it without examination, and though in a state of profound peace, without endeavouring to amend those parts they perceive are defective, dangerous to freedom, and destructive of the valuable principles of republican government—is truly humiliating. It is true there may be danger in delay; but there is danger in adopting the system in its present form; and I see the danger in either case will arise principally from the conduct and views of two very unprincipled parties in the United States—two fires, between which the honest and substantial people have long found themselves situated. One party is composed of little insurgents, men in debt, who want no law, and who want a share of the property of others; these are called levellers, Shayites, &c. The other party is composed of a few, but more dangerous men, with their servile dependents; these avariciously grasp at power and property; you may discover in all the actions of these men, an evident dislike to free and equal governments, and they will go systematically to work to change, essentially, the forms of government in this country; these are called aristocrates, morrisites, &c. &c. Between these two parties is the weight of the community; the men of middling property, men not in debt on the one hand, and men, on the other, content with republican governments, and not aiming at immense fortunes, offices, and power. In 1786, the little insurgents, the levellers, came forth, invaded the rights of others, and attempted to establish governments according to their wills. Their movements evidently gave encouragement to the other party, which, in 1787, has taken the political field, and with its fashionable dependents, and the tongue and the pen, is endeavouring to establish in great haste, a politer kind of government. These two parties, which will probably be opposed or united as it may suit their interests and views, are really insignificant, compared with the solid, free, and independent part of the community. It is not my intention to suggest, that either of these parties, and the real friends of the proposed constitution, are the same men. The fact is, these aristocrats support and hasten the adoption of the proposed constitution, merely because they think it is a stepping stone to their favourite object. I think I am well founded in this idea; I think the general politics of these men support it, as well as the common observation among them, That the proffered plan is the best that can be got at present, it will do for a few years, and lead to something better. The sensible and judicious part of the community will carefully weigh all these circumstances; they will view the late convention as a respectable assembly of men—America probably never will see an assembly of men of a like number, more respectable. But the members of the convention met without knowing the sentiments of one man in ten thousand in these states respecting the new ground taken. Their doings are but the first attempts in the most important scene ever opened. Though each individual in the state conventions will not, probably, be so respectable as each individual in the federal convention, yet as the state conventions will probably consist of fifteen hundred or two thousand men of abilities, and versed in the science of government, collected from all parts of the community and from all orders of men, it must be acknowledged that the weight of respectability will be in them—In them will be collected the solid sense and the real political character of the country. Being revisers of the subject, they will possess peculiar advantages. To say that these conventions ought not to attempt, coolly and deliberately, the revision of the system, or that they cannot amend it, is very foolish or very assuming. If these conventions, after examining the system, adopt it, I shall be perfectly satisfied, and wish to see men make the administration of the government an equal blessings to all orders of men. I believe the great body of our people to be virtuous and friendly to good government, to the protection of liberty and property; and it is the duty of all good men, especially of those who are placed as centinels to guard their rights—it is their duty to examine into the prevailing politics of parties, and to disclose them— while they avoid exciting undue suspicions, to lay facts before the people, which will enable them to form a proper judgment. Men, who wish the people of this country to determine for themselves, and deliberately to fit the government to their situation, must feel some degree of indignation at those attempts to hurry the adoption of a system, and to shut the door against examination. The very attempts create suspicions, that those who make them have secret views, or see some defects in the system, which, in the hurry of affairs, they expect will escape the eye of a free people.

What can be the views of those gentlemen in Pennsylvania, who precipitated decisions on this subject? What can be the views of those gentlemen in Boston, who countenanced the Printers in shutting up the press against a fair and free investigation of this important system in the usual way. The members of the convention have done their duty—why should some of them fly to their states—almost forget a propriety of behaviour, and precipitate measures for the adoption of a system of their own making? I confess candidly, when I consider these circumstances in connection with the unguarded parts of the system I have mentioned, I feel disposed to proceed with very great caution, and to pay more attention than usual to the conduct of particular characters. If the constitution presented be a good one, it will stand the test with a well informed people: all are agreed there shall be state conventions to examine it; and we must believe it will be adopted, unless we suppose it is a bad one, or that those conventions will make false divisions respecting it. I admit improper measures are taken against the adoption of the system as well as for it—all who object to the plan proposed ought to point out the defects objected to, and to propose those amendments with which they can accept it, or to propose some other system of government, that the public mind may be known, and that we may be brought to agree in some system of government, to strengthen and execute the present, or to provide a substitute. I consider the field of enquiry just opened, and that we are to look to the state conventions for ultimate decisions on the subject before us; it is not to be presumed, that they will differ about small amendments, and lose a system when they shall have made it substantially good; but touching the essential amendments, it is to be presumed the several conventions will pursue the most rational measures to agree in and obtain them; and such defects as they shall discover and not remove, they will probably notice, keep them in view as the ground work of future amendments, and in the firm and manly language which every free people ought to use, will suggest to those who may hereafter administer the government, that it is their expectation, that the system will be so organized by legislative acts, and the government so administered, as to render those defects as little injurious as possible.—Our countrymen are entitled to an honest and faithful government; to a government of laws and not of men; and also to one of their chusing—as a citizen of the country, I wish to see these objects secured, and licentious, assuming, and overbearing men restrained; if the constitution or social compact be vague and unguarded, then we depend wholly upon the prudence, wisdom and moderation of those who manage the affairs of government; or on what, probably, is equally uncertain and precarious, the success of the people oppressed by the abuse of government, in receiving it from the hands of those who abuse it, and placing it in the hands of those who will use it well.

In every point of view, therefore, in which I have been able, as yet, to contemplate this subject, I can discern but one rational mode of proceeding relative to it; and that is to examine it with freedom and candour, to have state conventions some months hence, which shall examine coolly every article, clause, and word in the system proposed, and to adopt it with such amendments as they shall think fit. How far the state conventions ought to pursue the mode prescribed by the federal convention of adopting or rejecting the plan in toto, I leave it to them to determine. Our examination of the subject hitherto has been rather of a general nature. The republican characters in the several states, who wish to make this plan more adequate to security of liberty and property, and to the duration of the principles of a free government, will, no doubt, collect their opinions to certain points, and accurately define those alterations and amendments they wish; if it shall be found they essentially disagree in them, the conventions will then be able to determine whether to adopt the plan as it is, or what will be proper to be done.

Under these impressions, and keeping in view the improper and unadvisable lodgment of powers in the general government, organized as it at present is, touching internal taxes, armies and militia, the elections of its own members, causes between citizens of different states, &c. and the want of a more perfect bill of rights, &c.—I drop the subject for the present, and when I shall have leisure to revise and correct my ideas respecting it, and to collect into points the opinions of those who wish to make the system more secure and safe, perhaps I may proceed to point out particularly for your consideration, the amendments which ought to be ingrafted into this system, not only in conformity to my own, but the deliberate opinions of others—you will with me perceive, that the objections to the plan proposed may, by a more leisure examination be set in a stronger point of view, especially the important one, that there is no substantial representation in the people provided for in a government, in which the most essential powers, even as to the internal police of the country, is proposed to be lodged.

I think the honest and substantial part of the community, will wish to see this system altered, permanency and consistency given to the constitution we shall adopt; and therefore they will be anxious to apportion the powers to the features and organization of the government, and to see abuse in the exercise of power more effectually guarded against. It is suggested, that state officers, from interested motives will oppose the constitution itself—I see no reason for this, their places in general will not be effected, but new openings to offices and places of profit must evidently be made by the adoption of the constitution in its present form.

Refutation of the "Federal Farmer": Timothy Pickering to Charles Tillinghast

Philadelphia, December 24, 1787

I acknowledged the receipt of your letter of Novr. 24th & in compliance with your request promised to write particularly my sentiments on the proposed constitution for the United States: but I expected my letter might be abridged, or superseded, by a publication of the debates in the convention of Pennsylvania, in which Mr. Wilson gave a satisfactory explanation of the plan, & convincing reasons for its adoption: this publication, however, I find will be delayed, by reason of the great length of the debates. I will therefore consider the subject as far as my leisure will permit; and as I know you possess great candour, & seek for *truth* above all things, I shall write with pleasure; and, if reasons can be offered which prove that the constitution will not *endanger*, but on the contrary, be the means of *preserving* the liberties of our country, I am sure you will give it your zealous support.—As your fears have been excited principally by the pamphlet you sent me, I will examine the chief parts of it; and if I show that the writer is chargeable with sophistry, with a want of candour, and with designed misrepresentations, you will give him up as one who under pretence of securing the freedom of the people, has very different objects in view; and tho' these may not be very obvious, yet we may be sure they exist: for *honest* intentions will put on no *disguise*.

I may first notice the art of the writer in assuming the title of The *Federal* Farmer & professing his "federal attachments" to prepossess his *federal* readers with an opinion that he *really wishes* to have established a *good federal government* for these states: but, Sir, I think it will appear that he is a *wolfe* in *sheep's* cloathing.—His next attempt is to prejudice his readers against the constitution, by exciting suspicions of the eminent characters by whom it was formed; suggesting that the leading men in the convention were of aristocratic principles & seized the opportunity of laying the foundation of one general *aristocratic* government for the United States; and at the same time affecting deeply to lament the non-attendance of a few members whose presence & influence would have prevented it. Who those non-attending members were, I know not: probably some were *necessarily* absent; others perhaps from too great an indifference about the important interests of their country, and whose absence therefore is not a subject for lamentation: at all events, it must be admitted that the attending members were fully competent to the task of forming a plan of government for the U.S.: and if we examine the characters of those who concurred in its adoption, we shall be satisfied that they aimed at forming a *good* one—the *best* indeed that could be agreed on.

Before I proceed to the plan itself let me remark another artifice of the *federal farmer*, and other opponents of the New Constitution, in raising a cry about *aristocracy*, as being (what it really is) the most oppressive kind of government; and then perpetually suggesting that the General Convention & the advocates of the constitution, designed & wished to introduce & establish that very government. But, my dear sir, be not alarmed with empty sounds. In the proposed constitution there is no foundation for an aristocracy: for its officers (including in that term as well the legislative as the executive branches) do not hold their places by *hereditary right*, nor *for life*, nor *by electing one another*; neither is *any portion* of *wealth* or *property* a necessary qualification. If a man has virtue & abilities, tho' not worth a shilling, he may be the *president* of the United States. *Does this savour of* ARISTOCRACY? On the contrary, does it not manifest the marked regard of the Convention to the equal rights of the people, without suffering mere *wealth* to hold the smallest preeminence over *poverty* attended with *virtue* and *abilities*. It deserves, indeed, particular notice, that while several of the state constitutions prescribe certain degrees of property as indispensable qualifications for offices, this which is proposed for the U.S. throws the door wide open for the entrance of *every* man who enjoys the confidence of his fellow citizens. We should also observe, that titles of nobility, a great stimulus to ambition, & the most odious as well as most dangerous distinction between the members of a community, are pointedly excluded from this system. If great *hereditary estates*, the foundation of *nobility*, are suffered to *continue* or to be *created* by entails it will be the fault, of the individual states, and not of the general government of the union. The laws of most, if not all, of the states admit the distribution of the property of a deceased citizen among all his children; and no *entails* ought to be permitted. And when all existing entails shall be broken, & future ones forbidden, we may make ourselves easy about aristocratic ambition. Great accumulations of wealth will then be rare, of short continuance, and consequently never dangerous.

The *federal farmer* describes three different forms of free government, under [   ] of which he says the United States may exist as a nation. The first is that which is at present established by the articles of confederation. The second is a government which might be grounded on the annihilation of the state governments, & a perfect union or consolidation of all the states under one entire government. The third will consolidate the states for certain national objects, and leave them severally distinct, independent republics as to internal police generally. The last is the form of government he would choose; and 'tis the last which has been chosen and recommended to the people by the general convention. The only difference, then, between them, should arise about the distribution of powers to be vested in the general government, & the governments of the several states. On this point we may expect men will differ: the general convention acknowledged the difficulty of drawing with precision the line between those rights which must be surrendered, & those which may be reserved. Let us now view their plan, & after a dispassionate consideration of it, seriously ask ourselves whether a better distribution of powers could be made? whether any are assigned to the national government which do not embrace national objects? & whether with less power the general government can preserve the union, establish justice, insure domestic tranquility, provide for the common defence & general welfare of the United States, & secure the blessings of liberty to ourselves and our posterity?

I shall not spend your time in descanting on one entire government for the United States, which would abolish all the state governments: for as such a government is not in contemplation, we have nothing to do with it. I will only remark, that as 'tis admitted by all, to be a form of government unsafe for a country so extensive as ours, the federal farmer and other opposers of the constitution, endeavour, by their bold, but unwarrantable assertions, to persuade their readers, not only that it will issue in such an entire government, but that its framers "proposed the partial consolidation with a view to collect all powers, ultimately in the United States into one entire government." This, indeed, is an extraordinary conclusion. The federal farmer admits the necessity of the "partial consolidation as the only plan of government which can secure the freedom & happiness of this people": and yet, when the Convention have proposed a *"partial* consolidation" he says they evidently designed thereby to effect ultimately *an entire* consolidation! (See page 253.)

In respect to the organization of the general government, the federal farmer, as well as other opposers, object to the smallness of the representation of the people in the House of Representatives; and uniformly reason upon the supposition that it will never consist of more than 65 members; which is the number it is to be composed of only until the actual enumeration of the people shall have been made. As soon as that shall be effected, the House of Representatives, reckoning one member for every 30 thousand of the people, will consist probably of at least one hundred members; and in 25 years more, of 200 members; and in half a century, it would consist of 400 members. It is true the Congress will possess a power of limiting the number of representatives, so that they shall never *exceed* one for every 30 thousand & they *may* be less; this power of regulating & limiting the number of representatives is properly vested in Congress; otherwise that House would in a century become a most unweildy body, and as very a mob as the British House of Commons. Such a power of regulating the number of the representatives in the legislature is not a novelty. In Pennsylvania, where the proposed Constitution has been so violently opposed, there is vested in the Legislature a similar power.—The capital error of all these objectors and which reduces all their reasoning to mere sophistry, is their assuming for granted *that our federal rulers will necessarily have interests sepirate from those of the people, and exercise the powers of government not only arbitrarily, but even wantonly.* But, sir, on what do they ground such wild surmises? Why they tell you that Congress will have power to regulate the elections to senators & representatives, and that possessing this power, they will exercise it to deprive the people of the freedom of election. The federal farmer says (page 260) "The general legislature *may* so regulate elections as to secure the choice of any particular description of men—it *may* make the whole state one district—make the capital, or any places in the state, the place or places of election"—& so forth, in the same chimerical strain. But does he,—does any man of common sense, really believe that the Congress will ever be guilty of so wanton an exercise of power? Will the immediate representatives of the people in Congress ever consent to so oppressive a regulation? For whose benefit would they do it? Would not the first attempt certainly exclude themselves? And would not the state legislatures at their next election of senators, as certainly reject every one who should give his assent to such a law? And if the president did not firmly give his qualified negative to it, would he ever again be placed in the chair of government? What other oppressive regulation can they make which will not immediately, or in a short time, affect *them* in common with their fellow citizens? What then have we to fear on this head?—But will no advantage arise from this *controuling* power of Congress? Yes, certainly. I say a *controuling* power, because a candid interpretation of that section in the constitution will show that it is intended and expected that the times, places & modes of electing senators & representatives should be regulated by the state legislatures; but that if any particular *state government* should be refractory, and in the pride of sovereignty, or influenced by any other improper motive, should either make no such regulations, or improper ones, then the Congress will have power to make such regulations as will insure to the *people* their rights of election, and *establish a uniformity in the mode of constituting the members of the Senate & House of Representatives.* If we give a loose to our imaginations, we may suppose that the State governments *may* abuse *their* power, and regulate these elections in such manner as would be highly inconvenient to the *people*, & injurious to the common interests of the States. And if such abuses should be attempted, will not the *people* rejoice that Congress have a *constitutional* power of correcting them?

The next objection is made to the constitution of the Senate, where the smallest state as "Delaware will have as much constitutional influence as the largest in the Union." This objection is made with an ill grace by those who pretend to be advocates for a *federal* in opposition to a *consolidated* government. The *federal farmer* confesses that "the senate is entirely on the federal plan." And tell me sir, without this equality of voice in the *senate* what *constitutional* means have the *small states*, of preserving that portion of independency which by this constitution they will retain. This reservation to each state of equal power in the *senate* is one striking proof that an entire consolidation or union of all the powers of government in the general legislature, was never intended: For in such a union of powers, the representation of each state in the senate should, like that in the House of Representatives be proportioned to the numbers of the people. But whether this equal power of each state in the Senate be proper or not what other provision could be made? The states represented in the General Convention were each sovereign & independent; and if the small states refused to yield that point, what was to be done? Was the union to be dissolved? — Notwithstanding this equality of power in the Senators of each state, have not the larger states made a great acquisition, by obtaining in the other branch of the legislature a representation proportioned to their strength & importance? How much more just will be their representation in the general government, by the proposed constitution, than it is now under the old articles of confederation? — In the choice of the president & Vice President the large states have also a voice proportioned to their numbers: unless in the case of the president no one candidate has a majority of the votes; for then the *federal* principle is again to operate, and the president is to be selected by the votes of the *states*, the representatives of each having one vote.—On this branch of the general government, the federal farmer makes this observation—"I suppose it was impracticable for the three large states, as they were called, to get the senate formed on any other principles: But this only proves, that we cannot form one general government on equal & just principles and that we ought not to lodge in it such extensive powers before we are convinced of the practicability of organizing it on just and equal principles."—Here we see the issue of all the objections of the federal farmer & other opposers of the Constitution: they go to the rejection of every form of an efficient government for the United States; and if these gentlemen could prevail, no such government would obtain, & the union would soon be dissolved: The fatal mischiefs that would result from such a dissolution need not be pointed out. I am happy however to find their opinions have so little influence. Two states have already unanimously adopted the Constitution. The opposition to it in Pennsylvania is evidently the opposition of a *State-Party*. This party is distinguished by the term *Constitutionalists*, which title they assumed as the warm advocates of the ill-arranged constitution of this state. Their opponents called themselves Republicans. And the politics of the state have been constantly vibrating as the one or the other party gained an ascendancy in the government. On the present question however the scene is greatly changed. Many, & those of the most sensible and worthy among the Constitutionalists, have decidedly declared themselves in favour of the proposed constitution, for the United States and the Republicans to a man (I believe) are its determined advocates. If it meets any opposition in the N. England states, it will be chiefly from the Shayites & Paper-Money-men: but their numbers & characters are alike contemptible.

But to return to the federal farmer. He mentions, as an objection, the eligibility of the members of Congress to offices civil and military, but without subjoining that the moment they accept any such offices they lose their seats in Congress. He objects also to the powers of the senate as too extensive, & thinks they will too much controul the president: and he even affects to tremble for the House of Representatives itself, as in danger of being oppressed by this Mighty Senate; (see page 265.) which is truly ridiculous. Can the Senate make war—raise armies, build navies, or *raise a shilling of money* without the House of Representatives? No! Where then is the danger that this House will be oppressed?—*But the Senate have in effect the power of conferring offices.* No such thing: they can only *approve* those whom the president shall *name* to offices; and the president is to be chosen mediately by the *people.* The president will have no dependence on the state *governments,* & therefore will feel no inducements to submit himself to *their* representatives. Even the federal farmer admits "that the election of the president & Vice president seems to be properly secured."

He objects to the powers of the judicial department, saying "in the Judges of the supreme court are lodged the *law,* the equity, and the *fact.*" These powers, he says, in well balanced governments are ever kept distinct. Why, sir, there are no such governments in the world, save the British, and those which have been formed on the British model, that is, the governments of the United States. Except in those governments, a court of equity, distinct from a court of law, is unknown. And among the U.S. two or three only I believe have such distinct courts of equity; in the rest, the courts of law possess also the powers of courts of equity for the most common & useful purposes. "It is (says the federal farmer) very dangerous to vest in the same judge power to decide on the law, and also general powers in equity; for if the law restrain him, he is only to step into his shoes of equity, and give what judgement his reason or opinion may dictate." Sir, this is all stuff. Read a few passages in Blackstone's commentaries and you will be convinced of it. "Equity (says he B. III. Ch. 27.)—is the *soul* & *spirit* of all law. *Positive* (or statute) law is *construed,* and *rational* law is *made,* by it. In *this,* equity is synonymous to Justice; in *that,* to the true sense & sound interpretation of the rule. But the very terms of a court of *equity* and a court of *law,* as contrasted to each other, are apt to confound & mislead us: as if the one judged without equity, & the other was not bound by any law. Whereas every definition or illustration to be met with which now draws a line between the two jurisdictions, by setting law & equity in

opposition to each other, will be found either totally erroneous, or erroneous to a certain degree." "Thus it is said that it
is the business of a court of equity in England to abate the
rigour of the Common Law. But no such power is contended
for." "It is also said, that a court of equity determines according to the spirit of the rule, and not according to the strict-
ness of the letter. But so also does a court of law. Both, for
instance, are equally bound, and equally profess, to interpret
statutes according to the true intent of the Legislature."—
"There is not a single rule of interpreting laws, whether equi-
tably or strictly, that is not equally used by the judges in the
courts both of law & equity."—"Each endeavours to fix and
adopt the true sense of the law in question; neither can enlarge, diminish, or alter that sense in a single tittle." Wherein
then, you will ask, consists the essential difference between
the two courts? Take Blackstone's answer. "It principally consists in the different modes of administering justice in each; *in
the mode of proof, the mode of trial, & the mode of relief.*"—From
him also you will learn, that an act of parliament, was passed
in the reign of Edward I (See Commentaries B III. Ch. 4)
making a provision which, by a little liberality in the Judges of
the courts of law "might have effectually answered all the purposes of a court of equity."—As our ideas of a court of equity
are derived from the English Jurisprudence, so doubtless the
Convention, in declaring that the judicial power shall extend
to all cases in *equity* as well as *law*, under the federal jurisdiction, had principally a reference to the *mode of administering
justice*, in cases of equity, agreeably to the practice of the court
of Chancery in England.

I intended, my dear sir, to have examined all the principal
objections of the federal farmer: but to do it particularly, I
find would oblige me to write a volume: and I see in every
page of his pamphlet so much disinginuity, I confess that I
lose my patience: neither have I time to treat the subject
much farther in detail. Let me observe generally, that the federal farmer, & other writers of the same stamp, upon reciting
the powers of the Congress artfully throw in expressions,
unduly to alarm their readers, with ideas that those powers
will be *arbitrarily* exercised.—Such as "Will & pleasure" at
Discretion—"Absolute power." &c. (In page 266.), he says

"a power to lay & collect taxes *at discretion*, is in itself of very great importance." This is very true; but what then? Does not the legislature of New-York, & of every other state, possess the power of taxing the people at *discretion*? at *will & pleasure*? and in this as well as many other things is not their power *absolute*? But the presumption is, that this *discretion*, *will & pleasure*, & *absolute power*, will be under the direction of *reason*, and this presumption is so well founded, that the people are, in fact, under no apprehensions of oppression from the exercise of such powers.

I mentioned the disingenuity of the federal farmer. In addition to the instances already noticed, take the following. In letter 3d. p. 259 referring to the proposed constitution, he says, "I wish the system adopted, with a *few* alterations; but those in my mind are essential ones." Attend then to his remarks on the system, and you will find he objects to *every* essential part. To the *smallness* of the house of representatives—To the *federal & small* representation of the States in the Senate—And to the *president* as "a new species of executive," and possessing too little power—To the *Judiciary* as vested with sundry powers which ought to be separated & exercised by different courts & bodies of men—And to the Congress, generally, as vested with too many powers. In a word, he objects to the *whole system* in the following passage, page 259. "I am fully convinced that we must organize the national government on *different principles*, and make the parts of it more efficient, and secure in it more effectually the different interests in the community; or else leave in the State governments some powers proposed to be lodged in it—at least till such an organization shall be found practicable." In page 264. he admits "the formation of the Senate & the smallness of the House (of representatives.) to be the result of our situation, & the actual state of things:" such, consequently, as if we have any general government at all, we *must* be contented with; yet immediately after, he endeavours to alarm us with the apprehensions of corruption in those assemblies, because *so few* may constitute a majority in each, and therefore easily "be influenced by bribes, offices & civilities"! —In page 265. he admits that the powers of regulating commerce, imposts, coin &c. *ought clearly* to be vested in Congress: yet in the next page joining the powers respecting coin and commerce with others he *says* they "will probably soon defeat the operations of the state laws & governments"! Thus he, like the other anti-federal writers, is perpetually conceding and retracting. They all know that the *people* of these states *feel* the necessity of an *efficient* federal government; & therefore they *affect* to desire the same thing: but in order to defeat the measure not only object to every material part of the system, but artfully start vain objects of fear & throw in here & there a sentence importing that such an efficient general government consistent with the liberties of the people is in the nature of things *impracticable*.

I will now as concisely as possible take notice of the powers of Congress, and enquire whether any which are improper or dangerous are proposed to be granted to them. But let me previously remark—That the *people* of the United States form *one nation*—that tis evidently their interest and desire to continue *one nation*—altho' for the more easy and advantageous management of the affairs of *particular districts*, the people have formed themselves into 13 separate communities, or states; that the *people* of these distinct states, having certain common & general interests, it is obviously necessary that one common & general government should be erected, to manage those interests for the best good of the whole; that as all power resides originally in the *people*, they have a right to make such a distribution of it as they judge their true interests require. Consequently, they may constitute such officers as they think best, and with such powers as they think proper to confer, for the management of the affairs of their *respective communities*; and at the same time appoint another set of officers with general powers to conduct the common concerns of *all the communities or states united*.

Let us now see whether a single power is proposed to be vested in the *general* government, which does not concern more than *a single* state.

The General Government will have power to *declare war*—to provide for the *common* defence, and *general* welfare of the United States; to *borrow money* on their credit; to raise armies—build navies—and to *make treaties* with foreign nations. Now when powers are given to accomplish any particular thing, it is the dictate of common sense that such other subordinate powers as are indispensably necessary to that end should also be given, either expressly or by fair implication. But without the power of direct taxation how can the general government with certainty provide for the common defence raise armies, build navies, or repay monies which it shall have borrowed? The imposts may be insufficient. Other sources of revenue therefore must be opened. "It will be said—it has been said—the Congress may make requisitions on the several States!"—True, and be denied! "But if any state refuses to furnish its quota let the Congress have the power of *compelling* payment to be made by such delinquent state."— And do you think sir this *compulsive* mode more eligible, than in the first instance to vest Congress with a *Constitutional* power of levying taxes for necessary national purposes? When a person has once refused what he ought to grant, do we not often see that from mere pride & obstinacy he persists in the refusal? States are composed of men, and are influenced by similar passions.—What if the 13 States were quite removed from the sea-coast, and revenues from imposts were consequently out of the question; at the same time their situation & circumstances should, as at present, require an intimate union, for their common good & security? How should the common treasury be supplied? We have had too melancholly proofs that *requisitions* on the 13 "sovereign & independent States" would be fruitless.—The Congress must then in such case have the power of direct taxation. And what would then be necessary for the *entire supplies* to the public treasury, may in our present situation be equally necessary to make good the *deficiencies* of the revenues arising from commerce. I therefore am willing, to submit to such direct taxation, whenever it shall be necessary to support the general government, & maintain the faith of the United States. And I am satisfied that as every such tax will equally affect the persons & estates of all the members of the general legislature, the power of levying it will be exercised with that prudence & propriety which we have a right to expect from wise and honest representatives— for if they are not wise and honest, it will be our own fault in choosing them; when we shall have no right to complain.

On a like principle it is proper that Congress should have

power to provide for organizing, arming, and disciplining the militia, and for calling it forth to execute the laws of the union, suppress insurrections, & repel invasions. As the militia of different states may serve together, the great advantages of uniformity in their organization, arms & discipline must be obvious to every man who is possessed of any degree of military knowledge. But this uniformity can be introduced & maintained only by the power of the general government. It is also equally necessary that Congress should have power to call forth the militia for the purposes expressed in the constitution. In the late war, pressing as was the common danger, we have been witnesses of the delays of states to furnish their contingents, and of their unequal exertions. If this power is vested in Congress, the calls will ever be proportioned, in time as well as extent, to the exigency of the service. Yet this power, useful & necessary as it is, has been objected to as dangerous, & in its nature oppressive; and therefore, it is concluded that it ought to remain with the *state legislatures*. But who are they? The *servants* of the *people*,—chosen by them to superintend the *local* concerns of their *particular states*. And who are the Congress?—Can you give a different answer? Are not *they* also the *servants* of the *people*,—chosen by them to superintend their *general* concerns in the *United States?*— Only bear always in your mind, sir, that the inhabitants of the United States are but *one people, one nation*, and all fears and jealousies about the annihilation of State governments will vanish. Some men pride themselves in their particular state sovereignties; and are extremely jealous that the general government of the United States will swallow them up. Ridiculous!—Do not the *people* constitute the *states*? Are not the *people* the *fountain* of *all power*? & Whether this flow in 13 distinct streams,—or in one larger stream, with thirteen branches, is not the *fountain* still the same? and the *Majesty* of the *People* undiminished?

These objectors make a loud out-cry about *standing armies*; as tho' a large and oppressive one, like the armies of the European nations, must be the necessary consequence of the adoption of this system: but this proceeds either from a want of discernment, or a design to excite a false alarm. We have a standing army at this hour—a small one indeed, & probably not adequate to the security of our frontiers; (tho' Congress have not the means of enlarging it, however necessary it may become:) And whilst we have frontiers to defend, and arsenals to secure, we must continue to have a standing army.—The fallacy lies here. In Europe large standing armies are kept up to maintain the power of their *hereditary monarchs*, who generally are *absolute*. In these cases the standing armies are instruments to keep the people in slavery. But remember that in the United States a standing army cannot be raised or kept up without the *consent* of the *people*, by their representatives in Congress—representatives whose powers will have very limited durations, and who cannot lay a single burthen on the people of which they and their children will not bear their proportion. The English (& no people have been more jealous of their liberty) have never gone farther than to declare that a standing army ought not to be kept up *without the consent of parliament*. It is very possible indeed that this consent may sometimes be improperly obtained, through the undue and corrupt influence of an *hereditary monarch*: But as we have not nor in the ordinary course of our affairs have reason to expect any such creature in the United States, we may make ourselves easy on this head.—On this subject I will add one remark—That vesting *Congress* with power to call out the militia, as the exigencies of the union may require, instead of being complained of as a grievance, demands the warmest approbation of those who are in dread of a standing army; for that efficient command of the militia will forever render it unnecessary to raise a permanent body of troops, excepting only the necessary guards requisite for the frontiers & arsenals.

There is but one other objection which I have time to notice. That respects the judicial powers. The federal farmer, and other objectors, say the causes between a state & citizens of another state—between citizens of different states—and between a state, or the citizens thereof, and the citizens or subjects of foreign states, should be left, as they now are, to the decision of the particular state courts. The other cases enumerated in the constitution, seem to be admitted as properly cognizable in the *federal* courts. With respect to all the former, it may be said generally, that as the local laws of the several states may differ from each other—as particular states may pass laws unjust in their nature, or partially unjust as they regard foreigners and the citizens of other states, it seems to be a wise provision, which puts it in the power of such foreigners & citizens to resort to a court where they may reasonably expect to obtain *impartial* justice. But as the courts of particular states will in these cases have a concurrent jurisdiction, so whilst they proceed with reasonable dispatch, & support their characters by upright decisions, they will probably be almost exclusively resorted to: But there is a particular & very cogent reason for securing to *foreigners* a trial, either in the first instance, or by appeal, in a *federal* court. With respect to *foreigners*, all the states form but *one nation*. This *nation* is responsible for the conduct of all its members towards foreign nations, their citizens & subjects; and therefore ought to possess the power of doing justice to the latter. Without this power, a single state, or one of its citizens, might embroil the whole union in a foreign war. The trial by jury in civil cases, I grant, is not explicitly secured by the constitution: but we have been told the reason of the omission; and to me it is satisfactory. In many of the civil causes subject to the jurisdiction of the federal courts, trial by jury would evidently be improper; in others, it was found impracticable in the convention to fix on the mode of constituting juries. But we may assure ourselves that the first Congress will make provision for introducing it in every case in which it shall be proper & practicable. Recollect that the Congress of 1775 directed jury trials in the cases of captures at sea: and that the inconveniences soon discovered in that mode of trial, obliged them to recommend an alteration, & to commit all admiralty causes to the decision of the judge alone. So if the Convention had positively fixed a trial by jury in all the civil cases in which it is contended that it ought to have been established,—it might have been found as highly inconvenient in practice as the case above stated; but being fixed by the *constitution*, the inconvenience must be endured (whatever mischief might arise from it) until the Constitution itself should be altered.

I have passed over unnoticed the other powers proposed to be vested in the Congress, because it seems to be generally admitted that they can properly be lodged no where else.

I now hope sir that I have presented you with such a view of the federal constitution, as will make it appear to you not that engine of tyranny which its enemies would fain persuade us it will prove. On the contrary, I hope you will be convinced that 'tis the best constitution we at present have any right to expect; & therefore that we ought readily to adopt it. Future experience may suggest improvements which may be engrafted into it. To satisfy you of *my* hearty approbation of it, I seriously assure you, that if I were now on my dying bed, & my sons were of mature age, my last words to them would be adopt this constitution.

P.S. If this letter serves in measure to remove your doubts & fears, perhaps it may produce the like effect on the minds of some other *candid* enquirers; and therefore you may use it as you think proper—but only as from a *friend*, without suffering *my name* to appear, as it is of too little consequence to add weight to my sentiment, except with an *intimate friend*.

"IS IT BEST FOR THE STATES TO UNITE, OR NOT TO UNITE?"

George Washington to Bushrod Washington

Mount Vernon, November 10, 1787.

Dear Bushrod: In due course of Post, your letters of the 19th. and 26th. Ult. came to hand and I thank you for the communications therein; for a continuation in matters of importance, I shall be obliged to you. That the Assembly would afford the People an opportunity of deciding on the proposed Constitution I had scarcely a doubt, the only question with me was, whether it would go forth under favourable auspices, or receive the stamp of disapprobation. The opponents I expected, (for it ever has been that the adversaries to a measure are more active than its Friends) would endeavor to stamp it with unfavourable impressions, in order to bias the Judgment that is ultimately to decide on it, this is evidently the case with the writers in opposition, whose objections are better calculated to alarm the fears, than to convince the Judgment, of their readers. They build their objections upon principles that do not exist, which the Constitution does not support them in, and the existence of which has been, by an appeal to the Constitution itself flatly denied; and then, as if they were unanswerable, draw all the dreadful consequences that are necessary to alarm the apprehensions of the ignorant or unthinking. It is not the interest of the major part of those characters to be convinced; nor will their local views yield to arguments, which do not accord with their present, or future prospects.

A Candid solution of a single question to which the plainest understanding is competent does, in my opinion, decide the dispute: namely is it best for the States to unite, or not to unite? If there are men who prefer the latter, then unquestionably the Constitution which is offered must, in their estimation, be wrong from the words, we the People to the signature inclusively; but those who think differently and yet object to parts of it, would do well to consider that it does not lye with any *one* State, or the *minority* of the States to superstruct a Constitution for the whole. The separate interests, as far as it is practicable, must be consolidated; and local views must be attended to, as far as the nature of the case will admit. Hence it is that every State has some objection to the present form and these objections are directed to different points, that which is most pleasing to one is obnoxious to another, and so vice versa. If then the Union of the whole is a desirable object, the componant parts must yield a little in order to accomplish it. Without the latter, the former is unattainable, for again I repeat it, that not a single State nor the minority of the States can force a Constitution on the Majority; but admitting the power it will surely be granted that it cannot be done without involving scenes of civil commotion of a very serious nature let the opponents of the proposed Constitution in this State be asked, and it is a question they certainly ought to have asked themselves, what line of conduct they would advise it to adopt, if nine other States, of which I think there is little doubt, should accede to the Constitution? would they recommend that it should stand single? Will they connect it with Rhode Island? or even with two others checkerwise and remain with them as outcasts from the Society, to shift for themselves? or will they return to their dependence on Great Britain? or lastly, have the mortification to come in when they will be allowed no credit for doing so?

The warmest friends and the best supporters the Constitution has, do not contend that it is free from imperfections; but they found them unavoidable and are sensible, if evil is likely to arise there from, the remedy must come hereafter; for in the present moment, it is not to be obtained; and, as there is a Constitutional door open for it, I think the People (for it is with them to Judge) can as they will have the advantage of experience on their Side, decide with as much propriety on the alterations and amendments which are necessary as ourselves. I do not think we are more inspired, have more wisdom, or possess more virtue, than those who will come after us.

The power under the Constitution will always be in the People. It is entrusted for certain defined purposes, and for a certain limited period, to representatives of their own chusing; and whenever it is executed contrary to their Interest, or not agreeable to their wishes, their Servants can, and undoubtedly will be, recalled. It is agreed on all hands that no government can be well administered without powers; yet the instant these are delegated, altho' those who are entrusted with the administration are no more than the creatures of the people, act as it were but for a day, and are amenable for every false step they take, they are, from the moment they receive it, set down as tyrants; their natures, one would conceive from this, immediately changed, and that they could have no other disposition but to oppress. Of these things, in a government constituted and guarded as *ours* is, I have no idea; and do firmly believe that whilst many *ostensible* reasons are assigned to prevent the adoption of it, the real ones are concealed behind the Curtain, because they are not of a nature to appear in open day. I believe further, supposing them pure, that as great evils result from too great Jealousy as from the want of it. We need look I think no further for proof of this, than to the Constitution, of some if not all of these States. No man is a warmer advocate for proper restraints and wholesome checks in every department of government than I am; but I have never yet been able to discover the propriety of placing it absolutely out of the power of men to render essential Services, because a possibility remains of their doing ill.

If Mr. Ronald can place the Finances of this Country upon so respectable a footing as he has intimated, he will deserve much of its thanks. In the attempt, my best wishes, I have nothing more to offer, will accompany him. I hope there remains virtue enough in the Assembly of this State to preserve inviolate public treaties and private Contracts; if these are infringed, farewell to respectability and safety in the Government.

I have possessed a doubt, but if any had existed in my breast, reiterated proofs would have convinced me of the impolicy of *all* commutable Taxes. If we cannot learn wisdom from experience, it is hard to say where it is to be found. But why talk of learning it; these things are *mere* Jobs by which few are enriched at the public expense; for whether premeditation, or ignorance, is the cause of this destructive scheme, it ends in oppression.

You have I find broke the Ice; the only advice I will offer to you on the occasion (if you have a mind to command the attention of the House) is to speak seldom, but to important Subjects, except such as particularly relate to your Constituents, and, in the former case make yourself *perfectly* master of the Subject. Never exceed a *decent* warmth, and submit your sentiments with diffidence. A dictatorial Stile, though it may carry conviction, is always accompanied with disgust. I am, &c.

"THE TREE OF LIBERTY MUST BE
REFRESHED FROM TIME TO TIME WITH
THE BLOOD OF PATRIOTS AND TYRANTS"

Thomas Jefferson to William Stephens Smith

Paris, November 13, 1787

DEAR SIR

I am now to acknolege the receipt of your favors of October the 4th. 8th. and 26th. In the last you apologize for your letters of introduction to Americans coming here. It is so far from needing apology on your part, that it calls for thanks on mine. I endeavor to shew civilities to all the Americans who come here, and who will give me opportunities of doing it: and it is a matter of comfort to know from a good quarter what they are, and how far I may go in my attentions to them.—Can you send me Woodmason's bills for the two copying presses for the M. de la fayette, and the M. de Chastellux? The latter makes one article in a considerable account, of old standing, and which I cannot present for want of this article.—I do not know whether it is to yourself or Mr. Adams I am to give my thanks for the copy of the new constitution. I beg leave through you to place them where due. It will be yet three weeks before I shall receive them from America. There are very good articles in it: and very bad. I do not know which preponderate. What we have lately read in the history of Holland, in the chapter on the Stadtholder, would have sufficed to set me against a Chief magistrate eligible for a long duration, if I had ever been disposed towards one: and what we have always read of the elections of Polish kings should have forever excluded the idea of one continuable for life. Wonderful is the effect of impudent and persevering lying. The British ministry have so long hired their gazetteers to repeat and model into every form lies about our being in anarchy, that the world has at length believed them, the English nation has believed them, the ministers themselves have come to believe them, and what is more

309

wonderful, we have believed them ourselves. Yet where does this anarchy exist? Where did it ever exist, except in the single instance of Massachusets? And can history produce an instance of a rebellion so honourably conducted? I say nothing of it's motives. They were founded in ignorance, not wickedness. God forbid we should ever be 20. years without such a rebellion. The people can not be all, and always, well informed. The part which is wrong will be discontented in proportion to the importance of the facts they misconceive. If they remain quiet under such misconceptions it is a lethargy, the forerunner of death to the public liberty. We have had 13. states independent 11. years. There has been one rebellion. That comes to one rebellion in a century and a half for each state. What country before ever existed a century and half without a rebellion? And what country can preserve it's liberties if their rulers are not warned from time to time that their people preserve the spirit of resistance? Let them take arms. The remedy is to set them right as to facts, pardon and pacify them. What signify a few lives lost in a century or two? The tree of liberty must be refreshed from time to time with the blood of patriots and tyrants. It is it's natural manure. Our Convention has been too much impressed by the insurrection of Massachusetts: and in the spur of the moment they are setting up a kite to keep the hen yard in order. I hope in god this article will be rectified before the new constitution is accepted.—You ask me if any thing transpires here on the subject of S. America? Not a word. I know that there are combustible materials there, and that they wait the torch only. But this country probably will join the extinguishers.— The want of facts worth communicating to you has occasioned me to give a little loose to dissertation. We must be contented to amuse, when we cannot inform. Present my respects to Mrs. Smith, and be assured of the sincere esteem of Dear Sir Your friend & servant,

TH: JEFFERSON

"MEN ARE AMBITIOUS, VINDICTIVE AND RAPACIOUS"

"Publius," The Federalist VI
[Alexander Hamilton]

Independent Journal (New York), November 14, 1787

To the People of the State of New-York.

The three last numbers of this Paper have been dedicated to an enumeration of the dangers to which we should be exposed, in a state of disunion, from the arms and arts of foreign nations. I shall now proceed to delineate dangers of a different, and, perhaps, still more alarming kind, those which will in all probability flow from dissentions between the States themselves, and from domestic factions and convulsions. These have been already in some instances slightly anticipated; but they deserve a more particular and more full investigation.

A man must be far gone in Utopian speculations who can seriously doubt, that if these States should either be wholly disunited, or only united in partial confederacies, the subdivisions into which they might be thrown would have frequent and violent contests with each other. To presume a want of motives for such contests, as an argument against their existence, would be to forget that men are ambitious, vindictive and rapacious. To look for a continuation of harmony between a number of independent unconnected sovereignties, situated in the same neighbourhood, would be to disregard the uniform course of human events, and to set at defiance the accumulated experience of ages.

The causes of hostility among nations are innumerable. There are some which have a general and almost constant operation upon the collective bodies of society: Of this description are the love of power or the desire of preeminence and dominion—the jealousy of power, or the desire of equality and safety. There are others which have a more circumscribed, though an equally operative influence, within their spheres:

Such are the rivalships and competitions of commerce between commercial nations. And there are others, not less numerous than either of the former, which take their origin intirely in private passions; in the attachments, enmities, interests, hopes and fears of leading individuals in the communities of which they are members. Men of this class, whether the favourites of a king or of a people, have in too many instances abused the confidence they possessed; and assuming the pretext of some public motive, have not scrupled to sacrifice the national tranquility to personal advantage, or personal gratification.

The celebrated Pericles, in compliance with the resentments of a prostitute,* at the expence of much of the blood and treasure of his countrymen, attacked, vanquished and destroyed, the city of the *Samnians*. The same man, stimulated by private pique against the *Megarensians*,† another nation of Greece, or to avoid a prosecution with which he was threatened as an accomplice in a supposed theft of the statuary *Phidias*,‡ or to get rid of the accusations prepared to be brought against him for dissipating the funds of the State in the purchase of popularity,§ or from a combination of all these causes, was the primitive author of that famous and fatal war, distinguished in the Grecian annals by the name of the *Pelopponesian* war; which, after various vicissitudes, intermissions and renewals, terminated in the ruin of the Athenian commonwealth.

The ambitious Cardinal who was Prime Minister to Henry VIIIth. permitting his vanity to aspire to the Tripple-Crown,‖ entertained hopes of succeeding in the acquisition of that splendid prize by the influence of the Emperor Charles Vth. To secure the favour and interest of this enterprising and powerful Monarch, he precipitated England into a war with France, contrary to the plainest dictates of Policy, and at the

---

*ASPASIA, vide PLUTARCH's life of Pericles.

†—— —— Idem.

‡—— —— Idem. Phidias was supposed to have stolen some public gold with the connivance of Pericles for the embellishment of the statue of Minerva.

§—— —— Idem.

‖ Worn by the Popes.

hazard of the safety and independence, as well of the Kingdom over which he presided by his councils, as of Europe in
general—For if there ever was a Sovereign who bid fair to
realise the project of universal monarchy it was the Emperor
Charles Vth. of whose intrigues Wolsey was at once the instrument and the dupe.

The influence which the bigottry of one female,* the pet-
ulancies of another,† and the cabals of a third,‡ had in the cotemporary policy, ferments and pacifications of a considerable
part of Europe are topics that have been too often descanted
upon not to be generally known.

To multiply examples of the agency of personal considerations in the production of great national events, either foreign or domestic, according to their direction would be an
unnecessary waste of time. Those who have but a superficial
acquaintance with the sources from which they are to be
drawn will themselves recollect a variety of instances; and
those who have a tolerable knowledge of human nature will
not stand in need of such lights, to form their opinion either
of the reality or extent of that agency. Perhaps however a reference, tending to illustrate the general principle, may with
propriety be made to a case which has lately happened among
ourselves. If SHAYS had not been a *desperate debtor* it is much
to be doubted whether Massachusetts would have been
plunged into a civil war.

But notwithstanding the concurring testimony of experience, in this particular, there are still to be found visionary, or
designing men, who stand ready to advocate the paradox of
perpetual peace between the States, though dismembered and
alienated from each other. The genius of republics (say they)
is pacific; the spirit of commerce has a tendency to soften the
manners of men and to extinguish those inflammable humours which have so often kindled into wars. Commercial
republics, like ours, will never be disposed to waste themselves in ruinous contentions with each other. They will be
governed by mutual interest, and will cultivate a spirit of mutual amity and concord.

*Madame De Maintenon.
†Dutchess of Marlborough.
‡Madame De Pompadoure.

Is it not (we may ask these projectors in politics) the true interest of all nations to cultivate the same benevolent and philosophic spirit? If this be their true interest, have they in fact pursued it? Has it not, on the contrary, invariably been found, that momentary passions and immediate interests have a more active and imperious controul over human conduct than general or remote considerations of policy, utility or justice? Have republics in practice been less addicted to war than monarchies? Are not the former administered by *men* as well as the latter? Are there not aversions, predilections, rivalships and desires of unjust acquisitions that affect nations as well as kings? Are not popular assemblies frequently subject to the impulses of rage, resentment, jealousy, avarice, and of other irregular and violent propensities? Is it not well known that their determinations are often governed by a few individuals, in whom they place confidence, and are of course liable to be tinctured by the passions and views of those individuals? Has commerce hitherto done any thing more than change the objects of war? Is not the love of wealth as domineering and enterprising a passion as that of power or glory? Have there not been as many wars founded upon commercial motives, since that has become the prevailing system of nations, as were before occasioned by the cupidity of territory or dominion? Has not the spirit of commerce in many instances administered new incentives to the appetite both for the one and for the other?—Let experience the least fallible guide of human opinions be appealed to for an answer to these inquiries.

Sparta, Athens, Rome and Carthage were all Republics; two of them, Athens and Carthage, of the commercial kind. Yet were they as often engaged in wars, offensive and defensive, as the neighbouring Monarchies of the same times. Sparta was little better than a well regulated camp; and Rome was never sated of carnage and conquest.

Carthage, though a commercial Republic, was the aggressor in the very war that ended in her destruction. Hannibal had carried her arms into the heart of Italy and to the gates of Rome, before Scipio, in turn, gave him an overthrow in the territories of Carthage and made a conquest of the Commonwealth.

Venice in latter times figured more than once in wars of

ambition; 'till becoming an object of terror to the other Italian States, Pope Julius the Second found means to accomplish that formidable league,* which gave a deadly blow to the power and pride of this haughty Republic.

The Provinces of Holland, 'till they were overwhelmed in debts and taxes, took a leading and conspicuous part in the wars of Europe. They had furious contests with England for the dominion of the sea; and were among the most persevering and most implacable of the opponents of Lewis XIV.

In the government of Britain the representatives of the people compose one branch of the national legislature. Commerce has been for ages the predominant pursuit of that country. Few nations, nevertheless have been more frequently engaged in war; and the wars, in which that kingdom has been engaged, have in numerous instances proceeded from the people.

There have been, if I may so express it, almost as many popular as royal wars. The cries of the nation and the importunities of their representatives have, upon various occasions, dragged their monarchs into war, or continued them in it contrary to their inclinations, and, sometimes, contrary to the real interests of the State. In that memorable struggle for superiority, between the rival Houses of *Austria* and *Bourbon* which so long kept Europe in a flame, it is well known that the antipathies of the English against the French, seconding the ambition, or rather the avarice of a favourite leader,† protracted the war beyond the limits marked out by sound policy and for a considerable time in opposition to the views of the Court.

The wars of these two last mentioned nations have in a great measure grown out of commercial considerations—The desire of supplanting and the fear of being supplanted either in particular branches of traffic or in the general advantages of trade and navigation.

From this summary of what has taken place in other countries, whose situations have borne the nearest resemblance to our own, what reason can we have to confide in those

*THE LEAGUE OF CAMBRAY, comprehending the Emperor, the King of France, the King of Arragon, and most of the Italian Princes and States.

†The Duke of Marlborough.

reveries, which would seduce us into an expectation of peace and cordiality between the members of the present confederacy, in a state of separation? Have we not already seen enough of the fallacy and extravagance of those idle theories which have amused us with promises of an exemption from the imperfections, weaknesses and evils incident to society in every shape? Is it not time to awake from the deceitful dream of a golden age, and to adopt as a practical maxim for the direction of our political conduct, that we, as well as the other inhabitants of the globe, are yet remote from the happy empire of perfect wisdom and perfect virtue?

Let the point of extreme depression to which our national dignity and credit have sunk—let the inconveniences felt every where from a lax and ill administration of government—let the revolt of a part of the State of North-Carolina—the late menacing disturbances in Pennsylvania and the actual insurrections and rebellions in Massachusetts declare——!

So far is the general sense of mankind from corresponding with the tenets of those, who endeavour to lull asleep our apprehensions of discord and hostility between the States, in the event of disunion, that it has from long observation of the progress of society become a sort of axiom in politics, that vicinity, or nearness of situation, constitutes nations natural enemies. An intelligent writer expresses himself on this subject to this effect—"NEIGHBOURING NATIONS (says he) are naturally ENEMIES of each other, unless their common weakness forces them to league in a CONFEDERATE REPUBLIC, and their constitution prevents the differences that neighbourhood occasions, extinguishing that secret jealousy, which disposes all States to aggrandise themselves at the expence of their neighbours."* This passage, at the same time points out the EVIL and suggests the REMEDY.

*Vide Principes des Negotiations par L'Abbe de Mably.

"Brutus" III

New York Journal, November 15, 1787

To the CITIZENS *of the* STATE *of* NEW-YORK.

In the investigation of the constitution, under your consideration, great care should be taken, that you do not form your opinions respecting it, from unimportant provisions, or fallacious appearances.

On a careful examination, you will find, that many of its parts, of little moment, are well formed; in these it has a specious resemblance of a free government—but this is not sufficient to justify the adoption of it—the gilded pill, is often found to contain the most deadly poison.

You are not however to expect, a perfect form of government, any more than to meet with perfection in man; your views therefore, ought to be directed to the main pillars upon which a free government is to rest; if these are well placed, on a foundation that will support the superstructure, you should be satisfied, although the building may want a number of ornaments, which, if your particular tastes were gratified, you would have added to it: on the other hand, if the foundation is insecurely laid, and the main supports are wanting, or not properly fixed, however the fabric may be decorated and adorned, you ought to reject it.

Under these impressions, it has been my object to turn your attention to the principal defects in this system.

I have attempted to shew, that a consolidation of this extensive continent, under one government, for internal, as well as external purposes, which is evidently the tendency of this constitution, cannot succeed, without a sacrifice of your liberties; and therefore that the attempt is not only preposterous, but extremely dangerous; and I have shewn, independent of this, that the plan is radically defective in a fundamental prin-

ciple, which ought to be found in every free government; to
wit, a declaration of rights.

I shall now proceed to take a nearer view of this system, to
examine its parts more minutely, and shew that the powers
are not properly deposited, for the security of public liberty.

The first important object that presents itself in the organization of this government, is the legislature. This is to be
composed of two branches; the first to be called the general
assembly, and is to be chosen by the people of the respective
states, in proportion to the number of their inhabitants, and
is to consist of sixty five members, with powers in the legislature to encrease the number, not to exceed one for every
thirty thousand inhabitants. The second branch is to be called
the senate, and is to consist of twenty-six members, two of
which are to be chosen by the legislatures of each of the
states.

In the former of these there is an appearance of justice, in
the appointment of its members—but if the clause, which
provides for this branch, be stripped of its ambiguity, it will
be found that there is really no equality of representation,
even in this house.

The words are "representatives and direct taxes, shall be apportioned among the several states, which may be included in
this union, according to their respective numbers, which shall
be determined by adding to the whole number of free persons, including those bound to service for a term of years, and
excluding Indians not taxed, three fifths of all other persons."—What a strange and unnecessary accumulation of
words are here used to conceal from the public eye, what
might have been expressed in the following concise manner.
Representatives are to be proportioned among the states respectively, according to the number of freemen and slaves inhabiting them, counting five slaves for three free men.

"In a free state," says the celebrated Montesquieu, "every
man, who is supposed to be a free agent, ought to be concerned in his own government, therefore the legislature
should reside in the whole body of the people, or their representatives." But it has never been alledged that those who are
not free agents, can, upon any rational principle, have any
thing to do in government, either by themselves or others. If

they have no share in government, why is the number of
members in the assembly, to be increased on their account? Is
it because in some of the states, a considerable part of the
property of the inhabitants consists in a number of their fellow men, who are held in bondage, in defiance of every idea
of benevolence, justice, and religion, and contrary to all the
principles of liberty, which have been publickly avowed in the
late glorious revolution? If this be a just ground for representation, the horses in some of the states, and the oxen in others, ought to be represented—for a great share of property in
some of them, consists in these animals; and they have as
much controul over their own actions, as these poor unhappy
creatures, who are intended to be described in the above recited clause, by the words, "all other persons." By this mode
of apportionment, the representatives of the different parts of
the union, will be extremely unequal; in some of the southern
states, the slaves are nearly equal in number to the free men;
and for all these slaves, they will be entitled to a proportionate share in the legislature—this will give them an unreasonable weight in the government, which can derive no additional strength, protection, nor defence from the slaves, but
the contrary. Why then should they be represented? What
adds to the evil is, that these states are to be permitted to
continue the inhuman traffic of importing slaves, until the
year 1808—and for every cargo of these unhappy people,
which unfeeling, unprincipled, barbarous, and avaricious
wretches, may tear from their country, friends and tender
connections, and bring into those states, they are to be rewarded by having an increase of members in the general
assembly. There appears at the first view a manifest inconsistency, in the apportionment of representatives in the senate,
upon the plan of a consolidated government. On every principle of equity, and propriety, representation in a government
should be in exact proportion to the numbers, or the aids
afforded by the persons represented. How unreasonable, and
unjust then is it, that Delaware should have a representation
in the senate, equal to Massachusetts, or Virginia? The latter
of which contains ten times her numbers, and is to contribute
to the aid of the general government in that proportion? This
article of the constitution will appear the more objectionable,

if it is considered, that the powers vested in this branch of the legislature are very extensive, and greatly surpass those lodged in the assembly, not only for general purposes, but, in many instances, for the internal police of the states. The other branch of the legislature, in which, if in either, a feint spark of democracy is to be found, should have been properly organized and established—but upon examination you will find, that this branch does not possess the qualities of a just representation, and that there is no kind of security, imperfect as it is, for its remaining in the hands of the people.

It has been observed, that the happiness of society is the end of government—that every free government is founded in compact; and that, because it is impracticable for the whole community to assemble, or when assembled, to deliberate with wisdom, and decide with dispatch, the mode of legislating by representation was devised.

The very term, representative, implies, that the person or body chosen for this purpose, should resemble those who appoint them—a representation of the people of America, if it be a true one, must be like the people. It ought to be so constituted, that a person, who is a stranger to the country, might be able to form a just idea of their character, by knowing that of their representatives. They are the sign—the people are the thing signified. It is absurd to speak of one thing being the representative of another, upon any other principle. The ground and reason of representation, in a free government, implies the same thing. Society instituted government to promote the happiness of the whole, and this is the great end always in view in the delegation of powers. It must then have been intended, that those who are placed instead of the people, should possess their sentiments and feelings, and be governed by their interests, or, in other words, should bear the strongest resemblance of those in whose room they are substituted. It is obvious, that for an assembly to be a true likeness of the people of any country, they must be considerably numerous.—One man, or a few men, cannot possibly represent the feelings, opinions, and characters of a great multitude. In this respect, the new constitution is radically defective.—The house of assembly, which is intended as a representation of the people of America, will not, nor cannot, in the nature of things, be a proper one—sixty-five men cannot be found in the United States, who hold the sentiments, possess the feelings, or are acquainted with the wants and interests of this vast country. This extensive continent is made up of a number of different classes of people; and to have a proper representation of them, each class ought to have an opportunity of choosing their best informed men for the purpose; but this cannot possibly be the case in so small a number. The state of New-York, on the present apportionment, will send six members to the assembly: I will venture to affirm, that number cannot be found in the state, who will bear a just resemblance to the several classes of people who compose it. In this assembly, the farmer, merchant, mecanick, and other various orders of people, ought to be represented according to their respective weight and numbers; and the representatives ought to be intimately acquainted with the wants, understand the interests of the several orders in the society, and feel a proper sense and becoming zeal to promote their prosperity. I cannot conceive that any six men in this state can be found properly qualified in these respects to discharge such important duties: but supposing it possible to find them, is there the least degree of probability that the choice of the people will fall upon such men? According to the common course of human affairs, the natural aristocracy of the country will be elected. Wealth always creates influence, and this is generally much increased by large family connections: this class in society will for ever have a great number of dependents; besides, they will always favour each other—it is their interest to combine—they will therefore constantly unite their efforts to procure men of their own rank to be elected—they will concenter all their force in every part of the state into one point, and by acting together, will most generally carry their election. It is probable, that but few of the merchants, and those the most opulent and ambitious, will have a representation from their body—few of them are characters sufficiently conspicuous to attract the notice of the electors of the state in so limited a representation. The great body of the yeoman of the country cannot expect any of their order in this assembly—the station will be too elevated for them to aspire to—the distance between the people and their representatives, will be so very great, that there is no probability that a farmer, however respectable, will be chosen—the mechanicks of every branch, must expect to be excluded from a seat in this Body—It will and must be esteemed a station too high and exalted to be filled by any but the first men in the state, in point of fortune; so that in reality there will be no part of the people represented, but the rich, even in that branch of the legislature, which is called the democratic.—The well born, and highest orders in life, as they term themselves, will be ignorant of the sentiments of the midling class of citizens, strangers to their ability, wants, and difficulties, and void of sympathy, and fellow feeling. This branch of the legislature will not only be an imperfect representation, but there will be no security in so small a body, against bribery, and corruption—It will consist at first, of sixty-five, and can never exceed one for every thirty thousand inhabitants; a majority of these, that is, thirty-three, are a quorum, and a majority of which, or seventeen, may pass any law—a majority of the senate, or fourteen, are a quorum, and eight of them pass any law—so that twenty-five men, will have the power to give away all the property of the citizens of these states—what security therefore can there be for the people, where their liberties and property are at the disposal of so few men? It will literally be a government in the hands of the few to oppress and plunder the many. You may conclude with a great degree of certainty, that it, like all others of a similar nature, will be managed by influence and corruption, and that the period is not far distant, when this will be the case, if it should be adopted; for even now there are some among us, whose characters stand high in the public estimation, and who have had a principal agency in framing this constitution, who do not scruple to say, that this is the only practicable mode of governing a people, who think with that degree of freedom which the Americans do—this government will have in their gift a vast number of offices of great honor and emolument. The members of the legislature are not excluded from appointments; and twenty-five of them, as the case may be, being secured, any measure may be carried.

The rulers of this country must be composed of very different materials from those of any other, of which history gives us any account, if the majority of the legislature are not, before many years, entirely at the devotion of the executive—and these states will soon be under the absolute domination of one, or a few, with the fallacious appearance of being governed by men of their own election.

The more I reflect on this subject, the more firmly am I persuaded, that the representation is merely nominal—a mere burlesque; and that no security is provided against corruption and undue influence. No free people on earth, who have elected persons to legislate for them, ever reposed that confidence in so small a number. The British house of commons consists of five hundred and fifty-eight members; the number of inhabitants in Great-Britain, is computed at eight millions—this gives one member for a little more than fourteen thousand, which exceeds double the proportion this country can ever have: and yet we require a larger representation in proportion to our numbers, than Great-Britain, because this country is much more extensive, and differs more in its productions, interests, manners, and habits. The democratic branch of the legislatures of the several states in the union consists, I believe at present, of near two thousand; and this number was not thought too large for the security of liberty by the framers of our state constitutions: some of the states may have erred in this respect, but the difference between two thousand, and sixty-five, is so very great, that it will bear no comparison.

Other objections offer themselves against this part of the constitution—I shall reserve them for a future paper, when I shall shew, defective as this representation is, no security is provided, that even this shadow of the right, will remain with the people.

Resolution of the Inhabitants of Pittsburgh

Pittsburgh Gazette, November 17, 1787

FRIDAY, November 9, 1787.
At a meeting of the inhabitants of Pittsburgh, at the house of Messrs. Tannehills, for the special purpose of taking the sense of this town with respect to the system of confederate government, proposed by the late convention at Philadelphia.
General JOHN GIBSON in the Chair.

It was considered that having had an opportunity of hearing on both sides the strictures which have been made upon this system of government, in conversation, in the Gazettes, and in other writings, on mature deliberation, we are of opinion, that it is the result of much political wisdom, good sense and candour in those who framed it; that we have no reason to expect any thing better from any other body of men assembled in convention; that from the necessity of *mutual concession* with the different states, it is not probable that any thing more equal could be formed; that our prosperity depends on our speedy adoption of some mode of government more efficient than that which we now possess; that of all people it becomes us of the western country more especially to desire an object of this kind, as from the weakness of Congress to take proper measures with the courts of Spain and Britain, we are on the one hand deprived of the advantages of the Mississippi trade, which is our natural right, and on the other, are liable to the incursions of the savages, the posts on the lakes not being yet delivered up according to treaty.

Resolved therefore unanimously. That it is our ardent wish and hope that this system of government may be speedily adopted.

Signed by order of the meeting,
JOHN GIBSON, Chairman.

"Philanthrop" to the Public

American Mercury (Hartford), November 19, 1787

To the PUBLIC.

The new proposed Constitution, being a system of great magnitude, and general discussion, as well as of universal concern, every individual has an undoubted right to offer his sentiments upon a subject so interesting to the community at large, tho' sorry indeed I am to discover occasion for further incentives to stimulate the people, to adopt with heart, and hand, a system so salutary, and so conducive to publick welfare, and more than sorry, am I that my abilities are not equal to the task of portraying the base designs, and wicked machinations of some of its opposers. None but those destitute of honour, & devoid of every spark of sensibility, could have the audacity to propagate groundless innuendos, with a view to impose on the generous credulity of weak minds, and thereby if possible produce anarchy and confusion in the state. Much pains is daily taken by artful misanthropists to evince that the adoption of the new constitution will deprive the people of all liberty, alledging that the grand legislature, or Congress, will then have power to oppress the people at pleasure; an idea so absurd, could never originate in the breast of an honest man, not destitute of reason. Is there a single clause in the constitution that deprives the people of any liberty which people in any part of the world do, or ought to possess? are not the people at large forever to remain the sole governours (under God) of the land we live in? are not the Congress and Senate servants of the people, chosen and instructed by them, because the whole body of the people cannot assemble at one place, to make and execute laws? and are not the Congress and Senate in regular rotation to return, and descend to the private station from whence they were elected by the people, and then, and there enjoy the blessings resulting from their good administration, with acclamations from their constituents, and a heart felt satisfaction which to a susceptible mind must be more ample reward than the possession of all the wealth in Peru? Or must they not upon the other hand, experience and participate all the evils attendant injudicious or iniquitous laws, and receive the execrations of thousands, and be deem'd to everlasting oblivion in the rank of mankind, never more to enjoy the confidence of the people, which must inevitably produce that horror and compunction of mind, only to be described by comparing their situation to the state of the damned? For my own part I am convinced that while Congress are appointed under the restrictions as limited in the new Constitution, were they as absolute as the Dey of Algiers, no fatal consequences could ever attend the community at large. Will any man of common sense suppose that the grand legislature of thirteen United States, can be less interested in the welfare happiness and prosperity of the country, than any other set of men whatever? Will their salaries for two or even for six years, (which seldom amounts to more than their expences) compensate for loss of character, and the ruin which they and their posterity must participate with the bulk of mankind, should their negociations produce ruinous consequences to their constituents? Every man of candour must believe that a Congress and Senate chosen conformably to the mode pointed out in the new Constitution, will exert every faculty, and strain every nerve to work out the salvation of their country, because it will be their interest so to do.

Let us for a moment call to view the most specious reason that can be urged by the advocates for anarchy and confusion, and the opposers to this glorious Constitution, and see what weight a rational man could give them: and let us in the first instance allow that all mankind are actuated by interested motives. The most plausible reason then that can be adduced for violation of faith, and prostitution of sentiments, is private interest; but surely real true self interest considered on a large extensive scale, is public good. Can the members of Congress, their friends, and posterity, thrive and flourish, in a country overwhelmed with misfortunes, and subjected thro' their management to some direful approaching catastrophe? They certainly cannot! their grandour, their peace and happiness, is

as much connected with, and as inseperable from the grandour, peace and happiness of the community at large, as that
of a husband and his beloved wife. The conjugal state might
with as much propriety be forbidden, and celibacy injoined
least the head of the family should commit acts of violence on
his offspring, and be incapable of governing his houshold, as
that the present Constitution should be rejected, least the
people selected to preside at the helm of affairs, should commit some flagrant act of injustice and thereby disgrace human
nature.

There is in my opinion no particular body, or description
of men, in north America, so deeply interested in the establishment of the new Constitution, as the Farmer. They of all
men will imediately experience the advantage resulting therefrom. Their taxes instead of being increased, will be lessoned,
and their produce will instantaneously (or very soon) rise in
value; as a field will then be opened for a more extensive
trade, than ever can take place while there is no stability in
government; the Merchant will then court the Farmer, and
the Farmer be encouraged to cultivate his lands.

That money must be raised, and that government must be
supported no men of common sense will deny. Should this
Constitution be adopted, the duties on imports, which is a
voluntary tax, will render needless, or at least lesson the direct
taxation of landed property; whereas at present, while we
have, as it were, no government, or at least no energy in government, duties of impost and excise are laid in the different
states, which serve only as a subterfuge for the (I cannot call
them Merchants) Pedler and Trader, to impose on the honest
farmer: because the Trader at present makes use of the Authority of (what is called) Government, to inhance the value
of his goods, by adding to the costs and charges, the whole
duty stipulated by our assemblys, whereas it is well known,
that the most sanctified among the Traders do not pay more
than one tenth of the duties they charge; so that while the
honest unwary people, are daily paying taxes, which in strict
justice should tend to lessen their foreign and domestic debt,
they are only enriching the Trader, who pockets the whole.

One proposition suggested, and artfully propagated by the
enemies of our country, and which is daily gaining ground,

among the weaker brethren, requires notice, and which I could wish to see discanted by some abler pen, as it really has, and if not refuted may have more weight in defeating the completion of this glorious Constitution, than any other consideration whatever: viz. It is alledged that the Southern States being entitled to send a larger number of delegates than the northern, they will have it in their power to carry measures into execution that may be peculiarly injurious to the Northern States; as though what would tend, under the proposed constitution, to the aggrandizement of the former, must inevitably involve the latter in ruin. This proposition is so big with absurdity, that I have not patience, nor even leisure at present to point out its falacy; but hope it may not be considered as chimerical; and that the worthy Landholder which appeared in the last American Mercury, will not suffer his talents to sleep upon this occasion.

In ardent expectation of seeing the new constitution speedily established, I remain on all occasions

PHILANTHROP.

"A Landholder" [Oliver Ellsworth] III

Connecticut Courant (Hartford), November 19, 1787

To the Holders and Tillers of Land.

GENTLEMEN, When we rushed to arms for preventing British usurpation, liberty was the argument of every tongue.

This word would open all the resources of the country and draw out a brigade of militia rapidly as the most decisive orders of a despotic government. Liberty is a word which, according as it is used, comprehends the most good and the most evil of any in the world. Justly understood it is sacred next to those which we appropriate in divine adoration; but in the mouths of some it means any thing, which will enervate a necessary government, excite a jealousy of the rulers who are our own choice, and keep society in confusion for want of a power sufficiently concentered to promote its good. It is not strange that the licentious should tell us a government of energy is inconsistent with liberty, for being inconsistent with their wishes and their vices, they would have us think it contrary to human happiness. In the state this country was left by the war, with want of experience in sovereignty, and the feelings which the people then had; nothing but the scene we had passed thro' could give a general conviction that an internal government of strength is the only means of repressing external violence, and preserving the national rights of the people against the injustice of their own brethren. Even the common duties of humanity will gradually go out of use, when the constitution and laws of a country, do not insure justice from the public and between individuals. American experience, in our present deranged state, hath again proved these great truths, which have been verified in every age since men were made and became sufficiently numerous to form into public bodies. A government capable of controling the whole, and bringing its force to a point is one of the prerequisites for national liberty. We combine in society, with an expectation, to have our persons and properties defended against unreasonable exactions either at home or abroad. If the public are unable to protect us against the unjust impositions of foreigners, in this case we do not enjoy our natural rights, and a weakness in government is the cause. If we mean to have our natural rights and properties protected, we must first create a power which is able to do it, and in our case there is no want of resources, but only of a civil constitution which may draw them out and point their force.

The present question is shall we have such a constitution or not? We allow it to be a creation of power; but power when necessary for our good is as much to be desired as the food we eat or the air we breathe. Some men are mightily afraid of giving power lest it should be improved for oppression; this is doubtless possible, but where is the probability. The same objection may be made against the constitution of every state in the union, and against every possible mode of government; because a power of doing good always implies a power to do evil if the person or party be disposed.

The right of the legislature to ordain laws binding on the people, gives them a power to make bad laws.

The right of the judge to inflict punishments, gives him both power and opportunity to oppress the innocent; yet none but crazy men will from thence determine that it is best to have neither a legislature nor judges.

If a power to promote the best interest of the people, necessarily implies a power to do evil, we must never expect such a constitution in theory as will not be open in some respects to the objections of carping and jealous men. The new Constitution is perhaps more cautiously guarded than any other in the world, and at the same time creates a power which will be able to protect the subject; yet doubtless objections may be raised, and so they may against the constitution of each state in the union. In Connecticut the laws are the constitution by which the people are governed, and it is generally allowed to be the most free and popular in the thirteen states. As this is the state in which I live and write, I will instance several things which with a proper colouring and a spice of jealousy appear most dangerous to the natural rights of the people, yet they never have been dangerous in practice, and are absolutely necessary at some times to prevent much greater evil.

The right of taxation or of assessing and collecting money out of the people, is one of those powers which may prove dangerous in the exercise, and which by the new constitution is vested solely in representatives chosen for that purpose. But by the laws of Connecticut, this power called so dangerous may be exercised by the selectmen of each town, and this not only without their consent but against their express will, where they have considered the matter, and judge it improper. This power they may exercise when and so often as they judge necessary! Three justices of the quorum, may tax a whole country in such sums as they think meet, against the express will of all the inhabitants. Here we see the dangerous power of taxation vested in the justices of the quorum and even in Select men, men whom we should suppose as likely to err and tyrannize as the representatives of three millions of people, in solemn deliberation, and amenable to the vengeance of their constituents, for every act of injustice. The same town officers have equal authority where personal liberty is concerned, in a matter more sacred than all the property in the world, the disposal of your children. When they judge fit, with the advice of one justice of the peace, they may tear them from the parents embrace, and place them under the absolute control of such masters as they please; and if the parents reluctance excites their resentment, they may place him and his property under overseers. Fifty other instances fearfull as these might be collected from the laws of the state, but I will not repeat them least my readers should be alarmed where there is no danger. These regulations are doubtless best, we have seen much good and no evil come from them. I adduced these instances to shew, that the most free constitution when made the subject of criticism may be exhibited in frightful colours, and such attempts we must expect against that now proposed. If my countrymen, you wait for a constitution which absolutely bars a power of doing evil, you must wait long, and when obtained it will have no power of doing good. I allow you are oppressed, but not from the quarter that jealous and wrong-headed men would insinuate. You are oppressed by the men, who to serve their own purposes would prefer the shadow of government to the reality. You are oppressed for want of a power which can protect commerce, encourage business, and create a ready demand for the productions of your farms. You are become poor, oppression continued will make wise men mad. The landholders and farmers have long borne this oppression, we have been patient and groaned in secret, but can promise for ourselves no longer; unless relieved madness, may excite us to actions we now dread.

"Publius," The Federalist VIII
[Alexander Hamilton]

New-York Packet, November 20, 1787

To the People of the State of New-York.

Assuming it therefore as an established truth that the several States, in case of disunion, or such combinations of them as might happen to be formed out of the wreck of the general confederacy, would be subject to those vicissitudes of peace and war, of friendship and enmity with each other, which have fallen to the lot of all neighbouring nations not united under one government, let us enter into a concise detail of some of the consequences, that would attend such a situation.

War between the States, in the first periods of their separate existence, would be accompanied with much greater distresses than it commonly is in those countries, where regular military establishments have long obtained. The disciplined armies always kept on foot on the continent of Europe, though they bear a malignant aspect to liberty and œconomy, have notwithstanding been productive of this signal advantage, of rendering sudden conquests impracticable, and of preventing that rapid desolation, which used to mark the progress of war, prior to their introduction. The art of fortification has contributed to the same ends. The nations of Europe are incircled with chains of fortified places, which mutually obstruct invasion. Campaigns are wasted in reducing two or three frontier garrisons, to gain admittance into an enemy's country. Similar impediments occur at every step, to exhaust the strength and delay the progress of an invader. Formerly an invading army would penetrate into the heart of a neighbouring country, almost as soon as intelligence of its approach could be received; but now a comparatively small force of disciplined troops, acting on the defensive with the aid of posts, is able to impede and finally to frustrate the enterprises of one much more considerable. The history of war, in that quarter of the globe, is no longer a history of nations subdued and empires overturned, but of towns taken and retaken, of battles that decide nothing, of retreats more beneficial than victories, of much effort and little acquisition.

In this country the scene would be altogether reversed. The jealousy of military establishments, would postpone them as long as possible. The want of fortifications leaving the frontiers of one State open to another, would facilitate inroads. The populous States would with little difficulty overrun their less populous neighbours. Conquests would be as easy to be made, as difficult to be retained. War therefore would be desultory and predatory. PLUNDER and devastation ever march in the train of irregulars. The calamities of individuals would make the principal figure in the events, which would characterise our military exploits.

This picture is not too highly wrought, though I confess, it would not long remain a just one. Safety from external danger is the most powerful director of national conduct. Even the ardent love of liberty will, after a time, give way to its dictates. The violent destruction of life and property incident to war—the continual effort and alarm attendant on a state of continual danger, will compel nations the most attached to liberty, to resort for repose and security, to institutions, which have a tendency to destroy their civil and political rights. To be more safe they, at length, become willing to run the risk of being less free.

The institutions alluded to are STANDING ARMIES, and the correspondent appendages of military establishments. Standing armies it is said are not provided against in the new constitution; and it is therefore inferred, that they may exist under it.* Their existence however from the very terms of the proposition, is, at most, problematical & uncertain. But standing armies, it may be replied, must inevitably result from a dissolution of the confederacy. Frequent war and constant

---

*This objection will be fully examined in its proper place, and it will be shown that the only natural precaution which could have been taken on this subject has been taken; and a much better one than is to be found in any constitution that has been heretofore framed in America, most of which contain no guard at all on this subject.

apprehension, which requires a state of as constant preparation, will infallibly produce them. The weaker States or confederacies, would first have recourse to them, to put themselves upon an equality with their more potent neighbours. They would endeavour to supply the inferiority of population and resources, by a more regular and effective system of defence, by disciplined troops and by fortifications. They would, at the same time, be necessitated to strengthen the executive arm of government; in doing which, their constitutions would acquire a progressive direction towards monarchy. It is of the nature of war to increase the executive at the expence of the legislative authority.

The expedients which have been mentioned, would soon give the States or confederacies that made use of them, a superiority over their neighbours. Small States, or States of less natural strength, under vigorous governments, and with the assistance of disciplined armies, have often triumphed over larger States, or States of greater natural strength, which have been destitute of these advantages. Neither the pride, nor the safety of the more important States, or confederacies, would permit them long to submit to this mortifying and adventitious inferiority. They would quickly resort to means similar to those by which it had been effected, to reinstate themselves in their lost pre-eminence. Thus we should in a little time see established in every part of this country, the same engines of despotism, which have been the scourge of the old world. This at least would be the natural course of things, and our reasonings will be the more likely to be just, in proportion as they are accommodated to this standard.

These are not vague inferrences drawn from supposed or speculative defects in a constitution, the whole power of which is lodged in the hands of the people, or their representatives and delegates, but they are solid conclutions drawn from the natural and necessary progress of human affairs.

It may perhaps be asked, by way of objection to this, why did not standing armies spring up out of the contentions which so often distracted the ancient republics of Greece? Different answers equally satisfactory may be given to this question. The industrious habits of the people of the present day, absorbed in the pursuits of gain, and devoted to the improvements of agriculture and commerce are incompatible with the condition of a nation of soldiers, which was the true condition of the people of those republics. The means of revenue, which have been so greatly multiplied by the encrease of gold and silver, and of the arts of industry, and the science of finance, which is the offspring of modern times, concurring with the habits of nations, have produced an intire revolution in the system of war, and have rendered disciplined armies, distinct from the body of the citizens, the inseparable companion of frequent hostility.

There is a wide difference also, between military establishments in a country, seldom exposed by its situation to internal invasions, and in one which is often subject to them, and always apprehensive of them. The rulers of the former can have no good pretext, if they are even so inclined, to keep on foot armies so numerous as must of necessity be maintained in the latter. These armies being, in the first case, rarely, if at all, called into activity for interior defence, the people are in no danger of being broken to military subordination. The laws are not accustomed to relaxations, in favor of military exigencies—the civil state remains in full vigor, neither corrupted nor confounded with the principles or propensities of the other state. The smallness of the army renders the natural strength of the community an overmatch for it; and the citizens, not habituated to look up to the military power for perfection, or to submit to its oppressions, neither love nor fear the soldiery: They view them with a spirit of jealous acquiescence in a necessary evil, and stand ready to resist a power which they suppose may be exerted to the prejudice of their rights. The army under such circumstances, may usefully aid the magistrate to suppress a small faction, or an occasional mob, or insurrection; but it will be unable to enforce encroachments against the united efforts of the great body of the people.

In a country, in the predicament last described, the contrary of all this happens. The perpetual menacings of danger oblige the government to be always prepared to repel it—its armies must be numerous enough for instant defence. The continual necessity for their services enhances the importance of the soldier, and proportionably degrades the condition of the citizen. The military state becomes elevated above the civil. The inhabitants of territories, often the theatre of war, are unavoidably subjected to frequent infringement on their rights, which serve to weaken their sense of those rights; and by degrees, the people are brought to consider the soldiery not only as their protectors, but as their superiors. The transition from this disposition to that of considering them as masters, is neither remote, nor difficult: But it is very difficult to prevail upon a people under such impressions, to make a bold, or effectual resistance, to usurpations, supported by the military power.

The kingdom of Great Britain falls within the first description. An insular situation, and a powerful marine, guarding it in a great measure against the possibility of foreign invasion, supercede the necessity of a numerous army within the kingdom. A sufficient force to make head against a sudden descent, till the militia could have time to rally and embody, is all that has been deemed requisite. No motive of national policy have demanded, nor would public opinion have tolerated a larger number of troops upon its domestic establishment. There has been, for a long time past, little room for the operation of the other causes, which have been enumerated as the consequences of internal war. This peculiar felicity of situation has, in a great degree, contributed to preserve the liberty, which that country to this day enjoys, in spite of the prevalent venality and corruption. If, on the contrary, Britain had been situated on the continent, and had been compelled, as she would have been, by that situation, to make her military establishments at home co-extensive with those of the other great powers of Europe, she, like them, would in all probability, be at this day a victim to the absolute power of a single man. 'Tis possible, though not easy, that the people of that island may be enslaved from other causes, but it cannot be by the powers of an army so inconsiderable as that which has been usually kept up in that kingdom.

If we are wise enough to preserve the Union, we may for ages enjoy an advantage similar to that of an insulated situation. Europe is at a great distance from us—Her colonies in our vicinity, will be likely to continue too much disproportioned in strength, to be able to give us any dangerous annoyance. Extensive military establishments cannot, in this position, be necessary to our security. But if we should be disunited, and the integral parts should either remain separated, or which is most probable, should be thrown together into two or three confederacies, we should be in a short course of time, in the predicament of the continental powers of Europe—our liberties would be a prey to the means of defending ourselves against the ambition and jealousy of each other.

This is an idea not superficial or futile, but solid and weighty. It deserves the most serious and mature consideration of every prudent and honest man of whatever party. If such men will make a firm and solemn pause, and meditate dispassionately on the importance of this interesting idea, if they will contemplate it, in all its attitudes, and trace it to all its consequences, they will not hesitate to part with trivial objections to a constitution, the rejection of which would in all probability put a final period to the Union. The airy phantoms that flit before the distempered imaginations of some of its adversaries, would quickly give place to the more substantial forms of dangers real, certain, and formidable.

A CONFEDERATE REPUBLIC: THE INTERNAL
ADVANTAGES OF A REPUBLICAN WITH THE
EXTERNAL FORCE OF A MONARCHICAL
GOVERNMENT

"Publius," The Federalist IX
[Alexander Hamilton]

Independent Journal (New York), November 21, 1787

To the People of the State of New-York.

A Firm Union will be of the utmost moment to the peace
and liberty of the States as a barrier against domestic faction
and insurrection. It is impossible to read the history of the
petty Republics of Greece and Italy, without feeling sensations of horror and disgust at the distractions with which they
were continually agitated, and at the rapid succession of revolutions, by which they were kept in a state of perpetual vibra-
tion, between the extremes of tyranny and anarchy. If they
exhibit occasional calms, these only serve as short-lived con-
trasts to the furious storms that are to succeed. If now and
then intervals of felicity open themselves to view, we behold
them with a mixture of regret arising from the reflection that
the pleasing scenes before us are soon to be overwhelmed by
the tempestuous waves of sedition and party-rage. If momentary rays of glory break forth from the gloom, while they
dazzle us with a transient and fleeting brilliancy, they at the
same time admonish us to lament that the vices of government should pervert the direction and tarnish the lustre of
those bright talents and exalted indowments, for which the
favoured soils, that produced them, have been so justly
celebrated.

From the disorders that disfigure the annals of those republics, the advocates of despotism have drawn arguments, not
only against the forms of republican government, but against
the very principles of civil liberty. They have decried all free
government, as inconsistent with the order of society, and
have indulged themselves in malicious exultation over its

friends and partizans. Happily for mankind, stupendous fabrics reared on the basis of liberty, which have flourished for ages, have in a few glorious instances refuted their gloomy sophisms. And, I trust, America will be the broad and solid foundation of other edifices not less magnificent, which will be equally permanent monuments of their errors.

But it is not to be denied that the portraits, they have sketched of republican government, were too just copies of the originals from which they were taken. If it had been found impracticable, to have devised models of a more perfect structure, the enlightened friends to liberty would have been obliged to abandon the cause of that species of government as indefensible. The science of politics, however, like most other sciences has received great improvement. The efficacy of various principles is now well understood, which were either not known at all, or imperfectly known to the ancients. The regular distribution of power into distinct departments—the introduction of legislative ballances and checks—the institution of courts composed of judges, holding their offices during good behaviour—the representation of the people in the legislature by deputies of their own election—these are either wholly new discoveries or have made their principal progress towards perfection in modern times. They are means, and powerful means, by which the excellencies of republican government may be retained and its imperfections lessened or avoided. To this catalogue of circumstances, that tend to the amelioration of popular systems of civil government, I shall venture, however novel it may appear to some, to add one more on a principle, which has been made the foundation of an objection to the New Constitution, I mean the ENLARGEMENT of the ORBIT within which such systems are to revolve either in respect to the dimensions of a single State, or to the consolidation of several smaller States into one great confederacy. The latter is that which immediately concerns the object under consideration. It will however be of use to examine the principle in its application to a single State which shall be attended to in another place.

The utility of a confederacy, as well to suppress faction and to guard the internal tranquillity of States, as to increase their external force and security, is in reality not a new idea. It has been practiced upon in different countries and ages, and has received the sanction of the most applauded writers, on the subjects of politics. The opponents of the PLAN proposed have with great assiduity cited and circulated the observations of Montesquieu on the necessity of a contracted territory for a republican government. But they seem not to have been apprised of the sentiments of that great man expressed in another part of his work, nor to have adverted to the consequences of the principle to which they subscribe, with such ready acquiescence.

When Montesquieu recommends a small extent for republics, the standards he had in view were of dimensions, far short of the limits of almost every one of these States. Neither Virginia, Massachusetts, Pennsylvania, New-York, North-Carolina, nor Georgia, can by any means be compared with the models, from which he reasoned and to which the terms of his description apply. If we therefore take his ideas on this point, as the criterion of truth, we shall be driven to the alternative, either of taking refuge at once in the arms of monarchy, or of splitting ourselves into an infinity of little jealous, clashing, tumultuous commonwealths, the wretched nurseries of unceasing discord and the miserable objects of universal pity or contempt. Some of the writers, who have come forward on the other side of the question, seem to have been aware of the dilemma; and have even been bold enough to hint at the division of the larger States, as a desirable thing. Such an infatuated policy, such a desperate expedient, might, by the multiplication of petty offices, answer the views of men, who possess not qualifications to extend their influence beyond the narrow circles of personal intrigue, but it could never promote the greatness or happiness of the people of America.

Referring the examination of the principle itself to another place, as has been already mentioned, it will be sufficient to remark here, that in the sense of the author who had been most emphatically quoted upon the occasion, it would only dictate a reduction of the SIZE of the more considerable MEMBERS of the Union; but would not militate against their being all comprehended in one Confederate Government. And this is the true question, in the discussion of which we are at present interested.

So far are the suggestions of Montesquieu from standing in opposition to a general Union of the States, that he explicitly treats of a CONFEDERATE REPUBLIC as the expedient for extending the sphere of popular government and reconciling the advantages of monarchy with those of republicanism.

"It is very probable (says he*) that mankind would have been obliged, at length, to live constantly under the government of a SINGLE PERSON, had they not contrived a kind of constitution, that has all the internal advantages of a republican, together with the external force of a monarchical government. I mean a CONFEDERATE REPUBLIC."

"This form of Government is a Convention, by which several smaller *States* agree to become members of a larger *one*, which they intend to form. It is a kind of assemblage of societies, that constitute a new one, capable of encreasing by means of new associations, till they arrive to such a degree of power as to be able to provide for the security of the united body."

"A republic of this kind, able to withstand an external force, may support itself without any internal corruption. The form of this society prevents all manner of inconveniencies."

"If a single member should attempt to usurp the supreme authority, he could not be supposed to have an equal authority and credit, in all the confederate states. Were he to have too great influence over one, this would alarm the rest. Were he to subdue a part, that which would still remain free might oppose him with forces, independent of those which he had usurped, and overpower him before he could be settled in his usurpation."

"Should a popular insurrection happen, in one of the confederate States, the others are able to quell it. Should abuses creep into one part, they are reformed by those that remain sound. The State may be destroyed on one side, and not on the other; the confederacy may be dissolved, and the confederates preserve their sovereignty."

*Spirit of Laws, Vol. I. Book IX. Chap. I.

"As this government is composed of small republics it enjoys the internal happiness of each, and with respect to its external situation it is possessed, by means of the association of all the advantages of large monarchies."

I have thought it proper to quote at length these interesting passages, because they contain a luminous abrigement of the principal arguments in favour of the Union, and must effectually remove the false impressions, which a misapplication of other parts of the work was calculated to make. They have at the same time an intimate connection with the more immediate design of this Paper; which is to illustrate the tendency of the Union to repress domestic faction and insurrection.

A distinction, more subtle than accurate has been raised between a *confederacy* and a *consolidation* of the States. The essential characteristic of the first is said to be, the restriction of its authority to the members in their collective capacities, without reaching to the individuals of whom they are composed. It is contended that the national council ought to have no concern with any object of internal administration. An exact equality of suffrage between the members has also been insisted upon as a leading feature of a Confederate Government. These positions are in the main arbitrary; they are supported neither by principle nor precedent. It has indeed happened that governments of this kind have generally operated in the manner, which the distinction, taken notice of, supposes to be inherent in their nature—but there have been in most of them extensive exceptions to the practice, which serve to prove as far as example will go, that there is no absolute rule on the subject. And it will be clearly shewn, in the course of this investigation, that as far as the principle contended for has prevailed, it has been the cause of incurable disorder and imbecility in the government.

The definition of a *Confederate Republic* seems simply to be, an "assemblage of societies" or an association of two or more States into one State. The extent, modifications and objects of the Fœderal authority are mere matters of discretion. So long as the separate organisation of the members be not abolished, so long as it exists by a constitutional necessity for local purposes, though it should be in perfect subordination to the general authority of the Union, it would still be, in fact and in theory, an association of States, or a confederacy. The proposed Constitution, so far from implying an abolition of the State Governments, makes them constituent parts of the national sovereignty by allowing them a direct representation in the Senate, and leaves in their possession certain exclusive and very important portions of sovereign power—This fully corresponds, in every rational import of the terms, with the idea of a Fœderal Government.

In the Lycian confederacy, which consisted of twenty three CITIES, or republics, the largest were intitled to *three* votes in the COMMON COUNCIL, those of the middle class to *two* and the smallest to *one*. The COMMON COUNCIL had the appointment of all the judges and magistrates of the respective CITIES. This was certainly the most delicate species of interference in their internal administration; for if there be any thing, that seems exclusively appropriated to the local jurisdictions, it is the appointment of their own officers. Yet Montesquieu, speaking of this association, says "Were I to give a model of an excellent confederate republic, it would be that of Lycia." Thus we perceive that the distinctions insisted upon were not within the contemplation of this enlightened civilian, and we shall be led to conclude that they are the novel refinements of an erroneous theory.

George Mason, "Objections to the Constitution"

circulated early October 1787, published in full
in the *Virginia Journal* (Alexandria), November 22, 1787

To the PRINTERS of the VIRGINIA JOURNAL
and ALEXANDRIA ADVERTISER.

Gentlemen, At this important crisis when we are about to determine upon a government which is not to effect us for a month, for a year, or for our lives: but which, it is probable, will extend its consequences to the remotest posterity, it behoves every friend to the rights and privileges of man, and particularly those who are interested in the prosperity and happiness of this country, to step forward and offer their sentiments upon the subject in an open, candid and independent manner. — Let the constitution proposed by the late Convention be dispassionately considered and fully canvassed. — Let no citizen of the United States of America, who is capable of discussing the important subject, retire from the field. — And, above all, let no one disseminate his objections to, or his reasons for approving of the constitution in such a manner as to gain partizans to his opinion, without giving them an opportunity of seeing how effectually his sentiments may be controverted, or how far his arguments may be invalidated. — For when a man of acknowledged abilities and great influence (and particularly one who has paid attention to the subject) *hands forth* his opinion, upon a matter of general concern, among those upon whom he has reason to think it will make the most favorable impression, without submitting it to the test of a public investigation, he may be truly said to take an undue advantage of his influence, and appearances would justify a supposition that he wished to effect, in a clandestine manner, that which he could not accomplish by an open and candid application to the public.

I expected, Gentlemen, that Col. Mason's objections to the proposed constitution would have been conveyed to the public, before this time, through the channel of your, or some other paper, but as my expectations, in that respect, have not yet been gratified, I shall take the liberty to send you a copy of them for publication, which I think must be highly acceptable to a number of your customers who have not had an opportunity of seeing them in manuscript.

"Objections to the Constitution of Government formed by the Convention.

"There is no declaration of rights; and the laws of the general government being paramount to the laws and constitutions of the several States, the declarations of rights in the separate States are no security. Nor are the people secured even in the enjoyment of the benefits of the common law, which stands here upon no other foundation than its having been adopted by the respective acts forming the constitutions of the several States.

"In the House of Representatives there is not the substance, but the shadow only of representation; which can never produce proper information in the Legislature, or inspire confidence in the people; the laws will therefore be generally made by men little concerned in, and unacquainted with their effects and consequences.*

"The Senate have the power of altering all money-bills, and of originating appropriations of money, and the salaries of the officers of their own appointment in conjunction with the President of the United States; although they are not the representatives of the people, or amenable to them.

"These with their other great powers (viz. their power in the appointment of ambassadors and other public officers, in making treaties, and in trying all impeachments) their influence upon and connection with the supreme executive from these causes, their duration of office, and their being a constant existing body almost continually sitting, joined with

---

*Col. Mason acknowledges that this objection was in some degree lessened by inserting the word *thirty* instead of *forty*, as it was at first determined, in the 3d clause of the 2d section of the 1st article.

their being one complete branch of the Legislature, will destroy any balance in the government, and enable them to accomplish what usurpations they please upon the rights and liberties of the people.

"The judiciary of the United States is so constructed and extended as to absorb and destroy the judiciaries of the several States; thereby rendering law as tedious, intricate and expensive, and justice as unattainable by a great part of the community, as in England, and enabling the rich to oppress and ruin the poor.

"The President of the United States has no constitutional council (a thing unknown in any safe and regular government) he will therefore be unsupported by proper information and advice; and will be generally directed by minions and favorites—or he will become a tool to the Senate—or a Council of State will grow out of the principal officers of the great departments; the worst and most dangerous of all ingredients for such a council in a free country; for they may be induced to join in any dangerous or oppressive measures, to shelter themselves, and prevent an inquiry into their own misconduct in office; whereas had a constitutional council been formed (as was proposed) of six members, viz. two from the eastern, two from the middle, and two from the southern States, to be appointed by vote of the States in the House of Representatives, with the same duration and rotation in office as the Senate, the Executive would always have had safe and proper information and advice, the President of such a council might have acted as Vice-President of the United States, pro tempore, upon any vacancy or disability of the chief Magistrate; and long continued sessions of the Senate would in a great measure have been prevented.

"From this fatal defect of a constitutional council has arisen the improper power of the Senate, in the appointment of public officers, and the alarming dependance and connection between that branch of the Legislature and the supreme Executive.

"Hence also sprung that unnecessary and dangerous officer the Vice-President; who for want of other employment is made President of the Senate; thereby dangerously blending the executive and legislative powers; besides always giving to some one of the States an unnecessary and unjust pre-eminence over the others.

"The President of the United States has the unrestrained power of granting pardons for treason; which may be some-times exercised to screen from punishment those whom he had secretly instigated to commit the crime, and thereby pre-vent a discovery of his own guilt.

"By declaring all treaties supreme laws of the land, the Ex-ecutive and the Senate have, in many cases, an exclusive power of legislation; which might have been avoided by proper distinctions with respect to treaties, and requiring the assent of the House of Representatives, where it could be done with safety.

"By requiring only a majority to make all commercial and navigation laws, the five southern States (whose produce and circumstances are totally different from that of the eight northern and eastern States) will be ruined; for such rigid and premature regulations may be made, as will enable the mer-chants of the northern and eastern States not only to demand an exorbitant freight, but to monopolize the purchase of the commodities at their own price, for many years: To the great injury of the landed interest, and impoverishment of the peo-ple: And the danger is the greater, as the gain on one side will be in proportion to the loss on the other. Whereas requiring two-thirds of the members present in both houses would have produced mutual moderation, promoted the general interest and removed an insuperable objection to the adoption of the government.

"Under their own construction of the general clause at the end of the enumerated powers, the Congress may grant mo-nopolies in trade and commerce, constitute new crimes, inflict unusual and severe punishments, and extend their power as far as they shall think proper; so that the State Legislatures have no security for the powers now presumed to remain to them; or the people for their rights.

"There is no declaration of any kind for preserving the lib-erty of the press, the trial by jury in civil causes; nor against the danger of standing armies in time of peace.

"The State Legislatures are restrained from laying export duties on their own produce.

"The general Legislature is restrained from prohibiting the further importation of slaves for twenty odd years; though such importations render the United States weaker, and more vulnerable, and less capable of defence.

"Both the general Legislature and the State Legislatures are expressly prohibited making ex post facto laws; though there never was nor can be a Legislature but must and will make such laws, when necessity and the public safety require them, which will hereafter be a breach of all the constitutions in the Union, and afford precedents for other innovations.

"This government will commence in a moderate aristocracy; it is at present impossible to foresee whether it will, in its operation, produce a monarchy, or a corrupt oppressive aristocracy; it will most probably vibrate some years between the two, and then terminate between the one and the other."

Many of the foregoing objections and the reasonings upon them, appear to be calculated more to alarm the fears of the people, than to answer any good or valuable purpose. — Some of them are raised upon so slender a foundation as would render it doubtful whether they were the production of Col. *Mason*'s abilities, if an incontestible evidence of their being so could not be adduced.

November 19, 1787.

A "Prolix" Comment on Mason's "Objections": James Madison to George Washington

New York, October 18, 1787

I have been this day honoured with your favor of the 10th instant, under the same cover with which is a copy of Col. Mason's objections to the Work of the Convention. As he persists in the temper which produced his dissent it is no small satisfaction to find him reduced to such distress for a proper gloss on it; for no other consideration surely could have led him to dwell on an objection which he acknowledged to have been in some degree removed by the Convention themselves—on the paltry right of the Senate to propose alterations in money bills—on the appointment of the vice President—President of the Senate instead of making the President of the Senate the vice President, which seemed to be the alternative—and on the *possibility*, that the Congress may misconstrue their powers & betray their trust so far as to grant monopolies in trade &c. If I do not forget too some of his other reasons were either not at all or very faintly urged at the time when alone they ought to have been urged; such as the power of the Senate in the case of treaties & of impeachments; and their duration in office. With respect to the latter point I recollect well that he more than once disclaimed opposition to it. My memory fails me also if he did not acquiesce in if not vote for, the term allowed for the further importation of slaves; and the prohibition of duties on exports by the States. What he means by the dangerous tendency of the Judiciary I am at some loss to comprehend. It never was intended, nor can it be supposed that in ordinary cases the inferior tribunals will not have final jurisdiction in order to prevent the evils of which he complains. The great mass of suits in every State lie between Citizen & Citizen, and relate to matters not of federal cognizance. Notwithstanding the stress laid on the necessity of a Council to the President I strongly suspect, tho I was a friend to the thing, that if such an one as Col. Mason proposed, had been established, and the power of the Senate in appointments to offices transferred to it, that as great a clamour would have been heard from some quarters which in general eccho his Objections. What can he mean by saying that the Common law is not secured by the new Constitution, though it has been adopted by the State Constitutions. The Common law is nothing more than the unwritten law, and is left by all the Constitutions equally liable to legislative alterations. I am not sure that any notice is particularly taken of it in the Constitutions of the States. If there is, nothing more is provided than a general declaration that it shall continue along with other branches of law to be in force till legally changed. The Constitution of Virga. drawn up by Col. Mason himself, is absolutely silent on the subject. An *ordinance* passed during the same Session, declared the Common law as heretofore & all Statutes of prior date to the 4 of James I. to be still the law of the land, merely to obviate pretexts that the separation from G. Britain threw us into a State of nature, and abolished all civil rights and obligations. Since the Revolution every State has made great inroads & with great propriety in many instances on this *monarchical* code. The "revisal of the laws" by a Comĩtte of wch. Col. Mason was a member, though not an acting one, abounds with such innovations. The abolition of the *right of primogeniture*, which I am sure Col. Mason does not disapprove, falls under this head. What could the Convention have done? If they had in general terms declared the Common law to be in force, they would have broken in upon the legal Code of every State in the most material points: they wd. have done more, they would have brought over from G. B. a thousand heterogeneous & antirepublican doctrines, and even the *ecclesiastical Hierarchy itself*, for that is a part of the Common law. If they had undertaken a discrimination, they must have formed a digest of laws, instead of a Constitution. This objection surely was not brought forward in the Convention, or it wd. have been placed in such a light that a repetition of it out of doors would scarcely have been hazarded. Were it allowed the weight which Col. M. may suppose it deserves, it would remain to be decided whether it be candid to arraign the

Convention for omissions which were never suggested to them—or prudent to vindicate the dissent by reasons which either were not previously thought of, or must have been wilfully concealed—But I am running into a comment as prolix, as it is out of place.

I find by a letter from the Chancellor (Mr. Pendleton) that he views the act of the Convention in its true light, and gives it his unequivocal approbation. His support will have great effect. The accounts we have here of some other respectable characters vary considerably. Much will depend on Mr. Henry, and I am glad to find by your letter that his favorable decision on the subject may yet be hoped for.—The Newspapers here begin to teem with vehement & virulent calumniations of the proposed Govt. As they are chiefly borrowed from the Pensylvania papers, you see them of course. The reports however from different quarters continue to be rather flattering.

Reply to Mason's "Objections": "Civis Rusticus"

Virginia Independent Chronicle (Richmond), January 30, 1788

(The following was written previous to the publication of that in Mr. Dixon's paper of the 5th instant, but not sent to the printer when written from want of a conveyance, the person who wrote it living at a distance from Richmond.)

To Mr. DAVIS.

The following "objections to the Constitution of Government formed by the Convention," are stated to be Col. Mason's.

I shall remark on them with that freedom which every person has a right to exercise on publications, but, with that deference, which is due to this respectable and worthy gentleman; to whose great and eminent talents, profound judgment, and strength of mind, no man gives a larger credit, than he, who presumes to criticise his objections—these, falling from so great a height, from one of such authority, may be supposed, if not taken notice of, to contain arguments unanswerable—not obtruding themselves on my mind in that forcible manner, I submit to the decision of the public, whether, what is now offered, contain declamation or reason; cavil, or refutation.

1st. "There is no declaration of rights; and the laws of the general government being paramount to the laws and constitutions of the several states, the declarations of rights in the separate states are no security. Nor are the people secured even in the enjoyment of the benefits of the common law, which stands here upon no other foundation than its having been adopted by the respective acts forming the constitutions of the several states.

2d. In the house of representatives there is not the substance, but the shadow only of representation; which can never produce proper information in the legislature, or inspire confidence in the people; the laws will therefore be generally made by men little concerned in, and unacquainted with their effects and consequences.

3d. The senate have the power of altering all money bills, and of originating appropriations of money and the salaries of the officers of their own appointment, in conjunction with the president of the United States; although they are not the representatives of the people, or amenable to them. These, with their other great power (viz. their power in the appointment of ambassadors and other public officers, in making treaties, and in trying all impeachments) their influence upon and connection with the supreme executive from these causes, their duration of office, and their being a constant existing body almost continually sitting, joined with their being one complete branch of the legislature, will destroy any balance in the government, and enable them to accomplish what usurpations they please upon the rights and liberties of the people.

4th. The judiciary of the United States is so constructed and extended as to absorb and destroy the judiciaries of the several states; thereby rendering law as tedious, intricate and expensive, and justice as unattainable by a great part of the community, as in England, and enabling the rich to oppress and ruin the poor.

5th. The president of the United States has no constitutional council (a thing unknown in any safe and regular government) he will therefore be unsupported by proper information and advice, and will be generally directed by minions and favorites—or will become a tool to the senate—or a council of state will grow out of the principal officers of the great departments; the worst and most dangerous of all ingredients for such a council in a free country: For they may be induced to join in any dangerous or oppressive measures, to shelter themselves and prevent an enquiry into their own misconduct in office; whereas had a constitutional council been formed (as was proposed) of six members, viz. two from the eastern, two from the middle, and two from the southern states, to be appointed by vote of the states in the House of Representatives, with the same duration and rotation in office as the senate, the executive would always have had safe and proper information and advice, the president of such a council might have acted as vice-president of the United States, pro tempore, upon any vacancy or disability of the chief magistrate, and long continued sessions of the senate would in a great measure have been prevented.

From this fatal defect of a constitutional council has arisen the improper power of the senate in the appointment of public officers, and the alarming dependance and connection between that branch of the legislature and the supreme executive.

6th. Hence also sprung that unnecessary and dangerous officer the vice-president, who for want of other employment is made president of the senate: Thereby dangerously blending the executive and legislative powers; besides always giving to some one of the states an unnecessary and unjust preeminence over the others.—The president of the United States has the unrestraining power of granting pardons for treason; which may be sometimes exercised to screen from punishment those whom he had secretly instigated to commit the crime, and thereby prevent a discovery of his own guilt.

7th. By declaring all treaties supreme laws of the land, the executive and the senate have, in many cases, an executive power of legislation, which might have been avoided by proper distinctions with respect to treaties, and requiring the assent of the house of representatives where it could be done with safety.

8th. By requiring only a majority to make all commercial and navigation laws, the five southern states (whose produce and circumstances are totally different from that of the eight northern and eastern states) will be ruined; for such rigid and premature regulations may be made, as will enable the merchants of the northern and eastern states not only to demand an exorbitant freight, but to monopolise on the purchase of the commodities at their own price, for many years, to the great injury of the landed interest, and impoverishment of the people: And the danger is the greater, as the gain on one side will be in proportion to the loss on the other: Whereas requiring two thirds of the members present in both houses would have produced mutual moderation, promoted the general interest, and removed an insuperable objection to the adoption of the government.

9th. Under their own construction of the general clause at the end of the enumerated powers, the Congress may grant monopolies in trade and commerce, constitute new crimes, inflict unusual and severe punishments, and extend their power as far as they shall think proper; so that the state legislatures have no security for the powers now presumed to remain to them; or the people for their rights.

10th. There is no declaration of any kind for preserving the liberty of the press, the trial by jury in civil causes; nor against the danger of standing armies in time of peace.

11th. The state legislatures are restrained from laying export duties on their produce.

12th. The general legislature is restrained from prohibiting the further importations of slaves for twenty odd years; though such importations render the United States weaker and more vulnerable, and less capable of defence.

13th. Both the general legislature and the state legislatures are expressly prohibited making expost facto laws; though there never was, nor can be a legislature but must and will make such laws, when necessity and the public safety require them; which will hereafter be a breach of all the constitutions in the union, and afford precedents for other invocations.

This government will commence in a moderate aristocracy; it is at present impossible to foresee whether it will, in its operation produce a monarchy, or a corrupt oppressive aristocracy, it will most probably vibrate some years between the two, and then terminate between the one and the other."

Ob. 1st. This objection proves too much, it goes against all sovereignty, "it being paramount to all laws of the several states, the declaration of rights in the separate states are no security," if the declaration of rights in the separate states be no security, which it is confessed are not repealed, neither would a general declaration of rights be any security, for the sovereign who made it could repeal it; "the very title of sovereignty shews the absurdity of an irrevocable law." The people have every security of enjoying the benefits of the common law, and all acts of parliament previous to the fourth of James the first, they ever had—they remain unrepealed, and are the palladium of the rights of the people: as long as *they* retain the spirit of freedom, these rights will exist, amidst the mighty shock of revolutions, the crush of power, the fall of colonies, and the rise of empires.

There are only five states in the union that have declarations of rights—the proposed government is thoroughly popular—the house of representatives are immediately chosen by the people, the senate mediately by their representatives *in Assembly*, and the president by electors, in such manner as the legislature of the state may direct—at the end of four years, he may, and will be removed from his situation, unless he discharge the duties of it, to the approbation of the people, and to the glory and advantage of America. A government thus constituted stands in need of no bill of rights; the liberties of the people never can be lost, until they are lost to themselves, in a vicious disregard of their dearest interests, a sottish indolence, a wild licentiousness, a dissoluteness of morals, and a contempt of all virtue.

2d. "The house of representatives is not numerous enough," and yet they exceed in number the present Congress: there was a time when these could acquire information, and why should not their successors? the number from this state will be ten, besides two senators; the number at present only five.—The reason of not augmenting the representation, I take to be this; the fear of augmenting the expences of government; and considering the condition of America, it is wise to pay a particular respect to this circumstance.

3d. "The senate have the power of altering money bills;" and why not? because the Lords in England, an hereditary aristocracy, have not, of late years, been permitted by the commons to exercise this power, shall the senate, a rotatory body, chosen by the representatives of the people, be deprived of this essential right of legislation? the people cannot be taxed, but, by the consent of their immediate representatives.

They can fix no salaries without the consent and approbation of the president: Here they are checked; if we suppose both these bodies colluding, (which would at once demonstrate their wickedness and folly) and setting salaries at an infinitely exorbitant pitch, and above services; will not the house of representatives reclaim against such measures, and refuse all grants of money, 'till these are altered, and redressed? Of this truly respectable part of the constitution, in my idea, there is not the least ground for apprehension or fear: they cannot take their seats, 'till thirty years of age: the presumption is not a violent one, that their integrity will be tried, and their abilities known and approved: most of them probably will be past, "the hey-day in the blood;" weaned from the intoxicating dissipation of youth, and the hot allurements of pleasure.

4th. The judiciary of the United States have *original* jurisdiction *only*, in all cases affecting ambassadors, other public ministers and consuls, and those in which a state shall be party—The convention has only crayoned the outlines, it is left to the Congress, to fill up and colour the canvas—To these able artists, the representatives of the states, the Wittenagemot of America (this task, the finishing of this piece) is left with great propriety—*It is taken for granted* by Mr. Mason that law will be rendered tedious and expensive, &c.— Let us pass over this begging of the question, and ask, what could this enlightened gentleman mean? by instancing England, as the place where justice is tedious and unattainable— "At the sittings in London and Middlesex there are not so few as eight hundred causes set down a year, and all disposed of; of these not more than twenty or thirty are ever afterwards heard of in the shape of special verdicts, special cases, &c.— Notwithstanding this immensity of business, it is notorious, that in consequence of method and a few rules, which have been laid down to prevent delay (even where the parties themselves would willingly consent to it) nothing now hangs in court—Upon the last day of the term there was not a single matter of any kind that remained undetermined" Burrow's Rep. 4th vol. p. 2583. May justice in America be always attainable as in England, and may it be administered here precisely as it is administered at Westminster-Hall! The rich here, as in all other countries, will have an advantage over the poor, in all cases where the services of eminent and learned men are to be commanded by the influence of money.

5th. Had the convention left the executive power indivisible, I am free to own it would have been better, than giving the senate a share in it; or had they left the power to the president of appointing his own privy council, upon each of whom for every measure be advised and carried, responsibility should have been fixed, this blending of what should be separate would have been avoided—The following conjecture may explain the reason of this: A jealousy of executive government; and a jealousy in the minor states, which made them anxious to add every weight to the scale of the senate, considering it as the inexpugnable barrier of their privileges, and the soul of their existence.

6th. The powers of the vice-president do not strike me as dangerous; he will seldom or ever have that devolution of power by the death, resignation, or inability of the president; and, if he should, he will exercise it for a short time—The president's having the unrestrained power of pardoning for treasons is another objection; and why? "it may be sometimes exercised to screen from punishment those whom he, (the president) had secretly instigated to commit the crime, and thereby prevent a discovery of his own guilt"—I appeal to this worthy gentleman himself, I appeal to the public, whether there be in this objection, more of validity and force, or chimera and imagination.

7th. The infraction of the present treaty shews the necessity of treaties having the force of laws—When any publicity of them will not be injurious to America, they will be submitted to the representatives in Congress. The King of England can make peace or declare war; can make treaties, but, whenever the Commons disapprove of the measures by which these have been brought about, we know the consequences—Col. Mason is too well read in parliamentary history, not to know what the effects would have been, had the Commons frowned on those of Hanover, Seville, &c. negociated in the administration of Sir Robert Walpole—The cast of the proposed constitution is surely more popular than the English.

8th. Our interest is variant, not opposite; different from, not contrary to, that of the eastern states: I confess, on this point I have had my fears: as a Virginian, it would be more to my mind not to have the possibility of restraint imposed on the free transport of our staple, but, as an American I would submit this to the general sense, rather than secede—If, as I believe, for I will not assert, the agricultural system in Pennsylvania prevail over the commercial, we need not fear monopolies in the carrying business, restrictions, and navigation acts. I believe too, but I will not assert, be this as it may,—that the representative Congress of the United States will not, in fifty years, make so large a sacrifice of the trade of Virginia on the altar of selfishness and monopoly, as her assembly has made of it, in four, on the altar of ignorance and absurd prejudice.

9th. The latter part of the answer to the 6th objection may suffice for this—Valeat quantum valere potest.

10th. "No declaration of the liberty of the press." Our Bill of Rights declares, and it is not repealed, that the freedom of the press is one of the great bulwarks of the liberty of the people, and never can be restrained, but by despotic power. The people of England have no other security for the liberty of the press, than we have—Their own spirit, and an act of parliament—their act of parliament *may* be repealed—our Bill of Rights *may* be repealed. Of that no man has any fear, of this no man need have, while this spirit is in the people—"This peculiar privilege must last (says a learned writer) as long as our government remains, in any degree, free and independent—it is seldom that liberty of any kind is lost at once—slavery has so frightful an aspect to men accustomed to freedom, that it must steal upon them by degrees, and disguise itself in a thousand shapes in order to be received—But, if the liberty of the press ever be lost, it will be lost at once.—The general laws against sedition and libelling are at present as strong as they can possibly be made, nothing can impose a further restraint, but, either clapping an imprimatur on the press, or giving to the court very large discretionary powers, to punish whatever displeases them—but these concessions would be such a bare faced violation of liberty, that they will probably be the last efforts of a despotic government—Hume's essay vol. i. p. 17."

The last efforts of a despotic government! Can we then a popular government, a guaranteed republic, fear this more under the proposed, than the present constitution?

A standing army without the consent of the representatives of the people in Congress there never can be: to their wisdom and their discretion we submit—Necessity may oblige America to raise an army—and who can judge of this necessity so well as Congress? Where can this power be more safely reposed? Dr. Smith (in his "Wealth of Nations," book 5. ch. 1.) is of opinion in some cases, that a standing army is not dangerous to liberty—of this the people of America will judge, and a people jealous of their liberty, vigiliant over executory magistracy, will oppose with their united voice this institution, when they discover its end to be usurpation and tyranny.

11th. Happy for Virginia, that this restraint is imposed. Laying duties on exports is the acme of impolicy, and has been the practice of our Assemblies.

12th. Not restraining for twenty years the importation of Africans will not effect us—This gives South-Carolina and Georgia that privilege, if it be their pleasure to avail themselves of it—Is not this objection, the excess of criticism?

13th. Ex post facto laws have ever been considered as abhorrent from liberty: necessity and public safety never can require them—"If laws do not punish an offender, let him go unpunished; let the legislature, admonished of the defect of the laws, provide against the commission of future crimes of the same sort—The escape of one delinquent can never produce so much harm to the community, as may arise from the infraction of a rule, upon which the purity of public justice, and the existence of civil liberty essentially depend"—Pæley's Principles of Moral Philosophy, vol. 2. p. 234. Octavo Ed.

14th. The last objection does not call for any particular animadversion—What the government may terminate in depends on the people—let them feel their importance, be alive to their own interests; elect those of the best abilities and character; keep a jealous eye over their representatives, and over judicial and executory magistracy; be disposed to reverence the authority of laws, yet active to detect and expose malversation and wrong measures: the proposed government will then, not only induce external consideration and respectability, but will have internal efficiency and permanence, and will ensure to the present and future generations, security of property, and peace, happiness, and liberty, the great end of political and civil society.

I have now finished, what I proposed to observe on these objections, and trust no person will conclude my design has been to condemn this respectable gentleman for not putting his signature to the constitution; on the contrary, thinking as he did, I commend him—The man of abilities, firmness, and integrity will dare to think, to judge, and act for himself, his principles have not the pliancy of his gloves, neither has he his mind to make up at every revolution of an hour: authority with him is not the guide to truth, nor does infallibility rest in numbers—He has a surer monitor; his own judgment and the dictates of his conscience of such stern matter is, if I am rightly informed, the mind of Mr. Mason composed, never yielding itself up, when convinced of its rectitude, at the arbitrium of the popular breath, nor giving into opinions that are not its own.

Dec. 29, 1787.

Answers to Mason's "Objections": "Marcus" [James Iredell] I–V

Norfolk and Portsmouth Journal (Virginia), February 20–March 19, 1788

I
FEBRUARY 20, 1788

MR. M'LEAN, *I beg the favour of you to publish in your paper, the following Answers to Mr. Mason's Objections to the New Constitution. Each objection is inserted in his own words (as taken from a printed newspaper) before the answer given to it, so that the merits of both will be fairly before the Public.—Nothing can be more easy than the business of objecting, and as mankind are generally much more apt to find fault than to approve its success is commonly proportionable; but I trust the good sense of America, at this awful period, will exert itself to judge coolly and impartially, especially as the dissenting gentlemen appear to differ as much from each other as from the respectable majority who have recommended the New Constitution to the public.—I am Sir, your very humble servant,*

The AUTHOR.

Answers to Mr. Mason's *Objections* to the New Constitution, Recommended by the late Convention at Philadelphia.

1st. Objection.

"There is no declaration of rights, and the laws of the general government being paramount to the laws and constitutions of the several States, the declarations of rights in the separate States are no security; nor are the people secured even in the enjoyment of the benefit of the common law, which stands here upon no other foundation than its having been adopted by the respective acts forming the constitutions of the several States."

Answer.

1. *As to the want of a Declaration of Rights.*

The introduction of these in England, from which the idea was originally taken, was in consequence of usurpations of the Crown, contrary, as was conceived, to the principles of their government. But there, no original constitution is to be found, and the only meaning of a declaration of rights in that country is, that in certain particulars specified, the Crown had no authority to act. Could this have been necessary, had there been a Constitution in being, by which it could have been clearly discerned whether the Crown had such authority or not? Had the people by a solemn instrument delegated particular powers to the Crown at the formation of their government, surely the Crown which in that case could claim under that instrument only, could not have contended for more power than was conveyed by it. So it is in regard to the new Constitution here: The future government which may be formed under that authority, certainly cannot act beyond the warrant of that authority. As well might they attempt to impose a King upon America, as go one step in any other respect beyond the terms of their institution. The question then only is, whether more power will be vested in the future government than is necessary for the general purposes of the Union. This may occasion a ground of dispute—but after expressly defining the powers that are to be exercised, to say that they shall exercise no other powers (either by a general or particular enumeration) would seem to me both nugatory and ridiculous. As well might a Judge when he condemns a man to be hanged, give strong injunctions to the Sheriff that he should not be beheaded.*

2. As to the common law, it is difficult to know what is meant by that part of the objection. So far as the people are now entitled to the benefit of the common law, they certainly

---

*It appears to me a very just remark of Mr. Wilson in his celebrated speech, that a Bill of Rights would have been dangerous, as implying that without such a reservation the Congress would have authority in the cases enumerated, so that if any had been omitted (and who would undertake to recite all the state and individual rights not relinquished by the new Constitution?) they might have been considered at the mercy of the general Legislature.

will have a right to enjoy it under the new constitution, till altered by the general Legislature, which even in this point has some cardinal limits assigned to it. What are most acts of Assembly but a deviation in some degree from the principles of the common law? The people are expressly secured (contrary to Mr. Mason's wishes) against *ex post facto* laws, so that the tenure of any property at any time held under the principles of the common law, cannot be altered by any act of the future general legislature. The principles of the common law, as they now apply, must surely always hereafter apply, except in those particulars in which express authority is given by this Constitution; in no other particular can the Congress have authority to change it, and I believe it cannot be shewn that any one power of this kind given is unnecessarily given, or that the power would answer its proper purpose if the Legislature was restricted from any innovations on the principles of the common law, which would not in all cases suit the vast variety of incidents that might arise out of it.

IId. Objection.

"In the House of Representatives there is not the substance but the shadow only of representation, which can never produce proper information in the Legislature, or inspire confidence in the people; the laws will therefore be generally made by men little concerned in, and unacquainted with, their effects and consequences."

Answer.

This is a mere matter of calculation. It is said the weight of this objection was in a great measure removed by altering the number of 40000 to 30000 constituents. To shew the discontented nature of man, some have objected to the number of representatives as being too large. I leave to every man's judgment whether the number is not sufficiently respectable, and whether if that number be sufficient it would have been right, in the very infancy of this government, to burthen the people with a great additional expence to answer no good purpose.*

---

*I have understood it was considered at the Convention, that the proportion of one Representative to 30,000 Constituents, would produce at the very first nearly the number that would be satisfactory to Mr. Mason. So that I

IIId. Objection.

"The Senate have the power of altering all money bills, and of originating appropriations of money, and the salaries of the officers of their own appointment, in conjunction with the President of the United States; although they are not the Representatives of the people, or amenable to them. These, with their other great powers (*viz.* their powers in the appointment of ambassadors and all public officers, in making treaties, and in trying all impeachments), their influence upon and connection with the Supreme Executive from these causes; their duration of office, and their being a constant existent body almost continually sitting, joined with their being one complete branch of the Legislature, will destroy any balance in the government, and enable them to accomplish what usurpations they please upon the rights and liberties of the people."

Answer.

This objection respecting the dangerous power of the Senate, is of that kind which may give rise to a great deal of gloomy prediction, without any solid foundation. An imagination indulging itself in chimerical fears, upon the disappointment of a favourite plan may point out danger arising from any system of government whatever, even if Angels were to have the administration of it; since I presume, none but the Supreme Being himself is altogether perfect, and of course every other species of beings may abuse any delegated portion of power. This sort of visionary scepticism therefore will lead us to this alternative, either to have no government at all, or to form the best system we can, making allowance for human imperfection. In my opinion, the fears as to the power of the Senate are altogether groundless, as to any probability of their being either able or willing to do any important mischief. My reasons are—

1. Because tho' they are not immediately to represent the people, yet they are to represent the Representatives of the people, who are annually chosen, and it is therefore probable,

---

presume this reason was wrote before the material alteration was made from 40,000 to 30,000, which is said to have taken place the very last day, just before the signature.

the most popular, or confidential persons in each State, will be elected members of the Senate.

2. Because one third of the Senate are to be chosen as often as the immediate Representatives of the people, and as the President can act in no case from which any great danger can be apprehended without the concurrence of two-thirds, let us think ever so ill of the designs of the President, and the danger of a combination of power among a standing body generally associated with him, unless we suppose every one of them to be base and infamous (a supposition, thank God, bad as human nature is, not within the verge of the slightest probability), we have reason to believe that the one third newly introduced every second year, will bring with them from the immediate body of the people a sufficient portion of patriotism and independence to check any exorbitant designs of the rest.

3. Because in their legislative capacity they can do nothing without the concurrence of the House of Representatives, and we need look no further than England for a clear proof of the amazing consequence which Representatives of the people bear in a free government. There the King (who is hereditary, and therefore not so immediately interested, according to narrow views of interest which commonly govern Kings, to consult the welfare of his people) has the appointment to almost every office in the government, many of which are of high dignity and great pecuniary value; has the creation of as many Peers as he pleases, is not restricted from bestowing places on the members of both Houses of Parliament, and has a direct negative on all bills, besides the power of dissolving the Parliament at his pleasure. In theory would not any one say this power was enormous enough to destroy any balance in the Constitution? Yet what does the history of that country tell us?—That so great is the natural power of the House of Commons (tho' a very imperfect representation of the people, and a large proportion of them actually purchasing their seats), that ever since the Revolution the Crown has continually aimed to corrupt them by the disposal of places and pensions; that without their hearty concurrence it found all the wheels of government perpetually clogged; and, that notwithstanding this, in great critical emergencies, the members have

broke through the trammels of power and interest, and, by speaking the sense of the people (tho' so imperfectly representing them) either forced an alteration of measures, or made it necessary for the Crown to dissolve them. If their power under these circumstances, is so great, what would it be if their Representation was perfect and their members could hold no appointments, and at the same time had a security for their seats? The danger of a destruction of the balance would be perhaps on the popular side, notwithstanding the hereditary tenure and weighty prerogatives of the Crown, and the permanent station and great wealth and consequence of the Lords. Our Representatives therefore, being an adequate and fair representation of the people, and they being expressly excluded from the possession of any places, and not holding their existence upon any precarious tenure must have vast influence; and considering that in every popular government the danger of faction is often very serious and alarming, if such a danger could not be checked in its instant operation by some other power more independent of the immediate passions of the people, and capable therefore of thinking with more coolness, the government might be destroyed by a momentary impulse of passion, which the very members who indulged it might for ever afterwards in vain deplore. The institution of the Senate seems well calculated to answer this salutary purpose. Excluded as they are from places themselves, they appear to be as much above the danger of personal temptation as they can be. They have no permanent interest as a body to detach them from the general welfare, since six years is the utmost period of their existence, unless their respective legislatures are sufficiently pleased with their conduct to re-elect them. This power of re-election is itself a great check upon abuse, because if they have ambition to continue members of the Senate, they can only gratify this ambition by acting agreeably to the opinion of their constituents. The House of Representatives, as immediately representing the people, are to originate all money bills. This I think extremely right, and it is certainly a very capital acquisition to the popular Representative. But what harm can arise from the Senate, who are nearly a popular Representative also, proposing amendments when those amendments must be concurred with by the original proposers? The wisdom of the Senate may sometimes point out amendments, the propriety of which the other House may be very sensible of, though they had not occurred to themselves. There is no great danger of any body of men suffering by too eager an adoption of any amendment proposed to any system of their own. The probability is stronger of their being too tenacious of their original opinion, however erroneous, than of their profiting by the wise information of any other persons whatever. Human nature is so constituted, and therefore I think we may safely confide in the admission of a free intercourse of opinion on the detail of business, as well as to taxation as to other points. Our House of Representatives surely could not have such reason to dread the power of a Senate circumstanced as ours must be, as the House of Commons in England the permanent authority of the Peers, and therefore a jealousy which may be well grounded in the one case, would be entirely ill directed in the other. For similar reasons, I dread not any power of originating appropriations of money as mentioned in the objection. While the concurrence of the other House must be had, and as that must necessarily be the most weighty in the government, I think no danger is to be apprehended. The Senate has no such authority as to awe or influence the House of Representatives, and it will be as necessary for one as for the other that proper active measures should be pursued. And in regard to appropriations of money, occasions for such appropriations may, on account of their concurrence with the executive power, occur to the Senate, which would not to the House of Representatives; and therefore if the Senate were precluded from laying any such proposals before the House of Representatives, the government might be embarrassed, and it ought ever to be remembered, that in our views of distant and chimerical dangers we ought not to hazard our very existence as a people, by proposing such restrictions as may prevent the exertion of any necessary power.—The power of the Senate in the appointment of Ambassadors, &c. is designed as a check upon the President.—They must be appointed in some manner. If the appointment was by the President alone, or by the President and a Privy Council (Mr. Mason's favourite plan), an objection to such a system would have appeared much more plausible. It would have been said that this was approaching too much towards Monarchical power, and if this new Privy Council had been like all I have ever heard of it would have afforded little security against an abuse of power in the President. It ought to be shewn by reason and probability (not bold assertion) how this concurrence of power with the President can make the Senate so dangerous. It is as good an argument to say that it will not, as that it will.* The power of making treaties is so important, that it would have been highly dangerous to vest it in the Executive alone, and would have been the subject of much greater clamour. From the nature of the thing, it could not be vested in the popular Representative. It must therefore have been provided for, with the Senate's concurrence, or the concurrence of a Privy Council (a thing which I believe nobody has been mad enough to propose), or the power, the greatest Monarchical power that can be exercised, must have been vested in a manner that would have excited universal indignation, in the President alone. As to the power of trying impeachments, let Mr. Mason shew where this power could more properly have been placed. It is a necessary power in every free government, since even the Judges of the Supreme Court of Judicature themselves may require a trial, and other public officers might have too much influence before an ordinary and common Court. And what probability is there that such a Court acting in so solemn a manner, should abuse its power (especially as it is wisely provided that their sentences shall extend only to removal from office and incapacitation) more than any other Court? The argument as to the possible abuse of power, as I have before suggested, will reach all delegation of power whatever, since all power may be abused where fallible beings are to execute it; but we must take as much caution as we can, being careful at the same time not to be too wise to do any thing at all. The bold assertions at the

*It seems, by the letter which has been published of Mr. Elseworth and Mr. Sherman, as if one reason of giving a share in these appointments to the Senate was, that persons in what are called the lesser States might have an equal chance for such appointments, in proportion to their merit, with those in the larger, an advantage that could only be expected from a body in which the States were equally represented.

end of this objection are mere declamation, and till some reason is assigned for them, I shall take the liberty to rely upon the reasons I have stated above, as affording a belief that the popular Representative must for ever be the most weighty in this government, and of course that apprehensions of danger from such a Senate are altogether ill founded.

(*To be continued.*)

II
FEBRUARY 27, 1788

Answers to Mr. Mason's *Objections* to the New Constitution, Recommended by the late Convention at Philadelphia.

IVth. Objection.

"The Judiciary of the United States is so constructed and extended, as to absorb and destroy the Judiciaries of the several States; thereby rendering law as tedious, intricate and expensive; and justice as unattainable by a great part of the community as in England; and enabling the rich to oppress and ruin the poor."

Answer.

Mr. Mason has here asserted, "That the Judiciary of the United States is so constructed and extended, as to absorb and destroy the Judiciaries of the several States." How is this the case? Are not the State Judiciaries left uncontrouled as to all the affairs of *that State only*? In this, as in all other cases, where there is a wise distribution, power is commensurate to its object. With the mere internal concerns of a State, Congress are to have nothing to do. In no case but where the Union is in some measure concerned, are the Fœderal Courts to have any jurisdiction. The State Judiciary will be a satellite waiting upon its proper planet: That of the Union like the sun, cherishing and preserving a whole planetary system.

In regard to a possible ill construction of this authority, we must depend upon our future Legislature in this case, as well as others, in respect to which it is impracticable to define every thing; that it will be provided for so as to occasion as little expence and distress to individuals as can be. In parting with the coercive authority over the States, as States, there must be a coercion allowed as to individuals. The former power no man of common sense can any longer seriously contend for: The latter is the only alternative. Suppose an objection should be made, that the future Legislature should not ascertain salaries, because they might divide among themselves and their officers all the revenue of the Union:* Will not every man see how irrational it is to expect that any government can exist, which is to be fettered in its most necessary operations, for fear of abuse?

Vth. Objection.

"The President of the United States, has no Constitutional Council (a thing unknown in any safe and regular government), he will therefore be unsupported by proper information and advice; and will generally be directed by minions and favorites—or he will become a tool to the Senate—or a Council of State will grow out of the principal officers of the great departments; the worst and most dangerous of all ingredients for such a Council in a free country; for they may be induced to join in any dangerous or oppressive measures; to shelter themselves, and prevent an enquiry into their own misconduct in office: Whereas, had a Constitutional Council been formed (as was proposed) of six Members, viz. two from the eastern, two from the middle, and two from the southern States; to be appointed by vote of the States in the House of Representatives, with the same duration and rotation of office as the Senate, the Executive would always have had safe and proper information and advice. The President of such a Council might have acted as Vice-President of the United States, *pro tempore*, upon any vacancy or disability of the Chief Magistrate; and long-continued Sessions of the Senate would,

---

*When I wrote the above, I had not seen Governor Randolph's letter: Otherwise, I have so great a respect for that gentleman's character, I should have treated with more deference an idea in some measure countenanced by him. One of his objections relates to the Congress fixing their own salaries. I am persuaded, upon a little reflection, that gentleman must think this is one of those cases where a trust must unavoidably be reposed. No salaries could certainly be fixed now, so as to answer the various changes in the value of money, that in the course of time must take place. And in what condition would the Supreme Authority be, if their very subsistence depended on an inferior power? An abuse in this case too, would be so gross, that it is very unlikely to happen; but if it should, it would probably prove much more fatal to the authors, than injurious to the people.

in a great measure have been prevented. From this fatal defect of a Constitutional Council, has arisen the improper power of the Senate, in the appointment of public officers, and the alarming dependence and connexion between that branch of the Legislature and the Supreme Executive. Hence also sprung that unnecessary and dangerous officer, the Vice-President; who, for want of other employment, is made President of the Senate; thereby dangerously blending the Executive and Legislative powers; besides always giving to some of the States an unnecessary and unjust pre-eminence over the others."

Answer.

Mr. Mason here reprobates the omission of a particular Council for the President, as a thing contrary to the example of all safe and regular governments. Perhaps there are very few governments now in being, deserving of that character, if under the idea of safety, he means to include safety for a proper share of personal freedom, without which their safety and regularity in other respects would be of little consequence to a people so justly jealous of liberty as I hope the people in America ever will be. Since however Mr. Mason refers us to such authority, I think I cannot do better than to select for the subject of our enquiry in this particular, a government which must be universally acknowledged to be the most safe and regular of any considerable government now in being (though I hope, America will soon be able to dispute that pre-eminence). Every body must know I speak of Great-Britain; and in this I think I give Mr. Mason all possible advantage; since, in my opinion, it is most probable he had Great-Britain principally in his eye when he made this remark. And in the very height of our quarrel with that country, so wedded were our ideas to the institution of a Council, that the practice was generally, if not universally followed, at the formation of our governments, though we instituted councils of a quite different nature; and so far as the little experience of the writer goes, have very little benefited by it. My enquiry into this subject shall not be confined to the actual present practice of Great-Britain. I shall take the liberty to state the constitutional ideas of Councils in England, as derived from their ancient laws subsisting long before the Union, not omitting however to shew what the present practice really is.—By the laws of England* the King is said to have four Councils. 1. The High Court of Parliament. 2. The Peers of the Realm. 3. His Judges. 4. His Privy Council.—By the first, I presume, is meant in regard to the making of laws; because the usual introductory expressions in most acts of Parliament, viz. "By the King's Most Excellent Majesty, by and with the advice and consent of the Lords Spiritual and Temporal, and Commons, &c." shew, that in a constitutional sense, they are deemed the King's laws, after a ratification in Parliament. The Peers of the Realm are, by their birth hereditary Counsellors of the Crown, and may be called upon for their advice either in time of Parliament, or when no Parliament is in being. They are called in some law books, *Magnum Concilium Regis*. (The King's Great Council). It is also considered the privilege of every particular Peer, to demand an audience of the King, and to lay before him any thing he may deem of public importance. The Judges, I presume, are called "A Council of the King," upon the same principle that the Parliament is, because the administration of justice is in his name, and the Judges are considered as his instruments in the distribution of it. We come now to the Privy Council, which I imagine, if Mr. Mason had any particular view towards England when he made this objection, was the one he intended as an example of a *Constitutional Council* in that kingdom. The Privy Council in that country is undoubtedly of very ancient institution; but it has one fixed property invariably annexed to it, that it is a mere creature of the Crown, dependent on its will both for number and duration, since the King may, whenever he thinks proper, discharge any particular Member, or the whole of it, and appoint another.† If this precedent is of moment to us, merely as a precedent, it should be followed in all its parts; and then what would there be in the regulation to prevent the President from being governed by "minions and favorites?" It would only be the means of rivetting them on constitutional ground. So far as precedents in England apply, the Peers being constitutionally the *Great Council of the King*, tho' also a

*See Coke's Commentary upon Littleton, 110. I. Blackstone's Commentaries, 227 and seq.

†I. Blackstone's Commentaries, 232.

part of the Legislature, we have reason to hope, that there is by no means, such gross impropriety as has been suggested, in giving the Senate, tho' a branch of the Legislature, a strong controul over the Executive. The only difference in the two cases is, that the Crown may or may not give this consequence to the Peers at its own pleasure; and accordingly we find, that for a long time past, this Great Council has been very seldom consulted: Under our Constitution, the President is allowed no option in respect to certain points, wherein he cannot act without the Senate's concurrence. But we cannot infer from any example in England, that a concurrence between the Executive and a part of the Legislature is contrary to the maxims of their government, since their government allows of such a concurrence whenever the Executive pleases. The rule therefore from the example of the freest government in Europe, that the Legislative and Executive powers must be altogether distinct, is liable to exceptions. It does not mean that the Executive shall not form a part of the Legislature (for the King who has the whole Executive authority, is one entire branch of the Legislature; and this, Montesquieu, who recognizes the general principle, declares is necessary): Neither can it mean (as the example above evinces) that the Crown must consult neither house as to any exercise of its Executive power: But its meaning must be, that one power shall not include *both authorities*: The King, for instance, shall not have the sole Executive, and sole Legislative authority also. He may have the former, but must participate the latter with the two Houses of Parliament. The rule also would be infringed were the three branches of the Legislature to share jointly the Executive power. But so long as the people's Representatives are altogether distinct from the Executive authority, the liberties of the people may be deemed secure. And in this point, surely there can be no manner of comparison between the provisions by which the independence of our House of Representatives is guarded, and the condition in which the British House of Commons is left exposed to every species of corruption.—But Mr. Mason says, for want of a Council, the President may become "a tool to the Senate." Why?—Because he cannot act without their concurrence. Would not the same reason hold for his being "a tool to the Council," if he could not act without their concurrence, supposing a Council was to be imposed upon him without his own nomination (according to Mr. Mason's plan)? As great care is taken to make him independent of the Senate; as I believe human precaution can provide. Whether the President will be a tool to any persons, will depend upon the man; and the same weakness of mind which would make him pliable to one body of controul, would certainly attend him with another. But Mr. Mason objects, if he is not directed by minions and favorites, nor becomes a tool of the Senate, "A Council of State will grow out of the principal officers of the great departments, the worst and most dangerous of all ingredients for such a Council, in a free country; for they may be induced to join in any dangerous or oppressive measures to shelter themselves, and prevent an inquiry into their own misconduct in office." I beg leave again to carry him to my old authority, England, and ask him what efficient Council they have there, but one formed of their great officers? Notwithstanding their important *constitutional Council*, every body knows that the whole movements of their government, where a Council is consulted at all, are directed by their *Cabinet Council*, composed entirely of the principal officers of the great departments: That when a Privy Council is called, it is scarcely ever for any other purpose than to give a formal sanction to the previous determinations of the other; so much so that it is notorious that not one time in a thousand one Member of the Privy Council, except a known adherent of administration, is summoned to it. But though the President, under our Constitution, may have the aid of the "principal officers of the great departments," he is to have this aid, I think, in the most unexceptionable manner possible. He is not to be assisted by a Council, summoned to a jovial dinner perhaps, and giving their opinions according to the nod of the President—but the opinion is to be given with the utmost solemnity, *in writing*. No after equivocation can explain it away. It must for ever afterwards speak for itself, and commit the character of the writer, in lasting colours either of fame or infamy, or neutral insignificance, to future ages, as well as the present. From those written reasons, weighed with care, surely the President can form as good a judgment as if they had been given by a dozen formal characters, carelessly met together on a slight appointment. And this further advantage would be derived from the proposed system (which would be wanting if he had constitutional advice to screen him) that the President must be *personally responsible* for every thing. For though an ingenious gentleman has proposed, that a Council should be formed, who should be responsible for *their opinions*; and the same sentiment of justice might be applied to these opinions of the great officers, I am persuaded it will in general be thought infinitely more *safe*, as well as more *just*, that the President who acts should be responsible for his *conduct*, following advice at his peril, than that there should be a danger of punishing any man for an erroneous opinion which might possibly be sincere. Besides the morality of this scheme, which may well be questioned, its inexpediency is glaring, since it would be so plausible an excuse, and the insincerity of it so difficult to detect; the hopes of impunity this avenue to escape, would afford, would nearly take away all dread of punishment. As to the temptations mentioned to the officers joining in dangerous or oppressive measures to shelter themselves, and prevent an enquiry into their own misconduct in office, this proceeds upon a supposition that the President and the great officers may form a very wicked combination to injure their country; a combination that in the first place it is utterly improbable, in a strong respectable government, should be formed for that purpose; and in the next, with such a government as this Constitution would give us, could have little chance of being successful, on account of the great superior strength, and natural and jealous vigilance of one at least, if not both the two weighty branches of Legislation. This evil however, of the possible depravity of *all public officers*, is one that can admit of no cure, since in every institution of government, the same danger in some degree or other must be risqued; it can only be guarded against by strong checks, and I believe it would be difficult for the objectors to our new Constitution, to provide stronger ones against any abuse of the Executive authority, than will exist in that. As to the Vice-President, it appears to me very proper he should be chosen much in the same manner as the President, in order that the States may be secure, upon any accidental loss by death or otherwise, of the President's service; of the services in the same important station of the man in whom they repose their second confidence. The complicated manner of election wisely prescribed, would necessarily occasion a considerable delay in the choice of another; and in the mean time the President of the Council, tho' very fit for the purpose of advising, might be very ill qualified, especially in a critical period, for an active executive department. I am concerned to see among Mr. Mason's other reasons, so trivial a one as the little advantage one State might accidentally gain by a Vice-President of their country having a seat, with merely a casting vote in the Senate. Such a reason is utterly unworthy that spirit of amity, and rejection of local views, which can alone save us from destruction. It was the glory of the late Convention, that by discarding such, they formed a general government upon principles that did as much honor to their hearts as to their understandings. God grant, that in all our deliberations, we may consider America as one body, and not divert our attention from so noble a prospect, to small considerations of partial jealousy and distrust. It is in vain to expect upon any system to secure an exact equilibrium of power for all the States. Some will occasionally have an advantage from the superior abilities of its Members; the field of emulation is however open to all. Suppose any one should now object to the superior influence of Virginia (and the writer of this is not a citizen of that State) on account of the high character of General Washington, confessedly the greatest man of the present age, and perhaps equal to any that has existed in any period of time: Would this be a reason for refusing a union with her, though the other States can scarcely hope for the consolation of ever producing his equal?

(*To be continued.*)

III
MARCH 5, 1788
Answers to Mr. Mason's *Objections* to the New Constitution, Recommended by the late Convention at Philadelphia.

VIth. Objection.
"The President of the United States, has the unrestrained power of granting pardons for treason, which may be some-

times exercised to screen from punishment those whom he had secretly instigated to commit the crime, and thereby prevent a discovery of his own guilt."

Answer.

Nobody can contend upon any rational principles, that a power of pardoning should not exist somewhere in every government, because it will often happen in every country, that men are obnoxious to a legal conviction, who yet are entitled, from some favorable circumstances in their case, to a merciful interposition in their favor. The advocates of monarchy have accordingly boasted of this, as one of the advantages of that form of government, in preference to a Republican; nevertheless this authority is vested in the Stadtholder in Holland, and I believe is vested in every Executive power in America. It seems to have been wisely the aim of the late Convention in forming a general government for America, to combine the acknowledged advantages of the British Constitution with proper Republican checks, to guard as much as possible against abuses; and it would have been very strange if they had omitted this which has the sanction of such great antiquity in that country, and if I am not mistaken, an universal adoption in America.* Those gentlemen who object to other parts of the Constitution, as introducing innovations, con-

*I have since found, that in the Constitutions of some of the States, there are much stronger restrictions on the Executive authority, in this particular, than I was aware of. In others the restriction only extends to prosecutions carried on by the General Assembly, or the most numerous branch of Legislature; or a contrary provision by law: Virginia is in the latter class. But when we consider how necessary it is in many cases to make use of accomplices to convict their associates, and what little regard ought in general to be paid to a guilty man swearing to save his own life, we shall probably think that the jealousies which (by prohibiting pardons before conviction) ever disabled the Executive authority from procuring unexceptionable testimony of this sort, may more fairly be ascribed to the natural irritation of the public mind at the time when the Constitutions were formed, than to an enlarged and full consideration of the whole subject. Indeed, it could scarcely be avoided, that when arms were first taken up in the cause of liberty, to save us from the immediate crush of arbitrary power, we should lean too much rather to the extreme, of weakening than of strengthening the Executive power in our own government. In England, the only restriction upon this power in the King, in case of Crown prosecutions (one or two slight cases excepted) is, that his pardon is not pleadable in bar of an impeachment; but he may pardon after

trary to long experience, with a very ill grace attempt to reject an experience so unexceptionable as this, to introduce an innovation (perhaps the first ever suggested) of their own. When a power is acknowledged to be necessary, it is a very dangerous thing to prescribe limits to it; for men must have a greater confidence in their own wisdom than I think any men are entitled to, who imagine they can form such exact ideas of all possible contingencies as to be sure that the restriction they propose will not do more harm than good. The probability of the President of the United States committing an act of treason against his country is very slight; he is so well guarded by the other powers of government, and the natural strength of the people at large must be so weighty, that in my opinion it is the most chimerical apprehension that can be entertained. Such a thing is however possible, and accordingly he is not exempt from a trial, if he should be guilty, or supposed guilty, of that or any other offence. I entirely lay out of the consideration, the improbability of a man honored in such a manner by his country, risquing, like General Arnold, the damnation of his fame to all future ages, though it is a circumstance of some weight in considering, whether, for the sake of such a remote and improbable danger as this, it would be prudent to abridge this power of pardoning in a manner altogether unexampled, and which might produce mischiefs, the extent of which, it is not perhaps easy at present to foresee. In estimating the value of any power it is possible to bestow, we have to chuse between inconveniences of some sort or other, since no institution of man can be entirely free from all. Let us now therefore consider some of the actual inconveniencies which would attend an abridgement of the power of the President in this respect. One of the great advantages attending a single Executive power is, the degree of secrecy and dispatch with which, on critical occasions, such a power can act. In war this advantage will often counter-ballance the want of many others. Now suppose, in the very

---

conviction, even on an impeachment; which is an authority not given to our President, who in cases of impeachment has no power either of pardoning or reprieving.

midst of a war of extreme consequence to our safety or prosperity, the President could prevail upon a gentleman of abilities to go into the enemy's country, to serve in the useful, but dishonorable character of a spy: Such are certainly maintained by all vigilant governments, and in proportion to the ignominy of the character, and the danger sustained in the enemy's country, ought to be his protection and security in his own. This man renders very useful services; perhaps, by timely information prevents the destruction of his country. Nobody knows of these secret services but the President himself; his adherence however to the enemy is notorious: He is afterwards intercepted in endeavouring to return to his own country, and having been perhaps a man of distinction before, he is proportionably obnoxious to his country at large for his supposed treason. Would it not be monstrous, that the President should not have it in his power to pardon this man? or that it should depend upon mere solicitation and favor, and perhaps, though the President should state the fact as it really was, some zealous partizan, with his jealousy constantly fixed upon the President, might insinuate that in fact the President and he were secret traitors together, and thus obtain a rejection of the President's application. It is a consideration also of some moment, that there is scarcely any accusation more apt to excite popular prejudice than the charge of treason. There is perhaps no country in the world where justice is in general more impartially administered than in England; yet let any man read some of the trials for treason in that country even since the Revolution, he will see sometimes a fury influencing the Judges, as well as the Jury, that is extremely disgraceful. There may happen a case in our country, where a man in reality innocent, but with strong plausible circumstances against him, would be so obnoxious to popular resentment, that he might be convicted upon very slight and insufficient proof. In such a case it would certainly be very proper for a cool, temperate man of high authority, and who might be supposed uninfluenced by private motives, to interfere, and prevent the popular current proving an innocent man's ruin. I know men who write with a view to flatter the people, and not to give them honest information, may misrepresent this account, as an invidious imputation on the usual impartiality of Juries. God knows, no man more highly reverences that blessed institution than I do: I consider them the natural safeguard of the personal liberties of a free people, and I believe they would much seldomer err in the administration of justice, than any other tribunal whatever. But no man of experience and candor will deny the probability of such a case as I have supposed, sometimes, tho' rarely happening; and whenever it did happen, surely so safe a remedy as a prerogative of mercy in the chief magistrate of a great country, ought to be at hand. There is little danger of an abuse of such a power, when we know how apt most men are in a Republican government, to court popularity at too great an expence, rather than to do a just and beneficent action, in opposition to strong prevailing prejudices, among the people. But, says Mr. Mason, "The President may sometimes exercise this power to screen from punishment those whom he had secretly instigated to commit the crime, and thereby prevent a discovery of his own guilt." This is possible, but the probability of it is surely too slight to endanger the consequences of abridging a power which seems so generally to have been deemed necessary in every well regulated government. It may also be questioned, whether, supposing such a participation of guilt, the President would not expose himself to greater danger by pardoning, than by suffering the law to have its course. Was it not supposed, by a great number of intelligent men, that Admiral Byng's execution was urged on to satisfy a discontented populace, when the Administration, by the weakness of the force he was entrusted with, were, perhaps the real cause of the miscarriage before Minorca? Had he been acquitted, or pardoned he could perhaps have exposed the real fault: As a prisoner under so heavy a charge, his recrimination would have been discredited as merely the effort of a man in despair to save himself from an ignominious punishment. If a President should pardon an accomplice, that accomplice then would be an unexceptionable witness. Before, he would be a witness with a rope about his own neck, struggling to get clear of it at all events. Would any men of understanding, or at least ought they to credit an accusation from a person under such circumstances?*

VIIth. Objection.

"By declaring all treaties supreme laws of the land, the Executive and the Senate have in many cases an exclusive power of legislation, which might have been avoided by proper distinctions with respect to treaties, and requiring the assent of the House of Representatives, where it could be done with safety."

Answer.

Did not Congress very lately unanimously resolve in adopting the very sensible letter of Mr. Jay, that a treaty when once made pursuant to the sovereign authority, *ex vi termini* became immediately the law of the land? It seems to result unavoidably from the nature of the thing, that when the constitutional right to make treaties is exercised, the treaty so made should be binding upon those who delegated authority for that purpose. If it was not, what foreign power would trust us? And if this right was restricted by any such fine checks as Mr. Mason has in his imagination, but has not thought proper to disclose, a critical occasion might arise, when for want of a little rational confidence in our own government, we might be obliged to submit to a master in an enemy. Mr. Mason wishes the House of Representatives to have some share in this business; but he is immediately sensible of the impropriety of it, and adds, "Where it could be done with safety." And how is it to be known whether it can be done with safety or not, but during the pendency of a negociation? Must not the President and Senate judge, whether it can be done with safety or not? If they are of opinion it is unsafe, and the House of Representatives of course not consulted, what becomes of this boasted check, since if it amounts to no more than that the President and Senate may consult the House of Representatives if they please, they may do this as well without such a provision as with it? Nothing

---

*The evidence of a man confessing himself guilty of the same crime, is undoubtedly admissible; but it is generally, and ought to be always viewed with great suspicion, and other circumstances should be required to corroborate it.

would be more easy than to assign plausible reasons after the negociation was over, to shew that a communication was unsafe, and therefore surely a precaution that could be so easily eluded, if it was not impolitic to the greatest degree, must be thought trifling indeed. It is also to be observed, that this authority so obnoxious in the new Constitution (which is unfortunate in having little power to please some persons, either as containing new things or old) is vested indefinitely and without restriction in our present Congress, who are a body constituted in the same manner as the Senate is to be; but there is this material difference in the two cases, that we shall have an additional check under the new system of a President of high personal character, chosen by the immediate body of the people.

(*To be continued.*)

IV

March 12, 1788

Answers to Mr. Mason's *Objections* to the New Constitution, Recommended by the late Convention at Philadelphia.

VIIIth. Objection.

"Under their own construction of the general clause at the end of the enumerated powers, the Congress may grant monopolies in trade and commerce, constitute new crimes, inflict unusual and severe punishments, and extend their power as far as they shall think proper; so that the State Legislatures have no security for the powers now presumed to remain to them, or the people for their rights. There is no declaration of any kind for preserving the Liberty of the Press—the Trial by Jury in civil cases—nor against the danger of standing armies in time of peace."

Answer.

The general clause at the end of the enumerated powers is as follows:—

"To make all laws which shall be necessary and proper for carrying into execution the *foregoing powers, and all other powers vested by this Constitution in the United States, or in any department or office thereof.*"

Those powers would be useless, except acts of Legislation could be exercised upon them. It was not possible for the Convention, nor is it for any human body, to foresee and provide for all contingent cases that may arise. Such cases must therefore be left to be provided for by the general Legislature, as they shall happen to come into existence. If Congress, under pretence of exercising the power delegated to them, should, in fact, by the exercise of any other power, usurp upon the rights of the different Legislatures, or of any private citizens, the people will be exactly in the same situation as if there had been an express provision against such power in particular, and yet they had presumed to exercise it. It would be an act of tyranny, against which no parchment stipulations can guard; and the Convention surely can be only answerable for the propriety of the powers given, not for the future virtues of all with whom those powers may be entrusted. It does not therefore appear to me, that there is any weight in this objection more than in others—but, that I may give it every fair advantage, I will take notice of every particular injurious act of power which Mr. Mason points out as exerciseable by the authority of Congress, under this general clause.

The first mentioned is, "That the Congress may grant monopolies in trade and commerce." Upon examining the Constitution, I find it expressly provided, "That no preference shall be given to the ports of one State over those of another;" and that "Citizens of each State shall be entitled to all privileges and immunities of citizens in the several States." These provisions appear to me to be calculated for the very purpose Mr. Mason wishes to secure. Can they be consistent with any monopoly in trade and commerce?* I apprehend therefore, under this expression must be intended more than is expressed; and if I may conjecture from another publication

*One of the powers given to Congress is, "To promote the progress of science and useful arts, by securing for limited times to authors and inventors, the exclusive right to their respective writings and discoveries." I am convinced Mr. Mason did not mean to refer to this clause. He is a gentleman of too much taste and knowledge himself to wish to have our government established upon such principles of barbarism as to be able to afford no encouragement to genius.

of a gentleman of the same State and in the same party of opposition, I should suppose it arose from a jealousy of the Eastern States, very well known to be often expressed by some gentlemen of Virginia. They fear, that a majority of the States may establish regulations of commerce which will give great advantage to the carrying trade of America, and be a means of encouraging New England vessels rather than old England.—Be it so.—No regulations can give such advantage to New England vessels, which will not be enjoyed by all other American vessels, and many States can build as well as New England, tho' not at present perhaps in equal proportion.* And what could conduce more to the preservation of the union, than allowing to every kind of industry in America a peculiar preference! Each State exerting itself in its own way, but the exertions of all contributing to the common security, and increasing the rising greatness of our country! Is it not the aim of every wise country to be as much the carriers of their own produce as can be? And would not this be the means in our own of producing a new source of activity among the people, giving to our own fellow citizens what otherwise must be given to strangers, and laying the foundation of an independent trade among ourselves, and of gradually raising a navy in America, which, however distant the prospect, ought certainly not to be out of our sight. There is no great probability however that our country is likely soon to enjoy so glorious an advantage. We must have treaties of commerce, because without them we cannot trade to other countries. We already have such with some nations—we have none with Great-Britain; which can be imputed to no other cause but our not having a strong respectable government to bring that nation to terms. And surely no man who feels for the honor of his country, but must view our present degrading commerce with that country with the highest indignation,

*Some might apprehend, that in this case as New England would at first have the greatest share of the carrying trade, that the vessels of that country might demand an unreasonable freight; but no attempt could be more injurious to them, as it would immediately set the Southern States to building, which they could easily do, and thus a temporary loss would be compensated with a lasting advantage to us. The very reverse would be the case with them; besides, that from that country alone there would probably be competition enough for freight to keep it upon reasonable terms.

and the most ardent wish to extricate ourselves from so disgraceful a situation. This only can be done by a powerful government, which can dictate conditions of advantage to ourselves, as an equivalent for advantages to them; and this could undoubtedly be easily done by such a government, without diminishing the value of any articles of our own produce; or if there was any diminution it would be too slight to be felt by any patriot in competition with the honor and interest of his country.

As to the constituting new crimes, and inflicting unusual and severe punishment, certainly the cases enumerated wherein the Congress are empowered either to define offences, or prescribe punishments, are such as are proper for the exercise of such authority in the general Legislature of the union. They only relate to "counterfeiting the securities and current coin of the United States; to piracies and felonies committed on the high seas, and offences against the law of nations, and to treason against the United States." These are offences immediately affecting the security, the honor or the interest of the United States at large, and of course must come within the sphere of the Legislative authority which is entrusted with their protection. Beyond these authorities Congress can exercise no other power of this kind, except in the enacting of penalties to enforce their acts of Legislation in the cases where express authority is delegated to them, and if they could not enforce such acts by the enacting of penalties, those powers would be altogether useless, since a legislative regulation without some sanction would be an absurd thing indeed. The Congress having, for these reasons, a just right to authority in the above particulars, the question is, whether it is practicable and proper to prescribe the limits to its exercise, for fear that they should inflict punishments unusual and severe? It may be observed in the first place, that a declaration against "cruel and unusual punishments," formed part of an article in the Bill of Rights at the Revolution in England, in 1688. The prerogative of the Crown having been grossly abused in some preceding reigns, it was thought proper to notice every grievance they had endured, and those declarations went to an abuse of power in the crown only, but were never intended to limit the authority of Parliament. Many of these articles of the

Bill of Rights in England, without a due attention to the difference of the cases, were eagerly adopted when our Constitutions were formed, the minds of men then being so warmed with their exertions in the cause of liberty, as to lean too much perhaps towards a jealousy of power to repose a proper confidence in their own government. From these articles in the State Constitutions, many things were attempted to be transplanted into our new Constitution, which would either have been nugatory or improper: This is one of them. The expressions "unusual and severe," or "cruel and unusual," surely would have been too vague to have been of any consequence, since they admit of no clear and precise signification. If to guard against punishments being too severe, the Convention had enumerated a vast variety of cruel punishments, and prohibited the use of any of them, let the number have been ever so great, an inexhaustible fund must have been unmentioned, and if our government had been disposed to be cruel, their invention would only have been put to a little more trouble. If to avoid this difficulty, they had determined, not negatively, what punishments should not be exercised, but positively what punishments should, this must have led them into a labyrinth of detail which in the original constitution of a government would have appeared perfectly ridiculous, and not left a room for such changes according to circumstances, as must be in the power of every Legislature that is rationally formed. Thus, when we enter into particulars, we must be convinced that the proposition of such a restriction would have led to nothing useful, or to something dangerous, and therefore that its omission is not chargeable as a fault in the new Constitution. Let us also remember, that as those who are to make those laws must, themselves be subject to them, their own interest and feelings will dictate to them not to make them unnecessarily severe; and that in the case of treason, which usually in every country exposes men most to the avarice and rapacity of government, care is taken that the innocent family of the offender shall not suffer for the treason of their relation. This is the crime with respect to which a jealousy is of the most importance, and accordingly it is defined with great plainness and accuracy, and the temptations to abusive prosecutions guarded against as much as possible. I now proceed to the three great cases:—The Liberty of the Press—The Trial by Jury in civil cases, and a Standing Army in time of peace.

The Liberty of the Press is always a grand topic for declamation; but the future Congress will have no other authority over this than to secure to authors for a limited time the exclusive privilege of publishing their works. This authority has long been exercised in England, where the press is as free as among ourselves, or in any country in the world, and surely such an encouragement to genius is no restraint on the liberty of the press, since men are allowed to publish what they please of their own; and so far as this may be deemed a restraint upon others it is certainly a reasonable one, and can be attended with no danger of copies not being sufficiently multiplied, because the interest of the proprietor will always induce him to publish a quantity fully equal to the demand— besides, that such encouragement may give birth to many excellent writings which would otherwise have never appeared.* If the Congress should exercise any other power over the press than this, they will do it without any warrant from this Constitution, and must answer for it as for any other act of tyranny.

In respect to the trial by jury in civil cases, it must be observed, it is a mistake to suppose, that such a trial takes place in all civil cases now. Even in the common law Courts, such a trial is only had where facts are disputed between the parties, and there are even some facts triable by other methods. In the Chancery and Admiralty Courts, in many of the States, I am told, they have no Juries at all. The States in these particulars differ very much in their practice from each other: A general declaration therefore to preserve the trial by Jury in all civil cases, would only have produced confusion, so that the Courts afterwards in a thousand instances would not have known how to have proceeded. If they had added "as heretofore accustomed," that would not have answered the purpose, because there has been no uniform custom about it. If therefore the Convention had interfered, it must have been by

---

*If this provision had not been made in the new Constitution, no author could have enjoyed such an advantage in all the United States, unless a similar law constantly subsisted in each of the States separately.

entering into a detail highly unsuitable to a fundamental constitution of government: If they had pleased some States, they
must have displeased others, by innovating upon modes of
administering justice perhaps endeared to them by habit, and
agreeable to their settled conviction of propriety. As this was
the case it appears to me it was infinitely better, rather than
endanger every thing by attempting too much, to leave this
complicated business of detail, to the regulation of the future
Legislature, where it can be adjusted coolly and at ease, and
upon full and exact information.—There is no danger of the
trial by Jury being rejected, when so justly a favorite of the
whole people. The Representatives of the people surely can
have no interest in making themselves odious for the mere
pleasure of being hated; and when a Member of the House of
Representatives is only sure of being so for two years, but
must continue a citizen all his life, his interest as a citizen, if
he is a man of common sense, to say nothing of his being a
man of common honesty, must ever be uppermost in his
mind. We know the great influence of the monarchy in the
British government, and upon what a different tenure the
Commons there have their seats in Parliament, from that prescribed to our Representatives. We know also, they have a
large standing army. It is in the power of the Parliament if
they dare to exercise it, to abolish the trial by jury altogether—but woe be to the man who should dare to attempt
it—it would undoubtedly produce an insurrection that would
hurl every tyrant to the ground who attempted to destroy
that great and just favorite of the English nation. We certainly
shall be always sure of this guard at least, upon any such act
of folly or insanity in our Representatives: They soon would
be taught the consequence of sporting with the feelings of a
free people. But when it is evident that such an attempt cannot be rationally apprehended, we have no reason to anticipate unpleasing emotions of that nature. There is indeed little
probability, that any degree of tyranny which can be figured
to the most discoloured imagination, as likely to arise out of
our government, could find an interest in attacking the trial
by Jury in civil cases; and in criminal ones, where no such
difficulties intervened as in the other, and where there might

be supposed temptations to violate the personal security of a citizen, it is sacredly preserved.

The subject of a standing army has been exhausted in so masterly a manner in two or three numbers of the Fœderalist (a work which I hope will soon be in every body's hands) that, but for the sake of regularity in answering Mr. Mason's objections, I should not venture upon the same topic; and shall only presume to do so, with a reference for fuller satisfaction to that able performance. It is certainly one of the most delicate and proper cases for the consideration of a free people, and so far as a jealousy of this kind leads to any degree of caution not incompatible with the public safety, it is undoubtedly to be commended. Our jealousy of this danger has descended to us from our British ancestors: In that country they have a monarch, whose power being limited, and at the same time his prerogatives very considerable, a constant jealousy of him is both natural and proper. The two last of the Stuarts having kept up a considerable body of standing forces in time of peace, for the clear and almost avowed purpose of subduing the liberties of the people, it was made an article of the Bill of Rights at the Revolution, "That the raising or keeping a standing army within the kingdom in time of peace, unless it be with the consent of Parliament, is against law;" but no attempt was made, or I dare say, ever thought of, to restrain the Parliament from the exercise of that right. An army has been since kept on foot annually by authority of Parliament, and I believe ever since the Revolution they have had some standing troops; disputes have frequently happened about the number, but I don't recollect any objection by the most zealous patriot, to the keeping up of any at all. At the same time, notwithstanding the above practice of an annual vote (arising from a very judicious caution) it is still in the power of Parliament to authorise the keeping up of any number of troops for any indefinite time, and to provide for their subsistence for any number of years: Considerations of prudence, not constitutional limits to their authority, alone restrain such an exercise of it. Our Legislature however will be strongly guarded, though that of Great Britain is without any check at all. No appropriations of money for military service can continue longer than two years. Considering the extensive services the general government may have to provide for upon this vast continent, no forces with any serious prospect of success, could be attempted to be raised for a shorter time. Its being done for so short a period, if there were any appearances of ill designs in the government, would afford time enough for the real friends of their country to sound an alarm; and when we know how easy it is to excite jealousy of any government, how difficult for the people to distinguish from their real friends, those factious men, who in every country are ready to disturb its peace for personal gratifications of their own, and those desperate ones to whom every change is welcome, we shall have much more reason to fear that the government may be overawed by groundless discontents, than that it should be able, if contrary to every probability such a government could be supposed willing, to effect any designs for the destruction of their own liberties, as well as those of their constituents: For surely we ought ever to remember, that there will not be a man in the government but who has been either mediately or immediately recently chosen by the people, and that for too limited a time to make any arbitrary designs, consistent with common sense, when every two years a new body of Representatives, with all the energy of popular feelings, will come to carry the strong force of a severe national controul, into every department of government; to say nothing of the one-third to compose the Senate, coming at the same time warm with popular sentiments from their respective Assemblies. Men may, to be sure, suggest dangers from any thing; but it may truly be said, that those who can seriously suggest the danger of a premeditated attack on the liberties of the people from such a government as this, could with ease assign reasons equally plausible for distrusting the integrity of any government formed in any manner whatever; and really it does seem to me, that all their reasons may be fairly carried to this position,—that in as much as any confidence in any men would be unwise, as we can give no power but what may be grossly abused, we had better give none at all, but continue as we are, or resolve into total anarchy at once, of which indeed, our present condition falls very little short. What sort of a government must that be, which, upon the most certain intelligence that hostilities were meditated against it, could take no method for its defence, till after a formal declaration, of war, or the enemy's standard was actually fixed upon the shore. The first has for some time been out of fashion; but if it had not, the restraint these gentlemen recommend, would certainly have brought it into disuse with every Power who meant to make war upon America. They would not be such fools as to give us the only warning we had informed them we would accept of, before we would take any steps to counteract their designs. The absurdity of our being prohibited from preparing to resist an invasion till after it had actually taken place,* is so glaring that no man can consider it for a moment without being struck with astonishment, to see how rashly, and with how little consideration gentlemen, whose characters are certainly respectable, have suffered themselves to be led away by so delusive an idea. The example of other countries, so far from warranting any such limitation of power, is directly against it. That of England is particularly noticed. In our present articles of Confederation there is no such restriction. It has been observed by the Fœderalist, that Pennsylvania and North-Carolina appear to be the only States in the union, which have attempted any restraint of the Legislative authority in this particular, and that their restraint appears rather in the light of a caution than a prohibition; but, that notwithstanding that, Pennsylvania had been obliged to raise forces in the very face of that article of her Bill of Rights. That great writer, from the remoteness of his situation, did not know that North-Carolina had equally violated her Bill of Rights in a similar manner. The Legislature of that State, in November 1786, passed an act for raising 201 men for the protection of a County called David-

---

*Those gentlemen who gravely tell us the militia will be sufficient for this purpose, do not recollect that they themselves do not desire we should rely solely on a militia in case of actual war, and therefore in the case I have supposed, they cannot be deemed sufficient even by themselves, for when the enemy landed it would undoubtedly be a time of war, but the misfortune would be, that they would be prepared—we not. Certainly all possible encouragement should be given to the training of our militia, but no man can really believe that they will be sufficient without the aid of any regular troops, in a time of foreign hostility. A powerful militia may make fewer regulars necessary, but will not make it safe to dispense with them altogether.

son County, against hostilities from the Indians; they were to continue for *two years* from the time of their first rendezvous, unless sooner disbanded by the Assembly; and were to be "subject to the same rules with respect to their government as were established in the time of the late war by the Congress of the United States, for the government of the Continental army:" These are the very words of the act. Thus, for the example of the only two countries in the world, that I believe ever attempted such a restriction, it appears to be a thing incompatible with the safety of government. Whether their restriction is to be considered as a caution or a prohibition, in less than five years after peace the caution has been disregarded, or the prohibition disobeyed.* Can the most credulous or suspicious man, require stronger proof of the weakness and impolicy of such restraints?

(*To be concluded in our next.*)

v

MARCH 19, 1788

Answers to Mr. Mason's *Objections* to the New Constitution, Recommended by the late Convention at Philadelphia.

(*Concluded from our last.*)

IXth. Objection.

"The State Legislatures are restrained from laying export duties on their own exports."

Answer.

Duties upon exports, though they may answer in some particulars a convenience to the country which imposes them, are certainly not things to be contended for, as if the very being of a State was interested in preserving them. Where there is a kind of monopoly this may sometimes be ventured upon, but even there perhaps more is lost by imposing such duties than is compensated for by any advantage. Where there is not a

---

*I presume we are not to be deemed in a state of war whenever any Indian hostilities are committed on our frontiers. If that is the case, I don't suppose we have had six years of peace since the first settlement of the country, or shall have for fifty years to come. A distinction between peace and war would be idle indeed, if it can be frittered away by such pretences as those.

species of monopoly no policy can be more absurd. The American States are so circumstanced, that some of the States necessarily export part of the produce of neighbouring ones. Every duty laid upon such exported produce, operates in fact as a tax by the exporting State upon the non-exporting State. In a system expressly formed to produce concord among all, it would have been very unwise to have left such a source of discord open; and upon the same principle, and to remove as much as possible every ground of discontent, Congress itself are prohibited from laying duties on exports, because by that means those States which have a great deal of produce to export, would be taxed much more heavily than those which have little or none for exportation.

Xth. Objection.

"The general Legislature is restrained from prohibiting the further importation of slaves for twenty odd years, though such importations render the United States weaker, more vulnerable, and less capable of defence."

Answer.

If all the States had been willing to adopt this regulation, I should, as an individual, most heartily have approved of it, because, even if the importation of slaves in fact rendered us stronger, less vulnerable, and more capable of defence, I should rejoice in the prohibition of it, as putting a stop to a trade which has already continued too long for the honor and humanity of those concerned in it. But as it was well known that South-Carolina and Georgia thought a further continuance of such importations useful to them, and would not perhaps otherwise have agreed to the new Constitution, those States which had been importing till they were satisfied, could not with decency have insisted upon their relinquishing advantages themselves had already enjoyed. Our situation makes it necessary to bear the evil as it is. It will be left to the future Legislatures to allow such importations or not. If any, in violation of their clear conviction of the injustice of this trade, persist in pursuing it, this is a matter between God and their own consciences. The interests of humanity will however have gained something by a prohibition of this inhuman trade, though at the distance of twenty odd years.

XIth. Objection.

"Both the general Legislature, and the State Legislatures are expressly prohibited making *ex post facto* laws, though there never was, nor can be a Legislature but must and will make such laws when necessity and the public safety require them; which will hereafter be a breach of all the Constitutions in the union, and afford precedents for other innovations."

Answer.

My ideas of liberty are so different from those of Mr. Mason, that in my opinion this very prohibition is one of the most valuable parts of the new Constitution. *Ex post facto* laws may some times be convenient, but that they are ever absolutely necessary I shall take the liberty to doubt, till that necessity can be made apparent. Sure I am, they have been the instrument of some of the grossest acts of tyranny that were ever exercised, and have this never failing consequence, to put the minority in the power of a passionate and unprincipled majority, as to the most sacred things; and the plea of necessity is never wanting where it can be of any avail. This very clause, I think, is worth ten thousand Declarations of Rights, if this the most essential right of all was omitted in them. A man may feel some pride in his security, when he knows that what he does innocently and safely to-day, according to the laws of his country, cannot be tortured into guilt and danger to-morrow. But if it should happen, that a great and overruling necessity, acknowledged and felt by all, should make a deviation from this prohibition excusable, shall we not be more safe in leaving the excuse for an extraordinary exercise of power to rest upon the apparent equity of it alone, than to leave the door open to a tyranny it would be intolerable to bear? In the one case every one must be sensible of its justice, and therefore excuse it: In the other, whether its exercise was just or unjust, its being lawful would be sufficient to command obedience. Nor would a case like that, resting entirely on its own bottom, from a conviction of invincible necessity, warrant an avowed abuse of another authority where no such necessity existed or could be pretended.

I have now gone through Mr. Mason's objections; one thing still remains to be taken notice of; his prediction, which he is pleased to express in these words: "This government will commence in a modern aristocracy; it is at present impossible to foresee, whether it will, in its operation, produce a monarchy or a corrupt oppressive aristocracy; it will most probably vibrate some years between the two, and then terminate in the one or the other." From the uncertainty of this prediction, we may hope Mr. Mason was not divinely inspired when he made it, and of course that it may as fairly be questioned as any of his particular objections. If my answers to his objections are in general solid, a very different government will arise from the new Constitution if the several States should adopt it, as I hope they will. It will not probably be too much to flatter ourselves with, that it may present a spectacle of combined strength in government; and genuine liberty in the people the world has never yet beheld. In the mean time our situation is critical to the greatest degree. Those gentlemen who think we may at our ease go on from one Convention to another, to try if all objections cannot be conquered by perseverance, have much more sanguine expectations that I can presume to form. There are critical periods in the fate of nations, as well as in the life of man, which are not to be neglected with impunity. I am much mistaken if this is not such a one with us. When we were at the very brink of despair, the late excellent Convention, with an unanimity that none could have hoped for, generously discarding all little considerations, formed a system of government which I am convinced can stand the nicest examination, if reason and not prejudice is employed in viewing it. With a happiness of thought, which in our present awful situation ought to silence much more powerful objections than any I have heard, they have provided in the very frame of government a safe, easy and unexceptionable method of correcting any errors it may be thought to contain. These errors may be corrected at leisure; in the mean time the acknowledged advantages likely to flow from this Constitution may be enjoyed. We may venture to hold up our head among the other powers of the world. We may talk to them with the confidence of an independent people, having strength to resent insults, and avail ourselves of all our natural advantages. We may be assured of once more beholding justice, order and dignity taking place of the present anarchical confusion prevailing almost every where, and drawing upon us universal disgrace. We may hope, by proper exertions of industry, to recover thoroughly from the shock of the late war, and truly to become an independent, great and prosperous people. But if we continue as we now are, wrangling about every trifle, listening to the opinion of a small minority in preference to a large and most respectable majority of the first men in our country, and among them some of the first in the world; if our minds in short, are bent rather on indulging a captious discontent, than bestowing a generous and well-placed confidence in those who we have every reason to believe are entirely worthy of it, we shall too probably present a spectacle for malicious exultation to our enemies, and melancholy dejection to our friends; and the honor, glory and prosperity which were just within our reach, will, perhaps be snatched from us for ever.

January, 1788.

"Cato" V

New York Journal, November 22, 1787

To the CITIZENS *of the State of* NEW-YORK.
In my last number I endeavored to prove that the language
of the article relative to the establishment of the executive of
this new government was vague and inexplicit, that the great
powers of the President, connected with his duration in office
would lead to oppression and ruin. That he would be governed by favorites and flatterers, or that a dangerous council
would be collected from the great officers of state;—that the
ten miles square, if the remarks of one of the wisest men,
drawn from the experience of mankind, may be credited,
would be the asylum of the base, idle, avaricious and ambitious, and that the court would possess a language and
manners different from yours; that a vice-president is as
unnecessary, as he is dangerous in his influence—that the
president cannot represent you, because he is not of your own
immediate choice, that if you adopt this government, you will
incline to an arbitrary and odious aristocracy or monarchy—
that the president possessed of the power, given him by this
frame of government differs but very immaterially from the
establishment of monarchy in Great-Britain, and I warned
you to beware of the fallacious resemblance that is held out to
you by the advocates of this new system between it and your
own state governments.

And here I cannot help remarking, that inexplicitness seems
to pervade this whole political fabric: certainty in political
compacts which Mr. Coke *calls the mother and nurse of repose
and quietness*, the want of which induced men to engage in
political society, has ever been held by a wise and free people
as essential to their security; as on the one hand it fixes barriers

which the ambitious and tyrannically disposed magistrate dare not overleap, and on the other, becomes a wall of safety to the community—otherwise stipulations between the governors and governed are nugatory; and you might as well deposit the important powers of legislation and execution in one or a few and permit them to govern according to their disposition and will; but the world is too full of examples, which prove that *to live by one man's will became the cause of all men's misery.* Before the existence of express political compacts it was reasonably implied that the magistrate should govern with wisdom and justice, but mere implication was too feeble to restrain the unbridled ambition of a bad man, or afford security against negligence, cruelty, or any other defect of mind. It is alledged that the opinions and manners of the people of America, are capable to resist and prevent an extension of prerogative or oppression; but you must recollect that opinion and manners are mutable, and may not always be a permanent obstruction against the encroachments of government; that the progress of a commercial society begets luxury, the parent of inequality, the foe to virtue, and the enemy to restraint; and that ambition and voluptuousness aided by flattery, will teach magistrates, where limits are not explicitly fixed to have separate and distinct interests from the people, besides it will not be denied that government assimilates the manners and opinions of the community to it. Therefore, a general presumption that rulers will govern well is not a sufficient security.—You are then under a sacred obligation to provide for the safety of your posterity, and would you now basely desert their interests, when by a small share of prudence you may transmit to them a beautiful political patrimony, which will prevent the necessity of their travelling through seas of blood to obtain that, which your wisdom might have secured:—It is a duty you owe likewise to your own reputation, for you have a great name to lose; you are characterised as cautious, prudent and jealous in politics; whence is it therefore, that you are about to precipitate yourselves into a sea of uncertainty, and adopt a system so vague, and which has discarded so many of your valuable rights:—Is it because you do not believe that an American can be a tyrant? If this be the case you rest on a weak basis, Americans are like other men in similar situations, when the manners and opinions of the community are changed by the causes I mentioned before, and your political compact inexplicit, your posterity will find that great power connected with ambition, luxury, and flattery, will as readily produce a Caesar, Caligula, Nero, and Domitian in America, as the same causes did in the Roman empire.

But the next thing to be considered in conformity to my plan, is the first article of this new government, which comprises the erection of the house of representatives and senate, and prescribes their various powers and objects of legislation. The most general objections to the first article, are that biennial elections for representatives are a departure from the safe democratical principles of annual ones—that the number of representatives are too few; that the apportionment and principles of increase are unjust; that no attention has been paid to either the numbers or property in each state in forming the senate; that the mode in which they are appointed and their duration, will lead to the establishment of an aristocracy; that the senate and president are improperly connected, both as to appointments, and the making of treaties, which are to become the supreme law of the land; that the judicial in some measure, to wit, as to the trial of impeachments is placed in the senate a branch of the legislative, and some times a branch of the executive: that Congress have the improper power of making or altering the regulations prescribed by the different legislatures, respecting the time, place, and manner of holding elections for representatives; and the time and manner of choosing senators; that standing armies may be established, and appropriation of money made for their support, for two years; that the militia of the most remote state may be marched into those states situated at the opposite extreme of this continent; that the slave trade, is to all intents and purposes permanently established; and a slavish capitation, or poll-tax, may at any time be levied—these are some of the many evils that will attend the adoption of this government.

But with respect to the first objection, it may be remarked that a well digested democracy has this advantage over all others, to wit, that it affords to many the opportunity to be advanced to the supreme command, and the honors they thereby enjoy fills them with a desire of rendering themselves worthy of them; hence this desire becomes part of their education, is matured in manhood, and produces an ardent affection for their country, and it is the opinion of the great Sidney, and Montesquieu that this is in a great measure produced by annual election of magistrates.

If annual elections were to exist in this government, and learning and information to become more prevalent, you never will want men to execute whatever you could design— Sidney observes *that a well governed state is as fruitful to all good purposes as the seven headed serpent is said to have been in evil; when one head is cut off, many rise up in the place of it.* He remarks further, that *it was also thought, that free cities by frequent elections of magistrates became nurseries of great and able men, every man endeavoring to excel others, that he might be advanced to the honor he had no other title to, than what might arise from his merit, or reputation,* but the framers of this *perfect government,* as it is called, have departed from this democratical principle, and established bi-ennial elections, for the house of representatives, who are to be chosen by the people, and sextennial for the senate, who are to be chosen by the legislatures of the different states, and have given to the executive the unprecedented power of making temporary senators, in case of vacancies, by resignation or otherwise, and so far forth establishing a precedent for virtual representation (though in fact, their original appointment is virtual) thereby influencing the choice of the legislatures, or if they should not be so complaisant as to conform to his appointment—offence will be given to the executive and the temporary members, will appear ridiculous by rejection; this temporary member, during his time of appointment, will of course act by a power derived from the executive, and for, and under his immediate influence.

It is a very important objection to this government, that the representation consists of so few; too few to resist the influence of corruption, and the temptation to treachery, against which all governments ought to take precautions—how guarded you have been on this head, in your own state constitution, and yet the number of senators and representatives proposed for this vast continent, does not equal those of your own state; how great the disparity, if you compare them with the aggregate numbers in the United States. The history of representation in England, from which we have taken our model of legislation, is briefly this, before the institution of legislating by deputies, the whole free part of the community usually met for that purpose, when this became impossible, by the increase of numbers, the community was divided into districts, from each of which was sent such a number of deputies as was a complete representation of the various numbers and orders of citizens within them; but can it be asserted with truth, that six men can be a complete and full representation of the numbers and various orders of the people in this state? Another thing may be suggested against the small number of representatives is, that but few of you will have the chance of sharing even in this branch of the legislature; and that the choice will be confined to a very few; the more complete it is, the better will your interests be preserved, and the greater the opportunity you will have to participate in government, one of the principal securities of a free people; but this subject has been so ably and fully treated by a writer under the signature of Brutus, that I shall content myself with referring you to him thereon, reserving further observations on the other objections I have mentioned, for my future numbers.

"Publius," The Federalist X [James Madison]

Daily Advertiser (New York), November 22, 1787

To the People of the State of New-York.

Among the numerous advantages promised by a well constructed Union, none deserves to be more accurately developed than its tendency to break and control the violence of faction. The friend of popular governments, never finds himself so much alarmed for their character and fate, as when he contemplates their propensity to this dangerous vice. He will not fail therefore to set a due value on any plan which, without violating the principles to which he is attached, provides a proper cure for it. The instability, injustice and confusion introduced into the public councils, have in truth been the mortal diseases under which popular governments have every where perished; as they continue to be the favorite and fruitful topics from which the adversaries to liberty derive their most specious declamations. The valuable improvements made by the American Constitutions on the popular models, both ancient and modern, cannot certainly be too much admired; but it would be an unwarrantable partiality, to contend that they have as effectually obviated the danger on this side as was wished and expected. Complaints are every where heard from our most considerate and virtuous citizens, equally the friends of public and private faith, and of public and personal liberty; that our governments are too unstable; that the public good is disregarded in the conflicts of rival parties; and that measures are too often decided, not according to the rules of justice, and the rights of the minor party; but by the superior force of an interested and over-bearing majority. However anxiously we may wish that these complaints had no foundation, the evidence of known facts will not permit us to deny that they are in some degree true. It will be found indeed, on a candid review of our situation, that

some of the distresses under which we labor, have been erroneously charged on the operation of our governments; but it
will be found, at the same time, that other causes will not
alone account for many of our heaviest misfortunes; and
particularly, for that prevailing and increasing distrust of
public engagements, and alarm for private rights, which are
echoed from one end of the continent to the other. These
must be chiefly, if not wholly, effects of the unsteadiness and
injustice, with which a factious spirit has tainted our public
administration.

By a faction I understand a number of citizens, whether
amounting to a majority or minority of the whole, who are
united and actuated by some common impulse of passion, or
of interest, adverse to the rights of other citizens, or to the
permanent and aggregate interests of the community.

There are two methods of curing the mischiefs of faction:
the one, by removing its causes; the other, by controling its
effects.

There are again two methods of removing the causes of
faction: the one by destroying the liberty which is essential to
its existence; the other, by giving to every citizen the same
opinions, the same passions, and the same interests.

It could never be more truly said than of the first remedy,
that it is worse than the disease. Liberty is to faction, what air
is to fire, an aliment without which it instantly expires. But it
could not be a less folly to abolish liberty, which is essential to
political life, because it nourishes faction, than it would be to
wish the annihilation of air, which is essential to animal life,
because it imparts to fire its destructive agency.

The second expedient is as impracticable, as the first would
be unwise. As long as the reason of man continues fallible,
and he is at liberty to exercise it, different opinions will be
formed. As long as the connection subsists between his reason
and his self-love, his opinions and his passions will have a
reciprocal influence on each other; and the former will be
objects to which the latter will attach themselves. The diversity in the faculties of men from which the rights of property
originate, is not less an insuperable obstacle to a uniformity of
interests. The protection of these faculties is the first object of
Government. From the protection of different and unequal

faculties of acquiring property, the possession of different degrees and kinds of property immediately results: and from the influence of these on the sentiments and views of the respective proprietors, ensues a division of the society into different interests and parties.

The latent causes of faction are thus sown in the nature of man; and we see them every where brought into different degrees of activity, according to the different circumstances of civil society. A zeal for different opinions concerning religion, concerning Government, and many other points, as well of speculation as of practice; an attachment to different leaders ambitiously contending for pre-eminence and power; or to persons of other descriptions whose fortunes have been interesting to the human passions, have in turn divided mankind into parties, inflamed them with mutual animosity, and rendered them much more disposed to vex and oppress each other, than to co-operate for their common good. So strong is this propensity of mankind to fall into mutual animosities, that where no substantial occasion presents itself, the most frivolous and fanciful distinctions have been sufficient to kindle their unfriendly passions, and excite their most violent conflicts. But the most common and durable source of factions, has been the various and unequal distribution of property. Those who hold, and those who are without property, have ever formed distinct interests in society. Those who are creditors, and those who are debtors, fall under a like discrimination. A landed interest, a manufacturing interest, a mercantile interest, a monied interest, with many lesser interests, grow up of necessity in civilized nations, and divide them into different classes, actuated by different sentiments and views. The regulation of these various and interfering interests forms the principal task of modern Legislation, and involves the spirit of party and faction in the necessary and ordinary operations of Government.

No man is allowed to be a judge in his own cause; because his interest would certainly bias his judgment, and, not improbably, corrupt his integrity. With equal, nay with greater reason, a body of men, are unfit to be both judges and parties, at the same time; yet, what are many of the most important acts of legislation, but so many judicial determinations, not indeed concerning the rights of single persons, but concerning the rights of large bodies of citizens; and what are the different classes of legislators, but advocates and parties to the causes which they determine? Is a law proposed concerning private debts? It is a question to which the creditors are parties on one side, and the debtors on the other. Justice ought to hold the balance between them. Yet the parties are and must be themselves the judges; and the most numerous party, or, in other words, the most powerful faction must be expected to prevail. Shall domestic manufactures be encouraged, and in what degree, by restrictions on foreign manufactures? are questions which would be differently decided by the landed and the manufacturing classes; and probably by neither, with a sole regard to justice and the public good. The apportionment of taxes on the various descriptions of property, is an act which seems to require the most exact impartiality; yet there is perhaps no legislative act in which greater opportunity and temptation are given to a predominant party, to trample on the rules of justice. Every shilling with which they over-burden the inferior number, is a shilling saved to their own pockets.

It is in vain to say, that enlightened statesmen will be able to adjust these clashing interests, and render them all subservient to the public good. Enlightened statesmen will not always be at the helm: Nor, in many cases, can such an adjustment be made at all, without taking into view indirect and remote considerations, which will rarely prevail over the immediate interest which one party may find in disregarding the rights of another, or the good of the whole.

The inference to which we are brought, is, that the *causes* of faction cannot be removed; and that relief is only to be sought in the means of controling its *effects*.

If a faction consists of less than a majority, relief is supplied by the republican principle, which enables the majority to defeat its sinister views by regular vote: It may clog the administration, it may convulse the society; but it will be unable to execute and mask its violence under the forms of the Constitution. When a majority is included in a faction, the form of popular government on the other hand enables it to sacrifice to its ruling passion or interest, both the public good and the rights of other citizens. To secure the public good, and private rights, against the danger of such a faction, and at the same time to preserve the spirit and the form of popular government, is then the great object to which our enquiries are directed: Let me add that it is the great desideratum, by which alone this form of government can be rescued from the opprobrium under which it has so long labored, and be recommended to the esteem and adoption of mankind.

By what means is this object attainable? Evidently by one of two only. Either the existence of the same passion or interest in a majority at the same time, must be prevented; or the majority, having such co-existent passion or interest, must be rendered, by their number and local situation, unable to concert and carry into effect schemes of oppression. If the impulse and the opportunity be suffered to coincide, we well know that neither moral nor religious motives can be relied on as an adequate control. They are not found to be such on the injustice and violence of individuals, and lose their efficacy in proportion to the number combined together; that is, in proportion as their efficacy becomes needful.

From this view of the subject, it may be concluded, that a pure Democracy, by which I mean, a Society, consisting of a small number of citizens, who assemble and administer the Government in person, can admit of no cure for the mischiefs of faction. A common passion or interest will, in almost every case, be felt by a majority of the whole; a communication and concert results from the form of Government itself; and there is nothing to check the inducements to sacrifice the weaker party, or an obnoxious individual. Hence it is, that such Democracies have ever been spectacles of turbulence and contention; have ever been found incompatible with personal security, or the rights of property; and have in general been as short in their lives, as they have been violent in their deaths. Theoretic politicians, who have patronized this species of Government, have erroneously supposed, that by reducing mankind to a perfect equality in their political rights, they would, at the same time, be perfectly equalized and assimilated in their possessions, their opinions, and their passions.

A Republic, by which I mean a Government in which the scheme of representation takes place, opens a different prospect, and promises the cure for which we are seeking. Let us examine the points in which it varies from pure Democracy, and we shall comprehend both the nature of the cure, and the efficacy which it must derive from the Union.

The two great points of difference between a Democracy and a Republic are, first, the delegation of the Government, in the latter, to a small number of citizens elected by the rest: secondly, the greater number of citizens, and greater sphere of country, over which the latter may be extended.

The effect of the first difference is, on the one hand to refine and enlarge the public views, by passing them through the medium of a chosen body of citizens, whose wisdom may best discern the true interest of their country, and whose patriotism and love of justice, will be least likely to sacrifice it to temporary or partial considerations. Under such a regulation, it may well happen that the public voice pronounced by the representatives of the people, will be more consonant to the public good, than if pronounced by the people themselves convened for the purpose. On the other hand, the effect may be inverted. Men of factious tempers, of local prejudices, or of sinister designs, may by intrigue, by corruption or by other means, first obtain the suffrages, and then betray the interests of the people. The question resulting is, whether small or extensive Republics are most favorable to the election of proper guardians of the public weal; and it is clearly decided in favor of the latter by two obvious considerations.

In the first place it is to be remarked that however small the Republic may be, the Representatives must be raised to a certain number, in order to guard against the cabals of a few; and that however large it may be, they must be limited to a certain number, in order to guard against the confusion of a multitude. Hence the number of Representatives in the two cases, not being in proportion to that of the Constituents, and being proportionally greatest in the small Republic, it follows, that if the proportion of fit characters, be not less, in the large than in the small Republic, the former will present a greater option, and consequently a greater probability of a fit choice.

In the next place, as each Representative will be chosen by a greater number of citizens in the large than in the small

Republic, it will be more difficult for unworthy candidates to practise with success the vicious arts, by which elections are too often carried; and the suffrages of the people being more free, will be more likely to centre on men who possess the most attractive merit, and the most diffusive and established characters.

It must be confessed, that in this, as in most other cases, there is a mean, on both sides of which inconveniencies will be found to lie. By enlarging too much the number of electors, you render the representative too little acquainted with all their local circumstances and lesser interests; as by reducing it too much, you render him unduly attached to these, and too little fit to comprehend and pursue great and national objects. The Federal Constitution forms a happy combination in this respect; the great and aggregate interests being referred to the national, the local and particular, to the state legislatures.

The other point of difference is, the greater number of citizens and extent of territory which may be brought within the compass of Republican, than of Democratic Government; and it is this circumstance principally which renders factious combinations less to be dreaded in the former, than in the latter. The smaller the society, the fewer probably will be the distinct parties and interests composing it; the fewer the distinct parties and interests, the more frequently will a majority be found of the same party; and the smaller the number of individuals composing a majority, and the smaller the compass within which they are placed, the more easily will they concert and execute their plans of oppression. Extend the sphere, and you take in a greater variety of parties and interests; you make it less probable that a majority of the whole will have a common motive to invade the rights of other citizens; or if such a common motive exists, it will be more difficult for all who feel it to discover their own strength, and to act in unison with each other. Besides other impediments, it may be remarked, that where there is a consciousness of unjust or dishonorable purposes, communication is always checked by distrust, in proportion to the number whose concurrence is necessary.

Hence it clearly appears, that the same advantage, which a

Republic has over a Democracy, in controling the effects of faction, is enjoyed by a large over a small Republic—is enjoyed by the Union over the States composing it. Does this advantage consist in the substitution of Representatives, whose enlightened views and virtuous sentiments render them superior to local prejudices, and to schemes of injustice? It will not be denied, that the Representation of the Union will be most likely to possess these requisite endowments. Does it consist in the greater security afforded by a greater variety of parties, against the event of any one party being able to out-number and oppress the rest? In an equal degree does the encreased variety of parties, comprised within the Union, encrease this security. Does it, in fine, consist in the greater obstacles opposed to the concert and accomplishment of the secret wishes of an unjust and interested majority? Here, again, the extent of the Union gives it the most palpable advantage.

The influence of factious leaders may kindle a flame within their particular States, but will be unable to spread a general conflagration through the other States: a religious sect, may degenerate into a political faction in a part of the Confeder-acy; but the variety of sects dispersed over the entire face of it, must secure the national Councils against any danger from that source: a rage for paper money, for an abolition of debts, for an equal division of property, or for any other improper or wicked project, will be less apt to pervade the whole body of the Union, than a particular member of it; in the same proportion as such a malady is more likely to taint a particular county or district, than an entire State.

In the extent and proper structure of the Union, therefore, we behold a Republican remedy for the diseases most incident to Republican Government. And according to the degree of pleasure and pride, we feel in being Republicans, ought to be our zeal in cherishing the spirit, and supporting the character of Federalists.

"A Countryman" [*Roger Sherman?*] II

New Haven Gazette (Connecticut), November 22, 1787

To the PEOPLE *of* Connecticut.

It is fortunate that you have been but little distressed with that torrent of impertinence and folly, with which the newspaper politicians have overwhelmed many parts of our country.

It is enough that you should have heard, that one party has seriously urged, that we should adopt the *New Constitution* because it has been approved by *Washington* and *Franklin*: and the other, with all the solemnity of apostolic address to *Men, Brethren, Fathers, Friends and Countrymen*, have urged that we should reject, as dangerous, every clause thereof, because that *Washington* is more used to command as a soldier, than to reason as a politician—*Franklin* is *old*—others are *young*—and *Wilson* is *haughty*. You are too well informed to decide by the opinion of others, and too independent to need a caution against undue influence.

Of a very different nature, tho' only one degree better than the other reasoning, is all that sublimity of *nonsense* and *alarm*, that has been thundered against it in every shape of *metaphoric terror*, on the subject of a *bill of rights*, the *liberty of the press, rights of conscience, rights of taxation and election, trials in the vicinity, freedom of speech, trial by jury*, and a *standing army*. These last are undoubtedly important points, much too important to depend on mere paper protection. For, guard such privileges by the strongest expressions, still if you leave the legislative and executive power in the hands of those who are or may be disposed to deprive you of them—you are but slaves. Make an absolute monarch—give him the supreme authority, and guard as much as you will by bills of right, your liberty of the press, and trial by jury;—he will find means either to take them from you, or to render them useless.

The only real security that you can have for all your important rights must be in the nature of your government. If you suffer any man to govern you who is not strongly interested in supporting your privileges, you will certainly lose them. If you are about to trust your liberties with people whom it is necessary to bind by stipulation, that they shall not keep a standing army, your stipulation is not worth even the trouble of writing. No bill of rights ever yet bound the supreme power longer than the *honey moon* of a new married couple, unless the *rulers were interested* in preserving the rights; and in that case they have always been ready enough to declare the rights, and to preserve them when they were declared.—The famous English *Magna Charta* is but an act of parliament, which every subsequent parliament has had just as much constitutional power to repeal and annul, as the parliament which made it had to pass it at first. But the security of the nation has always been, that their government was so formed, that at least *one branch* of their legislature must be strongly interested to preserve the rights of the nation.

You have a bill of rights in Connecticut (i.e.) your legislature many years since enacted that the subjects of this state should enjoy certain privileges. Every assembly since that time, could, by the same authority, enact that the subjects should enjoy none of those privileges; and the only reason that it has not long since been so enacted, is that your legislature were as strongly interested in preserving those rights as any of the subjects; and this is your only security that it shall not be so enacted at the next session of assembly: and it is security enough.

Your General Assembly under your present constitution are supreme. They may keep troops on foot in the most profound peace, if they think proper. They have heretofore abridged the trial by jury in some causes, and they can again in all. They can restrain the press, and may lay the most burdensome taxes if they please, and who can forbid? But still the people are perfectly safe that not one of these events shall take place so long as the members of the General assembly are as much interested, and interested in the same manner as the other subjects.

On examining the new proposed constitution, there can not be a question, but that there is authority enough lodged in the proposed federal Congress, if abused, to do the greatest injury. And it is perfectly idle to object to it, that there is no bill of rights, or to propose to add to it a provision that a trial by jury shall in no case be omitted, or to patch it up by adding a stipulation in favor of the press, or to guard it by removing the paltry objection to the right of Congress to regulate the time and manner of elections.

If you can not prove by the best of all evidence, viz. by the *interest of the rulers*, that this authority will not be abused, or at least that those powers are not more likely to be abused by the Congress, than by those who now have the same powers, you must by no means adopt the constitution:—No, not with all the bills of rights and all the stipulations in favour of the people that can be made.

But if the members of Congress are to be interested just as you and I are, and just as the members of our present legislatures are interested, we shall be just as safe, with even supreme power, (if that were granted) in Congress, as in the General Assembly. If the members of Congress can take no improper step which will not affect them as much as it does us, we need not apprehend that they will usurp authorities not given them to injure that society of which they are a part.

The sole question, (so far as any apprehension of tyranny and oppression is concerned) ought to be, how are Congress formed? how far are the members interested to preserve your rights? how far have you a controul over them?—Decide this, and then all the questions about their power may be dismissed for the amusement of those politicians whose business it is to catch flies, or may occasionally furnish subjects for *George Bryan's* POMPOSITY, or the declamations of *Cato*—*An Old Whig*—*Son of Liberty*—*Brutus*—*Brutus junior*—*An Officer of the Continental Army*,—the more contemptible *Timoleon*—and the residue of that rabble of writers.

"Americanus" [John Stevens, Jr.] II

Daily Advertiser (New York), November 23, 1787

Experience has produced ample conviction in the minds of all of us, that a Federal Government, which admits of an Independent Sovereignty in the States individually, can never be so construed as to command the resources, and bring into action the collective force of the nation. Indeed, had our situation been similar to that of the Swiss Cantons, the inconveniencies of such a confederation would probably not have been greatly felt. Inhabiting a country rough and mountainous throughout; so inaccessible that there can exist no motive to provoke hostilities either with their neighbours or amongst themselves—from poverty and remoteness from navigation rendered incapable of ever becoming commercial: Amongst a people thus circumstanced, there can happen but few occasions for national exertion. How widely does the country we possess differ from this—extending a length of two thousand miles along a sea coast, indented by innumerable harbours, and comprehending infinite variety with respect to soil, climate and product. From the natural consequences of such a situation, we feel at every turn the most pressing necessity for the vigorous and unremitted exertions of a National Government. The Convention have certainly acted wisely in throwing the Confederation totally aside, and erecting in its place an entire new fabric. This was a decisive boldness I had not looked for. I was therefore the more strongly impressed in its favor, when, for the first time, I saw this Constitution. The writings of those gentlemen in opposition to it, whatever effects they may have produced on others, have hitherto tended only to fix more firmly the sentiments I had imbibed in the first instance. For my own part, I must say, it has pleased me much, that some of these champions have shown themselves *openly* in the field of controversy—had they remained altogether *under cover*, and kept up only a sort of Indian fight, we must have remained in a great measure ignorant of their total strength. I have, however, a strong suspicion that Cato has nearly exhausted his quiver, and will be put to some difficulty to proceed without renewing the attack in the same quarter, or in other words, repeating the same story over again.

In his last number, he has urged his objections against "the Executive branch of this new System." The first paragraph of the 1st sect. of the 2d article, is thus expressed. "The Executive power shall be vested in a President of the United States of America. He shall hold his office during the term of four years, and, together with the Vice-President, chosen for the same term, be elected as follows." "This inexplicitness," he tells us, "perhaps may lead to an establishment for life." Cato must certainly be hard pushed for argument, when he can advance so paltry a cavil as this. Without a total change of sentiment in the majority of the people of these States, such "an establishment for life" could never be effected, though the words of the above quoted paragraph were much more inexplicit, than Cato pretends they are at present.

The comparison which he has thought to his purpose to institute between a BRITISH MONARCH and a PRESIDENT under the Constitution is surely unworthy of attention. It must excite ridicule and contempt in every man when he considers on one side, the dreadful catalogue of unnecessary, but dangerous, prerogatives, which, in the British Government, is vested in the Crown; and, on the other side, takes a view of the powers with which this Constitution has cloathed the President. Imperial dignity, and hereditary succession—constituting an independent branch of the Legislature—the creation of Peers and distribution of titles and dignities—the supremacy of a national church—the appointment of Arch-bishops and Bishops—the power of convening, proroguing, and dissolving the Parliament—the fundamental maxim that the King can do no wrong—to be above the reach of all Courts of law—to be accountable to no power whatever in the nation—his person to be sacred and inviolable—all these unnecessary, but dangerous prerogatives, independent of many others, such as the sole power of making war and peace—making treaties, leagues and alliances—the collection, management and expenditure of an immense revenue, deposited annually in the Royal Exchequer—with the appointment of an almost innumerable tribe of officers, dependent thereon—all these prerogatives, besides a great many more, which it is unnecessary to detail here, (none of all which are vested in the President) put together, form an accumulation of power of immense magnitude; but which, it seems, are only "immaterial incidents."

Let the arrangement and distribution of the executive branch, be what it may, whether it be split and divided into a variety of distinct parts—or put into commission and executed by a body of ten or twenty members, this however I will aver, and challenge Cato to gainsay it if he can, that every power which by this Constitution is vested in a President, is *indispensably necessary* to good Government, and must of consequence be entrusted somewhere. If Cato therefore, in the place of forming the above idle and ridiculous comparison, had pointed out to us in what manner the powers of the executive branch could have been modified, and distributed to more advantage, and with greater security to liberty, he had certainly done more to the purpose.

But you do not, Cato, deal fairly either with us or your friend Montesquieu. You institute a comparison between a King of England, and a President, and because you find that some of the powers necessarily vested in this President, and some of the prerogatives of that King are alike, you place them on a footing, and talk "of a President possessing the powers of a Monarch." But admitting that a President, and a King of England, were as like as two peas; this, however, will by no means serve your turn. Montesquieu is here speaking expressly of the Court of an absolute Monarch. What similitude Cato's ingenuity may discover between a President, and a King of Spain, or a Grand Monarch, I can form no conjecture.

But he quarrels too with the revisory power vested in the President. Of what strange heterogeneous materials are we poor mortals compounded! What Cato here reprobates, I must confess I esteem as one of the most excellent things in the Constitution.

But as Cato is so fond of Montesquieu as to quote him at every turn, and has attempted to establish his positions as "irrefragable axioms," it is surprising to me that he has never met, in the course of his reading in this favorite author, an authority exactly in point. With a view therefore, of easing his apprehensions respecting the dangerous powers of a President, I shall here transcribe it. "The Executive power ought to be in the hands of a Monarch, because this branch of Government having need of dispatch, is better administered by one than by many." He is here speaking of the Constitution of England, which he afterwards tells us is "the best that could possibly be imagined by men."

"The safety of the people in a Republic depends on the share or proportion they have in the Government." The justness of this proportion appears at first view so obvious, that the mind gives it its assent without a thought of examination. But notwithstanding this plausible appearance, it happens a little unfortunately for this pretty theory, that experience has afforded us the most ample proofs that the people themselves are totally unfit for the exercise of *any* of the powers of Government. They are obliged from necessity, to confide in others for the execution of these important trusts. Indeed good Government depends altogether on the proper delegation of the several powers thereof. I might here, after the example of our worthy Minister at the Court of Great-Britain, cause all the Republican Governments that have ever existed in the world, whether ancient or modern, to pass in review before my gentle readers. But in pity to them I shall refrain. I will resist the temptation though great, and forego this glorious opportunity (which may perhaps never offer again during the course of a long life) of displaying an immensity of erudition. Suffice it to say, that on such an investigation it would be found invariably, that exactly in proportion to "the share the people have in the Government," has anarchy, violence, and the most shocking outrages and enormities of every kind prevailed. All power however in a free Government, must be derived originally from the people. *But of themselves they are absolutely incapable of the exercise of any.* This is an "axiom," I will venture to assert, much more "irrefragable" than any Cato has yet thought fit to give us from Montesquieu's spirit of laws, but which, by the by, if it had suited his purpose, he might have found there.

What Montesquieu has said of Harrington may in some measure be applied to Cato and his coadjutors. "Harrington," says he, "in his Oceana, has also enquired into the utmost degree of liberty to which the *Constitution* of a State may be carried. But of him indeed it may be said, that for want of *knowing* the nature of *real* liberty, he busied himself in the pursuit of an *imaginary* one; and that he built a Chalcedon, tho' he had a Byzantium before his eyes."

Louis Guillaume Otto to Comte de Montmorin

New York, November 26, 1787

I received Dispatch No. 4. which You did me the honor of writing to me on the 31. of last August. The indulgence with which You deigned to receive my last reports can only encourage me to redouble my zeal and diligence.

The debates, My Lord, for and against the new Constitution continue to absorb public attention and while the individual States are preparing to call conventions in order to adopt or reject this new plan, the two parties abuse each other in the public papers with a rancor which sometimes does not even spare insults and personal invectives. As in these sorts of political commotions, the men and the issues usually disguise themselves so as to become unrecognizable, the partisans of the innovation are called *Federalists* and the others more commonly *Whigs*, although neither of these names has a direct relation to the object in question. This spirit of argument is even pushed to intolerance in regard to foreigners and they absolutely want us to take a side for or against the new Constitution. Some politicians trying to be shrewder than others have even suggested that this Constitution was bad since it was approved by foreign Ministers. According to one side Despotism will be the necessary consequence of the proposed Constitution; according to the others the united States will reach the summit of glory and power with this same Constitution. Indifferent Spectators agree that the new form of Government, well executed will be able to produce good results; but they also think that if the states really had the desire to be united the present Confederation would be adequate for all their needs. Meanwhile they are unable to conceal that after having excited this general ferment there is no longer a means to stop it, that the old edifice is almost destroyed, and that any fabric whatsoever must be substituted for it. In effect it was impossible to carry out a more violent coup to the authority of Congress, than in saying to all America, to the entire Universe, that this body is inadequate to the needs of the Confederation and that the united States have become the laughingstock of all the powers. This principle repeated over and over by all the Innovators seems as false as their spirits are excited; the united States held the place among nations which their youth and means assigned them; they are neither rich enough, populated enough, nor well established enough to appear with more luster and perhaps one ought to reproach them only for the impatience of anticipating their future grandeur.

The new Congress is not yet formed, My Lord; the delegates are arriving slowly and their deliberations will not be very important before the different States have given their opinions on the proposed Government. The task of this Assembly will then become very delicate; it will have to weigh without prejudice the opinions and modifications of the individual States, to judge if nine Members of the Confederation have indeed consented to it and to fix the time of the Elections for the new sovereign body. This process can only take place towards the middle of the following year if it can however be hoped to gather the vote of nine States.

That of Pensylvania, My Lord, was the most eager to elect Delegates to examine the Constitution. The Federalists there have a majority of two to one and although their deliberations have not yet ended it can almost be foreseen that the Constitution will be adopted. Other States are putting more circumspection and calmness into their proceedings; several Counties have even specifically recommended to their Delegates to examine the new plan in the greatest detail and not to allow themselves to be carried away by party spirit always detrimental in general affairs.

Until now only Virginia has articulated plausible reasons not to accede to it. One of the first measures proposed by the new Government would probably be the writing of a navigation act. The aim of this act could only be to give Americans a special advantage and perhaps an exclusive right in the exportation of tobacco and as the Virginians are hardly sailors they would find themselves entirely at the mercy of the New

England States which have been up to now the Peddlers for the Southerners. The competition of foreign nations would be banished from the new system and tobacco being much more susceptible of being taxed than commodities from other States, Virginia would certainly pay the largest portion of public revenue. It seems to be in the interest of Virginia to attract all the commercial nations to its ports, but it is important to the Northern States to insist on an exclusive navigation and they would almost always be in a large majority in the future Congress.

Be that as it may, My Lord, it still appears that only a foreign stimulus can restore energy to the federal Government, in whatever form is considered appropriate to reproduce it. The assessment of taxes and duties will be the stumbling block that will make the most well thought out plans fail unless the sudden appearance of an Enemy and an imminent danger rekindles that spirit of unanimity that formerly produced such grand results. But as this revolution is not absolutely necessary it would be unfortunate to buy possible advantages with real calamities.

"Brutus" IV

New York Journal, November 29, 1787

To *the* PEOPLE *of the State of* NEW-YORK.

There can be no free government where the people are not possessed of the power of making the laws by which they are governed, either in their own persons, or by others substituted in their stead.

Experience has taught mankind, that legislation by representatives is the most eligible, and the only practicable mode in which the people of any country can exercise this right, either prudently or beneficially. But then, it is a matter of the highest importance, in forming this representation, that it be so constituted as to be capable of understanding the true interests of the society for which it acts, and so disposed as to pursue the good and happiness of the people as its ultimate end. The object of every free government is the public good, and all lesser interests yield to it. That of every tyrannical government, is the happiness and aggrandisement of one, or a few, and to this the public felicity, and every other interest must submit.—The reason of this difference in these governments is obvious. The first is so constituted as to collect the views and wishes of the whole people in that of their rulers, while the latter is so framed as to separate the interests of the governors from that of the governed. The principle of self love, therefore, that will influence the one to promote the good of the whole, will prompt the other to follow its own private advantage. The great art, therefore, in forming a good constitution, appears to be this, so to frame it, as that those to whom the power is committed shall be subject to the same feelings, and aim at the same objects as the people do, who transfer to them their authority. There is no possible way to effect this but by an equal, full and fair representation; this, therefore, is the great desideratum in politics. However fair an appearance any government may make, though it may possess a thousand plausible articles and be decorated with ever so many ornaments, yet if it is deficient in this essential principle of a full and just representation of the people, it will be only like a painted sepulcher—For, without this it cannot be a free government; let the administration of it be good or ill, it still will be a government, not according to the will of the people, but according to the will of a few.

To test this new constitution then, by this principle, is of the last importance—It is to bring it to the touch-stone of national liberty, and I hope I shall be excused, if, in this paper, I pursue the subject commenced in my last number, to wit, the necessity of an equal and full representation in the legislature.—In that, I showed that it was not equal, because the smallest states are to send the same number of members to the senate as the largest, and, because the slaves, who afford neither aid or defence to the government, are to encrease the proportion of members. To prove that it was not a just or adequate representation, it was urged, that so small a number could not resemble the people, or possess their sentiments and dispositions. That the choice of members would commonly fall upon the rich and great, while the middling class of the community would be excluded. That in so small a representation there was no security against bribery and corruption.

The small number which is to compose this legislature, will not only expose it to the danger of that kind of corruption, and undue influence, which will arise from the gift of places of honor and emolument, or the more direct one of bribery, but it will also subject it to another kind of influence no less fatal to the liberties of the people, though it be not so flagrantly repugnant to the principles of rectitude. It is not to be expected that a legislature will be found in any country that will not have some of its members, who will pursue their private ends, and for which they will sacrifice the public good. Men of this character are, generally, artful and designing, and frequently possess brilliant talents and abilities; they commonly act in concert, and agree to share the spoils of their country among them; they will keep their object ever in view, and follow it with constancy. To effect their purpose, they will assume any shape, and, Proteus like, mould themselves into any form—where they find members proof against direct bribery or gifts of offices, they will endeavor to mislead their minds by specious and false reasoning, to impose upon their unsuspecting honesty by an affectation of zeal for the public good; they will form juntos, and hold out-door meetings; they will operate upon the good nature of their opponents, by a thousand little attentions, and seize them into compliance by the earnestness of solicitation. Those who are acquainted with the manner of conducting business in public assemblies, know how prevalent art and address are in carrying a measure, even over men of the best intentions, and of good understanding. The firmest security against this kind of improper and dangerous influence, as well as all other, is a strong and numerous representation: in such a house of assembly, so great a number must be gained over, before the private views of individuals could be gratified that there could be scarce a hope of success. But in the fœderal assembly, seventeen men are all that is necessary to pass a law. It is probable, it will seldom happen that more than twenty-five will be requisite to form a majority, when it is considered what a number of places of honor and emolument will be in the gift of the executive, the powerful influence that great and designing men have over the honest and unsuspecting, by their art and address, their soothing manners and civilities, and their cringing flattery, joined with their affected patriotism; when these different species of influence are combined, it is scarcely to be hoped that a legislature, composed of so small a number, as the one proposed by the new constitution, will long resist their force. A farther objection against the feebleness of the representation is, that it will not possess the confidence of the people. The execution of the laws in a free government must rest on this confidence, and this must be founded on the good opinion they entertain of the framers of the laws. Every government must be supported, either by the people having such an attachment to it, as to be ready, when called upon, to support it, or by a force at the command of the government, to compel obedience. The latter mode destroys every idea of a free government; for the same force that may be employed to compel obedience to good laws, might, and probably would be used to wrest from the people their constitutional liberties.—Whether it is practicable to have a representation for the whole union sufficiently numerous to obtain that confidence which is necessary for the purpose of internal taxation, and other powers to which this proposed government extends, is an important question. I am clearly of opinion, it is not, and therefore I have stated this in my first number, as one of the reasons against going into so an entire consolidation of the states—one of the most capital errors in the system, is that of extending the powers of the fœderal government to objects to which it is not adequate, which it cannot exercise without endangering public liberty, and which it is not necessary they should possess, in order to preserve the union and manage our national concerns; of this, however, I shall treat more fully in some future paper—But, however this may be, certain it is, that the representation in the legislature is not so formed as to give reasonable ground for public trust.

In order for the people safely to repose themselves on their rulers, they should not only be of their own choice. But it is requisite they should be acquainted with their abilities to manage the public concerns with wisdom. They should be satisfied that those who represent them are men of integrity, who will pursue the good of the community with fidelity; and will not be turned aside from their duty by private interest, or corrupted by undue influence; and that they will have such a zeal for the good of those whom they represent, as to excite them to be deligent in their service; but it is impossible the people of the United States should have sufficient knowledge of their representatives, when the numbers are so few, to acquire any rational satisfaction on either of these points. The people of this state will have very little acquaintance with those who may be chosen to represent them; a great part of them will, probably, not know the characters of their own members, much less that of a majority of those who will compose the fœderal assembly; they will consist of men, whose names they have never heard, and of whose talents and regard for the public good, they are total strangers to; and they will have no persons so immediately of their choice so near them, of their neighbours and of their own rank in life, that they can feel themselves secure in trusting their interests in their hands. The representatives of the people cannot, as they now do, after they have passed laws, mix with the people, and explain to them the motives which induced the adoption of any measure, point out its utility, and remove objections or silence unreasonable clamours against it.—The number will be so small that but a very few of the most sensible and respectable yeomanry of the country can ever have any knowledge of them: being so far removed from the people, their station will be elevated and important, and they will be considered as ambitious and designing. They will not be viewed by the people as part of themselves, but as a body distinct from them, and having separate interests to pursue; the consequence will be, that a perpetual jealousy will exist in the minds of the people against them; their conduct will be narrowly watched; their measures scrutinized; and their laws opposed, evaded, or reluctantly obeyed. This is natural, and exactly corresponds with the conduct of individuals towards those in whose hands they intrust important concerns. If the person confided in, be a neighbour with whom his employer is intimately acquainted, whose talents, he knows, are sufficient to manage the business with which he is charged, his honesty and fidelity unsuspected, and his friendship and zeal for the service of his principal unquestionable, he will commit his affairs into his hands with unreserved confidence, and feel himself secure; all the transactions of the agent will meet with the most favorable construction, and the measures he takes will give satisfaction. But, if the person employed be a stranger, whom he has never seen, and whose character for ability or fidelity he cannot fully learn—If he is constrained to choose him, because it was not in his power to procure one more agreeable to his wishes, he will trust him with caution, and be suspicious of all his conduct.

If then this government should not derive support from the good will of the people, it must be executed by force, or not executed at all; either case would lead to the total destruction of liberty.—The convention seemed aware of this, and have therefore provided for calling out the militia to execute the laws of the union. If this system was so framed as to command that respect from the people, which every good free government will obtain, this provision was unnecessary—the people would support the civil magistrate. This power is a novel one, in free governments—these have depended for the execution of the laws on the Posse Comitatus, and never raised an idea, that the people would refuse to aid the civil magistrate in executing those laws they themselves had made. I shall now dismiss the subject of the incompetency of the representation, and proceed, as I promised, to shew, that, impotent as it is, the people have no security that they will enjoy the exercise of the right of electing this assembly, which, at best, can be considered but as the shadow of representation.

By section 4, article 1, the Congress are authorized, at any time, by law, to make, or alter, regulations respecting the time, place, and manner of holding elections for senators and representatives, except as to the places of choosing senators. By this clause the right of election itself, is, in a great measure, transferred from the people to their rulers.—One would think, that if any thing was necessary to be made a fundamental article of the original compact, it would be, that of fixing the branches of the legislature, so as to put it out of its power to alter itself by modifying the election of its own members at will and pleasure. When a people once resign the privilege of a fair election, they clearly have none left worth contending for.

It is clear that, under this article, the fœderal legislature may institute such rules respecting elections as to lead to the choice of one description of men. The weakness of the representation, tends but too certainly to confer on the rich and *well-born*, all honours; but the power granted in this article, may be so exercised, as to secure it almost beyond a possibility of controul. The proposed Congress may make the whole state one district, and direct, that the capital (the city of New-York, for instance) shall be the place for holding the election; the consequence would be, that none but men of the most elevated rank in society would attend, and they would as certainly choose men of their own class; as it is true what the *Apostle Paul* saith, that "no man ever yet hated his own flesh, but nourisheth and cherisheth it."—They may declare that those members who have the greatest number of votes, shall be considered as duly elected; the consequence would be that the people, who are dispersed in the interior parts of the state, would give their votes for a variety of candidates, while any order, or profession, residing in populous places, by uniting their interests, might procure whom they pleased to be chosen—and by this means the representatives of the state may be elected by one tenth part of the people who actually vote. This may be effected constitutionally, and by one of those silent operations which frequently takes place without being noticed, but which often produces such changes as entirely to alter a government, subvert a free constitution, and rivet the chains on a free people before they perceive they are forged. Had the power of regulating elections been left under the direction of the state legislatures, where the people are not only nominally but substantially represented, it would have been secure; but if it was taken out of their hands, it surely ought to have been fixed on such a basis as to have put it out of the power of the fœderal legislature to deprive the people of it by law. Provision should have been made for marking out the states into districts, and for choosing, by a majority of votes, a person out of each of them of permanent property and residence in the district which he was to represent.

If the people of America will submit to a constitution that will vest in the hands of any body of men a right to deprive them by law of the privilege of a fair election, they will submit to almost any thing. Reasoning with them will be in vain, they must be left until they are brought to reflection by feeling oppression—they will then have to wrest from their oppressors, by a strong hand, that which they now possess, and which they may retain if they will exercise but a moderate share of prudence and firmness.

I know it is said that the dangers apprehended from this clause are merely imaginary, that the proposed general legislature will be disposed to regulate elections upon proper principles, and to use their power with discretion, and to promote the public good. On this, I would observe, that constitutions are not so necessary to regulate the conduct of good rulers as to restrain that of bad ones.—Wise and good men will exercise power so as to promote the public happiness under any form of government. If we are to take it for granted, that those who administer the government under this system, will always pay proper attention to the rights and interests of the people, nothing more was necessary than to say who should be invested with the powers of government, and leave them to exercise it at will and pleasure. Men are apt to be deceived both with respect to their own dispositions and those of others. Though this truth is proved by almost every page of the history of nations, to wit, that power, lodged in the hands of rulers to be used at discretion, is almost always exercised to the oppression of the people, and the aggrandizement of themselves; yet most men think if it was lodged in their hands they would not employ it in this manner.—Thus when the prophet *Elisha* told *Hazael*, "I know the evil that thou wilt do unto the children of Israel; their strong holds wilt thou set on fire, and their young men, wilt thou slay with the sword, and wilt dash their children, and rip up their women with child." Hazael had no idea that he ever should be guilty of such horrid cruelty, and said to the prophet, "Is thy servant a dog that he should do this great thing." Elisha, answered, "The Lord hath shewed me that thou shalt be king of Syria." The event proved, that Hazael only wanted an opportunity to perpetrate these enormities without restraint, and he had a disposition to do them, though he himself knew it not.

"A REVOLUTION WHICH HAS NO PARALLEL IN THE ANNALS OF HUMAN SOCIETY"

"Publius," The Federalist XIV
[James Madison]

New-York Packet, November 30, 1787

To the People of the State of New-York.

We have seen the necessity of the union as our bulwark against foreign danger, as the conservator of peace among ourselves, as the guardian of our commerce and other common interests, as the only substitute for those military establishments which have subverted the liberties of the old world; and as the proper antidote for the diseases of faction, which have proved fatal to other popular governments, and of which alarming symptoms have been betrayed by our own. All that remains, within this branch of our enquiries, is to take notice of an objection, that may be drawn from the great extent of country which the union embraces. A few observations on this subject will be the more proper, as it is perceived that the adversaries of the new constitution are availing themselves of a prevailing prejudice, with regard to the practicable sphere of republican administration, in order to supply by imaginary difficulties, the want of those solid objections, which they endeavor in vain to find.

The error which limits Republican Government to a narrow district, has been unfolded and refuted in preceding papers. I remark here only, that it seems to owe its rise and prevalence, chiefly to the confounding of a republic with a democracy: And applying to the former reasonings drawn from the nature of the latter. The true distinction between these forms was also adverted to on a former occasion. It is, that in a democracy, the people meet and exercise the government in person; in a republic they assemble and administer it by their representatives and agents. A democracy consequently will be confined to a small spot. A republic may be extended over a large region.

To this accidental source of the error may be added the

artifice of some celebrated authors, whose writings have had a great share in forming the modern standard of political opinions. Being subjects either of an absolute, or limited monarchy, they have endeavored to heighten the advantages or palliate the evils of those forms; by placing in comparison with them, the vices and defects of the republican, and by citing as specimens of the latter, the turbulent democracies of ancient Greece, and modern Italy. Under the confusion of names, it has been an easy task to transfer to a republic, observations applicable to a democracy only, and among others, the observation that it can never be established but among a small number of people, living within a small compass of territory.

Such a fallacy may have been the less perceived as most of the governments of antiquity were of the democratic species; and even in modern Europe, to which we owe the great principle of representation, no example is seen of a government wholly popular, and founded at the same time wholly on that principle. If Europe has the merit of discovering this great mechanical power in government, by the simple agency of which, the will of the largest political body may be concentered, and its force directed to any object, which the public good requires; America can claim the merit of making the discovery the basis of unmixed and extensive republics. It is only to be lamented, that any of her citizens should wish to deprive her of the additional merit of displaying its full efficacy on the establishment of the comprehensive system now under her consideration.

As the natural limit of a democracy is that distance from the central point, which will just permit the most remote citizens to assemble as often as their public functions demand; and will include no greater number than can join in those functions; so the natural limit of a republic is that distance from the center, which will barely allow the representatives of the people to meet as often as may be necessary for the administration of public affairs. Can it be said, that the limits of the United States exceed this distance? It will not be said by those who recollect that the Atlantic coast is the longest side of the union; that during the term of thirteen years, the representatives of the States have been almost continually assembled;

and that the members from the most distant States are not chargeable with greater intermissions of attendance, than those from the States in the neighbourhood of Congress.

That we may form a juster estimate with regard to this interesting subject, let us resort to the actual dimensions of the union. The limits as fixed by the treaty of peace are on the east the Atlantic, on the south the latitude of thirty-one degrees, on the west the Missisippi, and on the north an irregular line running in some instances beyond the forty-fifth degree, in others falling as low as the forty-second. The southern shore of Lake Erie lies below that latitude. Computing the distance between the thirty-one and forty-five degrees, it amounts to nine hundred and seventy-three common miles; computing it from thirty-one to forty-two degrees to seven hundred, sixty four miles and an half. Taking the mean for the distance, the amount will be eight hundred, sixty-eight miles and three-fourths. The mean distance from the Atlantic to the Missisippi does not probably exceed seven hundred and fifty miles. On a comparison of this extent, with that of several countries in Europe, the practicability of rendering our system commensurate to it, appears to be demonstratable. It is not a great deal larger than Germany, where a Diet representing the whole empire is continually assembled; or than Poland before the late dismemberment, where another national Diet was the depository of the supreme power. Passing by France and Spain, we find that in Great Britain, inferior as it may be in size, the representatives of the northern extremity of the island, have as far to travel to the national Council, as will be required of those of the most remote parts of the union.

Favorable as this view of the subject may be, some observations remain which will place it in a light still more satisfactory.

In the first place it is to be remembered, that the general government is not to be charged with the whole power of making and administering laws. Its jurisdiction is limited to certain enumerated objects, which concern all the members of the republic, but which are not to be attained by the separate provisions of any. The subordinate governments which can extend their care to all those other objects, which can be separately provided for, will retain their due authority and activity. Were it proposed by the plan of the Convention to abolish the governments of the particular States, its adversaries would have some ground for their objection, though it would not be difficult to shew that if they were abolished, the general government would be compelled by the principle of self-preservation, to reinstate them in their proper jurisdiction.

A second observation to be made is, that the immediate objects of the Fœderal Constitution is to secure the union of the Thirteen Primitive States, which we know to be practicable; and to add to them such other States, as may arise in their own bosoms or in their neighbourhoods, which we cannot doubt to be equally practicable. The arrangements that may be necessary for those angles and fractions of our territory, which lie on our north western frontier, must be left to those whom further discoveries and experience will render more equal to the task.

Let it be remarked in the third place, that the intercourse throughout the union will be daily facilitated by new improvements. Roads will every where be shortened, and kept in better order; accommodations for travellers will be multiplied and meliorated; and interior navigation on our eastern side will be opened throughout, or nearly throughout the whole extent of the Thirteen States. The communication between the western and Atlantic districts, and between different parts of each, will be rendered more and more easy by those numerous canals with which the beneficence of nature has intersected our country, and which art finds it so little difficult to connect and complete.

A fourth and still more important consideration is, that as almost every State will on one side or other, be a frontier, and will thus find in a regard to its safety, an inducement to make some sacrifices for the sake of the general protection; so the States which lie at the greatest distance from the heart of the union, and which of course may partake least of the ordinary circulation of its benefits, will be at the same time immediately contiguous to foreign nations, and will consequently stand on particular occasions, in greatest need of its strength and resources. It may be inconvenient for Georgia or the States forming our western or north eastern borders to send their representatives to the seat of government, but they would find it more so to struggle alone against an invading enemy, or even to support alone the whole expence of those precautions, which may be dictated by the neighbourhood of continual danger. If they should derive less benefit therefore from the union in some respects, than the less distant States, they will derive greater benefit from it in other respects, and thus the proper equilibrium will be maintained throughout.

I submit to you my fellow citizens, these considerations, in full confidence that the good sense which has so often marked your decisions, will allow them their due weight and effect; and that you will never suffer difficulties, however formidable in appearance or however fashionable the error on which they may be founded, to drive you into the gloomy and perilous scene into which the advocates for disunion would conduct you. Hearken not to the unnatural voice which tells you that the people of America, knit together as they are by so many chords of affection, can no longer live together as members of the same family; can no longer continue the mutual guardians of their mutual happiness; can no longer be fellow citizens of one great respectable and flourishing empire. Hearken not to the voice which petulantly tells you that the form of government recommended for your adoption is a novelty in the political world; that it has never yet had a place in the theories of the wildest projectors; that it rashly attempts what it is impossible to accomplish. No my countrymen, shut your ears against this unhallowed language. Shut your hearts against the poison which it conveys; the kindred blood which flows in the veins of American citizens, the mingled blood which they have shed in defence of their sacred rights, consecrate their union, and excite horror at the idea of their becoming aliens, rivals, enemies. And if novelties are to be shunned, believe me the most alarming of all novelties, the most wild of all projects, the most rash of all attempts, is that of rending us in pieces, in order to preserve our liberties and promote our happiness. But why is the experiment of an extended republic to be rejected merely because it may comprise what is new? Is it not the glory of the people of America, that whilst they have paid a decent regard to the opinions of former times and other nations, they have not suffered a blind veneration for antiquity, for custom, or for names, to overrule the suggestions of their own good sense, the knowledge of their own situation, and the lessons of their own experience? To this manly spirit, posterity will be indebted for the possession, and the world for the example of the numerous innovations displayed on the American theatre, in favor of private rights and public happiness. Had no important step been taken by the leaders of the revolution for which a precedent could not be discovered, no government established of which an exact model did not present itself, the people of the United States might, at this moment, have been numbered among the melancholy victims of misguided councils, must at best have been labouring under the weight of some of those forms which have crushed the liberties of the rest of mankind. Happily for America, happily we trust for the whole human race, they pursued a new and more noble course. They accomplished a revolution which has no parallel in the annals of human society: They reared the fabrics of governments which have no model on the face of the globe. They formed the design of a great confederacy, which it is incumbent on their successors to improve and perpetuate. If their works betray imperfections, we wonder at the fewness of them. If they erred most in the structure of the union; this was the work most difficult to be executed; this is the work which has been new modelled by the act of your Convention, and it is that act on which you are now to deliberate and to decide.

"Americanus" [*John Stevens, Jr.*] *III*

Daily Advertiser (New York), November 30, 1787

"It is natural for a Republic to have only a small territory." It may be thought by some an unpardonable piece of temerity in me to deny the truth of this maxim of the celebrated Civilian, in so decisive a tone as I have ventured to do in a former paper. To satisfy those therefore, whose delicacy may be hurt on this occasion, I hope I shall be able before I finish this paper to bring about a perfect reconciliation between the Baron and myself; and thus deprive Cato of the assistance of this powerful auxiliary, on this occasion at least. It is manifest from a variety of passages, that Montesquieu's idea of a Republic, was a Government in which the collective body of the people, as in Democracy, or of the nobles, as in Aristocracy, possessed a share in the management of public affairs: Thus he tells us "the people in whom the supreme power resides ought to have the management of every thing within their reach." "It is likewise a fundamental law in Democracies, that the people should have the sole power to enact laws." It is obvious that to collect the suffrages of a numerous people, scattered over a wide extent of country on every law, on every public measure, would be utterly impracticable. According therefore to his idea of a Republican Government, this maxim of his, that a Republic should be confined to a small territory, is certainly a very just one. Should I be able to prove that the Governments of these States are founded on principles totally different from those which Montesquieu here had in view, it will then be manifest that Cato has lugged him into a controversy in which he is no ways concerned.

The Republics of antiquity were chiefly Democratic, those of modern date are chiefly Aristocratic. As to Aristocracies we have nothing to do with them. But let us enquire a little into the nature and genius of the ancient Republics of Greece and Rome. Cato's maxim, "that the safety of the people in a

Republic depends on the share or proportion they have in the Government," seem to have been deemed by them indispensibly necessary; indeed, as they had no idea of appointing representatives to legislate for them, they had no other alternative; either the people collectively must retain to themselves a voice in the management of public affairs, or all pretensions to liberty must be resigned. To obviate the natural tendency of this radical defect in the frame of their Governments, they were under an absolute necessity of recurring to violent methods. To support these wretched institutions, the laws of nature herself were subverted. The life of a citizen was one continued effort of self-denial and restraint. Every social passion—all the finer feelings of the heart—the tender ties of parent and child—every enjoyment, whether of sentiment or of sense—every thing in short which renders life desirable, was relinquished. The Romans did not carry this system of self-denial to that extreme as was done by some of the Grecian States. They found however that a rigid attention to manners was indispensibly necessary. Magistrates were appointed for the express purpose of inspecting into the lives and conduct of every citizen—the public good superceded every consideration of a private nature—fathers condemned their own sons to the axe. Let it not be thought however that this exalted degree of patriotism—this rigid system of mortification and self-denial was the effect of choice; no! far from it! it was necessity that imposed it on them.—This magnanimous people saw plainly that their safety depended upon keeping up this austerity of manners. As from the very nature of this sort of Government there can be no regular checks established for preventing the abuse of power, the people are in a great measure constrained to rely on the patriotism and personal virtue of those citizens who compose the Government.

The Grecians and Romans have however infinite merit in subjecting themselves to so severe a discipline, in foregoing so many of the blessings and enjoyments of this life, for the sake of liberty.

The history of these States affords us very striking instances of the astonishing force of this passion of the human heart, when man is placed in a situation proper for displaying it.

Without a due attention to these distinctive properties of the Republics of antiquity, we cannot form an adequate idea of the immense advantages of a representative legislature. The people of Rome, of Sparta, &c. were obliged to keep a constant eye on the conduct of their rulers for this reason, and that they might be enabled to exercise their right of a personal vote on public affairs, it was absolutely necessary that the citizens be confined within a small compass.

But if matters can be so ordered, that by appointing Representatives, the people can have the business of the State transacted in a better manner than they can possibly do it themselves, there is then no determining what may be the extent of the state. Thus it will be found that the Government of the most extensive State of the Union, though greater perhaps than all the States of Greece put together, may be administered with infinitely more care and safety than was any one of them, though comprehended within the limits of a few square miles.

The major part of mankind are slaves to sound—the writings of a great man, who has distinguished himself in any of the walks of science, in a short time become "irrefragable axioms." Thus, thro' the indolence and inattention of some, and the knavery of others, error becomes at length so firmly established as to baffle, for a long time, the assaults of philosophy and truth.

And thus it is, that with those who suffer themselves to be carried away by a name, and attend not to things, the application Cato makes of Montesquieu's maxim to the Government of these States, would pass currently and without opposition. But this would be to sacrifice sense to sound with a vengeance.

The political institutions we have contrived and adopted in this new world differ as widely from the republics of the old, whether antient or modern, as does a well constructed edifice, where elegance and utility unite and harmonize, differ from a huge mishapen pile reared by Gothic ignorance and barbarity.

I have already remarked, that a Republic confined to a small territory, must, from its own nature, be incident to great inconvenience. Faction, instability, and frequent revolutions, are inherent properties. Besides, that its weakness exposes it to continual danger from the enterprizes of ambitious neighbours. What a capital improvement then is representation to a Republican Government. By this simple expedient can the sense of the people of an extensive Empire be collected with ease and certainty. By this admirable contrivance, the care and attention of Government is extended equally to every part—the wants and wishes of the most remote corners are known and attended to. But what is of infinite importance, a Government on this plan can be so constructed, as that the different parts of it shall form mutual checks on each other. This is not all, a number of lesser communities may be united under one head; and thus form an extensive Empire. But this new combination will give still greater security to liberty, because more checks will be added. The Government of the Union, and those of the States individually, will be watchful centinels on the conduct of each other. By this means the usurpations of power are guarded against, and liberty secured without the interference of the collective body of the people. Until this important discovery in the art of Government was made, the people themselves formed almost the only check on the Government. For, from the necessity of the case, the right of proposing new laws to the consideration of the people, necessarily devolved upon those who were entrusted with the execution of those laws. Now it may easily be conceived, that to counteract the sinister views of their rulers, it required the utmost circumspection in the people—indeed it was impossible, by the most active and vigilant attention to public officers, for the people to avoid being dupes to the artifices of designing men. This indeed is a business the people are by no means calculated for. Conscious of this inability, the Romans procured the establishment of tribunes, who were to be the guardians of the people's rights, and to defend their privileges against the power of the Senate and the Consuls. How well this expedient answered the end, history will inform us. All that train of unavoidable mischiefs, which necessarily attends the interference of the people in the management of public affairs, instantly vanish when we have recourse to a representative Legislature. Nothing more is then necessary to place liberty on the firmest basis, than the frequent recurrence of elections—that representation be ade-

quate and proportionate—and that the Representatives be
tied down from interfering in any shape, in the Executive
parts of Government, but confined absolutely to the business
of their mission, which should be Legislation solely. If these
things are attended to, the people need be under no apprehensions about the management of affairs. From the very
nature of things, these Representatives cannot fail of proving
the faithful and effectual guardians of the people. Here then
we have that grand desideratum, that has hitherto been wanting in all the popular Governments we are acquainted with,
that the people may repose confidence in Government, without danger of its being abused. As these Representatives are
chosen only for a short period, at the expiration of which,
they are again reduced to the level of their fellow-citizens; and
as, during their continuance in this service, they are absolutely
prohibited from interfering in any of the Executive branches
of the Government; thus it becoming impossible for them to
form an interest separate from that of the community at large,
they can have no motive whatever for betraying that of their
Constituents. A Government formed on this plan, requires in
the execution of it, none of those heroic virtues which we
admire in the antients, and to us are known only by story.
The sacrifice of our dearest interests, self-denial, and austerity
of manners, are by no means necessary. Such a Government
requires nothing more of its subjects than that they should
study and pursue merely their own true interest and happiness. As it is adapted to the ordinary circumstances of mankind, requiring no extraordinary exertions to support it, it
must of course be the more firm, secure and lasting. A Government thus founded on the broad basis of human nature,
like a tree which is suffered to retain its native shape, will
flourish for ages with little care or attention. But like this
same tree, if distorted into a form unnatural and monstrous,
will require the constant use of the pruning knife, and all the
art and contrivance of a skilful operator, to counteract the
efforts of nature against the violence which has been offered
her.

I would not however, wish it to be thought, that it is in
any degree my design to depreciate that amor patriæ, which is
a sentiment so natural to the human breast, and which, when

well directed, is capable of such glorious effects—but unfortunately for mankind, the majority possess it in a very gross degree. It is with them generally nothing more than a blind attachment to a party, or to the local interests of a narrow district.

"Agrippa" [*James Winthrop*] *III*

Massachusetts Gazette (Boston), November 30, 1787

To the PEOPLE.

It has been proved, from the clearest evidence, in two former papers, that a free government, I mean one in which the power frequently returns to the body of the people, is in principle the most stable and efficient of any kind; that such a government affords the most ready and effectual remedy for all injuries done to persons and the rights of property. It is true we have had a tender act. But what government has not some law in favour of debtors. The difficulty consists in finding one that is not more unfriendly to the creditors than ours. I am far from justifying such things. On the contrary I believe that it is universally true, that acts made to favour a part of the community are wrong in principle. All that is now intended is, to remark that we are not worse than other people in that respect which we most condemn. Probably the inquiry will be made, whence the complaints arise. This is easily answered. Let any man look round his own neighbourhood, and see if the people are not, with a very few exceptions, peaceable and attached to the government; if the country had ever within their knowledge more appearance of industry, improvement, and tranquillity; if there was ever more of the produce of all kinds together for the market; if their stock does not rapidly increase; if there was ever a more ready vent for their surplus; & if the average of prices is not about as high as was usual in a plentiful year before the war. These circumstances all denote a general prosperity. Some classes of citizens indeed suffer greatly. Two descriptions I at present recollect. The publick creditors form the first of these classes and they ought to, and will be, provided for. Let us for a moment consider their situation and prospects. The embarassments consequent upon a war, and the usual reduction of prices immediately after a war, necessarily occasioned a want of punctuality in publick payments. Still however the publick debt has been very considerably reduced, not by the dirty and delusive scheme of depreciation, but the nominal sum. Applications are continually making for purchases in our eastern and western lands. Great exertions are making for clearing off the arrears of outstanding taxes, so that the certificates for interest on the state debt have considerably increased in value. This is a certain indication of returning credit. Congress this year disposed of a large tract of their lands towards paying the principal of their debt. Pennsylvania has discharged the whole of their part of the continental debt. New-York has nearly cleared its state debt, and has located a large part of their new lands towards paying the continental demands. Other states have made considerable payments. Every day from these considerations the publick ability and inclination to satisfy their creditors increases. The exertions of last winter were as much to support publick as private credit. The prospect therefore of the publick creditors is brightening under the present system. If the new system should take effect without amendments, which however is hardly probable, the increase of expense will be death to the hopes of all creditors both of the continental and of the state. With respect however to our publick delays of payment we have the precedent of the best established countries in Europe.

The other class of citizens to which I alluded was the ship-carpenters. All agree that their business is dull; but as nobody objects against a system of commercial regulations for the whole continent, that business may be relieved without subverting all the ancient foundations and laws which have the respect of the people. It is a very serious question whether giving to Congress the unlimited right to regulate trade would not injure them still further. It is evidently for the interest of the state to encourage our own trade as much as possible. But in a very large empire, as the whole states consolidated must be, there will always be a desire of the government to increase the trade of the capital, and to weaken the extremes. We should in that case be one of the extremes, and should feel all the impoverishment incident to that situation. Besides, a jealousy of our enterprising spirit, would always be an inducement to cramp our exertions. We must then be impoverished or we must rebel. The alternative is dreadful.

At present this state is one of the most respectable and one of the most influential in the union. If we alone should object to receiving the system without amendments, there is no doubt but it would be amended. But the case is not quite so bad. New-York appears to have no disposition even to call a convention. If they should neglect, are we to lend our assistance to compel them by arms, and thus to kindle a civil war without any provocation on their part. Virginia has put off their convention till May, and appears to have no disposition to receive the new plan without amendments. Pennsylvania does not seem to be disposed to receive it as it is. The same objections are made in all the states, that the civil government which they have adopted and which secures their rights will be subverted. All the defenders of this system undertake to prove that the rights of the states and of the citizens are kept safe. The opposers of it agree that they will receive the least burdensome system which shall defend those rights. Both parties therefore found their arguments on the idea that these rights ought to be held sacred. With this disposition is it not in every man's mind better to recommit it to a new convention, or to Congress, which is a regular convention for the purpose, and to instruct our delegates to confine the system to the general purposes of the union, than to *endeavour* to force it through in its present form, and with so many opposers as it must have in every state on the continent. The case is not of such pressing necessity as some have represented. Europe is engaged and we are tranquil. Never therefore was an happier time for deliberation. The supporters of the measure are by no means afraid of insurrections taking place, but they are afraid that the present government will prove superiour to their assaults.

THE SOVEREIGNTY AND DIVERSITY
OF THE STATES WILL BE LOST

Samuel Adams to Richard Henry Lee

Boston, December 3, 1787

I am to acknowledge your several Favours of the 5th and 27 of October, the one by the Post and the other by our worthy Friend Mr Gerry. The Session of our General Court which lasted six Weeks, and my Station there requiring my punctual & constant Attendance, prevented my considering the *new* Constitution as it is already called, so closely as was necessary for me before I should venture an Opinion.

I confess, as I enter the Building I stumble at the Threshold. I meet with a National Government, instead of a fœderal Union of Sovereign States. I am not able to conceive why the Wisdom of the Convention led them to give the Preference to the former before the latter. If the several States in the Union are to become one entire Nation, under one Legislature, the Powers of which shall extend to every Subject of Legislation, and its Laws be supreme & controul the whole, the Idea of Sovereignty in these States must be lost. Indeed I think, upon such a Supposition, those Sovereignties ought to be eradicated from the Mind; for they would be Imperia in Imperio justly deemd a Solecism in Politicks, & they would be highly dangerous, and destructive of the Peace Union and Safety of the Nation. And can this National Legislature be competent to make Laws for the *free* internal Government of one People, living in Climates so remote and whose "Habits & particular Interests" are and probably always will be so different. Is it to be expected that General Laws can be adapted to the Feelings of the more Eastern & the more Southern Parts of so extensive a Nation? It appears to me difficult if practicable. Hence then may we not look for Discontent, Mistrust, Disaffection to Government and frequent Insurrections, which will require standing Armies to suppress them in one Place & another where they may happen to arise. Or if Laws could be made, adapted to the local Habits Feelings, Views & Interests of those distant Parts, would they not cause Jealousies of Partiality in Government which would excite Envy and other malignant Passions productive of Wars and fighting. But should we continue distinct sovereign States, confederated for the Purposes of mutual Safety and Happiness, each contributing to the fœderal Head such a Part of its Sovereignty as would render the Government fully adequate to those Purposes and *no more*, the People would govern themselves more easily, the Laws of each State being well adapted to its own Genius & Circumstances, and the Liberties of the United States would be more secure than they can be, as I humbly conceive, under the proposed new Constitution. You are sensible, Sir, that the Seeds of Aristocracy began to spring even before the Conclusion of our Struggle for the natural Rights of Men. Seeds which like a Canker Worm lie at the Root of free Governments. So great is the Wickedness of some Men, & the stupid Servility of others, that one would be almost inclined to conclude that Communities cannot be free. The few haughty Families, think *They* must govern. The Body of the People tamely consent & submit to be their Slaves. This unravels the Mystery of Millions being enslaved by the few! But I must desist—My weak hand prevents my proceeding further at present. I will send you my poor Opinion of the political Structure at another Time. In the Interim oblige me with your Letters; & present mine & Mrs A's best Regards to your Lady & Family, Colo Francis, Mr A. L. if with you, & other Friends.

P.S. As I thought it a Piece of Justice I have venturd to say that I had often heard from the best Patriots from Virginia that Mr G Mason was an early active & able Advocate for the Liberties of America,

"Agrippa" [James Winthrop] IV

Massachusetts Gazette (Boston), December 4, 1787

To the PEOPLE.

Having considered some of the principal advantages of the happy form of government under which it is our peculiar good fortune to live, we find by experience, that it is the best calculated of any form hitherto invented, to secure to us the rights of our persons and of our property, and that the general circumstances of the people shew an advanced state of improvement never before known. We have found the shock given by the war in a great measure obliterated, and the publick debt contracted at that time to be considerably reduced in the nominal sum. The Congress lands are fully adequate to the redemption of the principal of their debt, and are selling and populating very fast. The lands of this state, at the west, are, at the moderate price of eighteen pence an acre, worth near half a million pounds in our money. They ought, therefore, to be sold as quick as possible. An application was made lately for a large tract at that price, and continual applications are made for other lands in the eastern part of the state. Our resources are daily augmenting.

We find, then, that after the experience of near two centuries our separate governments are in full vigour. They discover, for all the purposes of internal regulation, every symptom of strength, and none of decay. The new system is, therefore, for such purposes, useless and burdensome.

Let us now consider how far it is practicable consistent with the happiness of the people and their freedom. It is the opinion of the ablest writers on the subject, that no extensive empire can be governed upon republican principles, and that such a government will degenerate to a despotism, unless it be made up of a confederacy of smaller states, each having the full powers of internal regulation. This is precisely the principle which has hitherto preserved our freedom. No instance can be found of any free government of considerable extent which has been supported upon any other plan. Large and consolidated empires may indeed dazzle the eyes of a distant spectator with their splendour, but if examined more nearly are always found to be full of misery. The reason is obvious. In large states the same principles of legislation will not apply to all the parts. The inhabitants of warmer climates are more dissolute in their manners, and less industrious, than in colder countries. A degree of severity is, therefore, necessary with one which would cramp the spirit of the other. We accordingly find that the very great empires have always been despotick. They have indeed tried to remedy the inconveniences to which the people were exposed by local regulations; but these contrivances have never answered the end. The laws not being made by the people, who felt the inconveniences, did not suit their circumstances. It is under such tyranny that the Spanish provinces languish, and such would be our misfortune and degradation, if we should submit to have the concerns of the whole empire managed by one legislature. To promote the happiness of the people it is necessary that there should be local laws; and it is necessary that those laws should be made by the representatives of those who are immediately subject to the want of them. By endeavouring to suit both extremes, both are injured.

It is impossible for one code of laws to suit Georgia and Massachusetts. They must, therefore, legislate for themselves. Yet there is, I believe, not one point of legislation that is not surrendered in the proposed plan. Questions of every kind respecting property are determinable in a continental court, and so are all kinds of criminal causes. The continental legislature has, therefore, a right to make rules *in all cases* by which their judicial courts shall proceed and decide causes. No rights are reserved to the citizens. The laws of Congress are in all cases to be the supreme law of the land, and paramount to the constitutions of the individual states. The Congress may institute what modes of trial they please, and no plea drawn from the constitution of any state can avail. This new system is, therefore, a consolidation of all the states into one large mass, however diverse the parts may be of which it is to be composed. The idea of an uncompounded republick, on an average, one thousand miles in length, and eight hundred in breadth, and containing six millions of white inhabitants all reduced to the same standard of morals, or habits, and of laws, is in itself an absurdity, and contrary to the whole experience of mankind. The attempt made by Great-Britain to introduce such a system, struck us with horrour, and when it was proposed by some theorists that we should be represented in parliament, we uniformly declared that one legislature could not represent so many different interests for the purposes of legislation and taxation. This was the leading principle of the revolution, and makes an essential article in our creed. All that part, therefore, of the new system, which relates to the internal government of the states, ought at once to be rejected.

"Publius," The Federalist XVI
[Alexander Hamilton]

New-York Packet, December 4, 1787

To the People of the State of New-York.

The tendency of the principle of legislation for States, or communities, in their political capacities, as it has been exemplified by the experiment we have made of it, is equally attested by the events which have befallen all other governments of the confederate kind, of which we have any account, in exact proportion to its prevalence in those systems. The confirmations of this fact will be worthy of a distinct and particular examination. I shall content myself with barely observing here, that of all the confederacies of antiquity, which history has handed down to us, the Lycian and Achæan leagues, as far as their remain vestiges of them, appear to have been most free from the fetters of that mistaken principle, and were accordingly those which have best deserved, and have most liberally received the applauding suffrages of political writers.

This exceptionable principle may as truly as emphatically be stiled the parent of anarchy: It has been seen that delinquencies in the members of the Union are its natural and necessary offspring; and that whenever they happen, the only constitutional remedy is force, and the immediate effect of the use of it, civil war.

It remains to enquire how far so odious an engine of government, in its application to us, would even be capable of answering its end. If there should not be a large army, constantly at the disposal of the national government, it would either not be able to employ force at all, or when this could be done, it would amount to a war between different parts of the confederacy, concerning the infractions of a league; in which the strongest combination would be most likely to prevail, whether it consisted of those who supported, or of those who resisted the general authority. It would rarely happen that the delinquency to be redressed would be confined to a single member, and if there were more than one, who had neglected their duty, similarity of situation would induce them to unite for common defence. Independent of this motive of sympathy, if a large and influential State should happen to be the aggressing member, it would commonly have weight enough with its neighbours, to win over some of them as associates to its cause. Specious arguments of danger to the common liberty could easily be contrived; plausible excuses for the deficiencies of the party, could, without difficulty be invented, to alarm the apprehensions, inflame the passions, and conciliate the good will even of those States which were not chargeable with any violation, or omission of duty. This would be the more likely to take place, as the delinquencies of the larger members might be expected sometimes to proceed from an ambitious premeditation in their rulers, with a view to getting rid of all external controul upon their designs of personal aggrandizement; the better to effect which, it is presumable they would tamper beforehand with leading individuals in the adjacent States. If associates could not be found at home, recourse would be had to the aid of foreign powers, who would seldom be disinclined to encouraging the dissentions of a confederacy, from the firm Union of which they had so much to fear. When the sword is once drawn, the passions of men observe no bounds of moderation. The suggestions of wounded pride, the instigations of irritated resentment, would be apt to carry the States, against which the arms of the Union were exerted to any extremes necessary to revenge the affront, or to avoid the disgrace of submission. The first war of this kind would probably terminate in a dissolution of the Union.

This may be considered as the violent death of the confederacy. Its more natural death is what we now seem to be on the point of experiencing, if the fœderal system be not speedily renovated in a more substantial form. It is not probable, considering the genius of this country, that the complying States would often be inclined to support the authority of the Union by engaging in a war against the non-complying States. They would always be more ready to pursue the milder course of putting themselves upon an equal footing with the delinquent members, by an imitation of their example. And the guilt of all would thus become the security of all. Our past experience has exhibited the operation of this spirit in its full light. There would in fact be an insuperable difficulty in ascertaining when force could with propriety be employed. In the article of pecuniary contribution, which would be the most usual source of delinquency, it would often be impossible to decide whether it had proceeded from disinclination, or inability. The pretence of the latter would always be at hand. And the case must be very flagrant in which its fallacy could be detected with sufficient certainty to justify the harsh expedient of compulsion. It is easy to see that this problem alone, as often as it should occur, would open a wide field for the exercise of factious views, of partiality and of oppression, in the majority that happened to prevail in the national council.

It seems to require no pains to prove that the States ought not to prefer a national constitution, which could only be kept in motion by the instrumentality of a large army, continually on foot to execute the ordinary requisitions or decrees of the government. And yet this is the plain alternative involved by those who wish to deny it the power of extending its operations to individuals. Such a scheme, if practicable at all, would instantly degenerate into a military despotism; but it will be found in every light impracticable. The resources of the Union would not be equal to the maintenance of an army considerable enough to confine the larger States within the limits of their duty; nor would the means ever be furnished of forming such an army in the first instance. Whoever considers the populousness and strength of several of these States singly at the present juncture, and looks forward to what they will become, even at the distance of half a century, will at once dismiss as idle and visionary any scheme, which aims at regulating their movements by laws, to operate upon them in their collective capacities, and to be executed by a coertion applicable to them in the same capacities. A project of this kind is little less romantic than that monster-taming spirit, which is attributed to the fabulous heroes and demi-gods of antiquity.

Even in those confederacies, which have been composed of

members smaller than many of our counties, the principle of legislation for sovereign States, supported by military coertion, has never been found effectual. It has rarely been attempted to be employed, but against the weaker members: And in most instances attempts to coerce the refractory and disobedient, have been the signals of bloody wars; in which one half of the confederacy has displayed its banners against the other half.

The result of these observations to an intelligent mind must be clearly this, that if it be possible at any rate to construct a Fœderal Government capable of regulating the common concerns and preserving the general tranquility, it must be founded, as to the objects committed to its care, upon the reverse of the principle contended for by the opponents of the proposed constitution. It must carry its agency to the persons of the citizens. It must stand in need of no intermediate legislations; but must itself be empowered to employ the arm of the ordinary magistrate to execute its own resolutions. The majesty of the national authority must be manifested through the medium of the Courts of Justice. The government of the Union, like that of each State, must be able to address itself immediately to the hopes and fears of individuals; and to attract to its support, those passions, which have the strongest influence upon the human heart. It must in short, possess all the means and have a right to resort to all the methods of executing the powers, with which it is entrusted, that are possessed and exercised by the governments of the particular States.

To this reasoning it may perhaps be objected, that if any State should be disaffected to the authority of the Union, it could at any time obstruct the execution of its laws, and bring the matter to the same issue of force, with the necessity of which the opposite scheme is reproached.

The plausibility of this objection will vanish the moment we advert to the essential difference between a mere NON COMPLIANCE and a DIRECT and ACTIVE RESISTANCE. If the interposition of the State-Legislatures be necessary to give effect to a measure of the Union, they have only NOT TO ACT or TO ACT EVASIVELY, and the measure is defeated. This neglect of duty may be disguised under affected but unsubstantial provisions, so as not to appear, and of course not to excite any alarm in the people for the safety of the constitution. The State leaders may even make a merit of their surreptitious invasions of it, on the ground of some temporary convenience, exemption, or advantage.

But if the execution of the laws of the national government, should not require the intervention of the State Legislatures; if they were to pass into immediate operation upon the citizens themselves, the particular governments could not interrupt their progress without an open and violent exertion of an unconstitutional power. No omissions, nor evasions would answer the end. They would be obliged to act, and in such a manner, as would leave no doubt that they had encroached on the national rights. An experiment of this nature would always be hazardous—in the face of a constitution in any degree competent to its own defence, and of a people enlightened enough to distinguish between a legal exercise and an illegal usurpation of authority. The success of it would require not merely a factious majority in the Legislature, but the concurrence of the courts of justice, and of the body of the people. If the Judges were not embarked in a conspiracy with the Legislature they would pronounce the resolutions of such a majority to be contrary to the supreme law of the land, unconstitutional and void. If the people were not tainted with the spirit of their State representatives, they, as the natural guardians of the constitution, would throw their weight into the national scale, and give it a decided preponderancy in the contest. Attempts of this kind would not often be made with liberty or rashness; because they could seldom be made without danger to the authors; unless in cases of a tyrannical exercise of the Fœderal authority.

If opposition to the national government should arise from the disorderly conduct of refractory, or seditious individuals, it could be overcome by the same means which are daily employed against the same evil, under the State governments. The Magistracy, being equally the Ministers of the law of the land, from whatever source it might emanate, would doubtless be as ready to guard the national as the local regulations from the inroads of private licentiousness. As to those partial commotions and insurrections which sometimes disquiet society, from the intrigues of an inconsiderable faction, or from sudden or occasional ill humours that do not infect the great body of the community, the general government could command more extensive resources for the suppression of disturbances of that kind, than would be in the power of any single member. And as to those mortal feuds, which in certain conjunctures spread a conflagration through a whole nation, or through a very large proportion of it, proceeding either from weighty causes of discontent given by the government, or from the contagion of some violent popular paroxism, they do not fall within any ordinary rules of calculation. When they happen, they commonly amount to revolutions and dismemberments of empire. No form of government can always either avoid or controul them. It is in vain to hope to guard against events too mighty for human foresight or precaution, and it would be idle to object to a government because it could not perform impossibilities.

ON THE ERRORS OF "CATO" AND
OF CELEBRATED WRITERS

"Americanus" [John Stevens, Jr.] IV

Daily Advertiser (New York), December 5 & 6, 1787

The investigation of the principles and probable tendency of the new plan of Government, is evidently the most important discussion that ever employed the pen or engaged the attention of man: The immense magnitude of the subject fills the mind with the most awful impressions. To suffer ourselves to be governed in a business of so interesting a nature by the maxims and principles of systematic writers, however celebrated, would be an unpardonable indiscretion. Let us avail ourselves of every light they can afford; but would it not be downright madness to shackle ourselves with maxims and principles which are clearly inapplicable to the nature of our political institutions? The path we are pursuing is new, and has never before been trodden by man. Our principal dependance, then, in this arduous business, must be derived from the resources of our own minds: As we can find no rule or precedent to which we can appeal, our determinations must result from the dispassionate but vigorous exertions of our own good sense and judgment. From this view of the subject I feel the incumbent weight on my shoulders. I am sensible how hard a task it is to root out and abolish errors sanctified and established by time and the reputation of celebrated writers.

In every science this rule must invariably hold good, that new combinations require new principles. Montesquieu tells us, "it is a fundamental law in Democracies, that the people should have the sole power to enact laws." From this fundamental law, all his reasonings, all his inferences on the nature of this species of Government are drawn. That a Republic should be confined to a small territory—heroic virtues—self-denial—and the sacrifice of our dearest interests are essentially necessary, and are consequences flowing immediately from the nature of this fundamental law. For, was the Government extensive, the people would find the exercise of their sovereignty impracticable, and was it not for the patriotism and self-denial of individuals, the public interest would be neglected or betrayed.

But has this law been established as a fundamental in the Constitution of any of our Governments? I believe Cato himself will not venture to answer this question in the affirmative. It is a fact notorious to all the world, to the unlearned as well as learned, that the people of these States have in no instance retained the exercise of sovereignty in their own hands; but have universally appointed representatives to legislate for them. Here then there obviously appears a most material and essential difference between the fundamental law of Democracy laid down by Montesquieu, and the fundamental law established in the several Constitutions of these States. From this difference of the fundamental law, there of course flow principles and consequences as different. And as we manifestly can have no recourse to precedent, our political institutions being founded upon a fundamental law altogether new in Republican government, the principles and consequences resulting therefrom must be sought after and discovered from our own experience, and from deductions drawn from the peculiar nature of these institutions.

Having, as I presume, cleared the question (as the mathematician does his equation from co-efficients) of these non-essentials, which can serve no other purpose but to perplex and embarrass our enquiries, I shall now proceed to the further consideration of Cato's objections; and glean up every sentence which carries the least shadow of an argument, and which has not yet been fully answered.

"This consolidated Republic cannot do without the aid of a standing army." It is readily admitted that a moderate military establishment will be necessary. But, "will not political security, and even the opinion of it, be extinguished?" By no means. There are various circumstances which will render it impossible for a standing army to become dangerous; provided these States continue United. The causes which require large military establishments in Europe, do not exist on this side the Atlantic. But why is the trifling force which it may be necessary for us to keep up, made so great a bug-bear of? Does not Great-Britain support a standing army vastly greater than we can ever have occasion for? Yet, if we go out of our own country, where shall we find more "political security;" less "force," less "violence," in the exercise of the powers of Government? But, "the malecontents in each State," who, as Cato informs us, "will *not be a few*, nor *the least important*, will be exciting factions against it." What will be the numbers of these malecontents, I know not. It will be sufficient if the majority in favor of the Constitution be clear and decided, which I sincerely hope, and firmly believe it will be. Indeed, should an Angel come down from Heaven, and present us with a Constitution of Government altogether spotless and free from blemish; should we not still have malecontents amongst us? Would there not be Cato's and Brutus's ready to disseminate groundless jealousies and vain fears? If a plan of Government must be rejected because some are opposed to it, is it not evident that none can ever be adopted? One remark, however, I must beg leave to address more immediately to Cato and his party: If there is any one "axiom in the science of politics," which may be deemed "irrefragable," it must certainly be this;—that in a free Government the majority must necessarily govern; and that, therefore, it becomes the indispensable duty of good citizens to acquiesce; to attempt an opposition by means of force and violence, would be to commit a crime of the blackest dye.

(*To be continued.*)

[*Concluded from yesterday's paper.*]

Cato insinuates that a large Republic is less capable of suppressing domestic insurrections than a small one. From what causes do insurrections generally arise? Some turbulent individual infuses jealousy and discontent into the minds of the people. But the personal influence of an individual cannot extend far. The contagion therefore must spread progressively, if it spreads at all; indeed, it can never happen but from some gross error in Government, that the great body of the people, spread over a large extent of country, can all be infected with this spirit of discontent at one and the same time.

The time that must necessarily be consumed in communicating the flame of sedition from one quarter of an extensive territory to another, will also give time to Government to collect her strength. The passion of the insurgents will cool—wild uproar will give place to calm reflection—negociation will ensue—matters will be accommodated, and peace restored. But should Government be drove to the disagreeable necessity of recurring to the use of arms; it will then be a matter of no small moment that, from the extent of her territories, she is able to collect her forces from parts remote from the scene of action. From hence, this capital advantage, among many others, will be derived; that, on the restoration of peace, harmony and cordial reconciliation will probably ensue, as personal resentment and rancor will not be engendered between parties who will of course be strangers to each other.

Cato tells us that the Government of small States will be more mild and also more vigorous than that of larger ones. But if it is true that small States ever have been, and from the nature of man ever must be the nurseries of parties, factions, discord, discontent, wild uproar, and seditious tumults; this observation of his must manifestly be erroneous. The characteristics of a *mild* Government are Liberty without Licentiousness, and Government without Tyranny; of a *vigorous* one, unanimity, consistency, and uniformity in its councils.

We are told that extent of territory, variety of climates, productions and commerce, difference of extent, and number of inhabitants, dissimilitude of interests, morals and politics, will render this consolidated Republican form of Government impracticable. But what is the drift and tendency of this mode of argumentation? It evidently militates with equal force against every species of general Government—call it by what name you will, whether Consolidation or Confederation, it matters not, all must be equally impracticable. Nay! this mode of argumentation leads immediately to consequences which I cannot suppose Cato could have had in contemplation. If diversity of interest arising from various contingencies, such as climate, productions, commerce, morals, politics, &c. &c. form invariable bars against the due exercise of the powers of Government; then, I say there is an end of every thing.

For, if the infinite number and variety of distinct and jarring interests, which necessarily prevail among the individuals of a society in a state of civilization cannot be controled and reconciled by the energetic exertions of the powers of Government, we must then relinquish all our ideas of the efficiency of Government as mere chimeras. The very end, purpose and design of all Government is to prevent the destructive effects of these clashing interests on the peace, security and happiness of society. Strange mode of argumentation! that the very circumstances which require and call aloud for all the energy of such an efficient Government as this constitution has delineated, should, by an unaccountable perversity of all the rules of just reasoning, be urged as an argument against the Constitution itself.

We are told that the strongest principle of Union exists between the members of the same family. The next general principle of Union is amongst citizens of the same state; but when we still enlarge the circle so as to comprehend the citizens of other States, affection and attachment are lost.—"Is it therefore, from certainty like this, reasonable to believe the inhabitants of Georgia or New-Hampshire will have the same obligations towards you as your own, and preside over your lives, liberties and property with the same care and attachment?" It is by no means necessary. The principles I have endeavored to establish as resulting from the nature of our Governments, form a sufficient answer to this question. This attachment to the particular interest of our own State, if too strong, becomes a very pernicious principle; and I view it as a capital advantage that the nature of our Governments renders it in a great measure unnecessary. It is sufficient that we have the most ample and clearest assurances which the nature of the thing will admit of, that the interests of the States individually can never be wantonly sacrificed. That the general interests of the Union should be first attended to and provided for, is but just and proper.

I come next to the consideration of Cato's fifth number, a great part of which is taken up with a long and labored harangue against trusting discretionary power in the hands of any man. Propriety of language, elegance of diction, and justness of remark, it must be allowed are by no means wanting here: but how these remarks apply to a Constitution in which the powers of Government are ascertained and defined with accuracy and precision, I am at a loss to conceive. From want of explicitness in this Constitution, he again urges the probability of a Monarchial establishment.

That the fecund womb of time may hereafter produce causes and events tending to such an establishment, is to be sure not impossible, but, in my opinion, very improbable. This inexplicitness which Cato complains of, can operate only as a drop to the bucket. A free people are not to be deprived of their liberty by logical refinements and mere verbal criticisms. To effect this purpose more efficacious means must be recurred to.

After revolving this subject in my own mind, in every light I can place it, I can see none of those dangerous consequences, apprehended by Cato, from investing the Executive power in the hands of a single person. The most effectual way, perhaps, of effacing these gloomy fears from our minds, is to compare the distribution of power made by this Constitution, with the distribution of power which has taken place in the Government of Great-Britain. It is a fact, universally admitted, that no people have ever enjoyed real liberty, in so eminent a degree, as do the people of England. But what an immense disparity is there between this celebrated Government, and the Constitution offered for our acceptance, with respect to the limitations and restrictions in favor of liberty! We find there an hereditary Monarch, invested with such an host of dangerous prerogatives as appears incompatible with any degree of liberty. He has the sole prerogative of making war and peace; of making treaties, leagues and alliances, on whatever condition he thinks proper; sends and receives Ambassadors; he forms a distinct branch of the Legislature; he has the sole command of the fleets and armies, with the appointment of all the offices and places dependent thereon, both military and civil; he alone can levy troops, equip fleets and build fortresses. He is the source of all the Judicial power in the State; he is the chief of all the tribunals, and the Judges are only his substitutes; every thing is transacted in his name; the judgments must be with his seal, and are executed by his officers. By a fiction in the law, he is looked upon as the universal proprietor of the kingdom. He can pardon offences. He is the fountain of honor, office and privilege; creates Peers of the realm, and distributes titles and dignities. He is the head and supreme governor of the national Church. In this capacity he appoints the Bishops, and the two Archbishops; he alone convenes, prorogues or dissolves the Convocation of the Clergy; his assent likewise is necessary to the validity of their acts. He is the Superintendent of Commerce; he has the prerogative of regulating weights and measures; he alone can coin money, and can give currency to foreign coin. He possesses the power of convening, proroguing and dissolving the Parliament; the collection, management and expenditure of an immense revenue, deposited annually in the Royal Exchequer, with the appointment of an almost innumerable tribe of officers dependent thereon. In fine, what seems to carry so many powers to the height, is its being a fundamental maxim, that THE KING CAN DO NO WRONG; he is above the reach of all Courts of law; he is accountable to no power whatever in the nation; and his person is sacred and inviolable.

In the next place, we find an hereditary Nobility, and an order of gownsmen totally dependent on the Crown, who form another distinct branch of the Legislature, and a Court of Judicature in cases of appeal. This body of Nobility are created and encreased at the will of the Crown. Here are then, two branches out of three of the Legislature, wholly independent of the people. The House of Commons are, to be sure, an elective body, and the only part of the Government in any degree dependent on the people. They form, however, a very imperfect representation of the collective body of the people. Out of 513, the number of Members sent by England to Parliament, the Boroughs and Cinque Ports send no less than 382. Some of these Boroughs contain but one voter; many of them not more than ten; and the major part of them less than one hundred. But if representation is so imperfect and unequal, there still remains a most capital defect, as to the frequency of elections, and the vague, uncertain footing this privilege of the people, so indispensibly necessary to liberty, stands upon. No fixed rule has been established for the duration of Parliament. But it is left to the discretion of Parliament itself to lengthen or shorten its own duration, as they in their wisdom shall judge expedient; and accordingly we find Parliaments to have been annual, triennial, septennial, duodennial, and octodennial. At present they are septennial.

When we consider maturely all these circumstances in the Government of Great-Britain, so unfriendly to liberty, instead of supposing them the freest people on earth (ourselves excepted) it must really appear wonderful, that any degree of liberty whatever can be supported. But it must add greatly to our surprise on this occasion, when we consider further, that this people, so celebrated for liberty, have emerged, by slow and almost imperceptible degrees, from a state of the vilest vassalage, to their present pre-eminent station among nations. Indeed the history of the rise and progress of liberty amongst this people, in circumstances so extremely unfavorable and adverse, has convinced me fully, that is is impossible to subjugate a numerous and free people, spread over a wide extent of country, without the intervention and concurrence of adventitious and extrinsic causes. The ordinary powers of a well constructed Government are inadequate to this purpose. Let not, therefore, my fellow-countrymen, the gloomy apprehensions of Cato fright your imaginations. Nothing surely can be more chimerical than this idea of the powers of a President finally degenerating into an establishment for life.

Richard Henry Lee to
Governor Edmund Randolph

Virginia Gazette (Petersburg), December 6, 1787

Copy of a letter from the Hon. Richard Henry Lee, *Esq; one of the Delegates from this State in Congress, to his Excellency the Governor.*

New-York, Oct. 16, 1787.

DEAR SIR, I was duly honored with your favor of September 17th, from Philadelphia, which should have been acknowledged long before now, if the nature of the business that it related to had not required time.

The establishment of the new plan of government, in its present form, is a question that involves such immense consequences to the present times and to posterity, that it calls for the deepest attention of the best and wisest friends of their country and of mankind. If it be found good after mature deliberation, adopt it, if wrong, amend it at all events, for to say (as many do) that a bad government must be established for fear of anarchy, is really saying that we must kill ourselves for fear of dying. Experience and the actual state of things, shew that there is no difficulty in procuring a general convention; the late one being collected without any obstruction: Nor does external war, or internal discord prevent the most cool, collected, full, and fair discussion of this all-important subject. If with infinite ease, a convention was obtained to prepare a system, why may not another with equal ease be procured to make proper and necessary amendments? Good government is not the work of a short time, or of sudden thought. From *Moses* to *Montesquieu* the greatest geniuses have been employed on this difficult subject, and yet experience has shewn capital defects in the system produced for the government of mankind. But since it is neither prudent or easy to make frequent changes in government, and as bad governments have been generally found the most fixed; so it becomes of the last consequence to frame the first establishment upon ground the most unexceptionable, and such as the best theories with experience justify; not trusting as our new constitution does, and as many approve of doing, to time and future events to correct errors, that both reason and experience in similar cases, point out in the new system. It has hitherto been supposed a fundamental maxim that in governments rightly balanced, the different branches of legislature should be unconnected, and that the legislative and executive powers should be separate:—In the new constitution, the president and senate have all the executive and two thirds of the legislative power. In some weighty instances (as making all kinds of treaties which are to be the laws of the land) they have the whole legislative and executive powers. They jointly, appoint all officers civil and military, and they (the senate) try all impeachments either of their own members, or of the officers appointed by themselves.

Is there not a most formidable combination of power thus created in a few, and can the most critic eye, if a candid one, discover responsibility in this potent corps? Or will any sensible man say, that great power without responsibility can be given to rulers with safety to liberty? It is most clear that the parade of impeachment is nothing to them or any of them—as little restraint is to be found, I presume from the fear of offending constituents.—The president is for four years duration and Virginia (for example) has one vote of thirteen in the choice of him, and this thirteenth vote not of the people, but electors, two removes from the people. The senate is a body of six years duration, and as in the choice of president, the largest state has but a thirteenth vote, so is it in the choice of senators.—This latter statement is adduced to shew that responsibility is as little to be apprehended from amenability to constituents, as from the terror of impeachment. You are, therefore, Sir, well warranted in saying, either a monarchy or aristocracy will be generated, perhaps the most grievous system of government may arise. It cannot be denied with truth, that this new constitution is, in its first principles, highly and dangerously oligarchic; and it is a point agreed that a government of the few, is, of all governments, the worst. The only check to be found in favor of the democratic principle in this system is, the house of representatives; which I believe may justly be called a mere shread or rag of representation: It being obvious to the least examination, that smallness of number and great comparative disparity of power, renders that house of little effect to promote good, or restrain bad government. But what is the power given to this ill constructed body? To judge of what may be for the general welfare, and such judgments when made, the acts of Congress become the supreme laws of the land. This seems a power co-extensive with every possible object of human legislation.—Yet there is no restraint in form of a bill of rights, to secure (what Doctor Blackstone calls) that residuum of human rights, which is not intended to be given up to society, and which indeed is not necessary to be given for any good social purpose.—The rights of conscience, the freedom of the press, and the trial by jury are at mercy. It is there stated, that in criminal cases, the trial shall be by jury. But how? In the state. What then becomes of the jury of the vicinage or at least from the county in the first instance, for the states being from 50 to 700 miles in extent? This mode of trial even in criminal cases may be greatly impaired, and in civil causes the inference is strong, that it may be altogether omitted as the constitution positively assumes it in criminal, and is silent about it in civil causes.—Nay, it is more strongly discountenanced in civil cases by giving the supreme court in appeals, jurisdiction both as to law and fact. Judge Blackstone in his learned commentaries, art. jury trial, says, it is the most transcendant privilege which any subject can enjoy or wish for, that he cannot be affected either in his property, his liberty, his person, but by the unanimous consent of 12 of his neighbours and equals. A constitution that I may venture to affirm has under providence, secured the just liberties of this nation for a long succession of ages.—The impartial administration of justice, which secures both our persons and our properties, is the great end of civil society. But if that be entirely *entrusted* to the magistracy, a select body of men, and those generally selected by the prince, or such as enjoy the highest offices of the state, these decisions in spite of their own natural integrity, will have frequently an involuntary bias towards those of their own rank and dignity. It is not to be expected from human nature, that the few should always be attentive to the good of the many. The learned judge further says, that every tribunal selected for the decision of *facts*, is a step towards establishing aristocracy; the most oppressive of all governments. The answer to these objections is, that the new legislature may provide remedies!—But as they may, so they may not, and if they did, a succeeding assembly may repeal the provisions.—The evil is found resting upon constitutional bottom, and the remedy upon the mutable ground of legislation, revocable at any annual meeting. It is the more unfortunate that this great security of human rights, the trial by jury, should be weakened in this system, as power is unnecessarily given in the second section of the third article, to call people from their own country in all cases of controversy about property between citizens of different states and foreigners, with citizens of the United States, to be tried in a distant court where the Congress may sit. For although inferior congressional courts may for the above purposes be instituted in the different states, yet this is a matter altogether in the pleasure of the new legislature, so that if they please not to institute them, or if they do not regulate the right of appeal reasonably, the people will be exposed to endless oppression, and the necessity of submitting in multitudes of cases, to pay unjust demands, rather than follow suitors, through great expence, to far distant tribunals, and to be determined upon there, as it may be, without a jury.—In this congressional legislature, a bare majority of votes can enact commercial laws, so that the representatives of the seven northern states, as they will have a majority, can by law create the most oppressive monopoly upon the five southern states, whose circumstances and productions are essentially different from theirs, although not a single man of these voters are the representatives of, or amenable to the people of the southern states. Can such a set of men be, with the least colour of truth called a representative of those they make laws for? It is supposed that the policy of the northern states will prevent such abuses. But how feeble, Sir, is policy when opposed to interest among trading people:—And what is the restraint arising from policy? Why that we may be forced by abuse to become ship-builders!—But how long will it be before a people of agriculture can produce ships sufficient to export such bulky commodities as ours, and of such extent; and if we had the ships, from whence are the seamen to come? 4000 of whom at least will be necessary in Virginia. In questions so liable to abuse, why was not the necessary vote put to two thirds of the members of the legislature? With the constitution, came from the convention so many members of that body to Congress, and of those too, who were among the most fiery zealots for their system, that the votes of three states being of them, two states divided by them, and many others mixed with them, it is easy to see that Congress could have little opinion upon the subject. Some denied our right to make amendments, whilst others more moderate agreed to the right, but denied the expediency of amending; but it was plain that a majority was ready to send it on in terms of approbation—my judgment and conscience forbid the last, and therefore I moved the amendments that I have the honor to send you inclosed herewith, and demanded the yeas and nays that they might appear on the journal. This seemed to alarm and to prevent such appearance on the journal, it was agreed to transmit the constitution without a syllable of approbation or disapprobation; so that the term unanimously only applied to the transmission, as you will observe by attending to the terms of the resolve for transmitting. Upon the whole, Sir, my opinion is, that as this constitution abounds with useful regulations, at the same time that it is liable to strong and fundamental objections, the plan for us to pursue, will be to propose the necessary amendments, and express our willingness to adopt it with the amendments, and to suggest the calling of a new convention for the purpose of considering them. To this I see no well founded objection, but great safety and much good to be the probable result. I am perfectly satisfied that you make such use of this letter as you shall think to be for the public good; and now after begging your pardon for so great a trespass on your patience, and presenting my best respects to your lady, I will conclude with assuring you, that I am with the sincerest esteem and regard, dear Sir, your most affectionate and obedient servant, RICHARD HENRY LEE.

POSTSCRIPT.

It having been found from universal experience, that the most express declarations and reservations are necessary to protect the just rights and liberty of mankind from the silent, powerful and ever active conspiracy of those who govern; and it appearing to be the sense of the good people of America, by the various bills or declarations of rights whereon the government of the greater number of states are founded. That such precautions are necessary to restrain and regulate the exercise of the great powers given to rulers. In conformity with these principles, and from respect for the public sentiment on this subject, it is submitted,—That the new constitution proposed for the government of the United States be bottomed upon a declaration or bill of rights, clearly and precisely stating the principles upon which this social compact is founded, to wit: That the rights of conscience in matters of religion ought not to be violated—That the freedom of the press shall be secured—That the trial by jury in criminal and civil cases, and the modes prescribed by the common law for the safety of life in criminal prosecutions, shall be held sacred—That standing armies in times of peace are dangerous to liberty, and ought not to be permitted, unless assented to by two-thirds of the members composing each house of the legislature under the new constitution—That the elections should be free and frequent; That the right administration of justice should be secured by the independency of the judges; That excessive bail, excessive fines, or cruel and unusual punishments, should not be demanded or inflicted; That the right of the people to assemble peaceably, for the purpose of petitioning the legislature, shall not be prevented; That the citizens shall not be exposed to unreasonable searches, seizure of their persons, houses, papers or property; and it is necessary for the good of society, that the administration of government be conducted with all possible maturity of judgment, for which reason it hath been the practice of civilized nations, and so determined by every state in the Union: That a council of state or privy council should be appointed to advise and assist in the arduous business assigned to the executive power. Therefore let the new constitution be so amended, as to admit the appointment of a privy council, to consist of eleven members chosen by the president, but responsible for the advice they may give. For which purpose the advice given shall be entered in a council book, and signed by the giver, in all affairs of great moment, and that the counsellors act under an oath of office. In order to prevent the dangerous blending of the legislative and executive powers, and to secure responsibility, the privy, and not the senate shall be joined with the president in the appointment of all officers, civil and military, under the new constitution; that the constitution be so altered as not to admit the creation of a vice-president, when duties as assigned may be discharged by the privy council, except in the instance of proceeding in the senate, which may be supplied by a speaker chosen from the body of senators by themselves, as usual, that so may be avoided the establishment of a great officer of state, who is sometimes to be joined with the legislature, and sometimes to administer the government, rendering responsibility difficult, besides giving unjust and needless preeminence to that state from whence this officer may have come. That such parts of the new constitution be amended as provide imperfectly for the trial of criminals by a jury of the vicinage, and to supply the omission of a jury trial in civil causes or disputes about property between individuals, whereby the common law is directed, and as generally it is secured by the several state constitutions. That such parts of the new constitution be amended, as permit the vexatious and oppressive callings of citizens from their own country, and all controversies between citizens of different states and between citizens and foreigners, to be tried in a far distant court, and as it may be without a jury, whereby in a multitude of cases, the circumstances of distance and expence may compel numbers to submit to the most unjust and ill-founded demand— That in order to secure the rights of the people more effectually from violation, the power and respectability of the house of representatives be increased, by increasing the number of delegates to that house, where the popular interest must chiefly depend for protection—That the constitution be so amended as to increase the number of votes necessary to determine questions in cases where a bare majority may be seduced by strong motives of interest to injure and oppress the minority of the community, as in commercial regulations, where advantage may be taken of circumstances to ordain rigid and premature laws, that will in effect amount to monopolies, to the great impoverishment of those states whose peculiar situation expose them to such injuries.

John Adams to Thomas Jefferson

London, December 6, 1787

The Project of a new Constitution, has Objections against it, to which I find it difficult to reconcile myself, but I am so unfortunate as to differ somewhat from you in the Articles, according to your last kind Letter.

You are afraid of the one—I, of the few. We agree perfectly that the many should have a full fair and perfect Representation.—You are Apprehensive of Monarchy; I, of Aristocracy.—I would therefore have given more Power to the President and less to the Senate. The Nomination and Appointment to all offices I would have given to the President, assisted only by a Privy Council of his own Creation, but not a Vote or Voice would I have given to the Senate or any Senator, unless he were of the Privy Council. Faction and Distraction are the sure and certain Consequence of giving to a Senate a Vote in the distribution of offices.

You are apprehensive the President when once chosen, will be chosen again and again as long as he lives. So much the better as it appears to me.—You are apprehensive of foreign Interference Intrigue, Influence.—So am I.—But, as often as Elections happen, the danger of foreign Influence recurs. the less frequently they happen the less danger.—and if the same Man may be chosen again, it is probable he will be, and the danger of foreign Influence will be less. Foreigners, seeing little Prospect will have less Courage for Enterprize.

Elections, my dear Sir, Elections to Offices which are great objects of Ambition, I look at with terror.—Experiments of this kind have been so often tryed, and so universally found productive of Horrors, that there is great Reason to dread them.

Mr Littlepage who will have the Honour to deliver this will tell you all the News.

"Agrippa" [*James Winthrop*] V

Massachusetts Gazette (Boston), December 11, 1787

To the PEOPLE.

In the course of inquiry it has appeared, that for the purposes of internal regulation and domestick tranquillity, our small and separate governments are not only admirably suited in theory, but have been remarkably successful in practice. It is also found, that the direct tendency of the proposed system, is to consolidate the whole empire into one mass, and, like the tyrant's bed, to reduce all to one standard. Though this idea has been started in different parts of the continent, and is the most important trait of this draft, the reasoning ought to be extensively understood. I therefore hope to be indulged in a particular statement of it.

Causes of all kinds, between citizens of different states, are to be tried before a continental court. This court is not bound to try it according to the local laws where the controversies happen; for in that case it may as well be tried in a state court. The rule which is to govern the new courts, must, therefore, be made by the court itself, or by its employers, the Congress. If by the former, the legislative and judicial departments will be blended; and if by the Congress, though these departments will be kept separate, still the power of legislation departs from the state in all those cases. The Congress, therefore, have the right to make rules for trying *all kinds* of *questions* relating to property between citizens of different states. The sixth article of the new constitution provides, that the continental laws shall be the supreme law of the land, and all judges in the separate states shall be bound thereby, any thing in the sititution or laws of any state to the contrary notwithstanding. All the state officers are also bound by oath to support this constitution. These provisions cannot be understood otherwise than as binding the state judges and other officers, to execute the continental laws in their own proper departments within the state. For all questions, other than those between citizens of the same state, are at once put within the jurisdiction of the continental courts. As no authority remains to the state judges, but to decide questions between citizens of the same state, and those judges are to be bound by the laws of Congress, it clearly follows, that all questions between citizens of the same state are to be decided by the general laws and not by the local ones.

Authority is also given to the continental courts, to try all causes between a state and its own citizens. A question of property between these parties rarely occurs. But if such questions were more frequent than they are, the proper process is not to sue the state before an higher authority; but to apply to the supreme authority of the state, by way of petition. This is the universal practice of all states, and any other mode of redress destroys the sovereignty of the state over its own subjects. The only case of the kind in which the state would probably be sued, would be upon the state notes. The endless confusion that would arise from making the estates of individuals answerable, must be obvious to every one.

There is another sense in which the clause relating to causes between the state and individuals is to be understood, and it is more probable than the other, as it will be eternal in its duration, and increasing in its extent. This is the whole branch of the law relating to criminal prosecutions. In all such cases, the state is plaintiff, and the person accused is defendant. The process, therefore, will be, for the attorney-general of the state to commence his suit before a continental court. Considering the state as a party, the cause must be tried in another, and all the expense of transporting witnesses incurred. The individual is to take his trial among strangers, friendless and unsupported, without its being known whether he is habitually a good or a bad man; and consequently with one essential circumstance wanting by which to determine whether the action was performed maliciously or accidentally. All these inconveniences are avoided by the present important restriction, that the cause shall be tried by a jury of the vicinity, and tried in the county where the offence was committed. But by the proposed *derangement*, I can call it by no softer name, a man must be ruined to prove his innocence. This is far from being a forced construction of the proposed form. The words appear to me not intelligible, upon the idea that it is to be a *system* of government, unless the construction now given, both for civil and criminal processes, be admitted. I do not say that it is intended that all these changes should take place within one year, but they probably will in the course of half a dozen years, if this system is adopted. In the mean time we shall be subject to all the horrors of a divided sovereignty, not knowing whether to obey the Congress or the state. We shall find it impossible to please two masters. In such a state frequent broils will ensue. Advantage will be taken of a popular commotion, and even the venerable forms of the state be done away, while the new system will be enforced in its utmost rigour, by an army. I am the more apprehensive of a standing army, on account of a clause in the new constitution which empowers Congress to keep one at all times; but this constitution is evidently such that it cannot stand any considerable time without an army. Upon this principle one is very wisely provided. Our present government knows of no such thing.

George Lee Turberville to James Madison

Richmond, Virginia, December 11, 1787

Will you excuse an abrupt tresspass upon your leizure—
which has its rise from a desire to promote the welfare of
Virginia & the Union a cause that has so long been the object of your pursuits—& that has already received so many
beneficial supports from your attention—& still expects to
receive so much future aid—from your Counsel—Assiduity
& patriotism—?

Tis not sir to draw from you—your opinions—but merely
to be informed of some parts of the Plan of Government proposed by the convention at Philadelphia—which appear
obscure to a Reader that I have ventured to interrupt you,
seeing that it is impossible to receive any information in the
circle here—but what manifestly bears ye Stamp of faction—
rancour—or intemperance—

Upon a question of Such importance—(on which perhaps
it may be my lot to have a Vote) you will therefore excuse me
for endeavoring to understand the subject as well as possible
to the end that I may be enabled to form cooly & deliberately—such an opinion of it as my best abilities—aided by
extreme attention—& all the information I can obtain—will
admit—without further apology therefore I will proceed to
mention such parts of the plan as appear obscure to me—
always premising that it is not my wish to draw from you
your own opinions, but only the reasonings thereon—& the
objects thereof that weighed with the convention—

The principal objection that the opponents bring forward
against this Constitution, is the total want of a Bill of
Rights—this they build upon as an essential—and altho' I
am satisfied that an enumeration of those priviledges which
we retained—wou'd have left floating in uncertainty a number of non enumerated contingent powers and priviledges—
either in the powers granted or in those retained—thereby

indisputably trenching upon the powers of the states—& of the Citizens—insomuch as those not specially retained might by just implication have been consider'd as surrender'd—still it wou'd very much assist me in my determination upon this subject if the sense of the Convention and their opinion upon it cou'd be open'd to me—

Another objection (and that I profess appears very weighty with me) is the want of a Council of State to assist the President—to detail to you the various reasons that lead to this opinion is useless. You have seen them in all the publications almost that pretend to analyse this system—most particularly in Colo. Masons   We have heard from *private persons* that a system of government was engrossed—which had an Executive council—and that the priviledge of importing slaves (another great evil) was not mention'd in it—but that a Coalition took place between the members of the small states —& those of the southern states—& they barter'd the Council for the Priviledge—and the present plan thus defective— owes it origin to this Junction—if this was the case it takes greatly off from the confidence that I ever conceived to be due to this Convention—such conduct wou'd appear rather like the attempt of a party to carry an interested measure in a state legislature than the production of the United Wisdom— Virtue—& Uprightness of America called together to deliberate upon a form of Government that will affect themselves & their latest Posterity.—

The operation of the Judiciary is a matter so far beyond the reach of most of our fellow Citizens that we are bounden to receive—& not to originate our opinions upon this branch of ye Federal government—Lawyers alone conceive themselves masters of this subject & they hold it forth to us *danger* & *distress* as the inevitable result of the new system—& that this will proceed from the immense power of the general Judiciary—which will pervade the states from one extremity to the other & will finally absorb—& destroy the state Courts— But to me their power seem's very fairly defined by the clauses that constitute them—& the mention of Juries, in criminal cases—seeming therefor by implication in civil cases—not to be allowed, is the only objection *I* have to this Branch—

Why shou'd the United states in Congress Assembled be enabled to fix on the places of choosing the Representatives?

Why shou'd the Laws of the Union operate agt. & super-cede—the state Constitutions?

Wou'd not an uniform duty—impost—or excise of £5. pr. hhd on Tobo. exported—throughout the United states—operate upon the tobo. states alone? & have not the U. S. the power of levying this impost?

Why shou'd the states be prevented from raising a Revenue by Duties or Taxes—on their own Exports? Are the states not bound down to direct Taxation for the support of their police & government?

Why was not that truely republican mode of forcing the Rulers or sovereigns of the states to mix after stated Periods with the people again—observed—as is the case with the present members of Congress—Governors of this state &c &c—?

For what Reason—or to answer what republican Veiw is it, that the way is left open for the importation of Negro slaves for twenty one Yrs?

May not the powers of the Congress from the clause which enables them to pass all Laws necessary to carry this system into effect—& that clause also which declares their Laws to be paramount to the Constitutions of the states—be so oper-ated upon as to annihilate the state Governments?

If the Laws of the United states are to be superior to the Laws & Constitutions of the several states, why was not a Bill of Rights affixed to this Constitution by which the Liberties of individuals might have been secured against the abuse of Fœderal Power?

If Treaties are to be the Laws of the Land and to supercede all laws and Constitutions of the states—why is the Ratifica-tion of them left to the senate & President—and not to the house of Representatives also?

These queries if satisfactorily answer'd will defeat all the at-tempts of the opposition—many of them I can readily answer to satisfy myself—but I still doubt whether my fondness for the new government may not make me as improper a Judge in its favor, as the rage of the opposition renders those who are under its influence inadequate to decide even agt. it—

You will I hope my good sir excuse this scrawl which is scarcely legible it has been written by peice meals—& as I cou'd snatch an opportunity from the hurry of business—& from the noise & clamour of the disputants at ye house in which I lodge—the Mail is just going out and I have not time—to add the detail of State politics—but as I have written on the subject of the federal Constitution—I will Just detain you for a moment on ye present Situation of it in this state—

The people in the Country generally for it—the doctrine of amendments exploded by them—the Assembly I fear agt. it—Mr. Henry—Mr. Harrison—Mr. smith—All the Cabells & Colo. Mason—agt. or at least favorer's of the Amendatory system—& notwithstanding our Resolutions of the 25th. of October—I fear we shall still pass some measure that may have an influence unwarrantable & derogatory. Mr. Henry has declared his intention (and perhaps this day may see his plan effectuated) of bringing in a bill for the purpose of promoting a second Convention at Philadelphia to consider amendments—& that the speakers of the two houses shou'd form a Committee of Correspondence to communicate with our sister states on that subject—You know the force of this wonderful mans oratory upon a Virginia house of Delegates—& I am sure will with me lament that that force shou'd be ever erroneously or injudiciously directed—

Much I hope sir that we shall have the assistance of your Counsel in the Convention—

My best regards to Mr. Carrington—Mr. Griffin & Mr. Brown if they have arrived—

"Publius," The Federalist XXI
[Alexander Hamilton]

Independent Journal (New York), December 12, 1787

To the People of the State of New-York.

Having in the three last numbers taken a summary review of the principal circumstances and events, which have depicted the genius and fate of other confederate governments; I shall now proceed in the enumeration of the most important of those defects, which have hitherto disappointed our hopes from the system established among ourselves. To form a safe and satisfactory judgment of the proper remedy, it is absolutely necessary that we should be well acquainted with the extent and malignity of the disease.

The next most palpable defect of the subsisting confederation is the total want of a SANCTION to its laws. The United States as now composed, have no powers to exact obedience, or punish disobedience to their resolutions, either by pecuniary mulcts by a suspension or divestiture of privileges, or in any other constitutional mode. There is no express delegation of authority to them to use force against delinquent members; and if such a right should be ascribed to the fœderal head, as resulting from the nature of the social compact between the States, it must be by inference and construction, in the face of that part of the second article, by which it is declared, that is, "each State shall retain every power, jurisdiction and right, not *expressly* delegated to the United States in Congress assembled." There is doubtless a striking absurdity in supposing that a right of this kind does not exist, but we are reduced to the dilemma either of embracing that supposition, preposterous as it may seem, or of contravening or explaining away a provision, which has been of late a repeated theme of the eulogies of those, who oppose the new constitution; and the want of which in that plan, has been the subject of much plausible animadversion and severe criticism. If we are unwilling to impair the force of this applauded provision, we shall be obliged to conclude, that the United States afford the extraordinary spectacle of a government, destitute even of the shadow of constitutional power to enforce the execution of its own laws. It will appear from the specimens which have been cited, that the American confederacy in this particular, stands discriminated from every other institution of a similar kind, and exhibits a new and unexampled phenomenon in the political world.

The want of a mutual guarantee of the State governments is another capital imperfection in the fœderal plan. There is nothing of this kind declared in the articles that compose it; and to imply a tacit guarantee from consideration of utility, would be a still more flagrant departure from the clause which has been mentioned, than to imply a tacit power of coertion, from the like considerations. The want of a guarantee, though it might in its consequences endanger the Union, does not so immediately attack its existence as the want of a constitutional sanction to its laws.

Without a guarantee, the assistance to be derived from the Union in repelling those domestic dangers, which may sometimes threaten the existence of the State constitutions, must be renounced. Usurpation may rear its crest in each State, and trample upon the liberties of the people; while the national government could legally do nothing more than behold its encroachments with indignation and regret. A successful faction may erect a tyranny on the ruins of order and law, while no succour could constitutionally be afforded by the Union to the friends and supporters of the government. The tempestuous situation, from which Massachusetts has scarcely emerged, evinces that dangers of this kind are not merely speculative. Who can determine what might have been the issue of her late convulsions, if the mal-contents had been headed by a Cæsar or by a Cromwell? Who can predict what effect a despotism established in Massachusetts, would have upon the liberties of New-Hampshire or Rhode-Island; of Connecticut or New-York?

The inordinate pride of State importance has suggested to some minds an objection to the principle of a guarantee in the fœderal Government; as involving an officious interference in the domestic concerns of the members. A scruple of this kind would deprive us of one of the principal advantages to be expected from Union; and can only flow from a misapprehension of the nature of the provision itself—It could be no impediment to reforms of the State Constitutions by a majority of the people in a legal and peaceable mode. This right would remain undiminished. The guarantee could only operate against changes to be effected by violence. Towards the prevention of calamities of this kind too many checks cannot be provided. The peace of society, and the stability of government, depend absolutely on the efficacy of the precautions adopted on this head. Where the whole power of the government is in the hands of the people, there is the less pretence for the use of violent remedies, in partial or occasional distempers of the State. The natural cure for an ill administration, in a popular or representative constitution, is a change of men. A guarantee by the national authority would be as much levelled against the usurpations of rulers, as against the ferments and outrages of faction and sedition in the community.

The principle of regulating the contributions of the states to the common treasury by QUOTAS is another fundamental error in the confederation. Its repugnancy to an adequate supply of the national exigencies has been already pointed out, and has sufficiently appeared from the trial which has been made of it. I speak of it now solely with a view to equality among the States. Those who have been accustomed to contemplate the circumstances, which produce constitutional wealth, must be satisfied that there is no common standard, or barometer, by which the degrees of it can be ascertained. Neither the value of lands nor the numbers of the people, which have been successively proposed as the rule of State contributions, has any pretension to being a just representative. If we compare the wealth of the United Netherlands with that of Russia or Germany or even of France; and if we at the same time compare the total value of the lands, and the aggregate population of that contracted district, with the total value of the lands, and the aggregate population of the immense regions of either of the three last mentioned countries, we shall at once discover that there is no comparison between the proportion of either of these two objects and that of the relative wealth of those nations. If the like parallel were to be run between several of the American States; it would furnish a like result. Let Virginia be contrasted with North-Carolina, Pennsylvania with Connecticut, or Maryland with New-Jersey, and we shall be convinced that the respective abilities of those States, in relation to revenue, bear little or no analogy to their comparative stock in lands or to their comparative population—The position may be equally illustrated by a similar process between the counties of the same State. No man who is acquainted with the State of New-York will doubt, that the active wealth of Kings County bears a much greater proportion to that of Montgomery, than it would appear to be, if we should take either the total value of the lands or the total numbers of the people as a criterion!

The wealth of nations depends upon an infinite variety of causes. Situation, soil, climate, the nature of the productions, the nature of the government, the genius of the citizens—the degree of information they possess—the state of commerce, of arts, of industry—these circumstances and many much too complex, minute, or adventitious, to admit of a particular specification, occasion differences hardly conceivable in the relative opulence and riches of different countries. The consequence clearly is, that there can be no common measure of national wealth; and of course, no general or stationary rule, by which the ability of a State to pay taxes can be determined. The attempt therefore to regulate the contributions of the members of a confederacy, by any such rule, cannot fail to be productive of glaring inequality and extreme oppression.

This inequality would of itself be sufficient in America to work the eventual destruction of the Union, if any mode of inforcing a compliance with its requisitions could be devised. The suffering States would not long consent to remain associated upon a principle which distributes the public burthens with so unequal a hand; and which was calculated to impoverish and oppress the citizens of some States, while those of others would scarcely be conscious of the small proportion of the weight they were required to sustain. This however is an evil inseparable from the principle of quotas and requisitions.

There is no method of steering clear of this inconvenience but by authorising the national Government to raise its own revenues in its own way. Imposts, excises and in general all duties upon articles of consumption may be compared to a fluid, which will in time find its level with the means of paying them. The amount to be contributed by each citizen will in a degree be at his own option, and can be regulated by an attention to his resources. The rich may be extravagant, the poor can be frugal. And private oppression may always be avoided by a judicious selection of objects proper for such impositions. If inequalities should arise in some States from duties on particular objects, these will in all probability be counterballanced by proportional inequalities in other States from the duties on other objects. In the course of time and things, an equilibrium, as far as it is attainable, in so complicated a subject, will be established every where. Or if inequalities should still exist they would neither be so great in their degree, so uniform in their operation, nor so odious in their appearance, as those which would necessarily spring from quotas upon any scale, that can possibly be devised.

It is a signal advantage of taxes on articles of consumption, that they contain in their own nature a security against excess. They prescribe their own limit; which cannot be exceeded without defeating the end proposed—that is an extension of the revenue. When applied to this object, the saying is as just as it is witty, that "in political arithmetic, two and two do not always make four." If duties are too high they lessen the consumption—the collection is eluded; and the product to the treasury is not so great as when they are confined within proper and moderate bounds. This forms a complete barrier against any material oppression of the citizens, by taxes of this class, and is itself a natural limitation of the power of imposing them.

Impositions of this kind usually fall under the denomination of indirect taxes, and must always constitute the chief part of the revenue raised in this country. Those of the direct kind, which principally relate to lands and buildings, may admit of a rule of apportionment. Either the value of land, or the number of the people may serve as a standard. The state of agriculture, and the populousness of a country, have been

considered as nearly connected with each other. And as a rule
for the purpose intended, numbers in the view of simplicity
and certainty, are entitled to a preference. In every country it
is an Herculean task to obtain a valuation of the land; in a
country imperfectly settled and progressive in improvement,
the difficulties are increased almost to impracticability. The
expence of an accurate valuation is in all situations a formidable objection. In a branch of taxation where no limits to the
discretion of the government are to be found in the nature of
things, the establishment of a fixed rule, not incompatible
with the end, may be attended with fewer inconveniencies
than to leave that discretion altogether at large.

"Americanus" [John Stevens, Jr.] V

Daily Advertiser (New York), December 12, 1787

Montesquieu's Spirit of Laws is certainly a work of great merit. The philanthropy and acuteness of observation which every page discloses, are evidences of the excellency of his heart, and the penetrative force of his understanding.—On an attentive perusal, however, of this celebrated performance, it will manifestly appear, that the main object of the author, and what he seems ever to have most at heart, was to mollify the rigors of Monarchy, and render this species of Government in some degree compatible with Liberty. No man ever had a juster claim to the grateful acknowledgments of his countrymen. But tho' his work has been of infinite service to his country, yet the principles he has endeavored to establish will by no means stand the test of the rigid rules of philosophic precision. It ever has been the fate of system mongers to mistake the productions of their own imaginations, for those of nature herself: And their works, instead of advancing the cause of truth, serve only as false guides, who are ever ready to mislead us and impede our progress. Tho' the Spirit of Laws contains a fund of useful and just observations on Government, yet, the systematic part of it is evidently defective. His general divisions of Government into different species—his definition of their several natures, and the principles he deduces from them, do not convey to the mind clear and distinct ideas of different qualities really existing in the nature of things.

To begin with his general divisions, he has divided Government into three species; Republican, Monarchial, and Despotic. His definitions of their several natures are as follows: "A Republican Government is that in which the body, or only a part of the people is possessed of the supreme power:

Monarchy, that in which a single person governs by fixed and established laws: A Despotic Government, that in which a single person directs every thing by his own will and caprice."

In the first definition are blended together two species of Government, evidently distinct in their natures. In the one, the supreme power, or the source of power, is in the body of the people; in the other, it is in a certain number of persons, be they more or less, who form a class of men distinct from the people at large. This is a distinction derived from the very nature of things. The one is in its nature a free Government, the other is in its nature Arbitrary or Despotic. The two last definitions are only modifications of the same species. It is a Government in which all power is centered in, or derived from a single person. In order to elucidate the propriety of this general division, he has endeavoured to establish certain principles, which are the different springs of action which set these different species of Government in motion. The principle of Republican Government is VIRTUE: That of Monarchy is HONOR: That of Despotic Government is FEAR. This is certainly a very fanciful piece of business. It is to be sure an ingenious conceit, by which he would endeavor to establish a distinction between an Arbitrary Monarch and a Despotic one. Notwithstanding this happy discovery of Montesquieu in favor of the Government of his native country, fear, I apprehend, is still the most predominant principle in this Government. A military establishment, consisting of two or three hundred thousand men, is a principle of action in Government a thousand times more energetic than this vague sentiment of honor. Is honor a principle of action sufficiently powerful to make a peasant (for instance) submit with chearfulness to all the grievous impositions by which the poor are so miserably oppressed?

The theory which Montesquieu has endeavored to establish, is certainly erroneous. His general divisions; his definitions of the natures of the different species of Government, and the principles which form the springs of action in each, are unsatisfactory.

The most obvious and natural general division, and which has prevailed universally 'till Montesquieu introduced this new theory, is into Democracy, Aristocracy and Monarchy.

In Democracy the supreme power is possessed by, or derived from the aggregate body of the people. In Aristocracy, this power is possessed by, or derived from a part only of the people. In Monarchy it is possessed by, or derived from a single person. This general division may be again subdivided. Democracy may be either pure, that is where the people govern themselves, or it may be representative, that is where they delegate the powers of Government to certain persons for a limited time. So too in Aristocracy, the supreme power may be exercised by the whole body of the Nobles, or intrusted to a certain number. Monarchy may be either a pure disposition where every thing depends immediately on the will of the Prince, or assume a milder aspect by the establishment of intermediate, subordinate, and dependent powers.

As to the principles which ensure obedience, and enable the Government to operate, they are universally the same in every species of Government, though compounded in various degrees.

1. Fear, or the dread of punishment. This is the simplest, most powerful, and of course the most universal motive of obedience amongst mankind, and is therefore principally depended upon in all arbitrary Governments.

2. Attachment. This arises from an infinite variety of circumstances, and becomes the more forceable in proportion to the moderation and freedom of the Government. Customs, manners, habits, prejudices, are the ordinary sources of this attachment. But what, among an enlightened people, ought to form the strongest motive of attachment to Government, arises from a conviction of its necessity and utility.

Montesquieu tells us that "ambition is pernicious in a Republic." So far is this from being true, that the fact is, that no Government so much requires the aid of this powerful spring to human actions. By ambition however, I do not mean that insatiate lust of domination and despotic sway, by which the annals of mankind have been so disgraced, but that laudable desire of excelling in whatever we undertake, which is the source of every excellence of which our nature is capable. Without the impulse of this noble passion, where would the people find men, who would cheerfully submit themselves to the toils, cares, and perplexities incident to the management of public affairs? Montesquieu may talk of virtue as the spring of action in a republican Government; but, I trust, its force would be found too feeble to produce great exertions without the aid of ambition. Can any man, who has a tolerable acquaintance of human nature, imagine that men would so eagerly engage in public affairs, from whence they can hope to derive no personal emolument, merely from the impulse of so exalted, so pure, so disinterested a passion as patriotism, or political virtue? No! it is ambition that constitutes the very life and soul of Republican Government. As fear and attachment insure obedience to Government, so does ambition set its wheels in motion.

The necessity of following Cato, naturally led me into an investigation of the nature and principles of Republican Government. Though an enquiry of this kind is not immediately necessary in the business at present agitating, yet it is intimately connected with it, and is certainly a very interesting speculation. I shall now proceed to make some remarks on Cato's fifth number.

The Constitution directs that the members to the House of Representatives be elected biennially. This departure from the good Democratic rule it seems does not meet with Cato's approbation. The question then is, whether this delegation of legislative power for the term of two years can prove any way dangerous to liberty. If Cato will permit us to reason from analogy on this point, I conceive there will not remain the least shadow of apprehension. For if, in the Government of England, such as I have described it, a septennial Parliament, forming so inadequate a representation of the nation, and in which too officers under Government are admitted to have seats, has proved however so firm a barrier in favor of liberty, what reasonable fears can be entertained against a biennial House of Representatives, who are restricted from holding any office under Government, and who form a just and equal representation of the great body of the people. If then there can be no room for apprehensions of danger from the establishment of biennial elections, we must allow at least that it is more convenient, and affords the members more time to acquire a knowledge of public affairs competent to the station they fill.

From the whole tenor of the passage in Cato's fifth number respecting the power given to the State Executives to make temporary appointment of Senators, we are led to suppose that this power has been placed in the executive of the general Government. The executive of the Federal Government, would indeed form a strange depository of a power of this nature. It is unnecessary for me to point out the different consequences resulting from this power being vested in a State or a Federal Executive. They are certainly too important to leave the matter in the least doubtful. Candor therefore required the utmost explicitness.

But what were the views of the Convention in vesting this temporary power in the executive of each State? Was it not evidently from a scrupulous attention to the interests of the States individually. This objection therefore does not come with a good grace from Cato, who is so great an advocate for State sovereignty. It is surely of the highest importance to the States individually that they be fully represented in an Assembly who have the power of forming treaties and alliances, appointing Ambassadors, and other public ministers and consuls, judges of the Supreme Court, and all other officers of the United States, whose appointments are not otherwise provided for.

But "it is an important objection to this Government, that the representation consists of so few." How "corruption" and "treachery" should ever prevail in an Assembly constituted as this is, I cannot even conjecture. In an Assembly framed on the plan of the present Congress, where the whole of the legislative and executive powers centre in a single body, in such an Assembly there might be some ground for apprehensions of this nature.

But what man could there be in the Government who could form a separate interest of such magnitude, as to induce him to have recourse to such vile means. Surely a President, whose term of office is so short, and whose powers are so limited, could have no object in view sufficiently important to recompence him for the disgrace and ignominy which would inevitably attend an action so atrocious. But admitting that every scruple of this nature was overcome, and that he had so far succeeded in his project as, contrary to all human probability, to corrupt a majority of the legislature to concur with him, could this business be kept a secret? Would not suspicion set the minority to work, and would there be a possibility of preventing a discovery of the plot? And would not the President and his corrupt majority be hurled from their stations and consigned to everlasting infamy? But experience is the safest guide. Let us once more appeal to the Government of Great-Britain. We find an hereditary Monarch, who pursues a permanent interest manifestly distinct from the community at large. An house of Peers wholly at his devotion. He possesses an infinite variety of means of influencing a majority of the house of Commons, which can never obtain in a Government upon the plan of that we have now before us. Notwithstanding all these unfavorable circumstances we can find few or no instances in which the general interest of the nation has been betrayed or neglected.

But what would be the consequence of a representation bearing any kind of proportion to that of a State Assembly? In all probability, in half a century more, these States will contain twenty millions of people, which number, according to the rule established by the Constitution, would require a house of representatives, consisting of near seven hundred members. An Assembly much larger than this, could not act with any tolerable convenience as one deliberative body.

"Another thing may be suggested against the small number of representatives is, that the choice will be confined to a very few." And so it would be was this number quadrupled. For what proportion would twenty four bear to the whole number of citizens in this State. But the fact is, that no Government, that has ever yet existed in the world, affords so ample a field, to individuals of all ranks, for the display of political talents and abilities. Here are no Patricians, who engross the offices of State. No man who has real merit, let his situation be what it will, need dispair. He first distinguishes himself amongst his neighbours at township and county meeting; he is next sent to the State Legislature. In this theatre his abilities, whatever they are, are exhibited in their true colors, and displayed to the views of every man in the State: from hence his ascent to a seat in Congress becomes easy and sure. Such a regular uninterrupted gradation from the chief men in a village, to the chair of the President of the United States, which this Government affords to all her citizens without distinction, is a perfection in Republican Government, heretofore unknown and unprecedented.

"Philadelphiensis [Benjamin Workman] IV

Freeman's Journal (Philadelphia), December 12, 1787

1 SAMUEL viii. 18. —*And ye shall cry out in that day, because of your* king *which ye shall have chosen you: and the Lord will not hear you in that day.*

My Fellow-Citizens, I do not write to inflame your minds, but to inform them. I do not write with a view to excite jealousies, and exhibit imaginary evils, but to promote your peace: I have no intentions of encouraging you to oppose or alter your present free government; but on the contrary, I advise you, yea, I entreat you, not to change it for one that is worse: if you cannot procure a better, why, be doing with the old bad one. Except you are tired of freedom; except you are determined to entail slavery on yourselves and your posterity, for God's sake reject with that dignity becoming freemen, that tyrannical system of government, the new constitution. If you adopt it in toto, you will lose every thing dear to freemen, and receive nothing in return but misery and disgrace. Were some additional powers for regulating commerce, and the *impost duties* for a limited time, granted to the present Congress; this would probably answer all our purposes: but before Congress should be vested with greater powers than they now have, their number ought at least to be tripled—suppose two hundred and sixty; that is, twenty members for each state. But this matter I shall leave for the discussion of our next federal convention; if we should have the good luck to see their high mightinesses once more *locked up in the Statehouse*, guarded by captain M'Clean's old battle-ax battalion.

Among the schemes and collusions that the friends of the new constitution have made use of to dupe the people into its adoption, that of making them believe that such a government would raise America to an eminent rank among the nations of the earth, seems to have been one of the most successful.—There is not a writer that I have seen on the subject, that has called the truth of this matter into question; no wonder then, that the less informed should be imposed upon; when men of more enlightened understandings seem even to have swallowed the bait.

No people in the world have more of the genuine *amor patriæ*, than the citizens of the United States; that noble ambition, that laudable love for the dignity and character of his country, is so implanted in the breast of an American, that he is willing not only to contribute generously and largely of his property, but likewise to expend his blood to support that government that should establish the national respectability of his country.—This truly grand principle is so copiously infused into the hearts of our countrymen, that, I really believe, there is scarce an inconvenience to which they would not cheerfully submit, provided this great point could be obtained. On this account then there are many who, although they are thoroughly persuaded, that the new constitution is defective in many striking and material instances, yet, through their national pride, would magnanimously overlook these, to have their country on a respectable footing as a nation. But ah, my fellow citizens, you are even disappointed here! It is a mere delusion! nothing but the basest deception; for, in the adoption of this constitution, we will probably lose that small portion of national character which we now enjoy, instead of gaining an accession to it. What compensation then are you to receive in return for the liberties and privileges belonging to yourselves and posterity, that you are now about to sacrifice at the altar of this *monster*, this *Colossus of despotism*. Why really the return you deserve, if you are mean enough to submit to be gulled after this manner, is *poverty, slavery* and *broken hearts*.—But probably, you will say, these are groundless conjectures, and we are perfectly convinced, that our new government, however it may be imperfect in some matters of an inferior nature, yet it must and will be *powerful*; yea, a government that will make its enemies tremble. If you mean by its enemies the helpless widow and orphan, the hard working husbandman, sunk down by labour and poverty, I grant it; but if you mean a foreign enemy, you insult your understanding. No, my friends, instead of becoming formidable, we will be the scorn and contempt of the whole world during the existence of this contemptible government. Let us take but a rational view of its strength and respectability, and then we shall see that we have really nothing to depend on in this new constitution, that can raise the national character of America, but on the contrary, we will sink into a state of insignificance and misery.

The number of inhabitants in the United States is now probably about three millions and an half.—These are scattered over a continent twelve hundred miles long and eight hundred broad. Now to keep such an extensive country in subjection to one general government, a *standing army* by far too numerous for such a small number of people to maintain, must and will be garrisoned in every district through the whole; and in case of emergency, the collecting of these scattered troops into one large body, to act against a foreign enemy, will be morally impossible. Besides they will have too much business on hand at their respective garrisons, *in awing the people*, to be spared for other purposes. There is no doubt, but to carry the arbitrary decrees of the federal judges into execution, and to protect the *tax gatherers* in collecting the revenue, will be ample employment for the military; indeed with all their strength and numbers, I am afraid, that they will find this a job of some difficulty, perhaps more than they will get through decently. Upon the whole I think it is pretty obvious, that our *standing army* will have *other fish to fry* than fighting a foreign enemy; there is work enough cut out for them of a domestic nature, without troubling them on other occasions. Moreover, such of them as might be brought into action, could not be depended upon; for they will principally consist of the purgings of the European prisons, and low ruffians bred among ourselves who do not love to work.—And who could suppose that such vile characters as these, should be trusted to protect our country, our wives, our daughters, and our little ones? No, my friends, God deliver us from such protectors!—Their mean souls wanting that *amor patriæ*, that love of virtue, that noble love for the welfare and happiness of their fellow men, which animates the man of courage, and constitutes him the soldier, would fail them at the approach of an enemy; yea, they would either fly ere the battle commenced, or submit on the first charge; and probably turn their arms against the country that expected their protection. What I advance here, are truths, founded on reason and the nature of things, and the experience of all ages affords ample examples for their illustration.

Very little need be said respecting the militia defending the country; perhaps what I have advanced in my last essay, is enough on that head; indeed the thing itself carries its own evidence along with it. A person that has judgment sufficient to compare two ideas together, must see, that an *oppressed people*, reduced to a state of abject vassalage, by a despotic government, will never voluntarily venture their lives for it.

When people are once slaves, it is a matter of little concern to them who are their masters.—The fable of the sensible ass is so pertinent to our purpose, that I cannot forbear reciting it:—"An old fellow was feeding an ass in a fine green meadow, and being alarmed by the sudden approach of the enemy, was impatient with the ass to put himself forward, and fly with all the speed he was able. The ass asked him, whether or no he thought the enemy would clap *two pair of panniers* upon his back? The man said, no, there was no fear of that. Why then, says the ass, I'll not stir an inch, for what is it to me who my master is, since I shall but carry my *panniers* as usual."

There is not the most distant hope, that we shall ever have a navy under this constitution which annihilates the state governments; for, if each state were to retain its *sovereignty*, I am well convinced, that we might have a considerable *fleet* in a few years; the larger states might each build a ship of the line every year, and the lesser states would furnish us with frigates; a noble emulation among the states would be the consequence, one state would vie with another, and public spirited individuals would contribute generously to raise the character of their own state. But this consolidation of all the states into one general government, renders this project impossible; the federal government having an unlimited power in taxation, which, no doubt, they will exercise to the utmost; leaves the states without the means of building even a *boat*. But had they money, they dare not use it for that purpose, for, Congress are to have an absolute power over the *standing army, navy,* and *militia*; so that it is out of the question, whether a particular state be, or be not, able to build a ship of war; she must meddle with no such matter; it only belongs to the emperor and our well born Congress to build and maintain a navy. Now, if we give ourselves time to think but for a moment, we must be convinced in our minds, that Congress having a large national debt already accumulated, the emperor, themselves, their judges, lawyers, revenue-collectors, dependants, flatterers, &c. &c. and above all, the *standing army*, at least double officered, to provide for, will find themselves at their wit's end, to devise *ways* and *means* for all these purposes. In short, the industry of three millions of people, were it all applied to this use, would be little enough.—Where then will the navy come from? Where will Congress find money even to build and maintain cutters to prevent smuggling on the extensive coast of America? No where, truly: such a supposition is farcical indeed; and should the new constitution be established, a federal navy is a mere finesse, an absolute nonentity.

The Congress must procure money to pay the *standing army punctually*, come of other matters what will; their very existence depends on this. For a neglect of payment might and really would cause a mutiny in the military, and then, down tumbles the federal constitution, whose *mighty basis* was said to be at the centre of the earth. The standing army will be its grand support—now, if this give way, the building itself will be instantly levelled to the ground. And heaven grant that Columbia may never see such another erected again on her domain. *Amen.*

"Brutus" V

New York Journal, December 13, 1787

To the PEOPLE of the State of NEW-YORK.

It was intended in this Number to have prosecuted the enquiry into the organization of this new system; particularly to have considered the dangerous and premature union of the President and Senate, and the mixture of legislative, executive, and judicial powers in the Senate.

But there is such an intimate connection between the several branches in whom the different species of authority is lodged, and the powers with which they are invested, that on reflection it seems necessary first to proceed to examine the nature and extent of the powers granted to the legislature.

This enquiry will assist us the better to determine, whether the legislature is so constituted, as to provide proper checks and restrictions for the security of our rights, and to guard against the abuse of power—For the means should be suited to the end; a government should be framed with a view to the objects to which it extends: if these be few in number, and of such a nature as to give but small occasion or opportunity to work oppression in the exercise of authority, there will be less need of a numerous representation, and special guards against abuse, than if the powers of the government are very extensive, and include a great variety of cases. It will also be found necessary to examine the extent of these powers, in order to form a just opinion how far this system can be considered as a confederation, or a consolidation of the states. Many of the advocates for, and most of the opponents to this system, agree that the form of government most suitable for the United States, is that of a confederation. The idea of a confederated government is that of a number of independent states entering into a compact, for the conducting certain general concerns, in which they have a common interest, leaving the management of their internal and local affairs to their separate governments. But whether the system proposed is of this nature cannot be determined without a strict enquiry into the powers proposed to be granted.

This constitution considers the people of the several states as one body corporate, and is intended as an original compact, it will therefore dissolve all contracts which may be inconsistent with it. This not only results from its nature, but is expressly declared in the *6th article* of it. The design of the constitution is expressed in the preamble, to be, "in order to form a more perfect union, to establish justice, insure domestic tranquility, provide for the common defence, promote the general welfare, and secure the blessings of liberty to ourselves and posterity." These are the ends this government is to accomplish, and for which it is invested with certain powers, among these is the power "to make all laws which are *necessary and proper* for carrying into execution the foregoing powers, and *all other* powers vested by this constitution in the government of the United States, or in any department or officer thereof." It is a rule in construing a law to consider the objects the legislature had in view in passing it, and to give it such an explanation as to promote their intention. The same rule will apply in explaining a constitution. The great objects then are declared in this preamble in general and indefinite terms to be to provide for the common defence, promote the general welfare, and an express power being vested in the legislature to make all laws which shall be necessary and proper for carrying into execution all the powers vested in the general government. The inference is natural that the legislature will have an authority to make all laws which they shall judge necessary for the common safety, and to promote the general welfare. This amounts to a power to make laws at discretion: No terms can be found more indefinite than these, and it is obvious, that the legislature alone must judge what laws are proper and necessary for the purpose. It may be said, that this way of explaining the constitution, is torturing and making it speak what it never intended. This is far from my intention, and I shall not even insist upon this implied power, but join issue with those who say we are to collect the idea of the powers given from the express words of the clauses granting them; and it will not be difficult to shew that the same authority is expressly given which is supposed to be implied in the forgoing paragraphs.

In the 1st article, 8th section, it is declared, "that Congress shall have power to lay and collect taxes, duties, imposts and excises, to pay the debts, and provide for the common defence, and general welfare of the United States." In the preamble, the intent of the constitution, among other things, is declared to be to provide for the common defence, and promote the general welfare, and in this clause the power is in express words given to Congress "to provide for the common defence, and general welfare."—And in the last paragraph of the same section there is an express authority to make all laws which shall be necessary and proper for carrying into execution this power. It is therefore evident, that the legislature under this constitution may pass any law which they may think proper. It is true the 9th section restrains their power with respect to certain objects. But these restrictions are very limited, some of them improper, some unimportant, and others not easily understood, as I shall hereafter shew. It has been urged that the meaning I give to this part of the constitution is not the true one, that the intent of it is to confer on the legislature the power to lay and collect taxes, &c. in order to provide for the common defence and general welfare. To this I would reply, that the meaning and intent of the constitution is to be collected from the words of it, and I submit to the public, whether the construction I have given it is not the most natural and easy. But admitting the contrary opinion to prevail, I shall nevertheless, be able to shew, that the same powers are substantially vested in the general government, by several other articles in the constitution. It invests the legislature with authority to lay and collect taxes, duties, imposts and excises, in order to provide for the common defence, and promote the general welfare, and to pass all laws which may be necessary and proper for carrying this power into effect. To comprehend the extent of this authority, it will be requisite to examine 1st. what is included in this power to lay and collect taxes, duties, imposts and excises.

2d. What is implied in the authority, to pass all laws which shall be necessary and proper for carrying this power into execution.

3d. What limitation, if any, is set to the exercise of this power by the constitution.

1st. To detail the particulars comprehended in the general terms, taxes, duties, imposts and excises, would require a volume, instead of a single piece in a news-paper. Indeed it would be a task far beyond my ability, and to which no one can be competent, unless possessed of a mind capable of comprehending every possible source of revenue; for they extend to every possible way of raising money, whether by direct or indirect taxation. Under this clause may be imposed a poll-tax, a land-tax, a tax on houses and buildings, on windows and fire places, on cattle and on all kinds of personal property:—It extends to duties on all kinds of goods to any amount, to tonnage and poundage on vessels, to duties on written instruments, news-papers, almanacks, and books:—It comprehends an excise on all kinds of liquors, spirits, wines, cyder, beer, &c. and indeed takes in duty or excise on every necessary or conveniency of life; whether of foreign or home growth or manufactory. In short, we can have no conception of any way in which a government can raise money from the people, but what is included in one or other of these general terms. We may say then that this clause commits to the hands of the general legislature every conceivable source of revenue within the United States. Not only are these terms very comprehensive, and extend to a vast number of objects, but the power to lay and collect has great latitude; it will lead to the passing a vast number of laws, which may affect the personal rights of the citizens of the states, expose their property to fines and confiscation, and put their lives in jeopardy: it opens a door to the appointment of a swarm of revenue and excise officers to prey upon the honest and industrious part of the community, eat up their substance, and riot on the spoils of the country.

2d. We will next enquire into what is implied in the authority to pass all laws which shall be necessary and proper to carry this power into execution.

It is, perhaps, utterly impossible fully to define this power.

The authority granted in the first clause can only be understood in its full extent, by descending to all the particular
cases in which a revenue can be raised; the number and
variety of these cases are so endless, and as it were infinite,
that no man living has, as yet, been able to reckon them up.
The greatest geniuses in the world have been for ages
employed in the research, and when mankind had supposed
that the subject was exhausted they have been astonished with
the refined improvements that have been made in modern
times, and especially in the English nation on the subject—If
then the objects of this power cannot be comprehended, how
is it possible to understand the extent of that power which
can pass all laws which shall be necessary and proper for
carrying it into execution? It is truly incomprehensible. A case
cannot be conceived of, which is not included in this power.
It is well known that the subject of revenue is the most difficult and extensive in the science of government. It requires
the greatest talents of a statesman, and the most numerous
and exact provisions of the legislature. The command of the
revenues of a state gives the command of every thing in
it.—He that has the purse will have the sword, and they that
have both, have every thing; so that the legislature having
every source from which money can be drawn under their
direction, with a right to make all laws necessary and proper
for drawing forth all the resource of the country, would have,
in fact, all power.

Were I to enter into the detail, it would be easy to shew
how this power in its operation, would totally destroy all
the powers of the individual states. But this is not necessary for those who will think for themselves, and it will be
useless to such as take things upon trust, nothing will awaken
them to reflection, until the iron hand of oppression compel
them to it.

I shall only remark, that this power, given to the federal
legislature, directly annihilates all the powers of the state legislatures. There cannot be a greater solecism in politics than
to talk of power in a government, without the command of
any revenue. It is as absurd as to talk of an animal without
blood, or the subsistence of one without food. Now the
general government having in their controul every possible

source of revenue, and authority to pass any law they may deem necessary to draw them forth, or to facilitate their collection; no source of revenue is therefore left in the hands of any state. Should any state attempt to raise money by law, the general government may repeal or arrest it in the execution, for all their laws will be the supreme law of the land: If then any one can be weak enough to believe that a government can exist without having the authority to raise money to pay a door-keeper to their assembly, he may believe that the state government can exist, should this new constitution take place.

It is agreed by most of the advocates of this new system, that the government which is proper for the United States should be a confederated one; that the respective states ought to retain a portion of their sovereignty, and that they should preserve not only the forms of their legislatures, but also the power to conduct certain internal concerns. How far the powers to be retained by the states shall extend, is the question; we need not spend much time on this subject, as it respects this constitution, for a government without the power to raise money is one only in name. It is clear that the legislatures of the respective states must be altogether dependent on the will of the general legislature, for the means of supporting their government. The legislature of the United States will have a right to exhaust every source of revenue in every state, and to annul all laws of the states which may stand in the way of effecting it; unless therefore we can suppose the state governments can exist without money to support the officers who execute them, we must conclude they will exist no longer than the general legislatures choose they should. Indeed the idea of any government existing, in any respect, as an independent one, without any means of support in their own hands, is an absurdity. If therefore, this constitution has in view, what many of its framers and advocates say it has, to secure and guarantee to the separate states the exercise of certain powers of government it certainly ought to have left in their hands some sources of revenue. It should have marked the line in which the general government should have raised money, and set bounds over which they should not pass, leaving to the separate states other means to raise supplies for the support of their governments, and to discharge their respective debts. To this it is objected, that the general government ought to have power competent to the purposes of the union; they are to provide for the common defence, to pay the debts of the United States, support foreign ministers, and the civil establishment of the union, and to do these they ought to have authority to raise money adequate to the purpose. On this I observe, that the state governments have also contracted debts, they require money to support their civil officers, and how this is to be done, if they give to the general government a power to raise money in every way in which it can possibly be raised, with such a controul over the state legislatures as to prohibit them, whenever the general legislature may think proper, from raising any money. It is again objected that it is very difficult, if not impossible, to draw the line of distinction between the powers of the general and state governments on this subject. The first, it is said, must have the power of raising the money necessary for the purposes of the union, if they are limited to certain objects the revenue may fall short of a sufficiency for the public exigencies, they must therefore have discretionary power. The line may be easily and accurately drawn between the powers of the two governments on this head. The distinction between external and internal taxes, is not a novel one in this country, it is a plain one, and easily understood. The first includes impost duties on all imported goods; this species of taxes it is proper should be laid by the general government; many reasons might be urged to shew that no danger is to be apprehended from their exercise of it. They may be collected in few places, and from few hands with certainty and expedition. But few officers are necessary to be imployed in collecting them, and there is no danger of oppression in laying them, because, if they are laid higher than trade will bear, the merchants will cease importing, or smuggle their goods. We have therefore sufficient security, arising from the nature of the thing, against burdensome, and intolerable impositions from this kind of tax. But the case is far otherwise with regard to direct taxes; these include poll taxes, land taxes, excises, duties on written instruments, on every thing we eat, drink, or wear; they take hold of every species of property, and come home to every man's house and packet. These are often so oppressive, as to grind the face of the poor, and render the lives of the common people a burden to them. The great and only security the people can have against oppression from this kind of taxes, must rest in their representatives. If they are sufficiently numerous to be well informed of the circumstances, and ability of those who send them, and have a proper regard for the people, they will be secure. The general legislature, as I have shewn in a former paper, will not be thus qualified, and therefore, on this account, ought not to exercise the power of direct taxation. If the power of laying imposts will not be sufficient, some other specific mode of raising a revenue should have been assigned the general government; many may be suggested in which their power may be accurately defined and limited, and it would be much better to give them authority to lay and collect a duty on exports, not to exceed a certain rate per cent, than to have surrendered every kind of resource that the country has, to the complete abolition of the state governments, and which will introduce such an infinite number of laws and ordinances, fines and penalties, courts, and judges, collectors, and excisemen, that when a man can number them, he may enumerate the stars of Heaven.

I shall resume this subject in my next, and by an induction of particulars shew, that this power, in its exercise, will subvert all state authority, and will work to the oppression of the people, and that there are no restrictions in the constitution that will soften its rigour, but rather the contrary.

"Publius," The Federalist XXII
[Alexander Hamilton]

New-York Packet, December 14, 1787

To the People of the State of New-York.

In addition to the defects already enumerated in the existing Fœderal system, there are others of not less importance, which concur in rendering it altogether unfit for the administration or the affairs of the Union.

The want of a power to regulate commerce is by all parties allowed to be of the number. The utility of such a power has been anticipated under the first head of our inquiries; and for this reason as well as from the universal conviction entertained upon the subject, little need be added in this place. It is indeed evident, on the most superficial view, that there is no object, either as it respects the interests of trade or finance that more strongly demands a Fœderal superintendence. The want of it has already operated as a bar to the formation of beneficial treaties with foreign powers; and has given occasions of dissatisfaction between the States. No nation acquainted with the nature of our political association would be unwise enough to enter into stipulations with the United States, by which they conceded privileges of any importance to them, while they were apprised that the engagements on the part of the Union, might at any moment be violated by its members; and while they found from experience that they might enjoy every advantage they desired in our markets, without granting us any return, but such as their momentary convenience might suggest. It is not therefore to be wondered at, that Mr. Jenkinson in ushering into the House of Commons a bill for regulating the temporary intercourse between the two countries, should preface its introduction by a declaration that similar provisions in former bills had been found to answer every purpose to the commerce of Great Britain, & that it would be prudent to persist in the plan until it should appear whether the American government was likely or not to acquire greater consistency.*

Several States have endeavoured by separate prohibitions, restrictions and exclusions, to influence the conduct of that kingdom in this particular; but the want of concert, arising from the want of a general authority, and from clashing, and dissimilar views in the States, has hitherto frustrated every experiment of the kind; and will continue to do so as long as the same obstacles to an uniformity of measures continue to exist.

The interfering and unneighbourly regulations of some States, contrary to the true spirit of the Union, have in different instances given just cause of umbrage and complaint to others; and it is to be feared that examples of this nature, if not restrained by a national controul, would be multiplied and extended till they became not less serious sources of animosity and discord, than injurious impediments to the intercourse between the different parts of the confederacy. "The commerce of the German empire,† is in continual trammels from the multiplicity of the duties which the several Princes and States exact upon the merchandizes passing through their territories; by means of which the fine streams and navigable rivers with which Germany is so happily watered, are rendered almost useless." Though the genius of the people of this country might never permit this description to be strictly applicable to us, yet we may reasonably expect, from the gradual conflicts of State regulations, that the citizens of each, would at length come to be considered and treated by the others in no better light than that of foreigners and aliens.

The power of raising armies, by the most obvious construction of the articles of the confederation, is merely a power of making requisitions upon the States for quotas of men. This practice, in the course of the late war, was found replete with obstructions to a vigorous and to an œconomical system of defence. It gave birth to a competition between the States,

*This as nearly as I can recollect was the sense of his speech in introducing the last bill.

†Encyclopedie *article* empire.

which created a kind of auction for men. In order to furnish the quotas required of them, they outbid each other, till bounties grew to an enormous and insupportable size. The hope of a still further increase afforded an inducement to those who were disposed to serve to procrastinate their inlistment; and disinclined them to engaging for any considerable periods. Hence slow and scanty levies of men in the most critical emergencies of our affairs—short inlistments at an unparalleled expence—continual fluctuations in the troops, ruinous to their discipline, and subjecting the public safety frequently to the perilous crisis of a disbanded army—Hence also those oppressive expedients for raising men which were upon several occasions practised, and which nothing but the enthusiasm of liberty would have induced the people to endure.

This method of raising troops is not more unfriendly to œconomy and vigor, than it is to an equal distribution of the burthen. The States near the seat of war, influenced by motives of self preservation, made efforts to furnish their quotas, which even exceeded their abilities, while those at a distance from danger were for the most part as remiss as the others were diligent in their exertions. The immediate pressure of this inequality was not in this case, as in that of the contributions of money, alleviated by the hope of a final liquidation. The States which did not pay their proportions of money, might at least be charged with their deficiencies; but no account could be formed of the deficiencies in the supplies of men. We shall not, however, see much reason to regret the want of this hope, when we consider how little prospect there is, that the most delinquent States will ever be able to make compensation for their pecuniary failures. The system of quotas and requisitions, whether it be applied to men or money, is in every view a system of imbecility in the union, and of inequality and injustice among the members.

The right of equal suffrage among the States is another exceptionable part of the confederation. Every idea of proportion, and every rule of fair representation conspire to condemn a principle, which gives to Rhode-Island an equal weight in the scale of power with Massachusetts, or Connecticut, or New-York; and to Delaware, an equal voice in the national deliberations with Pennsylvania or Virginia, or North-Carolina. Its operation contradicts that fundamental maxim of republican government, which requires that the sense of the majority should prevail. Sophistry may reply, that sovereigns are equal, and that a majority of the votes of the States will be a majority of confederated America. But this kind of logical legerdemain will never counteract the plain suggestions of justice and common sense. It may happen that this majority of States is a small minority of the people of America;* and two thirds of the people of America, could not long be persuaded, upon the credit of artificial distinctions and syllogistic subtleties, to submit their interests to the management and disposal of one third. The larger States would after a while revolt from the idea of receiving the law from the smaller. To acquiesce in such a privation of their due importance in the political scale, would be not merely to be insensible to the love of power, but even to sacrifice the desire of equality. It is neither rational to expect the first, nor just to require the last—the smaller States considering how peculiarly their safety and welfare depend on union, ought readily to renounce a pretension; which, if not relinquished would prove fatal to its duration.

It may be objected to this, that not seven but nine States, or two thirds of the whole number must consent to the most important resolutions; and it may be thence infered, that nine States would always comprehend a majority of the inhabitants of the Union. But this does not obviate the impropriety of an equal vote between States of the most unequal dimensions and populousness; nor is the inference accurate in point of fact; for we can enumerate nine States which contain less than a majority of the people;† and it is constitutionally possible, that these nine may give the vote. Besides there are matters of considerable moment detainable by a bare majority; and there are others, concerning which doubts have been entertained,

---

*New-Hampshire, Rhode-Island, New-Jersey, Delaware, Georgia, South-Carolina and Maryland, are a majority of the whole number of the States, but they do not contain one third of the people.

†Add New-York and Connecticut, to the foregoing seven, and they will still be less than a majority.

which if interpreted in favor of the sufficiency of a vote of seven States, would extend its operation to interests of the first magnitude. In addition to this, it is to be observed, that there is a probability of an increase in the number of States, and no provision for a proportional augmentation of the ratio of votes.

But this is not all; what at first sight may seem a remedy, is in reality a poison. To give a minority a negative upon the majority (which is always the case where more than a majority is requisite to a decision) is in its tendency to subject the sense of the greater number to that of the lesser number. Congress from the non-attendance of a few States have been frequently in the situation of a Polish Diet, where a single VOTE has been sufficient to put a stop to all their movements. A sixtieth part of the Union, which is about the proportion of Delaware and Rhode-Island, has several times been able to oppose an intire bar to its operations. This is one of those refinements which in practice has an effect, the reverse of what is expected from it in theory. The necessity of unanimity in public bodies, or of something approaching towards it, has been founded upon a supposition that it would contribute to security. But its real operation is to embarrass the administration, to destroy the energy of government, and to substitute the pleasure, caprice or artifices of an insignificant, turbulent or corrupt junto, to the regular deliberations and decisions of a respectable major- ity. In those emergencies of a nation, in which the goodness or badness, the weakness or strength of its government, is of the greatest importance, there is commonly a necessity for action. The public business must in some way or other go forward. If a pertinacious minority can controul the opinion of a majority respecting the best mode of conducting it; the majority in order that something may be done, must conform to the views of the minority; and thus the sense of the smaller number will over-rule that of the greater, and give a tone to the national proceedings. Hence tedious delays—continual negotiation and intrigue—contemptible compromises of the public good. And yet in such a system, it is even happy when such compromises can take place: For upon some occasions, things will not admit of accommodation; and then the mea- sures of government must be injuriously suspended or fatally defeated. It is often, by the impracticability of obtaining the concurrence of the necessary number of votes, kept in a state of inaction. Its situation must always favour of weakness—sometimes border upon anarchy.

It is not difficult to discover that a principle of this kind gives greater scope to foreign corruption as well as to domestic faction, than that which permits the sense of the majority to decide; though the contrary of this has been presumed. The mistake has proceeded from not attending with due care to the mischiefs that may be occasioned by obstructing the progress of government at certain critical seasons. When the concurrence of a large number is required by the constitution to the doing of any national act, we are apt to rest satisfied that all is safe, because nothing improper will be likely *to be done*; but we forget how much good may be prevented, and how much ill may be produced, by the power of hindering the doing what may be necessary, and of keeping affairs in the same unfavorable posture in which they may happen to stand at particular periods.

Suppose for instance we were engaged in a war, in conjunction with one foreign nation against another. Suppose the necessity of our situation demanded peace, and the interest or ambition of our ally led him to seek the prosecution of the war, with views that might justify us in making separate terms. In such a state of things, this ally of ours would evidently find it much easier by his bribes and intrigues to tie up the hands of government from making peace, where two thirds of all the votes were requisite to that object, than where a simple majority would suffice. In the first case he would have to corrupt a smaller number; in the last a greater number. Upon the same principle it would be much easier for a foreign power with which we were at war, to perplex our councils and embarrass our exertions. And in a commercial view we may be subjected to similar inconveniences. A nation, with which we might have a treaty of commerce, could with much greater facility prevent our forming a connection with her competitor in trade; tho' such a connection should be ever so beneficial to ourselves.

Evils of this description ought not to be regarded as imaginary. One of the weak sides of republics, among their numerous advantages, is that they afford too easy an inlet to foreign corruption. An hereditary monarch, though often disposed to sacrifice his subjects to his ambition, has so great a personal interest in the government, and in the external glory of the nation, that it is not easy for a foreign power to give him an equivalent for what he would sacrifice by treachery to the State. The world has accordingly been witness to few examples of this species of royal prostitution, though there have been abundant specimens of every other kind.

In republics, persons elevated from the mass of the community, by the suffrages of their fellow-citizens, to stations of great pre-eminence and power, may find compensations for betraying their trust, which to any but minds animated and guided by superior virtue, may appear to exceed the proportion of interest they have in the common stock, and to overbalance the obligations of duty. Hence it is that history furnishes us with so many mortifying examples of the prevalency of foreign corruption in republican governments. How much this contributed to the ruin of the ancient commonwealths has been already delineated. It is well known that the deputies of the United Provinces have, in various instances been purchased by the emissaries of the neighbouring kingdoms. The Earl of Chesterfield (if my memory serves me right) in a letter to his court, intimates that his success in an important negotiation, must depend on his obtaining a Major's commission for one of those deputies. And in Sweden, the parties were alternately bought by France and England, in so barefaced and notorious a manner that it excited universal disgust in the nation; and was a principal cause that the most limited monarch in Europe, in a single day, without tumult, violence, or opposition, became one of the most absolute and uncontrouled.

A circumstance, which crowns the defects of the confederation, remains yet to be mentioned—the want of a judiciary power. Laws are a dead letter without courts to expound and define their true meaning and operation. The treaties of the United States to have any force at all, must be considered as part of the law of the land. Their true import as far as respects individuals, must, like all other laws, be ascertained by judicial determinations. To produce uniformity in these determinations, they ought to be submitted in the last resort, to one SUPREME TRIBUNAL. And this tribunal ought to be instituted under the same authority which forms the treaties themselves. These ingredients are both indispensable. If there is in each State, a court of final jurisdiction, there may be as many different final determinations on the same point, as there are courts. There are endless diversities in the opinions of men. We often see not only different courts, but the Judges of the same court differing from each other. To avoid the confusion which would unavoidably result from the contradictory decisions of a number of independent judicatories, all nations have found it necessary to establish one court paramount to the rest—possessing a general superintendance, and authorised to settle and declare in the last resort, an uniform rule of civil justice.

This is the more necessary where the frame of the government is so compounded, that the laws of the whole are in danger of being contravened by the laws of the parts. In this case if the particular tribunals are invested with a right of ultimate jurisdiction, besides the contradictions to be expected from difference of opinion, there will be much to fear from the bias of local views and prejudices, and from the interference of local regulations. As often as such an interference was to happen, there would be reason to apprehend, that the provisions of the particular laws might be prefered to those of the general laws; for nothing is more natural to men in office, than to look with peculiar deference towards that authority to which they owe their official existence.

The treaties of the United States, under the present constitution, are liable to the infractions of thirteen different Legislatures, and as many different courts of final jurisdiction, acting under the authority of those Legislatures. The faith, the reputation, the peace of the whole union, are there continually at the mercy of the prejudices, the passions, and the interests of every member of which it is composed. Is it possible that foreign nations can either respect or confide in such a government? Is it possible that the People of America will longer consent to trust their honor, their happiness, their safety, on so precarious a foundation?

In this review of the Confederation, I have confined myself

to the exhibition of its most material defects; passing over those imperfections in its details, by which even a great part of the power intended to be confered upon it has been in a great measure rendered abortive. It must be by this time evident to all men of reflection, who can divest themselves of the prepossessions of preconceived opinions, that it is a system so radically vicious and unsound, as to admit not of amendment but by an entire change in its leading features and characters.

The organization of Congress, is itself utterly improper for the exercise of those powers which are necessary to be deposited in the Union. A single Assembly may be a proper receptacle of those slender, or rather fettered authorities, which have been heretofore delegated to the fœderal head; but it would be inconsistent with all the principles of good government, to intrust it with those additional powers which even the moderate and more rational adversaries of the proposed constitution admit ought to reside in the United States. If that plan should not be adopted; and if the necessity of union should be able to withstand the ambitious aims of those men, who may indulge magnificent schemes of personal aggrandizement from its dissolution; the probability would be, that we should run into the project of confering supplementary powers upon Congress as they are now constituted; and either the machine, from the intrinsic feebleness of its structure, will moulder into pieces in spite of our ill-judged efforts to prop it; or by successive augmentations of its force and energy, as necessity might prompt, we shall finally accumulate in a single body, all the most important prerogatives of sovereignty; and thus entail upon our posterity, one of the most execrable forms of government that human infatuation ever contrived. Thus we should create in reality that very tyranny, which the adversaries of the new constitution either are, or affect to be solicitous to avert.

It has not a little contributed to the infirmities of the existing fœderal system, that it never had a ratification by the PEOPLE. Resting on no better foundation than the consent of the several Legislatures, it has been exposed to frequent and intricate questions concerning the validity of its powers; and has in some instances given birth to the enormous doctrine of a right of legislative repeal. Owing its ratification to the law of a State, it has been contended, that the same authority might repeal the law by which it was ratified. However gross a heresy it may be, to maintain that *a party* to a *compact* has a right to revoke that *compact*, the doctrine itself has had respectable advocates. The possibility of a question of this nature, proves the necessity of laying the foundations of our national government deeper than in the mere sanction of delegated authority. The fabric of American Empire ought to rest on the solid basis of THE CONSENT OF THE PEOPLE. The streams of national power ought to flow immediately from that pure original fountain of all legitimate authority.

"Agrippa" [*James Winthrop*] *VI*

Massachusetts Gazette (Boston), December 14, 1787

To the PEOPLE.

To prevent any mistakes, or misapprehensions of the argument, stated in my last paper, to prove that the proposed constitution is an actual consolidation of the separate states into one extensive commonwealth, the reader is desired to observe, that in the course of the argument, the new plan is considered as an intire system. It is not dependent on any other book for an explanation, and contains no references to any other book. All the defences of it, therefore, so far as they are drawn from the state constitutions, or from maxims of the common law, are foreign to the purpose. It is only by comparing the different parts of it together, that the meaning of the whole is to be understood. For instance—

We find in it, that there is to be a legislative assembly, with authority to constitute courts for the trial of all kinds of civil causes, between citizens of different states. The right to appoint such courts necessarily involves in it the right of defining their powers, and determining the rules by which their judgment shall be regulated; and the grant of the former of those rights is nugatory without the latter. It is vain to tell us, that a maxim of common law requires contracts to be determined by the law existing where the contract was made: for it is also a maxim, that the legislature has a right to alter the common law. Such a power forms an essential part of legislation. Here, then, a declaration of rights is of inestimable value. It contains those principles which the government never can invade without an open violation of the compact between them and the citizens. Such a declaration ought to have come to the new constitution in favour of the legislative rights of the several states, by which their sovereignty over their own citizens within the state should be secured. Without such an express declaration the states are annihilated in reality upon receiving this constitution—the forms will be preserved only during the pleasure of Congress.

The idea of consolidation is further kept up in the right given to regulate trade. Though this power under certain limitations would be a proper one for the department of Congress; it is in this system carried much too far, and much farther than is necessary. This is, without exception, the most commercial state upon the continent. Our extensive coasts, cold climate, small estates, and equality of rights, with a variety of subordinate and concurring circumstances, place us in this respect at the head of the union. We must, therefore, be indulged if a point which so nearly relates to our welfare be rigidly examined. The new constitution not only prohibits vessels, bound from one state to another, from paying any duties, but even from entering and clearing. The only use of such a regulation is, to keep each state in complete ignorance of its own resources. It certainly is no hardship to enter and clear at the custom-house, and the expense is too small to be an object.

The unlimitted right to regulate trade, includes the right of granting exclusive charters. This, in all old countries, is considered as one principle branch of prerogative. We find hardly a country in Europe which has not felt the ill effects of such a power. Holland has carried the exercise of it farther than any other state; and the reason why that country has felt less evil from it is, that the territory is very small, and they have drawn large revenues from their colonies in the East and West Indies. In this respect, the whole country is to be considered as a trading company, having exclusive privileges. The colonies are large in proportion to the parent state; so that, upon the whole, the latter may gain by such a system. We are also to take into consideration the industry which the genius of a free government inspires. But in the British islands all these circumstances together have not prevented them from being injured by the monopolies created there. Individuals have been enriched, but the country at large has been hurt. Some valuable branches of trade being granted to companies, who transact their business in London, that city is, perhaps, the place of the greatest trade in the world. But Ireland, under such influence, suffers exceedingly, and is impoverished; and Scotland is a mere bye-word. Bristol, the second city in England, ranks not much above this town in population. These things must be accounted for by the incorporation of trading companies; and if they are felt so severely in countries of small extent, they will operate with ten-fold severity upon us, who inhabit an immense tract; and living towards one extreme of an extensive empire, shall feel the evil, without retaining that influence in government, which may enable us to procure redress. There ought, then, to have been inserted a restraining clause, which might prevent the Congress from making any such grant, because they consequentially defeat the trade of the out-ports, and are also injurious to the general commerce, by enhancing prices, and destroying that rivalship which is the great stimulous to industry.

Lawrence Taliaferro to James Madison

Rose Hill, Orange County, Virginia, December 16, 1787

I recd. your vary Frendly Letter from New york sumtime ago & Am Much Oblige to you for the Information you gave Me of My Nephu John Taliaferro at Princetown—I am sorry to inform you that the Federal Sistum is rufly Handeld by sum vary Able Men in this State tho. we have sum vary good & Able Men that are Frends to that & thear Cuntary & Wish it to be Adopted as spedily as Posable I am inform'd that that Excelent & good Man Genl. Washington has Offer'd himself for the Spring convention & it is the sincere Wish & desier of Myself & a Grate Many others that you will Also represent the Peopel of this County in the Spring Convention & we Earnestly Beg that you will be hear sum time before the Elextion for even those that are Oppos'd to the Federal Sistum wish to have an Opportunity of conversing with you on it—I dare say you will be gratly suppd. to hear that it is report'd that you Are Opos'd to the Sistum & I was told the other day that you ware Actually writing a Pece against it—I am a vary pore Penman & dont wish to take up two Much of you time in reding a Long Letter or I could give you a grat many More Instances of the Rancor of the Enemes to Peac & Good Goverment & will only repet our ernest desier that you will be hear a Week or two before the Elextion by which Menes I make no doubt but the Citisens of this state will be prevented from being led into an Error by a few Men that seme vary ernest in doing it—

"A Landholder" [Oliver Ellsworth] VII

Connecticut Courant (Hartford), December 17, 1787

To the Landholders and Farmers.

I have often admired the spirit of candour, liberality, and justice, with which the Convention began and completed the important object of their mission. "In all our deliberations on this subject," say they, "we kept steadily in our view, that which appears to us the greatest interest of every true American, the consolidation of our union, in which is involved our prosperity, felicity, safety, perhaps our national existence. This important consideration, seriously and deeply impressed on our minds, led each state in the Convention to be less rigid on points of inferior magnitude, than might otherwise have been expected; and thus the Constitution which we now present, is the result of a spirit of amity, and of that mutual deference and concession, which the peculiarity of our political situation rendered indispensible."

Let us, my fellow citizens, take up this constitution with the same spirit of candour and liberality; consider it in all its parts; consider the important advantages which may be derived from it, and the fatal consequences which will probably follow from rejecting it. If any objections are made against it, let us obtain full information on the subject, and then weigh these objections in the balance of cool impartial reason. Let us see, if they be not wholly groundless; But if upon the whole they appear to have some weight, let us consider well, whether they be so important, that we ought on account of them to reject the whole constitution. Perfection is not the lot of human institutions; that which has the most excellencies and fewest faults, is the best that we can expect.

Some very worthy persons, who have not had great advantages for information, have objected against that clause in the constitution, which provides, that *no religious Test shall ever be required as a qualification to any office or public trust under the United States.* They have been afraid that this clause is unfavourable to religion. But, my countrymen, the sole purpose and effect of it is to exclude persecution, and to secure to you the important right of religious liberty. We are almost the only people in the world, who have a full enjoyment of this important right of human nature. In our country every man has a right to worship God in that way which is most agreeable to his own conscience. If he be a good and peaceable citizen, he is liable to no penalties or incapacities on account of his religious sentiments; or in other words, he is not subject to persecution.

But in other parts of the world, it has been, and still is, far different. Systems of religious error have been adopted, in times of ignorance. It has been the interest of tyrannical kings, popes, and prelates, to maintain these errors. When the clouds of ignorance began to vanish, and the people grew more enlightened, there was no other way to keep them in error, but to prohibit their altering their religious opinions by severe persecuting laws. In this way persecution became general throughout Europe. It was the universal opinion that one religion must be established by law; and that all, who differed in their religious opinions, must suffer the vengeance of persecution. In pursuance of this opinion, when popery was abolished in England, and the church of England was established in its stead, severe penalties were inflicted upon all who dissented from the established church. In the time of the civil wars, in the reign of Charles I. the presbyterians got the upper hand, and inflicted legal penalties upon all who differed from them in their sentiments respecting religious doctrines and discipline. When Charles II. was restored, the church of England was likewise restored, and the presbyterians and other dissenters were laid under legal penalties and incapacities. It was in this reign, that a religious test was established as a qualification for office; that is, a law was made requiring all officers civil and military (among other things) to receive the Sacrament of the Lord's Supper, according to the usage of the church of England, written six months after their admission to office, under the penalty of 500l. and disability to hold the office. And by another statute of the same reign, no person was capable of being elected to any office relating to the government of any city or corporation, unless, within a twelvemonth before, he had received the Sacrament according to the rites of the church of England. The pretence for making these severe laws, by which all but churchmen were made incapable of any office civil or military, was to exclude the papists; but the real design was to exclude the protestant dissenters. From this account of test-laws, there arises an unfavourable presumption against them. But if we consider the nature of them and the effects which they are calculated to produce, we shall find that they are useless, tyrannical, and peculiarly unfit for the people of this country.

A religious test is an act to be done, or profession to be made, relating to religion (such as partaking of the sacrament according to certain rites and forms, or declaring one's belief of certain doctrines,) for the purpose of determining, whether his religious opinions are such, that he is admissible to a public office. A test in favour of any one denomination of christians would be to the last degree absurd in the United States. If it were in favour of either congregationalists, presbyterians, episcopalions, baptists, or quakers; it would incapacitate more than three fourths of the American citizens for any public office; and thus degrade them from the rank of freemen. There needs no argument to prove that the majority of our citizens would never submit to this indignity.

If any test-act were to be made, perhaps the least exceptionable would be one, requiring all persons appointed to office, to declare, at the time of their admission, their belief in the being of a God, and in the divine authority of the scriptures. In favour of such a test, it may be said, that one who believes these great truths, will not be so likely to violate his obligations to his country, as one who disbelieves them; we may have greater confidence in his integrity. But I answer: His making a declaration of such a belief is no security at all. For suppose him to be an unprincipled man, who believes neither the word nor the being of a God; and to be governed merely by selfish motives; how easy it is for him to dissemble? how easy is it for him to make a public declaration of his belief in the creed which the law prescribes; and excuse himself by calling it a mere formality? This is the case with the test-laws and creeds in England. The most abandoned characters partake of the sacrament, in order to qualify themselves for public employments. The clergy are obliged by law to administer the ordinance unto them; and thus prostitute the most sacred office of religion; for it is a civil right in the party to receive the sacrament. In that country, subscribing to the thirty-nine articles is a test for admission into holy orders. And it is a fact, that many of the clergy do this; when at the same time, they totally disbelieve several of the doctrines contained in them. In short, test-laws are utterly ineffectual; they are no security at all; because men of loose principles will, by an external compliance, evade them. If they exclude any persons, it will be honest men, men of principle, who will rather suffer an injury, than act contrary to the dictates of their consciences. If we mean to have those appointed to public offices, who are sincere friends to religion; we the people who appoint them, must take care to choose such characters; and not rely upon such cob-web barriers as test-laws are.

But to come to the true principle, by which this question ought to be determined: The business of civil government is to protect the citizen in his rights, to defend the community from hostile powers, and to promote the general welfare. Civil government has no business to meddle with the private opinions of the people. If I demean myself as a good citizen, I am accountable, not to man, but to God, for the religious opinions which I embrace, and the manner in which I worship the supreme being. If such had been the universal sentiments of mankind, and they had acted accordingly, persecution, the bane of truth and nurse of error, with her bloody axe and flaming hand, would never have turned so great a part of the world into a field of blood.

But while I assert the right of religious liberty; I would not deny that the civil power has a right, in some cases, to interfere in matters of religion. It has a right to prohibit and punish gross immoralities and impieties; because the open practice of these is of evil example and public detriment. For this reason, I heartily approve of our laws against drunkenness, profane swearing, blasphemy, and professed atheism. But in this state, we have never thought it expedient to adopt a test-law; and yet I sincerely believe we have as great a proportion of religion and morality, as they have in England, where every person who holds a public office, must be either a saint by law, or a hypocrite by practice. A test-law is the parent of hypocrisy, and the offspring of error and the spirit of persecution. Legislatures have no right to set up an inquisition, and examine into the private opinions of men. Test-laws are useless and ineffectual, unjust and tyrannical; therefore the Convention have done wisely in excluding this engine of persecution, and providing that no religious test shall ever be required.

Dissent of the Minority of the Pennsylvania Convention

Pennsylvania Packet (Philadelphia), December 18, 1787

The Address and Reasons of Dissent of the Minority
of the Convention of the State of Pennsylvania
to their Constituents.

It was not until after the termination of the late glorious contest, which made the people of the United States an independent nation, that any defect was discovered in the present confederation. It was formed by some of the ablest patriots in America. It carried us successfully through the war; and the virtue and patriotism of the people, with their disposition to promote the common cause, supplied the want of power in Congress.

The requisition of Congress for the five *per cent.* impost was made before the peace, so early as the first of February, 1781, but was prevented taking effect by the refusal of one state; yet it is probable every state in the union would have agreed to this measure at that period, had it not been for the extravagant terms in which it was demanded. The requisition was new moulded in the year 1783, and accompanied with an additional demand of certain supplementary funds for 25 years. Peace had now taken place, and the United States found themselves labouring under a considerable foreign and domestic debt, incurred during the war. The requisition of 1783 was commensurate with the interest of the debt, as it was then calculated; but it has been more accurately ascertained since that time. The domestic debt has been found to fall several millions of dollars short of the calculation, and it has lately been considerably diminished by large sales of the western lands. The states have been called on by Congress annually for supplies until the general system of finance proposed in 1783 should take place.

It was at this time that the want of an efficient federal government was first complained of, and that the powers vested in Congress were found to be inadequate to the procuring of the benefits that should result from the union. The impost was granted by most of the states, but many refused the supplementary funds; the annual requisitions were set at nought by some of the states, while others complied with them by legislative acts, but were tardy in their payments, and Congress found themselves incapable of complying with their engagements, and supporting the federal government. It was found that our national character was sinking in the opinion of foreign nations. The Congress could make treaties of commerce, but could not enforce the observance of them. We were suffering from the restrictions of foreign nations, who had shackled our commerce, while we were unable to retaliate: and all now agreed that it would be advantageous to the union to enlarge the powers of Congress; that they should be enabled in the amplest manner to regulate commerce, and to lay and collect duties on the imports throughout the United States. With this view a convention was first proposed by Virginia, and finally recommended by Congress for the different states to appoint deputies to meet in convention, "for the purposes of revising and amending the present articles of confederation, so as to make them adequate to the exigencies of the union." This recommendation the legislatures of twelve states complied with so hastily as not to consult their constituents on the subject; and though the different legislatures had no authority from their constituents for the purpose, they probably apprehended the necessity would justify the measure; and none of them extended their ideas at that time further than "revising and amending the present articles of confederation." Pennsylvania by the act appointing deputies expressly confined their powers to this object; and though it is probable that some of the members of the assembly of this state had at that time in contemplation to annihilate the present confederation, as well as the constitution of Pennsylvania, yet the plan was not sufficiently matured to communicate it to the public.

The majority of the legislature of this commonwealth, were at that time under the influence of the members from the city of Philadelphia. They agreed that the deputies sent by them to convention should have no compensation for their services, which determination was calculated to prevent the election of any member who resided at a distance from the city. It was in vain for the minority to attempt electing delegates to the convention, who understood the circumstances, and the feelings of the people, and had a common interest with them. They found a disposition in the leaders of the majority of the house to chuse themselves and some of their dependants. The minority attempted to prevent this by agreeing to vote for some of the leading members, who they knew had influence enough to be appointed at any rate, in hopes of carrying with them some respectable citizens of Philadelphia, in whose principles and integrity they could have more confidence; but even in this they were disappointed, except in one member: the eighth member was added at a subsequent session of the assembly.

The Continental convention met in the city of Philadelphia at the time appointed. It was composed of some men of excellent characters; of others who were more remarkable for their ambition and cunning, than their patriotism; and of some who had been opponents to the independence of the United States. The delegates from Pennsylvania were, six of them, uniform and decided opponents to the constitution of this commonwealth. The convention sat upwards of four months. The doors were kept shut, and the members brought under the most solemn engagements of secrecy.* Some of those who opposed their going so far beyond their powers, retired, hopeless, from the convention, others had the firmness to refuse signing the plan altogether; and many who did sign it, did it not as a system they wholly approved, but as the best that could be then obtained, and notwithstanding the time spent on this subject, it is agreed on all hands to be a work of haste and accommodation.

Whilst the gilded chains were forging in the secret conclave, the meaner instruments of despotism without, were busily employed in alarming the fears of the people with dangers which did not exist, and exciting their hopes of greater advantages from the expected plan than even the best government on earth could produce.

The proposed plan had not many hours issued forth from

---

*The Journals of the conclave are still concealed.

the womb of suspicious secrecy, until such as were prepared for the purpose, were carrying about petitions for people to sign, signifying their approbation of the system, and requesting the legislature to call a convention. While every measure was taken to intimidate the people against opposing it, the public papers teemed with the most violent threats against those who should dare to think for themselves, and *tar and feathers* were liberally promised to all those who would not immediately join in supporting the proposed government be it what it would. Under such circumstances petitions in favour of calling a convention were signed by great numbers in and about the city, before they had leisure to read and examine the system, many of whom, now they are better acquainted with it, and have had time to investigate its principles, are heartily opposed to it. The petitions were speedily handed into the legislature.

Affairs were in this situation when on the 28th of September last a resolution was proposed to the assembly by a member of the house who had been also a member of the federal convention, for calling a state convention, to be elected within *ten* days for the purpose of examining and adopting the proposed constitution of the United States, though at this time the house had not received it from Congress. This attempt was opposed by a minority, who after offering every argument in their power to prevent the precipitate measure, without effect, absented themselves from the house as the only alternative left them, to prevent the measure taking place previous to their constituents being acquainted with the business—That violence and outrage which had been so often threatened was now practised; some of the members were seized the next day by a mob collected for the purpose, and forcibly dragged to the house, and there detained by force whilst the quorum of the legislature, *so formed*, compleated their resolution. We shall dwell no longer on this subject, the people of Pennsylvania have been already acquainted therewith. We would only further observe that every member of the legislature, previously to taking his seat, by solemn oath or affirmation, declares, "that he will not do or consent to any act or thing whatever that shall have a tendency to lessen or abridge their rights and privileges, as declared in the constitution of this state." And that constitution which they are so solemnly sworn to support cannot legally be altered but by a recommendation of the council of censors, who alone are authorised to propose alterations and amendments, and even these must be published at least *six months*, for the consideration of the people.—The proposed system of government for the United States, if adopted, will alter and may annihilate the constitution of Pennsylvania; and therefore the legislature had no authority whatever to recommend the calling a convention for that purpose. This proceeding could not be considered as binding on the people of this commonwealth. The house was formed by violence, some of the members composing it were detained there by force, which alone would have vitiated any proceedings, to which they were otherwise competent; but had the legislature been legally formed, this business was absolutely without their power.

In this situation of affairs were the subscribers elected members of the convention of Pennsylvania. A convention called by a legislature in direct violation of their duty, and composed in part of members, who were compelled to attend for that purpose, to consider of a constitution proposed by a convention of the United States, who were not appointed for the purpose of framing a new form of government, but whose powers were expressly confined to altering and amending the present articles of confederation.—Therefore the members of the continental convention in proposing the plan acted as individuals, and not as deputies from Pennsylvania.* The assembly who called the state convention acted as individuals, and not as the legislature of Pennsylvania; nor could they or the convention chosen on their recommendation have authority to do any act or thing, that can alter or annihilate the constitution of Pennsylvania (both of which will be done by the new constitution) nor are their proceedings in our opinion, at all binding on the people.

*The continental convention in direct violation of the 13th article of the confederation, have declared, "that the ratification of nine states shall be sufficient for the establishment of this constitution, between the states so ratifying the same."—Thus has the plighted faith of the states been sported with! They had solemnly engaged that the confederation now subsisting should be inviolably preserved by each of them, and the union thereby formed, should be perpetual, unless the same should be altered by mutual consent.

The election for members of the convention was held at so early a period and the want of information was so great, that some of us did not know of it until after it was over, and we have reason to believe that great numbers of the people of Pennsylvania have not yet had an opportunity of sufficiently examining the proposed constitution.—We apprehend that no change can take place that will affect the internal government or constitution of this commonwealth, unless a majority of the people should evidence a wish for such a change; but on examining the number of votes given for members of the present state convention, we find that of upwards of *seventy thousand* freemen who are intitled to vote in Pennsylvania, the whole convention has been elected by about *thirteen thousand* voters, and though *two thirds* of the members of the convention have thought proper to ratify the proposed constitution, yet those *two thirds* were elected by the votes of only *six thousand and eight hundred* freemen.

In the city of Philadelphia and some of the eastern counties, the junto that took the lead in the business agreed to vote for none but such as would solemnly promise to adopt the system in *toto*, without exercising their judgment. In many of the counties the people did not attend the elections as they had not an opportunity of judging of the plan. Others did not consider themselves bound by the call of a set of men who assembled at the state-house in Philadelphia, and assumed the name of the legislature of Pennsylvania; and some were prevented from voting, by the violence of the party who were determined at all events to force down the measure. To such lengths did the tools of despotism carry their outrage, that in the night of the election for members of convention, in the city of Philadelphia, several of the subscribers (being then in the city to transact your business) were grossly abused, ill-treated and insulted while they were quiet in their lodgings, though they did not interfere, nor had any thing to do with the said election, but, as they apprehend, because they were supposed to be adverse to the proposed constitution, and would not tamely surrender those sacred rights, which you had committed to their charge.

The convention met, and the same disposition was soon manifested in considering the proposed constitution, that had been exhibited in every other stage of the business. We were prohibited by an express vote of the convention, from taking any question on the separate articles of the plan, and reduced to the necessity of adopting or rejecting *in toto.*—'Tis true the majority permitted us to debate on each article, but restrained us from proposing amendments.—They also determined not to permit us to enter on the minutes our reasons of dissent against any of the articles, nor even on the final question our reasons of dissent against the whole. Thus situated we entered on the examination of the proposed system of government, and found it to be such as we could not adopt, without, as we conceived, surrendering up your dearest rights. We offered our objections to the convention, and opposed those parts of the plan, which, in our opinion, would be injurious to you, in the best manner we were able; and closed our arguments by offering the following propositions to the convention.

1. The right of conscience shall be held inviolable; and neither the legislative, executive nor judicial powers of the United States shall have authority to alter, abrogate, or infringe any part of the constitution of the several states, which provide for the preservation of liberty in matters of religion.

2. That in controversies respecting property, and in suits between man and man, trial by jury shall remain as heretofore, as well in the federal courts, as in those of the several states.

3. That in all capital and criminal prosecutions, a man has a right to demand the cause and nature of his accusation, as well in the federal courts, as in those of the several states; to be heard by himself and his counsel; to be confronted with the accusers and witnesses; to call for evidence in his favor, and a speedy trial by an impartial jury of his vicinage, without whose unanimous consent, he cannot be found guilty, nor can he be compelled to give evidence against himself; and that no man be deprived of his liberty, except by the law of the land or the judgment of his peers.

4. That excessive bail ought not to be required, nor excessive fines imposed, nor cruel nor unusual punishments inflicted.

5. That warrants unsupported by evidence, whereby any

officer or messenger may be commanded or required to search suspected places, or to seize any person or persons, his or their property, not particularly described, are grievous and oppressive, and shall not be granted either by the magistrates of the federal government or others.

6. That the people have a right to the freedom of speech, of writing and publishing their sentiments, therefore, the freedom of the press shall not be restrained by any law of the United States.

7. That the people have a right to bear arms for the defence of themselves and their own state, or the United States, or for the purpose of killing game; and no law shall be passed for disarming the people or any of them, unless for crimes committed, or real danger of public injury from individuals; and as standing armies in the time of peace are dangerous to liberty, they ought not to be kept up: and that the military shall be kept under strict subordination to and be governed by the civil powers.

8. The inhabitants of the several states shall have liberty to fowl and hunt in seasonable times, on the lands they hold, and on all other lands in the United States not inclosed, and in like manner to fish in all navigable waters, and others not private property, without being restrained therein by any laws to be passed by the legislature of the United States.

9. That no law shall be passed to restrain the legislatures of the several states from enacting laws for imposing taxes, except imposts and duties on goods imported or exported, and that no taxes, except imposts and duties upon goods imported and exported, and postage on letters shall be levied by the authority of Congress.

10. That the house of representatives be properly increased in number; that elections shall remain free; that the several states shall have power to regulate the elections for senators and representatives, without being controuled either directly or indirectly by any interference on the part of the Congress; and that elections of representatives be annual.

11. That the power of organizing, arming and disciplining the militia (the manner of disciplining the militia to be prescribed by Congress) remain with the individual states, and that Congress shall not have authority to call or march any of

the militia out of their own state, without the consent of such state, and for such length of time only as such state shall agree.

That the sovereignty, freedom and independency of the several states shall be retained, and every power, jurisdiction and right which is not by this constitution expressly delegated to the United States in Congress assembled.

12. That the legislative, executive, and judicial powers be kept separate; and to this end that a constitutional council be appointed, to advise and assist the president, who shall be responsible for the advice they give, hereby the senators would be relieved from almost constant attendance; and also that the judges be made completely independent.

13. That no treaty which shall be directly opposed to the existing laws of the United States in Congress assembled, shall be valid until such laws shall be repealed, or made conformable to such treaty; neither shall any treaties be valid which are in contradiction to the constitution of the United States, or the constitutions of the several states.

14. That the judiciary power of the United States shall be confined to cases affecting ambassadors, other public ministers and consuls; to cases of admiralty and maritime jurisdiction; to controversies to which the United States shall be a party; to controversies between two or more states—between a state and citizens of different states—between citizens claiming lands under grants of different states; and between a state or the citizens thereof and foreign states, and in criminal cases, to such only as are expressly enumerated in the constitution, & that the United States in Congress assembled, shall not have power to enact laws, which shall alter the laws of descents and distribution of the effects of deceased persons, the titles of lands or goods, or the regulation of contracts in the individual states.

After reading these propositions, we declared our willingness to agree to the plan, provided it was so amended as to meet those propositions, or something similar to them: and finally moved the convention to adjourn, to give the people of Pennsylvania time to consider the subject, and determine for themselves; but these were all rejected, and the final vote was taken, when our duty to you induced us to vote against the proposed plan, and to decline signing the ratification of the same.

During the discussion we met with many insults, and some personal abuse; we were not even treated with decency, during the sitting of the convention, by the persons in the gallery of the house; however, we flatter ourselves that in contending for the preservation of those invaluable rights you have thought proper to commit to our charge, we acted with a spirit becoming freemen, and being desirous that you might know the principles which actuated our conduct, and being prohibited from inserting our reasons of dissent on the minutes of the convention, we have subjoined them for your consideration, as to you alone we are accountable. It remains with you whether you will think those inestimable privileges, which you have so ably contended for, should be sacrificed at the shrine of despotism, or whether you mean to contend for them with the same spirit that has so often baffled the attempts of an aristocratic faction, to rivet the shackles of slavery on you and your unborn posterity.

Our objections are comprised under three general heads of dissent, viz.

WE Dissent, first, because it is the opinion of the most celebrated writers on government, and confirmed by uniform experience, that a very extensive territory cannot be governed on the principles of freedom, otherwise than by a confederation of republics, possessing all the powers of internal government; but united in the management of their general, and foreign concerns.

If any doubt could have been entertained of the truth of the foregoing principle, it has been fully removed by the concession of *Mr. Wilson*, one of the majority on this question; and who was one of the deputies in the late general convention. In justice to him, we will give his own words; they are as follows, viz. "The extent of country for which the new constitution was required, produced another difficulty in the business of the federal convention. It is the opinion of some celebrated writers, that to a small territory, the democratical; to a middling territory (as Montesquieu has termed it) the monarchial; and to an extensive territory, the despotic form of government is best adapted. Regarding then the wide and almost unbounded jurisdiction of the United States, at first view, the hand of despotism seemed necessary to controul, connect, and protect it; and hence the chief embarrassment rose. For, we know that, altho' our constituents would chearfully submit to the legislative restraints of a free government, they would spurn at every attempt to shackle them with despotic power."—And again in another part of his speech he continues.—"Is it probable that the dissolution of the state governments, and the establishment of one *consolidated empire* would be eligible in its nature, and satisfactory to the people in its administration? I think not, as I have given reasons to shew that so extensive a territory could not be governed, connected, and preserved, but by the *supremacy of despotic power*. All the exertions of the most potent emperors of Rome were not capable of keeping that empire together, which in extent was far inferior to the dominion of America."

We dissent, secondly, because the powers vested in Congress by this constitution, must necessarily annihilate and absorb the legislative, executive, and judicial powers of the several states, and produce from their ruins one consolidated government, which from the nature of things will be *an iron handed despotism*, as nothing short of the supremacy of despotic sway could connect and govern these United States under one government.

As the truth of this position is of such decisive importance, it ought to be fully investigated, and if it is founded to be clearly ascertained; for, should it be demonstrated, that the powers vested by this constitution in Congress, will have such an effect as necessarily to produce one consolidated government, the question then will be reduced to this short issue, viz. whether satiated with the blessings of liberty; whether repenting of the folly of so recently asserting their unalienable rights, against foreign despots at the expence of so much blood and treasure, and such painful and arduous struggles, the people of America are now willing to resign every privilege of freemen, and submit to the dominion of an absolute government, that will embrace all America in one chain of despotism; or whether they will with virtuous indignation, spurn at the shackles prepared for them, and confirm their liberties by a conduct becoming freemen.

That the new government will not be a confederacy of states, as it ought, but one consolidated government, founded upon the destruction of the several governments of the states, we shall now shew.

The powers of Congress under the new constitution, are complete and unlimited over the *purse* and the *sword*, and are perfectly independent of, and supreme over, the state governments; whose intervention in these great points is entirely destroyed. By virtue of their power of taxation, Congress may command the whole, or any part of the property of the people. They may impose what imposts upon commerce; they may impose what land taxes, poll taxes, excises, duties on all written instruments, and duties on every other article that they may judge proper; in short, every species of taxation, whether of an external or internal nature is comprised in section the 8th, of article the 1st, viz. "The Congress shall have power to lay and collect taxes, duties, imposts, and excises, to pay the debts, and provide for the common defence and general welfare of the United States."

As there is no one article of taxation reserved to the state governments, the Congress may monopolise every source of revenue, and thus indirectly demolish the state governments, for without funds they could not exist, the taxes, duties and excises imposed by Congress may be so high as to render it impracticable to levy further sums on the same articles; but whether this should be the case or not, if the state governments should presume to impose taxes, duties or excises, on the same articles with Congress, the latter may abrogate and repeal the laws whereby they are imposed, upon the allegation that they interfere with the due collection of their taxes, duties or excises, by virtue of the following clause, part of section 8th, article 1st. viz. "To make all laws which shall be necessary and proper for carrying into execution the foregoing powers, and all other powers vested by this constitution in the government of the United States, or in any department or officer thereof."

The Congress might gloss over this conduct by construing

every purpose for which the state legislatures now lay taxes, to be for the *"general welfare,"* and therefore as of their jurisdiction.

And the supremacy of the laws of the United States is established by article 6th, viz. "That this constitution and the laws of the United States, which shall be made in pursuance thereof, and *all treaties* made, or which shall be made, under the authority of the United States, shall be the *supreme law* of the *land*; and *the judges in every state shall be bound thereby; any thing in the constitution or laws of any state to the contrary notwithstanding.*" It has been alledged that the words "pursuant to the constitution," are a restriction upon the authority of Congress; but when it is considered that by other sections they are invested with every efficient power of government, and which may be exercised to the absolute destruction of the state governments, without any violation of even the forms of the constitution, this seeming restriction, as well as every other restriction in it, appears to us to be nugatory and delusive; and only introduced as a blind upon the real nature of the government. In our opinion, "pursuant to the constitution," will be co-extensive with the *will* and *pleasure* of Congress, which, indeed, will be the only limitation of their powers.

We apprehend that two co-ordinate sovereignties would be a solecism in politics. That therefore as there is no line of distinction drawn between the general, and state governments; as the sphere of their jurisdiction is undefined, it would be contrary to the nature of things, that both should exist together, one or the other would necessarily triumph in the fullness of dominion. However the contest could not be of long continuance, as the state governments are divested of every means of defence, and will be obliged by "the supreme law of the land" *to yield at discretion.*

It has been objected to this total destruction of the state governments, that the existence of their legislatures is made essential to the organization of Congress; that they must assemble for the appointment of the senators and president general of the United States. True, the state legislatures may be continued for some years, as boards of appointment, merely, after they are divested of every other function, but the framers of the constitution foreseeing that the people will soon be disgusted with this solemn mockery of a government without power and usefulness, have made a provision for relieving them from the imposition, in section 4th, of article 1st, viz. "The times, places, and manner of holding elections for senators and representatives, shall be prescribed in each state by the legislature thereof; *but the Congress may at any time, by law make or alter such regulations; except as to the place of chusing senators.*"

As Congress have the controul over the time of the appointment of the president general, of the senators and of the representatives of the United States, they may prolong their existence in office, for life, by postponing the time of their election and appointment, from period to period, under various pretences, such as an apprehension of invasion, the factious disposition of the people, or any other plausible pretence that the occasion may suggest; and having thus obtained life-estates in the government, they may fill up the vacancies themselves, by their controul over the mode of appointment; with this exception in regard to the senators, that as the place of appointment for them, must, by the constitution, be in the particular state, they may depute some body in the respective states, to fill up the vacancies in the senate, occasioned by death, until they can venture to assume it themselves. In this manner, may the only restriction in this clause be evaded. By virtue of the foregoing section, when the spirit of the people shall be gradually broken; when the general government shall be firmly established, and when a numerous standing army shall render opposition vain, the Congress may compleat the system of despotism, in renouncing all dependance on the people, by continuing themselves, and children in the government.

The celebrated *Montesquieu*, in his Spirit of Laws, vol. 1, page 12th, says, "That in a democracy there can be no exercise of sovereignty, but by the suffrages of the people, which are their will; now the sovereigns will is the sovereign himself; the laws therefore, which establish the right of suffrage, are fundamental to this government. In fact, it is as important to regulate in a republic in what manner, by whom, and concerning what suffrages are to be given, as it is in a monarchy to know who is the prince, and after what manner he ought to govern." The *time, mode* and *place* of the election of representatives, senators and president general of the United States, ought not to be under the controul of Congress, but fundamentally ascertained and established.

The new constitution, consistently with the plan of consolidation, contains no reservation of the rights and privileges of the state governments, which was made in the confederation of the year 1778, by article the 2d, viz. "That each state retains its sovereignty, freedom and independence, and every power, jurisdiction and right, which is not by this confederation expressly delegated to the United States in Congress assembled."

The legislative power vested in Congress by the foregoing recited sections, is so unlimited in its nature; may be so comprehensive and boundless in its exercise, that this alone would be amply sufficient to annihilate the state governments, and swallow them up in the grand vortex of general empire.

The judicial powers vested in Congress are also so various and extensive, that by legal ingenuity they may be extended to every case, and thus absorb the state judiciaries, and when we consider the decisive influence that a general judiciary would have over the civil polity of the several states, we do not hesitate to pronounce that this power, unaided by the legislative, would effect a consolidation of the states under one government.

The powers of a court of equity, vested by this constitution, in the tribunals of Congress; powers which do not exist in Pennsylvania, unless so far as they can be incorporated with jury trial, would, in this state, greatly contribute to this event. The rich and wealthy suitors would eagerly lay hold of the infinite mazes, perplexities and delays, which a court of chancery, with the appellate powers of the supreme court in fact as well as law would furnish him with, and thus the poor man being plunged in the bottomless pit of legal discussion, would drop his demand in despair.

In short, consolidation pervades the whole constitution. It begins with an annunciation that such was the intention. The main pillars of the fabric correspond with it, and the concluding paragraph is a confirmation of it. The preamble begins with the words, "We the people of the United States," which is the style of a compact between individuals entering into a state of society, and not that of a confederation of states. The other features of consolidation, we have before noticed.

Thus we have fully established the position, that the powers vested by this constitution in Congress, will effect a consolidation of the states under one government, which even the advocates of this constitution admit, could not be done without the sacrifice of all liberty.

3. We dissent, Thirdly, Because if it were practicable to govern so extensive a territory as these United States includes, on the plan of a consolidated government, consistent with the principles of liberty and the happiness of the people, yet the construction of this constitution is not calculated to attain the object, for independent of the nature of the case, it would of itself, necessarily produce a despotism, and that not by the usual gradations, but with the celerity that has hitherto only attended revolutions effected by the sword.

To establish the truth of this position, a cursory investigation of the principles and form of this constitution will suffice.

The first consideration that this review suggests, is the omission of a BILL OF RIGHTS ascertaining and fundamentally establishing those unalienable and personal rights of men, without the full, free, and secure enjoyment of which there can be no liberty, and over which it is not necessary for a good government to have the controul. The principal of which are the rights of conscience, personal liberty by the clear and unequivocal establishment of the writ of *habeas corpus*, jury trial in criminal and civil cases, by an impartial jury of the vicinage or county; with the common law proceedings, for the safety of the accused in criminal prosecutions and the liberty of the press, that scourge of tyrants; and the grand bulwark of every other liberty and, privilege; the stipulations heretofore made in favor of them in the state constitutions, are entirely superceded by this constitution.

The legislature of a free country should be so formed as to have a competent knowledge of its constitutents, and enjoy their confidence. To produce these essential requisites, the representation ought to be fair, equal, and sufficiently numerous, to possess the same interests, feelings, opinions, and views, which the people themselves would possess, were they all assembled; and so numerous as to prevent bribery and undue influence, and so responsible to the people, by frequent and fair elections, as to prevent their neglecting or sacrificing the views and interests of their constitutents, to their own pursuits.

We will now bring the legislature under this constitution to the test of the foregoing principles, which will demonstrate, that it is deficient in every essential quality of a just and safe representation.

The house of representatives is to consist of 65 members; that is one for about every 50,000 inhabitants, to be chosen every two years. Thirty-three members will form a quorum for doing business; and 17 of these, being the majority, determine the sense of the house.

The senate, the other constituent branch of the legislature, consists of 26 members, being *two* from each state, appointed by their legislatures every six years—fourteen senators make a quorum; the majority of whom, eight, determines the sense of that body: except in judging on impeachments, or in making treaties, or in expelling a member, when two thirds of the senators present, must concur.

The president is to have the controul over the enacting of laws, so far as to make the concurrence of *two* thirds of the representatives and senators present necessary, if he should object to the laws.

Thus it appears that the liberties, happiness, interests, and great concerns of the whole United States, may be dependent upon the integrity, virtue, wisdom, and knowledge of 25 or 26 men.—How unadequate and unsafe a representation! Inadequate, because the sense and views of 3 or 4 millions of people diffused over so extensive a territory comprising such various climates, products, habits, interests, and opinions, cannot be collected in so small a body; and besides, it is not a fair and equal representation of the people even in proportion to its number, for the smallest state has as much weight in the senate as the largest, and from the smallness of the number to be chosen for both branches of the legislature; and from the mode of election and appointment, which is under the controul of Congress; and from the nature of the thing, men of the most elevated rank in life, will alone be chosen. The other orders in the society, such as farmers, traders, and mechanics, who all ought to have a competent number of their best informed men in the legislature, will be totally unrepresented.

The representation is unsafe, because in the exercise of such great powers and trusts, it is so exposed to corruption and undue influence, by the gift of the numerous places of honor and emolument, at the disposal of the executive; by the arts and address of the great and designing; and by direct bribery.

The representation is moreover inadequate and unsafe, because of the long terms for which it is appointed, and the mode of its appointment, by which Congress may not only controul the choice of the people, but may so manage as to divest the people of this fundamental right, and become self-elected.

The number of members in the house of representatives *may* be encreased to one for every 30,000 inhabitants. But when we consider, that this cannot be done without the consent of the senate, who from their share in the legislative, in the executive, and judicial departments, and permanency of appointment, will be the great efficient body in this government, and whose weight and predominancy would be abridged by an increase of the representatives, we are persuaded that this is a circumstance that cannot be expected. On the contrary, the number of representatives will probably be continued at 65, although the population of the country may swell to treble what it now is; unless a revolution should effect a change.

We have before noticed the judicial power as it would effect a consolidation of the states into one government; we will now examine it, as it would affect the liberties and welfare of the people, supposing such a government were practicable and proper.

The judicial power, under the proposed constitution, is founded on the well-known principles of the *civil law*, by which the judge determines both on law and fact, and appeals are allowed from the inferior tribunals to the superior, upon the whole question; so that *facts* as well as *law*, would be re-examined, and even new facts brought forward in the court of appeals; and to use the words of a very eminent Civilian—"The cause is many times another thing before the court of appeals, than what it was at the time of the first sentence."

That this mode of proceeding is the one which must be adopted under this constitution, is evident from the following circumstances:—1st. That the trial by jury, which is the grand characteristic of the common law, is secured by the constitution, only in criminal cases.—2d. That the appeal from both *law* and *fact* is expressly established, which is utterly inconsistent with the principles of the common law, and trials by jury. The only mode in which an appeal from law and fact can be established, is, by adopting the principles and practice of the civil law; unless the United States should be drawn into the absurdity of calling and swearing juries, merely for the purpose of contradicting their verdicts, which would render juries contemptible and worse than useless.—3d. That the courts to be established would decide on all cases *of law and equity*, which is a well known characteristic of the civil law, and these courts would have conusance not only of the laws of the United States and of treaties, and of cases affecting ambassadors, but of all cases of *admiralty and maritime jurisdiction*, which last are matters belonging exclusively to the civil law, in every nation in Christendom.

Not to enlarge upon the loss of the invaluable right of trial by an unbiassed jury, so dear to every friend of liberty, the monstrous expence and inconveniences of the mode of proceeding to be adopted, are such as will prove intolerable to the people of this country. The lengthy proceedings of the civil law courts in the chancery of England, and in the courts of Scotland and France, are such that few men of moderate fortune can endure the expence of; the poor man must therefore submit to the wealthy. Length of purse will too often prevail against right and justice. For instance, we are told by the learned judge *Blackstone*, that a question only on the property of an *ox*, of the value of *three* guineas, originating under the civil law proceedings in Scotland, after many interlocutory orders and sentences below, was carried at length from the court of sessions, the highest court in that part of Great Britain, by way of *appeal* to the house of lords, where the question of law and fact was finally determined. He adds, that no pique or spirit could in the court of king's bench or common pleas at Westminster, have given continuance to such a cause for a tenth part of the time, nor have cost a twentieth part of the expence. Yet the costs in the courts of king's bench and common pleas in England, are infinitely greater than those which the people of this country have ever experienced. We abhor the idea of losing the transcendant privilege of trial by jury, with the loss of which, it is remarked by the same learned author, that in Sweden, the liberties of the commons were extinguished by an aristocratic senate: and that *trial by jury* and the liberty of the people went out together. At the same time we regret the intolerable delay, the enormous expences and infinite vexation to which the people of this country will be exposed from the voluminous proceedings of the courts of civil law, and especially from the appellate jurisdiction, by means of which a man may be drawn from the utmost boundaries of this extensive country to the seat of the supreme court of the nation to contend, perhaps with a wealthy and powerful adversary. The consequence of this establishment will be an absolute confirmation of the power of aristocratical influence in the courts of justice; for the common people will not be able to contend or struggle against it.

Trial by jury in criminal cases may also be excluded by declaring that the libeller for instance shall be liable to an action of debt for a specified sum; thus evading the common law prosecution by indictment and trial by jury. And the common course of proceeding against a ship for breach of revenue laws by information (which will be classed among civil causes) will at the civil law be within the resort of a court, where no jury intervenes. Besides, the benefit of jury trial, in cases of a criminal nature, which cannot be evaded, will be rendered of little value, by calling the accused to answer far from home; there being no provision that the trial be by a jury of the neighbourhood or country. Thus an inhabitant of Pittsburgh, on a charge of crime committed on the banks of the Ohio, may be obliged to defend himself at the side of the Delaware, and so *vice versa*. To conclude this head: we observe that the judges of the courts of Congress would not be independent, as they are not debarred from holding other offices, during the pleasure of the president and senate, and as they may derive their support in part from fees, alterable by the legislature.

The next consideration that the constitution presents, is the undue and dangerous mixture of the powers of government: the same body possessing legislative, executive, and judicial powers. The senate is a constituent branch of the legislature, it has judicial power in judging on impeachments, and in this case unites in some measure the characters of judge and party, as all the principal officers are appointed by the president-general, with the concurrence of the senate and therefore they derive their offices in part from the senate. This may biass the judgments of the senators, and tend to screen great delinquents from punishment. And the senate has, moreover, various and great executive powers, viz. in concurrence with the president-general, they form treaties with foreign nations, that may controul and abrogate the constitutions and laws of the several states. Indeed, there is no power, privilege or liberty of the state governments, or of the people, but what may be affected by virtue of this power. For all treaties, made by them, are to be the "supreme law of the land; any thing in the constitution or laws of any state, to the contrary notwithstanding."

And this great power may be exercised by the president and 10 senators (being two-thirds of 14, which is a quorum of that body). What an inducement would this offer to the ministers of foreign powers to compass by bribery *such concessions* as could not otherwise be obtained. It is the unvaried usage of all free states, whenever treaties interfere with the positive laws of the land, to make the intervention of the legislature necessary to give them operation. This became necessary, and was afforded by the parliament of Great-Britain, in consequence of the late commercial treaty between that kingdom and France.—As the senate judges on impeachments, who is to try the members of the senate for the abuse of this power! And none of the great appointments to office can be made without the consent of the senate.

Such various, extensive, and important powers combined in one body of men, are inconsistent with all freedom; the celebrated Montesquieu tells us, that "when the legislative and executive powers are united in the same person, or in the same body of magistrates, there can be no liberty, because apprehensions may arise, lest the same monarch or *senate* should enact tyrannical laws, to execute them in a tyrannical manner."

"Again, there is no liberty, if the power of judging be not separated from the legislative and executive powers. Were it joined with the legislative, the life and liberty of the subject would be exposed to arbitrary controul; for the judge would then be legislator. Were it joined to the executive power, the judge might behave with all the violence of an oppressor. There would be an end of every thing, were the same man, or the same body of the nobles, or of the people, to exercise those three powers; that of enacting laws; that of executing the public resolutions; and that of judging the crimes or differences of individuals."

The president general is dangerously connected with the senate; his coincidence with the views of the ruling junto in that body, is made essential to his weight and importance in the government, which will destroy all independency and purity in the executive department, and having the power of pardoning without the concurrence of a council, he may skreen from punishment the most treasonable attempts that may be made on the liberties of the people, when instigated by his coadjutors in the senate. Instead of this dangerous and improper mixture of the executive with the legislative and judicial, the supreme executive powers ought to have been placed in the president, with a small independent council, made personally responsible for every appointment to office or other act, by having their opinions recorded; and that without the concurrence of the majority of the quorum of this council, the president should not be capable of taking any step.

We have before considered internal taxation, as it would effect the destruction of the state governments, and produce one consolidated government. We will now consider that subject as it affects the personal concerns of the people.

The power of direct taxation applies to every individual, as congress, under this government, is expressly vested with the authority of laying a capitation or poll tax upon every person to any amount. This is a tax that, however oppressive in its nature, and unequal in its operation, is certain as to its produce and simple in its collection; it cannot be evaded like the objects of imposts or excise, and will be paid, because all that a man hath will he give for his head. This tax is so congenial to the nature of despotism, that it has ever been a favorite under such governments. Some of those who were in the late general convention from this state, have long laboured to introduce a poll-tax among us.

The power of direct taxation will further apply to every individual as congress may tax land, cattle, trades, occupations, &c. to any amount, and every object of internal taxation is of that nature, that however oppressive, the people will have but this alternative, either to pay the tax, or let their property be taken, for all resistance will be vain. The standing army and select militia would enforce the collection.

For the moderate exercise of this power, there is no controul left in the state governments, whose intervention is destroyed. No relief, or redress of grievances can be extended, as heretofore, by them. There is not even a declaration of RIGHTS to which the people may appeal for the vindication of their wrongs in the court of justice. They must therefore, implicitly, obey the most arbitrary laws, as the worst of them will be pursuant to the principles and form of the constitution, and that strongest of all checks upon the conduct of administration, *responsibility to the people*, will not exist in this government. The permanency of the appointments of senators and representatives, and the controul the congress have over their election, will place them independent of the sentiments and resentment of the people, and the administration having a greater interest in the government than in the community, there will be no consideration to restrain them from oppression and tyranny. In the government of this state, under the old confederation, the members of the legislature are taken from among the people, and their interests and welfare are so inseparably connected with those of their constituents, that they can derive no advantage from oppressive laws and taxes, for they would suffer in common with their fellow citizens; would participate in the burthens they impose on the community, as they must return to the common level, after a short period; and notwithstanding every exertion of influence, every means of corruption, a necessary rotation excludes them from permanency in the legislature.

This large state is to have but ten members in that Congress which is to have the liberty, property and dearest concerns of every individual in this vast country at absolute command and even these ten persons, who are to be our only guardians; who are to supercede the legislature of Pennsylvania, will not be of the choice of the people, nor amenable to them. From the mode of their election and appointment they will consist of the lordly and high-minded; of men who will have no congenial feelings with the people, but a perfect indifference for, and contempt of them; they will consist of those harpies of power, that prey upon the very vitals; that riot on the miseries of the community. But we will suppose, although in all probability it may never be realized in fact, that our deputies in Congress have the welfare of their constituents at heart, and will exert themselves in their behalf, what security could even this afford; what relief could they extend to their oppressed constituents? To attain this, the majority of the deputies of the twelve other states in Congress must be alike well disposed; must alike forego the sweets of power, and relinquish the pursuits of ambition, which from the nature of things is not to be expected. If the people part with a responsible representation in the legislature, founded upon fair, certain and frequent elections, they have nothing left they can call their own. Miserable is the lot of that people whose every concern depends on the WILL and PLEASURE of their rulers. Our soldiers will become Janissaries, and our officers of government Bashaws; in short, the system of despotism will soon be compleated.

From the foregoing investigation, it appears that the Congress under this constitution will not possess the confidence of the people, which is an essential requisite in a good government; for unless the laws command the confidence and respect of the great body of the people, so as to induce them to support them, when called on by the civil magistrate, they must be executed by the aid of a numerous standing army, which would be inconsistent with every idea of liberty; for the same force that may be employed to compel obedience to good laws, might and probably would be used to wrest from the people their constitutional liberties. The framers of this constitution appear to have been aware of this great deficiency; to have been sensible that no dependence could be placed on the people for their support: but on the contrary, that the government must be executed by force. They have therefore made a provision for this purpose in a permanent STANDING ARMY, and a MILITIA that may be subjected to as strict discipline and government.

A standing army in the hands of a government placed so independent of the people, may be made a fatal instrument to overturn the public liberties; it may be employed to enforce the collection of the most oppressive taxes, and to carry into execution the most arbitrary measures. An ambitious man who may have the army at his devotion, may step up into the throne, and seize upon absolute power.

The absolute unqualified command that Congress have over the militia may be made instrumental to the destruction of all liberty, both public and private; whether of a personal, civil or religious nature.

First, the personal liberty of every man probably from sixteen to sixty years of age, may be destroyed by the power Congress have in organizing and governing of the militia. As militia they may be subjected to fines to any amount, levied in a military manner; they may be subjected to corporal punishments of the most disgraceful and humiliating kind, and to death itself, by the sentence of a court martial: To this our young men will be more immediately subjected, as a select militia, composed of them, will best answer the purposes of government.

Secondly, The rights of conscience may be violated, as there is no exemption of those persons who are conscientiously scrupulous of bearing arms. These compose a respectable proportion of the community in the state. This is the more remarkable, because even when the distresses of the late war, and the evident disaffection of many citizens of that description, inflamed our passions, and when every person, who was obliged to risque his own life, must have been exasperated against such as on any account kept back from the common danger, yet even then, when outrage and violence might have been expected, the rights of conscience were held sacred.

At this momentous crisis, the framers of our state constitution made the most express and decided declaration and stipulations in favour of the rights of conscience: but now when no necessity exists, those dearest rights of men are left insecure.

Thirdly, The absolute command of Congress over the milita may be destructive of public liberty; for under the guidance of an arbitrary government, they may be made the unwilling instruments of tyranny. The militia of Pennsylvania may be marched to New England or Virginia to quell an insurrection occasioned by the most galling oppression, and aided by the standing army, they will no doubt be successful in subduing their liberty and independency; but in so doing, although the magnanimity of their minds will be extinguished, yet the meaner passions of resentment and revenge will be increased, and these in turn will be the ready and obedient instruments of despotism to enslave the others; and that with an irritated vengeance. Thus may the militia be made the instruments of crushing the last efforts of expiring liberty, of riveting the chains of despotism on their fellow citizens, and on one another. This power can be exercised not only without violating the constitution, but in strict conformity with it; it is calculated for this express purpose, and will doubtless be executed accordingly.

As this government will not enjoy the confidence of the people, but be executed by force, it will be a very expensive and burthensome government. The standing army must be numerous, and as a further support, it will be the policy of this government to multiply officers in every department: judges, collectors, tax-gatherers, excisemen and the whole host of revenue officers will swarm over the land, devouring the hard earnings of the industrious. Like the locusts of old, impoverishing and desolating all before them.

We have not noticed the smaller, nor many of the considerable blemishes, but have confined our objections to the great and essential defects; the main pillars of the constitution: which we have shewn to be inconsistent with the liberty and happiness of the people, as its establishment will annihilate the state governments, and produce one consolidated government, that will eventually and speedily issue in the supremacy of despotism.

In this investigation, we have not confined our views to the interests or welfare of this state, in preference to the others. We have overlooked all local circumstances—we have considered this subject on the broad scale of the general good: we have asserted the cause of the present and future ages: the cause of liberty and mankind.

Nathaniel Breading
John Smilie
Richard Baird
Adam Orth
John A. Hanna
John Whitehill
John Harris
Robert Whitehill
John Reynolds
Jonathan Hoge
Nicholas Lutz

John Ludwig
Abraham Lincoln
John Bishop
Joseph Heister
Joseph Powel
James Martin
William Findley
John Baird
James Edgar
William Todd.

Reply to the Pennsylvania Minority:
"America" [Noah Webster]

Daily Advertiser (New York), December 31, 1787

To the DISSENTING MEMBERS of the
late CONVENTION of PENNSYLVANIA.

Gentlemen, Your long and elaborate publication, assigning
the reasons for your refusing to subscribe the ratification of
the NEW FEDERAL CONSTITUTION, has made its appearance in the public papers, and, I flatter myself, will be
read throughout the United States. It will feed the flame of
opposition among the weak, the wicked, the designing, and
the factious; but it will make many new converts to the proposed Government, and furnish the old friends of it with new
weapons of defence. The very attempt to excite uneasiness
and disturbance in a State, about a measure legally and constitutionally adopted, after a long and ample discussion in a
Convention of the people's Delegates, marks a disposition,
beyond all conception, obstinate, base, and politically wicked.
But *obstinacy* is the leading trait in your public characters, and,
as it serves to give *consistency* to your actions, even in error, it
cannot fail to procure you that share of respect which is paid
to the *firmness* of Satan and his fellow apostates, who, after
their expulsion from Heaven, had too much pride to *repent*
and *ask for a re-admission*. My address to you will not be so
lengthy as your publication; your arguments are *few*, altho'
your harangue is *long* and *insidious*.

You begin with telling the world, that *no defect was discovered in the present Confederation, till after the war*. Why did you
not publish the truth? You know, Gentlemen, that during six
years of the war, we had *no Confederation at all*. You know
that the war commenced in April, 1775, and that we had *no
Confederation* till March, 1781. You know (for some of you are
men of abilities and reading) or ought to know, a principle of
fear, in time of war, operates more powerfully in binding
together the States which have a common interest, than all
the parchment compacts on earth. Could we, then, discover

the defects of our present Confederation, with *two years'* experience only, and an enemy in our country? You know we could not.

I will not undertake to detect the falshood of every assertion, or the fallacy of all your reasoning on each article. In the most of them the public will anticipate any thing I could say, and confute your arguments as fast as they read them. But I must tell you, Gentlemen, that your reasoning against the *New Constitution* resembles that of Mr. Hume on miracles. You begin with some *gratis dicta*, which are denied; you assume *premises* which are *totally false*, and then reason on them with great address. Your whole reasoning, and that of all the opposers of the Federal Government, is built on this *false principle*, that the *Federal Legislature* will be a body *distinct from* and *independent* of the people. Unless your opposition is grounded on *that principle*, it stands on *nothing*; and on any *other* supposition, your arguments are but *declamatory nonsense*.

But the principle is false. The Congress, under the proposed Constitution, will have the *same interest* as the people — they are a *part* of the people — their interest is *inseparable* from that of the people; and this union of interest will eternally remain, while the right of election shall continue in the people. Over this right Congress will have no control: the time and manner of exercising that right are very wisely vested in Congress, otherwise a delinquent State might embarrass the measures of the Union. The safety of the public requires that the Federal body should prevent any particular delinquency; but the *right of election* is above their control: it *must* remain in the people, and be exercised once in two, four or six years. A body thus organized, with thirteen Legislatures watching their measures, and several millions of jealous eyes inspecting their conduct, would not be apt to betray their constituents. Yet this is not the best ground of safety. The first and almost only principle that governs men, is *interest. Love of our country* is a powerful auxiliary motive to patriotic actions; but rarely or never operates against *interest*. The only requisite to secure liberty, is to connect the *interest* of the *Governors* with that of the *governed*. Blend these interests — make them inseparable — and both are safe from voluntary invasion. How shall this union be formed? This question is answered. The union is formed by the equal principles on which the people of these States hold their property and their rights. But how shall this union of interests be perpetuated? The answer is easy—bar all perpetuities of estates—prevent any exclusive rights—preserve all preferment dependent on the choice of the people—suffer no power to exist independent of the people or their Representatives. While there exists no power in a State, which is independent on the will of the electors, the rights of the people are secure. The only barrier against tyranny, that is necessary in any State, is *the election of Legislators* by the yeomanry of that State. Preserve *that*, and every privilege is safe. The Legislators thus chosen to represent the people, should have all the power that the people would have, were they assembled in one body to deliberate upon public measures. The distinction between the powers of the *people* and of their *Representatives* in the Legislature, is as absurd in *theory*, as it proves pernicious in *practice*. A distinction, which has already countenanced and supported *one rebellion* in America; has prevented many *good* measures; has produced many *bad*; has created animosities in many States, and embarrassments in all. It has taught the people a lesson, which, if they continue to practise, will bring laws into contempt, and frequently mark our country with blood.

You object, Gentlemen, to the powers vested in Congress. Permit me, to ask you, where will you limit their powers? What bounds will you prescribe? You will reply, *we will reserve certain rights, which we deem invaluable, and restrain our rulers from abridging them*. But, Gentlemen, let me ask you, how will you define these rights? would you say, *the liberty of the Press shall not be restrained*? Well, what is this liberty of the Press? Is it an unlimited licence to publish *any thing and every thing* with impunity? If so, the Author, and Printer of any treatise, however obscene and blasphemous, will be screened from punishment. You know, Gentlemen, that there are books extant, so shockingly and infamously obscene and so daringly blasphemous, that no society on earth, would be vindicable in suffering the publishers to pass unpunished. You certainly know that such cases *have* happened, and *may* happen again—nay, you know that they are *probable*. Would not that indefinite expression, *the liberty of the Press*, extend to the justification of every *possible publication*? Yes, Gentlemen, you know, that under such a general licence, a man who should publish a treatise to *prove his maker a knave*, must be screened from legal punishment. I shudder at the thought!—But the truth must not be concealed. The Constitutions of several States *guarantee that very licence*.

But if you attempt to define the *liberty of the Press*, and ascertain what cases shall fall within that privilege, during the course of centuries, where will you *begin*? Or rather, where will you *end*? Here, Gentlemen, you will be puzzled. Some publications certainly *may* be a breach of civil law: You will not have the effrontery to deny a truth so obvious and intuitively evident. Admit that principle; and unless you can define precisely the cases, which are, and are not a breach of law, you have no right to say, the liberty of the Press shall not be restrained; for such a license would warrant *any breach of law*. Rather than hazard such an abuse of privilege, is it not better to leave the right altogether with your rulers and your posterity? No attempts have ever been made by a Legislative body in America, to abridge that privilege; and in this free enlightened country, no attempts could succeed, unless the public should be convinced that an abuse of it would warrant the restriction. Should this ever be the case, you have no right to say, that a future Legislature, or that posterity shall not abridge the privilege, or punish its abuses. The very attempt to establish a permanent, unalterable Constitution, is an act of consummate arrogance. It is a presumption that we have all possible wisdom—that we can foresee all possible circumstances—and judge for future generations, better than they can for themselves.

But you will say, that trial by jury, is an unalienable right, that ought not to be trusted with our rulers. Why not? If it is such a darling privilege, will not Congress be as fond of it, as their constituents? An elevation into that Council, does not render a man insensible to his privileges, nor place him beyond the necessity of securing them. A member of Congress is liable to all the operations of law, except during his attendance on public business; and should he consent to a law, annihilating any right whatever, he deprives himself, his family and estate, of the benefit resulting from that right, as well as his constituents. This circumstance alone, is a sufficient security.

But, why this outcry about juries? If the people esteem them so highly, why do they ever neglect them, and suffer the trial by them to go into disuse? In some States, *Courts of Admiralty* have no juries—nor Courts of Chancery at all. In the City-Courts of some States, juries are rarely or never called, altho' the parties may demand them; and one State, at least, has lately passed an act, empowering the parties to submit both *law* and *fact* to the Court. It is found, that the judgment of a Court, gives as much satisfaction, as the verdict of a jury, as the Court are as good judges of fact, as juries, and much better judges of law. I have no desire to abolish trials by jury, although the original design and excellence of them, is in many cases superseded.—While the people remain attached to this mode of deciding causes, I am confident, that no Congress can wrest the privilege from them.

But, Gentlemen, our legal proceedings want a reform. Involved in all the mazes of perplexity, which the chicanery of lawyers could invent, in the course of 500 years, our road to justice and redress is tedious, fatiguing and expensive. Our Judicial proceedings are capable of being simplified, and improved in almost every particular. For God's sake, Gentlemen, do not shut the door against improvement. If the people of America, should ever spurn the shackles of opinion, and venture to leave the road, which is so overgrown with briers and thorns, as to strip a man's cloaths from his back as he passes, I am certain they can devise a more easy, safe, and expeditious mode of administering the laws, than that which harrasses every poor mortal, that is wretched enough to want *legal* justice. In Pennsylvania, where very respectable merchants, have repeatedly told me, they had rather lose a debt of fifty pounds, than attempt to recover it by a legal process, one would think that men, who value liberty and property, would not restrain any Government from suggesting a remedy for such disorders.

Another right, which you would place beyond the reach of Congress, is the writ of *habeas corpus*. Will you say that this right may not be suspended in *any* case? You dare not. If it may be suspended in any case, and the Congress are to judge of the necessity, what security have you in a declaration in its favor? You had much better say nothing upon the subject.

But you are frightened at a standing army. I beg you, Gentlemen, to define a *standing army*. If you would refuse to give Congress power to raise troops, to guard our frontiers, and garrison forts, or in short, to enlist men for any purpose, then we understand you—you tie the hands of your rulers so that they cannot defend you against any invasion. This is protection indeed! But if Congress can raise a body of troops for a year, they can raise them for a *hundred years*, and your declaration against *standing armies* can have no other effect, than to prevent Congress from denominating their troops, a *standing army*. You would only introduce into this country, the English farce of mechanically passing an annual bill for the support of troops which are never disbanded.

You object to the indefinite power of taxation in Congress. You must then limit the exercise of that power by the sums of money to be raised; or leaving the sums indefinite, must prescribe the *particular mode* in which, and the *articles* on which the money is to be raised. But the sums cannot be ascertained, because the necessities of the States cannot be foreseen nor defined. It is beyond even *your* wisdom and profound knowledge, Gentlemen, to ascertain the public exigencies, and reduce them to the provisions of a Constitution. And if you would prescribe the mode of raising money, you will meet with equal difficulty. The different States have different modes of taxation, and I question much whether even *your* skill, Gentlemen, could invent a uniform system that should sit easy upon every State. It must therefore be left to experiment, with a power that can correct the errors of a system, and suit it to the habits of the people. And if no uniform mode will answer this purpose, it will be in the power of Congress to lay taxes in each State, according to its particular practice. But you know, Gentlemen, that an efficient Federal Government will render taxes unnecessary—*that it will ease the people of their burdens*, and *remove their complaints*, and therefore when you raise a clamor about the right of taxation, you must be guilty of the *basest design*—your hearts must be as *malignant* as your actions have been *insidious*. You know that requisitions on the States are ineffectual—That they cannot be rendered effectual, but by a compulsory power in Congress—You know that without an efficient power to raise money, Government cannot secure person, property or justice—Nay, you know further, that such power is as safely lodged in your *Representatives* in Congress, as it is in your *Representatives* in your distinct Legislatures.

You would likewise restrain Congress from requiring *excessive bail*, or imposing *excessive fines* and *unusual punishment*. But unless you can, in every possible instance, previously define the words *excessive* and *unusual*—if you leave the discretion of Congress to define them on occasion, any restriction of their power by a general indefinite expression, is a nullity—mere *formal nonsense*. What consummate arrogance must you possess, to presume you can *now* make *better* provision for the Government of these States, during the course of ages and centuries, than the future Legislatures can, on the spur of the occasion! Yet your whole reasoning on the subject implies this arrogance, and a presumption that you have a right to legislate for posterity!

But to complete the list of unalienable rights, you would insert a clause in your declaration, *that every body shall, in good weather, hunt on his own land, and catch fish in rivers that are public property*. Here, Gentlemen, you must have exerted the whole force of your genius! Not even the *all-important* subject of *legislating for a world* can restrain my laughter at this clause! As a supplement to that article of your bill of rights, I would suggest the following restriction:—"That Congress shall never restrain any inhabitant of America from eating and drinking, *at seasonable times*, or prevent his lying on his *left side*, in a long winter's night, or even on his back, when he is fatigued by lying on his *right*."—This article is of just as much consequence as the 8th clause of your proposed bill of rights.

But to be more serious, Gentlemen, you must have had in idea the forest-laws in Europe, when you inserted that article; for no circumstance that ever took place in America, could have suggested the thought of a declaration in favor of hunting and fishing. Will you forever persist in error? Do you not reflect that the state of property in America, is directly the reverse of what it is in Europe? Do you not consider, that the forest-laws in Europe originated in *feudal tyranny*, of which not a trace is to be found in America? Do you not know that in this country almost every farmer is Lord of his own soil? That instead of suffering under the oppression of a Monarch and Nobles, a class of haughty masters, totally independent of the people, almost every man in America is a *Lord himself*— enjoying his property in fee? Where then the necessity of laws to secure hunting and fishing? You may just as well ask for a clause, giving licence for every man to till *his own land*, or milk *his own cows*. The Barons in Europe procured forest-laws to secure the right of hunting on *their own land*, from the intrusion of those who had no property in lands. But the distribution of land in America, not only supersedes the necessity of any laws upon this subject, but renders them absolutely trifling. The same laws which secure the property in land, secure to the owner the right of using it as he pleases.

But you are frightened at the prospect of a *consolidation of the States*. I differ from you very widely. I am afraid, after all our attempts to unite the States, that contending interests, and the pride of State-Sovereignties, will either prevent our union, or render our Federal Government weak, slow and inefficient. The danger is all on this side. If any thing under Heaven now endangers our liberties and independence, it is that single circumstance.

You harp upon that clause of the New Constitution, which declares, that the laws of the United States, &c. shall be the supreme law of the land; when you know that the powers of the Congress are defined, to extend only to those matters which are in their nature and effects, *general*. You know, the Congress cannot meddle with the internal police of any State, or abridge its Sovereignty. And you know, at the same time, that in all general concerns, the laws of Congress must be *supreme*, or they must be *nothing*.

But the public will ask, who are these men that so violently oppose the New Constitution? I will tell them. You are the heads of that party, Gentlemen, which, on the celebration of a very glorious event in Philadelphia, at the close of the war, collected in a mob, and broke the windows of the Quakers, and committed the most detestable outrages, because their religion would not suffer them to illuminate their windows, and join in the rejoicings. You are the men, Gentlemen, that wrested the Charter from the Bank, without the least justifiable pretence; sporting with a grant which *you* had made, and which had never been forfeited. You are the men, that, without a show of right, took away the Charter of the University, and vested it in the hands of your own tools. Yes, Gentlemen, you are the men, who prescribed a test law and oath of abjuration in Pennsylvania, which excluded more than half the Citizens of the State from all Civil Offices. A law, which, had it not been altered by the efforts of more reasonable men, would have established you, and your adherents, as an Aristocratic junto, in all the offices and emoluments of the State. Could your base designs have been accomplished, *you* would have rioted in all the benefits of Government, and Pennsylvania would now, have been subject to as tyrannical an Aristocracy, as ever cursed Society. Such has been the uniformly infamous conduct of the men, who now oppose the best Constitution of Government, ever devised by human wisdom.

But the most bare-faced act of tyranny and wickedness, which has distinguished your political characters, remains to be mentioned. You are the men, Gentlemen, who have abandoned your parts of duty, and betrayed the constitutional rights of the State of Pennsylvania, by *seceding from the Legislature*, with the design of defeating the measures of a constitutional quorum of the House. Yes, Gentlemen, and to add to the infamy of your conduct, you have the audacity to *avow the intention*. Will you then attempt to palliate the crime, by saying it was *necessary?* Good Heavens! *necessary* that a State should be *ruled by a minority*! *necessary* that the sense of a legislature should be defeated by a junto, which had labored incessantly, for four years, to establish an *Aristocracy* in the State! The same principle which will vindicate you, will justify any *one* man in defeating the sense of the *whole* State. If a minority may prevent a law, one man may do it; but is this liberty? Is this your concern for the rights of the State? Dare you talk of rights, which you have so flagrantly invaded? Will the world expect *you* to be the guardians of privileges? No,

Gentlemen, they will sooner expect lessons of morality from the wheel-barrowed criminals, that clank their chains along your streets.

Do you know, Gentlemen, that you are treading in the steps of the Governors before the revolution? Do you know that from the first settlement of Pennsylvania, there was a contest between the people and the deputies of the proprietaries? And that when a Governor could not bring the Assembly to resign their rights, he would *prevail on certain members to leave the House*, and prevent their measures. Yes, Gentlemen, you are but following the precedents of your tyrannical Governors.* You have begun, and pursued, with unwearied perseverance, the same plan of Despotism which wrought the late revolution; and, with a calm, hypocritical phiz, pretend to be *anxious for the liberties of the people*.

These facts stare you in the face! They are *felt* in Pennsylvania—and *known* to the world! There is not a spot in the United States, where the solemnity of contracts and grants, has been so sacrilegiously violated—and the rights of men so wantonly and perseveringly abused, as by you and your junto in Pennsylvania—except only, in the little detestable corner of the Continent, called *Rhode-Island*. Thanks be to the Sovereign Ruler of events, you are checked in your career of tyranny—your power is dwindling into impotence—and your abuse of the respectable Convention, and of the friends of our Federal Union, will shroud you in oblivion, or accelerate your progress to merited contempt.

*See, a Review of the Constitution and Government of Pennsylvania, Page 24.

A Cumberland County Mutual Improvement Society Addresses the Pennsylvania Minority

Carlisle Gazette (Pennsylvania), January 2, 1788

Messieurs PRINTERS. By inserting the following in your useful gazette, you will oblige a number of your constant readers.

An Address to the Minority of the State Convention of Pennsylvania.

The history of mankind is pregnant with frequent, bloody and almost imperceptible transitions from freedom to slavery. Rome, after she had been long distracted by the fury of the patrician and plebeian parties, at length found herself reduced to the most abject slavery under a Nero, a Caligula, &c. The successive convulsions, which happened at Rome, were the immediate consequence of the aspiring ambition of a few great men, and the very organization and construction of the government itself. The republic of Venice, by the progressive and almost imperceptible encroachments of the nobles, has at length degenerated into an odious and permanent aristocracy. This we are convinced by indubitable demonstration, will be the final consequence of the proposed Federal Constitution; and because we prize the felicity and freedom of our posterity equally with our own, we esteem it our indispensible duty to oppose it with that determined resolution and spirit that becomes freemen. That fire for liberty which was kindled in every patriotic breast during the late glorious contention, though in a latent state, will be easily rekindled; and upon the contact of a very spark will devour by its direful explosion, not only the enemies of liberty, but both parties promiscuously. Discontent, indignation and revenge already begins to be visible in every patriotic countenance; and civil discord already raises her sneaky head: And we are well convinced that nothing less than a total recantation and annihilation of the proposed aristocratic delusion will appease the insulted and enraged defenders of liberty. If the lazy and great wish to ride, they may lay it down as an indubitable position or axiom, that the people of America will make very refractory and restiff hackneys. Although the designing and artful Federalists have effected their scheme so far as to have the constitution adopted in this state by surprize, notwithstanding the people are pretty generally convinced of their delusion, and little less than the lives of their betrayers will satiate their revenge. Not even the authority of the clergy, who seem generally to have been a set of men decidedly opposed to popular freedom, can give sanction to such a government. The people of America understand their rights better than, by adopting such a constitution, to rivet the fetters of slavery; or to sacrifice their liberty at the shrine of aristocracy or arbitrary government. We, the subscribers, are a society united for the express purpose of reciprocal or mutual improvement; we meet once a week, and political matters are frequently the subjects of litigation and debate. We have read and endeavoured fully to comprehend the proposed federal constitution; and also the arguments for and against it; and after mature deliberation, we unanimously acquiesce with, and cordially thank you the Minority in the late State Convention:—First, for your patriotic and spirited endeavours to support the drooping cause of liberty, and rights of your constituents: Secondly, for your integrity and firmness in stemming the torrent of popular clamour, insult and flattery: Thirdly, for your unanswerable, solid, and well-founded arguments and reason of dissent: Lastly, we rejoice to think that your names will shine illustriously in the page of history, and will be read with honour and grateful remembrance in the annals of fame; while the names of the majority, and their ignorant tools will be spurned and execrated by the succeeding generations as the pillars of slavery, tyranny and despotism.

James M'Cormick,	James Bell,
David Boyd,	Thomas Atchley,
William Gelson,	William Irvin,
James Irvin,	William Douglass,

Andrew Irvin,
Wm. Carothers sen.
William Addams,
Wm Carothers jun.
John Douglass,
Arch. Hamilton,
Joseph Junkin,
John Clandinen,
Thomas Henderson,
Robert Bell,
John Junkin,

John Walker,
William Greason,
David Walker,
Jonathan Walker,
John Buchanan,
Francis M'Guire,
John Armstrong,
Benj. Junkin,
John Carothers jun.
James Fleming,
Thomas Carothers.

Reply to the Pennsylvania Minority: "A Citizen of Philadelphia" [Pelatiah Webster]

Pennsylvania Gazette (Philadelphia), January 23, 1788

Messrs. HALL & SELLERS,

In the list of the signers of the protest of the minority of the Convention against the fœderal constitution, we find SIX—(and THREE of them the only speakers against it in the Convention) whose names are upon record as the friends of *paper money*, and the advocates for the late unjust *test-law* of Pennsylvania, which for near *ten* years excluded the *Quakers, Menonists, Moravians,* and several other sects scrupulous against war, from a representation in our government.

In the minutes of the second session of the Ninth General Assembly of the commonwealth of Pennsylvania, we find in the 212th page the following persons among the YEAS, who voted for the emission of paper money, which has, by its depreciation, so much injured the trade and manufactures of the state, and which, by impairing its funds, has weakened the strength of our government, and thereby destroyed the hopes and support of the public creditors. The persons are, *William Findley, John Smilie, Robert Whitehill, Adam Orth, Nicholas Lutz, Abraham Lincoln.*

In the 302d page of the same book, we find a report, declaring the Quakers, Moravians, &c. who, from conscientious scruples, declined taking part in the war, to be "enemies to liberty and the rights of mankind—British subjects, aliens and cowards—who had no share in the declaration of independence, in the formation of our constitution, or in establishing them by ARMS;" which report is agreed to, as appears in the list of the YEAS, by the same *William Findley, John Smilie, Robert Whitehill, Adam Orth, Nicholas Lutz, Abraham Lincoln.*

These men certainly are not in earnest, when they talk and write of *liberty*, and of the sacred rights of *conscience*. Their conduct contradicts all their speeches and publications; and if they were truly sensible of their folly and wickedness in opposing the new government, instead of trying to excite a civil war (in which they will bear no more part than they did in the late war with Great-Britain) they ought rather to acknowledge, with gratitude, the lenity of their fellow-citizens, in permitting them to live among us with impunity, after thus transgressing and violating the great principles of liberty, government and conscience.

In the Centinel, No. XI, we are told that General Washington (under God the deliverer of our country) is a poor creature, with many *constitutional* infirmities; and that he has, from ambitious motives, united with the *conspirators* of Delaware, Pennsylvania, New-Jersey and Connecticut, to enslave his country.—Can human nature sink so low as to be guilty of such base ingratitude to a man to whom America owes her independence and liberties? or will the more grateful sons of America suffer the author of such a declaration to continue to insult their opinions and feelings? There was a time, when the liberties of our country were at the mercy of this great and good man—There was a time when a defrauded and clamorous army, devoted to his will, and a Congress without power or credit, would have rendered it an easy matter for him to have established a monarchy in the United States. But how nobly did he behave in this alarming crisis of our affairs. He composed the turbulent and punished the mutinous spirit of the army. He strengthened by his influence the hands of Congress, and finally bequeathed, as his last legacy to his country, his parting advice, to form such a union as would for ever perpetuate her liberties.

In the same Centinel we are told, that *anarchy* and a *civil war* are less evils than the despotism (as he calls it) of the new government. It would be an affront to the understandings of my readers to controvert these two opinions—I shall only ask the author of them, whether he will risk himself, at the head of a company of his Carlisle *white* boys, in case he should succeed in his beloved scheme of exciting a civil war, or whether he would not rather shelter himself under a safe office, as he did during the late war, until the bloody storm was over?

The people of Pennsylvania have been so often told of *an appeal to arms*, when power and office (not liberty) were in danger, by the leaders of the old constitutional junto, that they now regard the threat no more than the scolding of the apple women in Market street, when they are disturbed by the country people on a market day. They remember how much these men boasted, and how little they did, during the late war. They know full well—that not only wealth, but that numbers—virtue, courage and military skill, are all on the fœderal side of the question in Pennsylvania. They know, that the brave and tried militia of Delaware and Jersey will not be neutral spectators of a contest in Pennsylvania, which involves in it the safety of a government, which they have unanimously and joyfully adopted. They, therefore, pity the poor madmen who spurn these threats, and anticipate no other consequence from their being carried further, than the certain ruin of two or three seditious individuals in the city of Philadelphia.

In a republic, the majority should certainly govern. Now a majority have decided in favour of the new constitution. The opposition to it after this, by a minority, is not only an attempt to establish an aristocracy, or a government of a *few* over the *many*, but it is downright rebellion.

But we are told, this majority have adopted a system of despotism. This is false;—for the new government is the best bulwark of freedom that ever was framed in the world. But I will suppose this was not the case, and that the new constitution was as bad as it is said to be. What then?—The minority are still bound to submit to it; for it is the choice of the *majority*, and they cannot be *free*, unless it be adopted. If it is rejected, then the majority, who are deprived of what they love and *prefer*, yield to the minority, which is contrary to every principle of democracy.

I wish the public creditors to look to themselves. The funding system of Pennsylvania is on its last legs. It cannot exist another year, without convulsing our state. All the distress, oppression, speculation, idleness, peculation in government, —and bankruptcies, not of merchants only, but of *tradesmen* and *farmers* (a thing unheard of before, and unknown in other countries) are owing to the funding law. Pennsylvania has assumed a million and an half of dollars in certificates, above her quota of the public debt. It is only by adopting the fœderal government that this enormous, unequal and oppressive burthen can be taken off our shoulders, and the state rescued out of the hands of speculators, sharpers and public defaulters. It is, moreover, only from a fœderal treasury that the public creditors, of all descriptions, can expect substantial and permanent justice.

"Publius," The Federalist XXIII
[Alexander Hamilton]

New-York Packet, December 18, 1787

To the People of the State of New-York.

The necessity of a Constitution, at least equally energetic with the one proposed, to the preservation of the Union, is the point, at the examination of which we are now arrived.

This enquiry will naturally divide itself into three branches — the objects to be provided for by a Fœderal Government — the quantity of power necessary to the accomplishment of those objects — the persons upon whom that power ought to operate. Its distribution and organization will more properly claim our attention under the succeeding head.

The principal purposes to be answered by Union are these — The common defence of the members — the preservation of the public peace as well against internal convulsions as external attacks — the regulation of commerce with other nations and between the States — the superintendence of our intercourse, political and commercial, with foreign countries.

The authorities essential to the care of the common defence are these — to raise armies — to build and equip fleets — to prescribe rules for the government of both — to direct their operations — to provide for their support. These powers ought to exist without limitation: *Because it is impossible to foresee or define the extent and variety of national exigencies, or the correspondent extent & variety of the means which may be necessary to satisfy them.* The circumstances that endanger the safety of nations are infinite; and for this reason no constitutional shackles can wisely be imposed on the power to which the care of it is committed. This power ought to be co-extensive with all the possible combinations of such circumstances; and ought to be under the direction of the same councils, which are appointed to preside over the common defence.

This is one of those truths, which to a correct and unprejudiced mind, carries its own evidence along with it; and may be obscured, but cannot be made plainer by argument or reasoning. It rests upon axioms as simple as they are universal. The *means* ought to be proportioned to the *end*; the persons, from whose agency the attainment of any *end* is expected, ought to possess the *means* by which it is to be attained.

Whether there ought to be a Fœderal Government intrusted with the care of the common defence, is a question in the first instance open to discussion; but the moment it is decided in the affirmative, it will follow, that that government ought to be cloathed with all the powers requisite to the complete execution of its trust. And unless it can be shewn, that the circumstances which may affect the public safety are reducible within certain determinate limits; unless the contrary of this position can be fairly and rationally disputed, it must be admitted, as a necessary consequence, that there can be no limitation of that authority, which is to provide for the defence and protection of the community, in any matter essential to its efficacy; that is, in any matter essential to the *formation, direction* or *support* of the NATIONAL FORCES.

Defective as the present Confederation has been proved to be, this principle appears to have been fully recognized by the framers of it; though they have not made proper or adequate provision for its exercise. Congress have an unlimited discretion to make requisitions of men and money—to govern the army and navy—to direct their operations. As their requisitions were made constitutionally binding upon the States, who are in fact under the most solemn obligations to furnish the supplies required of them, the intention evidently was, that the United States should command whatever resources were by them judged requisite to "the common defence and general welfare." It was presumed that a sense of their true interests, and a regard to the dictates of good faith, would be found sufficient pledges for the punctual performance of the duty of the members to the Fœderal Head.

The experiment has, however demonstrated, that this expectation was ill founded and illusory; and the observations made under the last head, will, I imagine, have sufficed to convince the impartial and discerning, that there is an absolute necessity for an entire change in the first principles of the system: That if we are in earnest about giving the Union energy and duration, we must abandon the vain project of legislating upon the States in their collective capacities: We must extend the laws of the Fœderal Government to the individual citizens of America: We must discard the fallacious scheme of quotas and requisitions, as equally impracticable and unjust. The result from all this is, that the Union ought to be invested with full power to levy troops; to build and equip fleets, and to raise the revenues, which will be required for the formation and support of an army and navy, in the customary and ordinary modes practiced in other governments.

If the circumstances of our country are such, as to demand a compound instead of a simple, a confederate instead of a sole government, the essential point which will remain to be adjusted, will be to discriminate the OBJECTS, as far as it can be done, which shall appertain to the different provinces or departments of power; allowing to each the most ample authority for fulfilling the objects committed to its charge. Shall the Union be constituted the guardian of the common safety? Are fleets and armies and revenues necessary to this purpose? The government of the Union must be empowered to pass all laws, and to make all regulations which have relation to them. The same must be the case, in respect to commerce, and to every other matter to which its jurisdiction is permitted to extend. Is the administration of justice between the citizens of the same State, the proper department of the local governments? These must possess all the authorities which are connected with this object, and with every other that may be allotted to their particular cognizance and direction. Not to confer in each case a degree of power, commensurate to the end, would be to violate the most obvious rules of prudence and propriety, and improvidently to trust the great interests of the nation to hands, which are disabled from managing them with vigour and success.

Who so likely to make suitable provisions for the public defence, as that body to which the guardianship of the public safety is confided—which, as the center of information, will best understand the extent and urgency of the dangers that threaten—as the representative of the WHOLE will feel itself most deeply interested in the preservation of every part—

which, from the responsibility implied in the duty assigned to it, will be most sensibly impressed with the necessity of proper exertions—and which, by the extension of its authority throughout the States, can alone establish uniformity and concert in the plans and measures, by which the common safety is to be secured? Is there not a manifest inconsistency in devolving upon the Fœderal Government the care of the general defence, and leaving in the State governments the *effective* powers, by which it is to be provided for? Is not a want of co-operation the infallible consequence of such a system? And will not weakness, disorder, an undue distribution of the burthens and calamities of war, an unnecessary and intolerable increase of expence, be its natural and inevitable concomitants? Have we not had unequivocal experience of its effects in the course of the revolution, which we have just accomplished?

Every view we may take of the subject, as candid enquirers after truth, will serve to convince us, that it is both unwise and dangerous to deny the Fœderal Government an unconfined authority, as to all those objects which are intrusted to its management. It will indeed deserve the most vigilant and careful attention of the people, to see that it be modelled in such a manner, as to admit of its being safely vested with the requisite powers. If any plan which has been, or may be offered to our consideration, should not, upon a dispassionate inspection, be found to answer this description, it ought to be rejected. A government, the Constitution of which renders it unfit to be trusted with all the powers, which a free people *ought to delegate to any government*, would be an unsafe and improper depository of the NATIONAL INTERESTS, wherever THESE can with propriety be confided, the co-incident powers may safely accompany them. This is the true result of all just reasoning upon the subject. And the adversaries of the plan, promulgated by the Convention, ought to have confined themselves to showing that the internal structure of the proposed government, was such as to render it unworthy of the confidence of the people. They ought not to have wandered into inflammatory declamations, and unmeaning cavils about the extent of the powers. The POWERS are not too extensive for the OBJECTS of Fœderal administration, or in other words, for the management of our NATIONAL INTERESTS; nor can any satisfactory argument be framed to shew that they are chargeable with such an excess. If it be true, as has been insinuated by some of the writers on the other side, that the difficulty arises from the nature of the thing, and that the extent of the country will not permit us to form a government, in which such ample powers can safely be reposed, it would prove that we ought to contract our views, and resort to the expedient of separate Confederacies, which will move within more practicable spheres. For the absurdity must continually stare us in the face of confiding to a government, the direction of the most essential national interests, without daring to trust it with the authorities which are indispensable to their proper and efficient management. Let us not attempt to reconcile contradictions, but firmly embrace a rational alternative.

I trust, however, that the impracticability of one general system cannot be shewn. I am greatly mistaken, if any thing of weight, has yet been advanced of this tendency; and I flatter myself, that the observations which have been made in the course of these papers, have sufficed to place the reverse of that position in as clear a light as any matter still in the womb of time and experience can be susceptible of. This at all events must be evident, that the very difficulty itself drawn from the extent of the country, is the strongest argument in favor of an energetic government; for any other can certainly never preserve the Union of so large an empire. If we embrace the tenets of those, who oppose the adoption of the proposed Constitution, as the standard of our political creed, we cannot fail to verify the gloomy doctrines, which predict the impracticability of a national system, pervading the entire limits of the present Confederacy.

"Publius," The Federalist XXIV
[Alexander Hamilton]

Independent Journal (New York), December 19, 1787

To the People of the State of New-York.

To the powers proposed to be conferred upon the Fœderal Government in respect to the creation and direction of the national forces—I have met with but one specific objection; which if I understand it right is this—that proper provision has not been made against the existence of standing armies in time of peace: An objection which I shall now endeavour to shew, rests on weak and unsubstantial foundations.

It has indeed been brought forward in the most vague and general form, supported only by bold assertions, without the appearance of argument—without even the sanction of theoretical opinions, in contradiction to the practice of other free nations, and to the general sense of America, as expressed in most of the existing constitutions. The propriety of this remark will appear the moment it is recollected that the objection under consideration turns upon a supposed necessity of restraining the LEGISLATIVE authority of the nation, in the article of military establishments; a principle unheard of except in one or two of our state constitutions, and rejected in all the rest.

A stranger to our politics who was to read our newspapers at the present juncture, without having previously inspected the plan reported by the Convention, would be naturally led to one of two conclusions—either that it contained a positive injunction, that standing armies should be kept up in time of peace, or that it vested in the EXECUTIVE the whole power of leveying troops, without subjecting his discretion in any shape to the controul of the legislature.

If he came afterwards to peruse the plan itself, he would be surprised to discover that neither the one nor the other was the case—that the whole power of raising armies was lodged in the *legislature*, not in the *executive*; that this legislature was to be a popular body consisting of the representatives of the people periodically elected—and that instead of the provision he had supposed in favour of standing armies, there was to be found, in respect to this object, an important qualification even of the legislative discretion, in that clause which forbids the appropriation of money for the support of an army for any longer period than two years: a precaution which, upon a nearer view of it, will appear to be a great and real security against the keeping up of troops without evident necessity.

Disappointed in his first surmise, the person I have supposed would be apt to pursue his conjectures a little further. He would naturally say to himself, it is impossible that all this vehement and pathetic declamation can be without some colorable pretext. It must needs be that this people, so jealous of their liberties, have in all the preceding models of the constitutions which they have established, inserted the most precise and rigid precautions on this point, the omission of which in the new plan has given birth to all this apprehension and clamour.

If under this impression he proceeded to pass in review the several State Constitutions, how great would be his disappointment to find that *two only* of them* contained an interdiction of standing armies in time of peace; that the other eleven had either observed a profound silence on the subject,

---

*This statement of the matter is taken from the printed collections of State Constitutions.—Pennsylvania and North-Carolina, are the two which contain the interdiction in these words—"As standing armies in time of peace are dangerous to liberty, *they ought not* to be kept up." This is in truth rather a *caution* than a *prohibition*. New-Hampshire, Massachusetts, Delaware and Maryland, have in each of their bills of rights a clause to this effect—"Standing armies are dangerous to liberty, and ought not to be raised or kept up *without the consent of the Legislature*"—which is a formal admission of the authority of the Legislature. NEW-YORK has no bill of her rights, and her constitution says not a word about the matter. No bills of rights appear annexed to the constitutions of the other States except the foregoing, and their constitutions are equally silent. I am told, however, that one or two States have bills of rights, which do not appear in this collection; but that those also recognize the right of the legislative authority in this respect.

or had in express terms admitted the right of the legislature to authorise their existence.

Still however he would be persuaded that there must be some plausible foundation for the cry raised on this head. He would never be able to imagine, while any source of information remained unexplored, that it was nothing more than an experiment upon the public credulity, dictated either by a deliberate intention to deceive or by the overflowings of a zeal too intemperate to be ingenuous. It would probably occur to him that he would be likely to find the precautions he was in search of in the primitive compact between the States—Here at length he would expect to meet with a solution of the enigma. No doubt he would observe to himself the existing confederation must contain the most explicit provisions against military establishments in time of peace; and a departure from this model in a favourite point has occasioned the discontent which appears to influence these political champions.

If he should now apply himself to a careful and critical survey of the articles of confederation, his astonishment would not only be increased but would acquire a mixture of indignation at the unexpected discovery that these articles instead of containing the prohibition he looked for, and though they had with jealous circumspection restricted the authority of the State Legislatures in this particular, had not imposed a single restraint on that of the United States. If he happened to be a man of quick sensibility or ardent temper, he could now no longer refrain from regarding these clamours as the dishonest artifices of a sinister and unprincipled opposition to a plan which ought at least to receive a fair and candid examination from all sincere lovers of their country! How else, he would say, could the authors of them have been tempted to vent such loud censures upon that plan, about a point in which it seems to have conformed itself to the general sense of America as declared in its different forms of government, and in which it has even superadded a new and powerful guard unknown to any of them? If on the contrary he happened to be a man of calm and dispassionate feelings —he would indulge a sigh for the frailty of human nature, and would lament that in a matter so interesting to the happiness of millions the true merits of the question should be perplexed and entangled by expedients so unfriendly to an impartial and right determination. Even such a man could hardly forbear remarking that a conduct of this kind has too much the appearance of an intention to mislead the people by alarming their passions rather than to convince them by arguments addressed to their understandings.

But however little this objection may be countenanced even by precedents among ourselves, it may be satisfactory to take a nearer view of its intrinsic merits. From a close examination it will appear that restraints upon the discretion of the Legislature in respect to military establishments in time of peace would be improper to be imposed, and if imposed, from the necessities of society would be unlikely to be observed.

Though a wide ocean separates the United States from Europe; yet there are various considerations that warn us against an excess of confidence or security. On one side of us and stretching far into our rear are growing settlements subject to the dominion of Britain. On the other side and extending to meet the British settlements are colonies and establishments subject to the dominion of Spain. This situation and the vicinity of the West-India islands belonging to these two powers create between them, in respect to their American possessions, and in relation to us, a common interest. The savage tribes on our Western frontier ought to be regarded as our natural enemies their natural allies; because they have most to fear from us and most to hope from them. The improvements in the art of navigation have, as to the facility of communication, rendered distant nations in a great measure, neighbours, Britain and Spain are among the principal maritime powers of Europe. A future concert of views between these nations ought not to be regarded as improbable—The increasing remoteness of consanguinity is every day diminishing the force of the family-compact between France and Spain. And politicians have ever with great reason considered the ties of blood as feeble and precarious links of political connection. These circumstances combined admonish us not to be too sanguine in considering ourselves as intirely out of the reach of danger.

Previous to the revolution, and ever since the peace, there has been a constant necessity for keeping small garrisons on our Western frontier. No person can doubt that these will continue to be indispensable, if it should only be against the ravages and depredations of the Indians. These garrisons must either be furnished, by occasional detachments from the militia, or by permanent corps in the pay of the government. The first is impracticable; and if practicable, would be pernicious. The militia would not long, if at all, submit to be dragged from their occupations and families to perform that most disagreeable duty in times of profound peace. And if they could be prevailed upon, or compelled to do it, the increased expence of a frequent rotation of service, and the loss of labour and disconcertion of the industrious pursuits of individuals, would form conclusive objections to the scheme. It would be as burthensome and injurious to the public, as ruinous to private citizens. The latter resource of permanent corps in the pay of government amounts to a standing army in the time of peace; a small one indeed, but not the less real for being small. Here is a simple view of the subject that shows us at once the impropriety of a constitutional interdiction of such establishments, and the necessity of leaving the matter to the discretion and prudence of the legislature.

In proportion to our increase in strength, it is probable, nay it may be said certain, that Britain and Spain would augment their military establishments in our neighbourhood. If we should not be willing to be exposed in a naked and defenceless condition to their insults or encroachments, we should find it expedient to increase our frontier garrisons in some ratio to the force by which our Western settlements might be annoyed. There are and will be particular posts the possession of which will include the command of large districts of territory and facilitate future invasions of the remainder. It may be added that some of those posts will be keys to the trade with the Indian nations. Can any man think it would be wise to leave such posts in a situation to be at any instant seized by one or the other of two neighbouring and formidable powers? To act this part, would be to desert all the usual maxims of prudence and policy.

If we mean to be a commercial people or even to be secure

on our Atlantic side, we must endeavour as soon as possible to have a navy. To this purpose there must be dock-yards and arsenals; and, for the defence of these, fortifications and probably garrisons. When a nation has become so powerful by sea, that it can protect its dock-yards by its fleets, this supersedes the necessity of garrisons for that purpose; but where naval establishments are in their infancy, moderate garrisons will in all likelihood be found an indispensable security against descents for the destruction of the arsenals and dock-yards and sometimes of the fleet itself.

"Philadelphiensis" [*Benjamin Workman*] V

Independent Gazetteer (Philadelphia), December 19, 1787

"This is true liberty, when free born men
  Having to advise the public may speak free;
  Which he who can, and will, deserves high praise;
  Who neither can, nor will, may hold his peace;—
  What can be juster in a state than this?"

My Fellow Citizens, If the arbitrary proceedings of the convention of Pennsylvania do not rouse your attention to the rights of yourselves and your children, there is nothing that I can say will do it. If the contempt and obloquy with which that body (whose legality even may be questioned) has treated your petitions, can not bring you to think seriously, what then will? When a few Demagogues despising every sense of order and decency, have rejected the petitions of the people, and in the most supercilious manner, triumphed over the freemen of America, as if they were their slaves, and they themselves their lords and masters. I say that if such barefaced presumption and arrogance, such tyrannical proceedings of the men, who, if acting constitutionally, were the servants of the people, be not sufficient to awaken you to a sense of your duty and interest, nothing less than the goad and the whip can succeed: your condition must be like that of the careless and insecure sinner, whom neither the admonitions nor entreaties of his friends, nor even the threatnings of awaiting justice, could reclaim or convince of his error; his reformation is neglected until it is too late, when he finds himself in a state of unutterable and endless woe.

It may be asserted with confidence, that besides the petitions that Mr. Whitehill presented to the convention from Cumberland county against the adoption of the new constitution, there is not a county or town in the state that should not have followed the example, if a reasonable time had been allowed for the petitions to come in. Now if we consider but for a moment how contemptuously the people were treated on this occasion, we may form some idea of the way in which they are hereafter to be governed by their *well born masters*. "The petitions being read from the chair. Mr. M'Kean said he was sorry that at this stage of the business so *improper* an attempt should be made; he hoped therefore that the petitions would not be *attended to*." (Pennsylvania Herald.) Where is the freeman in America that can tamely suffer such an insult to his dignity to pass with impunity; where is that pusillanimous wretch who can submit to this contumely? Is not this the language of Britain, in the years 1775 and 1776, renewed. What said George the third and his pampered ministers, more than this, to the petitions of America? Is it improper for freemen to petition for their rights? If it be; then I say that the impropriety consisted only in their not *demanding* them. Propriety requires that the people should approach their representatives with a becoming humility; but the governors of a free people must ever be considered as their servants, and are therefore bound to observe decency towards them, and to act according to their instructions and agreeably to conscience. If the petitions of the freemen of America, couched in decent and respectful terms, will not be attended to; then be it known, that their *demands* must and will be granted: If no better will do, the ultima ratio regum must secure to the people their rights. God in his providence has crowned them with success once already on this head; and their is little doubt, with the same assistance, but a second attempt will terminate just as much in favor of liberty.

The indignity offered to the people and their petitions, by the haughty lordlings of the convention, proclaims the chains of despotism already firmly riveted; like a herald it cries aloud, hush ye slaves, how dare you interrupt your *mighty rulers*, who alone have a divine right to establish constitutions and governments calculated to promote their own agrandizement and honor. Ah my friends, the days of a cruel Nero approach fast; the language of a monster, of a Caligula, could not be more imperious. I challenge the whole continent, the *well born and their parasites*, to show an instance of greater insolence than this, on the part of the British tyrant and his infernal junto, to the people of America, before our glorious revolution. My fellow citizens, this is an awful crisis; your situation is alarming indeed; yourselves and your petitions are despised and trampled under the feet of self-important nabobs; whose diabolical plots and secret machinations have been carried on since the revolution, with a view to destroy your liberties, and reduce you to a state of slavery and dependence; and alas! I fear they have found you off your guard, and taken you by surprise: these aspiring men have seized the government, and secured all power, as they suppose, to themselves, now openly browbeat you with their insolence, and assume majesty; and even treat you like menial servants, your representatives as so many conquered slaves, that, they intend to make pass under the yoke, as soon as leisure from their gluttony and rioting on the industry of the poor, shall permit them to attend such a pleasing piece of sport.

But I trust, these petty tyrants will soon find to their confussion, that their own imprudent zeal has defeated their designs. Providence has ordered, that they should begin to carry their arbitrary schemes too soon into execution, that, their boundless ambition should precipitate their destruction, and that the glory of God should be made perfect in the salvation of the poor. Blessed be his name, "He hath shewed strength with his arm; he hath scattered the proud in the imagination of their hearts. He hath put down the mighty from their seat, and exalted them of low degree. He hath filled the hungry with good things, and the rich he hath sent empty away." As a villain, who, secreted to rob and murder in the silent hour of night, issues forth from his lurking place before the people have retired to sleep, and thus frustrates his infernal design by impatience; so in like manner the lust of dominion has urged these despots on to the adoption of measures that will inevitably, and, I hope, immediately unhinge every part of their conspiracy against the rights of their fellow-men, and bring on themselves infamy and disgrace.

Figure to yourselves, my brethren, a man with a plantation just sufficient to raise a competency for himself and his dear little children; but by reason of the immoderate revenue necessary to support the *emperor*, the illustrious *well born*

Congress, the standing army, &c. &c. he necessarily fails in the payment of his *taxes*; then a hard-hearted federal officer seizes, and sells, his cows, his horses, and even the land itself must be disposed of to answer the demands of government: He pleads unfruitful seasons, his old age, and his numerous, and helpless family. But alas! these avail him nothing, his farm, his cattle, and his all are sold for less than half their value to his wealthy neighbour, already possessed of half the land in the county, to whom also himself and his children must become servants and slaves, or else perish with hunger and want. Do I exaggerate here? No truly. View the misery of the poor under the despotic governments of Europe and Asia, and then deny the truth of my position, if you can. It is a common saying among the poor of Indostan, that to lie is better than to stand, to sleep is better than to wake, but death is best of all; for it delivers them from the cruelty of their nabobs. Even in the freest country in Europe, a lady's lap-dog is more esteemed than the child of a poor man. O God, what a monster is man! that a dog should be nourished and pampered up by him with dainties; whilst a being, possessed of knowledge, reason, judgement, and an immortal soul, bought with no less a price than the blood of our divine Redeemer, should be driven from his door, without admitting him even for a moment to assuage his hunger with the crumbs that might fall from his table.

But the members of the Federal Convention were men who have been all tried in the field of action, say some; they have fought for American liberty: Then the more to their shame be it said; curse on the villain who protects virgin innocence only with a view that he may himself become the ravisher; so that if the assertion were true, it only turns to their disgrace; but as it happens it is not true, or at least only so in part: This was a scheme taken by the despots and their sycophants to biass the public mind in favor of the constitution; for the convention was composed of a variety of characters; ambitious men Jesuites, tories, lawyers, &c. formed the majority, whose similitude to each other, consisted only in their determination to lord it over their fellow citizens; like the rays that converging from every direction meet in a point, their sentiments and deliberations concentered in tyranny alone; they were unanimous in forming a government that should raise the fortunes and respectability of the *well born few*, and oppress the plebians.

"A CONSTITUTION . . . DICTATED BY
HEAVEN ITSELF"

Joseph Barrell to Nathaniel Barrell

Boston, December 20, 1787

When I heard you was chosen delegate to the Convention I was glad, because I esteemed you an honest man, and knew you a Sensible one, and from every conversation I ever had with you upon the subject, (if I am not much mistaken) you were always on the side of a Federal Government, I have therefore, upon all proper Occasions mentioned the delegate from Old York, and vouched for the honor and Justness of his Sentiments on this important subject; judge then my surprize when I am told, that my brother is the most decided *Antifederalest*, in the Eastern Country, and that he had declared in the Town Meeting, he would loose his right hand before he would acceed to the proposed Constitution; yet, notwithstanding this report, I still defend your Character as a Federalest, because I will not suppose you wish that confusion to the Continent wch. seems agreed on all hands will be the consequence of rejecting; and because I think you too independent to aim at popularity upon any score, much less by opposeing a System wch. almost every honest man approves and which will, I hope and beleive render its opposers at least contemptable—

I have never 'till now put my pen to paper on account of the proposed constitution, and I have never yet conceived it necessary for any one to do it, it needs only to be read with an unprejudiced mind to be approved; while on the other hand it has always appeard to me, that the Antifederal Writers, have clearly proved themselves, either wickedly selfish, or opposed to all good government; and I am clear to declare according to my poor abilities, I have never yet seen in print, or heard in Conversation, any weighty Objection that was founded in truth; perhaps you, or I, might wish some things alterd to suit this particular State, or our particular situation;

but shall the man, who is entrusted with this important appointment *for the general good*, be so absorb'd in self, or blinded by local situation, as to endeavour to destroy, or marr, a Fabrick designed for the happiness of Millions,? surely such a Wretch deserves the detestation of every man of honor; and can never be pleaseing to that Being, who governs with an eye to the happiness of all—

If I did not know your opposition to the late Revolution, was owing to Religious Scruples which I hope you have now dismissed, I should suppose your present opposition, sprung from the same cause and (as I can make every allowance for Religious Frensey) that might save me from the mortification I must suffer in ranking my brother amongst those Antifederal Writers, and opposers of this Excellent Constitution, who, as often as they are found out, appear the most contemptable, and wretched Characters, *"Vox Populi,"* if he had any regard to truth, would have appeared under the more suitable signature of *"Vox Diaboli,"* for he is known to be one Abraham Holmes of Rochester, a chief amongst the Insurgents, and who was obliged to quit the State for a Season, on Accot of a State Warrent; this fellow returning upon a general pardon, was sent by that town to disgrace them in General Court; and it need no skill in Physiognomy, to determine on the slightest glance of his detested person, that nothing good could come from him; Agrippa, & John deWit, are no doubt as respectable Characters, but be that as it may; I would ask the *impartial*, have *they* said any thing true and important against the proposed constitution? and if we go to the Southward, and look at the Objections of a Mason; what are they but such as would disgrace a Tyrant? viz. *"because the proposed constitution does not reserve a right in Congress to make retrospective Laws"*! a Cursed power, which the *most abandoned Despot* alone would wish to possess; and none but the most abject Slaves could possibly endure—and another, "that Congress should make no Navagation Laws unless 2/3ds should agree to them," when it is manifest, any Laws of this kind made by Congress, must be in favor of these Northern States, and thereby give the United States, a preferrence to the British, & effectually preventing the intention of their Mistaken Policy, and the Advantage they have

taken of our wretched Government, to render us contemptable in the eyes of those, who once respected the name of
America; this Idea alone I should think would fire your Soul,
to exert every nerve to adopt a Constitution, which if every
circumstance is taken into view, appears to be dictated by
Heaven itself; but if you are really opposed to it, I will suppose it is from Principal, and if so, I think this one consideration alone will induce you to adopt it, vizt. because the
present Confederation cannot be alterd, unless *all the 13 States*
agree and I was going to say *Heaven and Earth may pass away
before that event will take place!* While the Constitution now
proposed may be alterd when ever *Nine* States shall require it,
Is it not therefore better to adopt this Constitution (even if it was
not the best) *which may be alterd rather than to retain the
present Wretched System wch. never can?* —

I shall say no more at present, because I will not beleive
you so lost to every noble sentiment, as to oppose but from
principal, but if such should be the case, altho' I shall be glad
to see you as a brother, yet depend you will meet the most
pointed opposition from all your friends here, as an Antifederalest —

You will find inclosed a Medal wch was struck to commem-
orate, the first American Enterprize to the Pacific Ocean, If
you are Federal you will be pleased, but to the Antifederalists,
the man of Enterprize must be disgusting, nor can he wish
him success, nor upon his principals is success needfull, for
what is property without good government? —

Ezra Stiles: Pluses and Minuses
of the Constitution

Diary Entry, New Haven, Connecticut, December 24, 1787

24. Whether national Prejudices are prejudicial? Sen^rs. Snow fell yesterday about four Inches. Thaw to day.

Hon. Ab^m Baldwin of Augusta in Georgia, spent the Even^g with me. In May, 1785 he was elected President of the Univ^y in Georgia, then æt. 31. Two Academies are already established in that State subject to the Trustees of the University. One at Augusta another at   . The Coll. to be built at Louisville 50 M. West of Augusta on Ogeechee River. In the two Academies about 15 youth are already advanced in Latin & Greek to read Virgil, Horace & Homer & Atkinsons Navigation, & are already fit to be admitted into College. But the Classes are not yet formed in the College, but will soon be, & will be formed very much upon the N. Engld. mode of College Education.

We conversed on the new Constitution formed by the Convention. On w^c I have formed this as my Opinion. 1. That it is not the most pfect Constitution yet 2. That it is a very good one, & that it is advisable to adopt it. However 3. That tho' much of it will be pmanent & lasting, yet much of it will be hereafter altered by future Revisions. And 4. That the best one remains yet to be investigated.

When the Convention was proposed I doubted its Expediency. 1. Because I doubted whether our wisest Men had yet attained Light eno' to see & discern the best, & what ought finally to prevail. 2. Neither did I think the People were ripe for the Reception of the best one if it could be investigated. And yet 3. I did not doubt but Time & future Experience would teach, open & lead us to the best one. And tho' we have got a much better one than I expected, & a very good one, yet my Judg^t still remains as before. I think there is not Power enough yet given to Congress for firm Government. Neither can I see how far it is safe to surrender the powers of the States to the Imperial Body, without 1. prostrat^g the

Sovereignty of the particular States. 2. Without laying the Found[a] of the Presidents growing up into an uncontrollable & absolute Monarch. And yet I think the last as well guarded as possible: and I know not whether it is possible to vest Congress with Laws, Revenues, & Army & Navy, without endangering the Ruin of the interior Powers & Liberties of the States.

"Publius," The Federalist XXVII
[Alexander Hamilton]

New-York Packet, December 25, 1787

To the People of the State of New-York.

It has been urged in different shapes that a constitution of the kind proposed by the Convention, cannot operate without the aid of a military force to execute its laws. This however, like most other things that have been alledged on that side, rests on mere general assertion; unsupported by any precise or intelligible designation of the reasons upon which it is founded. As far as I have been able to divine the latent meaning of the objectors, it seems to originate in a pre-supposition that the people will be disinclined to the exercise of fœderal authority in any matter of an internal nature. Waving any exception that might be taken to the inaccuracy or inexplicitness of the distinction between internal and external, let us enquire what ground there is to pre-suppose that disinclination in the people? Unless we presume, at the same time, that the power of the General Government will be worse administered than those of the State governments, there seems to be no room for the presumption of ill-will, disaffection or opposition in the people. I believe it may be laid down as a general rule, that their confidence in and obedience to a government, will commonly be proportioned to the goodness or badness of its administration. It must be admitted that there are exceptions to this rule; but these exceptions depend so entirely on accidental causes, that they cannot be considered as having any relation to the intrinsic merits or demerits of a constitution. These can only be judged of by general principles and maxims.

Various reasons have been suggested in the course of these papers, to induce a probability that the General Government will be better administered than the particular governments: The principal of which reasons are that the extension of the spheres of election will present a greater option, or latitude of choice to the people, that through the medium of the State Legislatures, which are select bodies of men, and who are to appoint the members of the national Senate,—there is reason to expect that this branch will generally be composed with peculiar care and judgment: That these circumstances promise greater knowledge and more extensive information in the national councils: And that they will be less apt to be tainted by the spirit of faction, and more out of the reach of those occasional ill humors or temporary prejudices and propensities, which in smaller societies frequently contaminate the public councils, beget injustice and oppression of a part of the community, and engender schemes, which though they gratify a momentary inclination or desire, terminate in general distress, dissatisfaction and disgust. Several additional reasons of considerable force, to fortify that probability, will occur when we come to survey with a more critic eye, the interior structure of the edifice, which we are invited to erect. It will be sufficient here to remark, that until satisfactory reasons can be assigned to justify an opinion, that the fœderal government is likely to be administered in such a manner as to render it odious or contemptible to the people, there can be no reasonable foundation for the supposition, that the laws of the Union will meet with any greater obstruction from them, or will stand in need of any other methods to enforce their execution, than the laws of the particular members.

The hope of impunity is a strong incitement to sedition—the dread of punishment—a proportionately strong discouragement to it—will not the government of the Union, which, if possessed of a due degree of power, call to its aid the collective resources of the whole confederacy, be more likely to repress the *former* sentiment, and to inspire the *latter*, than that of a single State, which can only command the resources within itself? A turbulent faction in a State may easily suppose itself able to contend with the friends to the government in that State; but it can hardly be so infatuated as to imagine itself a match for the combined efforts of the Union. If this reflection be just, there is less danger of resistance from irregular combinations of individuals, to the authority of the confederacy, than to that of a single member.

I will in this place hazard an observation which will not be the less just, because to some it may appear new; which is, that the more the operations of the national authority are intermingled in the ordinary exercise of government; the more the citizens are accustomed to meet with it in the common occurrences of their political life; the more it is familiarised to their sight and to their feelings; the further it enters into those objects which touch the most sensible cords, and put in motion the most active springs of the human heart; the greater will be the probability that it will conciliate the respect and attachment of the community. Man is very much a creature of habit. A thing that rarely strikes his senses will generally have but little influence upon his mind. A government continually at a distance and out of sight, can hardly be expected to interest the sensations of the people. The inference is, that the authority of the Union, and the affections of the citizens towards it, will be strengthened rather than weakened by its extension to what are called matters of internal concern; and will have less occasion to recur to force in proportion to the familiarity and comprehensiveness of its agency. The more it circulates through those channels and currents, in which the passions of mankind naturally flow, the less will it require the aid of the violent and perilous expedients of compulsion.

One thing at all events, must be evident, that a government like the one proposed, would bid much fairer to avoid the necessity of using force, than that species of league contended for by most of its opponents; the authority of which should only operate upon the States in their political or collective capacities. It has been shewn, that in such a confederacy, there can be no sanction for the laws but force; that frequent delinquencies in the members, are the natural offspring of the very frame of the government; and that as often as these happen they can only be redressed, if at all, by war and violence.

The plan reported by the Convention, by extending the authority of the fœderal head to the individual citizens of the several States, will enable the government to employ the ordinary magistracy of each in the execution of its laws. It is easy to perceive that this will tend to destroy, in the common apprehension, all distinction between the sources from which they might proceed; and will give the Fœderal Government the same advantage for securing a due obedience to its authority, which is enjoyed by the government of each State; in addition to the influence on public opinion, which will result from the important consideration of its having power to call to its assistance and support the resources of the whole Union. It merits particular attention in this place, that the laws of the confederacy, as to the *enumerated* and *legitimate* objects of its jurisdiction, will become the SUPREME LAW of the land; to the observance of which, all officers legislative, executive and judicial in each State, will be bound by the sanctity of an oath. Thus the Legislatures, Courts and Magistrates of the respective members will be incorporated into the operations of the national government, *as far as its just and constitutional authority extends*; and will be rendered auxiliary to the enforcement of its laws.* Any man, who will pursue by his own reflections the consequences of this situation, will perceive that there is good ground to calculate upon a regular and peaceable execution of the laws of the Union; if its powers are administered with a common share of prudence. If we will arbitrarily suppose the contrary, we may deduce any inferrences we please from the supposition; for it is certainly possible, by an injudicious exercise of the authorities of the best government, that ever was or ever can be instituted, to provoke and precipitate the people into the wildest excesses. But though the adversaries of the proposed constitution should presume that the national rulers would be insensible to the motives of public good, or to the obligations of duty; I would still ask them, how the interests of ambition, or the views of encroachment, can be promoted by such a conduct?

*The sophistry which has been employed to show that this will tend to the distruction of the State Governments will, in its proper place, be fully detected.

Governor Edmund Randolph's Reasons for Not Signing the Constitution

Richmond, Virginia, December 27, 1787

TO THE PRINTER.

SIR, *The inclosed letter contains the reasons of his Excellency Governor Randolph for refusing his signature to the proposed Fœderal Constitution of Government submitted to the several states by the late Convention at Philadelphia. The manner in which we have obtained it, and the authority by which we convey it to the Public, through the channel of your Press, will be explained by the letter herewith sent to you, which, we request may precede his Excellency's letter to the Speaker of the House of Delegates in your publication of them.*

M. SMITH,   JOHN H. BRIGGS.
CHARLES M. THRUSTON.   MANN PAGE, jun.

To his Excellency EDMUND RANDOLPH, Esquire.

SIR,   *December 2, 1787.*

It has been reported in various parts of the state, that the reasons which governed you in your disapprobation of the proposed Fœderal Constitution, no longer exist; and many of the people of this Commonwealth have wished to know what objections could induce you to refuse your signature to a measure so flattering to many principal characters in America, and which is so generally supposed to contain the seeds of prosperity and happiness to the United States.

We are satisfied, sir, that the time is passed, when you might with propriety have been requested to communicate your sentiments to the General Assembly on this subject; but, as you have been pleased to favor us with your observations in private, and we conceive they would not only afford satisfaction to the public, but also be useful by the information and instruction they will convey, we hope, you can have no objection to enable us to make them public through the medium of the Press. We have the honor to be, with respectful esteem, Sir, your most obedient servants,

M. SMITH,   JOHN H. BRIGGS.
CHARLES M. THRUSTON,   MANN PAGE, jun.

To M. Smith, Charles M. Thruston, John H. Briggs, and Mann Page, jun. Esquires.

GENTLEMEN,   *December 10, 1787.*

Your favor of the second instant, requesting permission to publish my letter on the new Constitution, gives me an opportunity of making known my sentiments, which, perhaps I ought not to decline. It has been written ever since its date, and was intended for the General Assembly. But I have hitherto been restrained from sending it to them, by motives of delicacy arising from two questions depending before that body, the one respecting the Constitution, the other myself. At this day too I feel an unwillingness to bring it before the Legislature, lest in the diversity of opinion, I should excite a contest unfavorable to that harmony with which I trust the great subject will be discussed. I therefore submit the publication of the letter to your pleasure.

I beg leave however, to remind you, that I have only mentioned my objections to the Constitution in general terms, thinking it improper, and too voluminous, to explain them at full length. But it is my purpose to go at large into the Constitution when a fit occasion shall present itself.

I am, Gentlemen, with the greatest respect, your most obedient servant,   *EDMUND RANDOLPH*

A LETTER OF HIS EXCELLENCY EDMUND RANDOLPH, ESQUIRE, ON THE FEDERAL CONSTITUTION.

SIR,   RICHMOND, OCTOBER 10, 1787.

The Constitution, which I inclosed to the General Assembly in a late official letter, appears without my signature. This circumstance, although trivial in its own nature, has been rendered rather important to myself at least, by being misunderstood by some, and misrepresented by others—As I disdain to conceal the reasons for with-holding my subscription, I have always been, still am, and ever shall be, ready to proclaim them to the world. To the legislature therefore, by whom I was deputed to the Fœderal Convention, I beg leave now to address them; affecting no indifference to public opinion, but resolved not to court it by an unmanly sacrifice of my own judgment.

As this explanation will involve a summary, but general review of our fœderal situation, you will pardon me, I trust, although I should transgress the usual bounds of a letter.

Before my departure for the Convention, I believed, that the confederation was not so eminently defective, as it had been supposed. But after I had entered into a free communication with those, who were best informed of the condition and interest of each state; after I had compared the intelligence derived from them, with the properties which ought to characterize the government of our union, I became persuaded, that the confederation was destitute of every energy, which a constitution of the United States ought to possess.

For the objects proposed by its institution were, that it should be a shield against foreign hostility, and a firm resort against domestic commotion: that it should cherish trade, and promote the prosperity of the states under its care.

But these are not among the attributes of our present union. Severe experience under the pressure of war—a ruinous weakness, manifested since the return of peace—and the contemplation of those dangers, which darken the future prospect, have condemned the hope of grandeur and of safety under the auspices of the confederation.

In the exigencies of war indeed the history of its effects is short; the final ratification having been delayed until the beginning of the year 1781. But howsoever short, this period is distinguished by melancholy testimonies, of its inability to maintain in harmony the social intercourse of the states, to defend Congress against incroachments on their rights, and to obtain by requisitions supplies to the fœderal treasury or recruits to the fœderal armies. I shall not attempt an enumeration of the particular instances; but leave to your own remembrance and the records of Congress, the support of these assertions.

In the season of peace too not many years have elapsed;

and yet each of them has produced fatal examples of delinquency, and sometimes of pointed opposition to fœderal duties. To the various remonstrances of Congress I appeal for a gloomy, but unexaggerated narrative of the injuries, which our faith, honor and happiness have sustained by the failures of the states.

But these evils are past; and some may be lead by an honest zeal to conclude, that they cannot be repeated. Yes, sir; they will be repeated as long as the confederation exists, and will bring with them other mischiefs, springing from the same source, which cannot be yet foreseen in their full array of terror.

If we examine the constitutions, and laws of the several states, it is immediately discovered, that the law of nations is unprovided with sanctions in many cases, which deeply affect public dignity and public justice. The letter, however of the confederation does not permit Congress to remedy these defects, and such an authority, although evidently deducible from its spirit, cannot, without a violation of the second article, be assumed. Is it not a political phænomenon, that the head of the confederacy should be doomed to be plunged into war, from its wretched impotency to check offences against this law? And sentenced to witness in unavailing anguish the infraction of their engagements to foreign sovereigns?

And yet this is not the only grievous point of weakness. After a war shall be inevitable, the requisitions of Congress for quotas of men or money, will again prove unproductive and fallacious. Two causes will always conspire to this baneful consequence.

1. No government can be stable, which hangs on human inclination alone, unbiassed by the fear of coercion; and 2. from the very connection between states bound to proportionate contributions,—jealousies and suspicions naturally arise, which at least chill the ardor, if they do not excite the murmurs of the whole. I do not forget indeed, that by one sudden impulse our part of the American continent has been thrown into a military posture, and that in the earlier annals of the war, our armies marched to the field on the mere recommendations of Congress. But ought we to argue from a contest, thus signalized by the magnitude of its stake, that as

often as a flame shall be hereafter kindled, the same enthusiasm will fill our legions? or renew them, as they may be thinned by losses?

If not, where shall we find protection? Impressions, like those, which prevent a compliance with requisitions of regular forces, will deprive the American republic of the services of militia. But let us suppose, that they are attainable, and acknowledge, as I always shall, that they are the natural support of a free government. When it is remembered, that in their absence agriculture must languish; that they are not habituated to military exposures and the rigor of military discipline, and that the necessity of holding in readiness successive detachments, carries the expence far beyond that of inlistments—this resource ought to be adopted with caution.

As strongly too am I persuaded, that requisitions for money will not be more cordially received. For besides the distrust, which would prevail with respect to them also; besides the opinion, entertained by each state of its own liberality and unsatisfied demands against the United States, there is another consideration, not less worthy of attention. The first rule for determining each quota was the value of all land granted or surveyed, and of the buildings and improvements thereon. It is no longer doubted, that an equitable, uniform mode of estimating that value, is impracticable; and therefore twelve states have substituted the number of inhabitants under certain limitations, as the standard according to which money is to be furnished. But under the subsisting articles of the union, the assent of the thirteenth state is necessary, and has not yet been given. This does of itself lessen the hope of procuring a revenue for fœderal uses; and the miscarriage of the impost almost rivets our despondency.

Amidst these disappointments, it would afford some consolation, if when rebellion shall threaten any state, an ultimate asylum could be found under the wing of Congress. But it is at least equivocal, whether they can intrude forces into a state, rent asunder by civil discord, even with the purest solicitude for our fœderal welfare, and on the most urgent intreaties of the state itself. Nay the very allowance of this power would be pageantry alone, from the want of money and of men.

To these defects of Congressional power, the history of

man has subjoined others, not less alarming. I earnestly pray, that the recollection of common sufferings, which terminated in common glory, may check the sallies of violence, and perpetuate mutual friendship between the states. But I cannot presume, that we are superior to those unsocial passions, which under like circumstances have infested more ancient nations. I cannot presume, that through all time, in the daily mixture of American citizens with each other, in the conflicts for commercial advantages, in the discontents, which the neighborhood of territory has been seen to engender in other quarters of the globe, and in the efforts of faction and intrigue—thirteen distinct communities under no effective superintending controul (as the United States confessedly now are notwithstanding the bold terms of the confederation) will avoid a hatred to each other deep and deadly.

In the prosecution of this inquiry we shall find the general prosperity to decline under a system thus unnerved. No sooner is the merchant prepared for foreign ports with the treasures, which this new world kindly offers to his acceptance, than it is announced to him, that they are shut against American shipping, or opened under oppressive regulations. He urges Congress to a counter-policy, and is answered only by a condolence on the general misfortune. He is immediately struck with the conviction, that until exclusion shall be opposed to exclusion and restriction to restriction, the American flag will be disgraced. For who can conceive, that thirteen legislatures, viewing commerce under different relations, and fancying themselves, discharged from every obligation to concede the smallest of their commercial advantages for the benefit of the whole, will be wrought into a concert of action in defiance of every prejudice? Nor is this all:—Let the great improvements be recounted, which have inriched and illustrated Europe: Let it be noted, how few those are, which will be absolutely denied to the United States, comprehending within their boundaries the choicest blessings of climate, soil and navigable waters; then let the most sanguine patriot banish, if he can, the mortifying belief, that all these must sleep, until they shall be roused by the vigour of a national government.

I have not exemplified the preceding remarks by minute

details; because they are evidently fortified by truth, and the consciousness of United America. I shall therefore no longer deplore the unfitness of the confederation to secure our peace; but proceed, with a truly unaffected distrust of my own opinions, to examine what order of powers the government of the United States ought to enjoy? how they ought to be defended against incroachment? whether they can be interwoven in the confederation without an alteration of its very essence? or must be lodged in new hands? shewing at the same time the convulsions, which seem to await us from a dissolution of the union or partial confederacies.

To mark the kind and degree of authority, which ought to be confided to the government of the United States is no more than to reverse the description, which I have already given, of the defects of the confederation.

From thence it will follow, that the operations of peace and war will be clogged without regular advances of money, and that these will be slow indeed, if dependent on supplication alone. For what better name do requisitions deserve, which may be evaded or opposed, without the fear of coercion? But although coercion is an indispensable ingredient, it ought not to be directed against a state, as a state; it being impossible to attempt it except by blockading the trade of the delinquent, or carrying war into its bowels. Even if these violent schemes were eligible, in other respects both of them might perhaps be defeated by the scantiness of the public chest; would be tardy in their complete effect, as the expence of the land and naval equipments must be first reimbursed; and might drive the proscribed state into the desperate resolve of inviting foreign alliances. Against each of them lie separate unconquerable objections. A blockade is not equally applicable to all the states, they being differently circumstanced in commerce and in ports; nay an excommunication from the privileges of the union would be vain, because every regulation or prohibition may be easily eluded under the rights of American citizenship, or of foreign nations. But how shall we speak of the intrusion of troops? shall we arm citizens against citizens, and habituate them to shed kindred blood? shall we risque the inflicting of wounds, which will generate a rancour never to be subdued? would there be no room to fear, that an army accustomed to fight, for the establishment of authority, would salute an emperor of their own? Let us not bring these things into jeopardy. Let us rather substitute the same process, by which individuals are compelled to contribute to the government of their own states. Instead of making requisitions to the legislatures, it would appear more proper, that taxes should be imposed by the foederal head, under due modifications and guards: that the collectors should demand from the citizens their respective quotas, and be supported as in the collection of ordinary taxes.

It follows too, that, as the general government will be responsible to foreign nations, it ought to be able to annul any offensive measure, or inforce any public right. Perhaps among the topics on which they may be aggrieved or complain, the commercial intercourse, and the manner, in which contracts are discharged, may constitute the principal articles of clamour.

It follows too, that the general government ought to be the supreme arbiter for adjusting every contention among the states. In all their connections therefore with each other, and particularly in commerce, which will probably create the greatest discord, it ought to hold the reins.

It follows too, that the general government ought to protect each state against domestic as well as external violence.

And lastly it follows, that through the general government alone can we ever assume the rank, to which we are entitled by our resources and situation.

Should the people of America surrender these powers, they can be paramount to the constitutions, and ordinary acts of legislation, only by being delegated by them. I do not pretend to affirm, but I venture to believe, that if the confederation had been solemnly questioned in opposition to our constitution or even to one of our laws, posterior to it, it must have given way. For never did it obtain with us a higher ratification, than a resolution of Assembly in the daily form.

This will be one security against incroachment. But another not less effectual is, to exclude the individual states from any agency in the national government, as far as it may be safe, and their interposition may not be absolutely necessary.

But now, sir, permit me to declare, that in my humble

judgment the powers by which alone the blessings of a general government can be accomplished, cannot be interwoven in the confederation without a change of its very essence; or in other words, that the confederation must be thrown aside. This is almost demonstrable from the inefficacy of requisitions and from the necessity of converting them into acts of authority. My suffrage, as a citizen, is also for additional powers. But to whom shall we commit these acts of authority, these additional powers? To Congress?—When I formerly lamented the defects in the jurisdiction of Congress, I had no view to indicate any other opinion, than that the fœderal head ought not to be so circumscribed. For free as I am at all times to profess my reverence for that body, and the individuals, who compose it, I am yet equally free to make known my aversion to repose such a trust in a tribunal so constituted. My objections are not the visions of theory, but the result of my own observation in America, and of the experience of others abroad. 1. The legislative and executive are concentred in the same persons. This, where real power exists, must eventuate in tyranny. 2. The representation of the states bears no proportion to their importance. This is an unreasonable subjection of the will of the majority to that of the minority. 3. The mode of election and the liability to be recalled may too often render the delegates rather partizans of their own states, than representatives of the union. 4. Cabal and intrigue must consequently gain an ascendancy in a course of years. 5. A single house of legislation will some times be precipitate, perhaps passionate. 6. As long as seven states are required for the smallest, and nine for the greatest votes, may not foreign influence at some future day insinuate itself, so as to interrupt every active exertion? 7. To crown the whole, it is scarcely within the verge of possibility, that so numerous an assembly should acquire that secrecy, dispatch, and vigour, which are the test of excellence in the executive department.

My inference from these facts and principles is, that the new powers must be deposited in a new body, growing out of a consolidation of the union, as far as the circumstances of the states will allow. Perhaps, however, some may meditate its dissolution, and others partial confederacies.

The first is an idea awful indeed and irreconcileable with a very early, and hitherto uniform conviction, that without union we must be undone. For before the voice of war was heard, the pulse of the then colonies was tried and found to beat in unison. The unremitted labour of our enemies was to divide, and the policy of every Congress to bind us together. But in no example was this truth more clearly displayed, than in the prudence, with which independence was unfolded to the sight, and in the forbearance to declare it, until America almost unanimously called for it. After we had thus launched into troubles, never before explored, and in the hour of heavy distress, the remembrance of our social strength not only forbade despair, but drew from Congress the most illustrious repetition of their settled purpose to despise all terms, short of independence.

Behold then, how successful and glorious we have been, while we acted in fraternal concord. But let us discard the illusion, that by this success and this glory the crest of danger has irrecoverably fallen. Our governments are yet too youthful to have acquired stability from habit. Our very quiet depends upon the duration of the union. Among the upright and intelligent, few can read without emotion the future fate of the states, if severed from each other. Then shall we learn the full weight of foreign intrigue—Then shall we hear of partitions of our country. If a prince, inflamed by the lust of conquest, should use one state, as the instrument of enslaving others—if every state is to be wearied by perpetual alarms, and compelled to maintain large military establishments—if all questions are to be decided by an appeal to arms, where a difference of opinion cannot be removed by negotiation—in a word, if all the direful misfortunes, which haunt the peace of rival nations, are to triumph over the land—for what have we contended? Why have we exhausted our wealth? Why have we basely betrayed the heroic martyrs of the federal cause?

But dreadful as the total dissolution of the union is to my mind, I entertain no less horror at the thought of partial confederacies. I have not the least ground for supposing, that an overture of this kind would be listened to by a single state; and the presumption is, that the politics of the greater part of the states flow from the warmest attachment to an union of the whole. If however a lesser confederacy could be obtained, by Virginia, let me conjure my countrymen well to weigh the probable consequences, before they attempt to form it.

On such an event, the strength of the union would be divided into two or perhaps three parts. Has it so increased since the war as to be divisible? — and yet remain sufficient for our happiness?

The utmost limit of any partial confederacy, which Virginia could expect to form, would comprehend only the three southern states, and her nearest northern neighbour. But they, like ourselves, are diminished in their real force, by the mixture of an unhappy species of population.

Again may I ask, whether the opulence of the United States has been augmented since the war? This is answered in the negative by a load of debt, and the declension of trade.

At all times must a southern confederacy support ships of war, and soldiery. As soon would a navy move from the forest, and an army spring from the earth, as such a confederacy, indebted, impoverished in its commerce, and destitute of men, could, for some years at least provide an ample defence for itself.

Let it not be forgotten, that nations, which can inforce their rights, have large claims against the United States, and that the creditor may insist on payment from any one of them. Which of them would probably be the victim? The most productive and the most exposed. When vexed by reprisals or war, the southern states will sue for alliances on this continent or beyond sea. If for the former, the necessity of an union of the whole is decided. If for the latter, America will, I fear, re-act the scenes of confusion and bloodshed, exhibited among most of those nations, which have, too late, repented the folly of relying on auxiliaries.

Two or more confederacies cannot but be competitors for power. The ancient friendship between the citizens of America, being thus cut off, bitterness and hostility will succeed in its place. In order to prepare against surrounding danger, we shall be compelled to vest somewhere or other power approaching near to a military government.

The annals of the world have abounded so much with instances of a divided people, being a prey to foreign influence, that I shall not restrain my apprehensions of it, should our union be torn asunder. The opportunity of insinuating it will be multiplied in proportion to the parts, into which we may be broken.

In short, sir, I am fatigued with summoning up to my imagination the miseries, which will harrass the United States, if torn from each other, and which will not end, until they are superseded by fresh mischiefs under the yoke of a tyrant.

I come therefore to the last and perhaps only refuge in our difficulties, a consolidation of the union, as far as circumstances will permit. To fulfil this desirable object, the constitution was framed by the Fœderal Convention. A quorum of eleven states, and the only member from a twelfth have subscribed it; Mr. MASON of Virginia, Mr. GERRY of Massachusetts and myself having refused to subscribe.

Why I refused, would, I hope, be solved to the satisfaction of those, who know me, by saying that a sense of duty commanded me thus to act. It commanded me, sir, For believe me, that no event of my life ever occupied more of my reflection. To subscribe seemed to offer no inconsiderable gratification; since it would have presented me to the world, as a fellow-labourer with the learned and zealous statesmen of America. But it was far more interesting to my feelings, that I was about to differ from three of my colleagues; one of whom is, to the honor of the country, which he has saved, imbosomed in their affections, and can receive no praise from the highest lustre of language; the other two of whom have been long inrolled among the wisest and best lovers of the commonwealth; and the unshaken and intimate friendship of all of whom I have ever prized, and still do prize, as among the happiest of all my acquisitions. I was no stranger to the reigning partiality for the members, who composed the convention; and had not the smallest doubt, that from this cause, and from the ardor for a reform of government, the first applauses at least would be loud, and profuse. I suspected too, that there was something in the human breast, which for a time would be apt to construe a temperateness in politicks into an enmity to the union. Nay I plainly foresaw, that in the dissensions of parties, a middle line would probably be interpreted into a want of enterprize and decision. But these considerations, how seducing soever, were feeble opponents to the suggestions of my conscience. I was sent to exercise my judgment, and to exercise it was my fixed determination; being instructed by even an imperfect acquaintance with mankind, that self approbation is the only true reward, which a political career can bestow, and that popularity would have been but another name for perfidy, if to secure it, I had given up the freedom of thinking for myself.

It would have been a peculiar pleasure to me, to have ascertained, before I left Virginia, the temper and genius of my fellow-citizens, considered relatively to a government, so substantially differing from the confederation, as that, which is now submitted. But this was for many obvious reasons impossible: and I was thereby deprived of what I thought the necessary guides.

I saw however that the confederation was tottering from its own weakness, and that the sitting of the convention was a signal of its total insufficiency. I was therefore ready to assent to a scheme of government, which was proposed, and which went beyond the limits of the confederation, believing, that without being too extensive it would have preserved our tranquility, until that temper and that genius should be collected.

But when the plan which is now before the General Assembly, was on its passage through the convention, I moved, that the state-conventions should be at liberty to amend, and that a second general Convention should be holden to discuss the amendments, which should be suggested by them. This motion was in some measure justified by the manner, in which the confederation was forwarded originally, by Congress to the state-legislatures, in many of which amendments were proposed, and those amendments were afterwards examined in Congress. Such a motion was doubly expedient here, as the delegation of so much more power was sought for. But it was negatived. I then expressed my unwillingness to sign. My reasons were the following.

1. It is said in the resolutions, which accompany the constitution, that it is to be submitted to a convention of Delegates, chosen in each state by the people thereof, for their assent and ratification. The meaning of these terms is allowed universally to be, that the Convention must either adopt the constitution

in the whole, or reject it in the whole, and is positively forbidden to amend. If therefore I had signed, I should have felt myself bound to be silent as to amendments, and to endeavor to support the constitution without the correction of a letter. With this consequence before my eyes and with a determination to attempt an amendment, I was taught by a regard for consistency not to sign.

2. My opinion always was, and still is, that every citizen of America, let the crisis be what it may, ought to have a full opportunity to propose through his representatives any amendment, which in his apprehension tends to the public welfare—By signing I should have contradicted this sentiment.

3. A constitution ought to have the hearts of the people on its side. But if at a future day it should be burthensome, after having been adopted in the whole, and they should insinuate, that it was in some measure forced upon them, by being confined to the single alternative of taking or rejecting it altogether, under my impressions and with my opinions I should not be able to justify myself had I signed.

4. I was always satisfied, as I have now experienced, that this great subject, would be placed in new lights and attitudes by the criticism of the world, and that no man can assure himself, how a constitution will work for a course of years, until at least he shall have heard the observations of the people at large. I also fear more from inaccuracies in a constitution, than from gross errors in any other composition; because our dearest interests are to be regulated by it, and power, if loosely given, especially where it will be interpreted with great latitude, may bring sorrow in its execution. Had I signed with these ideas, I should have virtually shut my ears against the information, which I ardently desired.

5. I was afraid, that if the Constitution was to be submitted to the people, to be wholly adopted or wholly rejected by them, they would not only reject it, but bid a lasting farewell to the union. This formidable event I wished to avert, by keeping myself free to propose amendments, and thus, if possible, to remove the obstacles to an effectual government. But it will be asked, whether all these arguments were not well weighed in Convention. They were, sir, and with great

candor. Nay, when I called to mind the respectability of those, with whom I was associated, I almost lost confidence in these principles. On other occasions I should chearfully have yielded to a majority; on this the fate of thousands, yet unborn, enjoined me not to yield, until I was convinced—

Again may I be asked, why the mode pointed out in the Constitution for its amendment, may not be a sufficient security against its imperfections, without now arresting it in its progress?—My answers are, 1. that it is better to amend, while we have the Constitution in our power, while the passions of designing men are not yet enlisted and while a bare majority of the states may amend, than to wait for the uncertain assent of three fourths of the states. 2. That a bad feature in government becomes more and more fixed every day. 3. That frequent changes of a Constitution even if practicable ought not to be wished, but avoided as much as possible: and 4. That in the present case it may be questionable, whether, after the particular advantages of its operation shall be discerned, three fourths of the states can be induced to amend.

I confess, that it is no easy task, to devise a scheme which shall be suitable to the views of all. Many expedients have occurred to me, but none of them appear less exceptionable than this: that if our Convention should choose to amend, another federal Convention be recommended: that in that federal Convention the amendments proposed by this or any other state, be discussed; and if incorporated in the constitution or rejected, or if a proper number of the other states should be unwilling to accede to a second Convention, the constitution be again laid before the same state-conventions, which shall again assemble on the summons of the Executives, and it shall be either wholly adopted, or wholly rejected, without a further power of amendment. I count such a delay, as nothing in comparison with so grand an object; especially too as the privilege of amending must terminate after the use of it once.

I should now conclude this letter, which is already too long, were it not incumbent on me from having contended for amendments, to set forth the particulars, which I conceive to require correction. I undertake this with reluctance; because it is remote from my intentions to catch the prejudices or prepossessions of any man. But as I mean only to manifest, that I have not been actuated by caprice, and now to explain every objection at full length would be an immense labour, I shall content myself with enumerating certain heads, in which the constitution is most repugnant to my wishes.

The two first points are the equality of suffrage in the Senate, and the submission of commerce to a mere majority in the legislature, with no other check than the revision of the President. I conjecture that neither of these things can be corrected; and particularly the former; without which we must have risen perhaps in disorder.

But I am sanguine in hoping, that in every other, justly obnoxious clause, Virginia, will be seconded by a majority of the states. I hope, that she will be seconded 1. in causing all ambiguities of expression to be precisely explained: 2. in rendering the President ineligible after a given number of years: 3. in taking from him either the power of nominating to the judiciary offices, or of filling up vacancies which therein may happen during the recess of the senate, by granting commissions which shall expire at the end of their next session: 4. in taking from him the power of pardoning for treason, at least before conviction: 5. in drawing a line between the powers of Congress and individual states; and in defining the former; so as to leave no clashing of jurisdictions nor dangerous disputes: and to prevent the one from being swallowed up by the other, under the cover of general words, and implication: 6. in abridging the power of the Senate to make treaties the supreme laws of the land: 7. in providing a tribunal instead of the Senate for the impeachment of Senators: 8. in incapacitating the Congress to determine their own salaries: and 9. in limiting and defining the judicial power.

The proper remedy must be consigned to the wisdom of the convention: and the final step, which Virginia shall pursue, if her overtures shall be discarded, must also rest with them.

But as I affect neither mystery nor subtilty, in politics, I hesitate not to say, that the most fervent prayer of my soul is the establishment of a firm, energetic government; that the most inveterate curse, which can befal us, is a dissolution of the union; and that the present moment, if suffered to pass away unemployed, can never be recalled. These were my opinions, while I acted as a Delegate; they sway me, while I speak as a private citizen. I shall therefore cling to the union, as the rock of our salvation, and urge Virginia to finish the salutary work, which she has begun. And if after our best efforts for amendments they cannot be obtained, I scruple not to declare, (notwithstanding the advantage, which such a declaration may give to the enemies of my proposal,) that I will, as an individual citizen, accept the constitution; because I would regulate myself by the spirit of America.

You will excuse me, sir, for having been thus tedious. My feelings and duty demanded this exposition: for through no other channel could I rescue my omission to sign from misrepresentation, and in no more effectual way could I exhibit to the General Assembly an unreserved history of my conduct.

I have the honor, Sir, to be, with great respect, your most obedient servant,   EDMUND RANDOLPH.
The Honorable the Speaker
of the House of Delegates.

THE CONSTITUTION OR ANARCHY:
THE NEED TO RATIFY

George Washington to Charles Carter

Virginia Herald (Fredericksburg), December 27, 1787

Extract of a Letter, of a late Date, from the illustrious President of the late Federal Convention, to his Friend in Fredericksburg, Virginia—extracted from Mr. Green's Virginia Herald.

"I thank you for your kind Congratulation on my safe Return from the Convention, and am pleased that the Proceedings of it have met your Approbation.—My *decided* Opinion of the Matter is, that there is *no Alternative* between the *Adoption* of it and *Anarchy*. If one State (however important it may conceive itself to be) or a Minority of them, should suppose that they can dictate a Constitution to the Union (unless they have the Power of applying the *ultima Ratio* to good Effect) they will find themselves deceived. All the Opposition to it that I have yet seen, is, I must confess, addressed more to the Passions than to the Reason; and *clear I am*, if another Federal Convention is attempted, that the Sentiments of the Members will be *more* discordant or *less* accommodating than the last. In fine, that they will agree upon no general Plan. General Government is now *suspended by a Thread*, I might go further, and say it is *really at an End*, and what will be the Consequence of a fruitless Attempt to amend the one which is offered, before it is tried, or of the Delay from the Attempt, does not in my Judgment need the *Gift of Prophesy to predict*.

"I am not a blind Admirer (for I saw the Imperfections) of the Constitution I aided in the Birth of, before it was handed to the Public; but I am fully persuaded it is the *best that can be obtained at this Time*, that it is free from many of the Imperfections with which it is charged, and that *it* or *Disunion* is before us to choose from. If the first is our Election, when the Defects of it are experienced, a constitutional Door is opened for Amendments, and may be adopted in a peaceable Manner, without Tumult or Disorder."

THE DANGERS OF UNLIMITED TAXATION:
"GIVE! GIVE!"

"Brutus" VI

New York Journal, December 27, 1787

It is an important question, whether the general government of the United States should be so framed, as to absorb and swallow up the state governments? or whether, on the contrary, the former ought not to be confined to certain defined national objects, while the latter should retain all the powers which concern the internal police of the states?

I have, in my former papers, offered a variety of arguments to prove, that a simple free government could not be exercised over this whole continent, and that therefore we must either give up our liberties and submit to an arbitrary one, or frame a constitution on the plan of confederation. Further reasons might be urged to prove this point—but it seems unnecessary, because the principal advocates of the new constitution admit of the position. The question therefore between us, this being admitted, is, whether or not this system is so formed as either directly to annihilate the state governments, or that in its operation it will certainly effect it. If this is answered in the affirmative, then the system ought not to be adopted, without such amendments as will avoid this consequence. If on the contrary it can be shewn, that the state governments are secured in their rights to manage the internal police of the respective states, we must confine ourselves in our enquiries to the organization of the government and the guards and provisions it contains to prevent a misuse or abuse of power. To determine this question, it is requisite, that we fully investigate the nature, and the extent of the powers intended to be granted by this constitution to the rulers.

In my last number I called your attention to this subject, and proved, as I think, uncontrovertibly, that the powers given the legislature under the 8th section of the 1st article, had no other limitation than the discretion of the Congress. It was shewn, that even if the most favorable construction was given to this paragraph, that the advocates for the new constitution could wish, it will convey a power to lay and collect taxes, imposts, duties, and excises, according to the discretion of the legislature, and to make all laws which they shall judge proper and necessary to carry this power into execution. This I shewed would totally destroy all the power of the state governments. To confirm this, it is worth while to trace the operation of the government in some particular instances.

The general government is to be vested with authority to levy and collect taxes, duties, and excises; the separate states have also power to impose taxes, duties, and excises, except that they cannot lay duties on exports and imports without the consent of Congress. Here then the two governments have concurrent jurisdiction; both may lay impositions of this kind. But then the general government have supperadded to this power, authority to make all laws which shall be necessary and proper for carrying the foregoing power into execution. Suppose then that both governments should lay taxes, duties, and excises, and it should fall so heavy on the people that they would be unable, or be so burdensome that they would refuse to pay them both—would it not be necessary that the general legislature should suspend the collection of the state tax? It certainly would. For, if the people could not, or would not pay both, they must be discharged from the tax to the state, or the tax to the general government could not be collected.—The conclusion therefore is inevitable, that the respective state governments will not have the power to raise one shilling in any way, but by the permission of the Congress. I presume no one will pretend, that the states can exercise legislative authority, or administer justice among their citizens for any length of time, without being able to raise a sufficiency to pay those who administer their governments.

If this be true, and if the states can raise money only by permission of the general government, it follows that the state governments will be dependent on the will of the general government for their existence.

What will render this power in Congress effectual and sure in its operation is, that the government will have complete judicial and executive authority to carry all their laws into effect, which will be paramount to the judicial and executive authority of the individual states: in vain therefore will be all interference of the legislatures, courts, or magistrates of any of the states on the subject; for they will be subordinate to the general government, and engaged by oath to support it, and will be constitutionally bound to submit to their decisions.

The general legislature will be empowered to lay any tax they chuse, to annex any penalties they please to the breach of their revenue laws; and to appoint as many officers as they may think proper to collect the taxes. They will have authority to farm the revenues and to vest the farmer general, with his subalterns, with plenary powers to collect them, in any way which to them may appear eligible. And the courts of law, which they will be authorized to institute, will have cognizance of every case arising under the revenue laws, the conduct of all the officers employed in collecting them; and the officers of these courts will execute their judgments. There is no way, therefore, of avoiding the destruction of the state governments, whenever the Congress please to do it, unless the people rise up, and, with a strong hand, resist and prevent the execution of constitutional laws. The fear of this, will, it is presumed, restrain the general government, for some time, within proper bounds; but it will not be many years before they will have a revenue, and force, at their command, which will place them above any apprehensions on that score.

How far the power to lay and collect duties and excises, may operate to dissolve the state governments, and oppress the people, it is impossible to say. It would assist us much in forming a just opinion on this head, to consider the various objects to which this kind of taxes extend, in European nations, and the infinity of laws they have passed respecting them. Perhaps, if liesure will permit, this may be essayed in some future paper.

It was observed in my last number, that the power to lay and collect duties and excises, would invest the Congress with authority to impose a duty and excise on every necessary and convenience of life. As the principal object of the government, in laying a duty or excise, will be, to raise money, it is obvious, that they will fix on such articles as are of the most general use and consumption; because, unless great quantities of the article, on which the duty is laid, is used, the revenue cannot be considerable. We may therefore presume, that the articles which will be the object of this species of taxes will be either the real necessaries of life; or if not these, such as from custom and habit are esteemed so. I will single out a few of the productions of our own country, which may, and probably will, be of the number.

Cider is an article that most probably will be one of those on which an excise will be laid, because it is one, which this country produces in great abundance, which is in very general use, is consumed in great quantities, and which may be said too not to be a real necessary of life. An excise on this would raise a large sum of money in the United States. How would the power, to lay and collect an excise on cider, and to pass all laws proper and necessary to carry it into execution, operate in its exercise? It might be necessary, in order to collect the excise on cider, to grant to one man, in each county, an exclusive right of building and keeping cider-mills, and oblige him to give bonds and security for payment of the excise; or, if this was not done, it might be necessary to license the mills, which are to make this liquor, and to take from them security, to account for the excise; or, if otherwise, a great number of officers must be employed, to take account of the cider made, and to collect the duties on it.

Porter, ale, and all kinds of malt-liquors, are articles that would probably be subject also to an excise. It would be necessary, in order to collect such an excise, to regulate the manufactory of these, that the quantity made might be ascertained, or otherwise security could not be had for the payment of the excise. Every brewery must then be licensed, and officers appointed, to take account of its product, and to secure the payment of the duty, or excise, before it is sold. Many other articles might be named, which would be objects of this species of taxation, but I refrain from enumerating them. It will probably be said, by those who advocate this system, that the observations already made on this head, are calculated only to inflame the minds of the people, with the apprehension of dangers merely imaginary. That there is not the least reason to apprehend, the general legislature will exercise their power in this manner. To this I would only say, that these kinds of taxes exist in Great Britain, and are severely felt. The excise on cider and perry, was imposed in that nation a few years ago, and it is in the memory of every one, who read the history of the transaction, what great tumults it occasioned.

This power, exercised without limitation, will introduce itself into every corner of the city, and country—It will wait upon the ladies at their toilett, and will not leave them in any of their domestic concerns; it will accompany them to the ball, the play, and the assembly; it will go with them when they visit, and will, on all occasions, sit beside them in their carriages, nor will it desert them even at church; it will enter the house of every gentleman, watch over his cellar, wait upon his cook in the kitchen, follow the servants into the parlour, preside over the table, and note down all he eats or drinks; it will attend him to his bed-chamber, and watch him while he sleeps; it will take cognizance of the professional man in his office, or his study; it will watch the merchant in the counting-house, or in his store; it will follow the mechanic to his shop, and in his work, and will haunt him in his family, and in his bed; it will be a constant companion of the industrious farmer in all his labour, it will be with him in the house, and in the field, observe the toil of his hands, and the sweat of his brow; it will penetrate into the most obscure cottage; and finally, it will light upon the head of every person in the United States. To all these different classes of people, and in all these circumstances, in which it will attend them, the language in which it will address them, will be GIVE! GIVE!

A power that has such latitude, which reaches every person in the community in every conceivable circumstance, and lays hold of every species of property they possess, and which has no bounds set to it, but the discretion of those who exercise it. I say, such a power must necessarily, from its very nature, swallow up all the power of the state governments.

I shall add but one other observation on this head, which is this—It appears to me a solecism, for two men, or bodies of men, to have unlimited power respecting the same object. It contradicts the scripture maxim, which saith, "no man can serve two masters," the one power or the other must prevail, or else they will destroy each other, and neither of them effect their purpose. It may be compared to two mechanic powers, acting upon the same body in opposite directions, the consequence would be, if the powers were equal, the body would remain in a state of rest, or if the force of the one was superior to that of the other, the stronger would prevail, and overcome the resistance of the weaker.

But it is said, by some of the advocates of this system, "That the idea that Congress can levy taxes at pleasure, is false, and the suggestion wholly unsupported: that the preamble to the constitution is declaratory of the purposes of the union, and the assumption of any power not necessary to establish justice, &c. to provide for the common defence, &c. will be unconstitutional. Besides, in the very clause which gives the power of levying duties and taxes, the purposes to which the money shall be appropriated, are specified, viz. to pay the debts, and provide for the common defence and general welfare."* I would ask those, who reason thus, to define what ideas are included under the terms, to provide for the common defence and general welfare? Are these terms definite, and will they be understood in the same manner, and to apply to the same cases by every one? No one will pretend they will. It will then be matter of opinion, what tends to the general welfare; and the Congress will be the only judges in the matter. To provide for the general welfare, is an abstract proposition, which mankind differ in the explanation of, as much as they do on any political or moral proposition that can be proposed; the most opposite measures may be pursued by different parties, and both may profess, that they have in view the general welfare; and both sides may be honest in their professions, or both may have sinister views. Those who advocate this new constitution declare, they are influenced by a regard to the general welfare; those who oppose it, declare they are moved by the same principles; and I have no doubt but a number on both sides are honest in their professions; and yet nothing is more certain than this, that to adopt this constitution, and not to adopt it, cannot both of them be promotive of the general welfare.

It is as absurd to say, that the power of Congress is limited

*Vide an examination into the leading principles of the federal constitution, printed in Philadelphia, Page 34.

by these general expressions, "to provide for the common safety, and general welfare," as it would be to say, that it would be limited, had the constitution said they should have power to lay taxes, &c. at will and pleasure. Were this authority given, it might be said, that under it the legislature could not do injustice, or pursue any measures, but such as were calculated to promote the public good, and happiness. For every man, rulers as well as others, are bound by the immutable laws of God and reason, always to will what is right. It is certainly right and fit, that the governors of every people should provide for the common defence and general welfare; every government, therefore, in the world, even the greatest despot, is limited in the exercise of his power. But however just this reasoning may be, it would be found, in practice, a most pitiful restriction. The government would always say, their measures were designed and calculated to promote the public good; and there being no judge between them and the people, the rulers themselves must, and would always, judge for themselves.

There are others of the favourers of this system, who admit, that the power of the Congress under it, with respect to revenue, will exist without limitation, and contend, that so it ought to be.

It is said, "The power to raise armies, to build and equip fleets, and to provide for their support, ought to exist without limitation, because it is impossible to foresee, or to define, the extent and variety of national exigencies, or the correspondent extent and variety of the means which may be necessary to satisfy them."

This, it is said, "is one of those truths which, to correct and unprejudiced minds, carries its own evidence along with it. It rests upon axioms as simple as they are universal: the means ought to be proportioned to the end; the person, from whose agency the attainment of any end is expected, ought to possess the means by which it is to be attained."*

This same writer insinuates, that the opponents to the plan promulgated by the convention, manifests a want of candor, in objecting to the extent of the powers proposed to be vested

*Vide the Federalist, No. 23.

in this government; because he asserts, with an air of confidence, that the powers ought to be unlimited as to the object to which they extend; and that this position, if not self-evident, is at least clearly demonstrated by the foregoing mode of reasoning. But with submission to this author's better judgment, I humbly conceive his reasoning will appear, upon examination, more specious than solid. The means, says the gentleman, ought to be proportioned to the end: admit the proposition to be true it is then necessary to enquire, what is the end of the government of the United States, in order to draw any just conclusions from it. Is this end simply to preserve the general government, and to provide for the common defence and general welfare of the union only? certainly not: for beside this, the state governments are to be supported, and provision made for the managing such of their internal concerns as are allotted to them. It is admitted, "that the circumstances of our country are such, as to demand a compound, instead of a simple, a confederate, instead of a sole government," that the objects of each ought to be pointed out, and that each ought to possess ample authority to execute the powers committed to them. The government then, being complex in its nature, the end it has in view is so also; and it is as necessary, that the state governments should possess the means to attain the ends expected from them, as for the general government. Neither the general government, nor the state governments, ought to be vested with all the powers proper to be exercised for promoting the ends of government. The powers are divided between them—certain ends are to be attained by the one, and other certain ends by the other; and these, taken together, include all the ends of good government. This being the case, the conclusion follows, that each should be furnished with the means, to attain the ends, to which they are designed.

To apply this reasoning to the case of revenue; the general government is charged with the care of providing for the payment of the debts of the United States; supporting the general government, and providing for the defence of the union. To obtain these ends, they should be furnished with means. But does it thence follow, that they should command all the revenues of the United States! Most certainly it does not. For if so, it will follow, that no means will be left to attain other ends, as necessary to the happiness of the country, as those committed to their care. The individual states have debts to discharge; their legislatures and executives are to be supported, and provision is to be made for the administration of justice in the respective states. For these objects the general government has no authority to provide; nor is it proper it should. It is clear then, that the states should have the command of such revenues, as to answer the ends they have to obtain. To say, "that the circumstances that endanger the safety of nations are infinite," and from hence to infer, that all the sources of revenue in the states should be yielded to the general government, is not conclusive reasoning: for the Congress are authorized only to controul in general concerns, and not regulate local and internal ones; and these are as essentially requisite to be provided for as those. The peace and happiness of a community is as intimately connected with the prudent direction of their domestic affairs, and the due administration of justice among themselves, as with a competent provision for their defence against foreign invaders, and indeed more so.

Upon the whole, I conceive, that there cannot be a clearer position than this, that the state governments ought to have an uncontroulable power to raise a revenue, adequate to the exigencies of their governments; and, I presume, no such power is left them by this constitution.

"Publius," The Federalist XXX [Alexander Hamilton]

New-York Packet, December 28, 1787

To the People of the State of New-York.
It has been already observed, that the Fœderal Government ought to possess the power of providing for the support of the national forces; in which proposition was intended to be included the expence of raising troops, of building and equiping fleets, and all other expences in any wise connected with military arrangements and operations. But these are not the only objects to which the jurisdiction of the Union, in respect to revenue, must necessarily be empowered to extend—It must embrace a provision for the support of the national civil list—for the payment of the national debts contracted, or that may be contracted—and in general for all those matters which will call for disbursements out of the national treasury. The conclusion is, that there must be interwoven in the frame of the government, a general power of taxation in one shape or another.

Money is with propriety considered as the vital principle of the body politic; as that which sustains its life and motion, and enables it to perform its most essential functions. A complete power therefore to procure a regular and adequate supply of it, as far as the resources of the community will permit, may be regarded as an indispensable ingredient in every constitution. From a deficiency in this particular, one of two evils must ensue; either the people must be subjected to continual plunder as a substitute for a more elegible mode of supplying the public wants, or the government must sink into a fatal atrophy, and in a short course of time perish.

In the Ottoman or Turkish empire, the sovereign, though in other respects absolute master of the lives and fortunes of his subjects, has no right to impose a new tax. The consequence is, that he permits the Bashaws or Governors of provinces to pillage the people without mercy; and in turn squeezes out of them the sums of which he stands in need to satisfy his own exigencies and those of the State. In America, from a like cause, the government of the Union has gradually dwindled into a state of decay, approaching nearly to annihilation. Who can doubt that the happiness of the people in both countries would be promoted by competent authorities in the proper hands, to provide the revenues which the necessities of the public might require?

The present confederation, feeble as it is, intended to repose in the United States, an unlimited power of providing for the pecuniary wants of the Union. But proceeding upon an erroneous principle, it has been done in such a manner as entirely to have frustrated the intention. Congress by the articles which compose that compact (as has been already stated) are authorised to ascertain and call for any sums of money necessary, in their judgment, to the service of the United States; and their requisitions, if conformable to the rule of apportionment, are in every constitutional sense obligatory upon the States. These have no right to question the propriety of the demand—no discretion beyond that of devising the ways and means of furnishing the sums demanded. But though this be strictly and truly the case; though the assumption of such a right be an infringement of the articles of Union; though it may seldom or never have been avowedly claimed; yet in practice it has been constantly exercised; and would continue to be so, as long as the revenues of the confederacy should remain dependant on the intermediate agency of its members. What the consequences of this system have been, is within the knowledge of every man, the least conversant in our public affairs, and has been amply unfolded in different parts of these inquiries. It is this which has chiefly contributed to reduce us to a situation which affords ample cause, both of mortification to ourselves, and of triumph to our enemies.

What remedy can there be for this situation but, in a change of the system, which has produced it? In a change of the fallacious and delusive system of quotas and requisitions? What substitute can there be imagined for this *ignis fatuus* in finance, but that of permitting the national government to raise its own revenues by the ordinary methods of taxation, authorised in every well ordered constitution of civil government? Ingenious men may declaim with plausibility on any subject; but no human ingenuity can point out any other expedient to rescue us from the inconveniencies and embarrassments, naturally resulting from defective supplies of the public treasury.

The more intelligent adversaries of the new constitution admit the force of this reasoning; but they qualify their admission by a distinction between what they call *internal* and *external* taxation. The former they would reserve to the State governments; the latter, which they explain into commercial imposts, or rather duties on imported articles, they declare themselves willing to concede to the Fœderal Head. This distinction, however, would violate that fundamental maxim of good sense and sound policy, which dictates that every POWER ought to be proportionate to its OBJECT; and would still leave the General Government in a kind of tutelage to the State governments, inconsistent with every idea of vigor or efficiency. Who can pretend that commercial imposts are or would be alone equal to the present and future exigencies of the Union? Taking into the account the existing debt, foreign and domestic, upon any plan of extinguishment, which a man moderately impressed with the importance of public justice and public credit could approve, in addition to the establishments, which all parties will acknowledge to be necessary, we could not reasonably flatter ourselves, that this resource alone, upon the most improved scale, would even suffice for its present necessities. Its future necessities admit not of calculation or limitation; and upon the principle, more than once adverted to, the power of making provision for them as they arise, ought to be equally unconfined. I believe it may be regarded as a position, warranted by the history of mankind, that *in the usual progress of things, the necessities of a nation in every stage of its existence will be found at least equal to its resources.*

To say that deficiencies may be provided for by requisitions upon the States, is on the one hand, to acknowledge that this system cannot be depended upon; and on the other hand, to depend upon it for every thing beyond a certain limit. Those who have carefully attended to its vices and deformities as they have been exhibited by experience, or delineated in the course of these papers, must feel an invincible repugnancy to trusting the national interests, in any degree, to its operation. Its inevitable tendency, whenever it is brought into activity, must be to enfeeble the Union and sow the seeds of discord and contention between the Fœderal Head and its members, and between the members themselves. Can it be expected that the deficiencies would be better supplied in this mode, than the total wants of the Union have heretofore been supplied, in the same mode? It ought to be recollected, that if less will be required from the States, they will have proportionably less means to answer the demand. If the opinions of those who contend for the distinction which has been mentioned, were to be received as evidence of truth, one would be led to conclude that there was some known point in the œconomy of national affairs, at which it would be safe to stop, and say, thus far the ends of public happiness will be promoted by supplying the wants of government, and all beyond this is unworthy of our care or anxiety. How is it possible that a government half supplied and always necessitous, can fulfil the purposes of its institution—can provide for the security of—advance the prosperity—or support the reputation of the commonwealth? How can it ever possess either energy or stability, dignity or credit, confidence at home or respectability abroad? How can its administration be any thing else than a succession of expedients temporising, impotent, disgraceful? How will it be able to avoid a frequent sacrifice of its engagements to immediate necessity? How can it undertake or execute any liberal or enlarged plans of public good?

Let us attend to what would be the effects of this situation in the very first war in which we should happen to be engaged. We will presume for argument sake, that the revenue arising from the impost-duties answer the purposes of a provision for the public debt, and of a peace establishment for the Union. Thus circumstanced, a war breaks out. What would be the probable conduct of the government in such an emergency? Taught by experience that proper dependence could not be placed on the success of requisitions; unable by its own authority to lay hold of fresh resources, and urged by considerations of national danger, would it not be driven to the expedient of diverting the funds already appropriated from their proper objects to the defence of the State? It is not easy to see how a step of this kind could be avoided; and if it should be taken, it is evident that it would prove the destruction of public credit at the very moment that it was become essential to the public safety. To imagine that at such a crisis credit might be dispensed with, would be the extreme of infatuation. In the modern system of war, nations the most wealthy are obliged to have recourse to large loans. A country so little opulent as ours, must feel this necessity in a much stronger degree. But who would lend to a government that prefaced its overtures for borrowing, by an act which demonstrated that no reliance could be placed on the steadiness of its measures for paying? The loans it might be able to procure, would be as limited in their extent as burthensome in their conditions. They would be made upon the same principles that usurers commonly lend to bankrupt and fraudulent debtors; with a sparing hand, and at enormous premiums.

It may perhaps be imagined, that from the scantiness of the resources of the country, the necessity of diverting the established funds in the case supposed, would exist; though the national government should possess an unrestrained power of taxation. But two considerations will serve to quiet all apprehension on this head; one is, that we are sure the resources of the community in their full extent, will be brought into activity for the benefit of the Union; the other is, that whatever deficiencies there may be, can without difficulty be supplied by loans.

The power of creating new funds upon new objects of taxation by its own authority, would enable the national government to borrow, as far as its necessities might require. Foreigners as well as the citizens of America, could then reasonably repose confidence in its engagements; but to depend upon a government, that must itself depend upon thirteen other governments for the means of fulfilling its contracts, when once its situation is clearly understood, would require a degree of credulity, not often to be met with in the pecuniary transactions of mankind, and little reconcileable with the usual sharp-sightedness of avarice.

Reflections of this kind, may have trifling weight with men, who hope to see realized in America, the halcyon scenes of the poetic or fabulous age; but to those who believe we are likely to experience a common portion of the vicissitudes and calamities, which have fallen to the lot of other nations, they must appear entitled to serious attention. Such men must behold the actual situation of their country with painful solicitude, and deprecate the evils which ambition or revenge might, with too much facility, inflict upon it.

"Agrippa" [*James Winthrop*] *IX*

Massachusetts Gazette (Boston), December 28, 1787

To the PEOPLE.

We come now to the second and last article of complaint against the present confederation, which is, that Congress has not the sole power to regulate the intercourse between us and foreigners. Such a power extends not only to war and peace, but to trade and naturalization. This last article ought never to be given them; for though most of the states may be willing for certain reasons to receive foreigners as citizens, yet reasons of equal weight may induce other states, differently circumstanced, to keep their blood pure. Pennsylvania has chosen to receive all that would come there. Let any indifferent person judge whether that state in point of morals, education, energy is equal to any of the eastern states; the small state of Rhode-Island only excepted. Pennsylvania in the course of a century has acquired her present extent and population, at the expense of religion and good morals. The eastern states have, by keeping separate from the foreign mixtures, acquired their present greatness in the course of a century and an half, and have preserved their religion and morals. They have also preserved that manly virtue which is equally fitted for rendering them respectable in war, and industrious in peace.

The remaining power for peace and trade might perhaps be safely enough lodged with Congress under some limitations. Three restrictions appear to me to be essentially necessary to preserve the equality of rights to the states, which it is the object of the state governments to secure to each citizen. 1st. It ought not to be in the power of Congress either by treaty or otherwise to alienate part of any state without the consent of the legislature. 2d. They ought not to be able by treaty or other law to give any legal preference to one part above another. 3d. They ought to be restrained from creating any monopolies. Perhaps others may propose different regulations and restrictions. One of these is to be found in the old confederation, and another in the newly proposed plan. The third seems to be equally necessary.

After all that has been said and written on this subject, and on the difficulty of amending our old constitution so as to render it adequate to national purposes, it does not appear that any thing more was necessary to be done, than framing two new articles. By one a limited revenue would be given to Congress with a right to collect it, and by the other a limited right to regulate our intercourse with foreign nations. By such an addition we should have preserved to each state its power to defend the rights of the citizens, and the whole empire would be capable of expanding, and receiving additions without altering its former constitution. Congress, at the same time, by the extent of their jurisdiction, and the number of their officers, would have acquired more respectability at home, and a sufficient influence abroad. If any state was in such a case to invade the rights of the Union, the other states would join in defence of those rights, and it would be in the power of Congress to direct the national force to that object. But it is certain that the powers of Congress over the citizens should be small in proportion as the empire is extended; that, in order to preserve the balance, each state may supply by energy what is wanting in numbers. Congress would be able by such a system as we have proposed to regulate trade with foreigners by such duties as should effectually give the preference to the produce and manufactures of our own country. We should then have a friendly intercourse established between the states, upon the principles of mutual interest. A moderate duty upon foreign vessels would give an advantage to our own people, while it would avoid all the disadvantages arising from a prohibition, and the consequent deficiency of vessels to transport the produce of the southern states.

Our country is at present upon an average a thousand miles long from north to south, and eight hundred broad from the Missisippi to the Ocean. We have at least six millions of white inhabitants, and the annual increase is about two hundred and fifty thousand souls, exclusive of emigrants from

Europe. The greater part of our increase is employed in settling the new lands, while the older settlements are entering
largely into manufactures of various kinds. It is probable, that
the extraordinary exertions of this state in the way of industry
for the present year only, exceed in value five hundred thousand pounds. The new settlements, if all made in the same
tract of country, would form a large state annually; and the
time seems to be literally accomplished when a nation shall be
born in a day. Such an immense country is not only capable
of yielding all the produce of Europe, but actually does produce by far the greater part of the raw materials. The restrictions on our trade in Europe, necessarily oblige us to make
use of those materials, and the high price of labour operates
as an encouragement to mechanical improvements. In this
way we daily make rapid advancements towards independence
in resources as well as in empire. If we adopt the new system
of government we shall by one rash vote lose the fruit of the
toil and expense of thirteen years, at the time when the benefits of that toil and expense are rapidly increasing. Though the
imposts of Congress on foreign trade may tend to encourage
manufactures, the excise and dry tax will destroy all the beneficial effects of the impost, at the same time that they diminish
our capital. Be careful then to give only a limited revenue,
and the limited power of managing foreign concerns. Once
surrender the rights of internal legislation and taxation, and
instead of being respected abroad, foreigners will laugh at us,
and posterity will lament our folly.

Luther Martin, "The Genuine Information" I, II, VIII, IX, XII

Maryland Gazette (Baltimore), December 28, 1787 – February 8, 1788

I

December 28, 1787

Mr. HAYES, It was the wish of many respectable characters both in the House of Assembly, and others, that the information received from the Delegates to the late Convention, should be made public. — I have taken some pains, to collect together, the substance of the information, which was given on that occasion to the House of Delegates by Mr. Martin; by your inserting it in your paper, you will oblige A CUSTOMER.

Mr. MARTIN, when called upon, addressed the House nearly as follows:

Mr. SPEAKER, Since I was notified of the resolve of this Honourable House, that we should attend this day, to give information with regard to the proceedings of the late convention, my time has necessarily been taken up with business, and I have also been obliged to make a journey to the Eastern-Shore: These circumstances have prevented me from being as well prepared as I could wish, to give the information required — However, the few leisure moments I could spare, I have devoted to refreshing my memory, by looking over the papers and notes in my possession; and shall with pleasure, to the best of my abilities, render an account of my conduct.

It was not in my power to attend the convention immediately on my appointment — I took my seat, I believe, about the eighth or ninth of June. I found that Governor Randolph, of Virginia, had laid before the convention certain propositions for their consideration, which have been read to this House by my Honourable colleague, and I believe, he has very faithfully detailed the substance of the speech with which the business of the convention was opened, for though I was not there at the time, I saw notes which had been taken of it.—The members of the convention from the States, came there under different powers.

The greatest number, I believe under powers, nearly the same as those of the delegates of this State—Some came to the convention under the former appointment, authorising the meeting of delegates merely to regulate trade.—Those of Delaware were *expressly instructed to agree to no system which should take away from the States, that equality of suffrage secured by the original articles of confederation*. Before I arrived, a number of rules had been adopted to regulate the proceedings of the convention, by one of which, seven States might proceed to business, and consequently four States, the majority of that number, might eventually have agreed upon a system which was to effect the whole Union. By another, *the doors were to be shut*, and the *whole proceedings were to be kept secret*; and so far did this rule extend, that we were thereby prevented from corresponding with gentlemen in the different States upon the subjects under our discussion—a circumstance, Sir, which I confess, I greatly regretted—I had no idea that all the wisdom, integrity, and virtue of this State, or of the others, were centered in the convention—I wished to have corresponded freely, and confidentially, with eminent political characters in my own, and other States, not implicitly to be dictated to by them, but to give their sentiments due weight and consideration. So *extremely solicitous* were they, that their proceedings should not transpire, that *the members were prohibited even from taking copies of resolutions, on which the convention were deliberating, or extracts of any kind from the journals without formally moving for, and obtaining permission, by a vote of the convention for that purpose.*

You have heard, Sir, the resolutions which were brought forward by the honourable member from Virginia—let me call the attention of this House, to the conduct of Virginia, when our confederation was entered into—That State then proposed, and obstinately contended, *contrary to the sense of, and unsupported by the other States, for an inequality of suffrage* founded on *numbers, or some such scale,* which should give *her,* and certain other States, *influence in the Union over the rest*— pursuant to that spirit which then characterized her, and uniform in her conduct, the very second resolve, is calculated expressly for that purpose *to give her a representation proportioned to her numbers,* as if the *want of that* was the *principle defect* in our original system, and this alteration the great means of remedying the evils we had experienced under our present government.

The object of *Virginia* and *other large States, to increase their power and influence over the others,* did not escape observation—The subject, however, was discussed with great coolness in the committee of the whole House (for the convention had resolved itself into a committee of the whole to deliberate upon the propositions delivered in by the honourable member from Virginia). Hopes were formed, that the farther we proceeded in the examination of the resolutions, the better the House might be satisfied of the impropriety of adopting them, and that they would finally be rejected by a majority of the committee—If on the contrary, a majority should report in their favour, it was considered that it would not preclude the members from bringing forward and submitting any other system to the consideration of the convention; and accordingly, while those resolves were the subject of discussion in the committee of the whole House, a number of the members who disapproved them, were preparing *another system,* such as *they thought more conducive to the happiness and welfare of the States*—The propositions originally submitted to the convention having been debated, and undergone a variety of alterations in the course of our proceedings, the committee of the whole House by a *small majority* agreed to a *report,* which I am happy, Sir, to have in my power to lay before you—It was as follow:

1. *Resolved,* That it is the opinion of this committee, that a *national* government ought to be established, consisting of a supreme, legislative, judiciary and executive.

2. That the legislative ought to consist of *two branches*.

3. That the members of the first branch of the national legislature ought to be elected by the people of the several States, for the term of three years, to receive fixed stipends, by which they may be compensated for the devotion of their time to public service, to be paid out of the national treasury, to be ineligible to any office established by a particular State, or under the authority of the United States, except those particularly belonging to the functions of the first branch, during the term of service, and under the national government, for the space of one year after its expiration.

4. That the members of the second branch of the legislature ought to be chosen by the individual legislatures, to be of the age of thirty years at least, to hold their offices for a term sufficient to ensure their independency, namely, seven years, one third to go out biennially, to receive fixed stipends, by which they may be compensated for the devotion of their time to public service, to be paid out of the national treasury, to be ineligible to any office by a particular State, or under the authority of the United States, except those peculiarly belonging to the functions of the second branch, during the term of service, and under the national government, for the space of one year after its expiration.

5. That each branch ought to possess the right of originating acts.

6. That the national legislature ought to be empowered to enjoy the legislative rights vested in Congress by the confederation, and *moreover, to legislate in all cases to which the separate States are incompetent*, or in which the *harmony of the United States may be interrupted, by the exercise of individual legislation*; to *negative* all laws passed by the *several States*, contravening, in the *opinion* of the *legislature* of the *United States*, the articles of union, or any treaties subsisting under the authority of the Union.

7. That the *right of suffrage* in the *first* branch of the national legislature, *ought not to be according to the rule established in the articles of confederation*, but according to some equitable rate of representation, namely, *in proportion to the whole number of white, and other free citizens and inhabitants of every age, sex and condition, including those bound to servitude for a term of*

years, and three fifths of all other persons, not comprehended in the foregoing description, except Indians not paying taxes in each State.

8. That the *right of suffrage* in the *second branch* of the national legislature, *ought to be according to the rule established in the first.*

9. That a national executive be instituted to consist of a single person, *to be chosen by the national legislature* for the term of seven years, with power to carry into execution the national laws, *to appoint to offices* in cases not otherwise provided for, to be ineligible a second time, and to be removable on impeachment and conviction of malpractice or neglect of duty, to receive a fixed stipend, by which he may be compensated for the devotion of his time to public service—to be paid out of the national treasury.

10. That the national executive shall have a right to *negative any legislative act which shall not afterwards be passed, unless by two third parts of each branch of the national legislature.*

11. That a national judiciary be established, to consist of one supreme tribunal, the judges of which, to be appointed *by the second branch* of the national legislature, to hold their offices during good behaviour, and to receive punctually, at stated times, a fixed compensation for their services, in which no increase or diminution shall be made, so as to affect the persons actually in office at the time of such increase or diminution.

12. That the *national legislature* be empowered to *appoint inferior tribunals.*

13. That the jurisdiction of the *national* judiciary shall extend to cases which respect the collection of the national revenue; cases arising under the laws of the United States—impeachments of any national officer, *and questions which involve the national peace and harmony.*

14. *Resolved,* That provision ought to be made for the admission of States lawfully arising within the limits of the United States whether from a voluntary junction of government, territory, or otherwise, with the consent of a number of voices in the national legislature less than the whole.

15. *Resolved,* That provision ought to be made for the continuance of Congress, and their authority and privileges, until

a given day after the reform of the articles of union shall be adopted, and for the completion of all their engagements.

16. That a republican constitution and its existing laws ought to be guarranteed to each State by the United States.

17. That provision ought to be made for the amendment of the articles of union, whensoever it shall seem necessary.

18. That the legislative, executive and judiciary powers, within the several States, ought to be bound by oath to support the articles of the union.

19. That the amendments which shall be offered to the confederation by this convention, ought, at a proper time or times, after the approbation of Congress, to be submitted to an assembly or assemblies, recommended by the legislatures, to be expressly chosen by the people to consider and decide thereon.

These propositions, Sir, were *acceded to* by a *majority of the members of the committee*—a system by which the *large States were to have not only an inequality of suffrage in the first branch*, but also *the same inequality* in the *second branch*, or senate; however, it was not designed the second branch should consist of the same *number* as the first. It was proposed that the senate should consist of *twenty-eight members*, formed on the following scale—Virginia to send *five*, Pennsylvania and Massachusetts each *four*, South-Carolina, North-Carolina, Maryland, New-York, and Connecticut *two* each, and the States of New-Hampshire, Rhode-Island, Jersey, Delaware, and Georgia each of them *one*; upon this plan, the three large States, Virginia, Pennsylvania, and Massachusetts, would have *thirteen* senators out of *twenty-eight*, almost *one half of the whole number*—Fifteen senators were to be a quorum to proceed to business; those *three States* would, therefore, have *thirteen* out of that quorum. Having this inequality *in each branch* of the legislature, it must be evident, Sir, that *they would make what laws they pleased, however disagreeable or injurious to the other States*, and that *they would always prevent the other States from making any laws, however necessary and proper, if not agreeable to the views of those three States*—They were not only, Sir, by this system, to have such an undue superiority in making laws and regulations for the Union, but to have the same superiority in the *appointment* of the *president*, the *judges*, and all *other officers* of government. Hence, those three States would in reality have the appointment of the president, judges, and all the other officers. This president, and these judges, so appointed, we may be morally certain would be citizens of one of those three States; and the president, as appointed by them, and a citizen of one of them, would espouse their interests and their views, when they came in competition with the views and interests of the other States. This president, so appointed by the three large States, and so unduly under their influence, was to have a negative upon every law that should be passed, which, if negatived by him, was not to take effect, unless assented to by two thirds of each branch of the legislatures, a provision which deprived ten States of even the faintest shadow of liberty; for if they, by a miraculous unanimity, having all their members present, should outvote the other three, and pass a law contrary to their wishes, those three large States need only procure the president to negative it, and thereby prevent a possibility of its ever taking effect, because the representatives of those three States would amount to much more than one third (almost one half) of the representatives in each branch. And, Sir, this government, so organized with all this undue superiority in those three large States, was as you see to have a power of negativing the laws passed by every State legislature in the Union. Whether, therefore, laws passed by the legislature of Maryland, New-York, Connecticut, Georgia, or of any other of the ten States, for the regulation of their internal police, should take effect, and be carried into execution, was to depend on the good pleasure of the representatives of Virginia, Pennsylvania and Massachusetts.

This system of slavery, which bound hand and foot ten States in the Union, and placed them at the mercy of the other three, and under the most abject and servile subjection to them, was approved by a majority of the members of the convention, and reported by the committee.

On this occasion, the House will recollect, that the convention was resolved into a committee of the whole—of this committee Mr. Gorham was chairman—The honorable Mr. Washington was then on the floor, in the same situation with any other member of the convention at large, to oppose any system he thought injurious, or to propose any alterations or amendments he thought beneficial, to these propositions so reported by the committee, no opposition was given by that illustrious personage, or by the president of the State of Pennsylvania. They both appeared cordially to approve them, and to give them their hearty concurrence; yet this system, I am confident, Mr. Speaker, there is not a member in this house would advocate, or who would hesitate one moment in saying it ought to be rejected. I mention this circumstance in compliance with the duty I owe this honorable body, not with a view to lessen those exalted characters, but to shew how far the greatest and best of men may be led to adopt very improper measures, through error in judgment, State influence, or by other causes, and to shew that it is our duty not to suffer our eyes to be so far dazzled by the splendor of names, as to run blindfolded into what may be our destruction.

Mr. Speaker, I revere those illustrious personages as much as any man here. No man has a higher sense of the important services they have rendered this country. No member of the convention went there more disposed to pay a deference to their opinions; but I should little have deserved the trust this State reposed in me, if I could have sacrificed its dearest interests to my complaisance for their sentiments.

(To be continued.)

II

January 1, 1788

Mr. MARTIN's *Information to the House of Assembly, continued.*

When contrary to our hopes it was found, that a majority of the members of the convention had in the committee agreed to the system, I have laid before you, we then thought it necessary to bring forward the propositions, which such of us who disapproved the plan before had prepared— The members who had prepared these resolutions were principally of the Connecticut, New-York, Jersey, Delaware and Maryland delegations.—The honorable Mr. Patterson, of the Jerseys, laid them before the convention—of these propositions* I am in possession of a copy, which I shall beg leave to read to you.

These propositions were referred to a committee of the whole house.—Unfortunately the New-Hampshire delegation had not yet arrived, and the sickness of a relation of the honorable Mr. M'Henry, obliged him still to be absent, a circumstance, Sir, which I considered much to be regretted, as Maryland thereby was represented by only two delegates, and they unhappily differed very widely in their sentiments.

The result of the referrence of these last propositions to a committee, was a speedy and hasty determination to reject them—I doubt not, Sir, to those who consider them with attention, so sudden a rejection will appear surprising; but it may be proper to inform you, that on our meeting in convention, it was soon found there were among us three parties of very different sentiments and views.

One party, whose object and wish it was to abolish and annihilate all State governments, and to bring forward one general government over this extensive continent of a monarchical nature, under certain restrictions and limitations:— Those who openly avowed this sentiment were, it is true, but few, yet it is equally true, Sir, that there was a considerable number who did not openly avow it, who were by myself, and many others of the convention, considered as being in reality favourers of that sentiment, and acting upon those principles, covertly endeavouring to carry into effect what they well knew openly and avowedly could not be accomplished.

The second party was not for the abolition of the State governments, nor for the introduction of a monarchical government under any form; but they wished to establish such a system as would give their own States undue power and influence in the government over the other States.—A third party was what I considered truly federal and republican—This party was nearly equal in number with the other two, and were composed of the delegations from Connecticut, New-York, New-Jersey, Delaware, and in part from Maryland; also

*These will be inserted in some future number, with some remarks on them.

of some individuals from other representations.—This party, Sir, were for proceeding upon terms of *federal equality*; they were for taking our present *federal system* as the basis of their proceedings, and as far as experience had shewn us that there were defects, to remedy those defects, as far as experience had shewn that other powers were necessary to the federal government, to give those powers—They considered this, the object for which they were sent by their State, and what their States expected from them—They urged, that if after doing this, experience should shew that there still were defects in the system (as no doubt there would be) the same good sense that induced this convention to be called, would cause the States when they found it necessary to call another; and if that convention should act with the same moderation, the members of it would proceed to correct such errors and defects as experience should have brought to light—That by proceeding in this train, we should have a prospect at length of obtaining as perfect a system of federal government, as the nature of things would admit. On the other hand, if we, contrary to the purpose for which we were intrusted, considering ourselves as master-builders, too proud to amend our original government, should demolish it entirely, and erect a new system of our own, a short time might shew the new system as defective as the old, perhaps more so—Should a convention be found necessary again, if the members thereof acting upon the same principles, instead of amending and correcting its defects, should demolish that entirely, and bring forward a third system, that also might soon be found no better than either of the former, and thus we might always remain young in government, and always suffering the inconveniences of an incorrect, imperfect system.

But, Sir, the favourers of monarchy, and those who wished the total abolition of State governments, well knowing that a government founded on *truly federal principles*, the basis of which were the *Thirteen State governments, preserved in full force and energy*, would be destructive of their views; and knowing they were too weak in numbers, openly to bring forward their system, conscious also that the people of America would reject it if proposed to them, joined their interest with that party, who wished a system, giving *particular States* the *power* and *influence over the others*, procuring in return mutual sacrifices from them, in giving the government *great* and *undefined powers* as to its *legislative* and *executive*, well knowing that by *departing from a federal system*, they paved the way for their favourite object, the *destruction of the State governments*, and the *introduction of monarchy*—And hence, Mr. Speaker, I apprehend, in a great measure, arose the objections of those honorable members Mr. Mason and Mr. Gerry. In every thing that tended to give the *large States power* over the *smaller*, the *first* of those gentlemen could not forget he belonged to the *ancient dominion*, nor could the *latter* forget that he represented Old Massachusetts; that part of the system which tended to give those States power over the others, met with their *perfect approbation*; but when they viewed it charged with *such powers* as would *destroy all State governments*, their *own* as well as the *rest*—when they saw a president so constituted as to differ from a monarch, scarcely but in name, and having it in his power to become such in reality when he pleased; they being *republicans* and *federalists* as far as an attachment to their own States would permit them, they warmly and zealously opposed those parts of the system. From these different sentiments, and from this combination of interest, *I apprehend*, Sir, proceeded the fate of what was called the Jersey resolutions, and the report made by the committee of the whole house.

The Jersey propositions being thus rejected, the convention took up those reported by the committee, and proceeded to debate them by paragraphs—It was now that they who disapproved the report found it necessary to make a *warm* and *decided opposition*, which took place upon the discussion of the seventh resolution, which related to the *inequality* of representation in the *first* branch.—Those who advocated this inequality, urged, that when the articles of confederation were formed, it was *only* from *necessity* and *expediency* that the States were admitted *each* to have an *equal vote*; but that our situation was *now altered*, and therefore those States who considered it contrary to their interest, would *no longer abide* by it. They said no State ought to wish to have influence in government, except in proportion to what it contributes to it; that if it contributes but little, it ought to have but a small vote; that taxation and representation ought always to go together; that if one State had *sixteen times as many inhabitants* as another, or was *sixteen times as wealthy*, it ought to have *sixteen times as many votes*; that an inhabitant of Pennsylvania ought to have as much weight and consequence as an inhabitant of Jersey or Delaware; that it was contrary to the feelings of the human mind—what the *large States* would *never* submit to; that the *large States* would have *great objects* in view, in which they would never permit the *smaller States* to thwart them; that *equality of suffrage* was the rotten part of the constitution, and that this was a happy time to get clear of it. In fine, that it was the poison which contaminated our whole system, and the source of all the evils we experienced.

This, Sir, is the substance of the arguments, if arguments they can be called, which were used in favour of *inequality of suffrage.*—Those, who advocated the *equality of suffrage*, took the matter up on the original principles of government— They urged that all men considered in a state of nature, before any government formed, are equally free and independent, no one having any right or authority to exercise power over another, and this *without any regard to difference in personal strength, understanding, or wealth*—That when such individuals enter into government, they have *each* a right to an *equal voice* in its first formation, and afterwards have *each* a right to an *equal vote* in every matter which relates to their government—That if it could be done conveniently, they have a right to exercise it in person—Where it cannot be done in person but for convenience, representatives are appointed to act for them, *every person* has a *right* to an *equal vote* in choosing that representative who is entrusted to do for the whole, that which the whole, if they could assemble, might do in person, and in the transacting of which each would have an equal voice—That if we were to admit, because a man was *more wise, more strong,* or *more wealthy,* he should be entitled to *more votes* than another, it would be *inconsistent with the freedom and liberty* of *that other*, and would reduce him to *slavery*—Suppose, for instance, ten individuals in a state of nature, about to enter into government, *nine* of whom are *equally wise, equally strong,* and *equally wealthy,* the *tenth* is *ten times as wise*, ten times as *strong* or ten times as *rich*; if for this reason he is to have *ten votes* for *each vote of either of the others*, the *nine* might as well have *no vote at all*, since though the *whole nine* might assent to a measure, yet the *vote of the tenth* would *countervail*, and *set aside all their votes*—If this *tenth* approved of what *they* wished to adopt, it would be well, but if he disapproved, he could prevent it, and in the same manner he could carry into execution *any measure he wished contrary to the opinion of all the others, he* having *ten votes*, and the *other* all together *but nine*—It is evident, that on these principles, *the nine* would have *no will nor discretion of their own*, but must be *totally dependent* on the *will* and *discretion* of the *tenth*, to *him they* would be as *absolutely slaves* as *any negro* is to his *master.*—If *he* did not attempt to carry into execution any measures injurious to the *other nine*, it could only be said that *they* had a *good master*, they would not be the *less slaves*, because *they* would be *totally dependent* on the *will* of *another*, and not on *their own will*—They might not *feel their chains*, but they would notwithstanding *wear them*, and whenever their *master* pleased he might draw them so tight as to gall them to the bone. Hence it was urged the *inequality of representation*, or giving to one man more votes than another on account of his wealth, &c. was *altogether inconsistent with the principles of liberty*, and in the *same proportion as it should be adopted*, in favour of *one* or *more*, in *that proportion are the others inslaved*—It was urged that though every individual should have an equal voice in the government, yet, even then superiour wealth, strength or understanding, would give great and undue advantages to those who possessed them. That wealth attracts respect and attention; superior strength would cause the weaker and more feeble to be cautious how they offended, and to put up with small injuries rather than to engage in an unequal contest—In like manner superior understanding would give its possessor many opportunities of profiting at the expence of the more ignorant.—Having thus established these principles with respect to the *rights* of *individuals* in a *state of nature*, and what is due to *each* on entering into government, principles established by every writer on liberty, they proceeded to shew that *States*, when *once formed*, are considered *with respect* to *each other as individuals* in a state of nature—That, like individuals, each *State* is considered *equally free* and *equally independent*, the *one* having no right to exercise authority over the *other*, though more *strong*, *more wealthy*, or *abounding with more inhabitants*—That when a number of *States* unite themselves under a *federal government*, the *same principles apply* to *them* as when a *number* of *individual men* unite themselves under a *State government*—That every argument which shews *one man* ought not to have *more votes* than *another*, because he is *wiser, stronger* or *wealthier*, proves that *one State* ought not to have *more votes* than *another*, because it is *stronger, richer, or more populous*—And that by *giving one State*, or *one or two States more votes* than the *others*, the *others* thereby are *enslaved to such State or States*, having the *greater number of votes*, in the *same manner* as in the case before put of *individuals* where *one* has *more votes than the others*—That the reason why each individual man in forming a State government should have an equal vote is, because each individual before he enters into government is *equally free* and *independent*—So *each State*, when *States enter* into a *federal government*, are entitled to an *equal vote*, because before they entered into such federal government, *each State* was *equally free* and *equally independent*—That *adequate* representation of *men formed into a State government*, consists in *each man* having an *equal voice* either personally, or if by representatives, that he should have an equal voice in choosing the representative—So adequate representation of *States* in a *federal government*, consists in *each State* having an *equal voice* either in person or by its representative in every thing which relates to the federal government—That this *adequacy of representation* is *more important* in a *federal*, than in a *State* government, because the members of a State government, the *district* of which is *not very large*, have generally such a *common interest*, that laws can scarcely be made by *one* part *oppressive* to the *others*, without *their suffering in common*; but the *different States* composing an *extensive federal empire*, widely distant, *one* from the *other*, may have *interests so totally distinct*, that the *one* part might be greatly *benefited* by what would be *destructive* to the *other*.

They were not satisfied by resting it on principles; they also appealed to history—They shewed that in the amphyctionic confederation of the Grecian cities, *each city* however *different* in *wealth, strength,* and other *circumstances,* sent the same *number* of deputies, and had *each* an *equal voice* in every thing that related to the common concerns of Greece. It was shewn that in the seven provinces of the United Netherlands, and the confederated Cantons of Switzerland, *each Canton* and *each province* have an *equal vote,* although there are as great distinctions of wealth, strength, population, and extent of territory among those provinces and *those Cantons,* as among *these States.* It was said, that the maxim that taxation and representation ought to go together, was true so far, that no person ought to be *taxed* who is not *represented,* but not in the extent insisted upon, to wit, that the *quantum* of *taxation* and *representation* ought to be the *same*; on the contrary, the *quantum* of *representation* depends upon the quantum of *freedom,* and therefore *all,* whether *individual States,* or individual *men,* who are *equally free,* have a right to *equal representation* — That to those who insist that he who pays the greatest share of taxes, ought to have the greatest number of votes; it is a sufficient answer to say, that *this rule* would be *destructive* of the *liberty* of the *others,* and would render *them slaves* to the *more rich* and *wealthy* — That if one man pays *more taxes* than another, it is because he has *more wealth* to be protected by government, and he receives greater benefits from the government — So if one State pays more to the federal government, it is because as a State, she enjoys greater blessings from it; she has more wealth protected by it, or a greater number of inhabitants, whose rights are secured, and who share its advantages.

(*To be continued.*)

VIII

January 22, 1788

Mr. MARTIN's *Information to the House of Assembly, continued.*

It was urged that by this system, we were giving the general government full and absolute power to regulate commerce, under which general power it would have a right to *restrain,* or *totally prohibit* the *slave trade* — it must appear to the world absurd and disgraceful to the last degree, that we should *except* from the exercise of that power, the *only branch of commerce*, which is *unjustifiable in its nature*, and *contrary* to the *rights* of *mankind*—That on the contrary, we ought *rather to prohibit expressly* in our *constitution*, the *further importation* of *slaves*; and to *authorize* the general government from time to time, to make such regulations as should be thought most advantageous for the *gradual abolition* of *slavery*, and the *emancipation* of the *slaves* which are already in the States.

That *slavery* is *inconsistent* with the *genius* of *republicanism*, and has a tendency to *destroy* those *principles* on which it is *supported*, as it *lessens the sense* of the *equal rights* of *mankind*, and habituates us to *tyranny* and *oppression*.—It was further urged, that by this system of government, every State is to be protected both from *foreign invasion* and from *domestic insurrections*; that from this consideration, it was of the *utmost importance* it should have a power to restrain the importation of slaves, since in *proportion* as the number of slaves were encreased in any State, in the *same* proportion the State is *weakened* and *exposed* to foreign invasion, or domestic insurrection, and *by so much the less* will it be able to protect itself against *either*; and therefore will by so much the more, want aid from, and be a burthen to, the union.—It was further said, that as in this system we were giving the general government a power under the idea of national character, or national interest, to regulate even our *weights* and *measures*, and have prohibited all possibility of *emitting paper money*, and *passing instalment laws, &c.*—It must appear still more extraordinary, that we should prohibit the government from interfering with the slave trade, than which *nothing* could so *materially affect* both our *national honour* and *interest*.—These reasons influenced me both on the committee and in convention, most decidedly to oppose and vote against the clause, as it now makes a part of the system.

You will perceive, Sir, not only that the general government is prohibited from interfering in the slave trade *before* the year eighteen hundred and eight, but that there is no provision in the constitution that it shall *afterwards* be prohibited, nor any security that such prohibition will ever take place—and I think there is great reason to believe that if the importation of slaves is permitted until the year eighteen hundred and eight, it will not be prohibited afterwards—At *this time* we do not generally hold this commerce in so *great* abhorrence as we have done.—When our *own* liberties were at stake, we *warmly* felt for the *common rights of men*—The danger being thought to be past, which threatened ourselves, we are daily growing *more insensible* to those rights—In those States who have restrained or prohibited the importation of slaves, it is only done by legislative acts which may be repealed—When those States find that they must in their *national character* and *connection* suffer in the *disgrace*, and share in the *inconveniences* attendant upon that detestable and iniquitous traffic, they may be desirous also to share in the *benefits* arising from it, and the odium attending it will be greatly effaced by the sanction which is given to it in the general government.

By the next paragraph, the general government is to have a *power* of *suspending* the *habeas corpus act*, in cases of *rebellion* or *invasion*.

As the State governments have a power of suspending the habeas corpus act, in those cases, it was said there could be no good reason for giving such a power to the general government, since whenever the *State* which is invaded or in which an insurrection takes place, finds its safety requires it, *it* will make use of that power—*And* it was urged, that if we gave this power to the general government, it would be an engine of oppression in its hands, since whenever a State should oppose its views, however arbitrary and unconstitutional, and refuse submission to them, the general government may declare it to be *an act of rebellion*, and suspending the habeas corpus act, may *seize* upon the persons of those *advocates of freedom*, who have had *virtue* and *resolution* enough to excite the opposition, and may *imprison* them during its pleasure in the *remotest* part of the union, so that a citizen of Georgia might be *bastiled* in the furthest part of New-Hampshire—or a citizen of New-Hampshire in the furthest extreme to the south, cut off from their family, their friends, and their every connection—These considerations induced me, Sir, to give my negative also to this clause.

In this same section there is a provision that no preference shall be given to the ports of one State over another, and that vessels bound to or from one State shall not be obliged to enter, clear or pay duties in another.—This provision, as well as that which relates to the uniformity of impost duties and excises, was introduced, Sir, by the delegation of this State.—Without such a provision it would have been in the power of the general government to have compelled all ships sailing into, or out of the Chesapeak, to clear and enter at Norfolk or some port in Virginia—a regulation which would be extremely injurious to our commerce, but which would if considered merely as to the interest of the union, perhaps not be thought unreasonable, since it would render the collection of the revenue arising from commerce more certain and less expensive.

But, Sir, as the system is now reported, the general government have a *power* to *establish what ports they please in each State*, and to ascertain at what ports in every State ships shall clear and enter in such State, a power which *may* be so used as to *destroy* the *effect* of that provision, since by it may be established a port in such a place as shall be so *inconvenient* to the State as to render it *more eligible* for their shipping to clear and enter in *another* than in their *own State*; suppose, for instance the general government should determine that all ships which cleared or entered in Maryland, should clear and enter at George-Town, on Potowmack, it would oblige all the ships which sailed from, or was bound to, any other part of Maryland, to clear or enter in some port in *Virginia*. To prevent such a use of the power which the general government now has of *limiting the number of ports* in a State, and *fixing the place* or *places where they shall be*, we endeavoured to obtain a provision that the general government should only, in the first instance, have authority to ascertain the *number* of ports proper to be established in each State, and transmit information thereof to the several States, the legislatures of which, respectively, should have the power to fix the *places* where those ports should be, according to their idea of what would be most *advantageous* to the *commerce* of their State, and most for the *ease* and *convenience* of their *citizens*; and that the general government should not interfere in the establishment of the *places*, unless the legislature of the State should neglect or refuse so to do; but we could not obtain this alteration.

By the tenth section, every State is *prohibited* from *emitting bills of credit*—As it was reported by the committee of detail, the States were *only* prohibited from emitting them *without the consent of Congress*; but the convention was so *smitten* with the *paper money dread*, that they insisted the prohibition should be *absolute*. It was my opinion, Sir, that the States ought not to be *totally deprived of the right to emit bills of credit*, and that as we had *not given* an *authority* to the *general government* for that purpose, it was the *more necessary* to *retain* it in the *States*—I considered that *this State*, and *some others*, have *formerly received great benefit* from paper emissions, and that if public and private credit should once more be restored, such emissions may *hereafter* be *equally advantageous*; and further, that it is impossible to foresee that events may not take place which shall render paper money of *absolute necessity*; and it was my opinion, if this power was not to be exercised by a State without the permission of the general government, it ought to be satisfactory even to those who were the *most haunted* by the apprehensions of paper money; I, therefore, thought it my duty to vote against this part of the system.

The same section also, puts it out of the power of the States, to make any thing but gold and silver coin a tender in payment of debts, or to pass any law impairing the obligation of contracts.

I considered, Sir, that there might be times of such *great public calamities* and *distress*, and of such *extreme scarcity* of *specie* as should render it the *duty* of a government for the *preservation* of even the *most valuable part* of its citizens in some measure to interfere in their favour, by passing laws *totally* or *partially stopping* the courts of justice—or authorising the debtor to pay by *instalments*, or by delivering up his property to his creditors at a *reasonable* and *honest* valuation.—The times have been such as to render regulations of this kind necessary in most, or all of the States, to prevent the *wealthy creditor* and the *monied* man from *totally* destroying the *poor* though even *industrious* debtor—*Such times* may *again* arrive.—I therefore, voted against depriving the States of this power, a power which I am decided they ought to possess, but which I admit ought only to be exercised on very important and urgent occasions.—I apprehend, Sir, the principal cause of complaint among the people at large is, the public and private debt with which they are oppressed, and which, in the present scarcity of cash, threatens them with destruction, unless they can obtain so much indulgence in point of time that by industry and frugality they may extricate themselves.

This *government proposed*, I apprehend so *far from removing* will greatly *encrease* those complaints, since grasping in its all powerful hand the citizens of the respective States, it will by the imposition of the variety of *taxes, imposts, stamps, excises* and *other duties, squeeze* from them the little money they may acquire, the hard earnings of their industry, as you would squeeze the juice from an orange, till not a drop more can be extracted, and then let *loose* upon them, their *private creditors*, to whose *mercy* it *consigns* them, by *whom* their property is to be *seized upon* and *sold* in this *scarcity* of *specie at a sheriffs sale*, where nothing but *ready cash* can be received for a *tenth part* of its *value*, and *themselves* and their *families* to be consigned to *indigence* and *distress*, without *their governments* having a *power* to *give them a moment's indulgence*, however *necessary* it might be, and however *desirous* to grant them aid.

By this same section, every State is also prohibited from laying any imposts, or duties on imports or exports, without the permission of the general government.—It was urged, that as almost all sources of taxation were given to Congress it would be but reasonable to leave the States the power of bringing revenue into their treasuries, by laying a duty on exports if they should think proper, which might be so *light* as not to injure or discourage industry, and yet might be productive of considerable revenue—Also, that there might be cases in which it would be proper, for the purpose of encouraging manufactures, to lay duties to prohibit the exportation of raw materials, and even in addition to the duties laid by Congress on *imports* for the sake of *revenue*, to lay a duty to discourage the importation of particular articles into a State, or to enable the *manufacturer here* to supply us on as *good terms* as they could be obtained from a *foreign market*; however, the most we could obtain was, that this power might be exercised by the States with, and *only* with the consent of Congress, and subject to its controul—And so anxious were they to seize on *every shilling* of our money for the general government, that they insisted *even* the *little revenue* that might thus arise, should not be appropriated to the use of the respective States where it was collected, but should be paid into the treasury of the United States; and accordingly it is so determined.

(*To be continued.*)

IX

January 29, 1788

Mr. MARTIN's *Information to the House of Assembly, continued.*

The *second article*, relates to the executive—his mode of election—his powers—and the length of time he should continue in office.

On these subjects, there was a great diversity of sentiment—Many of the members were desirous that the president should be elected for seven years, and not to be eligible a second time—others proposed that he should not be absolutely ineligible, but that he should not be capable of being chosen a second time, until the expiration of a certain number of years—The supporter of the above propositions, went upon the idea that the best security for liberty was a limited duration and a rotation of office in the chief executive department.

There was a party who attempted to have the president appointed during good behaviour, without any limitation as to time, and not being able to succeed in that attempt, they then endeavoured to have him re-eligible without any restraint.—It was objected that the choice of a president to continue in office during good behaviour, would be at once rendering our system an elective monarchy—and, that if the president was to be re-eligible without any interval of disqualification, it would amount nearly to the same thing, since with the powers that the president is to enjoy, and the interest and influence with which they will be attended, he will be almost absolutely certain of being re-elected from time to time, as long as he lives—As the propositions were reported by the committee of the whole house, the president was to be chosen for seven years, and not to be eligible at any time after—In the same manner the proposition was agreed to in convention, and so was it reported by the committee of detail, although a variety of attempts were made to alter that part of the system by those who were of a contrary opinion, in which they repeatedly failed; but, Sir, by never losing sight of their object, and choosing a proper time for their purpose, they succeeded at length in obtaining the alteration, which was not made until within the last twelve days before the convention adjourned.

As the propositions were agreed to by the committee of the whole house, the president was to be appointed by the national legislature, and as it was reported by the committee of detail, the choice was to be made by ballot in such a manner, that the States should have an equal voice in the appointment of this officer, as they, of right, ought to have; but those who wished as far as possible to establish a *national* instead of a *federal* government, made repeated attempts to have the president chosen by the people at large; on this the sense of the convention was taken, I think not less than three times while I was there, and as often rejected; but within the last fortnight of their session, they obtained the alteration in the manner it now stands, by which the large States have a very undue influence in the appointment of the president.—There is no case where the States will have an equal voice in the appointment of the president, except where two persons shall have each an equal number of votes, and those a majority of the whole number of electors, a case very unlikely to happen, or where no person has a majority of the votes; in these instances the house of representatives are to choose by ballot, each State having an equal voice, but they are confined in the last instance to the five who have the greatest number of votes, which gives the largest States a very unequal chance of having the president chose under their nomination.

As to the vice-president, that great officer of government, who is in case of death, resignation, removal or inability of the president, to supply his place, and be vested with his powers, and who is officially to be the president of the senate, there is no provision by which a majority of the voices of the electors are necessary for his appointment, but after it is decided who is chosen president, that person who has the next greatest number of votes of the electors, is declared to be legally elected to the vice-presidency, so that by this system it is very possible, and not improbable, that he may be appointed by the electors of a *single large State*; and a very undue influence in the senate is given to that State of which the vice-president is a citizen, since in every question where the senate is divided that State will have two votes, the president having on those occasions a casting voice.—Every part of the system which relates to the vice-president, as well as the present mode of electing the president, was introduced and agreed upon after I left Philadelphia.

Objections were made to that part of this article, by which the president is appointed commander in chief of the army and navy of the United States, and of the militia of the several States, and it was wished to be so far restrained, that he should not command in person; but this could not be obtained.—The power given to the president of granting reprieves and pardons, was also thought extremely dangerous, and as such opposed—The president thereby has the power of pardoning those who are guilty of treason, as well as of other offences; it was said that no treason was so likely to take place as that in which the president himself might be engaged—the attempt to assume to himself powers not given by the constitution, and establish himself in regal authority—in which attempt a provision is made for him to secure from punishment the creatures of his ambition, the associates and abettors of his treasonable practices, by granting them pardons should they be defeated in their attempts to subvert the constitution.

To that part of this article also, which gives the president a right to *nominate*, and with the consent of the senate to appoint all the officers, civil and military, of the United States, there were considerable opposition—it was said that the person who *nominates*, will always in reality *appoint*, and that this was giving the president a power and influence which together with the other powers, bestowed upon him, would place him above all restraint and controul. In fine, it was urged, that the president as here constituted, was a king in every thing but the name—that though he was to be chosen but for a limited time, yet at the expiration of that time if he is not re-elected, it will depend entirely upon his own moderation whether he will resign that authority with which he has once been invested—that from his having the appointment of all the variety of officers in every part of the civil department for the union, who will be very numerous—in them and their connexions, relations, friends and dependants, he will have a formidable host devoted to his interest, and ready to support his ambitious views.—That the army and navy, which may be encreased without restraint as to numbers, the officers of which from the highest to the lowest, are all to be appointed by him and dependant on his will and pleasure, and commanded by him in person, will, of course, be subservient to his wishes, and ready to execute his commands; in addition to which, the militia also are entirely subjected to his orders—That these circumstances, combined together, will enable him, when he pleases, to become a king in *name*, as well as in substance, and establish himself in office not only for his own life, but even if he chooses, to have that authority perpetuated to his family.

It was further observed, that the only appearance of responsibility in the president, which the system holds up to our view, is the provision for impeachment; but that when we reflect that he cannot be impeached but by the house of delegates, and that the members of this house are rendered dependant upon, and unduly under the influence of the president, by being appointable to offices of which he has the sole nomination, so that without his favour and approbation, they cannot obtain them, there is little reason to believe that a majority will ever concur in impeaching the president, let his conduct be ever so reprehensible, especially too, as the final event of that impeachment will depend upon a different body, and the members of the house of delegates will be certain, should the decision be ultimately in favour of the president, to become thereby the objects of his displeasure, and to bar to themselves every avenue to the emoluments of government.

Should he, contrary to probability, be impeached, he is afterwards to be tried and adjudged by the senate, and without the concurrence of two-thirds of the members who shall be present, he cannot be convicted—This senate being constituted a privy council to the president, it is probable many of its leading and influential members may have advised or concurred in the very measures for which he may be impeached;

THE GENUINE INFORMATION XII

the members of the senate also are by the system, placed as unduly under the influence of, and dependent upon the president, as the members of the other branch, since they also are appointable to offices, and cannot obtain them but through the favour of the president—There will be great, important and valuable offices under this government, should it take place, more than sufficient to enable him to hold out the expectation of one of them to *each* of the senators— Under these circumstances, will any person conceive it to be difficult for the president always to secure to himself more than one-third of that body? Or, can it reasonably be believed, that a criminal will be convicted who is constitutionally empowered to bribe his judges, at the head of whom is to preside on those occasions the chief justice, which officer in his original appointment, must be *nominated* by the president, and will therefore, probably, be appointed not so much for his eminence in legal knowledge and for his integrity, as from favouritism and influence, since the president knowing that in case of impeachment the chief justice is to preside at his trial, will naturally wish to fill that office with a person of whose voice and influence he shall consider himself secure.—These are reasons to induce a belief that there will be but little probability of the president ever being either impeached or convicted; but it was also urged, that vested with the powers which the system gives him and with the influence attendant upon those powers, to him it would be but of little consequence whether he was impeached or convicted, since he will be able to set both at defiance.—These considerations occasioned a part of the convention to give a negative to this part of the system establishing the executive as it is now offered for our acceptance.

(To be continued.)

XII

February 8, 1788
Mr. MARTIN's *Information to the House of Assembly, concluded.*
 The part of the system, which provides that *no religious test* shall ever be required as a qualification to any office or public trust under the United States, was adopted by a very great

majority of the convention, and without much debate,—
however, there were some members *so unfashionable* as to
think that a *belief of the existence of a Deity*, and of a *state of
future rewards and punishments* would be some security for
the good conduct of our rulers, and that in a Christian country it would be at *least decent* to hold out some distinction
between the professors of Christianity and downright infi-
delity or paganism.

The seventh article declares, that the ratification of *nine
States* shall be sufficient for the establishment of this constitution between the States ratifying the same.

It was attempted to obtain a resolve that if seven States,
whose votes in the first branch should amount to a majority
of the representation in that branch, concured in the adoption
of the system, it should be sufficient, and this attempt was
supported on the principle, that a majority ought to govern
the minority;—but to this it was objected that although it
was true, after a constitution and form of government is
agreed on, in every act done under and consistent with that
constitution and form of government, the act of the majority,
unless otherwise agreed in the constitution, should bind
the minority, yet it was directly the *reverse* in *originally forming*
a constitution, or *dissolving it*—That in originally forming a
constitution, it was necessary that *every individual* should
agree to it to become bound thereby—and that when *once
adopted* it could not be *dissolved* by consent, unless with the
consent of *every individual* who was *party* to the original
agreement—That in forming our original federal government
every member of that government, that is each State, expressly
consented to it;—that it is a *part* of the *compact* made and
entered into in the *most solemn* manner, that there should be
no *dissolution* or *alteration* of that federal government without
the consent of *every State*, the members of, and parties to the
original compact; that therefore *no alteration* could be made
by the consent of a *part* of the States, or by the consent of
the *inhabitants* of a *part of the States*, which could either *release*
the States so consenting from the obligation they are under to
the other States, or which could in any manner become *obligatory* upon those States that should not ratify such alterations.—Satisfied of the *truth* of these positions, and not

holding ourselves at liberty to *violate* the *compact*, which this State had *solemnly entered into* with the others, by *altering* it in a *different* manner from that which by the same compact is provided and stipulated, a number of the members and among those the *delegation* of *this State* opposed the ratification of this system in *any other manner* than by the *unanimous consent* and agreement of *all the States*.

By our original articles of confederation any alterations proposed are in the first place to be *approved* by Congress.— Accordingly as the resolutions were originally adopted by the convention, and as they were reported by the committee of detail, it was proposed that this system should be laid before Congress *for their approbation*;—but, Sir, the warm advocates of this system fearing it would not meet with the approbation of Congress, and determined, even though Congress and the respective State legislatures should disapprove the same, to force it upon them, if possible, through the intervention of the people at large moved to strike the words "for their approbation" and succeeded in their motion; to which, it being directly in violation of the mode prescribed by the articles of confederation for the alteration of our federal government, a part of the convention, and myself in the number, thought it a duty to give a decided negative.

Agreeable to the articles of confederation entered into in the most *solemn* manner, and for the *observance* of which the States *pledged* themselves to each other, and called upon the *Supreme Being* as a *witness* and *avenger* between them, *no alterations* are to be made in those articles unless after they are approved by Congress, they are agreed to and ratified by the *legislature* of *every* State; but by the resolve of the convention this constitution is not to be ratified by the legislatures of the respective States, but is to be submitted to conventions chosen by the people, and if ratified by them is to be binding.

This resolve was opposed among others by the delegation of Maryland;—your delegates were of opinion that as the form of government proposed was, if adopted, most essentially to *alter* the *constitution* of *this State*, and as our constitution had pointed out a mode by which, and by which *only*, alterations were to be made therein, a convention of the people could not be called to agree to and ratify the said form of government without a *direct violation* of our constitution, which it is the duty of every individual in this State to protect and support;—in this opinion all your delegates who were attending were unanimous—I, Sir, opposed it also upon a more extensive ground—as being directly *contrary* to the mode of altering our federal government *established* in our original compact, and as such being a *direct violation* of the mutual faith plighted by the States to each other, I gave it my negative.

I also was of opinion that the States considered as States, in their political capacity, are the members of a federal government—That the States in their political capacity, or as sovereignties, are entitled, and *only entitled* originally to agree upon the form of, and submit themselves to, a federal government, and afterwards by mutual consent to dissolve or to alter it—That every thing which relates to the formation, the dissolution or the alteration of a *federal* government over States equally free, sovereign and independent is the *peculiar* province of the *States* in their *sovereign* or *political* capacity, in the same manner as what relates to forming alliances or treaties of peace, amity or commerce, and that the people at large in their individual capacity, have no more right to interfere in the one case than in the other—That according to these principles we originally acted in forming our confederation; it was the States as States, by their representatives in Congress, that formed the articles of confederation;—it was the States as States, by their legislatures, ratified those articles, and it was there established and provided that the States as States, that as by their legislatures, should agree to any alterations that should hereafter be proposed in the federal government, before they should be binding—and any alterations agreed to in any other manner cannot release the States from the obligation they are under to each other by virtue of the original articles of confederation.—The people of the different States never made any objection to the manner the articles of confederation were formed or ratified, or to the mode by which alterations were to be made in that government—with the rights of their respective States they wished not to interfere—Nor do I believe the people in their individual capacity would ever have expected or desired to have been appealed to on the present occasion, in violation of the rights of their respective States, if the favourers of the proposed constitution, imagining they had a better chance of forcing it to be adopted by a *hasty* appeal to the people at large, who could not be so good judges of the dangerous consequences, had not insisted upon this mode—Nor do these positions in the least interfere with the principle, that all power originates from the people, because when once the people have *exercised their power* in *establishing* and *forming* themselves into a *State government*, it never *devolves back* to them, nor have they a *right* to *resume* or *again to exercise that power* until such events take place as will amount to a *dissolution* of their *State government*:—And it is an established principle that a dissolution or alteration of a *federal* government doth not dissolve the *State* governments which compose it.—It was also my opinion that upon *principles of sound policy*, the agreement or disagreement to the proposed system ought to have been by the State legislatures, in which case, let the event have been what it would, there would have been but little prospect of the *public peace* being *disturbed* thereby—Whereas the attempt to force down this system, although Congress and the respective State legislatures should disapprove, by appealing to the people, and to procure its establishment in a manner totally unconstitutional, has a tendency to set the *State governments* and their *subjects* at *variance* with each other—to *lessen* the *obligations* of *government*—to *weaken* the *bands of society*—to introduce *anarchy* and *confusion*—and to *light* the *torch of discord and civil war* throughout this continent.—All these considerations weighed with me most forcibly against giving my assent to the mode by which it is resolved this system is to be ratified, and were urged by me in opposition to the measure.

I have now, Sir, in discharge of the duty I owe to this house, given such information as hath occured to me, which I consider most material for them to know; and you will easily perceive from this detail that a great portion of that time, which ought to have been devoted calmly and impartially to consider what alterations in our federal government would be most likely to procure and preserve the happiness of the union, was employed in a *violent struggle* on the one side to obtain *all power* and *dominion* in their own hands, and on the other to prevent it—and that the *aggrandizement* of particular States and particular individuals appears to have been much more the object sought after than the welfare of our country.

The interest of this State, not confined merely to itself, abstracted from all others, but considered relatively; and as far as was consistent with the common interest of the other States, I thought it my duty to pursue according to the best opinion I could form of it.

When I took my seat in the convention, I found them attempting to bring forward a system, which I was sure never had entered into the contemplation of those I had the honour to represent, and which upon the fullest consideration, I considered not only injurious to the interest and the rights of this State, but also incompatible with the political happiness and freedom of the States in general; from that time until my business compelled me to leave the convention, I gave it every possible opposition in every stage of its progression.—I opposed the system there with the same explicit frankness with which I have here given you a history of our proceedings, and an account of my own conduct, which in a particular manner I consider you as having a right to know—While there, I endeavoured to act as became a free man, and the delegate of a free State. Should my conduct obtain the approbation of those who appointed me, I will not deny it would afford me satisfaction; but to me that approbation was at most no more than a *secondary* consideration—my *first* was to *deserve* it;—left to myself to act according to the best of my discretion, my conduct should have been the same, had I been even sure your censure would have been my only reward, since I hold it sacredly my duty to dash the cup of poison, if possible, from the hand of a State or an individual, however anxious the one or the other might be to swallow it.

Indulge me, Sir, in a single observation further. There are persons who endeavour to hold up the idea that this system is only opposed by the officers of government—I, Sir, am in that predicament.—I have the honor to hold an appointment in this State. Had it been considered any objection, I presume I should not have been appointed to the convention—If it could have any effect on my mind, it would only be that of warming my heart with gratitude, and rendering me more anxious to promote the true interest of that State which has conferred upon me the obligation, and to heighten my guilt had I joined in sacrificing its essential rights—But, Sir, it would be well to remember, that this system is not calculated to *diminish* the *number* or the *value* of *offices*--on the contrary, if adopted, it will be productive of an enormous increase in their number—many of them will be also of great honour and emolument. Whether, Sir, in this variety of appointments and in the scramble for them, I might not have as good a prospect to advantage myself as many others is not for me to say—but this, Sir, I can say with truth, that so far was I from being influenced in my conduct by interest, or the consideration of office, that I would cheerfully resign the appointment I now hold—I would bind myself never to accept another either under the general government or that of my own State—I would do more, Sir, so destructive do I consider the present system to the happiness of my country, I would cheerfully sacrifice that share of property with which Heaven has blessed a life of industry,—I would reduce myself to indigence and poverty; and those who are dearer to me than my own existence I would entrust to the care and protection of that Providence who hath so kindly protected myself, if on *those terms only* I could procure my country to reject those chains which are forged for it.

"*The New Roof*" [*Francis Hopkinson*]

Pennsylvania Packet (Philadelphia), December 29, 1787

The roof of a certain mansion house was observed to be in a very bad condition, and insufficient for the purpose of protection from the inclemencies of the weather. This was matter of surprize and speculation, as it was well known the roof was not more than 12 years old, and therefore, its defects could not be ascribed to a natural decay by time. Altho' there were many different opinions as to the cause of this deficiency, yet all agreed that the family could not sleep in comfort or safety under it. It was at last determined to appoint some skilful architects to survey and examine the defective roof, to make report of its condition, and to point out such alterations and repairs as might be found necessary. These skilful architects, accordingly went into a thorough examination of the faulty roof, and found

1st. That the whole frame was too weak.

2d. That there were indeed 13 rafters, but that these rafters were not connected by any braces or ties, so as to form a union of strength.

3d. That some of these rafters were thick and heavy, and others very slight, and as the whole had been put together whilst the timber was yet green, some had warped outwards, and of course sustained an undue weight, whilst others warping inwards, had shrunk from bearing any weight at all.

4th. That the lathing and shingling had not been secured with iron nails, but only wooden pegs, which, shrinking and swelling by successions of wet and dry weather, had left the shingles so loose, that many of them had been blown away by the winds, and that before long, the whole would probably, in like manner, be blown away.

5th. That the cornice was so ill proportioned, and so badly put up, as to be neither of use, nor an ornament. And

6th. That the roof was so flat as to admit the most idle

servants in the family, their playmates and acquaintance to trample on and abuse it.

Having made these observations, these judicious architects gave it as their opinion, that it would be altogether vain and fruitless to attempt any alterations or amendments in a roof so defective in all points; and therefore proposed to have it entirely removed, and that a new roof of a better construction should be erected over the mansion house. And they also prepared and offered a drawing or plan of a new roof, such as they thought most excellent for security, duration, and ornament. In forming this plan they consulted the most celebrated authors in ancient and modern architecture, and brought into their plan the most approved parts, according to their judgments, selected from the models before them; and finally endeavoured to proportion the whole to the size of the building, and strength of the walls.

This proposal of a new roof, it may well be supposed, became the principal subject of conversation in the family, and the opinions upon it were various according to the judgment, interest, or ignorance of the disputants.

On a certain day, the servants of the family had assembled in the great hall to discuss this important point; amongst these was James the architect, who had been one of the surveyors of the old roof, and had a principal hand in forming the plan of a new one. A great number of the tenants had also gathered out of doors and crowded the windows and avenues to the hall, which were left open that they might hear the arguments for and against the new roof.

Now there was an old woman, known by the name of Margery, who had got a comfortable apartment in the mansion house. This woman was of an intriguing spirit, of a restless and inveterate temper, fond of tattle, and a great mischief maker. In this situation, and with these talents, she unavoidably acquired an influence in the family, by the exercise of which, according to her natural propensity, she had long kept the house in confusion, and sown discord and discontent amongst the servants. Margery, was, for many reasons, an irreconcileable enemy to the new roof, and to the architects who had planned it; amongst these, two reasons were very obvious—1st, The mantle piece on which her cups and platters were placed, was made of a portion of the great cornice, and she boiled her pot with the shingles that blew off from the defective roof: And 2dly, It so happened that in the construction of the new roof, her apartment would be considerably lessened. No sooner, therefore, did she hear of the plan proposed by the architects, but she put on her old red cloak, and was day and night trudging amongst the tenants and servants, and crying out against the new roof and the framers of it. Amongst these she had selected William, Jack, and Robert, three of the tenants, and instigated them to oppose the plan in agitation—she caused them to be sent to the great hall on the day of debate, and furnished them with innumerable alarms and fears, cunning arguments, and specious objections.

Now the principal arguments and objections with which Margery had instructed William, Jack, and Robert, were,

1st. That the architects had not exhibited a bill of scantling for the new roof, as they ought to have done; and therefore the carpenters, under pretence of providing timber for it, might lay waste whole forests, to the ruin of the farm.

2nd. That no provision was made in the plan for a trap door for the servants to pass through with water, if the chimney should take fire; and that, in case of such an accident, it might hereafter be deemed penal to break a hole in the roof for access to save the whole building from destruction.

3d. That this roof was to be guarded by battlements, which, in stormy seasons would prove dangerous to the family, as the bricks might be blown down and fall on their heads.

4th. It was observed that the old roof was ornamented with 12 pedestals ranged along the ridge, which were objects of universal admiration; whereas, according to the new plan, these pedestals were only to be placed along the eves of the roof, over the walls; and that a cupola was to supply their place on the ridge or summit of the new roof.—As to the cupola itself, some of the objecters said it was too heavy and would become a dangerous burthen to the building, whilst others alledged that it was too light and would certainly be blown away by the wind.

5th. It was insisted that the 13 rafters being so strongly braced together, the individual and separate strength of each rafter would be lost in the compounded and united strength of the whole; and so the roof might be considered as one solid mass of timber, and not as composed of distinct rafters, like the old roof.

6th. That according to the proposed plan, the several parts of the roof were so framed as to mutually strengthen and support each other, and therefore, there was great reason to fear that the whole might stand independent of the walls; and that in time the walls might crumble away, and the roof remain suspended in air, threatening destruction to all that should come under it.

To these objections, James the architect, in substance, replied,

1st. As to the want of a bill of scantling, he observed, that if the timber for this roof was to be purchased from a stranger, it would have been quite necessary to have such a bill, lest the stranger should charge in account more than he was entitled to; but as the timber was to be cut from our own lands, a bill of scantling was both useless and improper—of no use, because the wood always was and always would be the property of the family, whether growing in the forest, or fabricated into a roof for the mansion house—and improper, because the carpenters would be bound by the bill of scantling, which, if it should not be perfectly accurate, a circumstance hardly to be expected, either the roof would be defective for want of sufficient materials, or the carpenters must cut from the forest without authority, which is penal by the laws of the house.

To the second objection he said, that a trap door was not properly a part in the frame of a roof; but there could be no doubt but that the carpenters would take care to have such a door through the shingling, for the family to carry water through, dirty or clean, to extinguish fire either in the chimney or on the roof; and that this was the only proper way of making such a door.

3d. As to the battlements, he insisted that they were absolutely necessary for the protection of the whole house.—1st. In case of an attack by robbers, the family would defend themselves behind these battlements, and annoy and disperse the enemy.—2dly. If any of the adjoining buildings should take fire, the battlements would screen the roof from the destructive flames: and 3dly. They would retain the rafters in their respective places in case any of them should from rottenness or warping be in danger of falling from the general union, and injuring other parts of the roof; observing that the battlements should always be ready for these purposes, as there would be neither time or opportunity for building them after an assault was actually made, or a conflagration begun. As to the bricks being blown down, he said the whole was in the power of the family to repair or remove any loose or dangerous parts, and there could be no doubt but that their vigilance would at all times be sufficient to prevent accidents of this kind.

4th. With respect to the 12 pedestals he acknowledged their use and elegance; but observed that these, like all other things, were only so in their proper places, and under circumstances suited to their nature and design, and insisted that the ridge of a roof was not the place for pedestals, which, should rest on the solid wall, being made of the same materials and ought in propriety to be considered as so many projections or continuations of the wall itself, and not as component parts of the wooden roof. As to the cupola, he said that all agreed there should be one of some kind or other, as well for a proper finish to the building, as for the purposes of indicating the winds and containing a bell to sound an alarm in cases of necessity. The objections to the present cupola, he said, were too contradictory to merit a reply.

To the 5th objection he answered, That the intention really was to make a firm and substantial roof by uniting the strength of the 13 rafters; and that this was so far from annihilating the several rafters and rendering them of no use individually, that it was manifest from a bare inspection of the plan, that the strength of each contributed to the strength of the whole, and that the existence of each and all were essentially necessary to the existence of the whole fabric as a roof.

Lastly. He said, that the roof was indeed so framed that the parts should mutually support and check each other, but it was most absurd and contrary to the known laws of nature, to infer from thence that the whole frame should stand self supported in air, for however its component parts might be combined with respect to each other, the whole must necessarily rest upon and be supported by the walls. That the walls might indeed stand for a few years in a ruinous and uninhabitable condition without any roof, but the roof could not for a moment stand without the support of the walls; and finally, that of all dangers and apprehensions this of the roof's remaining when the walls are gone was the most absurd and impossible.

It was mentioned before, that, whilst this debate was carrying on in the great hall, the windows and doors were crowded with attendants. Amongst these was a half crazy fellow who was suffered to go at large because he was a harmless lunatic. Margery, however, thought he might be a serviceable engine in promoting opposition to the new roof. As people of deranged understandings are easily irritated, she exasperated this poor fellow against the architects, and fill'd him with the most terrible apprehensions from the new roof; making him believe that the architects had provided a dark hole in the garret, where he was to be chained for life. Having by these suggestions filled him with rage and terror, she let him loose among the crowd, where he roar'd and bawl'd to the annoyance of all bye-standers. This circumstance would not have been mentioned but for the opportunity of exhibiting the stile and manner in which a deranged and irritated mind will express itself—one of his rhapsodies shall conclude this narrative.—

"The new Roof! the new Roof! Oh! the new Roof!— Shall demagogues, despising every sense of order and decency, frame a new roof?—If such bare-faced presumption, arrogance and tyrannical proceeding will not rouse you, the goad and the whip—the goad and the whip should do it— but you are careless and insecure sinners, whom neither admonitions, entreaties and threatnings can reclaim—sinners consigned to unutterable and endless woe—Where is that pusillanimous wretch who can submit to such contumely—oh the *ultima Ratio Regium*: (He got these three Latin words from Margery.) oh *the ultima Ratio Regium*—oh! the days of Nero! ah! the days of Caligula! ah! the British tyrant and his infernal junto—glorious revolution—awful crisis—self-important nabobs—diabolical plots and secret machinations

—oh the architects! the architects—they have seized the government, secured power, brow beat with insolence and assume majesty—oh the architects! they will treat you as conquered slaves—they will make you pass under the yoke, and leave their gluttony and riot to attend the pleasing sport—oh that the glory of the Lord may be made perfect—that he would shew strength with his arm and scatter the proud in the imaginations of their hearts—blow the trumpet—sound an alarm—I will cry day and night—behold is not this my number five—attend to my words ye women labouring of child—ye sick persons and young children—behold—behold the lurking places, the despots, the infernal designs—lust of dominion and conspiracies—from battle and murder and from sudden death—good Lord deliver us.

Figure to yourselves, my good fellows, a man with a cow and a horse—oh the battlements, the battlements, they will fall upon his cow, they will fall upon his horse, and wound them, and bruise them and kill them, and the poor man will perish with hunger. Do I exaggerate?—no truly—Europe and Asia and Indostan deny it if you can—oh God! what a monster is man!—A being possessed of knowledge, reason, judgment and an immortal soul—what a monster is man! But the architects are said to be men of skill—then the more their shame—curse on the villains!—they are despots, sycophants, Jesuits, tories, lawyers—curse on the villains! We beseech thee to hear us—Lord have mercy on us—Oh!—Ah!—Ah!—Oh!"—

"Giles Hickory" [*Noah Webster*] *I*

American Magazine (New York), December 1787

One of the principal objections to the new Federal Constitution is, that it contains no *Bill of Rights*. This objection, I presume to assert, is founded on ideas of government that are totally false. Men seem determined to adhere to old prejudices, and reason *wrong*, because our ancestors reasoned *right*. A Bill of Rights against the encroachments of Kings and Barons, or against any power independent of the people, is perfectly intelligible; but a Bill of Rights against the encroachments of an elective Legislature, that is, against our *own* encroachments on *ourselves*, is a curiosity in government.

One half the people who read books, have so little ability to apply what they read to their own practice, that they had better not read at all. The English nation, from which we descended, have been gaining their liberties, inch by inch, by forcing concessions from the crown and the Barons, during the course of six centuries. *Magna Charta*, which is called the palladium of English liberty, was dated in 1215, and the people of England were not represented in Parliament till the year 1265. Magna Charta established the rights of the Barons and the clergy against the encroachments of royal prerogative; but the commons or people were hardly noticed in that deed. There was but one clause in their favor, which stipulated that, "no villain or rustic should, by any fine, be bereaved of his carts, plows and instruments of husbandry." As for the rest, they were considered as a part of the property belonging to an estate, and were transferred, as other moveables, at the will of their owners. In the succeeding reign, they were permitted to send Representatives to Parliament; and from that time have been gradually assuming their proper degree of consequence in the British Legislature. In such a nation, every law or statute that defines the powers of the crown, and circumscribes them within determinate limits, must be considered as a barrier to guard popular liberty. Every acquisition of freedom must be established as a *right*, and solemnly recognized by the supreme power of the nation; lest it should be again resumed by the crown under pretence of ancient prerogative; For this reason, the habeas corpus act passed in the reign of Charles 2d, the statute of the 2d of William and Mary, and many others which are declaratory of certain privileges, are justly considered as the pillars of English freedom.

These statutes are however not esteemed because they are unalterable; for the same power that enacted them, can at any moment repeal them; but they are esteemed, because they are barriers erected by the Representatives of the nation, against a power that exists independent of their own choice.

But the same reasons for such declaratory constitutions do not exist in America, where the supreme power is *the people in their Representatives*. The *Bills of Rights*, prefixed to several of the constitutions of the United States, if considered as assigning the reasons of our separation from a foreign government, or as solemn declarations of right against the encroachments of a foreign jurisdiction, are perfectly rational, and were doubtless necessary. But if they are considered as barriers against the encroachments of our own Legislatures, or as constitutions unalterable by posterity, I venture to pronounce them nugatory, and to the last degree, absurd.

In our governments, there is no power of legislation, independent of the people; no power that has an interest detached from that of the public; consequently there is no power existing against which it is necessary to guard. While our Legislatures therefore remain elective, and the rulers have the same interest in the laws, as the subjects have, the rights of the people will be perfectly secure without any declaration in their favor.

But this is not the principal point. I undertake to prove that a standing *Bill of Rights* is *absurd*, because no constitutions, in a free government, can be unalterable. The present generation have indeed a right to declare what *they* deem a *privilege*; but they have no right to say what the *next* generation shall deem a privilege. A State is a supreme corporation that never dies. Its powers, when it acts for itself, are at all times, equally extensive; and it has the same right to *repeal* a law this year, as it had to *make* it the last. If therefore our posterity are bound by our constitutions, and can neither amend nor annul them, they are to all intents and purposes our slaves.

But it will be enquired, have we then no right to say, that trial by jury, the liberty of the press, the habeas corpus writ and other invaluable privileges, shall never be infringed nor destroyed? By no means. We have the same right to say that lands shall descend in a particular mode to the heirs of the deceased proprietor, and that such a mode shall never be altered by future generations, as we have to pass a law that the trial by jury shall never be abridged. The right of Jury-trial, which we deem invaluable, may in future cease to be a privilege; or other modes of trial more satisfactory to the people, may be devised. Such an event is neither impossible nor improbable. Have we then a right to say that our posterity shall not be judges of their own circumstances? The very attempt to make *perpetual* constitutions, is the assumption of a right to control the opinions of future generations; and to legislate for those over whom we have as little authority as we have over a nation in Asia. Nay we have as little right to say that trial by jury shall be perpetual, as the English, in the reign of Edward the Confessor, had, to bind their posterity forever to decide causes by fiery Ordeal, or single combat. There are perhaps many laws and regulations, which from their consonance to the eternal rules of justice, will always be good and conformable to the sense of a nation. But most institutions in society, by reason of an unceasing change of circumstances, either become altogether improper or require amendment; and every nation has at all times, the right of judging of its circumstances and determining on the propriety of changing its laws.

The English writers talk much of the omnipotence of Parliament; and yet they seem to entertain some scruples about their right to change particular parts of their constitution. I question much whether Parliament would not hesitate to change, on any occasion, an article of Magna Charta. Mr. Pitt, a few years ago, attempted to reform the mode of representation in Parliament. Immediately an uproar was raised against the measure, as *unconstitutional*. The representation of the kingdom, when first established, was doubtless equal and wise; but by the increase of some cities and boroughs and the depopulation of others, it has become extremely *unequal*. In some boroughs there is scarcely an elector left to enjoy its privileges. If the nation feels no great inconvenience from this change of circumstances, under the old mode of representation, a reform is unnecessary. But if such a change has produced any national evils of magnitude enough to be felt, the present form of electing the Representatives of the nation, however *constitutional*, and venerable for its antiquity, may at any time be amended, if it should be the sense of Parliament. The *expediency* of the alteration must always be a matter of opinion; but all scruples as to the *right* of making it are totally groundless.

Magna Charta may be considered as a contract between two parties, the King and the Barons, and no contract can be altered but by the consent of both parties. But whenever any article of that deed or contract shall become inconvenient or oppressive, the King, Lords and Commons may either amend or annul it at pleasure.

The same reasoning applies to each of the United States, and to the Federal Republic in general. But an important question will arise from the foregoing remarks, which must be the subject of another paper.

"Agrippa" [James Winthrop] X

Massachusetts Gazette (Boston), January 1, 1788

To the PEOPLE.

Friends and Brethren,

It is a duty incumbent on every man, who has had opportunities for inquiry to lay the result of his researches on any matter of publick importance before the publick eye. No further apology will be necessary with the generality of my readers, for having so often appeared before them on the subject of the lately proposed form of government. It has been treated with that freedom which is necessary for the investigation of truth, and with no greater freedom. On such a subject, extensive in its nature, and important in its consequences, the examination has necessarily been long, and the topicks treated of have been various. We have been obliged to take a cursory, but not inaccurate view of the circumstances of mankind under the different forms of government to support the different parts of our argument. Permit me now to bring into one view the principal propositions on which the reasoning depends.

It is shewn from the example of the most commercial republick of antiquity, which was never disturbed by a sedition for above seven hundred years, and at last yielded after a violent struggle to a foreign enemy, as well as from the experience of our own country for a century and an half; that the republican, more than any other form of government is made of durable materials. It is shewn from a variety of proof, that one consolidated government is inapplicable to a great extent of country; is unfriendly to the rights both of persons and property, which rights always adhere together; and that being contrary to the interest of the extreme of an empire, such a government can be supported only by power, and that commerce is the true bond of union for a free state. It is shewn from a comparison of the different parts of the proposed plan, that it is such a consolidated government. By article 3, section 2, Congress are empowered to appoint courts with authority to try civil causes of every kind, and even offences against particular states; by the last clause of article 1, section 8, which defines their legislative powers, they are authorised to make laws for carrying into execution all the "powers vested by this constitution in the government of the United States, or in *any department* or officer thereof;" and by article 6, the judges in every state are to be bound by the laws of Congress. It is therefore a complete consolidation of all the states into one, however diverse the parts of it may be. It is also shewn that it will operate unequally in the different states, taking from some of them a greater share of wealth; that in this last respect it will operate more to the injury of this common-wealth than of any state in the union; and that by reason of its inequality it is subversive of the principles of a free government, which requires every part to contribute an equal proportion. For all these reasons this system ought to be rejected, even if no better plan was proposed in the room of it. In case of a rejection we must remain as we are, with trade extending, resources opening, settlements enlarging, manufactures increasing, and publick debts diminishing by fair payment. These are mighty blessings, and not to be lost by the hasty adoption of a new system. But great as these benefits are, which we derive from our present system, it has been shewn, that they may be increased by giving Congress a limited power to regulate trade, and assigning to them those branches of the impost on our foreign trade only, which shall be equal to our proportion of their present annual demands. While the interest is thus provided for, the sale of our lands in a very few years will pay the principal, and the other resources of the state will pay our own debt. The present mode of assessing the continental tax is regulated by the extent of landed property in each state. By this rule the Massachusetts has to pay one eighth. If we adopt the new system, we shall surrender the whole of our impost and excise, which probably amount to a third of those duties of the whole continent, and must come in for about a sixth part of the remaining debt. By this means we shall be deprived of the benefit arising from the largeness of our loans to the continent, shall lose our ability to satisfy the just demands on the state. Under the limitations of revenue and commercial regulation contained in these papers, the balance will be largely in our favour; the importance of the great states will be preserved, and the publick creditors both of the continent and state will be satisfied without burdening the people. For a more concise view of my proposal, I have thrown it into the form of a resolve supposed to be passed by the convention which is shortly to set in this town.

"Commonwealth of Massachusetts.

"Resolved, That the form of government lately proposed by a federal convention, held in the city of Philadelphia, is so far injurious to the interests of this commonwealth, that we are constrained by fidelity to our constituents to reject it; and we do hereby reject the said proposed form and every part thereof. But in order that the union of these states may, as far as possible, be promoted, and the federal business as little obstructed as may be, we do agree on the part of this commonwealth, that the following addition be made to the present articles of confederation.

XIV. The United States shall have power to regulate the intercourse between these states and foreign dominions, under the following restrictions; viz. 1st. No treaty, ordinance, or law shall alienate the whole or part of any state, without the consent of the legislature of such state. 2d. The United States shall not by treaty or otherwise give a preference to the ports of one state over those of another; nor, 3d. create any monopolies or exclusive companies; Nor, 4th, extend the privileges of citizenship to any foreigner. And for the more convenient exercise of the powers hereby, and by the former articles given, the United States shall have authority to constitute judicatories, whether supreme or subordinate, with power to try all piracies and felonies done on the high seas, and also all civil causes in which a foreign state, or subject thereof actually resident in a foreign country and not being British absentees, shall be one of the parties. They shall also have authority to try all causes in which ambassadours shall be concerned. All these trials shall be by jury and in some sea-port town. All imposts levied by Congress on trade shall be confined to foreign produce or foreign manufactures imported, and to foreign ships trading in our harbours, and all their absolute prohibitions shall be confined to the same articles. All imposts and confiscations shall be to the use of the state in which they shall accrue, excepting in such branches as shall be assigned by any state as a fund for defraying their proportion of the continental. And no powers shall be exercised by Congress but such as are expressly given by this and the former articles. And we hereby authorize our delegates in Congress, to sign and ratify an article in the foregoing form and words, without any further act of this state for that purpose, provided the other states shall accede to this proposition on their part on or before the first day of January, which will be in the year of our Lord 1790. All matters of revenue being under the controul of the legislature, we reccommend to the general court of this commonwealth, to devise, as early as may be, such funds, arising from such branches of foreign commerce, as shall be equal to our part of the current charges of the continent, and to put Congress in possession of the revenue arising therefrom, with a right to collect it, during such term as shall appear to be necessary for the payment of the principal of their debt, by the sale of the western lands."

By such an explicit declaration of the powers given to Congress, we shall provide for all federal purposes, and shall at the same time secure our rights. It is easier to amend the old confederation, defective as it has been represented, than it is to correct the new form. For with what ever view it was framed, truth constrains me to say, that it is insiduous in its form, and ruinous in its tendency. Under the pretence of different branches of the legislature, the members will in fact be chosen from the same general description of citizens. The advantages of a check will be lost, while we shall be continually exposed to the cabals and corruption of a British election. There cannot be a more eligible mode than the present, for appointing members of Congress, nor more effectual checks provided than our separate state governments, nor any system so little expensive, in case of our adopting the resolve just stated, or even continuing as we are. We shall in that case avoid all the inconvenience of concurrent jurisdictions, we shall avoid the expensive and useless establishments of the

Philadelphia proposition, we shall preserve our constitution and liberty, and we shall provide for all such institutions as will be useful. Surely then you cannot hesitate, whether you will chuse freedom or servitude. The object is now well defined. By adopting the form proposed by the convention, you will have the derision of foreigners, internal misery, and the anathemas of posterity. By amending the present confederation, and granting limited powers to Congress, you secure the admiration of strangers, internal happiness, and the blessings and prosperity of all succeeding generations. Be wise then, and by preserving your freedom, prove, that Heaven bestowed it not in vain. Many will be the efforts to delude the convention. The mode of judging is itself suspicious, as being contrary to the antient and established usage of the commonwealth. But since this mode is adopted, we trust, that the numbers of that venerable assembly will not so much regard the greatness of their power, as the sense and interest of their constituents. And they will do well to remember that even a mistake in adopting it, will be destructive, while no evils can arise from a total, and much less, probably, from such a partial rejection as we have proposed.

I have now gone through my reasonings on this momentous subject, and have bared the facts and deductions from them, which you will verify for yourselves. Personal interest was not my object, or I should have pursued a different line of conduct. Though I conceived that a man who owes allegiance to the state, is bound, on all important occasions, to propose such inquiries as tend to promote the publick good; yet I did not imagine it to be any part of my duty to present myself to the fury of those, who appear to have other ends in view. For this cause, and for this only, I have chosen a feigned signature. At present all the reports concerning the writer of these papers are merely conjectural. I should have been ashamed of my system, if it had needed such feeble support as the character of individuals. It stands on the firm ground of the experience of mankind. I cannot conclude this long disquisition better, than with a caution derived from the words of inspiration. *Discern the things of your peace now in the days thereof, before they be hidden from your eyes.*

"Publius," The Federalist XXXII–XXXIII [Alexander Hamilton]

Independent Journal (New York), January 2, 1788

To the People of the State of New-York.

Although I am of opinion that there would be no real danger of the consequences, which seem to be apprehended to the State Governments, from a power in the Union to controul them in the levies of money; because I am persuaded that the sense of the people, the extreme hazard of provoking the resentments of the State Governments, and a conviction of the utility and necessity of local administrations, for local purposes, would be a complete barrier against the oppressive use of such a power: Yet I am willing here to allow in its full extent the justness of the reasoning, which requires that the individual States should possess an independent and uncontrolable authority to raise their own revenues for the supply of their own wants. And making this concession I affirm that (with the sole exception of duties on imports and exports) they would under the plan of the Convention retain that authority in the most absolute and unqualified sense; and that an attempt on the part of the national Government to abrige them in the exercise of it would be a violent assumption of power unwarranted by any article or clause of its Constitution.

An intire consolidation of the States into one complete national sovereignty would imply an intire subordination of the parts; and whatever powers might remain in them would be altogether dependent on the general will. But as the plan of the Convention aims only at a partial Union or consolidation, the State Governments would clearly retain all the rights of sovereignty which they before had and which were not by that act *exclusively* delegated to the United States. This exclusive delegation or rather this alienation of State sovereignty would only exist in three cases; where the Constitution in express terms granted an exclusive authority to the Union; where it granted in one instance an authority to the Union and in another prohibited the States from exercising the like authority; and where it granted an authority to the Union, to which a similar authority in the States would be absolutely and totally *contradictory* and *repugnant*. I use these terms to distinguish this last case from another which might appear to resemble it; but which would in fact be essentially different; I mean where the exercise of a concurrent jurisdiction might be productive of occasional interferences in the *policy* of any branch of administration, but would not imply any direct contradiction or repugnancy in point of constitutional authority. These three cases of exclusive jurisdiction in the Fœderal Government may be exemplified by the following instances: The last clause but one in the 8th. section of the 1st. article provides expressly that Congress shall exercise *"exclusive legislation"* over the district to be appropriated as the seat of government. This answers to the first case. The first clause of the same section impowers Congress *"to lay and collect taxes, duties, imposts and excises"* and the 2d. clause of the 10th. section of the same article declares that *"no State shall* without the consent of Congress, *lay any imposts or duties on imports or exports* except for the purpose of executing its inspection laws." Hence would result an exclusive power in the Union to lay duties on imports and exports with the particular exception mentioned; but this power is abriged by another clause which declares that no tax or duty shall be laid on articles exported from any State; in consequence of which qualification it now only extends to the *duties on imports*. This answers to the second case. The third will be found in that clause, which declares that Congress shall have power "to establish an UNIFORM RULE of naturalization throughout the United States." This must necessarily be exclusive; because if each State had power to prescribe a DISTINCT RULE there could not be no UNIFORM RULE.

A case which may perhaps be thought to resemble the latter, but which is in fact widely different, affects the question immediately under consideration. I mean the power of imposing taxes on all articles other than exports and imports. This, I contend, is manifestly a concurrent and coequal authority in the United States and in the individual States. There is plainly no expression in the granting clause which makes that power *exclusive* in the Union. There is no independent clause or sentence which prohibits the States from exercising it. So far is this from being the case, that a plain and conclusive argument to the contrary is to be deduced from the restraint laid upon the States in relation to duties on imports and exports. This restriction implies an admission, that if it were not inserted the States would possess the power it excludes, and it implies a further admission, that as to all other taxes the authority of the States remains undiminished. In any other view it would be both unnecessary and dangerous; it would be unnecessary because if the grant to the Union of the power of laying such duties implied the exclusion of the States, or even their subordination in this particular there could be no need of such a restriction; it would be dangerous because the introduction of it leads directly to the conclusion which has been mentioned and which if the reasoning of the objections be just, could not have been intended; I mean that the States in all cases to which the restriction did not apply would have a concurrent power of taxation with the Union. The restriction in question amounts to what lawyers call a NEGATIVE PREGNANT; that is a *negation* of one thing and an *affirmance* of another; a negation of the authority of the States to impose taxes on imports and exports, and an affirmance of their authority to impose them on all other articles. It would be mere sophistry to argue that it was meant to exclude them *absolutely* from the imposition of taxes of the former kind, and to leave them at liberty to lay others *subject to the controul* of the national Legislature. The restraining or prohibitory clause only says, that they shall not *without the consent of Congress* lay such duties; and if we are to understand this in the sense last mentioned, the Constitution would then be made to introduce a formal provision for the sake of a very absurd conclusion; which is that the States *with the consent* of the national Legislature might tax imports and exports; and that they might tax every other article *unless controuled* by the same body. If this was the intention why not leave it in the first instance to what is alleged to be the natural operation of the original clause conferring a general power of taxation upon the Union? It is evident that this could not have been the intention and that it will not bear a construction of the kind.

As to a supposition of repugnancy between the power of taxation in the States and in the Union, it cannot be supported in that sense which would be requisite to work an exclusion of the States. It is indeed possible that a tax might be laid on a particular article by a State which might render it *inexpedient* that thus a further tax should be laid on the same article by the Union; but it would not imply a constitutional inability to impose a farther tax. The quantity of the imposition, the expediency or inexpediency of an increase on either side, would be mutually questions of prudence; but there would be involved no direct contradiction of power. The particular policy of the national and of the State systems of finance might now and then not exactly coincide, and might require reciprocal forbearances. It is not however a mere possibility of inconvenience in the exercise of powers, but an immediate constitutional repugnancy, that can by implication alienate and extinguish a pre-existing right of sovereignty.

The necessity of a concurrent jurisdiction in certain cases results from the division of the sovereign power; and the rule that all authorities of which the States are not explicitly divested in favour of the Union remain with them in full vigour, is not only a theoretical consequence of that division, but is clearly admitted by the whole tenor of the instrument which contains the articles of the proposed constitution. We there find that notwithstanding the affirmative grants of general authorities, there has been the most pointed care in those cases where it was deemed improper that the like authorities should reside in the States, to insert negative clauses prohibiting the exercise of them by the States. The tenth section of the first article consists altogether of such provisions. This circumstance is a clear indication of the sense of the Convention, and furnishes a rule of interpretation out of the body of the act which justifies the position I have advanced, and refutes every hypothesis to the contrary.

The last clause of the eighth section of the first article of the plan under consideration, authorises the national legislature "to make all laws which shall be *necessary* and *proper*, for carrying into execution *the powers* by that Constitution vested in the government of the United States, or in any department or officer thereof;" and the second clause of the sixth article declares, that "the Constitution and the Laws of the United States made *in pursuance thereof,* and the treaties made by their authority shall be the *supreme law* of the land; any thing in the constitution or laws of any State to the contrary notwithstanding."

These two clauses have been the sources of much virulent invective and petulant declamation against the proposed constitution, they have been held up to the people, in all the exaggerated colours of misrepresentation, as the pernicious engines by which their local governments were to be destroyed and their liberties exterminated—as the hideous monster whose devouring jaws would spare neither sex nor age, nor high nor low, nor sacred nor profane; and yet strange as it may appear, after all this clamour, to those who may not have happened to contemplate them in the same light, it may be affirmed with perfect confidence, that the constitutional operation of the intended government would be precisely the same, if these clauses were entirely obliterated, as if they were repeated in every article. They are only declaratory of a truth, which would have resulted by necessary and unavoidable implication from the very act of constituting a Fœderal Government, and vesting it with certain specified powers. This is so clear a proposition, that moderation itself can scarcely listen to the railings which have been so copiously vented against this part of the plan, without emotions that disturb its equanimity.

What is a power, but the ability or faculty of doing a thing? What is the ability to do a thing but the power of employing the *means* necessary to its execution? What is a LEGISLATIVE power but a power of making LAWS? What are the *means* to execute a LEGISLATIVE power but LAWS? What is the power of laying and collecting taxes but a *legislative power*, or a power of *making laws*, to lay and collect taxes? What are the proper means of executing such a power but *necessary* and *proper* laws?

This simple train of enquiry furnishes us at once with a test by which to judge of the true nature of the clause complained of. It conducts us to this palpable truth, that a power to lay and collect taxes must be a power to pass all laws *necessary* and *proper* for the execution of that power; and what does the unfortunate and calumniated provision in question do more than declare the same truth; to wit, that the national legislature to whom the power of laying and collecting taxes had been previously given, might in the execution of that power pass all laws *necessary* and *proper* to carry it into effect? I have applied these observations thus particularly to the power of taxation, because it is the immediate subject under consideration, and because it is the most important of the authorities proposed to be conferred upon the Union. But the same process will lead to the same result in relation to all other powers declared in the constitution. And it is *expressly* to execute these powers, that the sweeping clause, as it has been affectedly called, authorises the national legislature to pass all *necessary* and *proper* laws. If there is any thing exceptionable, it must be sought for in the specific powers, upon which this general declaration is predicated. The declaration itself, though it may be chargeable with tautology or redundancy, is at least perfectly harmless.

But SUSPICION may ask why then was it introduced? The answer is, that it could only have been done for greater caution, and to guard against all cavilling refinements in those who might hereafter feel a disposition to curtail and evade the legitimate authorities of the Union. The Convention probably foresaw that it has been a principal aim of these papers to inculcate that the danger which most threatens our political welfare, is, that the State Governments will finally sap the foundations of the Union; and might therefore think it necessary, in so cardinal a point, to leave nothing to construction. Whatever may have been the inducement to it, the wisdom of the precaution is evident from the cry which has been raised against it; as that very cry betrays a disposition to question the great and essential truth which it is manifestly the object of that provision to declare.

But it may be again asked, who is to judge of the *necessity* and *propriety* of the laws to be passed for executing the powers of the Union? I answer first that this question arises as well and as fully upon the simple grant of those powers, as upon the declaratory clause: And I answer in the second place, that the national government, like every other, must judge in the first instance of the proper exercise of its powers; and its constituents in the last. If the Fœderal Government should overpass the just bounds of its authority, and make a tyrannical use of its powers; the people whose creature it is must appeal to the standard they have formed, and take such measures to redress the injury done to the constitution, as the exigency may suggest and prudence justify. The propriety of a law in a constitutional light, must always be determined by the nature of the powers upon which it is founded. Suppose by some forced constructions of its authority (which indeed cannot easily be imagined) the Fœderal Legislature should attempt to vary the law of descent in any State; would it not be evident that in making such an attempt it had exceeded its jurisdiction and infringed upon that of the State? Suppose again that upon the pretence of an interference with its revenues, it should undertake to abrogate a land tax imposed by the authority of a State, would it not be equally evident that this was an invasion of that concurrent jurisdiction in respect to this species of tax which its constitution plainly supposes to exist in the State governments? If there ever should be a doubt on this head the credit of it will be intirely due to those reasoners, who, in the imprudent zeal of their animosity to the plan of the Convention, have laboured to invelope it in a cloud calculated to obscure the plainest and simplest truths.

But it is said, that the laws of the Union are to be the *supreme law* of the land. But what inference can be drawn from this or what would they amount to, if they were not to be supreme? It is evident they would amount to nothing. A LAW by the very meaning of the term includes supremacy. It is a rule which those to whom it is prescribed are bound to observe. This results from every political association. If individuals enter into a state of society the laws of that society must be the supreme regulator of their conduct. If a number of political societies enter into a larger political society, the laws which the latter may enact, pursuant to the powers entrusted to it by its constitution, must necessarily be supreme over those societies, and the individuals of whom they are composed. It would otherwise be a mere treaty, dependent on the good faith of the parties, and not a government; which is only another word for POLITICAL POWER AND SUPREMACY. But it will not follow from this doctrine that acts of the larger society which are *not pursuant* to its constitutional powers but which are invasions of the residuary authorities of the smaller societies will become the supreme law of the land. These will be merely acts of usurpation and will deserve to be treated as such. Hence we perceive that the clause which declares the supremacy of the laws of the Union, like the one we have just before considered, only declares a truth, which flows immediately and necessarily from the institution of a Fœderal Government. It will not, I presume, have escaped observation that it *expressly* confines this supremacy to laws made *pursuant to the Constitution*; which I mention merely as an instance of caution in the Convention; since that limitation would have been to be understood though it had not been expressed.

Though a law therefore for laying a tax for the use of the United States would be supreme in its nature, and could not legally be opposed or controuled; yet a law for abrogating or preventing the collection of a tax laid by the authority of a State (unless upon imports and exports) would not be the supreme law of the land, but an usurpation of power not granted by the constitution. As far as an improper accumulation of taxes on the same object might tend to render the collection difficult or precarious, this would be a mutual inconvenience not arising from a superiority or defect of power on either side, but from an injudicious exercise of power by one or the other, in a manner equally disadvantageous to both. It is to be hoped and presumed however that mutual interest would dictate a concert in this respect which would avoid any material inconvenience. The inference from the whole is—that the individual States would, under the proposed constitution, retain an independent and uncontroulable authority to raise revenue to any extent of which they may stand in need by every kind of taxation except duties on imports and exports. It will be shewn in the next paper that this CONCURRENT JURISDICTION in the article of taxation was the only admissible substitute for an intire subordination, in respect to this branch of power, of the State authority to that of the Union.

"Centinel" [Samuel Bryan] VIII

Independent Gazetteer (Philadelphia), January 2, 1788

TO THE PEOPLE OF PENNSYLVANIA.

Fellow Citizens, Under the benign influence of liberty, this country, so recently a rugged wilderness and the abode of savages and wild beasts, has attained to a degree of improvement and greatness, in less than two ages, of which history furnishes no parallel: It is here that human nature may be viewed in all its glory; man assumes the station designed him by the creation; a happy equality and independency pervades the community; it is here the human mind, untrammeled by the restraints of arbitrary power, expands every faculty: as the field to fame and riches is open to all, it stimulates universal exertion, and exhibits a lively picture of emulation, industry and happiness. The unfortunate and oppressed of all nations, fly to this grand asylum, where liberty is ever protected, and industry crowned with success.

But as it is by comparison only that men estimate the value of any good, they are not sensible of the worth of those blessings they enjoy, until they are deprived of them; hence from ignorance of the horrors of slavery, nations, that have been in possession of that rarest of blessings, liberty, have so easily parted with it: when groaning under the yoke of tyranny what perils would they not encounter, what consideration would they not give to regain the inestimable jewel they had lost; but the jealousy of despotism guards every avenue to freedom, and confirms its empire at the expence of the devoted people, whose property is made instrumental to their misery, for the rapacious hand of power seizes upon every thing; dispair presently succeeds, and every noble faculty of the mind being depressed, and all motive to industry and exertion being removed, the people are adapted to the nature of the government, and drag out a listless existence.

If ever America should be enslaved it will be from this cause, that they are not sensible of their peculiar felicity, that they are not aware of the value of the heavenly boon, committed to their care and protection, and if the present conspiracy fails, as I have no doubt will be the case, it will be the triumph of reason and philosophy, as these United States have never felt the iron hand of power, or experienced the wretchedness of slavery.

The conspirators against our liberties have presumed too much on the maxim that nations do not take the alarm, until they feel oppression: the enlightened citizens of America have on two memorable occasions convinced the tyrants of Europe that they are endued with the faculty of foresight, that they will jealously guard against the first introduction of tyranny, however speciously glossed over, or whatever appearance it may assume: It was not the mere amount of *the duty on stamps*, or *tea* that America opposed, they were considered as signals of approaching despotism, as precedents whereon the superstructure of arbitrary sway was to be reared.

Notwithstanding such illustrious evidence of the good sense and spirit of the people of these United States, and contrary to all former experience of mankind, which demonstrates that it is only by gradual and imperceptible degrees that nations have hitherto been enslaved, except in case of conquest by the sword; the authors of the present conspiracy are attempting to seize upon absolute power at one grasp, impatient of dominion they have adopted a decisive line of conduct, which, if successful, would obliterate every trace of liberty. I congratulate my fellow citizens that the infatuated confidence of their enemies has so blinded their ambition, that their defeat must be certain and easy, if imitating the refined policy of successful despots, they had attacked the citadel of liberty by sap, and gradually undermined its outworks, they would have stood a fairer chance of effecting their design; but in this enlightened age thus rashly to attempt to carry the fortress by storm, is folly indeed. They have even exposed some of their batteries prematurely, and thereby unfolded every latent view, for the unlimited power of taxation would alone have been amply sufficient for every purpose; by a proper application of this, the will and pleasure of the ruler would of course have become the supreme law of the land; therefore there was no use in portraying the ultimate object, by superadding the form to reality of supremacy in the following clause, viz. that which empowers the new congress to make all laws that may be necessary and proper for carrying into execution any of their powers, by virtue of which every possible law will be constitutional, as they are to be the sole judges of the propriety of such laws, that which ordains that their acts shall be the supreme law of the land, any thing in the laws or constitution of any state to the contrary notwithstanding; that which gives Congress the absolute controul over the time and mode of its appointment and election, whereby, independent of any other means, they may establish hereditary despotism; that which authorizes them to keep on foot at all times a standing army; and that which subjects the militia to absolute command—and to accelerate the subjugation of the people, trial by jury in civil cases and the liberty of the press are abolished.

So flagrant, so audacious a conspiracy against the liberties of a free people is without precedent. Mankind in the darkest ages have never been so insulted; even then, tyrants found it necessary to pay some respect to the habits and feelings of the people, and nothing but the name of a Washington could have occasioned a moment's hesitation about the nature of the new plan, or saved its authors from the execration and vengeance of the people, which eventually will prove an aggravation of their treason; for America will resent the imposition practised upon the unsuspicious zeal of her *illustrious deliverer*, and vindicate her character from the aspersions of these enemies of her happiness and fame.

The advocates of this plan have artfully attempted to veil over the true nature and principles of it with the names of those respectable characters that by consummate cunning and address they have prevailed upon to sign it, and what ought to convince the people of the deception and excite their apprehensions, is that with every advantage which education, the science of government and of law, the knowledge of history and superior talents and endowments, furnish the authors and advocates of this plan with, they have from its publication exerted all their power and influence to prevent all discussion of the subject, and when this could not be prevented they have constantly avoided the ground of argument and recurred to declamation, sophistry and personal abuse, but principally relied upon the magic of names. Would this have been their conduct, if their cause had been a good one? No, they would have invited investigation and convinced the understandings of the people.

But such policy indicates great ignorance of the good sense and spirit of the people, for if the sanction of every convention throughout the union was obtained by the means these men are practising; yet their triumph would be momentary, the favorite object would still elude their grasp; for a government founded on fraud and deception could not be maintained without an army sufficiently powerful to compel submission, which the *well born* of America could not speedily accomplish. However the complexion of several of the more considerable states does not promise even this point of success. The Carolinas, Virginia, Maryland, New-York and New-Hampshire have by their wisdom in taking a longer time to deliberate, in all probability saved themselves from the disgrace of becoming the dupes of this gilded bait, as experience will evince that it need only be properly examined to be execrated and repulsed.

The merchant, immersed in schemes of wealth, seldom extends his views beyond the immediate object of gain; he blindly pursues his seeming interest, and sees not the latent mischief; therefore it is, that he is the last to take the alarm when public liberty is threatened. This may account for the infatuation of some of our merchants, who, elated with the imaginary prospect of an improved commerce under the new government, overlook all danger: they do not consider that commerce is the hand-maid of liberty, a plant of free growth that withers under the hand of despotism, that every concern of individuals will be sacrificed to the gratification of the men in power, who will institute injurious monopolies and shackle commerce with every device of avarice; and that property of every species will be held at the will and pleasure of rulers.

If the nature of the case did not give birth to these well-founded apprehensions, the principles and characters of the authors and advocates of the measure ought. View the monopolising spirit of the principal of them. See him converting a bank, instituted for common benefit, to his own and creatures emolument, and by the aid thereof, controuling the credit of the state, and dictating the measures of government. View the vassalage of our merchants, the thraldom of the city of Philadelphia, and the extinction of that spirit of independency in most of its citizens so essential to freedom. View this Collosus attempting to grasp the commerce of America and meeting with a sudden repulse, in the midst of his immense career, receiving a shock that threatens his very existence. View the desperate fortunes of many of his co-adjutors and dependants, particularly the bankrupt situation of the principal instrument under the *great man* in promoting the new government, whose superlative arrogance, ambition and repacity, would need the spoils of thousands to gratify; view his towering aspect, he would have no bowels of compassion for the oppressed, he would *overlook* all their sufferings. Recollect the strenuous and unremitted exertions of these men, for years past, to destroy our admirable constitution, whose object is to secure equal liberty and advantages to all, and the great obstacle in the way of their ambitious schemes, and then answer, whether these apprehensions are chimerical, whether such characters will be less ambitious, less avaritious, more moderate, when the privileges, property, and every concern of the people of the United States shall lie at their mercy, when they shall be in possession of absolute sway?

Philadelphia; December 29, 1787.

"Brutus" VII

New York Journal, January 3, 1788

The result of our reasoning in the two preceeding numbers is this, that in a confederated government, where the powers are divided between the general and the state government, it is essential to its existence, that the revenues of the country, without which no government can exist, should be divided between them, and so apportioned to each, as to answer their respective exigencies, as far as human wisdom can effect such a division and apportionment.

It has been shewn, that no such allotment is made in this constitution, but that every source of revenue is under the controul of the Congress; it therefore follows, that if this system is intended to be a complex and not a simple, a confederate and not an entire consolidated government, it contains in it the sure seeds of its own dissolution.—One of two things must happen—Either the new constitution will become a mere *nudum pactum*, and all the authority of the rulers under it be cried down, as has happened to the present confederation—Or the authority of the individual states will be totally supplanted, and they will retain the mere form without any of the powers of government.—To one or the other of these issues, I think, this new government, if it is adopted, will advance with great celerity.

It is said, I know, that such a separation of the sources of revenue, cannot be made without endangering the public safety—"unless (says a writer) it can be shewn that the circumstances which may affect the public safety are reducible within certain determinate limits; unless the contrary of this position can be fairly and rationally disputed; it must be admitted as a necessary consequence, that there can be no limitation of that authority which is to provide for the defence and protection of the community, &c."*

*Federalist, No. 23.

The pretended demonstration of this writer will instantly vanish, when it is considered, that the *protection and defence* of the community is not intended to be entrusted *solely* into the hands of the general government, and by his own confession it ought not to be. It is true this system commits to the general government the protection and defence of the community against foreign force and invasion, against piracies and felonies on the high seas, and against insurrection among ourselves. They are also authorised to provide for the administration of justice in certain matters of a general concern, and in some that I think are not so. But it ought to be left to the state governments to provide for the protection and defence of the citizen against the hand of private violence, and the wrongs done or attempted by individuals to each other— Protection and defence against the murderer, the robber, the thief, the cheat, and the unjust person, is to be derived from the respective state governments.—The just way of reasoning therefore on this subject is this, the general government is to provide for the protection and defence of the community against foreign attacks, &c. they therefore ought to have authority sufficient to effect this, so far as is consistent with the providing for our internal protection and defence. The state governments are entrusted with the care of administring justice among its citizens, and the management of other internal concerns, they ought therefore to retain power adequate to the end. The preservation of internal peace and good order, and the due administration of law and justice, ought to be the first care of every government.—The happiness of a people depends infinitely more on this than it does upon all that glory and respect which nations acquire by the most brilliant martial atchievements—and I believe history will furnish but few examples of nations who have duly attended to these, who have been subdued by foreign invaders. If a proper respect and submission to the laws prevailed over all orders of men in our country; and if a spirit of public and private justice, oeconomy and industry influenced the people, we need not be under any apprehensions but what they would be ready to repel any invasion that might be made on the country. And more than this, I would not wish from them—A defensive war is the only one I think justifiable—I do not make these observations to prove, that a government ought not to be authorised to provide for the protection and defence of a country against external enemies, but to shew that this is not the most important, much less the only object of their care.

The European governments are almost all of them framed, and administered with a view to arms, and war, as that in which their chief glory consists; they mistake the end of government—it was designed to save mens lives, not to destroy them. We ought to furnish the world with an example of a great people, who in their civil institutions hold chiefly in view, the attainment of virtue, and happiness among ourselves. Let the monarchs in Europe, share among them the glory of depopulating countries, and butchering thousands of their innocent citizens, to revenge private quarrels, or to punish an insult offered to a wife, a mistress, or a favorite: I envy them not the honor, and I pray heaven this country may never be ambitious of it. The czar Peter the great, acquired great glory by his arms; but all this was nothing, compared with the true glory which he obtained, by civilizing his rude and barbarous subjects, diffusing among them knowledge, and establishing, and cultivating the arts of life: by the former he desolated countries, and drenched the earth with human blood: by the latter he softened the ferocious nature of his people, and pointed them to the means of human happiness. The most important end of government then, is the proper direction of its internal police, and œconomy; this is the province of the state governments, and it is evident, and is indeed admitted, that these ought to be under their controul. Is it not then preposterous, and in the highest degree absurd, when the state governments are vested with powers so essential to the peace and good order of society, to take from them the means of their own preservation?

The idea, that the powers of congress in respect to revenue ought to be unlimited, "because the circumstances which may affect the public safety are not reducible to certain determinate limits," is novel, as it relates to the government of the united states. The inconveniencies which resulted from the feebleness of the present confederation was discerned, and felt soon after its adoption. It was soon discovered, that a power to require money, without either the authority or means to enforce a collection of it, could not be relied upon either to provide for the common defence, the discharge of the national debt, or for support of government. Congress therefore, so early as February 1781, recommended to the states to invest them with a power to levy an impost of five per cent ad valorem, on all imported goods, as a fund to be appropriated to discharge the debts already contracted, or which should hereafter be contracted for the support of the war, to be continued until the debts should be fully and finally discharged. There is not the most distant idea held out in this act, that an unlimited power to collect taxes, duties and excises was necessary to be vested in the united states, and yet this was a time of the most pressing danger and distress. The idea then was, that if certain definite funds were assigned to the union, which were certain in their natures, productive, and easy of collection, it would enable them to answer their engagements, and provide for their defence, and the impost of five per cent was fixed upon for the purpose.

This same subject was revived in the winter and spring of 1783, and after a long consideration of the subject, and many schemes were proposed; the result was, a recommendation of the revenue system of April 1783; this system does not suggest an idea that it was necessary to grant the United States unlimitted authority in matters of revenue. A variety of amendments were proposed to this system, some of which are upon the journals of Congress, but it does not appear that any of them proposed to invest the general government with discretionary power to raise money. On the contrary, all of them limit them to certain definite objects, and fix the bounds over which they could not pass. This recommendation was passed at the conclusion of the war, and was founded on an estimate of the whole national debt. It was computed, that one million and an half of dollars, in addition to the impost, was a sufficient sum to pay the annual interest of the debt, and gradually to abolish the principal.—Events have proved that their estimate was sufficiently liberal, as the domestic debt appears upon its being adjusted to be less than it was computed, and since this period a considerable portion of the principal of the domestic debt has been discharged by the sale of the western lands. It has been constantly urged by Congress, and by individuals, ever since, until lately, that had this revenue been appropriated by the states, as it was recommended, it would have been adequate to every exigency of the union. Now indeed it is insisted, that all the treasures of the country are to be under the controul of that body, whom we are to appoint to provide for our protection and defence against foreign enemies. The debts of the several states, and the support of the governments of them are to trust to fortune and accident. If the union should not have occasion for all the money they can raise, they will leave a portion for the state, but this must be a matter of mere grace and favor. Doctrines like these would not have been listened to by any state in the union, at a time when we were pressed on every side by a powerful enemy, and were called upon to make greater exertions than we have any reason to expect we shall ever be again. The ability and character of the convention, who framed the proferred constitution, is sounded forth and reiterated by every declaimer and writer in its favor, as a powerful argument to induce its adoption. But are not the patriots who guided our councils in the perilous times of the war, entitled to equal respect. How has it happened, that none of these perceived a truth, which it is pretended is capable of such clear demonstration, that the power to raise a revenue should be deposited in the general government without limitation? Were the men so dull of apprehension, so incapable of reasoning as not to be able to draw the inference? The truth is, no such necessity exists. It is a thing practicable, and by no means so difficult as is pretended, to limit the powers of the general government in respect to revenue, while yet they may retain reasonable means to provide for the common defence.

It is admitted, that human wisdom cannot foresee all the variety of circumstances that may arise to endanger the safety of nations—and it may with equal truth be added, that the power of a nation, exerted with its utmost vigour, may not be equal to repel a force with which it may be assailed, much less may it be able, with its ordinary resources and power, to oppose an extraordinary and unexpected attack;—but yet every nation may form a rational judgment, what force will be competent to protect and defend it, against any enemy with which it is probable it may have to contend. In extraordinary attacks, every country must rely upon the spirit and special exertions of its inhabitants—and these extraordinary efforts will always very much depend upon the happiness and good order the people experience from a wise and prudent administration of their internal government. The states are as capable of making a just estimate on this head, as perhaps any nation in the world.—We have no powerful nation in our neighbourhood; if we are to go to war, it must either be with the Aboriginal natives, or with European nations. The first are so unequal to a contest with this whole continent, that they are rather to be dreaded for the depredations they may make on our frontiers, than for any impression they will ever be able to make on the body of the country. Some of the European nations, it is true, have provinces bordering upon us, but from these, unsupported by their European forces, we have nothing to apprehend; if any of them should attack us, they will have to transport their armies across the atlantic, at immense expence, while we should defend ourselves in our own country, which abounds with every necessary of life. For defence against any assault, which there is any probability will be made upon us, we may easily form an estimate.

I may be asked to point out the sources, from which the general government could derive a sufficient revenue, to answer the demands of the union. Many might be suggested, and for my part, I am not disposed to be tenacious of my own opinion on the subject. If the object be defined with precision, and will operate to make the burden fall any thing nearly equal on the different parts of the union, I shall be satisfied.

There is one source of revenue, which it is agreed, the general government ought to have the sole controul of. This is an impost upon all goods imported from foreign countries. This would, of itself, be very productive, and would be collected with ease and certainty.—It will be a fund too, constantly encreasing—for our commerce will grow, with the productions of the country; and these, together with our consumption of foreign goods, will encrease with our population. It is said, that the impost will not produce a sufficient sum to satisfy the demands of the general government; perhaps it would not. Let some other then, equally well defined, be assigned them:—that this is practicable is certain, because such particular objects were proposed by some members of Congress when the revenue system of April 1783, was agitated in that body. It was then moved, that a tax at the rate of ____ nine-tieths of a dollar on surveyed land, and a house tax of half a dollar on a house, should be granted to the United States. I do not mention this, because I approve of raising a revenue in this mode. I believe such a tax would be difficult in its collection, and inconvenient in its operation. But it shews, that it has heretofore been the sense of some of those, who now contend, that the general government should have unlimited authority in matters of revenue, that their authority should be definite and limitted on that head.—My own opinion is, that the objects from which the general government should have authority to raise a revenue, should be of such a nature, that the tax should be raised by simple laws, with few officers, with certainty and expedition, and with the least interference with the internal police of the states.—Of this nature is the impost on imported goods—and it appears to me that a duty on exports, would also be of this nature—and therefore, for ought I can discover, this would be the best source of revenue to grant the general government. I know neither the Congress nor the state legislatures will have authority under the new constitution to raise a revenue in this way. But I cannot perceive the reason of the restriction. It appears to me evident, that a tax on articles exported, would be as nearly equal as any that we can expect to lay, and it certainly would be collected with more ease and less expence than any direct tax. I do not however, contend for this mode, it may be liable to well founded objections that have not occurred to me. But this I do contend for, that some mode is practicable, and that limits must be marked between the general government, and the states on this head, or if they be not, either the Congress in the exercise of this power, will deprive the state legislatures of the means of their existence, or the states by resisting the constitutional authority of the general government, will render it nugatory.

"Publius," The Federalist XXXIV
[Alexander Hamilton]

New-York Packet, January 4, 1788

To the People of the State of New-York.

I flatter myself it has been clearly shewn in my last number, that the particular States, under the proposed Constitution, would have CO-EQUAL authority with the Union in the article of revenue, except as to duties on imports. As this leaves open to the States far the greatest part of the resources of the community, there can be no color for the assertion, that they would not possess means as abundant as could be desired for the supply of their own wants, independent of all external control. That the field is sufficiently wide will more fully appear when we come to advert to the inconsiderable share of the public expences, for which it will fall to the lot of the State governments to provide.

To argue upon abstract principles that this co-ordinate authority cannot exist, is to set up supposition and theory against fact and reality. However proper such reasonings might be to show that a thing *ought not to exist*, they are wholly to be rejected, when they are made use of to prove that it does not exist, contrary to the evidence of the fact itself. It is well known that in the Roman republic, the legislative authority in the last resort, resided for ages in two different political bodies; not as branches of the same legislature, but as distinct and independent legislatures; in each of which an opposite interest prevailed; in one the Patrician—in the other the Plebian. Many arguments might have been adduced to prove the unfitness of two such seemingly contradictory authorities, each having power to *annul* or *repeal* the acts of the other. But a man would have been regarded as frantic, who should have attempted at Rome to disprove their existence. It will readily be understood, that I allude to the COMI-TIA CENTURIATA and the COMITIA TRIBUTA. The former, in which the people voted by Centuries, was so arranged as to give a superiority to the Patrician interest: In the latter, in which numbers prevailed, the Plebian interest had an entire predominancy. And yet these two legislatures co-existed for ages, and the Roman republic attained to the utmost height of human greatness.

In the case particularly under consideration there is no such contradiction as appears in the example cited; there is no power on either side to annul the acts of the other. And in practice there is little reason to apprehend any inconvenience; because in a short course of time the wants of the States will naturally reduce themselves within *a very narrow compass*; and in the interim the United States will, in all probability, find it convenient to abstain wholly from those objects to which the particular states would be inclined to resort.

To form a more precise judgment of the true merits of this question, it will be well to advert to the proportion between the objects that will require a fœderal provision in respect to revenue; and those which will require a state provision. We shall discover that the former are altogether unlimited; and that the latter are circumscribed within very moderate bounds. In pursuing this inquiry, we must bear in mind, that we are not to confine our view to the present period, but to look forward to remote futurity. Constitutions of civil government are not to be framed upon a calculation of existing exigencies; but upon a combination of these, with the probable exigencies of ages, according to the natural and tried course of human affairs. Nothing therefore can be more fallacious, than to infer the extent of any power, proper to be lodged in the national government, from an estimate of its immediate necessities. There ought to be a CAPACITY to provide for future contingencies, as they may happen; and as these are illimitable in their nature, it is impossible safely to limit that capacity. It is true perhaps that a computation might be made, with sufficient accuracy to answer the purposes of the quantity of revenue requisite to discharge the subsisting engagements of the Union, and to maintain those establishments, which for some time to come, would suffice in time of peace. But would it be wise, or would it not rather be the extreme of folly to stop at this point, and to leave the government intrusted with the care of the national defence, in a state of absolute incapacity to provide for the protection of the community, against future invasions of the public peace by foreign war or domestic convulsions? If on the contrary, we ought to exceed this point, where can we stop short of an indefinite power of providing for emergencies as they may arise? Though it is easy to assert, in general terms, the possibility of forming a rational judgment of a due provision against probable dangers; yet we may safely challenge those who make the assertion to bring forward their data, and may affirm that they would be found as vague and uncertain as any that could be produced to establish the probable duration of the world. Observations confined to the mere prospects of internal attacks can deserve no weight, though even these will admit of no satisfactory calculation: but if we mean to be a commercial people, it must form a part of our policy to be able one day to defend that commerce. The support of a navy and of naval wars must baffle all the efforts of political arithmetic, admitting that we ought to try the novel and absurd experiment in politics of tying up the hands of government from offensive war founded upon reasons of state: Yet, certainly we ought not to disable it from guarding the community against the ambition or enmity of other nations. A cloud has been for some time hanging over the European world. If it should break forth into a storm, who can insure us that in its progress a part of its fury would not be spent upon us? No reasonable man would hastily pronounce that we are entirely out of its reach. Or if the combustible materials that now seem to be collecting, should be dissipated without coming to maturity; or if a flame should be kindled without extending to us, what security can we have, that our tranquility will long remain undisturbed from some other cause, or from some other quarter? Let us recollect that peace or war will not always be left to our option; that however moderate or unambitious we may be, we cannot count upon the moderation, or hope to extinguish the ambition of others. Who could have imagined, at the conclusion of the last war, that

France and Britain, wearied and exhausted as they both were, would so soon have looked with so hostile an aspect upon each other? To judge from the history of mankind we shall be compelled to conclude, that the fiery and destructive passions of war reign in the human breast with much more powerful sway than the mild and beneficent sentiments of peace; and that to model our political systems upon speculations of lasting tranquility is to calculate on the weaker springs of the human character.

What are the chief sources of expence in every government? What has occasioned that enormous accumulation of debts with which several of the European nations are oppressed? The answer plainly is, wars and rebellions—the support of those institutions which are necessary to guard the body politic against these two most mortal diseases of society. The expences arising from those institutions which are relative to the mere domestic police of a State—to the support of its legislative, executive and judicial departments, with their different appendages, and to the internal encouragement of agriculture and manufactures, (which will comprehend almost all the objects of state expenditure) are insignificant in comparison with those which relate to the national defence.

In the kingdom of Great-Britain, where all the ostentatious apparatus of monarchy is to be provided for, not above a fifteenth part of the annual income of the nation is appropriated to the class of expences last mentioned; the other fourteen fifteenths are absorbed in the payment of the interest of debts, contracted for carrying on the wars in which that country has been engaged, and in the maintenance of fleets and armies. If on the one hand it should be observed, that the expences incurred in the prosecution of the ambitious enterprizes and vain-glorious pursuits of a monarchy, are not a proper standard by which to judge of those which might be necessary in a republic; it ought on the other hand, to be remarked that there should be as great a disproportion, between the profusion and extravagance of a wealthy kingdom in its domestic administration, and the frugality and œconomy, which, in that particular, become the modest simplicity of republican government. If we balance a proper deduction from one side against that which it is supposed ought to be made from the other, the proportion may still be considered as holding good.

But let us advert to the large debt which we have ourselves contracted in a single war, and let us only calculate on a common share of the events which disturb the peace of nations, and we shall instantly perceive without the aid of any elaborate illustration, that there must always be an immense disproportion between the objects of Fœderal and State expenditures. It is true that several of the States separately are incumbered with considerable debts, which are an excrescence of the late war. But when these are discharged, the only call for revenue of any consequence, which the State Governments will continue to experience, will be for the mere support of their respective civil lists; to which, if we add all contingencies, the total amount in every State, ought not to exceed two hundred thousand pounds.

In framing a government for posterity as well as ourselves, we ought in those provisions which are designed to be permanent, to calculate not on temporary, but on permanent causes of expence. If this principle be a just one, our attention would be directed to a provision in favor of the State Governments for an annual sum of about 200,000 pounds; while the exigencies of the Union could be susceptible of no limits, even in imagination. In this view of the subject by what logic can it be maintained, that the local governments ought to command in perpetuity, an EXCLUSIVE source of revenue for any sum beyond the extent of 200,000 pounds? To extend its power further, in *exclusion* of the authority of the Union, would be to take the resources of the community out of those hands which stood in need of them for the public welfare, in order to put them in other hands, which could have no just or proper occasion for them.

Suppose then the Convention had been inclined to proceed upon the principle of a repartition of the objects of revenue between the Union and its members, in *proportion* to their comparitive necessities; what particular fund could have been selected for the use of the States, that would not either have been too much or too little; too little for their present, and too much for the future wants. As to the line of separation between external and internal taxes, this would leave to the States at a rough computation, the command of two thirds of the resources of the community, to defray from a tenth to a twentieth part of its expences; and to the Union, one third of the resources of the community, to defray from nine tenths to nineteen twentieths of its expences. If we desert this boundary, and content ourselves with leaving to the States an exclusive power of taxing houses and lands, there would still be a great disproportion between the *means* and the *end*; the possession of one third of the resources of the community, to supply at most one tenth of its wants. If any fund could have been selected and appropriated equal to and not greater than the object, it would have been inadequate to the discharge of the existing debts of the particular States, and would have left them dependent on the union for a provision for this purpose.

The preceding train of observations will justify the position which has been elsewhere laid down, that, "A CONCURRENT JURISDICTION in the article of taxation, was the only admissible substitute for an entire subordination, in respect to this branch of power, of the State authority to that of the Union." Any separation of the objects of revenue, that could have been fallen upon, would have amounted to a sacrifice of the great INTERESTS of the Union to the POWER of the individual States. The Convention thought the concurrent jurisdiction preferable to that subordination; and it is evident that it has at least the merit of reconciling an indefinite constitutional power of taxation in the Foederal Government, with an adequate and independent power in the States to provide for their own necessities. There remain a few other lights, in which this important subject of taxation will claim a further consideration.

Samuel Osgood to Samuel Adams

New York, January 5, 1788

I recd. your favor duely with its Enclosure which I forwarded by that worthy Gentlemans Brother.

you honor me, Sir, by requesting my Sentiments at this critical Moment—I will readily acknowledge, that I long labored to convince myself that the proposed System, would answer, for a Plan of general Government—That the extreme Necessity of a more efficient federal Government than the present—The Uncertainty of obtaining Amendments as well as the Delay, if they should be obtained, had some Weight on my Mind—The all important Reason with many for adopting the Plan without Amendments—is, that if we don't accept of the one proposed, we shall have none. This seems to allow that the Objections made against it, are good; the Plain Meaning of it, is then, that Despotism is better for us, than to remain as we are.

It would take me much Time, as well as Paper to arrange all my Ideas on this important Plan—It has scarcely been out of my Mind since it first made its Appearance—In combining, & comparing its various Parts, new Ideas are constantly occuring—And I am more & more perswaded, that it is a Plan, that the common People can never understand—That if adopted—the Scribes & Pharisees only will be able to interpret, & give it a Meaning.—

Mr. Wilsons Observation, so often repeated is true, "That what ever is not given is reserved."—But the great Question upon this is what is there of Consequence to the People that is not given.

The general Government will have the unlimited Power [   ] collecting Money immediately from the People—The most important Objects of this Government are to prevent foreign Wars, & to regulate the Commerce of the United States with foreign Nations—for these Objects, alone, the

People cannot & ought not to appropriate all their Revenue—It is said the State Legislatures are to [   ] that [   ]
[———] [———] the internal Police of the State will be a
Duty incumbent on them—It is undoubtedly true, that the
Happiness of the People, in this View, will depend as much
(if not more) on the State Legislatures, as on the general Government; & [   ] as they have no exclusive Revenue left
them; it may [   ] be said they have no Revenue at all—No
good Reason in my Opinion has, or can be assigned for placing the Legislatures in this absurd Situation; provided the
Intent is, that they shall continue for the Objects of internal
Police—The Absurdity in this Instance, made such an Impression on me, that I examined the Plan, to see if the general
Government was not furnished expressly with Powers to legislate in all possible Cases, & there[   ] to relieve the State
Legislatures from the Necessity of meeting at all for any Purposes of Legislation; & I am satisfied that this is a Fact.—The
Plan of complete consolidation by the proposed Instrument
could not be eff[   ] if the States retained exclusively a Part
of their Revenue. But as they Do not—it may be brot about;
& in a Way [   ] has not been handed to the public yet.—

The unlimited Power of exclusive Legislation is expressly
given to Congress, over a Place not exceeding ten Miles
Square—Here every Species of Legislation must be gone
into.—The Laws thus made, will be made in Pursuance of
the Constitution; & if so, they will be the supreme Law of the
Land, & the Judges in every State will be sworn to obey
them. It will not be in the Power of the Judge to discriminate,
& say, that one Law is confined to the Limits of ten Miles
Square, & that another Law pervades all the States: every
Law must be considered as a Law of the United States made
in Pursuance of the Constitution.—

The Judicial Power extends to all Cases of Law & Equity
arising under the Constitution &ca—The Extent of the Judicial Power is therefore, as indefinite & unlimited as Words can
make it—Where the united States are a Party against a State
the supreme Judicial Court have expressly original Jurisdiction—suppose then, any State should object to the exercise of
Power by Congress as infringing the Constitution of the
State, the legal Remedy is to try the Question before the

supreme Judicial Court—& they have Power, not confining themselves to the Letter of the general or State Constitutions, to consider & determine upon it, in Equity—This is in Fact leaving the Matter to the Judges of the supreme Judicial Court—They may by a Number of legal Decisions, make what Constitution they Please for the united States.—I am doubtful whether any Instance can be found, where a free People have voluntarily established, so great & so important, a supreme Judicial Court.—

A Legislature without corresponding Judicial Courts is of no Consequence to the People—That this must result from the System; that the State Legislatures will have no Judicial Courts, is not difficult to make apparent—The continental Judicial is to decide on Controversies between Citizens of different States—A Citizen of Masstts. commences Process against a fellow Citizen—Altho the Plaintiff is not in fact a Citizen of New hampshire, yet in Law he is so, & entitled to all the Priviledges & Immunities of a Citizen of New hampshire, one of which is to try a Massachusetts Man before a continental Court.—Therefore the ingenious Lawyer, will always make one appear before the Court as a Citizen in Law, & the other as a Citizen in fact—which will give the continental Court Cognizance of Controversies between two Citizens of the same State—What Use then for a State Judicial? of what Consequence will be the State Bill of Rights—The continental Judicial are not bound by it. I think, Sir, that the Judicial Net is spread; & it will not hereafter be said, we have toiled all Day and caught nothing.—We have traced the State Legislatures to a Situation, where they have neither Money at command, & their Judicial Courts striped of all Business— Suppose then it should be made a Question before the supreme Judicial Court of the united States, whether, in Equity, a State Legislature should be kept in Existence, for any other Purpose than mere Elections, which has neither Money, nor Judicial Courts—I believe no one can doubt what the Decision would be. The Framers of the Plan seem to have had this in View; for the Congress have expressly the Power of making or altering the Times & Manner of choosing the Senators. How far the Word "Manner" extends I know not—But I suppose, if Congress should determine, that the

People at large, or a certain Description of them, should vote on the Senators, it would only be altering the Manner of choosing them—If this be true, Congress will have the exclusive Right of pointing out the Qualification of the Voters for Senators, which will undoubtedly limit the States, to a small Number of Voters. —The Electors for a President stand upon the same precarious Ground—Whether they are to continue Electors for Life, or for one Choice, only, does not appear. It is apparent by attending to the 2d. Clause of the 2d. Article, that the Existence of the State Legislature is not necessary for the Purpose of choosing Electors.

The Supporters of the Plan have asserted that the Existence of the State Legislatures is secured, because they must meet for the Purpose of Organizing, from Time to Time, the general Government; that their Existence must necessarily be co extensive. But this I doubt of very much—Surely, in Equity, without the Existence of the State Legislatures, the continental Government must exist.—And not merely in Consequence of the Purse & the Sword, but in Consequence of the Equitable Powers of the Compact. But, Sir, if the above Reasoning is not fair, & well founded, tho' I do not see but it is —yet let us give the Supporters the Sum total of their Argument, the State Legislatures must exist, for the Purpose of Elections.—& is this all?—Then let us give them another Name—It is not fit that a Board of Electors Should be called a Legislature. I am, Sir, for a fair, explicit & efficient general Government—But I cannot consent, in this Way, to be conclaved out of a Bill of Rights.—This Government is expressly, by its admiring Advocates, to reach the Life Liberty & Property of the Individual Person of every one in the united States, capable of feeling the Government—Man is a weak, foolish Creature of Habit; governed by Instinct as other Animals; tame & docile; without Sagacity: therefore, tho' he dislikes it at first, Time will meliorate & soften his Savage Manners & Disposition; he will then bear the Chains quietly.—But, Sir, this is not true.—This mighty fabric will not give us an efficient Government for many years; the Supporters of it allow it; what will it do? It will be shut up in the ten Miles Square with very little Knowledge of its Operations, until by Bribery and Corruption, & an undue Use of the public Monies, Nabobs are created in each State; & then the Scenery will be changed; the Mask will be laid aside.—It has cost me many a Sleepless Night to find out the most obnoxious Part of the proposed Plan.—And I have finally fixed upon the exclusive Legislation in the Ten Miles Square.— This space is capable of holding two Millions of People— Here will the Wealth and Riches of every State center—And shall there be in the Bowels of the united States such a Number of People, brot up under the Hand of Despotism, without one Priviledge of Humanity, that they can claim; all must be Grace & favor to them.—Shall the supreme Legislature of the most enlightened People on the Face of the Earth; a People who have recently offered up,—upon the Altar of Freedom, near sixty thousand of their bravest Men, & near two hundred Millions of specie Dollars—be secluded from the World of Freemen; & seated down among Slaves & Tenants at Will?—And have not this supreme Legislature a Right to naturalize me there; whether I will or not? What means the establishing of an uniform Rule of Naturalization?—What does it mean in Equity? May not the sovereign of the Country, Grant exclusive Privilidges to all that are willing to be naturalized in that hallowed Spot?—What an inexhaustable Fountain of Corruption are we opening? The Revenue there collected will not belong to the united States.

Upon proper Principles, I wish the Legislature of the united States to have Ten Miles Square—But let the People settled there, have a Bill of Rights. Let them know that they are Freemen—Let them have the Liberty of Speech, of the Press, of Religion, &ca Let them when numerous enough be represented in the lower House.—Let the Revenue there collected be accounted for to the united States as other Revenue—Let the Laws made for the internal Police, have a partial & not a general Stile.—Mankind are too much disposed to barter away their Freedom for the Sake of Interest.—The deluded Philadelphians have however egregiously miscalculated. If the Ten Miles Square should be taken agreeably to their offer, one Mile above the northern Liberties of their City—a very few years will empty the City of Philadelphia—They will be naturally dazzled with the Splendor of the New Government & Insect like, be drawn to it.—

I have said, & I beleive if the new Government should take Place, it would prove true, that the first Rebellion against it, would break out in the Town of Boston.—Masstts. has about 400.000 Inhabitants—There is therefore now, one Representative [   ] 50.000—Boston has about 15. or 16.000 Inhabitants she has little Chance of sending one Representative to a Body, who are to regulate all their commercial Concerns.—

"The Republican" to the People

Connecticut Courant (Hartford), January 7, 1788

To the PEOPLE.

It is generally agreed, that the old articles of Confederation are inadequate to answer the great national purposes, for which they were designed. It is likewise generally agreed, that the new constitution is better adapted to answer these great purposes. All the objections which are made against it, are reducible to this single one; that it is dangerous to liberty. Say the opposers of it, if we adopt it, our liberties have no security. If this objection be well-founded, if the new Constitution does destroy the safe-guards of that liberty for which American blood and treasure has been lavished, let us exert every nerve to oppose it. God forbid, that we, my countrymen, who have maintained our liberties in spite of the seducing artifices, the hostile arms, and the horrid cruelties, which Britain has called into action for the purpose of enslaving us, should now through our folly surrender those precious rights, which God and nature have given to men. But on the other hand, if those patriotic citizens, whom we have chosen from among us, for their knowledge of government, love of liberty, and love of their country, have formed a plan of government, which, without endangering our liberties, is calculated to render us a great, respectable, and happy nation; let us not, through folly and ill-directed jealousy, reject this which is probably the only system for promoting our national felicity, which we shall ever have an opportunity of adopting. If we reject this system, which comes recommended to us by the unanimous assent of the ablest and best men, that the American continent could appoint; what reason or encouragement can there be for the States ever to appoint another convention? I use the expression *unanimous assent*, because those three gentlemen, who refused to subscribe to the Constitution, did so, not from substantial objections to it, but from partial considerations, which can have no weight with a free and enlightened people.

In answer to the objection before stated, I say, that adopting the new Constitution will not expose us to the loss of liberty; but the great barriers of liberty will still remain, and, in all human probability, will continue to be its security for ages and generations to come. The principal circumstances, which render liberty secure, are a spirit of liberty among the people—a general diffusion of knowledge—a general distribution of property—a militia of freemen—and a fair representation in the supreme Legislature.

The people of the United States possess in a high degree a spirit of liberty. This is a principle which is natural to the human mind. We love to have the command of our own actions and the direction of our own interests. Our minds rise with indignation against oppression and tyranny. These natural feelings have never been eradicated from our minds by subjection to the will of a tyrant. But that freedom with which the principles of liberty have been discussed, that ardour with which they have been inculcated upon the public minds, that long struggle for liberty which has called these principles into action, have so fixed and confirmed the spirit of liberty that it must and will long continue to be a ruling principle of our actions, and guard us against the encroachments of tyranny.

Another circumstance highly conducive to the security of liberty, is the general diffusion of knowledge among the great body of the people. The American citizens in general are by far better educated and more knowing than the people at large in other countries. And in those states where the people have heretofore had the fewest advantages for learning, they are setting up schools, and gaining fast in point of useful knowledge. This is a circumstance of the highest importance to a free people. For where the great body of the citizens are ignorant, and incapable of discerning their true interests, they may be duped by artful and factious men, and led to do things destructive to their own rights and liberties. But a sensible intelligent people, who have access to the sources of information, and are capable of discerning what measures are conducive to the public welfare, will not be easily induced to act contrary to their own interests, and destroy those rights and liberties which are the foundations of public happiness.

Another circumstance highly favourable to liberty, is the general distribution of property among the people at large. In most of the American states, property is more equally divided among the great body of the people, than it is in any other country. Our laws and customs, which divide great estates among all the children of the deceased owner; the way being open for industrious men, who are born to no inheritance, to acquire property; and the plenty and cheapness of land, will long cause property to be diffused among the people at large. The people do and will possess freeholds of their own; they can live comfortably and independently on their farms. Men in such a situation feel the dignity of human nature, and scorn to be dependent on the will of a tyrant. When they exercise the important right of choosing men to act for them in a public capacity, they will act independently; we may reasonably presume, they will choose those who will be faithful to their country.

It is a capital circumstance in favour of our liberty, that the people themselves are the military power of our country. In countries under arbitrary government, the people oppressed and dispirited, neither possess arms nor know how to use them. Tyrants never feel secure, until they have disarmed the people. They can rely upon nothing but standing armies of mercenary troops for the support of their power. But the people of this country have arms in their hands; they are not destitute of military knowledge; every citizen is required by Law to be a soldier; we are all martialed into companies, regiments, and brigades, for the defence of our country. This is a circumstance which encreases the power and consequence of the people; and enables them to defend their rights and priveleges against every invader.

If in addition to the advantages, which I have before mentioned, for maintaining liberty, a people have a free constitution of government, their liberties, are secured by the strongest barriers. The great distinction between a free and an arbitrary government is this; in the former the people give their assent to the Laws by which they are governed; in the latter, the laws are made by a power which they cannot controul. And the plain reason, why the former kind of government secures the rights and liberties of the people, is, that the people will not consent to laws which are oppressive to themselves. In a country of any considerable extent, the people cannot meet together in person to make Laws; consequently they must do it, if at all, by their representatives. Now if they have the privelege of electing representatives to act for them, if they have an opportunity of choosing a fair and adequate representation, and if no law can be made without the consent of these representatives, we may presume the people will be free from oppression; because their own interest will induce them to choose those who will be faithful to their country. The new constitution gives the people a fair opportunity to elect their representatives for the general Legislature. The state Legislatures are to make the regulations and arrangements for the choice, and to make the privelege still more secure, these regulations are subject to the revision of the general Legislature. The constitution expressly provides that the choice shall be by the people, which cuts off both from the general and state Legislatures the power of so regulating the mode of election, as to deprive the people of a fair choice. As to the number of representatives, it is certainly as great as it ought to be. It is greater than the numbers in Congress under the old confederation; and we never have found, that the number of members in Congress was so small as to occasion any danger or inconvenience. As our country grows more populous and wealthy, it will be proper to have a more numerous representation. Accordingly it is wisely provided in the new constitution, that the number of representatives shall increase as that of the people increases. Upon the whole, therefore I am warranted in saying, that there is full provision made in the new constitution for an adequate representation of the people.

Now as the people of the United States possess a spirit of liberty to induce them to maintain their rights; as there is such a diffusion of knowledge among them, as enables them to judge by what methods liberty is to be supported; as the people at large possess such a share of property as gives them the rank of independent freemen; as the people themselves are the military power of our country; these important supports of liberty, together with our choice of representatives in the lower branch of the Legislature, would secure our rights, even supposing the power of the president and Senate were vested in a king and body of Nobles independent of the people. I am justified in making this assertion, by the circumstances which the people of the United States are in, and by the experience of other nations. With all the advantages for maintaining the rights of a free people, which I have mentioned, and when no oppressive measures of government could be taken without the consent of our representatives, unless by an open violation of our constitutional rights, our liberties would stand firm. The people, we may safely presume, would choose men of abilities and integrity, who would withstand every attempt to undermine their liberties. The spirit of the people would oppose every open and direct attempt to enslave them. Experience likewise justifies my assertion. The people of England possess a political constitution similar to the one I have been describing, though, far inferior to it in the fairness of representation, and though their advantages for maintaining liberty are far inferior to those which I have mentioned as possessed by us; yet they have long maintained their liberties. Kings have attempted to tyrannize over them; but they brought one to the block and expelled another from his throne and kingdom. It is true, their liberties are now impaired; but it is by causes which I have not time to delineate, and which are not applicable to the political circumstances of this country. And impaired as their liberties are, their King still finds it necessary to submit to the public voice in the measures of his government.

But, my fellow citizens, it is not with us, as it is with other nations who have been called free, and have been said to enjoy the privileges of a free government. Other nations have been called free, if they have had only the privilege of choosing one branch of their legislature, and that in a very partial unequal manner. And such a privilege has ensured to them the blessings of a free government, until they become so degenerate and corrupt, that they had not virtue enough to keep alive the sacred flame of liberty. But we, besides electing the representatives in the federal legislature, choose the members of the senate in a manner which even the opposers of federal measures cannot, without self-contradiction, deny to be highly conducive to the safety of our liberties. These gentlemen say, that our liberties are safe in the hands of the state-legislatures. The state-legislatures appoint the senators; they will be faithful to the people; they will have better opportunities than the people to know the characters of those whom they appoint; therefore they will appoint men who breathe the very spirit of the state-legislatures, and consequently deserve the most unlimited confidence of the people. No encroachment can be made upon our liberties without their consent; they will withstand every encroachment; therefore they will afford full security for our liberties.

The President of the United States is to be appointed in a manner which is wisely adapted to concentrate the general voice of the people. He is an officer appointed by the people. If he wishes to be appointed again, he depends upon the people. He therefore will be the guardian of the liberties of the people. The president, the senate, the representatives, are all chosen by the people. They form a tripple wall around our liberties. In short, the constitution breathes the spirit of liberty. The people breathe the spirit of liberty. The state legislatures will still possess extensive powers; they will have great influence upon the general government; we ought to presume, they will be faithful to the people; their influence will therefore be in favour of liberty. We possess advantages superior to those of any other people to maintain our liberty. Therefore if we adopt the new constitution, if we will act like rational freemen, and choose men of abilities and integrity to carry this plan of government into execution, we may with reason expect, that our liberties and privileges will endure as long as is consistent with the instability of all human affairs. But if we reject this constitution, it must be upon the principle, that those, who are chosen by the people, are not fit to be trusted with the necessary powers of government. If this be a just principle, all our republican governments are but snares to enslave the people; a free government is impracticable; and we must adopt the gloomy idea, that anarchy or tyranny is the only alternative for men.

But, my fellow citizens, the prospect of human affairs is not so gloomy. Act out your native good sense; be not afraid to entrust men appointed by yourselves with the powers necessary for promoting your interest; learn the characters of those whom you appoint to places of trust and power; choose men who know what the public good requires; and have virtue to act accordingly; act rationally upon the great political subjects which are submitted to your consideration. Our national hopes are fast approaching to their grand crisis; the friends of liberty throughout the world have their eyes fixed upon us; if we have not wisdom and virtue enough to unite *government and liberty*; the cause of liberty must be given up for lost. We are a young, virtuous, and growing people; we have the good wishes of all mankind; nature has bountifully bestowed upon us the blessings of climate and soil; the extent of our country affords room for our rapid increase for ages to come; a wise system of government we want; a wise system of government is offered for our acceptance; receive the offered good; put it in practice with wisdom, moderation, and virtue; and you may become a great, flourishing and happy nation.

State of Connecticut, January 2, 1788.

Resolutions of the Tradesmen of the Town of Boston

Massachusetts Gazette (Boston), January 8, 1788

Boston, January 7, 1788.

AGREEABLE to an advertisement inserted in the papers of this day, the TRADESMEN of this town convened at Mason's-hall, Green Dragon, when John Lucas, Esquire, Paul Revere, Esquire, and Mr. Benjamin Russell, were chosen to draft certain resolutions, expressive of the sense of this body. The committee, after having retired for that purpose, returned, and reported the following—which, being read, was UNANIMOUSLY accepted, and ordered to be printed in the several publick papers—viz.

WHEREAS some persons, intending to injure the reputation of the tradesmen of this town, have asserted, that they were unfriendly and adverse to the adoption of the constitution of the United States of America, as proposed on the 17th September last, by the Convention of the United States assembled in Philadelphia: Therefore, to manifest the falsehood of such assertions, and to discover to the world our sentiments of the proposed frame of government,

Be it RESOLVED,

1. THAT such assertions are false and groundless; and it is the sense of this body, that all those, who propagate such reports, have no other view than the injury of our reputation, in the attainment of their own wicked purposes, on base and false grounds.

2. THAT, in the judgment of this body, the proposed frame of government, is well calculated to secure the liberties, protect the property, and guard the rights of the citizens of America; and it is our warmest wish and prayer that the same should be adopted by this commonwealth.

3. THAT, it is our opinion, if said constitution should be adopted by the United States of America, trade and navi-

gation will revive and increase, employ and subsistence will be afforded to many of our townsmen, who are now suffering from want of the necessaries of life; that it will promote industry and morality; render us respectable as a nation; and procure us all the blessings to which we are entitled from the natural wealth of our country; our capacity for improvement, from our industry, our freedom and independence.

4. THAT it is the sense of this body, that if the proposed frame of government should be rejected, the small remains of commerce yet left us, will be annihilated, the various trades and handicrafts dependent thereon, must decay; our poor will be increased, and many of our worthy and skilful mechanicks compelled to seek employ and subsistence in strange lands.

5. THAT, in the late election of delegates to represent this town in Convention, it was our design, and the opinion of this body, the design of every good man in town, to elect such men, and such only, as would exert their utmost ability to promote the adoption of the proposed frame of government in all its parts, without any conditions, pretended amendments, or alterations whatever: and that such, and such only, will truly represent the feelings, wishes, and desires of their constituents: and if any of the delegates of this town should oppose the adoption of said frame of government in gross, or under pretence of making amendments, or alterations of any kind, or of annexing conditions to their acceptance, such delegate or delegates will act contrary to their best interest, the strongest feelings, and warmest wishes of the Tradesmen of the town of Boston.

Per order   JOHN LUCAS.

After the above resolutions were passed, John Lucas, Esq. Mr. Joseph Clark, Paul Revere, Esq. Mr. Rhodes, Mr. William Boardman, Joshua Witherlee, Esq. and Captain David Spear, were appointed a standing-committee, to notify a meeting of the Tradesmen of this town in future. After which the meeting was dissolved.

It was with pleasure, says a correspondent, he observed the perfect order, unanimity, and intelligence, that pervaded the body of respectable Tradesmen which met last evening at the Green-Dragon. Notwithstanding the number exceeded three hundred and eighty, as appeared by an enumeration made at the time of their retiring from the Hall, as much regularity and propriety were discovered throughout all their proceedings, and deliberations, as ever were observed in any legislative body.

"Publius," The Federalist XXXVI
[Alexander Hamilton]

New-York Packet, January 8, 1788

To the People of the State of New-York.

We have seen that the result of the observations, to which the foregoing number has been principally devoted, is that from the natural operation of the different interests and views of the various classes of the community. Whether the representation of the people be more or less numerous, it will consist almost entirely of proprietors of land, of merchants and members of the learned professions, who will truly represent all those different interests and views. If it should be objected that we have seen other descriptions of men in the local Legislatures; I answer, that it is admitted there are exceptions to the rule, but not in sufficient number to influence the general complexion or character of the government. There are strong minds in every walk of life that will rise superior to the disadvantages of situation, and will command the tribute due to their merit, not only from the classes to which they particularly belong, but from the society in general. The door ought to be equally open to all; and I trust, for the credit of human nature, that we shall see examples of such vigorous plants flourishing in the soil of Fœderal, as well as of State Legislation; but occasional instances of this sort, will not render the reasoning founded upon the general course of things less conclusive.

The subject might be placed in several other lights that would lead all to the same result; and in particular it might be asked, what greater affinity or relation of interest can be conceived between the carpenter or blacksmith, and the linen manufacturer or stocking weaver, than between the merchant and either of them? It is notorious, that there are often as great rivalships between different branches of the mechanic or

manufacturing arts, as there are between any of the departments of labor and industry; so that unless the representative
body were to be far more numerous than would be consistent
with any idea of regularity or wisdom in its deliberations, it is
impossible that what seems to be the spirit of the objection
we have been considering, should ever be realised in practice.
But I forbear to dwell any longer on a matter, which has hitherto worn too loose a garb to admit even of an accurate inspection of its real shape or tendency.

There is another objection of a somewhat more precise
nature that claims our attention. It has been asserted that a
power of internal taxation in the national Legislature could
never be exercised with advantage, as well from the want of a
sufficient knowledge of local circumstances as from an interference between the revenue laws of the Union and of the
particular States. The supposition of a want of proper knowledge, seems to be entirely destitute of foundation. If any
question is depending in a State Legislature respecting one of
the counties which demands a knowledge of local details, how
is it acquired? No doubt from the information of the members of the county. Cannot the like knowledge be obtained in
the national Legislature from the representatives of each
State. And is it not to be presumed that the men who will
generally be sent there, will be possessed of the necessary
degree of intelligence, to be able to communicate that information? Is the knowledge of local circumstances, as applied to
taxation, a minute topographical acquaintance with all the
mountains, rivers, streams, high-ways and bye-paths in each
State, or is it a general acquaintance with its situation and
resources—with the state of its agriculture, commerce, manufactures—with the nature of its products and consump-
tions—with the different degrees and kinds of its wealth,
property and industry?

Nations in general, even under governments of the more
popular kind, usually commit the administration of their
finances to single men or to boards composed of a few individuals, who digest and prepare, in the first instance, the plans
of taxation, which are afterwards passed into laws by the
authority of the sovereign or Legislature.

Inquisitive and enlightened Statesmen are deemed every

where best qualified to make a judicious selection of the objects proper for revenue; which is a clear indication, as far as the sense of mankind can have weight in the question, of the species of knowledge of local circumstances requisite to the purposes of taxation.

The taxes intended to be comprised under the general denomination of internal taxes, may be subdivided into those of the *direct* and those of the *indirect* kind. Though the objection be made to both, yet the reasoning upon it seems to be confined to the former branch. And indeed, as to the latter, by which must be understood duties and excises on articles of consumption, one is at a loss to conceive what can be the nature of the difficulties apprehended. The knowledge relating to them, must evidently be of a kind that will either be suggested by the nature of the article itself, or can easily be procured from any well informed man, especially of the mercantile class. The circumstances that may distinguish its situation in one State from its situation in another must be few, simple, and easy to be comprehended. The principal thing to be attended to would be to avoid those articles which had been previously appropriated to the use of a particular State; and there could be no difficulty in ascertaining the revenue system of each. This could always be known from the respective codes of laws, as well as from the information of the members of the several States.

The objection when applied to real property, or to houses and lands, appears to have, at first sight, more foundation; but even in this view, it will not bear a close examination. Land taxes are commonly laid in one of two modes, either by *actual* valuations permanent or periodical, or by occasional assessments, at the discretion or according to the best judgment of certain officers, whose duty it is to make them. In either case the EXECUTION of the business, which alone requires the knowledge of local details, must be devolved upon discreet persons in the character of commissioners or assessors, elected by the people or appointed by the government for the purpose. All that the law can do must be to name the persons or to prescribe the manner of their election or appointment, to fix their numbers and qualifications; and to draw the general outlines of their powers and duties. And what is there in all this, that cannot as well be performed by the national Legislature as by a State Legislature? The attention of either can only reach to general principles; local details, as already observed, must be referred to those who are to execute the plan.

But there is a simple point of view in which this matter may be placed, that must be altogether satisfactory. The national Legislature can make use of *the system of each State within that State.* The method of laying and collecting this species of taxes in each State, can, in all its parts, be adopted and employed by the Fœderal Government.

Let it be recollected, that the proportion of these taxes is not to be left to the discretion of the national Legislature: but is to be determined by the numbers of each State as described in the second section of the first article. An actual census or enumeration of the people must furnish the rule; a circumstance which effectually shuts the door to partiality or oppression. The abuse of this power of taxation seems to have been provided against with guarded circumspection. In addition to the precaution just mentioned, there is a provision that "all duties, imposts and excises, shall be UNIFORM throughout the United States."

It has been very properly observed by different speakers and writers on the side of the Constitution, that if the exercise of the power of internal taxation by the Union, should be discovered on experiment, to be really inconvenient, the Fœderal Government may then forbear the use of it and have recourse to requisitions in its stead. By way of answer to this, it has been triumphantly asked, why not in the first instance omit that ambiguous power and rely upon the latter resource? Two solid answers may be given; the first is, that the exercise of that power, if convenient, will be preferable, because it will be more effectual; and it is impossible to prove in theory or otherwise than by the experiment that it cannot be advantageously exercised. The contrary indeed appears most probable. The second answer is, that the existence of such a power in the Constitution, will have a strong influence in giving efficacy to requisitions. When the States know that the Union can supply itself without their agency, it will be a powerful motive for exertion on their part.

As to the interference of the revenue laws of the Union, and of its members; we have already seen that there can be no clashing or repugnancy of authority. The laws cannot therefore in a legal sense, interfere with each other; and it is far from impossible to avoid an interference even in the policy of their different systems. An effectual expedient for this purpose will be mutually to abstain from those objects, which either side may have first had recourse to. As neither can *controul* the other, each will have an obvious and sensible interest in this reciprocal forbearance. And where there is an *immediate* common interest, we may safely count upon its operation. When the particular debts of the States are done away, and their expences come to be limited within their natural compass, the possibility almost of interference will vanish. A small land tax will answer the purposes of the States, and will be their most simple and most fit resource.

Many spectres have been raised out of this power of internal taxation to excite the apprehensions of the people—double sets of revenue officers—a duplication of their burthens by double taxations, and the frightful forms of odious and oppressive poll taxes, have been played off with all the ingenious dexterity of political legerdemain.

As to the first point, there are two cases, in which there can be no room for double sets of officers; one where the right of imposing the tax is exclusively vested in the Union, which applies to the duties on imports; and the other, where the object has not fallen under any State regulation or provision, which may be applicable to a variety of objects. In other cases, the probability is, that the United States will either wholly abstain from the objects pre-occupied for local purposes, or will make use of the State officers and State regulations, for collecting the additional imposition. This will best answer the views of revenue, because it will save expence in the collection, and will best avoid any occasion of disgust to the State governments and to the people. At all events, here is a practicable expedient for avoiding such an inconvenience; and nothing more can be required than to show that evils predicted do not necessarily result from the plan.

As to any argument derived from a supposed system of influence, it is a sufficient answer to say, that it ought not to be presumed; but the supposition is susceptible of a more precise answer. If such a spirit should infest the councils of the Union, the most certain road to the accomplishment of its aim would be to employ the State officers as much as possible, and to attach them to the Union by an accumulation of their emoluments. This would serve to turn the tide of State influence into the channels of the national government, instead of making fœderal influence flow in an opposite and adverse current. But all suppositions of this kind are invidious, and ought to be banished from the consideration of the great question before the people. They can answer no other end than to cast a mist over the truth.

As to the suggestion of double taxation, the answer is plain. The wants of the Union are to be supplied in one way or another; if to be done by the authority of the Fœderal Government, it will not be to be done by that of the State government. The quantity of taxes to be paid by the community, must be the same in either case; with this advantage, if the provision is to be made by the Union, that the capital resource of commercial imposts, which is the most convenient branch of revenue, can be prudently improved to a much greater extent under fœderal than under State regulation, and of course will render it less necessary to recur to more inconvenient methods; and with this further advantage, that as far as there may be any real difficulty in the exercise of the power of internal taxation, it will impose a disposition to greater care in the choice and arrangement of the means; and must naturally tend to make it a fixed point of policy in the national administration to go as far as may be practicable in making the luxury of the rich tributary to the public treasury, in order to diminish the necessity of those impositions, which might create dissatisfaction in the poorer and most numerous classes of the society. Happy it is when the interest which the government has in the preservation of its own power, coincides with a proper distribution of the public burthens, and tends to guard the least wealthy part of the community from oppression!

As to poll taxes, I, without scruple, confess my disapprobation of them; and though they have prevailed from an early period in those States* which have uniformly been the most tenacious of their rights, I should lament to see them introduced into practice under the national government. But does it follow because there is a power to lay them, that they will actually be laid? Every State in the Union has power to impose taxes of this kind; and yet in several of them they are unknown in practice. Are the State governments to be stigmatised as tyrannies because they possess this power? If they are not, with what propriety can the like power justify such a charge against the national government, or even be urged as an obstacle to its adoption? As little friendly as I am to the species of imposition, I still feel a thorough conviction, that the power of having recourse to it ought to exist in the Fœderal Government. There are certain emergencies of nations, in which expedients that in the ordinary state of things ought to be foreborn, become essential to the public weal. And the government from the possibility of such emergencies ought ever to have the option of making use of them. The real scarcity of objects in this country, which may be considered as productive sources of revenue, is a reason peculiar to itself, for not abridging the discretion of the national councils in this respect. There may exist certain critical and tempestuous conjunctures of the State, in which a poll tax may become an inestimable resource. And as I know nothing to exempt this portion of the globe from the common calamities that have befallen other parts of it, I acknowledge my aversion to every project that is calculated to disarm the government of a single weapon, which in any possible contingency might be usefully employed for the general defence and security.

*The New-England States.

Thomas B. Wait to George Thatcher

Portland, Maine, January 8, 1788

My dear friend—
Your kind letter of the 23d ultimo receiv'd.—
My opposition to the proposed plan of Continental Govt. does not, as you suppose, arise from *"violence of passion."*—

On reception of the Report of the Convention, I perused, and admired it:—Or rather, like many who still *think* they admire it, I loved Geo. Washington—I venerated Benj. Franklin—and therefore concluded that I must love and venerate all the works of their hands:—This, if you please my friend, was *"violence of passion"*—and to this very *violence of passion* will the proposed Constitution owe its adoption—i.e.— should the people ever adopt it. The honest and uninformed *freemen* of America entertain the same opinion of those two gentlemen as do European *slaves* of their Princes,—*"that they can do no wrong"*—

On the unprecedented Conduct of the Pennsylvania Legislature, I found myself disposed to lend an ear to the arguments of the opposition—not with an expectation of being convinced that the new Constitution was defective; but because I thought the minority had been ill used; and I felt a little curious to hear the particulars.

The address of the Seceders was like the Thunder of Sinai—it's lightnings were irresistable; and I was obliged to acknowledge, not only that the conduct of the majority was highly reprehensible, but that the Constitution itself might possibly be defective.—My mind has since been open to conviction—I have read & heard every argument, on either side, with a degree of candour, of which I never, on any other occasion, felt myself possessed—And, after this cool and impartial examination I am constrained—I repeat it, my dear friend—I am constrained to say, that I am dissatisfied with the proposed Constitution.—

Your arguments against the necessity of a Bill of Rights are ingenious; but, pardon me my friend, they are not convincing.—You have traced the origin of a Bill of Rights accurately.—The People of England, as you say, undoubtedly made use of a Bill of Rights to obtain their liberties of their soverigns; but is this an argument to prove that they ought not now to make use of Bills in defence of those liberties?— shall a man throw away his sword, and refuse to defend a piece of property, for no other reason than that his property was obtained by that very sword?—Bills of Rights have been the happy instruments of wresting the privileges and rights of the people from the hand of Despotism; and I trust God that Bills of Rights will still be made use of by the people of America to defend them against future encroachments of despotism—Bills of Rights, in my opinion, are the grand bulwarks of freedom.

But, say some, however necessary in state Constitutions, there can be no necessity for a Bill of Rights in the Continental plan of Govt.—because every Right is reserved that is not *expressly* given up—Or, in other words, Congress have no powers but those *expressly* given by that Constitution.—This is the *doctrine* of the *celebrated* Mr. Wilson; and as you, my friend, have declared it *orthodox*, be so good as to explain the meaning of the following Extracts from the Constitution— Art. I Sect. 9.—"The privilege of the writ of Habeas Corpus shall *not* be suspended &c."—"*No* bill of attainder or ex post facto law shall be passed."—"*No* money shall be drawn from the treasury" &c.—"*No* title of nobility shall be granted by the United states."—Now, how absurd—how grosly absurd is all this, if Congress, in reality, have no powers but those particularly specified in the Constitution!—

It will not do, my friend—for God's sake let us not deny self-evident propositions—let us not sacrifice the truth, that we may establish a favourite hypothesis;—in the present case, the liberties and happiness of a world may also be sacrificed.—

There is a certain darkness, duplicity and studied ambiguity of expression running thro' the whole Constitution which renders a Bill of Rights peculiarly necessary.—As it now stands but very few individuals do, or ever will understand it.—Consequently, Congress will be its own *interpreter*—The article respecting taxation and representation is neither more or less than a *puzling Cap*; and you, my friend, had the pleasure of *wearing* it, at my office, an hour or two—and then pulled it off, *just as wise* as when you put it on.—But you will now perhaps tell me that you can explain it entirely to my satisfaction—possibly you can; but that may not happen completely to satisfy Congress—if it should not, why they will put a different one,—one that may not satisfy *either you or me*—But Some persons have *guessed* the meaning to be this—that *taxation and representation should be in proportion to all the freemen and slaves in each state—counting five of the latter to three of the former*—If these were the ideas of the Convention, what a strange collection of words do we find in the Constitution to express them!—Who, in the name of God, but the *majority* of that honl. body, would ever have tho't of expressing like ideas in like words!—But bad as may be the *mode* of *expression*, the *ideas*, in my opinion, are worse—

By this *interpretation* the article in question is an egregious imposition on the northern states—Tell me, if you can, why a southern *negro*, in his present debased condition, is any more intitled to representation, than a northern *Bullock*?—Both are mere pieces of property—and nothing more!—The latter is equally a *free agent* with the former.—

O, for that social Evening you so kindly wish for!—I want prodigeously to see you:—But it grieves me that we do not think alike—You will, my dear Thatcher, I know you will alter your opinion—And I charitably conclude The only reason why you had not done it when you wrote me, was, that owing to the small pox, you had not attended to the arguments of the opposition.—

And now let me beseech you, not obstinately to defend your present notions of the new Constitution tho' they may be all the *ton* in the *great* world, till you have examined every argument that has been used against it—pay particular attention to the Debates of the Pennsylvania Convention; and I am certain that you must acknowledge if the Constitution is good, that it by no means appears so from any arguments made use of by the majority of that body—they are lighter than straws.—

How can you, after *perusing* the arguments of Crazy Jonathan, approve of the abolition of juries in civil causes—If the Genl. Court of this state are insurgents for depriving the subject of that right in 110 actions out of 120—what shall we say to the Constitution that evidently deprives the subject of that right altogether?—O, my good friend, that cursed Small pox has made a crazy Jonathan of you in good earnest.—But your life is spared—and I am happy—

Last Saturday week I did myself the pleasure of visiting your dear wife and family—and tarried till Monday noon—it was a godly season—had you been present, it had been a Paradise.—

Mrs. Thatcher shew'd me your P.S. wherein you charge all who do not think as you do with *sorcery, witch craft,* &c.—It pain'd me to the soul—I wanted to shed a tear; and had no one been present, I should certainly have given vent to a dozen—I wish, said I, to Mrs. T. that your good husband and myself could think alike—I wish, replied she, that I had not shewn you the P.—S.—or rather that you had agreed to think alike before you parted—or, added Tempy, that Uncle was now present to settle the difference—We all joined most heartily in the last wish—we almost made a prayer of it; but it was not heard—perhaps we did not ask in faith—Be this as it might—Politicks, from that moment, was consigned over to the wind, and not a soul of us would even lend an ear to its whistling. . . .

We continued as perfectly happy as was possible in the absence of our *friend*, our *Uncle* and our *father*, until sunday noon;—at which time Jeremiah Hill, Esq. made his appearance—from that time till after tea, (which we drank at his house) we eat and drank and talked politicks. The Squire, you must know, is a professed Constitutionalist—Silas and myself were *Anti's*—so we had nothing to do but fall at it *hammer & tongs*,—Had you been within hearing, you would have wished the new Constitution, or its advocate, or both, at the Devil—We *roasted* him—we *basted* him, till he became quite a *crisp*; and, had we tarried the evening, we should certainly have *devoured* him—We took pity upon, and left him directly after tea—returned to your house, and were again happy. . . .

You say nothing of a Post to Pownalboro'—The people at

the Eastward are amazingly impatient—It is an important period; and they are almost totally ignorant of every public transaction—Five Delegates in six, from these three Counties are opposed to the new plan of Cont. Government—Genl. Thompson and your *Brother* Widgery are warm in the opposition, and both are Conventioners—

Mr. Barnard's Contract for the year 1787,—hath expired— The Post-master Genl. has not renewed it for 1788—'tho' applied to by Mr. B.—We therefore have no Post from Portsmoth to this place—Mr. Barnard rides or *letteth it alone*, as he pleaseth.—Mr. Freeman is very uneasy on this account; and joins with me in requesting you to see the P. Mastr Genl. and to enquire into the matter—We are barbarously neglected, my friend.—

Your friend foever—

P.S.—your papers are sent weekly, sealed, directed, &c.—I am surprised that you have not recivd them. . . .

"Brutus" VIII

New York Journal, January 10, 1788

The next powers vested by this constitution in the general government, which we shall consider, are those, which authorise them to "borrow money on the credit of the United States, and to raise and support armies." I take these two together and connect them with the power to lay and collect taxes, duties, imposts and excises, because their extent, and the danger that will arise from the exercise of these powers, cannot be fully understood, unless they are viewed in relation to each other.

The power to borrow money is general and unlimited, and the clause so often before referred to, authorises the passing any laws proper and necessary to carry this into execution. Under this authority, the Congress may mortgage any or all the revenues of the union, as a fund to loan money upon, and it is probable, in this way, they may borrow of foreign nations, a principal sum, the interest of which will be equal to the annual revenues of the country.—By this means, they may create a national debt, so large, as to exceed the ability of the country ever to sink. I can scarcely contemplate a greater calamity that could befal this country, than to be loaded with a debt exceeding their ability ever to discharge. If this be a just remark, it is unwise and improvident to vest in the general government, a power to borrow at discretion, without any limitation or restriction.

It may possibly happen that the safety and welfare of the country may require, that money be borrowed, and it is proper when such a necessity arises that the power should be exercised by the general government.—But it certainly ought never to be exercised, but on the most urgent occasions, and then we should not borrow of foreigners if we could possibly avoid it.

The constitution should therefore have so restricted, the exercise of this power as to have rendered it very difficult for the government to practise it. The present confederation requires the assent of nine states to exercise this, and a number of the other important powers of the confederacy—and it would certainly have been a wise provision in this constitution, to have made it necessary that two thirds of the members should assent to borrowing money—when the necessity was indispensible, this assent would always be given, and in no other cause ought it to be.

The power to raise armies, is indefinite and unlimitted, and authorises the raising forces, as well in peace as in war. Whether the clause which impowers the Congress to pass all laws which are proper and necessary, to carry this into execution, will not authorise them to impress men for the army, is a question well worthy consideration? If the general legislature deem it for the general welfare to raise a body of troops, and they cannot be procured by voluntary enlistments, it seems evident, that it will be proper and necessary to effect it, that men be impressed from the militia to make up the deficiency.

These powers taken in connection, amount to this: that the general government have unlimitted authority and controul over all the wealth and all the force of the union. The advocates for this scheme, would favor the world with a new discovery, if they would shew, what kind of freedom or independency is left to the state governments, when they cannot command any part of the property or of the force of the country, but at the will of the Congress. It seems to me as absurd, as it would be to say, that I was free and independent, when I had conveyed all my property to another, and was tenant to will to him, and had beside, given an indenture of myself to serve him during life.—The power to keep up standing armies in time of peace, has been justly objected, to this system, as dangerous and improvident. The advocates who have wrote in its favor, have some of them ridiculed the objection, as though it originated in the distempered brain of its opponents, and others have taken pains to shew, that it is a power that was proper to be granted to the rulers in this constitution. That you may be enabled to form a just opinion on this subject, I shall first make some remarks, tending to prove, that this power ought to be restricted, and then animadvert on the arguments which have been adduced to justify it.

I take it for granted, as an axiom in politic, that the people should never authorise their rulers to do any thing, which if done, would operate to their injury.

It seems equally clear, that in a case where a power, if given and exercised, will generally produce evil to the community, and seldom good—and which, experience has proved, has most frequently been exercised to the great injury, and very often to the total destruction of the government; in such a case, I say, this power, if given at all, should if possible be so restricted, as to prevent the ill effect of its operation.

Let us then enquire, whether standing armies in time of peace, would be ever beneficial to our country—or if in some extraordinary cases, they might be necessary; whether it is not true, that they have generally proved a scourge to a country, and destructive of their liberty.

I shall not take up much of your time in proving a point, in which the friends of liberty, in all countries, have so universally agreed. The following extract from Mr. Pultney's speech, delivered in the house of commons of Great-Britain, on a motion for reducing the army, is so full to the point, and so much better than any thing I can say, that I shall be excused for inserting it. He says, "I have always been, and always shall be against a standing army of any kind; to me it is a terrible thing, whether under that of a parliamentary, or any other designation; a standing army is still a standing army by whatever name it is called; they are a body of men distinct from the body of the people; they are governed by different laws, and blind obedience, and an entire submission to the orders of their commanding officer, is their only principle; the nations around us, sir, are already enslaved, and have been enslaved by those very means; by means of their standing armies they have every one lost their liberties; it is indeed impossible that the liberties of the people in any country can be preserved where a numerous standing army is kept up. Shall we then take our measures from the example of our neighbours? No, sir, on the contrary, from their misfortunes we ought to learn to avoid those rocks upon which they have split.

"It signifies nothing to tell me that our army is commanded

by such gentlemen as cannot be supposed to join in any measures for enslaving their country; it may be so; I have a very good opinion of many gentlemen now in the army; I believe they would not join in any such measures; but their lives are uncertain, nor can we be sure how long they will be kept in command, they may all be dismissed in a moment, and proper tools of power put in their room. Besides, sir, we know the passions of men, we know how dangerous it is to trust the best of men with too much power. Where was a braver army than that under Jul. Cæsar? Where was there ever an army that had served their country more faithfully? That army was commanded generally by the best citizens of Rome, by men of great fortune and figure in their country, yet that army enslaved their country. The affections of the soldiers towards their country, the honor and integrity of the under officers, are not to be depended on. By the military law the administration of justice is so quick, and the punishment so severe, that neither the officer nor soldier dare dispute the orders of his supreme commander; he must not consult his own inclination. If an officer were commanded to pull his own father out of his house, he must do it; he dares not disobey; immediate death would be the sure consequence of the least grumbling: and if an officer were sent into the court of request, accompanied by a body of musketeers with screwed bayonets, and with orders to tell us what we ought to do, and how we were to vote: I know what would be the duty of this house; I know it would be our duty to order the officer to be hanged at the door of the lobby: but I doubt, sir, I doubt much, if such a spirit could be found in the house, or in any house of commons that will ever be in England.

"Sir, I talk not of imaginary things? I talk of what has happened to an English house of commons, from an English army; not only from an English army, but an army that was raised by that very house of commons, an army that was paid by them, and an army that was commanded by generals appointed by them; therefore do not let us vainly imagine, that an army, raised and maintained by authority of parliament, will always be submissive to them. If an army be so numerous as to have it in their power to overawe the parliament, they will be submissive as long as the parliament does nothing to

disoblige their favourite general; but when that case happens
I am afraid, that in place of the parliament's dismissing the
army, the army will dismiss the parliament."—If this great
man's reasoning be just, it follows, that keeping up a standing
army, would be the highest degree dangerous to the liberty
and happiness of the community—and if so, the general government ought not to have authority to do it; for no government should be empowered to do that which if done, would
tend to destroy public liberty.

"Mark Antony"

Independent Chronicle (Boston), January 10, 1788

"Here under leave of BRUTUS, *and the rest,*
(For Brutus is an honourable man;
So are they all, all honourable men,)
Come I to speak."——   JULIUS CÆSAR.

Mess'rs. ADAMS and NOURSE,

Among the various artifices of those who are opposed to the federal constitution or to any efficient plan of government, none is more natural, and perhaps none more successful, than to excite a jealousy between the inhabitants of the several States. Upon this plan the suggestions of Brutus, whose speculations have appeared in your paper, appear frequently to be founded. I particularly allude, at present, to his third number, in which he objects to the mode of representation proposed in the new constitution, expatiating largely upon an idea, at which the feelings of Freemen must reluct, that the system of slavery in the southern States, is patronized and encouraged by the proposed mode of representation. Such misrepresentations ought surely to be exposed. With many it is needless; but those who have perceived the futility of his observations, will excuse me for the sake of those who have not.

The equal voice of unequal States in Congress, is a well grounded objection of long standing, to the present Confederation. A new system therefore, which should not remedy this defect, would most surely be rejected by the larger States; while the minor States would feel alarmed at the reform, unless they were secured, by a provision in some measure conformable to the spirit of the confederation. In this dilemma, originating from opposite interests, human wisdom, perhaps, could not devise a happier expedient than the new frame of government proposes. A House of Representatives chosen by the States, according to their respective numbers, gives weight to the larger States, in some measure, proportioned to their magnitude; while the small States, are secured from the danger or the apprehension of being overborn by their more powerful confederates, by an equal voice in the Senate.

In this new construction of a House of Representatives, the number, which each State shall send, becomes an interesting question. The general answer is easy, that it ought to be in proportion to the supplies furnished to the public chest. This equitable rule has become a political maxim, which *Brutus* himself enforces when it suits his convenience. The next enquiry is, by what rule taxes shall be proportioned, which when ascertained, is also the rule of representation. The mode prescribed in the confederation, has long been esteemed injudicious and impracticable. It has not hitherto governed the Continental requisition; and if executed and observed, would probably prove unsatisfactory and unjust. Those who are acquainted with State *Valuations*, will concur with the above conclusions, especially when they calculate its operation among thirteen different powers. Some other rule of apportionment became indispensible. The number of inhabitants in each State, has obtained the preference to any other system: And for the combined advantages of simplicity, certainty, facility and equity, none probably can be found more eligible. Here a difficulty arises, with respect to the slaves in the southern States, nor would the difficulty be lessened probably if they were infranchised. Five of them are computed to be equal to three freemen. Their comparative value cannot be demonstrated; but it is acknowledged that they are not equal to free persons, in an estimation of this nature; and the ratio established, being the result of compromise, the presumption is in favour of its propriety.

This connected system of representation and taxation is thus expressed in the proposed Constitution: "Representatives and direct taxes shall be proportioned among the several States, which may be included within this Union, according to their respective numbers, which shall be determined by adding to the whole number of free persons, including those bound to service for a term of years, and excluding Indians

not taxed, three-fifths of all other persons." Few sentences I
believe of equal import, can be produced, so perspicuous and
comprehensive. But the critical *Brutus* is offended with its
construction, and, after suggesting its ambiguity, proceeds to
give us an abridged sense of it in his own superior style.
"What a strange and unnecessary accumulation of words (says
he) are here used, to conceal from the public eye, what might
have been expressed in the following concise manner—*Representatives are to be proportioned among the States respectively,
according to the number of freemen and slaves inhabiting them,
counting five slaves for three freemen?*" The charge of studied
concealment, which *Brutus* so illiberally suggests, is applicable
only to himself. It frequently happens that precision is lost in
conciseness; but *Brutus* has sacrificed the truth. The careful
reader will observe, that the article under consideration proportions representatives and taxes according to numbers. But
the pretended abridgment fabricated by *Brutus*, mentions
Representatives only. The difference is material. In the constitution, it is a fair and equitable establishment: As represented
by *Brutus*, one essential branch is omitted, upon which its
consistency depended, and being thus mutilated it has been
exposed to his objections. This artifice has in some measure
succeeded to his wishes, for some have been misled by his
suggestions. But, my countrymen, he deceives and abuses
you. For what has *Brutus* attacked? Is it the alteration of the
rule of apportioning taxes, from a valuation of property to
numbers? No.—His reason dictated, and probably his own
experience in public affairs, demonstrated the propriety of the
measure. Does he disapprove of the ratio between free persons and other persons, in this great political estimate? Upon
this matter he is silent. Does he condemn the proportion of
Representatives to taxes? No.—In the same performance,
when cavilling against the Senate he observes, "on every principle of equity and propriety, representation in a government,
should be in exact proportion to the numbers or aids, afforded by the persons represented"—The same principle applies to States, as to individuals in this respect; and if *Brutus*
had been honest, his abilities would have saved him from inconsistency. The number of persons, whatever their condition
or degree, being reckoned to any State, to render it charge-

able in the public contributions, in the same proportion ought that State to be represented. As the slaves are not personally chargeable with taxes, so they are not concerned in representation. But says *Brutus*, "Why is the number of members in the assembly, to be encreased on their account? Is it because in some of the States, a considerable part of the property of the inhabitants, consists in a number of their fellow men, who are held in bondage, in defiance of every idea of benevolence, justice, and religion, and contrary to all the principles of liberty, which have been publickly avowed, in the late glorious revolution? If this be a just ground of representation, the horses in some of the States, and the oxen in others, ought to be represented: for a great share of property in some of them consists in these animals;" &c. Is the man really misled, or does he only attempt to mislead others, and to avail himself of our strong disapprobation of slavery? The practice of slavery among our confederates ought to be regreted by us, but it is evidently beyond our controul. Do we in fact countenance or give encouragement to it, by consenting to this rule of apportionment, more than we should by concurring with another? Suppose for instance, Representatives and direct taxes were to be apportioned by a valuation, instead of numbers, and thirty thousand pounds property, should give one representative, instead of thirty thousand persons. If Virginia exceeded Massachusetts in the valuation, thirty thousand pounds, as it would bear its additional proportion of the public burdens, it would be entitled to an additional representation. For greater convenience and certainty, the rule of apportionment is changed from a valuation to numbers. Shall not the slaves be reckoned? The objection of the northern States has hitherto been, that they were not to be estimated nearer at par with the free. Virginia, we will suppose, is found to contain thirty thousand persons more than Massachusetts, reckoning slaves in the ratio proposed by the constitution. We all agree it ought to be proportionably chargeable in the federal contributions; shall it not have its proportionate representation? Having granted it in the former instance, with what pretence of equity or propriety can we deny it in the latter? And is slavery any more promoted or affected in one case than in the other? The number of persons, and of slaves, necessarily, among the rest, is fixed upon only as a criterion to determine each State's proportion in the public contributions, to which representation ought to be adequate. The sophistry of *Brutus* wholly arises from this circumstance; for if the proportion was determined by any other criterion, the States holding slaves would probably have as large a representation, as under the mode proposed. If they had not, it would be because their taxes were less, which could only evince, probably, that the criterion was not so certain or equitable as the one under consideration. *Brutus* has mentioned *horses* and *oxen*. If the number of those animals was the rule of apportionment of taxes, upon the principle above established, and which *Brutus* concedes, the representation of the States would in fact be according to the number of horses or oxen, found in them respectively; and it might then be said they were represented or that they increased the representation, in the same sense as *Brutus* suggests it respecting the slaves. In reality they have no concern in the representation, any further than they are used, with other persons, in a certain proportion, to determine the States proportion of taxes, from *which,* representation originating, as the effect from the cause, is therefore determined by the same rule. The representation is given to the State, and the Representatives are to be chosen, *by the electors of the most numerous branch of the State legislature,* according to the second article of the proposed federal constitution. In these elections the slaves have no part: and here we may feel a degree of regret, that in any quarter of the United States, such a proportion of our fellow creatures, should be deprived of a share of political and civil liberty. To this only do the objections of Brutus, and his warm declamations apply: for, whatever may be their intended operation, upon an entire view of the true sense of the article in question, part of which he has artfully suppressed, they evidently do not affect the proposed constitution.

The acts of power, which some of the States see fit to exercise with respect to their internal concerns, may be repugnant to our notions of justice; but shall we therefore refuse to confederate with them? *Brutus* himself surely, could not have this in contemplation. Does *Brutus* wish the slaves emancipated! It is a dictate of humanity, and we need no stimulus to join with him most cordially. But even in this laudible pursuit, we ought to temper the feelings of humanity with political wisdom. Great numbers of slaves becoming citizens, might be burdensome and dangerous to the Public. These inconveniencies ought to be regarded. *M. Montesquieu*, whom *Brutus* quotes, and whom we all revere, after mentioning the embarrassment of the Roman Senate, in this respect, sometimes limiting, at other times facilitating the infranchisement of slaves, with great modesty observes, "much less can I determine what ought to be the regulations of a good republic, in an affair of this kind; this depends on too many circumstances." Of this he is certain, that "their condition should be more favoured in the civil, than in the political State"—As federalists, and I think as patriots, we ought to agree with him. This subject doubtless engaged the attention of the late respectable Convention. But, in the immensity of their object, it was not their province to establish those minute provisions, which properly belong partly to federal, partly to State Legislation. They probably went as far as policy would warrant, or practicability allow. The friends to liberty and humanity, may look forward with satisfaction to the period, when slavery shall not exist in the United States; while the enlightened patriot will approve of the system, which renders its abolition gradual.

To return to *Brutus*, from whom I have in some measure wandered. I have endeavoured to expose the fallacy and futility of his objections, to a very important article of the proposed Constitution; whether his mistakes were willful or designed, let the impartial determine. Certain it is, that under a pretence of abbreviating the article, he has given a false and imperfect representation of it, and under that representation, has pointed a number of objections, calculated to engage the feelings of the people, but which do not apply to the article as it stands in the Constitution. The zeal of Brutus may have led him into error, and that zeal may be honest: But his apparent ability prevents me from supposing him inconscious of the fallacy of his own observations. He might consider that the number of those who read, is greater than of those who examine; and that the feelings of the people might be so engaged, as to mislead their judgment. If he was influenced by those considerations to urge conscious fallacies upon the public mind, the investigation of truth is not his object; his patriotism is pretension; his zeal suspicious, and as he writes with design, we ought to read with caution.

James Madison to
Governor Edmund Randolph

New York, January 10, 1788

My dear friend

I have put off writing from day to day for some time past, in expectation of being able to give you the news from the packet, which has been looked for every hour. Both the French & English have overstaid their usual time ten or 15 days, and are neither of them yet arrived. We remain wholly in the dark with regard to the posture of things in Europe.

I received two days ago your favor of Decr. 27. inclosing a copy of your letter to the Assembly. I have read it with attention, and I can add with pleasure, because the spirit of it does as much honor to your candour, as the general reasoning docs to your abilities. Nor can I believe that in this quarter the opponents to the Constitution will find encouragement in it. You are already aware that your objections are not viewed in the same decisive light by me as they are by you. I must own that I differ still more from your opinion that a prosecution of the experiment of a second Convention will be favorable even in Virginia to the object which I am sure you have at heart. It is to me apparent that had your duty led you to throw your influence into the opposite scale, that it would have given it a decided and unalterable preponderancy; and that Mr. Henry would either have suppressed his enmity, or been baffled in the policy which it has dictated. It appears also that the ground taken by the opponents in different quarters, forbids any hope of concord among them. Nothing can be farther from your views than the principles of different setts of men, who have carried on their opposition under the respectability of your name. In this State the party adverse to the Constitution, notoriously meditate either a dissolution of the Union, or protracting it by patching up the Articles of Confederation. In Connecticut & Massachussetts, the oppo-

744

sition proceeds from that part of the people who have a repugnancy in general to good government, to any substantial
abridgment of State powers, and a part of whom in Massts.
are known to aim at confusion, and are suspected of wishing
a reversal of the Revolution. The Minority in Pennsylva. as far
as they are governed by any other views than an habitual &
factious opposition, to their rivals, are manifestly averse to
some essential ingredients in a national Government. You are
better acquainted with Mr. Henry's politics than I can be, but
I have for some time considered him as driving at a Southern
Confederacy and as not farther concurring [   ] the plan of
amendments than as he hopes to render it subservient to his
real designs. Viewing the matter in this light, the inference
with me is unavoidable that were a second trial to be made,
the friends of a good constitution for the Union would not
only find themselves not a little differing from each other as
to the proper amendments; but perplexed & frustrated by
men who had objects totally different. A second Convention
would of course be formed under the influence, and composed in great measure of the members of opposition in the
several States. But were the first difficulties overcome, and the
Constitution re-edited with amendments, the event would
still be infinitely precarious. Whatever respect may be due to
the rights of private judgment, and no man feels more of it
than I do, there can be no doubt that there are subjects to
which the capacities of the bulk of mankind are unequal and
on which they must and will be governed by those with
whom they happen to have acquaintance and confidence. The
proposed Constitution is of this description. The great body
of those who are both for & against it, must follow the judgment of others not their own. Had the Constitution been
framed & recommended by an obscure individual, instead of
the body possessing public respect & confidence, there can
not be a doubt, that altho' it would have stood in the identical words, it would have commanded little attention from
most of those who now admire its wisdom. Had yourself,
Col. Mason, Col. R. H. L. Mr. Henry & a few others, seen
the Constitution in the same light with those who subscribed
it, I have no doubt that Virginia would have been as zealous
& unanimous as she is now divided on the subject. I infer

from these considerations that if a Government be ever adopted in America, it must result from a fortunate coincidence of leading opinions, and a general confidence of the people in those who may recommend it. The very attempt at a second Convention strikes at the confidence in the first; and the existence of a second by opposing influence to influence, would in a manner destroy an effectual confidence in either, and give a loose to human opinions; which must be as various and irreconcileable concerning theories of Government, as doctrines of Religion; and give opportunities to designing men which it might be impossible to counteract.

The Connecticut Convention has probably come to a decision before this; but the event is not known here. It is understood that a great majority will adopt the Constitution. The accounts from Massts. vary extremely according to the channels through which they come. It is said that S. Adams who has hitherto been reserved, begins to make open declaration of his hostile views. His influence is not great, but this step argues an opinion that he can calculate on a considerable party. It is said here, and I believe on good ground that N. Carolina has postponed her Convention till July, in order to have the previous example of Virga. Should N. Carolina fall into Mr. H——y's politics which does not appear to me improbable, it will endanger the Union more than any other circumstance that could happen. My apprehensions of this danger increase every day. The multiplied inducements at this moment to the local sacrifices necessary to keep the States together, can never be expected to co-incide again, and they are counteracted by so many unpropitious circumstances, that their efficacy can with difficulty be confided in. I have no information from S. Carolina or Georgia, on which any certain opinion can be formed of the temper of those States. The prevailing idea has been that both of them would speedily & generally embrace the Constitution. It is impossible however that the example of Virga. & N. Carolina should not have an influence on their politics. I consider every thing therefore as problematical from Maryland Southward.

I am surprised that Col. H. Lee who is a well-wisher to the Constitution should have furnished Wilkinson with the alarm concerning the Mississippi, but the political connections of the latter in Pena. would account for his biass on the subject.

We have no Congress yet. The number of Sts on the Spot does not exceed five. It is probable that a quorum will now be soon made. A Delegate from N. Hampshire is expected which will make up a representation from that State. The termination of the Connecticut Convention will set her delegates at liberty. And the Meeting of the Assembly of this State, will fill the vacancy which has some time existed in her Delegation.

Samuel Holden Parsons to William Cushing

Middletown, Connecticut, January 11, 1788

The ratification of the Constitution of Government proposed by the general convention was subscribed & completed
in this State last Thursday—the Numbers present were 168,
of which 40 only gave their negative—that humane Imperfection can be capable of establishing or framing a perfect
System of Government is not to be expected; and where different Interests are to be united and the Component Members of the general Government are so diverse in their
Manners & Habits as in the present case the difficulty is
greatly increasd—I am on these Considerations more surprised that the Delegates of the States have united in a System
which contains so few Imperfections than alarmed at the
powers granted in the Constitution to the Legislative, Executive, or judicial Departments—The Objection founded on the
want of a Bill of Rights appears to me to have no weight—
this Constitution is grounded on the Idea that the People are
the fountain of all Power, that no Dominion can rightfully be
exercised over them but by their consent, and that every Officer of Government is amenable to them in the exercise of the
Authorities granted—if this is a just Idea it is the Ruler who
must receive a Bill of Rights from the People & not they from
him—every power not granted rests where all power was before lodged—and establishing any other Bill of Rights would
be dangerous, as it would at least imply that nothing more
was left with the People than the Rights defined & securd in
such Bill of Rights—at the Time those Matters were so much
agitated in England, the King was suppos'd to be the fountain of all Power & every franchise the People possessed was
by his Gift & an Act of Grace & favor—the Reverse of this is
true here, and therefore no such Measure can be a proper
one——

—if the Union of the American States is necessary for their

748

Security, which I believe no Man will seriously deny, the only Inquiry that can fairly be made, by an honest Man, will be, does the propos'd plan grant such powers as if properly exercis'd will accomplish the best good and greatest Happiness of the Members? and are those Powers sufficiently guarded against an undue Use of them—or on the whole considering every attending Circumstance is as much political & civil Liberty Secured by this Constitution as we have reasonably to expect from a Constitution where so many different Interests are to be consulted, and in a case where a Union is necessary?—for myself, I believe, whatever answer may be given to the first Question, the powers granted are as great as the public Mind is prepared to give, and I hope properly administered may serve good purposes for a Time (I hope a long Time)—the Objects to which the Legislative powers extend are necessary to the Happiness and prosperity of the whole Territory; and such as no particular State can extend her Acts to so as to controul the conduct of Her Neighbours—

That the Means of securing the Welfare of the Community must be coextensive with the Objects to which the Legislature extends its Views I think must be admitted—If the Property & personal Service of the Individuals is necessary, under any given Circumstance, to Secure the Republic it is certain there must somewhere be lodged a Power to call them forth; as the Cases which may occur are so various, humane foresight so limited, and the Occasions may probably be so pressing as not to admit a Consultation of the People, it must be exercised at Discretion limited in the best manner we can to prevent abuse—to say the U.S. may have the Impost & Nothing more is not granting the Means of Protection, in the probable Cases which may occur; to devolve on them a Duty to protect & secure the States and deny them the Means is an Absurdity—I think we involve ourselves in unnecessary Doubts about our Security against an undue Use of the Powers granted by the Constitution by not clearly distinguishing between our present Condition and that of the People of G. Britain; there the Supreme executive is hereditary, he does not derive his powers from the Gift of the People; at least, if the contrary is true in *Theory* its practical Operation is not such; he there holds as his prerogative the Power of raising &

disbanding Armies, the Right to make War & Peace with many other very great & important Rights independant of any Controul; that the Armies are *his Armies*, and their Direction is solely by him without any Controul—the only Security the people there have, against the Ambition of a bad King is the power to deny Money, without which no Army can be kept up—here the Army when raisd is the Army of the People, it is they who raise & pay them it is they who judge of the Necessity of the Measure, tis they who are to feel the Burthens & partake the Benefits—to deny them the Power by their Representatives to raise Armies when they judge it necessary; to deny them the Right to command so much property as shall be necessary for all the Exigencies of the States is to require of them the Discharge of Duties they are totally unable to fulfil——

I think we are safe in the Exercise of those Powers by Congress; especially when Experience Shews us that a Body of Men raisd by the Legislature never did Set up the Legislative Authority as the Supreme Head independant of the People, but whenever any evil Effects have followed, it has been by Setting up an Individual in utter Extinction of the Legislative—it is therefore *our* Army and *our* Purse & not the Sword or purse of a King——

—if a Constitution is not to be establishd unless it is impossible to abuse the Powers given to the Destruction of the Community, I will venture to assert that *no* Government can ever be established—for the Delegation of Powers is necessary to the Being of Society, and it is impossible so to guard them that they may not be abused for a Time—an Assembly of a State, the Officers of a County or Town or of any smaller Community may betray the Confidence repos'd in them; and it is impossible to grant such powers as are necessary to do Us good without granting such as *may* do Us evil; our Security must rest in our frequently recurring back to the People the fountain of all power by our Elections—the contrary Opinion appears to involve a Suspicion that a Man becomes a Villain the Moment he is intrusted with power—if this so, in the Extent the Objection Supposes, it concludes against the propriety of establishing any Government in any possible Case——

—but it is said the Representation is too small, this is Matter of Opinion, on which Men will differ; if we look forward half a Century we shall probably see a Representation as large as will be found necessary or Convenient; and when we find so great a Difficulty in keeping up that Number under the present Confederation, it is not likely we shall think the propos'd Numbers too few, at present——

it is also objected that by Law Congress may alter the *Time, place,* & *Manner* of choosing Representatives and they may so abuse this Power as to destroy the free Election of the States—it appears to me proper that Congress should determine the *Time*, our Different Legislatures have on this Subject gone into different Practices, it is necessary all Elections should be in Season to attend the fœderal Legislature and expedient, at least, they should be in One Day throughout the Union this can only be done by the national Authority—it may be so that the present Places of holding Elections will be impossible for the Electors to be convened at; witness S. Carolina & Georgia in the late War, and even after this Constitution shall be ratified, it may happen that some one of the States in the Union may neglect or refuse to make any Law by which the Electors may be conven'd, a Variety of other Cases may occur in which it will be proper for Congress by their Acts to enable the Electors to exercise their undoubted Privileges—and when our own Experience has so often convincd Us of the Necessity of frequent Changes in the Manner of Elections to prevent Corruption, who can wish the Manner to be unalterably fixed?—the Qualifications of Electors is exclusively with the States and there it ought forever to rest.

As to the Executive Powers some appear to apprehend Danger, but when the President is created by the People, when he so often falls back to the State of a private Citizen, when he no possibility of gaining greater Emoluments during his Continuance in Office, & when there is Nothing of any great Importance in his Power *Solely* I think no Man of considerable Discernment can have fears from this Quarter unless he has also very weak Nerves——

The Judicial Powers, at first View, seemed to me the most exceptionable—but I believe it will always be admitted that the Judicial Powers of every State must be coextensive with

the Legislative—And I cannot find that the legislative powers
propos'd in this Constitution are extended to any Objects in
which the Nation are not immediately or mediately con-
cernd— the general Laws of Bankruptcy appear to be necessary both for Creditors & Debtors, and it appears reasonable
when conform'd to in One State they should be effectual to
secure the Debtor throughout the Union; those Acts may &
often do affect the Rights of Citizens of different States, to
guard which the Powers of particular States do not extend, it
is therefore proper that those should be regulated by some
Authority extending over all—the same apply in cases of
Captures & a variety of other Cases—perhaps, however, it
may be questioned whither an Appeal will lie from a *State
Court* to the *Supreme Fœderal Court* or from the inferior Fœderal Court only— if that is the Case the Jurisdiction is concurrent & in the Election of the Plaintiff to which he will
apply—if the Right is proper to be granted the guards
against abuse must be by Laws to regulate the Exercise of the
right—

Trial by Jury is said to be taken away—no such Inference
can be drawn from the Constitution—All civil were never
tried by Jury in this Country or in G.B. Admiralty Causes,
ecclesiastical, & Chancery Cases are of that Number; the
Mode of Ascertaining the Fact will be pointed out by Law,
and we cannot suppose Congress to divest themselves of all
good Sense as well as honesty so as to adopt Measures totally
repugnant to the Habits & feelings of the people as the Objection supposes—It appears to me that few Men will at this
time of Day reject the Idea of Coercion as necessary to a good
Government—the existence of those Principles of pure Virtue in the Members of the Community which are necessary
on the Ground of the Objectors, is not at this Time generally
believed— and the Want of it is the principal if not the only
Reason, why Government is necessary; this is a powerful Motive to induce Men to consent to be governed, but this consent would be of little avail unless, a Coercive Power to
compel Obedience was not also granted, and I think it must
appear much more eligible to carry home the punishment of
the Offence to the Person of the Transgressor by legal Decrees, than to exercise the power of the Sword against States

& Communities & involve the Innocent & guilty in one indiscriminate Scene of Distress—but this System tis said will
destroy the States Sovereignty or reduce Us to the necessity
of adopting the Absurd Position of *Imperium in Imperio*. I
admit it will & ought to *limit* the exercise of Sovereign Authority in the States & restrain it to fewer Objects—this must
be necessary if a Supreme Authority the last resort in any
matters—And the absurdity of Imperium in Imperio never
existed but where both Powers were coextensive in their
Objects.—A Town, City or County to some purposes have
complete legislative Powers, yet no Man supposes a State cannot exist under those Circumstances—A Congress have made
Laws to govern their Armies, but did we ever find any evil
Consequence flowing from it to weaken the Powers of civil
Government?

— In the new Constitution All Contracts are left as they
were in the old—this appears to me proper as we cannot if
we were desirous destroy all the Debt of the U.S. we have
other Powers to consult on this Subject—nor would it have
been well to have any new Ingagements on the Subject—the
Want of Power to establish religious Tests is a grievance in the
Minds of some; in addition to the very many & conclusive
Arguments against religious Tests—I am fully convincd of the
Expediency of incerting the exclusive Clause lest in future
Time by Construction such Right may be supposd to exist,
and under the Influence of the enthusiasm which has impeld
Men to the greatest Absurdities, we may in future *hang
Witches* or establish such Tests as would disgrace humane Nature— But what will become of the States who refuse their
Assent & are in the present Confederation? I answer we have
all broken that Covenant & it is now prostrate in the Dust &
no State can charge another with breaking these Covenants as
they have by common Consent dissolvd it—I have to apologize for troubling you; but can any the least Benefit be derivd
by new Arguments or old Ones plac'd in different Lights I
have a consciousness you will pardon me

"Publius," The Federalist XXXVII
[James Madison]

Daily Advertiser (New York), January 11, 1788

To the People of the State of New-York.

In reviewing the defects of the existing Confederation, and shewing that they cannot be supplied by a Government of less energy than that before the public, several of the most important principles of the latter fell of course under consideration. But as the ultimate object of these papers is to determine clearly and fully the merits of this Constitution, and the expediency of adopting it, our plan cannot be compleated without taking a more critical and thorough survey of the work of the Convention; without examining it on all its sides; comparing it in all its parts, and calculating its probable effects. That this remaining task may be executed under impressions conducive to a just and fair result, some reflections must in this place be indulged, which candor previously suggests. It is a misfortune, inseparable from human affairs, that public measures are rarely investigated with that spirit of moderation which is essential to a just estimate of their real tendency to advance or obstruct the public good; and that this spirit is more apt to be diminished than prompted, by those occasions which require an unusual exercise of it.—To those who have been led by experience to attend to this consideration, it could not appear surprising, that the act of the Convention which recommends so many important changes and innovations, which may be viewed in so many lights and relations, and which touches the springs of so many passions and interests, should find or excite dispositions unfriendly both on one side, and on the other, to a fair discussion and accurate judgment of its merits. In some, it has been too evident from their own publications, that they have scanned the proposed Constitution, not only with a predisposition to censure; but with a predetermination to condemn; as the language held by others betrays an opposite predetermination or bias, which must render their opinions also of little moment in the question. In placing however, these different characters on a level, with respect to the weight of their opinions, I wish not to insinuate that there may not be a material difference in the purity of their intentions. It is but just to remark in favor of the latter description, that as our situation is universally admitted to be peculiarly critical, and to require indispensibly, that something should be done for our relief, the predetermined patron of what has been actually done, may have taken his bias from the weight of these considerations, as well as from considerations of a sinister nature. The predetermined adversary on the other hand, can have been governed by no venial motive whatever. The intentions of the first may be upright, as they may on the contrary be culpable. The views of the last cannot be upright, and must be culpable. But the truth is, that these papers are not addressed to persons falling under either of these characters. They solicit the attention of those only, who add to a sincere zeal for the happiness of their country, a temper favorable to a just estimate of the means of promoting it.

Persons of this character will proceed to an examination of the plan submitted by the Convention, not only without a disposition to find or to magnify faults; but will see the propriety of reflecting that a faultless plan was not to be expected. Nor will they barely make allowances for the errors which may be chargeable on the fallibility to which the Convention, as a body of men, were liable; but will keep in mind that they themselves also are but men, and ought not to assume an infallibility in rejudging the fallible opinions of others.

With equal readiness will it be perceived, that besides these inducements to candor, many allowances ought to be made for the difficulties inherent in the very nature of the undertaking referred to the Convention.

The novelty of the undertaking immediately strikes us. It has been shewn in the course of these papers, that the existing Confederation is founded on principles which are fallacious; that we must consequently change this first foundation, and with it, the superstructure resting upon it. It has been shewn,

that the other confederacies which could be consulted as precedents, have been viciated by the same erroneous principles,
and can therefore furnish no other light than that of beacons,
which give warning of the course to be shunned, without
pointing out that which ought to be pursued. The most that
the Convention could do in such a situation, was to avoid the
errors suggested by the past experience of other countries, as
well as of our own; and to provide a convenient mode of
rectifying their own errors, as future experience may unfold
them.

Among the difficulties encountered by the Convention, a
very important one must have lain, in combining the requisite
stability and energy in Government, with the inviolable attention due to liberty, and to the Republican form. Without substantially accomplishing this part of their undertaking, they
would have very imperfectly fulfilled the object of their
appointment, or the expectation of the public: — Yet, that it
could not be easily accomplished, will be denied by no one,
who is unwilling to betray his ignorance of the subject.
Energy in Government is essential to that security against
external and internal danger, and to that prompt and salutary
execution of the laws, which enter into the very definition of
good Government. Stability in Government, is essential to national character, and to the advantages annexed to it, as well
as to that repose and confidence in the minds of the people,
which are among the chief blessings of civil society. An irregular and mutable legislation, is not more an evil in itself, than
it is odious to the people; and it may be pronounced with
assurance, that the people of this country, enlightened as they
are, with regard to the nature, and interested, as the great
body of them are, in the effects of good Government, will
never be satisfied, till some remedy be applied to the vicissitudes and uncertainties, which characterize the State administrations. On comparing, however, these valuable ingredients
with the vital principles of liberty, we must perceive at once,
the difficulty of mingling them together in their due proportions. The genius of Republican liberty, seems to demand on
one side, not only, that all power should be derived from the
people; but, that those entrusted with it should be kept in
dependence on the people, by a short duration of their

appointments; and, that, even during this short period, the trust should be placed not in a few, but in a number of hands. Stability, on the contrary, requires, that the hands, in which power is lodged, should continue for a length of time, the same. A frequent change of men will result from a frequent return of elections, and a frequent change of measures, from a frequent change of men: whilst energy in Government requires not only a certain duration of power, but the execution of it by a single hand. How far the Convention may have succeeded in this part of their work, will better appear on a more accurate view of it. From the cursory view, here taken, it must clearly appear to have been an arduous part.

Not less arduous must have been the task of marking the proper line of partition, between the authority of the general, and that of the State Governments. Every man will be sensible of this difficulty in proportion as he has been accustomed to contemplate and discriminate objects, extensive and complicated in their nature. The faculties of the mind itself have never yet been distinguished and defined, with satisfactory precision, by all the efforts of the most acute and metaphysical Philosophers. Sense, perception, judgment, desire, volition, memory, imagination, are found to be separated by such delicate shades, and minute gradations, that their boundaries have eluded the most subtle investigations, and remain a pregnant source of ingenious disquisition and controversy. The boundaries between the great kingdoms of nature, and still more, between the various provinces, and lesser portions, into which they are subdivided, afford another illustration of the same important truth. The most sagacious and laborious naturalists have never yet succeeded, in tracing with certainty, the line which separates the district of vegetable life from the neighboring region of unorganized matter, or which marks the termination of the former and the commencement of the animal empire. A still greater obscurity lies in the distinctive characters, by which the objects in each of these great departments of nature, have been arranged and assorted. When we pass from the works of nature, in which all the delineations are perfectly accurate, and appear to be otherwise only from the imperfection of the eye which surveys them, to the institutions of man, in which the obscurity arises as well from the object itself, as from the organ by which it is contemplated; we must perceive the necessity of moderating still farther our expectations and hopes from the efforts of human sagacity. Experience has instructed us that no skill in the science of Government has yet been able to discriminate and define, with sufficient certainty, its three great provinces, the Legislative, Executive and Judiciary; or even the privileges and powers of the different Legislative branches. Questions daily occur in the course of practice, which prove the obscurity which reigns in these subjects, and which puzzle the greatest adepts in political science. The experience of ages, with the continued and combined labors of the most enlightened Legislators and jurists, have been equally unsuccessful in delineating the several objects and limits of different codes of laws and different tribunals of justice. The precise extent of the common law, the statute law, the maritime law, the ecclesiastical law, the law of corporations and other local laws and customs, remain still to be clearly and finally established in Great-Britain, where accuracy in such subjects has been more industriously pursued than in any other part of the world. The jurisdiction of her several courts, general and local, of law, of equity, of admiralty, &c. is not less a source of frequent and intricate discussions, sufficiently denoting the indeterminate limits by which they are respectively circumscribed. All new laws, though penned with the greatest technical skill, and passed on the fullest and most mature deliberation, are considered as more or less obscure and equivocal, until their meaning be liquidated and ascertained by a series of particular discussions and adjudications. Besides the obscurity arising from the complexity of objects, and the imperfection of the human faculties, the medium through which the conceptions of men are conveyed to each other, adds a fresh embarrassment. The use of words is to express ideas. Perspicuity therefore requires not only that the ideas should be distinctly formed, but that they should be expressed by words distinctly and exclusively appropriated to them. But no language is so copious as to supply words and phrases for every complex idea, or so correct as not to include many equivocally denoting different ideas. Hence it must happen, that however accurately objects may be discriminated in themselves, and however accurately the discrimination may be considered, the definition of them may be rendered inaccurate by the inaccuracy of the terms in which it is delivered. And this unavoidable inaccuracy must be greater or less, according to the complexity and novelty of the objects defined. When the Almighty himself condescends to address mankind in their own language, his meaning, luminous as it must be, is rendered dim and doubtful, by the cloudy medium through which it is communicated. Here then are three sources of vague and incorrect definitions; indistinctness of the object, imperfection of the organ of conception, inadequateness of the vehicle of ideas. Any one of these must produce a certain degree of obscurity. The Convention, in delineating the boundary between the Federal and State jurisdictions, must have experienced the full effect of them all.

To the difficulties already mentioned, may be added the interfering pretensions of the larger and smaller States. We cannot err in supposing that the former would contend for a participation in the Government, fully proportioned to their superior wealth and importance; and that the latter would not be less tenacious of the equality at present enjoyed by them. We may well suppose that neither side would entirely yield to the other, and consequently that the struggle could be terminated only by compromise. It is extremely probable also, that after the ratio of representation had been adjusted, this very compromise must have produced a fresh struggle between the same parties, to give such a turn to the organization of the Government, and to the distribution of its powers, as would encrease the importance of the branches, in forming which they had respectively obtained the greatest share of influence. There are features in the Constitution which warrant each of these suppositions; and as far as either of them is well founded, it shews that the Convention must have been compelled to sacrifice theoretical propriety to the force of extraneous considerations.

Nor could it have been the large and small States only which would marshal themselves in opposition to each other on various points. Other combinations, resulting from a difference of local position and policy, must have created additional difficulties. As every State may be divided into different districts, and its citizens into different classes, which give birth to contending interests and local jealousies; so the different parts of the United States are distinguished from each other, by a variety of circumstances, which produce a like effect on a larger scale. And although this variety of interests, for reasons sufficiently explained in a former paper, may have a salutary influence on the administration of the Government when formed; yet every one must be sensible of the contrary influence which must have been experienced in the task of forming it.

Would it be wonderful if under the pressure of all these difficulties, the Convention should have been forced into some deviations from that artificial structure and regular symmetry, which an abstract view of the subject might lead an ingenious theorist to bestow on a Constitution planned in his closet or in his imagination? The real wonder is, that so many difficulties should have been surmounted; and surmounted with a unanimity almost as unprecedented as it must have been unexpected. It is impossible for any man of candor to reflect on this circumstance, without partaking of the astonishment. It is impossible for the man of pious reflection not to perceive in it, a finger of that Almighty hand which has been so frequently and signally extended to our relief in the critical stages of the revolution. We had occasion in a former paper, to take notice of the repeated trials which have been unsuccessfully made in the United Netherlands, for reforming the baneful and notorious vices of their Constitution. The history of almost all the great councils and consultations, held among mankind for reconciling their discordant opinions, assuaging their mutual jealousies, and adjusting their respective interests, is a history of factions, contentions, and disappointments; and may be classed among the most dark and degrading pictures which display the infirmities and depravities of the human character. If, in a few scattered instances, a brighter aspect is presented, they serve only as exceptions to admonish us of the general truth; and by their lustre to darken the gloom of the adverse prospect to which they are contrasted. In revolving the causes from which these exceptions result, and applying them to the particular instance before us, we are necessarily led to two important conclusions. The first is, that the Convention must have enjoyed in a very singular degree, an exemption from the pestilential influence of party animosities; the diseases most incident to deliberative bodies, and most apt to contaminate their proceedings. The second conclusion is, that all the deputations composing the Convention, were either satisfactorily accommodated by the final act; or were induced to accede to it, by a deep conviction of the necessity of sacrificing private opinions and partial interests to the public good, and by a despair of seeing this necessity diminished by delays or by new experiments.

"Agrippa" [*James Winthrop*] *XII*

Massachusetts Gazette (Boston), January 11, 15, 18, 1788

To the MASSACHUSETTS CONVENTION.

GENTLEMEN,

Suffer an individual to lay before you his contemplations on the great subject that now engages your attention. To you it belongs, and may Heaven direct your judgment, to decide on the happiness of all future generations as well as the present.

It is universally agreed, that the object of every just government is to render the people happy, by securing their persons and possessions from wrong. To this end it is necessary that there should be local laws and institutions; for a people inhabiting various climates will unavoidably have local habits and different modes of life, and these must be consulted in making the laws. It is much easier to adapt the laws to the manners of the people, than to make manners conform to laws. The idle and dissolute inhabitants of the south, require a different regimen from the sober and active people of the north. Hence, among other reasons, is derived the necessity of local governments, who may enact, repeal, or alter regulations as the circumstances of each part of the empire may require. This would be the case, even if a very great state was to be settled at once. But it becomes still more needful, when the local manners are formed, and usages sanctified by the practice of a century and an half. In such a case, to attempt to reduce all to one standard, is absurd in itself, and cannot be done but upon the principle of power, which debases the people, and renders them unhappy, till all dignity of character is put away. Many circumstances render us an essentially different people from the inhabitants of the southern states. The unequal distribution of property, the toleration of slavery, the ignorance and poverty of the lower classes, the softness of the climate, and dissoluteness of manners, mark their character.

Among us, the care that is taken of education, small and nearly equal estates, equality of rights, and the severity of the climate, renders the people active, industrious and sober. Attention to religion and good morals is a distinguishing trait in our character. It is plain, therefore, that we require for our regulation laws, which will not suit the circumstances of our southern brethren, and the laws made for them would not apply to us. Unhappiness would be the uniform product of such laws; for no state can be happy, when the laws contradict the general habits of the people, nor can any state retain its freedom, while there is a power to make and enforce such laws. We may go further, and say, that it is impossible for any single legislature so fully to comprehend the circumstances of the different parts of a very extensive dominion, as to make laws adapted to those circumstances. Hence arises in most nations of extensive territory, the necessity of armies, to cure the defect of the laws. It is actually under the pressure of such an absurd government, that the Spanish provinces have groaned for near three centuries; and such will be our misfortune and degradation, if we ever submit to have all the business of the empire done by one legislature. The contrary principle of local legislation by the representatives of the people, who alone are to be governed by the laws, has raised us to our present greatness; and an attempt on the part of Great-Britain, to invade this right, brought on the revolution, which gave us a separate rank among the nations. We even declared, that we would not be represented in the national legislature, because one assembly was not adequate to the purposes of internal legislation and taxation.

[*Remainder next Tuesday.*]

(*Concluded from our last.*)

To the MASSACHUSETTS CONVENTION.

GENTLEMEN,

The question then arises, what is the kind of government best adapted to the object of securing our persons and possessions from violence? I answer, a FEDERAL REPUBLICK. By this kind of government each state reserves to itself the right of making and altering its laws for internal regulation, and the right of executing those laws without any external restraint, while the general concerns of the empire are committed to an assembly of delegates, each accountable to his own constituents. This is the happy form under which we live, and which seems to mark us out as a people chosen of God. No instance can be produced of any other kind of government so stable and energetick as the republican. The objection drawn from the Greek and Roman states does not apply to the question. Republicanism appears there in its most disadvantageous form. Arts and domestick employments were generally committed to slaves, while war was almost the only business worthy of a citizen. Hence arose their internal dissensions. Still they exhibited proofs of legislative wisdom and judicial integrity hardly to be found among their monarchick neighbours. On the other hand we find Carthage cultivating commerce, and extending her dominions for the long space of seven centuries, during which term the internal tranquillity was never disturbed by her citizens. Her national power was so respectable, that for a long time it was doubtful whether Carthage or Rome should rule. In the form of their government they bore a strong resemblance to each other. Rome might be reckoned a free state for about four hundred and fifty years. We have then the true line of distinction between those two nations, and a strong proof of the hardy materials which compose a republican government. If there was no other proofs, we might with impartial judges risk the issue upon this alone. But our proof rests not here. The present state of Europe, and the vigour and tranquillity of our own governments, after experiencing this form for a century and an half, are decided proofs in favour of those governments which encourage commerce. A comparison of our own country, first with Europe and then with the other parts of the world, will prove, beyond a doubt, that the greatest share of freedom is enjoyed by the citizens, so much more does commerce flourish. The reason is, that every citizen has an influence in making the laws, and thus they are conformed to the general interests of the state; but in every other kind of government they are frequently made in favour of a part of the community at the expense of the rest.

The argument against republicks, as it is derived from the Greek and Roman states, is unfair. It goes on the idea that no other government is subject to be disturbed. As well might we conclude, that a limited monarchy is unstable, because, that under the feudal system, the nobles frequently made war upon their king, and disturbed the publick peace. We find, however, in practice, that limited monarchy is more friendly to commerce, because more friendly to the rights of the subject, than an absolute government; and that it is more liable to be disturbed than a republick, because less friendly to trade and the rights of individuals. There cannot, from the history of mankind, be produced an instance of rapid growth in extent, in numbers, in arts, and in trade, that will bear any comparison with our country. This is owing to what the friends of the new system, and the enemies of the revolution, for I take them to be nearly the same, would term *our extreme liberty*. Already, have our ships visited every part of the world, and brought us their commodities in greater perfection, and at a more moderate price, than we ever before experienced. The ships of other nations croud to our ports, seeking an intercourse with us. All the estimates of every party make the balance of trade for the present year to be largely in our favour. Already have some very useful, and some elegant manufactures got established among us, so that our country every day is becoming independent in her resources. Two thirds of the continental debt has been paid since the war, and we are in alliance with some of the most respectable powers of Europe. The western lands, won from Britain by the sword, are an ample fund for the principal of all our publick debts; and every new sale excites that manly pride, which is essential to national virtue. All this happiness arises from the freedom of our institutions and the limitted nature of our government; a government that is respected from principles of affection, and obeyed with alacrity. The sovereigns of the old world are frequently, though surrounded with armies, treated with insult; and the despotick monarchies of the east, are the most fluctuating, oppressive and uncertain governments of any form hitherto invented. These considerations are sufficient to establish the excellence of our own form, and the goodness of our prospects.

Let us now consider the probable effects of a consolidation of the separate states into one mass; for the new system extends so far. Many ingenious explanations have been given of it; but there is this defect, that they are drawn from maxims of the common law, while the system itself cannot be bound by any such maxims. A legislative assembly has an inherent right to alter the common law, and to abolish any of its principles, which are not particularly guarded in the constitution. Any system therefore which appoints a legislature, without any reservation of the rights of individuals, surrenders all power in every branch of legislation to the government. The universal practise of every government proves the justness of this remark; for in every doubtful case it is an established rule to decide in favour of authority. The new system is, therefore, in one respect at least, essentially inferiour to our state constitutions. There is no bill of rights, and consequently a continental law may controul any of those principles, which we consider at present as sacred; while not one of those points, in which it is said that the separate governments misapply their power, is guarded. Tender acts and the coinage of money stand on the same footing of a consolidation of power. It is a mere fallacy, invented by the deceptive powers of mr. Wilson, that what rights are not given are reserved. The contrary has already been shewn. But to put this matter of legislation out of all doubt, let us compare together some parts of the book; for being an independent system this is the only way to ascertain its meaning.

In article III. section 2, it is declared, that "the judicial power shall extend to all cases in law and equity arising under this constitution, the laws of the United States, and treaties made or which shall be made under their authority." Among the cases arising under this new constitution are reckoned, "all controversies between citizens of different states," which include all kinds of civil causes between those parties. The giving Congress a power to appoint courts for such a purpose is as much, there being no stipulation to the contrary, giving them power to legislate for such causes, as giving them a right to raise an army, is giving them a right to direct the operations of the army when raised. But it is not left to implication. The last clause of article I. section 8, expressly gives them power "to make all laws which shall be needful and proper for carrying into execution the foregoing powers, and all other powers vested by this constitution in the government of the United States, or in any department or officer thereof." It is, therefore, as plain as words can make it, that they have a right by this proposed form to legislate for all kinds of causes respecting property between citizens of different states. That this power extends to all cases between citizens of the same state, is evident, from the sixth article, which declares all continental laws and treaties to be the *supreme law* of the land, and that all state judges are bound thereby, *"any thing in the constitution or laws of any state to the contrary notwithstanding."* If this is not binding the judges of the separate states in their own office, by continental rules, it is perfect nonsense. There is then a complete consolidation of the legislative powers in all cases respecting property. This power extends to all cases between a state and citizens of another state. Hence a citizen, possessed of the notes of another state, may bring his action, and there is no limitation that the execution shall be levied on the publick property of the state, but the property of individuals is liable. This is a foundation for endless confusion and discord. This, right to try causes between a state and citizens of another state, involves in it all criminal causes; and a man who has accidentally transgressed the laws of another state, must be transported, with all his witnesses, to a third state, to be tried. He must be ruined to prove his innocence. These are necessary parts of the new system, and it will never be complete till they are reduced to practice. They effectually prove a consolidation of the states, and we have before shewn the ruinous tendency of such a measure.

By sect. 8, of article I. Congress are to have the unlimitted right to regulate commerce, external and *internal*, and may therefore create monopolies which have been universally injurious to all the subjects of the countries that have adopted them, excepting the monopolists themselves. They have also the unlimited right to imposts and all kinds of taxes, as well to levy as to collect them. They have indeed very nearly the same powers claimed formerly by the British parliament. Can we have so soon forgot our glorious struggle with that power, as to think a moment of surrendering it now? It makes no difference in principle whether the national assembly was elected for seven years or for six. In both cases we should vote to great disadvantage, and therefore ought never to agree to such an article. Let us make provision for the payment of the interest of our part of the debt, and we shall be fairly acquitted. Let the fund be an impost on our foreign trade, and we shall encourage our manufactures. But if we surrender the unlimitted right to regulate trade and levy taxes, imposts will oppress our foreign trade for the benefit of other states, while excises and taxes will discourage our internal industry. The right to regulate trade, without any limitations, will, as certainly as it is granted, transfer the trade of this state to Pennsylvania. That will be the seat of business and of wealth, while the extremes of the empire will, like Ireland and Scotland, be drained to fatten an overgrown capital. Under our present equal advantages, the citizens of this state come in for their full share of commercial profits. Surrender the rights of taxation and commercial regulation, and the landed states at the southward will all be interested in draining our resources; for whatever can be got by impost on our trade and excises on our manufactures, will be considered as so much saved to a state inhabited by planters. All savings of this sort ought surely to be made in favour of our own state; and we ought never to surrender the unlimitted powers of revenue and trade to uncommercial people. If we do, the glory of the state from that moment departs, never to return.

The safety of our constitutional rights consists in having the business of government lodged in different departments, and in having each part well defined. By this means each branch is kept within the constitutional limits. Never was a fairer line of distinction than what may be easily drawn between the continental and state governments. The latter provide for all cases, whether civil or criminal, that can happen ashore, because all such causes must arise within the limits of some state. Transactions between citizens may all be fairly included in this idea, even although they should arise in passing by water from one state to another. But the intercourse between us and foreign nations, properly forms the department of Congress. They should have the power of regulating trade under such limitations as should render their laws equal. They should have the right of war and peace, saving the equality of rights, and the territory of each state. But the power of naturalization and internal regulation should not be given them. To give my scheme a more systematick appearance, I have thrown it into the form of a resolve, which is submitted to your wisdom for amendment, but not as being perfect.

"Resolved, that the form of government proposed by the federal convention, lately held in Philadelphia, be rejected on the part of this commonwealth; and that our delegates in Congress are hereby authorised to propose on the part of this commonwealth, and, if the other states for themselves agree thereto, to sign an article of confederation, as an addition to the present articles, in the form following, provided such agreement be made on or before the first day of January, which will be in the year of our Lord 1790; the said article shall have the same force and effect as if it had been inserted in the original confederation, and is to be construed consistently with the clause in the former articles, which restrains the United States from exercising such powers as are not expressly given.

"XIV. The United States shall have power to regulate, whether by treaty, ordinance, or law, the intercourse between these states and foreign dominions and countries, under the following restrictions. No treaty, ordinance, or law shall give a preference to the ports of one state over those of another; nor 2d. impair the territory or internal authority of any state; nor 3d. create any monopolies or exclusive companies; nor 4th. naturalise any foreigners. All their imposts and prohibitions shall be confined to foreign produce and manufactures imported, and to foreign ships trading in our harbours. All imposts and confiscations shall be to the use of the state where they shall accrue, excepting only such branches of impost, as shall be assigned by the separate states to Congress for a fund to defray the interest of their debt, and their current charges. In order the more effectually to execute this and the former articles, Congress shall have authority to appoint courts, supreme & subordinate, with power to try all crimes, not relating to state securities, between any foreign state, or subject of such state, actually residing in a foreign country, and not being an absentee or person who has alienated himself from these states on the one part, and any of the United States or citizens thereof on the other part; also all causes in which foreign ambassadours or other foreign ministers resident here shall be immediately concerned, respecting the jurisdiction or immunities only. And the Congress shall have authority to execute the judgment of such courts by their own affairs. Piracies and felonies committed on the high seas shall also belong to the department of Congress for them to define, try, and punish, in the same manner as the other causes shall be defined, tried, and determined. All the before mentioned causes shall be tried by jury, and in some sea-port town. And it is recommended to the general court at their next meeting to provide and put Congress in possession of funds arising from foreign imports and ships sufficient to defray our share of the present annual expenses of the continent."

Such a resolve explicitly limitting the powers granted is the farthest we can proceed with safety. The scheme of accepting the report of the Convention, and amending it afterwards, is merely delusive. There is no intention among those who make the proposition to amend it at all. Besides, if they have influence enough to get it accepted in its present form, there is no probability, that they will consent to an alteration when possessed of an unlimited revenue. It is an excellence in our present confederation, that it is extremely difficult to alter it. An unanimous vote of the states is required. But this newly proposed form is founded in injustice, as it proposes that a fictitious consent of only nine states shall be sufficient to establish it. Nobody can suppose that the consent of a state is any thing more than a fiction, in the view of the federalists, after the mobbish influence used over the Pennsylvania convention. The two great leaders of the plan, with a modesty of Scotsmen, placed a rabble in the gallery to applaud their speeches, and thus supplied their want of capacity in the argument. Repeatedly were Wilson and M'Kean worsted in the argument by the plain good sense of Findly and Smilie. But reasoning or knowledge had little to do with the federal party. Votes were all they wanted by whatever means obtained. Means not less criminal have been mentioned among us. But votes that are bought can never justify a treasonable conspiracy. Better, far better, would it be to reject the whole, and remain in possession of present advantages. The authority of Congress to decide disputes between states is sufficient to prevent their recurring to hostility: and their different situation, wants and produce is a sufficient foundation for the most friendly intercourse. All the arts of delusion and legal chicanery will be used to elude your vigilance, and obtain a majority. But keeping the constitution of the state, and the publick interest in view, will be your safety.

[*We are obliged, contrary to our intention, to postpone the remainder of Agrippa till our next.*]

(*Concluded from our last.*)

To the MASSACHUSETTS CONVENTION.

GENTLEMEN,

To tell us that we ought to look beyond local interests, and judge for the good of the empire, is sapping the foundation of a free state. The first principle of a just government is, that it shall operate equally. The report of the convention is extremely unequal. It takes a larger share of power from some, and from others, a larger share of wealth. The Massachusetts will be obliged to pay near three times their present proportion towards continental charges. The proportion is now ascertained by the quantity of landed property, then it will be by the number of persons. After taking the whole of our standing revenue, by impost and excise, we must still be held to pay a sixth part of the remaining debt. It is evidently a contrivance to help the other states at our expense. Let us then be upon our guard, and do no more than the present confederation obliges. While we make that our beacon we are safe. It was framed by men of extensive knowledge and enlarged ability, at a time when some of the framers of the new plan were hiding in the forests to secure their precious persons. It was framed by men, who were always in favour of a limitted government, and whose endeavours Heaven has crowned with success. It was framed by men, whose idols were not power and high life, but industry and constitutional liberty, and who are now in opposition to this new scheme of oppression. Let us then cherish the old confederation like the apple of our eye. Let us confirm it by such limitted powers to Congress, and such an enlarged intercourse, founded on commerce and mutual want, with the other states, that our union shall outlast time itself. It is easier to prevent an evil than to cure it. We ought therefore to be cautious of innovations. The intrigues of interested politicians will be used to seduce even the elect. If the vote passes in favour of the plan, the constitutional liberty of our country is gone forever. If the plan should be rejected, we always have it in our power, by a fair vote of the people at large, to extend the authority of Congress. This ought to have been the mode pursued. But our antagonists were afraid to risk it. They knew that the plan would not bear examining. Hence we have seen them insulting all who were in opposition to it, and answering arguments only with abuse. They have threatened and they have insulted the body of the people. But I may venture to appeal to any man of unbiassed judgment, whether his feelings tell him, that there is any danger at all in rejecting the plan. I ask not the palsied or the jaundiced, nor men troubled with bilious or nervous affections, for they can see danger in every thing. But I apply to men who have no personal expectations from a change, and to men in full health. The answer of all such men will be, that never was a better time for deliberation. Let us then, while we have it in our power, secure the happiness and freedom of the present and future ages. To accept of the report of the convention, under the idea that we can alter it when we please, will be sporting with fire-brands arrows and death. It is a system which must have an army to support it, and there can be no redress but by a civil war. If, as the federalists say, there is a necessity of our receiving it, for heaven's sake let our liberties go without our making a formal surrender. Let us at least have the satisfaction of protesting against it, that our own hearts may not reproach us for the meanness of deserting our dearest interests.

Our present system is attended with the inestimable advantage of preventing unnecessary wars. Foreign influence is assuredly smaller in our publick councils, in proportion as the members are subject to be recalled. At present, their right to sit continues no longer than their endeavours to secure the publick interest. It is therefore not an object for any foreign power to give a large price for the friendship of a delegate in Congress. If we adopt the new system, every member will depend upon thirty thousand people, mostly scattered over a large extent of country, for his election. Their distance from the seat of government will make it extremely difficult for the electors to get information of his conduct. If he is faithful to his constituents, his conduct will be misrepresented, in order to defeat his influence at home. Of this we have a recent instance, in the treatment of the dissenting members of the late federal convention. Their fidelity to their constituents was their whole fault. We may reasonably expect similar conduct to be adopted, when we shall have rendered the friendship of the members valuable to foreign powers, by giving them a secure seat in Congress. We shall too have all the intrigues, cabals and bribery practised, which are usual at elections in Great-Britain. We shall see and lament the want of publick virtue; and we shall see ourselves bought at a publick market, in order to be sold again to the highest bidder. We must be involved in all the quarrels of European powers, and oppressed with expense, merely for the sake of being like the nations round about us. Let us then, with the spirit of freemen, reject the offered system, and treat as it deserves the proposition of men who have departed from their commission; and let us deliver to the rising generation the liberty purchased with our blood.

"Publius," The Federalist XXXVIII
[James Madison]

Independent Journal (New York), January 12, 1788

To the People of the State of New-York.

It is not a little remarkable that in every case reported by antient history, in which government has been established with deliberation and consent, the task of framing it has not been committed to an assembly of men; but has been performed by some individual citizen of pre-eminent wisdom and approved integrity. Minos, we learn, was the primitive founder of the government of Crete; as Zaleucus was of that of the Locrians. Theseus first, and after him Draco and Solon, instituted the government of Athens. Lycurgus was the Lawgiver of Sparta. The foundation of the original government of Rome was laid by Romulus; and the work compleated by two of his elective successors, Numa, and Tullus Hostilius. On the abolition of Royalty, the Consular administration was substituted by Brutus, who stepped forward with a project for such a reform, which he alledged had been prepared by Tullus Hostilius, and to which his address obtained the assent and ratification of the Senate and people. This remark is applicable to confederate governments also. Amphyction, we are told, was the author of that which bore his name. The Achæan League received its first birth from Achæus, and its second from Aratus. What degree of agency these reputed Lawgivers might have in their respective establishments, or how far they might be cloathed with the legitimate authority of the people, cannot in every instance be ascertained. In some, however, the proceeding was strictly regular. Draco appears to have been entrusted by the people of Athens, with indefinite powers to reform its government and laws. And Solon, according to Plutarch, was in a manner compelled by the universal suffrage of his fellow citizens, to take upon him the sole and absolute power of new modelling the Constitution. The proceedings under Lycurgus were less regular; but as far as the advocates for a regular reform could prevail, they all turned their eyes towards the single efforts of that celebrated patriot and sage, instead of seeking to bring about a revolution, by the intervention of a deliberative body of citizens. Whence could it have proceeded that a people jealous as the Greeks were of their liberty, should so far abandon the rules of caution, as to place their destiny in the hands of a single citizen? Whence could it have proceeded, that the Athenians, a people who would not suffer an army to be commanded by fewer than ten Generals, and who required no other proof of danger to their liberties than the illustrious merit of a fellow citizen should consider one illustrious citizen as a more eligible depository of the fortunes of themselves and their posterity, than a select body of citizens, from whose common deliberations more wisdom, as well as more safety, might have been expected? These questions cannot be fully answered without supposing that the fears of discord and disunion among a number of Counsellors, exceeded the apprehension of treachery or incapacity in a single individual. History informs us likewise of the difficulties with which these celebrated reformers had to contend; as well as of the expedients which they were obliged to employ, in order to carry their reforms into effect. Solon, who seems to have indulged a more temporising policy, confessed that he had not given to his countrymen the government best suited to their happiness, but most tolerable to their prejudices. And Lycurgus, more true to his object, was under the necessity of mixing a portion of violence with the authority of superstition; and of securing his final success, by a voluntary renunciation, first of his country, and then of his life. If these lessons teach us, on one hand, to admire the improvement made by America on the ancient mode of preparing and establishing regular plans of government; they serve not less on the other, to admonish us of the hazards and difficulties incident to such experiments, and of the great imprudence of unnecessarily multiplying them.

Is it an unreasonable conjecture that the errors which may be contained in the plan of the Convention are such as have resulted rather from the defect of antecedent experience on this complicated and difficult subject, than from a want of accuracy or care in the investigation of it; and consequently such as will not be ascertained until an actual trial shall have pointed them out? This conjecture is rendered probable not only by many considerations of a general nature, but by the particular case of the articles of confederation. It is observable that among the numerous objections and amendments suggested by the several States, when these articles were submitted for their ratification, not one is found which alludes to the great and radical error, which on actual trial has discovered itself. And if we except the observations which New-Jersey was led to make rather by her local situation than by her peculiar foresight, it may be questioned whether a single suggestion was of sufficient moment to justify a revision of the system. There is abundant reason nevertheless to suppose that immaterial as these objections were, they would have been adhered to with a very dangerous inflexibility in some States, had not a zeal for their opinions and supposed interests, been stifled by the more powerful sentiment of self-preservation. One State, we may remember, persisted for several years in refusing her concurrence, although the enemy remained the whole period at our gates, or rather in the very bowels of our country. Nor was her pliancy in the end effected by a less motive than the fear of being chargeable with protracting the public calamities, and endangering the event of the contest. Every candid reader will make the proper reflections on these important facts.

A patient who finds his disorder daily growing worse; and that an efficacious remedy can no longer be delayed without extreme danger; after coolly revolving his situation, and the characters of different physicians, selects and calls in such of them as he judges most capable of administering relief, and best entitled to his confidence. The physicians attend: The case of the patient is carefully examined: a consultation is held. They are unanimously agreed that the symptoms are critical, but that the case, with proper and timely relief, is so far from being desperate, that it may be made to issue in an improvement of his constitution. They are equally equanimous in prescribing the remedy by which this happy effect is to be produced. The prescription is no sooner made known however, than a number of persons interpose, and without denying the reality or danger of the disorder, assure the patient that the prescription will be poison to his constitution, and forbid him under pain of certain death to make use of it. Might not the patient reasonably demand before he ventured to follow this advice, that the authors of it should at least agree among themselves, on some other remedy to be substituted? and if he found them differing as much from one another, as from his first counsellors, would he not act prudently, in trying the experiment unanimously recommended by the latter, rather than in hearkening to those who could neither deny the necessity of a speedy remedy, nor agree in proposing one?

Such a patient, and in such a situation is America at this moment. She has been sensible of her malady. She has obtained a regular and unanimous advice from men of her own deliberate choice. And she is warned by others against following this advice, under pain of the most fatal consequences. Do the monitors deny the reality of her danger? No. Do they deny the necessity of some speedy and powerful remedy? No. Are they agreed, are any two of them agreed in their objections to the remedy proposed, or in the proper one to be substituted? Let them speak for themselves. This one tells us that the proposed constitution ought to be rejected, because it is not a confederation of the States, but a Government over individuals. Another admits that it ought to be a government over individuals, to a certain extent, but by no means to the extent proposed. A third does not object to the Government over individuals, or to the extent proposed, but to the want of a bill of rights. A fourth concurs in the absolute necessity of a bill of rights, but contends that it ought to be declaratory not of the personal rights of individuals, but of the rights reserved to the States in their political capacity. A fifth is of opinion that a bill of rights of any sort would be superfluous and misplaced and that the plan would be unexceptionable, but for the fatal power of regulating the times and places of election. An objector in a large State exclaims loudly against the unreasonable equality of representation in the Senate. An objector in a small State is equally loud against the dangerous inequality in the house of representatives. From this quarter we are alarmed with the amazing expence from the number of persons who are to administer the new Government. From another quarter, and sometimes from the same quarter, on another occasion, the cry is that the Congress will be but the shadow of a representation, and that the Government would be far less objectionable, if the number and the expence were doubled. A patriot in a State that does not import or export, discerns insuperable objections against the power of direct taxation. The patriotic adversary in a State of great exports and imports, is not less dissatisfied that the whole burden of taxes may be thrown on consumption. This Politician discovers in the constitution a direct and irresistible tendency to monarchy. That is equally sure, it will end in aristocracy. Another is puzzled to say which of these shapes it will ultimately assume, but sees clearly it must be one or other of them. Whilst a fourth is not wanting who with no less confidence affirms that the constitution is so far from having a bias towards either of these dangers, that the weight on that side will not be sufficient to keep it upright and firm against its opposite propensities. With another class of adversaries to the constitution, the language is that the legislative executive and judiciary departments are intermixed in such a manner as to contradict all the ideas of regular government, and all the requisite precautions in favour of liberty. Whilst this objection circulates in vague and general expressions, there are not a few who lend their sanction to it. Let each one come forward with his particular explanation and scarce any two are exactly agreed on the subject. In the eyes of one the junction of the Senate with the President in the responsible function of appointing to offices, instead of vesting this executive power in the executive, alone, is the vicious part of the organisation. To another, the exclusion of the house of representatives whose numbers alone could be a due security against corruption and partiality in the exercise of such a power, is equally obnoxious. With another, the admission of the President into any share of a power which must ever be a dangerous engine in the hands of the executive magistrate, is an unpardonable violation of the maxims of republican jealousy. No part of the arrangement according to some is more inadmissible than the trial of impeachments by the Senate, which is alternately a member both of the legislative and executive departments, when this power so evidently belonged to the judiciary department. We concur fully, reply others, in the objection to this part of the plan, but we can never agree that a reference of impeachments to the judiciary authority would be an amendment of the error. Our principal dislike to the organisation arises from the extensive powers already lodged in that department. Even among the zealous patrons of a council of State, the most irreconcilable variance is discovered concerning the mode in which it ought to be constituted. The demand of one gentleman is that the council should consist of a small number, to be appointed by the most numerous branch of the Legislature. Another would prefer a larger number, and considers it as a fundamental condition that the appointment should be made by the President himself.

As it can give no umbrage to the writers against the plan of the Fœderal Constitution, let us suppose that as they are the most zealous, so they are also the most sagacious of those who think the late Convention were unequal to the task assigned them, and that a wiser and better plan might and ought to be substituted. Let us further suppose that their country should concur both in this favorable opinion of their merits, and in their unfavorable opinion of the Convention, and should accordingly proceed to form them into a second Convention, with full powers and for the express purpose of revising and remoulding the work of the first. Were the experiment to be seriously made, though it requires some effort to view it seriously even in fiction, I leave it to be decided by the sample of opinions just exhibited, whether with all their enmity to their predecessors, they would in any one point depart so widely from their example, as in the discord and ferment that would mark their own deliberations; and whether the Constitution, now before the public, would not stand as fair a chance for immortality, as Lycurgus gave to that of Sparta, by making its change to depend on his own return from exile and death, if it were to be immediately adopted, and were to continue in force, not until a BETTER, but until ANOTHER should be agreed upon by this new assembly of Lawgivers.

It is a matter both of wonder and regret, that those who

raise so many objections against the new Constitution, should never call to mind the defects of that which is to be exchanged for it. It is not necessary that the former should be perfect; it is sufficient that the latter is more imperfect. No man would refuse to give brass for silver or gold, because the latter had some alloy in it. No man would refuse to quit a shattered and tottering habitation, for a firm and commodious building, because the latter had not a porch to it; or because some of the rooms might be a little larger or smaller, or the ceiling a little higher or lower than his fancy would have planned them. But waving illustrations of this sort, is it not manifest that most of the capital objections urged against the new system, lie with tenfold weight against the existing Confederation? Is an indefinite power to raise money dangerous in the hands of a fœderal government? The present Congress can make requisitions to any amount they please; and the States are constitutionally bound to furnish them; they can emit bills of credit as long as they will pay for the paper; they can borrow both abroad and at home, as long as a shilling will be lent. Is an indefinite power to raise troops dangerous? The Confederation gives to Congress that power also; and they have already begun to make use of it. Is it improper and unsafe to intermix the different powers of government in the same body of men? Congress, a single body of men, are the sole depository of all the fœderal powers. Is it particularly dangerous to give the keys of the treasury, and the command of the army, into the same hands? The Confederation places them both in the hands of Congress. Is a Bill of Rights essential to liberty? The Confederation has no Bill of Rights. Is it an objection against the new Constitution, that it empowers the Senate with the concurrence of the Executive to make treaties which are to be the laws of the land? The existing Congress, without any such controul, can make treaties which they themselves have declared, and most of the States have recognized, to be the supreme law of the land. Is the importation of slaves permitted by the new Constitution for twenty years? By the old, it is permitted for ever.

I shall be told that however dangerous this mixture of powers may be in theory, it is rendered harmless by the dependence of Congress on the States for the means of carrying them into practice: That however large the mass of powers may be, it is in fact a lifeless mass. Then say I in the first place, that the Confederation is chargeable with the still greater folly of declaring certain powers in the fœderal government to be absolutely necessary, and at the time rendering them absolutely nugatory: And in the next place, that if the Union is to continue, and no better government be substituted, effective powers must either be granted to or assumed by the existing Congress, in either of which events the contrast just stated will hold good. But this is not all. Out of this lifeless mass has already grown an excrescent power, which tends to realize all the dangers that can be apprehended from a defective construction of the supreme government of the Union. It is now no longer a point of speculation and hope that the Western territory is a mine of vast wealth to the United States; and although it is not of such a nature as to extricate them from their present distresses, or for some time to come, to yield any regular supplies for the public expences, yet must it hereafter be able under the proper management both to effect a gradual discharge of the domestic debt, and to furnish for a certain period, liberal tributes to the Federal Treasury. A very large proportion of this fund has been already surrendered by individual States; and it may with reason be expected, that the remaining States will not persist in withholding similar proofs of their equity and generosity. We may calculate therefore that a rich and fertile country, of an area equal to the inhabited extent of the United States, will soon become a national stock. Congress have assumed the administration of this stock. They have begun to render it productive. Congress have undertaken to do more; they have proceeded to form new States; to erect temporary Governments; to appoint officers for them; and to prescribe the conditions on which such States shall be admitted into the confederacy. All this has been done; and done without the least colour of constitutional authority. Yet no blame has been whispered; no alarm has been sounded. A GREAT and INDEPENDENT fund of revenue is passing into the hands of a SINGLE body of men, who can RAISE TROOPS to an INDEFINITE NUMBER, and appropriate money to their support for an INDEFINITE PERIOD OF TIME. And yet there are men who have not only been silent spectators of this prospect; but who are advocates for the system which exhibits it; and at the same time urge against the new system the objections which we have heard. Would they not act with more consistency in urging the establishment of the latter, as no less necessary to guard the Union against the future powers and resources of a body constructed like the existing Congress, than to save it from the dangers threatened by the present impotency of that assembly?

I mean not by any thing here said to throw censure on the measures which have been pursued by Congress. I am sensible they could not have done otherwise. The public interest, the necessity of the case, imposed upon them the task of overleaping their constitutional limits. But is not the fact an alarming proof of the danger resulting from a government which does not possess regular powers commensurate to its objects. A dissolution or usurpation is the dreadful dilemma to which it is continually exposed.

"Americanus" [*John Stevens, Jr.*] VI

Daily Advertiser (New York), January 12, 1788

We may take it for granted, I presume, that the public are, at this time, fully possessed of every objection which the opponents to the new Constitution are capable of urging. The far greater part of these objections have been dictated by interest, passion and prejudice. However a few individuals may *feel* themselves affected by the adoption of this Constitution, to every unprejudiced mind, it must be apparent, that the investigation of its tendency and probable operation, merely as it may affect the liberties of the people, are reducible to a very few leading points.

1st. Whether there is a practicability of carrying into execution a Republican Government, comprehending so large an extent of territory.

2d. Whether the liberties of the people will be safe, under the Constitution proffered to us by the late Convention.

Let us see how the dissenting minority of the Convention of Pennsylvania have argued on the first head. They lay it down as the necessary consequences of the adoption of this Constitution:

1st. That the Legislative, Executive and Judicial powers of the several States, will be annihilated.

2d. That from their ruins will be produced one consolidated Government, which, from the nature of things, will be an iron handed despotism.

With respect to the first position, all our conclusions must be founded on arguments, drawn from the nature and affections of mankind. This foundation, it is true, will admit of no higher evidence than probability: But, in this business, probability will fall little short of certainty itself.

It will readily be admitted, I presume, by all parties, that both the Federal and State Constitutions, are the mere creatures of the PEOPLE. Not only their original establishments, but the exercise and administration of these institutions, are dependent for their support and existence on the breath of the people. And, whilst property shall continue divided amongst the bulk of the people, it will be utterly impossible to wrest from them this SUPREMACY. We may safely admit as a fundamental truth, that an enlightened people can never be enslaved, merely by the instrumentality of the ordinary powers of a well constructed Government. To effect this purpose, the intervention of adventitious and extrinsic causes, are absolutely necessary.

From these premises, therefore, which reason and experience mutually concur to establish, I argue, that, from the affections and propensities of mankind, it is highly improbable that the people should acquiesce in, consent to, or permit the annihilation of the State Governments.

We are well assured that it is the principle of attraction which supports the universe. The moral world, as well as the physical, are equally subject to its laws. The operation of this principle has been discovered to be proportionate to the distances of bodies from each other. Thus, amongst mankind, its force is continually decreasing, as we recede from the centre. To make use of Cato's own words, "The strongest principle of union, resides within our own domestic walls. The ties of a parent exceed that of any other; as we depart from home, the next general principle of union is amongst citizens of the same State, where acquaintance, habits, and fortunes, nourish affection and attachment; enlarge the circle still further, and, as citizens of different States, though we acknowledge the same national denomination, we lose the ties of acquaintance, habits and fortunes, and thus, by degrees, we lessen in our attachments, till, at length, we no more than acknowledge a sameness of species." It is then sufficiently evident, that the attachment of the people to the Governments of their own States, individually, will be much stronger than to the Federal Government. And it follows, obviously, that to compass the annihilation of the State Governments, the Federal Head must be able to command, and support a force, equal to the united strength of the yeomanry of these States. I leave it to any man, whom party prejudices have not totally bereft of his senses, to calculate the chance against such an event ever happening.

The next consequence that will attend the adoption of this Constitution is, that from the ruins of the State Governments, will be produced one consolidated Government, which, from the nature of things, will be an iron handed despotism.

Having already proved, as I flatter myself, in the clearest manner the nature of the subject will admit of, that the premises of the above proposition are improbable to a degree amounting nearly to certainty; agreeably, therefore, to the strict rules of logic, I might content myself with denying the consequences deducible therefrom. But let me for a moment indulge the gentlemen in their apprehensions of ANNIHILA-TION, which, as it respects their own political consequence, may be [   ] enough; but which, as it respects the State Governments, is altogether *affectation*.

This consolidated Government will be an iron handed despotism. But how do they prove this? Montesquieu, somewhere in his spirit of laws, tells us, that "it is natural for a republic to have only a small territory." This is the sole proof or argument which the gentlemen have adduced in support of their general position from whence this *iron handed despotism* is inferred, viz. "that *a very extensive territory* cannot be governed on the principles of freedom, otherwise than by a confederation of republics."

But if the *ipse dixit* of Montesquieu is to be admitted as conclusive evidence on this point, his assertions on other points ought equally to govern our determinations. But will the gentlemen assent to the truth of the following positions? "Democratic and Aristocratic States are not in their own nature free." "The English is the best species of Constitution that could possibly be imagined by man." If they will not, they surely must allow us, equally with themselves, the privilege of *dissenting* to any other position of this celebrated writer, more especially should we be able to prove that it is no wise applicable to the matter in hand.

As this *iron handed despotism* is an inference, grounded on the passage of Montesquieu, first above cited, and indeed, has no other support; we might very fairly leave the matter to rest here, until the gentlemen produced other proofs, or, at least, until they signified their willingness to assent to every proposition contained in that author's book.

But, however the fact may be, respecting the just limits of a Republic; whether, from the nature of this species of Government, it must necessarily be confined within narrow bounds; or whether, by some *improvements in its Constitution*, it may be rendered capable of embracing a wide extent of territory—this, (as I flatter myself, I have proved in a former number) is evident—that, what Montesquieu has advanced on this subject, cannot be applied to the Constitution now under discussion. By this Constitution, *the sole power of enacting laws*, is vested in a representative body: Agreeably to Montesquieu, "it is a fundamental law in democracies, that the *people* should have *the sole power to enact laws*." Indeed, it is impossible to say to what extent of territory a Government, upon a Republican plan, may be carried, by means of this expedient of a *Representative* Legislature.

The gentlemen talk of "uniform experience," and "the opinion of the most celebrated writers on Government." This experience, and this opinion may be conclusive, for aught I know, against every Republican Government that has ever yet existed; if we except the Government of Great Britain, and those of the United States of America. But the fact is, that by an *improvement in their construction*, unknown before in Republican Governments, these have actually been rendered capable of comprehending *a very extensive territory*. When these gentlemen, therefore, shall have ascertained the precise distance, from whence it may be possible to send *representatives* to the seat of Government, they will then be able to describe the exact bounds of the territory, over which this species of Government is capable of being extended.

Tho' what is here advanced may, with truth, be deemed immaterial, as the probability of the State Governments ever being annihilated and absorbed by the general Government is so very small, yet I conceived it not amiss, to indulge the gentlemen with this concession, merely to shew them, that they may be confuted even on their own ground.

The next consideration is, *whether the liberties of the people will be safe under the Constitution proffered to us by the late Convention?*

To determine this very important question, I contend it is by no means necessary to go into a minute investigation of every part. It is amply sufficient for this purpose, if a few leading principles have been carefully attended to. Does a representation of the people proportionate to numbers, and whose election revolves statedly at short periods, form one independent branch of the Legislature? Is this representative body inhibited from interfering in the business of the Executive and Judicial departments? And lastly, are these departments provided with the means of defending themselves against such an interference? If these few cardinal points have been attended to and established, I say, so far as concerns the liberties of the people, every other provision to be found in this Constitution is of little importance. Establish these fundamentals, and we may safely give to Cato and Brutus, to the Centinel and the dissenting minority of the Convention of Pennsylvania, a chart blanche to fill up as they please. I will boldly venture to affirm, that though they might form a very turbulent and uneasy Government, it would be past their skill to fabricate one, which could wrest from the people of these States their liberties. An attentive review of the Government of Great-Britain, and the experience we have already had of our institutions, leave us no room to doubt the truth of this assertion. REPRESENTATION is the grand secret in the formation of republican Government. Provided that this right is secured and perpetuated—that its sources remain pure and uncontaminated—that Legislation constitutes its only business—and that elections are frequent and periodical, we need not be very solicitous on the score of liberty, with respect to the other constituent parts of Government. Experience has evinced beyond the possibility of doubt, between the Constitution of Pennsylvania, for instance, and that of Great Britain—the nearest approaches, perhaps, to pure democracy, on the one hand, and to absolute monarchy on the other, which this species of Government is capable of—I say, that between these extremes, a thousand combinations of the powers of government may be formed, and the liberties of the people still remain inviolate. That some of these possible combinations are calculated to carry Government to a much higher degree of perfection than others, will readily be admitted. But, provided what may be deemed essential to the security of liberty has been duly attended to, it certainly argues great arrogance and want of becoming deference to the opinions of others to quarrel with and reject a plan of Government, because, forsooth, it may not square exactly with *our* ideas of perfection.

It was not till the Revolution in England that any tolerable ideas of good Government were formed. Plato, Sir Thomas More and Harrington, before this period had amused themselves with forming visionary schemes of perfect Governments, but, for want of experimental knowledge, their plans are no better than romances, the extravagant sallies of an exuberant imagination. But it is principally from our own experience that we can derive just notions of the true foundations on which the liberties of the people rest. And can these gentlemen then, with any color of reason, flatter themselves that they can reach to the summit of perfection by an ascent so sudden and abrupt? No, my fellow-countrymen! Let us be thankful to an all-ruling Providence, which has enabled us to discover the *clue* by which we may finally extricate ourselves from that labyrinth of profound darkness and perplexity in which mankind have hitherto wandered, with only now and then a glimmering of light. Let us endeavor to make the best use we can of those important discoveries in the science of Government, which the revolution in England, and the late revolution amongst ourselves have opened to our view. Let us be content to leave to posterity, the glory and happiness of perfecting that plan of Government, which the united wisdom of those worthy patriots, who formed the late Convention, has proffered to us.

DEBATES IN THE STATE
RATIFYING CONVENTIONS

Pennsylvania, November 20 – December 15, 1787
Connecticut, January 3 – 9, 1788
Massachusetts, January 9 – February 7, 1788

James Wilson's Opening Address

November 24, 1787

Mr. WILSON. As the only member of this respectable body, who had the honor of a seat in the late Fœderal Convention, it is peculiarly my duty Mr. President, to submit to your consideration, the general principles that have produced the national Constitution, which has been framed and proposed by the assembled delegates of the United States, and which must finally stand or fall by the concurrent decision of this Convention, and of others acting upon the same subject, under similar powers and authority. To frame a Government for a single city or State, is a business both in its importance and facility, widely different from the task entrusted to the Fœderal Convention, whose prospects were extended not only to thirteen Independent and Sovereign States, some of which in territorial jurisdiction, population, and resource, equal the most respectable nations of Europe, but likewise to innumerable States yet unformed, and to myriads of citizens who in future ages shall inhabit the vast uncultivated regions of the continent. The duties of that body therefore, were not limitted to local or partial considerations, but to the formation of a plan commensurate with a great and valuable portion of the globe.

I confess, Sir, that the magnitude of the object before us, filled our minds with awe and apprehension. In Europe the opening and extending the navigation of a single river, has been deemed an act of imperial merit and importance; but how insignificant does it seem when we contemplate the scene that nature here exhibits, pouring forth the Potowmack, the Rapahannock, the Susquehanna, and other innumerable rivers, to dignify, adorn, and enrich our soil. But the magnitude of the object was equalled by the difficulty of accomplishing it, when we considered the uncommon dexterity and address that were necessary to combat and reconcile the jarring interests that seemed naturally to prevail, in a country, which presenting a coast of 1500 miles to the Atlantic, is composed of 13 distinct and Independant States, varying essentially in their situation and dimensions, and in the number and habits of their citizens. Their interests too, in some respects really different, and in many apparently so; but whether really or apparently, such is the constitution of the human mind, they make the same impression, and are prosecuted with equal vigour and perseverance. Can it then be a subject for surprize that with the sensations indispensably excited by so comprehensive and so arduous an undertaking, we should for a moment yield to despondency, and at length, influenced by the spirit of conciliation, resort to mutual concession, as the only means to obtain the great end for which we were convened? Is it a matter of surprize that where the springs of dissension were so numerous, and so powerful, some force was requisite to impel them to take, in a collected state, a direction different from that which separately they would have pursued?

There was another reason, that in this respect, encreased the difficulties of the Fœderal Convention—the different tempers and dispositions of the people for whom they acted. But, however widely they may differ upon other topics, they cordially agree in that keen and elevated sense of freedom and independence, which has been manifested in their united and successful opposition to one of the most powerful kingdoms of the world. Still it was apprehended by some, that their abhorrence of constraint, would be the source of objection and opposition; but, I confess, that my opinion, formed upon a knowledge of the good sense, as well as the high spirit of my Constituents, made me confident that they would esteem that government to be the best, which was best calculated eventually to establish and secure the dignity and happiness of their country. Upon this ground, I have occasionally supposed that my constituents have asked the reason for my assent to the several propositions contained in the plan before us. My answer, tho' concise, is a candid, and, I think a satisfactory one—because I thought them right; and thinking them right, it would be a poor compliment indeed to presume they could be disagreeable to my Constituents—a presumption that might occasion a retort to which I wish not to expose myself, as it would again be asked, "is this the opinion you entertain of those who have confided in your judgment? From what ground do you infer that a vote right in itself would be disagreeable to us?" and it might with justice be added, "this sentiment evinces that you deserved not the trust which we reposed in you." No Sir!—I have no right to imagine that the reflected rays of delegated power can displease by a brightness that proves the superior splendor of the luminary from which they proceed.

The extent of country for which the New Constitution was required, produced another difficulty in the business of the Fœderal Convention. It is the opinion of some celebrated writers, that to a small territory, the democratical, to a midling territory, (as Montesquieu has termed it) the monarchical, and, to an extensive territory, the despotic form of government, is best adapted. Regarding then, the wide and almost unbounded jurisdiction of the United States, at first view, the hand of despotism seemed necessary to controul, connect, and protect it; and hence the chief embarrasment arose. For, we knew that, although our Constituents would chearfully submit to the legislative restraints of a free government, they would spurn at every attempt to shackle them with despotic power.

In this dilemma, a Fœderal Republic naturally presented itself to our observation, as a species of government which secured all the internal advantages of a republic, at the same time that it maintained the external dignity and force of a monarchy. The definition of this form of government may be found in Montesquieu, who says, I believe, that it consists in assembling distinct societies, which are consolidated into a new body, capable of being encreased by the addition of other members;—an expanding quality peculiarly fitted to the circumstances of America.

But, while a Fœderal Republic, removed one difficulty, it introduced another, since there existed not any precedent to assist our deliberations; for, though there are many single governments, both ancient and modern, the history and principles of which are faithfully preserved, and well understood, a perfect confederation of independent states is a system hitherto unknown. The Swiss Cantons, which have often been mentioned in that light, cannot properly be deemed a Fœderal Republic, but merely a system of United States. The United Netherlands are also an assemblage of states; yet, as their proceedings are not the result of their combined decisions, but of the decisions of each state individually, their association is evidently wanting in that quality which is essential to constitute a Fœderal Republic. With respect to the Germanic Body, its members are of so disproportionate a size, their separate governments and jurisdictions so different in nature and extent, the general purpose and operation of their union so indefinite and uncertain, and the exterior power of the House of Austria so prevalent, that little information could be obtained or expected from that quarter. Turning then to ancient history, we find the Achæan and Lycian leagues, and the Amphyctionic council bearing a superficial resemblance to a Fœderal Republic; but of all these, the accounts which have been transmitted to us, are too vague and imperfect to supply a tolerable theory, and they are so destitute of that minute detail from which practical knowledge may be derived, that they must now be considered rather as subjects of curiosity, than of use or information.

Government, indeed, taken as a science, may yet be considered in its infancy; and with all its various modifications, it has hitherto been the result of force, fraud, or accident. For, after the lapse of six thousand years since the creation of the world, America now presents the first instance of a people assembled to weigh deliberately and calmly, and to decide leisurely and peacably, upon the form of government by which they will bind themselves and their posterity. Among the ancients, three forms of government seem to have been correctly known, the Monarchical, Aristocratical, and Democratical; but their knowledge did not extend beyond those simple kinds, though much pleasing ingenuity has occasionally been exercised, in tracing a resemblance of mixed government in some ancient institutions, particularly between them and the British Constitution. But, in my opinion, the result of these ingenious refinements does more honor to the moderns in discovering, than to the ancients in forming the similitude. In the work of Homer, it is supposed by his enthusiastic commentators, the seeds of every science are to be found; but, in truth, they are first observed in subsequent discoveries, and then the fond imagination transplants them to the book. Tacitus, who lived towards the close of that period, which is called ancient, who had read the history of all antecedent and cotemporary governments, who was perfectly competent to judge of their nature, tendency, and quality, Tacitus considers a mixed government as a thing rather to be wished than expected; and, if ever it did occur, it was his opinion, that it could not last long. One fact, however, is certain, that the ancients had no idea of representation, that essential to every system of wise, good, and efficient government. It is surprising, indeed, how very imperfectly, at this day, the doctrine of representation is understood in Europe. Even Great-Britain, which boasts a superior knowledge of the subject, and is generally supposed to have carried it into practice, falls far short of its true and genuine principles. For, let us enquire, does representation pervade the constitution of that country? No. Is it either immediately or remotely the source of the executive power? No. For it is not any part of the British constitution, as practised at this time, that the king derives his authority from the people. Formerly that authority was claimed by hereditary or divine right; and even at the revolution, when the government was essentially improved, no other principle was recognized, but that of an original contract between the sovereign and the people—a contract which rather excludes than implies the doctrine of representation. Again; Is the judicial system of England grounded on representation? No. For the judges are appointed by the king, and he, as we have already observed, derives not his majesty or power from the people. Lastly, then, let us review the legislative body of that nation, and even there, though we find representation operating as a check, it cannot be considered as a pervading principle. The lords, acting with hereditary right, or under an authority immediately communicated by regal prerogative, are not the representatives of the people, and yet they, as well as the sovereign, possess a negative power in the paramount business of legislation. Thus the vital principle of the British constitution is confined to a narrow corner, and the world has left to America the glory and happiness of forming a government, where representation shall at once supply the basis and the cement of the superstructure. For, representation, Sir, is the true chain between the people, and those to whom they entrust the administration of the government; and, though it may consist of many links, its strength and brightness, never should be impaired. Another, and perhaps the most important obstacle to the proceedings of the Fœderal Convention, arose in drawing the line between the national and the individual governments of the states.

On this point a general principle readily occurred, that whatever object was confined in its nature and operation to a particular State, ought to be subject to the separate government of the States, but whatever in its nature and operation extended beyond a particular State, ought to be comprehended within the Fœderal jurisdiction. The great difficulty, therefore, was the application of this general principle, for it was found impracticable to enumerate and distinguish the various objects to which it extended, and as the mathematics, only, are capable of demonstration, it ought not to be thought extraordinary that the Convention could not develope a subject, involved in such endless perplexity. If however, the proposed constitution should be adopted, I trust that in the theory there will be found such harmony, and in the practice such mutual confidence between the national and individual governments, that every sentiment of jealousy and apprehension will be effectually destroyed. But Sir, permit me to ask, whether on the ground of a union, the individual or the national government ought most to be trusted? For my part, I think it more natural to presume that the interest of each would be pursued by the whole, than the reverse of the proposition, that the several States would prefer the interest of the confederated body; for in the general government each is represented, but in the separate governments, only the separate States.

These difficulties, Mr. President, which embarrassed the Fœderal Convention, are not represented to enhance the merit of surmounting them, but with a more important view, to shew how unreasonable it is to expect that the plan of government, should correspond with the wishes of all the States, of all the citizens of any one state, or of all the citizens of the United continent. I remember well, Sir, the effect of those surrounding difficulties in the late Convention. At one time the great and interesting work seemed to be at a stand, at another it proceeded with energy and rapidity, and when at last, it was accomplished, many respectable members beheld it with wonder and admiration. But having pointed out the obstacles which they had to encounter, I shall now beg leave to direct your attention, to the end which the Convention proposed.

Our wants, imperfections, and weakness, Mr. President, naturally incline us to society; but it is certain, society cannot exist without some restraints. In a state of nature each individual has a right, uncontrouled, to act as his pleasure or his interest may prevail, but it must be observed that this licence extends to every individual, and hence the state of nature is rendered insupportable, by the interfering claims, and the consequent animosities of men, who are independant of every power and influence, but their passions and their will. On the other hand, in entering into the social compact, though the individual parts with a portion of his natural rights, yet, it is evident that he gains more by the limitation of the liberty of others, than he loses by the limitation of his own,—so that in truth, the aggregate of liberty is more in society, than it is in a state of nature.

It is then, Sir, a fundamental principle of society, that the welfare of the whole shall be pursued and not of a part, and the measures necessary to the good of the community, must consequently be binding upon the individuals that compose it. This principle is universally allowed to be just with respect to single governments, and there are instances in which it applies with equal force to independent Communities; for the situation and circumstances of states may make it as necessary for them, as for individuals, to associate. Hence, Mr. President, the important question arises—are such the situation and circumstances of the American States?

At this period, America has it in her power to adopt either of the following modes of Government: She may dissolve the individual sovereignty of the States, and become one consolidated empire; She may be divided into thirteen separate, independant, and unconnected Commonwealths; she may be erected into two or more confederacies; or, lastly, she may become one comprehensive Fœderal Republic.

Allow me, Sir, to take a short view of each of these suppositions. Is it probable that the dissolution of the State governments, and the establishment of one consolidated empire, would be eligible in its nature, and satisfactory to the people in its administration? I think not, as I have given reasons to shew that so extensive a territory could not be governed, connected, and preserved, but by the Supremacy of despotic power. All the exertions of the most potent Emperors of Rome were not capable of keeping that Empire together, which in extent was far inferior to the dominion of America. Would an independent, an unconnected situation, without any associating head, be advantageous or satisfactory? The consequences of this system would at one time expose the States to foreign insult and depredations, and, at another, to internal jealousy, contention, and war. Then let us consider the plan of two or more confederacies which has often been suggested, and which certainly presents some aspects more inviting than either of the preceeding modes, since the subjects of strife would not be so numerous, the strength of the confederates would be greater, and their interests more united. But even here when we fairly weigh the advantages and the disadvantages, we shall find the last greatly preponderating; the expences of government would be considerably multiplied, the seeds of rivalship and animosity would spring up, and spread the calamities of war and tumult through the country; for tho' the sources of rancour might be diminished, their strength, and virulence would probably be increased.

Of these three species of government, however, I must observe, that they obtained no advocates in the Fœderal Convention, nor can I presume that they will find advocates here, or in any of our sister states. The general sentiment in that body, and, I believe, the general sentiment of the citizens of America, is expressed in the motto which some of them have chosen, UNITE OR DIE; and while we consider the extent of the country, so intersected and almost surrounded with navigable rivers, so separated and detached from the rest of the world, it is natural to presume that Providence has designed us for an united people, under one great political compact. If this is a just and reasonable conclusion, supported by the wishes of the people, the Convention did right in proposing a single confederated Republic. But in proposing it, they were necessarily lead, not only to consider the situation, circumstances, and interests of one, two, or three states, but of the collective body; and as it is essential to society, that the welfare of the whole should be preferred to the accommodation of a part, they followed the same rule in promoting the national advantages of the Union, in preference to the separate advantages of the States. A principle of candor, as well as duty, lead to this conduct; for, as I have said before, no government, either single or confederated can exist, unless private and individual rights are subservient to the public and general happiness of the nation. It was not alone the state of Pennsylvania, however important she may be as a constituent part of the union, that could influence the deliberations of a Convention, formed by a delegation from all the United States, to devise a government adequate to their common exigencies, and impartial in its influence and operation. In the spirit of union, inculcated by the nature of their commission, they framed the constitution before us, and in the same spirit, they submit it to the candid consideration of their constituents.

Having made some remarks upon the nature and principles of civil society, I shall now take a cursory notice of civil liberty, which is essential to the well-being of civil government. The definition of civil liberty is, briefly, that portion of natural liberty which men resign to the government, and which then produces more happiness, than it would have produced if retained by the individuals who resign it;—still however leaving to the human mind, the full enjoyment of every privilege that is not incompatible with the peace and order of society. Here I am easily lead to the consideration of another species of liberty, which has not yet received a discriminating name, but which I will venture to term Fœderal liberty. This, Sir, consists in the agregate of the civil liberty which is surrendered by each state to the national government; and the same principles that operate in the establishment of a single society, with respect to the rights reserved or resigned by the individuals that compose it, will justly apply in the case of a confederation of distinct and Independent States.

These observations have been made, Mr. President, in order to preface a representation of the state of the union, as it appeared to the late Convention. We all know, and we have all felt, that the present system of confederation is inadequate to the government and the exigencies of the United States. Need I describe the contrasted scene which the revolution has presented to our view? On the one hand, the arduous struggle in the cause of liberty terminated by a glorious and triumphant peace; on the other, contention and poverty at home, discredit and disgrace abroad. Do we not remember what high expectations were formed by others and by ourselves, on the return of peace? And have those honorable expectations from our national character, been realized? No!—What then has been the cause of disappointment? Has America lost her magnanimity or perseverance? no. Has she been subdued by any high handed invasion of her liberties? still I answer no; for, dangers of that kind were no sooner seen, than they were repelled. But the evil has stolen in from a quarter little suspected, and the rock of Freedom, which stood firm against the attacks of a foreign foe, has been sapped and undermined by the licentiousness of our own citizens. Private calamity, and public anarchy have prevailed; and even the blessing of Independency has been scarcely felt or understood by a people who have dearly atchieved it.

Shall I, Sir, be more particular in this lamentable history? The commencement of peace, was likewise the commencement of our distresses and disgrace. Devoid of power, we could neither prevent the excessive importations which lately deluged the country, nor even raise from that excess a contribution to the public revenue; devoid of importance, we were unable to command a sale for our commodities in a foreign market; devoid of credit, our public securities were melting in the hands of their deluded owners, like snow before the Sun; devoid of dignity, we were inadequate to perform treaties on our own part, or to compel a performance on the part of a contracting nation. In short, Sir, the tedious tale disgusts me, and I fondly hope, it is unnecessary to proceed. The years of languor are over. We have seen dishonor and destruction, it is true, but we have at length penetrated the cause, and are now anxious to obtain the cure. The cause need not be specified by a recapitulation of facts; every act of Congress, and the proceedings of every State are replete with proofs in that respect, and all point to the weakness and imbecility of the existing Confederation; while the loud and concurrent voice of the people proclaims an efficient national government to be the only cure. Under these impressions, and with these views, the late Convention were appointed and met; the end which they proposed to accomplish, being to frame one national and efficient government, in which the exercise of beneficence, correcting the jarring interests of every part, should pervade the whole, and by which the peace, freedom, and happiness of the United States should be permanently ensured. The principles and means that were adopted by the Convention to obtain that end, are now before us, and will become the great object of our discussion. But on this point, as upon others, permit me to make a few general observations.

In all governments, whatever is their form, however they may be constituted, there must be a power established, from which there is no appeal—and which is therefore called absolute, supreme, and uncontroulable. The only question is, where that power is lodged?—a question that will receive different answers from the different writers on the subject. Sir William Blackstone says, it resides in the omnipotence of the British Parliament, or in other words, corresponding with the practice of that country, it is whatever the British Parliament pleases to do: So that when that body was so base and treacherous to the rights of the people as to transfer the legislative authority to Henry the eighth, his exercising that authority by proclamations and edicts, could not strictly speaking be termed unconstitutional, for under the act of Parliament his will was made the law, and therefore, his will became in that respect the constitution itself. But were we to ask some politicians who have taken a faint and inaccurate view of our establishments, where does this supreme power reside in the United States? They would probably answer, in their Constitutions. This however, tho' a step nearer to the fact, is not a just opinion; for, in truth, it remains and flourishes with the people; and under the influence of that truth we, at this moment, sit, deliberate and speak. In other countries, indeed the revolutions of government are connected with war, and all its concomitant calamities. But with us, they are considered as the means of obtaining a superior knowledge of the nature of government, and of accomplishing its end. That the supreme power therefore, should be vested in the people, is, in my judgment, the great panacea of human politics. It is a power paramount to every constitution, inalienable in its nature, and indefinite in its extent. For, I insist, if there are errors in government the people have the right not only to correct and amend them, but likewise totally to change and reject its form; and under the operation of that right, the citizens of the United States can never be wretched beyond retrieve, unless they are wanting to themselves.

Then let us examine, Mr. President, the three species of simple governments, which, as I have already mentioned, are the monarchical, aristocratical and democratical. In a monarchy, the supreme power is vested in a single person: in an aristocracy, it is possessed by a body, not formed upon the principle of representation, but enjoying their station by descent, by election among themselves, or in right of some personal or territorial qualification; and, lastly, in a democracy, it is inherent in the people, and is either exercised by themselves or by their representatives. Each of these systems has its advantages, and its disadvantages. The advantages of a monarchy are strength, dispatch, and unity: its disadvantages are expence, tyranny, and war. The advantages of an aristocracy are experience, and the wisdom resulting from education: its disadvantages are the disention of the governors, and the oppression of the people. The advantages of a democracy are liberty, caution, industry, fidelity, and an opportunity of bringing forward the talents and abilities of the citizens, without regard to birth or fortune: its disadvantages are disention and imbecility, for the assent of many being required, their exertions will be feeble, and their councils too soon discovered.

To obtain all the advantages, and to avoid all the inconveniences of these governments, was the leading object of the late Convention. Having therefore considered the formation and principles of other systems, it is natural to enquire, of what description is the Constitution before us? In its principles, Sir, it is purely democratical; varying indeed, in its form, in order to admit all the advantages, and to exclude all the disadvantages which are incidental to the known and established constitutions of government. But when we take an extensive and accurate view of the streams of power that appear through this great and comprehensive plan, when we contemplate the variety of their directions, the force and dignity of their currents, when we behold them intersecting, embracing, and surrounding the vast possessions and interests of the Continent, and when we see them distributing on all hands, beauty, energy and riches, still, however numerous and wide their courses, however diversified and remote the blessings they diffuse, we shall be able to trace them all to one great and noble source, THE PEOPLE.

Such, Mr. President, are the general observations with which I have thought it necessary to trouble you. In discussing the distinct propositions of the Fœderal Plan, I shall have occasion to apply them more particularly to that subject, but at present, I shall conclude with requesting the pardon of the Convention for having so long intruded upon their patience.

John Smilie Responds to Wilson on the Lack of a Bill of Rights

November 28, 1787

Mr. Smilie: I expected, Mr. President, that the honorable gentleman would have proceeded to a full and explicit investigation of the proposed system, and that he would have made some attempts to prove that it was calculated to promote the happiness, power, and general interests of the United States. I am sorry that I have been mistaken in this expectation, for surely the gentleman's talents and opportunities would have enabled him to furnish considerable information upon this important subject; but I shall proceed to make a few remarks upon those words in the preamble of this plan, which he has considered of so super-excellent a quality. Compare them, Sir, with the language used in forming the state constitution and however superior they may be to the terms of the great charter of England, still, in common candor, they must yield to the more sterling expressions employed in this act. Let these speak for themselves:

"That all men are born equally free and independent, and have certain natural, inherent and unalienable rights, amongst which are, the enjoying and defending life and liberty, acquiring, possessing and protecting property, and pursuing and obtaining happiness and safety.

"That the people of this state have the sole, exclusive and inherent right of governing and regulating the internal police of the same.

"That all power being originally inherent in, and consequently derived from the people; therefore all officers of government, whether legislative or executive, are their trustees and servants, and at all times accountable to them.

"That government is, or ought to be, instituted for the common benefit, protection and security of the people, nation or community; and not for the particular emolument or advantage of any single man, family, or set of men, who are a part only of that community: And that the community hath an indubitable, unalienable and indefeasible right to reform, alter or abolish government in such manner as shall be by that community judged most conducive to the public weal."

But the gentleman takes pride in the superiority of this short preamble when compared with magna charta; — why, Sir, I hope the rights of men are better understood at this day, than at the framing of that deed, and we must be convinced that civil liberty is capable of still greater improvement and extension, than is known even in its present cultivated state. True, Sir, the supreme authority naturally rests in the people, but does it follow, that therefore a declaration of rights would be superfluous? Because the people have a right to alter and abolish government, can it therefore be inferred that every step taken to secure that right would be superfluous and nugatory? The truth is, that unless some criterion is established by which it could be easily and constitutionally ascertained how far our governors may proceed, and by which it might appear when they transgress their jurisdiction, this idea of altering and abolishing government is a mere sound without substance. Let us recur to the memorable declaration of the 4th of July, 1776. Here it is said:

"When, in the course of human events, it becomes necessary for one people to dissolve the political bands which have connected them with another, and to assume among the powers of the earth, the separate and equal station to which the laws of nature's God entitle them, a decent respect to the opinions of mankind requires that they should declare the causes which impel them to the separation.

"We hold these truths to be self evident; that all men are created equal; that they are endowed by their Creator with certain unalienable rights; that among these are life, liberty, and the pursuit of happiness. That to secure these rights, governments are instituted among men, deriving their just powers from the consent of the governed; that whenever any form of government becomes destructive of these ends, it is the right of the people to alter or to abolish it, and to institute a new government, laying its foundation on such principles, and organizing its powers in such form, as to them shall seem most likely to effect their safety and happiness."

Now, Sir, if in the proposed plan, the gentleman can shew

any similar security for the civil rights of the people I shall certainly be relieved from a weight of objection to its adoption, and I sincerely hope, that as he has gone so far, he will proceed to communicate some of the reasons (and undoubtedly they must have been powerful ones,) which induced the late federal convention to omit a bill of rights, so essential in the opinion of many citizens to a perfect form of government.

James Wilson and John Smilie Debate the Need for a Bill of Rights

November 28, 1787

Mr. Wilson. Mr. President, we are repeatedly called upon to give some reason why a bill of rights has not been annexed to the proposed plan. I not only think that enquiry is at this time unnecessary and out of order, but I expect, at least, that those who desire us to shew why it was omitted, will furnish some arguments to shew that it ought to have been inserted; for the proof of the affirmative naturally falls upon them. But the truth is, Sir, that this circumstance, which has since occasioned so much clamour and debate, never struck the mind of any member in the late convention 'till, I believe, within three days of the dissolution of that body, and even then, of so little account was the idea, that it passed off in a short conversation, without introducing a formal debate, or assuming the shape of a motion. For, Sir, the attempt to have thrown into the national scale an instrument in order to evince that any power not mentioned in the constitution was reserved, would have been spurned at as an insult to the common understanding of mankind. In civil government it is certain, that bills of rights are unnecessary and useless, nor can I conceive whence the contrary notion has arisen. Virginia has no bill of rights, and will it be said that her constitution was the less free?

Mr. Smilie. I beg leave to observe, Mr. President, that although it has not been inserted in the printed volume of state constitutions, yet I have been assured by Mr. Mason, that Virginia has a bill of rights.

Mr. Wilson. I do not rely upon the information of Mr. Mason, or of any other gentleman on a question of this kind, but I refer to the authenticity of the volume which contains the state constitutions, and in that Virginia has no bill of rights. But, Sir, has South Carolina no security for her liberties? that state has no bill of rights. Are the citizens of the Eastern shore of the Delaware more secured in their freedom, or more enlightened on the subject of government than the citizens of the western shore? New Jersey has no bill of rights; New-York has none; Connecticut has none, and Rhode-Island has none. Thus, Sir, it appears from the example of other states, as well as from principle, that a bill of rights is neither an essential nor a necessary instrument in framing a system of government, since liberty may exist and be as well secured without it. But it was not only unnecessary, but on this occasion, it was found impracticable; for who will be bold enough to undertake to enumerate all the rights of the people? and when the attempt to enumerate them is made, it must be remembered that if the enumeration is not complete, every thing not expressly mentioned will be presumed to be purposely omitted. So it must be with a bill of rights, and an omission in stating the powers granted to the government, is not so dangerous as an omission in recapitulating the rights reserved by the people. We have already seen the origin of magna charta, and tracing the subject still further, we find the petition of rights claiming the liberties of the people, according to the laws and statutes of the realm, of which the great charter was the most material; so that here again recourse is had to the old source from which their liberties are derived, the grant of the king. It was not 'till the revolution that the subject was placed upon a different footing, and even then the people did not claim their liberties as an inherent right, but as the result of an original contract between them and the sovereign. Thus, Mr. President, an attention to the situation of England, will shew that the conduct of that country in respect to bills of rights, cannot furnish an example to the inhabitants of the United States, who by the revolution have regained all their natural rights, and possess their liberty neither by grant nor contract. In short, Sir, I have said that a bill of rights would have been improperly annexed to the federal plan, and for this plain reason, that it would imply that whatever is not expressed was given, which is not the principle of the proposed constitution.

Mr. Smilie. The arguments which have been urged, Mr. President, have not in my opinion, satisfactorily shewn that a bill of rights would have been an improper, nay, that it is not a necessary appendage to the proposed system. As it has been denied that Virginia possesses a bill of rights, I shall on that subject only observe, that Mr. Mason, a gentleman certainly of great information and integrity, has assured me that such a thing does exist, and I am persuaded, I shall be able at a future period to lay it before the convention. But, Sir, the state of Delaware has a bill of rights, and I believe one of the honourable members (Mr. M'Kean) who now contests the necessity and propriety of that instrument, took a very conspicuous part in the formation of the Delaware government. It seems however that the members of the federal convention were themselves convinced, in some degree, of the expediency and propriety of a bill of rights, for we find them expressly declaring that the writ of Habeas Corpus and the trial by jury in criminal cases shall not be suspended or infringed. How does this indeed agree with the maxim that whatever is not given is reserved? Does it not rather appear from the reservation of these two articles that every thing else, which is not specified, is included in the powers delegated to the government? This, sir, must prove the necessity of a full and explicit declaration of rights; and when we further consider the extensive, the undefined powers vested in the administrators of this system, when we consider the system itself as a great political compact between the governors and the governed, a plain, strong, and accurate, criterion by which the people might at once determine when, and in what instance, their rights were violated, is a preliminary, without which this plan ought not to be adopted. So loosely, so inaccurately are the powers which are enumerated in this constitution defined, that it will be impossible, without a test of that kind, to ascertain the limits of authority, and to declare when government has degenerated into oppression. In that event the contest will arise between the people and the rulers: "You have exceeded the powers of your office, you have oppressed us," will be the language of the suffering citizens. The answer of the government will be short—"We have not exceeded our power: you have no test by which you can prove it." Hence, Sir, it will be impracticable to stop the progress of tyranny, for there will be no check but the people, and their exertions must be futile and uncertain; since it will be difficult indeed, to communicate to them, the violation that has been committed, and their proceedings will be neither systematical nor unanimous. It is said, however, that the difficulty of framing a bill of rights was insurmountable: but, Mr. President, I can not agree in this opinion. Our experience, and the numerous precedents before us, would have furnished a very sufficient guide. At present there is no security, even for the rights of conscience, and under the sweeping force of the sixth article, every principle of a bill of rights, every stipulation for the most sacred and invaluable privileges of man, are left at the mercy of government.

"The Defect Is in the System Itself": Robert Whitehill on the Dangers of the Powers of Congress and the Illogic of the Habeas Corpus Clause

November 30, 1787

Mr. Whitehill. I confess, Mr. President, that after the full exercise of his eloquence and ingenuity, the honorable delegate to the late convention, has not removed those objections which I formerly submitted to your consideration, in hopes of striking indeed, from his superior talents and information, a ray of wisdom to illuminate the darkness of our doubts, and to guide us in the pursuit of political truth and happiness. If the learned gentleman, however, with all his opportunities of investigating this particular system, and with all his general knowledge in the science of government, has not been able to convert or convince us; far be it from me to impute this failure to the defects of his elocution, or the languor of his disposition. It is no impeachment of those abilities which have been eminently distinguished in the abstruse disquisitions of law, that they should fail in the insidious task of supporting, on popular principles, a government which originates in mystery, and must terminate in despotism. Neither can the want of success, Sir, be ascribed to the want of zeal; for, we have heard with our ears, and our eyes have seen, the indefatigable industry of the worthy member in advocating the cause which he has undertaken. But Mr. President, the defect is in the system itself,—there lies the evil which no argument can palliate, no sophistry can disguise. Permit me, therefore, Sir, again to call your attention to the principles which it contains, and for a moment to examine the ground upon which those principles are defended. I have said, and with encreasing confidence I repeat, that the proposed constitution must eventually annihilate the independant sovereignty of the several states. In answer to this, the forms of election for supplying the offices of the federal head have been recapitulated; it has

811

been thence inferred that the connection between the individual and the general governments is of so indissoluble a nature, that they must necessarily stand or fall together, and, therefore, it has been finally declared to be impossible, that the framers of this constitution, could have a premeditated design to sow in the body of their work, the seeds of its own destruction. But, Sir, I think it may be clearly proved, that this system contains the seeds of self-preservation, independent of all the forms referred to;—seeds which will vegitate and strengthen in proportion to the decay of state authority, and which will ultimately spring up and overshadow the thirteen commonwealths of America, with a deadly shade. The honorable member from the city has indeed, observed that every government should possess the means of its own preservation; and this constitution is possibly the result of that proposition. For, Sir, the first article comprises the grants of powers so superlative in their nature, and so unlimitted in their extent, that without the aid of any other branch of the system, a foundation rests upon this article alone, for the extension of the federal jurisdiction to the most extravagant degree of arbitrary sway. It will avail little to detect and deplore the encroachments of a government clothed in the plenitude of these powers; it will afford no consolation to reflect that we are not enslaved by the positive deriliction of our rights; but it will be well to remember, at this day, Sir, that, in effect, we rob the people of their liberties, when we establish a power, whose usurpations they will not be able to counteract or resist. It is not alone, however, the operative force of the powers expressly given to Congress that will accomplish their independence of the states, but we find an efficient auxiliary in the clause that authorizes that body "to make all laws which shall be necessary and proper for carrying into execution the foregoing powers, and all other powers vested by this constitution in this government of the United States, or in any department or office thereof." Hence, sir, if it should happen, as the honorable members from the city have presumed, that by the neglect or delinquency of the states, no place and manner, or an improper place and manner for conducting the elections should be appointed, will it not be said that the general government ought not for this reason to be destroyed? and will it

not therefore be necessary for carrying the powers of this constitution into execution, that the Congress should provide for
its elections in such manner as will prevent the federal business from being frustrated, by the listless or refractory disposition of the states individually? This event is in a great
measure provided for, indeed, by the plan itself; for, "the
Congress may (constitutionally) at any time by law make or
alter such regulations (that is the times, places, and manner of
holding elections prescribed in each state by the legislatures
thereof) except as to the places of choosing senators." If the
power here given was necessary to the preservation of the
proposed government, as the honorable members have contended, does it not, at the same time, furnish the means to act
independant of the connection, which has been so often represented, as the great security for the continuance of the state
sovereignties? Under the sanction of this clause, the senators
may hold their seats as long as they live, and there is no authority to dispossess them. The duration of the house of representatives may likewise be protracted to any period, since
the time and place of election will always be adapted to the
objects of the Congress, or its leading demagogues; and as
that body will ultimately declare what shall constitute the
qualification of its members, all the boasted advantages of
representation must terminate in idle form and expensive parade. If the voice of complaint should not then be silenced by
the dread of punishment, easy it is nevertheless to anticipate
the fate of petitions or remonstrances presented by the trembling hand of the oppressed, to the irritated and ambitious
oppressor. Solicitation will be answered by those statutes
which are to be the supreme law of the land, and reproach
will be overcome by the frown of insolent authority. This Mr.
President, is but a slight view of the calamities that will be
produced by the exercise of those powers, which the honorable members from the city have endeavored to persuade us,
it is necessary to grant to the new government, in order to
secure its own preservation, and to accomplish the objects of
the union. But in considering, Sir, what was necessary to the
safety and energy of the government, some attention ought
surely to have been paid to the safety and freedom of the
people. No satisfactory reason has yet been offered for the

omission of a bill of rights; but, on the contrary, the honorable members are defeated in the only pretext which they have been able to assign, that every thing which is not given is excepted, for we have shewn that there are two articles expressly reserved, the writ of Habeas Corpus, and the trial by jury in criminal cases, and we have called upon them, in vain, to reconcile this reservation with the tenor of their favourite proposition. For, if there was danger in the attempt to enumerate the liberties of the people, lest it should prove imperfect and defective, how happens it, that in the instances I have mentioned, that danger has been incurred? Have the people no other rights worth their attention, or is it to be inferred, agreeably to the maxim of our opponents, that every other right is abandoned? Surely, Sir, our language was competent to declare the sentiments of the people, and to establish a bar against the intrusions of the general government, in other respects as well as these; and when we find some privileges stipulated, the argument of danger is effectually destroyed; and the argument of difficulty, which has been drawn from the attempt to enumerate every right, cannot now be urged against the enumeration of more rights than this instrument contains. In short, Mr. President, it is our duty to take care that the foundation of this system is so laid, that the superstructure, which is to be reared by other hands, may not cast a gloom upon the temple of freedom, the recent purchase of our toil and treasure. When, therefore, I consider it as the means of annihilating the constitutions of the several states, and, consequently, the liberties of the people, I should be wanting to my constituents, to myself, and to posterity, did I not exert every talent with which Heaven has endowed me, to counteract the measures that have been taken for its adoption. That it was the design of the late federal convention to absorb and abolish the individual sovereignty of the states, I seek no other evidence but this system; for as the honorable delegate to that body has recommended, I am also satisfied to judge of the tree by its fruit. When, therefore, I behold it thus systematically constructed for the accomplishment of that object,— when I recollect the talents of those who framed it, I cannot hesitate to impute to them an intention corresponding with the principles and operation of their own work. Finally, Sir, that the dissolution of our state constitutions will produce the ruin of civil liberty is a proposition easy to be maintained, and which, I am persuaded, in the course of these debates, will be incontrovertibly established in the mind of every member, whose judgment is open to conviction, and whose vote has not been conclusively pledged for the ratification of this constitution, before its merits were discussed.

Benjamin Rush Speaks
Against a Bill of Rights

November 30, 1787

Doctor Rush. I believe, Mr. President, that of all the treaties which have ever been made, William Penn's was the only one, which was contracted without parchment; and I believe, likewise, it is the only one that has ever been faithfully adhered to. As it has happened with treaties, so, Sir, has it happened with bills of rights, for never yet has one been made which has not, at some period or other, been broken. The celebrated magna charta of England was broken over and over again, and these infractions gave birth to the petition of rights. If, indeed, the government of that country has not been violated for the last hundred years, as some writers have said, it is not owing to charters or declarations of rights, but to the balance which has been introduced and established in the legislative body. The constitution of Pennsylvania, Mr. President, is guarded by an oath, which every man employed in the administration of the public business, is compelled to take; and yet, sir, examine the proceedings of the council of censors, and you will find innumerable instances of the violation of that constitution, committed equally by its friends and enemies. In truth then, there is no security but in a pure and adequate representation; the checks and all the other desiderata of government, are nothing but political error without it, and with it, liberty can never be endangered. While the honorable convention, who framed this system, were employed in their work, there are many gentlemen who can bear testimony that my only anxiety was upon the subject of representation; and when I beheld a legislature constituted of three branches, and in so excellent a manner, either directly or indirectly, elected by the people, and amenable to them, I confess, Sir, that here I chearfully reposed all my hopes and confidence of safety. Civilians having taught us, Mr. President, that occupancy was the origin of property, I think, it may likewise be considered as the origin of liberty; and as we enjoy all our natural rights from a pre occupancy, antecedent to the social state, in entering into that state, whence shall they be said to be derived? would it not be absurd to frame a formal declaration that our natural rights are acquired from ourselves? and would it not be a more rediculous solecism to say, that they are the gift of those rulers whom we have created, and who are invested by us with every power they possess? Sir, I consider it as an honor to the late convention, that this system has not been disgraced with a bill of rights; though I mean not to blame, or reflect upon those states, which have encumbered their constitutions with that idle and superfluous instrument. One would imagine however, from the arguments of the opposition that this government was immediately to be administered by foreigners,—strangers to our habits and opinions, and unconnected with our interests and prosperity. These apprehensions, Sir, might have been excused while we were contending with Great Britain; but, at this time, they are applicable to all governments, as well as that under consideration; and the arguments of the honorable members are, indeed, better calculated for an Indian council fire, than the meridian of this refined and enlightened convention.

William Findley on the Constitution as a Plan for National Consolidation

December 1, 1787

On Saturday Mr. Findley delivered an eloquent and powerful speech to prove that the proposed plan of government amounted to a consolidation, and not a confederation of the states. Mr. Wilson had before admitted that if this was a just objection it would be strongly against the system; and, it seems, from the subsequent silence of all its advocates upon that subject (except Doctor Rush, who on Monday insinuated that he saw and rejoiced at the eventual annihilation of the state sovereignties) Mr. Findley has established his position. Previous to an investigation of the plan, that gentleman animadverted upon the argument of necessity, which had been so much insisted upon, and shewed that we were in an eligible situation to attempt the improvement of the federal government, but not so desperately circumstanced as to be obliged to adopt any system, however destructive to the liberties of the people, and the sovereign rights of the states. He then argued that the proposed constitution established a general government and destroyed the individual governments, from the following evidence taken from the system itself. 1st, In the Preamble, it is said, *We the People*, and not *We the States*, which therefore is a compact between individuals entering into society, and not between separate States enjoying independent power, and delegating a portion of that power for their common benefit. 2dly, That in the legislature each member has a vote, whereas in a confederation, as we have hitherto practised it, and from the very nature of the thing, a state can only have one voice, and therefore all the delegates of any state can only give one vote. 3d, The powers given to the federal body for imposing internal taxation will necessarily destroy the state sovreignties for there cannot exist two independent sovreign taxing powers in the same community, and the strongest will, of course, annihilate the weaker. 4th, The power given to regulate and judge of elections is a proof of a consolidation, for there cannot be two powers employed at the same time in regulating the same elections, and if they were a confederated body, the individual states would judge of the elections, and the general Congress would judge of the credentials which proved the election of its members. 5th, The judiciary power, which is co-extensive with the legislative, is another evidence of a consolidation. 6th, The manner in which the wages of the members is paid, makes another proof, and *lastly* the oath of allegiance directed to be taken establishes it incontrovertibly, for would it not be absurd that the members of the legislative and executive branches of a sovereign state should take a test of allegiance to another sovereign or independent body?

James Wilson Replies to Findley

December 1, 1787

The secret is now disclosed, and it is discovered to be a dread, that the boasted state sovereignties, will under this system be disrobed of part of their power. Before I go into the examination of this point, let me ask one important question—Upon what principle is it contended that the sovereign power resides in the state governments? the honorable gentleman has said only, that there can be no subordinate sovereignty. Now if there can not, my position is, that the sovereignty resides in the people, they have not parted with it; they have only dispensed such portions of power as were conceived necessary for the public welfare. This constitution stands upon this broad principle. I know very well, sir, that the people have hitherto been shut out of the fœderal government, but it is not meant that they should any longer be dispossessed of their rights. In order to recognize this leading principle, the proposed system sets out with a declaration, that its existence depends upon the supreme authority of the people alone. We have heard much about a consolidated government.—I wish the honorable gentleman would condescend to give us a definition of what he meant by it. I think this the more necessary, because I apprehend that the term, in the numerous times it has been used, has not always been used in the same sense. It may be said and I believe it has been said, that a consolidated government is such, as will absorb and destroy the governments of the several states. If it is taken in this view, the plan before us is not a consolidated government, as I shewed on a former day, and may, if necessary, shew further on some future occasion.—On the other hand, if it is meant, that the general government will take from the state governments their power in some particulars, it is confessed and evident, that this will be its operation and effect.

When the principle is once settled, that the people are the source of authority, the consequence is, that they may take from the subordinate governments powers with which they have hitherto trusted them, and place those powers in the general government, if it is thought that they will be productive of more good.—They can distribute one portion of power, to the more contracted circle, called state governments: they can also furnish another proportion to the government of the United States. Who will undertake to say, as a state officer, that the people may not give to the general government what powers, and for what purposes they please? how comes it, sir, that these state governments dictate to their superiors? to the majesty of the people? When I say the majesty of the people, I mean the thing and not a mere compliment to them. The honorable gentleman went a step further and said, that the state governments were kept out of this government altogether. The truth is, and it is a leading principle in this system, that not the states only, but the people also shall be here represented. And if this is a crime, I confess, the general government is chargeable with it; but I have no idea, that a safe system of power, in the government, sufficient to manage the general interest of the United States, could be drawn from any other source, or rested in any other authority than that of the people at large, and I consider this authority as the rock on which this structure will stand.—If this principle is unfounded, the system must fall. If honorable gentlemen, before they undertake to oppose this principle, will shew that the people have parted with their power to the state governments, then I confess I cannot support this constitution. It is asked can there be two taxing powers? Will the people submit to two taxing powers? I think they will, when the taxes are required for the public welfare, by persons appointed immediately by their fellow citizens.

But I believe this doctrine is a very disagreeable one to some of the state governments. All the objects that will furnish an encrease of revenue, are eagerly seised by them; perhaps this will lead to the reason why a state government, when she was obliged to pay only about an eighth part of the loan office certificates, should voluntarily undertake the payment of about one-third part of them. This power of taxation will be regulated in the general government upon equitable principles. No state can have more than her just proportion to discharge—no longer will government be obliged to assign her funds for the payment of debts she does not owe. Another objection has been taken, that the judicial powers are coextensive with the objects of the national government. So far as I can understand the idea of magistracy in every government, this seems to be a proper arrangement; the judicial department is considered as a part of the executive authority of government. Now, I have no idea that the authority should be restrained, so as not to be able to perform its functions with full effect. I would not have the legislature sit to make laws, which cannot be executed. It is not meant here that the laws shall be a dead letter; it is meant, that they shall be carefully and duly considered, before they are enacted; and that then they shall be honestly and faithfully executed. This observation naturally leads to a more particular consideration of the government before us. In order, sir, to give permanency, stability and security to any government, I conceive it of essential importance, that its legislature should be restrained; that there should not only be, what we call a *passive*, but an *active* power over it; for of all kinds of despotism, this is the most dreadful, and the most difficult to be corrected. With how much contempt have we seen the authority of the people, treated by the legislature of this state—and how often have we seen it making laws in one session, that have been repealed the next, either on account of the fluctuation of party, or their own impropriety.

This could not have been the case in a compound legislature; it is therefore proper to have efficient restraints upon the legislative body. These restraints arise from different sources: I will mention some of them. In this constitution they will be produced in a very considerable degree, by a division of the power in the legislative body itself. Under this system, they may arise likewise from the interference of those officers, who will be introduced into the executive and judicial departments. They may spring also from another source; the election by the people; and finally, under this constitution, they may proceed from the great and last resort—from the PEOPLE themselves. I say, under this constitution, the legislature may be restrained, and kept within its prescribed bounds, by the interposition of the judicial department. This I hope, sir, to explain clearly and satisfactorily. I had occasion, on a former day, to state that the power of the constitution was paramount to the power of the legislature, acting under that constitution. For it is possible that the legislature, when acting in that capacity, may transgress the bounds assigned to it, and an act may pass, in the usual *mode*, notwithstanding that trangression; but when it comes to be discussed before the judges—when they consider its principles, and find it to be incompatible with the superior power of the constitution, it is their duty to pronounce it void; and judges independent, and not obliged to look to every session, for a continuance of their salaries, will behave with intrepidity, and refuse to act the sanction of judicial authority. In the same manner, the president of the United States could shield himself, and refuse to carry into effect, an act that violates the constitution.

In order to secure the president from any dependence upon the legislature, as to his salary, it is provided, that he shall, at stated times, receive for his services, a compensation that shall neither be encreased nor diminished, during the period for which he shall have been elected, and that he shall not receive, within that period, any other emolument from the United States, or any of them.

To secure to the judges this independence, it is ordered that they shall receive for their services, a compensation which shall not be diminished during their continuance in office. The congress may be restrained, by the election of its constituent parts. If a legislature shall make a law contrary to the constitution, or oppressive to the people, they have it in their power, every second year, in one branch, and every sixth year in the other, to displace the men, who act thus inconsistent with their duty; and if this is not sufficient, they have still a further power; they may assume into their own hands, the alteration of the constitution itself—they may revoke the lease, when the conditions are broken by the tenant. But the most useful restraint upon the legislature, because it operates constantly, arises from the division of its power, among two branches, and from the qualified negative of the president upon both. As this government is formed, there are two sources from which the representation is drawn, though they both ultimately flow from the people. *States* now exist and others will come into existence; it was thought proper that they should be represented in the general government. But, gentlemen will please to remember, this constitution was not framed merely for the states; it was framed for the PEOPLE also; and the popular branch of the congress, will be the objects of their immediate choice.

The two branches will serve as checks upon each other; they have the same legislative authorities, except in one instance. Money bills must originate in the house of representatives. The senate can pass no law without the concurrence of the house of representatives; nor can the house of representatives, without the concurrence of the senate. I believe, sir, that the observation which I am now going to make, will apply to mankind in every situation; they will act with more caution, and perhaps more integrity, if their proceedings are to be under the inspection and control of another, than when they are not. From this principle, the proceedings of congress will be conducted with a degree of circumspection not common in single bodies, where nothing more is necessary to be done, than to carry the business through amongst themselves, whether it be right or wrong. In compound legislatures, every object must be submitted to a distinct body, not influenced by the arguments, or warped by the prejudices of the other. And, I believe, that the persons who will form the congress, will be cautious in running the risk, *with a bare majority*, of having the negative of the president put on their proceedings. As there will be more circumspection in forming the laws, so there will be more stability in the laws when made. Indeed one is the consequence of the other; for what has been well considered, and founded in good sense, will, in practice, be useful and salutary, and of consequence will not be liable to be soon repealed. Though two bodies may not possess more wisdom or patriotism, than what may be found in a single body, yet they will necessarily introduce a greater degree of precision. An indigested and inaccurate code of laws, is one of the most dangerous things that can be introduced into any government. The force of this observation is well known by every gentleman that has attended to the laws of this state. This, sir, is a very important advantage, that will arise from this division of the legislative authority.

I will proceed now to take some notice of a still further restraint upon the legislature—I mean the qualified negative of the president. I think this will be attended with very important advantages, for the security and happiness of the people of the United States. The president, sir, will not be a stranger to our country, to our laws, or to our wishes. He will, under this constitution, be placed in office as the president of the whole union, and will be chosen in such a manner that he may be justly stiled THE MAN OF THE PEOPLE; being elected by the different parts of the United States, he will consider himself as not particularly interested for any one of them, but will watch over the whole with paternal care and affection. This will be the natural conduct to recommend himself to those who placed him in that high chair, and I consider it as a very important advantage, that such a man must have every law presented to him, before it can become binding upon the United States. He will have before him the fullest information of our situation, he will avail himself not only of records and official communications, foreign and domestic, but he will have also the advice of the executive officers in the different departments of the general government.

If in consequence of this information and advice, he exercise the authority given to him, the effect will not be lost—he returns his objections, together with the bill, and unless two thirds of both branches of the legislature are *now* found to approve it, it does not become a law. But even if his objections do not prevent its passing into a law, they will not be useless; they will be kept together with the law, and, in the archives of congress, will be valuable and practical materials, to form the minds of posterity for legislation—if it is found that the law operates inconveniently or oppressively, the people may discover in the president's objections, the source of that inconvenience or oppression. Further, sir, when objections shall have been made, it is provided, in order to secure the greatest degree of caution and responsibility, that the votes of both houses shall be determined by yeas and nays, and the names of the persons, voting for and against the bill, shall be entered in the journal of each house respectively. Thus much I have thought proper to say, with regard to the distribution of the legislative authority, and the restraints under which it will be exercised.

The gentleman in opposition strongly insists, that the general clause at the end of the eighth section, gives to congress a power of legislating generally; but I cannot conceive by what means he will render the word susceptible of that expansion. Can the words, the congress shall have power to make all laws, which shall be necessary and proper to carry into execution the foregoing powers, be capable of giving them general legislative power?—I hope that it is not meant to give to congress merely an illusive shew of authority, to deceive themselves or constituents any longer. On the contrary, I trust it is meant, that they shall have the power of carrying into effect the laws, which they shall make under the powers vested in them by this constitution. In answer to the gentleman from Fayette (Mr. Smilie,) on the subject of the press, I beg leave to make an observation; it is very true, sir, that this constitution says nothing with regard to that subject, nor was it necessary, because it will be found, that there is given to the general government no power whatsoever concerning it; and no law in pursuance of the constitution, can possibly be enacted, to destroy that liberty.

I heard the honorable gentleman make this general assertion, that the Congress was certainly vested with power to make such a law, but I would be glad to know by what part of this constitution such a power is given? Until that is done, I shall not enter into a minute investigation of the matter, but shall at present satisfy myself with giving an answer to a question that has been put. It has been asked, if a law should be made to punish libels, and the judges should proceed under that law, what chance would the printer have of an acquittal? And it has been said he would drop into a den of devouring monsters.

I presume it was not in the view of the honorable gentleman to say there is no such thing as a libel, or that the writers of such ought not to be punished. The idea of the liberty of the press, is not carried so far as this in any country—what is meant by the liberty of the press is, that there should be no antecedent restraint upon it; but that every author is responsible when he attacks the security or welfare of the government, or the safety, character and property of the individual. With regard to attacks upon the public, the mode of proceeding is by a prosecution. Now if a libel is written, it must be within some one of the United States, or the district of congress. With regard to that district, I hope it will take care to preserve this as well as the other rights of freemen; for whatever district congress may chuse, the cession of it cannot be completed without the consent of its inhabitants. Now sir, if this libel is to be tried, it must be tried where the offence was committed; for under this constitution, as declared in the second section of the third article, the trial must be held in the state; therefore on this occasion it must be tried where it was published, if the indictment is for publishing; and it must be tried likewise by a jury of that state. Now I would ask, is the person prosecuted in a worse situation under the general government, even if it had the power to make laws on this subject, than he is at present under the state government? It is true, there is no particular regulation made, to have the jury come from the body of the county in which the offence was committed; but there are some states in which this mode of collecting juries is contrary to their established custom, and gentlemen ought to consider that this constitution was not meant merely for Pennsylvania. In some states the juries are not taken from a single county. In Virginia, the sheriff, I believe, is not confined, even to the inhabitants of the state, but is at liberty to take any man he pleases, and put him on the jury. In Maryland I think a sett of jurors serve for the whole Western Shore, and another for the Eastern Shore.

I beg to make one remark on what one gentleman has said, with respect to amendments being proposed to this constitution. To whom are the convention to make report of such amendments? He tells you, to the present congress. I do not wish to report to that body, the representatives only of the state governments; they may not be disposed to admit the people into a participation of their power. It has also been supposed, that a wonderful unanimity subsists among those who are enemies to the proposed system. On this point I also differ from the gentleman who made the observation. I have taken every pains in my power, and read every publication I could meet with, in order to gain information; and as far as I have been able to judge, the opposition is inconsiderable and inconsistent. Instead of agreeing in their objections, those who make them, bring forward such as are diametrically opposite. On one hand, it is said, that the representation in congress is too small; on the other, it is said to be too numerous. Some think the authority of the senate too great; some that of the house of representatives; and some that of both. Others draw their fears from the powers of the president; and like the iron race of Cadmus, these opponents rise, only to destroy each other.

James Wilson on the Slave-Trade Clause

December 3, 1787

Much fault has been found with the mode of expression, used in the first clause of the ninth section of the first article. I believe I can assign a reason, why that mode of expression was used, and why the term slave was not directly admitted in this constitution;—and as to the manner of laying taxes, this is not the first time that the subject has come into the view of the United States, and of the legislatures of the several states. The gentleman (Mr. Findley) will recollect, that in the present congress, the quota of the fœderal debt, and general expences, was to be in proportion to the value of LAND, and other enumerated property, within the states. After trying this for a number of years, it was found on all hands, to be a mode that could not be carried into execution. Congress were satisfied of this, and in the year 1783, recommended, in conformity with the powers they possess'd under the articles of confederation, that the quota should be according to the number of free people, including those bound to servitude, and excluding Indians not taxed. These were the very expressions used in 1783, and the fate of this recommendation was similar to all their other resolutions. It was not carried into effect, but it was adopted by no fewer than eleven, out of thirteen states; and it can not but be matter of surprise, to hear gentlemen, who agreed to this very mode of expression at that time, come forward and state it as an objection on the present occasion. It was natural, sir, for the late convention, to adopt the mode after it had been agreed to by eleven states, and to use the expression, which they found had been received as unexceptionable before. With respect to the clause, restricting congress from prohibiting the migration or importation of such persons, as any of the states now existing, shall think proper to admit, prior to the year 1808. The honorable gentleman says, that this clause is not only dark, but intended to grant to congress, for that time, the power to admit the importation of slaves. No such thing was intended; but I will tell you what was done, and it give me high pleasure, that so much was done. Under the present confederation, the states may admit the importation of slaves as long as they please; but by this article after the year 1808, the congress will have power to prohibit such importation, notwithstanding the disposition of any state to the contrary. I consider this as laying the foundation for banishing slavery out of this country; and though the period is more distant than I could wish, yet it will produce the same kind, gradual change, which was pursued in Pennsylvania. It is with much satisfaction I view this power in the general government, whereby they may lay an interdiction on this reproachful trade; but an immediate advantage is also obtained, for a tax or duty may be imposed on such importation, not exceeding ten dollars for each person; and, this sir, operates as a partial prohibition; it was all that could be obtained, I am sorry it was no more; but from this I think there is reason to hope, that yet a few years, and it will be prohibited altogether; and in the mean time, the new states which are to be formed, will be under the control of congress in this particular; and slaves will never be introduced amongst them. The gentleman says, that it is unfortunate in another point of view; it means to prohibit the introduction of white people from Europe, as this tax may deter them from coming amongst us; a little impartiality and attention will discover the care that the convention took in selecting their language. The words are, the *migration or* IMPORTATION of such persons, &c. shall not be prohibited by congress prior to the year 1808, but a tax or duty may be imposed on such IMPORTATION; it is observable here, that the term migration is dropped, when a tax or duty is mentioned; so that congress have power to impose the tax, only on those imported.

Robert Whitehill Replies to Wilson on the Slave-Trade Clause

December 3, 1787

Mr. PRESIDENT,

It has been said that Congress will have power, by the new constitution, to lay an impost on the *importation* of slaves, into these states; but that they will have no power to impose any tax upon the *migration* of Europeans. Do the gentlemen, sir, mean to insult our understandings, when they assert this? Or are they ignorant of the English language? If, because of their ignorance, they are at a loss, I can easily explain this clause for them—The words *"migration"* and *"importation,"* sir, being *connected* by the *disjunctive* conjunction *"or,"* certainly mean either migration, or importation; either the one, or the other; or both. Therefore, when we say "a tax may be laid upon such *importation*," we mean, either upon the *importation*, or *migration*; or upon both; for, because they are *joined together*, in the first instance, by the *disjunctive* conjunction *or*, they are both synonimous terms for the same thing—therefore, *"such importation,"* because the *comparative* word, *such*, is used, means both importation, and migration.

James Wilson's Summation and Final Rebuttal

December 11, 1787

MR. WILSON.

Morning Session

Three weeks have now elapsed since this convention met: Some of the delegates attended on Tuesday the 20th November; a great majority within a day or two afterwards, and all but one on the 4th day. We have been since employed in discussing the business for which we are sent here. I think it will now become evident to every person who takes a candid view of our discussions, that it is high time our proceedings should draw towards a conclusion. Perhaps our debates have already continued as long, nay, longer than is sufficient for every good purpose. The business which we were intended to perform, is necessarily reduced to a very narrow compass. The single question to be determined is, shall we assent to and ratify the constitution proposed?

As this is the first state whose convention has met on the subject, and as the subject itself is of very great importance not only to Pennsylvania, but to the United States, it was thought proper, fairly, openly and candidly, to canvass it. This has been done. You have heard, Mr. President, from day to day, and from week to week, the objections that could be offered from any quarter. We have heard those objections once—we have heard a great number of them repeated much oftener than once. Will it answer any valuable end, sir, to protract these debates longer? I suppose it will not. I apprehend it may serve to promote very pernicious and destructive purposes. It may perhaps be insinuated to other states, and even to distant parts of this state, by people in opposition to this system, that the expediency of adopting, is at most very doubtful, and that the business labours among the members of the convention.

This would not be a true representation of the fact; for there is the greatest reason to believe, that there is a very considerable majority, who do not hesitate to ratify the constitution. We were sent here to express the voice of our constituents on the subject, and I believe that many of them expected to hear the echo of that voice before this time.

When I consider the attempts that have been made on this floor, and the many misrepresentations of what has been said among us that have appeared in the public papers, printed in this city, I confess that I am induced to suspect that opportunity may be taken to pervert and abuse the principles on which the friends of this constitution act. If attempts are made here, will they not be repeated when the distance is greater, and the means of information fewer? Will they not at length produce an uneasiness, for which there is, in fact, no cause? Ought we not to prohibit any such uses being made of the continuance of our deliberations? We do not wish to preclude debate—of this our conduct has furnished the most ample testimony. The members in opposition have not been prevented a repetition of all their objections, that they could urge against this plan.

The honorable gentleman from Fayette (Mr. Smilie) the other evening claimed for the minority, the merit of contending for the rights of mankind; and he told us, that it has been the practice of all ages, to treat such minorities with contempt: he further took the liberty of observing, that if the majority had the power, they do not want the inclination to consign the minority to punishment. I know that claims, self-made, form no small part of the merit, to which we have heard undisguised pretences; but it is one thing to claim, and it is another thing, very different indeed, to support that claim. The minority, sir, are contending for the rights of mankind; what then are the majority contending for? If the minority are contending for the rights of mankind, the majority must be contending for the doctrines of tyranny and slavery. Is it probable that that is the case? Who are the majority in this assembly? Are they not the people? are they not the representatives of the people, as well as the minority? Were they not elected by the people as well as by the minority? Were they not elected by the greater part of the people? Have we a single right separate from the rights of the people? Can we forge fetters for others, that will not be clasped round our own limbs? Can we make heavy chains, that shall not cramp the growth of our own posterity? On what fancied distinction shall the minority assume to themselves the merit of contending for the rights of mankind?

Sir, if the system proposed by the late convention, and the conduct of its advocates, who have appeared in this house, deserve the declarations and insinuations that have been made concerning them—well may we exclaim—Ill fated America! thy crisis was approaching! perhaps it was come! Thy various interests were neglected—thy most sacred rights were insecure. Without a government! without energy! without confidence internally! without respect externally! the advantages of society were lost to thee! In such a situation, distressed but not despairing, thou desiredst to re-assume thy native vigour, and to lay the foundation of future empire! Thou selectedst a number of thy sons, to meet together for the purpose. The selected and honored characters met; but horrid to tell! they not only consented, but they combined in an aristocratic system, calculated and intended to enslave their country! Unhappy Pennsylvania! thou, as a part of the union, must share in its unfortunate fate! for when this system, after being laid before thy citizens, comes before the delegates selected by you for its consideration, there are found but three of the numerous members that have virtue enough to raise their voices in support of the rights of mankind! America, particularly Pennsylvania, must be ill starred indeed, if this is a true state of the case! I trust we may address our country in far other language.

Happy America! thy crisis was indeed alarming, but thy situation was not desperate. We had confidence in our country; though on which ever side we turned, we were presented with scenes of distress. Though the jarring interests of the various states, and the different habits and inclinations of their inhabitants, all lay in the way, and rendered our prospect gloomy, and discouraging indeed, yet such were the generous and mutual sacrifices offered up, that amidst forty two members, who represented twelve of the United States, there were only three who did not attest the instrument as a confirmation of its goodness—happy Pennsylvania! this plan has been laid before thy citizens for consideration, they have sent delegates to express their voice; and listen, with rapture listen! from only three opposition has been heard against it.

The singular unanimity that has attended the whole progress of their business, will in the minds of those considerate men, who have not had opportunity to examine the general and particular interest of their country, prove to their satisfaction, that it is an excellent constitution, and worthy to be adopted, ordained and established by the people of the United States.

After having viewed the arguments drawn from *probability*, whether this is a good or a bad system, whether those who contend for it, or those who contend against it, contend for the rights of mankind, let us step forward and examine the *fact*.

We were told some days ago, by the honorable gentleman from Westmoreland (Mr. Findley) when speaking of this system and its objects, that the convention, no doubt, thought they were forming a compact or contract of the greatest importance. Sir, I confess I was much surprised at so late a stage of the debate, to hear such principles maintained. It was matter of surprise to see the great leading principle of this system, still so very much misunderstood. "The convention, no doubt, thought they were forming a compact!" I cannot answer for what every member thought; but I believe it cannot be said, that they thought they were making a compact, because I cannot discover the least trace of a compact in that system. There can be no compact unless there are more parties than one. It is a new doctrine, that one can make a compact with himself. "The convention were forming compacts!" With whom? I know no bargains that were made there. I am unable to conceive who the parties could be. The state governments make a bargain with one another; that is the doctrine that is endeavoured to be established, by gentlemen in opposition, their state sovereignties wish to be represented! But far other were the ideas of the convention, and far other are those conveyed in the system itself.

As this subject has been often mentioned and as often misunderstood, it may not be improper to take some further notice of it. This, Mr. President, is not a government founded upon compact; it is founded upon the power of the people. They express in their name and their authority, *"We the People do ordain and establish,"* &c. from their ratification, and their ratification alone, it is to take its constitutional authenticity; without that, it is no more than *tabula rasa*.

I know very well all the common-place rant of state sovereignties, and that government is founded in original compact. If that petition was examined, it will be found not to acceed very well with the true principle of free government. It does not suit the language or genius of the system before us. I think it does not accord with experience, so far as I have been able to obtain information from history.

The greatest part of government have been founded on conquest; perhaps a few early ones may have had their origin in paternal authority. Sometimes a family united, and that family afterwards extended itself into a community. But the greatest governments which have appeared on the face of the globe, have been founded in conquest. The great empires of Assyria, Persia, Macedonia and Rome, were all of this kind. I know well that in Great-Britain, since the revolution, it has become a principle, that the constitution is founded in contract; but the form and time of that contract, no writer has yet attempted to discover. It was however recognised at the time of the revolution, therefore is politically true. But we should act very imprudently to consider our liberties as placed on such foundation.

If we go a little further on this subject, I think we see that the doctrine of original compact, cannot be supported consistently with the best principles of government. If we admit it, we exclude the idea of amendment; because a contract once entered into between the governor and governed, becomes obligatory, and cannot be altered but by the mutual consent of both parties. The citizens of United America, I presume do not wish to stand on that footing, with those to whom, from convenience, they please to delegate the exercise of the general powers necessary for sustaining and preserving the union. They wish a principle established, by the operation of which the legislatures may feel the direct authority of the people. The people possessing that authority, will continue to exercise it by amending and improving their own work. This constitution may be found to have defects in it; amendments hence may become necessary; but the idea of a government founded on contract, destroys the means of improvement. We hear it every time the gentlemen are up, "shall we violate the confederation, which directs every alteration that is thought necessary to be established by the state legislatures only." Sir, those gentlemen must ascend to a higher source; the people fetter themselves by no contract. If your state legislatures have cramped themselves by compact, it was done without the authority of the people, who alone possess the supreme power.

I have already shewn, that this system is not a compact or contract; the system itself tells you what it is; it is an ordinance and establishment of the people. I think that the force of the introduction to the work, must by this time have been felt. It is not an unmeaning flourish. The expressions declare, in a practical manner, the principle of this constitution. It is ordained and established by the people themselves; and we, who give our votes for it, are merely the proxies of our constituents. We sign it as their attornies, and as to ourselves, we agree to it as individuals.

We are told by honorable gentlemen in opposition, "that the present confederation should have been continued, but that additional powers should have been given to it: That such was the business of the late convention, and that they had assumed to themselves, the power of proposing another in its stead; and that which is proposed, is such an one as was not expected by the legislatures nor by the people." I apprehend this would have been a very insecure, very inadequate, and a very pernicious mode of proceeding. Under the present confederation, congress certainly do not possess sufficient power; but one body of men we know they are; and were they invested with additional powers, they must become dangerous. Did not the honorable gentleman himself tell us, that the powers of government, vested either in one man, or one body of men, formed the very description of tyranny? To have placed in the present, the legislative, the executive and judicial authority, all of which are essential to the general government, would indubitably have produced the severest despotism. From this short deduction, one of these two things must have appeared to the convention, and must appear to every man, who is at the pains of thinking on the subject. It was indispensably necessary, either to make a new distribution of the powers of government, or to give such powers to one body of men, as would constitute a tyranny. If it was proper to avoid tyranny, it becomes a requisite to avoid placing additional powers in the hands of a congress, constituted like the present; hence the conclusion is warranted, that a different organization ought to take place.

Our next enquiry ought to be, whether this is the most proper disposition and organization of the necessary powers. But before I consider this subject, I think it proper to notice one sentiment, expressed by an honorable gentleman from the county of Cumberland (Mr. Whitehill;) he asserts the extent of the government is too great, and this system cannot be executed. What is the consequence, if this assertion is true? It strikes directly at the root of the union.

I admit, Mr. President, there are great difficulties in adopting a system of good and free governments to the extent of our country. But I am sure that our interests as citizens, as states and as a nation, depend essentially upon an union. This constitution is proposed to accomplish that great and desirable end. Let the experiment be made; let the system be fairly and candidly tried, before it is determined that it cannot be executed.

I proceed to another objection; for I mean to answer those that have been suggested, since I had the honor of addressing you last week. It has been alleged by honorable gentlemen, that this general government possesses powers, for *internal* purposes, and that the general government cannot exercise internal powers. The honorable member from Westmoreland (Mr. Findley) dilates on this subject, and instances the opposition that was made by the colonies against Great-Britain, to prevent her imposing internal taxes or excises. And before the fœderal government will be able to impose the one, or obtain the other, he considers it necessary that it should possess power for every internal purpose.

Let us examine these objections; if this government does not possess internal as well as external power, and that power for internal as well as external purposes, I apprehend, that all that has hitherto been done, must go for nothing. I apprehend a government that cannot answer the purposes for which it is intended, is not a government for this country. I know that congress, under the present articles of confederation, possess no internal power, and we see the consequences; they can recommend; they can go further, they can make requisitions, but there they must stop. For as far as I recollect, after making a law, they cannot take a single step towards carrying it into execution. I believe it will be found in experience, that with regard to the exercise of internal powers, the general government will not be unnecessarily rigourous. The future collection of the duties and imposts, will, in the opinion of some, supercede the necessity of having recourse to internal taxation. The United States will not, perhaps, be often under the necessity of using this power at all; but if they should, it will be exercised only in a moderate degree. The good sense of the citizens of the United States, is not to be alarmed by the picture of taxes collected at the point of the bayonet. There is no more reason to suppose, that the delegates and representatives in congress, any more than the legislature of Pennsylvania, or any other state, will act in this manner. Insinuations of this kind, made against one body of men, and not against another, though both the representatives of the people, are not made with propriety, nor will they have the weight of argument. I apprehend the greatest part of the revenue will arise from external taxation. But certainly it would have been very unwise in the late convention to have omitted the addition of the other powers; and I think it would be very unwise in this convention, to refuse to adopt this constitution, because it grants congress power to lay and collect taxes, for the purpose of providing for the common defence and general welfare of the United States.

What is to be done to effect these great purposes, if an impost should be found insufficient? Suppose a war was suddenly declared against us by a foreign power, possessed of a formidable navy, our navigation would be laid prostrate, our imports must cease; and shall our existence as a nation, depend upon the peaceful navigation of our seas? A strong exertion of maratime power, on the part of an enemy, might deprive us of these sources of revenue in a few months.

It may suit honorable gentlemen, who live at the western extremity of this state, that they should contribute nothing, by internal taxes, to the support of the general government. They care not what restraints are laid upon our commerce; for what is the commerce of Philadelphia to the inhabitants on the other side the Alleghany Mountain? But though it may suit them, it does not suit those in the lower part of the state, who are by far the most numerous. Nor can we agree that our safety should depend altogether upon a revenue arising from commerce.

Excise may be a necessary mode of taxation; it takes place in most states already.

The capitation tax is mentioned as one of those that are exceptionable. In some states, that mode of taxation is used; but I believe in many, it would be received with great reluctance; there are one or two states, where it is constantly in use, and without any difficulties and inconveniences arising from it. An excise, in its very principles, is an improper tax, if it could be avoided; but yet it has been a source of revenue in Pennsylvania, both before the revolution and since; during all which time, we have enjoyed the benefit of free government.

I presume, sir, that the executive powers of government ought to be commensurate with the government itself, and that a government which cannot act in every part, is so far defective. Consequently it is necessary, that congress possess powers to tax internally, as well as externally.

It is objected to this system, that under it there is no sovereignty left in the state governments. I have had occasion to reply to this already; but I should be very glad to know at what period the state governments became possessed of the supreme power. On the principle on which I found my arguments, and that is the principle of this constitution, the supreme power resides in the people. If they chuse to indulge a part of their sovereign power to be exercised by the state governments, they may. If they have done it, the states were right in exercising it; but if they think it no longer safe or convenient, they will resume it, or make a new distribution, more likely to be productive of that good, which ought to be our constant aim.

The power both of the general government, and the state

governments, under this system, are acknowledged to be so many emanations of power from the people. The great object now to be attended to, instead of disagreeing about who shall possess the supreme power, is to consider whether the present arrangement is well calculated to promote and secure the tranquillity and happiness of our common country. These are the dictates of sound and unsophisticated sense, and what ought to employ the attention and judgment of this honorable body.

We are next told, by the honorable gentlemen in opposition (as indeed we have been from the beginning of the debates in this convention, to the conclusion of their speeches yesterday) that this is a consolidated government, and will abolish the state governments. Definitions of a consolidated government have been called for; the gentlemen gave us what they termed definition, but it does not seem, to me at least, that they have as yet expressed clear ideas upon that subject. I will endeavour to state their different ideas upon this point. The gentleman from Westmoreland (Mr. Findley) when speaking on this subject, says, that he means by a consolidation, that government which puts the thirteen states into one.

The honorable gentleman from Fayette (Mr. Smilie) gives you this definition: "What I mean by a consolidated government, is one that will transfer the sovereignty from the state governments, to the general government."

The honorable member from Cumberland (Mr. Whitehill) instead of giving you a definition, sir, tells you again, that "it is a consolidated government, and we have proved it so."

These, I think, sir, are the different descriptions given us of a consolidated government. As to the first, that it is a consolidated government, that puts the thirteen United States into one; if it is meant, that the general government will destroy the governments of the states, I will admit that such a government would not suit the people of America: It would be improper for *this* country, because it could not be proportioned to *its extent* on the principles of freedom. But that description does not apply to the system before you. This, instead of placing the state governments in jeopardy, is founded on their existence. On this principle, its organization depends; it must stand or fall, as the state governments are secured or ruined.

Therefore, though this may be a very proper description of a consolidating government, yet it must be disregarded as inapplicable to the proposed constitution. It is not treated with decency, when such insinuations are offered against it.

The honorable gentleman (Mr. Smilie) tells you, that a consolidating government, "is one that will transfer the sovereignty from the state governments to the general government." Under this system, the sovereignty is not in the possession of the state governments, therefore it cannot be transferred from them to the general government. So that in no point of view of this definition, can we discover that it applies to the present system.

In the exercise of its powers will be insured the exercise of their powers to the state government; it will insure peace and stability to them; their strength will encrease with its strength, their growth will extend with its growth.

Indeed narrow minds, and some such there are in every government—narrow minds, and intriguing spirits, will be active in sowing dissentions and promoting discord between them. But those whose understandings, and whose hearts are good enough to pursue the general welfare, will find, that what is the interest of the whole, must, on the great scale, be the interest of every part. It will be the duty of a state, as of an individual, to sacrifice her own convenience to the general good of the union.

The next objection that I mean to take notice of is, that the powers of the several parts of this government are not kept as distinct and independent as they ought to be. I admit the truth of this general sentiment. I do not think, that in the powers of the senate, the distinction is marked with so much accuracy as I wished, and still wish; but yet I am of opinion, that real and effectual security is obtained, which is saying a great deal. I do not consider this part as *wholly* unexceptionable; but even where there are defects in this system, they are improvements upon the old. I will go a little further; though in this system, the distinction and independence of power is not adhered to with entire theoretical precision, yet it is more strictly adhered to than in any other system of government in the world. In the constitution of Pennsylvania, the executive department exercises judicial powers, in the trial of public officers; yet a similar power in this system is complained of; at the same time the constitution of Pennsylvania is referred to, as an example for the late convention, to have taken a lesson by.

In New-Jersey, in Georgia, in South-Carolina, and in North Carolina, the executive power is blended with the legislative. Turn to their constitutions, and see in how many instances.

In North-Carolina, the senate and house of commons, elect the governor himself; they likewise elect seven persons, to be a council of state, to advise the governor in the execution of his office. Here we find the whole executive department under the nomination of the legislature, at least the most important part of it.

In South-Carolina, the legislature appoint the governor and commander in chief, lieutenant governor and privy council. "Justices of the peace shall be nominated by the legislature, and commissioned by the governor," and what is more, they are appointed during pleasure. All other judicial officers, are to be appointed by the senate and house of representatives. I might go further, and detail a great multitude of instances, in which the legislative, executive, and judicial powers are blended, but it is unnecessary; I only mention these to shew, that though this constitution does not arrive at what is called perfection, yet, it contains great improvements, and its powers are distributed with a degree of accuracy, superior to what is termed accuracy, in particular states.

There are four instances in which improper powers are said to be blended in the senate. We are told, that this government is imperfect, because the senate possess the power of trying impeachments. But here, sir, the senate are under a check, as no impeachment can be tried until it is made; and the house of representatives possess the sole power of making impeachments. We are told that the share which the senate have in making treaties, is exceptionable; but here they are also under a check, by a constituent part of the government, and nearly the immediate representative of the people, I mean the president of the United States. They can make no treaty without his concurrence. The same observation applies in the appointment of officers. Every officer must be nominated solely and exclusively, by the president.

Much has been said on the subject of treaties, and this power is denominated a blending of the legislative and executive powers in the senate. It is but justice to represent the favorable, as well as unfavorable side of a question, and from thence determine, whether the objectionable parts are of a sufficient weight to induce a rejection of this constitution.

There is no doubt, sir, but under this constitution, treaties will become the supreme law of the land; nor is there any doubt but the senate and president possess the power of making them. But though treaties are to have the force of laws, they are in some important respects very different from other acts of legislation. In making laws, our own consent alone is necessary. In forming treaties, the concurrence of another power becomes necessary; treaties, sir, are truly contracts, or compacts, between the different states, nations, or princes, who find it convenient or necessary to enter into them. Some gentlemen are of opinion, that the power of making treaties should have been placed in the legislature at large; there are, however, reasons that operate with a great force on the other side. Treaties are frequently, (especially in time of war,) of such a nature, that it would be extremely improper to publish them, or even commit the secret of their negociation to any great number of persons. For my part I am not an advocate for secrecy in transactions relating to the public; not generally even in forming treaties, because I think that the history of the diplomatique corps will evince, even in that great department of politics, the truth of an old adage, that "honesty is the best policy," and this is the conduct of the most able negociators; yet sometimes secrecy may be necessary, and therefore it becomes an argument against committing the knowledge of these transactions to too many persons. But in their nature treaties originate differently from laws. They are made by equal parties, and each side has half of the bargain to make; they will be made between us and the powers at the distance of three thousand miles. A long series of negociation will frequently precede them; and can it be the opinion of these gentlemen, that the legislature should be in session during this whole time? It well deserves to be remarked, that though the house of representatives possess no active part in making treaties, yet their legislative authority will be found to have strong restraining influence upon both president and senate. In England, if the king and his ministers find themselves, during their negociation, to be embarrassed, because an existing law is not repealed, or a new law is not enacted, they give notice to the legislature of their situation, and inform them that it will be necessary, before the treaty can operate, that some law be repealed, or some be made. And will not the same thing take place here? Shall less prudence, less caution, less moderation, take place among those who negotiate treaties for the United States, than among those who negotiate them for the other nations of the earth? And let it be attended to, that even in the making treaties the states are immediately represented, and the people mediately represented; two of the constituent parts of government must concur in making them. Neither the president nor the senate solely, can complete a treaty; they are checks upon each other, and are so balanced, as to produce security to the people.

I might suggest other reasons, to add weight to what has already been offered, but I believe it is not necessary; yet let me however add one thing, the senate is a favorite with many of the states, and it was with difficulty that these checks could be procured: it was one of the last exertions of conciliation, in the late convention, that obtained them.

It has been alleged, as a consequence of the small number of representatives, that they will not know as intimately as they ought, the interests, inclinations, or habits, of their constituents.

We find on an examination of all its parts, that the objects of this government are such, as extend beyond the bounds of the particular states. This is the line of distinction between this government, and the particular state governments.

This principle I had an opportunity of illustrating on a former occasion. Now when we come to consider the objects of this government, we shall find, that in making our choice of a proper character, to be a member of the house of representatives, we ought to fix on one, whose mind and heart are enlarged; who possesses a general knowledge of the interests of America, and a disposition to make use of that knowledge, for the advantage and welfare of his country. It belongs not to this government to make an act for a particular township, county, or state.

A defect in *minute* information, has not certainly been an objection in the management of the business of the United States; but the want of enlarged ideas, has hitherto been chargeable on our councils; yet even with regard to minute knowledge, I do not conceive it impossible to find eight characters, that may be very well informed as to the situation, interests and views, of every part of this state; and who may have a concomitant interest with their fellow citizens: they could not materially injure others, without affecting their own fortunes.

I did say, that in order to obtain that enlarged information in our representatives, a large district for election would be more proper than a small one. When I speak of large districts, it is not agreeable to the idea entertained by the honorable member from Fayette (Mr. Smilie) who tells you, that elections for large districts must be ill attended, because the people will not chuse to go very far on this business. It is not meant, sir, by me, that the votes should be taken at one place; no, sir, the elections may be held thro' this state, in the same manner as elections for members of the general assembly, and this may be done too without any additional inconvenience or expence.

If it could be effected all the people of the same society ought to meet in one place, and communicate freely with each other on the great business of representation. Though this cannot be done in fact, yet we find that it is the most favorite and constitutional idea. It is supported by this principle too, that every member is the representative of the whole community, and not of a particular part. The larger therefore the district is, the greater is the probability of selecting wise and virtuous characters, and the more agreeable it is to the constitutional principle of representation.

As to the objection, that the house of representatives may be bribed by the senate, I confess I do not see that bribery is an objection against *this system*; it is rather an objection against human nature. I am afraid that bribes in every government may be offered and received; but let me ask of the gentlemen who urge this objection, to point out where any power is given to bribe *under this constitution?* Every species of influence is guarded against as much as possible. Can the senate procure money to effect such design? All public monies must be disposed of by law, and it is necessary that the house of representatives originate such law. Before the money can be got out of the treasury, it must be appropriated by law. If the legislature had the effrontery to set aside three or four hundred thousand pounds for this purpose, and the people would tamely suffer it, I grant it might be done; and in Pennsylvania the legislature might do the same; for by a law, and that conformably to the constitution, they might divide among themselves what portion of the public money they pleased. I shall just remark, sir, that the objections, which have repeatedly been made, with regard to "the number of representatives being too small, and that they may possibly be made smaller: that the districts are too large, and not within the reach of the people; and that the house of representatives may be bribed by the senate." These objections come with an uncommon degree of impropriety, from those who would refer us back to the articles of confederation. For under those, the representation of this state cannot exceed seven members, and may consist of only two; and these are wholly without the reach or control of the people. Is there not also greater danger that the majority of such a body might be more easily bribed, than the majority of one, not only more numerous, but checked by a division of two or three distinct and independent parts? The danger is certainly better guarded against in the proposed system, than in any other yet devised.

The next objections which I shall notice, are, "that the powers of the senate are too great, that the representation therein is unequal, and that the senate, from the smallness of its number, may be bribed." Is there any propriety in referring us to the confederation on this subject? Because, in one or two instances, the senate possess more power than the house of representatives, are these gentlemen supported in their remarks, when they tell you they wished and expected more powers to be given to the present congress, a body certainly much more exceptionable than any instituted under this system?

"That the representation in the senate is unequal," I regret, because I am of opinion, the states ought to be represented according to their importance; but in this system there is considerable improvement; for the true principle of representation is carried into the house of representatives, and into the choice of the president; and without the assistance of one or the other of these, the senate is inactive, and can do neither good or evil.

It is repeated again and again, by the honorable gentlemen, "that the power over elections, which is given to the general government in this system, is a dangerous power." I must own I feel myself surprized that an objection of this kind should be persisted in, after what has been said by my honorable colleague in reply. I think it has appeared by a minute investigation of the subject, that it would have been not only unwise, but highly improper in the late convention, to have omitted this clause, or given less power, than it does over elections. Such powers, sir, are enjoyed by every state government in the United States. In some, they are of a much greater magnitude; and why should this be the only one deprived of them? Ought not these, as well as every other legislative body, to have the power of judging of the qualifications of its own members? "The times, places and manner of holding elections for representatives, may be altered by congress." This power, sir, has been shewn to be necessary, not only on some particular occasions, but even to the very existence of the fœderal government. I have heard some very improbable suspicions indeed, suggested with regard to the manner in which it will be exercised. Let us suppose it may be improperly exercised; is it not more likely so to be by the particular states, than by the government of the United States? because the general government will be more studious of the good of the whole, than a particular state will be; and therefore, when the power of regulating the time, place or manner of holding elections, is exercised by the congress, it will be to correct the improper regulations of a particular state.

I now proceed to the second article of this constitution, which relates to the executive department.

I find, sir, from an attention to the arguments used by the gentlemen on the other side of the house, that there are but few exceptions taken to this part of the system. I shall take notice of them, and afterwards point out some valuable qualifications, which I think this part possess in an eminent degree.

The objection against the powers of the president, is not that they are too many or too great, but to state it in the gentleman's own language, they are so trifling, that the president is no more than the *tool* of the senate.

Now, sir, I do not apprehend this to be the case, because I see that he may do a great many things, independent of the senate; and with respect to the executive powers of government in which the senate participate, they can do nothing without him. Now I would ask, which is most likely to be the tool of the other? Clearly, sir, he holds the helm, and the vessel can proceed neither in one direction nor another, without his concurrence. It was expected by many, that the cry would have been against the powers of the president as a monarchical power; indeed the echo of such sound was heard, some time before the rise of the late convention. There were men at that time determined to make an attack upon whatever system should be proposed, but they mistook the point of direction. Had the president possessed those powers, which the opposition on this floor are willing to consign him, of making treaties, and appointing officers, with the advice of a council of state, the clamor would have been, that the house of representatives, and the senate, were the *tools* of the monarch. This, sir, is but conjecture, but I leave it to those who are acquainted with the current of the politics pursued by the enemies to this system, to determine whether it is a reasonable conjecture or not.

The manner of appointing the president of the United States, I find is not objected to, therefore I shall say little on that point. But I think it well worth while, to state to this house, how little the difficulties, even in the most difficult part of this system, appear to have been noticed by the honorable gentlemen in opposition. The convention, sir, were perplexed with no part of this plan, so much as with the mode of choosing the president of the United States. For my own part, I think the most unexceptionable mode, next after the one prescribed in this constitution, would be that practised by the eastern states, and the state of New-York; yet if gentlemen object, that an 8th part of our country forms a district too large for elections, how much more would they object, if it was extended to the whole union? On this subject, it was the opinion of a great majority in convention, that the thing was impracticable; other embarrassments presented themselves.

Was the president to be appointed by the legislature? was he to continue a certain time in office, and afterward was he to become inelegible?

To have the executive officers dependent upon the legislative, would certainly be a violation of that principle, so necessary to preserve the freedom of republics, that the legislative and executive powers should be separate and independent. Would it have been proper, that he should be appointed by the senate? I apprehend, that still stronger objections could be urged against that—cabal—intrigue, corruption—every thing bad would have been the necessary concomitant of every election.

To avoid the inconveniences already enumerated, and many others that might be suggested, the mode before us was adopted. By it we avoid corruption, and we are little exposed to the lesser evils of party and intrigue; and when the government shall be organized, proper care will undoubtedly be taken to counteract influence even of that nature—the constitution, with the same view has directed, that the day on which the electors shall give their votes, shall be the same throughout the United States. I flatter myself the experiment will be a happy one for our country.

The choice of this officer is brought as nearly home to the people as is practicable; with the approbation of the state legislatures, the people may elect with only one remove; for "each state shall appoint, in such manner as the legislature thereof may direct, a number of electors equal to the whole number of senators and representatives, to which the state may be entitled in congress." Under this regulation, it will not be easy to corrupt the electors, and there will be little time or opportunity for tumult or intrigue. This, sir, will not be like the elections of a Polish diet, begun in noise and ending in bloodshed.

If gentlemen will look into this article, and read for themselves, they will find, that there is no well-grounded reason to suspect the president will be the *tool* of the senate. "The president shall be commander in chief of the army and navy of the United States, and of the militia of the several states, when called into the actual service of the United States. He may require the opinion in writing of the principal officers in each of the executive departments, upon any subject relative to the duties of their respective offices; and he shall have power to grant reprieves and pardons, for offences against the United States." Must the president, after all, be called the *tool* of the senate? I do not mean to insinuate, that he has more powers than he ought to have, but merely to declare, that they are of such a nature, as to place him above expressions of contempt.

There is another power of no small magnitude, entrusted to this officer: "He shall take care, that the laws be faithfully executed."

I apprehend, that in the administration of this government, it will not be found necessary for the senate always to sit. I know some gentlemen have insinuated and conjectured, that this will be the case, but I am inclined to a contrary opinion. If they had employment every day, no doubt but it might be the wish of the senate, to continue their session; but from the nature of their business, I do not think it will be necessary for them to attend longer than the house of representatives. Besides their legislative powers, they possess three others, viz. trying impeachments—concurring in making treaties, and in appointing officers. With regard to their power in making treaties, it is of importance, that it should be very seldom exercised—we are happily removed from the vortex of European politics, and the fewer, and the more simple our negotiations with European powers, the better they will be; if such be the case, it will be but once in a number of years, that a single treaty will come before the senate. I think, therefore, that on this account it will be unnecessary to sit constantly. With regard to the trial of impeachments, I hope it is what will seldom happen. In this observation, the experience of the ten last years support me. Now there is only left the power of concurring in the appointment of officers;—but care is taken, in this constitution, that this branch of business may be done without their presence—the president is authorised to fill up all vacancies, that may happen during the recess of the senate, by granting commissions, which shall expire at the end of their next session. So that on the whole the senate need not sit longer than the house of representatives, at the public expense; and no doubt if apprehensions are entertained of the senate, the house of representatives will not provide pay for them, one day longer than is necessary. But what (it will be asked) is this great power of the president? he can fill the offices only by temporary appointments. True; but every person knows the advantage of being once introduced into an office; it is often of more importance than the highest recommendation.

Having now done with the legislative and executive branches of this government, I shall just remark, that upon the whole of the executive, it appears that the gentlemen in opposition state nothing as exceptionable, but the deficiency of powers in the president; but rather seem to allow some degree of political merit in this department of government.

I now proceed to the judicial department; and here, Mr. President, I meet an objection, I confess I had not expected; and it seems it did not occur to the honorable gentleman (Mr. Findley) who made it, until a few days ago.

He alleges, that the judges, under this constitution, are not rendered sufficiently independent, because they may hold other offices; and though they may be independent as judges, yet their other office may depend upon the legislature. I confess, sir, this objection appears to me, to be a little wire-drawn in the first place; the legislature can appoint to no office, therefore the dependence could not be on them for the office, but rather on the president and senate; but then these cannot add the salary, because no money can be appropriated, but in consequence of a law of the United States. No sinecure can be bestowed on any judge, but by the concurrence of the whole legislature and of the president; and I do not think this an event that will probably happen.

It is true, that there is a provision made in the constitution of Pennsylvania, that the judges shall not be allowed to hold any other office whatsoever; and I believe they are expressly forbidden to set in congress; but this, sir, is not introduced as a principle into this constitution. There are many states in the union, whole constitutions do not limit the usefulness of their best men, or exclude them from rendering such services to their country, for which they are found eminently qualified. New-York, far from restricting their chancellor or judges of the supreme court, from a seat in congress, expressly provide for sending them there on extraordinary occasions. In Connecticut, the judges are not precluded from enjoying other offices. Judges from many states have sat in congress. Now it is not to be expected, that eleven or twelve states are to change their sentiments and practice on this subject, to accommodate themselves to Pennsylvania.

It is again alleged against this system, that the powers of the judges are too extensive; but I will not trouble you, sir, with a repetition of what I had the honor of delivering the other day; I hope the result of those arguments gave satisfaction, and proved that the judicial were commensurate with the legislative powers; that they went no further, and that they ought to go so far.

The laws of congress being made for the union, no particular state can be alone affected, and as they are to provide for the general purposes of the union, so ought they to have the means of making the provisions effectual, over all that country included within the union.

MR. WILSON.

Afternoon Session

I shall now proceed, Mr. President, to notice the remainder of the objections that have been suggested, by the honorable gentlemen who oppose the system now before you.

We have been told, sir, by the honorable member from Fayette (Mr. Smilie) "that the trial by jury was *intended* to be given up, and the civil law was *intended* to be introduced into its place, in civil cases."

Before a sentiment of this kind was hazarded, I think, sir, the gentleman ought to be prepared with better proof in its support, than any he has yet attempted to produce. It is a charge, sir, not only unwarrantable, but cruel; the idea of such a thing, I believe, never entered into the mind of a single member of that convention; and I believe further, that they never suspected there would be found within the United States, a single person that was capable of making such a charge. If it should be well founded, sir, they *must* abide by the consequences, but if (as I trust it will fully appear) it is ill founded, then he or they who make it, *ought* to abide by the consequences.

Trial by jury forms a large field for investigation, and numerous volumes are written on the subject; those who are well acquainted with it may employ much time in its discussion; but in a country where its excellence is so well understood, it may not be necessary to be very prolix, in pointing them out. For my part, I shall confine myself to a few observations in reply to the objections that have been suggested.

The member from Fayette (Mr. Smilie) has laboured to infer, that under the articles of confederation, the congress possessed no appellate jurisdiction; but this being decided against him, by the words of that instrument, by which is granted to congress the power of "establishing courts for receiving and determining, finally, appeals in all cases of capture;" he next attempts a distinction, and allows the power of appealing from the decisions of the judges, but not from the verdict of a jury; but this is determined against him also, by the practice of the states; for in every instance which has occurred, this power has been claimed by congress, and exercised by the court of appeals; but what would be the consequence of allowing the doctrine for which he contends: Would it not be in the power of a jury, by their verdict, to involve the whole union in a war? They may condemn the property of a neutral, or otherwise infringe the law of nations; in this case ought their verdict to be without revisal? Nothing can be inferred from this, to prove that trials by jury were intended to be given up. In Massachusetts, and all the eastern states, their causes are tried by juries, though they acknowledge the appellate jurisdiction of congress.

I think I am not now to learn the advantages of a trial by jury; it has excellencies that entitle it to a superiority over any other mode, in cases to which it is applicable.

Where jurors can be acquainted with the characters of the parties, and the witnesses, where the whole cause can be

brought within their knowledge and their view, I know no
mode of investigation equal to that by a jury; they hear every
thing that is alleged; they not only hear the words, but they
see and mark the features of the countenance; they can judge
of the weight due to such testimony; and moreover, it is a
cheap and expeditious manner of distributing justice. There is
another advantage annexed to the trial by jury; the jurors may
indeed return a mistaken, or ill founded verdict, but their
errors cannot be systematical.

Let us apply these observations to the objects of the judicial
department, under this constitution. I think it has been shewn
already, that they all extend beyond the bounds of any particular state; but further, a great number of the civil causes there
enumerated, depend either upon the law of nations, or the
marine law, that is, the general law of mercantile countries.
Now, sir, in such causes, I presume it will not be pretended
that this mode of decision ought to be adopted; for the law
with regard to them is the same here as in every other country, and ought to be administered in the same manner. There
are instances, in which I think it highly probable, that the trial
by jury will be found proper; and if it is highly probable that
it will be found proper, is it not equally probable, that it will
be adopted? There may be causes depending between citizens
of different states, and as trial by jury is known and regarded
in all the states, they will certainly prefer that mode of trial
before any other. The congress will have the power of making
proper regulations on this subject, but it was impossible for
the convention to have gone minutely into it; but if they
could, it must have been very improper, because alterations,
as I observed before, might have been necessary; and whatever the convention might have done would have continued
unaltered, unless by an alteration of the constitution. Besides;
there was another difficulty with regard to this subject. In
some of the states they have courts of chancery, and other
appellate jurisdictions, and those states are as attached to that
mode of distributing justice, as those that have none are to
theirs.

I have desired, repeatedly, that honorable gentlemen, who
find fault, would be good enough to point out what they
deem to be an improvement. The member from Westmore-

land (Mr. Findley) tells us, that the trial between citizens of different states, ought to be by a jury of that state in which the cause of action arose. Now it is easy to see, that in many instances, this would be very improper and very partial; for beside the different manner of collecting and forming juries in the several states, the plaintiff comes from another state; he comes a stranger, unknown as to his character or mode of life, while the other party is in the midst of his friends, or perhaps his dependants. Would a trial by jury in such a case ensure justice to the stranger? But again; I would ask that gentleman, whether, if a great part of his fortune was in the hands of some person in Rhode-Island, he would wish, that his action to recover it, should be determined by a jury of that country, under its present circumstances?

The gentleman from Fayette (Mr. Smilie) says, that if the convention found themselves embarrassed, at least they might have done thus much, they should have declared, that the substance should be secured by congress; this would be saying nothing unless the cases were particularized.

Mr. Smilie.

I said the convention ought to have declared, that the legislature should establish the trial by jury by proper regulations.

Mr. Wilson.

The legislature shall establish it by proper regulations! So after all, the gentleman has landed us at the very point from which we set out. He wishes them to do the very thing they have done, to leave it to the discretion of congress. The fact, sir, is, nothing more could be done.

It is well known, that there are some cases that should not come before juries; there are others, that in some of the states, never come before juries, and in these states where they do come before them, appeals are found necessary, the facts re-examined, and the verdict of the jury sometimes is set aside; but I think in all cases, where the cause has come originally before a jury, that the last examination ought to be before a jury likewise.

The power of having appellate jurisdiction, as to facts, has been insisted upon as a proof, "that the convention *intended* to give up the trial by jury in civil cases, and to introduce the civil law." I have already declared my own opinion on this point, and have shewn, nor merely, that it is founded on reason and authority. The express declaration of congress* is to the same purpose: They insist upon this power, as requisite to preserve the peace of the union; certainly, therefore, it ought always to be possessed by the head of the confederacy.

We are told, as an additional proof, that the trial by jury was intended to be given up, "that appeals are unknown to the common law; that the term is a civil law term, and with it the civil law is intended to be introduced." I confess I was a good deal surprized at this observation being made; for Blackstone, in the very volume which the honorable member (Mr. Smilie) had in his hand, and read us several extracts from, has a chapter entitled "of proceeding in the nature of appeals;" and in that chapter says, that the principal method of redress for erroneous judgments, in the king's courts of record, is by writ of error to some superior "*court of appeal.*"† Now, it is well known, that his book is a commentary upon the common law. Here then is a strong refutation of the assertion, "that appeals are unknown to the common law."

I think these were all the circumstances adduced to shew the truth of the assertion, that in this constitution, the trial by jury was *intended* to be given up by the late convention in framing it. Has the assertion been proved? I say not, and the allegations offered, if they apply at all, apply in a contrary direction. I am glad that this objection has been stated, because it is a subject upon which the enemies of this constitution have much insisted. We have now had an opportunity of investigating it fully, and the result is, that there is no foundation for the charge, but it must proceed from ignorance, or something worse.

I go on to another objection, which has been taken to this system, "that the expence of the general government and of the state governments, will be too great, and that the citizens will not be able to support them." If the state governments are to continue as cumbersome and expensive as they have

*Journals of congress. March 6, 1779.
†III. Blackstone, 406.

hitherto been, I confess it would be distressing to add to their expences, and yet it might be necessary; but I think I can draw a different conclusion on this subject, from more conjectures than one. The additional revenue to be raised by a general government, will be more than sufficient for the additional expence; and a great part of that revenue may be so contrived, as not to be taken from the citizens of this country; for I am not of opinion, that the consumer always pays the impost that is laid on imported articles; it is paid sometimes by the importer, and sometimes by the foreign merchant who sends them to us. Had a duty of this nature been laid at the time of the peace, the greatest part of it would have been the contribution of foreigners. Besides, whatever is paid by the citizens, is a voluntary *payment*.

I think, sir, it would be very easy and laudable, to lessen the expences of the state governments. I have been told, (and perhaps it is not very far from the truth) that there are *two thousand* members of assembly in the several states; the business of revenue is done in consequence of requisitions from congress, and whether it is furnished or not, it commonly becomes a subject of discussion. Now when this business is executed by the legislature of the United States, I leave it to those who are acquainted with the expence of long and frequent sessions of assembly, to determine the great saving that will take place. Let me appeal to the citizens of Pennsylvania, how much time is taken up in this state every year, if not every session, in providing for the payment of an amazing interest due on her funded debt. There will be many sources of revenue, and many opportunities for œconomy, when the business of finance shall be administered under one government; the funds will be more productive, and the taxes, in all probability, less burthensome than they are now.

I proceed to another objection, that is taken against the power given to congress, of raising and keeping up standing armies. I confess I have been surprized that this objection was ever made, but I am more so that it is still repeated and insisted upon. I have taken some pains to inform myself how the other governments of the world stand with regard to this power; and the result of my enquiry is, that there is not one which has not the power of raising and keeping up standing armies. A government without the power of defence! it is a solecism!

I well recollect the principle insisted upon by the patriotic body in Great-Britain; it is, that in time of peace, a standing army ought not to be kept up, without the consent of parliament. Their only apprehension appears to be, that it might be dangerous, was the army kept up without the concurrence of the representatives of the people. Sir, we are not in the millenium. Wars may happen—and when they do happen, who is to have the power of collecting and appointing the force then become immediately and indispensably necessary?

It is not declared in this constitution, that the congress *shall* raise and support armies. No, sir, if they are not driven to it by necessity, why should we suppose they would do it by choice, any more than the representatives of the same citizens, in the state legislatures? for we must not lose sight of the great principle upon which this work is founded. The authority here given to the general government, flows from the same source, as that placed in the legislatures of the several states.

It may be frequently necessary to keep up standing armies in time of peace. The present congress have experienced the necessity; and seven hundred troops are just as much a standing army as seventy thousand. The principle which sustains them is precisely the same. They may go further, and raise an army, without communicating to the public the purpose for which it is raised. On a particular occasion, they did this: When the commotions existed in Massachusetts, they gave orders for enlisting an additional body of two thousand men. I believe it is not generally known, on what a perilous tenure we held our freedom and independence at that period. The flames of internal insurrection were ready to burst out in every quarter; they were formed by the correspondents of some state officers (to whom an allusion was made on a former day) and from one end to the other of the continent, we walked on ashes, concealing fire beneath our feet; and ought congress to be deprived of power to prepare for the defence and safety of our country? Ought they to be restrained from arming, until they divulge the motive which induced them to arm? I believe the *power* of raising and keeping up an army, in time of peace, is essential to every government. No government can secure its citizens against dangers, internal and external, without possessing it, and sometimes carrying it into execution. I confess it is a power, in the exercise of which all wise and moderate governments will be as prudent and forbearing as possible. When we consider the situation of the United States, we must be satisfied, that it will be necessary to keep up some troops for the protection of the western frontiers, and to secure our interest in the internal navigation of that country. It will be not only necessary, but it will be œconomical on the great scale. Our enemies finding us invulnerable, will not attack us, and we shall thus prevent the occasion for larger standing armies. I am now led to consider another charge that is brought against this system.

It is said, that congress should not possess the power of calling out the militia, to execute the laws of the union, suppress insurrections and repel invasions, nor the president have the command of them, when called out for such purposes.

I believe any gentleman who possesses military experience will inform you, that men without an uniformity of arms, accoutrements and discipline, are no more than a mob in a camp; that in the field, instead of assisting, they interfere with one another. If a soldier drops his musquet, and his companion, unfurnished with one, takes it up, it is of no service, because his cartridges do not fit it. By means of this system, a uniformity of arms and discipline will prevail throughout the United States.

I really expected that for this part of the system at least, the framers of it would have received plaudits, instead of censures, as they here discover a strong anxiety to have this body put upon an effective footing, and thereby, in a great measure, to supercede the necessity of raising, or keeping up, standing armies.

The militia formed under this system, and trained by the several states, will be such a bulwark of internal strength, as to prevent the attacks of foreign enemies. I have been told, that about the year 1744, an attack was intended by France upon Massachusetts Bay, but was given up on reading the militia law of that province.

If a single state could deter an enemy from such attempts,

what influence will the proposed arrangement have upon the different powers of Europe!

In every point of view, this regulation is calculated to produce the best effects. How powerful and respectable must the body of militia appear, under general and uniform regulations! how disjointed, weak and inefficient are they at present! I appeal to military experience for the truth of my observations.

The next objection, sir, is a serious one indeed; it was made by the honorable gentleman from Fayette (Mr Smilie) "The convention knew this was not a free government, otherwise they would not have asked the powers of the purse and sword." I would beg to ask the gentleman, what free government he knows that has not the powers of both? there was indeed a government under which we unfortunately were for a few years past, that had them not, but it does not now exist. A government without those powers, is one of the improvements with which opposition wish to astonish mankind.

Have not the freest government those powers? and are they not in the fullest exercise of them? this is a thing so clear, that really it is impossible to find facts or reason more clear, in order to illustrate it. Can we create a government without the power to act; how can it act without the assistance of men? and how are men to be procured without being paid for their services? is not the one power the consequence of the other?

We are told, and it is the last and heaviest charge, "that this government is an aristocracy, and was *intended* so to be by the late convention;" and we are told (the truth of which is not disputed) that an aristocratical government is incompatible with freedom. I hope, before this charge is believed, some stronger reasons will be given in support of it, than any that have yet been produced.

The late convention were assembled to devise some plan for the security, safety and happiness of the people of the United States; if they have devised a plan, that robs them of their power, and constitutes an aristocracy, they are the parricides of their country, and ought to be punished as such. What part of this system is it that warrants the charge?

What is an aristocratic government? I had the honor of

giving a definition of it at the beginning of our debates; it is, sir, the government of a few over the many, elected by themselves, or possessing a share in the government by inheritance, or in consequence of territorial rights, or some quality independent of the choice of the people; this is an aristocracy, and this constitution is said to be an aristocratical form of government, and it is also said that it was intended so to be by the members of the late convention who framed it. What peculiar rights have been reserved to any class of men, on any occasion? does even the first magistrate of the United States draw to himself a single privilege, or security that does not extend to every person throughout the United States? Is there a single distinction attached to him in this system, more than there is to the lowest officer in the republic? Is there an office from which any one set of men whatsoever are excluded? Is there one of any kind in this system but is as open to the poor as to the rich? to the inhabitant of the country, as well as to the inhabitant of the city? and are the places of honor and emoluments confined to a few? and are these few the members of the late convention? Have they made any particular provisions in favor of themselves, their relations, or their posterity? If they have committed their country to the demon of aristocracy, have they not committed themselves also, with every thing they held near and dear to them?

Far, far other is the genius of this system. I have had already the honor of mentioning its general nature; but I will repeat it, sir. In its principle, it is purely democratical; but its parts are calculated in such manner, as to obtain those advantages also, which are peculiar to the other forms of government in other countries. By appointing a single magistrate, we secure strength, vigour, energy and responsibility in the executive department. By appointing a senate, the members of which are elected for six years, yet by a rotation already taken notice of, they are changing every second year, we secure the benefit of experience, while, on the other hand, we avoid the inconveniences that arise from a long and detached establishment. This body is periodically renovated from the people, like a tree, which, at the proper season, receives its nourishment from its parent earth.

In the other branch of the legislature, the house of representatives, shall we not have the advantages, of benevolence and attachment to the people, whose immediate representatives they are?

A free government has often been compared to a pyramid. This allusion is made with peculiar propriety in the system before you; it is laid on the broad basis of the people; its powers gradually rise, while they are confined, in proportion as they ascend, until they end in that most permanent of all forms. When you examine all its parts, they will invariably be found to preserve that essential mark of free governments—a chain of connection with the people.

Such, sir, is the nature of this system of government; and the important question at length presents itself to our view. Shall it be ratified, or shall it be rejected by this convention? In order to enable us still further to form a judgment on this truly momentous and interesting point, on which all we have or can have dear to us on earth, is materially depending, let us for a moment consider the consequences that will result from one or the other measure. Suppose we reject this system of government, what will be the consequence? Let the farmer say, he whose produce remains unasked for; nor can he find a single market for its consumption, though his fields are blessed with luxuriant abundance. Let the manufacturer and let the mechanic say, they can feel and tell their feelings. Go along the wharves of Philadelphia, and observe the melancholy silence that reigns. I appeal not to those who enjoy places and abundance under the present government; they may well dilate upon the easy and happy situation of our country. Let the merchants tell you, what is our commerce; let them say, what has been their situation, since the return of peace: An æra which they might have expected would furnish additional sources to our trade, and a continuance, and even an encrease to their fortunes. Have these ideas been realized, or do they not lose some of their capital in every adventure, and continue the unprofitable trade from year to year, subsisting under the hopes of happier times under an efficient general government? The ungainful trade carried on by our merchants, has a baneful influence on the interests of the manufacturer, the mechanic, and the farmer, and these I believe are the chief interests of the people of the United States.

I will go further—is there now a government among us that can do a single act, that a national government ought to do? Is there any power of the United States that can *command* a single shilling? this is a plain and a home question.

Congress may recommend, they can do more, they may require, but they must not proceed one step further.—If things are bad now, and that they are not worse, is only owing to hopes of improvement, or change in the system, will they become better when those hopes are disappointed? We have been told, by honorable gentlemen on this floor (Mr. Smilie, Mr. Findley and Mr. Whitehill) that it is improper to urge this kind of argument in favor of a new system of government, or against the old one: unfortunately, sir, these things are too severely felt to be omitted; the people feel them; they pervade all classes of citizens, and every situation from New-Hampshire to Georgia; the argument of necessity is the patriots defence, as well as the tyrant's plea.

Is it likely, sir, that, if this system of government is rejected, a better will be framed and adopted? I will not expatiate on this subject, but I believe many reasons will suggest themselves, to prove that such expectation would be illusory. If a better could be obtained at a future time; is there any thing essentially wrong in this? I go further, is there any thing wrong that cannot be amended more easily by the mode pointed out in the system itself, than could be done, by calling convention after convention, before the organization of the government. Let us now turn to the consequences that will result if we assent to, and ratify the instrument before you; I shall trace them as concisely as I can, because, I have trespassed already too long on the patience and indulgence of the house.

I stated on a former occasion one important advantage; by adopting this system, we become a NATION; at present we are not one. Can we perform a single national act? Can we do any thing to procure us dignity, or to preserve peace and tranquillity? can we relieve the distress of our citizens? can we provide for their welfare or happiness? The powers of our government are mere sound. If we offer to treat with a nation, we receive this humiliating answer. "You cannot in propriety of language make a treaty—because you have no power to execute it."

Can we borrow money? There are too many examples of unfortunate creditors existing, both on this and the other side of the Atlantic, to expect success from this expedient.—But could we borrow money, we cannot command a fund, to enable us to pay either the principal or interest; for, in instances where our friends have advanced the principal, they have been obliged to advance the interest also, in order to prevent the principal from being annihilated in their hands by depreciation. Can we raise an army? The prospect of a war is highly probable. The accounts we receive by every vessel from Europe, mention, that the highest exertions are making in the ports and arsenals of the greatest maritime powers; but, whatever the consequence may be, are we to lay supine? we know we are unable under the articles of confederation to exert ourselves, and shall we continue so, until a stroke be made on our commerce, or we see the debarkation of an hostile army on our unprotected shores? Who will guarantee that our property will not be laid waste, that our towns will not be put under contribution, by a small naval force, and subjected to all the horror and devastation of war? May not this be done without opposition, at least effectual opposition, in the present situation of our country? There may be safety over the Appelachian mountains, but there can be none on our sea coast. With what propriety can we hope our flag will be respected, while we have not a single gun to fire in its defence?

Can we expect to make internal improvement, or accomplish any of those great national objects, which I formerly alluded to, when we cannot find money to remove a single rock out of a river?

This system, sir, will at least make us a nation, and put it in the power of the union to act as such. We will be considered as such by every nation in the world. We will regain the confidence of our own citizens and command the respect of others.

As we shall become a nation, I trust that we shall also form a national character; and that this character will be adapted to the principles and genius of our system of government, as yet we possess none—our language, manners, customs, habits, and dress, depend too much upon those of other countries. Every nation in these respects should possess originality, there are not on any part of the globe finer qualities, for forming a national character, than those possessed by the children of America. Activity, perseverance, industry, laudable emulation, docility in acquiring information, firmness in adversity, and patience and magnanimity under the greatest hardships; from these materials, what a respectable national character may be raised! in addition to this character, I think there is strong reason to believe, that America may take the lead in literary improvements and national importance. This is a subject, which I confess, I have spent much pleasing time in considering. That language, sir, which shall become most generally known in the civilized world, will impart great importance over the nation that shall use it. The language of the United States will, in future times, be diffused over a greater extent of country, than any other that we now know. The French, indeed, have made laudable attempts toward establishing an universal language, but, beyond the boundaries of France, even the French language is not spoken by one in a thousand. Besides, the freedom of our country, the great improvements she has made and will make in the science of government, will induce the patriots and literati of every nation, to read and understand our writings on that subject, and hence it is not improbable that she will take the lead in political knowledge.

If we adopt this system of government, I think we may promise security, stability and tranquility to the governments of the different states. They will not be exposed to the danger of competition on questions of territory, or any other that have heretofore disturbed them. A tribunal is here founded to decide, justly and quietly, any interfering claim; and now is accomplished, what the great mind of Henry the IV. of France had in contemplation, a system of government, for large and respectable dominions, united and bound together in peace, under a superintending head, by which all their differences may be accommodated, without the distruction of the human race!! We are told by Sully, that this was the favorite pursuit of that good king during the last years of his life, and he would probably have carried it into execution, had not the dagger of an assassin deprived the world of his valuable life. I have, with pleasing emotion, seen the wisdom and benefi-cence of a less efficient power under the articles of confederation, in the determination of the controversy between the states of Pennsylvania and Connecticut; but, I have lamented, that the authority of congress did not extend to extinguish, entirely, the spark which has kindled a dangerous flame in the district of Wyoming.

Let gentlemen turn their attention to the amazing consequences which this principle will have in this extended country—the several states cannot war with each other; the general government is the great arbiter in contentions between them; the whole force of the union can be called forth to reduce an agressor to reason. What an happy exchange for the disjointed contentious state sovereignties!

The adoption of this system will also secure us from danger, and procure us advantages from foreign nations. This in our situation, is of great consequence. We are still an inviting object to one European power at least, and, if we cannot defend ourselves, the temptation may become too alluring to be resisted.—I do not mean, that, with an efficient government, we should mix with the commotions of Europe. No, sir, we are happily removed from them, and are not obliged to throw ourselves into the scale with any. This system will not hurry us into war, it is calculated to guard against it. It will not be in the power of a single man, or a single body of men, to involve us in such distress, for the important power of declaring war, is vested in the legislature at large;—this declaration must be made with the concurrence of the house of representatives; from this circumstance we may draw a certain conclusion, that nothing but our national interest can draw us into a war. I cannot forbear, on this occasion, the pleasure of mentioning to you the sentiments of the great and benevolent man whose works I have already quoted on another subject; Mr. Neckar, has adressed this country, in language important and applicable in the strictest degree to its situation and to the present subject. Speaking of war, and the great caution that all nations ought to use in order to avoid its calamities.— "AND you, rising nation, says he, whom generous efforts have freed from the yoke of Europe! let the universe be struck with still greater reverence at the sight of the privileges you have acquired, by seeing you continually employed for the public felicity: do not offer it as a sacrifice at the unsettled shrine of political ideas, and of the deceitful combinations of warlike ambition; avoid, or at least delay participating in the passions of our hemisphere; make your own advantage of the knowledge which experience alone has given to our old age, and preserve for a long time, the simplicity of childhood: in short, honor human nature, by shewing that when left to its own feelings, it is still capable of those virtues that maintain public order, and of that prudence which insures public tranquillity."

Permit me to offer one consideration more that ought to induce our acceptance of this system. I feel myself lost in the contemplation of its magnitude. By adopting this system, we shall probably lay a foundation for erecting temples of liberty, in every part of the earth. It has been thought by many, that on the success of the struggle America has made for freedom, will depend the exertions of the brave and enlightened of other nations.—The advantages resulting from this system, will not be confined to the United States, it will draw from Europe, many worthy characters, who pant for the enjoyment of freedom. It will induce princes, in order to preserve their subjects, to restore to them a portion of that liberty of which they have for many ages been deprived. It will be subservient to the great designs of providence, with regard to this globe; the multiplication of mankind, their improvement in knowledge, and their advancement in happiness.

Benjamin Rush on Morality and Government

December 12, 1787

. . . The important question was now called for, when Doctor Rush, requested the patience of the convention for a few minutes. He then entered into a metaphysical argument, to prove that the morals of the people had been corrupted by the imperfections of the government, and while he ascribed all our vices and distresses to the existing system, he predicted a milenium of virtue and happiness as the necessary consequence of the proposed constitution. To illustrate the depraved state of society, he remarked, among other things, the disregard which was notorious in matters of religion, so that between the congregation and the minister scarcely any communication or respect remained; nay, the Doctor evinced that they were not bound by the ties of common honesty, on the evidence of two facts, from which it appears that several clergymen had been lately cheated by their respective flocks of the wages due for their pastoral care and instruction. Doctor Rush then proceeded to consider the origin of the proposed system, and fairly deduced it from heaven, asserting that he as much believed the hand of God was employed in this work, as that God had divided the Red Sea to give a passage to the children of Israel, or had fulminated the ten commandments from Mount Sinai! Dilating sometime upon this new species of *divine right*, thus transmitted to the future governors of the union, he made a pathetic appeal to the opposition, in which he deprecated the consequences of any further contention, and pictured the honorable and endearing effects of an unanimous vote, after the full and fair investigation which the great question had undergone. "It is not, Sir, a majority, (continued the Doctor) however numerous and respectable, that can gratify my wishes—nothing short of an unanimous vote can indeed complete my satisfaction. And, permit me to add, were that event to take place, I could not preserve the strict bounds of decorum, but, flying to the other side of this room, I should cordially embrace every member, who has hitherto been in the opposition, as a brother and a patriot. Let us then, Sir, this night bury the hatchet, and smoke the calumet of peace!"

Robert Whitehill's Amendments
and the Final Vote

December 12, 1787

. . . Mr. Whitehill now rose, and having animadverted upon Doctor Rush's metaphysical arguments, and regretted that so imperfect a work should have been ascribed to God, he presented several petitions from 750 inhabitants of Cumberland county, praying, for the reasons therein specified, that the proposed constitution should not be adopted without amendments, and, particularly, without a bill of rights. The petitions being read from the chair, Mr. M'Kean said, he was sorry that at this stage of the business so improper an attempt should be made. He repeated that the duty of the convention was circumscribed to the adoption or rejection of the proposed plan, and such had certainly been the sense of the members when it was agreed that only one question could be taken on the important subject before us. He hoped, therefore, that the petitions would not be attended to. Mr. Whitehill then read, and offered as the ground of a motion for adjourning to some remote day, the consideration of the following articles, which he said, might either be taken, collectively, as a bill of rights, or, separately, as amendments to the general form of government proposed.

1. The rights of conscience shall be held inviolable, and neither the legislative, executive, nor judicial powers of the United States, shall have authority to alter, abrogate, or infringe any part of the constitutions of the several states, which provide for the preservation of liberty in matters of religion.

2. That in controversies respecting property, and in suits between man and man, trial by jury shall remain as heretofore, as well in the federal courts, as in those of the several states.

3. That in all capital and criminal prosecutions, a man has a right to demand the cause and nature of his accusation, as well in the federal courts, as in those of the several states; to be heard by himself or his council; to be confronted with the

accusers and witnesses, to call for evidence in his favor, and a speedy trial, by an impartial jury of the vicinage, without whose unanimous consent, he cannot be found guilty, nor can he be compelled to give evidence against himself; that no man be deprived of his liberty, except by the law of the land or the judgment of his peers.

4. That excessive bail ought not to be required, nor excessive fines imposed, nor cruel or unusual punishments inflicted.

5. That warrants unsupported by evidence, whereby any officer or messenger may be commanded or required to search suspected places, or to seize any person or persons, his or their property, not particularly described, are grievous and oppressive, and shall not be granted either by the magistrates of the federal government or others.

6. That the people have a right to the freedom of speech, of writing, and of publishing their sentiments, therefore, the freedom of the press shall not be restrained by any law of the United States.

7. That the people have a right to bear arms for the defence of themselves and their own state, or the United States, or for the purpose of killing game; and no law shall be passed for disarming the people or any of them, unless for crimes committed, or real danger of public injury from individuals; and as standing armies in the time of peace are dangerous to liberty, they ought not to be kept up: and that the military shall be kept under strict subordination to and be governed by the civil power.

8. The inhabitants of the several states shall have liberty to fowl and hunt in seasonable times, on the lands they hold, and on all other lands in the United States not inclosed, and in like manner to fish in all navigable waters, and others not private property, without being restrained therein by any laws to be passed by the legislature of the United States.

9. That no law shall be passed to restrain the legislatures of the several states, from enacting laws for imposing taxes, except imposts and duties on goods exported and imported, and that no taxes, except imposts and duties upon goods imported and exported, and postage on letters shall be levied by the authority of Congress.

10. That elections shall remain free, that the house of representatives be properly increased in number, and that the several states shall have power to regulate the elections for senators and representatives, without being controuled either directly or indirectly by any interference on the part of Congress, and that elections of representatives be annual.

11. That the power of organizing, arming and disciplining the militia, (the manner of disciplining the militia to be prescribed by Congress) remain with the individual states, and that Congress shall not have authority to call or march any of the militia out of their own state, without the consent of such state, and for such length of time only as such state shall agree.

12. That the legislative, executive, and judicial powers be kept separate, and to this end, that a constitutional council be appointed to advise and assist the President, who shall be responsible for the advice they give; (hereby, the senators would be relieved from almost constant attendance) and also that the judges be made compleatly independant.

13. That no treaties which shall be directly opposed to the existing laws of the United States in Congress assembled, shall be valid until such laws shall be repealed or made conformable to such treaty, neither shall any treaties be valid which are contradictory to the constitution of the United States, or the constitutions of the individual states.

14. That the judiciary power of the United States shall be confined to cases affecting ambassadors, other public ministers and consuls, to cases of admiralty and maritime jurisdiction, to controversies to which the United States shall be a party, to controversies between two or more states—between a state and citizens of different states—between citizens claiming lands under grants of different states, and between a state or the citizens thereof and foreign states, and in criminal cases, to such only as are expressly enumerated in the constitution, and that the United States in Congress assembled, shall not have power to enact laws, which shall alter the laws of descents and distributions of the effects of deceased persons, the title of lands or goods, or the regulation of contracts in the individual states.

15. That the sovereignty, freedom and independency of the

several states shall be retained, and every power, jurisdiction and right which is not by this constitution expressly delegated to the United States in Congress assembled.

Some confusion arose on these articles being presented to the chair, objections were made by the majority to their being officially read, and, at last, Mr. Wilson desired that the intended motion might be reduced to writing, in order to ascertain its nature and extent. Accordingly, Mr. Whitehill drew it up, and it was read from the chair in the following manner.

"That this Convention do adjourn to the   day of   next, then to meet in the city of Philadelphia, in order that the propositions for amending the proposed constitution may be considered by the people of this state; that we may have an opportunity of knowing what amendments or alterations may be proposed by other states, and that these propositions, together with such other amendments as may be proposed by other states, may be offered to Congress, and taken into consideration by the United States, before the proposed constitution shall be finally ratified."

As soon as the motion was read, Mr. Wilson said, he rejoiced that it was by this means ascertained upon what principles the opposition proceeded, for, he added, the evident operation of such a motion would be to exclude the people from the government and to prevent the adoption of this or any other plan of confederation. For this reason he was happy to find the motion reduced to certainty, that it would appear upon the journals, as an evidence of the motives which had prevailed with those who framed and supported it, and that its merited rejection would permanently announce the sentiments of the majority respecting so odious an attempt. Mr. Smilie followed Mr. Wilson, declaring that he too rejoiced that the motion was reduced to a certainty, from which it might appear to their constituents, that the sole object of the opposition was to consult with, and obtain the opinions of the people upon a subject, which they had not yet been allowed to consider. "If, exclaimed Mr. Smilie, those gentlemen who have affected to refer all authority to the people, and to act only for the common interest, if they are sincere, let them embrace this last opportunity to evince that sincerity.

They all know the precipitancy with which the measure has hitherto been pressed upon the state, and they must be convinced that a short delay cannot be injurious to the proposed government, if it is the wish of the people to adopt it; if it is not their wish, a short delay which enables us to collect their real sentiments, may be the means of preventing future contention and animosity in a community, which is, or ought to be equally dear to us all."—The question being taken on the motion, there appeared for it 23, against it 46.—The great and conclusive question was then taken, that "this convention do assent to and ratify the plan of federal government, agreed to and recommended by the late federal convention?" when the same division took place, and the yeas and nays being called by Mr. Smilie and Mr. Chambers, were as follow:

YEAS	YEAS
George Latimer	John Hubley
Benjamin Rush	Jasper Yates
Hilary Baker	Henry Slagle
James Wilson	Thomas Campbell
Thomas M'Kean	Thomas Hartley
William M'Pherson	David Grier
John Hunn	John Black
George Gray	Benjamin Pedan
Samuel Ashmead	John Arndt
Enoch Edwards	Stephen Balliott
Henry Wynkoop	Joseph Horsefield
John Barclay	David Deshler
Thomas Yardley	William Wilson
Abraham Stout	John Boyd
Thomas Bull	Thomas Scott
Anthony Wayne	John Nevill
William Gibbons	John Allison
Richard Downing	Jonathan Roberts
Thomas Cheyney	John Richards
John Hannum	F. A. Muhlenberg
Stephen Chambers	James Morris
Robert Coleman	Timothy Pickering
Sebastian Graff	Benjamin Elliot

NAYS	NAYS
John Whitehill	William Findley
John Harris	John Baird
John Reynolds	William Todd
Robert Whitehill	James Marshall
Jonathan Hoge	James Edgar
Nicholas Lutz	Nathaniel Breading
John Ludwig	John Smilie
Abraham Lincoln	Richard Bard
John Bishop	William Brown
Joseph Heister	Adam Orth
James Martain	John Andre Hannah
Joseph Powell	

This important decision being recorded, Mr. M'Kean moved that the convention do to-morrow proceed in a body to the court-house, there to proclaim the ratification, and that the Supreme Executive Council be requested to make the necessary arrangements for the procession on that occasion, which motion was agreed to, and the convention adjourned 'till the next morning at half past nine o'clock.

Oliver Ellsworth Defends the Taxing Power and Comments on Dual Sovereignties and Judicial Review

January 7, 1788

The paragraph which respects taxes, imposts and excises, was largely debated, by several Gentlemen.

Gen. Wadsworth objected against it, because it gave the power of the purse to the general Legislature; another paragraph gave the power of the sword; and that authority, which has the power of the sword and purse, is despotic. He objected against imposts and excises, because their operation would be partial and in favour of the southern States. Some other objections were likewise made against this Paragraph. In answer to them Mr. Ellsworth expressed himself nearly to the following effect.

Mr. President, This is a most important clause in the constitution; and the Gentlemen do well to offer all the objections which they have against it. Through the whole of this debate, I have attended to the objections which have been made against this clause; and I think them all to be unfounded. The clause is general; it gives the general Legislature "power to lay and collect taxes, duties, imposts and excises to pay the debts, and provide for the common defence and general welfare of the United States." There are three objections against this clause. *First*, that it is too extensive, it extends to all the objects of taxation; *secondly*, that it is partial; *thirdly*, that Congress ought not to have power to lay taxes at all.

The first objection is that this clause extends to all the objects of taxation. But, though it does extend to all, it does not extend to them exclusively. It does not say that Congress shall have all these sources of revenue, and the States none. All, excepting the impost, still lie open to the States. This State owes a debt, it must provide for the payment of it. So do all the other States. This will not escape the attention of Congress. When making calculations to raise a revenue, they will bear this in mind. They will not take away that which is necessary for the States. They are the head, and will take care that the members do not perish. The State debt, which now lies heavy upon us arose, from the want of powers in the federal system. Give the necessary powers to the national government, and the State will not be again necessitated to involve itself in debt for its defence in war. It will lie upon the national government to defend all the States, to defend all its members, from hostile attacks. The United States will bear the whole burden of war. It is necessary, that the power of the general Legislature should extend to all the objects of taxation, that Government should be able to command all the resources of the country; because no man can tell what our exigencies may be. Wars have now become rather war of the purse, than of the sword. Government must therefore be able to command the whole power of the purse; otherwise a hostile nation may look into our constitution, see what resources are in the power of Government, and calculate to go a little beyond us; then they may obtain a decided superiority over us, and reduce us to the utmost distress. A government, which can command but half its resources, is like a man with but one arm to defend himself.

The second objection is that the impost is not a proper mode of taxation; that it is partial to the southern States. I confess I am mortified, when I find gentlemen supposing that their delegates in convention were inattentive to their duty, and made a sacrifice of the interests of their constituents. If however the impost be a partial mode, this circumstance, high as my opinion of it is, would stagger my belief in it; for I abhor partiality. But I think there are three special reasons, why an impost is the best way of raising a national revenue.

The first is, it is the most fruitful and easy way. All nations have found it to be so. Direct taxation can go but little way towards raising a revenue. To raise money in this way, people must be provident; they must be constantly laying up money to answer the demands of the collector. But you cannot make people thus provident; if you would do any thing to purpose, you must come in when they are spending, and take a part with them. This does not take away the tools of a man's business, or the necessary utensils of his family: It only comes in, when he is taking his pleasure, and feels generous, when he is laying out a shilling for superfluities, it takes two-pence of it for public use, and the remainder will do him as much good as the whole. I will instance two facts, which shew how easily and insensibly a revenue is raised by indirect taxation. I suppose people in general are not sensible, that we pay a tax to the State of New-York. Yet it is an uncontrovertible fact, that we the people of Connecticut pay annually into the Treasury of New-York more than fifty Thousand Dollars. Another instance I will mention: One of our common river sloops pays in the West-Indies a Portage Bill of £.60. This is a tax which foreigners lay upon us and we pay it. For a duty laid upon our shipping which transports our produce to foreign markets, sinks the price of our produce, and operates as an effectual tax upon those who till the ground, and bring the fruits of it to market. All nations have seen the necessity and propriety of raising a revenue by indirect taxation, by duties upon articles of consumption. France raises a revenue of 24 Millions Sterling per annum, and it is chiefly in this way. 50 Millions of Livres they raise upon the single article of Salt. The Swiss cantons raise almost the whole of their revenue upon Salt. Those States purchase all the Salt which is to be used in the country; they sell it out to the people at an advanced price; the advance is the revenue of the country. In England the whole public revenue is about 12 Millions Sterling per annum. The land tax amounts to about 2 Millions, the window and some other taxes to about two millions more. The other 8 Millions is raised upon articles of consumption. The whole standing army of Great-Britain could not enforce the collection of this vast sum by direct taxation. In Holland their prodigious taxes amounting to forty shillings for each inhabitant, are levied chiefly upon articles of consumption. They excise every thing, not excepting even their houses of infamy.

The experiments, which have been made in our own country, shew the productive nature of indirect taxes. The imports into the United States amount to a very large sum. They never will be less, but will continue to increase for ages and centuries to come. As the population of our country increases, the imposts will necessarily increase. They will increase, because our citizens will choose to be farmers living independently on their free holds, rather than to be manufacturers, and work for a groat a day. I find by calculation, that a general impost of 5 per cent would raise the sum of £.245,000 per annum, deducting 8 per cent for the charges of collecting. A further sum might be deducted for smuggling, a business which is understood too well among us, and which is looked upon in too favourable a light. But this loss in the public revenue will be over balanced by the increase of importations. And a further sum may be reckoned upon some articles, which will bear a higher duty than the one recommended by Congress. Rum, instead of 4d. per Gallon, may be set higher, without any detriment to our health or morals. In England it pays a duty of 4s.6d. the Gallon. Now let us compare this source of revenue with our national wants. The interest of the Foreign debt is £.130,000 Lawful Money per annum. The expense of the civil list is £.37,000. There are likewise further expenses, for maintaining the Frontier posts, for the support of those who have been disabled in the service of the Continent, and some other contingencies, amounting together with the civil list to £.130,000. This sum added to the interest of the foreign debt will be £.260,000. The consequence follows, that the avails of the impost will pay the interest of the whole foreign debt, and nearly satisfy these current national expenses. But perhaps it will be said, that these paper calculations are overdone, and that the real avails will fall far short. Let me point out then what has actually been done. In only three of the States, in Massachusetts, New-York, and Pennsylvania, £.160 or 180,000 per annum have been raised by impost. From this fact we may certainly conclude, that, if a general impost should be laid, it would raise a greater sum than I have calculated. It is a strong argument in favor of an impost, that the collection of it will interfere less with the internal police of the States, than any other species of taxation. It does not fill the country with revenue officers, but is confined to the sea coast, and is chiefly a water operation. Another weighty reason in favour of this branch of revenue is, if we do not give it to Congress, the individual States will have it. It will give some States an opportunity of oppressing others, and destroy all harmony between them. If we would have the States friendly to each other, let us take away this bone of contention, and place it, as it ought in justice to be placed in the hands of the general government.

But says an honourable Gentleman near me, the impost will be a partial tax; the southern States will pay but little in comparison with the Northern. I ask, what reason is there for this assertion? Why says he, we live in a cold climate, and want warming. Do not they live in a hot climate, and want quenching? Until you get as far south as the Carolinas, there is no material difference in the quantity of cloathing which is worn. In Virginia they have the same course of cloathing, that we have. In Carolina, they have a great deal of cold, raw, chilly weather: even in Georgia, the river Savannah has been crossed upon the ice. And if they do not wear quite so great a quantity of cloathing in those States as with us; yet people of rank wear that which is of a much more expensive kind. In these States, we manufacture one half of our cloathing and all our tools of Husbandry; in those, they manufacture none, nor ever will. They will not manufacture, because they find it much more profitable to cultivate their lands which are exceedingly fertile. Hence they import almost every thing, not excepting the carriages in which they ride, the hoes with which they till the ground, and the Boots which they wear. If we doubt of the extent of their importations, let us look at their exports. So exceedingly fertile and profitable are their Lands, that a hundred large ships are every year loaded with rice and indigo from the single port of Charlestown. The rich returns of these cargoes of immense value will be all subject to the impost. Nothing is omitted, a duty is to be paid upon the blacks which they import. From Virginia their exports are valued at a million sterling per annum; the single article of tobacco amounts to seven or eight hundred thousand. How does this come back? not in money, for the Virginians are poor to a proverb in money. They anticipate their crops; they spend faster than they earn; they are ever in debt. Their rich exports return in eatables, in drinkables, in wearables. All these are subject to the impost. In Maryland their exports are as great in proportion as those in Virginia. The imports and exports of the southern States are quite as great in proportion as those of the northern. Where then exists this partiality, which has been objected? It exists no where but in the uninformed mind.

But there is one objection, Mr. President, which is broad enough to cover the whole subject. Says the objector, Congress ought not to have power to raise any money at all. Why? Because they have the power of the sword, and if we give them the power of the purse, they are despotic. But I ask, Sir, was there ever a government without the power of the sword and the purse? This is not a new coined phraise; but it is misapplied; it belongs to quite another subject. It was brought into use in Great-Britain, where they have a king vested with hereditary power. Here, say they, it is dangerous to place the power of the sword and the purse in the hands of one man, who claims an authority independent of the people. Therefore we will have a parliament. But the king and parliament together, the supreme power of the nation, they have the sword and the purse. And they must have both, else how could the country be defended? For the sword without the purse is of no effect, it is a sword in the scabbard. But does it follow, because it is dangerous to give the power of the sword and the purse to a hereditary prince, who is independent of the people, that therefore, it is dangerous to give it to the parliament, to congress which is your parliament, to men appointed by yourselves, and dependent upon yourselves? This argument amounts to this, you must cut a man in two in the middle, to prevent his hurting himself.

But says the Honourable objector, if Congress levy money, they must legislate. I admit it. Two Legislative powers, says he, cannot exist together in the same place. I ask, why can they not? It is not enough to say they cannot. I wish for some reason. I grant that both cannot legislate upon the same object, at the same time, and carry into effect Laws which are contrary to each other. But the constitution excludes every thing of this kind. Each Legislature has its province; their limits may be distinguished. If they will run foul of each other, if they will be trying who has the hardest head, it cannot be helped. The road is broad enough, but if two men will justle each other, the fault is not in the road. Two several Legislatures have in fact existed, and acted at the same time in the same territory. It is in vain to say, they cannot exist, when they actually have done it. In the time of the war we had an army. Who made the laws for the army? By whose authority were offenders tried and executed? Congress was the power. By their authority, a man was taken, tried, condemned and hanged, in this very town. He belonged to the army; he was a proper subject of military law; he deserted to the enemy; he deserved his fate. Wherever the army was, in whatever state, there congress had complete legislative, judicial and executive power. This very spot where we now are, is a city. It has complete legislative, judicial and executive powers. It is a complete state in miniature. Yet it breeds no confusion, it makes no scism. The city has not eat up the state, nor the state the city. But if this is a new city, if it has not had time to unfold its principles, I will instance the city of New-York, which is and long has been an important part of that state, it has been found beneficial, its powers and privileges have not clashed with the state. The city of London contains three or four times as many inhabitants as the whole state of Connecticut. It has extensive powers of government, and yet it makes no interference with the general government of the kingdom. This constitution defines the extent of the powers of the general government. If the general legislature should at any time overleap their limits, the judicial department is a constitutional check. If the United States go beyond their powers, if they make a law which the constitution does not authorise, it is void; and the judicial power, the national judges, who to secure their impartiality are to be made independent, will declare it to be void. On the other hand, if the states go beyond their limits, if they make a law which is an usurpation upon the general government, the law is void, and upright independent judges will declare it to be so. Still however, if the united states and the individual states will quarrel, if they want to fight, they may do it, and no frame of government can possibly prevent it. It is sufficient for this constitution, that, so far from laying them under a necessity of contending, it provides every reasonable check against it. But perhaps at some time or other there will be a contest, the states may rise against the general government. If this does take place, if all the states combine, if all oppose, the whole will not eat up the members, but the measure which is opposed to the sense of the people, will prove abortive. In republics, it is a fundamental principle, that the majority govern, and that the minority comply with the general voice. How contrary then to republican principles, how humiliating is our present situation. A single state can rise up, and put a *veto* upon the most important public measures. We have seen this actually take place, a single state has controuled the general voice of the union, a minority, a very small minority has governed us. So far is this from being consistent with republican principles, that it is in effect the worst species of monarchy.

Hence we see, how necessary for the union is a coercive principle. No man pretends the contrary. We all see and feel this necessity. The only question is, shall it be a coercion of Law, or a coercion of arms: There is no other possible alternative. Where will those who oppose a coercion of Law, come out? where will they end? A necessary consequence of their principles is a war of the States one against another. I am for coercion by Law, that coercion which acts only upon delinquent individuals. This constitution does not attempt to coerce sovereign bodies, States in their political capacity. No coercion is applicable to such bodies, but that of an armed force. If we should attempt to execute the Laws of the Union by sending an armed force against a delinquent State, it would involve the good and bad, the innocent and guilty, in the same calamity. But this legal coercion singles out the guilty individual, and punishes him for breaking the Laws of the union. All men will see the reasonableness of this, they will acquiesce, and say, let the guilty suffer. How have the morals of the people been depraved for the want of an efficient government which might establish justice and righteousness. For the want of this, iniquity has come in upon us like an overflowing flood. If we wish to prevent this alarming evil, if we wish to protect the good citizen in his right, we must lift up the standard of justice, we must establish a national government, to be enforced by the equal decisions of Law, and the peaceable arm of the magistrate.

Governor Samuel Huntington on the Need for Coercive National Power

January 9, 1788

The Convention got through with debating upon the constitution by sections. It was canvassed critically and fully. Every objection was raised against it, which the ingenuity and invention of its opposers could devise. The writer of this account could wish to exhibit to public view, though he is sensible he could do it but imperfectly, the whole of the debates upon this interesting subject; but they would be so exceedingly prolix, that he is obliged to give up any such attempt. Suffice it to say, that all the objections to the constitution vanished, before the learning and eloquence of a Johnson, the genuine good sense and discernment of a Sherman, and the Demosthenian energy of an Ellsworth.

After the Convention had finished debating upon the constitution by sections, Gen. Parsons, in order to bring up the subject for a general discussion, moved the grand question, "That this convention do assent to, ratify and adopt the Constitution reported by the convention of Delegates in Philadelphia on the 17th day of September A. D. 1787 and referred to the determination of this Convention by an act of General Assembly in October last."

This motion was seconded by Gen. Huntington. Upon the general discussion of the subject, His Excellency Gov. Huntington, expressed himself nearly as follows:

Mr. President, I do not rise to detain this convention for any length of time. The subject has been so fully discussed, that very little can be added to what has been already offered. I have heard, and attended with pleasure to what has been said upon this subject. The importance of it merited a full and ample discussion. It does not give me pain, but pleasure, to hear the sentiments of those gentlemen who differ from me. It is not to be expected from human nature, that we should all have the same opinion. The best way to learn the nature and effects of different systems of government, is not from theoretical dissertations, but from experience, from what has actually taken place among mankind. From this latter source of information it is, that mankind have obtained a more complete knowledge of the nature of government, than they had in ages past. It is an established truth that no nation can exist without a coercive power, a power to enforce the execution of its political regulations. There is such a love of liberty implanted in the human breast, that no nation ever willingly gave up its liberty. If they lose this inestimable birth-right of man, it is from a want not of will, but of the proper means, to support it. If we look into history, we shall find that the common avenue through which tyranny has entered in, and enslaved nations who were once free, has been their not supporting government. The great secret of preserving liberty is to lodge the supreme power so as to be well supported and not abused. If this could only be effected, no nation would ever lose its liberty. The history of mankind clearly shews, that it is dangerous to entrust the supreme power in the hands of one man. The same source of knowledge proves that it is not only inconvenient, but dangerous to liberty, for the people of a large community to attempt to exercise in person the supreme authority. Hence arises the necessity that the people should act by their representatives; but this method, so necessary for the support of civil liberty, is an improvement of modern times. Liberty however is not so well secured as it ought to be, when the supreme power is lodged in one body of representatives. There ought to be two branches of the legislature, that the one may be a check upon the other. It is difficult for the people at large to know when the supreme power is verging towards abuse, and to apply the proper remedy. But if the government be properly balanced, it will possess a renovating principle, by which it will be able to right itself. The constitution of the British nation affords us great light upon the subject of government. Learned men in other countries have admired it, but they thought it too fine spun to prove beneficial in practice. But a long trial has now shewn its excellence; and the difficulties which that nation now experiences, arise not from their constitution, but from other circumstances.

The author of nature has given to mankind a certain degree of insight into futurity. As far as we can see a probability that certain events will happen, so far we do well to provide and guard. But we may attempt to go too far; it is in vain to think of providing against every possible contingency. The happiness of civil society depends not merely upon their constitution of Government, but upon a variety of circumstances. One constitution may suit one particular nation exceedingly well; when a different one would suit another nation in different circumstances. Even among the American States there is such a difference in sentiments, habits, and customs, that a government, which would be very suitable for one, might not be agreeable to another.

I am fully of opinion, that the great council of the union must have a controuling power with respect to matters of national concern. There is at present an extreme want of power in the national government; and it is my opinion that this constitution does not give too much. As to the subject of representation, at first view it appears small; but upon the whole, the purposes of the union could not be so well answered by a greater number. It is impracticable to have the numbers of the representation as great, and the times of electing as frequent, as they are in our State Governments. Nor is this necessary for the security of liberty. It is sufficient, if the choice of representatives be so frequent, that they must depend upon the people, and that an inseparable connection be kept up between the electors and elected.

The state governments, I think, will not be endangered by the powers vested by this constitution in the general government. While I have attended in Congress, I have observed, that the members were quite as strenuous advocates for the rights of their respective states, as for those of the union. I doubt not but this will continue to be the case, and hence I infer that the general government will not have the disposition to encroach upon the states. But still the people themselves must be the chief support of liberty. While the great body of the freeholders are acquainted with the duties which they owe to their God, to themselves, and to men, they will remain free. But if ignorance and depravity should prevail, they will inevitably lead to slavery and ruin. Upon the whole view of this constitution, I am in favour of it, and think it bids fair to promote our national prosperity.

This is a new event in the history of mankind.—Heretofore, most governments have been formed by tyrants, and imposed on mankind by force. Never before did a people, in time of peace and tranquility, meet together by their representatives, and with calm deliberation frame for themselves a system of government. This noble attempt does honour to our country. While I express my sentiments in favour of this constitution, I candidly believe that the gentlemen who oppose it, are actuated by principles of regard to the public welfare. If we will exercise mutual candour for each other, and sincerely endeavour to maintain our liberties, we may long continue to be a free and happy people.

Letter to the Massachusetts Centinel by "Marcus" Objecting to Instructing the Delegates

January 9, 1788

Mr. RUSSELL,

The information in your last, that Sandwich had instructed their delegates to the Convention to vote against the adoption of the new Constitution, although the eligibility of such a measure, were demonstrated by the strongest arguments, must afford matter of surprize and astonishment to the rational part of the community.

When an alteration in the federal system is confessedly a desideratum in American politicks; — when in fact, we are reduced to the alternative of adopting a government which has efficiency, and a national controul, coextensive with our national concerns; or, of dwindling into insignificance, and becoming the scorn, and the derision of nations; it certainly becomes us as a wise and virtuous people coolly to deliberate upon the proposed plan of federal government. Conformably to this idea, our wise legislature called a Convention, to collect the wisdom and experience of the commonwealth, for cool deliberation, on a momentous subject, big with the fate of thirteen, independent, rising States. A convention was not called, it is presumed, blindly and absolutely to ratify, or to reject instantly the proposed Constitution; but previous to either, freely to discuss its merits, and the expediency, or inexpediency of adopting it. That the mode of instructing delegates absolutely to ratify, or to reject the Constitution, is repugnant to these sentiments, is extremely obvious: There can be no deliberation, or it can answer no valuable purpose, where the line of conduct is marked out by invincible predetermination. If a town decide upon the question, and their decision is binding upon their delegates, *they* can answer the purposes of carriers only, or be the mere mechanical echo of a party; and the design of the Convention, so far as respects them, is intirely frustrated. Were it the original intention of the legislature to submit the Constitution to the respective towns for their ratification, or rejection, the assembling a Convention would not only be needless, but absurd and injurious to the community. But as the design was evidently to collect a representation of the State, unshackled by particular, positive instructions, the proceedings of the town of Sandwich are highly reprehensible: They are insulting to their delegates, and injurious to the publick;—insulting to their delegates, because they suppose them incapable of acting alone, or unworthy of confidence;—injurious to the publick, because they load the Commonwealth with the expense of paying two men travel and attendence, when it can derive no benefit from their deliberation. As a majority of the electors were antifederal, they undoubtedly elected antifederal men. The only reason then for instructing them, must have arisen from their fears; their fears, that, as some men are open to conviction, the political creed of their delegates, might be shaken by the triumph of reason and truth over sophistry and errour. We sincerely regret this procedure of the good people of Sandwich, as it must, with their celebrated instructions to their representatives in the present court, remain an indelible stigma upon the character of the town.

Boston, Jan. 4, 1788

Fisher Ames on Biennial Elections and on the Volcano of Democracy

January 15, 1788

Mr. AMES. I do not regret, Mr. President, that we are not unanimous upon this question. I do not consider the diversity of sentiment which prevails, as an impediment in our way to the discovery of truth. In order that we may think alike upon this subject at last, we shall be compelled to discuss it, by ascending to the principles upon which the doctrine of representation is grounded.

Without premeditation, in a situation so novel, and awed by the respect which I feel for this venerable assembly, I distrust extremely my own feelings, as well as my competency to prosecute this inquiry. With the hope of an indulgent hearing, I will attempt to proceed. I am sensible, sir, that the doctrine of frequent elections, has been sanctified by antiquity; and is still more endeared to us by our recent experience, and uniform habits of thinking. Gentlemen have expressed their zealous partiality for it. They consider this as a leading question in the debate, and that the merits of many other parts of the constitution are involved in the decision. I confess, sir, and I declare that my zeal for frequent elections, is not inferior to their own. I consider it as one of the first securities for popular liberty, in which its very essence may be supposed to reside. But how shall we make the best use of this pledge and instrument of our safety? A right principle, carried to an extreme, becomes useless. It is apparent that a delegation for a very short term, as for a single day, would defeat the design of representation. The election in that case would not seem to the people to be of any importance, and the person elected would think as lightly of his appointment. The other extreme is equally to be avoided. An election for a very long term of years, or for life, would remove the member too far from the controul of the people, would be dangerous to liberty, and in fact repugnant to the purposes of the delegation. The truth as usual, is placed somewhere between the extremes, and I believe is included in this proposition: The term of election must be so long, that the representative may understand the interests of the people, and yet so limited, that his fidelity may be secured by a dependence upon their approbation.

Before I proceed to the application of this rule, I cannot forbear to premise some remarks upon two opinions, which have been suggested.

Much has been said about the people divesting themselves of power, when they delegate it to representatives; and that all representation is to their disadvantage, because it is but an image, a copy, fainter and more imperfect than the original, the people, in whom the light of power is primary and unborrowed, which is only reflected by their delegates.—I cannot agree to either of these opinions.—The representation of the people is something more than the people. I know, sir, but one purpose which the people can effect without delegation, and that is, to destroy a government. That they cannot erect a government is evinced by our being thus assembled, on their behalf. The people must govern by a majority, with whom all power resides. But how is the sense of this majority to be obtained? It has been said that a pure democracy is the best government for a small people who may assemble in person. It is of small consequence to discuss it, as it would be inapplicable to the great country we inhabit. It may be of some use in this argument, however, to consider, that it would be very burdensome, subject to faction and violence, decisions would often be made by surprise, in the precipitancy of passion, by men who either understand nothing, or care nothing about the subject; or by interested men, or those who vote for their own indemnity. It would be a government not by laws, but by men. Such were the paltry democracies of Greece and Asia Minor, so much extolled, and so often proposed as a model for our imitation. I desire to be thankful, that our people are not under any temptation, to adopt the advice. I think it will not be denied, that the people are gainers by the election of representatives. They may destroy, but they cannot exercise the powers of government, in person; but by their servants, *they* govern—they do not renounce their power—they do not sacrifice their rights—they become the true sovereigns of the country when they delegate that power, which they cannot use themselves, to their trustees.

I know, sir, that the people talk about the liberty of nature, and assert that we divest ourselves of a portion of it, when we enter into society. This is declamation against matter of fact. We cannot live without society; and as to liberty, how can I be said to enjoy that which another may take from me, when he pleases. The liberty of one depends not so much on the removal of all restraint, from him, as on the due restraint upon the liberty of others. Without such restraint, there can be no liberty—liberty is so far from being endangered or destroyed by this, that it is extended and secured. For I said, that we do not enjoy that, which another may take from us. But civil liberty cannot be taken from us, when any one may please to invade it: For we have the strength of the society of our side.

I hope, sir, that these reflections, will have some tendency to remove the ill impressions which are made by proposing to divest the people of their power.

That they may never be divested of it, I repeat that I am in favour of frequent elections. They who commend annual elections, are desired to consider, that the question is, whether biennial elections are a defect in the constitution: For it does not follow, because annual elections are safe, that biennial are dangerous: For both may be good. Nor is there any foundation for the fears of those, who say that if we who have been accustomed to chuse for one year only, now extend it to two, the next stride will be to five, or seven years, and the next for term of life: For this article, with all its supposed defects, is in favour of liberty. Being inserted in the constitution, it is not subject to be repealed by law. We are sure that it is the worst of the case.

It is a fence against ambitious encroachments, too high and too strong to be passed: In this respect, we have greatly the advantage of the people of England and of all the world. The law which limits their parliaments, is liable to be repealed.

I will not defend this article, by saying that it was a matter of compromise in the federal Convention: It has my entire approbation as it stands. I think that we ought to prefer, in this article, biennial elections to annual, and my reasons for this opinion, are drawn from these sources.

From the extent of the country to be governed.

The objects of their legislation.

And the more perfect security of our liberty.

It seems obvious, that men who are to collect in Congress from this great territory, perhaps from the bay of Fundy, or from the banks of the Ohio, and the shore of Lake Superior, ought to have a longer term in office, than the delegates of a single state, in their own legislature. It is not by riding post to and from Congress, that a man can acquire a just knowledge of the true interests of the union. This term of election, is inapplicable to the state of a country, as large as Germany, or as the Roman empire in the zenith of its power.

If we consider the objects of their delegation, little doubt will remain. It is admitted that annual elections may be highly fit for the state legislature. Every citizen grows up with a knowledge of the local circumstances of the state. But the business of the federal government will be very different. The objects of their power are few and national. At least two years in office will be necessary to enable a man to judge of the trade and interests of states which he never saw. The time I hope, will come, when this excellent country will furnish food, and freedom, (which is better than food, which is the food of the soul) for fifty millions of happy people. Will any man say that the national business can be understood in one year?

Biennial elections appear to me, sir, an essential security to liberty. These are my reasons.

Faction and enthusiasm are the instruments by which popular governments are destroyed. We need not talk of the power of an aristocracy. The people when they lose their liberties are cheated out of them. They nourish factions in their bosoms, which will subsist so long as abusing their honest credulity shall be the means of acquiring power. A democracy is a volcano, which conceals the fiery materials of its own destruction. These will produce an eruption, and carry desolation in their way. The people always mean right, and if time is allowed for reflection and information, they will do right. I would not have the first wish, the momentary impulse of the publick mind, become law. For it is not always the sense of the people, with whom, I admit, that all power resides. On great questions, we first hear the loud clamours of passion, artifice and faction. I consider biennial elections as a security that the sober, second thought of the people shall be law. There is a calm review of publick transactions, which is made by the citizens who have families and children, the pledges of their fidelity. To provide for popular liberty, we must take care that measures shall not be adopted without due deliberation. The member chosen for two years will feel some independence in his seat. The factions of the day will expire before the end of his term.

The people will be proportionally attentive to the merits of a candidate. Two years will afford opportunity to the member to deserve well of them, and they will require evidence that he has done it.

But, sir, the representatives are the grand inquisition of the union. They are by impeachment to bring great offenders to justice. One year will not suffice to detect guilt, and to pursue it to conviction: therefore they will escape, and the balance of the two branches will be destroyed, and the people oppressed with impunity. The senators will represent the sovereignty of the states. The representatives are to represent the people. The offices ought to bear some proportion in point of importance. This will be impossible if they are chosen for one year only.

Will the people then blind the eyes of their own watchmen? Will they bind the hands which are to hold the sword for their defence? Will they impair their own power, by an unreasonable jealousy of themselves?

For these reasons I am clearly of opinion, that the article is entitled to our approbation as it stands: and as it has been demanded, why annual elections were not preferred to biennial, permit me to retort the question, and to inquire in my turn, what reason can be given why, if annual elections are good, biennial elections are not better?

The enquiry in the latter part of Mr. Ames's speech, being directed to the Hon. Mr. ADAMS—that gentleman said, he only made the inquiry for information, and that he had heard sufficient to satisfy himself of its propriety.

A Sharp Exchange on the Powers of Congress and Its Probable Corruption

January 17, 1788

The 4th section still under deliberation.

Hon. Mr. TURNER. Mr. President, I am pleased with the ingenuity, of some gentlemen in defence of this section. I am so impressed with the love of our liberty so dearly bought, that I heartily acquiesce in compulsory laws, for the people ought to be obliged to attend to their interest. But I do not wish to give Congress a power which they can abuse; and, I wish to know whether such a power is not contained in this section? I think it is. I now proceed, sir, to the consideration of an idea, that Congress may alter the place for chusing representatives in the general Congress—they may order that it may be at the extremity of a state, and by their influence, may there prevail that persons may be chosen, who otherwise would not; by reason that a part of the qualified voters in part of the state, would be so incommoded thereby, as to be debarred from their right as much as if they were bound at home. If so, such a circumstance would militate against the constitution, which allows every man to vote. Altering the *place* will put it so far in the power of Congress, as that the representatives chosen will not be the true and genuine representatives of the people, but creatures of the Congress; and so far as they are so, so far are the people deprived of their rights, and the choice will be made in an irregular and unconstitutional manner. When this alteration is made by Congress—may we not suppose whose re-election will be provided for? Would it not be for those who were chosen before? The great law of self preservation will prevail. It is true, they might, one time in an hundred, provide for a friend, but most commonly for themselves. But, however honourable the convention may be who proposed this article, I think it is a genuine power for Congress to perpetuate themselves—a power that cannot be unexceptionally exercised in any case whatever:—Knowing the numerous arts, that de-

signing men are prone to, to secure their election, and perpetuate themselves, it is my hearty wish that a rotation may be
provided for. I respect and revere the convention who proposed this constitution. In order that the power given to
Congress may be more palatable, some gentlemen are pleased
to hold up the idea, that we may be blessed with sober, solid,
upright men in Congress. I wish that we may be favoured
with such rulers; but I fear they will not all, if most be the
best moral or political characters. It gives me pain, and I believe it gives pain to others, thus to characterize the country
in which I was born. I will endeavour to guard against any
injurious reflections against my fellow citizens. But they must
have their true characters, and if I represent them wrong, I
am willing to make concessions. I think that the operation of
paper money, and the practice of privateering, have produced
a gradual decay of morals—introduced pride—ambition—
envy—lust of power—produced a decay of patriotism, and
the love of commutative justice; and I am apprehensive these
are the invariable concommitants of the luxury, in which we
are unblessedly involved, almost to our total destruction. In
the lower ranks of people, luxury and avarice operate to the
want of publick duty and the payment of debts. These demonstrate the necessity of an energetick government: As people
become more luxurious, they become more incapacitated of
governing themselves. And are we not so? A like people, a
like prince: But suppose it should so happen, that the administrators of this constitution should be preferable to the corrupt mass of the people, in point of manners, morals, and
rectitude; power will give a keen edge to the principles I have
mentioned. Ought we not, then, to put all checks and con-
trouls on governours for the publick safety: therefore, instead
of giving Congress powers they *may* not abuse, we ought to
withold our hands from granting such, as *must* be abused if
exercised. This is a general observation. But to the point: At
the time of the restoration, the people of England were so
vexed, harassed and worn down, by the *anarchical* and confused state of the nation, owing to the commonwealth not
being well digested, that they took an opposite career; they
run mad with loyalty, and would have given Charles any
thing he could have asked—Pardon me, sir, if I say I feel the

want of an energetick government, and the dangers to which this dear country is reduced, as much as any citizen of the United States; but I cannot prevail on myself to adopt a government, which wears the face of power, without examining it. Relinquishing an *hair's breadth* in a constitution is a great deal; for by small degrees has liberty in all nations, been wrested from the hands of the people. I know great powers are necessary to be given to Congress, but I wish they may be well guarded.

Judge SUMNER, remarking on Gen. *Thompson's* frequent exclamation of *"O! my country!"* expressed from an apprehension that the Constitution would be adopted, said, *that* expression might be used with greater propriety, should this Convention reject it. The Hon. Gentleman then proceeded to demonstrate the necessity of the 4th sect.—the absurdity of the *supposition*, that Congress would remove the places of election to remote parts of the States;—combated the idea, that Congress would, when chosen, act as bad as possible—and concluded by asking, if a war should take place, (and it was supposable) if France and Holland should send an army to collect the millions of livres they have lent us in the time of our distresses, and that army should be in possession of the seat of government of any particular State, (as was the case when Lord *Cornwallis* ravaged Carolina) and the state legislature could not appoint the elections, is not a power to provide for such elections necessary to be lodged in the general Congress?

Mr. WIDGERY denied the statement of Dr. *Jarvis* (that every 30,000 persons can elect one representative) to be just, as the Constitution provides, that the number *shall not exceed* one to every 30,000—it did not follow, he thought that the 30,000 *shall* elect one. But admitting that they have a right to chuse one—we will suppose Congress should order an election to be in Boston in January, and from the scarcity of money, &c. not a fourth part could attend—would not three quarters of the people be deprived of their right?

Rev. Mr. WEST. I rise to express my astonishment at the arguments of some gentlemen against this section!—They have only started *possible* objections—I wish the gentlemen would shew us, that what they so much deprecate is *probable*.

Is it probable that we shall choose men to ruin us? Are we to object to all governments; and because power *may* be abused, shall we be reduced to anarchy and a state of nature? What hinders our state legislatures from abusing their power? They may violate the Constitution—they may levy taxes oppressive and intolerable, to the amount of all our property. An argument which proves too much, it is said, proves nothing. Some say, Congress may remove the place of elections to the State of South-Carolina; this is inconsistent with the words of the Constitution, which says, *"that the elections shall be prescribed in* each *State by the legislature thereof,"* &c. and that representation shall be apportioned according to numbers; it will frustrate the end of the Constitution—and is a reflection on the gentlemen who formed it. Can we, sir, suppose them so wicked, so vile, as to recommend an article so dangerous: Surely gentlemen who argue these *possibilities*, shew they have a very weak cause. That we may all be free from passions, prepossessions and party spirit, I sincerely hope, otherwise reason will have no effect. I hope there are none here but who are open to conviction, as it is the sured method to gain the suffrage of our consciences. The Hon. Gentleman from Scituate has told us, that the people of England, at the restoration, *on account of the inconveniencies of the confused state of the Commonwealth, run mad with loyalty.* If the gentleman means to apply this to us, we ought to adopt this Constitution—for if the people are *running mad* after an energetick government, it is best to stop now, as by his rule they may run further and get a worse one; therefore the gentleman's arguments turn right against himself. Is it possible that imperfect man can make a perfect Constitution. Is it possible that a frame of government can be devised by such weak and frail creatures, but what must savour of that weakness? Though there are some things that I do not like in this Constitution, yet I think it necessary that it should be adopted. For may we not rationally conclude, that the persons we shall chuse to administer it, will be in general good men?

Gen. THOMPSON. Mr. President, I have frequently heard of the abilities and fame of the learned and reverend gentleman last speaking, and now I am witness to them: but, sir, one thing surprizes me—it is, to hear the worthy gentleman insinuate that our federal rulers would undoubtedly be *good men*, and that therefore, we have little to fear from their being intrusted with all power—This, sir, is quite contrary to the common language of the clergy, who are continually representing mankind as reprobate and deceitful, and that we really grow worse and worse day after day. I really believe we do, sir, and I make no doubt to prove it before I sit down, from the old testament. When I consider the man that slew the lion and the bear, and that he was a man after *God's own heart*; when I consider his son, blessed with *all wisdom*—and the errors they fell into, I extremely doubt the infallibility of human nature. Sir, I suspect my own heart, and I shall suspect our rulers.

Dr. HOLTEN thought this paragraph necessary to a complete system of government. [*But the Hon. gentleman spoke so low that we could not hear him distinctly throughout.*]

Capt. SNOW. It has been said, Mr. President, that there is too much power delegated to Congress, by the section under consideration—I doubt it; I think power the hinge on which the whole Constitution turns. Gentlemen have talked about Congress moving the place of elections from Georgia to the Mohawk river, but I never can believe it. I will venture to conjecture we shall have some honest men in our Congress. We read that there were two who brought a *good report*, Caleb and Joshua—Now, if there are but two in Congress who are honest men, and Congress should attempt to do what the gentlemen say they will, (which will be *high treason*) they will bring a *report* of it—and I stand ready to leave my wife and family—sling my knapsack—travel westward—to cut their heads off. I, sir, since the war, have had commerce with six different nations of the globe, and I have enquired in what estimation America is held—and if I may believe good, honest, credible men, I find this country held in the same light by foreign nations, as a well behaved negro is, in a gentleman's family. Suppose, Mr. President, I had a chance to make a good voyage, but I tie my Captain up to such strict orders, that he can go to no other island to sell my vessel, although there is a certainty of his doing well: the consequence is, he returns, but makes a bad voyage, because he had not power enough to act his judgment: (for honest men do right:) Thus, sir, Congress cannot save us from destruction, because we tie their hands and give them no power; (I think people have lost their privileges by not improving them) and I like this power being vested in Congress as well as any paragraph in the Constitution: for as the man is accountable for his conduct, I think there is no danger. Now, Mr. President, to take all things into consideration, something more must be said, to convince me to the contrary.

[*Several other gentlemen went largely into the debate on the 4th section, which those in favour of it demonstrated to be necessary:* first, *as it may be used to correct a negligence in elections:* secondly, *as it will prevent the dissolution of the government by designing and refractory states:* thirdly, *as it will operate as a check, in favour of the people, against any designs of the federal Senate, and their constituents, the state legislatures, to deprive the people of their right of election: and* fourthly, *as it provides a remedy for the evil, should any state, by invasion, or other cause, not have it in its power to appoint a place, where the citizens thereof may meet to chuse their federal representatives. Those against it urged, that the power is unlimited and unnecessary.*——]

Major Martin Kinsley on
the Excessive Powers of Congress

January 21, 1788

Major KINGSLEY. Mr. President, after so much has been said on the powers to be given to Congress, I shall say but a few words on the subject. By the articles of confederation the people have three checks on their delegates in Congress; the annual election of them, their rotation, and the power to recall any, or all of them, when they see fit: in view of our federal rulers, they are the servants of the people: in the new constitution, we are deprived of annual elections, have no rotation, and cannot recall our members; therefore our federal rulers will be masters and not servants. I will examine what powers we have given to our masters. They have power to lay and collect all taxes, duties, imposts and excises; raise armies, fit out navies, to establish themselves in a federal town of ten miles square, equal to four middling townships, erect forts, magazines, arsenals, &c. — Therefore, should the Congress be chosen of designing and interested men, they can perpetuate their existence, secure the resources of war; and the people will have nothing left to defend themselves with. Let us look into ancient history. — The Romans, after a war, thought themselves safe in a government of ten men, called the Decemviri: these ten men were invested with all powers, and were chosen for three years. By their arts and designs they secured their second election; but finding, from the manner in which they had exercised their power, they were not able to secure their third election, they declared themselves masters of Rome, impoverished the city, and deprived the people of their rights. It has been said that there was no such danger here; I will suppose they were to attempt the experiment, after we have given them all our money, established them in a federal town, given them, the power of coining money, and raising a standing army; and to establish their arbitrary government; what resources have the people left? I cannot see any. — The parliament of England was first chosen annually;

they afterwards lengthened their duration to three years; and from triennial they became septennial. The government of England has been represented as a good and happy government, but some parts of it, their greatest political writers much condemn: especially that of the duration of their Parliaments: Attempts are yearly made to shorten their duration, from septennial to triennial; but the influence of the ministry is so great, that it has not yet been accomplished. From this duration, bribery and corruption are introduced. Notwithstanding they receive no pay, they make great interest for a seat in Parliament, one or two years before its dissolution, and give from five to twenty guineas, for a vote; and the candidates sometimes expend from 10,000l to .30,000l. Will a person throw away such a fortune—and waste so much time, without the probability of replacing such a sum with interest? Or can there be security in such men? Bribery may be introduced here as well as in Great-Britain—and Congress may equally oppress the people—because we cannot call them to an account; considering that there is no annual election—no rotation—no power to recall them, provided for.

Thomas Dawes, Jr., on Legitimate Standing Armies

January 24, 1788

Mr. DAWES observed, upon the authority of Congress to raise and support armies, that all the objections which had been made by gentlemen against *standing* armies, were inapplicable to the present question; which was, that as there must be an authority somewhere, to raise and support armies, whether that authority ought to be in Congress. As Congress are the *legislature* upon the proposed plan of government, in them only, said he, should be lodged the power under debate. Some gentlemen seem to have confused ideas about *standing armies*: That the legislature of a country should not have power to raise armies, is a doctrine he never heard before. Charles II. in England, kept in pay an army of five thousand men, and James II. augmented them to thirty thousand. This occasioned a great and just alarm through the nation; and accordingly when William III. came to the throne, it was declared to be unconstitutional to raise or keep a standing army in time of peace, *without the consent of the legislature*. Most of our own State constitutions have borrowed this language from the English declaration of rights; but none of them restrain their legislatures from raising and supporting armies. Those who never objected to such an authority in Congress, as vested by the old Confederation, surely ought not to object to such a power in a Congress, where there is to be a new branch of representation, arising immediately from the people, and which branch alone must originate those very grants that are to maintain the army. When we consider that this branch is to be elected every two years, there is great propriety in its being restrained from making any grants in support of the army for a longer space than that of their existence. If the election of this popular branch were for seven years, as in England, the same men who would make the first grant, might also the second and third, for the continuance of the army; and such an acquaintance might exist between the representatives in Congress and the leaders of the army, as might be unfavourable to liberty. But the wisdom of the late Convention has avoided this difficulty. The army must expire of itself in two years after it shall be raised, unless renewed by representatives, who at that time will have just come fresh from the body of the people. It will share the same fate as that of a temporary law, which dies at the time mentioned in the act itself, unless revived by some future legislature.

Amos Singletary and Jonathan Smith on "Leviathan" Swallowing Up "Us Little Folks" and on the Danger of Anarchy

January 25, 1788

Hon. Mr. SINGLETARY. Mr. President, I should not have troubled the Convention again, if some gentlemen had not called upon them that were on the stage in the beginning of our troubles, in the year 1775. I was one of them—I have had the honour to be a member of the court all the time, Mr. President, and I say, that if any body had proposed such a Constitution as this, in that day, it would have been thrown away at once—it would not have been looked at. We contended with Great-Britain—some said for a three-penny duty on tea, but it was not that—it was because they claimed a right to tax us and bind us in all cases whatever. And does not this Constitution do the same? does it not take away all we have—all our property? does it not lay *all* taxes, duties, imposts and excises? and what more have we to give? They tell us Congress won't lay dry taxes upon us, but collect all the money they want by impost. I say there has always been a difficulty about impost. Whenever the General Court was a going to lay an impost they would tell us it was more than trade could bear, that it hurt the fair trader, and encouraged smuggling; and there will always be the same objection; they won't be able to raise money enough by impost and then they will lay it on the land, and take all we have got. These lawyers, and men of learning, and monied men, that talk so finely and gloss over matters so smoothly, to make us poor illiterate people swallow down the pill, expect to get into Congress themselves; they expect to be the managers of this Constitution and get all the power and all the money into their own hands, and then they will swallow up all us little folks, like the great *Leviathan*, Mr. President, yes, just as the whale swallowed up *Jonah*. This is what I am afraid of; but I won't say any more at present, but reserve the rest to another opportunity.

Hon. Mr. SMITH. Mr. President, I am a plain man and get my living by the plough. I am not used to speak in publick, but I beg your leave to say a few words to my brother plough-joggers in this house. I have lived in a part of the country where I have known the worth of good government by the want of it. There was a black cloud that rose in the east last winter, and spread over the west.—[*Here Mr.* Widgery *interrupted. Mr. President, I wish to know what the gentleman means by the* east.] I mean, sir, the county of Bristol; the cloud rose there and burst upon us, and produced a dreadful effect. It brought on a state of *anarchy*, and that leads to *tyranny*. I say it brought anarchy. People that used to live peaceably, and were before good neighbours, got distracted and took up arms against government. [*Here Mr.* Kingsley *called to order, and asked what had the history of last winter to do with the Constitution? Several gentlemen, and among the rest the Hon. Mr.* Adams, *said the gentleman was in order—let him go on in his own way.*] I am a going, Mr. President, to shew you, my brother farmers, what were the effects of anarchy, that you may see the reasons why I wish for good government. People, I say took up arms, and then if you went to speak to them, you had the *musket of death* presented to your breast. They would rob you of your property, threaten to burn your houses; oblige you to be on your guard night and day; alarms spread from town to town; families were broke up; the tender mother would cry, O my son is among them! What shall I do for my child! Some were taken captive, children taken out of their schools and carried away. Then we should hear of an *action*, and the poor prisoners were *set in the front*, to be killed by their own friends. How dreadful, how distressing was this! Our distress was so great that we should have been glad to catch at any thing that looked like a government for protection. Had any person, that was able to protect us, come and set up his standard we should all have flocked to it, even if it had been a *monarch*, and that monarch might have proved a tyrant, so that you see that anarchy leads to tyranny, and better have *one* tyrant than so many at once.

Now, Mr. President, when I saw this Constitution, I found

that it was a cure for these disorders. It was just such a thing as we wanted. I got a copy of it and read it over and over. I had been a member of the Convention to form our own state Constitution, and had learnt something of the checks and balances of power, and I found them all here. I did not go to any lawyer, to ask his opinion, we have no lawyer in our town, and we do well enough without. I formed my own opinion, and was pleased with this Constitution. My honourable old daddy there (*pointing to Mr.* Singletary) won't think that I expect to be a Congress-man, and swallow up the liberties of the people. I never had any post, nor do I want one, and before I am done you will think that I don't deserve one. But I don't think the worse of the Constitution because lawyers, and men of learning and monied men, are fond of it. I don't suspect that they want to get into Congress and abuse their power. I am not of such a jealous make; they that are honest men themselves are not apt to suspect other people. I don't know why our constituents have not as good a right to be as jealous of us, as we seem to be of the Congress, and I think those gentlemen who are so very suspicious, that as soon as a man gets into power he turns rogue, had better look *at home*.

We are by this Constitution allowed to send *ten* members to Congress. Have we not more than that number fit to go? I dare say if we pick out ten, we shall have another ten left, and I hope ten times ten, and will not these be a check upon those that go; Will they go to Congress and abuse their power and do mischief, when they know that they must return and look the other ten in the face, and be called to account for their conduct? Some gentlemen think that our liberty and property is not safe in the hands of monied men, and men of learning, I am not of that mind.

Brother farmers, let us suppose a case now—suppose you had a farm of 50 acres, and your title was disputed, and there was a farm of 5000 acres joined to you that belonged to a man of learning, and his title was involved in the same difficulty; would not you be glad to have him for your friend, rather than to stand alone in the dispute? Well, the case is the same, these lawyers, these monied men, these men of learning, are all embarked in the same cause with us, and we must all swim or sink together; and shall we throw the Constitution overboard, because it does not please us alike? Suppose two or three of you had been at the pains to break up a piece of rough land, and sow it with wheat—would you let it lay waste, because you could not agree what *sort* of a fence to make? would it not be better to put up a fence that did not please every one's fancy rather than not fence it at all, or keep disputing about it, until the wild beast came in and devoured it. Some gentlemen say, don't be in a hurry—take time to consider, and don't take a leap in the dark.—I say take things in time—gather fruit when it is ripe. There is a time to sow and a time to reap; we sowed our seed when we sent men to the federal convention, now is the harvest, now is the time to reap the fruit of our labour, and if we don't do it now I am afraid we never shall have another opportunity.

Abraham Holmes and Christopher Gore on the Possible Abuses of the Federal Judiciary

January 30, 1788

Mr. HOLMES. Mr. President, I rise to make some remarks on the paragraph under consideration, which treats of the judiciary power.

It is a maxim universally admitted, *that the safety of the subject consists in having a right to a trial as free and impartial as the lot of humanity will admit of.*—Does the Constitution make provision for such a trial? I think not: For in a criminal process a person shall not have a right to insist on a trial in the vicinity where the fact was committed, where a jury of the peers would, from their local situation, have an opportunity to form a judgment of the *character* of the person charged with the crime, and also to judge of the *credibility* of the witnesses. There a person must be tried by a jury of strangers—a jury who *may be* interested in his conviction; and where he *may*, by reason of the distance of his residence from the place of trial, be incapable of making such a defence, as he is in justice intitled to, and which he could avail himself of, if his trial was in the same county where the crime is said to have been committed.

These circumstances, as horrid as they are, are rendered still more dark and gloomy, as there is no provision made in the Constitution to prevent the Attorney-General from filing information against any person, whether he is indicted by the grand jury or not; in consequence of which the most innocent person in the Commonwealth may be taken by virtue of a warrant issued in consequence of such information, and dragged from his home, his friends, his acquaintance, and confined in prison, until the next session of the court, which has jurisdiction of the crime with which he is charged (and how frequent those sessions are to be, we are not yet informed of) and after long, tedious and painful imprisonment, though acquited on trial, may have no possibility to obtain any kind of satisfaction for the loss of his liberty, the loss of his time, great expenses and perhaps cruel sufferings.

But what makes the matter still more alarming is that as the model of criminal process is to be pointed out by Congress, and they have no constitutional check on them, except that the trial is to be by a *jury*, but who this jury is to be, how qualified, where to live, how appointed, or by what rules to regulate their procedure, we are ignorant of as yet;—whether they are to live in the county where the trial is;—whether they are to be chosen by certain districts;—or whether they are to be appointed by the sheriff *ex officio*;—whether they are to be for one session of the Court only, or for a certain term of time, or for good behaviour, or during pleasure; are matters which we are intirely ignorant of as yet.

The mode of trial is altogether indetermined—whether the criminal is to be allowed the benefit of council; whether he is to be allowed to meet his accuser face to face: whether he is to be allowed to confront the witnesses and have the advantage of cross examination we are not yet told.

These are matters of by no means small consequence, yet we have not the smallest constitutional security, that we shall be allowed the exercise of these privileges, neither is it made certain in the Constitution, that a person charged with a crime, shall have the privileges of appearing before the court or jury which is to try them.

On the whole, when we fully consider this matter, and fully investigate the powers granted—explicitly given, and especially delegated, we shall find Congress possessed of powers enabling them to institute judicatories, little less inauspicious than a certain tribunal in Spain, which has long been the disgrace of Christendom—I mean that diabolical institution the INQUISITION.

What gives an additional glare of horrour to these gloomy circumstances, is the consideration that Congress have to ascertain, point out, and determine, what kind of punishments shall be inflicted on persons convicted of crimes; they are no where restrained from inventing the most cruel and unheard of punishments, and annexing them to crimes, and there is no constitutional check on them, but that RACKS and GIBBETS, may be amongst the most mild instruments of their discipline.

There is nothing to prevent Congress from passing laws which shall compel a man who is accused or suspected of a crime, to furnish evidence against himself, and even from establishing laws which shall order the court to take the charge exhibited against a man for truth, unless he can furnish evidence of his innocence.

I do not pretend to say Congress *will* do this, but sir, I undertake to say that Congress (according to the powers proposed to be given them by the Constitution) *may* do it; and if they do not, it will be owing *intirely*—I repeat it, it will be owing *intirely* to the GOODNESS of the MEN, and not in the *least degree* owing to the GOODNESS of the CONSTITUTION.

The framers of our State Constitution, took particular care to prevent the General Court from authorizing the judicial authority to issue a warrant against a man for a crime, unless his being guilty of the crime was supported by oath of affirmation, prior to the warrants being granted; why it should be esteemed so much more safe to intrust Congress with the power of enacting laws, which it was deemed so unsafe to intrust our state legislature with, I am unable to conceive.

Mr. GORE—observed in reply to Mr. HOLMES—that it had been the uniform conduct of those in opposition to the proposed form of government, to determine, in every case where it was possible that the administrators thereof could do wrong, that they would do so, although it were demonstrable that such wrong would be against their own honour and interest, and productive of no advantage to themselves—On this principle alone have they determined that the trial by jury would be taken away in civil cases—when it had been clearly shewn, that no words could be adopted, apt to the situation and customs of each state in this particular—Jurors are differently chosen in different states, and in point of qualification the laws of the several states are very diverse—not less so, in

the causes and disputes which are intitled to trial by jury—
what is the result of this—that the laws of Congress may, and
will be conformable to the local laws in this particular, although the Constitution could not make an universal rule
equally applying to the customs and statutes of the different
states—very few governments, (certainly not this) can be interested in depriving the people of trial by jury in questions of
meum et tuum—in criminal cases alone, are they interested
to have the trial under their own controul—and in such cases
the Constitution expressly stipulates for trial by jury—but
then says the gentleman from Rochester (*Mr. Holmes*) to the
safety of life it is indispensibly necessary the trial of crimes
should be in the vicinity—and the vicinity is construed to
mean county—this is very incorrect, and gentlemen will see
the impropriety by referring themselves to the different local
divisions and districts of the several states—but further, said
the gentleman, the idea that the jury coming from the neighbourhood, and knowing the character and circumstances of
the party in trial, is promotive of justice, on reflection will
appear not founded in truth—if the jury judge from any
other circumstances, but what are part of the cause in question, they are not impartial—The great object is to determine
on the real merits of the cause uninfluenced by any personal
considerations—if therefore the jury could be perfectly ignorant of the person in trial, a just decision would be more
probable—from such motives did the wise Athenians so constitute the fam'd Areopagus, that when in judgment, this
court should sit at midnight and in total darkness, that the
decision might be on the thing, and not on the person—further, said the gentleman, it has been said, because the constitution does not expressly provide for an indictment by grand
jury in criminal cases, therefore some officer under this government will be authorized to file informations and bring any
man to jeopardy of his life, and indictment by grand jury will
be disused—if gentlemen who pretend such fears, will look
into the constitution of Massachusetts, they will see that no
provision is therein made for an indictment by grand jury, or
to oppose the danger of an attorney general filing informations, yet no difficulty or danger has arisen to the people of

this Commonwealth, from this defect, if gentlemen please to call it so—if gentlemen would be candid and not consider that wherever Congress may possibly abuse power, that they certainly will, there would be no difficulty in the minds of any in adopting the proposed constitution.

General William Heath on Slavery

January 30, 1788

Gen. HEATH. Mr. President—By my indisposition, and absence, I have lost several important opportunities; I have lost the opportunity of expressing my sentiments with a candid freedom, on some of the paragraphs of the system, which have lain heavy on my mind. I have lost the opportunity of expressing my warm approbation on some of the paragraphs. I have lost the opportunity of asking some questions for my own information, touching some of the paragraphs, and which naturally occurred, as the system unfolded. I have lost the opportunity of hearing those judicious, enlightening, and convincing arguments, which have been advanced during the investigation of the system,—this is my misfortune, and I must bear it. The paragraph respecting the migration or importation of such persons, as any of the States now existing shall think proper to admit, &c. is one of those considered during my absence, and I have heard nothing on the subject, save what has been mentioned this morning, but I think the gentlemen who have spoken, have carried the matter rather too far on both sides,—I apprehend that it is not in our power to do any thing for, or against, those who are in slavery in the southern States. No gentleman within these walls detests every idea of slavery more than I do: It is generally detested by the people of this Commonwealth,—and I ardently hope that the time will soon come, when our brethren in the southern States will view it as we do, and put a stop to it, but to this we have no right to compel them. Two questions naturally arise if we ratify the Constitution, shall we do any thing by our act to hold the blacks in slavery—or shall we become partakers of other men's sins. I think neither of them: Each State is sovereign and independent to a certain degree, and they have a right, and will regulate their own internal affairs, as to themselves appears proper; and shall we refuse to eat, or to drink, or to be united, with those who do not think, or act, just as we do, surely not. We are not in this case partakers of other mens sins, for in nothing do we voluntarily encourage the slavery of our fellow men, a restriction is laid on the federal government, which could not be avoided and a union take place: The federal Convention went as far as they could, the migration or importation, &c. is confined to the States now *existing only*, new States cannot claim it. Congress by their ordinance for erecting new States, some time since, declared, that the new States shall be republican, and that there shall be no slavery in them. But whether those in slavery in the southern States, will be emancipated after the year 1808, I do not pretend to determine, I rather doubt it.

Charles Jarvis on the Amendment Procedure: An Irrefutable Argument for Ratification

January 30, 1788

Dr. JARVIS. Mr. President—I cannot suffer the present article to be passed, without rising to express my entire and perfect approbation of it—Whatever may have been my private opinion of any other part, or whatever faults or imperfections I have remarked, or fancied I have seen, in any other instance, here, sir, I have found complete satisfaction—this has been a resting place, on which I have reposed myself in the fullest security, whenever a doubt has occurred, in considering any other passage in the proposed Constitution. The Hon. Gentleman last speaking, has called upon those persons who are opposed to our receiving the present system, to show another government in which such a wise precaution has been taken, to secure to the people the right of making such alterations and amendments in a peaceable way, as experience shall have proved to be necessary.—Allow me to say, sir, as far as the narrow limits of my own information extend, I know of no such example—In other countries, sir, unhappily for mankind, the history of their respective revolutions have been written in blood; and it is in this only that any great or important change in our political situation, has been effected, without publick commotions—When we shall have adopted the Constitution before us, we shall have in this article an adequate provision for all the purposes of political reformation. If in the course of its operation, this government shall appear to be too severe, here are the means by which this severity may be attempered and corrected;—if, on the other, it shall become too languid in its movements, here again we have a method designated, by which a new portion of health and spirit may be infused in the Constitution.

There is, sir, another view which I have long since taken of this subject, which has produced the fullest conviction in my own mind, in favour of our receiving the government which we have now in contemplation—Should it be rejected, I beg gentlemen would observe, that a concurrence of all the States must be had before a new Convention can be called to form another Constitution:—But the present article provides, upon nine States concurring in any alteration or amendment to be proposed, either by Congress, or any future Convention, that this alteration shall be a part of the Constitution, equally powerful and obligatory with any other part. If it be alledged that this union is not likely to happen, will it be more likely, that an union of a greater number of concurring sentiments may be had, as must be, in case we reject the Constitution in hopes of a better—But that this is practicable, we may safely appeal to the history of this country as a proof, in the last twenty years. We have united against the British—we have united in calling the late federal Convention—and we may certainly unite again in such alterations as in reason shall appear to be important for the peace and happiness of America.

In the Constitution of this State the article providing for alterations is limitted in its operation to a given time; but in the present Constitution, the article is perfectly at large, unconfined to any period, and may admit of measures being taken, in any moment after it is adopted. In this point it has undoubtedly the advantage. I shall not sit down, sir, without repeating, that as it is clearly more difficult for twelve States to agree to another Convention, than for nine to unite in favour of amendments, so it is certainly better to receive the present Constitution in the hope of its being amended, than it would be to reject it altogether, with, perhaps, the vain expectation of obtaining another more agreeable than the present—I see no fallacy in the argument, Mr. President, but if there is, permit me to call upon any gentleman to point it out, in order that it may be corrected—for at present it seems to me of such force as to give me entire satisfaction.

The Reverend Daniel Shute and
Colonel William Jones on Religious Tests
and Christian Belief

January 31, 1788

Rev. Mr. SHUTE. Mr. President—To object to the latter part of the paragraph under consideration, which excludes a religious test, is, I am sensible, very popular; for the most of men, some how, are rigidly tenacious of their own sentiments in religion, and disposed to impose them upon others as the *standard* of truth. If in my sentiments, upon the point in view, I should differ from some in this honourable body, I only wish from them the exercise of that candour, with which true religion is adapted to inspire the honest and well-disposed mind.

To establish a religious test as a qualification for offices in the proposed Federal Constitution, appears to me, sir, would be attended with injurious consequences to some individuals, and with no advantage to the *whole*.

By the injurious consequences to individuals, I mean, that some, who in every other respect, are qualified to fill some important post in government, will be excluded by their not being able to stand the religious test—which I take to be a privation of part of their civil rights.

Nor is there to me any conceivable advantage, sir, that would result in the *whole* from such a test. Unprincipled and dishonest men will not hesitate to subscribe to *any thing*, that may open the way for their advancement, and put them into a situation the better to execute their base and iniquitous designs. Honest men alone, therefore, however well qualified to serve the publick, would be excluded by it, and their country be deprived of the benefit of their abilities.

In this great and extensive empire, there is and will be a great variety of sentiments in religion among its inhabitants. Upon the plan of a religious test, the question I think must be, who shall be excluded from national trusts? Whatever

919

answer bigotry may suggest, the dictates of candour and equity, I conceive, will be *none*.

Far from limiting my charity and confidence to men of my own denomination in religion, I suppose, and I believe, sir, that there are worthy characters among men of every other denomination—among the Quakers—the Baptists—the Church of England—the Papists—and even among those who have no other guide, in the way to virtue and heaven, than the dictates of natural religion.

I must therefore think, sir, that the proposed plan of government, in this particular, is wisely constructed: That as all have an equal claim to the blessings of the government under which they live, and which they support, so none should be excluded from them for being of any particular denomination in religion.

The presumption is, that the eyes of the people will be upon the faithful in the land, and from a regard to their own safety, will chuse for their rulers, men of known abilities—of known probity—of good moral characters. The apostle Peter tells us, that God is no respecter of persons, but in every nation he that feareth him and worketh righteousness, is *acceptable* to him—And I know of no reason, why men of such a character, in a community, of whatever denomination in religion, *ceteris paribus*, with other suitable qualifications, should not be *acceptable* to the people, and why they may not be employed, by them, with safety and advantage in the important offices of government.—The exclusion of a religious test in the proposed Constitution, therefore, clearly appears to me, sir, to be in favour of its adoption.

Colonel JONES (*Bristol*) thought, that the rulers ought to believe in God or Christ—and that however a test may be prostituted in England, yet he thought if our publick men were to be of those who had a good standing in the church, it would be happy for the United States—and that a person could not be a good man without being a good Christian.

John Hancock Proposes Ratification, with Amendments Recommended to "Quiet the Apprehensions of Gentlemen"

January 31, 1788

When the Convention met in the afternoon,

His Excellency the PRESIDENT observed, that a motion had been made and seconded, that this Convention do assent to, and ratify, the Constitution which had been under consideration—and that he had in the former part of the day intimated his intention of submitting a proposition to the consideration of the Convention. My motive, says he, arises from my earnest desire to this Convention, my fellow-citizens and the publick at large, that this Convention may adopt such a form of government, as may extend its good influences to every part of the United States, and advance the prosperity of the whole world. His situation, his Excellency said, had not permitted him to enter into the debates of this Convention.—It however, appeared to him necessary, from what had been advanced in them, to adopt the form of government proposed; but, observing a diversity of sentiment in the gentlemen of the Convention, he had frequently had conversation with them on the subject; and from this conversation, he was induced to propose to them, whether the introduction of some general amendments would not be attended with the happiest consequences: For that purpose he should, with the leave of the Hon. Convention, submit to their consideration a proposition, in order to remove the doubts, and quiet the apprehensions of gentlemen; and if in any degree the object should be acquired, he should feel himself perfectly satisfied. He should therefore, submit them—for he was, he said, unable to go more largely into the subject, if his abilities would permit him, relying on the candour of the Convention to bear him witness, that his wishes for a good constitution were sincere. [*His Excellency then read his proposition.*] This gentlemen, concluded his Excellency, is the proposition which I had to make; and I submit it to your consideration, with the sincere wish, that it may have a tendency to promote a spirit of union.

Samuel Adams Supports Hancock's Proposition

January 31, 1788

Hon. Mr. ADAMS. Mr. President—I feel myself happy in contemplating the idea, that many benefits will result from your Excellency's conciliatory proposition, to this commonwealth and to the United States; and I think it ought to precede the motion made by the gentleman from Newbury-Port; and to be at this time considered by the Convention. I have said, that I have had my doubts of this Constitution—I could not digest every part of it, as readily as some gentlemen; but this, sir, is my misfortune, not my fault. Other gentlemen have had their doubts, but, in my opinion the proposition submitted, will have a tendency to remove such doubts, and to conciliate the minds of the convention, and the people without doors. This subject, sir, is of the greatest magnitude, and has employed the attention of every rational man in the United States: but the minds of the people are not so well agreed on it as all of us could wish. A proposal, of this sort, coming from Massachusetts, from her importance, will have its weight. Four or five states have considered and ratified the constitution as it stands; but we know there is a diversity of opinion even in these states, and one of them is greatly agitated. If this Convention should particularize the amendments necessary to be proposed, it appears to me it must have weight in other States where Conventions have not yet met. I have observed the sentiments of gentlemen on the subject, as far as Virginia; and I have found that the objections were similar, in the news papers, and in some of the Conventions.—Considering these circumstances, it appears to me that such a measure will have the most salutary effect throughout the union.—It is of the greatest importance, that *America* should still be united in sentiment. I think I have not been heretofore unmindful of the advantage of such an union. It is essential that the people should be united in the federal government, to withstand the common enemy, and to preserve their valuable rights and liberties. We find in the great

State of Pennsylvania, one third of the Convention are opposed to it: should there then be large minorities in the several states, I should fear the consequences of such disunion.

Sir, there are many parts of it I esteem as highly valuable, particularly the article which empowers Congress to regulate commerce, to form treaties &c. For want of this power in our national head, our friends are grieved, and our enemies insult us. Our ambassadour at the court of London is considered as a mere cypher, instead of the representative of the United States.—Therefore it appears to me, that a power to remedy this evil should be given to Congress, and the remedy applied as soon as possible.

The only difficulty on gentlemen's minds is, whether it is best to accept this Constitution on conditional amendments, or to rely on amendments in future, as the Constitution provides. When I look over the article which provides for a revision, I have my doubts. Suppose, sir, nine states accept the Constitution without any conditions at all; and the four states should wish to have amendments, where will you find nine States to propose, and the legislatures of nine States to agree, to the introduction of amendments—Therefore it seems to me, that the expectation of amendments taking place at some future time, will be frustrated. This method, if we take it, will be the most likely to bring about the amendments, as the Conventions of New-Hampshire, Rhode-Island, New-York, Maryland, Virginia, and South-Carolina, have not yet met. I apprehend, sir, that these States will be influenced by the proposition which your Excellency has submitted, as the resolutions of Massachusetts have ever had their influence. If this should be the case, the necessary amendments would be introduced more early, and more safely. From these considerations, as your Excellency did not think it proper to make a motion, with submission, I move, that the paper read by your Excellency, be now taken under consideration, by the Convention.

Samuel Nasson's "Pathetick Apostrophe" to Liberty, and Judge Increase Sumner's Reply

February 1, 1788

Mr. NASSON. Mr. President—I feel myself happy, that your Excellency has been placed by the free suffrages of your fellow-citizens, at the head of this government: I also feel myself happy, that your Excellency has been placed in the chair of this Hon. Convention: And I feel a confidence, that the proposition submitted to our consideration yesterday by your Excellency, has for its object the good of your country: But, sir, as I have not had an opportunity leisurely to consider it, I shall pass it over, and take a short view of the Constitution at large, which is under consideration, though my abilities, sir, will not permit me to do justice to my feelings—or to my constituents. Great-Britain, sir, first attempted to enslave us, by declaring her laws supreme, and that she had a right to bind us in all cases whatever. What, sir, roused the Americans to shake off the yoke preparing for them?—It was this measure, the power to do which we are now about giving to Congress—And here, sir, I beg the indulgence of this hon. body, to permit me to make a short apostrophe to Liberty.— Oh! Liberty—thou greatest good—thou fairest property! with thee I wish to live—with thee I wish to die! Pardon me if I drop a tear on the peril to which she is exposed: I cannot, sir, see this brightest of jewels tarnished! a jewel worth ten thousand worlds! And shall we part with it so soon?—Oh, No. Gentlemen ask, can it be supposed, that a Constitution so pregnant with danger, could come from the hands of those who framed it? Indeed, sir, I am suspicious of my own judgment, when I contemplate this idea—when I see the list of illustrious names annexed to it:—But, sir, my duty to my constituents, obliges me to oppose the measure they recommend, as obnoxious to their liberty and safety.

When, sir, we dissolved the political bands which connected us with Great-Britain, we were in a state of nature—we then formed and adopted the Confederation, which

925

must be considered as a sacred instrument; this confederated us under one head, as sovereign and independent States. Now, sir, if we give Congress power to dissolve that Confederation, to what can we trust? If a nation consent thus to treat their most solemn compacts, who will ever trust them? Let us, sir, begin with this Constitution, and see what it is—and first, "We the People of the United States, do," &c. If this, sir, does not go to an annihilation of the state governments, and to a perfect consolidation of the whole union, I do not know what does. What! shall we consent to this? Can 10, 20, or 100 persons in this State, who have taken the oath of allegiance to it, dispense with this oath. Gentlemen may talk as they please of dispensing in certain cases with oaths; but, sir, with me they are sacred things: We are under oath; we have sworn that Massachusetts is a sovereign and independent State—How then, can we vote for this Constitution, that destroys that sovereignty?

The Hon. Col. VARNUM begged leave to set the worthy gentleman right—The very oath, he said, which the gentleman has mentioned, provides an exception for the power to be granted to Congress.

Well, continued Mr. NASSON, to go on—Mr. President— Let us consider the Constitution without a Bill of Rights. When I give up any of my natural rights, it is for the security of the rest: But here is not one right secured, although many are neglected.

With respect to biennial elections, the paragraph is rather loosely expressed; I am a little in favour of our ancient custom. Gentlemen say they are convinced that the alteration is necessary: It may be so: When I see better, I will join with them.

To go on. Representation and taxation to be apportioned according to numbers. This, sir, I am opposed to; it is unequal. I will shew an instance in point—We know for certainty, that in the town of Brooklyn, persons are better able to pay their taxes, than in the parts I represent: Suppose the tax is laid on polls: Why the people of the former place will pay their tax ten times as easy, as the latter—thus helping that part of the community, which stands in the least need of help: On this footing the poor pay as much as the rich: And in this a way is laid, that five slaves shall be rated no more than three children. Let gentlemen consider this—a farmer takes three small orphans, on charity, to bring up—they are bound to him—when they arrive at 21 years of age, he gives each of them a couple suits of clothes, a cow, and two or three young cattle—we are rated as much for these, as a farmer in Virginia is for five slaves, whom he holds for life— they and their posterity—the male and the she ones too. The senate, Mr. President, are to be chosen two from each State. This, sir, puts the smaller States on the footing with the larger—when the States have to pay according to their numbers—New-Hampshire does not pay a fourth part as much as Massachusetts. We must, therefore, to support the *dignity* of the union, pay four times as much as New-Hampshire, and almost fourteen times as much as Georgia— who, we see, are equally represented with us.

The term, sir, for which the senate is chosen, is a griev- ance—it is too long to trust any body of men with power: It is impossible but that such men will be tenacious of their places; they are to be raised to a lofty eminence, and they will be loth to come down; and in the course of six years, may by management, have it in their power to create officers, and obtain influence enough, to get in again, and so for life.— When we felt the hand of British oppression upon us, we were so jealous of rulers, as to declare them eligible but for three years in six. In this Constitution we forget this princi- ple. I, sir, think that rulers ought at short periods, to return to private life, that they may know how to feel for, and regard their fellow creatures. In six years, sir, and at a great distance, they will quite forget them.

> *"For time and absence cure the purest love"*

We are apt to forget our friends, except when we are convers- ing with them.

We now come, sir, to the 4th section. Let us see—the times, places and manners of holding elections, shall be pre- scribed in each State by the legislature thereof. No objections to this: but, sir, after *the flash of lightening comes the peal of thunder*; "but Congress may at any time, alter them, &c." Here it is, Mr. President: this is the article which is to make Congress omnipotent. Gentlemen say, this is the greatest beauty of the Constitution—this is the great security for the people—this is the all in all. Such language have I heard in this house: but, sir, I say, by this power Congress may, if they please, order the election of federal representatives for Massachusetts, to be at Great-Barrington, or Machias: And at such a time too, as shall put it in the power of a few artful, and designing men, to get themselves elected at their pleasure.

The 8th sect. Mr. President, provides that Congress shall have power to lay and collect taxes, duties, imposts, excises, &c. We may, sir, be poor; we may not be able to pay these taxes, &c.—we must have a little meal, and a little meat, whereon to live; and save a little for a rainy day: But what follows? Let us see. To raise and support armies. Here, sir, comes the key to unlock this cabinet: Here is the mean by which you will be made to pay your taxes? But will ye, my countrymen, submit to this. Suffer me, sir, to say a few words on the fatal effects, of standing armies, that bane of republican governments! A standing army! Was it not with this that Cæsar passed the *Rubicon*, and laid prostrate the liberties of his country? By this has seven eighths of the once free nations of the globe, been brought into bondage! Time would fail me, were I to attempt to recapitulate the havock made in the world, by standing armies. Britain attempted to inforce her arbitrary measures, by a standing army. But, sir, we had patriots then who alarmed us of our danger—who shewed us the serpent, and bid us beware of it. Shall I name them? I fear I shall offend your Excellency? But I cannot avoid it? I must. We had an HANCOCK, an ADAMS, and a WARREN—our sister States too, produced a RANDOLPH a WASHINGTON, a GREENE, and a MONTGOMERY, who lead us in our way—Some of these have given up their lives in defence of the liberties of their country; and my prayer to God is, that when this race of illustrious patriots, shall have bid adieu to the world; that from their dust, as from the sacred ashes of the Phœnix, another race may arise, who shall take our posterity by the hand, and lead them to trample on the necks of those who shall dare to infringe on their liberties—Sir, had I a voice like Jove, I would proclaim it throughout the world—and had I an arm like Jove, I would hurl from the globe those villains that would dare attempt to establish in our country a standing army. I wish, sir, that the gentlemen of Boston, would bring to their minds the fatal evening of the 5th of March 1770—when by standing troops they lost five of their fellow townsmen—I will ask them what price can atone for their lives? What money can make satisfaction for the loss? The same causes produces the same effects. An army may be raised on pretence of helping a friend, or many pretences might be used; that night, sir, ought to be a sufficient warning against standing armies, except in cases of great emergency—they are too frequently used for no other purpose than dragooning the people into slavery, but I beseech you, my countrymen, for the sake of your posterity, to act like those worthy men, who have stood forth in defence of the rights of mankind; and shew to the world, that you will not submit to tyranny. What occasion have we for standing armies? We fear no foe—If one should come upon us, we have a militia, which is our bulwark. Let Lexington witness that we have the means of defence among ourselves. If during the last winter there was not much alacrity shewn by the militia, in turning out, we must consider that they were going to fight their countrymen. Do you, sir, suppose, that had a British army invaded us at that time, that such supineness would have been discovered. No, sir, to our enemies dismay, and discomfort, they would have felt the contrary: But against deluded, infatuated men they did not wish to exert their valour or their strength. Therefore, sir, I am utterly opposed to a standing army, in time of peace.

The paragraph that gives Congress power to suspend the writ of habeas corpus, claims a little attention—This is a great bulwark—a great privilege indeed—we ought not, therefore, to give it up, on any slight pretence. Let us see — how long it is to be suspended? As long as rebellion or invasion shall continue. This is exceeding loose. Why is not the time limitted, as in our Constitution? But, sir, its design would then be defeated—It was the intent, and by it we shall give up one of our greatest privileges. Mr. N. concluded by saying, he had much more to say, but as the House were impatient, he should sit down for the present, to give other gentlemen an opportunity to speak.

Judge SUMNER, adverting to the pathetick apostrophe of

the gentlemen last speaking, said, he could with as much sincerity apostrophize—Oh! Government! thou greatest good! thou best of blessings!—with thee I wish to live—with thee I wish to die.—Thou art as necessary to the support of the political body, as meat and bread are to the natural body. The learned Judge then turned his attention to the proposition submitted by the President, and said, he sincerely hoped, that it would meet the approbation of the Convention, as it appeared to him a remedy for all the difficulties, which gentlemen in the course of the debates had mentioned. He particularized the objections that had been started; and shewed that their removal was provided for in the proposition: And concluded by observing, that the probability was very great, that if the amendents proposed were recommended by this Convention, that they would, on the meeting of the first Congress, be adopted by the general government.

Isaac Backus on Religion and the State, Slavery, and Nobility

February 4, 1788

Rev. Mr. BACKUS. Mr. President, I have said very little in this honourable Convention; but I now beg leave to offer a few thoughts upon some points in the Constitution proposed to us. And I shall begin with the exclusion of any religious test. Many appear to be much concerned about it, but nothing is more evident, both in reason, and in the holy scriptures, than that religion is ever a matter between God and individuals; and therefore no man or men can impose any religious test, without invading the essential prerogatives of our Lord Jesus Christ. Ministers first assumed this power under the Christian name; and then Constantine approved of the practice, when he adopted the profession of Christianity, as an engine of state-policy. And let the history of all nations be searched, from that day to this, and it will appear that the imposing of religious tests hath been the greatest engine of tyranny in the world. And I rejoice to see so many gentlemen who are now giving in the rights of conscience, in this great and important matter. Some serious minds discover a concern lest, if all religious tests should be excluded, the Congress would hereafter establish Popery, or some other tyrannical way of worship. But it is most certain, that no such way of worship can be established, without any religious test.

Much, sir, hath been said, about the importation of slaves into this country. I believe that, according to my capacity, no man abhors that wicked practice more than I do, and would gladly make use of all lawful means, towards the abolishing of slavery in all parts of the land.—But let us consider where we are, and what we are doing. In the articles of confederation, no provision was made to hinder the importation of slaves into any of these States; but a door is now opened, hereafter to do it; and each State is at liberty now to abolish slavery as soon as they please. And let us remember our former connection with Great-Britain, from whom many in our land think we ought not to have revolted: How did they carry on the slave-trade! I know that the Bishop of Gloucester, in an annual sermon in London, in February, 1766, endeavoured to justify their tyrannical claims of power over us, by casting the reproach of the slave-trade upon the Americans. But at the close of the war, the Bishop of Chester, in an annual sermon, in February, 1783, ingenuously owned, that their nation is the most deeply involved in the guilt of that trade, of any nation in the world; and also, that they have treated their slaves in the West-Indies, worse than the French or Spaniards have done theirs.—Thus slavery grows more and more odious through the world;—and, as an honourable gentleman said some days ago, "Though we cannot say, that slavery is struck with an apoplexy, yet we may hope it will die with a consumption." And a main source, sir, of that iniquity, hath been an abuse of the covenant of circumcision, which gave the seed of Abraham to destroy the inhabitants of Canaan, and to take their houses, vineyards, and all their estates as their own; and also to buy and hold others as servants. And as christian privileges are much greater than those of the Hebrews were, many have imagined that they had a right to seize upon the lands of the heathen, and to destroy or enslave them as far as they could extend their power. And from thence the mystery of iniquity carried many into the practice of making *merchandise of slaves and souls of men*. But all ought to remember, that when God promised the land of Canaan to Abraham and his seed, he let him know that they were not to take possession of that land, until the *iniquity of the Amorites was full*; and then they did it under the immediate direction of heaven; and they were as real executors of the judgment of God upon those heathens, as any person ever was an executor of a criminal justly condemned. And in doing it they were not allowed to invade the lands of the Edomites, who sprang from Esau, who was not only of the seed of Abraham, but was born at the same birth with Israel; and yet they were not of that church. Neither were Israel allowed to invade the lands of the Moabites, or of the children of Ammon, who were of the seed of Lot. And no officer in Israel had any legislative power, but such as were immediately inspired. Even David, the man after God's own heart, had no legislative power, but only as he was inspired from above; and he is expressly called a *Prophet* in the New Testament. And we are to remember that Abraham and his seed, for four hundred years, had no warrant to admit any strangers into that church, but by buying of him as a servant, with money. And it was a great privilege to be bought, and adopted into a religious family for seven years, and then to have their freedom. And that covenant was expressly repealed in various parts of the New-Testament; and particularly in the first epistle to the Corinthians, wherein it is said, *Ye are bought with a price; therefore glorify God in your body, and in your spirit, which are God's. And again, circumcission is nothing, and uncircumcission is nothing, but the keeping of the commandments of God. Ye are bought with a price, be not ye the servants of men.* Thus the gospel sets all men upon a level; very contrary to the declaration of an honourable gentleman in this house "That the Bible was contrived for the advantage of a particular order of men."

Another great advantage, sir, in the Constitution before us, is its excluding all titles of nobility, or hereditary sucession of power; which hath been a main engine of tyranny in foreign countries. But the American revolution was built upon the principle, that all men are born with an equal right to liberty and property, and that officers have no right to any power but what is fairly given them by the consent of the people. And in the Constitution now proposed to us, a power is reserved to the people, constitutionally to reduce every officer again to a private station; and what a guard is this against their invasion of others rights, or abusing of their power! Such a door is now opened, for the establishing of righteous government, and for securing equal liberty, as never was before opened to any people upon earth.

Charles Jarvis Supports Hancock's Strategy on Amendments

February 4, 1788

Dr JARVIS. Mr. President—The objections which gentlemen have made to the form of ratification which has been submitted by your Excellency, have arisen, either from a doubt of our having a right to propose alterations; or, from the supposed improbability that any amendments recommended by this assembly, will ever become a part of the federal system.—If we have no right, sir, to propose alterations, there remains nothing further to be attempted, but take the final question independent of the propositions for amendment—But, I hope the mere assertion of any one is not to operate as an argument in this assembly; and we are yet waiting for evidence to prove this very singular position which has been so often repeated—If we have a right, sir, to receive, or reject the Constitution, surely we have an equal authority to determine in what way this right shall be exercised—It is a maxim, I believe universally admitted, that in every instance, the manner in which every power is to be exerted, must be in its nature discretionary with that body to which this power is delegated—If this principle be just, sir, the ground which has been taken to oppose your Excellency's proposal by disputing the right of recommending alterations, must be necessarily relinquished:—But gentlemen say, that they find nothing about amendments in the commission under which they are acting, and they conceive it neither agreeable to the resolution of the legislature, nor to the sense of their constituents, that such a scheme should be adopted:—Let us inquire then, sir, under what authority we are acting; and to what tribunal we are amenable: Is it then, sir, from the late federal Convention, that we derive our authority? Is it from Congress, or is it even from the legislature itself—It is from neither, sir—we are convened in right of the people, as their immediate representatives, to execute the most important trust which it is possible to receive, and we are accountable in its execution, to God

934

only, and our own consciences.—When gentlemen assert then, that we have no right to recommend alterations, they must have ideas strangely derogatory to the influence and authority of our constituents, whom we have the honour of representing:—But should it be thought there was even a part of the people who conceived we were thus restricted as to the forms of our proceedings, we are still to recollect that their aggregate sense, on this point, can only be determined by the voices of the majority in this Convention. The arguments of those gentlemen, who oppose any propositions of amendments, amount simply to this, sir, that the whole people of Massachusetts, assembled by their delegates, on the most solemn and interesting occasion, are not at liberty to resolve in what form this trust shall be executed.—When we reflect seriously and cooly on this point, I think, sir we shall doubt no longer.

But with respect to the prospect of these amendments, which are the subject of discussion, being adopted by the first Congress, which shall be appointed under the new Constitution, I really think, sir, that it is not only far from being improbable, but is in the highest degree likely. I have thought long and often, on the subject of amendment, and I know no way in which they could be more likely to succeed.—If they were made conditional to our receiving the proposed Constitution, it has ever appeared to me, that a conditional amendment must operate as a total rejection. As so many other States have received the Constitution, as it is, how can it be made to appear, that they will not adhere to their own resolutions; and should they remain as warmly and pertinaciously attached to their opinion, as we might be decidedly in favour of our own sentiments, a long and painful interval might elapse before we should have the benefit of a federal Constitution. I have never yet heard an argument to remove this difficulty: Permit me to inquire of gentlemen what reason we have to suppose that the States which have already adopted the Constitution will suddenly consent to call a new Convention at the request of this State: Are we going to expose the Commonwealth to the disagreeable alternative of being forced into a compliance, or of remaining in opposition, provided nine others should agree to receive it. As highly as some persons talk of the force of this State, I believe we should be but a feeble power, unassisted by others, and detached from the general benefit of a national government. We are told, that under the blessing of Providence, we may do much—It is very true, sir, but it must be proved, that we shall be most likely to secure the approbation of Heaven by refusing the proposed system.

It has been insinuated, sir, that these amendments have been artfully introduced to lead to a decision which would not otherwise be had—Without stopping to remark on the total want of candour in which such an idea has arisen, let us inquire whether there is even the appearance of reason to support this insinuation. The propositions are annexed, it is true, to the ratification; but the assent is complete and absolute without them. It is not possible it can be otherwise understood by a single member in this Hon. body—Gentlemen, therefore, when they make such an unjust observation, do no honour to the sagacity of others. Supposing it possible that any single member can be deceived by such a shallow artifice, permit me to do justice to the purity of intention in which they have arisen, by observing, that I am satisfied nothing can be farther from your Excellency's intentions. The propositions are general and not local; they are not calculated for the peculiar interest of this State, but with indiscriminate justice comprehend the circumstances of the individual on the banks of the Savannah, as well as of the hardy and industrious husbandman on the margin of the Kennebeck: Why then they should not be adopted, I confess I cannot conceive. There is one of them in a particular manner which is very agreeable to me. When we talk of our wanting a bill of rights to the new Constitution, the first article proposed must remove every doubt on this head—as by positively securing what is not expressly delegated, it leaves nothing to the uncertainty of conjecture, or to the refinements of implication; but is an explicit reservation of every right and privilege which are nearest and most agreeable to the people. There has been scarcely an instance where the influence of Massachusetts has not been felt and acknowledged in the union—In such a case, her voice will be heard, sir; and I am fully in sentiment if these amendments are not engrafted on the Constitution, it will be our own fault—the remaining seven States will have our example before them, and there is a high probability that they, or at least some of them, will take our conduct as a precedent, and will perhaps assume the same mode of procedure. Should this be the fact, their influence will be united to our's. But your delegates will besides be subject to a perpetual instruction until its object is completed; and it will be always in the power of the people and the legislature to renew those instructions. But if they should fail, we must then acquiesce in the decision of the majority, and this is the known condition on which all free governments depend.

Would gentlemen who are opposed to the Constitution wish to have no amendments? This does not agree with their reiterated objections to the proposed system: Or are they afraid, sir, that these propositions will secure a larger majority? On such an occasion, we cannot be too generally united. The Constitution is a great political experiment—The amendments have a tendency to remove many objections which have been made to it—and I hope, sir, when it is adopted, that they will be annexed to the ratification in the manner which your Excellency has proposed.

Nathaniel Barrell, a *"Plain Husbandman,"* Warns of the Passion for Power, but Favors Ratification

February 5, 1788

Mr. BARRELL. [*of York*] Awed in the presence of this august assembly—conscious of my inability to express my mind fully on this important occasion—and sensible how little I must appear in the eyes of those giants in rhetorick, who have exhibited such a pompous display of declamation:—Without any of those talents calculated to draw attention—without the pleasing eloquence of Cicero, or the blaze of Demosthenian oratory, I rise, Sir, to discharge my duty to my constituents, who I know expect something more from me than meerly a silent vote. With no pretensions to talents above the simple language adapted to the line of my calling, the plain husbandman, I hope the gentlemen who compose this hon. body, will fully understand me when I attempt to speak my mind of the Federal Constitution as it now stands.—I wish, Sir, to give my voice for its amendment before it can be salutary for our acceptance—because, Sir, notwithstanding the Wilsonian oratory and all the learned arguments I have seen written—notwithstanding the many laboured speeches I have heard in its defence, and after the best investigation I am able to give this subject, I fear it is pregnant with baneful effects, although I may not live to feel them.

Because, Sir, as it now stands, Congress will be vested with more extensive powers than ever Great-Britain exercised over us, too great in my opinion to intrust with any class of men, let their talents or virtues be ever so conspicuous, even though composed of such exalted amiable characters as the great Washington: For while we consider them as men of like passions, the same spontaneous, inherent thirst for power with ourselves—great and good as they may be, when they enter upon this all-important charge, what security can we have that they will continue so?—And, Sir, were we sure they would continue the faithful guardians of our liberties, and prevent any infringement on the privileges of the people—what assurance can we have that such men will always hold the reins of government—that their successors will be such?—History tells us Rome was happy under Augustus—though wretched under Nero, who could have no greater power than Augustus—and yet this same Nero, when young in government, could shed tears on signing a death warrant, though afterwards became so callous to the tender feelings of humanity, as to behold with pleasure Rome in flames.

Because, Sir, I think that six years is too long a term for any set of men to be at the helm of government:—For in that time they may get so firmly rooted, and their influence be so great as to continue themselves for life.

Because, Sir, I am not certain we are able to support the additional expense of such a government.

Because, Sir, I think a continental collector will not be so likely to do us justice in collecting the taxes, as collectors of our own.

Because, Sir, I think a frame of government on which all laws are founded, should be so simple and explicit, that the most illiterate may understand it, whereas this appears to me so obscure and ambiguous that the most capacious mind cannot fully comprehend it.

Because, Sir, the duties of excise and impost, and to be taxed besides, appears too great a sacrifice—and when we have given them up, what shall we have to pay our own debts, but a dry tax.

Because, Sir, I do not think this will produce the efficient government we are in pursuit of.

Because, Sir, they fix their own salaries without allowing any controul.

And because, Sir, I think such a government may be disagreeable to men with the high notions of liberty, we Americans have.

And, Sir, I could wish this Constitution had not been in some parts of the continent hurried on like the driving of Jehu very furiously, for such important transactions should be without force, and with cool deliberation.—These, Sir, were my objections, and those of my constituents, as they occur to my memory—some of which have been removed in the course of the debates, by the ingenious reasonings of the speakers—I wish I could say the whole were.—But after all, there are some yet remain on my mind, enough to convince me, excellent as this system is, in some respects it needs alterations, therefore I think it becomes us as wise men, as the faithful guardians of the people's rights, and as we wish well to posterity, to propose such amendments as will secure to us and ours that liberty, without which life is a burthen.

Thus, Sir, have I ventured to deliver my sentiments, in which is involved those of my constituents, on this important subject, cautiously avoiding every thing like metaphysical reasoning, least I should invade the prerogative of those respectable gentlemen of the law, who have so copiously displayed their talents on this occasion. But, Sir, although you may perceive by what I have said, that *this* is not in my view, the most perfect system I could wish—yet as I am possessed with an assurance that the proposed amendments will take place—as I dread the fatal effects of anarchy—as I am convinced the Confederation is essentially deficient, and that it will be more difficult to amend that, than to reform this—and as I think *this Constitution* with all its imperfections, is *excellent* compared with that—and that it is the best Constitution we can now obtain—as the greatest good I can do my country at present, I could wish for an adjournment, that I might have an opportunity to lay it before my constituents with the arguments which have been used in the debates, which have eased my mind, and I trust would have the effect on theirs, so as heartily to join me in ratifying the same:—But, Sir, if I cannot be indulged on this desirable object, I am almost tempted to risque their displeasure and adopt it without their consent.

John Hancock's Final Observations: "We Must All Rise or Fall Together"

February 6, 1788

GENTLEMEN,

Being now called upon to bring the subject under debate to a decision, by bringing forward the question—I beg your indulgence to close the business with a few words. I am happy that my health has been so far restored, that I am rendered able to meet my fellow-citizens, as represented in this Convention. I should have considered it was one of the most distressing misfortunes of my life, to be deprived of giving my aid and support to a system, which if amended (as I feel assured it will be) according to your proposals, cannot fail to give the people of the United States, a greater degree of political freedom, and eventually as much national dignity, as falls to the lot of any nation on the earth. I have not since I had the honour to be in this place, said much on the important subject before us: All the ideas appertaining to the system, as well those which are against as for it, have been debated upon with so much learning and ability, that the subject is quite exhausted.

But you will permit me, gentlemen, to close the whole with one or two general observations. This I request, not expecting to throw any new light upon the subject, but because it may possibly prevent uneasiness and discordance, from taking place amongst us and amongst our constituents.

That a general system of government is indispensably necessary to save our country from ruin, is agreed upon all sides. That the one now to be decided upon has its defects, all agree; But when we consider the variety of interests, and the different habits of the men it is intended for, it would be very singular to have an entire union of sentiment respecting it. Were the people of the United States to delegate the powers proposed to be given, to men who were not dependent on them frequently for elections—to men whose interests either from rank, or title, would differ from that of their fellow-citizens in common, the task of delegating authority would be vastly more difficult; but as the matter now stands, the powers reserved by the people render them secure, and until they themselves become corrupt, they will always have upright and able rulers. I give my assent to the Constitution in full confidence that the amendments proposed will soon become a part of the system—these amendments being in no wise local, but calculated to give security and ease alike to all the States, I think that all will agree to them.

Suffer me to add, that let the question be decided as it may, there can be no triumph on the one side, or chagrin on the other—Should there be a great division, every good man, every one who loves his country, will be so far from exhibiting extraordinary marks of joy, that he will sincerely lament the want of unanimity, and strenuously endeavour to cultivate a spirit of conciliation, both in Convention, and at home. The people of this Commonwealth, are a people of great light —of great intelligence in publick business—They know that we have none of us an interest separate from theirs—that it must be our happiness to conduce to theirs—and that we must all rise or fall together—They will never, therefore, forsake the first principle of society, that of being governed by the voice of the majority; and should it be that the proposed form of government should be rejected, they will zealously attempt another. Should it by the vote now to be taken be ratified, they will quietly acquiesce, and where they see a want of perfection in it, endeavour in a constitutional way to have it amended.

The question now before you is such as no nation on earth, without the limits of America, have ever had the privilege of deciding upon. As the Supreme Ruler of the Universe has seen fit to bestow upon us this glorious opportunity, let us decide upon it—appealing to him for the rectitude of our intentions—and in humble confidence that he will yet continue to bless and save our country.

The Form of the Ratification of Massachusetts

February 6, 1788

COMMONWEALTH of MASSACHUSETTS.
In convention of the delegates of the people of the commonwealth of Massachusetts, Feb. 6, 1788.

The convention having impartially discussed, and fully considered, the constitution for the United States of America, reported to Congress, by the convention of delegates from the United States, of America, and submitted to us, by a resolution of the General Court of the said commonwealth, passed the twenty fifth day of October last past; and acknowledging with grateful hearts the goodness of the Supreme Ruler of the universe, in affording the people of the United States, in the course of his Providence, an opportunity, deliberately and peaceably, without fraud or surprise, of entering into an explicit and solemn compact with each other, by assenting to and ratifying a new constitution, in order to form a more perfect union, establish justice, insure domestick tranquillity, provide for the common defence, promote the general welfare, and secure the blessings of liberty to themselves, and their posterity—DO, in the name and in behalf of the people of the commonwealth of Massachusetts, ASSENT to and RATIFY the said *constitution, for the United States of America.*

And as it is the opinion of this convention, that certain amendments and alterations in the said constitution, would remove the fears, and quiet the apprehensions of many of the good people of this commonwealth, and more effectually guard against an undue administration of the federal government, the convention do therefore recommend, that the following alterations and provisions be introduced into the said constitution:

First. That it be explicitly declared, that all powers, not expressly delegated by the aforesaid constitution, are reserved to the several states, to be by them exercised.

Secondly. That there shall be one representative to every thirty thousand persons, according to the census mentioned in the constitution, until the whole number of the representatives amounts to two hundred.

Thirdly. That Congress do not exercise the powers vested in them by the 4th sect. of the 1st art. but in cases when a state neglect or refuse to make regulations therein mentioned, or shall make regulations subversive of the rights of the people, to a free and equal representation in Congress, agreeably to the constitution.

Fourthly, That Congress do not lay direct taxes, but when the monies arising from the impost and excise are insufficient for the publick exigencies; nor then, until Congress shall have first made a requisition upon the states, to assess, levy and pay their respective proportions of such requisition, agreeably to the census fixed in the said constitution, in such way and manner as the legislature of the state shall think best,—and in such case, if any state shall neglect or refuse to pay its proportion, pursuant to such requisition, then Congress may assess and levy such states proportion, together with interest thereon, at the rate of six per cent. per annum, from the time of payment prescribed in such requisition.

Fifthly. That Congress erect no company of merchants with exclusive advantages of commerce.

Sixthly. That no person shall be tried for any crime by which he may incur an infamous punishment, or loss of life, until he be first indicted by a grand jury, except in such cases as may arise in the government and regulation of the land and naval forces.

Seventhly. The supreme judicial federal court shall have no jurisdiction of causes between citizens of different states, unless the matter in dispute, whether it concerns the reality or personality, be of the value of three thousand dollars, at the least: Nor shall the federal judicial powers extend to any actions between citizens of different states where the matter in dispute, whether it concerns the reality or personality, is not of the value of fifteen hundred dollars, at the least.

Eighthly. In civil actions, between citizens of different states, every issue of fact, arising in actions at common law, shall be tried by a jury, if the parties, or either of them, request it.

Ninthly. Congress shall, at no time, consent, that any person, holding an office of trust or profit, under the United States, shall accept of a title of nobility, or any other title or office, from any king, prince, or foreign state.

And the Convention do, in the name and in behalf of the people of this commonwealth, enjoin it upon their representatives in Congress, at all times, until the alterations and provisions aforesaid have been considered, agreeably to the fifth article of the said constitution, to exert all their influence, and use all reasonable and legal methods to obtain a ratification of the said alterations and provisions in such manner as is provided in the said article.

And that the United States in Congress assembled may have due notice of the assent and ratification of the said constitution by this Convention—It is

RESOLVED, That the assent and ratification aforesaid be engrossed on parchment, together with the recommendation and injunction aforesaid, and with this resolution; and that his excellency JOHN HANCOCK, esquire, president, and the honourable WILLIAM CUSHING, esquire, vice-president, of this Convention, transmit the same, countersigned by the secretary of the Convention, under their hands and seals, to the United States in Congress assembled.

(Signed) JOHN HANCOCK, President,
WILLIAM CUSHING, Vice-President.

(Countersigned)
GEORGE RICHARDS MINOT, Sec'y.

APPENDIX

The Declaration of Independence

The Articles of Confederation

*Letter from the Constitutional Convention
to the President of Congress*

*Resolutions of the Convention
Concerning the Ratification and
Implementation of the Constitution*

The Constitution

The Declaration of Independence

In CONGRESS, July 4, 1776.
The unanimous Declaration
of the thirteen united States of America,

When in the Course of human events, it becomes necessary for one people to dissolve the political bands which have connected them with another, and to assume among the powers of the earth, the separate and equal station to which the Laws of Nature and of Nature's God entitle them, a decent respect to the opinions of mankind requires that they should declare the causes which impel them to the separation.— We hold these truths to be self-evident, that all men are created equal, that they are endowed by their Creator with certain unalienable Rights, that among these are Life, Liberty and the pursuit of Happiness.— That to secure these rights, Governments are instituted among Men, deriving their just powers from the consent of the governed,— That whenever any Form of Government becomes destructive of these ends, it is the Right of the People to alter or to abolish it; and to institute new Government, laying its foundation on such principles and organizing its powers in such form, as to them shall seem most likely to effect their Safety and Happiness. Prudence, indeed, will dictate that Governments long established should not be changed for light and transient causes; and accordingly all experience hath shewn, that mankind are more disposed to suffer, while evils are sufferable, than to right themselves by abolishing the forms to which they are accustomed. But when a long train of abuses and usurpations, pursuing invariably the same Object evinces a design to reduce them under absolute Despotism, it is their right, it is their duty, to throw off such Government, and to provide new Guards for their future security.— Such has been the patient sufferance of these Colonies; and such is now the necessity which constrains them to alter their former Systems of Government. The history of the present King of Great Britain is a history of repeated injuries and usurpations, all having in direct object the establishment of an absolute Tyranny over these States. To prove this, let Facts be submitted to a candid world.— He has refused his

949

Assent to Laws, the most wholesome and necessary for the public good.—He has forbidden his Governors to pass Laws of immediate and pressing importance, unless suspended in their operation till his Assent should be obtained; and when so suspended, he has utterly neglected to attend to them. —He has refused to pass other Laws for the accommodation of large districts of people, unless those people would relinquish the right of Representation in the Legislature, a right inestimable to them and formidable to tyrants only.—He has called together legislative bodies at places unusual, uncomfortable, and distant from the depository of their public Records, for the sole purpose of fatiguing them into compliance with his measures.—He has dissolved Representative Houses repeatedly, for opposing with manly firmness his invasions on the rights of the people.—He has refused for a long time, after such dissolutions, to cause others to be elected; whereby the Legislative powers, incapable of Annihilation, have returned to the People at large for their exercise; the State remaining in the mean time exposed to all the dangers of invasion from without, and convulsions within.—He has endeavoured to prevent the population of these States; for that purpose obstructing the Laws for Naturalization of Foreigners; refusing to pass others to encourage their migrations hither, and raising the conditions of new Appropriations of Lands.—He has obstructed the Administration of Justice, by refusing his Assent to Laws for establishing Judiciary powers —He has made Judges dependent on his Will alone, for the tenure of their offices, and the amount and payment of their salaries.—He has erected a multitude of New Offices, and sent hither swarms of Officers to harrass our people, and eat out their substance.—He has kept among us, in times of peace, Standing Armies without the Consent of our legislatures.—He has affected to render the Military independent of and superior to the Civil power.—He has combined with others to subject us to a jurisdiction foreign to our constitution, and unacknowledged by our laws; giving his Assent to their Acts of pretended Legislation:—For Quartering large bodies of armed troops among us:—For protecting them, by a mock Trial, from punishment for any Murders which they should commit on the Inhabitants of these States:—For calling off our Trade with all parts of the world:—For imposing Taxes on us without our Consent:—For depriving us in many cases, of the benefits of Trial by Jury:—For transporting us beyond Seas to be tried for pretended offences—For abolishing the free System of English Laws in a neighbouring Province, establishing therein an Arbitrary government, and enlarging its Boundaries so as to render it at once an example and fit instrument for introducing the same absolute rule into these Colonies:—For taking away our Charters, abolishing our most valuable Laws and altering fundamentally the Forms of our Governments:—For suspending our own Legislatures, and declaring themselves invested with power to legislate for us in all cases whatsoever.—He has abdicated Government here, by declaring us out of his Protection and waging War against us.—He has plundered our seas, ravaged our Coasts, burnt our towns, and destroyed the Lives of our people.—He is at this time transporting large Armies of foreign Mercenaries to compleat the works of death, desolation and tyranny, already begun with circumstances of Cruelty & perfidy scarcely paralleled in the most barbarous ages, and totally unworthy the Head of a civilized nation.—He has constrained our fellow Citizens taken Captive on the high Seas to bear Arms against their Country, to become the executioners of their friends and Brethren, or to fall themselves by their Hands.—He has excited domestic insurrections amongst us, and has endeavoured to bring on the inhabitants of our frontiers, the merciless Indian Savages, whose known rule of warfare, is an undistinguished destruction of all ages, sexes and conditions. In every stage of these Oppressions We have Petitioned for Redress in the most humble terms: Our repeated Petitions have been answered only by repeated injury. A Prince, whose character is thus marked by every act which may define a Tyrant, is unfit to be the ruler of a free people. Nor have We been wanting in attentions to our Brittish brethren. We have warned them from time to time of attempts by their legislature to extend an unwarrantable jurisdiction over us. We have reminded them of the circumstances of our emigration and settlement here. We have appealed to their native justice and magnanimity, and we have conjured them by the ties of our common kindred to disavow these usurpations, which, would inevitably interrupt our connections and correspondence They too have been deaf to the voice of justice and of consanguinity. We must, therefore, acquiesce in the necessity, which denounces our Separation, and hold them, as we hold the rest of mankind, Enemies in War, in Peace Friends.—

We, therefore, the Representatives of the united States of America, in General Congress, Assembled, appealing to the Supreme Judge of the world for the rectitude of our intentions, do, in the Name, and by Authority of the good People of these Colonies, solemnly publish and declare, That these United Colonies are, and of Right ought to be Free and Independent States; that they are Absolved from all Allegiance to the British Crown, and that all political connection between them and the State of Great Britain, is and ought to be totally dissolved; and that as Free and Independent States, they have full Power to levy War, conclude Peace, contract Alliances, establish Commerce, and to do all other Acts and Things which Independent States may of right do.—And for the support of this Declaration, with a firm reliance on the protection of divine Providence, we mutually pledge to each other our Lives, our Fortunes and our sacred Honor.

John Hancock

Josiah Bartlett
Wm Whipple
Saml Adams
John Adams
Robt Treat Paine
Elbridge Gerry
Step. Hopkins
William Ellery
Roger Sherman
Saml Huntington
Wm Williams
Oliver Wolcott
Matthew Thornton
Wm Floyd
Phil. Livingston
Fran^s. Lewis
Lewis Morris
Richd Stockton
Jno Witherspoon
Fra^s. Hopkinson
John Hart
Abra Clark
Robt Morris
Benjamin Rush
Benj. Franklin
John Morton
Geo Clymer
Ja^s. Smith
Geo. Taylor
James Wilson
Geo. Ross

Cæsar Rodney
Geo Read
Tho M:Kean
Samuel Chase
W^m. Paca
Thos. Stone
Charles Carroll of Carrollton
George Wythe
Richard Henry Lee
Th Jefferson
Benj Harrison
Th^s Nelson Jr.
Francis Lightfoot Lee
Carter Braxton
Wm Hooper
Joseph Hewes
John Penn
Edward Rutledge
Thos Heyward Junr
Thomas Lynch Junr.
Arthur Middleton
Button Gwinnett
Lyman Hall
Geo Walton

The Articles of Confederation

To all to whom these Presents shall come, we the under signed Delegates of the States affixed to our Names send greeting. Whereas the Delegates of the United States of America in Congress assembled did on the fifteenth day of November in the Year of our Lord One Thousand Seven Hundred and Seventy seven, and in the Second Year of the Independence of America agree to certain articles of Confederation and perpetual Union between the States of New-hampshire, Massachusetts-bay, Rhodeisland and Providence Plantations, Connecticut, New York, New Jersey, Pennsylvania, Delaware, Maryland, Virginia, North-Carolina, South-Carolina and Georgia in the Words following, viz, "Articles of Confederation and perpetual Union between the States of Newhampshire, Massachusetts-bay, Rhodeisland and Providence Plantations, Connecticut, New-York, New-Jersey, Pennsylvania, Delaware, Maryland, Virginia, North-Carolina, South-Carolina and Georgia.

Article I. The Stile of this confederacy shall be "The United States of America."

Article II. Each state retains its sovereignty, freedom and independence, and every Power, Jurisdiction and right, which is not by this confederation expressly delegated to the United States, in Congress assembled.

Article III. The said states hereby severally enter into a firm league of friendship with each other, for their common defence, the security of their Liberties, and their mutual and general welfare, binding themselves to assist each other, against all force offered to, or attacks made upon them, or any of them, on account of religion, sovereignty, trade, or any other pretence whatever.

Article IV. The better to secure and perpetuate mutual friendship and intercourse among the people of the different states in this union, the free inhabitants of each of these states, paupers, vagabonds and fugitives from Justice excepted, shall be entitled to all privileges and immunities of free citizens in the several states; and the people of each state shall have free ingress and regress to and from any other state, and shall enjoy therein all the privileges of trade and commerce, subject to the same duties, impositions and restrictions as the inhabitants thereof respectively, provided that such restriction shall not extend so far as to prevent the removal of property imported into any state, to any other state of which the Owner is an inhabitant; provided also that no imposition, duties or restriction shall be laid by any state, on the property of the united states, or either of them.

If any Person guilty of, or charged with treason, felony, or other high misdemeanor in any state, shall flee from Justice, and be found in any of the united states, he shall upon demand of the Governor or executive power, of the state from which he fled, be delivered up and removed to the state having jurisdiction of his offence.

Full faith and credit shall be given in each of these states to the records, acts and judicial proceedings of the courts and magistrates of every other state.

Article V. For the more convenient management of the general interests of the united states, delegates shall be annually appointed in such manner as the legislature of each state shall direct, to meet in Congress on the first Monday in November, in every year, with a power reserved to each state, to recal its delegates, or any of them, at any time within the year, and to send others in their stead, for the remainder of the Year.

No state shall be represented in Congress by less than two, nor by more than seven Members; and no person shall be capable of being a delegate for more than three years in any term of six years; nor shall any person, being a delegate, be capable of holding any office under the united states, for which he, or another for his benefit receives any salary, fees or emolument of any kind.

Each state shall maintain its own delegates in a meeting of the states, and while they act as members of the committee of the states.

In determining questions in the united states, in Congress assembled, each state shall have one vote.

Freedom of speech and debate in Congress shall not be impeached or questioned in any Court, or place out of Congress, and the members of congress shall be protected in their persons from arrests and imprisonments, during the time of their going to and from, and attendance on congress, except for treason, felony, or breach of the peace.

Article VI.   No state without the Consent of the united states in congress assembled, shall send any embassy to, or receive any embassy from, or enter into any conferrence, agreement, alliance or treaty with any King prince or state; nor shall any person holding any office of profit or trust under the united states, or any of them, accept of any present, emolument, office or title of any kind whatever from any king, prince or foreign state; nor shall the united states in congress assembled, or any of them, grant any title of nobility.

No two or more states shall enter into any treaty, confederation or alliance whatever between them, without the consent of the united states in congress assembled, specifying accurately the purposes for which the same is to be entered into, and how long it shall continue.

No state shall lay any imposts or duties, which may interfere with any stipulations in treaties, entered into by the united states in congress assembled, with any king, prince or state, in pursuance of any treaties already proposed by congress, to the courts of France and Spain.

No vessels of war shall be kept up in time of peace by any state, except such number only, as shall be deemed necessary by the united states in congress assembled, for the defence of such state, or its trade; nor shall any body of forces be kept up by any state, in time of peace, except such number only, as in the judgment of the united states, in congress assembled, shall be deemed requisite to garrison the forts necessary for the defence of such state; but every state shall always keep up a well regulated and disciplined militia, sufficiently armed and accoutred, and shall provide and constantly have ready for use, in public stores, a due number of field pieces and tents, and a proper quantity of arms, ammunition and camp equipage.

No state shall engage in any war without the consent of the united states in congress assembled, unless such state be actually invaded by enemies, or shall have received certain advice of a resolution being formed by some nation of Indians to invade such state, and the danger is so imminent as not to admit of a delay, till the united states in congress assembled can be consulted: nor shall any state grant commissions to any ships or vessels of war, nor letters of marque or reprisal, except it be after a declaration of war by the united states in congress assembled, and then only against the kingdom or state and the subjects thereof, against which war has been so declared, and under such regulations as shall be established by the united states in congress assembled, unless such state be infested by pirates, in which case vessels of war may be fitted out for that occasion, and kept so long as the danger shall continue, or until the united states in congress assembled shall determine otherwise.

Article VII. When land-forces are raised by any state for the common defence, all officers of or under the rank of colonel, shall be appointed by the legislature of each state respectively by whom such forces shall be raised, or in such manner as such state shall direct, and all vacancies shall be filled up by the state which first made the appointment.

Article VIII. All charges of war, and all other expences that shall be incurred for the common defence or general welfare, and allowed by the united states in congress assembled, shall be defrayed out of a common treasury, which shall be supplied by the several states, in proportion to the value of all land within each state, granted to or surveyed for any Person, as such land and the buildings and improvements thereon shall be estimated according to such mode as the united states in congress assembled, shall from time to time direct and appoint. The taxes for paying that proportion shall be laid and levied by the authority and direction of the legislatures of the several states within the time agreed upon by the united states in congress assembled.

Article IX. The united states in congress assembled, shall have the sole and exclusive right and power of determining on peace and war, except in the cases mentioned in the sixth article—of sending and receiving ambassadors—entering into treaties and alliances, provided that no treaty of commerce shall be made whereby the legislative power of the respective states shall be restrained from imposing such imposts and duties on foreigners, as their own people are subjected to, or from prohibiting the exportation or importation of any species of goods or commodities whatsoever—of establishing rules for deciding in all cases, what captures on land or water shall be legal, and in what manner prizes taken by land or naval forces in the service of the united states shall be divided or appropriated—of granting letters of marque and reprisal in times of peace—appointing courts for the trial of piracies and felonies committed on the high seas and establishing courts for receiving and determining finally appeals in all cases of captures, provided that no member of congress shall be appointed a judge of any of the said courts.

The united states in congress assembled shall also be the last resort on appeal in all disputes and differences now subsisting or that hereafter may arise between two or more states concerning boundary, jurisdiction or any other cause whatever; which authority shall always be exercised in the manner following. Whenever the legislative or executive authority or lawful agent of any state in controversy with another shall present a petition to congress stating the matter in question and praying for a hearing, notice thereof shall be given by order of congress to the legislative or executive authority of the other state in controversy, and a day assigned for the appearance of the parties by their lawful agents, who shall then be directed to appoint by joint consent, commissioners or judges to constitute a court for hearing and determining the matter in question: but if they cannot agree, congress shall name three persons out of each of the united states, and from the list of such persons each party shall alternately strike out one, the petitioners beginning, until the number shall be reduced to thirteen; and from that number not less than seven, nor more than nine names as congress shall direct, shall in the presence of congress be drawn out by lot, and the persons whose names shall be so drawn or any five of them, shall be commissioners or judges, to hear and finally determine the controversy, so always as a major part of the judges who shall hear the cause shall agree in the determination: and if either party shall neglect to attend at the day appointed, without shewing reasons, which congress shall judge sufficient, or being present shall refuse to strike, the congress shall proceed to nominate three persons out of each state, and the secretary of congress shall strike in behalf of such party absent or refusing; and the judgment and sentence of the court to be appointed, in the manner before prescribed, shall be final and conclusive; and if any of the parties shall refuse to submit to the authority of such court, or to appear or defend their claim or cause, the court shall nevertheless proceed to pronounce sentence, or judgment, which shall in like manner be final and decisive, the judgment or sentence and other proceedings being in either case transmitted to congress, and lodged among the acts of congress for the security of the parties concerned: provided that every commissioner, before he sits in judgment, shall take an oath to be administered by one of the judges of the supreme or superior court of the state, where the cause shall be tried, "well and truly to hear and determine the matter in question, according to the best of his judgment, without favour, affection or hope of reward:" provided also that no state shall be deprived of territory for the benefit of the united states.

All controversies concerning the private right of soil claimed under different grants of two or more states, whose jurisdictions as they may respect such lands, and the states which passed such grants are adjusted, the said grants or either of thcm being at the same time claimed to have originated antecedent to such settlement of jurisdiction, shall on the petition of either party to the congress of the united states, be finally determined as near as maybe in the same manner as is before prescribed for deciding disputes respecting territorial jurisdiction between different states.

The united states in congress assembled shall also have the sole and exclusive right and power of regulating the alloy and value of coin struck by their own authority, or by that of the respective states—fixing the standard of weights and measures throughout the united states—regulating the trade and managing all affairs with the Indians, not members of any of the states, provided that the legislative right of any state within its own limits be not infringed or violated—establishing and regulating post-offices from one state to another, throughout all the united states, and exacting such postage on the papers passing thro' the same as may be requisite to defray the expences of the said office—appointing all officers of the land forces, in the service of the united states, excepting regimental officers—appointing all the officers of the naval forces, and commissioning all officers whatever in the service of the united states—making rules for the government and regulation of the said land and naval forces, and directing their operations.

The united states in congress assembled shall have authority to appoint a committee, to sit in the recess of congress, to be denominated "A Committee of the States," and to consist of one delegate from each state; and to appoint such other committees and civil officers as may be necessary for managing the general affairs of the united states under their direction—to appoint one of their number to preside, provided that no person be allowed to serve in the office of president more than one year in any term of three years; to ascertain the necessary sums of Money to be raised for the service of the united states, and to appropriate and apply the same for defraying the public expences—to borrow money, or emit bills on the credit of the united states, transmitting every half year to the respective states an account of the sums of money so borrowed or emitted,—to build and equip a navy—to agree upon the number of land forces, and to make requisitions from each state for its quota, in proportion to the number of white inhabitants in such state; which requisition shall be binding, and thereupon the legislature of each state shall appoint the regimental officers, raise the men and cloath, arm and equip them in a soldier like manner, at the expence of the united states, and the officers and men so cloathed, armed and equipped shall march to the place appointed, and within the time agreed on by the united states in congress assembled: But if the united states in congress assembled shall, on consideration of circumstances judge proper that any state should not raise men, or should raise a smaller number than its quota, and that any other state should raise a greater number of men than the quota thereof, such extra number shall be raised, officered, cloathed, armed and equipped in the same manner as the quota of such state, unless the legislature of such state shall judge that such extra number cannot be safely spared out of the same, in which case they shall raise officer, cloath, arm and equip as many of such extra number as they judge can be safely spared. And the officers and men so cloathed, armed and equipped, shall march to the place appointed, and within the time agreed on by the united states in congress assembled.

The united states in congress assembled shall never engage in a war, nor grant letters of marque and reprisal in time of peace, nor enter into any treaties or alliances, nor coin money, nor regulate the value thereof, nor ascertain the sums and expences necessary for the defence and welfare of the united states, or any of them, nor emit bills, nor borrow money on the credit of the united states, nor appropriate money, nor agree upon the number of vessels of war, to be built or purchased, or the number of land or sea forces to be raised, nor appoint a commander in chief of the army or navy, unless nine states assent to the same: nor shall a question on any other point, except for adjourning from day to day be determined, unless by the votes of a majority of the united states in congress assembled.

The congress of the united states shall have power to adjourn to any time within the year, and to any place within the united states, so that no period of adjournment be for a longer duration than the space of six Months, and shall publish the Journal of their proceedings monthly, except such parts thereof relating to treaties, alliances or military operations, as in their judgment require secrecy; and the yeas and nays of the delegates of each state on any question shall be entered on the Journal, when it is desired by any delegate; and the delegates of a state, or any of them, at his or their request shall be furnished with a transcript of the said Journal, except such parts as are above excepted, to lay before the legislatures of the several states.

Article X. The committee of the states, or any nine of them, shall be authorized to execute, in the recess of congress, such of the powers of congress as the united states in congress assembled, by the consent of nine states, shall from time to time think expedient to vest them with; provided that no power be delegated to the said committee, for the exercise of which, by the articles of confederation, the voice of nine states in the congress of the united states assembled is requisite.

Article XI. Canada acceding to this confederation, and joining in the measures of the united states, shall be admitted into, and entitled to all the advantages of this union: but no other colony shall be admitted into the same, unless such admission be agreed to by nine states.

Article XII. All bills of credit emitted, monies borrowed and debts contracted by, or under the authority of congress, before the assembling of the united states, in pursuance of the present confederation, shall be deemed and considered as a charge against the united states, for payment and satisfaction whereof the said united states, and the public faith are hereby solemnly pledged.

Article XIII. Every state shall abide by the determinations of the united states in congress assembled, on all questions which by this confederation are submitted to them. And the Articles of this confederation shall be inviolably observed by every state, and the union shall be perpetual; nor shall any alteration at any time hereafter be made in any of them; unless such alteration be agreed to in a congress of the united states, and be afterwards confirmed by the legislatures of every state.

And Whereas it hath pleased the Great Governor of the World to incline the hearts of the legislatures we respectively represent in congress, to approve of, and to authorize us to ratify the said articles of confederation and perpetual union. Know Ye that we the undersigned delegates, by virtue of the power and authority to us given for that purpose, do by these presents, in the name and in behalf of our respective constituents, fully and entirely ratify and confirm each and every of the said articles of confederation and perpetual union, and all and singular the matters and things therein contained: And we do further solemnly plight and engage the faith of our respective constituents, that they shall abide by the determinations of the united states in congress assembled, on all questions, which by the said confederation are submitted to them. And that the articles thereof shall be inviolably observed by the states we respectively represent, and that the union shall be perpetual. In Witness whereof we have hereunto set our hands in Congress. Done at Philadelphia in the state of Pennsylvania the ninth Day of July in the Year of our Lord one Thousand seven Hundred and Seventy-eight, and in the third year of the independence of America.

Josiah Bartlett John Wentworth Junr August 8th 1778	On the Part & behalf of the State of New Hampshire
John Hancock Samuel Adams Elbridge Gerry Francis Dana James Lovell Samuel Holten	On the part and behalf of the State of Massachusetts Bay
William Ellery Henry Marchant John Collins	On the part and behalf of the State of Rhode-Island and Providence Plantations
Roger Sherman Samuel Huntington Oliver Wolcott Titus Hosmer Andrew Adams	on the Part and behalf of the State of Connecticut
Jas. Duane Fras. Lewis Wm: Duer. Gouvr. Morris	On the Part and Behalf of the State of New York

Jno Witherspoon
Nathl. Scudder
} On the Part and in Behalf
of the State of New
Jersey Novr. 26. 1778.—

Robt Morris.
Daniel Roberdeau
Jona: Bayard Smith.
William Clingan
Joseph Reed　July 1778
} On the part and behalf
of the State of
Pennsylvania

Thos M:Kean　Feby 22, 1779
John Dickinson　May 5th– 1779
Nicholas Van Dyke,
} On the part & behalf
of the State of
Delaware

John Hanson　March 1st, 1781
Daniel Carroll　do
} on the part and behalf
of the State of Maryland

Richard Henry Lee
John Banister
Thomas Adams
Jno Harvie
Francis Lightfoot Lee
} On the Part and Behalf
of the State of
Virginia

John Penn, July 21st 1778
Corns. Harnett
Jno. Williams
} on the part and Behalf
of the State of No.
Carolina

Henry Laurens.
William Henry Drayton
Jno. Mathews
Richd. Hutson
Thos: Heyward Junr:
} On the part & behalf
of the State of
South-Carolina

Jno Walton　24th. July 1778
Edwd. Telfair.
Edwd Langworthy.
} On the part & behalf
of the State of Georgia

Letter from the Constitutional Convention to the President of Congress

In Convention, September 17, 1787.

SIR, WE have now the honor to submit to the consideration of the United States in Congress assembled, that Constitution which has appeared to us the most adviseable.

The friends of our country have long seen and desired, that the power of making war, peace and treaties, that of levying money and regulating commerce, and the correspondent executive and judicial authorities should be fully and effectually vested in the general government of the Union: but the impropriety of delegating such extensive trust to one body of men is evident—Hence results the necessity of a different organization.

It is obviously impracticable in the foederal government of these States; to secure all rights of independent sovereignty to each, and yet provide for the interest and safety of all—Individuals entering into society, must give up a share of liberty to preserve the rest. The magnitude of the sacrifice must depend as well on situation and circumstance, as on the object to be obtained. It is at all times difficult to draw with precision the line between those rights which must be surrendered, and those which may be reserved; and on the present occasion this difficulty was encreased by a difference among the several States as to their situation, extent, habits, and particular interests.

In all our deliberations on this subject we kept steadily in our view, that which appears to us the greatest interest of every true American, the consolidation of our Union, in which is involved our prosperity, felicity, safety, perhaps our national existence, This important consideration, seriously and deeply impressed on our minds, led each State in the Convention to be less rigid on points of inferior magnitude, than might have been otherwise expected; and thus the Constitution, which we now present, is the result of a spirit of amity, and of that mutual deference and concession which the peculiarity of our political situation rendered indispensible.

That it will meet the full and entire approbation of every State is not perhaps to be expected; but each will doubtless consider, that had her interests been alone consulted, the consequences might have been particularly disagreeable or injurious to others; that it is liable to as few exceptions as could reasonably have been expected, we hope and believe; that it may promote the lasting welfare of that country so dear to us all, and secure her freedom and happiness, is our most ardent wish.

With great respect, WE have the honor to be SIR, Your Excellency's most Obedient and humble servants.

> George Washington, President.
> By unanimous Order of the
> Convention

Resolutions of the Convention Concerning the Ratification and Implementation of the Constitution

In Convention Monday September 17th. 1787.

Present The States of New Hampshire, Massachusetts, Connecticut, Mr. Hamilton from New York, New Jersey, Pennsylvania, Delaware, Maryland, Virginia, North Carolina, South Carolina and Georgia.

RESOLVED, That the preceeding Constitution be laid before the United States in Congress assembled, and that it is the Opinion of this Convention, that it should afterwards be submitted to a Convention of Delegates, chosen in each State by the People thereof, under the Recommendation of its Legislature, for their Assent and Ratification; and that each Convention assenting to, and ratifying the Same, should give Notice thereof to the United States in Congress assembled.

Resolved, That it is the Opinion of this Convention, that as soon as the Conventions of nine States shall have ratified this Constitution, the United States in Congress assembled should fix a Day on which Electors should be appointed by the States which shall have ratified the same, and a Day on which the Electors should assemble to vote for the President, and the Time and Place for commencing Proceedings under this Constitution. That after such Publication the Electors should be appointed, and the Senators and Representatives elected: That the Electors should meet on the Day fixed for the Election of the President, and should transmit their Votes certified, signed, sealed and directed, as the Constitution requires, to the Secretary of the United States in Congress assembled, that the Senators and Representatives should convene at the Time and Place assigned; that the Senators should appoint a President of the Senate, for the sole Purpose of receiving, opening and counting the Votes for President; and, that after he shall be chosen, the Congress, together with the President, should, without Delay, proceed to execute this Constitution.

By the Unanimous Order of the Convention
W. Jackson Secretary.   Go: Washington Presidt.

The Constitution

[The footnotes in this appendix, keyed to the line number on the page, indicate portions of the Constitution that have been altered by subsequent amendment.]

We the People of the United States, in Order to form a more perfect Union, establish Justice, insure domestic Tranquility, provide for the common defence, promote the general Welfare, and secure the Blessings of Liberty to ourselves and our Posterity, do ordain and establish this Constitution for the United States of America.

Article. I.

Section. 1. All legislative Powers herein granted shall be vested in a Congress of the United States, which shall consist of a Senate and House of Representatives.

Section. 2. The House of Representatives shall be composed of Members chosen every second Year by the People of the several States, and the Electors in each State shall have the Qualifications requisite for Electors of the most numerous Branch of the State Legislature.

No Person shall be a Representative who shall not have attained to the Age of twenty five Years, and been seven Years a Citizen of the United States, and who shall not, when elected, be an Inhabitant of that State in which he shall be chosen.

Representatives and direct Taxes shall be apportioned among the several States which may be included within this Union, according to their respective Numbers, which shall be determined by adding to the whole Number of free Persons, including those bound to Service for a Term of Years, and excluding Indians not taxed, three fifths of all other Persons. The actual Enumeration shall be made within three Years after the first Meeting of the Congress of the United States, and within every subsequent Term of ten Years, in such Manner as

968.25–30 Representatives . . . other Persons.] Changed regarding representation by the Fourteenth Amendment; changed regarding taxation by the Sixteenth Amendment.

they shall by Law direct. The Number of Representatives shall not exceed one for every thirty Thousand, but each State shall have at Least one Representative; and until such enumeration shall be made, the State of New Hampshire shall be entitled to chuse three, Massachusetts eight, Rhode-Island and Providence Plantations one, Connecticut five, New-York six, New Jersey four, Pennsylvania eight, Delaware one, Maryland six, Virginia ten, North Carolina five, South Carolina five, and Georgia three.

When vacancies happen in the Representation from any State, the Executive Authority thereof shall issue Writs of Election to fill such Vacancies.

The House of Representatives shall chuse their Speaker and other Officers; and shall have the sole Power of Impeachment.

Section. 3.   The Senate of the United States shall be composed of two Senators from each State, chosen by the Legislature thereof, for six Years; and each Senator shall have one Vote.

Immediately after they shall be assembled in Consequence of the first Election, they shall be divided as equally as may be into three Classes. The Seats of the Senators of the first Class shall be vacated at the Expiration of the second Year, of the second Class at the Expiration of the fourth Year, and of the third Class at the Expiration of the sixth Year, so that one third may be chosen every second Year; and if Vacancies happen by Resignation, or otherwise, during the Recess of the Legislature of any State, the Executive thereof may make temporary Appointments until the next Meeting of the Legislature, which shall then fill such Vacancies.

No Person shall be a Senator who shall not have attained to the Age of thirty Years, and been nine Years a Citizen of the United States, and who shall not, when elected, be an Inhabitant of that State for which he shall be chosen.

The Vice President of the United States shall be President of the Senate, but shall have no Vote, unless they be equally divided.

969.16–17   chosen by the Legislature thereof,] Changed by the Seventeenth Amendment.

969.25–29   and if Vacancies . . . Vacanies.] Changed by the Seventeenth Amendment.

The Senate shall chuse their other Officers, and also a President pro tempore, in the Absence of the Vice President, or when he shall exercise the Office of President of the United States.

The Senate shall have the sole Power to try all Impeachments. When sitting for that Purpose, they shall be on Oath or Affirmation. When the President of the United States is tried, the Chief Justice shall preside: And no Person shall be convicted without the Concurrence of two thirds of the Members present.

Judgment in Cases of Impeachment shall not extend further than to removal from Office, and disqualification to hold and enjoy any Office of honor, Trust or Profit under the United States: but the Party convicted shall nevertheless be liable and subject to Indictment, Trial, Judgment and Punishment, according to Law.

Section. 4. The Times, Places and Manner of holding Elections for Senators and Representatives, shall be prescribed in each State by the Legislature thereof; but the Congress may at any time by Law make or alter such Regulations, except as to the Places of chusing Senators.

The Congress shall assemble at least once in every Year, and such Meeting shall be on the first Monday in December, unless they shall by Law appoint a different Day.

Section. 5. Each House shall be the Judge of the Elections, Returns and Qualifications of its own Members, and a Majority of each shall constitute a Quorum to do Business; but a smaller Number may adjourn from day to day, and may be authorized to compel the Attendance of absent Members, in such Manner, and under such Penalties as each House may provide.

Each House may determine the Rules of its Proceedings, punish its members for disorderly Behaviour, and, with the Concurrence of two thirds, expel a Member.

Each House shall keep a Journal of its Proceedings, and from time to time publish the same, excepting such Parts as may in their Judgment require Secrecy; and the Yeas and

970.23   be on . . . December,] Changed by the Twentieth Amendment.

Nays of the Members of either House on any question shall, at the Desire of one fifth of those Present, be entered on the Journal.

Neither House, during the Session of Congress, shall, without the Consent of the other, adjourn for more than three days, nor to any other Place than that in which the two Houses shall be sitting.

Section. 6.   The Senators and Representatives shall receive a Compensation for their Services, to be ascertained by Law, and paid out of the Treasury of the United States. They shall in all Cases, except Treason, Felony and Breach of the Peace, be privileged from Arrest during their Attendance at the Session of their respective Houses, and in going to and returning from the same; and for any Speech or Debate in either House, they shall not be questioned in any other Place.

No Senator or Representative shall, during the Time for which he was elected, be appointed to any civil Office under the Authority of the United States which shall have been created, or the Emoluments whereof shall have been encreased during such time; and no Person holding any Office under the United States, shall be a Member of either House during his Continuance in Office.

Section. 7.   All Bills for raising Revenue shall originate in the House of Representatives; but the Senate may propose or concur with Amendments as on other Bills.

Every Bill which shall have passed the House of Representatives and the Senate shall, before it become a Law, be presented to the President of the United States; If he approve he shall sign it, but if not he shall return it, with his Objections to that House in which it shall have originated, who shall enter the Objections at large on their Journal, and proceed to reconsider it. If after such Reconsideration two thirds of that House shall agree to pass the Bill, it shall be sent, together with the Objections, to the other House, by which it shall likewise be reconsidered, and if approved by two thirds of that House, it shall become a Law. But in all such Cases the Votes of both Houses shall be determined by yeas and Nays, and the Names of the Persons voting for and against the Bill shall be entered on the Journal of each

House respectively. If any Bill shall not be returned by the President within ten Days (Sundays excepted) after it shall have been presented to him, the Same shall be a Law, in like Manner as if he had signed it, unless the Congress by their Adjournment prevent its Return, in which Case it shall not be a Law.

Every Order, Resolution, or Vote to which the Concurrence of the Senate and House of Representatives may be necessary (except on a question of Adjournment) shall be presented to the President of the United States; and before the Same shall take Effect, shall be approved by him, or being disapproved by him, shall be repassed by two thirds of the Senate and House of Representatives, according to the Rules and Limitations prescribed in the Case of a Bill.

Section. 8.   The Congress shall have Power To lay and collect Taxes, Duties, Imposts and Excises, to pay the Debts and provide for the common Defence and general Welfare of the United States; but all Duties, Imposts and Excises shall be uniform throughout the United States;

To borrow Money on the credit of the United States;

To regulate Commerce with foreign Nations, and among the several States, and with the Indian Tribes;

To establish an uniform Rule of Naturalization, and uniform Laws on the subject of Bankruptcies throughout the United States;

To coin Money, regulate the Value thereof, and of foreign Coin, and fix the Standard of Weights and Measures;

To provide for the Punishment of counterfeiting the Securities and current Coin of the United States;

To establish Post Offices and post Roads;

To promote the Progress of Science and useful Arts, by securing for limited Times to Authors and Inventors the exclusive Right to their respective Writings and Discoveries;

To constitute Tribunals inferior to the supreme Court;

To define and punish Piracies and Felonies committed on the high Seas, and Offences against the Law of Nations;

To declare War, grant Letters of Marque and Reprisal, and make Rules concerning Captures on Land and Water;

To raise and support Armies, but no Appropriation of Money to that Use shall be for a longer Term than two Years;

To provide and maintain a Navy;

To make Rules for the Government and Regulation of the land and naval Forces;

To provide for calling forth the Militia to execute the Laws of the Union, suppress Insurrections and repel Invasions;

To provide for organizing, arming, and disciplining, the Militia, and for governing such Part of them as may be employed in the Service of the United States, reserving to the States respectively, the Appointment of the Officers, and the Authority of training the Militia according to the discipline prescribed by Congress;

To exercise exclusive Legislation in all Cases whatsoever, over such District (not exceeding ten Miles square) as may, by Cession of particular States, and the Acceptance of Congress, become the Seat of the Government of the United States, and to exercise like Authority over all Places purchased by the Consent of the Legislature of the State in which the same shall be, for the Erection of Forts, Magazines, Arsenals, dock-Yards, and other needful Buildings; —And

To make all Laws which shall be necessary and proper for carrying into Execution the foregoing Powers, and all other Powers vested by this Constitution in the Government of the United States, or in any Department or Officer thereof.

Section. 9.   The Migration or Importation of such Persons as any of the States now existing shall think proper to admit, shall not be prohibited by the Congress prior to the Year one thousand eight hundred and eight, but a Tax or duty may be imposed on such Importation, not exceeding ten dollars for each Person.

The Privilege of the Writ of Habeas Corpus shall not be suspended, unless when in Cases of Rebellion or Invasion the public Safety may require it.

No Bill of Attainder or ex post facto Law shall be passed.

No Capitation, or other direct, Tax shall be laid, unless in

Proportion to the Census or Enumeration herein before directed to be taken.

No Tax or Duty shall be laid on Articles exported from any State.

No Preference shall be given by any Regulation of Commerce or Revenue to the Ports of one State over those of another: nor shall Vessels bound to, or from, one State, be obliged to enter, clear, or pay Duties in another.

No Money shall be drawn from the Treasury, but in Consequence of Appropriations made by Law; and a regular Statement and Account of the Receipts and Expenditures of all public Money shall be published from time to time.

No Title of Nobility shall be granted by the United States: And no Person holding any Office of Profit or Trust under them, shall, without the Consent of the Congress, accept of any present, Emolument, Office, or Title, of any kind whatever, from any King, Prince, or foreign State.

Section. 10.   No State shall enter into any Treaty, Alliance, or Confederation; grant Letters of Marque and Reprisal; coin Money; emit Bills of Credit; make any Thing but gold and silver Coin a Tender in Payment of Debts; pass any Bill of Attainder, ex post facto Law, or Law impairing the Obligation of Contracts, or grant any Title of Nobility.

No State shall, without the Consent of the Congress, lay any Imposts or Duties on Imports or Exports, except what may be absolutely necessary for executing it's inspection Laws: and the net Produce of all Duties and Imposts, laid by any State on Imports or Exports, shall be for the Use of the Treasury of the United States; and all such Laws shall be subject to the Revision and Controul of the Congress.

No State shall, without the Consent of Congress, lay any Duty of Tonnage, keep Troops, or Ships of War in time of Peace, enter into any Agreement or Compact with another State, or with a foreign Power, or engage in War, unless actually invaded, or in such imminent Danger as will not admit of delay.

973.38–974.2 No Capitation . . . taken.] Changed by the Sixteenth Amendment.

Article. II.

Section. 1.   The executive Power shall be vested in a President of the United States of America. He shall hold his Office during the Term of four Years, and, together with the Vice President, chosen for the same Term, be elected, as follows

Each State shall appoint, in such Manner as the Legislature thereof may direct, a Number of Electors, equal to the whole Number of Senators and Representatives to which the State may be entitled in the Congress: but no Senator or Representative, or Person holding an Office of Trust or Profit under the United States, shall be appointed an Elector.

The Electors shall meet in their respective States and vote by Ballot for two Persons, of whom one at least shall not be an Inhabitant of the same State with themselves. And they shall make a List of all the Persons voted for, and of the Number of Votes for each; which List they shall sign and certify, and transmit sealed to the Seat of the Government of the United States, directed to the President of the Senate. The President of the Senate shall, in the Presence of the Senate and House of Representatives, open all the Certificates, and the Votes shall then be counted. The Person having the greatest Number of Votes shall be the President, if such Number be a Majority of the whole Number of Electors appointed; and if there be more than one who have such Majority, and have an equal Number of Votes, then the House of Representatives shall immediately chuse by Ballot one of them for President; and if no Person have a Majority, then from the five highest on the List the said House shall in like Manner chuse the President. But in chusing the President, the Votes shall be taken by States, the Representation from each State having one Vote; A quorum for this Purpose shall consist of a Member or Members from two thirds of the States, and a Majority of all the States shall be necessary to a Choice. In every Case, after the Choice of the President, the Person having the greatest Number of Votes of the Electors shall be the Vice President. But if there should remain two or more who have equal

Votes, the Senate shall chuse from them by Ballot the Vice President.

The Congress may determine the Time of chusing the Electors, and the Day on which they shall give their Votes; which Day shall be the same throughout the United States.

No Persons except a natural born Citizen, or a Citizen of the United States, at the time of the Adoption of this Constitution, shall be eligible to the Office of President; neither shall any Person be eligible to that Office who shall not have attained to the Age of thirty five Years, and been fourteen Years a Resident within the United States.

In Case of the Removal of the President from Office, or of his Death, Resignation, or Inability to discharge the Powers and Duties of the said Office, the Same shall devolve on the Vice President, and the Congress may by Law provide for the Case of Removal, Death, Resignation or Inability, both of the President and Vice President, declaring what Officer shall then act as President, and such Officer shall act accordingly, until the Disability be removed, or a President shall be elected.

The President shall, at stated Times, receive for his Services, a Compensation, which shall neither be encreased nor diminished during the Period for which he shall have been elected, and he shall not receive within that Period any other Emolument from the United States, or any of them.

Before he enter on the Execution of his Office, he shall take the following Oath or Affirmation:—"I do solemnly swear (or affirm) that I will faithfully execute the Office of President of the United States, and will to the best of my Ability, preserve, protect and defend the Constitution of the United States."

Section. 2.   The President shall be Commander in Chief of the Army and Navy of the United States, and of the Militia of the several States, when called into the actual Service of the United States; he may require the Opinion, in writing, of the principal Officer in each of the executive Departments, upon any Subject relating to the Duties of their respective Offices,

975.14–976.2   The Electors . . . Vice President.] Changed by the Twelfth Amendment.

976.12–19   In Case . . . elected.] Changed by the Twenty-fifth Amendment.

and he shall have Power to grant Reprieves and Pardons for Offences against the United States, except in Cases of Impeachment.

He shall have Power, by and with the Advice and Consent of the Senate, to make Treaties, provided two thirds of the Senators present concur; and he shall nominate, and by and with the Advice and Consent of the Senate, shall appoint Ambassadors, other public Ministers and Consuls, Judges of the supreme Court, and all other Officers of the United States, whose Appointments are not herein otherwise provided for, and which shall be established by Law: but the Congress may by Law vest the Appointment of such inferior Officers, as they think proper, in the President alone, in the Courts of Law, or in the Heads of Departments.

The President shall have Power to fill up all Vacancies that may happen during the Recess of the Senate, by granting Commissions which shall expire at the End of their next Session.

Section. 3.   He shall from time to time give to the Congress Information of the State of the Union, and recommend to their Consideration such Measures as he shall judge necessary and expedient; he may, on extraordinary Occasions, convene both Houses, or either of them, and in Case of Disagreement between them, with Respect to the Time of Adjournment, he may adjourn them to such Time as he shall think proper; he shall receive Ambassadors and other public Ministers; he shall take Care that the Laws be faithfully executed, and shall Commission all the Officers of the United States.

Section. 4.   The President, Vice President and all civil Officers of the United States, shall be removed from Office on Impeachment for, and Conviction of Treason, Bribery, or other high Crimes and Misdemeanors.

Article. III.

Section. 1.   The judicial Power of the United States, shall be vested in one supreme Court, and in such inferior Courts as the Congress may from time to time ordain and establish. The Judges, both of the supreme and inferior Courts, shall hold their Offices during good Behaviour, and shall, at stated Times, receive for their Services, a Compensation, which shall not be diminished during their Continuance in Office.

Section. 2.   The judicial Power shall extend to all Cases, in Law and Equity, arising under this Constitution, the Laws of the United States, and Treaties made, or which shall be made, under their Authority;—to all Cases affecting Ambassadors, other public Ministers and Consuls;—to all Cases of admiralty and maritime Jurisdiction;—to Controversies to which the United States shall be a Party;—to Controversies between two or more States—between a State and Citizens of another State;—between Citizens of different States,—between Citizens of the same State claiming Lands under Grants of different States, and between a State, or the Citizens thereof, and of foreign States, Citizens or Subjects.

In all Cases affecting Ambassadors, other public Ministers and Consuls, and those in which a State shall be Party, the supreme Court shall have original Jurisdiction. In all the other Cases before mentioned, the supreme Court shall have appellate Jurisdiction, both as to Law and Fact, with such Exceptions, and under such Regulations as the Congress shall make.

The Trial of all Crimes, except in Cases of Impeachment, shall be by Jury; and such Trial shall be held in the State where the said Crimes shall have been committed; but when not committed within any State, the Trial shall be at such Place or Places as the Congress may by Law have directed.

Section. 3.   Treason against the United States, shall consist only in levying War against them, or in adhering to their Enemies, giving them Aid and Comfort. No Person shall be convicted of Treason unless on the Testimony of two Witnesses to the same overt Act, or on Confession in open Court.

The Congress shall have Power to declare the Punishment of Treason, but no Attainder of Treason shall work Cor-

978.12–16   between a State . . . Subjects] Jurisdiction over suits brought against states by citizens of another state, or by foreigners, was addressed by the Eleventh Amendment.

ruption of Blood, or Forfeiture except during the Life of the Person attainted.

Article. IV.

Section. 1. Full Faith and Credit shall be given in each State to the public Acts, Records, and judicial Proceedings of every other State. And the Congress may by general Laws prescribe the Manner in which such Acts, Records and Proceedings shall be proved, and the Effect thereof.

Section. 2. The Citizens of each State shall be entitled to all privileges and Immunities of Citizens in the several States.

A Person charged in any State with Treason, Felony, or other Crime, who shall flee from Justice, and be found in another State, shall on Demand of the executive Authority of the State from which he fled, be delivered up, to be removed to the State having Jurisdiction of the Crime.

No Person held to Service or Labour in one State, under the Laws thereof, escaping into another, shall, in Consequence of any Law or Regulation therein, be discharged from such Service or Labour, but shall be delivered up on Claim of the Party to whom such Service or Labour may be due.

Section. 3. New States may be admitted by the Congress into this Union; but no new State shall be formed or erected within the Jurisdiction of any other State; nor any State be formed by the Junction of two or more States, or Parts of States, without the Consent of the Legislatures of the States concerned as well as of the Congress.

The Congress shall have Power to dispose of and make all needful Rules and Regulations respecting the Territory or other Property belonging to the United States; and nothing in this Constitution shall be so construed as to Prejudice any Claims of the United States, or of any particular State.

979.17–22 No Person . . . due.] Changed by the Thirteenth Amendment.

Section. 4. The United States shall guarantee to every State in this Union a Republican Form of Government, and shall protect each of them against Invasion; and on Application of the Legislature, or of the Executive (when the Legislature cannot be convened) against domestic Violence.

Article. V.

The Congress, whenever two thirds of both Houses shall deem it necessary, shall propose Amendments to this Constitution, or, on the Application of the Legislatures of two thirds of the several States, shall call a Convention for proposing Amendments, which, in either Case, shall be valid to all Intents and Purposes, as Part of this Constitution, when ratified by the Legislatures of three fourths of the several States, or by Conventions in three fourths thereof, as the one or the other Mode of Ratification may be proposed by the Congress; Provided that no Amendment which may be made prior to the Year One thousand eight hundred and eight shall in any Manner affect the first and fourth Clauses in the Ninth Section of the first Article; and that no State, without its Consent, shall be deprived of it's equal Suffrage in the Senate.

Article. VI.

All Debts contracted and Engagements entered into, before the Adoption of this Constitution, shall be as valid against the United States under this Constitution, as under the Confederation.

This Constitution, and the Laws of the United States which shall be made in Pursuance thereof; and all Treaties made, or which shall be made, under the Authority of the United States, shall be the supreme Law of the Land; and the Judges in every State shall be bound thereby, any Thing in the Constitution or Laws of any State to the Contrary notwithstanding.

The Senators and Representatives before mentioned, and the Members of the several State Legislatures, and all executive and judicial Officers; both of the United States and of the several States, shall be bound by Oath or Affirmation, to support this Constitution; but no religious Test shall ever be required as a Qualification to any Office or public Trust under the United States.

Article. VII.

The Ratification of the Conventions of nine States, shall be sufficient for the Establishment of this Constitution between the States so ratifying the Same.

DONE in Convention by the Unanimous Consent of the States present the Seventeenth Day of September in the Year of our Lord one thousand seven hundred and Eighty seven and of the Independance of the United States of America the Twelfth In Witness whereof We have hereunto subscribed our Names,

Attest William Jackson Secretary

Go: Washington—Presidt.
and deputy from Virginia

Delaware
Geo: Read
Gunning Bedford junr
John Dickinson
Richard Bassett
Jaco: Broom

Maryland
James McHenry
Dan of St Thos. Jenifer
Danl Carroll

Virginia
John Blair—
James Madison Jr.

North Carolina
Wm. Blount
Richd. Dobbs Spaight.
Hu Williamson

South Carolina
J. Rutledge
Charles Cotesworth
  Pinckney
Charles Pinckney
Pierce Butler

Georgia
William Few
Abr Baldwin

New Hampshire
John Langdon
Nicholas Gilman

Massachusetts
Nathaniel Gorham
Rufus King

Connecticut
Wm: Saml. Johnson
Roger Sherman

New York . . . . Alexander Hamilton

New Jersey
Wil: Livingston
David Brearley
Wm. Paterson.
Jona: Dayton

Pensylvania
B Franklin
Thomas Mifflin
Robt Morris
Geo. Clymer
Thos. FitzSimons
Jared Ingersoll
James Wilson
Gouv. Morris

ARTICLES in Addition to, and Amendment of, the Constitution of the United States of America, proposed by Congress, and ratified by the Legislatures of the several States, pursuant to the fifth Article of the original Constitution.

Article I.

Congress shall make no law respecting an establishment of religion, or prohibiting the free exercise thereof; or abridging the freedom of speech, or of the press; or the right of the people peaceably to assemble, and to petition the Government for a redress of grievances.

Article II.

A well regulated Militia, being necessary to the security of a free State, the right of the people to keep and bear Arms, shall not be infringed.

Article III.

No Soldier shall, in time of peace be quartered in any house, without the consent of the Owner, nor in time of war, but in a manner to be prescribed by law.

Article IV.

The right of the people to be secure in their persons, houses, papers, and effects, against unreasonable searches and seizures, shall not be violated, and no Warrants shall issue, but upon probable cause, supported by Oath or affirmation, and particularly describing the place to be searched, and the persons or things to be seized.

Article V.

No person shall be held to answer for a capital, or otherwise infamous crime, unless on a presentment or indictment of a Grand Jury, except in cases arising in the land or naval forces, or in the Militia, when in actual service in time of War or public danger; nor shall any person be subject for the same offence to be twice put in jeopardy of life or limb; nor shall be compelled in any criminal case to be a witness against himself, nor be deprived of life, liberty, or property, without due process of law; nor shall private property be taken for public use, without just compensation.

Article VI.

In all criminal prosecutions, the accused shall enjoy the right to a speedy and public trial, by an impartial jury of the State and district wherein the crime shall have been committed, which district shall have been previously ascertained by law, and to be informed of the nature and cause of the accusation; to be confronted with the witnesses against him; to have compulsory process for obtaining witnesses in his favor, and to have the Assistance of Counsel for his defence.

Article VII.

In Suits at common law, where the value in controversy shall exceed twenty dollars, the right of trial by jury shall be preserved, and no fact tried by a jury, shall be otherwise re-examined in any Court of the United States, than according to the rules of the common law.

Article VIII.

Excessive bail shall not be required, nor excessive fines imposed, nor cruel and unusual punishments inflicted.

Article IX.

The enumeration in the Constitution, of certain rights, shall not be construed to deny or disparage others retained by the people.

Article X.

The powers not delegated to the United States by the Constitution, nor prohibited by it to the States, are reserved to the States respectively, or to the people.

Articles I.–X. proposed to the states by Congress, September 25, 1789
Ratification completed, December 15, 1791
Ratification declared, March 1, 1792

Article XI.

The Judicial power of the United States shall not be construed to extend to any suit in law or equity, commenced or prosecuted against one of the United States by Citizens of another State, or by Citizens or Subjects of any Foreign State.

Proposed to the states by Congress, March 4, 1794
Ratification completed, February 7, 1795
Ratification declared, January 8, 1798

Article XII.

The Electors shall meet in their respective states, and vote by ballot for President and Vice-President, one of whom, at least, shall not be an inhabitant of the same state with themselves; they shall name in their ballots the person voted for as President, and in distinct ballots the person voted for as Vice-President, and they shall make distinct lists of all persons voted for as President, and of all persons voted for as Vice-President, and of the number of votes for each, which lists they shall sign and certify, and transmit sealed to the seat of the government of the United States, directed to the President of the Senate;—The President of the Senate shall, in the presence of the Senate and House of Representatives, open all the certificates and the votes shall then be counted;—The person having the greatest number of votes for President, shall be the President, if such number be a majority of the whole number of Electors appointed; and if no person have such majority, then from the persons having the highest numbers not exceeding three on the list of those voted for as President, the House of Representatives shall choose immediately, by ballot, the President. But in choosing the President, the votes shall be taken by states, the representation from each state having one vote; a quorum for this purpose shall consist of a member or members from two-thirds of the states, and a majority of all the states shall be necessary to a choice. And if the House of Representatives shall not choose a President whenever the right of choice shall devolve upon them, before the fourth day of March next following, then the Vice-President shall act as President, as in the case of the death or other constitutional disability of the President.—The person having the greatest number of votes as Vice-President, shall be the Vice-President, if such number be a majority of the whole number of Electors appointed, and if no person have a majority, then from the two highest numbers on the list, the Senate shall choose the Vice-President; a quorum for the purpose shall consist of two-thirds of the whole number of Senators, and a majority of the whole number shall be necessary to a choice. But no person constitutionally ineligible to the office of President shall be eligible to that of Vice-President of the United States.

Proposed to the states by Congress, December 9, 1803
Ratification completed, June 15, 1804
Ratification declared, September 25, 1804

Article XIII.

SECTION 1. Neither slavery nor involuntary servitude, except as a punishment for crime whereof the party shall have been duly convicted, shall exist within the United States, or any place subject to their jurisdiction.
SECTION 2. Congress shall have power to enforce this article by appropriate legislation.

Proposed to the states by Congress, January 31, 1865
Ratification completed, December 6, 1865
Ratification declared, December 18, 1865

Article XIV.

SECTION 1. All persons born or naturalized in the United States, and subject to the jurisdiction thereof, are citizens of the United States and of the State wherein they reside. No

985.2–7   And if . . . President.—] Changed by the Twentieth Amendment.

State shall make or enforce any law which shall abridge the privileges or immunities of citizens of the United States; nor shall any State deprive any person of life, liberty, or property, without due process of law; nor deny to any person within its jurisdiction the equal protection of the laws.

SECTION 2.   Representatives shall be apportioned among the several States according to their respective numbers, counting the whole number of persons in each State, excluding Indians not taxed. But when the right to vote at any election for the choice of electors for President and Vice President of the United States, Representatives in Congress, the Executive and Judicial officers of a State, or the members of the Legislature thereof, is denied to any of the male inhabitants of such State, being twenty-one years of age, and citizens of the United States, or in any way abridged, except for participation in rebellion, or other crime, the basis of representation therein shall be reduced in the proportion which the number of such male citizens shall bear to the whole number of male citizens twenty-one years of age in such State.

SECTION 3.   No person shall be a Senator or Representative in Congress, or elector of President and Vice President, or hold any office, civil or military, under the United States, or under any State, who, having previously taken an oath, as a member of Congress, or as an officer of the United States, or as a member of any State legislature, or as an executive or judicial officer of any State, to support the Constitution of the United States, shall have engaged in insurrection or rebellion against the same, or given aid or comfort to the enemies thereof. But Congress may by a vote of two-thirds of each House, remove such disability.

SECTION 4.   The validity of the public debt of the United States, authorized by law, including debts incurred for payment of pensions and bounties for services in suppressing insurrection or rebellion, shall not be questioned. But neither the United States nor any State shall assume or pay any debt or obligation incurred in aid of insurrection or rebellion

986.13–14   male inhabitants . . . twenty-one years of age] Regarding voting rights and sex, see the Nineteenth Amendment; regarding voting rights and age, see the Twenty-sixth Amendment.

against the United States, or any claim for the loss or emancipation of any slave; but all such debts, obligations and claims shall be held illegal and void.

SECTION 5.   The Congress shall have power to enforce, by appropriate legislation, the provisions of this article.

Proposed to the states by Congress, June 13, 1866
Ratification completed, July 9, 1868
Ratification declared, July 28, 1868

Article XV.

SECTION 1.   The right of citizens of the United States to vote shall not be denied or abridged by the United States or by any State on account of race, color, or previous condition of servitude.

SECTION 2.   The Congress shall have power to enforce this article by appropriate legislation.

Proposed to the states by Congress, February 26, 1869
Ratification completed, February 3, 1870
Ratification declared, March 30, 1870

Article XVI.

The Congress shall have power to lay and collect taxes on incomes, from whatever source derived, without apportionment among the several States, and without regard to any census or enumeration.

Proposed to the states by Congress, July 12, 1909
Ratification completed, February 3, 1913
Ratification declared, February 25, 1913

Article XVII.

The Senate of the United States shall be composed of two Senators from each State, elected by the people thereof, for six years; and each Senator shall have one vote. The electors in each State shall have the qualifications requisite for electors of the most numerous branch of the State legislatures.

When vacancies happen in the representation of any State in the Senate, the executive authority of such State shall issue writs of election to fill such vacancies: *Provided,* That the legislature of any State may empower the executive thereof to make temporary appointments until the people fill the vacancies by election as the legislature may direct.

This amendment shall not be so construed as to affect the election or term of any Senator chosen before it becomes valid as part of the Constitution.

Proposed to the states by Congress, May 13, 1912
Ratification completed, April 8, 1913
Ratification declared, May 31, 1913

Article XVIII.

SECTION 1.   After one year from the ratification of this article the manufacture, sale, or transportation of intoxicating liquors within, the importation thereof into, or the exportation thereof from the United States and all territory subject to the jurisdiction thereof for beverage purposes is hereby prohibited.

SEC. 2.   The Congress and the several States shall have concurrent power to enforce this article by appropriate legislation.

SEC. 3.   This article shall be inoperative unless it shall have been ratified as an amendment to the Constitution by the legislatures of the several States, as provided in the Constitution, within seven years from the date of the submission hereof to the States by the Congress.

Proposed to the states by Congress, December 18, 1917
Ratification completed, January 16, 1919
Ratification declared, January 29, 1919

Article XIX.

The right of citizens of the United States to vote shall not be denied or abridged by the United States or by any State on account of sex.

Congress shall have power to enforce this article by appropriate legislation.

Proposed to the states by Congress, June 4, 1919
Ratification completed, August 18, 1920
Ratification declared, August 26, 1920

988.10–23   Article XVIII. . . . Congress] Repealed by the Twenty-first Amendment.

Article XX.

SECTION 1.   The terms of the President and Vice President shall end at noon on the 20th day of January, and the terms of Senators and Representatives at noon on the 3d day of January, of the years in which such terms would have ended if this article had not been ratified; and the terms of their successors shall then begin.

SEC. 2.   The Congress shall assemble at least once in every year, and such meeting shall begin at noon on the 3d day of January, unless they shall by law appoint a different day.

SEC. 3.   If, at the time fixed for the beginning of the term of the President, the President elect shall have died, the Vice President elect shall become President. If a President shall not have been chosen before the time fixed for the beginning of his term, or if the President elect shall have failed to qualify, then the Vice President elect shall act as President until a President shall have qualified; and the Congress may by law provide for the case wherein neither a President elect nor a Vice President elect shall have qualified, declaring who shall then act as President, or the manner in which one who is to act shall be selected, and such person shall act accordingly until a President or Vice President shall have qualified.

SEC. 4.   The Congress may by law provide for the case of the death of any of the persons from whom the House of Representatives may choose a President whenever the right of choice shall have devolved upon them, and for the case of the death of any of the persons from whom the Senate may choose a Vice President whenever the right of choice shall have devolved upon them.

SEC. 5.   Sections 1 and 2 shall take effect on the 15th day of October following the ratification of this article.

SEC. 6.   This article shall be inoperative unless it shall have been ratified as an amendment to the Constitution by the legislatures of three-fourths of the several States within seven years from the date of its submission.

Proposed to the states by Congress, March 2, 1932
Ratification completed, January 23, 1933
Ratification declared, February 6, 1933

Article XXI.

SECTION 1.   The eighteenth article of amendment to the Constitution of the United States is hereby repealed.

SECTION 2.   The transportation or importation into any State, Territory, or possession of the United States for delivery or use therein of intoxicating liquors, in violation of the laws thereof, is hereby prohibited.

SECTION 3.   This article shall be inoperative unless it shall have been ratified as an amendment to the Constitution by conventions in the several States, as provided in the Constitution, within seven years from the date of the submission hereof to the States by the Congress.

Proposed to the states by Congress, February 20, 1933
Ratification completed, December 5, 1933
Ratification declared, December 5, 1933

Article XXII.

SECTION 1.   No person shall be elected to the office of the President more than twice, and no person who has held the office of President, or acted as President, for more than two years of a term to which some other person was elected President shall be elected to the office of the President more than once. But this Article shall not apply to any person holding the office of President when this Article was proposed by the Congress, and shall not prevent any person who may be holding the office of President, or acting as President, during the term within which this Article becomes operative from holding the office of President or acting as President during the remainder of such term.

SEC. 2.   This article shall be inoperative unless it shall have been ratified as an amendment to the Constitution by the legislatures of three-fourths of the several States within seven years from the date of its submission to the States by the Congress.

Proposed to the states by Congress, March 21, 1947
Ratification completed, February 27, 1951
Ratification declared, March 1, 1951

Article XXIII.

SECTION 1.   The District constituting the seat of Government of the United States shall appoint in such manner as the Congress may direct:

A number of electors of President and Vice President equal to the whole number of Senators and Representatives in Congress to which the District would be entitled if it were a State, but in no event more than the least populous State; they shall be in addition to those appointed by the States, but they shall be considered, for the purposes of the election of President and Vice President, to be electors appointed by a State; and they shall meet in the District and perform such duties as provided by the twelfth article of amendment.

SEC. 2.   The Congress shall have power to enforce this article by appropriate legislation.

Proposed to the states by Congress, June 17, 1960
Ratification completed, March 29, 1961
Ratification declared, April 3, 1961

Article XXIV.

SECTION 1.   The right of citizens of the United States to vote in any primary or other election for President or Vice President, for electors for President or Vice President, or for Senator or Representative in Congress, shall not be denied or abridged by the United States or any State by reason of failure to pay any poll tax or other tax.

SEC. 2.   The Congress shall have power to enforce this article by appropriate legislation.

Proposed to the states by Congress, August 27, 1962
Ratification completed, January 23, 1964
Ratification declared, February 4, 1964

Article XXV.

SECTION 1.   In case of the removal of the President from office or of his death or resignation, the Vice President shall become President.

SEC. 2.   Whenever there is a vacancy in the office of the Vice President, the President shall nominate a Vice President who shall take office upon confirmation by a majority vote of both Houses of Congress.

SEC. 3. Whenever the President transmits to the President pro tempore of the Senate and the Speaker of the House of Representatives his written declaration that he is unable to discharge the powers and duties of his office, and until he transmits to them a written declaration to the contrary, such powers and duties shall be discharged by the Vice President as Acting President.

SEC. 4. Whenever the Vice President and a majority of either the principal officers of the executive departments or of such other body as Congress may by law provide, transmit to the President pro tempore of the Senate and the Speaker of the House of Representatives their written declaration that the President is unable to discharge the powers and duties of his office, the Vice President shall immediately assume the powers and duties of the office as Acting President.

Thereafter, when the President transmits to the President pro tempore of the Senate and the Speaker of the House of Representatives his written declaration that no inability exists, he shall resume the powers and duties of his office unless the Vice President and a majority of either the principal officers of the executive department or of such other body as Congress may by law provide, transmit within four days to the President pro tempore of the Senate and the Speaker of the House of Representatives their written declaration that the President is unable to discharge the powers and duties of his office. Thereupon Congress shall decide the issue, assembling within forty-eight hours for that purpose if not in session. If the Congress, within twenty-one days after receipt of the latter written declaration, or, if Congress is not in session, within twenty-one days after Congress is required to assemble, determines by two-thirds vote of both Houses that the President is unable to discharge the powers and duties of his office, the Vice President shall continue to discharge the same as Acting President; otherwise, the President shall resume the powers and duties of his office.

Proposed to the states by Congress, July 6, 1965
Ratification completed, February 10, 1967
Ratification declared, February 23, 1967

Article XXVI.

SECTION 1.   The right of citizens of the United States, who are eighteen years of age or older, to vote shall not be denied or abridged by the United States or by any State on account of age.

SEC. 2.   The Congress shall have power to enforce this article by appropriate legislation.

Proposed to the states by Congress, March 23, 1971
Ratification completed, July 1, 1971
Ratification declared, July 5, 1971

Article XXVII.

No law, varying the compensation for the services of the Senators and Representatives, shall take effect, until an election of Representatives shall have intervened.

Proposed to the states by Congress, September 25, 1789
Ratification completed, May 7, 1992
Ratification declared, May 18, 1992

Biographical Notes

Speakers, Writers, and Letter Recipients

JOHN ADAMS (1735–1826)   Born October 30, 1735, in Braintree, Massachusetts, eldest son of Susanna Boylston and John Adams (a farmer), and second cousin of Samuel Adams. After graduating from Harvard College in 1755, taught school in Worcester, Massachusetts, and took up the study of law; admitted to the Boston bar in November 1758. Married Abigail, daughter of the minister William Smith of Weymouth, Massachusetts, in October 1764. Though opposed to mob action, took active role against Stamp Act in 1765. Rode circuits around state as law practice grew. Moved to Boston in 1768, where he successfully defended John Hancock against a smuggling charge that year. Elected delegate to the Massachusetts General Court from Boston in 1770. With Josiah Quincy, successfully defended British soldiers Captain Preston and his men in October–November 1770 against charges of murder in the controversial "Boston Massacre" case. Exhausted by town life, moved back to Braintree in 1771 but soon returned to Boston and his expanding law practice. Elected to the First Continental Congress in 1774; served on various committees. Elected to the provincial congress and became a member of the council. Served in the Second Continental Congress 1775–78 where he nominated George Washington to be commander-in-chief of the Continental Army in 1775. Published pamphlet *Thoughts on Government* in January 1776 and urged the other colonies to institute new governments. Seconded Richard Henry Lee's motion for independence and served on the committee with Jefferson, Franklin, Robert R. Livingston, and Roger Sherman to prepare draft; signed the Declaration of Independence. With Franklin, took leading role on committee to draft a plan of treaties with foreign countries. Elected to the Board of War; with Franklin and Edward Rutledge, met with Lord Howe on Staten Island in fruitless conciliatory negotiation. Formed alliances and friendships with the Lees of Virginia, Benjamin Rush, and Jefferson, among others. Elected to replace Silas Deane as commissioner (with Franklin and Arthur Lee) to the court of France in November 1777. Arrived in Paris with son John Quincy in April 1778; returned to America in August 1779. Served in convention to frame Massachusetts constitution based largely on his plan, but before draft was completed was sent by Congress to Europe to negotiate peace and commercial treaty with Great Britain. Arrived in Paris in February 1780, distrusted Franklin and had falling-out with French foreign minister Vergennes; went to Holland to try to get loans. Appointed minister to Holland by Congress in December 1780; August 1782, named minister plenipotentiary to the United Provinces, negotiated loan and signed treaty of amity and commerce. Returned to France in time to help Franklin and Jay (whose efforts he supported) complete final elements of treaty; signed provisional peace accord with England in November 1782 (final treaty was signed in September 1783). Negotiated further loans in Holland. Joined by his family in France in 1784, was appointed first U.S. minister to Britain and served 1785–88. In London he wrote three-volume *Defence of the Constitutions of the United States* (1787–88), in which he criticized many American state constitutions as lacking in stability. He praised the new U.S. Constitution, though he still desired more stability and order than it seemed to promise. As vice-president of the United States under Washington, April 1789–March 1797, he supported Washington and helped Hamilton pass his financial measures. Elected president as a Federalist in 1796, he was angered by Hamilton's efforts against him in the election; retained Washington's cabinet. Appointed John Marshall, Charles Cotesworth Pinckney, and Elbridge Gerry to a special mission to France 1797–98, resulting in the infuriating XYZ Affair. Prepared for possible war with France, increasing the army and navy and naming Washington to command; was forced by Washington to accept Hamilton as second in command (with Charles Cotesworth Pinckney third). Engaged in an undeclared naval war with France, 1798–1800. Signed Alien and Sedition Acts. After hearing that France would respond favorably, appointed William Vans Murray, Oliver Ellsworth, and William R. Davie to second peace mission in 1799, despite disagreement with his cabinet (peace with France was concluded in September 1800). Learned that some members of his cabinet were taking instructions from Hamilton; confronted McHenry, secretary of war, who resigned, and Pickering, who refused to resign and remained until May 1800 when Adams fired him (Wolcott was another Hamiltonian but Adams was unaware of his role). Appointed John Marshall secretary of state to replace Pickering and, in January 1801, appointed him Chief Justice of the U.S. Supreme Court (for a while he occupied both positions). Partly because of the enmity of Hamilton and his friends and the consequent split in the Federalist party, lost the election to Jefferson in 1800. When Congress reorganized the judiciary system in 1801, Adams made a large number of lifetime appointments before leaving office, angering Jefferson. Retired to his farm in Quincy (part of old Braintree) in 1801. With Benjamin Rush as mediator, renewed correspondence with Jefferson in 1812. Served as presidential elector for James Monroe in 1821. Died in Quincy, Massachusetts, July 4, 1826.

SAMUEL ADAMS (1722–1803) Born September 27, 1722, in Boston, son of Mary Fifield and Samuel Adams (a prosperous Boston brewer and real estate owner who was active in civic affairs and who had established a land bank that was later destroyed by Governor Thomas Hutchinson). Graduated from Harvard College in 1740 and studied law briefly. Went into business, but was not successful. In 1749, married Elizabeth Checkley, who died in 1757, leaving him with two children. Married Elizabeth Wells in 1764. Became one of the most active members of the committee of correspondence of the Sons of Liberty during the Stamp Act crisis. Organized town meetings and wrote pamphlets and articles throughout the period leading up to the Revolution. Frequently corresponded with the Lees of Virginia, John Lamb of New York, and many others. Appointed tax collector of Boston. Elected to the Massachusetts General Court 1765–74. Served with his second cousin John Adams in the Continental Congress from 1774 to 1782 (when he resigned). Supported independence from an early date. Seconded nomination of George Washington as commander-in-chief of Continental Army. Signed the Declaration of Independence. Was a member of the committee that drafted Articles of Confederation in 1776. Member of the Massachusetts state constitutional convention 1779–80. President of the state senate in 1781. Supported suppression of Shays' Rebellion by the militia. Served as a delegate to Massachusetts ratifying convention of 1788, despite the death of his only son on January 17. Reluctant at first to support the Constitution, at the end of the convention threw his influence behind John Hancock's crucial call for amendments subsequent to ratification. Elected lieutenant governor in 1789, defeating Benjamin Lincoln; reelected annually through 1793. Elected governor for three terms, 1794–97. Died in Boston on October 2, 1803.

FISHER AMES (1758–1808)   Born April 9, 1758, in Dedham, Massachusetts, son of Deborah Fisher and Nathaniel Ames (innkeeper, doctor, almanac maker, and publisher). Graduated from Harvard College in 1774. Served briefly with the militia. Taught country school in Dedham area, read Greek and Latin classics, and began study of law on his own in 1777. Entered law offices of William Tudor in Boston, completed his studies, and was admitted to the Suffolk bar in 1781. Returned to Dedham and opened his own practice. Wrote and published the "Lucius Junius Brutus" essays in October 1786 and the "Camillus" essays in March 1787, urging that Shays' Rebellion be put down by armed force and stressing the need for a stronger central government. Represented Dedham in the Massachusetts General Court and in the Massachusetts ratifying convention in 1788, where he supported ratification. Elected to U.S. House of Representatives in 1789, defeating Samuel Adams. Served in the first four Congresses 1789–97, where he supported Hamilton's construction of the Constitution in favor of powerful central government and eloquently defended Jay's Treaty with England in 1796. In July 1792, he married Frances Worthington of Springfield, Massachusetts, with whom he had seven children. One of the most influential Federalists, he considered himself a republican but not a democrat, feeling that the two had little in common. Was horrified by the French Revolution and felt its excesses were caused by too much democracy. Retained political influence after his retirement from Congress, and with George Cabot, Hamilton, and Oliver Wolcott, attempted to elect Charles Cotesworth Pinckney, rather than John Adams, president in 1800. Practiced law, and experimented with the breeding of dairy cattle and hogs and the culture of fruit trees. Became the first non-cleric chosen to be president of Harvard College, though his health compelled him to decline the post. Died at Dedham, July 4, 1808.

JOHN ARMSTRONG (1717–1795)   Born October 13, 1717, in Brookborough Parish, County Fermanagh, Ireland, son of James Armstrong. Married Rebecca Lyon of Enniskillen in the same county (their son, General John

Armstrong, an aide to Mercer and Horatio Gates and the author of the Newburgh Addresses of 1783, married a sister of Robert R. Livingston; served as diplomat under Jefferson and as secretary of war under Madison). They moved to the Cumberland district in Pennsylvania. Armstrong, as surveyor, laid out the town of Carlisle. Served successfully in French and Indian War as captain and lieutenant colonel. Commissioned brigadier general in the Continental Army in May 1776, and then major general and commander of the Pennsylvania militia. Served in the Continental Congress 1779–80. Supported ratification of the Constitution. When Washington wrote him (letter of April 25, 1788), Armstrong was retired and living in Carlisle, Pennsylvania, where he died on March 9, 1795.

ISAAC BACKUS (1724–1806)   Born January 20, 1724, in Norwich, Connecticut, son of Elizabeth Tracy and Samuel Backus (farmer and owner of the Backus Iron Works). Attended seven years of public school in winter. Became a Separatist from the New England standing church in 1746 (a movement influenced by the teachings of Jonathan Edwards); he felt called to preach. Offered ministerial post in established church, but decided instead to form his own Separatist group in the precinct of Titicut (part of the towns of Middleborough and Bridgewater, Massachusetts) in 1748. Married Susanna Mason of Rehoboth in 1749 (with whom he had nine children) and bought a farm in Middleborough in 1750. To support growing family, also acted as agent for brother Elijah's ironworks and sold books when traveling. After controversies among the Separatists over infant baptism, Backus became a Baptist, and was named minister of the Middleborough First Baptist Church in 1756. Continued itinerant preaching throughout New England, mainly on horseback. Appointed a trustee of the first Baptist college, Rhode Island College (later Brown University), founded by James Manning in 1765. In 1767 helped organize the Warren Baptist Association to protect the group from persecution by civil authorities. Supported the Revolution from an early date. Advocated religious liberty and the separation of church and state. Became one of the most important and prolific Baptist leaders in New England, and his parish of Middleborough became the strongest Baptist community in Massachusetts. Delegate from Middleborough to Massachusetts ratifying convention of 1788, where he was one of the few Baptists to support ratification. In 1789, visited Baptist congregations in Virginia and North Carolina. Approved Jefferson and Madison's stand on religious freedom, and voted, as did most New England Baptists, for Jefferson in 1800 and 1804. He died on November 20, 1806.

JOSEPH BARRELL (1739–1804)   Born in Boston, son of Ruth Greene and John Barrell (a wealthy Boston merchant and shipowner) and brother of Nathaniel Barrell. Joseph Barrell went into business in Boston. He was one of the merchants who responded to Benjamin Lincoln's request for a loan of money to be used to suppress Shays' Rebellion. He helped organize the joint stock company that sent the first two American ships to the Pacific Northwest in 1787, one of which, the *Columbia*, was the first Boston ship to travel around the world 1787–90. Barrell made a fortune in the East India trade. He was a director of the Boston branch of the Bank of the United States. In 1792 he moved to Pleasant Hill, a country estate designed by Charles Bulfinch, and devoted himself to experimental agriculture. He was married three times and the father of twenty children.

NATHANIEL BARRELL (1732–1831)   Born in Boston, son of Ruth Greene and John Barrell (wealthy Boston merchant and shipowner). Nathaniel Barrell engaged in business in Portsmouth, New Hampshire, in the 1750s. In 1758, he married Sally Sayward, only child of Jonathan Sayward, with whom he had eleven children. In 1759, he was a lieutenant in General Wolfe's expedition against Quebec. From 1760 to 1763, he was in London, where he was presented to George III. He returned to Portsmouth and served in the provincial council of New Hampshire from 1763 to 1765. In 1764, he adopted the doctrines of Robert Sandeman and John Glass, which stressed obedience to civil authority and forbade taking up arms. During the Stamp Act crisis in 1765, the Sandemanians came under suspicion of being Tories and their church in Portsmouth was destroyed by rioters. Barrell suffered losses, closed his business in Portsmouth, and moved to York, district of Maine, to the estate of his father-in-law, who was also suspected of Tory sympathies. He took no part in political or military affairs during the Revolution. At the town meeting in 1787 to elect delegates to the Massachusetts ratifying convention, Barrell spoke vehemently against ratification, saying "he would sooner lose his Arm than put his Assent to the new proposed Constitution," and was elected one of two delegates from York. His reading of Pelatiah Webster's *The Weakness of Brutus Exposed*, and the efforts of his brother Joseph Barrell, George Thatcher, and others, induced him to change his mind, and he spoke and voted in favor of ratification. He afterwards served one term as representative from York in the General Court in 1794. He died April 3, 1831, at the age of 99.

GEORGE BRYAN (1731–1791)   Born August 11, 1731, in Dublin, Ireland, son of Sarah Dennis and Samuel Bryan (merchant). Immigrated to Philadelphia, Pennsylvania, in 1752. Formed partnership with James Wallace in importing company and in 1755 opened his own company. Married Elizabeth Smith in April 1757. Became associated with the Scots-Irish Presbyterians of Philadelphia, and in 1764 was elected with Thomas Willing to represent that city in the state assembly as members of the Proprietary party, defeating Benjamin Franklin and Joseph Galloway, who were supported by those preferring a Royal charter. Appointed judge of orphans' court and court of common pleas. Delegate to the Stamp Act Congress in 1765. Defeated for reelection to assembly in 1765. Signed non-importation agreements and continued judicial service. Appointed naval officer of the port of Philadelphia in 1776. Elected to Pennsylvania Supreme Executive Council and chosen vice-president, serving 1777–79. Named to commission to settle the boundary dispute between Virginia and Pennsylvania in 1779. Elected to state assembly in 1779 and helped draft and pass act for abolition of slavery. Appointed judge of the supreme court of Pennsylvania in 1780, where he served until his death. Elected to state council of censors in 1784. Supported revocation of the Bank of North America's charter in 1785. Was widely credited with having written the "Centinel" essays, which are now believed to have been written by his son, Samuel. A supporter of the state constitution of 1776 and a leading Antifederalist, he was a delegate to the convention at Harrisburg in September 1788, which recommended amendments to the Constitution. He died January 27, 1791.

SAMUEL BRYAN (1759–1821)   Born September 30, 1759, in Philadelphia, eldest son of Elizabeth Smith and George Bryan, provincial politician and judge of supreme court (see above). Assisted father in business and public affairs and lived in his house in Philadelphia. Appointed secretary of state council of censors in 1784. Served as clerk of state assembly from 1784 to 1786. In October 1787, during Pennsylvania ratifying convention, began secret authorship of "Centinel" columns, published in Philadelphia newspapers *Independent Gazetteer* and *Freeman's Journal*, opposing ratification. Series continued through November 1789; after federal Constitution was adopted, unsuccessfully defended the Pennsylvania constitution of 1776 against the new state constitution, which was ultimately adopted. In December 1790, was unsuccessful candidate for post of clerk of state senate and for appointment as secretary of commonwealth. In July 1795, Governor Thomas Mifflin appointed him state register general. Moved in 1799 to Lancaster, the new state capital. Governor Thomas McKean appointed him state comptroller general in 1801, and removed him from office in 1805. Unsuccessful candidate for collector of port of Philadelphia and state treasurer in 1807. In 1809, moved back to Philadelphia and became register of wills, serving until his death, in Chester County, on October 6, 1821.

CHARLES CARTER, JR. (1733–1796)   Born in King George County, Virginia, in 1733, son of Mary Walker and Colonel Charles Carter of Cleve. Nephew of Colonel Landon Carter of Sabine Hall and brother-in-law of Charles Carter of Corotoman and Shirley. Lived on a plantation at Nanzatico, King George County; later moved to Ludlow, in Stafford County, dividing his time between the plantation and a town house in Fredericksburg. Married Elizabeth Chiswell. Elected to Virginia House of Burgesses from King George County 1756–68 and 1769–71, and from Stafford County 1772–76. Joined the Virginia Association in summer of 1774 with rank of colonel; produced saltpeter during the war. He represented Stafford in the first four Revolutionary state conventions, 1774–76, in the house of delegates, 1776–79 and 1782–84, and was sheriff of Stafford, 1779–82. Elected to the state senate in 1789 and then elected to the council of state.

TENCH COXE (1755–1824)   Born May 22, 1755, in Philadelphia, son of Mary Francis and William Coxe (merchant). Attended College of Philadelphia (now University of Pennsylvania) and studied law. Entered father's business and in 1776 became a partner in firm of Coxe, Furman & Coxe. Resigned from the Pennsylvania militia in 1776, joined the British Army under Howe, and returned with them to Philadelphia in 1777. After the departure of the British, Coxe was arrested by the patriots, paroled, and joined the patriot cause. He was married twice, first to Catherine McCall of Philadelphia, who died without children, and then to Rebecca, daughter of Charles Coxe of New Jersey, with whom he had children. He was a delegate to the Annapolis Convention in 1786 and to the Continental Congress in 1787 and 1788. Wrote pamphlets in support of the proposed Constitution. Appointed assistant secretary of the treasury in 1789. Appointed commissioner of revenue in 1792 and served until his removal by John Adams in 1797. Became a staunch Republican. Appointed purveyor of public supplies by Jefferson in 1803 and held office until it was abolished in 1812. Remained friends with Jefferson and Madison for the rest of his life. Coxe believed in economic development through manufacturing, tariffs, and the free flow of interstate commerce. He encouraged cotton production and manufacturing, and purchased extensive tracts in western Pennsylvania coal fields. He died in Philadelphia on July 16, 1824.

WILLIAM CUSHING (1732–1810)   Born March 1, 1732, in Scituate, Massachusetts, son of Mary Cotton and John Cushing (member of the Massachusetts Governor's Council and a superior court judge). Graduated from Harvard College in 1751 and taught school for a year at Roxbury, Massachusetts. Studied law in the offices of Jeremiah Gridley of Boston and was admitted to the bar in 1755. Practiced law in Scituate until 1760, when he received appointment as register of deeds and judge of probate in the new county of Lincoln, in the district of Maine. In 1772, his father retired as superior court judge in Massachusetts and Cushing took his place. In 1774, when the assembly asked judges to accept their salaries from the colonial treasury rather than from the Crown, Cushing and three other judges accepted; only Chief Justice Oliver refused and was impeached. Cushing married Hannah Phillips of Middletown, Connecticut, in 1774; they had no children. When the Revolutionary council of state took over the government of Massachusetts in 1775, it retained Cushing as a member of the new supreme judicial court. John Adams was appointed chief justice but never served, and Cushing presided as senior justice in his absence until Adams's resignation in 1777. Cushing was appointed chief justice of the Massachusetts Supreme Judicial Court in 1777 and served until 1789. He was a member of the Massachusetts state constitutional convention in 1779–80. He was vice-president of the Massachusetts ratifying convention in 1788 and presided while John Hancock remained indisposed. A Federalist, he supported ratification, and was a presidential elector for Washington in 1789. Appointed by Washington in 1789 associate justice of the United States Supreme Court, where he served until his death. During Jay's mission to England, Cushing acted as chief justice in his absence. When John Jay resigned as chief justice in 1795 and the nomination of Edward Rutledge was rejected by the Senate, Washington offered the post to Cushing, who declined it on grounds of ill health. He died in Scituate on September 13, 1810.

NATHAN DANE (1752–1835)   Born December 29, 1752, in Ipswich, Massachusetts, son of Abigail Burnham and Daniel Dane (farmer). Attended common schools and graduated from Harvard College in 1778. Read law with Judge William Wetmore at Salem and taught school at Beverly, Massachusetts. Married Mrs. Mary Brown in November 1779. Admitted to the bar in 1782. Practiced law in Beverly and was elected to state house of representatives 1782–85. Delegate to the Continental Congress from 1785 to 1788. Helped draft the Northwest Ordinance and prepared the article prohibiting slavery north of the Ohio River. Opposed the Constitution when it was first reported and was unsuccessful candidate for delegate to Massachusetts ratifying convention. By July 1788, when ratification was assured, he supported the Constitution, with subsequent amendments, and his letters to Melancton Smith helped secure ratification in New York. In 1790, 1791, and 1794–97, he was elected to the state senate. In 1812, with Joseph Story and Judge William Prescott, he revised and published the Massachusetts Colonial and Provincial Laws. Presidential elector for DeWitt Clinton in 1812. Delegate to the Hartford Convention in 1814. Elected delegate to state constitutional convention of 1820, but his deafness prevented his attendance. In 1823, he published his *General Abridgment and Digest of American Law, with Occasional Notes and Comments* (8 volumes). Died in Beverly, February 15, 1835.

THOMAS DAWES, JR. (1757–1825)   Born in Boston, Massachusetts, July 8, 1757, son of Hannah Blake and Thomas Dawes (mechanic, architect, politician, and Revolutionary leader). Attended Latin School in Boston and Harvard College, where he graduated in 1777. Published "The Law Given at Sinai: A Poem" (1777) and "An Oration Delivered March 5, 1781," commemorating the Boston Massacre. Member of state constitutional convention of 1780. In 1781, married Peggy Greenleaf, with whom he had sixteen children, including the poet Rufus Dawes (born 1803). Member of the Board of Directors of the Massachusetts Bank. Published "An Oration Delivered July 4, 1787." Delegate from Boston to Massachusetts ratifying convention of 1788, where he supported ratification. Appointed judge of probate for Suffolk County in 1790. Appointed judge of supreme court of Massachusetts in 1792 and served until 1803. A presidential elector in 1792, 1796, and 1800, supported Washington and Adams. Judge of municipal court in Boston from 1803 to 1823. Member of the Academy of Arts and Sciences. Died at Boston July 22, 1825.

JOHN DICKINSON (1732–1808)   Born November 8, 1732, on father's estate Crosiadoré near Trappe, Talbot County, Maryland, son of Mary Cadwalader of Philadelphia and Samuel Dickinson of Talbot County, Maryland. Family moved to estate near Dover, Delaware, in 1740. Dickinson studied law in Philadelphia under John Moland in 1750. Went to the Middle Temple in London to continue his studies from 1753 to 1757. Admitted to the bar in Pennsylvania in 1757. Served in the Delaware state assembly 1760–61 and became speaker. Elected from Philadelphia to Pennsylvania State Assembly in 1762 and 1764. Supported the Proprietary party in Pennsylvania and opposed Franklin's Royalist party; feared a royal charter granted by the British ministry would be worse than proprietary control. Defeated for reelection in 1764. Delegate to the Stamp Act Congress in New York in 1765, where he drafted the Declaration of Rights. Took James Wilson as law student in 1766. Wrote and published the influential series *Letters from a Farmer in Pennsylvania*, 1767–68, in support of the colonial cause. Supported Non-Importation Agreements. Elected to Pennsylvania State Assembly in 1770, and served until 1776. In July 1770, he married Mary, daughter of Isaac Norris (wealthy merchant and leader of the Quaker party of Philadelphia). Was chairman of the Philadelphia committee of correspondence in 1774. Member of the First Continental Congress; served only one week in October 1774, during which time he wrote a petition to the king and the address to the people of Canada. Member of Second Continental Congress in 1775. Wrote second petition to the king, still hoping for reconciliation; also wrote a large part of the "Declaration of the Causes of taking up Arms." Voted against separation from Great Britain and did not sign Declaration of Independence. As chairman of committee wrote June draft of the Articles of Confederation in July. Joined his militia regiment at Elizabethtown, but resigned when he was not reelected to the next Continental Congress. Resigned from Pennsylvania State Assembly in 1776. Elected to Continental Congress from Delaware in November 1776, but declined to serve. When the British Army advanced on Philadelphia, he left for his estate in Delaware. Took part in battle of Brandywine in September 1777. Elected to Continental Congress from Delaware in 1779 and took his seat but resigned that same year. President of state of Delaware 1782–83. President of the Pennsylvania executive council 1783–85. With Benjamin Rush, in 1783 helped found and endow Dickinson College in Carlisle, Pennsylvania, donating extensive library he had inherited from his father-in-law. Delegate from Delaware to the Annapolis Convention in 1786 and Constitutional Convention in Philadelphia in 1787. Wrote "Fabius" letters supporting ratification. Presided at the Delaware constitutional convention in 1792. Received LL.D. from the College of New Jersey (now Princeton) in 1796. Wrote further "Fabius" letters in 1797, supporting American alliance with France. Remained friendly to Jefferson. Published *The Political Writings of John Dickinson* in 1801. Died in Wilmington, Delaware, February 14, 1808.

OLIVER ELLSWORTH (1745–1807)   Born in Windsor, Connecticut, April 29, 1745, son of Jemima Leavitt and David Ellsworth. His father intended him for the ministry and sent him to Yale in 1762. After two years he left Yale for the College of New Jersey (now Princeton), where he graduated in 1766. Studied for the ministry with John Smalley of New Britain for less than a year. Studied law with Matthew Griswold and Jesse Root and taught school. Admitted to the bar in 1771. Married Abigail Wolcott of East Windsor in 1772. Finding it difficult to earn money in law, he supported himself by farming and woodchopping. Moved in 1775 to Hartford, where his practice soon increased. Representative in general assembly in 1775 and 1776. Justice of the peace and state's attorney for Hartford County in 1777. Delegate from Connecticut to the Continental Congress 1777–83. By the time Noah Webster came to study law in his offices in 1779, Ellsworth had between 1,000 and 1,500 cases a year. Member of the governor's council 1780–85. Judge of the Connecticut Superior Court 1785–89. Delegate from Connecticut to the Constitutional Convention in Philadelphia in 1787, although he left before the signing. Strongly supported ratification in the Connecticut ratifying convention. Wrote the Federalist "Landholder" essays, which were widely republished. A member of the U.S. Senate 1789–96, drafted the Judiciary Act of 1789, which set up the federal court system. Strongly supported Hamilton's fiscal policies. After Jay resigned as chief justice, Rutledge's nomination was rejected by the Senate, and Cushing declined the post, Ellsworth was appointed by Washington to be Chief Justice of the U.S. Supreme Court, where he served from 1796 until 1800. Appointed by Adams to the peace commission to France to meet with Napoleon, 1799–1800, he took along his son Oliver Ellsworth, Jr., as secretary. Ellsworth's health was affected by the arduous journey, and he resigned from U.S. Supreme Court in 1800. Returned from Europe to Windsor, Connecticut, in 1801. Served on governor's council 1801–07. Presidential elector for Charles Cotesworth Pinckney in 1804. Became interested in agriculture and contributed a column, "Farmer's Repository," to the *Connecticut Courant*. Died in Windsor on November 26, 1807.

WILLIAM FINDLEY (1741–1821)   Born in 1741 of Scots-Irish Presbyterian parents in northern Ireland. Attended parish schools. Immigrated in 1762, first to Philadelphia, then to the Scots-Irish settlement near Waynesboro (now Franklin County), Pennsylvania. Worked as a weaver and taught school. Married in 1769 and bought a farm. During the Revolution, he entered the army as a private and rose to the rank of captain. After the war he moved to Westmoreland County to a farm near present-day Latrobe. Member of the Pennsylvania council of censors in 1783. Represented county in general assembly in 1785 and 1786. Delegate from Westmoreland County to Pennsylvania ratifying convention in 1787, where he vigorously opposed ratification. Attended the Antifederalist convention in Harrisburg in 1788. Delegate to state constitutional convention of 1789–90, where he chaired the drafting committee, and supported Wilson's plan for direct election of the executive and both houses. Member state supreme executive council in 1789 and 1790. Elected to state house of representatives in 1790–91. Elected to U.S. House of Representatives for four terms, 1791–99. Consistently represented interests of frontier communities and was instrumental in establishing first Ways and Means Committee. Played prominent role in mediating the Whiskey Rebellion of 1794 and met with Washington in Carlisle. Published *History of the Insurrection in the Four Western Counties of Pennsylvania* in 1796. Elected to state senate 1799–1803. Elected to U.S. House of Representatives seven more terms, 1803–17, where he supported policies of Jefferson and Madison. Died at Unity Township near Greensburg, Pennsylvania, April 5, 1821.

BENJAMIN FRANKLIN (1706–1790) Born January 17, 1706, in Boston, son of Abiah Folger and Josiah Franklin (a candle and soap maker who had emigrated from England in 1683). Attended Boston Grammar School 1714–15 and George Brownell's English school 1715–16. Worked in his father's shop, and was apprenticed to his brother James Franklin's printing business in 1718, where he worked on newspapers *The Boston Gazette* and *New-England Courant*, which published his anonymous "Silence Dogood" letters. In 1723, he ran away to New York, but failed to find work and moved on to Philadelphia. Encouraged by Governor William Keith to open a printing shop, he sailed for London in 1724 to purchase materials. In London, he worked as a typesetter and published *A Dissertation on Liberty and Necessity, Pleasure and Pain* in 1725. Returned to Philadelphia in 1726 and worked as clerk, bookkeeper, and printer. Bought newspaper *The Pennsylvania Gazette* in 1729, which became most widely read paper in colonies. Published *A Modest Enquiry into the Nature and Necessity of a Paper Currency* in 1729. Son William Franklin born out of wedlock to unidentified mother around 1730. Formed common-law union with Deborah Read Rogers, who had been deserted by her husband and with whom he had a son (died 1736) and daughter. Became Freemason, organized Library Company of Philadelphia, published German-language newspaper *Philadelphische Zeitung*, and *Poor Richard's Almanack*. Proposed first fire protection society and system of night watchmen for Philadelphia. Printed George Whitfield's journals and sermons, paper currency of Pennsylvania and New Jersey, and *General Magazine* (first in colonies). Designed Franklin stove in winter of 1740–41. Published *A Proposal for Promoting Useful Knowledge* in 1743, leading to founding of American Philosophical Society. Experimented with electricity beginning in 1745, and proved that lightning was form of electricity in 1750. Elected to Common Council of Philadelphia in 1748, alderman in 1751, and member of Pennsylvania Assembly in 1751. Appointed deputy postmaster general of North America in 1753. Negotiated treaty at Carlisle with Ohio Indians. Drew first known American political cartoon, a snake cut in sections with legend "Join or Die," in 1754. Attended Albany Congress on frontier defense and proposed a plan for colonial union. Arranged supplies and transport for General Braddock's expedition against Fort Duquesne, drafted militia bill passed by assembly in 1755, and organized frontier defenses. Elected member of Royal Society of London in 1756. Appointed Pennsylvania agent to England in 1757, and sailed to London, where his acquaintances eventually included David Hume, Samuel Johnson, Captain James Cook, Lord Granville, Joseph Priestley, James Boswell, and Adam Smith. Returned to Philadelphia in 1762. Denounced massacre of Christian Indians in Lancaster County by "Paxton Boys," who subsequently marched on Philadelphia, were met by Franklin, and dispersed. Elected speaker of assembly in 1764. Helped organize opposition to Stamp Act. Defeated for reelection to assembly in 1764, and was appointed colonial agent in London. Philadelphia house threatened by mob protesting Stamp Act. Examined by House of Commons regarding colonial resistance in 1766, and his answers helped lead to repeal of Stamp Act. Became colonial agent for Georgia, New Jersey, and Massachusetts. In 1772,

he clandestinely acquired letters of Massachusetts governor Thomas Hutchinson and lieutenant governor Peter Oliver recommending repressive measures
and relayed them to Thomas Cushing, who laid them before provincial assembly, exacerbating crisis in Boston. Involved in several unsuccessful attempts to
reconcile colonies with Britain. Returned to Philadelphia in 1775 and was chosen
delegate to Second Continental Congress, where he was active on many committees, including the one that drafted Declaration of Independence. Advocated proportional representation in debates over Articles of Confederation.
Named commissioner to France (with Silas Deane and Arthur Lee) and assumed post in December 1776. Negotiated French aid to colonies and treaty
of alliance. Became sole minister to France in September 1778. Responding
to Vergennes' complaints that John Adams's letters to him were insulting,
sent copies of their correspondence to Congress in 1780, contributing to
Adams's hostility to Franklin and to France. Appointed (with Jefferson, John
Adams, John Jay, and Henry Laurens) to negotiate peace with Great Britain
in 1781; treaty was eventually signed September 3, 1783. Negotiated treaties
with European powers, including Prussia (signed July 9, 1785). Returned to
Philadelphia in September 1785 and was elected president of Pennsylvania Supreme Executive Council. Named president of Pennsylvania Abolition Society
in 1787. Served as Pennsylvania delegate to Constitutional Convention in Philadelphia, where he was both an active participant and a conciliating presence.
Retired as president of state executive council in 1788, ending public career.
Continued efforts for abolition of slavery, including petitions presented to
Congress in 1789 and 1790. Died in Philadelphia on April 17, 1790.

ELBRIDGE GERRY (1744–1814)   Born July 17, 1744, at Marblehead, Massachusetts, son of Elizabeth Greenleaf of Boston and Thomas Gerry (English
shipmaster who settled in America and became a merchant). Graduated from
Harvard College in 1762. Joined his father and two older brothers in successful shipping business in Marblehead. Elected representative to the Massachusetts General Court in 1772. Influenced by Samuel Adams and became active
in state politics. When the Boston port was closed, used Marblehead as base
to receive supplies for the beleaguered city. Elected to the provincial congress
in 1774–76. Helped raise troops and procure munitions and supplies. Delegate with John Adams to the Second Continental Congress in 1776. Favored
independence before arriving, and signed the Declaration of Independence.
Maintained friendships with Samuel and John Adams and with Jefferson and
Madison even during the extremely partisan 1790s. Delegate to Continental
Congress 1776–81 and 1782–85, and was an active member except for the years
1780–83, when he returned to trade and privateering and served in the state
assembly. In January 1786, he married Ann Thompson, daughter of a New
York merchant, with whom he had three sons and four daughters who survived him. Retired from business with a comfortable income from invest-
ments in government securities and real estate. Delegate from Massachusetts
to Constitutional Convention in Philadelphia in 1787, where he actively participated but refused to sign or support the Constitution, which he thought

gave the federal government too much power. Gerry was not elected to the Massachusetts ratifying convention, but his advice was solicited by that body and by the state legislature. Elected to the U.S. House of Representatives in the first and second Congresses and served 1789–93. Presidential elector for John Adams in 1796. Appointed by Adams in 1797 to diplomatic mission to France, with Marshall and C. C. Pinckney, which led to XYZ Affair. Remained in France until 1798, after the other two returned home in disgust. Unsuccessful Democratic candidate for governor of Massachusetts in 1801, 1802, and 1803. Presidential elector for Jefferson in 1804. Elected governor of Massachusetts in 1810 and 1811. Defeated for a third term after extreme redistricting of state that gave rise to term "gerrymandering." Elected vice-president of the United States under Madison in 1812, served until his death in Washington, D.C., on November 23, 1814.

CHRISTOPHER GORE (1758–1827)   Born in Boston, Massachusetts, September 21, 1757, son of Frances Pinkney and John Gore (artisan who was prosecuted and banished as a Loyalist in 1776 and restored to citizenship in 1787). Attended Boston Latin school and Harvard College, graduating in 1776 (in class with George Thatcher). In April 1776, joined artillery regiment of brother-in-law Thomas Craft; commissioned an officer in October. Worked as regimental clerk until 1778. Studied law with Judge John Lowell and passed the bar in 1778. Established lucrative practice. Married Rebecca, daughter of Boston financier Edward Payne, in November 1785 (they had no children). Made fortune in government certificate and bond speculation. Was a director of the Massachusetts Bank 1785–92. Delegate from Boston to Massachusetts ratifying convention in 1788. Elected to state house of representatives from Boston in 1788 and 1789. Appointed first U.S. Attorney for Massachusetts in 1789 and served until 1796. Supported policies of Hamilton and became a director of the Boston branch of the Bank of the United States 1792–94. Appointed in 1796 (with William Pinkney) commissioner to England under Jay Treaty to negotiate war claims, and remained in England until 1804, serving as chargé d'affaires in 1803 and 1804. Accepted Daniel Webster as law student and clerk, and sponsored his admission to bar in 1805. Built fine country seat, Gore Place, in Waltham, Massachusetts, in 1804 (retired there in 1816), maintaining a house in Boston as well. Elected to state senate for 1806 and 1807 and to state house of representatives in 1808. Led Massachusetts fight against the Embargo Act. Elected governor of Massachusetts in 1809. Defeated for reelection in 1810 by Elbridge Gerry, and was unsuccessful candidate again in 1811. His tour of the state in 1809 in richly upholstered open carriage accompanied by liveried coachmen and outriders was cited as one cause of his defeat. Invested money in bridges, locks, and canals. Filled vacant seat in U.S. Senate from 1813 to 1816, when he resigned. Vigorously attacked the War of 1812 and Madison's administration. Presidential elector in 1816 for Federalist ticket of King and Howard. Overseer and fellow of Harvard College from 1810 to 1820. Died March 1, 1827, in Boston, leaving bulk of estate (nearly $100,000) to Harvard College.

ALEXANDER HAMILTON (1755–1804) Born January 11, 1755 (Hamilton later said he was born in 1757), in Nevis, in the West Indies, son of Rachel Fawcett Lavien (daughter of a French Huguenot physician and wife of John Lavien, a German merchant from whom she was divorced in 1758) and James Hamilton (younger son of the Laird of Cambuskeith, The Grange, Ayrshire, Scotland). Moved to St. Croix in 1765; father deserted mother, and she opened small store to support the family (she died in 1769). Hamilton clerked in counting house of Cruger and Beekman, 1766–72, and so impressed his employers and the Reverend Hugh Knox (who published letter by Hamilton about hurricane in 1772) that they sent him to America in October 1772 to obtain an education. Stayed with the William Livingston family while studying at Dr. Barber's preparatory school in Elizabethtown, New Jersey. President Witherspoon of the College of New Jersey (now Princeton) refused his request to take an accelerated course, and he entered King's College (now Columbia) in 1773. Defended Boston Tea Party in speech and in newspaper and became pamphleteer for the patriot cause. Appointed captain of artillery by the provincial congress of New York, in March 1776. Campaigned in Long Island, Manhattan, and New Jersey. He quickly won the confidence of Washington and became the general's aide in 1777 with a promotion to lieutenant colonel. Took part in battles at Brandywine, Germantown, and Monmouth. With John Laurens, was witness against General Charles Lee at his court martial. Wintered with army at Valley Forge and Morristown. Acted as interpreter between Washington and French officers. Married Elizabeth, daughter of General Philip Schuyler, in December 1780. Given a command under Lafayette in 1781 and led successful attack on British redoubt at Yorktown. An early advocate of a strong national government, wrote pamphlets and sent letters to the Continental Congress suggesting plans for a national bank and a continental convention to strengthen government. Studied law in Albany under several lawyers, including Robert Troup, who became a lifelong friend, and passed the bar in early summer 1782. Appointed receiver for continental taxes for New York in 1782. Elected to the Continental Congress 1782–83, where he worked closely with Madison and superintendent of finance Robert Morris. Helped start and became a director of the Bank of New York in 1784 (it began operations immediately, but was not chartered until 1792). Elected to the New York Assembly in 1786. Attended Annapolis Convention on interstate commerce, where he drafted the call for a Constitutional Convention to meet in Philadelphia in May 1787. Elected delegate, with John Lansing and Robert Yates (both of whom opposed strong national government), to the Constitutional Convention in Philadelphia in 1787, where he argued for strong national government modeled on the English system with a president and senate elected for life. Signed Constitution. As "Publius," with James Madison and John Jay, published a series of articles called *The Federalist*, defending the Constitution. Elected to Continental Congress in early 1788, and to the New York ratifying convention in Poughkeepsie, where he continued his advocacy. Appointed secretary of the treasury by Washington in 1789 with support of Madison and Robert Morris. Began vigorous and controversial program for assumption of state debts, creation of national bank, and support for manufactures. Dismayed by Madison's opposition to the assumption bill, finally made a deal with Jefferson and Madison to have the capital located on the Potomac in exchange for their help. Became a major figure in Washington's administration. Awarded honorary degrees from Dartmouth, Harvard, and Columbia, and a new college was named after him. Began bitter rivalry with Thomas Jefferson in cabinet. Accompanied Washington to western Pennsylvania in 1794 and took leading role in suppression of Whiskey Rebellion. Defended Jay's Treaty with England in 1795, though not happy with all its provisions, and was attacked by hostile crowds. Retired as secretary of the treasury in January 1795 for financial reasons. Continued active in politics, advising Washington and helping draft his "Farewell Address." In 1796 tried to influence election vote to make Thomas Pinckney president rather than John Adams. In autumn 1797, published confession of adulterous affair to establish that he had not indulged in any financial wrongdoing while secretary of the treasury. Was consulted on all policies by members of Adams's cabinet, Thomas Pickering, James McHenry, and Oliver Wolcott. When war tensions increased with France, was appointed major general, second in command to Washington, despite Adams's protest. Angry attack, *Letter from Alexander Hamilton concerning the Public Conduct and Character of John Adams, Esq., President of the United States*, published in newspapers in 1800 to Federalists' dismay. Returned to law practice when war threat was over. Son Philip killed in a duel in November 1801 fought with a Jeffersonian lawyer. Used influence to prevent Aaron Burr from becoming governor of New York and was challenged to duel by him. Accepted challenge and was shot by Burr in Weehawken, New Jersey, on July 11, 1804. Died in New York City on July 12, 1804.

JOHN HANCOCK (1737–1793)   Born January 12, 1737, in Braintree, Massachusetts, son of Mary Hawke and John Hancock (pastor of the Congregational church at Braintree). His father died in 1748, and Hancock was adopted by his childless uncle, Thomas Hancock (Boston's wealthiest merchant). Graduated from Harvard in 1754 and entered his uncle's business. In 1760, he went to England for a year to learn British mercantile practices. Became partner in the firm in 1763, and inherited the business when his uncle died in 1764. Elected to provincial house of representatives from Boston in 1765, with James Otis, Samuel Adams, and Thomas Cushing. In 1768, he was accused of smuggling wine, and was successfully defended by John Adams. Subsequently allied himself with Samuel Adams and devoted himself almost entirely to Revolutionary politics. Served in Massachusetts General Court through 1772. Elected in 1774 to the first provincial congress and was elected president of it. Delegate to Second Continental Congress in 1775, elected its president after resignation of Peyton Randolph. One of two Americans (Samuel Adams was the other) exempted from British amnesty offer in 1775. In August 1775, married Dorothy Quincy, with whom he had one son who died in childhood (1787). Reelected president of Continental Congress in 1776, served until his resignation in October 1777. First signer of the Declaration of Independence. Member of Massachusetts state constitutional convention in 1780. Enormously popular in Massachusetts, he was elected the state's first governor in 1780, and reelected to four successive terms through 1785. Resigned as governor in January 1785, but was elected again in 1787 and reelected the next six years. President of the Massachusetts ratifying convention in 1788, though he neither attended nor revealed how he would vote until the convention's final week. When he arrived he urged ratification with amendments to be considered once the new government was in place. Hancock died in office as governor on October 8, 1793.

WILLIAM HEATH (1737–1814)   Born March 2, 1737, in Roxbury, Massachusetts, son of Elizabeth Payson and Samuel Heath (farmer). He married Sarah Lockwood of Cambridge in April 1759. Heath turned his attention to military affairs as the crisis between Britain and the colonies escalated and in 1770 wrote a series of newspaper essays urging the people of Massachusetts to revive their militias. In 1761, and from 1771 to 1774, Heath served in the Massachusetts General Court and was later a member of the provincial congress. He was appointed brigadier general of militia in February 1775 and was promoted to major general at Bunker Hill. In 1776 he was appointed major general in the Continental Army. After the war, Heath returned to his farm in Roxbury, and helped organize the Society of the Cincinnati. He was elected delegate from Roxbury to the Massachusetts ratifying convention, where he supported ratification. He served in the state senate 1791–92, and became a judge of probate. Elected lieutenant governor in 1806, but declined to serve. Voted for Jefferson as presidential elector in 1804 and for DeWitt Clinton in 1812. He died January 24, 1814.

PATRICK HENRY (1736–1799)   Born May 29, 1736, in Hanover County, Virginia, son of Sarah Winston and John Henry, from Aberdeen, Scotland (vestryman of the Anglican church, justice of the peace, colonel in the militia, and owner of a plantation). Studied Latin with his father and enjoyed reading Latin classics. Became storekeeper in Hanover County. Married Sarah Shelton in 1754, and the couple worked a 300-acre plantation. When their house and furniture burned, Henry again tried storekeeping unsuccessfully in 1757. He began study of law and was admitted to the bar after little training, in 1760. Continued study on his own and became one of Virginia's foremost lawyers. Became a freeholder in Louisa County and was elected from that district to the Virginia House of Burgesses in 1765. During Stamp Act crisis, took active role in overcoming objections of representatives from Tidewater region. From 1765 to 1770, continued to gain influence and exercise power in the assembly. Delegate from Virginia to the First Continental Congress in 1774. Helped organize and took part in the Revolutionary conventions in Virginia 1774–76, delivering his famous speech with the words "give me liberty or give me death" to the state convention in March 1775. In April 1775, when he learned that Lord Dunmore, the governor, had seized the ammunition of the colony at Williamsburg, he delayed his attendance at the Second

Continental Congress, marched on Williamsburg with militia from Hanover, and returned the munitions to colonial control. In 1776, took part in drafting of new Virginia constitution and passage of resolution authorizing Continental Congress to declare independence. Elected governor of Virginia for three terms 1776–79 and two terms 1784–86. Though they had earlier been friends, Henry turned against Thomas Jefferson after Jefferson's two terms as governor (1779–81). After death of his first wife (in 1775), married Dorothy Dandridge. Following the war, Henry favored forgiving and restoring the Loyalists in Virginia and opposed Madison's effort to separate church and state. Declined appointment to the Constitutional Convention in Philadelphia in 1787. Delegate to Virginia ratifying convention in 1788, where he strongly opposed ratification. His influence in the state legislature gave him control over the election of senators from Virginia in 1788, and he prevented James Madison's election to the Senate and made his election to the House of Representatives difficult. Argued in the courts against payment of British foreign debts. In 1791, the father of many children and grandchildren and not in good health, he retired from politics and law to his new plantation, Red Hill, on the Staunton River. Declined to serve in the U.S. Senate, as Washington's secretary of state, and as chief justice of the Supreme Court. Became increasingly conservative and hostile to Jefferson, Madison, and many of his old supporters. Elected as a Federalist to the Virginia House of Delegates in 1799, but died before serving, on June 6, 1799.

JEREMIAH HILL (1747–1820)   Born April 30, 1747, in Biddeford, district of Maine, son of Sarah Smith and Jeremiah Hill (sawmill owner). Entered Harvard College in 1766; was expelled in 1768 for breaking a tutor's windows. Returned to Biddeford and in 1772 married Mary Emery, with whom he had at least twelve children. In May 1775, he was captain in Colonel Scammon's Maine regiment, and according to tradition he commanded a company at Bunker Hill. Appointed captain in the 18th Continental Infantry in 1776 and served with it two years, including at the battle of Saratoga. In 1779, he was appointed adjutant general under Solomon Lovell of the expedition of Massachusetts militia against the British outpost at Castine, Maine, on the Penobscot River. After storming outlying British batteries, the expedition was defeated by a British fleet with reinforcements. Remained in the army until the end of 1783 and became a member of the Society of the Cincinnati. Held various town offices in Biddeford and was justice of the peace for York County. Elected representative to the Massachusetts General Court in 1787 and 1788. Hill afterwards became collector of impost and excise for York, collector of the port of Biddeford and Saco, inspector of the port, collector of revenue, and collector of customs. He was also appointed judge of quorum and court of common pleas. Elected representative from Biddeford in the Massachusetts General Court in 1809 and 1812–14. Died at Biddeford on June 11, 1820.

ABRAHAM HOLMES (1754–1839)   Born June 9, 1754, in Rochester, Massachusetts. Associated with patriotic and Antifederalist Otis family of Barnstable and Freeman family of Sandwich. Delegate from Rochester to Massachusetts ratifying convention in 1788, where he opposed ratification. Self-educated in law, Holmes served as president of local court of sessions. Admitted to the Plymouth County bar in 1800. Delegate to the Massachusetts state constitutional convention of 1820. Member of the Massachusetts Executive Council from 1821 to 1823. Died September 7, 1839. Father of Charles Jarvis Holmes (1790–1859), Massachusetts lawyer and politician.

FRANCIS HOPKINSON (1737–1791)   Born October 2, 1737, in Philadelphia, son of English parents Mary Johnson and Thomas Hopkinson (successful lawyer, political and civic leader). First graduate of College of Philadelphia (now University of Pennsylvania) in 1757. Learned to play harpsichord in 1754 and performed in public by 1757. Composed music and wrote poems. Studied law under provincial attorney general Benjamin Chew and was admitted to the bar of the supreme court of Pennsylvania in 1761. Appointed collector of customs at Salem, New Jersey, in 1763. Visited England in 1766 to seek political advancement through influence of friends and relatives, but was unsuccessful. Became friends there with Benjamin Franklin and Benjamin West and returned in 1767. In 1768, married Ann Borden of Bordentown, New Jersey. Opened shop for English imported dry goods, and became collector of customs at New Castle, Delaware. Moved to Bordentown, New Jersey, and resumed successful practice of law. Member of provincial council 1774–76. Delegate from New Jersey to the Continental Congress in 1776. Signed Declaration of Independence. Designed state seal of New Jersey, other seals, and the American flag in 1777. During the Revolution he wrote pamphlets and political satires and served on various war boards. Judge of the admiralty court of Pennsylvania 1779–89. Member of the New Jersey ratifying convention of 1787, where he strongly supported ratification. Organized parade and ratification celebration in Philadelphia on July 4, 1788. Appointed judge of United States District Court for Eastern Pennsylvania in 1789. Died suddenly on May 9, 1791.

SAMUEL HUNTINGTON (1731–1796)   Born July 3, 1731, in Windham, Connecticut, son of Mehetable Thurston and Nathaniel Huntington (farmer and clothier). Apprenticed to a cooper at sixteen. Studied Latin and law on his own. Admitted to the bar in 1758 and began practice in Norwich, Connecticut. Married Martha Devotion in 1761; they had no children of their own and adopted two children of his brother Joseph, who had married the sister of his wife. Represented Norwich in the Connecticut General Assembly in 1765. Appointed king's attorney for Connecticut and justice of the peace 1765–75. Elected in 1775 to the upper house, where he served until 1784. Appointed judge of superior court in 1775, appointed chief justice in 1784. Delegate from Connecticut to the Continental Congress 1776–84. Signed Declaration of Independence. Elected president of Congress when Jay left on diplomatic mission in 1779, and served until resigning the post in 1781. Lieutenant governor of Connecticut in 1785. Governor of Connecticut 1786–96.

Member of the Connecticut ratifying convention, where he supported ratification. Served as presidential elector in 1789 and 1792. Died at Norwich on January 5, 1796.

JAMES IREDELL (1751–1799)   Born October 5, 1751, in Lewes, England, son of Margaret McCulloh and Francis Iredell (Bristol merchant). Iredell went to Edenton, North Carolina, as British comptroller of customs in 1768. Studied law with Samuel Johnston and married Johnston's sister, Hannah, in July 1773. Admitted to the bar in 1771. Collector of the port of Edenton 1774–76. Wrote articles in support of the American cause, but hoped that differences could be resolved and there would be no need to separate from England. Drafted law establishing state court system in 1776. Appointed judge of superior court in 1777. Elected state attorney general 1779–81. Elected to the council of state in 1787, which appointed him to compile and revise the state's laws, a work he completed in 1791. A fervent Federalist, Iredell wrote "Marcus" letters supporting adoption of the Constitution. Delegate from Edenton to North Carolina ratifying convention of 1788, where he led unsuccessful effort for ratification. In 1790, he owned over 4,500 acres of land and eight slaves. Appointed in 1790 by Washington to the U.S. Supreme Court, with responsibility to ride the southern circuit. Took James Wilson into his home when Wilson was trying to salvage his financial status and was hiding from creditors. Iredell's health was weakened by the strenuous work and hard circuit traveling; he died at his home in Edenton on October 20, 1799.

WILLIAM IRVINE (1741–1804)   Born November 3, 1741, near Enniskillen, County Fermanagh, Ulster province, Ireland, to a family of Scots descent. Educated at Trinity College, Dublin. Studied medicine and served as surgeon on British ship during Seven Years War. Moved to Carlisle, Pennsylvania, in 1764, where he practiced medicine and married Anne Callender. Member of the provincial convention in Philadelphia in 1774 that declared for American independence. At the start of the Revolution, he raised a regiment and was appointed colonel. Participated in expedition against Canada. Captured at Trois Riviéres and paroled; officially exchanged in May 1778. Participated in battle of Monmouth in June 1778. Appointed brigadier general in the Continental Army in 1779, served until 1783. Received land grant from Pennsylvania in 1785 as reward for his military service. Elected delegate from Pennsylvania to Continental Congress 1786–88. Supported adoption of the Constitution. Delegate to Pennsylvania state constitutional convention 1789–90. Elected to U.S. House of Representatives, served 1793–95. As major general and commander of state troops, he helped suppress the Whiskey Rebellion in western Pennsylvania in 1794. Appointed superintendent of military stores at Philadelphia in 1800. President of the Pennsylvania Society of the Cincinnati from 1801 until his death. Died in Philadelphia on July 29, 1804.

CHARLES JARVIS (1748–1807)   Born October 26, 1748, in Boston, Massachusetts, son of Sarah Church and Leonard Jarvis (wealthy merchant). Graduated from Harvard College in 1766. Studied medicine with Dr. William Lee Perkins and Dr. Joseph Gardner in Boston and continued his studies in London. Returned from England by 1769 and married Mary Clapham. After her death, he married Mary Pepperrell Sparhawk of Kittery in 1773. Became a distinguished doctor. Active member of the Sons of Liberty during the 1770s. Allied with Samuel Adams and John Hancock, although many of his in-laws and relatives were Loyalists. Active in civic and political affairs during the Revolution. Member of the Massachusetts state constitutional convention. Delegate from Boston to Massachusetts ratifying convention of 1788, where he supported ratification, though he later became distrustful of men in power. In 1788, he began long career as justice of the peace, and was elected to the state house of representatives 1788–97. Called "the bald eagle of the Boston seat" because of his baldness and sharpness in debate. He refused to stand for the first congressional elections. In 1794, he ran unsuccessfully for Congress as a Republican against his former protégé Fisher Ames. Attacked the Jay Treaty in 1795. Retired from state house of representatives in 1797, but was elected again in 1801 and defeated for reelection in 1802. At the urging of Samuel Adams, Jefferson appointed Jarvis physician and surgeon at the Charlestown Marine Hospital in 1802. He died in Boston, November 15, 1807.

JOHN JAY (1745–1829)   Born December 12, 1745, in New York City, son of Mary Van Cortlandt of Dutch ancestry and Peter Jay (wealthy merchant of French Huguenot descent). Soon after his birth, the family moved to farm at Rye, Westchester County. Four older brothers and sisters suffered mental or physical problems. Tutored at home and attended New Rochelle grammar school taught by French-speaking pastor of the Huguenot church, Peter Stouppe. Graduated from King's College (now Columbia University) in 1764, and became close friend of classmate Robert R. Livingston. Studied law in offices of Benjamin Kissam and was admitted to the bar in 1768. Entered into partnership with Livingston until 1771. Clerk of boundary commission to settle dispute between New Jersey and New York 1769–70. In April 1774, he married Sarah Van Brugh, daughter of William Livingston, an early supporter of colonial cause. In May 1774, as member of committee to draft response to closing of Boston port, called for meeting of delegates from all colonies to consult on course of action. Elected delegate from New York to First Continental Congress, traveled to Philadelphia in September 1774 with William Livingston, delegate from New Jersey. Signed the Association Agreement on non-importation and wrote *Address to the People of Great Britain*. In New York, he worked on committees to enforce the Association Agreements, organized a convention to elect delegates to the Second Continental Congress when the provincial assembly refused. Elected to both Revolutionary provincial congress and appointed to committee of safety. Attended Second Continental Congress in 1775 still hoping for reconciliation. Took active part in Congress, supporting measures for defense and apprehension of Tories. Served on secret committee of foreign correspondence and discouraged states from sending further petitions to the king. Commissioned colonel of regiment of state militia. Left Continental Congress in late April 1776 to return to New York because of the ill health of his wife and parents. Elected to New York provincial congress and authorized state delegation to sign Declaration of Independence. During British invasion of New York, served with Gilbert Livingston, Robert R. Livingston, and Robert Yates on secret committee to defend Hudson River from British naval incursions. Chairman of secret committee for detecting conspiracies, served with various members, including Melancton Smith. Moved family from Rye to Fishkill, New York, as British and Loyalists approached. Helped draft New York state constitution in 1777. Elected member of state council of safety. Appointed state chief justice in 1777 (resigned in August 1779). Elected president of Continental Congress in December 1778. Appointed by Congress minister plenipotentiary to Spain in September 1779, took his family with him and served from January 1780 to May 1782, though frustrated by lack of progress. Sent in June 1782 to join Franklin in Paris to negotiate terms of peace with England (other American commissioners, John Adams and Henry Laurens, arrived much later; Adams became a strong Jay supporter and helped with final details). The delegation did not follow Congress's orders to negotiate treaty under aegis of France and carried on the negotiations with England alone; resulting treaty was more favorable than expected, but Robert R. Livingston, secretary of foreign affairs in Congress, was unhappy that France had not been more involved in negotiations, and friendship with him cooled. Visited England before returning home in 1784 to find that Continental Congress had appointed him secretary of foreign affairs, a position he held 1785–89. He reorganized and strengthened the office; angered southern states when he recommended signing a treaty with Spain that would give up free navigation of the Mississippi for a period of 25 years. In 1785, he was a founder and became first president of the New York Society for Promoting the Manumission of Slaves, with Alexander Hamilton as one of its counselors. Jay had owned slaves, which he purchased and set free after a certain period. Convinced by diplomatic problems under the Confederation that a stronger central government was necessary. Wrote five of the *Federalist* papers. Supported ratification in the New York ratifying convention, and helped win over some Antifederalists by agreeing to write a circular letter to other states in support of a convention to propose amendments. Appointed by Washington as the first Chief Justice of the U.S. Supreme Court in 1789. Continued to act as secretary of foreign affairs in the new government until Jefferson's return from France in 1790. Received honorary LL.D. degree from Harvard College in 1790. Unsuccessful Federalist candidate for governor of New York in 1792, when accusations of fraud were made against Clinton. In April 1794, when war with England seemed likely, he was appointed minister plenipotentiary to England. Returned to United States in 1795 after signing treaty that was strongly attacked by many Americans. Resigned as Chief Justice in June 1795. Elected governor of New York and served two terms 1795–1801. In April 1799 signed bill for emancipation of slaves. Retired to his farm at Bedford, Westchester County, 40 miles from New York City; he was often consulted on matters of policy by many old friends and occasionally took part in meetings with them. He died on May 17, 1829, the last survivor of those who had attended the First Continental Congress.

THOMAS JEFFERSON (1743–1826)   Born April 13, 1743, at Shadwell, Goochland County (now Albemarle), Virginia, son of Jane Randolph and Peter Jefferson (surveyor, landowner, mapmaker, and magistrate). After death of mother's cousin, William Randolph, his father managed Randolph plantation at Tuckahoe on James River. Attended plantation school at Tuckahoe and Latin school conducted by the Reverend William Douglas at Shadwell from 1752 to 1758. After father died in 1757, attended school of the Reverend James Maury in Fredericksville 1758–60. Attended College of William and Mary from 1760 to 1762 and studied with mathematics professor William Small. In 1762, began study of law under George Wythe. Inherited 2,750 acres from father's estate in 1764. Admitted to Virginia bar in 1767 and began practice of law. In 1769, began building Monticello, country seat near Charlottesville, Virginia. Elected to house of burgesses from Albemarle County in 1769, and served until its dissolution in 1776. In 1772, he married Martha Wayles Skelton, with whom he had six children, four of whom died in childhood. In 1773, inherited large tracts of land and large debts from estate of father-in-law, John Wayles. Active in organizing resistance to British authority and committees of correspondence, and in 1774 published *A Summary View of the Rights of British America*. In 1775 and 1776, served as Virginia delegate to Continental Congress in Philadelphia, where he drafted the Declaration of Independence, adopted July 4, 1776. He also drafted a new state constitution for Virginia, which was not adopted. Elected to Virginia House of Delegates from Albemarle County in 1776, served until 1779. Elected governor of Virginia in 1779; reelected in 1780. During Benedict Arnold's invasion of Virginia in 1781, he organized colonial defenses and narrowly escaped capture by British troops under General Tarleton (his conduct was later investigated and exonerated by house of delegates). His wife died in 1782. Appointed by Congress commissioner to negotiate peace with Great Britain in 1782, but because of extreme cold and ice, was unable to leave Philadelphia to take up post. Served in Continental Congress 1783–84. Appointed in 1784 to join John Adams and Benjamin Franklin as minister to negotiate treaties with European powers. In 1785, succeeded Franklin as minister to France (post held until 1789) and published *Notes on the State of Virginia* in Paris. He received a copy of proposed Constitution in November 1787 and supported its ratification, but urged Madison and others to add a bill of rights. Published *Observations on the Whale-Fishery* in 1788. Attended sessions of Estates General at Versailles, and witnessed riots and massacres in Paris July–September 1789. Returned to America in 1790 and was appointed first secretary of state in Washington's administration. Opposed formation of national bank as unconstitutional in 1791, but Washington was convinced by secretary of treasury Alexander Hamilton to sign bill chartering it. In 1792, private note referring to "political heresies" of Vice-President John Adams was published without authorization as preface to Thomas Paine's *Rights of Man*. Disputes with Hamilton continued over removal of British troops from western posts, continuation of treaty obligations with French republic, and retaliation against discriminatory British trade policies. Resigned as secretary of state at the end of 1793 and returned to farming at Monticello. Denounced Jay's Treaty in 1795 and was seen as the leader of opposition to Federalist policies. Elected vice-president of the United States in 1796, finishing second to John Adams in electoral balloting. In 1797, he assumed leadership of Republican party. In 1798, he worked to prevent war with France following revelations of XYZ Affair and drafted Kentucky Resolutions (passed by Kentucky legislature) declaring Alien and Sedition Acts unconstitutional. In 1800, he ran the first national campaign for president between organized political parties and defeated John Adams. When Republican vice-presidential candidate Aaron Burr received the same number of electoral votes as Jefferson, election was thrown into the House of Representatives, which elected Jefferson president on 36th ballot. Published *A Manual of Parliamentary Practice* in 1801. Inaugurated as president in March 1801. Dispatched naval squadron to Mediterranean to protect American vessels against Barbary pirates. Encouraged Republicans to repeal Judiciary Act of 1801, enacted by lame-duck Federalists to expand federal court system. Sent James Monroe as minister plenipotentiary on special mission to join American minister Robert R. Livingston in France to negotiate purchase of New Orleans and free navigation of the Mississippi, resulting in Louisiana Purchase; treaty concluded in 1803. Commissioned Meriwether Lewis and William Clark to explore Louisiana Purchase; their expedition returned in 1806. Reelected president in landslide in 1804. Called for impeachment and removal of Supreme Court Justice Samuel Chase, who was acquitted by Senate in 1805. Concluded peace treaty with Tripoli in 1805 and maintained American neutrality in European war. Succeeded in passage of Non-Importation Act of 1806 to apply commercial pressure on Great Britain. In November 1806, he issued proclamation warning against the Burr conspiracy to separate western territories and attack Mexico. Burr, defended by Edmund Randolph and Luther Martin, was acquitted of charges of treason in 1807 trial with John Marshall presiding. In 1807, he refused to submit Monroe-Pinckney Treaty with Britain to Senate because of lack of guarantee against impressment and more open trade agreement. After incident in which HMS *Leopard* fired on, disabled, and boarded USS *Chesapeake*, he had the Embargo Act passed in December 1807, suspending all foreign commerce. Declined requests to seek third term as president. Signed Non-Intercourse Act in March 1809, repealing embargo and restoring trade with all nations except England and France. Retired to Monticello in 1809, kept up a large correspondence, and continued his efforts to establish system of general education. In 1811, he published a translation of Destutt de Tracy's *A Commentary and Review of Montesquieu's Spirit of the Laws*. Resumed correspondence with John Adams, leading to a reconciliation in 1812. In 1814, he sold his library to the United States; it became foundation of Library of Congress. In 1817–19, he was instrumental in founding University of Virginia at Charlottesville. In

1820, he denounced the Missouri Compromise, predicting it would exacerbate sectional rivalries. In 1823, he warmly approved the message that outlined the Monroe Doctrine, declaring western hemisphere closed to European expansion. Among his unpublished works were an *Autobiography*, *The Life and Morals of Jesus of Nazareth*, and *Anas* (a collection of memoranda from his government service). Died at Monticello, July 4, 1826.

WILLIAM JONES (1724–1811)   Born in Ireland, Jones came to Bristol, district of Maine, with his family in 1730. He worked as a joiner and taught school. Withdrew from the local Presbyterian church when it became Congregational and published a scathing attack on local Presbyterian and Congregational clergy and later on the Methodists. Delegate from Bristol to Massachusetts ratifying convention of 1788, where he opposed ratification. At the convention, on January 19, 1788, he moved that a fast be held to ask the "advice of God" on the Constitution. In his later years, he was often heard to say that "he could have made a better Constitution himself."

MARTIN KINSLEY (1754–1835)   Born June 2, 1754, in Bridgewater, Massachusetts. Graduated from Harvard College in 1778. Studied medicine. Purveyor of supplies for Continental Army. Town treasurer of Hardwick, Massachusetts, from 1787 to 1792. Lost commission as major in Massachusetts militia for sympathizing with Shays' Rebellion in 1787. Member state house of representatives from Hardwick in 1787, 1788, 1790–92, and 1794–96. Delegate from Hardwick to Massachusetts ratifying convention of 1788, where he opposed ratification. Moved to Hampden, district of Maine, in 1797. Member state house of representatives from Hampden 1801–04 and 1806. Member of Massachusetts Executive Council in 1810 and 1811. Judge of court of common pleas in 1811; judge of probate court. Member state senate in 1814. Elected to U.S. House of Representatives in 1818. Defeated for reelection in 1820. Died in Roxbury, Massachusetts, June 20, 1835.

MARQUIS DE LAFAYETTE (1757–1834)   Born September 6, 1757, in Chavaniac, Auvergne, France, son of Marie Louise Julie de la Rivire and Gilbert Marquis de Lafayette (colonel in the French grenadiers who died in battle in 1759). Taken to Paris for education in 1768. Mother and grandfather died in 1770, and he inherited a large income and decided to pursue a military career. Arranged marriage to Marie Adrienne Françoise de Noailles took place in April 1774. Learned of American colonists' uprising in 1775 and was moved to help their cause. With the German professional soldier John Kalb, he contracted with American agents Silas Deane and Arthur Lee to be received into the Continental Army in 1776. Arrived in his own ship on the coast of South Carolina in June 1777 and proceeded to Philadelphia to meet with the Continental Congress. At first rebuffed, he offered to serve at his own expense as a volunteer. Appointed major general but not given a command (Kalb was finally made a brigadier general and died fighting under Gates against Cornwallis in 1780). Appointed to Washington's staff, and they began lifelong friendship. In his first battle at Brandywine he was slightly wounded in the leg but rejoined Washington after a month. Appointed to command of division of Virginia light troops by Congress in December 1777. Fought in various battles and enjoyed great popularity among the Americans. When the French joined the war, he helped maintain good relations between the two countries. Returned to France early in 1779 on leave of absence and was greeted with great acclaim. Urged France to send troops and naval forces. Returned to America in 1780 and resumed command of Virginia division. Worked closely with Washington, acted as intermediary between French and American armies, and took part in the defeat of Cornwallis. Embarked for France in late December 1781. Received with great enthusiasm and continued to support the American cause. Prepared to return to America, but when he learned of signing of preliminary articles of peace, he returned to his home in Auvergne. Named his son George Washington Lafayette. Made a member of the Society of the Cincinnati. Became spokesman for republican ideas in France. Revisited America in 1784 and found a warm welcome wherever he went. In France, he continued to advocate American causes and worked for the abolition of slavery and the restoration of rights to French Protestants. Often consulted with Jefferson. Took leading part in early years of the French Revolution. By 1792, he was forced to flee the country and was captured by the Austrians and imprisoned at Olmutz, where he remained in prison until 1797. Remained in exile with his family until 1799, then returned to France and settled at La Grange, 40 miles from Paris. The French Revolution had destroyed his fortune, but he remained a believer in representative government. Made triumphal tour of America at the invitation of President Monroe in 1824. Took part in the July 1830 revolution in France. Continued his support of America. Died May 20, 1834.

ARTHUR LEE (1740–1792)   Born December 21, 1740, at Stratford, in Westmoreland County, Virginia, son of Hannah Ludwell and Thomas Lee. (Was brother of Richard Henry, Francis Lightfoot, and William Lee and first cousin once removed of Henry Lee.) Studied at Eton in 1754 and at the University of Edinburgh, where he took a medical degree and was first in his class in 1764. Practiced medicine in Williamsburg, Virginia, in 1767–68. Returned to England in 1769 to study law at Lincoln's Inn and Middle Temple. Became assistant to Benjamin Franklin as colonial agent for Massachusetts and New Jersey. With brother William, became active in London politics and friend of John Wilkes and classmate James Boswell. Became member of the American Philosophical Society and the Royal Society. Admitted to the bar in London in 1775. Wrote radical pamphlets and secretly corresponded with the Continental Congress. Appointed in October 1776 with Silas Deane and Benjamin Franklin to negotiate treaty and aid from France. Lee suspected (as British archives have since confirmed) that Deane's secretary, Edward Bancroft, was a spy for England, with Deane's assistance. Arranged, with the help of his brothers in Congress, for Deane's return to America after the treaty was signed in February 1778. Lee also suspected Franklin. Recalled to America in the fall of 1779 on the basis of Deane's report. Returned in late 1780 and was elected to the Virginia House of Delegates. Delegate from Virginia to the Continental Congress 1781–84. Member of commission to negotiate Indian treaties at Fort Stanwix in October 1784 and Fort McIntosh in January 1785. Appointed to the treasury board of the Continental Congress; held that position until the new government took power. Opposed ratification of the Constitution. Purchased estate, Lansdowne, in Middlesex County, Virginia, in 1791, and retired there. Died, unmarried, at Lansdowne on December 12, 1792.

HENRY ("LIGHT-HORSE HARRY") LEE (1756–1818)   Born July 29, 1756, at Leesylvania, near Dumfries, Prince William County, Virginia, son of Lucy Grymes and Henry Lee. (Was first cousin once removed of Arthur, Francis Lightfoot, Richard Henry, and William Lee.) Graduated from the College of New Jersey (now Princeton) in 1773, where he became friends with fellow student James Madison. Abandoned plans to study law in London at Middle Temple. Appointed captain in Theodorick Bland's regiment of Virginia cavalry in 1776. In 1777, with his company, he joined the Continental Army. Established lasting friendship with Washington. Promoted to major in January 1778 and commanded forces of cavalry and three of infantry, known as "Lee's Legion." Fought successfully in many engagements, including raid of Paulus Hook, and was promoted to lieutenant colonel in 1780. Joined Greene's command in the South, where he led Legion in Pyle's Massacre, the battles of Guilford Courthouse and Eutaw Springs, and the siege of Yorktown, where he witnessed the surrender of Cornwallis on October 19, 1781. Took leave from the army in February 1782. Married second cousin Matilda Lee, heiress of Stratford, in 1782, with whom he had two children who survived him. Helped found the Society of the Cincinnati in 1783. Elected to Virginia House of Delegates in 1785. Delegate from Virginia to the Continental Congress 1785–89. Member of the Virginia ratifying convention of 1788, where he supported ratification. Elected governor of Virginia in 1791 and served 1792–94. Appointed brigadier general and commander of Virginia troops to suppress the Whiskey Rebellion in western Pennsylvania in 1794. Wife Matilda died in 1790 and he married Anne Hill Carter, daughter of Charles Carter of Shirley, in 1793 (their fifth child was Robert E. Lee). Activated as major general in the United States Army in 1798. Elected as a Federalist to the U.S. House of Representatives for one term 1799–1801. Wrote the resolutions read by Marshall on the death of Washington in 1799, describing him as "first in war, first in peace, and first in the hearts of his countrymen." Retired to Stratford and engaged in land speculations. Imprisoned for debt 1809–10 and wrote *Memoirs of the War in the Southern Department of the United States* (published in 1812). Moved with family to Alexandria in 1810, surviving on wife's trust fund. Seriously injured in Baltimore riot in 1812 while attempting to help friend who published the *Federal Republican*, an anti-administration paper. Went to the West Indies in 1813 to recover failing health. Returned to the United States when he realized he was close to death. Died before reaching home on March 25, 1818, on Cumberland Island, Georgia.

RICHARD HENRY LEE (1732–1794)   Born January 20, 1732, at Machodoc in Westmoreland County, Virginia, son of Hannah Ludwell and Thomas Lee. (Was brother of Francis Lightfoot, William, and Arthur Lee, and first cousin once removed to Henry Lee.) Family moved to new home of Stratford around 1740. Tutored at home. Sent to England for education in 1744 and completed course at academy at Wakefield. Returned to Virginia in 1753. Became justice of the peace in Westmoreland County and member of the Virginia House of Burgesses in 1758. Married Anne Aylett of Westmoreland County in December 1757. Established residence at Chantilly, neighboring estate to Stratford. Took active role in colonial affairs and made strong anti-slavery speech in 1759 (later he was briefly involved in slave trade). Initially sought position of tax collector, but subsequently led protests against the Stamp Act in 1765 and corresponded with John Lamb, Samuel Adams, and others. Continued in the forefront of protests against taxation by Parliament. He was strong in appearance, but suffered from epilepsy and a left hand maimed in a hunting accident. Wife Ann died in 1768 and in 1769 he married Anne Gaskins Pinckard, widow of Thomas Pinckard (he had nine children with his two wives). Worked closely with Patrick Henry and Thomas Jefferson in the house of burgesses. Organized committees of correspondence in 1773. Delegate from Virginia to First and Second Continental Congresses in 1774 and 1775. Became lifelong friend of Samuel and John Adams. Delegate to Continental Congress in 1776, where he made the motion for independence from England (seconded by John Adams). Signed the Declaration of Independence. Signed the Articles of Confederation and convinced Virginia to surrender its claims on western lands, which made possible their ratification by all 13 states. Resigned from Continental Congress in failing health in 1779. Elected to the Virginia House of Delegates in 1780. Delegate from Virginia to Continental Congress in 1784–87; elected president of Congress in 1784. Took the lead in passage of the Northwest Ordinance, establishing basis on which new states were to be admitted and prohibiting slavery north of the Ohio River. Declined to be a delegate to the Constitutional Convention in Philadelphia in 1787. Member of Virginia ratifying convention of 1788, where he took leading role in opposing ratification. Elected to U.S. Senate in 1789, where he actively supported adoption of the Bill of Rights. Resigned from Senate in October 1792 in poor health. Died at Chantilly on June 19, 1794.

JAMES MADISON (1749–1812)   Born August 27, 1749, near Staunton, Virginia, son of Agatha Strother, of King George County, and John Madison. He was a cousin of President James Madison. When he was very young, his family moved to Madison Hall in Augusta (now Rockingham) County. Graduated from the College of William and Mary in 1771 and studied law with George Wythe (though admitted to the bar, he never practiced). From 1773 to 1775, he taught natural philosophy and mathematics at the college. Went to England in 1775 to continue studies and was ordained in the ministry of the Church of England. On his return to Williamsburg in 1777, he was elected president of the College of William and Mary and professor of natural and moral philosophy (positions he held for the rest of his life). A patriot during the Revolution, he was appointed chaplain of the Virginia House of Delegates in 1777. As captain of militia, he saw active service in the war on several occasions. In 1779, married Sarah Tate, with whom he had two children who survived him. He became friends with Jefferson when Jefferson was in Williamsburg as governor, and together they discussed what could be done to improve the college. Toward the end of the war, the college was disrupted when it was occupied first by the British and then by the French and Continental armies. Appointed to commission to define the boundaries between Virginia and Pennsylvania; later made the surveys from which *A Map of Virginia formed from Actual Surveys*, known as "Madison's Map," was drawn. Began teaching Adam Smith's *Wealth of Nations* at the college in 1784. Member of the American Philosophical Society. Consecrated the first Episcopal bishop of Virginia in 1790, but college duties allowed him only two months a year to attend to the affairs of the Episcopal church (which underwent major changes as a result of the disestablishment of Virginia churches, brought about through efforts of his friend Jefferson and cousin Madison). He died in Williamsburg on March 6, 1812.

JAMES MADISON (1751–1836)   Born March 16, 1751, across the Rappahannock River from Port Royal, oldest son of Nelly Conway and James Madison. Family moved when he was an infant to the site of Montpelier in Orange County, Virginia. After education at home, attended boarding school of Donald Robertson (Scots graduate of Aberdeen and Edinburgh universities) 1762–67. Continued study at home with Thomas Martin (a minister boarding at his house) in 1768 before entering the College of New Jersey (now Princeton) in 1769. Studied under college president, John Witherspoon, and graduated in 1771. Fellow students included Philip Freneau and Hugh Henry Brackenridge. Continued at college another year before returning to Virginia in 1773. In late 1774, became a member of committee of safety for Orange County, chaired by his father and including neighbors Lawrence Taliaferro and Joseph Spencer. Active in raising men and materials to defend against British invasion. Appointed colonel of militia of Orange County under command of father, but never took part in fighting. Member of Virginia convention of 1776 that framed new state government and instructed delegates to the Continental Congress to vote for independence. Strengthened George Mason's wording of freedom of religion clause in state declaration of rights. Elected to Virginia House of Delegates in October 1776 and met Jefferson for the first time. Worked with Jefferson to disestablish church in Virginia. Lost election to legislature in 1777 when he refused to supply the traditional barrel of liquor for voters. Appointed to council of state and held that position January 1778–80. Lived with cousin, the Reverend James Madison. Elected delegate from Virginia to Continental Congress in December 1779 and began attendance in Philadelphia in March 1780. Took active part in questions of cession of western lands. Served on many foreign committees and supported Robert R. Livingston over Arthur Lee for foreign secretary in 1781. Supported Robert Morris's efforts to stabilize Continental finances. With James Wilson, attempted to establish a Library of Congress and drafted list of books needed. Met Hamilton in Congress and worked closely with him to strengthen central government. Wrote address to the states on means of ridding country of debt (published as pamphlet). Left Congress in October 1783, discouraged by its inability to achieve national power: one state was able to block any important national measure, and there seemed no way to finance the repayment of internal and external debts. Elected from Orange County to state house of delegates 1784–87. Traveled with Lafayette to Fort Stanwix to witness Indian treaty in summer of 1784. Elected member of the American Philosophical Society in January 1785. Wrote "Memorial and Remonstrance," petition used to defeat Patrick Henry's tax assessment bill for state support of Christian churches. Secured passage of Jefferson's bill for religious liberty. Attended Annapolis Convention in 1786 and, with Hamilton and others, issued call for a convention of states to be held in Philadelphia in May 1787 to form a new plan of government for the United States. Elected delegate to Continental Congress, where he upheld right of free navigation on the Mississippi River, which was threatened by Jay's negotiations with the Spanish envoy Gardoqui. Delegate to the Constitutional Convention in Philadelphia in 1787, where he drafted the Virginia plan presented to the convention by Randolph. Played major role in guiding the work of the convention and returned to the Continental Congress in New York to aid transmittal of Constitution to the states. Wrote *Federalist* papers (with Hamilton and Jay) to assist the ratification struggle in New York. Awarded LL.D. degree from College of New Jersey (now Princeton). Returned to Orange County and won election to the Virginia ratifying convention of June 1788, where he led the fight for ratification against opposition led by Patrick Henry. Influence of Henry prevented his election to U.S. Senate. Elected to U.S. House of Representatives in 1789, defeating James Monroe. Advised Washington and wrote his inaugural address, then drafted the response from Congress and Washington's reply to it. Played important role in establishing the new government, including defining the duties and title of the president and the creation of departments of foreign affairs, treasury, and war. Introduced Bill of Rights amendments in June 1789 and guided their passage through Congress. In 1790, with Jefferson, made agreement with Hamilton to locate permanent capital on the Potomac River and to credit Virginia for payments on the general war debt. In return, he arranged support in Congress for Hamilton's assumption bill, which he thought unfair to Virginia. Fought unsuccessfully against creation of national bank, which he regarded as unconstitutional. When the federal government moved to Philadelphia, helped Jefferson convince Freneau to start the *National Gazette* there to counter Hamilton's journal. Wrote articles using term "Republican Party" to describe his and Jefferson's supporters (Hamiltonians were using the term "Federalists"). In 1793, learned that he had been made a "Citizen of France" (with Hamilton and Washington) by the National Assembly. Entered pamphlet war against Hamilton over president's right to declare neutrality and other issues. Married widow Dolley Payne Todd, of Quaker descent (she had one son by previous marriage), in September 1794. Attacked Jay's Treaty in 1795. Submitted Jefferson's name for election as president in 1796 to Republican caucus in Congress. Retired from Congress in 1797 and declined to seek Virginia governorship. Returned to Montpelier to farm and experiment with scientific agriculture. Drafted the Virginia Resolutions opposing the Alien and Sedition Acts in 1798. Appointed secretary of state by Jefferson in 1801 and served until 1809. Issued instructions to Robert R. Livingston for negotiations with France concerning cession of New Orleans and navigation rights on Mississippi River. Wrote the instructions to Monroe, who was sent as minister plenipotentiary to join Livingston's negotiations and sign treaty. Elected first president of the American Board of Agriculture in 1803. In 1806, wrote pamphlet *An Examination of the British Doctrine, which subjects to capture a Neutral Trade Not Open in Time of Peace*, protesting interference with American shipping. Supported Non-Importation Act to apply commercial pressure against Great Britain. With Jefferson, disapproved of treaty with England negotiated by Monroe and William Pinkney and decided not to submit it to the Senate in 1807. Elected president in 1808, defeating George Clinton, Charles Cotesworth Pinckney, and James Monroe. Efforts to raise money for defense were defeated in Congress in 1810. Annexed part of West Florida to the United States. Attempted to negotiate peaceful resolutions to attacks on American shipping by both England and France during Napoleonic Wars. When French appeared to concede some shipping rights, he appointed Joel Barlow minister to France in 1811. Continued efforts to avert crisis with England. Reinstated non-intercourse when England refused to rescind the Orders of Council aimed at American shipping. Dismissed Robert Smith as secretary of state when he learned Smith was conspiring against the administration (Madison had written all diplomatic correspondence himself because of Smith's incompetence). Appointed James Monroe secretary of state. Continued efforts to get Congress to strengthen national defenses. British repeal of Orders in Council arrived too late to prevent Congress from declaring war on England in June 1812. Viciously attacked by Federalist newspapers, but maintained freedom of press and speech throughout the war. Reelected president in 1812 despite setbacks in war. Reluctantly appointed John Armstrong secretary of war on advice of secretary of treasury Albert Gallatin. Appointed William Jones secretary of the navy. Throughout the war, naval victories cheered national prospects. Appointed new generals and reorganized army. Dismayed by disaffection of New England. Appointed John Quincy Adams, Albert Gallatin, and James A. Bayard as peace commissioners when Russia offered to mediate a settlement with England; this mediation was superseded by direct negotiation, and Madison added Henry Clay and Jonathan Russell to the commission. Became dissatisfied with Armstrong after examining his correspondence and ensured promotion of Andrew Jackson and Jacob Brown to higher ranks than Armstrong had recommended. Washington, D.C., captured and burned by British on August 24, 1814, despite Madison's previous warnings. Dismissed Armstrong as secretary of war and replaced him with

Monroe (who continued as acting secretary of state as well). News of peace treaty and Andrew Jackson's victory at New Orleans was received in February 1815. Delivered message to Congress asking for adequate regular army and gradual build-up of navy. Sought and received declaration of war against the Dey of Algiers on February 25, 1815. Appointed Alexander J. Dallas secretary of the treasury and was pleased with his service. Suggested amendment to the Constitution to allow the building of roads and canals. Signed bill creating the second Bank of the United States in April 1816. Refused to run for third term as president in 1816. Left Washington for the last time in April 1817 and traveled part of the way home by steamboat. Tended his farm and was appointed to the board of visitors of Jefferson's Central College (University of Virginia), where he helped choose professors. Worked on codification of English common law into statutes for the American states at request of Jeremy Bentham. Became active member of the American Colonization Society, organized in 1816. Continued active interest in political affairs, carried on large correspondence, responded to frequent requests for advice, and entertained many visitors. Prepared his notes on the debates in the Philadelphia convention of 1787 for publication after his death. After Jefferson's death, became rector of the college. Attended Virginia constitutional convention in Richmond 1829–30. During debates over nullification and state rights that began in 1830, wrote numerous letters and articles supporting union and clarifying intent of Constitution and his own work. Became last survivor of the Philadelphia convention in 1833. Died at Montpelier on June 27, 1836.

JOHN MARSHALL (1755–1835)   Born September 24, 1755, in a log cabin near Germantown in western Prince William County (Fauquier County after 1759) in the Virginia backcountry, son of Mary Randolph Keith and Thomas Marshall (land surveyor, employee and friend of George Washington, member of the house of burgesses in 1759, and sheriff of Fauquier County in 1765). Family moved before Marshall was ten years old to a frame house 30 miles west in a valley of the Blue Ridge Mountains, and they moved again to a larger house in 1773. Educated by his parents, by James Thompson, a Scots deacon, and by Archibald Campbell (who also taught James Monroe). In May 1775, Marshall was appointed lieutenant of the Culpeper Minute Men and fought the Loyalists at Great Bridge. In 1776, he enlisted in the Continental Army and served as a lieutenant in the Third Virginia Regiment under his father, its major. In late 1776, he was promoted and transferred to the Fifteenth Virginia Line. Took part in the battle of Brandywine, September 11, 1777, and spent the winter of 1777–78 at Valley Forge. Fought in battle of Monmouth under General Charles Lee, June 28, 1778, and was part of Henry Lee's light infantry that raided Paulus Hook, August 19, 1779. Appointed deputy judge advocate and captain. In 1780, while still in the army, he attended George Wythe's lectures on law at William and Mary College for six weeks (his only formal legal training), received his license to practice (signed by Governor Jefferson), and was admitted to the bar in Fauquier County in August 1780. Awaited orders to return to active duty, but none came and he resigned his commission in 1781. Elected to the state assembly from Fauquier County, where he had established his law practice, and served in 1782 and 1784–85. Served as member of the council of state, but retired from that position when he realized it hurt his law practice. In January 1783, he married Mary Willis Ambler of Yorktown, daughter of Rebecca Burwell and state treasurer Jacquelin Ambler, with whom he had six children who reached maturity. Became a member of the Society of the Cincinnati. One of his close friends was assemblyman James Monroe who had shared many of his war experiences. Did not seek election to the assembly 1785, but returned as a delegate from Henrico County 1787–88. Led the successful effort in 1787 to send the Constitution to a state convention without binding instructions. Delegate to the Virginia ratifying convention in 1788, where he strongly advocated ratification and made a speech defending federal judicial power. Reelected to house of delegates 1789–90, but did not run again until 1795. Maintained close friendship with George Mason and other Antifederalists despite political disagreements. Supported the Jay Treaty and the policies of Hamilton and Washington, but declined appointment as attorney general in 1795. Accepted John Adams's appointment as minister plenipotentiary (with Charles Cotesworth Pinckney and Elbridge Gerry) on the ill-fated XYZ peace mission to France 1797–98. Though the mission was not successful, it brought him national recognition when the ministers' dispatches were published. Elected to U.S. House of Representatives 1799–1800, where he acted as a moderate Federalist, voting in support of John Adams to send the second peace mission to France and for partial repeal of the Sedition Act. John Adams appointed him to replace the dismissed Thomas Pickering as secretary of state in 1800 and appointed him Chief Justice of the U.S. Supreme Court early in 1801 (he continued to act as secretary of state until Adams's term was over). He served as Chief Justice until 1835 and spoke for the court in cases such as *Marbury* v. *Madison, McCulloch* v. *Maryland, Cohens* v. *Virginia,* and *Gibbons* v. *Ogden.* Marshall repeatedly affirmed the supremecy of the Constitution over states, broadly interpreted its contract, commerce, and "necessary and proper" clauses, and established the power of the supreme court to judge the constitutionality of state laws and state court decisions. Wrote *The Life of George Washington* (5 volumes, 1804–07). Presided at trial of Aaron Burr (defended by Edmund Randolph and Luther Martin) for treason in circuit court in Richmond in 1807. He opposed the War of 1812. Died in Philadelphia on July 6, 1835.

LUTHER MARTIN (c. 1748–1826)   Born near Piscataway, New Jersey, February 9, 1748 (the date usually given), son of Hannah and Benjamin Martin (farmer). Attended the grammar school of the College of New Jersey (now Princeton) before entering the college in 1761; graduated in 1766. In 1767, he became schoolmaster in Queenstown, Maryland, where he remained until 1770, using the law library of one his pupil's father, Solomon Wright. From 1770 until 1771, he was schoolmaster at Onancock, Accomac County, Virginia, while continuing study of law. Admitted to the bar in Virginia in

1771. Settled in Somerset County, Maryland, and built up a lucrative practice of law. Served on committee to enforce boycott of British goods in 1774 and represented county in provincial congress at Annapolis. Was appointed attorney general of Maryland by Governor Thomas Johnson on the recommendation of Samuel Chase in 1778; moved to Baltimore and served until 1805. Served briefly with Baltimore Light Dragoons in 1781. In December 1783, married Maria Cresap, with whom he had two surviving daughters. Elected delegate from Maryland to Continental Congress in 1784, but did not serve. Elected delegate to the Constitutional Convention in Philadelphia in 1787, where he helped draft New Jersey plan for revising the Articles of Confederation. He bitterly and unsuccessfully opposed the Constitution in the Maryland ratifying convention. In 1797, launched public attacks on Thomas Jefferson, whose *Notes on the State of Virginia* had implicated Martin's father-in-law, Captain Michael Cresap, in the 1774 murder of family of a Mingo chief. Eventually became a staunch Federalist and anti-Jeffersonian. In 1805, defended Justice Samuel Chase in impeachment trial. With Edmund Randolph, defended Aaron Burr at his trial for treason before John Marshall in federal circuit court in Richmond in 1807. He was chief judge of the court of oyer and terminer for Baltimore County from 1813 until 1816; was appointed again as state attorney general in 1818. He was an attorney for Maryland in *McCulloch* v. *Maryland* (Marshall court ruled against him), against Daniel Webster, William Wirt, and William Pinkney in 1819. Forced to retire in 1822 because of ill-health, the legislature enacted an annual $5 fee on all attorneys for his support (repealed in 1823). In poor health and straitened financial condition, he was taken in by Aaron Burr in New York City in 1823, where he lived until his death on July 10, 1826.

GEORGE MASON (1725–1792)   Born in 1725 in the Northern Neck of Virginia, son of Ann Thomson and George Mason. Father died when Mason was ten years old, and he was brought up under the guardianship of John Mercer of Marlborough, Stafford County (lawyer and the owner of a large library). Educated by private tutors and by his own reading. In April 1750, married Anne Eilbeck of Mattawoman, Charles County, Maryland, with whom he had nine children. They moved to new home, Gunston Hall, at Dogue's Neck on the Potomac River below Alexandria near Washington's home at Mount Vernon. Mason acted as his own steward and attended the needs of his plantation. He was active in Fairfax County politics, served as trustee of the new town of Alexandria from 1754 until its incorporation in 1779 and as justice on the county court 1747–89. Took part in Truro Parish church activities 1748–85. Though he never became a professional lawyer, he was often asked for advice on public law. From 1752 to 1773, he was a member and treasurer of the Ohio Company for promoting western settlement. Elected to Virginia House of Burgesses in 1758, served until 1761. In 1766, he wrote an open letter to London merchants seeking repeal of the Stamp Act. Wife Anne died in 1773. Washington, also a member of the house of burgesses, would often consult with Mason before going to Williamsburg and ask him to write opinions on various issues. In 1774, Mason drafted the Fairfax Resolves that were eventually adopted by the Continental Congress. Member of the state Revolutionary conventions of 1775 and 1776 and a member of the state committee of safety in 1775. In 1776, he drafted much of the new Virginia state constitution, including its Declaration of Rights. Served in Virginia House of Delegates 1776–81, 1786–87 (absent), and 1787–88. Elected delegate from Virginia to the Continental Congress in 1777, but did not attend. Helped arrange the cession of the Northwest Territory by Virginia to the Confederation and the disestablishment of religion in Virginia. Though a slaveholder himself, consistently opposed the slave trade and denounced slavery. Married Sarah Brent in April 1780. Attended meeting at Mount Vernon in 1785 to coordinate support of Potomac navigation project by Virginia and Maryland. This meeting indirectly led to calling of the Annapolis Convention in 1786, which he did not attend. Chosen delegate from Virginia to the Constitutional Convention in Philadelphia in 1787, where he supported a more effective federal government, but ultimately refused to sign the Constitution. Delegate to Virginia ratifying convention of 1788, where he strongly opposed ratification without prior amendments. In 1790, the Virginia legislature elected him to the U.S. Senate, but he declined to serve. Died at Gunston Hall on October 7, 1792.

ARMAND-MARC, COMTE DE MONTMORIN-SAINT-HÉREM (1745–1792) Born October 13, 1745, in Paris, France, into an aristocratic family. In 1768 he became gentleman-in-waiting to the dauphin. In 1774, on the accession of Louis XVI, he was appointed minister to the archbishop of Treves. In 1777, he was appointed ambassador to the court of Charles III of Spain, where he successfully negotiated Spanish war assistance against England and befriended John Jay. Returned to France in 1783 and was appointed *commandant* of Brittany. Served there until 1787, when he succeeded Vergennes as foreign minister of France and was named to the Assembly of Notables. As foreign minister in 1787, he unsuccessfully advocated financial and military support for French partisans in the Netherlands. In 1788, he became involved with finance minister Necker in domestic affairs. In June 1789, he and Necker advised the king to pursue moderate constitutional reforms, but Louis XVI rejected their plan, overruled the decrees of the Third Estate, and, on July 11, dismissed Montmorin and the entire Necker ministry. On July 14, 1789, a popular uprising in Paris attacked and seized the Bastille, forcing Louis to recall Montmorin and Necker. After Necker's forced retirement in September 1790, Montmorin became the leading minister and allied himself with the comte de Mirabeau to preserve the monarchy, but his efforts to pursue a moderate course were attacked by both radicals and royalists. After the death of Mirabeau in April 1791, the king and queen made secret plans to escape France and raise an army of invasion. Montmorin unwittingly signed the false passports they used in their abortive flight in June, and although he was cleared of complicity in their flight, his reputation and credibility suffered. He continued in office until November 1791, when he resigned; he continued to advise the king and queen without success. In July 1792, he was publicly accused by Brissot and others of conspiring against the revolution. After the attack on the Tuileries in August 1792, he went into hiding, but was betrayed, arrested, and sent to the Abbaye prison, where he was impaled and hacked to death on September 2, 1792, during the September Massacres.

ELÉONORE FRANÇOIS ELIE, MARQUIS DE MOUSTIER (1751–1817)   Born May 15, 1751, at Paris, France, of an ancient and noble family. Attended Jesuit college at Heidelberg, completed military apprenticeship at Besançon, and, in 1768, was commissioned underlieutenant in the Royal-Navarre regiment. His brother-in-law, the marquis de Clermont d'Amboise, ambassador to Portugal, took him to Lisbon in 1769, where he became secretary. Accompanied his uncle to Naples in 1775. In 1778, he was made minister to the Elector of Treves. In 1783, he was sent as minister to London to resolve difficulties resulting from the Spanish intervention in the recent war. In 1787, he replaced La Luzerne as minister to the United States, where he served until 1789, when he returned to Paris. He became minister to Prussia in 1790, and in September 1791 was recalled and offered the post of foreign minister by Louis XVI. He declined, fearing his monarchical principles would further compromise the king's position, and accepted briefly the post of ambassador at Constantinople. Almost immediately, he joined the brothers of Louis XVI in exile, and was commissioned by them to negotiate with Prussia and England for intervention on behalf of the Bourbons. His secret correspondence fell into the hands of the revolutionaries and was used as evidence in the condemnation of himself and Louis XVI. After the failure of the Prussian invasion in 1792, he lived in England until 1796, and in Prussia until 1806, working for the restoration of the Bourbon monarchy. He returned to England in 1806 to escape the French occupation of Prussia, and remained there until the restoration of 1814, when he returned to France. He retired to Bailli, near Versailles, where he resided until his death, of apoplexy, on February 1, 1817.

SAMUEL NASSON (1744–1800)   Born in New Hampshire on February 14, 1744. Learned the saddler trade. Became a storekeeper in York, Maine, before the start of the Revolution. Enlisted in the Maine regiment of Massachusetts militia in May 1775. Joined the Continental Army and served in the siege of Boston and the battle of Long Island in 1776, achieving the rank of major. In 1778, he settled in Sanford, York County, Maine, where he was active in local affairs, serving as selectman, town clerk, and treasurer, and helping to organize a Congregational church. He was married first to Mary Ball Shores and subsequently to Mrs. Joanna Tilden Moulton. In 1787 Sanford's town meeting at first voted not to send a delegate to the Massachusetts ratifying convention, but at a second meeting elected Nasson as delegate. He was one of the more active participants opposing ratification without prior amendments at the convention in 1788. He was a member of the Massachusetts house of representatives 1788–89, during which time he took an important part in deciding how Massachusetts would choose presidential electors and United States representatives and senators. Though forced to compromise on many issues, succeeded in passing requirement that representatives live in the districts they represented. Afterward, Nasson was an unsuccessful candidate for various state offices. He died on August 28, 1800.

SAMUEL OSGOOD (1748–1813)　　　Born February 14, 1748, in Andover, Massachusetts, son of Sarah Sprague Johnson and Peter Osgood. Graduated from Harvard in 1770 and entered his brother Peter's business. Delegate to the Essex Convention in 1774. Enlisted in and became captain of Andover Minute Men at the outbreak of the Revolution. Appointed aide-de-camp to General Artemas Ward and promoted to major. Served eight months and resigned with the rank of colonel in February 1776. He married Martha Brandon of Cambridge in January 1775 (they had no children). Appointed justice of the peace in Essex County in January 1776. Member of the provincial congress in 1776, 1779, and 1780. Wife Martha died in 1778. Delegate to Massachusetts constitutional convention in 1779–80. Elected to the state senate in 1780. Delegate from Massachusetts to the Continental Congress 1781–84 during which time he served on many important committees. Appointed cashier of the Massachusetts Bank and a fellow of the American Academy of Arts and Sciences. Elected to state house of representatives. In 1785, he was appointed to the three-man Confederation board of treasury, with Walter Livingston and Arthur Lee, and moved to New York, where he served until September 1789. In 1786, he married Maria Bowne Franklin, widow of Walter Franklin of New York and connected through marriage with the Clinton family. Though he opposed the Constitution, Osgood served as postmaster general in Washington's cabinet from 1789 to 1791. He resigned that office when the government moved to Philadelphia. In 1800, he was elected to the New York Assembly and was chosen speaker. Organized a free school for the poor in New York and helped to found the American Academy of Fine Arts. Supported Jefferson (a friend since his time in the Continental Congress) for president in 1800. Jefferson appointed him supervisor of internal revenue for New York in 1802 and naval officer of the port of New York in 1803, a position he held until his death on August 12, 1813.

LOUIS-GUILLAUME OTTO, COMTE DE MOSLOY (1754–1817)　　　Born August 7, 1754, at Kork, Grand Duchy of Bade, son of the chancellor to the Landgrave of Hesse-Darmstadt. Attended Protestant University in Strasbourg, where he studied languages and law. In 1776, became private secretary to La Luzerne, French minister to Bavaria. Accompanied La Luzerne to United States in 1779, and became secretary of the legation. Returned to France and was appointed chargé d'affaires to America, replacing Marbois and serving under the comte de Moustier (who arrived in 1787). Married Elizabeth Livingston, daughter of Peter Van Brugh Livingston, in March 1787. After she died giving birth to a son (who survived) in December 1787, he married America-Françes, daughter of French consul in New York J. Hector St. John Crèvecoeur, in April 1790 at a wedding attended by Jefferson and others. They had one daughter. Otto returned to France in 1792, assumed a post in the foreign ministry, and allied himself with the Girondins. He was removed after the revolution of May 31, 1793, and imprisoned in the Luxembourg until July 1794. He retired to Lesches until 1798, when he became secretary to the ambassador to Berlin, Abbe Sieyes. In 1799, he became chargé d'affaires at Berlin and successfully forestalled a Prussian war against France. In 1800, he was sent to London to negotiate an exchange of prisoners, and was then appointed minister plenipotentiary and engaged in preliminary peace negotiations that laid groundwork for Treaty of Amiens. In 1802, he was replaced as minister to England and offered the post of minister to the United States, which he refused because of his wife's ill-health. Appointed minister to Munich in 1803; successfully prevented Bavarian alliance with Austria, Russia, and England. Warned Napoleon of impending Austrian occupation of Bavaria, leading to French victory at Austerlitz in 1805. Named counselor of state and officer of Legion of Honor, created comte de Mosloy. In 1809, became ambassador to Vienna and negotiated marriage of Napoleon and Archduchess Marie-Louise. Replaced by Narbonne as ambassador to Austria in 1813; became minister of state. Initially supported the Restoration of 1814, but was excluded from the council of state by influence of Tallyrand. After Napoleon's return to France in March 1815, served as undersecretary of state for foreign affairs. After Waterloo, was dispatched to England to negotiate for Napoleon's security, but was denied passport and could not leave Calais. Lived in retirement until his death in Paris, on November 9, 1817.

SAMUEL HOLDEN PARSONS (1737–1789)   Born May 14, 1737, in Lyme, Connecticut, son of Phebe Griswold and Jonathan Parsons (a minister and close friend of George Whitefield). In 1746, when problems arose over father's preaching, the family moved to Newburyport, Massachusetts. Graduated from Harvard in 1756 and returned to Lyme to study law under his uncle, Matthew Griswold. Admitted to the bar in Connecticut in 1759 and began practice in Lyme. In September 1761, he married Mehetable Mather, with whom he had seven children who lived to adulthood. Elected to the state assembly in 1762; served almost continuously until 1774, when he moved to New London. Became an officer in the militia in 1770 and supported independence from an early date. Appointed colonel of the 6th Connecticut Regiment and took part in capture of Fort Ticonderoga in 1775. Participated in siege of Boston and was transferred to New York and commissioned brigadier general in the Continental Army in 1776. Promoted to major general before he retired in 1782. After the war, he settled in Middletown, Connecticut, and served in the state legislature. Named commissioner in 1785 to settle Indian land claims in the Northwest. In 1786, he was president of the Connecticut Society of the Cincinnati. In 1787 he was elected director of the Ohio Company and appointed judge in the Northwest Territory. Member of the Connecticut ratifying convention of 1788, where he supported ratification. In 1788 he went to Adelphia (now Marietta), Ohio, to develop land claims; lived as a frontiersman. While returning from a trip to the Western Reserve, in which he had land interests, his canoe overturned in the rapids of Big Beaver River, and he died on November 17, 1789.

EDMUND PENDLETON (1721–1803)   Born September 9, 1721, in Caroline County, Virginia, son of Mary Taylor and Henry Pendleton. His father died the year he was born and his mother remarried. Apprenticed at age 14 to Benjamin Robinson, clerk of the court of Caroline. Became clerk to the vestry of St. Mary's Parish in 1737. Appointed clerk of the Caroline court martial in 1740. Admitted to the local bar in 1741. In 1742, he married Elizabeth Roy, who died within the year in childbirth. In June 1743, he married Sarah Pollard, with whom he had no children. Admitted to practice before the general court in 1745. Appointed justice of the peace for Caroline County in 1751. Elected to the Virginia House of Burgesses in 1752 and served until 1774. Opposed Patrick Henry's resolutions during the Stamp Act crisis (as he had opposed him on other issues), but opened his court without the use of stamps and stated that parliament had no constitutional authority to pass the act. In 1773, he was a member of Virginia's committee of correspondence. Delegate from Virginia to the First Continental Congress in 1774. Member of all of Virginia's Revolutionary conventions and president of two of them in 1775. President of state committee of safety 1775–76. Hoped that a compromise with Britain was still possible, but drafted the resolves instructing Virginia's delegates in the Continental Congress to propose independence. With Jefferson and George Wythe, he was placed on a committee to revise the laws of Virginia; he opposed Jefferson's programs for disestablishment of the church and abolition of primogeniture and entail. Elected first speaker of the new Virginia House of Delegates and appointed presiding judge of the court of chancery. When the supreme court of appeals was organized in 1779, became its first president and held that position until his death. Presided at the Virginia ratifying convention of 1788, where he warmly supported ratification. Though an old friend of Washington, he disapproved of the administration's financial and foreign policies and allied himself with the Jeffersonian Republicans. He died in Richmond, on October 26, 1803.

HENRY PENDLETON (1750–1789)   Born in 1750 in Culpeper County, Virginia, son of Nathaniel Greene Pendleton and nephew of Edmund Pendleton. With his brother Nathaniel, joined the Culpeper Minute Men when the Revolution began. Moved to South Carolina and was appointed judge of court of common pleas in 1776. Taken prisoner, he apparently violated parole and left Charleston in 1780 because of threats by Loyalists and refugees there. Fought under Nathaniel Greene at battle of Eutaw Springs in September 1781. Returned to Charleston and was taken prisoner again March 26, 1782. Originated the County Court Act of South Carolina and was one of three judges appointed to revise the laws of the state in 1785. Delegate to South Carolina ratifying convention in 1788, where he supported ratification. Declined to stand for election to U.S. House of Representatives in 1788. Died in the Greenville District of South Carolina on January 10, 1789.

TIMOTHY PICKERING (1745–1829)   Born July 17, 1745, in Salem, Massachusetts, son of Mary Wingate and Timothy Pickering. Graduated from Harvard College in 1763. Returned to Salem and became a clerk in the office of the register of deeds for Essex County, where he continued to work for ten years. In 1766, commissioned lieutenant in the Essex County militia. Studied military history on his own. Studied law and was admitted to the bar in 1768. Elected register of deeds in 1774. Active as Revolutionary publicist and pamphleteer. Appointed colonel in the 1st Regiment of Essex County militia in February 1775. Published pamphlet *An Easy Plan of Discipline for a Militia* (1775), which became standard manual for Massachusetts and other states until replaced by the manual of Baron von Steuben. In April 1776, he married Rebecca White (born in Bristol, England), with whom he had ten children. Commanded Massachusetts contingent that joined Washington in New York and took part in the winter campaigns of 1776–77 in New Jersey. Appointed adjutant general of the Continental Army May 1777 and served until January 1778. Appointed in November 1777 to newly organized board of war. Appointed quartermaster general in 1780 and served until 1783. After the war, he remained in Philadelphia and engaged in mercantile business. In 1787, he was commissioned by Pennsylvania to organize new county of Luzerne and moved his family to land he owned in the Wyoming Valley. Became involved in land-title disputes between Connecticut and Pennsylvania settlers. Delegate from Luzerne County to Pennsylvania ratifying convention of 1787, where he supported ratification. Delegate to state constitutional convention of 1789–90. Appointed federal commissioner to negotiate with Seneca Indians in 1790 and subsequently with other tribes. Appointed postmaster general in Washington's cabinet in 1791. Appointed secretary of war in January 1795 and secretary of state in August 1795, after Edmund Randolph was forced to resign. Fervently supported Hamilton's wing of Federalist party and often consulted with him. Remained as secretary of state under John Adams, but vehemently disagreed with him over policy toward revolutionary France; Pickering favored declaring war after the XYZ Affair, while Adams favored waiting and eventually negotiated an agreement with the French. Dismissed by Adams in May 1800, he returned to his farm in Pennsylvania. Considered a leading member of the Federalist party, friends purchased his lands and enabled him to return to Massachusetts, where he rented farms, first in Danvers and then at Wenham. Elected to the U.S. Senate 1803–11; strongly opposed the Louisiana Purchase and the Embargo Act. Served on Massachusetts Executive Council 1812–13. Elected to U.S. House of Representatives 1813–17. Continued a bitter opponent of Jefferson and Madison and was one of the most prominent leaders who advocated New England's secession before and during the War of 1812. In 1820, he moved back to Salem, where he died on January 29, 1829.

CHARLES COTESWORTH PINCKNEY (1746–1825)   Born February 25, 1746, in Charleston, South Carolina, son of Elizabeth Lucas (who helped bring indigo cultivation to South Carolina) and Charles Pinckney (chief justice of the province). Brother of Thomas Pinckney (1750–1828) and second cousin of Charles Pinckney (1757–1824). Family moved to England in 1753, when his father was appointed agent of the colony to London. Remained in England after his parents returned to America in 1758 (where his father soon died). Educated at Westminster and Christ Church College, Oxford, attended lectures of William Blackstone, and was admitted to the Middle Temple in 1764. Admitted to the English bar in 1769; practiced briefly before continuing his studies in France. Returned to America in late 1769 and was immediately elected to the colonial assembly. Admitted to the South Carolina bar in early 1770. Married Sarah Middleton, daughter of the second president of the Continental Congress and sister of Arthur Middleton, signer of the Declaration of Independence. Became acting attorney general for Camden, Georgetown, and the Cheraws in 1773. Served in the provincial congress 1775–76, where he advocated disestablishment of the church and served on various committees and the council of safety. Joined the militia and was appointed ranking major when the South Carolina 1st Regiment was organized. Promoted to colonel by September 1776. Appointed aide to Washington and took part in the battles of Brandywine and Germantown in 1777. In 1778 he took part in the campaign in Florida and the unsuccessful siege in Savannah. Taken prisoner after surrender of Charleston in 1780, was exchanged in 1782 and rejoined army; was discharged as brigadier general in 1783. Joined the Society of the Cincinnati (became its third president general in 1805). Elected to the lower house in 1778 and 1782. President of the state senate in 1779. Wife Sarah died in 1784, and he married Mary, daughter of Benjamin Stead. Delegate from South Carolina to the Constitutional Convention of 1787, where he opposed religious tests and proposed that Senate have power to ratify treaties. Delegate to South Carolina ratifying convention, where he supported ratification. Declined Washington's offers to appoint him U.S. Supreme Court justice, secretary of war, and secretary of state. In 1796, he succeeded Monroe as minister to France, but when he arrived he was not formally received and was forced to leave. He was one of the American peace commissioners (with Elbridge Gerry and John Marshall) appointed by Adams in 1797 for mission to France in what became known as the XYZ Affair, and he shared Marshall's view of the proceedings. In 1798, when war with France threatened, he was commissioned major general under Washington and Hamilton (discharged in June 1800). Unsuccessful Federalist candidate for vice-president in 1800 and unsuccessful Federalist candidate for president in 1804 and 1808. Helped found South Carolina College in 1801 and Charleston Bible Society in 1810. He lived at his plantation, Belmont, and in Charleston. Died in Charleston on August 16, 1825.

EDMUND RANDOLPH (1753–1813) Born August 10, 1753, at Tazewell Hall, near Williamsburg, Virginia, only son of Ariana Jenings and John Randolph (former king's attorney for Virginia). Graduated from the College of William and Mary, studied law with his father, and was admitted to the Virginia bar in 1774. His father left Virginia with Lord Dunmore and other Loyalists in 1775, and Randolph was taken into the home of his uncle, Peyton Randolph, who was the first president of the Continental Congress. In August 1775, he joined the army in Cambridge, Massachusetts, and was appointed aide-de-camp by Washington. Hearing of his uncle's death, he returned to Virginia. In August 1776, he married Elizabeth, daughter of Robert Carter and sister of George Nicolas, and had four children with her. Youngest member of the Virginia convention that adopted the first state constitution. Served as mayor of Williamsburg, clerk of the house of delegates, and attorney general of Virginia. Delegate from Virginia to the Continental Congress 1779–82. Governor of Virginia 1786–88. Delegate to the Annapolis Convention in 1786. Delegate to the Constitutional Convention in Philadelphia in 1787, where he proposed Virginia plan (drafted by Madison) but refused to sign the Constitution as written. Explained his reasons for refusing in a widely publicized letter. As delegate to Virginia ratifying convention in 1788, he surprised many by supporting ratification. Appointed the first attorney general of the United States by Washington in 1789 and served until 1794, during which time Washington relied on him to mediate differences between Jefferson and Hamilton. Appointed secretary of state in 1794 after Jefferson's retirement. Forced to resign in August 1795 after a letter written by retiring French minister Fauchet appeared to implicate Randolph in disloyal behavior (it was intercepted by the English and brought to Washington's attention by members of the cabinet). Randolph published a pamphlet defending himself in 1795. Moved to Richmond and resumed practice of law. He was senior counsel (with Luther Martin) for Aaron Burr during his trial for treason in federal circuit court before John Marshall in 1807. He died on September 12, 1813.

DAVID REDICK (d. 1805) Born in Ireland. Settled in western Pennsylvania. Admitted to the bar in Washington County, Pennsylvania, in 1782 and became one of western Pennsylvania's leading attorneys. Represented county in state legislature. Opposed the charter of the Bank of North America in 1785. Elected from Washington County to the Pennsylvania Supreme Executive Council in 1786 and served as vice-president of that body in 1788. Elected to the American Philosophical Society in January 1789. Delegate to state constitutional convention of 1789–90, where he supported Wilson in drawing up the state's new constitution. On October 9, 1794, during the Whiskey Rebellion, Redick and William Findley met with President Washington at Carlisle, Pennsylvania, to present the case of the insurgents. They failed to prevent federal intervention, and militia under Hamilton, Henry Lee, and Daniel Morgan occupied the western part of the state. Redick corresponded with Jefferson, but he became a Federalist in the late 1790s. He died in 1805.

BENJAMIN RUSH (1746–1813) Born January 4, 1746, in Byberry Township, outside of Philadelphia, son of Susanna Hall Harvey and her second husband, John Rush (gunsmith and farmer who died in 1751). Attended academy run by Samuel Finley, his mother's sister's husband, in West Nottingham in 1753. Entered College of New Jersey (now Princeton) in spring of 1759 and graduated in 1760. Studied medicine with John Redman, the leading physician in Philadelphia, from February 1761 to July 1766. Attended medical lectures at the College of Philadelphia (now University of Pennsylvania). Attended Edinburgh University and received M.D. degree in 1768. Helped convince Witherspoon to become president of the College of New Jersey in 1768. Spent five months in London in further study of medicine and became a friend of Franklin. Returned to Philadelphia and opened medical practice in 1769. Became the first professor of chemistry at the College of Philadelphia. Elected to the American Philosophical Association. In 1774 (and 1803) helped found the Pennsylvania Society for Promoting the Abolition of Slavery. Met delegates to the First and Second Continental Congresses and became friend of John Adams and Thomas Jefferson. Married Julia, daughter of Richard Stockton, trustee of College of New Jersey and a signer of the Declaration of Independence. He had many children, and six sons and three daughters survived him. Elected to the provincial congress. Delegate from Pennsylvania to the Continental Congress in 1776, where he signed the Declaration of Independence. Not reelected to Continental Congress because of his expressed dislike for the new Pennsylvania constitution. Served as surgeon general in the Continental Army in 1777, but resigned after his complaints to Washington about conditions and medical treatment were not heeded. Joined staff of the Pennsylvania Hospital in 1783. With John Dickinson, helped found Dickinson College in Carlisle, Pennsylvania. Supported various reform movements, including temperance, women's education, and improved treatment for the indigent sick. In 1787, he helped found the Philadelphia College of Physicians. Delegate to Pennsylvania ratifying convention of 1787, where he strongly supported ratification. With James Wilson, campaigned successfully for a new state constitution in 1789. Continued to teach and occupy various chairs after the College of Philadelphia merged with the University of the State of Pennsylvania to become the University of Pennsylvania in 1791. Member of Pennsylvania Democratic Society 1794. Resigned from Philadelphia College of Physicians after dispute over treatment of yellow fever in 1794. Pioneered studies of insanity and wrote *Medical Inquiries and Observations Upon the Diseases of the Mind* (1812). Supported Jefferson for president in 1796. Appointed treasurer of the U.S. mint by John Adams in November 1797 and retained that position until his death. Helped bring about reconciliation between Jefferson and Adams in 1812. Died in Philadelphia on April 19, 1813.

ROGER SHERMAN (1721–1793)   Born April 19 (old style), 1721, in Newton, Massachusetts, son of Mehetabel Wellington and William Sherman (shoemaker and farmer). Family moved to Stoughton (now Canton), Massachusetts, in 1723. Educated in common schools and read widely on his own. Worked on his father's farm and learned the shoemaker's craft. Father died in 1741. Moved to New Milford, Connecticut, where his older brother William lived, in 1743. In 1745, he was appointed surveyor for New Haven County (and for Litchfield County after it was was organized in 1752) and served until 1758. With his brother, owned the town's only store, and became its sole owner by 1756. Began buying land with money earned from surveying. Became a juryman, exciseman, town clerk pro tem, clerk of the church, deacon, school committeeman, and agent to the assembly on town business. Married Elizabeth Hartwell in November 1749, with whom he had seven children. Published a series of almanacs 1750–61. Admitted to the bar in Litchfield in 1754. Represented New Milford in the Connecticut General Assembly in 1755 and 1757–61. Appointed justice of the county court and commissary for the Connecticut troops in 1759. Wife Elizabeth died in 1760. In 1761, he moved to New Haven and became a merchant, importing goods and selling books to Yale students. Married Rebecca Prescott in May 1763, with whom he had eight children. Representative from New Haven to the lower house of the state legislature 1764–66 and an assistant to the upper house in 1766. Appointed justice of the peace in 1765. Appointed judge of the superior court of Connecticut in May 1766 and held office until 1789. Treasurer of Yale College 1765–76; received honorary degree in 1768. Sold his business in 1772 because of his public offices. Did not support activities of the Sons of Liberty. Delegate from Connecticut to First Continental Congress in 1774, where he denied the supremacy of parliament and signed the Association Agreement. Delegate to Continental Congress 1774–81 and 1783–84; served on committees that drafted the colonial Declaration of Rights and the Declaration of Independence, the Articles of Confederation, and other state papers. Member of the Connecticut Council of Safety 1777–79 and 1782. With Richard Law, he revised the statutory laws of Connecticut in 1783. Mayor of New Haven, 1784–86. Delegate from Connecticut to the Constitutional Convention in Philadelphia in 1787, where he took active part in arranging the Connecticut compromise. Delegate to Connecticut ratifying convention of 1787, where he supported ratification. Wrote newspaper essays in support of Constitution. Only person to sign all the important documents in the course of creating the national government. Elected to the U.S. House of Representatives in 1789, giving up his seat on the supreme court of Connecticut. Elected to the U.S. Senate in 1791. He died in New Haven on July 23, 1793.

DANIEL SHUTE (1722–1802)   Born July 19, 1722, in Malden, Massachusetts, son of Mary Waite and John Shute. Entered Harvard College in 1739 and graduated in 1743. Kept school in Chelmsford and in 1746 was ordained minister of newly organized South Parish in Hingham. Espoused a Liberal or Arminian form of Congregationalism, tending toward Unitarianism. In 1753 he married Mary Cushing of Hingham (died 1756), with whom he had two children. In 1758 he was appointed chaplain in Massachusetts regiment in unsuccessful expedition against Ticonderoga and in Mohawk Valley, where he contracted smallpox. In 1763 he married Deborah Cushing of Pembroke. Supplemented minister's salary by preparing students for college, among them the sons of John Hancock and Benjamin Lincoln. Became prosperous and built a handsome mansion in Hingham. Opposed the Stamp Act, but his election sermon in 1768 was critical of James Otis's defense of smugglers. Elected delegate from Hingham to state constitutional convention of 1780. Elected delegate (with Benjamin Lincoln) to Massachusetts ratifying convention of 1788, where he argued in favor of clause prohibiting religious tests; voted for ratification. Awarded D.D. degree from Harvard College in 1790. With Henry Ware, published *A Compendious and Plain Catechism* (1794). By 1798, he had lost his sight and retired from the pulpit. He died in Hingham on August 31, 1802.

AMOS SINGLETARY (1721–1806)   Born in September 1721, the first male child born in recently settled Sutton, Massachusetts, fourth son and sixth child of Mary Greele and John Singletary. Educated at home. In 1742, married Mary Curtis of Topsfield, with whom he had nine children. Operated gristmill and served as justice of the peace and justice of quorum, one of the duties of which was to administer the debtor's oath. Represented Sutton in provincial congress for four years during Revolution. Member Massachusetts House of Representatives four times, and state senator twice. Delegate to Massachusetts ratifying convention of 1788, where he opposed ratification.

JOHN SMILIE (1742–1812)   Born in northern Ireland in 1742. Attended common schools. Moved to Lancaster County, Pennsylvania, in 1760. Member of provincial conferences of 1775 and 1776. Served as private in Pennsylvania regiment 1776–77. Assemblyman from Lancaster County 1778–80. Moved to Westmoreland County, Pennsylvania, in 1781. Delegate to state council of censors in 1783 and 1784, where he opposed revision of the 1776 state constitution. Assemblyman from newly formed Fayette County 1784–86. Supported revocation of charter of Bank of North America. Member state supreme executive council 1786–89. Delegate from Fayette County to Pennsylvania ratifying convention of 1787, where he opposed ratification. Attended convention at Harrisburg in 1788. Member of state constitutional convention in 1789–90; supported James Wilson's draft. Served in state senate 1790–92. Elected to U.S. House of Representatives 1793–95. Member state house of representatives 1795–98. Jeffersonian-Republican presidential elector in 1796. Elected to U.S. House of Representatives in 1798; reelected seven times. Became close to Madison and helped move Republican programs through Congress. Served until his death in Washington, D.C., on December 30, 1812.

JONATHAN SMITH (c. 1740–1802)   Smith moved to Lanesborough, Massachusetts, from Litchfield, Connecticut, in 1770. Married Esther Bacon. Held many important town offices, including selectman and assessor, and was several times representative in the Massachusetts General Court. Member of committees of public safety and correspondence. Colonel in Berkshire regiment of Massachusetts militia. Delegate to the 1780 state constitutional convention. Delegate to Massachusetts ratifying convention of 1788, where he spoke and voted in favor of ratification. Died September 9, 1802.

MELANCTON SMITH (1744–1798)   Born May 7, 1744, in Jamaica, Long Island, New York, son of Elizabeth Bayles and Samuel Smith. Educated at home. Became storekeeper in Poughkeepsie, Dutchess County, New York, where he began to buy land. Helped organize the Washington Hollow Presbyterian Church in 1769. After the death of his wife, Sarah Smith, in 1770, he married Margaret, daughter of Richbill Mott, in 1771; they had three children. One of ten delegates from Dutchess County to the first provincial congress in 1775. In June 1775, organized and was captain of the first company of minutemen in Dutchess County, with duty to detect Loyalist conspiracies. Appointed on December 20, 1776, major in command of all New York ranger companies. Appointed high sheriff of the county in 1777 and 1779. Bought confiscated Loyalist lands, became a substantial landowner, and speculated in government securities and bonds. With Governor George Clinton's support, became commissary agent for the army. Appointed by Washington in 1782 to commission to settle disputes between army and contractors at West Point and elsewhere. Moved to New York City in 1784 and became a merchant and a lawyer. Delegate from New York to the Continental Congress 1785-88. Because New York City, a Federalist stronghold, would not send him to the New York ratifying convention in 1788, Smith sought and won election from Dutchess County. He consistently opposed the Constitution without amendments, but, in a move of great importance to ratification, finally agreed to give his support after Federalists promised to incorporate a bill of rights and news of ratification by Virginia and New Hampshire reached New York. Part of the compromise consisted of a circular letter, written by John Jay, sent to other states asking for a second Constitutional Convention. Elected to the legislature in 1791. Worked for Clinton's reelection as governor in 1792 and was appointed circuit judge. Died during yellow fever outbreak in New York City, on July 29, 1798.

WILLIAM STEPHENS SMITH (1755–1816)   Born in New York City, on November 8, 1755, son of Margaret Stephens (of Loyalist parents) and John Smith (wealthy merchant). Graduated from College of New Jersey (now Princeton) in 1774 and began study of law with Samuel Jones of New York. Joined the Continental Army as aide to General John Sullivan with the rank of major in August 1776 and took part in the battle of Long Island. Fought at Harlem Heights (where he was wounded), Throgs Neck, and White Plains, and joined the retreat through New Jersey in the fall of 1776. Served at battle of Trenton and became lieutenant colonel in William R. Lee's regiment. Served under Putnam in New York in 1777, fought at Monmouth and Newport in 1778, fought under Sullivan against the Six Nations in 1779, and at Springfield in 1780. Served under Lafayette as inspector and adjutant to corps of light infantry. Appointed aide-de-camp to Washington in July 1781 and took part in the siege of Yorktown. Supervised British evacuation of New York in 1783. Appointed secretary of legation in London in 1785, where he met John Adams's daughter, Abigail, whom he married in June 1786 and with whom he had three children. Accompanied Francisco de Miranda on tour of Continent. Visited Prussia and undertook diplomatic mission to Spain and Portugal. Returned to America in 1788 and engaged in land speculation. Helped found the New York Society of the Cincinnati; elected its secretary in 1790 and president in 1795. Appointed by Washington marshal of the district of New York in 1789 and later supervisor of the revenue and surveyor of the port. Served in the state assembly for three years. Became involved with Miranda's attempt to make Venezuela independent. Went bankrupt and was put in prison in 1806 for debt and for aiding South American revolutionaries on U.S. soil. Retired to Hamilton, Madison County, New York. Elected to U.S. House of Representatives in 1812. Died at Lebanon, Madison County, on June 10, 1816.

ISAAC SNOW (1714–1799)   Born February 11, 1714, at Truro, Massachusetts, son of Elizabeth Ripley and John Snow, Jr. Moved to Harpswell, district of Maine, before 1740. Married Apphia Atwood, with whom he had at least two sons. In 1776 fitted out privateer schooner *America* (ten guns, 80 men) and was commissioned captain September 16, 1776. Privateer sailed to Boston, was sold and refitted for 16 guns, and Snow was commissioned first lieutenant under captain Daniel McNeill on April 17, 1777. Delegate from Harpswell to Massachusetts ratifying convention of 1788, where he supported ratification. Died at St. Georges, district of Maine, in 1799.

JOHN STEVENS, JR.   (1749–1838)   Born in New York City in 1749, son of Elizabeth (daughter of James Alexander) and John Stevens (ship owner and merchant with extensive land holdings and political interests in New Jersey). Grew up at Perth Amboy, New Jersey. Received tutoring at home and at Kenersley's College near Woodbridge. Joined family in New York in 1762. Entered King's College (now Columbia) in 1766 and graduated in 1768. Admitted to the New York bar in 1771, but never practiced law. Joined his father in New Jersey political work and acted occasionally as special aide to Governor William Franklin. At the outbreak of the Revolution, commissioned captain in the New Jersey militia and appointed a loan office collector. New Jersey state treasurer 1777–83 and state surveyor general 1782–83. Married Rachel (daughter of John Cox of Bloomsbury, New Jersey) in October 1782, and they had seven children who survived him, including several who became successful inventors. In 1784, he bought a large tract of land (including most of present-day Hoboken) at auction. Lived in New York in winter and at his Hoboken estate, Castle Point, in summer. In 1787 and 1788 wrote "Americanus" essays supporting ratification of the Constitution. Attended demonstration of steamboat by John Fitch and James Rumsey on the Delaware River in 1788 and began serious study of its prospects. Urged friends in Congress to pass the first patent law in April 1790. With his brother-in-law Robert R. Livingston, Nicholas J. Roosevelt, and others, built experimental steamboats 1797–1800. Became consulting engineer for the Manhattan Company, organized by Livingston, Burr, and others to supply city with fresh water and act as a bank. Installed steam pump for company and continued to develop steam-powered engines and build boats. Robert Fulton, Roosevelt, and Livingston were granted a monopoly on steamboat traffic on the Hudson River in 1807. Stevens developed the first ocean-going steamboat and operated steamboats on the Delaware and the Connecticut Rivers and ferries to

Hoboken and elsewhere. Began to consider use of steam engine for railroad in 1810 and lobbied states to open ways. Received charter from New Jersey legislature to build railroad from Trenton to New Brunswick in 1815. Organized unsuccessful Pennsylvania Railroad with charter from state legislature in 1823. In 1825, to prove the viability of the steam locomotive, he built a model for demonstrations on his Hoboken estate. It was the first steam locomotive in the United States. Formed Camden & Amboy Railroad Company in 1830. He died in Hoboken on March 6, 1838.

EZRA STILES (1727–1795)   Born November 29 (old style), 1727, in North Haven (then part of New Haven), Connecticut, son of Kezia (daughter of Edward Taylor of Westfield, Massachusetts) and Isaac Stiles (Congregational minister). Mother died following his birth. His father married Esther Hooker (daughter of Samuel Hooker, Jr., of Hartford) in 1728. Educated at home. Attended Yale College and graduated in 1746. Received license to preach in 1749. Became a tutor at Yale, but uncertain about some elements of Christian doctrine, began study of law. Experimented with electrical apparatus sent to the college by Franklin, leading to a long friendship with him. Admitted to the bar in November 1753. In 1754 traveled to Newport, Boston, New York, and Philadelphia and attended Quaker, Episcopal, Dutch Reformed, and Roman Catholic services. In 1755 became pastor of the Second Congregational Church of Newport, Rhode Island. Appointed librarian of Redwood Library in Newport in 1756, giving him the opportunity to continue his studies. In February 1757 married Elizabeth, daughter of John Hubbard of New Haven, and they had five children who survived him. Supported Manning's efforts to establish the Baptist Rhode Island College (now Brown University) in 1763. Awarded D.D. degree from Edinburgh in 1765 and membership in the American Philosophical Society in 1768, both sponsored by Franklin. Wife Elizabeth died in 1775. Tensions in wartime Newport caused him to move his family to Dighton, Massachusetts, in March 1776. In May 1777 he accepted post at the First Church in Portsmouth, New Hampshire. Considered one of the most learned men in New England, Stiles was elected president of Yale in September 1777. Accepted post in March 1778 and moved in July to New Haven, where he spent the remainder of his life. He strongly supported colonial rights throughout the Revolutionary period. He married Mary, daughter of Benjamin Cranston of Newport and widow of William Checkley, in October 1782. Became the first president of the Connecticut Society for the Abolition of Slavery in 1790. Died in New Haven on May 12, 1795.

INCREASE SUMNER (1746–1799)   Born November 27, 1746, in Roxbury, Massachusetts, son of Sarah (daughter of Robert Sharp of Brookline and first cousin of John Adams's mother) and Increase Sumner (prosperous farmer). Attended Roxbury Grammar School (later Roxbury Latin), where he studied under William Cushing and Joseph Warren. Graduated from Harvard in 1767. Taught school in Roxbury for two years and studied law under Samuel

Quincy, solicitor general of the province. Admitted to the bar in 1774 and opened successful practice in Roxbury. Disapproved of British colonial policies, but took no part in the Revolution. Elected to the provincial congress 1776–79. In September 1779 married Elizabeth, daughter of William Hyslop, a Boston merchant of Scots descent, with whom he had a son and two daughters who survived him. Member of the Massachusetts convention of 1777–78 that drafted a constitution rejected by the voters. Member of the state constitutional convention of 1779–80. Elected to the state senate 1780–82. Appointed to the Massachusetts Supreme Judicial Court in 1782. Delegate to the Massachusetts ratifying convention of 1788, where he strongly supported ratification. Member of the board of trustees of Roxbury Latin, the Society for Propagating the Gospel among the Indians, and the American Academy of Arts and Sciences. Devoted himself to farming and the advancement of agriculture. An extremely popular Federalist, he was elected governor for three terms 1797–99. He died in Roxbury on June 7, 1799.

LAWRENCE TALIAFERRO (1734–1798)   Born December 3, 1734, son of Elizabeth (daughter of John Hay) and Francis Taliaferro. In 1758 married Mary Jackson, with whom he had three children who survived him. After her death, he married Sarah, daughter of Baldwin Dade, in February 1774, and they had seven children who survived. Served with James Madison on the committee of safety for Orange County 1774–76. Colonel of militia and Culpeper Minute Men (of which Thomas Marshall was captain and John Marshall, his son, lieutenant) September 1775–April 1776. Lived at Rose Hill, Orange County, Virginia, and was justice of the peace for Orange County. Died April 8, 1798.

GEORGE THATCHER (1754–1824)   Born April 12, 1754, in Yarmouth, Massachusetts, son of Anner Lewis and Lieutenant Peter Thatcher. Prepared for college under minister Timothy Hilliard of Barnstable. Graduated from Harvard College in 1776 (in class with Christopher Gore). Served one cruise on privateer. Studied law under Shearjashub Bourne of Cape Cod. Admitted to bar in 1778. Moved to York, district of Maine, and commenced practice. Settled at Biddeford in 1782 and took over practice from James Sullivan. Elected to Massachusetts General Court. In July 1784, married Sarah Savage of Weston, Massachusetts, with whom he had ten children. Delegate from Massachusetts to Continental Congress in 1787. Supported ratification of the Constitution and corresponded with delegates to Massachusetts ratifying convention, journalists, and office-holders, including Christopher Gore, Nathaniel Barrell, Rufus King, Samuel Nasson, William Widgery, Samuel Thompson, Nathan Dane, Samuel Otis, Jeremiah Hill, and Thomas Wait. Elected to U.S. House of Representatives in 1789 and reelected for five more terms through 1801. Judge in Maine district 1792–1800. Associate judge of Massachusetts Supreme Court 1800–20. Delegate to Maine constitutional convention in 1819. Judge of Maine Supreme Court 1820–24. About 1815, he began to spell his name "Thacher." Died in Biddeford, Maine, April 6, 1824.

SAMUEL THOMPSON (1735–1797)   Born in Brunswick, district of Maine, March 22, 1735, son of Reliance Hinkley and James Thompson. Selectman for Brunswick in 1768, 1770, and 1771. In 1774, became lieutenant colonel of militia, then colonel. On May 9, 1775, directed the capture at Falmouth of Captain Henry Mowatt of British sloop-of-war *Canceaux*, who was subsequently released on parole (Mowatt returned five months later and destroyed much of Falmouth by naval bombardment). On February 8, 1776, appointed brigadier general of Cumberland County militia. Head of the district committee of safety and representative to provincial congress in 1776. Moved to Topsham, Maine, about 1784 and was elected to the Massachusetts General Court as representative 1784–88 and 1790–94 and as senator in 1797. Earned considerable wealth (over $35,000 when he died). Delegate from Topsham to Massachusetts ratifying convention of 1788, where (with other delegates from the Maine region) he strongly opposed ratification, objecting to its provision for a standing army, infrequent elections, and acceptance of slavery. Unlike many other minority delegates, Thompson continued to oppose ratification after the Massachusetts convention. He died in Topsham in 1797.

CHARLES TILLINGHAST (c. 1748–1795)   A New York City distiller and merchant, Tillinghast married the oldest daughter of John Lamb and was allied with New York City's Sons of Liberty and Revolutionary leaders. During the war he was assistant to Hugh Hughes, deputy quartermaster general of Continental Army, and secured vessels for the evacuation from Long Island in 1776. In October 1788, became secretary of the New York Federal Republican Society, organized with his father-in-law and Melancton Smith, which distributed Antifederalist literature and agitated for a second federal convention. Served in the customs house until his death in the yellow fever epidemic of 1795.

GEORGE LEE TURBERVILLE (1760–1798)   Born September 7, 1760, son of Martha Lee and George Turberville of Westmoreland County. Educated in England. Captain in the 15th Virginia Regiment in 1776. Major and aide-de-camp to General Charles Lee in 1778. In 1781, served under Baron von Steuben during the invasion of Virginia until they had a strong disagreement and Turberville resigned. Married Bettie Tayloe Corbin. A planter and a neighbor and friend of Washington, Tuberville was elected from Richmond County to Virginia House of Delegates 1785–89. He was defeated in election to be delegate to Virginia ratifying convention in 1788. Sheriff of Richmond County in 1798. Died at Epping, Richmond County, March 26, 1798.

CHARLES TURNER (1732–1818)   Born at Scituate, Massachusetts, September 3, 1732, son of Eunice James and Charles Turner. Attended Harvard College and graduated in 1752. Joined church at Truro in 1752 and began to preach. In 1753 declined offer of pastorship, returned to Harvard, and practiced law briefly. In 1754 accepted call from church at Duxbury, where he was ordained in 1755. In 1757 married Mary Rand, with whom he had at least six children. Proponent of Liberal Congregationalism and early advocate of separation from England. Preached election sermon May 26, 1773, which offended Governor Hutchinson by its statement of Whig principles. Served on committees of correspondence and was harrassed by Tories and British sympathizers. Resigned as minister of Duxbury in 1775 and moved to Scituate. Elected state representative in 1780 and state senator 1783–88. Elected delegate to Massachusetts ratifying convention of 1788, where he initially opposed ratification over issue of annual elections, but changed his mind and spoke and voted for ratification with recommended amendments. Appointed chaplain of prison at Castle Island 1789–93. In 1791 moved to Turner (named in his honor in 1786), district of Maine, where he owned 23,000 acres. Continued to preach and became minister of First Church of Turner in 1803. Served as justice of the peace. Was an outspoken Federalist during the 1790s, but was a presidential elector for Jefferson in 1804. Died in Turner on August 10, 1818.

JOSEPH BRADLEY VARNUM (1750–1821)   Born January 29, 1750, in Dracut, Middlesex County, Massachusetts, son of Hannah Mitchell and Samuel Varnum. Attended common schools, but was mainly self-educated. Became a farmer and joined local militia, elected captain in 1770. Married Molly (daughter of Jacob Butler of Pelham, New Hampshire) in January 1773; they had 12 children. Present at the battle of Lexington in April 1775. Captain of the Dracut Minute Men, January 1776–April 1777. Served in campaigns against Burgoyne in 1777 and in Rhode Island in 1778. Elected to the state house of representatives 1780–84. Member of the state senate 1786–88 and 1795. Served with militia in suppression of Shays' Rebellion 1786–87. Appointed colonel of militia in 1787. Delegate from Dracut to the Massachusetts ratifying convention of 1788, where he supported ratification. Elected in 1795 to the U.S. House of Representatives; reelected eight times, serving 1795–1811. Speaker of the House of Representatives, 1807–11. Appointed brigadier general of militia in 1802 and major general in 1805. Unsuccessful Republican candidate for lieutenant governor in 1809. Resigned from House to take seat in the U.S. Senate 1811–17. Elected president pro tempore of the Senate in 1813 and was acting vice-president after death of Elbridge Gerry. Supported the Embargo Act and the War of 1812 (the only New Englander in Congress who supported the war) and opposed slavery and the slave trade. Lost election for governor to Caleb Strong in 1813. Appointed justice of the court of common pleas and chief justice of the court of general sessions 1811–15. Elected again to the state senate 1817–21. In 1818, he owned a farm of 500 acres. Delegate to the 1820 state constitutional convention. Helped found the Massachusetts Peace Society. Withdrew from Congregational church and became a Baptist. Died in Dracut on September 21, 1821.

JAMES WADSWORTH (1730–1817)   Born in Durham, Connecticut, July 8, 1730. Attended Yale College and graduated in 1748. Studied law and was admitted to bar. Served as militia officer 1752–79. Town clerk of Durham 1756–86. Delegate from Durham to state house of representatives 1759–85 (speaker 1784–85) and 1788–89. Justice of the peace for New Haven County

1761–86 and 1788–91 and justice of quorum 1773–78. Member council of safety 1777–82. Major general of state militia 1777–79. Judge of New Haven County court 1778–89. Delegate to Hartford Convention in 1780. Delegate from Connecticut to the Continental Congress 1783–86. Member state executive council 1785–89. State comptroller 1786–87. Delegate to Connecticut ratifying convention in 1788, where he opposed ratification. Refused reappointment to New Haven County court in 1789 rather than take the oath to uphold the Constitution. Died in Durham on September 22, 1817.

THOMAS BAKER WAIT (1762–1830)   Born in Saugus, Massachusetts, in 1762. Worked for the Boston *Independent Chronicle*. In 1784, married Betsy Smith, with whom he had at least two sons. Moved to Falmouth (now Portland), district of Maine, where he established (with Benjamin Titcomb) *Falmouth Gazette and Weekly Advertiser*, first newspaper in Maine. Was petitioner for incorporation of Portland in 1785. In 1786 paper became *Cumberland Gazette*, published by Wait alone, and in 1792 it became the *Eastern Herald*. A supporter of George Thatcher, Wait was physically assaulted by Thatcher's political opponents during the congressional campaign of 1792. Transferred paper to John Kelse Baker in 1796. He moved to Boston and collected and published *State Papers and Publick Documents of the United States* (8 volumes, 1814–15). He died in Boston in 1830.

BUSHROD WASHINGTON (1762–1829)   Born June 5, 1762, in Westmoreland County, Virginia, son of Hannah Bushrod of Bluefield, Virginia, and John Augustine Washington, younger brother of George Washington. Studied under a tutor in the home of Richard Henry Lee. Graduated from William and Mary College in 1778. Enlisted in the Continental Army as a private and was present at the surrender of Cornwallis at Yorktown in 1781. Studied law in Philadelphia under James Wilson. Admitted to the bar in Virginia; opened practice in Alexandria. Married Julia Ann Blackburn (daughter of Thomas Blackburn of Rippon Lodge, a former aide to Washington) in 1785; they had no children. Elected to the Virginia House of Delegates in 1787. Delegate to the Virginia ratifying convention in 1788, where he supported ratification. Moved to Richmond in 1790 because of his growing law practice. Among his many law students was Henry Clay. Appointed by John Adams in 1798 to succeed James Wilson on the U.S. Supreme Court, where he served until his death. George Washington left him his library, public and private papers, and Mount Vernon estate, where he moved after the death of Martha Washington in 1802. He favored the abolition of slavery and in 1816 was elected the first president of the American Colonization Society, but he sold 54 Mount Vernon slaves to Louisiana because he said their repeated attempts at escape made their retention unprofitable. He died in Philadelphia on November 26, 1829.

GEORGE WASHINGTON (1732–1799)   Born February 22, 1732, at Wakefield, Westmoreland County, Virginia, eldest son of Mary Ball and Augustine

Washington (who had two sons from a previous marriage). Family moved in 1735 to Little Hunting Creek, Stafford County, on the Potomac River and later to Ferry Farm, King George County, on the Rappahannock River. Father died in 1743, and Washington lived six years with relatives, including his half-brothers Augustine, in Westmoreland County, and Lawrence, at Mount Vernon. Attended school and studied mathematics and surveying. In 1748, accompanied James Genn to survey lands for Lord Fairfax in Shenandoah Valley. Appointed surveyor for Culpeper County in 1749. Accompanied half-brother Lawrence to Barbados and contracted smallpox before return to Virginia. Lawrence died in 1752, leaving Mount Vernon to him after his wife's death (she moved out and left it to him). Appointed adjutant general of Virginia militia, with rank of major. Commissioned in November 1753 to carry ultimatum demanding evacuation of French posts in Ohio territory and to meet with chiefs of the Six Nations. Traveled overland to forks of Ohio, held council with Six Nations at Logstown, and then proceeded to Fort Le Boeuf on Lake Erie, where he delivered message to French commander. Returned to Virginia in January 1754 and wrote report published in London as *The Journal of Major George Washington* in 1754. Commissioned lieutenant colonel of militia and sent to occupy forks of Ohio in April 1754. Finding French already in possession, built Fort Necessity near Great Meadows, Pennsylvania. Skirmished with French and signed armistice in July 1754. Resigned from militia in late 1754. Appointed aide-de-camp to General Braddock on British expedition against Fort Duquesne at forks of Ohio in 1755. Taken ill, but rejoined army the day before it was surprised by French and Indians at the Monongahela on July 9, 1755. Two horses were shot from under him and four bullets passed through his coat during battle. British force retreated to Great Meadows. Death of Braddock ended his appointment as aide-de-camp. Appointed colonel and commander-in-chief of Virginia forces in fall 1755, with responsibility for defense of the frontier. Defeated for election to Virginia House of Burgesses in 1755 and 1757. Traveled to Boston in February 1756 to resolve status of colonial military commissions. In 1758, cooperated with British general John Forbes in expedition against Fort Duquesne, which French forces abandoned on their approach in November 1758. Resigned from militia. Elected burgess from Frederick County in 1758 and reelected annually through 1774. Married Martha Dandridge Custis, wealthy widow of Daniel Parke Custis, in January 1759, and became farmer and planter at Mount Vernon. An early supporter of patriot causes, often enlisted his neighbor George Mason to write resolutions. Elected delegate from Virginia to First Continental Congress in 1774. Chosen commander of militia of five Virginia counties. Elected delegate to Second Continental Congress in 1775, where on June 15 he was unanimously elected commander-in-chief of all Continental forces. Traveled to Cambridge and assumed command of forces surrounding Boston in early July. Secured authorization from Continental Congress to bombard Boston, and by March 5, 1776, had brought captured cannon from Ticonderoga and entrenched them on Dorchester Heights. British evacuated Boston on March 17, 1776. At request of Congress, moved army to New York to defend against expected British invasion under Howe. Outflanked and defeated by British and Hessians at battle of Long Island on August 27, 1776. Evacuated Brooklyn on August 30 and New York City on September 12, 1776. Withdrew army to Harlem Heights, where it defeated British assault on September 16. Retreated to White Plains, and repulsed British attack on October 28. Forced to abandon Fort Lee, New Jersey, on November 20. Retreated with army to Newark, then New Brunswick, and finally to west bank of Delaware River in early December. British occupied Amboy, New Brunswick, Princeton, and Trenton, and went into winter quarters. On December 25, 1776, Washington led 2,400 troops across Delaware River and surprised and defeated Hessian forces at Trenton. Recrossed Delaware, but returned to Trenton on December 30. British counterattack on January 2, 1777, trapped Washington and army against Delaware River. Americans withdrew under cover of darkness, eluded opposing British forces, and advanced to Princeton, where they defeated smaller British force on January 3. Took army into winter quarters in Watchung Mountains near Morristown. British retreated to New Brunswick and Amboy. Trained and reorganized army into five divisions under major generals Greene, Sullivan, Stephen, Lincoln, and Stirling. Appointed marquis de Lafayette and Alexander Hamilton to his staff in 1777. Skirmished with British army in June 1777 but declined to be drawn into major battle. British evacuated New Jersey and began expedition against Philadelphia by way of Chesapeake Bay. Moved army south of Philadelphia to block British advance. Fought battle of Brandywine on September 11, 1777. British occupied Philadelphia on September 23. Washington attacked British force at Germantown, Pennsylvania, on October 4, but was driven back by reinforcements. British withdrew to Philadelphia. Informed of efforts involving Major General Thomas Conway to replace him as commander-in-chief with Horatio Gates, recent victor at Saratoga. Took army into winter quarters at Valley Forge, where Baron von Steuben was employed in drilling and training. Repeatedly appealed to Continental Congress and the states for provisions and supplies for ill-equipped and malnourished army. Supported proposal to grant Continental officers half pay for life. New British commander Clinton began overland evacuation from Philadelphia in June 1778. Washington followed, intercepted British, and fought inconclusive battle of Monmouth on June 28, 1778. British continued retreat to New York. Washington followed to White Plains and commenced land blockade. In 1779, British advanced up Hudson River and captured uncompleted American fort at Stony Point on June 1. Appointed Anthony Wayne to command attack that recaptured fort on July 16, halting British advance. Focus of British actions shifted to South, and Washington continued to occupy positions around New York City and plan attack in cooperation with French forces under Rochambeau. In August 1781, French and Continental armies were combined near New York City when Washington learned that French admiral De Grasse had sailed for Chesapeake Bay to drive off British fleet and trap Cornwallis and British Army at Yorktown, Virginia. Leaving half of Continental Army to hold British in New York, Washington proceeded with other half and French Army to join forces under Lafayette at Yorktown. Washington detoured to Mount Vernon for first visit home in six years. Armies assembled outside Yorktown by September 15, 1781, and commenced successful siege. British army surrendered October 19, 1781, ending major military operations of Revolution. Cornwallis declined to attend surrender, and Washington delegated Benjamin Lincoln to accept sword from British subordinate. Led troops back to Newburgh, New York. Adopted two of wife's orphaned grandchildren. Sent memorial to Congress regarding treatment of army veterans in December 1782 and addressed meeting of potentially rebellious officers at Newburgh in March 1783, stressing patience and duty. Sent circular letter to states seeking justice for officers and men and recommending union of states under federal head. After preliminary peace treaty was signed, Washington fixed the date for cessation of hostilities on April 19, 1783 (anniversary of battle of Lexington). Occupied New York as British evacuated on November 25. Traveled to Annapolis to meet with Continental Congress and resigned as commander-in-chief December 23, 1783. Retired to private life at Mount Vernon. Visited lands on Kanawha and Ohio rivers in 1784 and became president of Potomac Company to develop navigation routes to western rivers. Secured passage of bills in Maryland and Virginia legislatures to perform survey, create joint-stock company, and undertake construction. Meeting at Mount Vernon indirectly led to convention of states to discuss interstate commerce at Annapolis in 1786, which called for Constitutional Convention to be held in 1787. Attempted to restore financial condition of estate, but declined to sell slaves "because I am principled against this kind of traffic." Named to Virginia delegation to Constitutional Convention in Philadelphia in 1787 and was unanimously elected president of the convention. Signed and transmitted proposed Constitution to Continental Congress in September 1787. Supported ratification through private letters and advised James Madison and others. Unanimously elected first president of United States by electors from ten states on February 4, 1789. Inaugurated in New York on April 30, 1789. Appointed Thomas Jefferson secretary of state, Alexander Hamilton secretary of treasury, and Henry Knox secretary of war. Appointments to Supreme Court included successive chief justices John Jay, John Rutledge, and Oliver Ellsworth, and associate justices William Cushing, James Wilson, James Iredell, and Samuel Chase. Wished to retire after first term but was convinced to serve again. Unanimously reelected president by electors from fifteen states in 1792. Issued proclamation of neutrality in European wars on April 22, 1793. Disturbed by growing dissension between Jefferson and Hamilton, relied on Randolph as intermediary, and after Jefferson's retirement, appointed Randolph in his place. Called out militia to suppress Whiskey Rebellion in western Pennsylvania in fall of 1794 and led troops in person. Met with emissaries William Findley and David Redick at Carlisle before army under Hamilton, Henry Lee, and Daniel Morgan occupied western Pennsylvania. Pardoned all insurgents who took oath of allegiance. Denounced Democratic Societies for their alleged role in the rebellion. Pinckney Treaty with Spain in 1795 secured navigation rights on Mississippi River. Appointed John Jay to negotiate differences with Great Britain and though disappointed with elements of it, succeeded in having Jay's Treaty ratified despite opposition. Refused to supply papers relating to treaty to House of Representatives on grounds it had no constitutional role in ratification. Despite wish to avoid party factionalism, found his administration increasingly supported by Federalists and attacked by Republicans. After Hamilton's retirement, continued to rely on him for advice; asked him to help write "Farewell Address," published in September 1796; was succeeded as president by John Adams in 1797. Retired to Mount Vernon. On July 3, 1798, appointed lieutenant general and commander-in-chief of army being raised in expectation of war with France. Insisted on Hamilton as second in command over Adams's objections. Died at Mount Vernon after brief illness (cynache trachealis) on December 14, 1799. Congress immediately adopted resolutions, delivered by John Marshall and written by Henry Lee, declaring him "first in war, first in peace, and first in the hearts of his countrymen" and making February 22 a national holiday. French armies and British fleets flew flags at half-mast. His will granted freedom to Mount Vernon slaves after his wife's death and provided endowment for a national university.

NOAH WEBSTER (1758–1843)   Born October 16, 1758, in West Hartford, Connecticut, son of Mercy Steele and Noah Webster (farmer, justice of the peace, and deacon of the Congregational church). Enjoyed reading at an early age and attended local schools. Attended Yale College and graduated in 1778, though his father had to mortgage his farm to make this possible. Worked as a teacher and clerk and read law under several lawyers. Admitted to the bar in Hartford in 1781. Taught school in Goshen, New York, and prepared a spelling book, the first in a series of publications that included a grammar and a reader, together forming his *Grammatical Institute of the English Language* (changed to *American Language* in later editions). The difficulty of securing copyrights from thirteen separate state governments helped convince him of the need for an effective national government, and he became an active pamphleteer in the Federalist cause. Traveled to various states to obtain copyrights and earned a living by teaching, holding singing schools, and lecturing. Met Benjamin Franklin in Philadelphia in 1786 and discussed a favorite project of simplified spelling. Coined the terms "fœderal" and "antifœderal" for opposing political factions in 1786. Moved to New York to edit the new *American Magazine* in 1787, but the venture did not succeed. Published articles under various pseudonyms ("America," "Giles Hickory," "A Citizen of America") supporting ratification of the Constitution. Moved back to Hartford in 1788 to practice law. Married Rebecca Greenleaf (daughter of William Greenleaf, a Boston merchant) in Boston in October 1789 and eventually had seven children who survived him. Practiced law in Hartford until 1793, when prominent Federalists persuaded him to move to New York and edit a daily newspaper *The Minerva* (later *Commercial Advertiser*) and semi-weekly *The Herald* (later *Spectator*). He remained a Federalist all his life; strongly defended Adams against Hamilton in 1800. In New York, he continued to write on various subjects, including political economy and medicine. In 1803 he moved to New Haven and began work on his dictionary. Published first edition of his *Dictionary of the English Language* in 1806 and the larger *American Dictionary of the English Language* in 1828. Moved to Amherst, Massachusetts, in 1812 and helped found Amherst College in 1821. Served in Massachusetts legislature in 1815 and 1819. Returned to New Haven in 1822. Traveled in France and England to do research in lexicography 1824–25. Died in New Haven on May 28, 1843.

PELATIAH WEBSTER   (1726–1795)   Born November 24, 1726, in Lebanon, Connecticut, son of Joanna Crowfoot Smith and Pelatiah Webster. Graduated from Yale College in 1746. Studied theology and began preaching in Greenwich, Massachusetts, where he was ordained pastor in December 1749. He married widow Ruth Kellogg of Suffield, Connecticut, in September 1750, and they had five children. Moved to Philadelphia in 1755 and became a merchant. In 1776 he began to write essays on political economy, arguing against paper currency and the funding of the war by loans rather than taxation. While carrying cargo to Boston in 1777, he was captured by the British and held prisoner for several weeks in Newport. Jailed during the British occupation of Philadelphia in 1778; his property was confiscated (he later recovered most of it). After the war he continued writing on economic policy and published in 1783 one of the earliest pamphlets calling for a stronger national union. After death of his first wife, he married Rebecca Hunt in Boston in October 1785 (she died in 1793). Published pamphlets strongly supporting ratification of the Constitution. He died in Philadelphia on September 2, 1795.

SAMUEL WEST   (1730–1807)   Born March 3, 1730 (old style), in Yarmouth, Massachusetts, son of Ruth Jenkins and Sackfield West (medical practicioner and preacher). Moved at early age to Barnstable, Massachusetts, and studied with minister Joseph Green. Attended Harvard College on scholarship and graduated in 1754. Kept school at Falmouth, Massachusetts. In 1758, was candidate for ministerial post at Tisbury, on Martha's Vineyard; declined post in 1759 and preached briefly at Plymouth. In 1760 began 43-year pastorate at Acushnet or Dartmouth (after 1787, New Bedford), Massachusetts. In 1768 married Experience Howland of Plymouth, with whom he had at least one son. Widely respected for his piety and learning, he was often supported by the charity of Boston merchants. Elected to American Philosophical Society in 1768 and helped found American Academy of Arts and Sciences. Known as "Doctor West" or "Pater West," he was described as six feet, 200 pounds, perpetually disheveled, absent-minded, eccentric, and argumentative. An early advocate of Whig politics, he joined the army after Bunker Hill and served as chaplain for several months. In September 1775 deciphered captured coded letter from former Harvard classmate Benjamin Church, physician general of Continental Army, informing British of colonial defenses (Church was cashiered and imprisoned). Wrote many pieces supporting colonial cause for newspapers and preached election sermon in 1776. He was an Arminian or

Liberal Congregationalist and regarded the events of 1775 as the fulfillment of Biblical prophecies and the beginning of the millennium. Delegate from Dartmouth to state constitutional convention in 1779; published "Irenaeus" articles in Boston newspapers. Delegate from New Bedford to Massachusetts ratifying convention in 1788, where he supported ratification and privately urged former classmate Governor John Hancock to "come forth to save it, even if you are borne in men's arms—even at the sacrifice of your life." Wife Experience died in 1789, and in 1790 he married Louisa Hathaway Jenne (died 1797). In 1793 published *Essays on Liberty and Necessity*, arguing against New Light denial of free will. Close friend of Ezra Stiles and John Adams. Received S.T.D. from Harvard in 1793. Retired from pastorate in June 1803 and lived with son in Tiverton, Rhode Island, until his death on September 24, 1807.

ROBERT WHITEHILL (1738–1813)　Born July 21, 1738, in the Pequea settlement, Lancaster, Pennsylvania, son of Rachel Cresswell and James Whitehill (born in northern Ireland and settled in Pennsylvania in 1723). Received a good elementary education, studied under the Reverend Francis Alison, and read on his own. Married Eleanor (daughter of Adam Reed, an early western Pennsylvania settler) in 1765. In 1770 bought 440 acres of land in Lauther Manor (now Cumberland County) and built the area's first stone house two miles from the Susquehanna (near Harrisburg), where he lived for the rest of his life. Member of the county committee of safety 1774–75; favored independence by spring 1776. With George Bryan, helped draft the Pennsylvania constitution of 1776. Elected to the assembly 1776–78, 1783–87, and 1797–1801. Member of the state council of safety in 1777. Member of the state supreme executive council December 1779–November 1781. Member of the council of censors 1783–84, where he opposed revision of the state constitution. In 1785, he led the fight to revoke the charter of the Bank of North America. A strong Antifederalist, he was a delegate to the Pennsylvania ratifying convention of 1787, where he led the opposition to ratification. Attended the Antifederalist Harrisburg Convention in 1788. Delegate to the state constitutional convention of 1789–90, where he opposed changing the 1776 constitution and refused to sign the new state constitution. Elected to the state senate 1801–05. Elected to the U.S. House of Representatives four terms 1805–13, where he supported the policies of the Jeffersonian Republicans. He died at Lauther Manor on April 7, 1813.

WILLIAM WIDGERY (c. 1753–1822)　Born probably in Devonshire, England, about 1753. Immigrated with parents to Philadelphia and attended common schools. Engaged in shipbuilding. Served as lieutenant of a privateer during Revolution. Settled in New Gloucester, district of Maine, studied law, and was admitted to bar about 1790. Served in Massachusetts House of Representatives 1787–93 and 1795–97 and in state senate in 1794. Elected delegate to Massachusetts ratifying convention from New Gloucester in 1788, helped lead opposition to ratification, but after ratification said he would now support the Constitution. Served as selectman of New Gloucester 1789–90 and 1794–95. Member of state executive council 1806 and 1807. Elected as Republican to U.S. House of Representatives, served 1811 to 1813; supported War of 1812. Defeated for reelection; appointed judge of court of common pleas in 1813 and served until 1821. Died in Portland, Maine, July 31, 1822.

JAMES WILSON (1742–1798)   Born September 14, 1742, in Caskardy, Fifeshire, Scotland, son of Alison Lansdale and William Wilson (farmer and Associate Presbyterian). Educated for the ministry, attended the local grammar school, and entered St. Andrews United College on a scholarship in November 1757. Forced to leave school after his father's death, became a private tutor. Went to Edinburgh to learn bookkeeping and merchant accounting from Thomas Young. Sailed to America in fall 1765. Hired as Latin tutor in the College of Philadelphia (now University of Pennsylvania) in February 1766. Began study of law with John Dickinson in 1766. Admitted to the bar in Reading, Pennsylvania, where he began practice in 1767. Extended practice to surrounding counties and, in April 1769, was admitted to practice before the Pennsylvania supreme court. Moved to Carlisle, Pennsylvania, in fall 1770. Married Rachel (daughter of William Bird, a wealthy ironmaster from Birdsboro, near Reading) in November 1771; they had six children. Law practice grew, and in 1773 he began speculation in land, which he continued for the rest of his life. Became head of committee of correspondence and was elected to the first provincial convention in Philadelphia, July 1774. Published "Considerations on the Nature and Extent of the Legislative Authority of the British Parliament" (written in 1768, but now revised), maintaining colonies' allegiance to king while denying parliament's authority over them. Elected to provincial convention again in January 1775. Elected delegate to the Second Continental Congress, May 1775. Appointed to permanent committee of Indian affairs and was made one of three commissioners for the middle colonies. Traveled to Fort Pitt in August. Reelected to Continental Congress in November 1775. Active on many committees, serving with John and Samuel Adams, Patrick Henry, Richard Henry Lee, Franklin, and others. Initially favored delay of vote on independence in 1776, but was one of the three out of seven delegates from Pennsylvania who voted for it on July 2. Elected member of the Board of War. Consistently argued in Congress for a more powerful central government. Opposed the Pennsylvania state constitution of 1776; was not reelected to Continental Congress by the assembly in September 1777. Continued opposition to 1776 state constitution and organized attempts to have it changed, writing articles in the paper, sending out petitions, and communicating with friends around the state. No longer comfortable in Carlisle, where most of the people supported the 1776 constitution, moved to Philadelphia after the evacuation of the British in 1778. Defended Tories in court and developed new legal concept of treason; reputation as lawyer continued to grow. With help of friends, defended his house from angry mob in fall 1779. People on both sides were killed, and Wilson was forced to leave the city for over a week (in March 1780, a general pardon was issued to all concerned). With Robert Morris and Thomas Willing, attempted to create the Bank of Philadelphia to stabilize the currency, but the assembly refused to support it. Helped Robert Morris, appointed by Congress as superintendent of Continental finances, create the Bank of North America, chartered by Congress in 1781 (later chartered by Pennsylvania as well), becoming a subscriber, member of the Board of Trustees, and its attorney. Accepted Bushrod Washington as law student in his office. Successfully defended Pennsylvania's claims to the Wyoming Valley against Connecticut. Served in Continental Congress 1783–87, but was often absent on other affairs. Continued to enlarge land holdings and various business enterprises. Successfully defended (after initial defeat) the Bank of North America 1785–87. Elected to the American Philosophical Society in 1786. Wife Rachel died in 1786. Delegate from Pennsylvania to the Constitutional Convention in Philadelphia in 1787, where he was one of the most influential members, and to the Pennsylvania ratifying convention of 1787, where he led the Federalist forces for ratification. The new Pennsylvania constitution drafted in the state's constitutional convention 1789–90 was primarily Wilson's work, incorporating his idea of direct election of both houses of the legislature and governor (he was aided by Findley, Redick, and Smilie in getting his version passed). Appointed by Washington to the U.S. Supreme Court in 1789. Became the first professor of law in the College of Philadelphia; gave his first lecture in December 1790, and continued until 1791. Married Hannah Gray of Boston in September 1793. Disappointed when he was not appointed chief justice after Jay's resignation in 1795. Continued land speculations and efforts to build industrial community at Wilsonville, Pennsylvania, with borrowed money. The depression of 1796–97 made it impossible to meet his obligations, and he left Philadelphia (still retaining his position on Supreme Court) for Burlington, New Jersey, where he was arrested for debt in 1797. Released on bail raised by his son, he went south hoping to sell some of his land there. Stayed with fellow Supreme Court justice James Iredell in Edenton, North Carolina, until he was arrested again. Released on bail; took room in the Horniblow tavern next to the courthouse, where he died on August 21, 1798.

JAMES WINTHROP (1752–1821)   Born March 28, 1752, in Cambridge, Massachusetts, son of Rebecca Townsend and John Winthrop (Harvard mathematician). Graduated from Harvard in 1769 and became librarian in 1770. Fought at battle of Bunker Hill in June 1775, where he was slightly wounded. Appointed register of probate for Middlesex. Passed over for his late father's professorship in 1779 (and again in 1788) because of his eccentricities. In 1780 encouraged students to rebel against the college president. Became an early member of the American Academy of Arts and Sciences, but embarrassed the Academy by publishing fallacious solutions to mathematical problems in their journal. In 1786–87 he was a volunteer in the forces sent to suppress Shays' Rebellion. Resigned as college librarian in 1787 when forced by the college to choose between that post and his job as register of probate. Received an honorary M.A. degree from Dartmouth in 1787. Author of Antifederalist essays published under pseudonym "Agrippa." Appointed judge of common pleas for Middlesex in 1791. Surveyed the area for a proposed Cape Cod canal and was a promoter of the West Boston Bridge and the Middlesex Canal. Presidential elector for Jefferson in 1804. Helped found the Massachusetts Historical Society. Spent remaining years writing on theological and astronomical subjects. He never married. Became overseer of Allegheny College, founded by his friend Timothy Alden, and left the college his large library. Awarded LL.D. degree from Allegheny College in 1817. Died in Cambridge on September 26, 1821.

BENJAMIN WORKMAN   Emigrated from Dublin, Ireland, to Philadelphia in 1784. Became mathematics tutor at the University of Pennsylvania 1784–88. Wrote mathematics and geography textbooks and published *Father Tammany's Almanac* (1786–99). Was probably the author of twelve Antifederalist "Philadelphiensis" articles published in 1787–88.

Chronology of Events, 1774–1804

<table>
<tr><td>1774</td><td>In response to the Boston Tea Party of December 16, 1773, the British Parliament passes four laws that become known in the American colonies as the Coercive Acts. The Boston Port Act, which receives royal assent on March 31, closes Boston harbor, effective June 1, until "peace and obedience to the laws" is restored in the town and its people pay for the destroyed tea. Massachusetts Government Act, signed May 20, abrogates Massachusetts' 1691 royal charter by removing power of appointing the governor's council from the elected assembly and giving it to the king. Act also gives the royal governor power to appoint (or nominate, for the king's assent) all provincial judges and sheriffs, makes the sheriffs responsible for choosing jury panels, and severely restricts town meetings. Administration of Justice Act, signed May 20, allows trials of those accused of committing capital crimes while enforcing the law or collecting revenue to be removed to Britain or Nova Scotia. Quartering Act, signed June 2, allows quartering of troops in occupied dwellings throughout the colonies. (Quebec Act, signed June 22, establishes civil government for Quebec without an elected legislature, grants Roman Catholic Church the right to collect tithes, and potentially extends the province's borders to the Mississippi and Ohio rivers; it is viewed as a hostile measure by many colonists.) General Thomas Gage, commander-in-chief of British forces in North America, is commissioned as royal governor of Massachusetts and arrives in Boston on May 13; British troops begin landing in the city in mid-June.</td></tr>
</table>

May–Sept.   Calls for an intercolonial congress to propose common measures of resistance are made in Providence, Philadelphia, New York, and Williamsburg, Virginia, May 17–27. Delegates to the congress are chosen in 12 colonies, June 15–August 25, either by the elected assembly, a committee of correspondence chosen by the assembly, special meetings of town or county representatives, or by a convention called by members of the elected assembly after its dissolution by the royal governor. Meeting of parish delegates in Georgia on August 10 votes against sending delegates to the congress, although it does adopt a declaration of rights and chooses a committee of correspondence. Unable to enforce the law outside of Boston, Gage begins fortifying the city on September 3.

Sept.   Congress (later known as First Continental Congress) opens in Philadelphia on September 5 and is eventually attended by 56 delegates. Peyton Randolph (a delegate from Virginia) is unanimously elected president (presiding officer) of the Congress and Charles Thomson (who is not a delegate) is chosen as its secretary. (Thomson will serve until the end of the Second Continental Congress in 1789.) John Adams (Massachusetts) asks if each colony is to have an equal vote, or whether voting should be made proportional to the population or property of each colony. Patrick Henry (Virginia) proposes that voting be made proportional to free population, while John Jay (New York) and others support giving each colony one vote. Congress adopts rule giving each colony a single vote and makes its proceedings secret.

On September 17 Congress endorses Suffolk County Resolves, recently adopted by a convention in Massachusetts, which declare that no obedience is due the Coercive Acts and advocate measures of resistance, including the formation of a provincial congress, nonpayment of taxes, the boycott of British goods, and weekly militia training. Joseph Galloway (Pennsylvania) submits plan on September 28 for a union between Great Britain and the colonies that would create "an inferior and distinct branch of the British legislature" for the government of the "general affairs" of America. Each colonial assembly would send delegates to serve on a grand council for three-year terms, while a president-general, chosen by the king, would have an absolute veto over the council's acts. Measures pertaining to the colonies could originate in either the American council or the British Parliament, but the assent of both bodies would be required to make them law. The plan is defeated by a 6–5 vote (proposal is expunged from official journal on October 22).

Oct.

On October 14 Congress adopts series of declarations and resolves that denounce the Coercive Acts and Quebec Act as "impolitic, unjust, and cruel, as well as unconstitutional," call for the repeal of several other laws passed since 1763, protest the dissolution of elected assemblies and the royal appointment of colonial councils, and condemn the keeping of a standing army in the colonies in peacetime, without the consent of colonial legislatures, as "against law." The resolves enumerate rights that the colonists are entitled to under "the immutable laws of nature," the English constitution, and their colonial charters, including life, liberty, and property, the right to the common law of England, the right to trial by a local jury, and the right to assemble and petition the king. They assert that none of these rights can be taken from the colonists without the consent of their own legislatures, and

claim for the colonial legislatures an "exclusive power of legislation . . . in all cases of taxation and internal polity,"
subject only to royal veto, while "cheerfully" consenting to
acts of Parliament that regulate external commerce for the
benefit of the whole empire.

Oct.

Congress votes on October 18 to create Continental Association, modeled on Virginia Association formed in early August. Its articles pledge the colonies to discontinue the slave
trade and cease importing goods from Great Britain, Ireland,
and the East and West Indies after December 1, 1774, to cease
consuming British goods after March 1, 1775, and, if necessary, to cease all exports (excluding rice) to Britain, Ireland,
and the West Indies after September 10, 1775. The Association
is to be enforced by elected town, city, and county committees, which will punish violators by publicity and boycott.
After preparing addresses to the British people and to the
king, Congress calls on the people of the colonies to elect
deputies to provincial congresses, which in turn will elect delegates to a second Congress, called for May 10, 1775. Congress
adjourns October 26.

Nov.–Dec.

By the end of the year, provincial congresses or conventions have been formed in eight colonies. (Provincial congresses will meet in New York in April 1775 and Georgia in
July 1775. In Pennsylvania the assembly continues under its
1701 proprietary charter until June 1776. Connecticut and
Rhode Island continue to govern themselves under their
royal charters, which grant them a high degree of autonomy, including the right to elect their own governors.)

1775

On February 9 Parliament declares Massachusetts to be in rebellion. The House of Commons endorses on February 27 a
conciliatory proposal by ministry of Lord North, under
which Parliament would refrain from laying revenue taxes
upon the colonies if the colonial assemblies agree to levy their
own taxes to support imperial defense. General Gage receives
orders from ministry on April 14 (written January 27 but not
dispatched until March 13) directing him to use force against
the Massachusetts rebels. Revolutionary War begins when
British attempt to destroy military supplies at Concord leads
to fighting with militia at Lexington, Concord, and along the
road back to Boston on April 19. Massachusetts forces begin
siege of city.

May–June

Second Continental Congress meets in Philadelphia on
May 10, with every state except Georgia present. Peyton Randolph is reelected president; after he returns to Virginia for
meeting of its assembly, John Hancock (Massachusetts) is

elected on May 24 (14 men serve as president of the Congress between 1774 and 1789). Massachusetts provincial congress asks Congress for advice on establishing a government during the conflict with Great Britain. Congress responds on June 9 by recommending that the colony elect a new assembly and council to govern itself until the crown agrees to abide by the 1691 charter (new Massachusetts legislature meets in late July, with the council serving as the executive). Congress votes on June 14 to form a Continental army. John Adams nominates George Washington (a Virginia delegate) as its commander, and he is unanimously approved on June 15 (Washington assumes command in Cambridge, Massachusetts, on July 3). To finance army, Congress votes on June 22 to issue of $2 million in paper money not backed by specie and pledges that the "12 Confederated Colonies" will redeem the issue (decides on July 29 that each colony will assume a share of the debt in proportion to its population).

July–Aug.   Provincial congress meets in Georgia on July 4 and elects delegates to the Second Congress. On July 5 Congress approves the Olive Branch Petition, a conciliatory message to George III drafted by John Dickinson (Pennsylvania), and on July 6 adopts the Declaration of the Causes and Necessities of Taking Up Arms, drafted by Thomas Jefferson (Virginia) and rewritten by Dickinson. Declaration disavows intention to establish American independence, but asserts that colonists are "resolved to die freemen rather than to live slaves" and states that "foreign assistance is undoubtedly attainable" for the colonial cause. Congress appoints commissioners to negotiate with Indians, July 19, establishes a post office department headed by Benjamin Franklin (Pennsylvania), July 26, and rejects Lord North's proposal for conciliation, July 31, before adjourning on August 2. George III rejects Olive Branch Petition and on August 23 proclaims American colonies to be in rebellion (news reaches Congress on November 9).

Sept.–Dec.   Delegates from Georgia join Congress when it reconvenes September 12. Congress begins organizing a navy in October, appoints on November 29 five-member Committee of Correspondence to establish contact with foreign supporters (becomes Committee for Foreign Affairs on April 17, 1777), and on December 6 disavows allegiance to Parliament. British rule continues to collapse throughout the 13 colonies; in Virginia, militia defeats force under Lord Dunmore, the royal governor, at Great Bridge on December 9 (Dunmore will destroy much of Norfolk and retreat to ships in Chesapeake Bay). George III signs Prohibitory Act on December 23, closing off commerce with America and making American ships and crews subject to seizure by the Royal Navy.

1776 On advice of Congress, New Hampshire provincial congress adopts form of government for the colony on January 5.

Jan. *Common Sense*, pamphlet by Thomas Paine denouncing monarchical rule and advocating an independent American republic, is published in Philadelphia on January 10 (an expanded edition appears February 14); it sells tens of thousands of copies and is widely discussed throughout the colonies.

Mar.–Apr. Congress votes on March 3 to send Silas Deane to Europe to buy military supplies. British garrison evacuates Boston on March 17 and sails to Nova Scotia. South Carolina provincial congress adopts a plan of government on March 26. Congress opens American ports to all nations except Britain on April 6. North Carolina provincial congress authorizes its delegates on April 12 to vote in Congress for independence, while reserving for North Carolina the "sole and exclusive right" of forming its own constitution and laws.

May At the urging of his foreign minister the comte de Vergennes, Louis XVI of France authorizes clandestine support of the American insurgents on May 2. (After his arrival in Paris on July 7, Silas Deane will work with Vergennes and Pierre de Beaumarchais in arranging covert shipments of arms, supplies, and money; effort is soon joined by Spain.)

May–June Rhode Island legislature disavows allegiance to George III on May 4. Under leadership of John Adams and Richard Henry Lee (Virginia), Congress recommends on May 10 that each of the "United Colonies" form a government and on May 15 calls for royal authority in the colonies to be "totally suppressed." On May 15 Virginia convention (successor to the convention called by the assembly after its dissolution by Lord Dunmore in 1774) instructs its delegates in Congress to propose a declaration of independence and the formation of a confederation; it also appoints a committee to prepare a declaration of rights and constitution for Virginia. Following these instructions, Richard Henry Lee submits resolution in Congress on June 7, declaring that "these United Colonies are, and of right ought to be, free and independent States," urging the formation of foreign alliances, and recommending the preparation and transmission of "a plan of confederation" to the colonies for their approval. John Dickinson, James Wilson (Pennsylvania), Robert R. Livingston (New York), and others argue that an immediate declaration of independence would be premature. Congress postpones decision and refers resolution on independence to a committee of five (Franklin, John Adams, Livingston, Jefferson, and Roger Sherman, a Connecticut delegate) on June 11; Jefferson begins drafting a declaration. On June 12 resolution to form an American confederation is submitted to a committee of 13, consisting of one representative from each colony; its chairman, John Dickinson, begins drafting confederation plan.

June

Virginia convention adopts a declaration of rights, drafted by George Mason, on June 12, and a state constitution, drafted largely by George Mason and containing preamble written by Jefferson, on June 29.

July

On July 1 Congress resumes debate on Lee's independence resolution and approves it on July 2, severing all political ties with Great Britain. After revising Jefferson's draft (changes include deletion of passage condemning slave trade), Congress adopts the Declaration of Independence on July 4.

Dickinson committee submits draft of twenty "Articles of Confederation and Perpetual Union" on July 12, under which the states would "enter into a firm League of Friendship" for their "common Defence, the Security of their Liberties, and their mutual and general Welfare." Each state is to retain such of its current laws as it thinks fit, and to have exclusive power over its "internal police, in all matters that shall not interfere with the Articles of Confederation." Inhabitants of each state are to enjoy reciprocal rights, liberties, privileges, and immunities in the other states, including those pertaining to trade. Each state has one vote in Congress, which is to have sole power over foreign affairs, war and peace, admiralty and prize courts, coining money, settling disputes among the states, setting the boundaries of states, including those whose colonial charters claim lands extending to the South Sea (Pacific Ocean), establishing new territories, and maintaining a postal service, while the states retain all taxing power and are allowed to lay import and export duties, subject to treaties made by Congress with foreign states. Common expenses are to be paid out of a central treasury, supported by requisitions on the states, apportioned according to population and levied by the state legislatures. A Council of State, consisting of one delegate from each state, is to manage the general affairs of the Confederation. Troops are to be requisitioned from the states in proportion to their white inhabitants. Major issues are to require approval of nine states, lesser issues seven, and amendments to the Articles must be approved by every state legislature. Delegates to Congress are to be annually appointed by the state legislatures, and may be recalled at any time.

July–Aug.   Congress begins debating draft Articles on July 22. Franklin, John Adams, James Wilson, and Benjamin Rush (Pennsylvania) argue that representation of the states in Congress should be made proportional to their population. Samuel Chase (Maryland) moves amendment to count only whites when apportioning treasury requisitions, contending that slaves should be treated as property, not persons, and that it is unfair to tax southern property while exempting northern property. His amendment is defeated in a 7–5 vote along sectional lines on August 1, with Delaware supporting the proposal and Georgia divided. Delegates from states with western land claims oppose giving Congress power to set state boundaries (Massachusetts, Connecticut, Virginia, North and South Carolina, and Georgia have charter claims, while New York has a claim based on a treaty with the Iroquois Confederacy). Congress has revised draft of Articles printed on August 20, but then postpones further debate.

Aug.–Sept.   British troops land on Long Island, August 22, and win battle there on August 27, beginning series of American defeats in the New York region. On September 26 Congress appoints Franklin, Jefferson, and Silas Deane as commissioners to negotiate treaties with European powers. (Franklin arrives in Paris on December 21; Jefferson declines position and is replaced by Arthur Lee, who is already in Europe.)

Nov.–Dec.   Fort Washington in upper Manhattan surrenders to the British on November 16, and Fort Lee, New Jersey, is evacuated November 20, beginning Washington's retreat across New Jersey. Congress adjourns session in Philadelphia December 12 and meets in Baltimore on December 20 (will reconvene in Philadelphia on March 12, 1777). Washington's army crosses the Delaware on the night of December 25 and defeats Hessians at Trenton on the morning of December 26.

July–Dec.   States continue to frame and adopt their own constitutions, including New Jersey, July 2, Delaware, September 20, Pennsylvania, September 28, Maryland, November 9, and North Carolina, December 18. (After its adoption the Pennsylvania constitution becomes the focus of a continuing political struggle within the state between its "Constitutionalist" supporters and "Republican" opponents. Connecticut and Rhode Island revise their colonial charters to eliminate references to royal authority; Connecticut adopts its first state constitution in 1818, Rhode Island in 1842.)

1777   Georgia convention adopts state constitution on February 5 (convention had been elected in October 1776 to draw up a plan of government).

April   When Congress resumes discussion of the draft Articles on
                April 18, Thomas Burke (North Carolina) moves the adop-
                tion of a new article declaring that each state "retains its sov-
                ereignty, freedom and independence, and every Power,
                Jurisdiction and right, which is not by this confederation ex-
                pressly delegated to the United States, in Congress assem-
                bled." The amendment is carried in late April over the
                opposition of James Wilson and Richard Henry Lee.
                     New York convention (successor to its provincial congress)
                adopts state constitution on April 20 (none of the state con-
                stitutions adopted in 1776–77 are submitted to the people for
                ratification).

May–July   On May 5 the Massachusetts legislature asks the towns to
                grant it the power at the next election to frame a constitu-
                tion; the towns agree, and on June 17 the new legislature re-
                solves itself into a constitutional convention and appoints a
                drafting committee. Vermont adopts constitution on July 8
                that forbids slavery and declares the state independent from
                both Great Britain and New York (Vermont will not join the
                United States until 1791).

Sept.–Oct.   Congress ends session in Philadelphia on September 18
                (British occupy the city on September 25) and reconvenes in
                York, Pennsylvania, on September 30 (will remain there until
                June 27, 1778). In series of votes on the draft Articles of Con-
                federation, Congress defeats on October 7 amendments to
                make state representation in Congress proportional to popu-
                lation or to contributions to the central treasury; approves on
                October 14 amendment that changes the basis for apportion-
                ing financial requisitions from a state's population to the
                value of its land and improvements; and votes on October 15
                to remove from Congress the power to determine western
                state boundaries.

Oct.   After series of defeats, British army under General John
                Burgoyne surrenders to Americans under General Horatio
                Gates at Saratoga, New York, on October 17 (news of victory
                strengthens position of the comte de Vergennes, who advo-
                cates an open French alliance with the United States).

Oct.–Nov.   Congress further amends draft Articles, limiting the power
                of congressional commerce treaties to restrict state imposts
                and replacing the proposed Council of State with a Commit-
                tee of the States, to sit only when Congress is in recess. A
                procedure is established for submitting boundary disputes be-
                tween the states to commissioners selected by Congress, but
                the commissioners will have no power to enforce their rul-
                ings, and no state may be deprived of its territory for the
                benefit of the United States. On November 15 Congress ap-

proves revised Articles of Confederation and submits them to the state legislatures for ratification. The Maryland legislature instructs its congressional delegates on December 22 to secure an amendment to the Articles restoring congressional power to fix western state boundaries. (Advocates of congressional control over state boundaries argue that the land west of the Appalachians will be won from the British and Indians only by the common sacrifice of all the states, and assert that the "landless" states need western land to give as bounties to their soldiers. Opponents of congressional control charge that land speculators, who include many prominent Maryland and Pennsylvania political leaders, are seeking to protect their purchases from being invalidated by the Virginia legislature, which has the strongest claim to authority over the territory northwest of the Ohio River.)

Dec.   Washington begins winter encampment at Valley Forge, Pennsylvania, and appeals to Congress for supplies (will repeatedly ask Congress and the states for money and supplies throughout the war, often with meager results). Issues of Continental paper currency reach $38 million.

1778   American commissioners in Paris sign two treaties with France on February 6. Under their terms, France recognizes the independence of the United States and receives commercial privileges in American markets. In the event that French recognition of the United States leads to war between France and Great Britain, France and the United States pledge to fight and negotiate as allies, with the aim of securing complete American independence. France also renounces all claims to Canada and to land east of the Mississippi in return for an American commitment to help defend French possessions in the West Indies.

Feb.   New Hampshire legislature calls on February 26 for the election of a special convention to draw up a state constitution, which will then be submitted to town meetings and take effect if approved by three-fourths of the state's voters (convention meets on June 10). Massachusetts legislature submits proposed constitution, which lacks a bill of rights, to the town meetings on February 28 for ratification by two-thirds of the freemen; it is eventually rejected by vote of 9,972 to 2,083.

Mar.   South Carolina general assembly approves on March 19 a new constitution to replace the temporary form of government adopted in 1776.

Apr.–Dec.   French fleet sails from Toulon for America on April 11 (it arrives off Delaware Bay on July 8). By April 25 ten states have ratified the Articles; Maryland, New Jersey, and Delaware continue to oppose ratification because of the western land dispute. War breaks out between Britain and France after their naval forces clash in the English Channel on June 17. From June 22 to June 25, Congress considers and rejects 37 motions for changes or amendments to the Articles of Confederation proposed by seven state legislatures. Eight of the ratifying states sign the Articles on July 9 (the other two ratifying states sign by July 24). New Jersey legislature ratifies the Articles of Confederation on November 20. British capture Savannah, Georgia, on December 29, as the major theater of war shifts to the south.

1779   With more than $100 million in circulation, Continental currency trades for specie at 8–1. Delaware legislature ratifies the Articles of Confederation on February 1.

Feb.– June   Massachusetts legislature asks the towns on February 20 if special elections should be held for a new constitutional convention, independent of the legislature (towns agree, and convention meets on September 1). New Hampshire convention elected in 1778 submits proposed constitution to town meetings on June 5; it is rejected by a majority of the voters.

June– Sept.   After entering into alliance with France, Spain declares war on Great Britain on June 21 (Spain does not recognize American independence). After months of debate, Congress approves on August 14 minimum terms to be sought when peace negotiations begin; they include independence, evacuation of British forces, borders extending to the Mississippi in the west and the 31st parallel in the south, and free navigation of the Mississippi (navigation right is especially sought by southerners), but not the protection of fishing rights off Newfoundland (which is of special importance to New England delegates). On September 1 Congress resolves to limit emissions of Continental paper money at $200 million (total issues have reached $160 million). John Jay, president of the Congress, sends circular letter to the states on September 13 urging them to collect taxes in order to pay their requisitions into the common treasury. Congress appoints John Adams as peace negotiator and Jay envoy to Spain on September 27. (During his stay in Madrid from January 1780 to May 1782, Jay will be unable to secure Spanish recognition of American independence, negotiate treaties of alliance or commerce, or secure a significant loan.)

Oct.– Dec.   Autumn session of Virginia legislature ends state taxation of Anglicans in support of their own church and considers two proposed bills concerning religion. One would establish

Christianity in Virginia and levy a general assessment in its support, with taxpayers choosing which denomination their taxes would go to; the other, drafted by Jefferson in 1777, protects the free exercise of "religious opinions or belief" while forbidding taxation to support any religion. Neither law is passed.

1780   Continental currency trades for specie at 40–1. New York legislature offers on February 1 to cede its western lands, claimed through treaty with the Iroquois, to Congress (cession is accepted by Congress in October 1782). An act for the gradual abolition of slavery is passed by the Pennsylvania legislature on March 1 (gradual emancipation laws will be passed in Connecticut and Rhode Island in 1784).

Mar.   Massachusetts convention submits new constitution, drafted mainly by John Adams, to the towns on March 2 for ratification. (The constitution is approved by the towns, declared ratified on June 16, and takes effect on October 25, 1780.)

Mar.–Oct.   Congress approves plan on March 18 for retiring existing Continental currency, valued by the plan at 40–1 against specie, and replacing it with $10 million in new paper money (plan fails, and by spring 1781 Continental paper money has ceased to circulate). British take 5,000 prisoners when American garrison at Charleston, South Carolina, surrenders on May 12 (the largest American capitulation of the war). American force under Horatio Gates is routed by British and Loyalists at Camden, South Carolina, on August 16; Americans retreat to Hillsborough, North Carolina. Treachery of Benedict Arnold is revealed on September 25. Connecticut cedes most of its western lands on October 10 (cession is accepted in 1786). Congress grants Continental officers half-pay pensions for life on October 21.

1781   Pennsylvania Continental regiments mutiny on January 1 over pay and enlistments (negotiations with Pennsylvania state government end mutiny on January 8, the largest of several Continental mutinies in 1780–81). Virginia legislature offers on January 2 to cede to Congress its lands northwest of the Ohio River, on the condition that new states be eventually formed out of the territory and that purchases made from the Indians by land companies be voided (cession is supported by Jefferson, Madison, and Richard Henry Lee).

Jan.–Mar.   Congress begins establishment of executive departments with the creation of the Department of Foreign Affairs on January 10 (executive duties had previously been carried out by various committees of Congress). The Chevalier de la Luzerne, French minister to the United States, responds to pleas from Maryland for French naval protection against British raids in the Chesapeake Bay by urging Maryland to ratify the Articles; the Maryland legislature approves them on February 2. Congress votes February 3 to ask states for power to levy a 5 percent impost on imports in order to pay for the war; measure requires approval of all 13 state legislatures. Departments of War and Finance are established by Congress, February 6, and Robert Morris, a wealthy Pennsylvania merchant, is named superintendent of finance on February 20. Maryland delegates sign the Articles of Confederation on March 1, completing their ratification.

Mar.–May   On March 16 James Madison (Virginia), James Duane (New York), and James Varnum (Rhode Island) propose amending the Articles to give Congress the power to coerce states that defy Congress or fail to fulfill their requisitions (proposal is referred to committee and is never approved). Robert Morris takes office on May 14 after successfully demanding the power to control his subordinates. On May 26 he wins congressional approval for the chartering of a national bank (Bank of North America, first commercial bank in the United States, is chartered December 31) and begins to ease financial crisis with the help of French loans and subsidies and a large Dutch loan guaranteed by France.

May   After American victory at Cowpens, South Carolina (January 17) and drawn battle at Guilford Courthouse, North Carolina (March 15), Lord Cornwallis decides to strengthen British position in the Carolinas by attacking Virginia, a major source of supplies for American forces in the South. On May 20 Cornwallis reaches Petersburg, Virginia, and begins his Virginia campaign.

June   Second convention meets in New Hampshire in June and submits to the voters a new proposed constitution, which calls for indirect election of the state house of representatives; it is rejected.

June–Aug.   Congress names Franklin, Jay, Henry Laurens, and Jefferson as additional peace negotiators (Jefferson declines) and on June 15 revises its instructions, making independence and the preservation of the French alliance the only essential peace terms and requiring the negotiators to take no action without the "knowledge and concurrence" of French ministers and to "govern" themselves by "their advice and opinion." On August 10 Congress chooses Robert R. Livingston over Arthur Lee to be secretary for foreign affairs (French

| | envoy La Luzerne actively supports revision of instructions and Livingston's election). |
| Sept.–Oct. | French naval victory in Chesapeake Bay on September 5 prevents evacuation of army under Cornwallis from its base at Yorktown, Virginia. American and French armies under Washington and Rochambeau begin siege of Yorktown on September 28. Cornwallis surrenders on October 19, ending major fighting in the Revolutionary War. General Benjamin Lincoln becomes secretary at war on October 30. Morris moves to restore national finances to a specie basis, while states begin confronting problem of their war debts and the depreciation of their own wartime paper money issues. |

1782

After the House of Commons votes against continuing the war in America, Lord North resigns as prime minister on March 20. The new ministry of Lord Rockingham opens peace negotiations with Benjamin Franklin in Paris on April 12 (Franklin conducts negotiations independently of the French, despite his congressional instructions).

Feb.–Apr.

In response to uncertainty regarding congressional power to charter a bank, Robert Morris and his allies obtain a state charter for the Bank of North America from the Pennsylvania legislature. With states failing to meet their requisitions, Morris ceases paying interest on Continental loan office certificates (the major form of outstanding federal debt) and tells public creditors that payments cannot be resumed unless the impost is adopted. (Loan officers later begin issuing certificates for interest due, and in April 1784 Congress votes to allow states to pay part of their requisitions with these certificates.)

June–Dec.

New Hampshire convention reconvenes in June and revises the constitution rejected by the towns in 1781 (it is resubmitted in August but again fails to win approval). New York legislature approves in July a resolution, probably drafted by Alexander Hamilton, calling for a national convention to give Congress the power to raise money. Rhode Island refuses on November 1 to ratify the amendment levying the 5 percent impost, which 11 other states have agreed to (Georgia had not yet considered the measure); when Virginia repeals its ratification of the impost on December 7, the measure lapses. Maryland legislature adopts law allowing Maryland holders of Continental loan office certificates to exchange them for state securities.

Nov.

Franklin, John Adams, John Jay, and Henry Laurens sign preliminary peace treaty with Great Britain in Paris on

November 30 (agreement is to be implemented after Anglo-French treaty is negotiated). Its terms provide for: a cessation of hostilities; the evacuation of British forces from American territory; British recognition of an independent United States with borders extending north to the Great Lakes, west to the Mississippi, and south to the 31st parallel; the honoring of debts owed to creditors in the other country; the recognition of American fishing rights off Canada; and a pledge that Congress would "earnestly recommend" to the state legislatures the restoration of the rights and properties of Loyalists.

Dec.

On December 30 a special commission, formed by Congress at Pennsylvania's request to rule on the long-standing dispute between Pennsylvania and Connecticut over the Wyoming Valley in northeastern Pennsylvania, awards jurisdiction to Pennsylvania while recommending that land claims of Connecticut settlers in the region be recognized.

1783

On January 6 Congress receives memorial from Continental Army officers protesting the failure of Congress to pay them and asking that they receive several years' full pay in lieu of the lifetime pensions at half pay granted in 1780. Britain, France, and Spain sign preliminary peace agreement on January 20 (Britain proclaims an end to hostilities on February 4). Robert Morris tells Congress on January 24 that he will resign as superintendent of finance on May 31; Congress begins debating new financial measures and Morris continues in office. Anonymous address is circulated among Continental officers camped at Newburgh, New York, on March 10, denouncing congressional inaction on pay and inciting the army to defy Congress if its demands are not met. Washington condemns the address at an assembly held on March 15 and calls upon his officers to express their loyalty to Congress; they adopt a resolution doing so. Congress commutes officers' pensions to five years full pay on March 22, ratifies the preliminary peace treaty on April 15, and approves on April 18 a new plan for restoring public credit. It calls for levying specific excise duties and a general 5 percent impost for 25 years in order to pay the interest and principal on the national war debt. Collectors of the revenue are to be appointed by the states but would be removable by Congress, and the income collected is to be credited to each state's requisition quota. The plan also calls on the states to pay an additional $1.5 million annually for 25 years toward the discharge of the debt. A proposed amendment to the Articles, submitted to the states on April 18, changes the basis for apportioning requisitions from property to population, with "other persons" (slaves) counted as three-fifths of whites. Financial measure is opposed by Alexander Hamilton (New York), who favors stronger revenue measures, and by the Rhode Island delegates, who oppose any national impost.

May–June   On May 26 Congress furloughs Continental troops who enlisted for the duration of the war. Robert R. Livingston resigns as secretary for foreign affairs on June 5. Washington sends circular letter to state governors and legislatures on June 8, urging adoption of the congressional finance measures and the strengthening of the federal union. Pennsylvania soldiers from the Continental Army surround the State House in Philadelphia, where Congress and the Pennsylvania executive council are meeting, on June 21 and demand back pay. When the Pennsylvania council declines to use the militia to restore order, Congress leaves the city and reconvenes in Princeton, New Jersey, on June 26.

June   New Hampshire convention submits fourth proposed constitution to the voters in June (it is declared ratified on October 31 and goes into effect in June 1784).

July–Sept.   British government issues order on July 2 closing West Indian ports to American shipping and forbidding importation of American produce (Britain will also restrict ability of American ships to enter British ports). Final peace treaty between Great Britain and the United States of America is signed in Paris on September 3 (terms are similar to those of preliminary agreement of November 30, 1782).

Oct.–Nov.   Unable to agree on a single site for a permanent seat of government, Congress votes on October 7 to establish a "federal town" on the Delaware, near Trenton, New Jersey, then approves on October 20 the creation of a second capital on the Potomac, near Georgetown, Maryland, intending to alternate sessions between the two sites. Session in Princeton adjourns November 4 and Congress reconvenes in Annapolis, Maryland, on November 26, planning to move between Annapolis and Trenton until permanent capitals are ready.

Nov.–Dec.   Benjamin Lincoln resigns as secretary at war on November 12. British evacuate New York City on November 25 and Washington leads his troops into the city later in the day. Washington has farewell meeting with his officers on December 4 and then goes to Annapolis, where he addresses Congress on December 23 before resigning his commission.

1784   Congress ratifies final peace treaty on January 14 and calls on states to rescind confiscations of Loyalist property and repeal laws blocking the collection of debts owed British creditors. On March 1 Congress accepts Virginia's cession of its western land north of the Ohio and begins considering a proposal, written by Jefferson, for governing the territory. The plan would create ten new states, each not less than 100 or more than 150 miles square. Their free male inhabitants would temporarily adopt the constitution and laws of one of the original states, and then hold a constitutional convention when the state's free population reached 20,000. When a new state's free population equaled that of the smallest original state, it would join the Confederation on an equal basis, with a single vote in Congress. Each new state would be required to have a republican form of government and to assume a share of the federal debt, and slavery and involuntary servitude would be forbidden in all of the new states after 1800. After deleting the antislavery provision and making minor changes, Congress adopts the plan on April 23 (proposal is forwarded to the states in 1785 along with ordinance on western land sales). On April 30 Congress asks the states to grant it the power to regulate foreign commerce for 15 years so that it can respond to British trade restrictions. John Jay is appointed secretary for foreign affairs on May 7 (will not assume office, vacant since the resignation of Robert R. Livingston in June 1783, until December 21). After the Pennsylvania assembly tries to evict Connecticut settlers from the Wyoming Valley, fighting breaks out in May between settlers and Pennsylvania troops. On June 26 Spain orders the lower Mississippi closed to American navigation until the boundaries of Louisiana and West Florida are settled (the Spanish do not recognize the American frontiers established by the 1783 Anglo-American peace treaty).

June   In *Rutgers* v. *Waddington* Alexander Hamilton argues before the New York Mayor's Court on June 29 that the terms of the 1783 peace treaty are binding on the states and that a New York state law allowing suits against Loyalists should be voided by the court for violating the treaty. Chief Judge James Duane declares that while states cannot "alter or abridge" a treaty ratified by Congress, it would be "subversive of all government" for the court to reject a legislative enactment. The court then issues a ruling favorable to the defendant, asserting that the legislature could not have intended to violate the treaty and that judges should interpret the law accordingly (decision is criticized by the legislature and is widely debated in the press).

Sept.–Dec.   Second session of the Pennsylvania Council of Censors condemns the assembly's actions in the Wyoming Valley, and on September 15 the assembly votes to restore lands to settlers dispossessed in May. Autumn session of Virginia legislature considers new bill for levying a general assessment in support of the Christian religion. It is supported by Patrick Henry, Richard Henry Lee, and Edmund Pendleton, but opposed by James Madison, who succeeds on December 24 in postponing its final consideration until the fall of 1785.

Nov.–Dec.   Robert Morris leaves office as superintendent of finance on November 1 and is eventually replaced by a three-man Board of Treasury (board does not begin work until spring 1785). Congress convenes in Trenton on November 1 and adjourns on December 24 after deciding to meet in New York City until capital on banks of the Delaware is built (holds first session in New York on January 11, 1785, and will continue to meet there for the remainder of the Confederation).

1785   United States defaults on its French loans (will continue with difficulty to make interest payments on Dutch loans negotiated by John Adams in 1782 and 1784). On February 4 the Society for Promoting the Manumission of Slaves is formed in New York, with John Jay as its president and Alexander Hamilton as one of its counselors. (When Hamilton proposes that members begin by freeing their own slaves, the members decline, and the society will concentrate on protecting freed slaves and educating black children.) Congress appoints John Adams as the first American minister to Great Britain on February 24 and names Thomas Jefferson minister to France on March 10, replacing Franklin, who is planning to return to America (Adams and Jefferson are already in Europe, where they have been attempting to negotiate commercial treaties with continental governments). General Henry Knox is appointed secretary at war on March 8, filling position vacant since November 1783.

Mar.   Pennsylvania assembly votes on March 16 to assume payment of the interest on the national debt owed to Pennsylvanians, who own approximately one-third of the domestic national debt. The assumption measure, which is to be funded by selling public lands, levying £200,000 in annual taxes, and issuing £150,000 in paper money, is opposed by advocates of a stronger national government, including Robert Morris and John Dickinson, but is supported by many public creditors. (By the end of 1786 six other states issue paper money. In South Carolina and Pennsylvania, it cannot be used to pay private debts; in New York it can be used to pay creditors who sue; and in North Carolina, Georgia, New Jersey, and Rhode Island, it circulates as full legal tender. Issues are proposed in the other states, and in Maryland the senate defeats paper money bills that pass the house of delegates in December 1785 and December 1786.)

Mar.   Commissioners appointed by the Virginia and Maryland legislatures meet at Mount Vernon, March 25–28, to discuss disputes over navigation of the Potomac River and Chesapeake Bay. After reaching agreement on several commercial and financial measures, the commissioners write to the Pennsylvania executive council, proposing that Pennsylvania join in plans to link the Potomac and Ohio valleys by canals.

Mar.–May   On March 28 Congress begins considering proposed amendment to the Articles giving Congress permanent power to regulate commerce (measure is never approved for submission to the states). Congress passes ordinance for the disposal of western lands on May 20. It calls for surveying townships, six miles square, which will be divided for sale into 640-acre lots at minimum price of $1 an acre. One lot per township is to be reserved for supporting public education (proposal to reserve another lot for supporting the religion of the majority of the township inhabitants is narrowly defeated).

June   In late June Madison writes a "Memorial and Remonstrance" attacking the proposed Virginia bill for a general assessment in support of religion. Memorial is anonymously circulated with the help of George Mason and is signed by over 1,500 people (nearly 11,000 people sign petitions opposing the bill before the October 1785 legislative session opens, and the measure fails to win passage).

July–Dec.   John Adams writes Jay that a commercial treaty with Britain is impossible unless the states adopt uniform retaliatory measures against discriminatory British trading practices. Jay begins talks with Spanish envoy Diego de Gardoqui in July and is instructed by Congress on August 25 to negotiate a treaty recognizing American navigation rights on the Mississippi and the southwestern frontiers established in the 1783 peace treaty. In September the Constitutionalist majority in the Pennsylvania assembly repeals the charter of the Bank of North America and establishes a state loan office to issue paper money to farmers. On November 30 John Adams formally demands the evacuation of British garrisons from the Northwest in compliance with the 1783 treaty. Maryland legislature approves on December 5 agreement reached at Mount Vernon conference and proposes that Delaware join Maryland, Virginia, and Pennsylvania in an interstate navigation compact (Mount Vernon agreement is also ratified by Virginia legislature).

1786   In Virginia Madison wins passage on January 16 of revised version of the statute on religious freedom drafted by Jefferson in 1777 and first debated in 1779. (Madison writes to Jefferson that he hopes "this Country" has "extinguished for ever the ambitious hope of making laws for the human mind.") On January 21 the Virginia legislature calls for a general meeting of the states to consider adopting a uniform system of commercial regulations and appoints five commissioners to attend.

Feb.–May   A committee investigating finances reports to Congress on February 3 that only $2.4 million of the $15.6 million requisitioned from the states since October 1, 1781, has been received. British government informs John Adams on February 28 that they will not evacuate northwestern garrisons until Americans fulfill their treaty obligations to pay British creditors and compensate Loyalists. Pennsylvania and New York legislatures vote to assume principal on national debt owed their citizens, allowing them to exchange federal certificates for state securities. On May 4 the New York legislature approves the 1783 impost while refusing Congress the power to remove state-appointed collectors and insisting that New York paper money be accepted in payment of impost duties; Congress rejects these conditions on August 23. (By summer 1786 the other 12 states have approved the impost, although Pennsylvania vote is conditioned on supplementary funds being provided by all 13 states, a condition Pennsylvania legislature will refuse to drop despite congressional plea in September 1786. Every state except New Hampshire and Rhode Island has ratified the amendment to the Articles changing the basis for apportioning requisitions from property to population. All 13 states have granted Congress the power to regulate commerce for 15 years, but in varying forms that must be reconciled before the power can be exercised.)

May   Rhode Island legislature issues £100,000 in paper money in May and makes it legal tender for all debts. When creditors refuse to accept the money, the legislature establishes penalties for not accepting the money and denies trial by jury to those sued under the act.

July   Farmers in Massachusetts, burdened by debt and requirement to pay rising taxes in specie, petition the legislature for paper money and laws to suspend home and farm foreclosures. The legislature fails to pass significant relief measures before adjourning on July 8, but does grant supplemental funds requested by Congress in 1783 (tax burden is already high due to effort by the state government to quickly pay off its war debt).

Aug.

Jay reports to Congress on August 3 on the terms of a tentative Spanish-American commercial treaty he has negotiated with Gardoqui and recommends that the United States forgo its claim to free navigation of the Mississippi for 25 or 30 years in return for Spanish agreement to the treaty. On August 7, a 12-man committee of the Congress reports seven amendments to the Articles, drafted by Charles Pinckney (South Carolina), Nathan Dane (Massachusetts), and William Samuel Johnson (Connecticut), which would give Congress the power to regulate foreign and interstate commerce and directly levy taxes in states that failed to meet their requisitions, establish a seven-member federal judicial court, and reduce to 11 the number of states needed to approve future federal revenue measures. Amendments are not considered by the full Congress, which begins debating the proposed Jay-Gardoqui treaty. With all of the southern states opposed, on August 29 Congress votes 7–5 (Delaware is absent) to repeal its 1785 instructions requiring Jay to obtain free navigation of the Mississippi (because nine states are needed to ratify a treaty, the negotiations do not progress).

Aug.– Sept.

In Hatfield, Massachusetts, 50 Hampshire County towns meet, August 22–25, and adopt resolutions calling for the abolition of the state senate, reapportionment of the state house of representatives, issuing paper money, a reduction in court fees, changes in the court and tax systems, and moving the state capital from Boston (other county conventions make similar demands). The convention appeals against mob action, but on August 29 armed men prevent a court from sitting at Northampton. Court sessions are also broken up at Worcester, September 5, and Concord and Great Barrington, September 12, in an attempt to block further foreclosures.

Sept.

Convention called by Virginia legislature in January 1786 to consider new commercial regulations meets in Annapolis, September 11–14, and is attended by 12 commissioners from New York, New Jersey, Delaware, Pennsylvania, and Virginia (representatives from New Hampshire, Massachusetts, Rhode Island, and North Carolina do not arrive in time, and Georgia, South Carolina, Connecticut, and Maryland do not appoint delegates). With only five states represented, the meeting does not consider specific proposals regarding commerce, but does unanimously adopt a report, drafted by Hamilton, for transmission to Congress and all 13 states. It proposes that every state appoint representatives to meet in Philadelphia on May 14, 1787, to "devise such further provisions as shall appear to them necessary to render the constitution of the Fœderal Government adequate to the exigencies of the Union; and to report an Act for that purpose" to Congress for its approval, and then to the legislatures of every state for their unanimous confirmation. (Congress receives the report on September 20, refers it to a committee on October 11, and takes no further action before its session ends on November 3.)

In *Trevett* v. *Weeden* the Rhode Island superior court of judicature is asked to void the state's paper money enforcement act because it unconstitutionally abridges the fundamental right to trial by jury guaranteed by the Rhode Island colonial charter (which serves as the state constitution). Court rules on September 25 that it lacks jurisdiction over the case, effectively making the statute unenforceable. (When newspapers report that several of the judges delivered opinions holding the law unconstitutional, the court is summoned before a special session of the legislature and accused of subverting the legislative power; however, a motion to remove the judges fails, and the enforcement act is repealed.)

Sept.–Oct.   Massachusetts governor James Bowdoin orders 600 militiamen under General William Shepard to protect the sitting of the supreme judicial court at Springfield, where they are confronted on September 26 by 500 insurgents, led by former Revolutionary War captain Daniel Shays, who are trying to prevent indictments from being issued for previous court disruptions. (Although Shays never becomes the sole leader of the Massachusetts insurgents, the rebellion becomes associated with him throughout the country.) The court adjourns without taking action. When Congress sends Secretary at War Knox to Massachusetts to investigate the rebellion, Knox reports to Congress, Washington, and others that the insurgents number 12,000–15,000 and seek the common distribution of all property. Although it lacks power under the Articles to intervene in domestic disturbances, Congress authorizes Knox on October 20 to raise 1,340 troops and protect the federal arsenal at Springfield from the rebels, publicly claiming that the troops are to fight Indians along the Ohio River (federal troops are never used and their real purpose soon becomes known). Massachusetts rebels continue to block court sittings in the fall (crowds also resist debt collection in rural areas of New Hampshire, Pennsylvania, Maryland, Virginia, and South Carolina in 1786–87).

Nov.–Dec.   Legislatures appoint delegates to the Philadelphia convention in New Jersey, November 23, Virginia, December 4, and Pennsylvania, December 30 (in Virginia Patrick Henry and Richard Henry Lee will decline appointment).

1787   Delegates to the Philadelphia convention are appointed by legislatures in North Carolina, January 6, and New Hampshire, January 17. In New York the legislature adopts on January 26 a comprehensive law, drafted by John Lansing, that lists the rights and privileges of citizens.

Jan.–Apr.   Massachusetts governor James Bowdoin calls for 4,400 militia to assemble under General Benjamin Lincoln and suppress Shays' rebels. When Shays attempts to seize the Springfield arsenal on January 25, militia under Shepard open fire and kill four rebels. Lincoln pursues the insurgents to Petersham and scatters them on February 4. Shays and other leaders flee to Vermont, and the organized insurrection ends (five men are killed in skirmish near Sheffield on February 27, and unrest continues in western Massachusetts until June). Massachusetts legislature passes disqualification act on February 16, barring most rebels from holding office, voting, or serving as jurors for three years. In April elections in Massachusetts Governor Bowdoin is overwhelmingly defeated by John Hancock. Bowdoin and Hancock eventually pardon 14 men condemned to death for treason and murder during the rebellion (two rebels are hanged for burglary). The new legislature does not levy a direct tax in 1787 and adopts measures that give some relief to debtors.

Feb.–Mar.   Delaware legislature appoints delegates to the Philadelphia convention on February 3 and instructs them not to agree to any change in the equality of state representation in Congress. New session of Congress, designated to meet on November 6, 1786, achieves first regular quorum on February 12 and resumes consideration of the Annapolis report. On February 21 it calls for a convention to meet in Philadelphia on May 14 for "the sole and express purpose of revising the Articles of Confederation" and directs that proposed changes be submitted to Congress for its approval. Delegates are appointed in Massachusetts, March 3, New York, March 6, and South Carolina, March 8; in Massachusetts and New York they are instructed by the legislature to limit the convention to revising the Articles. On March 14 Rhode Island legislature refuses to elect delegates (will again decline on May 5 and June 16, despite efforts of legislators from trading towns of Newport and Providence to have state represented).

Mar.–Apr.   While attending Congress in the spring, Madison writes a memorandum, "Vices of the Political System of the United States," and outlines principles for a new plan of government in letters to Jefferson, Edmund Randolph, and Washington.

May   In *Bayard* v. *Singleton* the North Carolina supreme court voids a state law requiring the dismissal of recovery suits brought against owners of confiscated Loyalist property, ruling that it violates the right to trial by jury protected by the state constitution.

Connecticut legislature elects convention delegates on May 17 and instructs them only to revise the existing Articles. Maryland legislature elects delegates on May 26. (Of the 74 delegates chosen by 12 states, 55 will attend the convention at one time or another.)

On May 14 the convention meets in Philadelphia but fails to achieve a quorum. Virginia delegates caucus while waiting for the convention to begin. Quorum is achieved on May 25, when seven state delegations are present (delegations from Connecticut and Massachusetts achieve voting quorum on May 28, Georgia on May 31, Maryland on June 2, and New Hampshire delegates, possibly delayed by lack of funds, arrive on July 23; not all delegations will maintain a voting quorum throughout the convention). George Washington is unanimously elected president of the convention and a committee (Hamilton, Charles Pinckney, George Wythe) is appointed to prepare rules. Convention adopts rules, May 28–29, that make their deliberations secret, give each state delegation a single vote, let questions be decided by a majority of states present, and allow for the reconsideration of matters already voted on.

On May 29 Virginia governor Edmund Randolph opens the main deliberations by giving a speech on the defects of the Confederation and presenting 15 resolutions, drafted by the Virginia caucus, which incorporate many of Madison's ideas (resolutions become known as the Virginia plan). The resolutions propose establishing a national legislature with two branches, in which states would be represented and vote in proportion either to their "quotas of contribution" or to their free population. The first branch is to be elected by the people of the states and would be subject to rotation in office and recall, while the second branch is to be elected by the first branch, choosing from nominees submitted by the respective state legislatures. Each branch would have the right to originate legislation. The national legislature would have all of the powers of the existing Congress, as well as the power to "legislate in all cases to which the separate

States are incompetent," to veto all state laws which it thinks unconstitutional, and "to call forth the force of the Union" against any state failing to fulfill its national obligations. A national executive would be chosen by the national legislature and exercise the executive rights vested in Congress under the Articles of Confederation. The executive would be ineligible for reelection (its term, as well as those of both branches of the legislature, are left unspecified in the resolutions). A national judiciary, with both supreme and inferior tribunals, is to be chosen by the legislature and serve for good behavior (for life, unless removed for misconduct); its jurisdiction would include impeachment of national officers and "questions which may involve the national peace and harmony." The executive and members of the judiciary would form a council of revision with power to examine and veto all acts of the national legislature (including vetoes of state laws); the council's veto could be overridden by an unspecified vote in each legislative branch. New states could be admitted by a less than unanimous vote in the legislature and a "Republican Government" would be guaranteed by the United States to each state. The resolutions also call for continuing the present Congress until the new government takes power, establishing an amendment procedure for the new "Articles of Union" not involving the national legislature, and submitting the new plan of government to special assemblies chosen by the people after it has been approved by Congress. After Randolph speaks, Charles Pinckney (South Carolina) submits his own plan for a new government, and the convention adjourns.

On May 30 the convention resolves itself into a committee of the whole with Nathaniel Gorham (Massachusetts) presiding and begins debating the Virginia resolutions (the Pinckney plan is never discussed by the convention). The first resolution, calling for the Articles of Confederation to be "corrected & enlarged," is challenged by Gouverneur Morris (Pennsylvania), who says that the remaining Virginia resolutions are incompatible with the Articles. Charles Cotesworth Pinckney (South Carolina, a second cousin of Charles Pinckney) and Elbridge Gerry (Massachusetts) question whether the convention has the authority to discuss a system not founded on the principles of the Confederation. After further debate, a resolution calling for establishing "a *national* Government" consisting of "a *supreme* Legislative, Executive & Judiciary" is approved, 6–1. Debate then turns to how representation in the national legislature should be apportioned, but the matter is postponed when George

Read (Delaware) reminds the convention that his delegation has been instructed not to change the equality of state representation provided for by the Articles.

On May 31 the delegates agree to establish a bicameral legislature and begin debating whether the first branch should be elected by the people. Roger Sherman (Connecticut) and Gerry speak against popular election, which is supported by George Mason (Virginia), James Wilson (Pennsylvania), and Madison, and then approved by a 6–2 vote. A debate over the method of electing the second branch, which Wilson suggests should also be chosen by the people, reaches no conclusion.

June

On June 1 the committee of the whole debates the national executive. Wilson moves that it be a single person and is opposed by Randolph, who favors a plural executive; the question is postponed. Wilson also favors having the executive elected by the people, saying that he wishes to make both legislative branches and the executive as independent of the state legislatures as possible. The committee votes 5–4 to create a seven-year term for the executive. On June 2 Wilson proposes that the people vote for electors who will then choose the executive. His motion is defeated, 8–2, and the committee then approves, 8–2, election of the executive by the national legislature. John Dickinson (Delaware) seeks to make the executive removable on request of a majority of the state legislatures, arguing that it is necessary to preserve a role for the states under the new plan. He is opposed by Madison and Wilson and the motion is rejected, 9–1. A single executive is approved, 7–3, on June 4, and Gerry then moves that the executive be given veto power, subject to legislative override. Wilson and Hamilton argue in favor of an absolute veto, but are opposed by Benjamin Franklin, Sherman, Madison, Mason, and others. An executive veto, subject to override by a two-thirds majority in each legislative chamber, is approved 8–2 (override majority is increased to three-fourths on August 15, then changed back to two-thirds on September 12).

On June 6 Charles Pinckney moves for reconsideration of the popular election of the first branch and proposes that it be chosen instead by the state legislatures. During the ensuing debate Madison supports popular election and says that it will help limit the power of the state governments. He argues that in republics there is always a danger of a united majority oppressing a minority, and that the only remedy is to enlarge the republic, increasing the number of contending interests and factions and thus reducing the chances and opportunity for a single oppressive majority to emerge. Pinckney's motion is defeated, 8–3. Dickinson moves on June 7 that the second branch (now referred to as the Senate) be elected by the state legislatures. Wilson again advocates popular election, but the motion is carried 10–0.

When discussion of representation in the national legislature resumes on June 9, New Jersey delegates David Brearly and William Paterson warn that proportional representation will allow Massachusetts, Pennsylvania, and Virginia to dominate the new government. Paterson says that the people of the smaller states will never accept a scheme that abolishes the state equality they possess under the Confederation. On June 11 Roger Sherman proposes that representation in the first branch be in proportion to free population while in the Senate each state would have one vote. His motion for equality in the Senate is defeated, 6–5, with Massachusetts, Pennsylvania, Virginia, North Carolina, South Carolina, and Georgia opposed and Connecticut, New York, New Jersey, Delaware, and Maryland supporting.

On June 13 the committee of the whole ends its deliberations and an amended version of the Virginia plan is prepared in the form of 19 resolutions. It provides for the first branch of the legislature to be elected by the people for three-year terms and the second branch to be chosen by the state legislatures for seven-year terms. Representation of both branches is to be in proportion to the free population and three-fifths of "other persons" (slaves). The national legislature will elect a single executive to serve for a single seven-year term, and the supreme tribunal of the national judiciary will be appointed by the Senate.

William Paterson asks for an adjournment on June 14 so that an alternate plan can be prepared (plan is drafted by New Jersey delegation, along with delegates from Connecticut, New York, Delaware, and Maryland). On June 15 Paterson presents nine resolutions that call for giving the existing Congress power to directly levy imposts and stamp taxes, regulate foreign and interstate trade, and appoint an executive. Congress would also be able to collect requisitions from noncomplying states. A federal judiciary would rule on cases involving foreigners, treaties, and federal trade regulation and revenue collection. All acts of Congress and treaties would be "the supreme law of the respective States" to which "the Judiciary of the several States shall be bound thereby in their decisions, any thing in the respective laws of the Individual States to the contrary notwithstanding." The executive would have the power to compel a state to obey federal law.

On June 16 the convention again resolves into a committee

of the whole. John Lansing (New York) supports the New
Jersey plan, saying that it sustains the sovereignty of the states
while the Virginia plan destroys state sovereignty. He insists
that the convention has no power to supersede the Articles
and therefore the states will never adopt the Virginia plan.
Wilson replies with a detailed defense of the Virginia plan
and says that the convention has the authority to "*conclude
nothing*, but to be at liberty to *propose any thing*."

On June 18 Alexander Hamilton speaks for several hours,
praising the British constitution as the best in the world, and
presenting his own plan for creating an elected assembly,
serving for three years, and a Senate, elected for life by electors chosen by the people. A single executive would also serve
for life after being indirectly elected by the people and would
have an absolute veto. The Senate would have the sole power
to declare war, and the national legislature would establish
the courts in each state. All state governors would be appointed by the national government and have an absolute
veto over legislation in their states.

On June 19 Madison argues that the New Jersey plan will
not "remedy the evils" of the Confederation, which include:
violations of treaties; encroachments on federal authority;
states trespassing against one another; the threat of insurrection by armed minorities, or by minorities of voters allied
with "those whose poverty disqualifies them from the suffrage"; the injustice, impotence, and instability of many of
the state laws; and the influence of foreign powers within the
Union. Madison warns that if the Articles are merely
amended to give the Confederation coercive power against
recalcitrant members, national power will be used against the
weaker states but not against the stronger, and that if the
union dissolves for the lack of a new plan, the 13 states either
will remain independent and sovereign or will form two or
more smaller confederacies. In the first case, Madison predicts
that the smaller states will be unable to defend themselves
against their larger neighbors; in the second, the larger members of the new confederacies will offer the smaller states no
better concessions than does the Virginia plan. After Madison finishes, the committee of the whole votes, 7–3, to adhere
to the Virginia plan rather than the New Jersey plan, with
New York, New Jersey, and Delaware opposed and Maryland
divided.

Debate returns to the place of the states in the new system.
Rufus King (Massachusetts) says that the states under the
Confederation are not fully sovereign because they cannot
make war, peace, or foreign alliances. On June 20 Oliver Ells-

worth (Connecticut) proposes that the phrase "national government" in the first amended resolution be changed to "Government of the United States," and the convention unanimously agrees. John Lansing moves to preserve the Congress as it exists under the Confederation. George Mason says that the people will not give additional power to a Congress they do not directly elect. The Virginia plan does not ask the people to surrender power, but to transfer it from their state representatives to national representatives that they will directly choose. Luther Martin (Maryland) insists that the federal government was instituted to support the state governments, arguing that when the people of America separated from Britain, they chose to form 13 separate sovereignties instead of incorporating themselves into one. The Lansing motion is defeated, 6–4. On June 21 Wilson argues that the state and national governments have a shared interest, while Madison again warns that the encroachment of the states on federal authority is more likely and more dangerous than the reverse. The convention then changes the terms of the first legislative branch from three to two years.

On June 25 Charles Pinckney delivers a long speech on the nature of American society, agreeing with Hamilton's praise of the British constitution, but arguing that a similar constitution could not be introduced for many centuries in America, where there is greater equality than in any other country. Pinckney doubts an aristocracy will ever develop in America, since the landowners, merchants, and professional men, though divided in their pursuits, have common political interests, and are mutually dependent. On June 26 Madison again discusses the diversity of interests in America and argues that a Senate serving for long terms will help protect minorities against majority oppression. Gerry opposes long senatorial terms, predicting that the people will reject any system that approaches monarchy. The convention approves, 7–4, a six-year term, with one-third of the Senate chosen every two years.

Luther Martin speaks for several hours on the nature of government, June 27–28, again contending that the general government is meant to preserve state governments, not to govern individuals, and says that he would rather see partial confederacies than a government instituted according to the Virginia plan. Madison replies, citing ancient history and the fates of modern confederacies, and argues that the dissimilar interests of Massachusetts, Pennsylvania, and Virginia make it unlikely that they will combine to oppress the smaller states. Franklin reviews the "small progress" made in five weeks, and sees in it "a melancholy proof of the imperfection of the Human Understanding." He asks how it is that the delegates, "groping . . . in the dark to find political truth, and scarce able to distinguish it when presented to us" had not thought to call on "the Father of lights to illuminate our understandings." Franklin moves that sessions open with prayer, led by Philadelphia clergy. Hamilton worries that calling in clergy would alert the public to the dissensions within the convention. Hugh Williamson (North Carolina) says the convention has no funds. Randolph proposes that a sermon be preached on July 4, and prayers given each morning subsequently. No action is taken on the proposal.

June–July

On June 29 William Samuel Johnson (Connecticut) says the convention is divided between those who see the states as political societies and those who see them as districts of individual citizens. He urges that the two ideas be combined, with the people represented in one branch of the legislature and the states in the other. His position is not supported. The convention votes 6–4 in favor of proportional representation in the first branch, with Connecticut, New York, New Jersey, and Delaware opposed and Maryland divided. Hamilton, thinking the convention will never produce a strong enough constitution, returns to New York (will resume regular attendance on September 6). Debate on representation continues on June 30, when Gunning Bedford (Delaware) warns that if the large states dissolve the Confederation, the smaller states will find foreign allies. On July 2 Oliver Ellsworth moves that each state have a single vote in the Senate. The convention splits 5–5, with Connecticut, New York, New Jersey, Delaware, and Maryland voting yes and Georgia divided. Charles Cotesworth Pinckney proposes that a committee consisting of one member from each state be appointed to work out a compromise. The proposal is supported by Sherman, Gouverneur Morris, Randolph, and Gerry, opposed by Madison and Wilson, and approved, 10–1, with only Pennsylvania voting no. A committee is elected and the convention adjourns (committee members include Franklin, Gerry, Ellsworth, Paterson, Mason, and Luther Martin).

July

On July 5 the committee reports a compromise proposal. In the first branch of the legislature, each state would have one representative for every 40,000 people (with slaves counted as three-fifths of free citizens); in the second branch, each state would have an equal vote. All money bills would originate in the first branch, and they could not be altered or amended in the second. A new committee is appointed to propose an exact apportionment of the first branch. Its report distributes 56 members among the 13 states. Paterson objects to counting slaves as people, saying that they are treated as property and that including them in apportionment indirectly encourages the slave trade. A second committee is appointed and proposes a new apportionment calling for 65 members. Rufus King says it favors the South and describes the greatest difference of interests as being between the southern and New England states, not the large and small ones. Charles Cotesworth Pinckney says the proposed apportionment favors the North, which will be able to regulate trade to its own advantage. New York delegates Robert Yates and John Lansing, who believe the convention has authority only to amend the Articles, leave after the July 10 session, and their state is no longer represented.

In New York the Continental Congress adopts on July 13 the Northwest Ordinance for governing the territory beyond the Ohio River. Largely drafted by Nathan Dane (Massachusetts) and based in part on Jefferson's plan of 1784, the new law gives Congress the power to appoint a governor, secretary, and three judges for the territory. When the territorial population includes 5,000 adult free males, a territorial legislature will be formed, consisting of an elected house of representatives and a council appointed by Congress from nominees submitted by the elected territorial representatives. Between three and five states will eventually be formed from the territory, each to be admitted on full equality with the existing states when its population reaches 60,000. Slavery is prohibited in the territory, and its inhabitants are entitled to freedom of "peaceable" worship, the writ of habeas corpus, trial by jury, judicial proceedings according to the common law, and protection from immoderate fines and cruel and unusual punishments. The ordinance also provides for the return of fugitive slaves and forbids the making of laws interfering with valid existing private contracts.

As the debate over representation continues in the Philadelphia convention on July 14, Madison and Wilson restate their opposition to state equality in the Senate. On July 16 an amended compromise resolution is proposed, calling for a regular census to help reapportion the first branch according to population (with slaves counted as three-fifths of whites), requiring money bills to originate in the first branch and not be changed in the second, and giving each state an equal vote in the Senate. It is approved, 5–4, with Pennsylvania, Virginia, South Carolina, and Georgia opposed, and Massachusetts divided. Delegates from the larger states caucus but are unable to agree on a plan for reversing the vote, and when Gouverneur Morris moves on July 17 for reconsideration of the compromise, his motion is not seconded.

The convention begins considering other resolutions reported by the committee of the whole on June 13. Gouverneur Morris and Sherman argue that giving the national legislature power to veto state laws is unnecessary and offensive to the states. Madison defends it as essential to the "efficacy & security" of the new government, but the proposed legislative veto is rejected, 7–3.

Debate turns to whether the national legislature should elect the executive. Gouverneur Morris warns that the executive would become "the mere creature" of the legislature under such a system, and favors election by the people at large. He is supported by Wilson, but opposed by Sherman, Charles Pinckney, and Mason, who says that it would be as "unnatural" to refer the choice of the executive to the people as it would be to "refer a trial of colours to a blind man." Mason argues that the extent of the country would make it impossible for the people to judge the qualifications of candidates. A motion in favor of election by the people is defeated, 9–1. Gouverneur Morris advocates making the executive eligible for reelection as an incentive for good behavior; reeligibility is approved, 6–4.

On July 18 the convention votes 6–2 against having the national judiciary appointed by the executive, then divides, 4–4, on a proposal for the executive to appoint judges with the advice and consent of the Senate. Debate on the executive resumes on July 19, when Madison argues that the executive must be independent of the legislature and favors his indirect election by special electors. Ellsworth moves that the executive be chosen by electors and the convention approves, 6–3; it then votes, 8–2, in favor of the electors being chosen by the state legislatures. The convention also approves a six-year executive term.

On July 21 Wilson and Madison propose that the national judiciary share veto power with the executive. Wilson advocates giving the judiciary power to block laws that are unwise but not unconstitutional, while Madison argues that a shared veto will strengthen the check on legislative power. Gerry opposes the measure, saying it will create an alliance between the executive and judiciary. The motion is defeated, 4–3, and the convention votes, 6–3, in favor of having the Senate appoint judges.

On July 23 the convention debates resolution calling for ratification of the new Constitution by special conventions elected by the people. Ellsworth and Paterson propose submitting the Constitution to the state legislatures. Randolph argues that state legislatures are too often influenced by local demagogues who will be threatened by the new Constitution; Mason and Madison also strongly support ratification by conventions. The Ellsworth motion is defeated, 8–3. Convention then approves, 10–1, giving each state two senators, with each senator having an individual vote.

On July 24 the convention reconsiders the election of the executive and approves election by the national legislature, 7–4, reversing its vote of July 19. Reconsideration of reeligibility leads to suggestions that the executive serve for terms of 11, 15, or 20 years. Further discussion of the executive is postponed, and a committee of detail (John Rutledge of South Carolina, Randolph, Gorham, Ellsworth, and Wilson) is elected and instructed to draft a Constitution. After debating the executive without resolution on July 25, the convention votes, 7–3, in favor of a single seven-year term on July 26. It then submits 23 resolutions derived from the Virginia plan to the committee of detail, which also receives texts of the Pinckney and New Jersey plans, and adjourns until August 6.

July–Aug.   Randolph prepares a draft Constitution, which is examined by the committee, rewritten by Wilson, and again reviewed by the committee. The draft reported by the committee draws on the materials submitted by the convention, as well as state constitutions, the Articles of Confederation, and resolutions in the Continental Congress. It is divided into a preamble and 23 articles, with the preamble beginning "We the People of the States of . . ." and then listing all 13 states. In place of the general definition of legislative power given in the amended Virginia resolutions, the draft Constitution enumerates 17 powers to be vested in the new Congress and also gives the legislature power "to make all laws that shall be necessary and proper" for executing both its enumerated powers and all other powers given to the government of the United States by the Constitution. (The draft also lists several prohibitions on the powers of the states, and includes an article defining the judicial power of the United States.) Copies are printed and distributed to the delegates when the convention reconvenes on August 6.

Aug.   The convention begins a detailed examination and revision of the draft on August 7. Gouverneur Morris proposes uniformly restricting suffrage in elections for the House of

Representatives to freeholders; his amendment is defeated, 7–1, as several delegates argue that it would be impossible to establish an acceptable uniform property qualification. On August 10 the convention votes 7–3 to remove a draft clause giving Congress power to establish uniform property requirements for its own members.

Debate on enumerated legislative powers begins on August 16. Clause giving Congress power to regulate foreign and interstate commerce is unanimously approved. When the convention considers the power to "make war," Charles Pinckney suggests restricting it to the Senate, saying that it will be better qualified than the House of Representatives to judge foreign affairs. Pierce Butler (South Carolina) recommends giving the power to the president, who "will not make war but when the Nation will support it." Madison and Gerry move to replace "make" with "declare," leaving to the president "the power to repel sudden attacks." Their motion is approved, 8–1. Madison and Charles Pinckney each propose an additional list of legislative powers on August 18, and on August 20 Pinckney submits another list, which includes several enumerated restrictions on legislative power; their recommendations are referred to the committee of detail (some of the Madison and Pinckney recommendations are incorporated in the final Constitution). The "necessary and proper" clause is unanimously adopted on August 20.

Luther Martin moves on August 21 to give Congress the power to tax or to prohibit the importation of slaves and calls the slave trade "dishonorable to the American character." Rutledge replies that the question is one of interest, not religion and humanity. Ellsworth says that the "morality or wisdom" of slavery should be left to the states. On August 22 Sherman supports the draft clause forbidding interference with the slave trade. Mason condemns slavery and warns that "providence punishes national sins, by national calamities." He calls for giving the government power to prevent the increase of slavery. Ellsworth replies that morality would suggest freeing slaves already in the country and predicts that an increasing number of poor white laborers will eventually cause slavery to disappear. Rutledge says that North Carolina, South Carolina, and Georgia will never agree to a constitution prohibiting the slave trade. Gouverneur Morris recommends referring the question to a committee, along with draft clauses prohibiting Congress from taxing exports and requiring a two-thirds majority to pass navigation acts (laws regulating maritime commerce). He suggests, "These things may form a bargain among the Northern & Southern States." A committee consisting of a delegate from each state is chosen.

The convention resumes its review of the draft Constitution and adopts a clause forbidding Congress from passing bills of attainder or ex post facto laws (prohibition is extended to the states on August 28). An amended version of the "supreme law" clause, first introduced in the New Jersey plan, is unanimously adopted on August 23.

The convention debates on August 25 the committee report on the slave trade and navigation acts, which recommends that Congress should have the power to end the slave trade after 1800 and to tax the importation of slaves until then. It also recommends striking the draft clause requiring a two-thirds majority to pass navigation laws. Charles Cotesworth Pinckney moves that the slave trade be protected until 1808. Madison objects that 20 years of importation would be "dishonorable," but the motion is approved, 7–4, with New Jersey, Pennsylvania, Delaware, and Virginia opposed. Sherman and Madison object to taxing imported slaves, since it acknowledges that people can be property. King, John Langdon (New Hampshire), and Charles Cotesworth Pinckney say this is the price of securing eventual prohibition of the slave trade. On August 29 the convention debates making navigation laws subject to a simple majority. Mason says that this will make the southern states, who will be a minority in both the House and Senate, subject to the commercial interest of the majority. Madison argues that agricultural interests in the interior of the commercial states, as well as the admission of new agricultural western states, will prevent abuse of the power to make commercial laws. The convention votes 7–4 against a two-thirds majority, with Maryland, Virginia, North Carolina, and Georgia opposed, and then unanimously approves adding a fugitive-slave clause to the Constitution.

After unanimously voting to prohibit religious tests for holding office under the new Constitution, the convention debates how many state ratifications should be sufficient to begin the new government. Wilson recommends seven, Randolph nine, Sherman ten, and Daniel Carroll (Maryland) says that all 13 states must agree to dissolve the Articles of Confederation before the Constitution can go into effect. On August 31 the convention votes to make the ratification of nine states sufficient. Gouverneur Morris says that the Constitution must be ratified quickly, before state officials can intrigue against it; Luther Martin says the people will not ratify it unless they are hurried into it by surprise.

Mason tells the convention that he would sooner chop off his right hand than sign the Constitution as it stands. Sherman proposes the election of a committee consisting of one delegate from each state to report on postponed matters. The committee is chosen, with David Brearly (New Jersey) as its chairman; members include King, Sherman, Gouverneur Morris, Dickinson, and Madison.

Sept.

On September 4 the committee reports an amended article regarding the president, who will now serve for four years and be eligible for reelection. Presidential electors will be chosen in each state in a manner determined by the state legislature, and each state will have electors equal in number to its senators and representatives. Each elector will vote for two candidates, one of whom must not be a resident of their state. If no candidate receives a majority of electoral votes, or if there is a tie, the Senate is to choose a president from among the top five recipients of electoral votes. The candidate receiving the second-highest number of votes will become vice-president.

On September 5 Charles Pinckney says electors will not have sufficient knowledge of the "fittest men" and will vote for an eminent man from their own state. The resulting dispersion of electoral votes will lead to appointment by the Senate, who will repeatedly elect the same man. Mason fears that the proposed system will lead to the president and Senate forming a coalition to subvert the Constitution. Gouverneur Morris believes electors will choose "characters eminent & generally known" when voting for men from out of state, and that this will contribute to electoral majorities. A proposal by Wilson to have both houses of Congress choose the president when there is no electoral majority is defeated, 7–3. Madison and Williamson move that one-third of the electoral vote be sufficient to elect a president; they are defeated, 9–2. Randolph and Wilson warn that giving a role in presidential elections to the Senate will lead to its becoming an aristocracy. On September 6 the convention votes 9–2 in favor of having electors choose the president. Williamson suggests having both houses elect the president when there is no electoral majority, voting by state and not as individuals. Sherman then suggests giving the power to the House of Representatives, with the members from each state having one vote; his motion is seconded by Mason and approved, 10–1.

On September 7 the convention considers other proposals by the committee on postponed matters. It defeats, 10–1, a motion by Wilson to let the House of Representatives share treaty-making power with the Senate and then approves presidential power to make appointments with the advice and consent of the Senate. Mason proposes establishing a six-member council of state to advise the president; his motion, seconded by Franklin, is defeated 8–3. On September 8 the convention approves making a two-thirds majority in the Senate necessary to ratify treaties and gives the Senate power to amend money bills, which must still originate in the House. A committee of style (William Samuel Johnson, Gouverneur Morris, Madison, Hamilton, and King) is appointed to prepare a finished text of the Constitution. Convention debates draft clause on amendments, which provides for calling a convention if two-thirds of the state legislatures seek an amendment. Hamilton advocates giving Congress the power to initiate amendments. Madison moves that amendments be proposed by Congress when two-thirds of both houses deem them necessary or when two-thirds of the state legislatures apply for them, and then be ratified by either three-fourths of the state legislatures, or by conventions in three-fourths of the states. His motion is approved, 9–1. Hamilton proposes submitting the Constitution to the Continental Congress for approval before it is transmitted to the states. Wilson disagrees, warning that the Congress may refuse its assent, and the proposal is defeated.

On September 12 the committee of style submits its draft Constitution, consisting of a preamble and seven articles (much of the final wording is attributed to Gouverneur Morris). The preamble, rewritten by Morris, now begins "We, the People of the United States," and introduces language describing the purpose of the Constitution ("to form a more perfect union . . ."). The committee of style draft also includes a clause prohibiting states from impairing the obligation of contracts, which will be adopted without debate.

Mason and Gerry recommend that a bill of rights be prepared. Sherman says that the Constitution does not repeal state declarations of rights, which will still be in force and sufficient to secure the rights of the people. Mason answers that the laws of the United States are to be paramount to state bills of rights. The convention votes unanimously against preparing a bill of rights. On September 13 the committee of style reports two resolutions concerning the ratification and implementation of the Constitution (they are sent to Congress on September 17, along with a letter drafted by the committee and signed by Washington). The convention rejects on September 14 a motion by Madison to give Congress limited power to grant charters of incorporation benefiting the interest of the United States. On September 15 Mason objects to the power given to Congress regarding amendments. The convention unanimously votes to give two-thirds of the state legislatures power to call a convention to propose amendments.

Randolph, Mason, and Gerry then express their reservations (other delegates opposed to the Constitution have already left the convention). Randolph proposes that state ratifying conventions be able to submit amendments for consideration by a second general convention. If this procedure is not adopted, Randolph will not sign the Constitution and may oppose it in Virginia. Mason and Gerry also support a second convention. Mason believes the government being created will turn into either a monarchy or a tyrannical aristocracy and supports a second convention. Gerry specifically objects to the reeligibility of the Senate, control by Congress over places of elections and its own compensation, the possibility that monopolies could be established, the representation of three-fifths of the slaves as if they were freemen, and the vice-president being made head of the Senate, mixing executive and legislative powers. He adds that the rights of citizens are threatened by the power of the legislature "to make what laws they may please to call necessary and proper," to raise armies and money without limit, and to establish courts capable of trying civil cases without juries. The motion by Randolph proposing a second convention is unanimously defeated, and the convention then unanimously adopts the amended Constitution and orders it engrossed.

On September 17, with the engrossed Constitution ready to be signed, Benjamin Franklin rises with a written speech, which James Wilson reads. Franklin confesses that he does not entirely approve of the Constitution at present, but doubts that he will never change his mind. He urges unanimous support of the Constitution and hopes that future thoughts be turned to its good administration. Franklin presents a form of signing, drafted by Gouverneur Morris in the hope of gaining the signatures of the three dissenters, that asks delegates to sign as witnesses to the adoption of the Constitution "by the unanimous consent of the States present." Gorham, King, and Carroll move one final amendment, proposing that the number of representatives not exceed one for every 30,000 people, instead of the 40,000 presently called for. Washington rises from the chair and for the first time gives his sentiments on a question before the convention, supporting the amendment, despite its lateness, in the hope that it will remove a possible objection to the

Constitution. The amendment is adopted without opposition. Randolph apologizes to Franklin, but says he cannot sign the Constitution. He believes it will be rejected, and by withholding his name he will be able to take steps "consistent with the public good" in the ensuing confusion. Gouverneur Morris and Hamilton reply that they will support the Constitution despite their reservations and see anarchy as the only alternative to its adoption. Franklin asks Randolph, whom he commends for bringing the basic plan forward in May, to reconsider and sign. Randolph says he cannot sign, and warns that attempting to obtain unconditional ratification will produce anarchy and convulsion. Gerry sees a civil war ensuing, especially in Massachusetts, where two parties, one devoted to democracy and the other to the opposite extreme, already confront each other and will collide in the struggle over the Constitution. The convention adopts the form of signing proposed by Franklin and orders the convention journals deposited in the custody of Washington. (The journals are first published in 1819; Madison's notes of the debates, the fullest account by a participant, are posthumously published in 1840.) All of the 41 delegates present, except Gerry, Randolph, and Mason, then sign (Dickinson signs by proxy). Toward the close of the signing Franklin observes that during sessions he had often been unable to tell whether the sun painted on the back of the chair Washington presided from had been "rising or setting: But now at length I have the happiness to know that it is a rising and not a setting Sun." When the signing is completed, the convention dissolves itself.

The Constitution is read in Congress on September 20, and on September 26 debate begins on the ratification procedure proposed by the Constitutional Convention. Richard Henry Lee proposes amendments, but Congress unanimously resolves on September 28 to send the Constitution, along with the resolutions and letter accompanying it, to the state legislatures for submission to conventions elected by the people.

Press debate on the Constitution begins in Philadelphia, where a favorable commentary appears on September 19 and a critical article is published on September 26. (Supporters of the Constitution become known as Federalists and opponents as Antifederalists; most newspapers in the United States support the Federalists.) The first of seven Antifederalist letters by "Cato" appears in New York on September 27 (series runs until January 3, 1788).

Sept.–Oct.   In Pennsylvania the Constitution is supported by Republicans (opponents of the 1776 state constitution) and opposed by Constitutionalists (supporters of the 1776 state constitution). In Philadelphia the Federalist majority in the state assembly calls on September 28 for a state ratifying convention and proposes electing the convention in October. Antifederalist assemblymen object to the early date and prevent a quorum by boycotting the afternoon session (assembly is scheduled to adjourn on September 29; elections for a new assembly are to be held on October 9). On September 29 Federalists order the sergeant at arms to look for absentees, and with the help of a mob two Antifederalists are forcibly brought to the State House. With the necessary two-thirds quorum achieved, the assembly calls for the convention to be elected on November 6 and to meet on November 20. An address from 16 of the "seceding" Antifederalists is published on October 2, attacking the Federalists for their tactics and criticizing the Philadelphia convention for abandoning the Articles of Confederation.

Oct.   Samuel Bryan of Philadelphia publishes the first of his 18 Antifederalist "Centinel" essays in Philadelphia on October 5 (series runs until April 9, 1788). James Wilson defends the Constitution in a speech delivered in the State House Yard in Philadelphia on October 6 (printed version is widely circulated and is the subject of several Antifederalist replies as the press debate intensifies).

In New York the first of 16 Antifederalist essays by "Brutus" appears on October 18 (series runs until April 10, 1788). The first number of *The Federalist* appears in New York on October 27 under the name "Publius" (of the 85 essays published through May 28, 1788, Hamilton writes 51, Madison 29, and John Jay 5; the series appears in several New York newspapers and is collected in two volumes published on March 22 and May 28, 1788). While in New York, Madison corresponds with leading Federalists in Pennsylvania, Massachusetts, and Virginia, as well as with Edmund Randolph, whom he hopes to persuade to support ratification in Virginia.

Oct.–Nov.   On October 17 the Connecticut legislature calls for a ratifying convention to meet on January 3, 1788 (election is held November 12). Massachusetts legislature calls on October 25 for convention to meet on January 9, 1788 (elections are held November 19, 1787–January 7, 1788). Georgia legislature calls on October 26 for convention to meet on December 25 (elections are held December 4–5). Virginia legislature calls on October 31 for a convention to meet on June 2, 1788 (elections are held March 3–27, 1788). New Jersey legislature calls on November 1 for a convention to meet on December 11 (elections are held November 27–December 1).

Nov.   On November 3 a letter from Elbridge Gerry to the Massachusetts legislature explaining why he did not sign the Constitution is published in Boston. Five "Letters from the
Federal Farmer to the Republican" are published as a pamphlet on November 8; it becomes one of the most widely
circulated Antifederalist publications. Delaware legislature
calls on November 10 for a convention to meet on December
3 (election is held on November 26).

              Pennsylvania ratifying convention achieves quorum on No-
vember 21 and begins debate on November 24, with James
Wilson serving as the main Federalist advocate and Robert
Whitehill, William Findley, and John Smilie leading the opposition. On November 26 convention rejects, 44–24, an
Antifederalist motion to allow voting on individual articles
of the Constitution.

Nov.–Dec.   George Mason's objections to the Constitution, which
have been circulating privately since early October, are published November 21. Luther Martin attacks the Constitution
in a speech before the Maryland legislature on November 29
and gives an account of the proceedings of the Constitutional Convention (expanded version of speech is published
in 12 installments, December 28, 1787–February 8, 1788, and
in pamphlet form as "The Genuine Information" in April
1788). Maryland legislature calls on December 1 for a convention to meet April 21, 1788 (elections are held April 7,
1788). North Carolina legislature calls on December 6 for a
convention to meet on July 21, 1788 (elections are held
March 28–29).

Dec.   On December 7 Delaware convention votes 30–0 to ratify
the Constitution. Robert Whitehill submits 15 amendments to
the Pennsylvania convention on December 12 and proposes
that the convention adjourn so that the people may have time
to consider them. His motion is defeated, 46–23, and the
Constitution is then ratified, 46–23. An "Address and Reasons of Dissent," signed by 21 members of the minority, is
published on December 18 and widely circulated. (Antifederalists continue to oppose ratification in Pennsylvania, and in
March 1788 petitions signed by over 6,000 people in rural
counties are submitted to the assembly, asking it to reject ratification; the assembly takes no action.)

              Virginia legislature passes law on December 12 authoriz-
ing the Virginia ratifying convention to communicate with
other states regarding amendments to the Constitution. At
the request of the legislature, Governor Randolph transmits
copies of the bill to each state on December 27. (Letter does
not reach Antifederalist New York governor George Clinton

until March 7, 1788; during the ratification contest, some Antifederalists accuse Federalists of tampering with the mails.)

New Hampshire legislature calls on December 14 for a convention to meet on February 13, 1788 (elections are held December 31, 1787–February 12, 1788).

New Jersey convention votes to ratify, 38–0, on December 18.

Jefferson writes to Madison from Paris on December 20, expressing his unhappiness with the lack of a bill of rights in the Constitution and the reeligibility of the president.

On December 27 Virginia governor Edmund Randolph publishes his reasons for not signing the Constitution.

Georgia convention votes to ratify the Constitution, 26–0, on December 31.

1788   Connecticut convention votes to ratify, 128–40, on January 9. Massachusetts convention meets in Boston on January 9, with delegates from the coastal towns generally favoring ratification and delegates from rural counties generally opposed; convention includes delegates from the Maine district. Convention elects Governor John Hancock, who has remained publicly neutral on ratification, as its president, though William Cushing serves as presiding officer while Hancock remains confined with an attack of gout; his absence is seen by some delegates as a political maneuver. On January 14 the convention votes to consider the Constitution clause by clause and begins debate.

South Carolina house of representatives debates Constitution, January 16–19, and unanimously votes to call convention to meet on May 12 (elections are held April 11–12). House votes, 76–75, to hold convention in Charleston (Federalists are strongest in coastal lowlands, while Antifederalists are concentrated in the western uplands).

On January 24 Antifederalists in the Massachusetts convention propose ending the clause-by-clause debate and bringing the entire Constitution to a vote. Samuel Adams says that while he is troubled by some parts of the Constitution, he believes it should be fully considered; the motion for an immediate vote is defeated. Convinced that ratification without amendments of some kind is impossible, Federalist leaders reach agreement with Hancock on a compromise proposal. On January 31 Hancock gives a speech to the convention supporting ratification and recommending nine amendments for adoption by Congress and the states after the Constitution goes into effect. Samuel Adams supports Hancock's proposal and suggests that it will set an example for other states that have yet to ratify.

Feb.   New York legislature calls on February 1 for a convention to meet on June 17 (elections are held April 29–May 3, with the suffrage extended to all male freemen over 21).

A committee of the Massachusetts convention reports on February 4 a revised form of the amendments proposed by Hancock. On February 6 Hancock calls for conciliation in his final speech to the convention, which then votes, 187–168, to ratify the Constitution and recommend nine subsequent amendments.

New Hampshire convention meets on February 13. Federalists hope it will follow example of Massachusetts, but when they discover that many delegates have been instructed by their towns to vote against ratification, they move for an adjournment until June 18. Motion is carried, 56–51, and convention adjourns on February 22.

Mar.   Rhode Island legislature votes on March 1 to hold a popular referendum on the Constitution instead of a ratifying convention. Most Federalists boycott the vote, held in the towns on March 24, and the Constitution is rejected by 2,711 to 239.

In Virginia the result of convention elections, held March 3–27, is uncertain, with a small number of uncommitted delegates seen as likely to determine the outcome.

Apr.   Maryland convention votes on April 26 to ratify the Constitution, 63–11, before tabling amendments proposed by Antifederalists.

May   New York governor George Clinton writes to Randolph on May 8, proposing that the Virginia and New York conventions communicate regarding amendments (when Randolph receives the letter, he and the Virginia council of state decide that it should first be sent to the legislature, and it does not become public until June 26, after the Virginia convention has voted). New York Antifederalist John Lamb writes to Virginia Antifederalists George Mason, Patrick Henry, William Grayson, and Richard Henry Lee on May 18, proposing that Antifederalists in New York, Virginia, and New Hampshire work together to secure amendments before ratification. (Mason, Henry, and Grayson reply favorably on June 9, enclosing a list of proposed amendments, but the response of the New York Antifederalists does not reach Virginia until after its convention votes on ratification.)

South Carolina convention votes on May 23 to ratify the Constitution, 149–73, and recommends four subsequent amendments. With eight states having ratified, only one more ratification is necessary to bring the Constitution into effect, although both Federalists and Antifederalists anticipate that a union without Virginia and New York will be impracticable. Counting of ballots in New York in late May confirms election of 46 Antifederalists and 19 Federalists to the state ratifying convention; all of the Federalists are from New York City or neighboring counties, leading to speculation that the southern counties will secede from the state if the convention rejects the Constitution.

June

Virginia convention meets in Richmond on June 2 (convention includes 14 delegates from the Kentucky district). The convention unanimously elects Edmund Pendleton, a supporter of the Constitution, as president, and then votes on June 3 to consider the Constitution clause by clause in a committee of the whole chaired by Federalist George Wythe (clause-by-clause discussion is moved by Mason and supported by Madison; committee procedure allows Pendleton to join debate). On June 4 Patrick Henry and George Mason attack the Constitution while Edmund Randolph announces that he now supports ratification with recommended subsequent amendments. Madison gives his first extended speech on June 6 and becomes the leading Federalist advocate; other Federalist speakers include Pendleton, George Nicholas, Henry Lee, and John Marshall, while Grayson, John Tyler, Benjamin Harrison, and James Monroe join Mason and Henry in opposing unconditional ratification. Madison also continues correspondence with Hamilton in New York (Hamilton believes prior ratification by Virginia is essential to winning ratification in New York).

New York ratifying convention meets in Poughkeepsie on June 17 and elects Governor George Clinton as its president. On June 19 it approves proposal by Federalist Robert R. Livingston to consider the Constitution clause by clause and begins debate, with Hamilton leading the Federalists and Melancton Smith the Antifederalists.

New Hampshire convention begins second session on June 18 and on June 21 votes, 57–47, to ratify the Constitution and recommend 12 subsequent amendments. Federalists send news of ratification by express rider to New York convention.

Virginia convention ends clause-by-clause consideration on June 23. George Wythe proposes on June 24 that the convention ratify the Constitution and recommend the subsequent adoption of amendments. Henry introduces an alternate resolution, calling for the submission of amendments to other states for their consideration before the Constitution is ratified, and warns of the dangers of unconditional ratification in a speech which concludes during a violent thunderstorm. On

June 25 the Henry resolution is defeated, 88–80, and the Wythe resolution is approved, 89–79. The convention adopts a form of ratification on June 27 that recommends the adoption of 40 amendments and then adjourns.

July   Continental Congress receives New Hampshire act of ratification on July 2. With the necessary nine states having ratified the Constitution, the Congress appoints committee to draft an ordinance for putting it into effect by holding elections for the new government.

Express messenger brings news of Virginia ratification to New York convention on July 2. Convention ends its clause-by-clause debate on July 7. After Antifederalists caucus, John Lansing proposes a form of ratification on July 10 that includes explanatory, conditional, and recommended amendments. John Jay responds on July 11 by proposing unconditional ratification with explanatory and recommended amendments. The convention debates whether a conditional ratification would be accepted by Congress, with Antifederalist leader Melancton Smith expressing doubts on July 17 that conditional ratification is possible. Lansing proposes resolution on July 23 calling for ratification "upon condition" that specified measures be taken. Antifederalist Samuel Jones moves that "upon condition" be replaced by "in full confidence." Smith supports Jones, and the Jones motion is approved, 31–29. On July 24 Lansing proposes that New York reserve the right to secede from the new union if certain amendments are not adopted. After reading a letter from Madison expressing opinion that conditional ratification will leave New York out of the union, Hamilton proposes that the convention send a circular letter to the other states calling for a second general convention to consider amendments. On July 25 Jay reads a circular letter he has written with Lansing and Smith (draft is mainly the work of Jay, who plays a leading role in negotiating a compromise ratification with the Antifederalists). The letter is unanimously approved and the Lansing motion on secession is defeated, 31–28, with Smith, Jones, Gilbert Livingston, and other Antifederalists again voting with the Federalists. The final form of ratification, including explanatory and recommended amendments, is approved, 30–27, on July 26.

July–Aug.   North Carolina convention meets in Hillsborough on July 21, with Antifederalists holding a clear majority (convention includes five delegates from Tennessee, then part of North Carolina). Although the convention votes to consider the Constitution clause by clause, the Antifederalists generally refrain from engaging the Federalists in debate. On July 30

Antifederalist leader Willie Jones proposes that the convention withhold ratification of the Constitution and submit amendments to a second general convention. His resolution is approved, 183–83, on August 2, and the convention adjourns on August 4.

Sept.   Pennsylvania Antifederalists meet at Harrisburg, September 3–6, to propose amendments to the Constitution.

Sept.–Oct.   After prolonged debate over where the new government should meet, Continental Congress passes election ordinance on September 13 that sets dates for choosing presidential electors (January 7, 1789), electing the president (February 4, 1789), and beginning the new government (March 4, 1789), and retains New York City as the capital. (Senators and representatives are elected in the 11 ratifying states, September 30, 1788–July 16, 1789, with Federalists winning majorities in both houses.) Continental Congress achieves its last quorum on October 10.

Oct.   John Lamb, Melancton Smith, and eight other Antifederalists form Federal Republican Society in New York on October 30; society circulates letters within the state urging the election of representatives to the new Congress committed to amending the Constitution and corresponds with Antifederalists in other states in effort to procure a second general convention and to have George Clinton elected vice-president.

Nov.   The Virginia legislature elects Antifederalists Richard Henry Lee and William Grayson to the new Senate on November 8 after Patrick Henry opposes Madison's election, and on November 20 it requests that the new Congress call a second constitutional convention.

North Carolina legislature calls on November 30 for a second state ratifying convention to meet on November 16, 1789.

1789   On January 7 presidential electors are chosen in every ratifying state except New York, where dispute between Federalist and Antifederalist chambers of legislature prevents their election (electors are chosen by the voters in four states, nominated by the voters and chosen by the legislature in two states, elected by the legislature in three states, and chosen by the governor and council in one state). Madison runs against James Monroe for seat in House of Representatives from Virginia, promising to work in Congress for amendments protecting essential rights and debating the Constitution with Monroe at joint appearances throughout the district, which includes several Antifederalist counties. On February 2 Madison wins the election, 1,308–972. Electors meet in their states on February 4 and vote for two candidates in balloting for president. George Washington receives votes from all 69 electors and is elected president, and John Adams, with 34 votes, is elected vice-president (John Jay receives nine votes, and 26 votes are scattered among nine other candidates).

Feb.   On February 5 New York state legislature passes resolution calling for a second convention to consider amendments.

Mar.–Apr.   Continental Congress holds last session on March 2, attended by secretary Charles Thomson and a single delegate from New York. First Federal Congress convenes on March 4. Quorum is achieved in both houses on April 6 and electoral votes are counted. George Washington takes the oath of office as the first president of the United States on April 30.

May   After studying the amendments proposed by the state ratifying conventions, Madison tells the House of Representatives on May 4 that he will introduce amendments during the current session. Calls by the Virginia and New York legislatures for a second general convention are laid before the House, May 5–6.

On May 19 Madison proposes the creation of a Department of Foreign Affairs (later renamed the Department of State), Department of the Treasury, and Department of War. House debates whether executive officers subject to Senate confirmation can be dismissed by the president without the consent of the Senate. Madison argues that full presidential power to remove officials is implied in Article II of the Constitution, and the House adopts his position in 34–20 vote. (Legislation organizing the three executive departments is enacted July 27–September 2. Alexander Hamilton is confirmed as secretary of the treasury on September 11, Henry Knox as secretary of war on September 12, and Thomas Jefferson as secretary of state on September 26; Jefferson takes office on March 22, 1790, following his return from France.)

June   On June 8 Madison moves that the House begin considering amendments. Roger Sherman and other Federalists argue that adopting revenue measures and organizing the government is more important than changing the Constitution, which should be tested by experience before being altered. Madison refers to the widespread demands for a bill of rights made during ratification and argues that it is better for Congress to propose specific amendments than to have the entire Constitution reconsidered. He then recommends incorporating into the text of the Constitution a series of changes, most of which are intended to protect individual rights (proposals include adding new declarations of general principles to the preamble). After Madison presents his amendments, Federalists again argue that their consideration is premature, while

Elbridge Gerry says that the House should consider the full range of amendments proposed by the state conventions; the House postpones action on amendments. (Madison's proposals will be criticized by some Antifederalists, including George Mason, as a diversionary measure designed to forestall attempts to change the structure and powers of the new government.)

July—Aug.   On July 21 Madison again raises question of amendments. The House votes to refer his proposals of June 8, along with all of the amendments proposed by the state ratifying conventions, to an 11-member select committee whose members include Sherman and Madison. On July 28 the committee reports the June 8 Madison proposals in slightly altered form, and the House begins considering them on August 13. Gerry moves on August 18 that they also consider amendments recommended by the state conventions, but his motion is defeated, 34–18. South Carolina Antifederalist Thomas Tudor Tucker moves that amendment reserving "powers not delegated" to the states be changed to read "powers not expressly delegated." Madison objects, arguing that "it was impossible to confine a Government to the exercise of express powers; there must necessarily be admitted powers by implication, unless the constitution descended to recount every minutia." The motion is defeated. Tucker then proposes consideration of 17 amendments altering the powers and structure of the government; this motion is also defeated. Roger Sherman proposes on August 19 that the amendments be added as separate articles at the end of the Constitution, leaving the original text unaltered. His motion is approved, and on August 22 Sherman and two others are appointed to arrange the amendments. They report 17 articles on August 24 that are substantially similar to Madison's original proposals (revisions to preamble are omitted), and the House sends them to the Senate.

Aug.   On August 22 and August 24 President Washington visits the Senate chamber to ask for its advice concerning instructions for commissioners negotiating a treaty with southern Indians. When senators request that he put his questions in writing, Washington complies, but never again returns to ask the Senate for its advice.

Sept.   Senate begins its consideration of the amendments on September 2 and sends its version to the House on September 9. In the Senate version the 17 articles are reduced to 12 by combining some provisions and eliminating an article on the separation of powers and an article forbidding states from infringing the right to jury trial in criminal cases, "the rights of conscience," or the freedom of speech and the press (described by Madison as "the most valuable amendment of the lot"). The Senate also weakens the clause forbidding the establishment of religion. A conference committee, whose six members include Madison, Sherman, and senators Oliver Ellsworth and William Paterson, reports a compromise between the House and Senate versions on September 23 that closely follows the Senate version but restores the prohibition against congressional establishment of religion. It is approved by the House, 37–14, on September 24 and by the Senate on September 25; the 12 amendments are then submitted to the states for ratification.

Judiciary Act, largely drafted by Senator Oliver Ellsworth, becomes law on September 24. It implements Article III of the Constitution by creating a three-tiered federal judiciary, consisting of 13 district courts (one for each of the 11 states that have ratified, with additional courts for the Kentucky district of Virginia and the Maine district of Massachusetts), three circuit courts (in which cases will be heard in each district by two supreme court justices and the district court judge), and a supreme court, consisting of a chief justice and five associate justices (Chief Justice John Jay and five associate justices are confirmed on September 26). The act defines the original and appellate jurisdiction of the federal courts and specifies that cases in the state courts concerning the Constitution, treaties, or laws of the United States must first be decided by a state's highest court before being appealed to the United States Supreme Court. Appeals of state cases are restricted to instances where the state courts rule against the validity of a treaty or federal law; where they rule in favor of a state law that has been challenged as being contrary to the Constitution, treaties, or federal laws; or where they deny the validity of a right or privilege claimed under the Constitution, treaties, or federal law. The act also establishes the office of Attorney General of the United States; Edmund Randolph becomes attorney general on September 26 (Department of Justice is not established until 1870).

Nov.– Dec.   On November 20 New Jersey ratifies all but the second of the proposed amendments (requiring that no law varying congressional compensation can take effect without an election of Representatives having intervened). Second North Carolina convention ratifies the Constitution, 194–77, on November 21 and proposes amendments. Virginia house of delegates approves all 12 amendments on November 30, but Antifederalists in the state senate, who hope to obtain an amendment barring direct taxation by the federal government, oppose ratification. Georgia legislature rejects proposed amendments, but all 12 amendments are ratified by Maryland, December 19, and North Carolina, December 22.

1790   Secretary of the Treasury Hamilton submits a report on public credit to the House on January 14. It calls for funding the $54 million national debt and for federal assumption of $25 million of debt incurred by the states during the Revolutionary War (Hamilton believes assumption will strengthen the allegiance of state creditors to the new union). Holders of depreciated Continental securities will be able to exchange them for new interest-paying bonds at face value, and import and excise taxes will be levied to pay interest on the debt.

Jan.–Feb.   On January 17 the Rhode Island legislature narrowly approves bill calling a ratifying state convention. South Carolina ratifies all 12 proposed amendments on January 18, New Hampshire ratifies all but the second on January 25, and Delaware ratifies all but the first (regulating the numbers of representatives as the population increases, so that there eventually would be not more than one representative for every 50,000 persons, and no fewer than 200 representatives) on January 28. Massachusetts senate approves all but the first two amendments on January 29, and the state house of representatives approves all but the first, second, and twelfth on February 2; however, the two chambers fail to vote on a bill giving joint approval to any amendments, and Massachusetts does not report its partial ratification to the federal government. (Connecticut also fails to ratify the amendments.)

Feb.   Madison opposes Hamilton's funding measure for the national debt, arguing that it rewards speculators and unfairly denies compensation to those original holders of Continental securities, including many impoverished war veterans, who were forced to sell at depreciated prices. He favors discrimination between original and subsequent creditors, which Hamilton opposes as impractical and likely to undermine confidence in federal securities. The House rejects discrimination, 36–13, on February 22 and turns to consideration of assumption of state debts.

Feb.–Mar.   On February 24 New York ratifies all but the second proposed amendment. Pennsylvania ratifies all but the first two proposed amendments March 10.

Mar.–Apr.   Madison leads opposition in the House of Representatives to plan for assuming state debts, arguing that it unfairly discriminates against states, such as Virginia, that have already paid much of their war debt, or believe that they will be creditors of the federal government when Revolutionary War finances are finally settled. Assumption measure is defeated, 31–29, on April 12.

May–June   On May 13 the Senate passes a bill embargoing all trade between the 12 ratifying states and Rhode Island. Rhode Island convention votes to ratify the Constitution, 34–32, on May 29, and proposes a bill of rights and amendments; on June 7 the Rhode Island legislature ratifies all but the second of the 12 amendments proposed by Congress.

June–July   On June 2 House sends bill for funding the national debt to the Senate without assumption measure. In late June, Jefferson, Hamilton, and Madison agree that in exchange for southern support of the assumption measure, northern members of Congress will support moving the capital to Philadelphia for ten years and then permanently establishing it along the Potomac in 1800. The Senate sends bills for moving the capital and for assuming the state debts to the House in July, where they are passed by narrow margins. Virginia house of delegates adopts resolutions in early November condemning assumption of state debts as an exercise of powers not given to the federal government by the Constitution.

Dec.   Congress meets in Philadelphia on December 6. Hamilton submits report to the House on December 14 calling for the chartering of a national bank; the bank would be funded by the government and private investors, receive government deposits, assist the treasury and loan it money, and issue bank notes backed by specie.

1791   Bill chartering Bank of the United States passes Senate on January 20. It is opposed in the House by Madison, who argues that the Constitution does not specifically grant Congress the power to incorporate a bank, and that because the federal government can execute constitutionally specified powers such as collecting taxes and borrowing money without a bank, its incorporation cannot be considered "necessary" under the "necessary and proper" clause. The House passes the bill, 39–20 (all but one of the dissenting votes are from the five southern states). Unsure of the constitutionality of the bank bill, Washington asks Randolph and Jefferson for advisory opinions, then gives them to Hamilton for rebuttal while asking Madison to draft a veto message. In his opinion, Jefferson also finds no specific or general power in the Constitution to incorporate a bank, and argues that while a bank would be "convenient" for executing specified powers, it is not indispensable and therefore not "necessary." Hamilton submits his opinion to Washington on February 23, arguing that "necessary" means useful, not indispensable, and that the "necessary and proper" clause gives Congress implied power to adopt any measure clearly useful in executing a specified power, as long as the measure is not specifically prohibited by the Constitution. Washington signs the bank bill on February 25. Excise tax on distilled spirits, proposed by Hamilton as part of 1790 funding plan, becomes law on March 3.

Mar.–Apr.   Vermont is admitted to the Union on March 4. Before leaving on an extended tour of the South, Washington suggests on April 4 that Jefferson, Hamilton, Knox, and Adams meet in his absence.

Nov.   On November 3 Vermont ratifies all 12 proposed amendments. Antifederalists in Virginia state senate end their opposition, and on December 15 Virginia ratifies all 12 amendments, completing ratification of the third through the twelfth proposed amendments, which become the first ten amendments to the Constitution. (First proposed amendment, concerning apportionment of the House, remains unratified. Second proposed amendment, restricting congressional pay increases, is ratified by six states in 1789–91, by one state in 1873 and one state in 1978, and by 31 states in 1983–92; on May 7, 1992, it becomes the Twenty-seventh Amendment to the Constitution.)

Dec.   On December 5 Hamilton submits a report on manufactures to the House. It advocates encouraging domestic industry by government subsidies and protective tariffs, and finds constitutional authority for spending public funds on manufacturing subsidies in a broad interpretation of the general welfare clause. (Congress implements little of the proposed program, and Madison challenges Hamilton's broad construction as leading to the creation of a federal government of unlimited powers.)

Dec.   Washington begins meeting with Jefferson, Hamilton, Knox, and Randolph to discuss policy (term "cabinet" comes into use by 1793).

1792   On April 5 Washington uses the veto power for the first time, disapproving a bill apportioning representatives on the grounds that it unconstitutionally gives some states more than one representative for every 30,000 persons. The House sustains the veto, and on April 14 a new bill, apportioning representatives on a different basis, becomes law (measure increases the size of the House from 67 to 101).

Mar.–June   After Congress passes law on March 23 giving federal circuit courts responsibility for hearing Revolutionary War pension claims, Chief Justice Jay and justices Cushing, Wilson, Blair, and Iredell express opinion in letters to Washington that the law infringes upon the constitutional independence of the judicial branch, since it requires federal courts to perform nonjudicial duties and subjects their decisions to the nonjudicial review of the secretary of war and the Congress. (In 1793 Congress passes a new pension law that relieves the courts from hearing claims.)

May   On May 2 a militia act becomes law, authorizing the president to call forth state militias in case of insurrection against federal authority, or when a state calls for aid.

June   Kentucky is admitted to the Union on June 1.

June–July   In *Champion and Dickason* v. *Casey*, the U.S. Circuit Court for the district of Rhode Island rules in June that a state law giving debtors a three-year extension in paying their creditors violates the constitutional prohibition against state laws impairing the obligation of contracts (Article I, section 10). On July 11 the state of Georgia is summoned to respond in *Chisholm* v. *Georgia*, a suit brought before the U.S. Supreme Court by a South Carolina executor seeking payment for military supplies bought by Georgia commissioners in 1777. Georgia refuses to contest the suit, claiming that as a sovereign state it cannot be sued without its consent.

Aug.–Dec.   Continuing conflict over foreign and domestic policy between Jefferson and Hamilton becomes increasingly public as each writes or encourages newspaper attacks on the other. Washington tries unsuccessfully to mediate the feud, but does agree to serve a second term at the urging of Hamilton, Jefferson, Madison, and others. In the electoral balloting on December 5 Washington is reelected with the votes of all 132 electors, and Adams is reelected vice-president with 77 votes (George Clinton receives 50 electoral votes, Jefferson four, and Aaron Burr one).

1793   In a 4–1 decision, the Supreme Court rules on February 18 for the plaintiff in *Chisholm* v. *Georgia*, affirming that Article III, section 2 of the Constitution gives federal courts jurisdiction over suits brought against a state by a citizen of another state. An amendment intended to overturn the decision is introduced in both houses of Congress by February 20.

Apr.   Washington calls cabinet meeting on April 19 after learning that the revolutionary French republic has declared war on Great Britain. After Hamilton and Jefferson advocate opposing views, Washington decides to maintain the 1778 treaty of alliance with France (which does not obligate the United States to join France in an offensive war) while issuing a proclamation of neutrality (published April 22). When proclamation is challenged on constitutional grounds by supporters of France, Hamilton defends it in "Pacificus" newspaper articles, arguing that Article II of the Constitution gives the president broad general powers, including the power to negotiate and interpret treaties and to determine new courses in foreign affairs. At the urging of Jefferson, Madison replies in "Helvidius" articles, arguing that the power to interpret treaties and proclaim neutrality is constitutionally vested in Congress. (Controversy over neutrality and relations with France contribute to emergence of two political parties, with supporters of Madison and Jefferson calling themselves Republicans and supporters of Hamilton continuing to call themselves Federalists.)

July   Washington writes to Jay on July 18, asking for the advice of the Supreme Court on 29 legal issues relating to the 1778 treaty of alliance with France. In its reply the court declines to give an advisory opinion, stating that its proper role is restricted to ruling on actual disputes brought before it by litigation.

Dec.   Jefferson resigns as secretary of state, effective December 31 (although Jefferson is succeeded by Randolph, Hamilton becomes Washington's leading adviser on foreign policy).

1794   On March 4 Congress proposes the Eleventh Amendment to the states for ratification. Framed in reaction to *Chisholm* v. *Georgia*, the amendment removes from federal jurisdiction any suit "commenced or prosecuted" against a state by the citizen of another state, or by a foreigner.

Apr.–May   Tensions arising from British seizures of American ships trading with the French West Indies and from British trade with Indians along the northwest frontier result in growing anticipation of an Anglo-American war. In effort to avoid hostilities, Washington nominates Jay on April 16 to serve as a special envoy to Britain. After receiving instructions drafted mainly by Hamilton, Jay sails May 12 (arrives in England on June 8).

Aug.–Sept.   Resistance to excise tax on distilled spirits leads to widespread violence against federal officials in western Pennsylvania during summer. Washington issues proclamation on August 7, calling for the insurgents to disperse and summoning 15,000 militiamen into service, and a second proclamation on September 24, calling for suppression of the insurrection. When the federal force marches into western Pennsylvania, the "Whiskey Rebellion" collapses without further bloodshed. (Two men are later convicted of treason, but are pardoned by Washington.)

Nov.   On November 19 Jay signs treaty in London. Its terms include evacuation of British garrisons from frontier posts in the northwestern United States (a provision of the 1783 peace treaty never carried out by Britain), and establishment of commissions to resolve British claims against American debtors and American claims against British seizures of American commerce.

1795   Hamilton resigns as secretary of the treasury on January 31 (will continue to advise Washington on major issues). Ratification of the Eleventh Amendment is completed on February 7 (amendment is not declared to be in effect until January 8, 1798).

June–Aug.   Washington calls special session of the Senate for June 8. After secret debate, Senate votes, 20–10, on June 24 to ratify Jay's Treaty on condition that article concerning trade with British West Indies is renegotiated. Text of treaty is given to Republican newspaper and published July 1. Treaty is widely attacked for failing to secure American neutral rights, to protect American seamen from impressment, or to obtain compensation for slaves evacuated by the British at the end of the Revolutionary War, and for pledging to keep American ports open to British commerce. Despite misgivings, Washington signs treaty on August 18. Randolph resigns as secretary of state on August 19 after being accused by Washington of soliciting a bribe from the French; with the departure of Randolph, the cabinet becomes entirely Federalist.

1796   Supreme Court rules on March 7 in *Ware* v. *Hylton* that under the supremacy clause of Article VI of the Constitution, a wartime Virginia law allowing the discharge of British debts with paper currency is invalid because it contravenes provision of the 1783 peace treaty calling for payment of British debts at full sterling value. On March 8 the Supreme Court rules for the first time on the constitutionality of a congressional act, deciding in *Hylton* v. *United States* that a federal tax on carriages is an excise tax, not a direct tax, and thus does not have to be apportioned according to population as provided for in Article I, section 9.

Mar.–Apr.   Republicans in the House move to have documents relating to the negotiation of Jay's Treaty submitted by the president, arguing that because the treaty regulates commerce and requires appropriations for its implementation, the House has a constitutional right to examine the merits of the treaty. On March 24 the House calls for the papers in 62–37 vote. Washington replies on March 30, withholding the papers on

the grounds that the House has no constitutional role in ratifying treaties and asserting an executive right to maintain the
confidentiality of diplomatic correspondence. After an intense
debate, House votes 51–48 on April 30 to appropriate money
for implementation of the treaty.

June   Tennessee is admitted to the Union on June 1.

Sept.–Dec.   Washington makes public his decision not to seek a third
term when his farewell address is published on September 19.
In the presidential election, Federalist candidate John Adams
receives 71 electoral votes and is elected president, while Jefferson, the Republican candidate, receives 68 electoral votes
and becomes vice-president. (Federalist Thomas Pinckney receives 59 votes, Republican Aaron Burr 30, and nine other
candidates receive 48 electoral votes.)

1797   Relations with France worsen as French navy increases its
seizures of American ships trading with Britain. On May 31
Adams appoints Charles Cotesworth Pinckney, John Marshall, and Elbridge Gerry as commissioners to negotiate
treaty with France. When the commission arrives in Paris in
October, it is approached by three French diplomatic agents
(referred to in later dispatches as X, Y, and Z), who solicit
$240,000 bribe as precondition for negotiations, but the
American commissioners refuse to pay.

1798   Adams submits dispatches from American commissioners in
France to Congress on April 3, and the Federalist Senate
orders their publication. Revelation of "XYZ Affair" causes
popular furor against France. Administration and Congress
take measures to strengthen the navy (Department of the
Navy is established May 3) and army (Washington is named
its commander and chooses Hamilton as his second in command; Adams reluctantly accepts Hamilton's appointment)
while levying a direct property tax to finance war prepara-
tions. Unsure of winning majority support, Adams does not
ask Congress for a declaration of war against France, but
Congress does adopt measure on July 9 authorizing the navy
and privateers to capture armed French ships (limited naval
war with France begins in 1798).

July   Congress also adopts series of alien acts and a sedition act.
The three alien acts, passed June 18–July 6, extend the period
required for naturalization from five to 14 years and give the
president power to expel or, in time of declared war, to imprison dangerous aliens (no one is expelled under these laws,
and in 1802 the five-year naturalization period is restored).
Sedition act, which becomes law on July 14 after passing the

House by 44–41 vote, establishes criminal penalties for unlawfully opposing the execution of federal laws and makes publication of "false, scandalous, and malicious writing" attacking the federal government, the president, or the Congress a crime punishable by up to two years in prison and a fine not exceeding $2,000. (The act departs from the English common law of seditious libel by allowing defendants to offer the truth of their statements as a defense and by permitting juries to determine if statements are libelous under the law. During the Adams administration ten Republican editors and printers are convicted under the act in trials conducted by sometimes openly partisan Federalist judges.)

Oct.–Dec.   Jefferson secretly drafts resolutions attacking the Alien and Sedition Acts and shows them to Madison, who secretly drafts a second set of more moderate resolutions. Kentucky legislature adopts the Jefferson resolutions in modified form on November 10, and the Virginia legislature adopts the Madison resolutions as originally written on December 24. Both sets of resolutions condemn the Alien and Sedition Acts as unconstitutional and assert the right of states to determine the constitutionality of congressional acts.

Nov.   Kentucky resolutions describe the Constitution as a "compact" made by the states that gives the federal government only the powers definitely delegated to it, and deny that the federal government is the "exclusive or final judge" of its own powers. They assert that constitutionally each state "has an equal right to judge for itself" when the federal government has exceeded its delegated powers and to determine "the mode and measure of redress." Declaring the Alien and Sedition Acts to be "void, and of no force" for asserting unenumerated powers reserved to the states by the Tenth Amendment, the resolutions also denounce the alien acts for violating the independence of the judiciary and constitutional guarantees of due process and trial by jury and assert that the sedition act violates the First Amendment by giving the federal government power to punish press libels, a power constitutionally reserved to the states. The Kentucky resolutions conclude by asking the other states to unite in seeking repeal of the Alien and Sedition Acts.

Dec.   Virginia resolutions also describe the Constitution as a "compact" created by the states under which the federal government can exercise only enumerated powers. When the federal government dangerously exercises powers not granted to it by the Constitution, the resolutions assert that the states "have the right, and are in duty bound, to interpose for arresting the progress of the evil" and maintaining the liberties of the people. The resolutions denounce the alien acts for violating the separation of powers and describe the sedition act as a violation of the First Amendment. They conclude by asking the other states to join in declaring the acts unconstitutional and in working to preserve the liberties of the people.

1799   Adams nominates William Vans Murray as special envoy to France on February 18 in attempt to negotiate end to Franco-American hostilities (Oliver Ellsworth and William Davie are later named as additional negotiators). Peace overture splits Federalist party into Adams and Hamilton factions.

Nov.   In response to Kentucky and Virginia resolutions of 1798, legislatures of Delaware, Rhode Island, Massachusetts, New York, Connecticut, New Hampshire, and Vermont adopt resolutions declaring that only the federal courts have the power to determine the constitutionality of federal laws; some of the resolutions also defend the sedition act. On November 14 the Kentucky legislature adopts a second set of resolutions, declaring its attachment to the union and reaffirming its opposition to the Alien and Sedition Acts. The new resolutions assert that the states which formed the Constitution are "sovereign and independent," with the power to judge violations of it, and that "a nullification, by those sovereignties, of all unauthorized acts done" under the Constitution "is the rightful remedy" for such violations. (Jefferson's original 1798 draft for the Kentucky resolutions, first published in 1832 during the South Carolina nullification crisis, declared that states have a "natural right" to "nullify of their own authority" all unconstitutional "assumptions of power by others" within their own state limits.)

1800   Virginia house of delegates adopts on January 7 a report drafted by Madison on the response to the 1798 Virginia resolutions. In the report Madison writes that the people of the states, "in their highest sovereign capacity," ratified the Constitution and are thus parties to the compact creating the federal government, and that there "can be no tribunal above" the states "to decide in the last resort" whether the compact has been violated. Rejecting claims that under the First Amendment Congress is prohibited only from imposing prior restraints upon the press and therefore can pass laws punishing seditious libels, Madison asserts that the federal government is "destitute" of authority to punish the press, and argues that English doctrines of seditious libel are inappropriate in America, where the executive and legislature are responsible to the people and may justifiably incur their "hatred" and "contempt" by failing to discharge the public trust. (Opposition to the Alien and Sedition Acts becomes major Republican issue in the 1800 election campaign.)

May   Adams forces the resignation of Secretary of War James McHenry on May 6 and dismisses Secretary of State Timothy Pickering on May 12 for allying themselves with Hamilton and opposing his reelection (Adams appoints John Marshall to replace Pickering). Hamiltonian Federalists are further angered by Adams when he pardons John Fries, a Pennsylvania auctioneer condemned to death for treason, on May 21 against the unanimous opinion of his cabinet (Fries had been convicted of leading an armed band to free prisoners jailed for resisting the 1798 federal property tax).

Sept.   American negotiators in France sign treaty on September 30 ending undeclared naval war with France and suspending 1778 treaty of alliance. (When the Senate ratifies the treaty on condition that the 1778 treaty be completely abrogated, France refuses to pay compensation for seizures of American ships; amended treaty goes into effect on December 21, 1801.)

Nov.   Congress meets for the first time in new capital city of Washington on November 17.

Dec.   In the presidential election Jefferson and Republican vice-presidential candidate Aaron Burr each receive 73 electoral votes, Adams 65, Federalist vice-presidential candidate Charles Cotesworth Pinckney 64, and John Jay one electoral vote (tie is the result of Republican electors evenly dividing their two votes between Jefferson and Burr in order to preserve alliance between Virginia and New York Republican parties and to prevent election of a Federalist vice-president). The tie forces the presidential election into the Federalist-controlled House of Representatives. Although many Federalists prefer Burr over Jefferson, Hamilton considers Burr to be more dangerous and urges Federalists to elect Jefferson.

1801   Adams nominates Secretary of State John Marshall to be Chief Justice of the Supreme Court on January 20 (confirmed by the Senate on January 27, Marshall serves in both positions for remainder of the Adams administration).

Feb.   Official counting of electoral vote at joint session of Congress on February 11 confirms expected tie. House of Representatives immediately begins voting for president, with each state delegation having one vote as provided for by Article II, section 1. First ballot gives eight states for Jefferson, six for Burr, and two divided, leaving Jefferson one state short of the nine needed for a majority. Deadlock continues through 35 ballots; on the 36th ballot, held February 17, Jefferson receives the votes of ten states, Burr four, and two states cast blank ballots (Burr becomes vice-president).

Feb.–Mar.   New judiciary act is signed by Adams on February 13, reducing the size of the Supreme Court (after the next vacancy occurs) from six justices to five, relieving Supreme Court justices from circuit duty, creating six judicial circuits and 16 circuit court judges, and establishing five new judicial districts; the act also significantly expands federal jurisdiction. Adams and the Federalist Senate begin rapidly filling new judgeships with Federalists, with some appointees receiving their commissions on March 3; expansion of judicial power and appointments angers Jefferson and the Republicans.

Mar.–Dec.   Jefferson gives conciliatory inaugural address on March 4 and quickly pardons all persons convicted under the sedition act, which had expired on March 3. (During the Jefferson administration several Federalist editors will be prosecuted under state laws for seditious libel.) Jefferson also withholds the commissions of 17 of the 42 justices of the peace for the District of Columbia who were appointed and confirmed to five-year terms after Adams learned of his defeat in the 1800 election, but whose signed and sealed commissions remained undelivered when Jefferson took office (Jefferson believes that the number of appointments was excessive). In December William Marbury, one of the 17 justices of the peace who did not receive his commission, asks the U.S. Supreme Court to issue a writ of mandamus commanding Madison, now secretary of state, to deliver the commission (the Supreme Court is authorized to issue writs of mandamus as part of its original jurisdiction by section 13 of the 1789 judiciary act). The Court orders Madison to show cause why the writ should not be issued.

1802   Encouraged by Jefferson, Republicans in Congress move on January 6 to repeal the judiciary act of 1801 and abolish the newly created circuit judgeships. Federalists denounce the repeal bill as an unconstitutional threat to the independence of the judiciary, since it would remove from office judges appointed for good behavior. Republicans argue that since Article III, section 1 gives Congress the power to establish inferior federal courts, Congress also has the power to abolish them. Some Federalists predict that the Supreme Court will hold the repeal law unconstitutional, while some Republicans deny that the court has the power to determine the unconstitutionality of congressional acts, and criticize the show-cause order issued by the court in the pending case of *Marbury* v. *Madison* as an unconstitutional intrusion by the judiciary into the actions of the executive branch. Repeal measure becomes law on March 8. Congress then passes new judiciary act on April 23 that abolishes the June term of the Supreme Court (postponing until February 1803 any decision in *Marbury* v. *Madison* and on the constitutionality of the repeal act) and returns the Supreme Court justices to circuit duty.

1803   On February 24 the Supreme Court delivers its decision in *Marbury* v. *Madison*, holding an act of Congress unconstitutional for the first time. Chief Justice Marshall, speaking for a unanimous court, rules that Marbury is legally entitled to both his commission and a writ of mandamus commanding its delivery, and that the secretary of state is bound by the law to obey such a writ, but that the Supreme Court cannot issue the writ because section 13 of the 1789 judiciary act, giving the Supreme Court power to issue writs of mandamus as part of its original jurisdiction, unconstitutionally expanded the original jurisdiction of the court beyond the limits specified in Article III, section 2. In his opinion, Marshall defends the power of the judiciary to declare acts of Congress unconstitutional, writing that if the Constitution is to be a "superior paramount law, unchangeable by ordinary means," then legislative acts repugnant to the Constitution must be held void by the courts. In *Stuart* v. *Laird*, decided March 2 with Marshall not participating, the Supreme Court upholds the repeal of the 1801 judiciary act against a challenge that does not raise the question of whether Congress can remove judges appointed for good behavior.

Mar.   Ohio is admitted to the union on March 1.

May–Oct.   American negotiators in Paris sign treaty on May 2 purchasing Louisiana from France. Because the Constitution does not provide for the acquisition of foreign territory, Jefferson drafts an amendment authorizing the purchase, but then reluctantly agrees to having the acquisition approved under the existing treaty-making power when advisers warn him that questioning the constitutionality of the treaty could jeopardize its ratification (Senate ratifies treaty October 20).

Dec.   Twelfth Amendment, providing for separate balloting by the electors for president and vice-president, is proposed to the states on December 9.

1804   Ratification of the Twelfth Amendment by the states is completed on June 15 and the amendment is proclaimed in effect by Secretary of State Madison on September 17. (No further amendments to the Constitution will be made until the Thirteenth Amendment, abolishing slavery, is proposed and ratified in 1865 at the close of the Civil War.)

Notes on State Constitutions, 1776–90

VIRGINIA The Virginia convention (successor to the convention called in 1774 after the royal governor dissolved the assembly) adopted a declaration of rights, drafted by George Mason, on June 12, 1776, and a constitution, drafted largely by Mason, on June 29, 1776. The declaration of rights asserted that men have certain inherent rights and that all power is derived from the people. It called for the separation of powers in the state government and enumerated essential rights, including trial by a local jury, the ability to confront witnesses, freedom from the compulsion to give evidence, and the prohibition of excessive bails and fines, cruel and unusual punishments, and general search warrants. Declaration of rights also stated that no man should be deprived of his liberty "except by the law of the land, or the judgment of his peers," that freedom of the press should not be restrained and that all men are equally entitled to the free exercise of religion (draft of clause on religion was revised in convention by James Madison). The constitution established a bicameral general assembly, consisting of a house of delegates, elected annually and possessing the sole power to initiate legislation, and a senate, whose members served four-year terms. (Constitution retained existing property qualification for voting, which required adult males to own 25 acres of settled land or its town equivalent.) The senate had to approve all bills passed by the house and could propose amendments to pending laws, with the exception of money bills, which it was required to accept or reject without alteration. Both chambers annually elected the governor, who served as the executive with the advice of an eight-man council of state, also chosen by the legislature. The governor could serve for only three consecutive terms and had no veto over legislation. State judges were appointed by the general assembly and held their offices during "good behavior" (for life, unless removed for misconduct). State officials were prohibited from being elected to the legislature (prohibition against officials sitting in the legislature was adopted by other states in their constitutions). No provision was made for amending the constitution or distinguishing it from ordinary legislation.

NEW JERSEY Provincial congress, which had been elected to serve as an ordinary legislature, adopted constitution on July 2, 1776. It did not contain a separate declarations of rights, but did protect the right to trial by jury, grant religious toleration, and forbid the establishment of any particular religious sect, although officeholders were required to be Protestants. The constitution established a general assembly and a legislative council, both elected annually. Council members were required to own £1,000 property and members of the assembly £500, while ownership of £50 property was needed to vote. The council could accept or reject, but not alter, money bills passed by the general assembly. A governor was elected annually by a joint ballot of the legislature and had no veto power. All significant appointments were made by the legislature, with judges serving for fixed terms. Some articles of the constitution were declared unannulable, leaving the remainder capable of being changed by ordinary legislation.

DELAWARE   A convention elected for the purpose of framing a new government adopted a declaration of rights on September 11 and a constitution on September 20, 1776. The declarations of rights, similar to those adopted in Virginia and already framed in Pennsylvania, was declared to be unalterable. The constitution established a bicameral legislature elected by adult male taxpayers, with the house of assembly serving for one year and the council serving for three years. A president was elected by a joint ballot of the legislature for three years and was advised by a four-member privy council, with each chamber choosing two members. There was no executive veto. Judges were chosen by the legislature and served for good behavior, while other officials were appointed by the president and council. Officeholders were required to be Christians. While some articles of the constitution were declared unannulable, others could be changed by five-sevenths of the assembly and seven-ninths of the council.

PENNSYLVANIA   A convention elected in July 1776 for the purpose of framing a plan of government approved a state constitution on September 28, 1776, that included a declaration of rights, similar to the one adopted in Virginia but adding a statement that the people have a right to freedom of speech. Legislative powers were vested in a unicameral general assembly, elected by all male taxpayers over 21 and by non-taxpaying sons of freeholders over 21 (the widest suffrage adopted by any state). The assembly was elected annually and no member could serve more than four years in seven; delegates to the Continental Congress were also subject to rotation in office. Assembly members were required to believe in one God and the divine inspiration of the Old and New Testaments. Whenever possible, proposed laws were to be held over to the next session to allow for public discussion before their final enactment. A 12-member executive council was to be elected by the freemen, and two of its members were to be chosen as its president and vice-president by a joint ballot of the assembly and council. The council had no veto power. Supreme court judges served for seven-year terms. Every seven years an elected council of censors would review the actions of the state government and determine if the constitution has been violated. A two-thirds vote of the censors could propose amendments and call for a new convention to consider them, but the assembly had no power to change the constitution.

After its adoption the constitution became the focus of a continuing political struggle within the state between its "Constitutionalist" supporters and "Republican" opponents. The first council of censors, elected in October 1783, began meeting in November to review the state government. Amendments to the 1776 constitution advocated by the Republicans included creating a bicameral legislature, establishing a single executive with a limited veto, appointing judges for terms of good behavior, and abolishing rotation in office. Although the Republicans outnumbered Constitutionalists on the council, they did not have the two-thirds majority required to call a new convention.

In September 1789 the Republicans succeeded in having the assembly call a new constitutional convention. It met from November 24 until February 26, 1790, and drafted a constitution which established a bicameral legislature, replaced the executive council with a governor elected by the voters and possessing a limited veto, and tenured judges for good behavior. It also contained a new bill of rights, which included a provision on freedom of the press, drafted by James Wilson, that allowed juries in libel cases to determine both facts and law. The new constitution was adopted on September 2, 1790.

MARYLAND A convention elected for the purpose of framing a new government adopted a declaration of rights and a constitution on November 9, 1776. The declarations of rights contained provisions similar to those of the Virginia and Pennsylvania declarations, as well as a prohibition against bills of attainder. The constitution established a bicameral legislature, with the house of delegates elected annually by voters with 50 acres freehold or £30 property and the senate indirectly elected by an electoral college. Delegates were required to own £500 property and senators £1,000; all officeholders were required to be Christians. Money bills could be accepted or rejected by the senate but not altered by them. The governor and a five-member council were elected by a joint ballot of the legislature. There was no executive veto, but the governor and council did appoint judges, who served for good behavior, as well as other state officials. Changes to the constitution could be made by a majority of the legislature voting in two consecutive sessions.

NORTH CAROLINA Convention elected to frame a new government adopted a declaration of rights, similar to those of other states, and a constitution on December 18, 1776. The constitution established a house of commons and a senate, both elected annually. Taxpayers could vote for the house of commons, while ownership of 50 acres was needed to vote in senate elections. Members of the house of commons were required to own 100 acres and senators had to own 300 acres. The legislature elected a governor and seven-member council annually. There was no executive veto, and the legislature appointed judges, who served for good behavior, as well as other state officials. Officeholding was restricted to Protestants. No provision was made for amending the constitution.

GEORGIA A convention elected in October 1776 to draw up a plan of government adopted a constitution on February 5, 1777. Legislative power was vested in a unicameral assembly, elected annually, whose members were required to be Protestants owning 250 acres of land or £250 of property. The assembly annually elected a governor, who served for only one year out of three and had no veto or pardoning power, an advisory executive council, chosen from among the assembly members, and a state chief justice. Clergymen were forbidden to sit in the legislature, and the Anglican church was disestablished. The constitution protected the free exercise of religion unless "it be repugnant to the peace and safety of the State," freedom of the press, the right to trial by jury, and the principle of habeas corpus, while forbidding excessive fines or bail. Amendments could be made only by a convention petitioned for by a majority of the voters in a majority of the counties.

In November 1788 a convention framed a new state constitution, which was ratified and amended by subsequent conventions in January and May 1789. The new constitution created a house of representatives, elected for one year, and a senate, elected for three years; the governor, elected by the legislature for a two-year term, could veto legislation, but his veto could be overridden by a two-thirds majority in both chambers.

NEW YORK A convention acting as the state legislature adopted a constitution on April 20, 1777. Legislative power was vested in an assembly, elected annually by males with £20 freehold, and a senate, whose members served four-year terms and were elected by males with £100 freehold; voters qualified for senate elections also chose the governor, who served for three years. Each year the assembly elected four senators to a council of appointment, on which the governor had the deciding vote. The governor, chancellor, and supreme court judges formed a council of revision, which could veto legislation; a two-thirds majority in both legislative chambers could override the veto. The chancellor and judges of the supreme court held office during good behavior until they retired at age 60. Clergymen were forbidden to hold state office. Liberty of conscience and the right to trial by jury and to counsel in criminal cases were protected, but there was no separate declaration of rights. No provision was made for amending the constitution.

SOUTH CAROLINA The general assembly approved a new constitution on March 19, 1778, to replace the temporary form of government adopted in 1776. It established a senate and house of representatives, both of which served for two years. Appropriation bills had to originate in the house, and could be rejected, but not altered, by the senate; all other legislation could be drafted or amended in either chamber. Senators were required to have £2,000 freehold, while representatives, as well as all voters, had to be free white males over 21, owning 50 acres of land or a town lot of equivalent value. The legislature jointly elected a governor, lieutenant governor, and eight privy councilors, all of whom were required to have a £10,000 freehold, and who served for two years before becoming ineligible for the same office for the next four years. There was no executive veto. Judges were chosen by a joint legislative ballot and served for good behavior. All officeholders were required to be Protestants, and the "Christian Protestant religion" was established in the state. A majority of both legislative chambers could alter the constitution.

MASSACHUSETTS   A specially elected convention submitted a constitution, drafted mainly by John Adams, to the towns for ratification on March 2, 1780; it was approved and went into effect on October 25, 1780. The first article of its declaration of rights proclaimed that "All men are born free and equal" and have "natural" and "unalienable" rights regarding life, liberty, and property (in several cases tried in 1781 and 1783, Massachusetts judges and juries found slavery incompatible with this article; in 1790 the census reported that there were no longer any slaves in Massachusetts). Article II protected religious "profession or beliefs" against persecution, while Article III allowed the legislature to mandate public support for Protestant denominations, effectively continuing the establishment of the Congregational church. Other articles required that reasonable compensation be given for property taken for public use, protected individuals against being compelled to accuse or furnish evidence against themselves, prohibited unreasonable searches and seizures, bills of attainder, cruel and unusual punishments, ex post facto laws, and excessive fines and bail, guaranteed criminal defendants the right to confront witnesses and to trial by jury, and established the right of the people to assemble, instruct their representatives, and petition the legislature. The "Frame of Government" established a senate and a house of representatives, both elected annually by males over 21 who earned £3 a year from freehold property or had £60 in total property. Senators were required to have £300 freehold or £600 total property, representatives £100 freehold or £200 property. The senate was apportioned among districts according to assessed value of taxable property, while the house of representatives was apportioned according to population. All money bills originated in the house, but could be altered in the senate. The governor, elected annually by the voters, was required to have £1000 freehold, and, like the senators and representatives, had to be a declared Christian. Legislation could be vetoed by the governor, but a two-thirds majority in both legislative chambers could override his veto. The governor appointed all judicial officials and sheriffs, with the advice and consent of nine counselors jointly elected by the legislature from among those chosen to be senators. Judges served for good behavior. A new constitutional convention would be called in 1795 if two-thirds of the electors voted in favor of amendment in a referendum.

NEW HAMPSHIRE   An elected convention submitted a constitution to the towns in June; it was declared ratified on October 31 and went into effect in June 1784. It was closely modeled on the 1780 Massachusetts constitution, although the property qualifications for officeholders were lower than in Massachusetts and every male over 21 who paid a poll tax could vote. Executive power was vested in the president of the state, who presided over and voted in the senate, but lacked a veto over legislation.

CONNECTICUT and **RHODE ISLAND** revised their colonial charters (granted in 1662 and 1663) in 1776 to eliminate references to royal authority. In both states the governor, deputy governor, and council (which served as the upper house of the legislature) were annually elected by the freemen. The lower house of the legislature was elected by the towns twice a year in Connecticut and annually in Rhode Island. There was no executive veto in either state, and in both states judges were annually chosen by the legislature. Connecticut adopted its first state constitution in 1818, Rhode Island in 1842.

Note on the Texts

This volume collects the texts of newspaper articles, essays, pamphlets, private letters, diary entries, and speeches written or delivered during the debate over ratification of the Constitution from September 17, 1787, to February 6, 1788. The first section of the volume includes 123 pieces written, delivered, or printed as part of the general ratification debate between September 17, 1787, and January 12, 1788 (some items printed in the press after January 1788 are included here because they were written in direct response to earlier items). The second section contains speeches from, and letters pertaining to, the ratifying conventions held in Pennsylvania, Connecticut, and Massachusetts between November 20, 1787, and February 6, 1788.

Most items in the first section and a few in the second are taken from *The Documentary History of the Ratification of the Constitution*, published by the State Historical Society of Wisconsin, Madison, Wisconsin. This set of volumes is the most comprehensive collection ever made of the debates representing all viewpoints and presenting texts drawn from original documents, including manuscripts of private letters and notes, articles that appeared in newspapers, broadsides, and pamphlets, and the printed and manuscript records of state ratification conventions. The materials are gathered from the holdings of hundreds of libraries, historical societies, and private collections. Under the editorship of John P. Kaminski and Gaspare J. Saladino, the texts are unmodernized literal reproductions, maintaining the eighteenth-century spelling, punctuation, and word usage of the originals. The project consists of an introductory volume, *Constitutional Documents and Records, 1776–1787* (edited by Merrill Jensen, the project's first editor), and two multi-volume series: *Ratification of the Constitution by the States* (eventually to include 13 volumes), focusing on the public and private debates in the individual states as well as the debates in the state ratifying conventions, and *Commentaries on the Constitution: Public and Private* (eventually to include 5 volumes), which is a chronological arrangement, day by day, of the public and private commentaries from all thirteen states.

In the present volume the texts from the *Documentary History* follow those established by Kaminski and Saladino except for a few changes in editorial procedure. Words crossed out with a line through them have been deleted here. Bracketed editorial conjectural readings, in cases where the original text was damaged or difficult to read, are accepted without brackets when that reading seems the

only possible one; otherwise the missing words are indicated by a
bracketed space, i.e., [   ]. The editors of the *Documentary History*
also use angle brackets to indicate parts of articles that various other
newspapers excerpted and printed for their own use; these brackets
have been omitted in the present volume. In cases where the texts of
the early printings used as sources have been corrected or revised in
later printings (for example, *The Federalist*) or by publication of errata, the editors of the *Documentary History* give the later correction
in a footnote or insert the correction in brackets next to the original
word; this volume deletes the error and prints the corrected word in
the text without brackets.

The texts in the present volume that are not in the *Documentary*
History (many of them are scheduled for future *Documentary History*
volumes) are taken from the best alternative sources, whenever possible from original appearances in newspapers, pamphlets, or early
accounts of the state ratifying conventions. For instance, the texts of
the debates in the Pennsylvania ratifying convention are from the
Pennsylvania Herald and the *Independent Gazetteer*, which printed
versions prepared by Alexander J. Dallas from shorthand descriptions; the pamphlet edition of James Wilson's opening speech (also
transcribed by Dallas); and *Debates of the Convention, of the State of*
Pennsylvania on the Constitution, Proposed for the Government of the
United States, compiled and edited by Thomas Lloyd, published in
Philadelphia February 7, 1788 (this volume did not include any Antifederalist material). The texts of the debates in the Massachusetts
ratifying convention are from *Debates, Resolutions and Other Proceed-*
ings of the Convention of the Commonwealth of Massachusetts, Convened
at Boston, on the 9th of January, 1788, and Continuing until the 7th of
February Following, for the Purpose of Assenting to and Ratifying the
Constitution Recommended by the Grand Federal Convention. Together
with the Yeas and Nays on the Decision of the Grand Question. To Which
the Federal Constitution Is Prefixed, prepared by Benjamin Russell and
published in Boston March 18, 1788. The texts of some letters in the
first section are from *The Papers of James Madison: Volume 10, 27 May*
1787–3 March 1788, edited by Robert A. Rutland, Charles F. Hobson,
William M. E. Rachal, and Fredrika J. Teute (Chicago: University of
Chicago Press, 1977). The text of one letter is from *The Writings of*
George Washington, 1745–1799, volume 29, edited by John C. Fitzpatrick (Washington, D.C.: U.S. Government Printing Office, 1939),
and the text of one other letter is from the *Papers of Thomas Jefferson*
[7 August 1787–31 March 1788], volume XII, edited by Julian P. Boyd
(Princeton: Princeton University Press, 1955). The text of Ezra Stiles'
diary entry of December 24, 1787, is from *The Literary Diary of Ezra*

Stiles, edited by Franklin Bowditch Dexter (New York: Charles Scribner's Sons, 1901). The texts of two letters are printed from the original holograph manuscripts.

The following is a list of all the writings included in this volume, in the order of their appearance, giving the source of each text. The *Documentary History* is abbreviated as *DHRC*, and the volume and page number follow. When the article is from *Commentaries on the Constitution: Public and Private*, the item number assigned by that edition is also given (for example, CC:356).

LIST OF SOURCES

Benjamin Franklin's Speech, September 17, 1787. *DHRC*, XIII (1981), 213–14 (CC:77A), based on manuscript in Cornell University Libraries addressed to Daniel Carroll.

"Z" Replies to Franklin's Speech, December 6, 1787. *DHRC*, XIV (1983), 358–60 (CC:323), based on Boston *Independent Chronicle*, December 6, 1787.

Alexander Hamilton's Conjectures About the New Constitution, September 1787. *DHRC*, XIII (1981), 277–78 (CC:115), based on manuscript in Hamilton Papers, Library of Congress.

"A Revolution Effected by Good Sense and Deliberation," September 24, 1787. *DHRC*, XIII (1981), 224–26 (CC:91), based on New York *Daily Advertiser*, September 24, 1787.

David Redick to William Irvine, September 24, 1787. Holograph manuscript, recipient's copy, William Irvine Papers, The Historical Society of Pennsylvania, Philadelphia. Printed by permission of The Historical Society of Pennsylvania.

Strictures on the Proposed Constitution, September 26, 1787. *DHRC*, XIII (1981), 243–45 (CC:97), based on Philadelphia *Freeman's Journal*, September 26, 1787.

"An American Citizen" [Tench Coxe] I, September 26, 1787. *DHRC*, XIII (1981), 247–51 (CC:100A), based on Philadelphia *Independent Gazetteer*, September 26, 1787.

"An American Citizen" [Tench Coxe] II, September 28, 1787. *DHRC*, XIII (1981), 264–66 (CC:109), based on Philadelphia *Independent Gazetteer*, September 28, 1787.

"An American Citizen" [Tench Coxe] III, September 29, 1787. *DHRC*, XIII (1981), 272–73 (CC:112), based on Philadelphia *Independent Gazetteer*, September 29, 1787.

"Cato" I, September 27, 1787. *DHRC*, XIII (1981), 255–57 (CC:103), based on *New York Journal*, September 27, 1787.

Reply to "Cato" I: "Cæsar" I, October 1, 1787. *DHRC*, XIII (1981), 287–88 (CC:121), based on New York *Daily Advertiser*, October 1, 1787.

Rebuttal to "Cæsar" I: "Cato" II, October 11, 1787. *DHRC*, XIII (1981), 369–72 (CC:153), based on *New York Journal*, October 11, 1787.

James Madison to George Washington, September 30, 1787. *DHRC*, XIII (1981), 275–76 (CC:114), based on recipient's copy, Washington Papers, Library of Congress.

Richard Henry Lee to George Mason, October 1, 1787. *DHRC*, XIII (1981), 281–82 (CC:117), based on recipient's copy, Mason Papers, Library of Congress.

Rev. James Madison to James Madison, c. October 1, 1787. *DHRC*, XIII (1981), 283–85 (CC:118B), based on recipient's copy, Madison Papers, Library of Congress.

"Southwark," October 3, 1787. *Pennsylvania Gazette*, October 3, 1787.

"Centinel" [Samuel Bryan] I, October 5, 1787. *DHRC*, XIII (1981), 328–36 (CC:133), based on Philadelphia *Independent Gazetteer*, October 5, 1787.

James Wilson's Speech at a Public Meeting, October 6, 1787. *DHRC*, XIII (1981), 339–44 (CC:134), based on *Pennsylvania Herald*, October 9, 1787.

Reply to Wilson's Speech: "A Democratic Federalist," October 17, 1787. *DHRC*, XIII (1981), 387–92 (CC:167), based on *Pennsylvania Herald*, October 17, 1787.

Reply to Wilson's Speech: "Centinel" [Samuel Bryan] II, October 24, 1787. *DHRC*, XIII (1981), 457–68 (CC:190), based on Philadelphia *Freeman's Journal*, October 24, 1787.

Reply to Wilson's Speech: "Cincinnatus" [Arthur Lee] I, November 1, 1787. *DHRC*, XIII (1981), 530–33 (CC:222), based on *New York Journal*, November 1, 1787.

Reply to Wilson's Speech: "An Officer of the Late Continental Army" [William Findley?], November 6, 1787. Philadelphia *Independent Gazetteer*, November 6, 1787.

Rebuttal to "An Officer of the Late Continental Army": "Plain Truth," November 10, 1787. Philadelphia *Independent Gazetteer*, November 10, 1787.

Reply to Wilson's Speech: "Cincinnatus" [Arthur Lee] V, November 29, 1787. *DHRC*, XIV (1983), 303–10 (CC:307), based on *New York Journal*, November 29, 1787.

"An Old Whig" [George Bryan et al.] I, October 12, 1787. *DHRC*, XIII (1981), 376–79 (CC:157), based on Philadelphia *Independent Gazetteer*, October 12, 1787.

"Marcus," October 15, 1787. *DHRC*, XIII (1981), 383–84 (CC:162), based on New York *Daily Advertiser*, October 15, 1787.

"A Citizen of America" [Noah Webster], October 17, 1787. *An Examination into the Leading Principles of the Federal Constitution . . .* (Philadelphia, 1787).

"Brutus" I, October 18, 1787. *DHRC*, XIII (1981), 412–21 (CC:178), based on *New York Journal*, October 18, 1787.

The Weaknesses of Brutus Exposed: "A Citizen of Philadelphia" [Pelatiah Webster]: November 8, 1787. *DHRC*, XIV (1983), 64–74 (CC:244), based on *The Weaknesses of Brutus Exposed: or, Some Remarks in Vindication of the*

Constitution Proposed by the Late Federal Convention, against the Objections and Gloomy Fears of That Writer (Philadelphia, 1787).

A Political Dialogue, October 24, 1787. *DHRC*, XIII (1981), 455–57 (CC:189), based on *Massachusetts Centinel*, October 24, 1787.

James Madison to Thomas Jefferson, October 24, 1787. *The Papers of James Madison: Volume 10, 27 May 1787–3 March 1788*, edited by Robert A. Rutland, Charles F. Hobson, William M. E. Rachal, and Fredrika J. Teute (Chicago: The University of Chicago Press, 1977), 206–19, based on recipient's copy, Jefferson Papers, Library of Congress. Copyright 1977 The University of Chicago Press; reprinted by permission.

Thomas Jefferson Replies to Madison, December 20, 1787. *The Papers of James Madison: Volume 10*, 335–39, based on recipient's copy, Madison Papers, Library of Congress. Copyright 1977 The University of Chicago Press; reprinted by permission.

"Cato" III, October 25, 1787. *DHRC*, XIII (1981), 473–77 (CC:195), based on *New York Journal*, October 25, 1787.

"Publius," The Federalist I [Alexander Hamilton], October 27, 1787. *DHRC*, XIII (1981), 494–97 (CC:201), based on New York *Independent Journal*, October 27, 1787.

"John Humble," October 29, 1787. Philadelphia *Independent Gazetteer*, October 29, 1787.

"Americanus" [John Stevens, Jr.] I, November 2, 1787. New York *Daily Advertiser*, November 2, 1787.

Elbridge Gerry to the Massachusetts General Court, November 3, 1787. *DHRC*, XIII (1981), 548–50 (CC:227A), based on *Massachusetts Centinel*, November 3, 1787.

Reply to Elbridge Gerry: "A Landholder" [Oliver Ellsworth] IV, November 26, 1787. *DHRC*, XIV (1983), 231–35 (CC:295), based on *Connecticut Courant*, November 26, 1787.

A Further Reply to Elbridge Gerry: "A Landholder" [Oliver Ellsworth] V: December 3, 1787. *DHRC*, XIV (1983), 334–38 (CC:316), based on *Connecticut Courant*, December 3, 1787.

Letters from the "Federal Farmer" to "The Republican," November 8, 1787. *DHRC*, XIV (1983), 18–54 (CC:242), based on *Observations Leading to a Fair Examination of the System of Government Proposed by the Late Convention; and to Several Essential and Necessary Alterations in It. In a Number of Letters from the Federal Farmer to the Republican* (1787).

Refutation of the "Federal Farmer": Timothy Pickering to Charles Tillinghast, December 24, 1787. *DHRC*, XIV (1983), 193–205 (CC:288C), based on file copy, Pickering Papers, Massachusetts Historical Society.

George Washington to Bushrod Washington, November 10, 1787. *Writings of George Washington 1745–1799*, edited by John C. Fitzpatrick. (Washington, D.C.: U.S. Government Printing Office, 1939), XXIX.

Thomas Jefferson to William Stephens Smith, November 13, 1787. *Papers of Thomas Jefferson* [7 August 1787–31 March 1788], edited by Julian P. Boyd

(Princeton: Princeton University Press, 1955), XII, 349–51. Copyright 1955 Princeton University Press; reprinted by permission.

"Publius," The Federalist VI [Alexander Hamilton], November 14, 1787. *DHRC*, XIV (1983), 97–101 (CC:257), based on New York *Independent Journal*, November 14, 1787.

"Brutus" III, November 15, 1787. *DHRC*, XIV (1983), 119–24 (CC:264), based on *New York Journal*, November 15, 1787.

Resolution of the Inhabitants of Pittsburgh, November 17, 1787. *DHRC*, XIV (1983), 136 (CC:270A), based on *Pittsburgh Gazette*, November 17, 1787.

"Philanthrop" to the Public, November 19, 1787. Hartford *American Mercury*, November 19, 1787.

"A Landholder" [Oliver Ellsworth] III, November 19, 1787. *DHRC*, XIV (1983), 139–41 (CC:272), based on *Connecticut Courant*, November 19, 1787.

"Publius," The Federalist VIII [Alexander Hamilton], November 20, 1787. *DHRC*, XIV (1983), 142–46 (CC:274), based on *New-York Packet*, November 20, 1787.

"Publius," The Federalist IX [Alexander Hamilton], November 21, 1787. *DHRC*, XIV (1983), 158–63 (CC:277), based on New York *Independent Journal*, November 21, 1787.

George Mason, "Objections to the Constitution," circulated early October 1787, published in full November 22, 1787. *DHRC*, XIV (1983), 152–53 (CC:276B), based on *Virginia Journal*, November 22, 1787.

A "Prolix" Comment on Mason's "Objections": James Madison to George Washington, October 18, 1787. *DHRC*, XIII (1981), 408–09 (CC:176), based on recipient's copy, Washington Papers, Library of Congress.

Reply to Mason's "Objections": "Civis Rusticus," January 30, 1788. *DHRC*, VIII (1988), 331–39, based on *Virginia Independent Chronicle*, January 30, 1788.

Answers to Mason's "Objections": "Marcus" [James Iredell] I, February 20, 1788. *DHRC*, XVI (1986), 163–69 (CC:548), based on *Norfolk and Portsmouth Journal*, February 20, 1788.

Answers to Mason's "Objections": "Marcus" [James Iredell] II, February 27, 1788. *DHRC*, XVI (1986), 242–48 (CC:571), based on *Norfolk and Portsmouth Journal*, February 27, 1788.

Answers to Mason's "Objections": "Marcus" [James Iredell] III, March 5, 1788. *DHRC*, XVI (1986), 322–26 (CC:596), based on *Norfolk and Portsmouth Journal*, March 5, 1788.

Answers to Mason's "Objections": "Marcus" [James Iredell] IV, March 12, 1788. *DHRC*, XVI (1986), 379–87 (CC:616), based on *Norfolk and Portsmouth Journal*, March 12, 1788.

Answers to Mason's "Objections": "Marcus" [James Iredell] V, March 19, 1788. *DHRC*, XVI (1986), 427–29 (CC:630), based on *Norfolk and Portsmouth Journal*, March 19, 1788.

"Cato" V, November 22, 1787. *DHRC*, XIV (1983), 182–85 (CC:286), based on *New York Journal*, November 22, 1787.

"Publius," The Federalist X [James Madison], November 22, 1787. *DHRC*,

XIV (1983), 175–81 (CC:285), based on New York *Daily Advertiser*, November 22, 1787.

"A Countryman" [Roger Sherman?] II, November 22, 1787. *DHRC*, XIV (1983), 172–74 (CC:284), based on *New Haven Gazette*, November 22, 1787.

"Americanus" [John Stevens, Jr.] II, November 23, 1787. New York *Daily Advertiser*, November 23, 1787.

Louis Guillaume Otto to Comte de Montmorin, November 26, 1787. *DHRC*, XIV (1983), 229–31 (CC:294), based on recipient's copy (translation), Correspondance Politique, États-Unis, Vol. 32, 401–04, Archives du Ministère des Affaires Étrangères, Paris, France.

"Brutus" IV, November 29, 1787. *DHRC*, XIV (1983), 297–303 (CC:306), based on *New York Journal*, November 29, 1787.

"Publius," The Federalist XIV [James Madison], November 30, 1787. *DHRC*, XIV (1983), 313–17 (CC:310), based on *New-York Packet*, November 30, 1787.

"Americanus" [John Stevens, Jr.] III, November 30, 1787. New York *Daily Advertiser*, November 30, 1787.

"Agrippa" [James Winthrop] III, November 30, 1787. *Massachusetts Gazette*, November 30, 1787.

Samuel Adams to Richard Henry Lee, December 3, 1787. *DHRC*, XIV (1983), 333–34 (CC:315), based on recipient's copy, Lee Papers, American Philosophical Society, Philadelphia.

"Agrippa" [James Winthrop] IV, December 4, 1787. *Massachusetts Gazette*, December 4, 1787.

"Publius," The Federalist XVI [Alexander Hamilton], December 4, 1787. *DHRC*, XIV (1983), 339–43 (CC:317), based on *New-York Packet*, December 4, 1787.

"Americanus" [John Stevens, Jr.] IV, December 5–6, 1787. New York *Daily Advertiser*, December 5 & 6, 1787.

Richard Henry Lee to Governor Edmund Randolph, December 6, 1787. *DHRC*, XIV (1983), 366–72 (CC:325), based on Petersburg *Virginia Gazette*, December 6, 1787.

John Adams to Thomas Jefferson, December 6, 1787. *DHRC*, XIV (1983), 473–74 (Appendix II), based on recipient's copy, Jefferson Papers, Library of Congress.

"Agrippa" [James Winthrop] V, December 11, 1787. *Massachusetts Gazette*, December 11, 1787.

George Lee Turberville to James Madison, December 11, 1787. *DHRC*, XIV (1983), 405–08 (CC:338), based on recipient's copy, Madison Collection, New York Public Library.

"Publius," The Federalist XXI [Alexander Hamilton], December 12, 1787. *DHRC*, XIV (1983), 414–18 (CC:341), based on New York *Independent Journal*, December 12, 1787.

"Americanus" [John Stevens, Jr.] V, December 12, 1787. New York *Daily Advertiser*, December 12, 1787.

"Philadelphiensis" [Benjamin Workman] IV, December 12, 1787. *DHRC*, XIV (1983), 418–21 (CC:342), based on Philadelphia *Freeman's Journal*, December 12, 1787.

"Brutus" V, December 13, 1787. *DHRC*, XIV (1983), 422–28 (CC:343), based on *New York Journal*, December 13, 1787.

"Publius," The Federalist XXII [Alexander Hamilton], December 14, 1787. *DHRC*, XIV (1983), 436–44 (CC:347), based on *New-York Packet*, December 14, 1787.

"Agrippa" [James Winthrop] VI, December 14, 1787. *Massachusetts Gazette*, December 14, 1787.

Lawrence Taliaferro to James Madison, December 16, 1787. *DHRC*, IX (1990), 597, based on recipient's copy, Madison Papers, Library of Congress.

"A Landholder" [Oliver Ellsworth] VII, December 17, 1787. *DHRC*, XIV (1983), 448–52 (CC:351), based on *Connecticut Courant*, December 17, 1787.

Dissent of the Minority of the Pennsylvania Convention, December 18, 1787. *DHRC*, XV (1984), 13–34 (CC:353), based on *Pennsylvania Packet*, December 18, 1787.

Reply to the Pennsylvania Minority: "America" [Noah Webster], December 31, 1787. *DHRC*, XV (1984), 194–201 (CC:399), based on New York *Daily Advertiser*, December 31, 1787.

A Cumberland County Mutual Improvement Society Addresses the Pennsylvania Minority, January 2, 1788. *DHRC*, XV (1984), 228–30 (CC:408), based on *Carlisle Gazette*, January 2, 1788.

Reply to the Pennsylvania Minority: "A Citizen of Philadelphia" [Pelatiah Webster], January 23, 1788. *Pennsylvania Gazette*, January 23, 1788.

"Publius," The Federalist XXIII [Alexander Hamilton], December 18, 1787. *DHRC*, XV (1984), 4–7 (CC:352), based on *New-York Packet*, December 18, 1787.

"Publius," The Federalist XXIV [Alexander Hamilton], December 19, 1787. *DHRC*, XV (1984), 39–43 (CC:355), based on New York *Independent Journal*, December 19, 1787.

"Philadelphiensis" [Benjamin Workman] V, December 19, 1787. *DHRC*, XV (1984), 44–47 (CC:356), based on Philadelphia *Independent Gazetteer*, December 19, 1787.

Joseph Barrell to Nathaniel Barrell, December 20, 1787. *DHRC*, XV (1984), 49–51 (CC:358), based on recipient's copy, Sandeman-Barrell Papers, Massachusetts Historical Society.

Ezra Stiles: Pluses and Minuses of the Constitution, December 24, 1787. *The Literary Diary of Ezra Stiles, D.D., LL.D., President of Yale College*, edited by Franklin Bowditch Dexter, (New York: Charles Scribner's Sons, 1901), III.

"Publius," The Federalist XXVII [Alexander Hamilton], December 25, 1787. *DHRC*, XV (1984), 95–98 (CC:378), based on *New-York Packet*, December 25, 1787.

Governor Edmund Randolph's Reasons for Not Signing the Constitution,

December 27, 1787. *DHRC*, XV (1984), 123–34 (CC:385), based on *[Edmund Randolph and the Constitution]* (1787) (pamphlet sent by Randolph to Washington and Madison; title page missing).

George Washington to Charles Carter, December 27, 1787. *DHRC*, VIII (1988), 277–78, based on *Maryland Journal*, January 1, 1788 (*Virginia Herald* of December 27, 1787, not located).

"Brutus" VI, December 27, 1787. *DHRC*, XV (1984), 110–17 (CC:384), based on *New York Journal*, December 27, 1787.

"Publius," The Federalist XXX [Alexander Hamilton], December 28, 1787. *DHRC*, XV (1984), 160–64 (CC:391), based on *New-York Packet*, December 28, 1787.

"Agrippa" [James Winthrop] IX, December 28, 1787. *Massachusetts Gazette*, December 28, 1787.

Luther Martin, "The Genuine Information" I, December 28, 1787. *DHRC*, XV (1984), 150–55 (CC:389), based on Baltimore *Maryland Gazette*, December 28, 1787.

Luther Martin, "The Genuine Information" II, January 1, 1788. *DHRC*, XV (1984), 204–10 (CC:401), based on Baltimore *Maryland Gazette*, January 1, 1788.

Luther Martin, "The Genuine Information" VIII, January 22, 1788. *DHRC*, XV (1984), 433–37 (CC:467), based on Baltimore *Maryland Gazette*, January 22, 1788.

Luther Martin, "The Genuine Information" IX, January 29, 1788. *DHRC*, XV (1984), 494–97 (CC:484), based on Baltimore *Maryland Gazette*, January 29, 1788.

Luther Martin, "The Genuine Information" XII, February 8, 1788. *DHRC*, XVI (1986), 89–93 (CC:516), based on Baltimore *Maryland Gazette*, February 8, 1788.

"The New Roof" [Francis Hopkinson], December 29, 1787. *DHRC*, XV (1984), 181–88 (CC:394), based on *Pennsylvania Packet*, December 29, 1787.

"Giles Hickory" [Noah Webster] I, December 1787. *American Magazine*, December 1787.

"Agrippa" [James Winthrop] X, January 1, 1788. *Massachusetts Gazette*, January 1, 1788.

"Publius," The Federalist XXXII-XXXIII [Alexander Hamilton], January 2, 1788. *DHRC*, XV (1984), 217–23 (CC:405), based on New York *Independent Journal*, January 2, 1788.

"Centinel" [Samuel Bryan] VIII, January 2, 1788. *DHRC*, XV (1984), 231–34 (CC:410), based on Philadelphia *Independent Gazetteer*, January 2, 1788.

"Brutus" VII, January 3, 1788. *DHRC*, XV (1984), 234–40 (CC:411), based on *New York Journal*, January 3, 1788.

"Publius," The Federalist XXXIV [Alexander Hamilton], January 4, 1788. *DHRC*, XV (1984), 259–63 (CC:416), based on *New-York Packet*, January 4, 1788.

Samuel Osgood to Samuel Adams, January 5, 1788. *DHRC*, XV (1984), 263–67 (CC:417), based on recipient's copy, Adams Papers, New York Public Library.

"The Republican" to the People, January 7, 1788. *Connecticut Courant*, January 7, 1788.

Resolutions of the Tradesmen of the Town of Boston, January 8, 1788. *DHRC*, XV (1984), 292–95 (CC:424C), based on *Massachusetts Gazette*, January 8, 1788.

"Publius," The Federalist XXXVI [Alexander Hamilton], January 8, 1788. *DHRC*, XV (1984), 302–07 (CC:426), based on *New-York Packet*, January 8, 1788.

Thomas B. Wait to George Thatcher, January 8, 1788. *DHRC*, XV (1984), 284–87 (CC:422), based on recipient's copy, Thatcher Papers, Chamberlain Collection, Boston Public Library.

"Brutus" VIII, January 10, 1788. *DHRC*, XV (1984), 335–38 (CC:437), based on *New York Journal*, January 10, 1788.

"Mark Antony," January 10, 1788. Boston *Independent Chronicle*, January 10, 1788.

James Madison to Governor Edmund Randolph, January 10, 1788. *DHRC*, XV (1984), 326–28 (CC:432), based on recipient's copy, Madison Papers, Library of Congress.

Samuel Holden Parsons to William Cushing, January 11, 1788. Holograph manuscript, recipient's copy, Cushing Family Papers, Massachusetts Historical Society. Courtesy of Massachusetts Historical Society.

"Publius," The Federalist XXXVII [James Madison], January 11, 1788. *DHRC*, XV (1984), 343–48 (CC:440), based on New York *Daily Advertiser*, January 11, 1788.

"Agrippa" [James Winthrop] XII, January 11, 15, 18, 1788. *Massachusetts Gazette*, January 11, 15, 18, 1788.

"Publius," The Federalist XXXVIII [James Madison], January 12, 1788. *DHRC*, XV (1984), 353–59 (CC:442), based on New York *Independent Journal*, January 12, 1788.

"Americanus" [John Stevens, Jr.] VI, January 12, 1788. New York *Daily Advertiser*, January 12, 1788.

PENNSYLVANIA RATIFYING CONVENTION

James Wilson's Opening Address, November 24, 1787. *The Substance of a Speech Delivered by James Wilson, Esq. Explanatory of the General Principles of the Proposed Federal Constitution . . .* , compiled and edited by Alexander J. Dallas (Philadelphia, 1787), 3–10.

John Smilie Responds to Wilson, November 28, 1787. *Pennsylvania Herald*, December 8, 1787.

James Wilson and John Smilie, November 28, 1787. *Pennsylvania Herald*, December 12, 1787.

Robert Whitehill, November 30, 1787. *Pennsylvania Herald*, December 29, 1787.

Benjamin Rush, November 30, 1787. *Pennsylvania Herald*, January 5, 1788.

William Findley, December 1, 1787. *Pennsylvania Herald*, December 5, 1787.

James Wilson Replies to Findley, December 1, 1787. *Debates of the Convention, of the State of Pennsylvania on the Constitution, Proposed for the Government of the United States*, complied and edited by Thomas Lloyd (Philadelphia, 1788), 49–55.

James Wilson on the Slave-Trade Clause, December 3, 1787. *Debates of the Pennsylvania Convention* (1788), 57–59.

Robert Whitehill, December 3 1787. Philadelphia *Independent Gazetteer*, December 6, 1787.

James Wilson's Summation and Final Rebuttal, December 11, 1787. *Debates of the Pennsylvania Convention*, (1788), 100–35.

Benjamin Rush, December 12, 1787. *Pennsylvania Herald*, December 15, 1787.

Robert Whitehill's Amendments and the Final Vote, December 12, 1787. *Pennsylvania Herald*, December 15, 1787.

CONNECTICUT RATIFYING CONVENTION

Oliver Ellsworth, January 7, 1788. *DHRC*, XV (1984), 273–79 (CC:420), based on *Connecticut Courant*, January 14, 1788.

Samuel Huntington, January 9, 1788. *DHRC*, XV (1984), 312–15 (CC:428), based on *Connecticut Courant*, January 14, 1788.

MASSACHUSETTS RATIFYING CONVENTION

Letter to the *Massachusetts Centinel* by "Marcus," January 9, 1788. *Massachusetts Centinel*, January 9, 1788.

Fisher Ames, January 15, 1788. *Debates, Resolutions and Other Proceedings of the Convention of the Commonwealth of Massachusetts, Convened at Boston, on the 9th of January, 1788, and Continuing until the 7th of February Following, for the Purpose of Assenting to and Ratifying the Constitution Recommended by the Grand Federal Convention. Together with the Yeas and Nays on the Decision of the Grand Question. To Which the Federal Constitution Is Prefixed*, edited by Benjamin Russell (Boston, 1788), 30–35.

A Sharp Exchange, January 17, 1788. *Debates of Massachusetts Convention*, 56–61.

Major Martin Kinsley, January 21, 1788. *Debates of Massachusetts Convention*, 91–93.

Thomas Dawes, Jr., January 24, 1788. *Debates of Massachusetts Convention*, 132–33.

Amos Singletary and Jonathan Smith, January 25, 1788. *Debates of Massachusetts Convention*, 136–40.

This volume presents the texts of the documents chosen for inclusion here without change, except for the correction of typographical errors or slips of the pen and the modernization of the use of quotation marks (only beginning and ending quotation marks are provided here, instead of placing a quotation mark at the beginning of every line of a quoted passage). The other conventional features of eighteenth-century spelling and punctuation (including the use of italics for proper names and large and small capitals for emphasis) have been preserved. The following is a list of typographical errors corrected, cited by page and line number: 7.33, will *act*; 50.15, Assembly.; 97.13, you; 105.7, truble; 106.30, effors; 109.19, entirey; 109.39, *branches*; 112.9, diciplining; 112.20, *Article*.; 112.35, America.; 138.2, ara; 139.14, epuitable; 153.5, diroct; 154.36, partrician; 166.6, extends for by, the; 229.4, were were; 230.12, opject; 242.37, not in an executive; 327.20, lands;; 327.37, shoulst; 328.11, agranstizment; 416.10, The; 419.10, eyes.; 466.27, (and Virginia for example) has; 469.8, constitution came from the convention, so; 492.7, one; 518.19, to small too be; 518.32, system; 629.5, scenes; 629.33, advantages; 636.24, Massaschusetts; 673.17, cussory; 675.23, intercouse; 675.32, Sates; 717.5, 1787; 728.17, But, say you, some however; 739.36, represented—; 797.8, attenion; 805.21, 1786; 805.21, said.; 805.26, the the; 821.21, scoure;

822.17, concive; 824.36, introduded; 827.32, cconvention; 830.5, dispositian; 837.28, people.; 839.2, puposes; 841.25, government.; 846.34, agreeble; 849.7, gentlemen's; 849.20, tiwe; 849.22, phssessed; 861.15, goyernment; 864.39, hmiliating; 866.17, boundares; 889.25, convenion; 895.3, damours; 902.30, een; 903.7, or triennial; 905.7, temporay; 908.40, to together; 909.5, ap; 913.17, gentlemen; 915.27, southren; 932.11, odoius; 932.17, inhabitats; 932.20, the of. Error corrected fourth printing: 460.7, the the (*LOA*).

Notes

In the notes below, the reference numbers denote page and line of this volume (the line count includes headings). No note is made for information found in common desk-reference books such as *Webster's Ninth Collegiate* and *Webster's Biographical* dictionaries. Footnotes within the text were part of the original documents. Quotations from Shakespeare are keyed to *The Riverside Shakespeare*, ed. G. Blakemore Evans (Boston: Houghton Mifflin, 1974). Quotations from the Bible are keyed to the King James Version. Quotations from William Blackstone's *Commentaries on the Laws of England* are keyed to the first edition (4 vols., 1765–69; University of Chicago facsimile edition, 1979). For historical and biographical background see Chronology of Events and Biographical Notes in this volume. For further historical information and references to other studies, see the following volumes in *The Documentary History of the Ratification of the Constitution* (Madison: State Historical Society of Wisconsin): *Constitutional Documents and Records, 1776–1787* (vol. I, 1976), ed. Merrill Jensen, *Ratification of the Constitution by the States—Pennsylvania* (II, 1976), ed. Jensen, *Delaware, New Jersey, Georgia, Connecticut* (III, 1978), ed. Jensen, *Virginia* (VIII–X, 1988–92), ed. John P. Kaminski and Gaspare J. Saladino, and *Commentaries on the Constitution, Public and Private* (XIII–XVI, 1981–86), ed. Kaminski and Saladino; *The Papers of James Madison* (vols. 1–10, Chicago: University of Chicago Press, 1962–1977; vols. 11–17, Charlottesville: University Press of Virginia, 1977–91), ed. Robert A. Rutland et. al.; *The Records of the Federal Convention* (3 vols.; New Haven: Yale University Press, 1911), ed. Max Farrand; *Supplement to Max Farrand's The Records of the Federal Convention* (New Haven: Yale University Press, 1987), ed. James H. Hutson and Leonard Rapport; *Encyclopedia of the American Constitution* (4 vols.; New York: Macmillan Publishing Company, 1986), ed. Leonard W. Levy, Kenneth L. Karst, Dennis J. Mahoney; *The Federalist* (Middletown: Wesleyan University Press, 1961), ed. Jacob E. Cooke; *The Federal and State Constitutions, Colonial Charters, and Other Organic Laws of the States, Territories, and Colonies* (7 vols.; Washington, D.C.: Government Printing Office, 1909), ed. Francis N. Thorpe; Gaspare J. Saladino, "The Bill of Rights; A Bibliographic Essay" in *The Bill of Rights and the States: The Colonial and Revolutionary Origins of American Liberties* (Madison: Madison House Publishers, Inc., 1992), ed. Patrick T. Conley and John P. Kaminski; and Bernard Bailyn, "The Ideological Fulfillment of the American Revolution" in *Faces of Revolution: Personalities and Themes in the Struggle for American Independence* (New York: Alfred A. Knopf, Inc., 1990). The scholarship of the *The Documentary History of the Ratification of the Constitution* has been an essential aid in the preparation of this volume.

DEBATES IN THE PRESS AND IN PRIVATE CORRESPONDENCE

3.3–4   *Speech . . . Convention*] This speech was read for the 82-year-old Franklin by James Wilson just before the final votes were taken in the convention.

3.16–20   *Steele . . . Wrong.*] The mock dedication to Pope Clement XI of Urbano Cerri, *An Account of the state of the Roman Catholic Religion* (1715) by Bishop Benjamin Hoadley. It includes the quote "You are Infallible, and We always in the Right," p. ii.

3.30–31   if well administered] Alluding to Alexander Pope, *An Essay on Man* (1733–34), Epistle III, ll. 303–4: "For Forms of Government let fools contest; / Whate'er is best administered is best."

5.1–3   Then the Motion . . . accordingly.] Though the speech failed in its purpose of gaining the signatures of all the delegates (of the delegates present, Edmund Randolph and George Mason of Virginia and Elbridge Gerry of Massachusetts refused to sign), it led to the inclusion in the Constitution the form of signing, phrased by Gouverneur Morris and moved by Franklin: "done in Convention by the Unanimous Consent of the States present . . . In Witness whereof We have hereunto subscribed our Names." Madison commented that this "ambiguous form" had been drawn up by Morris "in order to gain the dissenting members, and put into the hands of Docr. Franklin that it might have the better chance of success." Franklin's speech was reprinted in almost every state, a total of 36 times before mid-February 1788. For a sharp criticism of the term "unanimous," see Richard Henry Lee to Edmund Randolph, December 6, 1787, page 469.20–25 in this volume.

6.2   "Z" . . . Speech] One of several negative replies to Franklin's concluding speech after it was published in the *Boston Gazette* on December 3. Some were bitter and vituperative. An anonymous writer in the *Massachusetts Gazette* of December 14, for example, said that Franklin—the "doubting Doctor," an "enfeebled sage," an "aged delegate," his mind worn out with philosophical, theological, and political researches—proved the wisdom of retiring before a "second childhood has weakened all the principles of manhood." Out of "tenderness to the infirmities of age" or respect for Franklin's former accomplishments as patriot and philosopher, "the puerile speech" should have been left "concealed beneath the roof where the liberties of America have been relinquished."

7.11–12   Dr. *Mayhew* . . . skies?] Cf. *Observations on the Charter and Conduct of the Society for the Propagation of the Gospel in Foreign Parts* (1763). The Reverend Jonathan Mayhew (1720–66), pastor of West Church, Boston, had been a leading polemicist in the struggle to prevent the establishment of an Anglican episcopate in America in the early 1760s. He identified religious freedom with freedom from civil tyranny.

7.19   act of uniformity] The Act of Uniformity (1662) required all clergymen in the realm to subscribe to the precepts of the Church of England.

8.6–7   *shed a tear,*] A verse mocking Franklin's supposed emotion on signing the Constitution had appeared in the Antifederalist *Boston American Herald* November 19: "The worn-out Sage too full his joy to speak, / The puerile tear stole down his wrinkl'd cheek; / He paused a moment—but alas, too late, / He lent his Signet to his Country's fate, / He grasped the trembling quil and signed his name, / And damn'd the Laurels of his former fame."

9.1–2   *Alexander Hamilton's* . . . *Constitution*] Hamilton did not publish and is not known to have circulated this private memorandum.

12.1–3   *"A Revolution* . . . September 24, 1787] This is the first original commentary on the Constitution known to have been published in New York.

12.30   "the *mutual* . . . *amity,*"] See "Letter from the Constitutional Convention to the President of Congress," page 965.36 in this volume.

13.33   *"watch and pray."*] Mark 13:33, 14:38; Matthew 26:41; Colossians 4:2.

15.21–23   power to collect . . . Civil causes] See Art. I, sec. 8, par. 4, page 972.23–25 in this volume, on the establishment of uniform rules for naturalization; Art. I, sec. 9, par. 1, page 973.28–33, on the free importation of "such Persons" (slaves) until 1808, giving Congress the right to tax each one up to ten dollars; and Art. III, sec. 2 (page 978.24–28), which mandates jury trials for criminal cases under federal jurisdiction but not in civil cases (a deliberate omission, reversed in the Seventh Amendment).

17.1   *Strictures* . . . *Constitution*] This anonymous piece is the first published criticism of the Constitution known to have appeared in the United States.

18.22   Fort Pitt.] At Pittsburgh. Formerly Fort Duquesne, it was burned by retreating French troops in 1758 during the Seven Years War, then rebuilt by the British and named Fort Pitt.

19.2–3   poll-taxes . . . emigrate,] The "Eastern States" referred to the states of New England. High taxes in Massachusetts, Connecticut, and

Rhode Island had spurred migration into Vermont (where the population tripled in the 1780s), Maine, New York State, and the Ohio River Valley.

19.12–13   Starve . . . Courts.]   Under English law, the jury of twelve men was kept without "meat, drink, fire, or candle, unless by permission of the judge, till they are all unanimously agreed." (William Blackstone, *Commentaries on the Laws of England*, 4 vols., 1765–69, Bk. 3, ch. 23, p. 375.)

20.3–28.2   *"An American . . . III*]   These were the first of almost 30 essays Tench Coxe published in defense of the Constitution. Coxe added a fourth "American Citizen" essay in late October, and the whole set was widely circulated in reprint form.

31.3   *"Cato"*]   The author of the seven "Cato" papers is unknown. Once assumed to have been Governor George Clinton, it is now speculated that the writer may have been Abraham Yates, Jr., the prominent New York state senator and delegate to Congress who had chaired the drafting of the state's constitution. The papers emanated from the New York Antifederalists against whom *The Federalist Papers* were principally directed. This first "Cato" paper was widely reprinted and responded to. Among the many replies to "Cato" were "Cæsar" I (page 34 in this volume) and John Stevens, Jr.'s, seven "Americanus" papers, six of which are reprinted in this collection; the first (page 227 in this volume) was a specific reply to "Cato" I.

34.2   *"Cæsar" I*]   The writer of this and a second "Cæsar" paper, published on October 17, is unknown. They were once attributed to Hamilton, but his authorship is now doubted.

36.4   the American Fabius]   The analogy of George Washington to the Roman general Quintus Fabius Maximus Verrucosus (d. 203 B.C.), whose strategy of exhaustive attrition finally wore down the strength of the invading Carthaginian army in Italy (Second Punic War, 218–201 B.C.), was commonly made—intended as a compliment to Washington's prudence, his concern for the welfare of his soldiers, and his heroism in saving his country with a minimum of fighting.

37.2   *Rebuttal*]   This reply to "Cæsar" I in turn elicited at least two published responses.

37.5–10   *"Remember . . . children."*]   Joseph Addison, *Cato* (1713), a dramatic tragedy in which the republican Cato commits suicide rather than submit to the dictator Caesar, III.i.

39.39   This resolution]   Adopted February 21, 1787; see Chronology of Events.

42.5   my arrival]   On September 24, 1787.

42.8   R.H.L. and Mr. Dane]   Richard Henry Lee of Virginia and Nathan Dane.

42.13–15   Resolution . . . *Government*]   See Chronology, February 21, 1787.

43.6   Col. M— . . . Me—Smith]   George Mason (see "Objections to the Constitution," page 345 in this volume) and Melancton Smith (see Biographical Notes).

44.21   Genl. Pinkney]   Charles Cotesworth Pinckney.

45.21   13th . . . Confederation]   See Articles of Confederation, page 962 in this volume.

45.33   moved the Amendments]   Lee had proposed 14 amendments constituting a bill of rights that covered most of the provisions in the eventual first ten amendments. For Lee's criticism of the structure of the proposed government and his proposal for amendments, see Lee to Randolph, page 465 in this volume.

46.20   Mr. Stone]   Probably Thomas Stone (1743–Oct. 5, 1787), state senator from Charles County, Maryland, who was elected as a delegate to the Constitutional Convention but declined to serve because his wife was seriously ill. Stone had served in the Continental Congress and was a signer of the Declaration of Independence.

46.23–27   Chancelor Pendleton . . . Judge Pendleton]   Chancellor Edmund Pendleton, president of the Virginia Supreme Court of Appeals, and his nephew Henry Pendleton, a justice of the South Carolina Court of Common Pleas.

48.5   Mr. Blair.]   John Blair (1732–1800), eminent Virginia jurist, was a delegate to the Constitutional Convention. He would vote to ratify in the Virginia convention.

50.10–11   Messrs. Bryan, . . . Nicholson,]   George Bryan (see Biographical Notes); his son-in-law Jonathan Bayard Smith (1742–1812), prothonotary and justice of the Court of Common Pleas of Philadelphia; and John Nicholson (1757–1800), Pennsylvania comptroller.

52.3   "*Centinel*"]   Eighteen "Centinel" essays, published through April 5, 1788, circulated throughout the states in newspaper, pamphlet, and broadside form, the first essay most widely of all. At the time, Samuel Bryan's father, George, was thought to be the author.

54.23   the two men]   Washington and Franklin.

54.35   Mr. Adams's treatise,]   John Adams, *Defence of the Constitutions of Government of the United States of America against the attack of M. Turgot* (vols. 1–2, 1787; vol. 3, 1788), a collection of constitutional documents and commentaries on various republics and on American state constitutions, emphasized the value of strong executives. Adams wrote the first volume (published in England, Jan. 1787) in 1786 while serving as minister to England, and sent copies to John Jay, Benjamin Franklin, Thomas McKean, Benjamin Rush, Tench Coxe, David Ramsay, Thomas Jefferson, Philip Mazzei, and Richard Price, and another hundred copies to Cotton Tufts for distribution in Massachusetts. Copies for sale arrived in April 1787, excerpts were printed in the *Pennsylvania Mercury* from May 11 to November 2, and American editions were printed in May and June. Madison, in a letter to Jefferson dated June 1787, wrote of the book: "Men of learning will find nothing new in it. Men of taste many things to criticize. And men without either not a few things, which they will not understand. It will nevertheless be read, and praised, and become a powerful engine in forming the public opinion." Neither Adams nor the book are mentioned in records of the Constitutional Convention, and there is no evidence that it influenced the writing or ratification of the Constitution in any significant way.

62.26–29   "WHO'S . . . OFFENDED."] Cf. Brutus's speech in Shakespeare's *Julius Caesar*, III.ii.29–30, 32–34.

63.3   *Wilson's . . . Meeting*] Delivered at a public meeting in the Pennsylvania State House Yard held to nominate candidates to the Pennsylvania state assembly. Wilson's speech proved to be the single most influential and most frequently cited document in the entire ratification debate. Written by one of the acknowledged architects of the Constitution, it confronted some of the most controversial and vulnerable points, such as the absence of a bill of rights, and its argument that under the Constitution the people retain all powers not explicitly given to the government became the intellectual focus of much of the debate. The speech was published in an "extra" edition of the *Pennsylvania Gazette* on October 29 and by the end of the year it had appeared in 34 newspapers in 27 towns across 12 states. It would be cited hundreds of times in the public prints and in the state convention debates. George Washington helped to disseminate the speech in Virginia, believing it effectively answered George Mason's "Objections," a document of equal importance on the Antifederalist side, which was being widely circulated in manuscript (see page 345 and note in this volume). The six documents that follow are a sampling of the writings the speech touched off.

66.2–3   cantonments . . . Ohio.] After the Revolutionary War the Continental Congress kept a few hundred troops along the frontier, where settlers faced Indian attacks sometimes instigated by the British, who continued to maintain outposts in the northern and western United States.

68.26   funding law] See Chronology, March 1785 and February–May 1786.

71.23–24   The case . . . *Zenger*] In the famous New York trial of 1735, John Peter Zenger (1697–1746), printer of the anti-administration *New York Weekly Journal*, was accused of seditious libel for printing derogatory remarks about the royal governor, William Cosby. Andrew Hamilton, who defended Zenger, attempted to introduce proof that the printed statements were true and argued that if they were true, Zenger should be acquitted. His arguments were disallowed by Justice James DeLancey, in accordance with English law, which held that truth was no defense against a charge of seditious libel, in part because such libels could cause a breach of the public peace. Ignoring DeLancey's instructions to consider only whether the statements in question had actually been printed by Zenger, the jury followed Hamilton's plea to consider itself competent to decide matters of law as well as of fact, and returned a verdict of not guilty. The decision is considered a landmark in establishing freedom of the press in America.

72.5–9   difference . . . *feigned issue.*] An arranged lawsuit involving the fact in dispute. For example, if a court of equity was unable to determine if "A" was the lawful heir of "B," it would be arranged for two individuals to wager money over whether "A" was the lawful heir. The two "bettors" would then disagree over the facts of their wager, and use their dispute as the basis for a lawsuit that would bring the question of "A" and "B" before a jury. (Blackstone, *Commentaries on the Laws of England*, Bk. III, ch. 27, p. 452.)

73.38–74.1   Clayton's . . . shift,] Ward's case (1636) was recorded by John Clayton in *Reports and Pleas of Assises at Yorke* (London, 1651). Charged with battery, the constable was convicted of a misdemeanor in the York court of assizes; the search was invalidated. (Assizes were periodical sessions of the superior courts in English counties for trial of criminal and civil issues.)

74.26   *Burgh* . . . disquisitions] James Burgh's *Political Disquisitions* (3 vols., Great Britain, 1774–75; Philadelphia, 1775) was one of the most influential pre-Revolutionary political and moral tracts, read by the colonists as a textbook of liberal ideas. Burgh (1714–75), born in Scotland, was a political and religious reformer in England.

76.19   *Venetian* aristocracy,] By the 18th century, Venice had become isolationist and stagnant under an aristocracy devoted to personal ambition and the preservation of ancestral traditions. Its main governing body, the Council of Ten (a doge and 16 members), had been instituted in 1310 to punish crimes against the state, but over time had increased its power through the use of secret police and the restriction of the suffrage to members of the oligarchy. (The republic would fall to Napoleon and the last doge would be deposed in 1797.)

78.26–29   *Montesquieu* . . . Empire] *The Spirit of the Laws* (1748), Vol. I, Bk. XIV, ch. 13, and *Considerations on the Causes of the Greatness of the Romans and Their Decline* (1734), ch. 9.

78.31   Farmer's Letters] John Dickinson's influential *Letters from a Farmer in Pennsylvania to the Inhabitants of the British Colonies* (*Pennsylvania Chronicle*, 1767–68; pamphlet collection, 1768).

84.17–27   "The policy . . . citizens."] Cf. *Commentaries on the Laws of England*, Bk. III, ch. 23, pp. 378–80.

84.30   *Forsey* against *Cunningham*] In *Forsey* v. *Cunningham* (1764), after damages for assault and battery had been awarded Forsey, Cunningham demanded that the supreme court of New York review matters not only of law and procedure but also of fact—the exclusive province of juries. The lieutenant governor, Cadwallader Colden, who had been battling with the legal establishment for years, backed Cunningham, and over the fierce objections of lawyers in New York, New Jersey, and Pennsylvania, obtained the support of the Privy Council in London. When the New York supreme court refused to proceed, and its stand was backed by the colonial assembly and the threat of mob action, the British authorities relented, limiting appeals to charges of errors in law.

87.13–15   "When . . . liberty."] *The Spirit of the Laws*, Vol. I, Bk. XI, ch. 6.

92.3   *"Cincinnatus"* [*Arthur Lee*]] Although a hostile piece in the Federalist *Pennsylvania Gazette* of November 21, 1787, suggested that Richard Henry Lee was the author of the "Cincinnatus" papers, William Shippen, Jr., and John Paradise, both relatives of the Lees by marriage, later attributed them to his brother, Arthur Lee. (Arthur Lee's ten "Monitor's Letters," 1769, directed against the British government, are similar to the "Cinncinatus" attacks on the Federalists.) Six "Cincinnatus" essays were published, Nov. 1–Dec. 6, 1787, all devoted to refuting Wilson's speech. "Cincinnatus" I was attacked point by point in "Anti-Cincinnatus" (Northampton, Mass., *Hampshire Gazette*, December 19).

93.10   *your mob*] See Chronology, September 1787.

93.11   *reptile Doctor*] Probably Benjamin Rush.

94.39   Peter Zenger] See note 71.23–24.

95.27–29   Zenger's . . . Woodfall;] In the case of the printer Henry Sampson Woodfall (1770), accused of seditious libel, the jury exceeded the limits of its traditional role (to determine only the fact of publication) and declared in effect that Woodfall was not guilty as charged. Lord Chief Justice Mansfield ruled that a new trial was necessary. Woodfall (1739–1805) was the publisher of the pseudonymous *Letters of Junius* (*London Public Advertiser*, Jan. 1769–Jan. 1772; collected edition, 1772).

98.29   Mr. W——] James Wilson.

98.38   STAMP ACT]   In 1785 Massachusetts, under Governor James Bowdoin, imposed a stamp tax on legal documents, newspapers, and almanacs.

101.40   *West . . . Valerius.*]   Benjamin West and Charles Willson Peale (or his brother, James). "Valerius" may be a reference to the first-century Roman historian Valerius Maximus, or to a pseudonymous pamphleteer, unidentified.

102.37–38   publication . . . *Pinckney,*]   *Observations on the Plan of Government Submitted to the Federal Convention* (New York, 1787), by Charles Pinckney (1757–1824), second cousin of Charles Cotesworth Pinckney and also a delegate from South Carolina to the Constitutional Convention. The pamphlet was published in October and reprinted, sometimes in part, in seven newspapers.

106.9–12   "It is . . . *President's letter.*]   From George Washington's letter as president of the Constitutional Convention transmitting the Constitution to the president of the Continental Congress, page 965.15–17 in this volume.

111.38   my letter to Timothy,]   In a letter in the October 30 *Philadelphia Independent Gazetteer,* "Plain Truth" had replied to "Timothy Meanwell's" attack on the Constitution for its lack of a bill of rights and for the "21 year" perpetuation of the slave trade. Likening this attack on Art. I, sec. 9 (the slave-trade provisions) to the arguments of "deistical and profane writers" opposed to "the dictates of Jesus Christ" who interpret a Biblical phrase, apply it to a "foreign subject," and believe they have proved a basic inconsistency, "Plain Truth" contended that the eventual prohibition, not the temporary continuation, of the trade was the important development, and that the whole document anticipated the eventual abolition of slavery. In rebuttal "Timothy Meanwell" pointed out that the language only made prohibition possible after 1808, not mandatory—to which "Plain Truth" replied that there was nothing in the clause that in any way affected the prohibition of the slave trade already in effect in ten states. (The "Timothy Meanwell" letters were printed in the *Independent Gazetteer* on October 29 and November 3, the second "Plain Truth" on November 7.)

113.6–17   "In all . . . indispensable."]   See page 965.27–38 in this volume.

115.34   shame . . . blush!]   *Hamlet,* III.iv.81.

117.21–22   Dr. Panegyric]   Probably Benjamin Rush.

118.12–13   a member . . . convention]   Probably Gouverneur Morris, who on August 31 had urged all speed in ratification to prevent a buildup of opposition by state officeholders who might feel threatened by the Constitution.

119.15–16   read Mr. Locke]   Cf. John Locke, *Two Treatises on Government* (1690), Second Treatise.

119.19–35   Barbeyrac's . . . magistrates."]   *Le Droit de la Nature et des Gens* (1706), Jean de Barbeyrac's translation of German juror and historian Samuel von Pufendorf's *De jure naturae et gentium* (1672; *On the Law of Nature and of Nations*), Vol. II, Bk. VII, ch. IV, sec. 1.

120.21   do.]   Ditto.

122.3   *George Bryan et al.*]   The eight "Old Whig" essays, which ran through February 7, 1788, were probably written by a group of Philadelphia Antifederalists led by George Bryan.

127.25   credit of the States]   This read "creditors of the States" in eight of the 11 reprints of the essay.

127.29   Cincinnati.]   The controversial Society of the Cincinnati, an association of officers of the Continental Army, was formed at the suggestion of General Henry Knox in June 1783, and Washington was its first president. Named for the Roman hero Cincinnatus, its stated purpose was to raise funds to protect officers and their families from hardship and to promote closer ties among the states. Membership would be inherited through the eldest son, but when there was no direct descendant, other relatives were eligible. The Cincinnati were widely attacked as a hereditary military aristocracy capable of overthrowing constitutional government. At the May 1784 general meeting, Washington urged the abolition of hereditary membership and other changes designed to allay public apprehensions about the society. His proposal was submitted to the state societies for their approval; the societies were still considering these changes during the ratification debate of 1787–88. After the Constitution was adopted, the Cincinnati became less controversial.

127.35   *Citation Laws.]   The Law of Citation (A.D. 426) was an effort to bring order into the chaos of imperial Roman law. It listed the five major legal authorities who thereafter would be acceptable for citation in the law courts.

129.3   "A Citizen . . . Webster]   Written at the request of Thomas Fitz-Simons, a Federalist delegate to the Constitutional Convention, and dedicated to Benjamin Franklin, this 55–page pamphlet was written by Webster on October 8 and 9, and published under the title *An Examination into the Leading Principles of the Federal Constitution Proposed by the Late Convention Held at Philadelphia. With Answers to the Principal Objections that Have Been Raised Against the System.* It had a wide sale in Pennsylvania and elsewhere and was excerpted in newspapers in Connecticut, Massachusetts, and Rhode Island. Antifederalist replies ridiculed Webster's show of learning and his defense of both the slave trade and general welfare clauses of the Constitution, but Federalists heaped praise on it, and an advertisement in the *Norfolk and*

Portsmouth Journal, April 30, 1788, described it as "a fit companion to the Federalist."

129.12–14   Fohi . . . Mango Capac;]   Fohi, or Foh, is a Chinese name for Buddha. According to legend Romulus, founder and monarch of Rome, established the senate and induced the Romans to preserve peace and promote the public good for their mutual interest. After a reign of 40 years he mysteriously vanished and became the god Quirinus. In his *History of the United States* (1832) Webster wrote that Mango Capac (also called Manco Capac, fl. A.D. 1200), traditional founder of the Inca dynasty in Peru, was a man of "superior genius" who "collected the wandering tribes into a social union, instructed them in the useful arts, curbed their passions, enacted salutary laws, made a judicious distribution of lands, and directed them to be tilled; in short, he laid the foundation of a great and prosperous empire." According to some stories, he was descended from the sun.

129.24   Zamolxis and Odin,]   According to one legend, Zamoxlis, or Zalmoxis, a native of Getae (sometimes identified as in Thrace, sometimes with modern Romania and Transylvania), was the slave and disciple of Pythagorus. He later returned to his homeland and civilized its people, and was deified after his death. In Norse mythology the supreme god Odin established the laws that govern the universe and the destiny of mortals.

132.38   *Federal Town*]   In 1783 Congress considered creating two federal districts, one on the Potomac River, the other on the Delaware, thus satisfying both southern and northern interests. This plan was defeated, though both sites were visited by a congressional committee.

133.38–134.14   expel . . . state.*]   In Pennsylvania's Wyoming District a veritable war had raged for twenty years between the colonial and state authorities and settlers from Connecticut, who claimed possession of the territory. In 1782 Congressional arbitration awarded the area to Pennsylvania which, after another period of violence, confirmed the Connecticut settlers in their titles to the land. The Pennsylvania legislature, torn between factions for and against the constitution of 1776, had first granted, then annulled, and then restored the corporate charter of the Bank of North America. The Constitutionalists had sought to block the convening of the state's ratifying convention by absenting themselves from the assembly in sufficient numbers to defeat a quorum. The sergeant at arms, backed by a Federalist mob, forcibly returned enough of the "seceding" members to validate the vote. See "Cincinnatus" I, page 93 and note 93.10.

134.20–22   Georgia . . . altering it;]   In late 1788 Georgia did revise its constitution of 1777, replacing its unicameral legislature with a bicameral body and its governor and council with a fairly strong single executive.

137.10–14   The constitution . . . Middleton.]   These references to Roman history and to the views of Philip Dormer Stanhope (1694–1773), Earl of Chesterfield, and René, l'Abbé de Vertot (1655–1735), Lord John Hervey

(1696–1743), and Conyers Middleton, D.D., (1683–1750), are in Nathaniel Hooke's *Observations . . . Concerning the Senate of Ancient Rome* (London, 1758). Hervey, a Roman Catholic priest, published several works on the Roman senate and became embroiled in a controversy with the stridently anti-papal Middleton, author of *Treatise on the Roman Senate* (1747); the argument is recorded in *Letters from Lord Hervey and Doctor Middleton concerning the Roman Senate* (1778).

137.19–21 "Mais . . . Romains.] "But as Romulus had chosen the first senators himself he reserved the right of naming, as he pleased, their successors," Gabriel Bonnot, Abbé de Mably (1709–85) *Observations sur les Romains*, ch. 1, a well-known book that had been available in English translation since 1751.

137.34–35 "Les familles . . . senat."] "The families who were descendants of the two hundred senators whom Romulus had created,—believed they had the sole right of entry into the senate," ch. 1.

137.39 A. U. C.] *Ab urbe condita*, or, *Anno urbis conditae*: From the year of the founding of the city (i.e., Rome, 753 B.C.).

138.28–33 Hannibal . . . proscriptions] Rome fought the Carthaginian general Hannibal during the Second Punic War (218–201 B.C.). After a period of civil war, the general Lucius Cornelius Sulla, or Sylla, became dictator in 82 B.C. and began publishing "proscription" lists of his enemies. Thousands were proscribed and then killed; their estates were confiscated and sold at auction. In 81 B.C. Sulla filled the vacancies in the senate and raised its number to 600.

138.40 See Vertot, . . . Middleton] Vertot's *Histoire des revolutions romaines* and Middleton's *Treatise on the Roman Senate* (1747). For Mably, see note 137.19–21.

142.36–42 Vell. . . . sunt."] Velleius Paterculus (c. 19 B.C.–after A.D. 30), *Historiae Romanae*; the Latin is translated: "Gradually, then, by taking back into the state those who either had not taken up arms or had laid them down in good time, power was reestablished."

143.27–28 Montesquieu . . . Romains,] *Considerations on the Causes of the Greatness of the Romans and Their Decline* (1734).

154.38–39 *"Quod . . . Tit. Liv.] "Because no plebeian has the auspices, and that is the reason the decemvirs have forbidden intermarriages, lest the auspices be confounded by the uncertain standing of those born to them" (Loeb translation), the argument offered in the 5th century B.C. against plebeians being chosen consuls. *Ab Urbe condita* (*The Annals of the Roman People*) by Livy (Titus Livius, 59 B.C.–A.D. 17) was the most extensive narrative of the Roman republic available in the 18th century.

155.37–39 *Auguriis . . . dirimerentur.] "Auguries and the augural priesthood so increased in honour that nothing was afterwards done, in the field or at home, unless the auspices had first been taken: popular assemblies, musterings of the army, acts of supreme importance—all were put off when the birds refused their consent" (Loeb translation; I, 36, in most modern editions).

156.17–26 "Thus . . . people."] Walter Moyle (1672–1721), *An Essay upon the Constitution of the Roman Government* (post. pub. 1721). Moyle was an English republican whose writings were influential in the development of America's revolutionary ideology.

157.39 "Ne quis . . . possideret."] "No one may own more than 500 measures of land." A jugera is 28,000 square feet.

158.12–13 *virtue . . . Laws*] In the "Author's Explanatory Notes" to Vol. I, Montesquieu defined virtue as "the love of one's country, that is, the love of equality. It is not a moral, not a Christian, but a political virtue, and it is the spring which sets the republican government in motion, as honor is the spring which gives motion to monarchy. Hence it is that I have distinguished the love of one's country, and of equality, by the appellation of political virtue. My ideas are new, and therefore I have been obliged to find new words, or give new acceptations of old terms, to convey my meaning."

158.41 *Political Sketches*] Six essays entitled *Political Sketches, inscribed to His Excellency John Adams* written by William Vans Murray (?1760–1803) of Maryland while studying law in London (1784–87). Murray's essays had been published as a pamphlet when the Constitutional Convention was still in session and reprinted in the Philadelphia *American Museum* a few weeks before Webster wrote this pamphlet. Murray had attacked Montesquieu's famous, and almost universally respected, belief that "virtue," which he took to mean ascetic self-denial, was necessarily the basis of any free republican state. Webster himself had briefly anticipated Murray's attack on this central axiom of traditional political thought in an earlier pamphlet of his own, *Sketches of American Policy* (1785), p. 24n.

164.3 *"Brutus"*] The author of the sixteen Antifederalist "Brutus" essays (*New York Journal*, October 18, 1787–April 10, 1788) is not known. They were possibly written by Robert Yates or Abraham Yates, Jr.

170.33 chap. xvi] In Book VIII.

171.5–6 same opinion . . . Beccarari.] Cesare Bonesana, Marchese di Beccaria, *Essay on Crimes and Punishments* (Milan, or Livorno, 1764; English translation, 1767), an argument against capital punishment and gross maltreatment of prisoners that stimulated action for penal reform throughout Western Europe. In chapter 6 Beccaria attempted to reduce Montesquieu's strictures against republics of large size "to mathematical exactness." In chapter 26 he discussed the problem in terms of probable outcomes.

176.3   *"The Weaknesses . . . Exposed"*]   This 23–page pamphlet, subtitled *"or, some Remarks in Vindication of the Constitution Proposed by the Late Federal Convention, against the Objections and Gloomy Fears of that Writer,"* was one of a number of replies to "Brutus" I. The first twenty pages were reprinted in the *New York Daily Advertiser* in four installments, November 20 to December 1. Webster had written several earlier tracts under the same pseudonym.

190.2–3   beware . . . Pharisees.]   The leaven refers to false doctrines, or hypocritical teachings, in Matthew 16:6, 11–12, Mark 8:15, and Luke 12:1.

192.4   *Madison to Thomas Jefferson*]   This letter is one of Madison's most careful and comprehensive interpretations of the Constitution, and is in some ways more revealing of his true view of the document than anything he would write for *The Federalist.*

192.8   Commodore Jones]   John Paul Jones.

192.14   Col. Carrington]   Edward Carrington (1749–1810), a Virginia delegate to the Continental Congress.

192.27   W.H. B.F.]   William Hay (c. 1749–c. 1826) of Virginia, and Benjamin Franklin.

193.1–2   Ubbo's book]   Ubbo Emmius, *Graecorum Respublicae*, the third volume, printed separately in 1632, of *Vetus Graecia* (1636).

193.4   *Encyclopedie*]   *Encyclopédie méthodique* (1781–1832), edited by Charles Panckoucké (1736–93), and later by his daughter, Thérèse Charlotte Agasse, was a rearrangement by subject in alphabetical order of *L'Encyclopédie, ou Dictionnaire Raisonné, des Arts et des Métiers* (1751–76), a dictionary of the universal knowledge of the time in the arts, sciences, trades, etc., edited by Diderot, and included articles by Montesquieu, Rousseau, Voltaire, D'Alembert, Jaucourt, Marmontel, and others.

194.18–19   Randolph . . . head]   Edmund Randolph of Virginia favored a three-man executive drawn from different parts of the country. He and John Blair voted against a single executive on June 4; George Mason, another opponent, was absent. For debates on the executive, see Chronology, June 1, 1787, ff.

196.5–7   As I . . . subject.]   In a letter dated March 19, 1787.

196.7–202.11   Such a check . . . general interests.]   This passage fully develops one of Madison's most cherished ideas. He had believed from the start that only a congressional veto over state legislation—and not judicial review—could guarantee individual and minority rights, and he was still smarting from the convention's rejection of that idea. In correspondence the previous summer he had failed also to convince his close friend and political ally Jefferson, then minister in France, of the wisdom of such a provision. When he tried in this letter to convince his friend of the correctness of the principles underlying the Constitution and of its pragmatic value to the nation, he returned to his defeated idea, attempting once again to persuade him that it was right, in the abstract at least. Madison made a copy of this section, presumably for later use. Though the defeated idea of a congressional veto was thereafter dropped from Madison's writings, the interest-group justification for extended republics that he had developed to support it became the heart of *The Federalist X* (page 404 in this volume) and *LI.* Other passages of the letter too, in essence if not in wording, were carried over into Madison's contributions to *The Federalist*, especially in nos. XXXVII, XLV, and XLVI. In writing the letter Madison drew heavily on his pre-convention memoranda that summarized his intense study of the failings of the Articles of Confederation and his careful analysis of all known confederacies, historical and contemporary—his "Vices of the Political System of the United States" and "Notes on Ancient and Modern Confederacies."

196.12   imperia in imperio.] Governments within a government (from the Latin proverb "imperium in imperio"—a government within a government).

196.23–29   Lycian . . . Helvetic System.] In his "Notes on Ancient and Modern Confederacies," Madison quotes Strabo on the confederated republic of Lycia, formed around 169 B.C. in southwest Asia Minor. According to Strabo, it was composed of 23 cities which managed their own domestic affairs and participated in a common council that deliberated on the affairs of Lycia. The cities were grouped in three ranks, and according to rank had either one, two, or three votes in the council, and also made contributions and performed other duties proportionate to their rank. The council chose a Lychiarch, or chief of the republic, and other magistrates, and established courts of justice. The Amphyctionic League, founded near Anthela in Thermopolae, was formed, Madison notes from various sources, to protect and defend the united cities, protect the Temple, and see that the water courses of the cities were never diverted. It first included from 10 to 12 cities, but was later enlarged to include all of Greece. Each city sent one deputy to the Amphyctionic Council to attend particularly to religious matters, and another to attend to civil and criminal matters affecting individuals, with both deciding general questions affecting the League. The Council was first organized around the Temple of Demeter, but later also met alternately at Delphi, where it was associated with the Temple of Apollo. (Although the Amphyctionic Council's purpose was originally both political and religious, it chiefly administered the temples and their property and conducted the Pythian Games.) The First Achaean League (5th–4th cent. B.C.), a confederation of cities on the Gulf of Corinth, was formed as a protection against pirates. The Second Achaean League, originally four cities, was founded around 280 B.C. primarily under the leadership of Aratus, who brought many of the principal Greek cities into the confederation; votes were proportional to the size and importance of the cities but, Madison noted from Polybius, the members "enjoyed a perfect equality, each of them sending the same number of delegates to the senate." It was dissolved in 147 B.C. after losing a war with Rome. The Helvetic Confederacy (Helvetia was the Latin name for present-day Switzerland) emerged when the forest cantons of Schwyz, Uri, and Unterwalden formed an anti-Hapsburg league in 1291, and by 1352 were joined by Bern and four other cantons. By 1513 the League included 13 cantons.

202.40–203.3   Mr. Wythe . . . Gerry]   George Wythe (1726–1806), professor of law at William and Mary College and a supporter of the Constitution; James McClurg (1746–1823), a Richmond physician; George Mason; and Elbridge Gerry of Massachusetts. For Mason's objections and a selection of replies to them, see page 345 ff. in this volume; for Governor Randolph's, page 595, and for Gerry's, page 231.

204.19   The Governour's party]   The governor of New York was George Clinton, an opponent of unconditional ratification of the Constitution.

204.34–36   Mr. Chase . . . Paca]   Samuel Chase (1741–1811), lawyer, merchant, and representative from Baltimore in the Maryland House of Delegates, and attorney William Paca (1740–99), Maryland's governor from 1782 to 1785, both signers of the Declaration of Independence. At the Maryland ratifying convention, April 21–29, 1788, Chase opposed the Constitution, and Paca, who proposed a number of amendments, voted to ratify it. Chase later became a fervent Federalist and, in 1796, a justice of the United States Supreme Court. In 1804 he was impeached by the Jeffersonian Republicans for his partisan conduct while serving on the circuit court bench. He was acquitted by the Senate in 1805 (Luther Martin served as his chief defense counsel).

204.38–205.1   letter . . . Pendleton]   Washington's letter of October 16, 1787, and Edmund Pendleton's of October 8.

205.2–3   Innes and Marshall]   Both James Innes (1754–98), the attorney general of Virginia, and John Marshall, the future Chief Justice of the Supreme Court, would vote in favor of ratification.

205.4–5   Mercer . . . Page]   James Mercer (1736–93), lawyer and judge of the Virginia General Court; Arthur Lee (see Biographical Notes); and Mann Page, Jr., (c. 1749–c. 1810), planter and lawyer, a member of the Virginia House of Delegates, the half-brother of John Page.

205.23   Mr. Dane]   See note 42.8.

205.28   plan with amendments]   See Lee to Randolph, page 465 in this volume.

205.34–36   Mr. Adams . . . reappointment]   John Adams had been the United States minister in London since 1785. Jefferson was reappointed minister to France on October 12.

205.38–206.2   *made . . . scruples.*]   The italicized words were written in a cipher that Jefferson sent to Madison from Europe on May 11, 1785.

206.8   Mr. Jay]   John Jay was then the United States secretary of foreign affairs.

206.31   Broome . . . Burke]   In a letter dated August 2, 1787, Jefferson had asked Madison for help in locating the property of John Burke, the brother of Thomas Burke of Ireland, who had died on passage from Jamaica or St. Eustatius to New York in 1785. The cash and property John Burke had on board was believed to have "come to the hands of" John Broome, a New York merchant. Jefferson was acting on behalf of Thomas Burke's wife, who was living in France.

206.35   Speech . . . C. P.]   Charles Pinckney of South Carolina. For the August 1786 debate over navigation of the Mississippi, see Chronology.

206.40   Musæum, Magazine,]   Philadelphia journals, *The American Museum* (January 1787–92) and *The Columbian Magazine, or Monthly Miscellany* (September 1786–92).

207.30–33   Stuart . . . P. Carrington.]   In a letter dated October 21, concerned in part with the calling of the state ratifying convention, Archibald Stuart (1757–1832), lawyer and member of the Virginia House of Delegates, wrote that Patrick Henry "has on all Occasions however foreign his subject attempted to give the Constitution a side blow. Its friends are equally warm in its support & never fail to pursue him through all his Windings." The others he mentions are William Nelson, Jr. (c. 1759–1813), lawyer and member of the house of delegates; attorney St. George Tucker (1752–1827), who represented the state at the Annapolis Convention in 1786; John Taylor (1753–1824), lawyer and former member of the house of delegates, who would become a leader of the Republicans; Paul Carrington (1733–1818), chief justice of the Virginia General Court, who, as delegate from Charlotte County to the state convention would vote for ratification; and William Cabell (1730–98) and Samuel Jordan Cabell (1756–1818), members of the house of delegates from Amherst County who would vote against ratification in the convention.

209.14   cyphered paragraph]   See page 205.38–206.2 and note.

209.20–21   Thos. Burke's case]   See page 206.31 and note. On September 17, Jefferson had written Madison that John Burke's "56 pounds," and perhaps his other belongings, had "been paid into the hands of a capt. William S. Browne of Providence" by Broome, and asked Madison to make further inquiries.

209.29   M. Bourgoin]   French miniaturist François Bourgoin, who had come to America that autumn hoping to establish himself in Philadelphia.

209.34   mr. Hopkinson.]   Francis Hopkinson.

210.33–37   To say . . . Audience]   See page 63 and note 63.3 in this volume.

212.25–26   rebellion in Massachusetts]   For Shays' Rebellion in western Massachusetts (1786–87), see Chronology, July–October 1786 and January–April 1787.

215.13–28   Montesquieu . . . monarchy.]   *The Spirit of the Laws*, Vol. I, Bk. III, ch. 16.

216.3–4   Locke . . . *compact*.]   See note 119.15–16.

216.5–7   *Political . . . security*]   *The Spirit of the Laws*, Vol. I, Bk. XI, ch. 2.

216.22–23   *property . . . consist*]   See note 119.15–16.

216.33   lost Vermont and Frankland]   New York claims to land in Vermont, which declared itself independent in 1777, were not finally resolved until 1791, when Vermont entered the Union. North Carolina had temporarily detached its western territory as the "state" of Franklin (1785–88), which would eventually be incorporated into the new state of Tennessee.

219.3   *The Federalist*]   By December 12, *The Federalist I* had been reprinted in nine newspapers in New York, Massachusetts, Rhode Island, Pennsylvania, and Virginia. The *Federalist* essays, Madison wrote, "were written most of them in great haste, and without any special allotment of the different parts of the subject to the several writers. . . . It frequently happened that whilst the printer was putting into type the parts of a number, the following parts were under the pen, & to be finished in time for the press." Yet the resulting 85 essays (the longest series by far of all those written in the ratification debate), even at the time of their publication, were praised as a masterpiece of political theory—in Jefferson's words "the best commentary on the principles of government which ever was written." But not all contemporaries, not even all the Federalists, agreed. Rufus King thought Oliver Ellsworth's "Landholder" essays (see pages 234, 239, 329, and note 234.3) more effective than the *Federalist* essays, and the Federalist judge Alexander Contee Hanson, formerly Washington's private secretary and soon to be chancellor of the state of Maryland, while acknowledging that *The Federalist* (collected in 2 vols., March–May 1788) displayed deep penetration and were ingenious and elaborate, found them sophistical in some places, painfully obvious in others, and throughout, prolix and tiresome. He could not get through them, he said; they do not "force the attention rouze the passions, or thrill the nerves." He thought his own short pamphlet, *Remarks on the Proposed Plan of a Federal Government, Addressed to the Citizens of the United States, by Aristides* (January 1788), dedicated to Washington, though perhaps inferior to *The Federalist* as an abstract treatise on government, "as an occasional pamphlet" was "superior" and "more serviceable." The *Federalist* essays, all addressed to "The

People of the State of New-York," were first published from October 27, 1787, to May 28, 1788; Hamilton wrote 51 of them, Madison, 29, and John Jay, 5.

227.6   Cato]   "Cato" III; see pages 214–18 and notes in this volume. This first "Americanus" essay set out the central theme of the seven-paper series: that Americans must not be confined in their thinking to the principles inherited from the past and formulated by over-respected European writers who could not have imagined what conditions in America would be like. Throughout the series, doctrines of Montesquieu, the most respected political theorist of the 18th century, were the special target of attack. Other Federalists attacked these doctrines differently, but one way or another, they believed, certain received ideas had to be refuted if the Constitution was to be intellectually acceptable; Stevens' attacks were perhaps the most direct and the most disrespectful of tradition.

230.15   *argumentum ad populum*]   An argument to the people (i.e., appealing to popular feeling or prejudice).

231.2–4   *Elbridge Gerry . . . Court*]   Gerry's statement was reprinted by every Massachusetts newspaper and by at least 31 newspapers in 11 other states; it also appeared in two pamphlet anthologies and *The American Museum*. Justifying the refusal to sign the Constitution by someone known to be an advocate of a stronger central government, it was felt to be an extremely damaging to the Federalist cause and was widely attacked. Gerry came under personal attack as well. His motives, his conduct in the convention, and his procedure in publishing this statement were all called into question.

234.3   *"A Landholder"*]   Thirteen "Landholder" essays were published simultaneously in the Hartford *Courant* and *American Mercury* (I–IX weekly from November 5 to December 31, 1787, and X–XIII, March 3 to 24, 1788) and were widely reprinted (see also note 219.3). Elbridge Gerry published a rebuttal to Ellsworth on January 5, 1788, and later that month Gerry was defended by the Maryland Antifederalist Luther Martin, who had left the Constitutional Convention in early September.

237.13–14   Whether . . . substituted?"]   Compare page 232.28–30.

243.23–30   Rhode-Island . . . Rhode-Island]   For Rhode Island, see Chronology, May and September 1786; for Shays' Rebellion, see July–October 1786 and January–April 1787.

245.3   *Letters . . . Republican"*]   This 40–page pamphlet, titled *Observations Leading to a Fair Examination of the System of Government Proposed by the Late Convention; and to Several Essential and Necessary Alterations in It. In a Number of Letters from the Federal Farmer to the Republican*, circulated almost everywhere in the states, and by early January was in its fourth printing. Early in May 1788, 13 more letters were published in a separate pamphlet, *An Additional Number of Letters from the Federal Farmer . . .*; the individual letters it contained were dated from December 25 to January 25. Antifederalists praised the letters: the first series, one Antifederalist printer wrote, *"breathes the pure, uncontaminated air of Republicanism, as well as the celebrated spirit of the year 1775."* Hamilton, in the *The Federalist LXVIII*, March 12, 1788, said it was the "most plausible" of the Antifederalist polemics, and Edward Carrington wrote Jefferson, in Paris, that the letters were the best of their kind in print. Despite their extremely wide circulation, the "Federal Farmer" letters were not elaborately refuted by the Federalists, though some rebuttals appeared. Contemporary opinion attributed the series to Richard Henry Lee, and today some consider Melancton Smith the author, but there is little substantiation for either. "The Republican" to whom the letters are ostensibly addressed was probably New York's Antifederalist governor, George Clinton.

246.5–6   Pope's . . . best."] See note 3.30–31.

251.1–2   had they all attended] In all, 19 elected delegates did not attend the Constitutional Convention; all but five of them formally declined to accept their appointments and resigned. Among those who chose not to attend were Charles Carroll of Carrollton (Maryland), Henry Laurens (South Carolina), and Patrick Henry and Richard Henry Lee (Virginia).

251.13   Eleven states met] Rhode Island chose not to elect delegates to the convention. New York's vote was counted until early July when two of the state's three delegates left the convention. New Hampshire's delegates did not arrive until late July.

280.1   well born, . . . Adams calls them,] John Adams, *Defence of the Constitutions of Government of the United States of America against the attack of M. Turgot*, Vol. I, Preface.

281.36–37   perpetual . . . Dickinson.] See note 78.31; no. 11, February 8, 1768.

284.30   morrisites] The followers of Robert Morris (1734–1806), the powerful Pennsylvania merchant and banker, superintendent of finance under the Continental Congress (1781–84) and a signer of the Declaration of Independence (see also note 689.39–40), and of Gouverneur Morris (1752–1816), the New York lawyer and politician, who was a member of the Continental Congress and assistant to Robert Morris when he was superintendent of finance. Both Morrises had attended the Constitutional Convention and were ardent Federalists associated with the mercantile, creditor interests and with the establishment in the middle colonies.

286.15–16   Boston . . . press] In October some Boston printers had refused to publish pseudonymous Antifederalist material unless they were given the writers' true identities. Assailed as a flagrant violation of the freedom of the press, the refusal to print such pieces created an uproar not only in Massachusetts but in other states as well, especially Connecticut, Rhode Island, New York, and Pennsylvania. The practice was soon dropped, but at least one

Federalist printer, when publishing Antifederalist views, gave unequal weight to Federalist rebuttals.

289.6–8   letter . . . constitution]   Tillinghast had asked Pickering, then a delegate to the Pennsylvania ratifying convention, for his opinion of the views of the "Federalist Farmer." Pickering wrote back on December 6 that he would reply more fully as soon as he had time, but declared that the "Federal Farmer" was "not a fair reasoner; and like all other opposers . . . alarms himself & would alarm his readers with imaginary fears."

289.10   publication of the debates]   The *Philadelphia Independent Gazetteer* of December 3 had announced William Lloyd's proposal to publish the debates of the Pennsylvania ratifying convention. (The convention adjourned on December 15, and Lloyd published the speeches of Federalists James Wilson and Thomas McKean on February 7, 1788.)

292.21   (See page 253.)]   Originally, "(See page 10)"; all of Pickering's references to page numbers of the *Federal Farmer* pamphlet have been changed to correspond to this volume.

304.12–15   If this letter . . . proper]   On January 27, 1788, Tillinghast sent a copy of Pickering's letter to New York Antifederalist Hugh Hughes, noting that although Pickering obviously expected him to have it printed, he refused to do so. (Pickering's letter was not published until the 20th century.)

307.25–35   Mr. Ronald . . . Taxes;]   William Ronald (d. 1793), a member of the Virginia House of Delegates, had been appointed to head a committee to amend the revenue laws. Legislation that would make tobacco and securities acceptable for payment of taxes was pending in Virginia. Also before the Assembly were proposals to delay payment of debts owed the British, which the peace treaty had guaranteed, and bills for the relief of private debtors. Ronald voted with the majority on making tobacco receivable, and on delaying payment of the British debts. Elected a delegate in 1788 to the Virginia ratifying convention from an Antifederalist county, he took no part in the convention debates, but voted to ratify the Constitution.

309.4   *William Stephens Smith*]   Smith, John Adams' son-in-law, was then the secretary of the American legation in London, and a frequent correspondent of Jefferson. This letter and one of the same date to Adams, written after a first reading of the Constitution, were the most critical of the many statements Jefferson made on the subject. Though he eventually came to appreciate the document's strengths and modified his criticism (see Madison's letter to Jefferson, page 192, and note 196.7–202.11 in this volume, and Jefferson to Madison, page 209), he never gave up his conviction that the reelectability of the president was a mistake.

309.16–17   M. de Chastellux]   François-Jean, Marquis de Chastellux (1734–88), author and military commander.

310.3   instance of Massachusets?]   Shays' Rebellion.

313.23   If SHAYS . . . *debtor*] For a different interpretation of Shays' Rebellion, see Jefferson's letter of November 13, page 310 in this volume.

313.39   Dutchess of Marlborough] Lady Sarah Churchill (1660–1744).

315.34–35   trade and navigation. / From this] The following was inserted when the *Federalist* essays were collected under Hamilton's direction in two volumes (March and May 1788) by John and Archibald M'Lean: "and sometimes even the more culpable desire of sharing in the commerce of other nations without their consent.

"The last war but two between Britain and Spain sprang from the attempts of the English merchants, to prosecute an illicit trade with the Spanish main. These unjustifiable practices on their part produced severities on the part of the Spaniards, towards the subjects of Great Britain, which were not more justifiable; because they exceeded the bounds of a just retaliation, and were chargeable with inhumanity and cruelty. Many of the English who were taken on the Spanish coasts were sent to dig in the mines of Potosi; and by the usual progress of a spirit of resentment, the innocent were after a while confounded with the guilty in indiscriminate punishment. The complaints of the merchants kindled a violent flame throughout the nation, which soon broke out in the house of commons, and was communicated from that body to the ministry. Letters of reprisal were granted and a war ensued, which in its consequences overthrew all the alliances that but twenty years before had been formed, with sanguine expectations of the most beneficial fruits."

315.38–39   LEAGUE . . . States.] The League of Cambrai (1508–10) included the Holy Roman Emperor Maximilian I, Louis XII of France, Ferdinand V of Aragon and several Italian city states. It was joined by Pope Julius II.

316.15–16   North-Carolina . . . Pennsylvania] See notes 133.38–134.14 and 216.33.

318.34–38   "In a free . . . representatives."] Cf. *The Spirit of the Laws*, Vol. I, Bk. XI, ch. 6.

324.9   JOHN GIBSON] Gibson (1740–1822) was major general of militia and a judge of the court of common pleas in Pennsylvania. He had been a frontier soldier and an Indian trader, served as a colonel in the Continental Army, and would be a delegate to the state convention (1789–90) that revised the Pennsylvania constitution of 1776.

326.13–14   Dey of Algiers,] Since 1671, Algeria had been governed by deys who ruled for life and were chosen by local civilian, military, and pirate leaders.

328.15–16   Landholder . . . Mercury] See note 234.3.

341.12–13   When Montesquieu . . . republics,] *The Spirit of the Laws*, Vol. I, Bk. VIII, ch. 16.

344.18–20   "Were I . . . Lycia."]   Bk. IX, ch. 3.

345.4–5   *"Objections to the Constitution"*]   After the committee of style submitted the draft Constitution to the Philadelphia Convention on September 12, 1787, George Mason and Elbridge Gerry unsuccessfully moved to have a bill of rights drafted and added to the proposed document. Intending to present a formal protest to the convention, Mason wrote out the first version of his objections on the back of his printed copy of the draft Constitution, but then became discouraged at the haste with which the majority of the delegates were concluding the proceedings and decided to withhold them. (Mason, Gerry, and Edmund Randolph did speak in the convention on September 15, explaining why they would not sign the Constitution.) By mid-October 1787 manuscript copies of Mason's original objections were being privately circulated in several states. On October 7, Mason sent a revised and enlarged version to Washington (see note 63.3), who passed a copy on to Madison. Washington then arranged for the reprinting in Virginia of James Wilson's speech of October 6, hoping it would counteract the influence of Mason's opposition (Wilson's speech appeared in the *Virginia Independent Chronicle*, October 24). By late November Federalists felt it necessary to have Mason's manuscript published so that it could be publicly discussed and refuted. It first appeared in the *Massachusetts Centinel* on November 21, but without the paragraph on navigation laws (see note 348.5–29). The next day the full version appeared in the *Virginia Journal*. Mason's "Objections" had a vast circulation in both the shortened form (reprinted in 21 newspapers) and in the full version, which appeared in newspapers, broadsides, and pamphlet anthologies. The publication of the document touched off a huge storm of responses. Few defenses of the "Objections" appeared in print, but despite the highly critical responses, it remained one of the central documents of the ratifying debate.

345.10–346.10   Gentlemen, . . . manuscript.]   The introduction and concluding statement (page 349.21–27) are by Tobias Lear (1762–1816), Washington's private secretary (1785–92, later his military secretary, 1798–99, then consul to Algiers, 1803–12). Washington did not know that the essay was going to be printed.

348.4–8   "The President . . . guilt.]   One of several respondents to this paragraph, "An Impartial Citizen," V (Petersburg *Virginia Gazette*, February 28, 1788), observed that any power can be abused, that every power will injure someone in some way, that all states have such a power, that all learned authorities justify it, that it properly should rest in the hands of a single supreme executive, and that it is perfectly consistent with democracy.

348.15–29   "By requiring . . . government."]   This paragraph was not in the "Objections" printed in the *Massachusetts Centinel* (November 21), but was printed in that paper on December 19 in an "extract of a letter to the Printer . . . from his correspondent at New-York, dated Dec. 7, 1787," which began: "The copy of the objections . . . which I sent you a few weeks since,

I obtained from a certain antifederal character, in this city—who, it since appears, like a true antifederalist, omitted one objection, which was the principal in Col. Mason's mind—and which he well knew, would, if published in the northern States, be an inducement to them to accept the Constitution. I shall only remark on this his Machiavelian conduct—that the enemies to the Federal plan, ought no longer to complain of deception—The article omitted, and which you may rely, is authentick, is as follows . . . "

351.16–18   *ordinance . . . land,*] The ordinance passed by the Virginia Revolutionary convention in 1776 made England's common law, general statutes and acts of parliament made in aid of the common law prior to 1607 (the fourth year of the reign of James I, and the year the Jamestown colony was founded) as well as Virginia's own laws and resolutions, the rule of decision in the state's courts.

352.6   letter . . . Pendleton)]   See note 204.38–205.1.

353.6   *Mr. Dixon's paper*]   John Dixon's Richmond *Virginia Gazette and Independent Chronicle.*

353.32–354.3   2d. . . . consequences.]   "Civis Rusticus" ignores Mason's qualifying footnote, page 346.37–39 in this volume.

355.21–22   executive power]   In Mason's "Objections," this reads "exclusive power."

356.22   invocations]   In Mason's "Objections," this reads "innovations."

356.35–38   The people . . . unrepealed]   See note 351.16–18.

357.3–4   declarations of rights]   Delaware, Maryland, Massachusetts, New Hampshire, North Carolina, Pennsylvania, and Virginia had declarations of rights in the constitutions they had adopted since 1776, and Connecticut had incorporated an act containing a declaration of rights into the modified colonial charter that served as its constitution.

358.6   "the hey-day in the blood;"]   *Hamlet*, III.iv.69: ". . . at your age / The heyday in the blood is tame, it's humble / And waits upon the judgment."

358.30–31   Burrow's Rep.]   James Burrow, *Reports of Cases Argued and Adjudged in the Court of King's Bench in the time of Lord Mansfield* (1756–72).

360.9   Valeat . . . potest.]   A Latin proverb, literally, "Let it have such value, or power, as it (intrinsically) possesses," i.e., "Let it pass for what it is worth."

360.33   Hume's essay]   David Hume, "Of the Liberty of the Press" in *Essays Moral, Political and Literary* (1741; 3d corrected edition, 1748).

361.24–25   Pæley's . . . Philosophy,]   William Paley, *Principles of Moral and Political Philosophy* (first pub. 1785), Bk. VI, ch. 8 ("On the Administration of Justice").

363.5   *"Marcus" . . . I – V*]   James Iredell published his five-part rebuttal of Mason's "Objections" at weekly intervals in Virginia beginning February 20, 1788. On March 27 the pieces were reprinted together as a pamphlet, in Newbern, North Carolina.

364.34–35   Mr. Wilson . . . speech]   See page 63 in this volume.

370.35–36   letter . . . Sherman,]   The letter two of Connecticut's delegates to the Constitutional Convention, Oliver Ellsworth and Roger Sherman, sent to Connecticut governor Samuel Huntington transmitting the Constitution (the letter was printed in 24 newspapers in five states).

372.30   Governor Randolph's letter]   See page 595 in this volume.

374.38   Coke's . . . Littleton]   *The First Part of the Institutes of the Laws of England. Or, a Commentary upon Littleton* (1628), Bk. II, ch. 10, sec. 164.

375.20–21   Montesquieu . . . necessary)]   *The Spirit of the Laws*, Bk. XI, ch. 6.

376.33–34   opinion . . . *in writing*]   Art. II, sec. 2.

382.28–31   Admiral Byng's . . . Minorca.]   Rear Admiral John Byng (1704–57) was sent in 1755 to save the British Mediterranean base on the island of Minorca from anticipated attack. Byng reached Minorca in May 1756 after the outbreak of the Seven Years War and found the island already under attack by the French. He ordered his fleet to attack the French naval force, but the engagement ended inconclusively when the French successfully withdrew. Byng then decided that his force was not sufficient to either renew the attack on the French fleet or protect Minorca, and he abandoned the island and returned to Gibraltar, outraging popular opinion in Britain. The ministry under the duke of Newcastle had Byng court-martialed. He was acquitted of charges of cowardice and treachery, but found guilty of neglect of duty in battle which, under the newly revised Articles of War, demanded the death sentence. Although the court did not expect the sentence to be carried out and recommended mercy, Byng was shot on March 14, 1757. Shortly before his execution, Byng said, "They make a precedent of me such as admirals hereafter may feel the effects," which Voltaire echoed in *Candide* (1759), where he wrote that in England "it is thought desirable to kill an admiral from time to time to encourage the others."

383.12–14   letter . . . land?]   In a report to the Continental Congress on October 13, 1786, Secretary for Foreign Affairs John Jay proposed a resolution that treaties could not be limited or interpreted by states because, once ratified by Congress, "they become, by virtue of the Confederation, part of the law of the land" and are both independent of the "will and power of the

Legislatures" and obligatory and binding on them. *Ex vi termini* means "from the force of the term," i.e., from the meaning of the term itself.

384.8–9   is vested . . . Congress,]   The Articles of Confederation (IX) vested the exclusive treaty-making power in Congress, but allowed an individual state to impose duties on foreign nationals equivalent to those their governments imposed on the state's citizens.

385.33–386.3   publication . . . Eastern States,]   R. H. Lee to Randolph (see page 468.27 ff. in this volume).

387.35   Bill . . . 1688]   In the Glorious Revolution of 1688, James II, the Catholic Stuart king of England, was deposed and driven into French exile. A new parliament was elected, and on February 13, 1689, it offered the throne to the Protestant Dutch prince William of Orange and his wife, Mary, the Protestant daughter of James II, on the condition that they agree to a declaration of right drawn up by parliament. William and Mary accepted, and the provisions of the declaration were incorporated in the "Act declaring the Rights and Liberties of the Subject and Setleing the Succession of the Crowne," commonly known as the Bill of Rights, which became law on December 16, 1689. The Bill of Rights established a line of royal succession, barred Catholics from the throne, denounced the abuses of James II, and declared that the crown could not legally suspend or dispense with laws, levy money, or keep a standing army in peacetime without the consent of parliament. It also called for free elections to parliament, frequent holdings of parliament, freedom of speech in parliament, proclaimed the right of subjects to petition the king, and declared that excessive bail and fines ought not to be imposed and that cruel and unusual punishments ought not to be inflicted. Among the abuses the Bill of Rights was directed against was the use of torture by Tudor and early Stuart monarchs, who frequently employed royal prerogatives such as privy council warrants to order crown officers to torture prisoners suspected of treason. Such torture was ruled to be illegal under the common law by the judges trying the assassin Felton in 1628, and by 1689 torture was widely condemned on both legal and humanitarian grounds. Growing sentiment against cruel and unusual punishment also helped mitigate the severity of penalties that were proscribed by law (e.g., it increasingly became the practice to let condemned traitors hang until they were dead, thus sparing them the pain of being disembowelled while alive).

393.21   the Fœderalist]   Number XXV.

397.2   modern aristocracy]   In Mason's "Objections," "moderate aristocracy." The error was corrected in the "Marcus" pamphlet.

399.5   "Cato" V]   For "Cato's" first three papers published September 27, October 11, and October 25, see pages 31, 37, 214 in this volume. For John Stevens, Jr.'s, reply to "Cato" V, see "Americanus" V, page 487 in this volume.

399.8   my last number]   "Cato" IV appeared in the *New York Journal* on November 8.

399.15   ten miles square] The proposed federal district.

399.32–33   Mr. Coke . . . *quietness*] *The Second Part of the Institutes of the Laws of England* (4th ed., London, 1671), "Proeme."

400.8–9   *to live . . . misery.*] Richard Hooker, *Of the Laws of Ecclesiastical Politie*, Bk. I (1594), ch. 10, sec. 5.

402.5–6   Sidney . . . magistrates.] Algernon Sidney, *Discourses concerning Government* (posthumously published, 1698), Vol. II, ch.2, sec. 21, and Montesquieu's *The Spirit of the Laws*, Vol. I, Bk. II, ch. 3.

402.10–17   Sidney . . . *reputation*] *Discourses concerning Government*, Vol. II, ch. 2, secs. 23, 28.

402.22–23   executive . . . temporary senators] "Publius" (Alexander Hamilton) in *The Federalist LXVII* (March 11, 1788) charged "Cato" with purposely misrepresenting the third paragraph of Article II, section 2, in order to suggest that the president would have the power to fill vacancies in the Senate occurring during its recess. "Publius" then cited Article I, section 3, paragraphs 1 and 2, which provide for the temporary appointment of senators by the executive of the state they represent. See pages 977.5–10, 14–17, and 969.15–17, 25–29 in this volume.

403.21   Brutus] "Brutus" III, page 317 in this volume.

404.3   *Federalist X*] Madison's first and posthumously most famous contribution to the series. For its origins, see page 196.7–202.11 and note.

414.30–31   *George Bryan's . . . Old Whig*] Some thought George Bryan was the author of the "Centinel" essays; see also note 122.3 to "The Old Whig."

416.8   his last number] "Cato" IV, *New York Journal*, November 8. ("Cato" V appeared the day before "Americanus" II was printed.)

417.28–32   "of a President . . . Monarch.] "Cato" IV, loosely quoting from Montesquieu on the qualities of the court of a monarch (*The Spirit of the Laws*, Bk. III, ch. 5.), cites *"ambition with idleness—baseness with pride—the thirst of engagements—contempt of civil duties—hope from the magistrates weakness; but, above all, the perpetual ridicule of virtue."*

418.7–12   "The Executive power . . . by men."] *The Spirit of the Laws*, Vol. I, Bk. XI, chs. 6 and 8.

418.13–14   "The safety . . . Government."] "Cato" IV.

419.4–10   "Harrington," . . . eyes."] *The Spirit of the Laws*, Vol. I, Bk. XI, ch. 6. In *The Commonwealth of Oceana* (1656), James Harrington presented his plan for an ideal republic.

420.2–3   *Louis . . . Montmorin*] This letter is one of a series of reports sent by the French chargé d'affaires in the United States, Louis-Guillaume

Otto, to his superior in Paris, the Comte de Montmorin, minister of foreign affairs and minister of marine.

424.12   my last number] November 25, page 317 in this volume.

426.7–8   my first number] October 18, page 164 in this volume.

428.38–39   *Apostle Paul . . . cherisheth it.*"] Ephesians 5:29.

430.13–20   *Elisha . . . Syria.*"] 2 Kings 8:12–13.

431.25–26   preceding papers] *The Federalist IX* and *X*, pages 339 and 404 in this volume.

431.30   former occasion.] *The Federalist X.*

437.4   "It is . . . territory."] *The Spirit of the Laws*, Vol. I, Bk. VIII, ch. 16.

437.6–7   Civilian] Professor, practitioner, or student of civil law.

437.17–20   "the people . . . enact laws."] *The Spirit of the Laws*, Vol. I, Bk. II, ch. 2.

443.3   *"Agrippa"*] Winthrop's 18-part "Agrippa" series began on November 23 and appeared at short intervals until February 5. These papers probably had less impact politically than the more widely known Antifederalist writings that emanated from powerful political groups in Philadelphia and New York.

443.12   tender act] An act legalizing the discharge of debts contracted in specie with payments of goods, especially farmers' crops. Winthrop is probably referring to Massachusetts' one-year tender act passed in June 1787.

446.3   *Samuel . . . Lee*] Samuel Adams' gradual and reluctant shift from the Antifederalism of this private letter and his public declaration of January 3 (see note 717.2) to his last-minute, critical vote for ratification in the Massachusetts convention after it agreed to propose amendments was one of the decisive developments that made the adoption of the Constitution possible.

446.5–7   Favours . . . Gerry.] In a letter dated October 27, Lee had written: "Our mutual friend Mr. Gerry furnishes me with an opportunity of writing to you without danger of my letter being stopt on its passage, as I have some reason to apprehend has been the case with letters written by me and sent by the Post—Under this impression it is, that I send you herewith a Copy of my letter to you of the 5th of this month." Lee also wrote that he would be returning from New York to Virginia on November 4th, and instructed Adams to send his reply to "our friend Mr. Osgood of the Treasury here," who would forward the letter "*safely.*" When Osgood received Adams'

December 3 letter, he gave it to Arthur Lee (also on the Board of Treasury), who got it to his brother on "the last of January."

446.8   my Station there,]   Adams was president of the Massachusetts senate 1787–88.

447.27   Colo Francis, Mr A. L.]   Lee's brothers Francis Lightfoot Lee and Arthur Lee.

448.4   December 4,]   The paper was misdated December 3.

451.15–16   Lycian and Achæan leagues,]   See note 196.23–29.

455.29   liberty]   Changed to "levity" in reprintings in New York and the M'Lean edition.

457.29–30   "it is a fundamental . . . laws."]   See note 437.17–20.

458.32–459.21   "This consolidated . . . "irrefragable,"]   The quotations in this paragraph are conflated from "Cato" III, page 214 ff. in this volume.

461.18–23   "Is it . . . attachment?"]   From "Cato" III.

465.2–3   *Richard . . . Randolph*]   When the Constitution was transmitted to Congress in late September 1787, Richard Henry Lee, then a Virginia delegate, decided that the Constitution was unacceptable as proposed and offered amendments along lines suggested by George Mason. After Congress transmitted the Constitution to the states for ratification, Lee began circulating copies of his amendments, and wrote Governor Edmund Randolph of Virginia, who had himself refused to sign the Constitution, to explain his views. Lee's proposed amendments were published on November 16, and then on December 6 the amendments appeared together with the letter to Randolph in the *Virginia Gazette*. (That issue is not known to be extant, but the letter and amendments appeared verbatim in the *Pennsylvania Packet*, December 20.) Widely reprinted, the letter was a matter of great concern to Federalists and touched off the publication of numerous essays in reply, which concentrated on thwarting Lee's proposal to call a second convention to draft a bill of rights. That idea was not original with Lee, though his letter greatly stimulated it; it constituted one of the most serious threats the Federalists faced. After Governor Randolph publicly supported the idea (see page 595 ff. in this volume), Madison wrote to him, with some concern, in an attempt to dissuade him (page 744 ff.).

465.20–21   kill . . . dying.]   Typical of the many responses to Lee's letter to Randolph were the three essays by "Cassius" (authorship unknown) that appeared in the *Virginia Independent Chronicle*, April 2, 9, 23, 1788. In the third letter "Cassius" responded specifically to Lee's formulation that to accept a bad government for fear of anarchy would be to kill oneself for fear of dying. Lee's remark assumes, "Cassius" wrote, that Virginia had the choice of creating a better constitution than the one that had been written in Philadelphia, or that the defective Articles of Confederation could somehow be redeemed, or that a new national convention, whose members would be bound by public instructions, could do better than the Constitutional Convention, whose members, meeting in secrecy, had been able to make necessary concessions free from public scrutiny.

467.13–16   Blackstone . . . purpose.]   Cf. *Commentaries on the Laws of England*, Bk. I, ch. 1, p. 125.

467.28–32   it is the most . . . equals.]   Bk. III, ch. 23, p. 379.

469.8–9   members . . . Congress,]   Lee had declined his appointment to the Constitutional Convention on the grounds that membership in both the Convention and Congress would involve a conflict of interests.

473.2   *John . . . Jefferson*]   In this letter Adams replies to a letter Jefferson had sent him on November 13. There were things in the Constitution, Jefferson had written, that staggered his disposition to approve of the convention's work: The House would be inadequate to perform its duties, and the president "seems a bad edition of a Polish king. He may be reelected from 4. years to 4. years for life. reason & experience prove to us that a chief magistrate, so continuable, is an officer for life. when one or two generations shall have proved that this is an office for life, it becomes on every succession worthy of intrigue, of bribery, of force, & even of foreign interference. it will be of great consequence to France & England to have America governed by a Galloman or Angloman. once in office, & possessing the military force of the union, without either the aid or check of a council, he would not be easily dethroned; even if the people could be induced to withdraw their votes from him. I wish that at the end of the 4. years they had made him for ever ineligible a second time. indeed I think all the good of this constitution might have been couched in three or four new articles to be added to the good, old, & venerable fabrick, which should have been preserved even as a religious relique."

473.33   Mr Littlepage]   Lewis Littlepage (1762–1892) of Virginia, chamberlain of Stanislaus II, king of Poland (1764–95), on a commission for the king, returned to Paris by late December.

478.12   in Colo. Masons]   Page 345 ff. in this volume.

480.12   Mr. Henry . . . Cabells]   For Patrick Henry, see Biographical Notes. Benjamin Harrison (1726–91), a former governor of Virginia (1782–84), believed that the Constitution needed a bill of rights; he would vote for ratification in the Virginia convention (June 2–27, 1788). Meriwether Smith (1730–94) of Essex County, a former member of the Continental Congress (1778–9, 1781), had helped draft Virginia's declaration of rights. He believed the Constitution should be amended before ratification. William

(1730–98) and Samuel (1756–1818) Cabell, delegates from Amherst County, would, like Smith and Henry, vote against ratification in the Virginia convention.

480.14–15   Resolutions . . . October] Resolutions by the Virginia House of Delegates to convene a state ratifying convention, subsequently passed on October 25 and concurred in by the senate on October 31. John Marshall and other Federalists successfully prevented an attempt by Henry and Mason to explicitly give the convention power to propose amendments.

480.19–21   Convention . . . Correspondence] On December 12 the Virginia legislature passed a bill authorizing the Virginia ratifying convention to communicate with other states, or state conventions, concerning the proposed Constitution. The legislature directed Governor Randolph on December 27 to send a copy of the law to the other states.

480.28–29   Mr. Carrington . . . Brown] Edward Carrington, Cyrus Griffin, and John Brown had been elected Virginia delegates to the Continental Congress in October.

482.31   tempestuous situation] Shays' Rebellion; see Chronology, July–October 1786 and January–April 1787.

487.34–488.3   "A Republican . . . caprice."] Vol. I, Bk. II, ch. 1.

489.30–31   "ambition . . . Republic."] Vol. I, Bk. III, ch. 7.

494.3   "Philadelphiensis] Workman's 12 "Philadelphiensis" essays were denounced as the work of "a half crazy fellow . . . a harmless lunatic" (Francis Hopkinson), of a "young inexperienced stranger . . . bellowing and braying like a wild asses colt" (Tench Coxe). The essays, which ran in the Independent Gazetteer and Freeman's Journal from November 7, 1787, to April 9, 1788, were widely reprinted in Pennsylvania. Their tone was mocked in Hopkinson's "New Roof" (see pages 667–68 and notes in this volume).

506.9   former paper] "Brutus" III and IV, pages 317 and 423 in this volume.

507.31–32   a bill . . . countries,] The bill, which became law in 1787, continued the original American Intercourse Act of 1783. Charles Jenkinson, later the Earl of Liverpool, was then president of the Board of Trade.

508.39   Encyclopedie article empire.] Diderot's L'Encyclopédie, Vol. V; see note 193.4.

510.24–26   nine States, . . . resolutions;] Article X of the Articles of Confederation.

513.23   Earl of Chesterfield] The 4th Earl of Chesterfield (Philip Dormer Stanhope) was British minister to the Netherlands, 1728–32.

513.26–31   in Sweden, . . . opposition,]   By the middle of the 18th century
Swedish politics was increasingly dominated by two rival parties, the expan-
sionist Hats, who were financially supported by France, and the more pacific
Caps, who were subsidized by Britain, Russia, and Denmark. The factions
contended for supremacy in the *Riksdag* (parliament), which was divided into
four estates, representing the nobles, clergy, burghers, and peasants. In February 1771, Gustavus III succeeded to the throne and won French support for
increasing the power of the Swedish monarchy. On June 25, 1771, Gustavus
addressed the *Riksdag* and appealed for reconciliation between the increasingly factious Hats and Caps, but the then-dominant Caps rejected his plea
and sought to further limit royal prerogative in the interest of pursuing a
pro-Russian policy. After first securing two key fortresses, Gustavus had his
guard officers arrest the council of state in Stockholm on August 19, 1772. The
Stockholm garrison and many of the townspeople supported the royal coup
d'etat, and on August 21 the *Riksdag* accepted a new constitution giving
the monarch power to appoint state officials. Gustavus then dissolved the
Riksdag, which did not reconvene until 1778. The transformation of Sweden
from a constitutional monarchy to an autocratic state was repeatedly used by
American writers as an example of the fragility of liberty and the potential for
a once-free people to become the abject subjects of a tyrant and to "kiss their
chains."

521.7–18   "In all . . . indispensible."]   See page 965.27–28 in this volume.

524.6   test . . . holy orders]   See note 7.19.

526.1–2   *Dissent . . . Convention*]   The publication of the views of 21 of
the 23 opponents of ratification in the Pennsylvania ratifying convention resolved an issue that went back to the first days of that meeting. During the
first sessions the Antifederalists, drawing on a provision of the Pennsylvania
constitution, moved that the convention journal include statements any member wished to submit explaining his vote on a divided issue. The Federalists,
who had little use for this provision in the state constitution and who feared
delays, unusual expense, and the stimulation of opposition in the population
at large, defeated the move. The opponents of ratification turned to the public press and published this statement of their arguments. The "Address and
Reasons," probably written by Samuel Bryan, author of the "Centinel" papers, appeared first in the *Pennsylvania Packet* six days after the convention
voted, and thereafter was reprinted in 13 newspapers in the North and South,
and circulated also in pamphlet, magazine, and broadside form. Federalists
feared the impact of this comprehensive statement of opposition, fought to
keep it from circulating in Massachusetts, where it might influence that state's
convention (to convene on January 9), and replied to it at length. Among the
many Federalist responses were Tench Coxe's eight "Philanthropos" essays,
"Americanus" VI (January 12), and Noah Webster's reply, page 553 in this
volume. The document undoubtedly stimulated the general desire for amendments and helped precipitate that issue in the critical form that faced the

Massachusetts convention in late January: whether to ratify and merely recommend subsequent amendments, or to make ratification contingent on the acceptance of prior amendments.

528.12–13   one . . . eighth member]   The one delegate from the Constitutionalist party was Jared Ingersoll; the eighth member, added on March 28, 1787, was Benjamin Franklin.

528.21–22   constitution . . . commonwealth.]   The 1776 Pennsylvania state constitution.

529.7–8   *tar and feathers*]   On September 28, 1787, the *Independent Gazetteer* carried an item in which an anonymous author warned an "anonymous scribbler, in the Freeman's Journal" who had criticized the Constitution that an "incensed people" might "honor him with a coat of TAR and FEATHERS" if he continued to "sow dissension among the weak, the credulous, and the ignorant." The same author signed himself "Tar and Feathers" in another item, October 2, in which he attacked the objections of "Fair Play" to the September 28 piece.

529.18–19   member of the house]   Philadelphia assemblyman George Clymer (1739–1813), a signer of the Declaration of Independence and merchant who had helped establish the Bank of North America in 1781; he would be elected to the U.S. House of Representatives in 1788.

535.35–536.17   "The extent . . . America."]   From James Wilson's convention speech of November 24, with italics added.

535.39   (as Montesquieu termed it)]   *The Spirit of the Laws*, Vol. I, Bk. VIII, ch. 20; see also I, VIII, chs. 16–19.

539.33   Spirit . . . vol. 1]   Bk. II, ch. 2.

544.35–545.5   *Blackstone . . . expence.*]   *Commentaries on the Laws of England*, Bk. III, ch. 24, p. 392n.

545.9–12   remarked . . . together.]   *Commentaries*, Bk. III, ch. 23, p. 381. The issue of jury trials in Sweden was referred to by others during the ratification debates.

546.33   late commercial treaty]   The Treaty of Navigation and Commerce, September 26, 1786, stated that its terms would be effective in Britain when legislation gave Britons "the Advantages which are granted to them by the present Treaty."

546.40–547.16   Montesquieu . . . individuals."]   *The Spirit of the Laws*, Vol. I, Bk. XI, ch. 6.

554.9   Hume on miracles]   *Enquiry concerning Human Understanding* (1748), especially Section 10—"Of Miracles." Hume's famous argument against the possibility of miracles, offensive to traditional Christians convinced of the literal truth of the Scriptures like Webster, assumed that natural laws underlie all natural phenomena and that what passed for miracles were only the manifestations of laws as yet not discovered.

554.10   *gratis dicta*]   Gratuitous assertions.

560.37–561.12   that party . . . reasonable men]   The references are to a series of episodes in Pennsylvania's history traceable in part to the Constitutionalist party: the breaking of windows of those who failed to illuminate them on days of military victory and other important celebrations; the Constitutionalist-controlled Assembly's revocation, in 1785, of the charter granted by the state in 1782 to the Republican-controlled Bank of North America; and the Assembly's confiscation of the College of Philadelphia's charter and the transformation of the College into a state university. See also note 566.11.

562.28–29   Review . . . 24.]   Richard Jackson, *An Historical Review of the Constitution and Government of Pennsylvania* (London 1759), regarding the dismissal in 1688 of the Provincial Council, on grounds of "Animosities and Dissentions" among its members, by the deputy governor of Pennsylvania acting for proprietor William Penn.

563.19–21   Venice . . . aristocracy.]   See note 76.19.

566.9   THREE]   William Findley, John Smilie, and Robert Whitehill.

566.11   *test-law*]   In September 1776 the convention that adopted the Pennsylvania state constitution declared that all voters in the forthcoming election would have to take an oath to uphold the new constitution. The oath was protested by opponents of the constitution, who believed it was designed to prevent those seeking amendments from voting, and by Quakers, who held religious scruples against swearing oaths. In June 1777 the Pennsylvania assembly passed a test law requiring all white male inhabitants of the state to abjure loyalty to George III, pledge allegiance to Pennsylvania as a sovereign state, and promise to expose all disloyal conspiracies. Those failing to take the oath were forbidden to vote, hold office, serve as jurors, sue for collection of debts, sell or transfer land, and were liable to be disarmed. The oath was widely resisted by Quakers, Mennonites, Moravians, and other pacifist sects who believed it would oblige them to fight in defense of the state, as well as by those who did not want to abjure allegiance to the crown. In the fall of 1777 several Quakers who had been arrested on suspicion of disloyalty were exiled to Virginia after refusing to take the oath (they were permitted to return nearly a year later). In 1778 the assembly passed two additional test laws: the first prohibited men in trades or professions who failed to take the oath from practicing, and the second barred anyone who failed to produce a certificate proving that he had taken the oath by June 1, 1778, from voting. (Disputes over whether voters had taken the oath, or whether the disqualification was being enforced, continually recurred in Pennsylvania elections.) In September 1784 the Republicans (opponents of the 1776 constitution) introduced a bill in the legislature to revise the test laws, but its passage was blocked when a minority of 19 Constitutionalists left the assembly chamber and prevented a quorum. An act was passed in March 1786, allowing all those previously disqualified to regain full citizenship by taking a new oath abjuring allegiance to the king, swearing allegiance to the state, and testifying that they had not voluntarily aided British forces after July 1776. The requirement to abjure royal allegiance was abolished in March 1787 and in March 1789 the oath of allegiance to the state, which was still protested by Quakers and Mennonites, was repealed.

567.12   Centinel, No. XI] Appeared on January 16 in the Philadelphia papers *Independent Gazette* and *Freeman's Journal*.

571.31–32   "the common . . . welfare."] See Articles of Confederation, Article VIII.

576.27–39   State Constitutions . . . collection;] Probably *The Constitutions of the Several Independent States of America*, ed. Francis Bailey (Philadelphia, 1781, reprinted in Boston, 1785, New York, 1786). It did not include Virginia's declaration of rights, which stated that standing armies in peacetime "should be avoided, as dangerous to liberty."

581.4   *"Philadelphiensis" . . . V*] For Francis Hopkinson's use of "Philadelphiensis" in "New Roof," see pages 667.9–668.27 and notes in this volume.

581.6–10   "This . . . this?"] The verses, from Euripides, were translated by Milton and printed on the title page of *Areopagitica; a speech of Mr. John Milton for the liberty of the unlicenc'd printing, to the Parliament of England* (1644).

581.32–34   petitions . . . Cumberland county] Robert Whitehill had presented petitions from the county declaring that the Constitution not be adopted without a bill of rights (see page 871.4–17 in this volume).

582.6   M'Kean] Thomas McKean (1734–1817), a signer of the Declaration of Independence, was Pennsylvania's chief justice and an active Federalist in the state's ratifying convention.

583.24–28   "He hath . . . away."] Luke 1:51–53.

586.3   *Joseph . . . Barrell*] The attitudes of the Barrell brothers to the Constitution and to ratification were typical of those of many Americans. Nathaniel Barrell initially opposed the Constitution, but then, as he explained in his speech in the Massachusetts ratifying convention (page 938 in this volume) he changed his opinion. These documents reflect the diverse initial reception and then the growing approval of the Constitution, which would culminate within a few years in admiration bordering on reverence.

586.10–11   delegate . . . York] On December 3, Nathaniel Barrell had been elected delegate from York to the Massachusetts convention.

587.16–19   "*Vox Populi*,". . . Holmes]   The essays of "*Vox Populi*" appeared in the *Massachusetts Gazette* on October 30 and November 6, 13, 16, and 23. Abraham Holmes (1754–1839), the state representative to whom Barrell attributes them, would vote against ratification in the Massachusetts convention.

587.25–26   Agrippa & John deWit,]   A series of five Antifederalist papers by "John De Witt" appeared in the *Boston American Herald* October 22, 29, November 5, 19, and December 3, 1787. For "Agrippa," see note 443.3.

588.23   first American . . . Ocean,]   In September 1787 Joseph Barrell and five other Massachusetts merchants, hoping to open a fur trade with China, sent the *Columbia Rediviva* and *Lady Washington* under captains John Kendrick (c. 1740–94) and Robert Gray (1755–1806) to the Pacific Northwest. The ships rounded Cape Horn and reached Vancouver Island in 1788. On July 30, 1789, the *Columbia*, commanded by Gray, set sail for China carrying sea-otter furs; it returned to Boston August 10, 1790, becoming the first ship carrying an American flag to sail around the world.

589.6   Hon. Ab^mBaldwin]   Abraham Baldwin (1754–1807), delegate from Georgia to Congress and a signer of the Constitution, had graduated from Yale and been a tutor there and served as a chaplain in the Continental Army. He moved to Georgia after being admitted to the bar in Connecticut in 1783.

589.18   We conversed . . . Constitution]   In a December 21, 1787, diary entry, Stiles describes the "Accot of the whole Progress in Convention" that Baldwin had given him.

592.8   And that / they will be less]   In the M'Lean edition of *The Federalist* (1788) "on account of the extent of the country from which those, to whose direction they will be committed, will be drawn" was inserted.

593.30–34   It has been shewn]   In Hamilton's *The Federalist XV* and *XVI* (page 451 in this volume).

595.3–4   *Governor . . . Constitution*]   Virginia's Governor Edmund Randolph, when he refused to sign the Constitution, explained that in due time he would make his objections public, and that he was undecided whether or not in the end he would favor ratification. The fact that so prominent a figure, known to favor a stronger government, had refused to sign buoyed the hopes of the Antifederalists, but the Federalists, through correspondence and discussions with Randolph, had reason to hope that he would decide in favor of the Constitution. He was pressed on both sides to explain himself, and, after much delay, he did, in response to a formal request by four Antifederalist members of the state's house of delegates. He allowed them to make public a letter of explanation he had addressed to the speaker of the house of delegates but had never sent. That letter, preceded by the brief correspondence with the four delegates, was published as a 16-page pamphlet on December 27 that was frequently reprinted in full or in part in newspapers throughout the states.

595.17–18   *M. SMITH . . . PAGE, jun.*]   Members of the house of delegates: John Howell Briggs of Sussex County, Charles Mynn Thruston (1738–1812) of Frederick County, and Mann Page, Jr. (c. 1749–1803), of Spotsylvania and Gloucester counties. For Meriwether Smith, see note 480.12.

598.19   the second article]   Of the Articles of Confederation

599.20–23   The first . . . thereon.]   Articles of Confederation, VIII.

599.25–27   twelve states . . . furnished.]   The amendment to the Articles of Confederation proposed to Congress in April 1783 by 1787 had been ratified by every state except Rhode Island and New Hampshire.

613.32   last number]   Page 499 in this volume.

617.1   excise on cider]   Parliament's adoption of an excise tax on cider in 1763 was followed by rioting and was a cause of the resignation of prime minister John Stuart, 3d Earl of Bute.

617.38–39   "no . . . masters,"]   Matthew 6:24.

618.39–40   an examination . . . constitution]   Noah Webster's pamphlet, page 129 in this volume.

631.4   *Luther . . . Information"*]   Luther Martin's account of the Constitutional Convention, which was titled *"Mr. Martin's Information to the House of Assembly"* when it appeared serially in the *Maryland Gazette*, was an extension of a speech he delivered on November 29 in response to the Maryland House of Delegates' request that the state's delegates to Philadelphia provide "information of the proceedings" of the convention. With additional essays and letters, it was printed as a 93-page pamphlet titled *The Genuine Information, Delivered to the Legislature of the State of Maryland* in April 1788. Martin's essays created a storm of controversy. Antifederalists praised Martin for having "laid open the conclave, exposed the dark scene within . . . and illustrated the machinations of ambition," and they defended him against "the rage of the conspirators" now determined, they said, to destroy him. ("Centinel" XIV, *Philadelphia Independent Gazetteer*, February 5, 1788.) Some Federalists vilified him personally and described his essay as a tissue of misunderstanding, misinterpretation, and outright lies. But other Federalists were not alarmed by Martin's "*imaginary* treasons and *unexecuted* plots" (*Maryland Gazette*). Martin, Madison said, was a "noisy" adversary but not a "formidable" one. Washington's secretary, Tobias Lear, in a letter to John Langdon, April 3, 1788, said Martin's character was "so infamous that anything advanced by him . . . would bias the people in favor of it." As they predicted, Martin's "Genuine Information" did little to impede ratification. Maryland's convention voted approval 63–11, on April 26, 1788, after only five days of discussion. Martin's polemics continued, but ultimately he became reconciled to the Constitution, and, in part because of his intense hatred of Jefferson, ended a "bulldog of federalism." The five segments presented here appear together because they are clearly part of a single composition divided up for publication, and because they bear no particular relation to the events of the time of their publication.

632.1–4　　　Randolph . . . colleague] The Virginia Resolutions (also known as the Virginia Plan), presented May 29, 1787, were read to the Maryland House of Delegates by James McHenry on November 29.

638.4–5　　　president . . . Pennsylvania.] Benjamin Franklin.

638.30–639.1　　the propositions . . . propositions*] The New Jersey, or Paterson, Plan was submitted to the convention on June 15. Martin did not include them in the newspaper series or the pamphlet, but they were printed in the *Maryland Gazette* on February 15, 1788, three days after his last installment appeared, and reprinted in the Philadelphia *Independent Gazetteer* (February 23) and in *The American Museum* magazine in April.

639.4–5　　New-Hampshire . . . arrived] Delegates John Langdon and Nicholas Gilman arrived on July 23.

639.8　　two delegates] Martin and Daniel of St. Thomas Jenifer.

641.27　　those reported by the committee] The amended version of the Virginia Resolutions approved by the committee of the whole on June 13, 1787. On June 19 the convention voted to consider them, not the New Jersey Resolutions, as the basis for the new plan of government.

647.3　　*common rights of men*] The slave trade was prohibited by the First Continental Congress in October 1774 and by the Second in April 1776.

647.36　　my negative . . . clause.] The Maryland delegation voted for the clause, which was adopted on August 28, 1787.

657.18–19　　moved to strike . . . motion;] Gouverneur Morris and Charles Pinckney made the motion, and it was adopted 8–3 on August 31, with Maryland in the minority.

662.3　　"*The New Roof*"] Published first in Pennsylvania, "The New Roof" was reprinted in newspapers from Vermont to South Carolina; in Maryland some readers of that state's *Gazette* found it a relief from Luther Martin's "Genuine Information" then running serially. Several of the reprints included explanatory notes; they are noted below, taken from the sources in which they first appeared.

662.5–6　　The roof . . . condition,] "The old Confederation" (footnote in Hopkinson's *Miscellaneous Essays and Occasional Writings*, posthumously published, 1792, Vol. II).

662.19　　whole . . . weak.] "No coercive power in the confederation" (*Federal Gazette*, Philadelphia, January 1, 1789).

662.20   13 rafters]   "Separate sovereignities" (*Federal Gazette*).

662.23–24   some . . . slight,]   "The states bearing unequal proportions of the public burthens, yet all equally represented in Congress, and having equal votes in forwarding or retarding public measures" (*Federal Gazette*).

662.29   wooden pegs]   "Paper Currency" (*Miscellaneous Essays and Occasional Writings*).

662.29–30   shrinking . . . weather,]   "Miserable state of finance, and the fluctuating value of paper money" (*Federal Gazette*).

662.34   cornice . . . proportioned,]   "Our situation, *as a nation*, neither respectable nor efficient." (*Federal Gazette*).

662.36–663.2   the roof . . . abuse it.]   "The federal government became contemptible" (*Federal Gazette*); "Want of dignity in government" (*Miscellaneous Essays and Occasional Writings*).

663.21   certain day . . . assembled]   "Meeting of the citizens of Philadelphia, at the state house, October 6, 1787" (*The American Museum*, August 1788); see page 63 and note in this volume.

663.23   James]   "J***s W*l**n, Esq" (New York *Daily Advertiser*, January 9, 1788).

663.29–20   Margery]   "George Bryan, the 4th Judge" (*Independent Gazetteer*, Philadelphia, January 4, 1788); to which the August *American Museum* added: "the reputed author of the pieces signed 'CENTINEL'" (see notes 52.3, 414.30–31). When the *Independent Gazetteer* printed "The New Roof," "Margery" was changed to "Margery, the midwife, . . ." On January 23, the paper printed a response from "An Old Woman" who wrote that she was "highly insulted by your endeavouring to make the world believe that a creature whose character is too contemptible to be considered as *a man*, must of course be regarded as *a woman*," and another from "Deborah Woodcock" who identified herself as a midwife and wrote that she was "exceedingly hurt" by the linking of "Margery" to her highly respected occupation. On January 26, the newspaper ran a letter from "Amicus" that accused Hopkinson of having written both pieces in an effort to call attention to his original essay.

664.9   William . . . Robert,]   "William Findley, John Smilie and Robert Whitehill" (*Independent Gazetteer*); to which *The American Museum* added "three members of the convention of the state of Pennsylvania, appointed to examine and decide upon the new constitution."

664.16   bill of scantling]   "Bill of Rights" (*Vermont Gazette*, Bennington, January 28, 1788).

664.20–24   no . . . destruction]   "No provision being made to secure the Liberty of the Press" (*Vermont Gazette*).

664.20–21   trap door]   "Liberty of the Press" (*Miscellaneous Essays and Occasional Writings*).

664.25   battlements]   "The standing army" (*Vermont Gazette*).

664.30   12 pedestals]   "Trial by jury" (*Federal Gazette*).

664.30–31   12 . . . admiration;]   "Juries" (*Vermont Gazette*).

664.33   a cupola]   "The presidentship of the United States" (*Federal Gazette*).

664.39–665.2   13 . . . whole]   "That the separate sovereignties of the states would be absorbed by the general union" (*Federal Gazette*).

665.8–11   whole . . . under it.]   "That it would be a consolidated government, and might exist independent of the people or the states" (*Miscellaneous Essays and Occasional Writings*; a similar footnote was first made in the *Federal Gazette*).

667.9–668.27   It was mentioned . . . Oh!"—]   Hopkinson struck out the final three paragraphs when "The New Roof" was published in the *Federal Gazette*. Benjamin Rush thought this "a judicious and laudable omission," since "the force and beauty of the allegory were diminished, by a conclusion which was beneath the dignity" of the work. The last three paragraphs, which parody Benjamin Workman's exaggerated style in his "Philadelphiensis" essays, Rush wrote, "had no immediate connection" with the rest of the piece. But when Hopkinson prepared "The New Roof" for inclusion in his *Miscellaneous Essays* the parody of Workman was restored.

667.11–13   a half . . . lunatic.]   "A furious writer under the signature of *Philadelphiensis*" (*Miscellaneous Essays and Occasional Writings*). The "half crazy fellow" was noted as "Philadelphiensis" in the *Independent Gazetteer*.

667.27   "The new Roof!]   "This fustian is a burlesque of a paper published under the signature of PHILADELPHIENSIS; the original is subjoined, taken from the Independent Gazetteer of Dec. 19, 1787. I had it in my power afterwards to detect and expose the real name of the author of these inflamatory publications, which put a stop to the productions of PHILADELPHIENSIS. He was an Irish schoolmaster, who had not been more than two years in the country, and who, without either property or reputation in America, endeavoured, under the cover of a fictitious signature, not only to enflame the people against the plan of government proposed by America's best patriot's and most able statesmen; but even ventured to abuse and vilify such characters as GENERAL WASHINGTON, Dr. Franklin, and the gentlemen who composed the general convention, calling them in the public papers, *villains* and *conspirators*" (*Miscellaneous Essays and Occasional Writings*). For "Philadelphiensis" V, see page 581 in this volume. Hopkinson, writing under the pseudonym A.B., had identified "Philadelphiensis" as "BENJAMIN WORKMAN, one of the *well-born tutors in the University of Pennsylvania*" in the *Independent Gazetteer*, March 11, 1788, three days after "Philadelphiensis" XI appeared; his letter ignited a furious newspaper debate among them and their supporters.

669.2   *"Giles Hickory"*]   Noah Webster wrote four "Giles Hickory" papers for his *American Magazine* attacking common principles of Revolutionary thought that might constitute limitations on the will of the people. He was aware that some of these arguments contradicted in part the views he had expressed earlier in his *Sketches of American Policy* (1785).

669.19–24   *Magna Charta . . . deed.*]   Webster refers to the view, first asserted by the 17th-century royalists to undermine the House of Commons' claim to being immemorial, hence anterior to kingship, that there was no record of a Commons until the 49th year of the reign of Henry III (1265).

670.5   statute . . . Mary]   The Habeas Corpus Act (1679), passed to prevent imprisonment without proper legal authority, detailed the methods of obtaining a writ of habeas corpus and imposed penalties on government officers who did not comply with writs that had been issued. The Bill of Rights (1689) provided that unreasonable bail ought not be required.

677.38–39   *Discern . . . eyes.*]   Cf. Luke 19:42.

678.3   *Federalist XXXII – XXXIII*]   Numbered XXXI when it appeared in the *Independent Journal*, this essay was divided into two essays on the advice of Alexander Hamilton, numbered XXXII and XXXIII, when *The Federalist Papers* were collected in the M'Lean edition (2 vols., March–May, 1788). In that first collected edition, essay XXXV became essay XXIX (Hamilton placing it by topic rather than date), requiring a change in the numbering of the subsequent essays. This volume uses the numbering of the M'Lean edition, which has become standard.

681.38   The last clause]   In the M'Lean edition, essay XXXIII starts here, introduced by an added sentence: "The residue of the argument against the provisions in the Constitution, in respect to taxation, is ingrafted upon the following clauses."

689.39–40   him . . . bank]   Robert Morris was a founder of the Bank of North America in 1781 (see also note 284.30). In 1782 he had the bank chartered in Pennsylvania, but in September 1785 the charter was revoked by the Pennsylvania Assembly. Morris was often accused by his enemies of using public office for private gain.

690.11   *great man*]   James Wilson had defended the Bank of North America.

697.4–6   moved . . . house,]   In a plan proposed to Congress, March 20, 1783, by Alexander Hamilton and James Wilson; it was rejected 7–4.

698.4   *The Federalist XXXIV*]   Originally, No. XXXII; see note 678.3.

700.20   naval wars / must baffle]   In the *New York Independent Journal* (January 5), the *New York Journal* (January 8), and the M'Lean edition, "would involve contingencies that" was inserted.

700.20–21   arithmetic, admitting]   In the printings noted above, "arithmetic" ended the sentence and "Admitting . . ." began a new paragraph.

703.18–21   "A CONCURRENT . . . Union."]   Hamilton is quoting from his previous paper, page 685.37–40 in this volume.

704.5–6   Enclosure . . . Brother.]   See note 446.5–7.

704.28–29   Mr. Wilsons . . . reserved."]   From his October 6 speech, page 64.10–11 in this volume.

708.35–37   Philadelphians . . . offer]   The Pennsylvania convention had voted on December 15, 1787, to cede to the new Congress under the Constitution a tract of land not to exceed ten miles square.

710.34–35   *unanimous . . . gentlemen*]   See note 5.1–3.

717.2   *Resolutions of the Tradesmen*]   It was clear from the beginning that the support of such economic interest groups as the urban artisans might be crucial to the adoption of the Constitution, and the Boston tradesmen, with their tradition of political activism, were particular targets of concern. Federalists and Antifederalists bombarded the Boston tradesmen with arguments in broadsides, handbills, and newspaper squibs, emphasizing the dangers or benefits of the Constitution to the future of the town's economy and its workers' welfare. The controversy came to center on the election of delegates to the state ratifying convention, which was to meet on January 9. At a caucus of the town's delegates on January 3, Samuel Adams, whose role was to be crucial and whose doubts about the Constitution had been expressed privately earlier (see Adams to Lee, page 446 and note 446.3), publicly declared himself opposed to ratification, and the word spread that the town's tradesmen in general were opposed. To counter that rumor, an open meeting of tradesmen was convened on January 7 and attended by about 380 people. Their resolutions, in full or in part, were reprinted widely in the northern and middle states. Federalists were delighted, hoping that the Boston tradesmen had set an example that would be followed elsewhere. (Their action was, in fact, followed by similar groups in other towns.) There is no evidence of how the tradesmen's resolutions influenced Samuel Adams; his only son was very ill at this time and died on January 17. He fell silent, and when at the climactic moment of the Massachusetts convention, on January 31, he finally declared his position, it was to support ratification with recommended amendments, a move that probably made ratification possible.

717.8   Mason's-hall, Green Dragon,]   The Green Dragon Tavern, bought by St. Andrew's Lodge of Freemasons before the American Revolution, had been a center of Revolutionary activity (Paul Revere and John Hancock, among other leaders of the Revolution, were lodge members).

717.8–9 Lucas . . . Russell] Lucas was Massachusetts commissary of pensioners, Revere a goldsmith, and Russell was the printer of the *Massachusetts Centinel*.

718.31–33 Clark . . . Spear] Clark was a shipwright, Jacob Rhodes a shipbuilder, Bordman a hatter, Witherle a coppersmith, and Spear was a cooper.

720.3 *XXXVI*] Originally, No. XXXIV.

726.30 defence and security.] In the M'Lean edition, a final paragraph was added: "I have now gone through the examination of those powers proposed to be conferred upon the federal government; which relate more peculiarly to its energy, and to its efficiency for answering the great and primary objects of union. There are others, which though omitted here, will in order to render the view of the subject more complete, be taken notice of under the next head of our enquiries. I flatter myself the progress already made will have sufficed to satisfy the candid and judicious part of the community, that some of the objections which have been most strenuously urged against the Constitution, and which were most formidable in their first appearance, are not only destitute of substance, but if they had operated in the formation of the plan, would have rendered it incompetent to the great ends of public happiness and national prosperity. I equally flatter myself that a further and more critical investigation of the system will serve to recommend it still more to every sincere and disinterested advocate for good government; and will leave no doubt with men of this character of the propriety and expediency of adopting it. Happy will it be for ourselves, and most honorable for human nature, if we have wisdom and virtue enough, to set so glorious an example to mankind!"

728.20–22 Congress . . . Wilson;] See page 64.4–7 in this volume.

729.30 the small pox] After being inoculated against small pox, Thatcher had suffered from a form of the disease, but had fully recovered around the end of December.

729.36 Debates . . . Convention] Wait had published some of the convention debates in his Portland *Cumberland Gazette* on December 20 and 27, 1787.

730.1–4 Crazy . . . 120—] "Crazy Jonathan," IV (*Cumberland Gazette*, October 4, 1787), inveighed against the Massachusetts law that he said allowed justices to assess damages "in 110 causes out of 120." (Wait's paper printed nine "Crazy Jonathan" essays from September 13 to November 15, 1787.)

730.20 Tempy] Temperance Hedge, Thatcher's niece.

730.29   Jeremiah Hill,]   Hill (1747–1820) was a Biddeford merchant, local official, and representative in the Massachusetts state legislature.

730.32   Silas]   Silas Lee (1760–1814), a graduate of Harvard, was a law student of Thatcher's and Temperance Hedge's future husband.

731.5   Thompson . . . Widgery]   Samuel Thompson, a militia general, and William Widgery, a lawyer, were both state representatives.

734.20   Mr. Pultney's speech]   Delivered in the House of Commons in 1732 and frequently reprinted. William Pulteney (1684–1764) was a leader of the Whig opposition to Sir Robert Walpole (1676–1745), first lord of the treasury and chancellor of the exchequer, 1721–42, and an ally of the former Tory leader Viscount Bolingbroke (1678–1751). Pulteney and Bolingbroke were both frequent contributors to *The Craftsman*, an anti-ministry journal founded in 1726 that attacked Walpole for his plan to fund the national debt and for using "corruption" and "influence," in the form of royal appointments and patronage, to maintain parliamentary support for his ministry. Pulteney was made Earl of Bath following the fall of the Walpole government in 1742, but played little role in politics after 1743.

735.9–14   braver army . . . country.]   In a series of campaigns fought 58–50 B.C., the Roman army under Julius Caesar conquered most of Gaul, drove the Germanic tribes back to the Rhine, and raided Britain. Caesar hoped to become consul for 48 B.C., but when the senate, which favored his rival Pompey, ordered him to surrender his military command before becoming consul, he refused, fearing that as a private citizen he would be vulnerable to political attack. In January 49 B.C. he led his army across the Rubicon, a small river dividing Italy from Cisalpine Gaul, defying the senate and precipitating a civil war. In 46 B.C. Caesar was made dictator for ten years, and in January 44 B.C., dictator for life; he was assassinated on March 15, 44 B.C.

735.32–33   English house . . . army]   At the outbreak of the English Civil War in 1642 parliament raised an army to fight Charles I. Reorganized as the New Model Army in 1645 under the leadership of Thomas Fairfax and Oliver Cromwell, by 1648 the parliamentary army had come increasingly under the influence of religious Independents, hostile to the Presbyterian party in parliament, and had also abandoned hope of a reconciliation with the king. Acting under the orders of the army council, Colonel Thomas Pride led troops into the House of Commons on December 6, 1648, and arrested or excluded about 140 Presbyterian members. The remaining members, who became known as the Rump parliament, then agreed under army pressure to establish a court to try the king for treason. Following the execution of Charles I on January 30, 1649, England was proclaimed a commonwealth, governed by parliament through a council of state. Tensions between the army and parliament persisted, and on April 20, 1653, Cromwell, now commander-in-chief of the army, led soldiers into the House of Commons and forcibly dissolved the Rump parliament after accusing it of corruption. A Nominated (also known as "Barebones") parliament was then created and dissolved by the army, and on December 16, 1653, Cromwell became Lord Protector of the Commonwealth for life. Before his death in 1658 Cromwell used his constitutional power as Lord Protector to dissolve two parliaments elected under the commonwealth. In 1660 a new parliament reached an agreement with Charles II under which the monarchy was restored. See also note 897.35.

737.6–9   "*Here . . .* CÆSAR.]   Shakespeare, from Mark Antony's speech at Caesar's funeral (III.ii.81–84) in which Antony undermines Brutus's presumed patriotism in murdering Caesar; italics and small capitalization added.

737.15–18   Brutus . . . third number]   "Brutus" III (page 317 in this volume) had been reprinted in the Boston *Independent Chronicle* on December 13.

738.14–15   The   mode . . . confederation]   Articles   of   Confederation, VIII.

738.35–739.1   "Representatives . . . persons."]   Art. I, sec. 2. "Mark Antony" is the first known explicit Federalist defense of the three-fifths clause in the public commentaries; *The Federalist* turned to the issue a month later (no. LIV).

742.5–13   *Montesquieu, . . .* State"—]   *The Spirit of the Laws*, Vol. I, Bk. XV, ch. 17.

744.13   letter to the Assembly]   See page 596 in this volume.

745.37   R. H. L.]   Richard Henry Lee.

746.38–747.1   Col. H. Lee . . . Mississippi,]   In his December 27 letter, Randolph had written that James Wilkinson, a leader in the district of Kentucky, would presumably sway the region to vote against the Constitution in the Virginia ratifying convention. Wilkinson, he wrote, was "rivetted by Colo. Harry Lee, declaring to him, that the surrender of the Mississippi would probably be among the early acts of the new congress." (For Jay's negotiations with the Spanish for rights to the Mississippi, see Chronology, July–August 1785 and August 1786.) Wilkinson (1757–1825), a leader of the region of Kentucky, through deception and political manipulation just short of treachery, had in 1787 obtained an exclusive trading monopoly for New Orleans markets from the Spanish.

754.2   *The Federalist XXXVII*]   Originally, No. XXXVI; see note 678.3.

760.5   a former paper]   *The Federalist X*, page 404 in this volume.

760.23–24   a former paper]   *The Federalist XX*, December 11, 1787.

762.3–5   XII . . . CONVENTION]   "Agrippa" XII was apparently written as one essay and then because of its length published in three installments. It was the first of a sub-series of five essays all addressed, unlike his earlier essays, to the Massachusetts convention (nos. XIII to XVI would run in the

Gazette from January 22 to February 5.) See also page 443 and note 443.3 in this volume.

774.21–22 prepared by Tullus Hostilius,] This reference to Tullus Hostilius was corrected to Servius Tullius in the M'Lean edition of *The Federalist*. Servius Tullius, sixth of the legendary kings of Rome (6th cent. B.C.), is referred to by Montesquieu as a liberal constitutional reformer. Tullus Hostilius (7th cent. B.C.), was believed to have been a warrior king. (Both are thought to be actual historical figures.) The first reference to Tullus Hostilius (774.18) was not changed in the M'Lean edition.

774.19–20 Consular . . . Brutus] According to legend, Lucius Junius Brutus (6th cent. B.C.), traditional founder of the Roman Republic, ousted the Tarquins and vested the power previously held by kings in consuls chosen from patrician families.

774.12–13 Minos . . . Zaleucus] According to legend, Minos, king of Crete, gave laws to his subjects around 1406 B.C. He was called throughout Greece "the favorite of the gods" and "the wise legislator." Zaleucus (c. 650 B.C.), lawgiver of the Greek colony of Locri in southwest Italy, was said to have first codified the Greek laws and was known as a severe yet humane legislator.

774.24–25 Amphyction . . . Achæus] See note 196.23–29. According to legend, the Achaeans were descendants of Achaeus, originally of Thessaly, who fled to Peloponnesus after accidentally killing a man.

774.33–34 according to Plutarch] In his *Lives*, Solon (c. 630–560 B.C.), returning from his travels to find Athens rent by dissension, was unanimously elected archon and sovereign legislator and instituted wise reforms in every department of the state, including laws that were fair to the poor.

775.6 deliberative . . . citizens.] According to early writers, Lycurgius (9th cent. B.C.), traditional founder of the constitution and social and military systems of Sparta, consulted the Oracle of Delphi before attempting to institute reforms in the disordered state. The approval of the oracle engendered wide popular support for all his reforms.

776.11 New-Jersey] In June 1778 the New Jersey legislature recommended an amendment to the Articles of Confederation consigning the regulation of foreign trade to the federal government (having no major ports of its own, the state was subject to New York and Pennsylvania laws and imposts). The proposal was rejected by the Continental Congress, 6–3.

776.20–21 One state . . . concurrence,] The Articles were adopted by Congress on November 15, 1777; Maryland did not ratify them until March 1, 1781.

781.28 Congress . . . stock.] For the Northwest Ordinance, see Chronology, July 13, 1787.

783.19–20   dissenting . . . Pennsylvania]   "Dissent of the Minority of the Pennsylvania Convention," page 526 in this volume.

784.21–31   Cato's . . . species."]   "Cato" III, page 217.40–218.9 in this volume.

785.16–18   Montesquieu . . . territory."]   Vol. I, Book VIII, ch. 16.

785.28–30   "Democratic . . . man."]   *The Spirit of the Laws*, Vol. I, Bk. XI, ch. 4 and ch. 8.

786.11–12   "it is . . . *laws*.]   Vol. I, Bk. II, ch. 2.

788.5   Revolution in England]   See note 387.35.

DEBATES IN THE STATE RATIFYING CONVENTIONS

791.1   PENNSYLVANIA RATIFYING CONVENTION]   Pennsylvania's ratifying convention was the first to convene, and the proceedings were tumultuous from the start. The great struggle that had convulsed the state since the adoption of the state constitution of 1776 and that had divided the political population into antagonistic parties spilled over into the ratification controversy. The so-called Constitutionalists, committed to the autonomy and supremacy of a popularly elected state legislature free of executive or judicial restraints, feared the imposition of an exterior authority whose laws, treaties, and judicial decisions would be supreme. The anti-Constitutionalists, or Republicans, fearful of the continuation of a legislative supremacy that could destroy economic stability, the sanctity of contract, and minority rights and security, viewed the federal Constitution as a blessing that would rescue the state, and the nation, from demagoguery and ruin. The lines between the Constitutionalist-Antifederalist minority, whose convention delegates were drawn largely from the western counties, and the Federalist majority, led by the eastern social and economic establishment, were tightly drawn.

791.3–4   *Opening . . . November 24, 1787*]   November 24 was the first day of actual discussion in the convention. Wilson's speech was summarized in the local newspapers on November 28, the same day a fuller version, prepared from the notes of Alexander J. Dallas, was published in a pamphlet; the pamphlet is printed here. Like the newspaper summaries, the pamphlet was reprinted and circulated widely throughout the states and within a month 19 newspapers in eight states outside of Pennsylvania had reprinted one or another version of the speech. The Federalists heaped praise on Wilson's learning, elegance, and reasoning ("The Powers of Demosthenes & Cicero seem'd to be united in this able Orator"—Francis Hopkinson to Thomas Jefferson, December 14, 1787), while the Antifederalists claimed Wilson had tried to establish principles by "mazes of sophistry" that existed "only in his own fertile imagination" ("Centinel" V). Thomas Lloyd, who had objected to the accuracy of the Dallas version, published his own version of Wilson's speech in his *Debates of the Convention of the State of Pennsylvania, on the Constitution,*

Proposed for the Government of the United States. The Speeches of Thomas M'Kean & James Wilson, Esquires; In Which They Have Unfolded the Principles . . . of the Constitution (February 7, 1788).

793.14   (as Montesquieu has termed it)]   See note 535.39.

793.29   Montesquieu . . . members;]   *The Spirit of the Laws*, Vol. I, Bk. IX, ch. 1.

794.7–8   Germanic Body,]   The Holy Roman Empire. In *The Federalist XIX* (December 8) Madison (assisted by Hamilton) had commented at length on the chaotic structure of the German empire, which he called, politically, "a monster" : "The fundamental principle, on which it rests, that the empire is a community of sovereigns; that the Diet is a representation of sovereigns; and that the laws are addressed to sovereigns; render the empire a nerveless body, incapable of regulating its own members; insecure against external dangers; and agitated with unceasing fermentations in its own bowels." He documented "the impossibility of maintaining order, and dispensing justice among these sovereign subjects" of the empire with reference to French and German historians.

794.14–15   Achæan . . . Amphyctionic]   See note 196.23–29.

795.22–25   revolution . . . people]   In 1689 parliament offered William and Mary the throne on the condition that they acknowledge the rights and liberties later included in the Bill of Rights (see note 387.35). In his *Commentaries*, Bk. I, ch. 6, Blackstone wrote that the Revolution of 1688 made clear the existence of a longstanding, unwritten "original contract" between the king and the people, under which the king pledged to govern his people according to law in return for their allegiance. Blackstone added that the terms of the contract were further specified by a 1689 act establishing new coronation oaths, which made it the duty of the king to govern by the statutes of parliament and the common law, to "execute judgment in mercy," and to maintain the established Protestant religion.

797.10–24   Our wants, . . . nature.]   In February 1788, Jefferson, Thomas Paine, and Lafayette met privately in Paris in what Lafayette called a small ratifying convention of their own. After Paine returned to England he wrote Jefferson a letter in response to Wilson's speech:

"After I got home, being alone and wanting amusement I sat down to explain to myself (for there is such a thing) my Ideas of natural and civil rights and the distinction between them. I send them to you to see how nearly we agree.

"Suppose 20 persons, strangers to each other, to meet in a Country not before inhabited. Each would be a sovereign in his own natural right. His will would be his Law, but his power, in many cases, inadequate to his right, and the consequence would be that each might be exposed, not only to each other, but to the other nineteen.

"It would then occur to them that their condition would be much improved, if a way could be devised to exchange that quantity of danger into so much protection, so that each individual should possess the strength of the whole number.

"As all their rights, in the first case, are natural rights, and the exercise of those rights supported only by their own natural individual power, they would begin by distinguishing between these rights they could individually exercise fully and perfectly and those they could not.

"Of the first kind are the rights of thinking, speaking, forming and giving opinions, and perhaps all those which can be fully exercised by the individual without the aid of exterior assistance, or in other words, rights of personal competency. Of the second kind are those of personal protection of acquiring and possessing property, in the exercise of which the individual natural power is less than the natural right.

"Having drawn this line they agree to retain individually the first Class of Rights or those of personal Competency; and to detach from their personal possession the second Class, or those of defective power and to accept in lieu thereof a right to the whole power produced by a condensation of all the parts. These I conceive to be civil rights or rights of Compact, and are distinguishable from Natural rights, because in the one we act wholly in our own person, in the other we agree not to do so, but act under the guarantee of society.

"It therefore follows that the more of those imperfect natural rights, or rights of imperfect power we give up and thus exchange the more security we possess, and as the word liberty is often mistakenly put for security Mr. Wilson has confused his Argument by confounding the terms.

"But it does not follow that the more natural rights of *every kind* we resign the more security we possess, because if we resign those of the first class we may suffer much by the exchange, for where the right and the power are equal with each other in the individual naturally they ought to rest there.

"Mr. Wilson must have some allusion to this distinction or his position would be subject to the inference you draw from it.

"I consider the individual sovereignty of the states retained under the Act of Confederation to be of the second class of rights. It becomes dangerous because it is defective in the power necessary to support it. It answers the pride and purpose of a few Men in each State, but the State collectively is injured by it."

(From *The Papers of Thomas Jefferson*, Vol. 13, Julian P. Boyd, editor. Copyright 1956 by Princeton University Press. Reprinted by permission.)

799.25–34   Having . . . society.]   See note 797.10–24.

801.26–27   Blackstone . . . Parliament]   *Commentaries on the Laws of England*, Book I, ch. 2, p. 156.

804.20–805.3   "That all . . . weal."]   Articles I, III, IV, and V of the declaration of rights in the Pennsylvania state constitution (1776).

807.23–27   Virginia . . . constitutions,] Virginia adopted a declaration of rights on June 12, 1776, and a constitution on June 29. See also note 576.27–39.

808.3   Connecticut has none,] See note 357.34.

808.19   petition of rights] The Petition of Right was presented to Charles I by parliament on June 7, 1628. Citing precedents from the Middle Ages, the petition condemned several recent actions by the king as being against established law, including the exacting of a loan from the people without the consent of parliament and the imprisonment of those refusing to pay, the forced quartering of soldiers in private homes, the execution by military courts of men resisting impressment into the army, and the assertion that royal commands alone provided legal justification for imprisonment without trial or hearing. The petition asked that the king cease levies on his subjects without the consent of parliament and that he observe previously recognized rights and liberties, including the right of every freeman not to be punished without "due process of law." Charles reluctantly assented to the petition and dissolved parliament on June 26. When parliament met early in 1629 and attempted to take further action against the king's use of the royal prerogative, Charles dissolved it and did not summon another until lack of money forced him to do so in 1640. The conflict between Charles and parliament then intensified, leading to the outbreak of the English Civil War in 1642.

808.23–24   revolution . . . footing,] See note 387.35.

808.26–27   original . . . sovereign.] See note 795.22–25.

811.7–8   honorable delegate] James Wilson.

812.12–13   honorable member] James Wilson.

812.31   the clause] Article I, section 8.

812.36   honorable members] Thomas McKean and James Wilson.

813.6–10   "the Congress . . . senators."] Cf. Article I, sec. 4.

814.34   honorable delegate] James Wilson.

816.34   Civilians] See note 437.6–7.

818.1–2   *William Findley . . . Consolidation*] This version of Findley's speech was published in the *Pennsylvania Herald* and *Pennsylvania Packet* on Wednesday, December 5, and was widely reprinted; outside of Pennsylvania, it appeared in at least 13 newspapers.

818.10–12   (except . . . sovereignties)] On December 5 the *Pennsylvania Packet* quoted Benjamin Rush in convention, December 3, as saying, ". . . this passion for separate sovereignty had destroyed the Grecian union.

This plurality of sovereignty is in politics what plurality of gods is in reli--
gion—it is the idolatry, the heathenry, of government."

820.8–9   honorable gentleman]   William Findley.

821.35–38   a state . . . one-third part]   As part of its obligation to the
Continental Congress, Pennsylvania was required to pay one-eighth of the
cost of funding the national debt held in the form of loan certificates. In 1785,
in an elaborate deal among the various interests, the state legislature voted to
fund all certificates held by Pennsylvanians (which amounted to perhaps one-
third of the total) and to pay for this benefit to bondholders by levying a
general tax, issuing paper money (some of which was set aside for a land
bank), and selling off western lands. Many merchants, especially those associated with the Bank of North America, and conservatives opposed the act
because of the paper money provision.

828.11–12   iron . . . other.]   According to legend, when Cadmus sowed
the teeth of a dragon in a Boeotian plain (later the city of Thebes), armed
men rose from the ground, then turned their arms against one another until
all but five were slain.

829.7   manner . . . taxes]   Article I, section 2, par. 3.

829.20   These were . . . 1783,]   The errata in Lloyd's *Debates in the Pennsylvania Convention* noted that this phrase should be deleted.

831.1–2   *Robert Whitehill . . . Clause*]   Reported by "Puff" (said to be
Benjamin Rush) as "Substance of a speech . . ." in an article in the *Independent Gazetteer* (December 6).

832.5   Morning Session]   Jasper Yeates noted that Wilson began this summation at 10:22 and broke off at 1:00 P.M.

837.34   honorable gentleman]   William Findley.

848.9   honorable gentleman,]   Thomas McKean.

849.7   gentleman's]   John Smilie's.

853.26   Afternoon Session]   Yeates noted that Wilson resumed speaking at
4:10 P.M. and continued for two hours.

864.17   tyrant's plea.]   On December 5, William Findley had said, "To
state the danger of refusing this plan is improper. It is the tyrant's plea: take
this or nothing."

866.30–35   Henry the IV . . . Sully,]   Maximilien de Béthune, duc de
Sully, minister of Henry IV (1553–1610), wrote about the king's plan to form
a federation of European states in the last book of his memoirs, *Économies
royales* (1638).

867.1–5   controversy . . . Wyoming.] For the Wyoming Valley and the
Trenton Decree see Chronology, December 1782, May–September, 1784, and
James Wilson in the Biographical Notes.

867.36–868.8   "AND . . . tranquillity."] *A Treatise on the Administration
of the Finances of France . . . by Mr. Necker* (Thomas Mortimer, trans., London, 1785), III, 441.

869.1   *Benjamin Rush . . . Government*] Published in the *Pennsylvania
Herald*, December 15. Rush's speech created a storm of controversy because of
its conclusion that ratification was the will of heaven. Alexander Dallas
(1759–1817), the editor of the *Pennsylvania Herald*, called it a "new species of
divine right." Dallas's summary was denounced by the convention's shorthand
reporter, Thomas Lloyd (1756–1827), as "a gross misrepresentation," and Dallas called Lloyd's criticism a "*gross falsehood.*" Rush promoted the republica-
tion of Lloyd's version (*Pennsylvania Gazette, Independent Gazetteer,* and
Pennsylvania Packet, December 19) in New York and Boston. On December
29, the *Independent Gazetteer* ran both versions of the speech side by side with
remarks by "P.Q." who wrote: "I cannot for my life and soul, find any difference in the features of either of these bantlings which have been laid at the
Doctor's door." Rush represented himself, sardonically, as unaffected by the
uproar ("as a fool & a madman I am you know *Scandal proof* in Pennsylvania"), but the speech undoubtedly contributed to the bitterness of the developing struggle. Federalist attacks on this and other Dallas versions of the
debates published in the *Herald* and on Dallas himself resulted in the cancel-
lation of about 100 subscriptions. In early January 1788 Dallas was dismissed
as editor of the paper, and it ceased publication after February 14. A lawyer
from the West Indies who had come to Pennsylvania to serve as *Herald* editor
in 1783, Dallas was later secretary of Pennsylvania (1790–1801), U.S. district
attorney for the Eastern District of Pennsylvania (1801–14), and secretary of
the treasury (1814–16) under Madison.

877.1   CONNECTICUT RATIFYING CONVENTION]   Throughout the 1780s
Connecticut's politics had been bitterly divided between a mercantile-
landholding elite and an agrarian faction, with the agrarians often demanding
new measures and a restructuring of the state's constitution—the original
royal charter of 1662 relieved of British control. In the early 1780s the state's
seesawing politics served the interests of both groups, but with so little consistency that no particular outcome resulted on any given issue. In 1783, when
the state legislature proved unresponsive, a convention was held to protest
Congress's proposed five-year pensions for Continental Army officers and to
demand a comprehensive reform of the state's political and constitutional
system. The lower chamber of the legislature then rejected the council's support of the proposed continental impost, and the first steps were taken to
separate the judicial function from the legislative and executive. Soldiers' scrip
was declared receivable for payment of taxes, the towns limited their collection of unpaid taxes, and some kinds of farm animals were no longer taxed.

The result was that the severe economic pressure that precipitated Shays' Rebellion in Massachusetts was avoided in Connecticut. But the conservative forces were still very active. The continental impost was finally approved, laws were passed favoring the state's mercantile interests, and though the legislature ignored the call for the Annapolis Convention and debated at length whether or not it should send delegates to the Constitutional Convention, in the end it elected two of its three delegates (William Samuel Johnson and Oliver Ellsworth) from among those known to favor greater federal power. The third delegate, Roger Sherman, while he supported popular interests at home and would favor the small states in the debates in Philadelphia, was capable of reaching compromises on important issues. After the convention ended, Sherman and Ellsworth were able to argue convincingly that the Constitution was by no means a dangerous departure. The strong backing of these representatives of opposite ends of the state's political spectrum, together with the newspapers' unanimous support of ratification, and above all the general recognition that federal control of commerce would free the state from New York's economic dominance and remove some of the tax burden from the farmers, helped bring popular opinion decisively to the side of ratification. By the end of 1787 ratification was almost certain, and there was little need for strenuous debating when the convention met. Only seven speeches, all reported by Hartford lawyer Enoch Perkins, are known to be extant.

877.3–5   *Oliver . . . Review*] From a report in the *Connecticut Courant* (January 14, 1788; also printed in the Hartford *American Mercury* January 14); the report was reprinted in other newspapers in Connecticut, New York, Pennsylvania, South Carolina, and Maryland by the end of February.

877.7   The paragraph] Article I, sec. 8, first paragraph.

883.22–32   This constitution . . . be so.] This presentation of the structural role of judicial review was the clearest that had yet appeared (it would be months before *The Federalist* would assess the issue). Ellsworth would act on the principles he set forth here as the main author of the Judiciary Act of 1789, and later became the Chief Justice of the U.S. Supreme Court.

885.1–2   *Governor Samuel Huntington . . . Power*] From the *Connecticut Courant*, January 14, 1788. The report was reprinted in the *American Mercury* on the same day and in other newspapers in Connecticut, New York, Pennsylvania, and Maryland by the end of February.

885.13   Johnson] William Samuel Johnson (1727–1819) of Stratford, a lawyer and signer of the Constitution and member of the Continental Congress (1784–87), had been elected president of the reconstituted Columbia College in May 1787 and served until 1800 (his father, the Rev. Samuel Johnson, had been its first president when it was founded as King's College in 1754). Johnson had been a delegate to the Stamp Act Congress of 1765, Connecticut

Agent in London (1767–71), member of the Connecticut legislature (1761–66, 1771–75), and would serve as U.S. senator, 1789–91.

885.17   Gen. Parsons] Samuel Holden Parsons.

885.24   Gen. Huntington] Jedediah Huntington (1743–1818), a business-man and alderman of Norwich, had been a brigadier general in the Continental Army and was breveted major general at the close of the war.

889.1   MASSACHUSETTS RATIFYING CONVENTION] The outcome of the Massachusetts convention (with 364 delegates, the largest of the conventions) was a decisive turning point in the adoption of the Constitution. If Massachusetts had not ratified when and how it did, the Constitution might not have been adopted. Before the Massachusetts convention met, five of the necessary nine states had ratified, but only one (Pennsylvania) was a major state. Ahead lay New York, Virginia, Maryland, and the Carolinas. The loss of either New York or Virginia would probably doom the Union under the Constitution even if the requisite nine states ratified, and Antifederalist sentiment was building up everywhere. It was assumed that a majority of the Massachusetts convention, led, in spirit at least, by Elbridge Gerry, was firmly opposed. It was assumed also that Samuel Adams was opposed, and it was known that the president of the convention, Governor John Hancock, was at least uncommitted and that he had developed one of his periodic attacks of gout, which he said kept him from attending the meetings. He was inactive through the debates of January, and Adams' position was still unclear. The Federalists mobilized all the rhetorical talent available for the debates, and found occasional support from delegates from some of the towns who had to defy their constituents' opinions to favor ratification. The effectiveness of the Federalists' speakers and of their political maneuvers mounted steadily. The commercial, political, and legal establishment in the eastern counties held firm; the tradesmen (artisans) in the larger towns were reliable; minority religious leaders like Isaac Backus rallied to the cause. But many of the mid-state and western constituencies were firmly Antifederalist (18–20 delegates were said to be veterans of Shays' rebel army). After three weeks of heated debates, the sides were quite evenly balanced. The outcome would turn on the question of amendments. The Federalist leadership, in Massachusetts as elsewhere, was determined to oppose all amendments and gain an unconditional ratification. The Antifederalists insisted on ratifying only with prior amendments, which might be submitted to the other states and refined and reconciled in some kind of second constitutional convention. At the end of January Federalist leaders decided that unconditional ratification was not possible, and after caucusing they reached an agreement with Hancock to have him support ratification with recommendatory, not conditional, amendments. In return the Federalists promised to support his reelection as governor, and may have also promised to support him for president if Virginia rejected the Constitution and Washington became ineligible (whether these promises influenced Hancock's decision is unknown). After adjustments in committee, Hancock's amendments were submitted to the convention, which on February 6 voted ratification as proposed. The vote was 187–168 and there is no doubt that Hancock's personal influence and the Federalists' partial concession on amendments provided the small margin of victory. Massachusetts' ratification was quickly publicized throughout the nation. Washington, concerned about what might happen in Virginia, called Massachusetts' ratification "a severe stroke" to the Antifederalists in his state, and told Madison that it "will have a powerful operation on the Minds of men who are not actuated more by disappointment, passion and resentment, than they are by moderation, prudence & candor." Madison, who was dubious of amendments in any form, agreed, and even Jefferson, who in February had urged that only nine states ratify while the remaining four remain outside the union in order to secure amendments, now agreed that "the plan of Massachusetts is far preferable, and will I hope be followed by those who are yet to decide." The Massachusetts formula of ratification with recommended subsequent amendments would be followed in the closely divided conventions in Virginia and New York. "The decision of Massachusetts," the Virginia Federalist Edward Carrington wrote, "is perhaps the most important event that ever took place in America, as upon her in all probability depended the fate of the Constitution." Hancock, who had been elected governor in 1787 with an overwhelming majority, was reelected in April 1788 without opposition.

889.8–9   instructed their delegates] The question of whether delegates to the ratifying convention should be bound by the instructions of their constituencies was difficult and highly controversial in several states. Instructions to representatives, or mandates, as they were sometimes called, had been common in the legislative history of a number of states; in Massachusetts mandates had been used irregularly since the 17th century. The issue had entered into the Revolutionary controversy when the British argued that the colonies were "virtually" represented in parliament as was any British community, whether or not it was an electoral constituency, since representatives were not elected as legal ambassadors of the interests of their several narrow constituencies but as general negotiators seeking to achieve the good of the whole. Actual representation thus acquired during the Revolution an ideological quality it had lacked before. The question of whether or not an elected delegate should be bound by instructions remained vital whenever contested issues arose in politics.

893.29   this article] Article I, sec. 2.

895.38   Mr. ADAMS] Samuel Adams.

896.4   4th section] Of Article I.

897.35   restoration] After the death of Oliver Cromwell on September 3, 1658, his son Richard succeeded him as Lord Protector of the Commonwealth, but proved unable to command the loyalty of either the army or of the Rump parliament (see note 735.32–33), which reassembled on May 7, 1659.

Cromwell abdicated as Lord Protector on May 25, 1659, and parliament assumed the government of the Commonwealth, although ultimate power still lay with the army, which forcibly dissolved parliament in October 1659. General George Monck resolved to bring an end to "sword government" by restoring parliamentary rule and marched his troops south from Scotland, entered London on February 3, 1660, and eventually brought about the election of a new parliament. The new Convention parliament of April 1660 was dominated by Royalists and Presbyterians willing to restore Charles II to the throne. Despite the opposition of some Presbyterians, who wanted to negotiate terms for the restoration, parliament proclaimed Charles king on May 8, 1660, solely on the basis of his previous declaration in favor of a general amnesty, liberty of conscience, fair settlement of land disputes, and full payment of money owed to the army. Monck supported the restoration, and Charles II entered London on May 29, 1660.

900.8–10   man . . . wisdom]   David (1 Samuel 13:14 and 17:35–36), and his son Solomon, to whom God gave wisdom (e.g. 1 Kings 4:29–34; 2 Chronicles 9:22–23).

906.9   the court]   Massachusetts General Court.

907.8–9   black cloud . . . west.]   A reference to Shays' Rebellion.

908.8–9   honourable old daddy]   Amos Singletary was 67, Jonathan Smith 48.

910.6   paragraph under consideration]   Article III, sect. 2, par. 3.

917.4–5   present article]   Article V.

918.18–19   Constitution . . . time;]   The Massachusetts constitution of 1780 provided (Chap. VI, Art. 10) that if in 1795 the state voters, by a two-thirds majority, favored amendments, a convention would be convened to deliberate on the proposed changes.

919.6–7   paragraph . . . religious test,]   Article VI, par. 3.

920.19–22   Peter . . . to him—]   Acts 10:34–35.

920.30   (Bristol)]   In the district of Maine.

921.9–10   former . . . proposition]   Hancock attended the convention for the first time on January 30 but did not speak. On the morning of January 31, after the convention had finished discussing the Constitution by paragraphs and while other Federalists were still in caucus preparing a list of amendments (they began caucusing on January 30), Theophilus Parsons made a motion to ratify, after which Hancock announced that he would present a proposition in the afternoon that would "remove the objections of some gentlemen." (Parsons, 1750–1813, a lawyer and representative of Newburyport in the Massachusetts House and a Federalist leader at the convention, had previously spoken with Hancock concerning ratification with amendments.) Tension was extremely high when at 3 P.M. Hancock appeared before the meeting packed with spectators and delivered his address.

921.19–24   to adopt . . . amendments]   For the form of ratification, see page 943 in this volume.

923.7   motion . . . Newbury-Port;]   Theophilus Parsons.

924.5–6   article . . . treaties;]   Article I, sec. 8; see also Article II, sec. 2.

924.8   Our ambassador . . . London]   John Adams.

924.16–17   article . . . revision,]   Article V.

926.35–36   Brooklyn, . . . represent]   Brookline is a suburb of Boston; Nasson represented Sanford in the district of Maine.

928.5   Great-Barrington, or Machias]   Great Barrington in Berkshire County, western Massachussetts, and Machias, in the southeast corner of the district of Maine.

928.19–20   Caesar passed the *Rubicon*]   See note 735.9–14.

929.1–3   standing army . . . 1770]   All but two regiments of British troops, sent to Boston to maintain order and enforce the Townshend Acts in September 1768, were withdrawn in 1769. On March 5, 1770, a mob of about 60 persons attacked a sentry, and ten soldiers of the 29th Regiment under the command of Captain Thomas Preston came to his rescue (soldiers had been harassed by gangs since their arrival in the city). Without orders, some of the soldiers opened fire on the crowd, wounding eight and killing five (three died immediately); their funerals occasioned a large patriotic demonstration and the incident became known as the "Boston massacre." Captain Preston and his men were brought to trial to pacify public outrage; they were defended by John Adams and Josiah Quincy. Two were convicted of manslaughter, branded on the hand, and discharged; the rest were acquitted on grounds of self-defense.

929.19–21   last winter . . . countrymen]   A reference to Shays' Rebellion.

932.2–7   Bishop . . . 1783]   The sermons of William Warburton (1698–1799), Bishop of Gloucester, and Beilby Porteus (1731–1808), Bishop of Chester, were delivered to the Anglican Church's Society for the Propagation of the Gospel. Porteus, an English-born son of American parents, was committed to reconciliation between the two countries, and to the abolition of the slave trade and of slavery. He became Bishop of London in 1787. Warburton was the author of among other books *Alliance between Church and State or, the Necessity and Equity of an Established Religion and a Test Law* (1736), which had gained him favor with the crown. He was frequently involved in theological and literary controversies.

932.12–15   gentleman . . . consumption."] Thomas Dawes, Jr., in the Massachusetts convention, January 18.

938.12–14   duty . . . vote.] On Barrell and his constituency's views in York, Maine, see page 586.10–16.

939.36–37   like . . . furiously,] 2 Kings 9:20. Reference is to Federalist campaign for quick ratification in Pennsylvania.

945.26   GEORGE RICHARDS MINOT] Minot (1758–1802) of Boston, a lawyer, was clerk of the state house of representatives and author of *History of the Insurrections in Massachusetts* (1788).

Index

Further information on persons marked with an asterisk (*) is given in the Biographical Notes section.

CATALOGING INFORMATION

The Debate on the Constitution
 Edited by Bernard Bailyn

 (The Library of America ; 62)
 Includes bibliographical references and indexes.
 Contents: Debates in the press and in private correspondence,
September 17, 1787–January 12, 1788; Debates in the state ratifying
conventions: Pennsylvania, Connecticut, Massachusetts.
  1. Federalist. 2. United States—Constitutional history.
3. United States—Politics and government—1783–1789. I. Title.
II. Series.
JK155.D33   1993   92-25449
342.73'029—dc20
[347.30229]
ISBN 0-940450-42-9 (alk. paper)

This book is set in 10 point Linotron Galliard,
a face designed for photocomposition by Matthew Carter
and based on the sixteenth-century face Granjon. The paper
is acid-free Ecusta Nyalite and meets the requirements for permanence of the American National Standards Institute. The binding
material is Brillianta, a 100% woven rayon cloth made by
Van Heek-Scholco Textielfabrieken, Holland. The composition is by Haddon Craftsmen, Inc., and The
Clarinda Company. Printing and binding
by R. R. Donnelley & Sons Company.
Designed by Bruce Campbell.

THE LIBRARY OF AMERICA SERIES

The Library of America fosters appreciation and pride in America's literary heritage by publishing, and keeping permanently in print, authoritative editions of its best and most significant writing. An independent nonprofit organization, it was founded in 1979 with seed money from the National Endowment for the Humanities and the Ford Foundation.

1. Herman Melville, *Typee, Omoo, Mardi* (1982)
2. Nathaniel Hawthorne, *Tales and Sketches* (1982)
3. Walt Whitman, *Poetry and Prose* (1982)
4. Harriet Beecher Stowe, *Three Novels* (1982)
5. Mark Twain, *Mississippi Writings* (1982)
6. Jack London, *Novels and Stories* (1982)
7. Jack London, *Novels and Social Writings* (1982)
8. William Dean Howells, *Novels 1875–1886* (1982)
9. Herman Melville, *Redburn, White-Jacket, Moby-Dick* (1983)
10. Nathaniel Hawthorne, *Collected Novels* (1983)
11. Francis Parkman, *France and England in North America*, vol. I (1983)
12. Francis Parkman, *France and England in North America*, vol. II (1983)
13. Henry James, *Novels 1871–1880* (1983)
14. Henry Adams, *Novels, Mont Saint Michel, The Education* (1983)
15. Ralph Waldo Emerson, *Essays and Lectures* (1983)
16. Washington Irving, *History, Tales and Sketches* (1983)
17. Thomas Jefferson, *Writings* (1984)
18. Stephen Crane, *Prose and Poetry* (1984)
19. Edgar Allan Poe, *Poetry and Tales* (1984)
20. Edgar Allan Poe, *Essays and Reviews* (1984)
21. Mark Twain, *The Innocents Abroad, Roughing It* (1984)
22. Henry James, *Essays, American & English Writers* (1984)
23. Henry James, *European Writers & The Prefaces* (1984)
24. Herman Melville, *Pierre, Israel Potter, The Confidence-Man, Tales & Billy Budd* (1985)
25. William Faulkner, *Novels 1930–1935* (1985)
26. James Fenimore Cooper, *The Leatherstocking Tales*, vol. I (1985)
27. James Fenimore Cooper, *The Leatherstocking Tales*, vol. II (1985)
28. Henry David Thoreau, *A Week, Walden, The Maine Woods, Cape Cod* (1985)
29. Henry James, *Novels 1881–1886* (1985)
30. Edith Wharton, *Novels* (1986)
31. Henry Adams, *History of the United States during the Administrations of Jefferson* (1986)
32. Henry Adams, *History of the United States during the Administrations of Madison* (1986)
33. Frank Norris, *Novels and Essays* (1986)
34. W. E. B. Du Bois, *Writings* (1986)
35. Willa Cather, *Early Novels and Stories* (1987)
36. Theodore Dreiser, *Sister Carrie, Jennie Gerhardt, Twelve Men* (1987)
37. Benjamin Franklin, *Writings* (1987)
38. William James, *Writings 1902–1910* (1987)
39. Flannery O'Connor, *Collected Works* (1988)
40. Eugene O'Neill, *Complete Plays 1913–1920* (1988)
41. Eugene O'Neill, *Complete Plays 1920–1931* (1988)
42. Eugene O'Neill, *Complete Plays 1932–1943* (1988)
43. Henry James, *Novels 1886–1890* (1989)
44. William Dean Howells, *Novels 1886–1888* (1989)
45. Abraham Lincoln, *Speeches and Writings 1832–1858* (1989)
46. Abraham Lincoln, *Speeches and Writings 1859–1865* (1989)
47. Edith Wharton, *Novellas and Other Writings* (1990)
48. William Faulkner, *Novels 1936–1940* (1990)
49. Willa Cather, *Later Novels* (1990)
50. Ulysses S. Grant, *Personal Memoirs and Selected Letters* (1990)